Heinrich Barth

Sammlung und Bearbeitung Central Afrikanischer Vokabularien

Heinrich Barth

Sammlung und Bearbeitung Central Afrikanischer Vokabularien

ISBN/EAN: 9783741159626

Manufactured in Europe, USA, Canada, Australia, Japa

Cover: Foto ©Andreas Hilbeck / pixelio.de

Manufactured and distributed by brebook publishing software (www.brebook.com)

Heinrich Barth

Sammlung und Bearbeitung Central Afrikanischer Vokabularien

Sammlung und Bearbeitung
Central-Afrikanischer Vokabularien

von

Heinrich Barth.

Erste Abtheilung.

Umfassendere Vokabularien der Kanúri-, Téda-, Hausa-, Fulfúlde-, Sońyai-, Lógoné-, Wándalá-, Bágrimma- und Maba-Sprachen.

Einleitung, Kap. 1—6. Fürwörter. Partikeln. Zahlwörter. Zeitwörter.

Collection
of
vocabularies of Central-African languages

compiled and analysed

by

Henry Barth, C. B. D. C. L.

I^st part.

Larger vocabularies of the Kanúri-, Téda-, Hausa-, Ful-fúl-de-, Sońyai-, Logone-, Wándalá-, Bágrimma- and Mába-languages.

Introductory Remarks chap. 1—6. Pronouns. Particles. Numerals. Verbs.

Gotha: Justus Perthes.
1862.

Einleitung.

Introductory Remarks.

Einleitung.

Erstes Kapitel.

Indem ich es mir angelegen sein lasse, nicht allein den Sprachforscher von Fach, sondern auch Denjenigen für die hier veröffentlichte Sammlung Afrikanischer Vokabularien zu interessiren, der entweder für die verschiedenen Stadien der menschlichen Kulturgeschichte eine lebendige Theilnahme hegt oder meiner Reise in's Besondere und ihren Ergebnissen mit Interesse gefolgt ist, beginne ich diese Einleitung mit einigen ganz allgemeinen Bemerkungen, um theils meinen Standpunkt zu dem hier gebotenen Material zu erklären, theils eine, wenn ich so sagen darf, pragmatische Geschichte der Ansammlung desselben zu liefern. Dies betrifft aber nur meine grösseren Vokabularien, bei den kürzeren werde ich nur an der geeigneten Stelle angeben, wo und unter welchen Umständen jedes von ihnen niedergeschrieben ist.

Viele haben mich gefragt, wie ich es auf meiner mehr als fünfjährigen Afrikanischen Reise, die sich über ein Ländergebiet von grösserer Ausdehnung als Europa erstreckte, angefangen habe, mich mit diesem Gewirr der mannichfachsten Völkerschaften zu verständigen. Nichts ist natürlicher als eine solche Frage. Denn, wenn schon sonst die Sprache das einzige Mittel richtiger Erkenntniss und friedlichen, freundlichen Verkehrs im Menschenleben ist, wie könnte denn der unbeschützte, ganz ausschliesslich auf seine eigene Energie und sein moralisches Übergewicht angewiesene Reisende in solchen Gegenden und unter solchen Völkerschaften dieses Mittels entbehren! Denn diese Naturvölker betrachten ganz natürlich den zu ihnen kommenden, wie vom Himmel herabgefallenen weissen Fremdling mit tiefstem Argwohn, bevor sie sich davon überzeugt haben, dass dieses wunderbare Wesen, dessen ganzes Auftreten, dessen Farbe, Erscheinung, Lebensweise und Thätigkeit so grundverschieden von dem ihrigen ist, — zumal wenn er gekommen ist, Land und Leute zu erforschen — dieselben menschlichen Gefühle und ähnliche, wenn auch nicht dieselben, Grundsätze hat, wie sie.

Wie habe ich es nun gemacht? Kannte ich vorher wenigstens die hauptsächlichsten der im Inneren Afrika's geredeten Sprachen? Mitnichten. Das Innere Afrika's hatte überhaupt meinen früheren Studien fern gelegen, deren fast ausschliesslicher Wahlplatz das klassische Becken des Mittelmeeres mit seinen in geographischer, wie historischer und ethnographischer Beziehung so reich gegliederten Küstenlandschaften gewesen war. Wäre ich zur Zeit, als die Theilnahme Deutscher Gelehrten an der Expedition Richardson's durch die Herren *v. Bunsen*, *Carl Ritter* und *Petermann* angeregt wurde, schon über der Bearbeitung des zweiten Abschnittes meiner ersten dreijährigen Reise gewesen, der mich mit Vorder-Asien beschäftigt hätte, dem Hauptziel meiner jugendlichen Reiseentwürfe, ich wäre wol kaum in diese Laufbahn eingetreten. Da mich aber die Ausarbeitung meiner Reise durch das Nord-Afrikanische Gestadeland, besonders in Folge der grossen Ausbreitung des Nord-Afrikanischen Stammes der Mázig oder Berbern, weiter in das Innere hineingeführt hatte, so war mir selbst das ferner gelegene Binnenland, an das mich vorher nur Namen wie Park und Lander knüpften, vom historischen Gesichtspunkte aus anziehend und interessant geworden. Ich hatte mich aber, abgesehen von der Berber-Sprache, mit den Sprachen jener Landschaften keineswegs beschäftigt; auch wäre es von geringer Bedeutung gewesen, da die damals vorliegenden Proben jener Sprachen, von

Introductory Remarks.

Chapter the first.

I think best, to begin this Introduction into my collection of African vocabularies with some account of the manner, in which they were made. For it is my ardent desire, to give some clear insight into the character of this collection and to explain the way, how I myself got through the difficulties arising from the variety of languages, not only to the professional linguist, but even to those, who either may take a sincere interest in the various phases of human society in general or who may have followed with some sort of concern my own travels in those distant countries. For a great many circumstances must remain unintelligible to the public at large, before the traveller has explained his way of proceeding step for step. However such an explanation concerns only my more complete vocabularies, while with regard to the shorter ones I shall only say in the proper place, where each of them was written down.

Thus, many have asked me, how I succeeded during my long African exploration, lasting more than five years and comprising a vaster extent of country than the whole surface of Europe, to deal with that host of different languages and make myself understood, and nothing is more natural than a question such as this. For, while the language in general is the only means of knowledge as well as of peaceable and friendly intercourse, how could the unprotected traveller be without it, placed as he is among savage and uncivilized tribes and dependent entirely upon his own energy and his personal moral ascendancy! For these tribes cannot but look upon the white stranger, who suddenly appears before them, as if he were fallen from the sky, and regard him with the most profound suspicion, before they become convinced, that this wonderful being has the same human feelings as themselves and similar, if not the same, principles of action notwithstanding the total difference of his colour, his appearance, his manner of living and his unintelligible and apparently absurd and foolish activity, especially if he is come, to explore the country, lay down its physical features and describe the people.

What is now my own case? How was it, that I succeeded? Have I been acquainted at least from the beginning with the principal of the languages spoken in the Interior of Africa? Not at all. On the contrary, the Interior of Africa altogether had been far remote from the range of my former studies, the almost exclusive object of which had been the classical basin of the Mediterranean with its border countries so richly and differently organized and the various nations, which have here developed their individual character in the course of history. Indeed, Providence herself lead me to that new sphere of activity and study. For, if at the time, when it was proposed by the Chevalier *Bunsen* and by Mr. *Petermann* and furthered by my dear lamented friend and teacher *Carl Ritter*, that some German savant should take part in the expedition undertaken by Mr. Richardson, I had been occupied already with the second section of my first travel, it is scarcely probable, that I should ever have entered upon this African career, as the second part of my former travel would have carried me to Asia, the principal object of the travelling projects of my youth, while in consequence of the wide expansion of the North-African race of the Mázigh or Berber my studies of the objects connected with the first part of my journey had familiarized me with even the far Interior of that continent which formerly had been before my mind only in connection

Seetzen, Burckhardt, Denham und anderen Reisenden gesammelt, abgesehen von Schön's auch noch sehr kurzer und unvollkommener Arbeit über die Hausa-Sprache [1]), nur spärliche und theils verfälschte Brocken waren, in welche Klasse besonders die Sprachproben in den zum Gebrauch der grossen, unglücklichen Niger-Expedition veröffentlichten Vokabularien gehören. Koelle hatte damals, im Winter 1849, sein tief eindringendes Studium der Bórnu- oder Kanúri-Sprache in Sierra Leone erst begonnen, und dass seine Arbeiten auf diesem Felde [2]) nicht einige Jahre früher erschienen sind, hat allerdings meinen linguistischen Arbeiten einen grossen Nachtheil gebracht, da sie von dieser Basis ausgehend ungleich weiter gefördert sein würden. Was ich an Koelle's Bórnu-Arbeiten auszusetzen habe, wird weiter unten besprochen werden. Koelle's Polyglotta [3]) dagegen würde mir, selbst wenn sie damals schon herausgegeben worden wäre, wenigstens für Sprachstudien nur wenig genützt haben, da diese Musterkarte Afrikanischer Sprachen zum grossen Theil fehlerhaft und unzuverlässig ist, wie das nach den Verhältnissen, unter denen der hochverdiente, unermüdliche und einsichtsvolle Missionär diese Wortlisten von Sklaven, die zum Theil vor vielen Jahren ihr Heimathland verlassen und seitdem mit einzelnen Individuen der verschiedensten Stämme in dem linguistischen Babel von Sierra Leone zusammengelebt hatten, abfragte, kaum anders möglich ist. Auch sind der Sprachproben zu wenige, um von irgend praktischem Nutzen zu sein.

So trat ich also gegen Ende des J. 1849 meine Reise, ausser einem leichten Einblick in den grammatischen Bau der Berber-Sprache, nur mit einer, sowol durch Lektüre als besonders durch langen praktischen Gebrauch, mir angeeigneten Kenntniss des Arabischen an, gab mich aber, sobald ich den Gegenstand einmal aufgenommen hatte, demselben mit Lust und Liebe und dem feurigsten Eifer hin, und ein Jeder, der fremde Länder besucht hat, weiss, wie unendlich leichter man sich da deren Sprachen aneignet, als im langweiligen Studium ohne lebendigen Anhalt daheim. Und wie viel mehr ist das bei barbarischen Sprachen der Fall, die durchaus keine Literatur besitzen und des geschichtlichen Anhalts ermangeln!

Vom volksthümlichen Arabisch also ausgehend, dessen Gebiet wir von Tripoli bis Mursuk zu durchschneiden hatten, verschaffte ich mir mit Hülfe der uns von der Küste her begleitenden, jenen inneren Landschaften angehörenden, befreiten Neger-Sklaven durch Niederschreiben und Auswendiglernen eine Kenntniss der gewöhnlichsten Ausdrücke in der Hausa- und Kanúri-Sprache. Da jedoch unser Weg nicht die gerade Richtung nach Bórnu verfolgen, sondern eine grosse südwestliche Abbiegung durch das Gebiet der Tauárek oder Imōšay zuerst nach den Hausa-Staaten nehmen sollte, wurde die Kanúri-Sprache bald für's Erste ganz bei Seite gelassen, während sonst für das Erlernen gerade dieser Sprache in Fezān das reichste Feld sich geboten hätte. Denn das alte Phazania war eben der ursprüngliche Sitz der Garamanten, eines, wie es scheint, mit Kanúri und Tédā eng verwandten Stammes, dem erst seit der Hälfte des siebenten Jahrhunderts n. Chr. Berberische und Arabische Volkselemente aufgepfropft worden sind. Ja, ich will hier vorläufig meine Vermuthung aussprechen, dass Phazania (Ɵaḍā-nin) das Land der Tédā bezeichnet.

---

[1]) Vocabulary of the Haussa language by the Rev. J. Fr. Schön. London 1843. 8°. Part I. English and Haussa. Part II. Haussa and English and phrases and specimens of translations, to which are prefixed the grammatical elements of the Haussa language.

[2]) a) African Native Literature or proverbs, tales, fables and historical fragments in the Kanuri or Bornu language, to which are added a translation of the above and a Kanuri-English vocabulary by Rev. S. W. Koelle. London 1854. — b) Grammar of the Bórnu or Kánuri language by Rev. S. W. Koelle. London 1854.

[3]) Polyglotta Africana, or a comparative vocabulary of nearly three hundred words and phrases in more than one hundred distinct African languages [d. h. in 100 dialektischen Idiomen von etwa dreissig verschiedenen Sprachen] by the Rev. S. W. Koelle. London 1854.

with the names of Park and Lander. But even then I had not made any acquaintance with the languages of Central Negroland, and that would scarcely have been possible, as very scanty and far from reliable documents were at that time before the public; I mean the short vocabularies collected by Seetzen, Burckhardt, Denham and other travellers, only the Rev. Schön's little work on the Hausa-language [1]) making a slight exception, though even the latter was very short and incomplete. The Rev. Koelle just at that period, in the winter 1849, had begun in Sierra Leone his diligent and accurate study of the Bórnu- or Kanúri-language and, no doubt, my own labours have suffered great damage from the circumstance, that his works [2]) on this subject were not brought out some years earlier, as, proceeding from this base, they would have made infinitely greater progress. The remarks I have to offer with regard to Koelle's labours on the Kanúri-language, will be developed further on. As for his Polyglotta [3]), it would have been of very little avail to me, at least in linguistical respect, even if it had then been out, as this „paper of patterns" of African languages, if I may so call it, in a great many cases is far from reliable, as it was scarcely possible otherwise, considered the circumstances, under which these short lists of words were made, the indefatigable and highly meritorious missionary being obliged to rely entirely upon the authority of slaves, many of whom had been dragged from their native country many years before and had since partialy forgotten their own idiom in the constant intercourse with slaves of other tribes in that linguistic Babel of Sierra Leone, the home of so many liberated slaves from all parts of Africa. Besides the specimens are too scanty, to be of any practical avail.

Thus, towards the close of the year 1849 I entered upon my long and dangerous African journey with nothing, but an insight into the grammatical structure of the Berber-language and a good knowledge of the Arabic, acquired as well by reading as especially through long practical use. However, as soon as I had once taken up the matter, I applied myself to the study of African languages with the greatest energy and enthusiasm, and any body, who has visited foreign countries, knows from experience, how infinitely more easy it is, there to acquire a foreign tongue, than at home without any practical application and immediate use. And how much more must this be the case with regard to barbarous languages, such as these!

Proceeding therefore from the vulgar Arabic, the territory of which we had to traverse as far as Murzuk, I immediately with the assistance of those of the liberated Negro-slaves in our company, who were natives of Bórnu and Hausa, began to form some superficial acquaintance with the most common terms of those languages. But, as our route was not to follow the straight direction towards Bórnu, but was to take a great south-westerly roundabout-way through the territory of the Tawárek or Imóshay towards the Hausa-states, the study of the Kanúri-language was soon relinquished, although the country of Fezzán, where we made a longer stay, offered the greatest facility for acquiring that very language. For the Phazania in ancient times was the original seat of the Garamantes, a tribe apparently related to or perhaps comprising the two tribes of the Téda and the Kanúri, upon whom from the second half of the seventh century downwards the Berber and Arabic elements have been engrafted. Nay, I here already express my opinion, that the name Phazania or rather Θaḍa-nia means nothing, but the country of the Téda.

---

1) Vocabulary of the Haussa language by the Rev. J. Fr. Schön. London 1843. 8°. Part I. English and Haussa. Part II. Haussa and English and phrases and specimens of translations, to which are prefixed the grammatical elements of the Haussa language.

2) a) African Native Literature or proverbs, tales, fables and historical fragments in the Kanuri or Bornu language, to which are added a translation of the above and a Kanuri-English vocabulary by Rev. S. W. Koelle. London 1854. — b) Grammar of the Bórnu or Kánuri language by Rev. S. W. Koelle. London 1854.

3) Polyglotta Africana, or a comparative vocabulary of nearly three hundred words and phrases in more than one hundred distinct African languages (that is to say, in one hundred dialectical idioms of about thirty different languages) by the Rev. S. W. Koelle. London 1854.

So bemühte ich mich, sobald wir Fezzán verliessen, seit Anfang Juni 1850, unablässig, mich der Te-mášiγ-t oder Mášiγ-Sprache, und zwar des von den Kél-owī gesprochenen Dialektes derselben, so wie des Hausa zu bemeistern. Aber das letztere überwog, sobald wir Ghât hinter uns hatten, entschieden, indem es sich als die schon in dem Berglande Asben, wenigstens bei denjenigen Stämmen, mit denen wir schon durch das Zusammenreisen vom Brunnen Karáda aus (Reisen, Th. I, S. 272), 27. Juli 1850, in Berührung kamen, im grösseren Verkehr vorwiegende Sprache erwies, während der Berberische Dialekt eben in Folge dieses Umstandes weniger rein war, und dazu kam die leichte, schnell fassliche Bildungsweise des Hausa und sein schöner, vokalreicher Klang, so dass es bald meine Lieblingssprache wurde. So kam es, dass mein Verzeichniss von Mášiγ-Wörtern und Phrasen, im Dialekt der Kél-owī, sehr unvollständig blieb, weshalb ich ihn in meinem, am Ende des fünften Bandes der Reisen veröffentlichten, Vokabular des Dialektes der Auelimmiden ganz unberücksichtigt gelassen habe. In Bezug auf die Hausa-Sprache stellte es sich aber nun immer entschiedener heraus, dass der Dialekt, den Schön am untersten Laufe des Niger studirt hatte, von dem in den nördlicheren Hausa-Ländern üblichen ein verschiedener ist. Während ich mich also im Mášiγ nur in den gewöhnlichsten Alltagsphrasen auszudrücken wusste, trotzdem dass ich mitunter auf Leute traf, mit denen ich nur in dieser Mundart verkehren konnte, lernte ich schon während unseres mehr als dreimonatlichen Aufenthaltes im Alpenlande Asben die Hausa-Sprache ziemlich fliessend sprechen, so dass ich ohne Dolmetscher sogar mit dem Herrn von A'gades mich einigermassen unterhalten konnte.

Nur während meines zwanzigtägigen Aufenthaltes in der Stadt A'gades selbst ward dieses Studium zeitweilig und leicht unterbrochen von einem ersten, aber überaus interessanten Einblick in den hier gesprochenen, allerdings unreinen Dialekt der Sonγai-Sprache, indem ich hier die für die gesammte Ethnographie Nord-Afrika's so wichtige Entdeckung der Identität der in A'gades und der am mittleren Niger geredeten Sprache machte; aber selbst mein Vokabular des Emghédesi machte ich nur durch Vermittelung des Hausa und hatte auch so wieder vielfache Gelegenheit, meine Kenntniss des letzteren zu ergänzen. Eine solche unablässige Ergänzung fand dann Statt, wie wir, von der nackten Hochfläche der Wüste herabsteigend, allmählich die wirthbareren Landschaften der Hausaua betraten, wo ich dann, von meinen Europäischen Gefährten getrennt und ganz allein auf den treuen und geselligen Gadāre (Reis. Th. II, S. 2) mich verlassend, über Kátsena die bedeutende Handelsstadt Kanō, den jetzigen Glanzpunkt der Hausa-Welt, erreichte und hier einen ungefähr einmonatlichen Aufenthalt machte.

Allerdings konnte ich nicht lange genug in jedem der Hauptorte der Hausa-Provinzen bleiben, um die Dialekt-Unterschiede der Sprache zu erfassen, aber, wäre es mir damals vergönnt gewesen, noch ein halbes Jahr auf Hausa-Boden zu verweilen, so würde ich mich der Sprache mit allen ihren feinsten Eigenthümlichkeiten vollkommen bemeistert haben. Aber das ist nicht das Loos des Forschungs-Reisenden in so ausgedehnten Ländermassen. Schon in den ersten Tagen des April 1851 sollte ich in der Hauptstadt Bórnu's mit Herrn Richardson zusammentreffen, und dass ich nicht Einen Tag länger zögerte, war ein Glück für das ganze Schicksal unserer Expedition, weil der bisherige Leiter derselben mittlerweile den Strapazen erlegen war und so die Interessen derselben ohne alle Vertretung gelassen hatte.

So musste ich also das mir so eben heimisch gewordene Gebiet der formenreichen und geschmeidigen Hausa-Sprache, in dem ich mich schon ganz zu Hause fühlte, verlassen und sah mich gezwungen, sofort das Gebiet einer grundverschiedenen Sprache zu betreten. Denn dass das Kanóri in seinen Wurzelwörtern und seinen ursprünglichen Redetheilen grundverschieden vom Hausa ist, wird Jeder erkennen, der meinen weiteren Untersuchungen folgt, wiewol die reichere und früher ausgebildete Hausa-Sprache, wie ich selbst zeigen

Thus, from the beginning of June 1850, when we left Fezzān, I applied myself with great energy to the learning of the To-māšiy-t or, as I shall further on call it, Māšiy-language and especially that dialect of it which is spoken by the Kēl-owī, and to that of the Hausa-language. But the latter began to predominate decidedly, as soon as we left Ghāt behind us, as the Hausa-idiom proved to be the prevailing language already in the territory of Asben, at least with regard to the general intercourse, especially with those people, with whom we came into contact already since the well of Karāda, July 27, 50 (Tr. and D. I, p. 248), while the Berber-idiom spoken in that province from this very reason is less pure; and moreover the easy character and the rich development of the Hausa-idiom caused it soon to be a favorite with me. However, with regard to the Hausa-language it became more and more evident, that the dialect, which the Rev. Schön had made the object of his study on the lower course of the Niger, was very different from that spoken in the northern districts of the Hausa-provinces. Thus it happened, that my vocabulary of the Kēl-owī dialect of the Berber-idiom remained very imperfect and that, while I was only capable of expressing myself in the common phrases of daily life, whenever I met a Tarki or Amōšay of pure blood, who did not but understand the Māšiy-idiom, I already during our stay in the mountainous country of Asben learned to speak the Hausa-language with tolerable fluency, so that I was able to converse even with the Sultan of A'gades without the assistance of an interpreter.

Only during my stay in the latter town this study was interrupted for a while and but very slightly by a first and highly interesting insight into the peculiar idiom here spoken, which I discovered to be a rather corrupted and impure dialect of the Soṅyai-language, the identity of the language spoken here with that spoken on the middle course of the Niger being a fact of the highest importance for the whole ethnography of North-Africa. But even my vocabulary of the Emgédesi-language I made only with the assistance and by means of the Hausa-language, and thus had frequent opportunity of improving my knowledge of the latter. Such an uninterrupted improving then took place, as descending gradually from the sterile and elevated level of the desert we entered upon the more fertile tracts of the Hausa-states, when, separated from my companions and relying almost entirely upon the communicative and cheerful old Hausa-slave Gadžāre (see Tr. and D. II, p. 2 and 4), by way of Kátsena I reached Kanō, the chief ornament and emporium of the Hausa-states at the present time, where I made a stay of a little more than a month.

Indeed, although I did not spend enough time in the single places, that I might have become fully aware of the dialectical differences of the idiom spoken in each of them, yet, if I had at that time been enabled to spend half a year longer among the Hausa-people, I should have become fully master of the language with all its finest peculiarities. But such is not the lot of an African explorer, who is dependent last of all upon his own inclination. For already in the very beginning of April I had stipulated with Mr. Richardson to meet him in the capital of Bórnu and the event proved, that the fate of our whole expedition was dependent upon my not lingering a moment longer, the Director of the expedition having meanwhile succumbed to the fatigues of the journey and its interests being thus left without being taken care of.

Thus therefore I was obliged to turn my back upon the territory of the Hausa-language so rich in forms and so pleasant to the ear, in which I had begun to feel quite at home, and to enter abruptly the territory of a totally different idiom. For, that the Kanúri is totally different from the Hausa in all its principal elements and original forms of speech, any body will acknowledge, who looks over the colums of the two languages with some care and attention, although I myself am about to show a few pages further on, what a considerable

wurde, vielfachen Einfluss auf die weitere Vervollkommnung der ersteren, besonders in Beziehung auf Verbalformen wie auf Partikeln, geübt hat. Dass bei einem solchen Charakter dieser beiden Sprachen, ganz abgesehen von den anderswo entwickelten historischen Verhältnissen, die Ableitung des Namens Kanúri vom Namen der Stadt und Landschaft Kanō, wie dies einer der Englischen Kritiker meiner Forschungen gethan hat, grundverkehrt ist, versteht sich von selbst. Dies wollte ich hier bei Gelegenheit von Kanō schon im Voraus bemerken.

So musste ich denn also dem geistig schon gewonnenen Sprachgebiet den Rücken kehren, ja das mit Mühe Gelernte absichtlich zu vergessen suchen, um mich mit vollem Eifer auf ein neues Feld zu werfen und so die Kanúri-Sprache zu erlernen. Denn nichts ist schrecklicher für den verlassenen Reisenden unter solchen Naturmenschen und zumal unter so gänzlich mittellosen Verhältnissen, wie ich mich damals befand, als von der Sprache der Leute, mit denen er verkehrt, nicht wenigstens das Nöthigste zu verstehen. Ja ich hatte damals gar keinen Dolmetscher zur Seite, wie überhaupt nie, sondern nur einen einzigen Diener als Factotum, den treuen, aber ungebildeten Mohammed aus Ghatrōn von fast reinem Tédā-Geblüt und des Arabischen nur wenig mächtig, dagegen aber mit der, seiner eigenen nahe verwandten, Kanúri-Sprache leidlich vertraut. So widmete ich mich also unter der besten Lehrerin, der eisernen Nothwendigkeit, eifrig dem Erlernen des Kanúri. In der Hauptstadt selbst aber angekommen fand ich nicht die volle Gelegenheit, die zu diesem Zweck wünschenswerth gewesen wäre. Denn einerseits war Kūkana mit seiner jetzigen Dynastie der Kanemíin und unter der Vesierschaft Hadj Beśír's damals so recht der Sitz Arabischer Afterbildung geworden, andererseits war gerade damals der Zusammenfluss ferner und einigermassen gebildeter Pilger auf ihrem Rückwege von Mekka oder dem Hinweg dahin so gross, dass ich diese glänzende Gelegenheit zur Gewinnung neuen geographischen Materials von grösster Bedeutung nicht vorübergehen lassen konnte, so dass schon aus diesen beiden Gründen meine Studien in der Kanúri-Sprache nicht eben grosse Fortschritte machten.

Dazu kam nun aber meine projektirte und mit Eifer im Auge behaltene Reise nach Adamaua. In jener ursprünglich unter dem Namen Fúmbinā begriffenen, aber von sehr verschiedenen Stämmen bewohnten und von den Fúl-be eroberten Landschaft konnte mir die Kenntniss des Kanúri so gut wie gar nichts nützen und ich musste Alles daran setzen, mich mit dem in jenen Landschaften, wenigstens von der herrschenden Klasse, gesprochenen Ful-fúl-de- oder, wie ich es ferner aus weiterhin auszuführenden Gründen nennen will, Fúl-Idiom einigermassen bekannt zu machen. Schon in Kátsena und Kanō, wo die Fúl-be ebenfalls den herrschenden Stamm bilden, hatte ich angefangen, dieser Sprache einige Aufmerksamkeit zu schenken, aber ihr, abgesehen von später aufgenommenen Wörtern, der Haussa-Sprache so unendlich fern liegendes Glossar und ihre gänzlich verschiedene grammatische Konstruktion hatten mich abgeschreckt. Mit um so grösserem Eifer machte ich mich dagegen jetzt daran, sobald — Anfang Mai 1851 — jene Reise bestimmt vor mir lag, da sie mir die Aussicht eröffnete, längere Zeit in von jenem Stamme bewohnten Landschaften mich aufzuhalten, wo ich nur mit Hülfe dieser Sprache hoffen konnte, etwas Tüchtiges zu leisten, und ich hatte an dem in meinen Reisen, Th. II, S. 433, erwähnten Mohámmedu einen höchst aufgeweckten und bereitwilligen Lehrmeister.

Hier bildete nun wieder die Haussa-Sprache die leichte Vermittlerin und sie ging Hand in Hand mit der Kanúri-Sprache, da mein Geleitsreiter, der Kaschella Bíllama (Reis. Th. II, S. 435), ausser Fúl nur diese Sprache verstand, und zwar in sehr schöner, reiner Form. So schritt mein Vokabular der Fúl-Sprache rasch vorwärts und ich ward wenigstens fähig, sehr viel von dem Gehörten zu verstehen, wenn ich auch nur sehr stümperhaft sprechen konnte. Aber dieses Studium sollte nicht lange währen; denn, als der in Yola residirende Statthalter von Adamaua mich schon nach drei Tagen aus der Hauptstadt zurückwies, liess ich vorläufig die Beschäftigung

influence the Hausa-language, which must have been developed at a much earlier period, has evidently exercised as well upon many verbal forms, as upon other parts of the language of Bórnu. And I make use of this opportunity for pointing out the absurdity of derivating the name of the Kanúri-language from the name of the town or province of Kanó, as one of the critics of my researches has done, even if we look only at the character of the idiom and leave all the historical relations out of the question.

On thus leaving the territory of the idiom, with which I had become familiarized, I was even obliged to try to forget what I had achieved to learn with great pains, in order to apply myself with all possible energy, and with an unprejudiced mind, to my new field. For nothing is more provoking to the unprotected traveller among people in such a state of nature and especially, if he himself be so badly provided as I then was, than not to be able to converse with them in their own language, at least with regard to the common occurrences of daily life. For neither then, nor at any other period of my travels, had I any interpreter as such, having at that time one single servant as a factotum for all kinds of service, Mohammed, a native of Ghatrón of almost pure Tédá-blood, and very little versed in good Arabic, while he was tolerably well acquainted with the Kanúri-language. I therefore betook myself to my new task under the best mistress necessity, but when arrived in the capital of the Bórnu empire did not find that opportunity of learning the Kanúri-language, which would have been desirable. For on the one hand Kukawa, with its present dynasty of the Kánemíyin and with Hadj Beshír as vizier at the head of the government, at that period was justly to be called the seat of a second hand copy of Arab civilization, while at the same time just at that moment the conflux of pilgrims from distant countries, some of them on their return from, others on their way to Mecca, was so great, that I could not allow to pass by this splendid opportunity of obtaining new geographical material of the utmost importance; the result of these two circumstances being, that my study of the Kanúri-language at that time did not make that progress, which they might otherwise have made.

But to the circumstances mentioned we must still add the project of my journey to Adamawa, cherished with great zeal and never left out of sight. Now, in that province, comprised originally under the name of Fúmbina and inhabited by a great many different tribes, but at present conquered by the Fúl-be, the knowledge of the Kanúri-language could be of no avail to me; and I was obliged to endeavour by all means, to make acquaintance and become familiarized with the Ful-fúl-de- or Fúl-language, such as it is spoken in that province, at least by the dominating class. Already in Kátsena and Kano, where the Fúl-be constitute likewise the dominating class, I had begun to dedicate some time to a preparatory knowledge of this language, but the difference of its glossary from that of the Hausa-idiom, if we do not take into regard words introduced at a later period, and its entirely peculiar grammatical construction had then deterred me from its study. But with the greater zeal I now applied myself to the latter, as soon as — beginning of May 1851 — the said journey lay distinctly before me, as it opened to me the prospect, that I might be allowed to make a longer stay in a country occupied and ruled by that tribe, where nothing but the knowledge of this very language could enable me, to make full use of the opportunity offered to me; and I found a very clever and communicative master in Mohámmedu, the person mentioned Tr. II p. 340.

Here again the Hausa-language together with the Kanúri constituted the supple medium of recognition, for my escort, the kashélla Bíllama (Tr. II, p. 352), besides Fúl understood nothing but the latter idiom, and in a very pure form. Thus my vocabulary of the Fúl made steady progress, and I learnt to understand at least a good deal of the household talk of the people, and could keep up a short conversation. But the study thus commenced was not to last long; for, as soon as the governor of Adamawa, who had his residence in Yóla, sent me back after a three day's stay, I again relinquished the study of this language, and the sequel

mit der Fúl-Sprache wieder liegen; auch war es wol gut, dass ich dem in Adamaua gesprochenen Dialekt nicht mehr Aufmerksamkeit schenkte, weil er, wie sich später ergab, ausserordentlich viele Idiotismen und Barbarismen enthält.

Also schon von diesem Tage an, dem 4ten Juni 1852, beschäftigte ich mich, so weit mein in Folge der längst eingetretenen Regenzeit leidender, durch fehlgeschlagene Hoffnungen noch mehr geschwächter körperlicher Zustand und die Strapazen der bei ungeheuerer Wasserfluth durch höchst unsichere Gegenden gemachten Reise es gestatteten, wiederum auf das Eifrigste mit der Kanúri-Sprache, und der gefällige und gebildete Kaschella verbesserte und ergänzte mein Glossar und meine Phrasensammlung mit der grössten Freude. Dieses Studium setzte ich dann in Kúkaua fort und hatte hier nun neben Bilama die beiden, den vornehmsten Ständen angehörigen und mit der in diesen Ländern höchsten Bildung begabten, Männer, Hadž Edris (Reisen, Th. III, S. 135) und Sittna Makarémma (Th. II, S. 374) zu Lehrern, aber leider war der Letztere ein höchst widerlicher alter Gauner und durchtriebener Schurke, sonst hätte ich von diesem Häftling der alten reinen Kanúri-Dynastie der Séfua das schönste Kanúri lernen und so Koelle's Arbeit besser controliren können.

Es folgte dann, vom 11ten September 1851 an, mein leidensvoller, unglücklicher Zug nach Kánem; auch er hielt sich auf Bórnu-Gebiet, wenn auch mit einem etwas abweichenden Dialekt; aber theils waren meine Kräfte durch immerwährendes Fieber und oft fürchterliche Märsche gänzlich erschöpft, theils war unsere Umgebung, wildes Kriegsvolk, so ungebildet und dazu meist Araber, weniger Kanúri und Kánem-bu, und die Letzteren noch dazu wenig mittheilsam, dass meine Fortschritte in der Kenntniss dieser Sprache während dieses Zeitraumes überaus gering waren.

Dagegen legte ich während unseres Aufenthaltes in Kánem zuerst Hand an ein Glossar der **Tédā-Sprache**, da wir auf diesem Zuge mit einigen der südlichen Abtheilungen dieses, über ungeheuere Strecken ausgebreiteten, Volksstammes, der seit alten Zeiten hier in Kánem sass (Reis. Th. III, S. 445, 456), fortwährend in Berührung traten, und es war sehr Schade, dass ich nicht Kraft und Zeit genug besass, diese Gelegenheit weiter auszubeuten und besonders mehr Phrasen und Geschichten, die wahre Quintessenz solcher linguistischer Studien, aus dem Munde dieser Eingeborenen niederzuschreiben, da, wie sich in der Folge ergab, dieser südliche Dialekt von dem nördlichen, mit dem ich später in Berührung kam und dem mein Gatroner angehörte, im Glossar wenigstens, ausserordentliche Abweichungen zeigt und im Ganzen wol viel reiner als der andere ist. Das Gesammtergebniss dieser meiner ersten Bekanntschaft mit der Tédā-Sprache war die klare Erkenntniss, dass diese Sprache in ihren Wurzeln mit der Kanúri-Sprache eng verwandt sei, und ich gab dieser Überzeugung Ausdruck in einem Briefe an Herrn Prof. Richard Lepsius, den ich später noch einmal näher berühren werde.

Eifriger, als auf diesem Zuge, wurde meine Kenntniss des Kanúri gefördert auf dem unmittelbar darauf folgenden Zuge in das Musgu-Land, der bis Anfang Februar 1852 dauerte und wo mir der oben erwähnte Hadž Edris wiederum zur Seite stand. Hier vervollkommnete ich denn mein Glossar der Kanúri-Sprache in der Weise, dass ich meinem Lehrer für jedes noch nicht in meinem Verzeichnisse stehende Wort oder Ausdruck einen Preis aussetzte. Zum Niederschreiben von Erzählungen war auch hier im Kriegslager keine Musse. Aber, was mein Glossar des Kanúri betrifft, so ist dasselbe, wenigstens was die ganze Lebenssphäre des Volkes angeht, keineswegs so unvollständig, als man auf den ersten Blick denken könnte, wenn auch einige Ausdrücke aus der höchsten Geistessphäre fehlen. Aber im Ganzen ist dies ein wich-

proved, that I had not foregone much by not paying more attention to the dialect spoken in Adamawa, as it turned out to contain a great many instances of idiotism and barbarism.

From this day onward, the 4th of June 1852, the Kanúri-language again constituted the chief medium of my conversation and even of my study, as far as my constitution allowed it, suffering greatly as I was in consequence of the many fatigues of the journey, and still more debilitated by mental anxiety and disappointment. While thus passing through territories infested by hostile tribes, and inundated by the heavy rains of the season, the communicative and well educated kašella corrected and completed my glossary and my collection of Kanúri-phrases most cheerfully. This study I afterwards continued in Kúkawa, where, besides Bíllama, I had two principal masters, and authorities, both of them belonging to the highest rank of society in these countries, and both possessing the highest culture of mind of which these people are capable; one of these persons was the Hadž Edrís (Tr. III, p. 148), the other Šitima Makarémma (Tr. II, p. 289); the latter being the more clever of the two, and capable of rendering greater service in this respect, as he belonged to the court of the old Kanúri-dynasty of the Séfua, but being such a despicable old rogue and so very exacting, that I could not make all the use of him which it would have been desirable.

Then followed from the 11th Sept. 1851 my wearisome and unfortunate expedition to Kánem, offering new opportunities of improving the knowledge of this language, notwithstanding a slight dialectical difference of the idiom spoken in that province. But on the one hand my physical strength, affected by a lasting attack of ague, became totally exhausted by heavy marches sometimes of extraordinary length, on the other our company on this expedition consisted of people of such an uncivilized character, being most of them the wildest set of freebooters and moreover of Arab extraction, while only a small number were Kanúri or Kánem-bú and even these not very communicative, that I made scarcely any progress in the knowledge of the Kanúri during this period.

Thus, almost the only linguistical profit, which I derived from my stay in Kánem, was the commencement of a glossary of the Tédā-language, we having come in contact on this expedition with some of the southernmost divisions of this tribe, scattered over immense tracts of country and settled in Kánem since the remotest times (Tr. III, p. 482, 492); and it was a great pity, that I did not possess strength and time enough, to be able to derive all the profit possible from this opportunity, and especially to write down from the mouth of the natives a greater number of stories, and phrases, the nerve and essence of such linguistical studies. For this southern dialect of the Tédā-language proved afterwards, when I came in contact with the northern one, which was also the language spoken by my servant from Ghatrón, to differ greatly from the latter, at least as far as regards the glossary, and on the whole it may be much purer. The chief general result of this my first acquaintance with the Tédā-language was the full conviction, that this language was intimately related to the Kanúri-language with regard to its roots; and I expressed this opinion accompanied by a few general remarks in a letter addressed to Mr. Lepsius, which I shall have occasion to mention once more further on.

More zealously, than on this expedition, my knowledge of the Kanúri was furthered on the immediately following expedition into the Musgu-country, which lasted till beginning of February 1852. Here, while the above mentioned Hadž Edrís was again at my side, I perfected my glossary of the Kanúri-language in such a way, that I gave some slight recompense to my teacher for every correction, or every new term or phrase, which he was able to offer me for my vocabulary, but as for writing down stories the camp-life offered very little leisure. But thus much I dare say, that my glossary of the Kanúri, at least with regard to the sphere of daily life of the people, is not at all so incomplete and defective, as some people might fancy, even if some terms belonging to mental conception are wanting. I must lay stress upon this

tiger Punkt bei dem Vergleich meiner Sammlung mit Koelle's Arbeiten, und da ich leider die letzteren im Lande noch nicht selbst controliren konnte, erwarte und hoffe ich, dass ein späterer Forscher, dem es vergönnt sein mag, Bórnu zu besuchen, und der auf diese Untersuchung eingehen will, finden wird, dass Koelle sehr viele idiomatische Ausdrücke hat, die im eigentlichen Bórnu nicht bekannt oder wenigstens zur Zeit nicht im Gebrauch sind. Auch ich habe ja Hunderte von Ausdrücken, die bei Koelle fehlen, obgleich ich selbst nicht unterlassen will, anzuführen, dass Koelle selbst sein Vokabular als in keiner Weise vollständig ansieht, wie denn schon seine Grammatik viele Ausdrücke, besonders Verba, enthält, die im Vokabular fehlen. Aber der hochverdiente Missionar selbst ist schon einem derartigen Einwande entgegengekommen durch die treffenden Bemerkungen, die er in dieser Beziehung (S. V der Vorrede zu seiner Grammatik) macht, indem er ausdrücklich angibt, dass die Sprache seiner Grammatik (und seines Vokabulars) dasjenige Kanúri (derjenige Dialekt des Kanúri) sei, wie es in der grossen Provinz Gasir gesprochen werde, oder vielmehr wie es gesprochen worden wäre zur Zeit, als sein Dolmetscher (die einzige ganz individuelle Autorität, aus deren Munde er in fünfjähriger Geistes-Pumpwerkstätte in Sierra Leone seine Arbeiten komponirte) seine Heimath verlassen habe, d. h. um das Jahr 1812. Seitdem habe eine neue Dynastie aus Kánum — so schreibt er statt Kánem — die alte Kanúri-Dynastie verdrängt, so dass die heutige Hofsprache Bórnu's der Kanum-Dialekt sei, der einigermassen von dem Kanúri seiner Grammatik abweiche, und weniger rein zu sein scheine als letzteres, das er als die Sprache der herrschenden Klasse, als die eigentliche National-Sprache des Landes betrachtet.

Anlass zu solcher Bemerkung gab Koelle wol, der auch in seiner Polyglotta auf meine Sammlungen Rücksicht nimmt, was ich später zu berühren Gelegenheit haben werde, ein oberflächlicher Einblick in mein Vokabular, das ich schon vor meiner Abreise von Bórnu nach Timbuktu im Herbst 1853 an Ritter v. Bunsen schickte, der es zuerst Englischen Sprachforschern, wie Mr. Latham, und den Missionaren mittheilte und dann an Herrn Prof. Lepsius nach Berlin schickte. Ich wollte hier diesen Punkt nur im Allgemeinen berühren, indem ich darauf ausdrücklich hinweisen muss, dass meine Sammlung nicht nach einem oder mehreren einzelnen Individuen bloss niedergeschrieben, sondern im täglichen Gebrauch in den verschiedensten Provinzen des Bórnu-Reiches controlirt wurde; weiter unten, bei den Bemerkungen des zweiten Kapitel's, werde ich Gelegenheit haben, den Punkt im Allgemeinen zu besprechen, wie wir bei den linguistischen Arbeiten von Missionaren trotz des unschätzbaren Vorzugs derselben in grammatischer Vollständigkeit, wie sie nur in langem Stillleben an Einem Orte zu erzielen und den stets erregten und beunruhigten Reisenden und Entdeckern völlig unmöglich ist, doch immer den Nachtheil im Auge behalten müssen, dass sie nicht diejenige Sprache darstellen, wie sie im Grossen und Ganzen im Munde des Volkes lebt, sondern wie sie in einem mehr oder minder beschränkten Dialekt im Munde weniger Individuen klingt, und zwar solcher, auf welche sie, die sprachgebildeten Europäer, selbst direkten intellektuellen Einfluss in langem geistigen Verkehr geübt haben. Und nun vergleiche man damit den maasslos abweichenden Unterschied der Dialekte einer durch Schrift nicht fixirten Sprache. Wir können also wol mit Recht und ohne Anmassung den Grundsatz aufstellen, dass sich die Arbeiten der Missionare und Reisenden gegenseitig ergänzen und verbessern können und sollen.

Auf diesem Músgu-Feldzug war es auch, wo ich mein Glossar der Wándalá-Sprache, die in dem von Denham, der in Bórnu üblichen Aussprache gemäss, Mándara genannten, jetzt in ganz enge Grenzen umschränkten Ländchen im Süden des Tsád gesprochen wird, aus dem Munde eines aufgeweckten Sklaven jener Nation und durch Vermittelung der Kanúri-Sprache

point, which is of great importance, and which nobody must lose sight of, when comparing my labours with those of Koelle's, and as I myself was not able to control among the natives each word of the vocabulary of the latter, as it was then not yet published, I hope and expect, that some future traveller, who may have the good fortune of visiting Bórnu, and who may enter upon this enquiry, will find, that Koelle's books contain a good many idiomatical terms not known in Bórnu Proper, or at least not now in common use. I myself on the other hand have some hundreds of terms, which are wanting in Koelle; though I must not omit to state, that Koelle himself does probably not look upon his vocabulary as in any way complete, as he himself has many words in his grammar, which are wanting in the latter. And the highly meritorious missionary himself has obviated and anticipated an objection like the preceding one by the striking remarks, which he himself has exposed (in the preface to his grammar, p. V), stating distinctly, that the language of his grammar (and, we may add, of his vocabulary too) is the Kanúri, „as it is spoken in the large province of Gasir" or perhaps more correctly, as it was spoken there at the time, „when his interpreter left his home", that is to say, about the year 1812, and this single individual person, we must not forget, was the sole authority, from the mouth of whom through an uninterrupted labour of five years the Rev. Koelle wrote down and composed his works. Since that period a new dynasty originating from Kānem — it is thus he writes the name of Kānem — dispossessing the old Kanúri-dynasty, came to the throne of Bórnu, the consequence being, as he says, „that the court language of Bórnu at the present day is the Kānem-dialect, which somewhat differs from, and seems to be less pure than the Kanúri" (of his grammar), which he looks upon as the language of the ruling class and therefore as the national language of the country.

The first motive and inducement for making such remarks the Rev. Koelle may have found in a superficial knowledge of my own vocabularies, although he does not mention them distinctly, while, as I shall have opportunity of remarking with regard to the language of the Yédina or Búdduma, he mentions expressly my collection of shorter vocabularies, both collections having been forwarded by me to the Chevalier Bunsen before my leaving Bórnu for Timbuktu in November 1853, and the Chevalier having shewn them to the English linguists, such as Mr. Latham, and the missionaries, before he sent them to Mr. Lepsius of Berlin. Here I wanted only to touch on this point in general, while I must call the attention of the reader distinctly to the point, that my Kanúri-vocabulary has not merely been written down from the mouth of one or more individuals, but has been controlled by the daily use of common life in the different provinces of the Bórnu empire. In the second chapter I shall have the opportunity of illustrating the general remark, how the linguistical labours of the missionaries, with a very few exceptions, use to have the defect, that they do not represent the languages, such as they live in the mouth of the people, but such as they are spoken in one peculiar dialect of more or less circumscribed limits by a few individuals, who, we must well remark, have long been worked upon by the intellectual influence of the missionaries; at the same time no body will deny, that the labours of these indefatigable men have an inestimable advantage in grammatical perfection, such as is only obtainable in the course of a long and quiet residence in one place, while it is quite out of the question for the dangerous and nomadic life of a traveller and explorer. But the right way seems to be, that the labours of both should tend to supply and correct each other, for the traveller will be able to represent many features, which must escape the missionary, especially if we take into regard the enormous discrepancy of dialects of a language, the use of which is not fixed by writing.

It was likewise on my expedition to the Músgu-country, that I wrote down my vocabulary of the Wándalā-idiom from the mouth of a slave of that nation through the medium of the Kanúri-language. That idiom is spoken by the inhabitants of the Wándalā- or Mándara-country, as it is generally known in Europe on the authority of Capt. Denham, a very small

niederschrieb. Dieses geschah langsam und wohlbedächtig im Beisein und unter Kontrole des obengenannten Hadž Edris und das Glossar ward später mittelst anderer Individuen jenes Stammes mehrfach kontrolirt und zuverlässig befunden [1].

Das Kanúri blieb neben dem Arabischen auch meine gewöhnliche Umgangssprache auf meiner Reise nach Bagirmi und während meines längeren Aufenthaltes daselbst, vom 4ten März bis zum 20sten August 1852, sowie während meines nachherigen Aufenthaltes in der Hauptstadt Bórnu's und auf meiner Reise bis Zinder am Ende desselben Jahres.

In Bagirmi nun verfertigte ich, vorzüglich mit Hülfe des gesinnungstüchtigen Patrioten und einsichtsvollen, frommen Mannes Bu-Bekr aus Bákada (Reis. Th. III, S. 299) ein sehr vollständiges und zuverlässiges Glossar der Bagirmi-Sprache, schrieb eine grosse Menge Phrasen, wie ich sie mir als Norm vorgezeichnet hatte, aus dem gewöhnlichen Reiseleben auf, um besonders Reisenden praktischen Nutzen zu gewähren und hatte selbst angefangen, mich der Sprache geistig etwas zu bemeistern und mir einen Einblick in ihren grammatischen Bau zu verschaffen, als das unverständige Benehmen der Einwohner oder vielmehr der Landesregierung gegen mich mir auch die Sprache verleidete.

Ich will schon an dieser Stelle angeben, dass Denham's kurzes Vokabular der Bégrimma-Sprache, das er als solches gibt [2], ziemlich richtig ist, während auch die wenigen Sprachproben, die er in Karnak Lógone niederschrieb [3] und für Lógone ausgab, gar nicht dem Lógone, sondern dem Bégrimma angehören, wogegen, was Koelle in seiner Polyglotta (XII, C, 3) für Bégrimma ausgibt, zum grossen Theil reines Haussa ist, indem der junge Sklave, aus dessen Munde er es niederschrieb, „der einzige Repräsentant seines Stammes in Sierra Leone" [4], seine Muttersprache offenbar und ganz natürlich zum grossen Theil vergessen hatte und dafür Wörter gab, die er von seinen Haussa-Kameraden gelernt.

In Más-eña, der Hauptstadt Bagirmi's, verfasste ich auch mein Glossar der Mába-Sprache, allerdings fast einzig und allein aus dem Munde eines einzigen Individuums, aber dieses war ein höchst aufgeweckter und zuverlässiger Mann, der Fáki Ibrahim, der sich zum Gelehrten auszubilden suchte, und ich betrieb diese Arbeit mit grosser Musse und Bedächtigkeit. Aber allerdings gibt dies Vokabular nicht die ganze Fülle der lebenden Volkssprache, und ich wünsche nichts sehnlicher, als dass dieselbe nun von Herrn Munzinger, dem Theilnehmer an der Heuglin'schen Expedition, im Falle sie auch nur leidlichen Erfolg hat, in ihrer ganzen Fülle erforscht werden möge. Bei Aufnahme dieses Vokabulars war die Arabische Sprache die Vermittlerin. Da nun Ibrahim dem besonderen Stamme der A'bu Sarib [5] angehörte, schrieb ich unter seiner Leitung auch mein kurzes Glossar dieser letzteren Sprache, die vom Mába ganz verschieden ist.

Dagegen ward das Niederschreiben des Vokabulars der Lógone-Sprache, das auch auf diese Reise fällt, durch das Kanúri vermittelt, und zwar waren meine Haupt-Autoritäten dabei ein sehr gemüthliches, gefälliges Ehepaar, das sich gegenseitig vervollständigte und ergänzte und bei mehrfacher Kontrole sich als vollkommen zuverlässig erwies. Nur muss

---

1) Mit den betreffenden Wörtern meines Glossars stimmen die von Denham gegebenen, ungefähr 80 an Zahl (Appendix XIX), im Ganzen ziemlich überein. Auffallend sind nur die Ausdrücke für 1 und 2: mtaqaa (mtake) und sardah; mtake erinnert an tek im Mába.

2) Denham and Clapperton, Tr. and Disc. II, Appendix N. XVIII. Begharmi vocabulary, taken from the mouth of the late Sultan's son, now a slave of the Sheikh of Bornou. — Seetzen's kurzes Verzeichniss von Begirma-Wörtern (in Vater's Sprachensammlungen S. 345) ist, abgesehen von den Zahlen, schlecht. Dagegen ist sein Verzeichniss von Wörtern und Redensarten aus der Sprache von Mobba (Mába), ebenda S. 305 ff., im Ganzen ziemlich richtig.

3) Denham and Clapperton, Travels and Discoveries, I, S. 336 ff.

4) Polyglotta, Introductory Remarks p. 17.

5) Über die A'bu Sarib s. Reis. und Entd., Anhang zu Bd. III, S. 509 f.

and limited territory to the south of lake Tsâd. I took down this vocabulary with care and diligence in the presence and under the control of the above mentioned Hadž Edrís, and had afterwards repeated opportunity of controlling it with other persons, when it was found correct and exact [1]).

The Kanúri together with the Arabic remained my common medium of conversation also on my journey to Bagírmi and during my stay in that country from the 4th of March till the 20th of August 1852, as well as during my further stay in the capital of Bórnu and on my journey to Zinder towards the end of that year.

In Bagírmi therefore I composed, especially with the assistance of the excellent patriot and the very intelligent and pious Bu-Bakr from Bákada (Tr. III, p. 339), a very complete and reliable glossary of the Bágrimma-language, wrote a good many phrases, such as I had marked them out, as being the most common object of conversation on a journey, and most useful to travellers, and I had even begun, to master a little the language and to procure me an insight into its grammatical structure, when the suspicious and imprudent behaviour of the inhabitants, or rather of the government against me made me relinquish that study.

Already in this place I will state, that the short vocabulary of the Bágrimma-language, given as such by Capt. Denham [2]), in general is correct, and what he heard in Kurnak Lógoné too and whence he concluded the similarity or identity of the language of Lógoné [3]) with that of Bagírmi, belonged likewise to this idiom and not to that of Lógoné at all, while, what Rev. Koelle gives in his Polyglotta (XII, C, 3) under the name of Bágrimma, mostly consists of pure Hausa-elements, the young slave, from the mouth of whom he wrote down his specimens, being, as Koelle says [4]), „the only representant of his tribe in Sierra Leone", having very naturally forgotten the greater part of his native idiom and adopted instead terms, which he had learnt from his Hausa-comrades.

In Más-eña, the capital of Bagírmi, I composed also the vocabulary of the Mába-language, indeed almost exclusively from the mouth of one single individual, but this individual being a very clever and reliable person, the fakih Ibrahim, who visited the Western countries of Negroland, in order to acquire the highest possible degree of Mussulman learning, and I absolved this work with leisure and diligence. But, no doubt, this vocabulary can by no means give a correct idea of the living language of the people, and I express my ardent wish, that in this respect, as well as in so many others, regarding the ethnological state of this quarter of Africa, Mr. Werner Munzinger, who accompanies the Heuglin-expedition, may add largely to our store of knowledge. In taking down this vocabulary the Arabic served as the starting point. But the above mentioned Ibrahím belonging to the particular tribe of the A'bū Sărib [5]), I wrote down from his mouth also a short glossary of the latter idiom, which, as we shall see, is totally distinct from the Mába-language.

While in this instance the Arabic served as the medium, in writing down the vocabulary of the Lógonē-idiom, which was likewise completed during this journey, I started from the Kanúri and used as chief authorities a very cheerful and communicative old couple, who completed and corrected each other, and on repeated occasions, when I had an opportunity of controlling, what

[1]) The words given by Capt. Denham (about 80 in number) in the XIXth appendix to his Narrative in general, besides differences in spelling, agree well with the corresponding ones in my vocabulary; only the terms for „one" and „two" disagree entirely, he giving mtaque (mtaka) for the first and cardah for the latter.

[2]) Denham and Clapperton, Tr. and Disc. II, Appendix no. XVIII. Begharmi vocabulary, taken from the mouth of the late Sultan's son, now a slave of the Sheikh of Bornou. — The short glossary of this language by Seetzen, in the „Sprachensammlungen" of Vater p. 248, is incorrect with the exception of the numerals, while on the other hand the collection of words made by him of the Mába-, or as he spells, Mobba-idiom and published p. 300 ff. of the same book in general is tolerably correct.

[3]) Denham and Clapperton, Travels and Discoveries, I, p. 236 ff.

[4]) Polyglotta, Introductory Remarks p. 17.

[5]) With regard to the A'bū Sărib see Tr. and Disc. III, Appendix p. 542.

ich bedauern, dass ich dieser Sprache insbesondere nicht mehr Zeit widmen konnte, da, so unwichtig sie auch bei der Kleinheit und politischen Nichtigkeit des Ländchens ist, sie doch einerseits durch ihre verwandtschaftlichen Beziehungen zu anderen Sprachen, besonders zum Hausa, wie sie sich durch meine Arbeiten ergeben werden, sowie andererseits als ein ausführlicheres Beispiel der grossen Gruppe der Mass-Sprachen, von deren übrigen Abtheilungen oder Dialekten ich sonst nur kürzere Vokabularien besitze, grosses Interesse zu verdienen scheint und wol dazu berufen sein mag, einige der wichtigsten Fragen in Betreff dieses wunderbaren Sprachenknäuels Central-Afrika's zu lösen.

So habe ich also im Ganzen genommen länger als zwei Jahre das Kanúri zu meiner hauptsächlichen Verkehrssprache gemacht, mit bald grösserem, bald geringerem Eifer es zu beherrschen gesucht, und ich kann wol sagen, dass ich diese Sprache leidlich richtig gesprochen habe, obgleich sie so gut wie das Hausa, das seiner reichen, leicht fortbildenden Lebenskraft, sowie seines grossen Vokalreichthums halber einmal meine Vorliebe auf das Entschiedenste gewonnen hatte und deshalb oft auch auf anderen Gebieten bei mir vorwog, wo ich mit Hausa-Leuten in Berührung kam. Jener Zeitraum von zwei Jahren schliesst übrigens auch meinen letzten Aufenthalt in Bórnu unmittelbar vor meiner Rückkehr nach Europa ein, der fast 6 Monate umfasste, aber mir dennoch nur wenig Gelegenheit bot, die noch etwa vorhandenen Lücken auszufüllen, da ich damals einerseits vollständig erschöpft war, andererseits vor Heimweh fast verging.

Mit meiner Ankunft in Badamóni am 22sten December 1852, auf meinem Zuge nach Timbúktu, betrat ich wiederum zu meiner grossen Freude das Gebiet der Hausa-Sprache und verkehrte in ihr nicht allein bis zu meiner Ankunft am Niger, den 20sten Juni 1853, bis wohin sie meine fast ausschliessliche Verkehrssprache blieb, und während meiner Rückreise von Sai bis zum Eintritt in Bórnu, von Anfang August bis Anfang December 1854, sondern auch während meiner ganzen übrigen Reise, da ich mit dem Zaberma-Burschen Sambo und mit dem freigelassenen Hausa-Knaben Dýrregu oder Dórugu ausschliesslich, mit dem Margi-Burschen A'bbega vorzugsweise in dieser Sprache verkehrte.

Diese beiden Freigelassenen, über die ich schon in meinen Reisen mehr gesagt habe (Th. IV, S. 9 f.), würden mir auch in Europa bei Ausarbeitung meiner Vokabularien von grossem Nutzen gewesen sein; aber leider konnte ich mich die erste Zeit nach meiner Rückkehr in England nicht mit linguistischen Studien befassen, da ich erst meine geographischen Resultate ausarbeiten musste, und während dieser Zeit zogen der Missionar Schön und seine Freunde es vor, mir diese Leute, die ich mit vielen Kosten und mit Unannehmlichkeiten aller Art nach Europa gebracht hatte, um bei ferneren Afrikanischen Expeditionen nützlich zu sein, und die ich ihnen mit grösster Freude friedlich überlassen hatte, mit Hinterlist und Gewalt aus den Händen zu reissen. So hat denn das Publicum die Vervollkommnung dieser Hausa-Studien von Herrn Schön zu fordern, dem diese schöne Gelegenheit, seine Hausa-Studien zu vervollkommnen, zu Theil geworden ist. Auch hat er schon einen guten Theil der Biblischen Bücher mit Hülfe Dýrregu's in die Hausa-Sprache übersetzt und steht diesen Augenblick im Begriff, eine vollständige Grammatik derselben herauszugeben, aber gegen seine Schreibweise habe ich viel einzuwenden, da er die bei seinen früheren unvollkommenen Studien einmal angenommenen falschen Grundsätze nicht hat aufgeben wollen. Natürlich war mein Leben bei meinen mühsamen Reisen und unzähligen anderen Beschäftigungen zu unruhig, um auch nur in dieser Sprache zahlreiche lange Geschichten niederzuschreiben und sie bis auf den Grund zu erforschen.

Sobald der Nutzen des Hausa beim alltäglichen Verkehr mit den Leuten, unter denen ich weilte, aufhörte, legte ich mich mit Eifer auf das Erlernen einerseits des Sońγai, andererseits des Ful-fúl-de oder Fūl. Aber einem auch nur mittelmässigen Erfassen der ersteren Sprache

they had stated, proved, that their information was of a most reliable character. I only regret, that I was prevented from giving more time to the study of this language, as notwithstanding the very limited territory, in which it is spoken, and the entire insignificance of the country in political respect: yet, in consequence of its alliences and relations with other languages, especially the Hausa, as I hope to prove in a future chapter, and in its character as a more elaborate specimen of the large group of the Masai-languages, of which great and important branch I have only a few short glossaries of some of the other dialects, this language seems to merit a considerable interest, and may be destined to solve one day some of the most difficult questions with regard to that wonderfully entangled coil of Central-African languages.

Thus, taken altogether, the Kanúri-idiom during a period of more than two years constituted preeminently my medium of conversation with the natives, I endeavouring, according to circumstances and the state of my health, with more or less zeal, to master the language with all its peculiarities, and I dare say, that I spoke it with a tolerable degree of accuracy and fluency, although never so well as the Hausa, which, on account of its copious as well as forcible and flexible character and from its richness in vowels, had once for all won my special predilection, which was the reason, why I preferred conversing in this idiom, whenever I came in contact with Hausa-people. The period of two years, however, includes also my last stay in Bórnu immediately before my return to Europe, comprising a space of about six months, but offering to me very little opportunity of filling out the vacancies and defects still existing in my knowledge as well as in my vocabulary, totally exhausted as I was at the time, and lingering with the most ardent desire after my return to Europe.

With my arrival at Badamúni on my journey to Timbúktu, on the 22nd Dec. 1853, I again, to my sincere satisfaction, entered the territory of the Hausa-language, and used it almost exclusively as a means of conversation till the 20th June 1853, when I arrived at the Niger, and likewise during my home-journey from Say till my arrival at the frontiers of Bórnu, from beginning of August till beginning of December 1854. But even during the whole of my journey to Timbúktu and back I conversed in this language exclusively, as well with my Zaberma-servant Sambo as with the Hausa-boy Dyrregu or Dórugu, and even mostly with the Marghi-lad A'bbega.

The two last mentioned liberated slaves, with regard to whom I have said more in my Travels (IV, p. 9 f.), would have rendered me great service in my linguistical studies even after my return to Europe, if other people had not crossed my intentions. For in the commencement I was not able to apply myself to this class of labours, as I was obliged, to work out my geographical material, and meanwhile the Rev. Schön and his friends preferred obtaining by artifice and violence, what they might have obtained much easier by fair means, and thus to take out of my hands those people, whom to my great inconvenience and expense I had brought to Europe, that they might be useful on future expeditions. Thus the public has a right to expect the perfection of these Hausa-studies from the Rev. Schön, to whose lot this excellent opportunity of perfecting his Hausa-labours has fallen. And I am glad to say, that with the assistance of Dyrregu he has succeeded in translating into the Hausa-language a good part of the Holy Records, and is now about to publish a new edition of his grammar. But I have much to say against his way of spelling; and I regret, that he has not chosen to give up errors, which he had committed at a former period from very imperfect materials. Of course, my life as a traveller and explorer under most dangerous circumstances and, involved as it was in all sorts of mental and material occupations left me too little of repose and tranquillity, to penetrate to the bottom of these linguistical studies.

As soon, as the Hausa-language ceased to serve as my general means of conversation with the people, with whom I had to deal, I applied myself with great zeal to the learning of the Soñyai on the one and the Ful-fúl-de or Fūl on the other hand. But two

wirkten leider besonders zwei Umstände entgegen. Erstlich war ich, wie ich in dem Berichte meiner Reise (Th. IV, S. 252) erwähnt, nicht im Stande, mir ein aufgewecktes Individuum des Sonyai-Stammes zum steten Begleiter zu gewinnen, und zweitens ist in den Landschaften, die ich durchzogen und besucht habe, die Volksthümlichkeit dieses Stammes seit mehr als zwei Jahrhunderten dermaassen unterdrückt worden, dass die Sprache, anstatt sich fortzubilden, von der Ausbildung, die sie unzweifelhaft einst schon erreicht hatte, als das Sonyai-Reich den ersten Rang unter den Königreichen des Negerlandes einnahm, weit zurückgeschritten ist. Wenn wir daher auch schon jetzt wol mit Recht behaupten können, dass diese Sprache von allen denen, die ich in dieser Sammlung behandle, die ärmste und roheste ist, so müssen wir doch, ehe wir ein vollständiges Urtheil über sie fällen, abwarten, bis wir umfassendere Proben von demjenigen Idiom erhalten, das noch jetzt in den eng umgränzten freien Ursitzen dieses Stammes (Reis. V, S. 732) gesprochen wird.

Fast am rohesten und am meisten ausgeartet scheint der jetzige Dialekt der einheimischen Bevölkerung Túmbutu's oder Timbúktu's zu sein, wo die Mischung mit anderen Stämmen und der grosse Verkehr, so wie das Vorwiegen des Máśiy auf der einen Seite, in Folge des mächtigen Umsichgreifens jenes Stammes gleich nach Zertrümmerung des Sonyai-Reiches, und des Arabischen auf der anderen Seite, in Folge des frühen Vorwiegens gelehrter Bestrebungen, die Timbúktu schon im fünfzehnten Jahrhundert zum Range einer höchst einflussreichen theologischen Fakultät erhoben, vielleicht nie eine reine Ausbildung erlaubte. Und mein überaus bewegter und unruhiger Aufenthalt in dieser Stadt, während dessen die Eingeborenen sich von mir fern halten mussten, gestattete mir durchaus keine ruhige Beschäftigung mit der Sprache.

In A'gades war aller Wahrscheinlichkeit nach der Sonyai-Stamm nicht von Ursprung an heimisch, sondern es ward hier, gleichwie im Nachbarstädtchen Tegidda, nur in Folge der Eroberungen und des grossen organisatorischen Talentes des Sonyai-Herrschers Hadj Muhammed A'skia an die Stelle der vertriebenen oder vernichteten Berber-Bevölkerung eine zahlreiche Kolonie gepflanzt, die bis auf die Gegenwart den Hauptkern der städtischen Bevölkerung jenes merkwürdigen Ortes bildet. Da nun der hier gesprochene Dialekt, das Emgédesi, grosse Mischung mit der Berber-Sprache erlitten hat, besonders mit dem von den umwohnenden Kel-ói gesprochenen Auraṡíe, so habe ich aus dem während meines Aufenthaltes in jener Stadt verfassten Glossar[1]) nur solche Ausdrücke in diese Sammlung aufgenommen, die ich auch in anderen Landschaften in Gebrauch gefunden habe. Überhaupt ist dieses Vokabular der Sonyai-Sprache in den verschiedensten Landschaften des einst weit ausgedehnten, jetzt jämmerlich zerrissenen Reiches und mit vielen Unterbrechungen zu Stande gekommen; denn ich fand kein einziges Individuum dieses Stammes so offen mittheilend und geistig aufgeweckt, dass ich mich mit ihm hätte auf längere Zeit sprachlich beschäftigen können.

Meine Hauptautoritäten, abgesehen von einzelnen gelegentlichen Verbesserungen und Ergänzungen, sind folgende: der oben erwähnte Sambo, ein Mischling des Fúl- und Sonyai-Stammes aus Zaberma, der Berber-Mischling Schéicho aus Waláta (Reis. IV, S. 260 f.), Dádoh, ein mit sehr

[1]) Dieses Emgédesi-Vokabular ward zuerst veröffentlicht in meinem Berichte über A'gades in der Zeitschrift der K. Geogr. Gesellschaft zu London, Bd. XXII, und darauf in den Monatsberichten der Gesellsch. für Erdkunde, 1852.

circumstances in particular prevented my mastering the first of these two languages with some degree of perfection. In the first instance, as I have stated in the Narrative of my Travels (IV, p. 249), I was not able to attach to myself as a constant companion or servant some clever individual of the Soñyai-tribe, and secondly, in those districts through which my journey lay, the nationality of this tribe has been suppressed for the last two centuries to such a degree, that the language instead of making progress in developping that richness of forms and expression which, no doubt, it once possessed, when the Soñyai-empire stood foremost among the kingdoms of Negroland, has steadily gone backwards. Therefore, although we may already now suppose with some degree of certainty, that of all those languages, which I treat in this collection, the Soñyai-idiom is the poorest and less cultivated, yet, before we give a wellfounded judgement in this instance, we must wait till we get more numerous specimens of that dialect of this idiom, which even at the present time is spoken within the narrow limits of the seats of the as yet independent section of this tribe (Tr. IV, p. 246, 652 f.).

Perhaps the rudest and most degraded of these dialects of the Soñyai-language is that spoken at the present time by the inhabitants of the town of Tumbutu or Timbúktu, and I suppose the reason to be the mixture with other tribes, which was there greater than in other places, and the extensive trade and commerce, which settled there, as well as the predominating influence of the Mañiy element on the one hand, in consequence of the political importance of that tribe being immoderately strengthened by the destruction of the Soñyai-empire, and of the Arabic on the other, in consequence of the early preponderance of learned studies, which elevated the town of Timbúktu to the rank of a most influential theological faculty as early as the XVth century, all these various influences not allowing the native idiom, which they were not able to vivify, to develop and perfect its own individual character. Besides, my stay in the town and its neighbourhood, being accompanied by the most harassing circumstances, which frightened the natives away from me, did not allow me a quiet study of the language.

As far as regards A'gades, the Soñyai-tribe according to all probability was not indigenous in that town from its origin, just as was the case with the neighbouring town Tegídda, but became settled there in consequence of the conquests and the grand talent of organization and colonization possessed by that eminent Soñyai-ruler Hadj Mohammed A'skia, who in order to fill the place of the Berber-inhabitants, whom he had driven out or annihilated, transplanted to that place a considerable colony of his own people, who till the present day constitute the principal portion of the inhabitants of the town. The Emgédesi however, the dialect which is there spoken, having been greatly spoiled by intermixture with the Berber-language, especially with the Auraytye, the dialect spoken by the neighbouring tribe of the Kél-owi, I have only introduced into this vocabulary such terms of the glossary made during my stay in A'gades *), as I found afterwards to be used also in other districts or provinces of the Soñyai-empire. Altogether the various parts of this vocabulary of the Soñyai-language have successively been written down and with sundry long interruptions in the different districts and provinces of this once very extensive, but now greatly distracted empire, for I did not find one single individual belonging to this tribe of such open and communicative disposition, and of such a mental capacity, that I could have pursued with him for a longer time such linguistical labours.

If we do not take into account occasional corrections or additions, my chief authorities are the following: the above mentioned Sambo, a native of Zaberma and hybrid of the Fúl- and Soñyai-nation, the Berber-hybrid 'Amer Walâti (Tr. IV, p. 283), Dádeb, an individual of

---

*) This Emgédesi-vocabulary was first published together with my report on A'gades in the Journal of the R. Geogr. Soc. of London vol. XXII and thence passed into the „Monatsberichte" of the Geogr. Soc. at Berlin 1851.

geringer Arabischer Bildung ausgestatteter Soñyai aus Tímbutu, und A'bd-llahi, der aufgeweckte Gouverneur der unabhängigen Stadtgemeinde Tiñge (Reis. IV, S. 321). Von Letzterem hätte ich seiner eigenen Persönlichkeit halber, so wie in Anbetracht des hier noch ziemlich rein gesprochenen Soñyai, am meisten lernen können, wenn es mir vergönnt gewesen wäre, dort länger zu verweilen. So ist wol, wie gesagt, trotz des im Ganzen fast vierzehnmonatlichen Aufenthaltes, den ich auf dem weit ausgedehnten Gebiete dieser Sprache zwischen A'gades und dem Thale Fógha auf der einen und Tímbutu auf der anderen Seite machte, das Soñyai, besonders in grammatischer Beziehung, am ungenügendsten in meiner Sammlung vertreten; auch fehlt es ganz an allen individuellen Ausdrücken, die von feinem Auffassungsvermögen zeugen, wie z. B. die verschiedenartigsten Laute der Thiere in dieser Sprache, so viel ich davon kennen lernte, nur als ein monotones Schreien alle durch denselben Ausdruck dargestellt werden.

Schon bevor ich noch den Niger bei der Stadt Sai erreichte, in Kátsena, nahm ich meine Fúl-Studien wieder mit Eifer vor, machte auch oft einen Anlauf, die Sprache praktisch zu beherrschen, wurde jedoch darin durch das ausserordentlich Unterbrochene, wie in den Gebieten, die ich von Gando an zu durchziehen hatte, das Fúl zur Anwendung kam, an grösseren Fortschritten gehindert, während selbst unter den in den Hausa-Städten angesiedelten Fúl-be die Hausa-Sprache als die leichtere und fliessendere im Umgang stets weiter um sich greift. Noch in Sarayámo, am südlichsten Arm des grossen Wassernetzes des mittleren Niger, musste ich ziemlich viel in dieser Sprache verkehren, dann aber trat sie durch die offene Feindschaft, welche die Fúl-be von Másina gegen mich zu hegen anfingen, ganz zurück, und dies war für das Studium dieser Sprache ein grosser Verlust, weil es höchst interessant und wichtig gewesen wäre, unter den sehr abweichenden Dialekten dieser Sprache den in Másina üblichen in leidlicher Vollständigkeit zu vertreten, um zwischen Sókoto und Fúta-Djálo ein Zwischenglied zu haben. Während nämlich der Missionar Reichardt seine noch nicht veröffentlichten Studien[1] der Fúl-Sprache eben in dem Dialekte von Fúta-Djálo gemacht hat, wurde mein Vokabular dieser Sprache besonders erst während meines zweiten Aufenthaltes in Sókoto im September und Oktober 1854 vervollständigt, und bei diesem Dialekt ist der Einfluss der Hausa-Sprache sehr gross; aber genau, zuverlässig und in gewisser Beziehung reich ist mein Vokabular der Fúl-Sprache doch.

Zweites Kapitel.

Einige allgemeine Bemerkungen über meine Vokabularien.

Ich gehe nun zu einigen allgemeinen Bemerkungen in Betreff der Vokabularien und der durch sie vertretenen Sprachen über.

Meine Sammlung hat den doppelten Zweck, einerseits Sprachgelehrten und Ethnographen ein ziemlich reiches Material und einen ersten leidlich umfassenden Einblick in eine ein grosses Ländergebiet umfassende Anzahl von Sprachen dieses bis dahin, zumal in dieser Hinsicht, so wenig gekannten Erdtheiles zu gewähren, andererseits aber auch ihnen sowol wie besonders auch etwaigen Reisenden in jene Länder eine Übersicht der den ganzen Lebenskreis dieser Völker am meisten kennzeichnenden und beschreibenden Ausdrücke in geistiger wie materieller Beziehung vorzuführen.

[1] Reichardt hat, so viel mir bekannt, bisher nur ein A-B-C-Buch publicirt: „Primer of the Fulah-language by the Rev. C. L. Reichardt". Berlin 1859.

the native Soñyai-population of Tímbuktu, endowed with a very limited amount of Arabic learning, and finally Bá-Bakr, the clever and communicative governor of the independent community of Tiñge (Tr. IV, p. 310). From the latter, on account of his own personal disposition as well, as with regard to the rather pure character of the Soñyai-dialect there spoken, I might have learnt most, if circumstances had allowed me to make a longer stay in that place. Thus, although on the whole I spent nearly a period of fourteen months in the very extensive territory of this Soñyai-language, inclosed between A'gades and the valley of Fógha on the one and Timbúktu on the other hand, nevertheless the Soñyai, especially in grammatical respect, probably forms the weakest part of my whole collection. It is moreover wanting entirely in individual expressions, such as bear testimony to an acute sense of perception and distinction of the people; thus for instance the most different sounds of animals in the Soñyai-language, as far as I could make out, are all regarded and expressed as one uniform mode of crying.

Already in Kátsena, long before I reached the Niger at the town of Sai, I took up once more my Fúl-studies with great zeal; and from thence onward even repeatedly made an occasional attempt at dominating the language for the practical use of conversation, but the way in which the dominion of the Fúl-be is continually broken and interrupted on that road, did not allow me a fair exercise, while among those sections of this tribe settled in the Hausa-cities the Hausa-language as the easier and more fluent idiom becomes always of greater influence. However, even in Sarayámo, situated to the south of Timbúktu on the southern-most branch of the complicated net-work of the middle course of the Niger, I still had to converse a good deal in this language, when in consequence of the open hostility exercised against me by the Fúl-be of Másina it was entirely put aside; and this, no doubt, was a severe loss to the knowledge of this language in general, as it would have been rather interesting and important, to have a tolerably good vocabulary of the dialect used in the province of Másina, in order to serve among the different dialects of this language as a connecting link between the dialect of Sókoto and that of Futa Djalo. For, while the Rev. Reichardt has made his studies[*] in this language particularly from the latter dialect, my vocabulary of the Fúl-language was especially perfected and enriched during my second stay in Sókoto, September and October 1854, and with this dialect the influence of the Hausa-idiom is undoubtedly very powerful, a great many new words having been borrowed from it and having supplanted old indigenous terms. Nevertheless my vocabulary of this idiom, as far as it goes, is accurate and reliable and even in many respects tolerably complete.

Chapter the second.

A few general remarks on the whole of my vocabularies.

I now proceed to make a few general remarks with regard to my vocabularies and the languages represented by them.

My collection pursues a twofold purpose. For, while it intends giving to the linguist and ethnographer a tolerably copious material of, and a somewhat comprehensive insight into, a larger number of languages comprising a vast extent of territory, formerly very little known in this respect, on the other hand it purposes giving to them, but principally to the traveller in those regions, a general view of the whole sphere of life of those people in material as well as in mental respect, circumstantiated by the individual terms used with regard to each object.

---

*) The Rev. Reichardt has, as far as is known to me, published as yet nothing, but a Primer: „Primer of the Fulah-language by the Rev. C. L. Reichardt". Berlin 1859.

Der erste Zweck begründet meine Anordnung in die grossen Redegruppen, von denen die 1ste die Fürwörter, Partikeln und Zahlwörter umfasst, die 2te die Zeitwörter, die 3te die Nennwörter, die 4te die Eigenschaftswörter und Adverbien und die 5te Phrasen. Indem ich dieser Anordnung folgte, war es keineswegs meine Ansicht, damit die Meinung auszudrücken, dass die Fürwörter die erste und ursprüngliche geistige Sprachidee des Menschen wäre, im Gegentheil, fast immer sind sie, wie ich das bei den einzelnen Sprachen nachzuweisen versucht habe, spätere Bildungen, theils aus eigenen nationalen Elementen komponirt, theils aber auch sogar erst aus fremden Sprachen herübergenommen. Aber doch bilden unzweifelhaft diese Redetheile die einfachsten Elemente bei den nun einmal fertigen Sprachen. In Betreff der Zeitwörter und Nennwörter will ich hier eine andere allgemeine Bemerkung machen, die ich ebenfalls wieder bei den einzelnen Sprachen besonders begründen werde. Die Zeitwörter, wie sie uns jetzt vorliegen, sind fast insgesammt späte Bildungen und erst durch Zusammensetzung mit einem Hülfszeitwort entstanden; aber doch ist der infinitive Verbalbegriff meist das Ursprüngliche, von dem das Nennwort sowol wie die spätere Verbalform abgeleitet ist. Bei mehreren dieser Sprachen, besonders aber bei der Kandri-Sprache werde ich die ursprünglichen Wortformen abzulösen suchen, und so werden wir auch hier sehen, dass diese ursprünglichsten Begriffe des Menschen, die in der Sprache zum Ausdruck gekommen, einsilbig sind. Es werden nun Viele einen Einwand dagegen erheben, dass ich bei den Zeitwörtern die erste Person der unbestimmten Zeit *) als massgebend angenommen habe; hätte ich aber die der ursprünglichen Form entschieden viel näher liegende dritte Person gewählt, so würde das in denjenigen Sprachen, mit welchen ich nur eine ganz oberflächliche Kenntniss erlangt habe, zahlreiche Irrthümer hervorgerufen haben. Auch habe ich die Form der dritten Person sehr häufig neben der ersten angegeben.

Mit dem zweiten Zweck steht die Anordnung der Vokabularien nach Sachen in Zusammenhang, indem das Verzeichniss der Nennwörter, vom Allgemeinsten, Gott und der Natur, ausgehend durch Thier- und Pflanzenwelt zum Menschen übergeht und ihn zuerst in seinen körperlichen und geistigen, dann in seinen häuslichen, politischen und kaufmännischen Beziehungen darstellt. Etwas verschieden ist die Anordnung der Zeitwörter, indem ich hier die Erscheinungen der Natur und Handlungen der Thiere, als meist durch mangelhafte, unpersönliche Verbalformen ausgedrückt, ans Ende gestellt habe; die übrigen Zeitwörter aber gehen von der Geburt und Erzeugung des Menschen aus, umfassen dann seine gewöhnlichen körperlichen und geistigen Funktionen und gehen so zu den individuelleren Handlungen über. Diese Anordnung schien die zweckmässigste, und das Auffinden einzelner Ausdrücke soll durch Übersichten der grossen Klassen der Wörter am Ende des Werkes erleichtert werden. An eine alphabetische Anordnung war bei einer Zusammenstellung neun verschiedener einheimischer Sprachen, die wiederum in zwei Europäische übertragen werden sollten, nicht zu denken.

Natürlich hat die hier gewählte Anordnung ihre grossen Schwächen; dabei ist der Nachtheil einer der hauptsächlichsten, dass die Ausdrücke in den verschiedenen, einander gegenüberstehenden Sprachen oft sehr mannichfaltig abweichende Bedeutungen haben, die nicht in einer Spalte als ihnen allen gemeinsam zusammengestellt werden konnten. Diesem Mangel suchte ich durch Erläuterungen in den Anmerkungen so viel wie möglich abzuhelfen, indem ich auch in den Anmerkungen bei Gelegenheit begriffsverwandter Wörter meist solche Ausdrücke gab, die ich nur in wenigen der aufgeführten Sprachen erfahren hatte. Bei diesem Mangel, der jedoch bei Vokabularien, die trotz eines ansehnlichen Umfanges auf gründliche Vollständigkeit nicht den geringsten Anspruch machen, überhaupt sehr zurücktritt, hatte diese Anordnung den grossen Vortheil, dass

*) Im Allgemeinen habe ich da, wo in einer Sprache ein anderes Tempus gewählt ist, es besonders angemerkt.

The first purpose has caused me to arrange each language into five classes of words, the 1st of which comprises the pronouns, particles and numerals, the 2nd the verbs, the 3rd the nouns, the 4th the adjectives and adverbs and the 5th a number of phrases. While choosing this arrangement, I did not at all intend to give it as my opinion, that the pronouns were the first and original mental conception of man, as expressed by language; on the contrary, almost all of them are of recent formation, as I shall endeavour to prove under the head of each language, and, while part of them are indeed derived from national elements, others have even been borrowed from foreign languages. But, nevertheless, these parts of speech undoubtedly constitute the most simple elements of the languages, such as they are now. With regard to the verbs and nouns I here shall make another general remark, which I have endeavoured likewise to prove by more individual arguments with regard to each single language. The verbs, such as they are now before our eyes, almost all of them are of late formation and have been formed by adding an auxiliary verb to the original root, such as is the case also in many other languages, but the infinitive tense of the verb in most cases is the root, from whence both, the noun as well as the more recent verbal form, have been derived. Now, with regard to several of these languages, but the Kanúri in particular, I shall endeavour to disclose the original verbal roots, and thus we shall see, that also in this case the first and most original notions of man, as expressed by speech, are monosyllables. Many of course will object against my having chosen the first person of the indefinite tense [1]) as representant of the verb, but, if I had taken the 3rd pers. sing., which, no doubt, approaches much closer to the original form, that would have caused a great many errors in those languages, with which I have become only superficially acquainted. I have also indicated, as often as possible, the form of the 3rd pers. beside that of the first.

With the second object the arrangement of my vocabularies according to categories of a material import is intimately related, the list of nouns commencing from the terms of the most general import, such as God and the principal natural phenomena, then by way of the animal and vegetable kingdom proceeding to describe man, first with its physical and mental operation and further on in his domestical, political and other relations. With respect to the arrangement of the verbs there is this difference, that I have placed the natural phenomena and actions of animals at the end, because mostly expressed by defective and impersonal verbal forms, but, as for the other verbs, they follow the same arrangement, beginning with the begetting and procreating of man, then comprising his common physical as well as mental functions, and thus proceeding to his actions of a more individual character. This arrangement appeared to be the best, and I intend facilitating the finding of single expressions by an index of the various classes of words at the end of the collection. An alphabetical arrangement was of course out of the question in a vocabulary representing nine different foreign languages, which were to be translated into two different European idioms.

No doubt, the order here chosen has some very great inconveniences, especially as the various terms in the different languages, here appearing in parallel order, often convey a very different notion and it not being possible, to place such a notion as corresponding to all these terms together. This inconvenience and defect I endeavoured to obviate, as much as possible, by explanations given in the notes, where I chose likewise to insert such terms of a similar meaning, as I could only express in a few of the languages. This is certainly a defect, which cannot well be avoided, but it is of less consequence in a collection of vocabularies, which, although of considerable extent, nevertheless do not make the slightest pretence to absolute completeness; but, on the other hand, this arrangement had the great advantage, that it offered

---

[1]) In general, with an occasional exception, where an other tense has been represented, it has been distinctly remarked.

begriffsverwandte Wörter stets zusammengestellt werden konnten, und dieser Vortheil kann nicht hoch genug angeschlagen werden, wenn man, wie das mein Hauptbestreben war, einen Einblick in die geistige Schöpferwerkstätte dieser Völker sich zu verschaffen sucht. So war es auch viel leichter und zweckmässiger, die jedesmaligen Stammwurzeln nach bester Einsicht abzusondern, indem sich sehr oft eine Verwandtschaft in Wörtern verschiedener Sprachen zeigt, die allmählich eine verschiedene Bedeutung angenommen haben, wie z. B. das Wort foto für „Sonne" und „Gott" in mehreren Dialekten des Kótoko unzweifelhaft identisch ist mit dem jetzt nur für „Feuer" gebrauchten Ausdruck podu im Bágrimma, indem hier der Islam die ursprüngliche Beziehung zwischen Feuer, Sonne und Gott zurückgedrängt hat, wo dann andere Wörter für die beiden letzteren Begriffe untergeschoben sind, wie auch der Ausdruck kau, „Sonne", im Kanúri einige Verwandtschaft mit kannu, „Feuer", zeigt. Eben so ging es mit dem vom Arabischen [illegible], „einstimmen", „zufrieden sein", abgeleiteten Ausdrucke in den verschiedenen Sprachen, Kanúri ardi-nískin (S. 54, N. 7), Haussa ua-t erde, ná-yirdá (S. 52, N. 14), Tédā ardí-kení-n [in negativer Form] (S. 62, N. 7). Die möglichste Absonderung der Wurzel war ebenfalls ein anderes Hauptbestreben von meiner Seite, weil man so die allmähliche Entstehung der Wörter und die Verwandtschaft der Ausdrücke unter einander, wo solche existirt, dem aufmerksamen Leser schon ohne weiteren Kommentar ziemlich klar vor Augen hält.

Schon im ersten Kapitel habe ich darauf aufmerksam gemacht, wie meine Vokabularien, wenigstens die neun umfassenderen, von denen ich hier nur spreche, im Ganzen darin einen völligen Gegensatz gegen ähnliche Arbeiten der Missionare bilden, dass sie nicht einen bestimmten Dialekt der Sprachen, sondern die Sprachen im Grossen und Ganzen, wie sie im Munde des Volkes leben, darstellen. Ich habe deshalb, wo mehrere sehr verschiedene Ausdrücke in den verschiedenen Dialekten neben einander herliefen, die Städte oder Landschaften, wo sie im Gebrauch sind, mit dem betreffenden Anfangsbuchstaben bezeichnet, worüber das Nähere im Folgenden unter den einzelnen Sprachen. Von Koelle im Besonderen habe ich schon gesprochen, ich will daher nur ein Wort über Schön's erste Arbeit sagen. Dieses erste Vokabular nebst kurzer Grammatik der Haussa-Sprache verfasste Schön auf der grossen unglücklichen Niger-Expedition, wo er das eigentliche Haussa-Land gar nicht berührte, sondern nur Provinzen, wie besonders das längs des Niger sich hinziehende Küstenland von Nūpe und Yóruba, wo diese Sprache zum Theil als Verkehrssprache dient. Jetzt freilich hat er in meinem freigelassenen Haussa-Burschen Dórregu die wirklich im Munde des Volkes lebende Sprache erhalten, obgleich seine früher einmal angenommenen Provincialismen und direkten Irrthümer ihm nicht gestatten, daraus den möglichen Nutzen in ganzer Fülle zu ziehen. Ich will hier noch ein anderes, eben so deutlich ausgesprochenes, Beispiel zur Erläuterung dieses Satzes anführen. Dies betrifft die vortreffliche Arbeit von Riis über die Odši- oder vielmehr Tši- oder Otši-Sprache. Diese Sprache begreift die Sprache des bedeutenden Asante-Reiches nebst mehreren umliegenden Provinzen; Riis dagegen abstrahirte seine Arbeit, wie er selbst offen erklärt, ganz allein von dem in der kleinen Landschaft Akuapim, und zwar zunächst in dessen Hauptorte Akropong, gesprochenen Dialekte, indem er nur gelegentlich auf einzelne Abweichungen des Asante-Dialekts hinweisen konnte ¹). Und, wie der Missionar mit klarer Einsicht in der unten angeführten Stelle selbst auseinandersetzt, wie anders gestaltet sich nun die Sprache als lebende

---

¹) H. N. Riis: Elemente des Akwapim-Dialekts der Odschi-Sprache. Basel 1853. Ich setze die ganze sehr bedeutende Stelle hierher (Vorwort S. IX): „Kehren wir nun zu der Odschi-Sprache zurück, so wird dieselbe also in dem südlichen Theil des Asante-Reichs, ferner in Fante, in Ahim, in Akwapim und Akwam gesprochen. Bei einer verhältnissmässig so grossen Ausdehnung kann es nicht fehlen, dass bedeutende Dialekt-Verschiedenheiten stattfinden; doch sind diese keineswegs so gross, dass sie ein erhebliches Hinderniss im gegenseitigen Verkehr der verschiedenen Völkerschaften bilden. Wir haben der Untersuchung dieser Verhältnisse keine besondere Aufmerksamkeit zuwenden können, und namentlich sind uns die Dialekts-Eigenthümlichkeiten von Fante, Ahim und Akwam ganz unbekannt geblieben, nicht zu reden von den verschiedenen Provinzen des Asante-Reiches. Da Asante das herrschende Glied des Odschi-Stammes, seine Hauptstadt der Mittelpunkt eines in den grossartigsten Verhältnissen entwickelten Negerlebens ist, und da die Ausbildung der Sprache glei-

the facility of placing side by side words of a related import, and this advantage is not to be valued high enough, if we endeavour to obtain an insight into the laboratory of mental production of these people, which indeed formed one of my chief purposes. Thus it was also much easier, and more adapted to the purpose, to separate and set forth the root of each word according to the best of my intelligence. For very often there is a close affinity between words of different languages, which gradually have adopted a somewhat different notion, as the term fete, in several dialects of the Kótoko-language meaning „sun" and „god", is undoubtedly identical with the term podu in Bágrimma, although the latter is now only used for „fire", the Mohammedan influence having destroyed the original relation between „fire", „sun" and „god" in the Bágrimma-language and new terms having been substituted for the two latter notions, while the Kanúri-term kau meaning „sun" still shows some affinity with kannu, „fire". In a like manner we see the Arabic term رضي, „to consent", „be content", appear in various words of the different languages, which gradually have received a different notion, as in Kanúri ardi-nískin (p. 55, note 7), in Hausa na-I ordá, ná-yirdā (p. 53, note 14), in Tédā in the negative form ardí-kuní-n (p. 63, note 7). The setting forth of the roots again formed another of my chief pursuits, because we thus best become aware of the gradual formation of the words and their affinity, even without a commentary being added in each case.

Already in the first chapter I have called the attention of the reader to the point, that my vocabularies, at least the larger ones, constitute a striking contrast to similar labours of the missionaries, because they do not represent a distinct and single dialect of each language, but each language in its general character and features, such as it lives in the mouth of the people. On this account, where several distinct terms belonging to different dialects go side by side, I have indicated the towns or districts, where each is spoken, by the initial letter of their respective name, on which head the following chapters are to give some further particulars. I have already spoken of the Rev. Koelle and I shall say more of him further on; here I must say a word of the first labour of the Rev. Schön. That rough sketch of a vocabulary and short grammar of the Hausa-language was compiled by the missionary in the course of that unfortunate and disastrous Niger-expedition, when he did not even reach the Hausa-country, but touched only on provinces, such as particularly the districts of Nupe and Yóruba, stretching along the banks of the Kwara, where the Hausa-idiom has been adopted as the language of commerce and intercourse. At present he has received through the Hausa-boy Dórugu specimens of the language, such as it is used by the natives of Hausa Proper, but the provincialisms and errors, which he had once adopted in the course of his former labours, do not allow him, to derive from this source all the advantage possible. But I shall here give another very distinct and clear example, whereby to illustrate, what I have said. This concerns the excellent labour of the missionary Riis on the Otši- or rather Tši- or Otši-language. This idiom comprises the language of the whole Asante kingdom, with several of the circumjacent provinces, while the material on which Riis worked, as he himself openly and freely acknowledges, consisted in nothing but the dialect spoken in the small district Akwapim or rather in the town of Akropong, the capital of the latter, he not being able but to refer occasionally to single deviations of the dialect as spoken in Asante Proper [1]). And now,

[1]) H. N. Riis: Elemente des Akwapim-Dialekts der Odschi- (Otši-) Sprache. Basel 1853 (the English edition I have not at my disposition). I here insert the whole passage of the preface p. IX: „If we now return to the Otši-language, we see, that it is spoken in the southern portion of the Asante-empire, moreover in Fante, in Akim, in Akwapim and Akwam. With a language spread over a territory of relatively so great an extent it cannot but be the case, that considerable differences of dialect exist; however, these are not of such importance, as to form an obstacle of any great consequence in the mutual intercourse of the various tribes amongst each other. We have not been able to pay particular attention to the inquiry into these relations, and the distinguishing features of the dialects spoken in the provinces of Fante, Akim and Akwam have especially remained unknown to us, leaving quite out of the question the dialects spoken in the various provinces of Asante Proper. But Asante being the dominating member of the Otši-tribe and its capital forming the centre of a state of

nach den grossartigeren Verhältnissen des Regierungssitzes von den Anschauungen einer entlegenen Provinz mit ihrem kleinen beengten Gesichtskreise.

Ich muss hier aber noch eine wichtige Bemerkung in Bezug auf Dialektverschiedenheiten machen. Gewiss müssen Dialektverschiedenheiten bei durch Schrift nicht fixirten Sprachen, wie diese Afrikanischen sind, im Allgemeinen sehr gross sein. Wir müssen hier aber wohl unterscheiden und dürfen nicht alle diese Sprachen ohne Unterschied in dieser Beziehung von einem und demselben Gesichtspunkte aus betrachten. Vor Allem zeigt sich der Unterschied zwischen solchen Sprachen, die I) einem noch blühenden und mächtigen und mehr oder minder concentrirten Reiche angehören, wie Bórnu, und II) solchen, die a) entweder von einem, über ungeheure, schwer zu passirende, Länderstrecken ausgebreiteten Stamm, wie die Imōšay und Tédā, gesprochen werden, oder b) α. von einer Nation, die, nachdem sie ein grosses Ländergebiet erobert, verkommen, wie die Soñγai und Kitoko, oder b) β. in mehrere besondere Reiche zerstückelt ist, wie die weit ausgebreitete Nation der Fúl-be. Denn es versteht sich von selbst, dass in einem Reiche, wo eine gewisse, wenn auch auf losen, feudalähnlichen Verhältnissen beruhende Centralisation und ein ansehnlicher Verkehr und Austausch zwischen den einzelnen Theilen Statt findet, die Verschiedenheit der Dialekte der herrschenden Sprache nicht so gross sein kann. Dies schliesst natürlich nicht aus, dass ein solches Reich wie Bórnu, nicht noch viele ganz abweichende Dialekte, ja selbst grundverschiedene Sprachen in den nur halb unterworfenen Landschaften und Provinzen in sich begreift. Ich rede hier nur von der herrschenden Sprache. Auch auf die meisten Sprachen der noch mehr oder weniger unabhängigen heidnischen Fürstenthümer findet der oben unter II, b, β. aufgestellte Grundsatz Anwendung; denn ich hege keinen Zweifel, dass, wenn wir eine Geschichte dieses Völkerknäuels besässen, wir klare Einsicht gewinnen würden, wie sich diese kleinen Staaten aus grösseren Gruppen stets mehr und mehr zerstückelt haben, und diese einmal so zerstückelten Völkerschaften gehen in Folge der unter ihnen einmal angefachten und von ihren Gegnern, den Moslemin, genährten Feindschaft stets mehr und mehr auseinander.

Während schon so meine Sammlung manchen Vortheil vor den Arbeiten der Missionare voraus hat, selbst abgesehen von dem Umstande, dass sie umfassende Vokabularien mehrerer Sprachen enthält, die den Europäern bisher kaum durch ganz kurze Glossarien bekannt geworden waren, darf ich bei dieser Betrachtung wol einen Punkt hervorheben, der den Nutzen meiner Vokabularien wol ganz besonders herausstellt; während nämlich im Allgemeinen die Mannichfaltigkeit der Unterschiede noch unendlich vermehrt wird durch die verschiedene Auffassung verschiedener Personen, biete ich hier dem gelehrten Publikum eine umfassende Sammlung vieler Sprachen[1], alle mit demselben Ohr aufgefasst und mit derselben Hand nieder-

eben Schritt hält mit der Gestaltung aller Lebensverhältnisse, die sich in ihr alsbald abspiegeln, so ist zu erwarten, dass das hier gesprochene Idiom manche Vorzüge vor denen der übrigen Stammgenossen hat, und dasselbe muss daher jedenfalls als der Hauptdialekt betrachtet werden. Eine Erforschung der Sprache vom rein linguistischen Standpunkte aus würde sich daher, ohne über die Wahl zu säumen, diesem Dialekte zugewandt haben. Uns haben die Umstände und der dringend praktische Zweck genöthigt, davon abzugehen und unsere ganze Aufmerksamkeit auf den in Akwapim und zunächst in dessen Hauptort Akropong gesprochenen Dialekt zu richten, und wir haben nur gelegentlich auf einzelne Abweichungen des Asante-Dialekts hinweisen können". Ich will nur fragen, ob der wirklich praktische Zweck erfüllt werden kann, wenn man sich dem Studium eines untergeordneten Dialektes zuwendet, während doch das einzig Praktische nur sein kann, die heiligen Bücher in den allgemein gültigen Hauptdialekt des Landes zu übersetzen.

[1] Vergl. die einsichtsvolle Bemerkung von Bleek in Betreff der Nama-Dialekte in Sir George Grey's library I, 1. p. 11. „Leichte dialektische Unterschiede mögen zwischen den Sprachen der verschiedenen Namaqua-Stämme zu bemerken sein, aber sie sind wahrscheinlich weniger hervorragend, als die Verschiedenheit der Orthographie uns glauben machen könnte."

let us take into regard, as the missionary himself has explained in the passage adduced in the foot note, how differently a language becomes developed in the midst of a capital with its manifold relations from what is the case in a distant province with its narrow sphere of life.

However, I must here make a remark of some importance with regard to dialectical differences of a language. No doubt, dialectical differences in languages the use of which has not been fixed by writing, such as these African idioms, must in general be very great indeed. But in this respect we must not consider all these languages from one and the same point of view, but, on the contrary, must make a distinction of the following kind. Above all there is a marked distinction between such idioms, which I) belong to an empire such as Bórnu, that is to say a country, as yet flourishing, and powerful to a certain extent, and endowed with a certain degree of centralization, and II) such idioms, which are a) either spoken by nations or tribes scattered over an immense extent of country, especially, if it be of a desert character and where intercourse is very difficult, such as the Imóšay and Tédā-tribes, or such as belonging to a nation, b, α) which, after having conquered and occupied a vast territory, has itself sunk from its power, and has been conquered by other tribes like the Sofiyui and Kótoko or which b, β) has been broken up, and split into several independent kingdoms, like the far-spread nation of the Fúl-be. For we may easily understand, how in an empire with a certain degree of centralization, based upon relations of a somewhat feudal nature, and favouring a considerable degree of commerce, and intercourse between its various parts, the difference of dialects of the dominating language cannot be so very great, although this uniformity of the dominating idiom by no means excludes the existence of a great many dialects, or even idioms of a totally different stock, spoken in provinces and districts only partially subdued. The case exemplified under II b, β. relates likewise to the languages, and idioms spoken in the pagan countries, which are in a more or less subjected condition; for I do not entertain the least doubt, that, if we did possess a history of this most intricate coil of languages, we should obtain a clear insight into the manner, how these small estates have been formed by the breaking up of larger national groups; and we see even at the present time, how these tribes, once isolated and split, constantly separate more and more from each other, in consequence of the hostility engendered and nourished among them by the Mohammedans.

Thus I have shown, that my collection of vocabularies has in some respect a great advantage over the labours of the missionaries, even without taking into regard, that it contains several vocabularies of languages scarcely known to Europeans through very short glossaries, but I have still to lay stress upon another point. For, while in general the manifold nature of differences and divergencies between various dialects of languages not fixed by writing is still augmented in an extraordinary manner by the way in which persons of a different state of capability catch the sound of language [1]), I here offer to the public a voluminous collection of nine different idioms, the sound of which was caught by the same ear and which were

Negro-life developed on the grandest scale and the developing of the language going hand in hand with the developing of all relations of life, which cannot but be necessarily reflected by the forms of speech, we must expect, that the idiom here spoken has many advantages over the dialects spoken in the other provinces; and the dialect of Asante Proper must, therefore, be considered as the principal dialect (of the whole group). From a purely linguistical point of view, therefore, the study of this language, without hesitating a moment with regard to the object of its choice, would necessarily have applied itself to this dialect. But we have been forced by circumstances and by the exigency of the practical object, which we had in view, to deviate from this principle, and to apply our whole attention and study to the dialect spoken in the district of Akwapim, and particularly in its chief place Akropong, while we have only been able to take into regard occasionally single instances of disagreement of the Asante-dialect". I have given the whole passage, which explains the object in question in the most liberal manner and I only put the question, whether the really practical object may possibly be obtained, if instead of translating the holy writ into the chief and dominating dialect of the country, the missionary applies himself to the study of a subordinate dialect.

[1]) Compare the intelligent remark made by Mr. Bleek with regard to the Nama-dialects, Grey's library, vol. I, 1. p. 11. „There may be slight dialectical differences observable between the different Namaqua-tribes, but they are probably less prominent than the variety of orthography would induce us to suppose."

geschrieben, und wenn schon hierdurch die beziehungsweise richtige Auffassung der Sprachen sicher gestellt ist, so habe ich ihr noch durch eine durchgeführte Accentuirung eine ungleich grössere Richtigkeit gegeben, so dass ich hoffen kann, dass der Europäer, der die von mir niedergeschriebenen Worte vor dem Eingeborenen ausspricht, auch sogleich verstanden wird, was von sehr wenigen ähnlichen Sammlungen gesagt werden kann. Und diese Vortheile werden bestehen, wenn auch Einzelnes allmählich viel genauer von Anderen ausgeführt werden wird. So hat zwar der Kapitän Hanoteau jetzt auch angefangen, die Te-mâšiy-t- oder Mâšiy-Sprache eingehender zu behandeln, aber, wie er die Worte ohne ihre richtige Betonung lässt, so wird mein Vokabular dieser Sprache, veröffentlicht am Ende des 5ten Bandes meiner Reisen, besonders zu praktischem Gebrauch sich sicher bewähren [1], obgleich ich damals, mit anderen Arbeiten beschäftigt, leider noch nicht mit der möglichen Sorgfalt in Auseinanderhaltung der Wurzeln verfuhr.

Wir haben nun einen anderen Punkt zu betrachten. Unzweifelhaft musste der Islam mit seinem reichen Ideenkreis und den beiden grammatisch und lexikalisch schon reich entwickelten Sprachen, vermittelst deren er an diese Völkerschaften des Binnenlandes herantrat, dem Arabischen auf der einen und dem Berberischen oder Mâšiy auf der anderen Seite, einen unbegränzten Einfluss auf alle neun in meinen grösseren Vokabularien vertretenen Sprachen ausüben, zumal da sie zu jener Zeit, allen Anzeichen zu Folge, in lexikalischer, ganz besonders aber in grammatikalischer Beziehung noch sehr wenig entwickelt waren. Nichts würde interessanter und belehrender sein, als wenn wir Proben dieser Sprachen vor der Zeit hätten, als sie mit jenen Sprachen und Ideen in Berührung kamen, um sie mit ihrem jetzigen Zustande zu vergleichen. Jetzt müssen wir a posteriori rückwärts gehen, um zu versuchen, auszuscheiden, was Neues in diese Sprachen durch jenen Prozess hineingetragen wurde. In lexikalischer Beziehung lässt sich die berührte Frage leicht beantworten und folgendes sind im Allgemeinen die Kreise von Ausdrücken, welche in diese Sprachen auf jene Weise, besonders aus dem Arabischen, eingeführt wurden; zuerst natürlich die Ausdrücke der Gottesreligion, deren ethische Anschauungen die früheren unbestimmten Gefühle von natürlichen und dämonischen Kräften, wovon ich in den Anmerkungen zu dem betreffenden Theile des Glossars mehr sagen werde, vertraten oder wenigstens verdunkelten; dann die Ausdrücke von Zeitbegriffen, einer gewissen Bildungsstufe, wie heirathen, lesen, schreiben und die damit zusammenhängenden Gegenstände, begrüssen u. s. w., dann gewisse Ausdrücke der Kleidung, Waffen, Kriegskunst überhaupt, vom Bauwesen, Handel und vieles Andere. In manchen Fällen gelang es natürlich den Eingeborenen, für die ihnen früher unbekannten Gegenstände oder Ideen nach Analogie schon besessener Wörter neue lebendige Ausdrücke zu bilden, aber hierin war unter diesen Völkern nach ihrem mehr oder minder lebhaften Naturell ein grosser Unterschied, und die Haussa-Leute haben hierin in Folge ihrer lebhaften Phantasie einen entschiedenen Vorzug vor den Kanûri. In grammatischer Beziehung ist natürlich die genaue Ergründung des Einflusses des Arabischen, besonders aber des Berberischen ungleich schwieriger und zweifelhafter. Ich habe kaum einen Zweifel, dass die Sprachen vor jener Berührung weder Declination noch Conjugation besassen, sondern die infinitive oder substantive Verbalwurzel einfach an einen Gegenstand oder eine Person anknüpften. Das werden wir bei den meisten derselben bei ihrer

[1] Ich will hier nur anführen, einen wie falschen Eindruck schon der Name der Sprache in der von Hanoteau angenommenen Form T a m a c h e ḳ machen muss, wo das erste a (vielmehr als unbedeutendes ă) dem zweiten langen Grundvokal â ganz gleich steht.

written down by the same hand. And, while already on this account the right conception of the languages in their relative individuality is fully secured, I have still made another step in advance towards representing each word with its own natural sound by applying a consistent system of accents; and I thus have reason to hope, that the European who pronounces one of the words as written down by me, in the presence of a native, will be easily understood, a presumption which is by no means to be entertained of most collections of the kind. And these advantages of my collection will remain, although in single respects others with more leisure and with a more limited range of study will not fail to add materially to the inquiry. Thus Mr. Hanoteau has already begun to enter into a deeper study of the Temāšiy-t- or Māšiy-language, but, as he leaves the words without the right accentuation, my vocabulary of that language, published at the end of the 5th volume of my Travels, will prove of considerable practical use*), although, taken up at the same time with geographical subjects, I did not apply to its publication all the care which I would have bestowed upon it with more leisure.

We have now to consider another point. There cannot be the least doubt but, that the Islam with its wide sphere of new ideas, as represented by the Berber and Arabic languages, by means of which it came in contact and overwhelmed these pagan tribes of the Interior, at least from a mental point of view, undeveloped as these languages were at that time in a grammatical, as well as glossarial respect, exercised more or less an unbounded influence upon all the nine languages represented by my larger vocabularies. Nothing, therefore, would be more interesting and instructive, than, if we possessed specimens of these languages, such as they were before the time, when they came in contact with those languages, and the ideas represented by them, in order to compare the character, they then presented, with their present condition. But, this not being possible, we now are reduced to proceed a posteriori in order to try to eliminate again the new elements which have thus been introduced into these languages. Such an inquiry is not so difficult, as it might seem; and the following are in general the categories of terms, and expressions, which have thus been borrowed by these languages, especially from the Arabic: first, the terms regarding the religion of the one God, the ethic ideas and conceptions of which took the place of, and obliterated the former indistinct feeling of natural and demoniacal powers, of which I shall have occasion to say more in the notes appended to the part of the glossary in question, then the terms regarding a certain estate of civilization, such as marrying, reading, writing and the objects having relation thereto, sections of time, and phrases of salutation, and of good breeding, then the terms relating to dress, instruments, and the art of warfare, as well as architecture, commerce, and so on. In some cases, indeed the natives were so happy as to form indigenous terms for naming the new objects from their own stock of linguistical material, and from the analogy of objects, or actions already expressed by their language, but in this respect there proved to be a considerable difference between the various tribes according to their more or less lively and vivacious character, and the Hausa-people have a most decided advantage in this regard before the Kanúri. But, while the question with regard to the influence of the Arabic- and Berber-languages upon the Negro-idioms here concerned, is not so difficult to be solved in connection with the glossary, this inquiry offers very considerable difficulties, if we consider the grammatical part of the language. As for myself, I have scarcely any doubt, that these Negro-idioms, before their being regenerated by the contact with these more civilized languages, possessed neither the forms of declension, nor those of conjugation, but merely the infinitive verbal root brought into connection with some object or sort of pronoun, as is still the case in the vulgar idiom of the Téda-people.

*) I here only adduce as an example the manner in which Mr. Hanoteau spells the name of the language viz Tamachek instead of Te-māšiy-t, the first a in his manner of writing being seemingly of the same character as the second while it is a mere mute.

einzelnen Besprechung im vierten Kapitel fast ganz deutlich erkennen. Ja selbst bei den Verbalwurzeln kann man oft wegen Ableitung von Fremdwörtern unsicher sein, und man erkennt nicht auf den ersten Blick, was aus dem Arabischen bloss äusserlich eingeführt ist [1]).

Jedoch in Beziehung auf die grammatische Einwirkung auf die Neger-Sprachen steht das Arabische weit hinter dem Berberischen zurück, ja kommt fast gar nicht in Betracht, und davon ist der einfache Grund der, dass das Arabische nur von einzelnen Individuen vertreten war, von denen die Eingeborenen zwar viele neue Ausdrücke für Dinge lernen konnten, die ihnen früher unbekannt gewesen waren, deren Rede aber auf ihre Sprache im Allgemeinen wenig Einfluss üben konnte, besonders da auch die Religionsschriften nur von einer kleinen Zahl Auserwählter verstanden wurde, während die Berber-Sprache in dem Munde einer ganzen Nation lebte; denn das muss man festhalten, dass, abgesehen von der wirklich Arabischen oder vielmehr Süa-Bevölkerung [2]) die Kenntniss des Arabischen bei der grossen Menge sich auf das mechanische Auswendiglernen der wichtigsten Gebetformeln und einiger Redensarten der Begrüssung beschränkt. Eben jene Vertretung der Berber- oder Mášiy-Sprache durch eine ganze Nation ist auch der Grund, weshalb in dem Grade der Beeinflussung durch das Berberische ein so gewaltiger Unterschied zwischen den hier aufgeführten Sprachen ist, der zum grossen Theil durch die früheren Wohnsitze der sie redenden Völker sich leicht erklärt. So beruht auch der offenbar grosse Einfluss, den die Berber-Sprache auf das Hausa ausgeübt hat, nach meiner Ansicht vielleicht ausschliesslich auf den früheren Wohnsitzen des Hausa-Volkes, ungleich weiter nach Norden, in Asben und selbst nördlicher, wo sie, ehe ihre Sprache ganz entwickelt war, etwa schon seit dem achten Jahrhundert unserer Zeitrechnung mit dem Mášiy in lebendige Berührung und wol selbst mit dem Mášiy-Stamme in nationale Vermischung traten. Auch die Kanúri allerdings hatten einst nördlichere Sitze, aber mehr im östlichen Theile der Wüste, wo die Berbern keinen direkten Einfluss auf sie ausüben konnten. Dagegen scheint, wie ich das bei der besonderen Besprechung der Kanúri-Sprache weiter ausführen werde, die Hausa-Sprache sehr bedeutenden Einfluss auf die Verbalbildung des Kanúri geübt zu haben, gleichwie sie ausserordentlichen Einfluss auf die Pronominalbildung des Lógone ausübte, wenn wir die letztere Erscheinung nicht durch eine unmittelbare Einwirkung der Berber-Sprache erklären wollen. Ich werde die Spuren eines Einflusses des Mášiy auf diese Sprachen, so weit er mir zur Gewissheit wurde, in einem besonderen Kapitel zusammenstellen.

Ich wollte diesen Punkt hier nur andeuten, indem ich ihn zur näheren Besprechung einem folgenden Kapitel überlasse, und füge nur noch hinzu, dass für Hinweisung auf die ursprünglichen Sitze dieser Völkerschaften ihre Bezeichnungen der Himmelsgegenden von grosser Bedeutung sind, obgleich bei Erklärung derselben vorerst noch mancher Zweifel übrig bleiben muss. Alle solche individuelle Beziehungen sind bei vorurtheilsfreier Berücksichtigung dieser Sprachen in verwandtschaftlicher Beziehung von grosser Bedeutung. So zum Beispiel wäre es grundfalsch, die Ausdrücke für „Rind" in diesen Sprachen als Beweis ihrer Verwandtschaft anzuführen, da das Rind, wie ich anderswo [3]) ausgeführt, von zwei verschiedenen Himmelsgegenden her bei diesen Völkern eingeführt wurde, oder die Verwandtschaft des Kanúri mit

[1]) Ich führe hier als Beispiel an die Ausdrücke für „ich verspotte" in K. ng-i sumbar, F. múde-sumbe und S. ége-sumbe, S. 78, N. 6 des Vokabulars, deren Ursprung aus dem Arabischen, nämlich von سبّ, ich, als ich jene Partie durchsah, nicht erkannte, jetzt aber keinen Zweifel daran habe. Die Einschiebung des m vor b in Worten, die aus der Arabischen Sprache herübergenommen sind, haben wir in vielen anderen Beispielen, wie gleich im Tédâ-Wort kambu, „das Grab", von قبر.

[2]) Reisen, Th. II, S. 438.

[3]) Reisen, Th. III, S. 200.

And, that such was the case with all of them, I hope to demonstrate, when I come to speak of each language singly in chapter the fourth. Nay, even with regard to the verbal roots we may often have reason to hesitate, and may not always recognize at first sight what has merely been borrowed from the Arabic [1]).

However, as far as regards the grammatical influence exercised upon the Negro-languages, the Arabic must needs cede the preeminence to the Berber-idiom, the reason being simply, because the Arabic was represented only by single individuals, from whom the natives of Negroland learnt many new terms of objects, formerly unknown to them, but whose conversation could have little influence upon their language in general, while the Berber-language was living in the mouth of a whole nation. For we must not forget, that the religious writings of the Arabs are only understood by a small number of individuals, among the natives of Negroland, and that, with one or two exceptions, in a most superficial manner while, if we do not take into account the really Arabic or rather Súa native population [2]), the common people even in the Mohammedan states know nothing of Arabic with the exception of the most simple, and necessary forms of prayer, and a few short phrases of salutation. This is also the reason why, with regard to the influence exercised by the Berber-idiom, there is a paramount difference between the languages here represented, which preeminently depends upon the place, where these tribes had formerly their seats; and the great influence exercised by the Berber-idiom upon the Hausa-language, according to my opinion, is based almost exclusively upon the seats of the Hausa-people having been situated in former times much farther to the north, in the country of Asben, and even more northerly, where at an early period, from the VIIIth century of our era downwards, when their language was not yet quite developed, they came into the most intimate contact, and even entered in some localities into a state of national intermixture with the Másiy-nation. No doubt, the Kanúri also once were settled much farther to the North, but rather in the Eastern portion of the desert, where the Berber-tribes exercised very little direct influence upon them. But on the other hand, as I shall have full opportunity of developing, when I come to speak of the Kanúri-language in particular, the Hausa-language appears to have influenced to a considerable degree the verbal formation of the Kanúri-language, while it exercised paramount influence upon the pronominal formation of the Lógoné-idiom, if we do not prefer to explain the latter phenomenon by means of an immediate influence of the Berber-language upon the latter. As for the specimens of such an influence, exercised by this idiom upon the languages represented in my vocabularies, as far as I have become aware of it, especially with regard to the glossary, I shall collect them under one general head.

These points I wanted only here to touch upon, leaving them, as for more diligent inquiry, to a following chapter, and only adding the remark, that with regard to the making out the original seats of tribes, the names which they give to the various quarters of the world, are of great importance, although in explaining their signification a great deal of doubt must remain. But altogether we must never lose out of sight such individual relations, when we want to consider without prejudice the ethnographical question. Thus, for instance, it would be perfectly wrong, to cite the terms for „cattle" in these languages as a proof of their affinity and relationship, the cattle, as I have explained elsewhere [3]), having been introduced

---

[1]) I have adduced as an instance the terms for „I scoff, deride", in the Hausa-, Fúl- and Sonyai-languages, H. na-i sambar, F. mâde-sambe, S. ága-sambe, which, when going over the page 76, note 3 of my glossary, I did not become aware of, that they are most probably derived from the Arabic [illegible]; of the inserting of an m before the b in words thus borrowed from the Arabic we find numerous instances as in the Tédâ-word kumbe, „the grave" from قبر.

[2]) In my Travels vol. II, p. 335, III, p. 136.

[3]) Travels III, p. 236.

dem Wándalá auf den Umstand zu begründen, dass das erstere manche den Ackerbau betreffenden Ausdrücke von letzterem angenommen hat; während sich diese Übereinstimmung ganz einfach aus dem materiellen Verhältniss erklärt, dass die Kanúri, aus wüsteren Gegenden in die fruchtbare Zone einwandernd, diese Ausdrücke von dem ihnen benachbarten Ackerbauvolk entlehnten. Ähnlich verhält es sich aber mit vielen anderen Ausdrücken. Die Hausa z. B. haben den Ausdruck nōno für „Milch" mit den Mandingo gemein in Folge ganz eigenthümlicher Verhältnisse in Bezug auf das besondere Verhältniss der Viehzucht.

Diese Betrachtung führt mich auf die Besprechung eines die Kulturgeschichte angehenden Punktes. Meine Vokabularien nämlich ergeben, neben anderen zahlreichen, für die inneren Kulturverhältnisse jener Völker wichtigen Resultate, z. B. die höchst interessanten Ergebnisse, dass Pferd und Esel im nördlichen Binnen-Afrika, wenigstens von sehr alter Zeit her, einheimisch waren, ebenso wie die Katze, der Hund dagegen erst in späterer Zeit von Nord-Ost eingeführt wurde. Ebenso scheint sich durch diese Wörtersammlungen die höchst interessante Frage über Reis und Tabak zu entscheiden, nämlich, dass ersterer, wenigstens seit uralter Zeit, einheimisch, letzterer trotz des Eindruckes, den ich selbst durch den starken Anbau dieser Pflanze bei den Negervölkern erhalten, in Übereinstimmung mit der hergebrachten Ansicht nicht einheimisch sei, da fast alle Sprachen sonderbarer Weise den mit unserem Europäischen, den Arabern ganz fremden Ausdruck zusammenhängenden Namen tába aufweisen; diese Form als tabbá hat auch die Yóruba-Sprache, durch deren Vermittelung er wahrscheinlich seit dem XVten Jahrh. von der Süd-West-Küste in das Innere eindrang. Auch ergeben diese Vokabularien anscheinend das merkwürdige Resultat, dass die Adansonia digitata, jener für diese Binnen-Afrikanischen Länder so charakteristische Baum, wenigstens in der ganzen Ländergruppe von Bagírmi bis Hausa, also vom Fittri-See bis fast zum Niger oder Kuara, nicht einheimisch war, sondern aus einer und derselben Gegend eingeführt wurde, während der ihm in dieser Ländergruppe beigelegte Name identisch ist mit dem schon bei den alten Egyptern vorkommenden.

Bei jeder Betrachtung verwandtschaftlicher Verhältnisse muss man stets vor Augen behalten, dass Sprachen eine allgemeine Ideen- und Principienverwandtschaft haben können, ohne eine thatsächliche Verwandtschaft zu besitzen, dass das ganz besonders von Völkerschaften gilt, die so ziemlich auf einer und derselben Stufe der Bildung stehen und deren ganze Lebensanschauung auf Ackerbau basirt ist. So ist der Kulturunterschied bei diesen Afrikanischen Völkerschaften keineswegs so gross, wie bei den Amerikanischen Völkern, wo Pritchard *) aus diesem Grunde die Anwendung eines solchen Princips zurückwies. Am Schlusse meiner gesammten linguistischen Sammlungen soll in einem übersichtlichen Abschnitt die Frage wegen Gruppirung dieser Völkerschaften und der Zusammenordnung ihrer Sprachen abgehandelt und durch ein Kartenblatt erläutert werden; aber auf theorisirende Zusammenstellungen lasse ich mich nicht ein und überlasse diese den Sprachforschern höherer Gattung. Mein Standpunkt ist der des Geographen und Ethnographen und ich halte mich nur an Fakten.

Drittes Kapitel.

Die in den Vokabularien angenommene Schreibweise.

Die Schreibweise, die bei diesen Sprachen anzuwenden ist, ist eine in vielen einzelnen Punkten schwierige Frage. Denn diese Sprachen besitzen selbst kein eigenthümliches Alphabet und benutzen das ihnen mit dem Islam bekannt gewordene Arabische Alphabet in der Mogrebinischen oder el Warsh genannten Schreibweise mit ganz wenigen Ausnahmen nur, um

*) Prichard in Report of the British association. 1847. p. 251.

into Central-Negroland, partly from the West, partly from the East; and the same is the case with many other objects, as the Kanúri, for instance, have the terms regarding the cultivation of the ground in common with the Wándala, because, immigrating into the fertile districts from more desert tracts, they borrowed these terms from their neighbours. Thus, the Hausa-people having the term nōno for milk in common with the Mandingo-people, constitutes a particular case of harmony between these two languages, which is based upon circumstances of a totally exceptional character.

This consideration leads me to speak of a point, which regards rather the history of civilization, than that is of any linguistical import; but altogether my glossary contains a vast material, highly interesting for the history and state of civilization of these regions. Thus it appears to prove, that the horse and ass have been indigenous in the Northern part of Central-Africa since very remote times, the same as the cat, while the dog most probably was introduced at a later period; in the same manner my vocabulary seems to decide the interesting question with regard to the origin of rice and tobacco to that effect, that rice was indigenous, while tobacco, notwithstanding the impression, the very extensive cultivation of this plant with the Negro-tribes made upon me at the time, in harmony with the preconceived idea of its American origin, would appear, not to be indigenous, as almost all languages represented in my vocabulary have the name tābu which, curious as it is, taken into regard the situation of these tribes, far in the Interior, is intimately connected with our European term, while the Arabic term is of a totally different character. The Yóruba also has this term in the form tubā́. To mention another question of considerable interest, these vocabularies seem to prove, that the Adansonia digitata, that is to say, that very tree which seems to be most characteristic of the countries of Central-Negroland, is not indigenous, and did not originally grow in that whole extent of country, bounded to the East by the Fittri, and towards the West nearly approaching the Niger, and comprising Bagírmi, Bórnu and Hausa with the neighbouring smaller states, but, that it was introduced into these countries from one and the same quarter, and was called by a name identical with the one given to it by the ancient Egyptians.

However, in considering relations of linguistic affinity we must never lose sight of the fact, that languages may have a general identity of ideas and principles without being allied with each other by real affinity, and that such a harmony is especially applicable to nations or tribes, which occupy about the same degree of civilization, while their whole sphere of life is based on agriculture, and circumscribed by the regularly recurring periods of seasons. Thus, the difference of character among these tribes, if we discard the Tédu-tribe, is by no means so great as with the indigenous tribes of America, where Pritchard [1]) on this account has rejected the above principle as not applicable. At the end of the whole of my linguistical collection the question, how these tribes and their languages are to be grouped together, shall be treated in a comprehensive manner, and be illustrated by a map; but I shall leave to linguists of a higher order all what belongs to theoretical views, my point of view being entirely that of a geographer and ethnographer, wholly depending upon facts.

Chapter the third.

The orthography adopted in these vocabularies.

It is a question of considerable intricacy and difficulty, with regard to many single points, how to write these African languages. For these languages neither possess an indigenous alphabet of their own, nor do they make use of the Arabic alphabet, which has become known to them in the Moghrebine form called el Warsh, but for compositions in the Arabic,

[1]) Pritchard in Report of the British association. 1847. p. 251.

eben Arabisch zu schreiben, und nicht ihre eigene Sprache. So, wenn ein eingeborener Koiām oder Bewohner von Díkōa oder sonst einer Stadt in Bórnu einem anderen Landsmanne in Múniō oder Udjé, oder wo sonst her, eine schriftliche Botschaft geben will, wendet er sich an einen ausdrücklich von dieser Beschäftigung lebenden Schreiber oder einen Mállem, d. h. einen mehr oder weniger beschränkten sogenannten Gelehrten (der Moslimischen heiligen Schrift), sagt ihm in seiner Muttersprache, was er schreiben soll, und überlässt es dann diesem Herrn, den so angegebenen Sinn in halb verständlichem Arabisch auszudrücken, das er nicht einmal, wenn vorgelesen, controlliren kann, wenn er nicht gerade selbst einige Brocken Arabisch versteht. Jene wenigen, eben erwähnten Ausnahmen, dass nämlich das Arabische zuweilen auch zum Niederschreiben in eingeborener Sprache abgefasster Redestücke verwandt werde, beziehen sich fast ausschliesslich auf das Niederschreiben einheimischer Gesänge oder Lieder, wie das z. B. in den Schriften des Sultan Bello von Sókoto ganz gewöhnlich ist, dass seinen in Arabischer Sprache abgefassten Bericht seiner Heerzüge ein in seiner angeborenen Fulfúlde-Sprache abgefasstes, aber wie der übrige Text des Schriftstückes mit Arabischer Schrift geschriebenes, Kriegslied unterbricht.

Nun haben allerdings die Missionare der Englischen Church missionary Society an der Westküste von Afrika neuerdings die Ansicht aufgestellt, dass die Anwendung Arabischer Schrift auf jene einheimischen Sprachen allgemeine Anwendung finden könne und haben Grundzüge einiger Sprachen und selbst längere Sprachproben in dieser Weise drucken lassen. Das hat aber nach meiner Ansicht keinen Sinn. Erstlich ist es unendlich schwer, ja in vielen Fällen unmöglich, die Worte der einheimischen Sprachen Arabisch zu schreiben und muss Vieles beim Lesen geistiger Ergänzung und Muthmassung überlassen bleiben, zweitens, wenn sich der Missionar nur an diejenigen wenden will, die der Arabischen Lektüre, besonders mit aller Fülle ihrer Schreibzeichen, völlig mächtig sind, gebraucht er die einheimischen Sprachen gar nicht, sondern kann sich, so wie in Arabischer Schrift, so auch in Arabischer Sprache an die Eingeborenen wenden, da der Hauptzweck doch in der Bekanntmachung mit den Büchern unserer heiligen Schrift besteht. Nun gar für Europäer diese fremden und schwer aufzufassenden Sprachen noch wiederum in einer, dem Europäer sowohl wie dem Afrikaner, fremden Schrift geben zu wollen, obgleich sie einige der Haupteigenthümlichkeiten wiederzugeben nicht im Stande ist, halte ich für verkehrt.

Ich habe also mit voller Überzeugung, den einzig richtigen Weg einzuschlagen, Europäische Schrift für diese Vokabularien gewählt, obgleich auch wir in Einer Sprache wenigstens nicht alle die hierzu nöthigen Laute besitzen. Da ich nun bei den einzelnen Sprachen in den folgenden Kapiteln auf die Frage wegen einzelner Laute zurückkommen muss, will ich hier nur ein Verzeichniss der gebrauchten Laute und Zeichen geben und einige wenige allgemeine Bemerkungen hinzufügen. Ich will nur noch aussprechen, dass es mein Bestreben war, dem von Herrn Prof. Lepsius vertretenen, gewiss unzweifelhaften, Prinzipe gemäss, stets einen Laut durch ein Zeichen auszudrücken.

Laute, die keiner weiteren Erklärung bedürfen, sondern gesprochen werden wie im Deutschen, mit Ausnahme des v, w, y und z, die wie im Englischen gesprochen werden, sind folgende:

b, d, f, g, h, k, l, m, n, p, r, s (= unserem ß in „fleissig"), t, v (E. „virgin"), w (E. „we"), y (E. „yes"), z (E. „zeal" = unserem s in „sich", „sehr").

Dem h verwandt habe ich noch, jedoch selten, zuweilen ein ḥ angewandt, das dem Arabischen ح gleichkommt. Denn in diesen nicht durch Schrift fixirten Sprachen sind so feine Unterschiede sehr unsicher. Dann aber χ = dem Arabischen خ und unserem ch.

Eben so habe ich neben k gebraucht ḳ = dem Arabischen ق, unserem q, dessen Gebrauch ausser vor u dem Engländer zumal unerträglich ist. Über die eigenthümliche wandelbare Natur des k werde ich weiter unten zu 18 noch Einiges beibringen.

and not in their own idiom if we do not take into account a very few exceptions. Thus, if a native Koyām, or an inhabitant of Dikwa, or of any other town or district of Bórnu, wants to send a written message to any countryman of his, may he live in Múnio, Udže or, wherever it may be, he applies either to one of the scribes who make this occupation their livelihood, or to a mállem, that is to say, a scripturist (of the Mohammedan creed) of a more or less limited degree of learning, informs him in his native idiom, what he has to write, and then leaves it to the ability of this gentleman, to express the matter in an half intelligible Arabic, as well as he is able, for very rarely the informant and customer understands enough of Arabic, in order to see that, what he wants, has been really and truely expressed by the scribe, when the latter reads to him what he has written. As for those few exceptions on which I touched above of the Arabic alphabet being occasionally applied to the writing of any discourse composed in any native language, they refer almost exclusively to the writing of native songs, as for instance we see in the writings of the late Sultan Bello of Sókoto, whose account of his several warlike expeditions, composed in the Arabic language, is frequently interrupted by a war- or triumphal song composed in his native Fūl- or Ful-fúl-de-idiom, but written like the rest of the composition with the Arabic alphabet.

Now, the missionaries of the Church Missionary Society, stationed on the West-coast of Africa, have recently supposed, that they might and ought to apply the Arabic alphabet to the writing of these native languages, and have already begun to print in this manner primers of some such languages, and even longer compositions. But such a proceeding, according to my opinion, has no practical use. For, first of all, it is extremely difficult, nay in many cases even impossible, to write the words of the native African languages with Arabic characters, and a great many peculiarities, which cannot be expressed, must remain to be supplied by the reader; secondly, if the missionary takes into account only those individuals, who are entirely masters of the Arabic reading, including a knowledge of all the subordinate signs of writing, he does not need at all the native languages, but may as well address the natives in the Arabic idiom, and not only in Arabic writing the principal object of all their labours consisting in making the Natives acquainted with the contents of our Holy writ. But, if Europeans be concerned, I take it to be a gross mistake, to represent these African languages, which are by no means easily to be mastered, in a sort of characters not less strange to the African idioms, than to the European, and which do not by far suffice for rendering intelligible some of the most peculiar features of those languages.

It is, therefore, from a full conviction of taking the only right way, that I have chosen European characters for representing these languages, although none of the European languages singly does possess all the sounds necessary for this purpose. Being obliged to come back to several questions regarding this subject, when speaking of each language singly in the following chapters, I here, in giving a complete list of the sounds employed in my vocabulary, add only a few general remarks. I first beg to say, that I have adopted the chief principle of Prof. Lepsius's alphabetical system, viz that of representing each sound by one individual sign, although I have not adopted all the signs, such as he has proposed.

Letters, which need no further explanation, and are sounded as in English, are the following:

b, d, f, g (as in „give"), h, k, l, m, n, p, r, s, t, v, w, y, z.

Besides h I have occasionally used, but rather rarely an ḥ, corresponding to the Arabic ح, for in these illiterate languages such niceties of distinction are rather uncertain. The Arabic خ, which in English is generally represented by kh, but which it was peremptorily necessary to represent by one sign, I have given by χ.

Besides k, the Arabic ك, I have occasionally used ḳ, corresponding to the Arabic ق, where such a distinction could be made with some degree of certainty, especially where the k sound is changed into a g. About the change of k into the English ch I shall speak further on.

Neben f und p habe ich noch zuweilen ein aspirirtes ṕ gebraucht, das dem Griechischen φ gänzlich entspricht, und das am leichtesten den besonders in Kanúri unaufhörlichen Übergang von p, ja selbst b in f kennzeichnet.

Neben n habe ich ŋ gebraucht, um den dumpfen Laut wie im Englischen Worte „king" = „König", anzuzeigen, und ausserdem den Spanischen Nasal-Laut ñ, der in manchen Afrikanischen Sprachen sehr gewöhnlich ist, obgleich er sich oft richtiger in ny auflöst, so z. B. H. mu mu-nyi von (na yi, „ich mache", nicht mu mu-ñi und im F. nyáma, nicht ñáma, „die Speise", weil Imp. yaŋg, „iss". Der Grund, weshalb ich das von Lepsius gewählte Zeichen ń nicht annehmen konnte, ist einfach der, weil ich den Accent zu anderen Zwecken benutze und weil ein solcher doppelter Gebrauch leicht Missverständnisse veranlasst, wie denn Koelle gerade das n mit dem Accent in ganz anderem Sinne gebraucht.

Neben r gebrauche ich γ, um einen eigenthümlichen Mittellaut zwischen r und g darzustellen. Dieser Mittellaut ist unseren Europäischen Sprachen im Bewusstsein fremd, aber faktisch doch oft gebraucht [1]); es ist der Laut, den die Araber غ schreiben. Dieser Laut erfährt einerseits je nach Natur der ihn umgebenden Laute und andererseits nach dialektischer Mundart von Landschaft und Gegend mannichfache Modificationen. Es ist entschieden, dass er schon in Algerien und dem Maghreb überhaupt sich wirklich dem r-Laut mehr nähert, als dem g-Laut, weshalb man die jetzt bei den Franzosen übliche Schreibweise nicht vom ursprünglich Arabischen Standpunkt aus betrachten muss. Dass der Buchstabe einen solchen Charakter in der Máśiγ-Sprache hat, sollte man von vorn herein nicht annehmen, da die Imóśay nur Ein Zeichen für ع und غ haben; und doch waltet gerade in vielen Ausdrücken und Namen der Máśiγ-Sprache der r-Laut sehr vor, wovon ich schon anderswo (Reis. Th. I, S. 255) als Beispiel den Ausdruck imyäd aufgestellt habe, den die Araber in [illegible] verwandelt haben, wo also das einfache r die Stelle des γ vertritt. Es ist also klar, dass, obgleich auch das Zeichen γ willkürlich ist, dieser Laut nicht dem χ in der Schreibweise durch irgend eine Abwandelung desselben, wie ein χ' eng angeschlossen werden kann. Der Missionar Koelle selbst, der in seiner Grammatik und seinem Vokabular der Kanúri-Sprache diesen Laut nicht hat, wendet ihn in seiner ein Jahr früher, 1853, erschienenen Polyglotta vielfach an unter dem bei ihm sehr zu beachtenden Zeichen γ, und zwar nicht allein bei anderen Afrikanischen Sprachen, sondern selbst bei blossen Dialekt-Abweichungen der Bórnu- oder Kanúri-Sprache, wie er z. B. das Wort für Regen, das er in Kanúri selbst délâgò schreibt, im Dialekt von Ngurū délâγu und in dem von Kánem délâγè schreibt (S. 90). Auch in der Gurma-Mosi-Gruppe ist das γ vollkommen sicher; denn, obgleich ich allerdings sonst die diesen Sprachen angehörenden Wörter, die Koelle in seiner Polyglotta mit γ gibt, mit g niedergeschrieben habe, stimmen wir Beide in boγa, „Ziege" und baγa, „Hund" völlig überein. Von der Sonγai-Sprache in's Besondere werde ich weiterhin sprechen. Hier will ich nur ein höchst belehrendes Beispiel für die Auffassung des غ von den Afrikanischen Stämmen im Allgemeinen anführen. Dies ist die Weise, wie sie das Arabische Wort غفر „verzeihen" verschiedentlich aufgefasst und umgewandelt haben; denn, während die Hausaua einen einfachen g-Laut erfasst zu haben scheinen, indem sie gáferta daraus machten, die Wándalá es durch háhera wiedergeben, hörte ich im Kanúri deutlich die Form grabáŋgena, und im Lógonē, obgleich diese Sprache ein besonderes γ hat, gráifera, während die Bágrimma-Sprache den nun einmal deutlich hervortretenden r-Laut ganz umstellte und gábraga daraus machte. Dagegen fassten die Fúl-be den Laut, wie etwa das griechische γ in γέγραφα auf und machten γáfaku oder

[1]) Ich fand z. B. wenn ich Maurische Araber, wie selbst den gelehrten Scheich el Bakai, eine Schaar Europäische Wörter mit Arabischer Schrift schreiben liess, dass sie r vor m oder b stets mit غ schrieben, wie arm, arbre, armour u. s. w.

Besides f, and p, and as an intermediate sound between both, I have made use of a p̓, corresponding to the Greek φ, and which is best fitted for showing the constant change of p, and even of b, into f.

Besides n I have made use of ṅ, to indicate the sound as in „king", and of the Spanish nasal ñ, which is common to several African languages, but in the use of which great precaution is necessary, as in many cases it is more correctly dissolved into ny, as for instance the Fulfúlde-word nyāma, „food" cannot be written ñāma, as it is derived from yā, „to eat", imp. yaṅg, just the same as ma-nyī in Hausa cannot be written mañī, as it is derived from yī, „to make". The reason, why I did not adopt ń, in order to express this nasal n was, because I use the sign of the accent for other purposes.

As a middling sound between r and g I use γ, corresponding to the Arabic غ and even not so foreign to European languages, as is generally thought, although we have not become fully conscious of its character *). This sound, however, in African languages is greatly modified, not only according to the nature of other sounds, with which it comes in contact, but also according to the country where the language is spoken. Thus there can be no doubt, that even in Algeria and in the Moghreb in general it really approaches more closely the sound of r, than the g, and we must therefore not judge of the way of writing this sound, usual with the French of Algeria, from a point of view, peculiar to the pure Arabic. That the letter has such a sound in the Māšiγ- or Te-māšiγ-t-language, we should not be inclined to conclude a priori, the Māšiγ or Imōšaγ having only one sign to express ع and غ, and nevertheless in many words or names, belonging to this idiom, and spelled with a γ, the r sound prevails in the most decided manner, of which I have shown an instance in the name imγāḍ, changed by the Moghrebian Arabs into [illegible], the simple ر taking the place of the γ (Tr. and Disc. I, p. 234). If, nevertheless, I have chosen the sign γ to express this sound, it is merely from want of anything better, and more expressive, and I did by no means thereby intend to imply, that it is to be pronounced like the γ in the modern Greek γέγραφα; but, at least, it seems to be preferable to the sign χ', which Lepsius has especially recommended. The Rev. Koelle himself, in whose grammar and vocabulary of the Kanúri-language this sound is not to be found, makes repeated use of it in his Polyglotta, which was published only one year previous to the other publications, and not only in words belonging to other languages, but even in such, as belong to mere dialects of the Kanúri-idiom, as, for instance, he writes the term dĕlāgĕ (in Kanúri Proper) dĕlāγu in the dialect of Ngurū, and dĕlāγĕ in that of Kānem (p. 90), and this sign γ which he employs is very remarkable, if we take into account, what I have just said. Even in the group of the Gurma- and Mosi-idioms the γ is perfectly established by Koelle's testimony, combined with my own, drawn as they are from so very different quarters; for, while I have written with a g most other words belonging to these languages, which Koelle in his Polyglotta has spelled with an γ, both of us agree as to the spelling of the term boγa, „goat" and baγa, „dog". I say here nothing of the Soṅγai-language, of which I shall speak further on, but I will mention in this place a circumstance, which is very instructive with regard to the manner, in which the idioms of Central-Negroland have caught the sound of the Arabic غ as brought to them by the Moghrebines, I mean the way, how they spell the word غفر, „to pardon"; for, while the Hausa-people seem to have understood the غ as a simple g sound, and have thence made gáferta, and in a similar manner the Wándalā-people kábora, in Kanúri I heard distinctly the form grabáṅgena, and in Lógoné gráffera, although this idiom has most decidedly the sound γ, while the Bágrimma changed the word entirely by transposing

*) Thus I found, that the Moors of Negroland, including even the learned Sheikh el Bakay, whenever I made them write European words in Arabic letters, rendered the r before m or b by غ, as in erm, arbre, armoir, and so on.

yáffaku darans. S. S. 78, N. 1. Ich habe bei diesem Worte absichtlich den wandelbaren Laut durch die entsprechendsten Buchstaben wiederzugeben gesucht und das Zeichen y nicht angewandt, wie denn die Art der Auffassung der Eingeborenen deutlich zu zeigen scheint, dass sie den Laut hier selbst nicht wie ein ẹ verstanden. Leider hat die Soṅyai-Sprache das Fremdwort nicht aufgenommen.

Neben s habe ich š gebraucht, entsprechend dem Deutschen sch.

Neben t, obgleich selten, habe ich das verstärkte t, ṭ = dem Arabischen ط gebraucht und diesen Buchstaben hätte ich wol noch häufiger anwenden können, wie ich denn in meinem Te-mášiγ-t-Vokabular in der Verwechselung dieser beiden Laute vielfach geirrt habe. Aber wir sehen, wie im Deutschen t und d in gewissen Dialekten der Volkssprache gar nicht unterschieden werden können und wie sollte das dann in diesen illiteraten Sprachen möglich sein.

Das aspirirte t, gleich dem Englischen th, habe ich durch θ gegeben, um die Identität mit dem Griechischen bekannten Zeichen ϑ darzustellen.

Neben z habe ich, den von Herrn Prof. Lepsius entwickelten Grundsätzen gemäss, ž gebraucht, um das Französische j wie in „jour" darzustellen.

Als Doppelkonsonanten habe ich gebraucht, ausser ks = x, (ds), dz, dž, ts und tš.

Über dz, ts ist nichts weiter zu sagen, als dass das dz gesprochen wird wie in fremden Namen, z. B. Dzungarei u. s. w., ts, wie unser z in „zerreissen".

Aber eine längere Betrachtung erfordert der Doppellaut dž und tš. dž entspricht in den meisten Fällen dem Arabischen ج, ja wird sogar meist nur in Wörtern gebraucht, die daraus abgeleitet sind, ich konnte ihn aber aus folgenden Gründen nicht mit ǵ oder in sonst einer Abwandelung von g geben. Denn erstlich finden sich gerade in den aus dem Arabischen in diese Neger-Sprachen eingeführten Ausdrücken stets Abweichungen des dž-Lautes in dz, ds ja ts, wie džennu, dzennu, tsonna, „Paradies"; džehénnem, dschénnem, „Hölle". Dann ist diese Trennung der Laute gut, um den verbalen Übergang des dž in ts zu zeigen; so wird aus dem Kanúri-Wort džeg-nískin in der 3ten Pers. Sing. tséh-tšin.

Allerdings könnten diese Beispiele Manchem nichts Anderes zu beweisen scheinen, als dass diese Völker den fremden Arabischen Laut nicht richtig aufzufassen vermochten, aber manche andere Betrachtungen führen dahin, das dž wie einen mit d componirten Laut in diesen Sprachen anzusehen, z. B. ist das Fúl-Wort džūl-ō, „Moslim", Plur. džūl-be wol sicherlich abgeleitet von dūl, mĕdo-dūl-na, „ich beschneide". Dann hat es auch noch einen ganz besonderen Vortheil, diesen componirten Laut dem einfachen ž an die Seite zu stellen. dž aufgelöst als Reduplication erscheint in džodžum. S. 34. N. 15.

Noch schwieriger als der dž-Laut ist tš. Man hat über diesen Laut sehr gestritten, und zumal die Engländer, die ihn in der merkwürdigen Form ch in cheese, church u. s. w. besitzen. Allerdings gibt es auch in den Afrikanischen Sprachen viele Fälle und besonders im Soṅyai, wo man lieber eine abgewandelte Form von k, als tš nehmen möchte, um diesen Laut darzustellen, aber doch lässt es sich in einer Zusammenstellung mehrerer Sprachen nicht durchführen: das würde Ungleichheiten hervorrufen, anstatt Alles nach einem und demselben Princip zu ordnen. Denn dieser Laut liegt eben zwischen k und ts in der Mitte und kann in der Schrift nur ungenügend dargestellt werden. Im Fúl geht tš in s über, tšādum, Plur. sādi.

Ich muss hier auch ein Wort über den häufigen Vorschlag des n oder ṅ vor g und zuweilen auch vor d und des m vor b sagen: ṅgāla, ṅgilla, nda, ye-mbúri-ekin. Ein solcher Vorschlag findet sich nicht allein in vielen anderen Afrikanischen und Asiatischen Sprachen, sondern auch in europäischen. In Bezug auf ṅg aber kann man zuweilen zweifelhaft sein, ob das n nicht vielmehr eine besondere Silbe in, un, als einen blossen Vorschlag bildet und das möchte ich eigentlich in den Fällen annehmen, wo z. B. Koelle einen Accent auf das ṅg setzt, was widersinnig aussieht. So gleich ṅgō, „siehe", ist wol ohne Zweifel falsch und wird viel richtiger úṅgō geschrieben, da Koelle selbst das Zeitwort wúṅgin hat, zu dem es

the sound r, which had been once expressed distinctly, and thus writing gábraga. On the other hand the Fúl-be really seized the sound as something like the modern Greek γ in γάγγρα, making γáfaku or γáffaku. See my glossary p. 78, note 4.

Besides s I have made use of š, in order to express by one sign the English sh.

Besides t, although rarely, I have employed the stronger ṭ, which perhaps ought sometimes to have taken the place of d, as in my Te-mášiγ-t I have repeatedly been misled in this respect, but, if even in European languages t and d are interchanged in different dialects, and cannot be distinguished by pronunciation, what must be the case with these illiterate languages.

Moreover, in order to express th, I have made use of the sign θ, as most closely approaching to the Greek ϑ.

Besides z, in conformity with the arguments developed by Prof. Lepsius, I have employed ž, in order to represent the French j in jour.

As for double consonants, I have employed, besides ks = x, (ds), dz, dž, ts and tš.

dz is known to the English only from foreign names, such as Dzoungaria; ts, as in the common Chinese names Tsa, Tsuṅg. But we are obliged to dwell longer on the double consonants dž and tš. dž in most cases corresponds to the Arabic ج, nay, is even employed almost exclusively in words derived from the Arabic, although from the following reasons I was prevented from using a sign derived from g, such as ǵ.

First, in those very terms, which have been introduced into these Negro-idioms from the Arabic, there occur constantly dialectical differences, through which the dž sound is changed into dz (ds), and even ts, such as dženna, dzenna, tsenna, „paradise", džehénnem, dzehénnem, „hell". But in other cases, likewise, dž is changed into ts, as in the Kanúri-verb džeg-ìskin, 3rd pers. sing. tsak-tšin.

Cases, like these, may seem to argue to some persons merely as so many proofs of the Africans not being able to pronounce correctly the foreign sound, but other arguments lead me to think, that they considered it as a double sound, composed of d (or even t) and s or z, as for instance the Fúl-term džul-o, „moslim", plur. djúl-be is most probably derived from dúl, médo-dúl-na, „I circumcise". We have also cases of dž being reduplicated, and dissolved, as in the Bágrimma-term dzodžum, „he is born" (gl. p. 34, note 15). Besides, there is a considerable advantage in employing dž, in order to place this composite sound side by side with the sound ž.

Still more difficult, than the sound dž is tš, and the English especially, who possess this very sound in the form ch („cheese", „church" and so on) object greatly against the use of it. No doubt, even in African languages, but especially in the Sońγai-idiom, there are many cases, where we should prefer a sign derived from k instead of a sign composed of t and š, but it would be very difficult and even impossible to use two different signs, according as in each case this sound has been derived from k or t. It is indeed a sound, which lies midways between k and t, and which in writing can only be insufficiently expressed. But in Fulfúlde there is a decided preponderating of t in this sound, as tš in the plural form in many instances is changed into s, tšódum, for instance, making sódi.

I must here add a word about the prefixing of n or ṅ before g and sometimes, but rarely, before d, and of m before b, such as ṅgúla, ṅgilla, nda, yo-mbári-skin. This is a feature common to many African, Asiatic and even European languages, but we may sometimes doubt, whether these combinations do not form really independent syllables by themselves. Thus Koelle writes ṅgo, „behold, here"; but, as there is the verb wúṅgin, „I see, I behold", it is more correct to write úṅgo. In this respect I was especially uncertain with regard to several words in the Tédá-language. If we had all these words written by the natives in Arabic characters, we should not be left in a doubt. Thus they write the name

den einfachen Imperativ bildet. Besonders unsicher war ich in dieser Hinsicht bei manchen Wörtern der Tédâ-Sprache. In dieser Beziehung würde die Art, wie die Eingeborenen selbst diese Wörter mit Arabischer Schrift schreiben, oft Aufklärung geben, wie sie denn den Namen der Stadt Ngala [illegible] schreiben, wodurch sie hinreichend zu erkennen geben, dass die beiden ersten Buchstaben Einen Laut bilden, so ungeeignet auch das [illegible] sein mag, diesen letzteren darzustellen.

In Betreff der Vokale a, e, i, o, u, ü = ö habe ich den feinen Unterschied, den Koelle gemäss den von Prof. Lepsius aufgestellten Regeln in seiner Grammatik (s. Kapitel II, §. 7) und in seinem Wörterbuche der Kanúri-Sprache eingeführt hat, nicht anwenden können und er selbst wäre sicherlich nicht dazu gekommen, hätte er seine Resultate von der lebenden Sprache eines ganzen Volkes ableiten wollen, anstatt von einem einzigen Individuum, dem er fünf Jahre lang die Zwangsjacke Europäischer Intelligenz und Verstandesregeln anlegte. Seine eigene Unsicherheit im Allgemeinen ist S. 10 der Gr. ziemlich deutlich ausgesprochen, besonders in dem Satze „neither can the line of demarcation between *o* and *e* be so distinctly drawn".

Ich unterscheide nur die kurzen Vokale, die weiter keiner Bezeichnung bedürfen, und die von Natur langen â, ê, î, û, ü oder die durch wandelbare Accente betonten á, é, í, ú, ǘ. Als Doppelvokale habe ich nur ai und ei, oi, au. Über ai, das ich ungleich häufiger als ei anwende, werde ich bei Gelegenheit der Kanúri-Sprache einiges Nähere sagen. Das von Koelle gebrauchte ui gehört nach meiner festen Überzeugung zwei Silben an und ou habe ich gleichfalls nicht anwenden können.

Viertes Kapitel.

Nähere Betrachtung der einzelnen in der Sammlung vertretenen Sprachen.

Die Kanúri-Sprache; manna Kanúri.

Bei der Kanúri-Sprache kann ich mich in Anbetracht der eingehenden und gründlichen Arbeiten des Missionar's Koelle kurz fassen, indem ich mich bestimmt auf solche Punkte beschränke, in denen ich in Bezug auf das, was ich oben S. XXIV gesagt habe, von meinem Standpunkt als Reisender, der die Sprache in ihrer lebendigen Existenz an sich nicht allein, sondern auch besonders im Zusammenhang mit den Nachbarsprachen aufgefasst hat, die Ansichten des Missionar's berichtigen oder ergänzen zu können glaube, indem ich hier noch einmal mein Bedauern ausdrücke, dass ich diese tiefen und eingehenden Studien meinen Forschungen nicht zu Grunde legen konnte, sondern selbst von den ersten Rudimenten anfangen musste. Vielleicht wird noch einmal ein anderer Reisender oder Missionar den ganzen Vortheil von unseren beiden, so unabhängig von einander gemachten, Arbeiten ziehen können.

Vorerst will ich einige Bemerkungen über meine Schreibweise dieser Sprache in's Besondere zusammenstellen, indem ich nur ein Wort über den Namen Kanúri vorausschicke.

Kanúri ist nach meiner festen Überzeugung der eigentliche Nationalname der Leute und Sprache von Bórnu — der, wie ich schon oben S. VIII behauptet, nichts in aller Welt mit dem Namen der Stadt Kano zu thun hat, sondern die ursprüngliche Form des Namens Kanemri war[1]); Bórnu oder Bórno dagegen, der zuerst bei Ebn Batúta um die Mitte des XIVten

---

[1]) Wir besitzen noch ganz deutliche Beweise, dass die Endung auf am, om, um in den meisten Kanúri-Wörtern, wie in sôlam, „Zange", nicht ursprünglich, sondern in bezüglich später Zeit hinzugefügt sind — siehe den Abschnitt, der die Verwandtschaft der Kanúri- und Tédâ-Sprache behandelt. In Betreff der Endung ri kann es allerdings nicht zweifelhaft sein, dass, wie Koelle in seiner Grammatik §. 43 sagt, diese Endung von Eigennamen Adjektive bildet zur Bezeichnung verschiedener Menschenklassen. Auch hat er nicht Unrecht, wenn er unter Nr. 3 den Namen Kanúri, Kanú-ri eben als Beispiel zu dieser Regel citirt. Dies erhält ferner meine Bestätigung durch den Vergleich dieser Namensform Kanú-ri mit dem Namen Kání-kó, der den Bornauern von den Asu-Leuten gegeben wird, wenn wir damit wieder den Namen Mallinkè, d. h. Malle-n-kê vergleichen, der die Einwohner von Melle bezeichnet. Von diesem Gesichtspunkte aus müssen wir also allerdings denjenigen entschuldigen, der aus Unkenntniss des historischen Thatbestandes den Namen Kanú-ri von der Stadt Kanó ableitet.

of the town Ngála, نغال, implying thereby, that the ng forms one sound, although the غ is scarcely the right sign for expressing it.

With regard to the vowels a, e, i, o, u, ų (= ue) I have not been able to carry through the nice distinctions, which the Rev. Koelle, adopting the principles of Mr. Lepsius, has introduced into his grammar (see chapter II, §. 7) as well, as into his vocabulary, of the Kanúri-language, and I am sure, the missionary himself would rather have hesitated in adopting such a complicated system of writing an illiterate language, if he had worked upon the living idiom of a whole nation, instead of abstracting all his rules from the pronunciation of a single individual, whom he was holding during five years under the control of European theories and of European schematizing. However, his own uncertainty in general is sufficiently expressed in the passage (§. 10 of the grammar), where he says „neither can the line of demarcation between e and e be so distinctly drawn". The vowels are to be pronounced as in Italian.

As for myself, I only distinguish between the short vowels, which need no further distinction, and the long ones by origin ā, ō, ī, ū, ų̄, or as distinguished by a moveable accent, á, é, í, ú, ų́. As for diphthongs, I use only ai, ei, oi and au. ui, looked upon as a diphthong by Koelle, according to my firm opinion, does not bear this character, but constantly belongs to two different syllables; nor have I found any reason for using his ou. With regard to the diphthong ai, which I use much more frequently than ei, I shall say something more, when I come to speak of the Kanúri-language in particular.

Chapter the fourth.

A few remarks with regard to each of the languages represented in this vocabulary.

The Kanúri-idiom; manna Kanúri.

With regard to the Kanúri-language, considering the profound and accurate study, which the Rev. Koelle has made of this language, I may limit my remarks to such points, where I think myself capable of correcting, or improving upon, the opinion stated by that meritorious labourer on this field. This divergency of opinion is based, as I have already stated in general p. XXV, on my character as a traveller, in which I have not only studied each of these languages singly as the idiom of a whole nation in the daily intercourse of the people, but do look upon the whole of these languages as the idioms of neighbouring tribes, exercising more or less influence one upon the other. But I have to repeat in this place my deep regret, that I was not enabled to base my own labours upon those of my contemporary, but was obliged to begin myself from the very first rudiments. May we hope, that a succeeding traveller or missionary will have the advantage of both our labours, thus independently made.

First I shall make a few remarks with regard to the name Kanúri, and shall then say something more about my way of spelling the words belonging to this language in particular.

Kanúri, according to my firm opinion, is the proper national name of the people and language of Bórnu which, as I have already stated p. IX, has nothing to do with the name of the town of Kanō, but probably is derived from the original form of the name Kánem-ri [1]); the

[1]) We have still the most distinct proofs, that the termination in em, am, am in most Kanúri-words such as télam, „tongue", was not original — see the chapter treating of the affinity between the Kanúri- and Tédā-idioms. — As for the suffix ri, it certainly cannot be doubtful, whether, as Koelle says (gr. §. 43), it forms adjectives of names for different classes of men, and he is quite right, when in n° 3 he cites Kanúri (Kanū-ri) as an example. This is still further illustrated and proved by comparing this form Kanú-ri with the name Kánl-bé given to the people of Bórnu by the Aba-people, taking likewise regard to the name Mellinkē i. e. Melle-n-kē, signifying the inhabitants of Melle. We may therefore well excuse a person, who has no knowledge of the historical state of the question, if he derives this name from that of the town of Kanō.

Jahrhunderts erscheint, ist der politische Name, der erst aufkam im Gegensatz zu demjenigen der Bulāla¹). Diese Ansicht erhält dadurch ihre bestimmte Bestätigung, dass die Tédā, die sich in jener politischen Zerstückelung an die Bulāla anschlossen, die Kanúri neben der weiter unten zu besprechenden Benennung Túguba nur mit anna Bórno bezeichnen; anna heisst „Leute", „Volk".

Meine Abweichung von Koelle's Schreibweise in bloss alphabetischer Beziehung berührt besonders zwei Punkte von Bedeutung. Der erste betrifft die zusammengesetzten Konsonanten tš und dž. Koelle sagt ausdrücklich (Grammatik §. 8, S. 12), dass die Kanúri-Sprache das dž allem Anschein nach von tš nicht bestimmt unterschieden habe. Das ist aber entschieden nur ein individueller Fehler seiner alleinigen Autorität 'Ali Eisāmi; denn ich sehe es nicht einmal für eine provinzielle Eigenthümlichkeit an, ausser in so fern es Koelle selbst betrifft, da das Ohr eines Süd-Deutschen entschieden weniger geeignet ist, den Unterschied zwischen diesen Lauten aufzufassen, als dasjenige eines Nord-Deutschen; denn, wenn ich selbst auch oben S. XXXVIII angegeben, dass in den aus dem Arabischen eingeführten Wörtern dž häufig mit dz und ts abwechsele, so findet eine solche Unbestimmtheit doch eben nur bei diesen eingeführten, der Sprache eigentlich fremden, Wörtern Statt. In den einheimischen Wörtern aber muss man diese Laute, so gut wie andere nahe liegende, auf das Bestimmteste von einander getrennt halten, und kein Kanúri, der nicht durch lange Abwesenheit von der Heimath viele charakteristische Züge seiner Sprache vergessen hätte, würde verstehn, wenn man den Mund dši statt tši nennte. Eine solche Verwechselung dieser und der verwandten Laute findet nun aber bei Koelle im höchsten Grade Statt, indem er z. B. tšé statt džé, „Tau", „Bindfaden", dzúmgin oder tsúmgin statt zumgin oder vielmehr zum-nískin, tšéni statt žéni, „Schöpflöffel", tšéna statt žéna, „Messer", tšíre statt žíre, „wahr", tsóga statt zóga, „Mütze" schreibt.

Diese verschiedenen Laute habe ich mit möglichster Schärfe auseinander gehalten und widerspreche auf das Entschiedenste dem oben angeführten Ausspruche Koelle's, dass es scheine, als wenn die Kanúri-Sprache dž von tš nicht unterschieden habe. Übrigens bewährt sich auch in Betreff des Kanúri die oben als allgemein aufgestellte Regel, dass tš zuweilen aus einem palatalen k oder g entstanden ist, aber lange nicht so häufig, wie z. B. im Sonyai.

Die zweite Abweichung von allgemeinerer Bedeutung in meiner Schreibweise betrifft besonders den Doppelvokal ai. Fast immer, wo ich mich dieses Doppelvokals bedient habe, wird der Leser bei Koelle ei finden und er gebraucht den ersten nur ganz ausnahmsweise, wie er denn bei keíga, „Gesang" angibt, dass es auch kaíga gesprochen werde, aber selten. So feine Unterscheidungen zu machen hielt Koelle sich berechtigt, da er doch sein Material in Sierra Leone, 200 Deutsche Meilen von Bórnu, aus dem Munde eines einzigen Eingeborenen sammelte, der 23 Jahre aus dem Heimathlande abwesend gewesen war; und dennoch kann nichts deutlicher sein, als z. B. das a in mai, „König", und den davon abgeleiteten Wörtern, das sich auch dem ma, „Person", natürlich anschliesst, und so schreibt Koelle in seiner Polyglotta selbst das Wort in den Dialekten von Múnio und Ngúrū.

In Betreff der von Koelle angewandten mannichfaltigen Vokal-Unterschiede habe ich schon oben S. XL meine Meinung ausgesprochen. Dass ferner die Kanúri-Sprache dem Anheben eines Wortes mit u abgeneigt sein sollte, wie Koelle sagt (Gr. §. 31), habe ich nicht gefunden und habe deshalb ganz ruhig ū, u-ma geschrieben u. s. w. Wenn sie den Namen 'Omar Wumar aussprechen, so ist das ganz etwas Anderes, da dies Wort mit einem ع anfängt.

Auch wird man in meiner Schreibweise eine grosse Abweichung in Betreff der Assimilation oder des Überganges der Konsonanten von den von Koelle (in §. 14 seiner Gr.) aufgestellten Regeln bemerken, indem bei mir keineswegs r hinter g in r oder hinter k in k übergeht,

¹) Siehe Reise Th. II, S. 304.

name of **Bórnu** or **Bórno** on the other hand, which appears for the first time in Ebn Batúta's Narrative, about the middle of the XIVth century, is the **political** name, which originated in the splitting of the Kanúri dynasty into two hostile factions, when the name Borno was given to one of them in opposition to that of Buláln being born by the other [1]). This opinion receives especial confirmation from the fact of the Téda, who followed the party of the Buláfe, calling the Kanúri-people, besides the name **Túguba** (Tr. III, p. 491), which I shall endeavour to explain further on, by the name **anna** (people) **Bórno**.

The manner, in which my way of writing deviates from that of Koelle's in merely alphabetical respect, regards especially two points of some importance. One of these considers the double consonants **tš** and **dž**. With regard to these sounds Koelle says distinctly in his grammar §. 8, p. 12 „the Kanúri-language does not seem to have developed **dž** as distinguished from **tš**", but that is decidedly an individual mistake of 'Ali Eisámi's, Koelle's only authority, for I do not even consider it as a provincial divergency, except in so far as the ear of a native of Southern Germany is much less capable of catching the difference of these sounds, than that of a native of Northern Germany. For, although I myself have stated previously (p. XXXIX), that in those words, which have been borrowed from the Arabic, **dž** is frequently interchanged with **ds** and **ts**, nevertheless such an uncertainty with regard to this sound only takes place in terms of foreign import, while with regard to indigenous Kanúri-terms we must keep these sounds, as well as others of a similar character, totally distinct. Thus no Kanúri man, who has not been absent from his native country for a long range of years, as 'Ali Eisámi was, would be able to understand a person who pronounces **dži** instead of **tši**, „month". But such an interchange of these totally distinct sounds is found in Koelle's works to a very wide extent, for he writes **tšó** instead of **džó**, „rope, cord", **dzúmgin** and **tsúmgin** instead of **súmgin** or rather **sum-nískin**, **tšéni** instead of **žéni**, „a scooping spoon", **tšénd** instead of **žéna**, „knife", **tšíré** instead of **žíré**, „true", **tsóga** instead of **sóga**, „cup" and so on.

These different sounds I have kept asunder with all possible distinctness and once more plainly contradict the statement of Koelle's, that „the Kanúri-language does not seem to have developed **dž** as distinguished from **tš**". In another respect the statement made above from a general point of view, that **tš** has sometimes been derived from a **k** or **g**, finds its application also in the Kanúri-language, but not by far so generally, as is the case with the Sobyai-language.

A second difference of more general import between my way of writing and that of Koelle's regards the diphthong **ai**, and the reader may take it as a general rule, that wherever I use **ai**, Koelle uses **ei**, while he employs the **ai** scarcely ever, one exception constituting the form **kaiga**, which form he states expressly to be used but rarely besides **keiga**, „song". Distinctions of such nicety Koelle thought himself authorized to make in Sierra Leone, at a distance of many hundred miles from Bórnu, from the mouth of one single native, who had been absent from his native country twenty three years. But nothing is more distinct, than, for instance, the **a** in **mai**, „king" and in the words thence derived.

As for the many distinctions employed by Koelle with regard to the character of the vowels, I have given my opinion already before (p. XLI); in this place I have to contradict his statement (gr. §. 31), that the language is averse to commencing words with **u**, for, if they pronounce a name like 'Omar, beginning with an ع, Wumar, that is quite a different affair, but I heard them distinctly pronounce **ū**, **ū-ma** and so on.

The reader will also observe a great difference between my way of writing and that of Koelle's with regard to the assimilation or identification of consonants, as I am not able to acknowledge the correctness of the rules established by him (gr. §. 14), and therefore do

---

[1]) See Travels and Disc. vol. II, p. 289.

ebenso n hinter l keineswegs auch in l, r hinter m keineswegs auch in m, sondern, wie ich in der wirklichen, lebendigen Aussprache des Volkes jeden Konsonanten ganz klar und deutlich aussprechen hörte, so halte ich es auch für richtig, ihn in der Schrift wiederzugeben und widerspreche Koelle, der diese Konsonanten in solchem Zusammenstoss „unvereinbar" (incompatible) nennt.

Den γ-Laut hat weder Koelle, noch ich im Kanúri, aber ich habe schon angeführt (S. XXXVI), dass Koelle ihn in seiner Polyglotta in anderen einfachen Dialekt-Abweichungen dieser Sprache hat; das würde er jedoch später vielleicht auch unterlassen haben.

Einige Wörter schreiben Koelle und ich so verschieden, dass man sie auf den ersten Blick kaum wird identificiren können, so ich h a m - s u, „kalt", Koelle á m s a ŋ. Ich hatte selbst grosse Mühe, viele meiner Wörter in seinen Büchern wiederzufinden. Wer von uns der Wahrheit näher gekommen ist, wird die Zeit lehren, vorläufig hoffe ich, dass meine Autorität schon jetzt von einiger Bedeutung sein wird.

Ich gehe nun zu einigen Bemerkungen in Betreff der Sprache selbst über.

Dass Koelle selbst schon auf bedeutende Abweichungen der Sprache von dem von ihm vertretenen Material Rücksicht genommen, und wie er sie zu erklären versucht hatte, habe ich schon oben S. XII ausgeführt. Auch bewährt sich diese Erklärung in einigen Fällen wirklich durch den Vergleich mit der Tédā-Sprache. So z. B. steht Koelle's Form ŋ g ą l a (oder doch vielmehr n g á l a), „gut", „schön", der Tédā-Form g a l l e oder g á l e näher als mein ṅ g i l l a, was die jetzt gebräuchliche populäre Form des Wortes ist. Vergleiche auch S. 92, N. 2 zu s o m - n í s k i n. Auch manche jetzt übliche Verbalformen mögen neuerer Bildung sein, wie mein w e l t - í s k i n (S. 66), eine Form, die Koelle gar nicht kennt und die vielleicht erst von dem von w é l ü g i n oder w ö l ö g i n abgeleiteten Substantiv w é l t e (Koelle w ə l t e) gebildet ist. Daraus können sich jedoch nicht alle Unterschiede erklären und ich empfehle künftigen Reisenden diese Punkte so, wie auch genau darauf Acht zu geben, ob z. B. folgende Abstraktiva wirklich im Gebrauch sind, wie k ę r r á g o, „Liebe", n ę m - b ō t e, „Schlaf" (dies wol gewiss nicht), n ę m g ō t e, „das Ergreifen", n ę m k á m t e, „ein Schnitt", n ę́ m k a m, „Menschlichkeit" (gewiss nicht). Ich glaube nämlich, dass, wie ich schon oben angedeutet, durch den langen Druck, den Koelle's geistige Pumpmaschine auf das Gehirn und die Auffassungsweise 'Ali's üben musste, dieser selbst aus blosser Analogie und nach bloss m ö g l i c h e r Formation sehr viele Wörter gebildet hat, die gar nicht existiren, ja auch nicht vor 50 Jahren im Kanúri existirt haben. Allerdings ist solche Fortbildung der Sprache für ein wirksames Verkehren der Missionare in ihrem Bekehrungswerk unumgänglich nöthig und ist nicht zu tadeln, so lange es sich innerhalb der Gränzen der Sprache hält, aber wenigstens sollten die Missionare stets angeben, wo sie ein neues Wort entweder selbst gebildet haben oder von ihren Schülern haben bilden lassen.

Ich gehe nun zu einigen grammatischen Betrachtungen über.

In Betreff des Pronomen Personale stimme ich Koelle völlig bei (Grammatik §. 31), der als Kennzeichen der 1sten Person u (ich bemerke hier nur, dass u auch im Altegyptischen als Bezeichnung der 1sten Person vorkommen soll, Bunsen V, 81) oder überhaupt einen Vokal; als Zeichen der 2ten n und für die 3te s angibt, aus denen die Plural- (eigentlich Dual-)Form durch ein angehängtes n d i, „zwei" gebildet sei. Dies wird besonders klar, wenn wir dieses n d i mit dem entsprechenden Altegyptischen t i vergleichen (Bunsen V, 81), obgleich die äussere Ähnlichkeit bloss zufällig ist. Das diesen einfachen Lauten angehängte m a aber hat Koelle nicht erfasst: es heisst „Person" (s. Vorb. S. 2, N. 1) und erläutert sehr schön, wie auch die Form ó k é i n - n i, für „ich selbst", den Satz Bunsen's V, S. 38 von der Bildung der Fürwörter auf Grund der Persönlichkeit.

Auch die Bildung des Pronomen Possessivum scheint Koelle nicht erfasst zu haben und das rührt von dem Umstande her, der überhaupt auf sein grammatisches Studium einen höchst

not change r behind g into an r, or behind k into k, or n after l into l likewise, or r behind m into m, but on the contrary, as I heard each consonant clearly and distinctly pronounced by the people, so I think it right to express them by writing, and I distinctly contradict Koelle, who calls these consonants incompatible, when thus meeting together.

The y sound appears neither in Koelle's nor in my own vocabulary of the Kandri-idiom, but I have already stated p. XXXVII, that Koelle employs it in his Polyglotta in dialectical variations of this very idiom, although a year later he perhaps would have suppressed this sound.

Altogether some words, as written by myself and by Koelle, look so differently, that the reader will have difficulty to recognise their identity, as for instance my ham-su and Koelle's ámāso, and I myself had considerable difficulty in finding my words even in his vocabulary. Who of us two has approached nearer to truth, time will decide, but, I hope, that as for accentuation in general, my authority will predominate even now.

I now proceed to make a few remarks with regard to the language itself.

Already p. XIII I have stated, that Koelle himself has taken into account the fact, that considerable variation of the linguistical material collected by him might prove to exist, and how he has endeavoured to explain such a circumstance. And I have to acknowledge, that in certain cases, what he says, finds a confirmation from a comparison with the Tóda-language. Thus his form ñgąla (ṅgála), „good, fine", approaches much closer to the Tóda-form galle or gálo, than my form ṅgilla, which, however, is the popular form at present used. Compare also p. 92, note 2 with regard to sem-nfekin. Some verbal forms also, which are now generally used, may be of mere modern formation, such as my welt-fskin (vocabulary p. 66), while I have never heard the forms wólṅgin or wólṅgin, given by Koelle. From this point of view, however, all differences cannot be well explained, and I therefore recommend to future travellers, to pay especial attention to these points, and also to see, whether abstract nouns like the following are really used, kęrrágo, „love", nęmbóte, „sleep", nǫmgote, „seizure", nemkámto, „a cut", nǫ́mkam, „humanity". That several of these words are never used, and have never been used neither, I am quite sure, and it is my firm belief, that Koelle by exercising a long and continued pressure on the mental powers of his scholar and teacher — for 'Ali was both —, and by inuring him to the theoretical laws of the structure of a language, made him form many words from mere analogy, and which may possibly be used, but which never have been used. Of course, for a missionary, who wants to prepare the way for converting the Natives, it is a peremptory law to form a great many new words, in order to be able to translate the Holy writ into the language of the Natives, but we must expect or rather exact from him, that he states, whenever he has formed a form by himself or has got it formed by his scholar, instead of introducing it into the vocabulary simply and silently as an example illustrative of the very grammatical rule, he wants to establish.

I now proceed first to making a few grammatical remarks.

With regard to the personal pronoun I agree perfectly with Koelle, who states (gr. § 31) as his opinion, that the characteristic sign of the first person is u, or a vowel in general, that of the second n, and of the third s, and that the plural (properly a dual-form) has been formed by adding ndi to these characteristic signs. This case, becomes much clearer by comparing ndi with the corresponding ti of the ancient Egyptian, where it is the sign of the dual. (Bunsen V, p. 81). But, as for the termination ma, which in many cases is added to these simple pronominal signs, it has not been seized by Koelle; it means „person, individual" (vocab. p. 13, note 1), and may serve as an illustration of what Bunsen says (Egypt vol. V, p. 38, German ed.), with regard to the formation of the pronouns.

While thus Koelle appears to have tolerably well seized the nature of the personal pronoun, the same cannot be said of the possessive pronoun, and the reason is his perfect unacquaintance with the grammatical structure of the languages of the neighbouring countries, espe-

nachtheiligen Einfluss geübt hat, dass er nämlich mit dem Charakter der Nachbar-Sprachen Bórnu's, besonders des Hausa, vollkommen unbekannt war.

Das Pronomen Possessivum ist nämlich unzweifelhaft durch Einwirkung des Berberischen beziehenden n entstanden, oder direkt durch das identische Altegyptische en als Genitiv-Verhältniss (Bunsen I, 355), das häufig bei Zusammensetzung mit dem Substantiv abgeworfen wird, hier aber jenen pronominalen Zeichen vorgesetzt wurde.

n-u, n-i: ni, „von mir, mein"[1], ὁ ἐμός,
n-n, n-m } num, „von dir, dein",
n-si: nisé, „von ihm, sein"[2],
n-a-ndi: ndé, „von uns, unser,
n-n-ndi: ndō, „von euch, euer",
n-sa-ndi: nisá, „von ihnen, ihr".

So erklärt es sich auch, warum diese possessiven Formen dem Subjekt nur folgen können.

Was nun die andere Form des Pronomen Possessivum mit kaké, Koelle káge, betrifft (S. 4 meines Vokabular's), so ist kaké offenbar ursprünglich ein Nomen, das „Sache", „Besitz" bedeutet, vielleicht verwandt mit dem H. agō; in der ersten Person ist das possessive Suffixum ni nur populärer Weise weggelassen, so dass kaké allein „mein" bedeutet.

Zu der Bildung und Etymologie von Substantiven, wie Koelle sie §. 26, S. 21 ausführt, kann ich noch Einiges hinzu bemerken und hierzu gibt eben auch der Vergleich mit den benachbarten Sprachen vielfachen Anlass, wie ich im Vokabular bei den einzelnen Fällen ausführen werde. Hier will ich nur bemerken, dass wir z. B. sehen, wie die Bildung der Substantive mit einem vorgesetzten ka oder kon beziehungsweise ziemlich jung ist. So können wir aus der völligen Übereinstimmung des Kanúri-Wortes ka-gálā, „die Amtseinsetzung" (bei Koelle kágalla) mit garā in Bágrimma, wenn wir die politische Abhängigkeit Bagirmi's von Bórnu in Betracht ziehen, schliessen, dass die Bágrimma-Sprache dieses Wort aufnahm, als es auch im Kanúri noch nicht den Vorsatz ka hatte, und dies kann wol kaum so lange her sein. Von demselben Gesichtspunkte aus muss ich Koelle darin widersprechen, dass kām, „Person", das Ursprüngliche sei, wovon der irreguläre Plur. ām gebildet worden (§. 28); hingegen bin ich überzeugt, dass ām als das Allgemeinere, das Ursprüngliche und kām daraus vermittelst ke, ka das Abgeleitete war. Ich will hier nur noch bemerken, dass das Zeichen des Dativs ro an das Egyptische or, r erinnert (Bunsen I, 355).

Dann muss ich Koelle widersprechen, wenn er es als allgemein gültige Regel aufstellt, dass das Eigenschaftswort auf ma im Plur. sich stets in bū verwandle (§. 40, 4). Allerdings sagt man nur Kānem-bū, Plur. von Kānem-ma, der Bewohner von Kānem, aber Bórnu-bū, „die Bórnu-Leute", habe ich nie gehört und dass ma häufig mit einem Plur. verbunden ist, zeigen zur Genüge schon die volleren Formen des Pronomen Possessivum mit ma, also ándi-ma, „wir", néndi-ma, „ihr", séndi-ma, „sie" (Vokab. S. 2) und das so ganz gewöhnliche sem-ma, „ganz", „alle", also in der Verbindung mit sū, „sie", sū sem-ma, „sie alle", da doch ma unterschieden nur dieselbe adjektive Endung, sem oder sam die Wurzel ist.

Ich will nur noch, soweit es sich auf Stammes- oder Völker-Verhältnisse bezieht, hinzufügen, dass dieser Redetheil ma in der Pluralform bū, besonders lebhaft an die Kafir-Wurzel mo, Plur. ba oder be erinnert, mit dem Unterschiede, dass letztere nur als Präfixum gebraucht wird, also mo-tšuana, „ein Mann aus dem Tschuana-Volk", Plur. be-tšuana, während das

---

[1] Ich muss hier nicht übergehen, dass durch ein unglückliches Übersehen S. 44 ein á bei der Form ā-ma ná-nia in meine Abschrift gekommen ist, während es in meinem Original-Manuskript gar nicht steht, und dass danach also auch Note 1 zu verbessern ist, die auf der falschen Form ná-ndia beruht.

[2] Das n in nisé ist also das Ursprüngliche und wird hinter einem Konsonanten nur gewöhnlich ausgestossen.

cially the Hausa, a want which has exercised an unfavourable influence upon his whole study of the Kanúri-language, otherwise so eminently profound.

The possessive pronoun, therefore, I have no doubt, has been formed by prefixing the Berber-sign n, which is identical with the en of the ancient Egyptians (Bunsen I, 335), indicative of reference and possession to the characteristic sign of the personal pronoun:

n-u, n-i: ni, „of me, my" [1]), ὁ ἐμοῦ.
n-n / n-m } num, „of thee, thy",
n-s: ntsé, „of him, his" [2]),
n-a-ndi: ndó, „of us, our",
n-n-ndi: ndō, „of you, your",
n-sa-ndi: ntsá, „of them, their".

In this manner it is easily explained, why these pronouns are nothing but suffixes.

With regard to the fuller form of the possessive pronoun with kakē (p. 4 of my vocabulary — Koelle kágo) I am sure, that kakē was originally a noun, indicative of possession and possibly related to the Hausa-word agō, the possessive suffix ni being thrown off in the first person.

To the remarks made by Koelle with regard to the formation, and the etymology of substantives (gr. §. 26, p. 21), I am able to make some additions of consequence, especially from a comparison with the neighbouring languages, as I shall have opportunity of further developing in my vocabulary. In this place I will only remark, that we have distinct proofs of the relatively recent formation of the substantives by prefixing ka or ken to the root. Thus, for instance, from the perfect identity of the Kanúri-term ka-gála, „the act of installation" (Koelle kágalla) with gará in Bágrimma, taking into account the state of political dependence upon Bornu in which Bagírmi was kept, we may draw the conclusion, that the Bágrimma borrowed this word from the Kanúri-language, when it had not yet received the prefix ka. From the same point of view I cannot agree with Koelle, who looks upon the singular kām, „a person" as the original form, from whence the plural am has been derived (gr. §. 28), while I am convinced, that am, „people" (T. auna), was the original notion, from which kam was formed by prefixing ke or ka, „one of the people". I only want to add, that ro, the sign of the dative case, reminds one of er in the ancient Egyptian.

I have also to oppose Koelle's statement, when he puts forth as a general rule (§. 40, 4), that the adjectives ending in ma form bū in the plural. No doubt, Kánem-bū appears to be the only right plural form of Kánem-ma, meaning „the inhabitant of Kánem", but Bórnu-bū, „the Bórnu-people", I have never heard, although this might be an antiquated form; we have, however, most common plural forms with ma, such as the fuller form of the personal pronoun ándi-ma „we", nóndi-ma, „you", sándi-ma, „they" (vocab. p. 2), and likewise the adjective sem-ma, „all", even in connection with sū, „they", sū sem-ma, „all of them"; the ma in all these cases being the same form of termination, and sam or sem being the root of sem-ma.

I want only to add, that the term ma, plur. bū, as far as it serves to represent relations of tribes or nationalities, reminds one very strikingly of the Kafir-root mo, plur. ba or be, the difference being, that the latter is only used as a prefix, as in the name mo-tšuāna, „an individual of the Tšuāna tribe", plur. bo-tšuāna, while the Kanúri ma is a suffix.

---

[1]) I here must observe, that through an unfortunate oversight a d has crept into my copy of the form ā-ma sá-ala (p. 64), while my original Mscr. has nothing of the kind, and that in consequence also note 1 which is based on the wrong form sá-ndis, has to be corrected.

[2]) The n in the form ntsé, therefore, is original and is only thrown off, when following after a consonant.

Kanúri ma nur als Suffixum gebraucht wird, also Kánem-ma, „ein Mann von Kánem", Plur. Kánem-bū. Man erklärt sich die Veränderung des m in b wol am leichtesten daraus, dass ma dem Altegyptischen Nachsatz pa, „Mann", „Mensch", entspricht. Auch ist es interessant, dass in der Sprache der benachbarten Yédina oder Búduma ma, „Sklave" heisst.

Diese Punkte, wo ich von Koelle abweiche, sind von nicht weit reichender Bedeutung; ungleich wichtiger dagegen und die ganze Entwickelung der Sprache berührend, sind meine von Koelle's Darstellung und Regeln abweichenden Ansichten in Betreff der Formen des Zeitwortes und der ganzen historischen Entwickelung dieses Redetheiles. Allerdings gründen sich meine Ansichten in dieser Beziehung ganz vorzugsweise auf meine Kenntniss des Hausa und Tédā, während Koelle alle seine Sprach-Studien ganz ausserhalb des Gebietes aller dieser Sprachen in seiner Studirstube in Sierra Leone machte. Besonders der Vergleich der Tédā-Sprache, deren Kenntniss ich allerdings erst angebahnt habe, muss über das ganze Wesen des Kanúri andere Ansichten verbreiten und halte ich deshalb ein ergründendes Studium dieser Sprache für höchst bedeutend.

Gleich bei dem oberflächlichsten Vergleich meines Vokabular's mit demjenigen Koelle's wird man finden, dass ich fast durchgängig diejenigen Zeitwörter, die er auf ṅgin endigen lässt, mit der Endung skin, fskin oder afskin gebe. Sucht man nun in seiner Grammatik sich über diese Formen zu belehren, so findet man gar Manches darüber, aber aus Allem, was Koelle sagt, leuchtet deutlich hervor, dass er selbst sich über diese Fragen nicht klar geworden ist.

So hat Koelle in einzelnen Augenblicken eine Ahnung von dem wirklichen Verhältniss dieser Formen, dann aber wird wieder Alles verwischt. Jedoch zweifele ich nicht, dass, wenn er alle die Verba, die ich mit der Endung auf skin gebe, in dieser Form gehört hätte, er wol selbst zu anderen Resultaten gekommen sein würde. So erwähnt er im §. 54 die beiden Formen skin und ṅgin als bestimmt getrennte Klassen und vergleicht sie im §. 63 ganz richtig mit der aktiven und medialen Form in der Griechischen Sprache; auch führt er das weiter aus, indem er sagt, „dass der ursprüngliche Unterschied wol der gewesen sei, dass die Verba auf ṅgin eine in sich abgeschlossene Bedeutung gehabt hätten ohne weiteres Bedürfniss eines Objektes, dagegen Verba auf skin eine transitive und nach Aussen gerichtete Handlung anzeigten". Auch er hält §. 64 die Form auf skin für die ältere, glaubt aber, dass sie viel enger und in mehr organischer Weise als blosse personale Endung mit der Wurzel des Zeitwortes zusammenhänge, während er ṅgin als eigentlich unabhängige Verbalform betrachten will. Dass es aber für die, eine aktive und transitive Bedeutung enthaltenden, Zeitwörter ebenso gut eine volle Hülfszeitform (ni-skin) gäbe, wie für diejenigen mit passiver Bedeutung (ṅgin), hoffe ich auf überzeugende Weise zeigen zu können, besonders wenn wir die entsprechenden Ausdrücke in der Hausa-Sprache heranziehen und festhalten, wie die letztere fast in denselben Breitegraden wie die Kanúri-Sprache, nur etwas westlicher, sich fast gleichzeitig entwickelte.

Ich stelle also folgende zwei Sätze auf:

I) Alle diejenigen Kanúri-Zeitwörter endigten ursprünglich auf skin, af-skin, die eine aktive oder transitive Thätigkeit anzeigten;

II) nur die Zeitwörter endigten auf ṅgin, die einen passiven oder zurückbeziehenden Zustand bezeichneten.

I. Die Zeitwörter auf skin und af-skin.

Bei dieser Klasse müssen wir zuerst die beiden angedeuteten Unterabtheilungen, von deren einer Koelle gar keine Ahnung gehabt hat, streng von einander scheiden, denn die

as, for instance, Kānem-ma, „an individual from Kānem", plur. Kānem-bū. The change of the m into b we may illustrate, I think, to a certain degree by comparing ma with the ancient Egyptian pe, „human being".

These points, in which I disagree with Koelle, are of little consequence; but of much greater importance, and affecting the whole character, and the formation of the language, are the divergencies of my views from his with regard to the forms and to the development of the verb. No doubt, my views in this respect are principally based upon my knowledge of the Tédā- and Hausa-languages, while the Rev. Koelle has studied the Kanúri-language exclusively during his residence in Sierra Leone, far beyond the borders of all these languages. It is especially the comparison with the Téda-language, the character of which I have certainly not but slightly begun to disclose, which is destined to open up other views with regard to the real character of the Kanúri-idiom, and it is on this account especially, that I think a thorough study of the former of the utmost importance.

Already at a first superficial glance at my vocabulary, while comparing it with Koelle's labours, the reader will find, that my Kanúri-verbs almost constantly terminate in skin, ískin or nískin, while he makes them terminate in ṅgin. Now, if a person wants to inform himself in Koelle's grammar with regard to these forms, he will find there a good deal of material, but it will soon appear to him, that the author, notwithstanding his profound studies, had never become quite clear himself on this important point.

Thus the Rev. Koelle in some passages appears to have divined to a certain degree the true state of the question, and the real relation of these forms, while in others he has mixed up the most different arguments. However, I have no doubt, that, if he had heard all those verbs terminating in skin, which I give with this form, he would have arrived at a different result. Thus in §. 54 he mentions the two forms as denoting distinctly separated classes, and in §. 63 he compares them very truely with the active, and middle form of the ancient Greek, and to this opinion he gives further development, when he says „the difference was probably this, that verbs in ṅgin expressed a notion complete in itself, and not needing the complement of an object; whereas verbs in skin expressed a transitive or outwardly operating direction of the verbal energy". He himself states his opinion in §. 64, that the form in skin may be of greater antiquity, but at the same time he thinks, that it is a mere personal termination, and much more closely and organically connected with the verbal root, while, according to his opinion, the form ṅgin bears rather the character of an originally independent and separate word. As for myself, I hope, to be able to prove, that the Kanúri-verbs contain a distinct class, denoting originally a transitive action, and formed by the aid of the full and originally independent auxiliary verb ní-skin, while all the verbs terminating in ṅgin originally conveyed either a reflective or a passive meaning. While endeavouring to prove this fact, I shall take constant regard to the Hausa-idiom, which developed its forms of speech in close proximity to the Kanúri, and almost under the same latitude, and at the same period.

I therefore put these two axioms:

I. All those Kanúri-verbs, which contained an active, or transitive meaning, originally terminated in skin, and ní-skin;

II. only those Kanúri-verbs, which contained a passive or reflective meaning, originally terminated in ṅgin.

I. The verbs in skin and ní-skin.

In considering this class of verbs we must first of all distinguish between, and keep asunder, the two subdivisions indicated in the heading, of one of which, although it is by far the more important one, Koelle has had no idea whatever. For, while the form skin

Endung auf skin scheint allerdings nichts zu sein, als eine blosse Verbal-Endung der ersten Person, die folgendermassen abgewandelt wird:

1ste Person Sing.	. . . skin	Plur.	yen,
2te „ „	. . . . . min	„	wi,
3te „ „	. . . . . tse	„	tsa,

nískin aber, obgleich selbstständig kaum gebraucht [1]), ist ein für sich selbstständiges Hülfszeitwort, „ich mache", in dem das n mit Umwandelung des dazu gehörenden Vokal-Lautes (ne, ni, nu, Imp. nē) in allen Personen ursprünglich als Wurzel in Verbindung mit obiger Personal-Form stehen bleibt und nur bei der 3ten Person des Singular und Plural in späterer Form verloren geht:

1ste Person Sing.	. . ni-skin	. . Plur.	ni-yen,
2te „ „	. . nç-min	. . „	nu-wi,
3te „ „	. . tse-nyin	. . „	tsa-nyin,
	(später tšin)	. .	(später tsei).

a) Die einfache Verbalform auf skin (rík, erík im Tédā; vergleiche das Hülfszeitwort iri des Alt-Egyptischen), ist offenbar sehr allmählich und unter den mannichfaltigsten Einflüssen gebildet worden. Ohne mich weiter auf Muthmassungen einzulassen, will ich nur angeben, dass nach meiner Überzeugung auch im Kanúri die erste Person ursprünglich auf k endete, also wahrscheinlich sik lautete, wo s das aktive, auch in der Berber-Sprache so häufig vertretene Zeichen ist, k dem dort als Endung erscheinenden y entspricht; dass s das charakteristische Zeichen dieser Form ist, sieht man am deutlichsten aus der Form des Futurums sono im Vergleich zu der Präsens-Form gono von der passiven Form in ńgin. Das n, in ward, meiner Meinung zufolge, erst hinzugefügt, nachdem die zweite Person auf min gebildet war, die einer Genitiv-Form sehr ähnlich sieht. Die eigenthümliche, so ganz abweichende, sonst ganz unerklärliche 3te Pers. tse erklärt sich auf das schönste durch einen Vergleich mit der entsprechenden Tédā-Form ke; tsé-bu-i, „er isst", im Kanúri ganz identisch mit dem Tédā ke-bū, ja wir haben selbst im Tédā sogar eine dialektische Nebenform mit te, tse-bū; ebenso dieselbe Person im Plural. Das eigentliche Zeichen der Thätigkeit in dieser Verbal-Endung scheint i zu sein.

b) Das Hülfszeitwort ní-skin, Imp. nē, ist wol ohne Zweifel durch den Einfluss des Hausa entstanden, wo ne, na das Hülfszeitwort ist, nur mit dem Unterschiede, dass hier die Vokal-Veränderung nach der Person durch ein Präfix geschieht, ni í-na, „ich bin thuend"; kai ká-na u. s. w. Auf die Wortbildung hat aber wol noch Einfluss gehabt das Beispiel des in der Hausa-Sprache gebrauchten Hülfszeitwortes yi, „machen", 1ste Person Sing. Präs. na-ī, wie denn z. B. das Kanúri karińg-nískin wörtlich dem Hausa-Ausdruck na-ī kūsa entspricht, „ich mache nahe", d. h. „ich nähere mich" (im Hausa gibt es auch den entsprechenden Ausdruck für das Gegentheil na-ī nēsa, „ich mache fern", d. h. „ich entferne mich"); ebenso der mit Hülfe dieses Hülfszeitwortes dem Arabischen (von رضى) entlehnte Ausdruck für „ich bin zufrieden", K. ardi-nískin, H. wörtlich na-ī (oder na-yi) ordā, contrahirt náyerdā. Ja fast noch deutlicher und vielleicht das beste Beispiel zur Beleuchtung des aufgestellten Satzes ist der Kanúri-Ausdruck manna-nískin (Koelle mannńgin), „ich mache Worte, rede", da es nach Hauptbegriff und Verbalform eine wörtliche Übertragung der Hausa-Phrase na-ī mágana ist.

---

1) Und doch gibt es nach Koelle ein solches selbstständiges ní-skin (bei ihm ágfa, i. q. nyskin, „ich sage") und es ist möglich, dass dies als die erste Handlung angesehen ist. Ich selbst aber bin unsicher über die Ableitung von Jue mit der Bedeutung „er sagte", von einem solchen ní-skin.

indeed does not seem to be any thing else, but a verbal termination of the first person sing., which is conjugated in the following manner:

1st pers. sing.	. . . skin . . .	plur. yen,
2nd „ „	. . . min . . .	„ wi,
3rd „ „	. . . tse . . .	„ tsa;

ní-skin, although it is not now used by itself*), nevertheless originally was an independent auxiliary verb with the meaning „I make", and of which the n (ne, ni, nu, imp. né), accompanied by a vowel, such as corresponds to the nature of the following sound, originally remained unchanged in all persons, in connection with the above personal termination, and was only lost in the 3rd person sing. and plur. in a later form, thus:

1st pers. sing.	. . . ni-skin . . .	plur. ni-yen,
2nd „ „	. . . ne-min . . .	„ nu-wi,
3rd „ „	. . . tse-nyin . . .	„ tsa-nyin,
	(later form tšin) . .	(later form tsei).

a) As for the simple inflectional form in skin, corresponding to the Téda-form rík, erík (compare the auxiliary verb iri of the ancient Egyptian), it appears to have been formed very gradually, and under very different influences. However, without entering upon further questions of a conjectural character, I will only state, that according to my firm believe the form of the 1st person originally terminated in k, so that it was most probably sik, in which form the s had the active power, which is so frequently exhibited in the verbal forms of the Mádiý-language, while k corresponded to the g or γ sound. That s is the characteristic sign of this form is most clearly demonstrated by sono, the form of the future, when compared with gono, the corresponding form of the verb in ǹgin. As for the final n or in, it seems to me to have only been added at a later period, when min, which has altogether the appearance of a genitive case, had been introduced to represent the 2nd person. As for tse, the peculiar prefix form of the 3rd pers. sing., it is now fully explained by a comparison with the corresponding Téda-form ke, as tsó-bu-i, „he is eating" is perfectly identical, as well with regard to the root, as to the form, with the Téda ke-bū; nay, we have even in Téda another form with te, tse-bū. The same is the case with the 3rd pers. plur. The vowel i seems to be the proper sign of activity in this verbal form.

b) As for the auxiliary verb ní-skin, imp. nó, it appears to me intimately connected with, and perhaps derived from, the Hausa no, na, the only difference being, that with the latter, the pronominal form being prefixed, na remains unchanged, thus ni í-na; kai ká-na etc. But besides, another auxiliary Hausa-verb, viz yí, 1st person-sing. pres. na-í, which expresses the transitive „making" more distinctly, seems to have exercised considerable influence upon many words composed with the aid of the Kanúri auxiliary verb ní-skin, as, for instance, the Kanúri-term káriñg-nískin is verbally identical with the Hausa-term na-í kūsa, „I make near" i. e. „I approach", while in the Hausa-idiom even the opposite term na-i nésa, „I make distant" i. q. „I withdraw" is in frequent use; in the same manner the Kanúri-term ardi-nískin, „I am content", which with the aid of the auxiliary verb has been formed from the Arabic رضى, is verbally identical with the Hausa-term na-i erdā, or in a contracted form náyerdā. But a still more striking example, and which perhaps best illustrates, at least in a practical respect, what I want to prove, is the Kanúri-term manna-nískin, „I make a speech, speak", as it corresponds exactly with the Hausa-term na-í mágana, as well with regard to the identity of the substantive, as with regard to the verbal form.

*) According to Koelle, who derives the verbal form tse, „he said" from a verb ágin or neskin, that is, ní-skin we should have an instance of such an independent use of the latter verb with the original notion of „speaking", but I myself am not certain as to the correctness of the root.

Als Beispiele der blossen Personal-Endung auf skin gebe ich hier die einfachen Begriffe:

bá-skin, „ich besteige", dí-skin, „ich thue", bú-skin, „ich esse",
yá-skin, „ich trinke", lí-skin, „ich bringe hervor", nú-skin, „ich sterbe",
tá-skin, „ich halte", yí-skin, „ich gebe", rú-skin, „ich sehe".

Das Hülfszeitwort ní-skin finden wir erstlich componirt mit monosyllaben verbalen Begriffen, oder abstracten Nennwörtern, oder onomatopoëtischen Lauten, wie folgende Beispiele zeigen:

le-nískin, „ich mache le", „ich gehe",
len-nískin, „ich mache len" oder vielleicht eigentlich let, „ich schlafe".
tši-nískin, wahrscheinlich eigentlich „ich mache, erhebe den Fuss", ši, „ich breche auf",
fú-nískin, „ich mache Wind, blase, athme",
sá-nískin, „ich mache sa" (onomatopoëtisch), erschüttere, treffe",
tua-nískin, „ich mache eine Pause", tuso, „ruhe mich aus",
bobó-nískin, „ich mache bobó", „rufe",
lólo-nískin, „ich mache lólo", „zittere (vor Kälte)".

Ebenso die von Arabischen substantivischen Begriffen abgeleiteten Zeitwörter, wie das oben angeführte ardí-nískin:

kará-nískin, „ich mache Lektüre, lese",
gúl-níshin, „ich mache Rede, sage",
sudžúd-nískin, „ich mache die Niederwerfung, werfe mich nieder im Gebet",
sálá-nískin, „ich mache Gebet, bete",
wolo-nískin, „ich mache die Abwaschung, wasche mich vor dem Gebet",
súm-nískin, „ich mache die Fasten, faste",
láfia-níshin, „ich mache (den Gruss)", el áfia, „Wohlsein", d. h. „ich frage, ob Alles wohl ist".

Dann in Verbindung mit adverbialen oder adjektiven Begriffen:

dá-nískin, „ich mache aufrecht, stehe",
far-nískin, „ich mache über, mache hoch", d. h. „ich springe", „tanze" (Vokab. S. 60), dann aber auch „ich mache (unterst) zu oberst", d. h. „ich zerstöre" (S. 98),
fi-nískin, „ich mache voll, bereit, fertig", daher die verschiedensten individuellen Beziehungen, „ich ziehe (das Schwert)" S. 96, „ich erbreche" S. 44, „lasse (einen Wind)" S. 46, „lege (das Ei)" S. 110, in der 3ten Person fi-tšin, „es regnet, der Regen fällt" S. 120 [1]):
ré-níshin, „ich mache entzwei, theile",
tar-níshin, „ich mache auseinander, breite aus, trockene",
fog-nískin, „ich mache zusammen, verbinde",
kárińg-níshin, „ich mache nahe, nähere mich",
deri-níshin, „ich mache rund, gehe umher".

Interessant, und belehrend über den eigentlichen Charakter des Hülfszeitwortes ní-skin ist auch der Vergleich mit dem etwas stärkeren dí-skin, „ich thue, vollbringe", von einer die menschliche Thätigkeit kennzeichnenden Wurzel, die auch der ganzen Gruppe Indo-Germanischer Sprachen gemeinsam ist. Vergleiche auch das Türkische dyr-mek. So haben wir einige zusammengesetzte Begriffe, die eben so gut mit dí-skin, wie mit ní-skin gebildet werden können, wie:

---

[1]) Koelle hat von dieser einfachen Wortbildung und Ableitung von so einfachen Grundbegriffen keine Ahnung und macht deshalb besondere Zeitwörter daraus, pingin und pingin. Ich habe übrigens jetzt keinen Zweifel mehr, dass von eben diesem fi auch die Zehnerzahlen im Kanúri gebildet sind, fi-ndi, „zwei Volle", nämlich zwei volle Zahlen der 10 Finger, fi-nsko, „drei Volle" u. s. w. Das war mir S. 8, N. 8 noch nicht klar geworden. Wie wenig Koelle auf diese einfache Wortbildung eingegangen ist, zeigt z. B. sein pérégin, „ich fege, reinige", d. h. feren-níshin, „ich mache eben", obgleich er selbst férné schreibt. S. Vokab. S. 106, N. 4. Vergl. auch Koelle's zwei Zeitwörter tárágin mit meinem Vokabular S. 103, N. 1.

As instances of the termination in skin I here give the following verbs:

bá-skin, „I mount", dí-skin, „I do", bú-skin, „I eat",
tá-skin, „I hold, seize", lí-skin, „I produce", nú-skin, „I die",
yá-skin, „I drink", yí-skin, „I give", rá-skin, „I see".

As for the auxiliary verb ní-skin, we find it first composed with monosyllabic verbal roots, or with abstract nouns, or with onomatopoetical sounds, as the following instances may serve to show:

lē-nískin, „I make lē", „walk, go",
len-nískin, „I make len", perhaps originally lot, „I sleep",
tĕl-nískin, probably originally „I make, raise the foot", kl, „I start",
fū-nískin, „I make wind, blow, respire",
sā-nískin, „I make sā" (an onomatopoetical sound), „strike",
tus-nískin, „I make a pause", tusū, „repose",
bobō-nískin, „I make bobō", „call",
ldlō-nískin, „I make lólō", „tremble (from cold)".

The same sort of composition we find with substantive notions, derived from the Arabic, such as ardi-nískin:

karā-nískin, „I make lecture, read",
gūl-nískin, „I make a word, say",
sudžūd-nískin, „I make, perform the prostration, prostrate myself in prayer",
sdlā-nískin, „I make prayer, I pray",
wolo-nískin, „I perform the washing before the prayer",
sūm-nískin, „I perform the fasting, I fast",
láfia-nískin, „I make (the common salutation)", el áfia, „well being", „ask, if all is well".

Further we find the auxiliary verb ní-skin combined with adverbs or adjectives:

dā-nískin, „I make upright, I stand",
far-nískin, „I make up, over, high", therefore „I jump, dance" (vocab. p. 60), „I make (undermost) uppermost", i. q. „I destroy" (p. 96),
fi-nískin, „I make ready, complete", therefore in the different individual relations „I draw" (the sword) p. 96, „I vomit" (p. 44), „I let (a fart)" p. 16, „I lay (an egg)" p. 110 and in the 3rd person fi-tšin (the rain) „falls", „it is raining, p. 120 *).
rē-nískin, „I make asunder (in two), divide, split",
tar-nískin, „I make asunder, spread out, dry",
fog-nískin, „I make together, join",
kūring-nískin, „I make near, approach",
deri-nískin, „I make round, walk about".

Interesting also as conveying much information with regard to the original character of the auxiliary verb ní-skin is a comparison of the latter with the more expressive verb dí-skin, „I do", „perform", a verb which is in itself highly interesting, as it is almost identical with the corresponding root, proper to almost the whole group of the Indo-Germanic idioms. Thus in the Kanúri-idiom we have some composite terms with dí-skin, as well as with ní-skin, such as

---

*) Koelle has no idea of such original notions, and of the natural way of composition in this manner, wherefore, as in most similar cases, also here he makes two separate verbs plngin and plágin. As for me, I do not now doubt, as I did, when writing vocab. p. 3, note 6, that even the terms designating the tenths of the numbers, from twenty onward, are derived from the same fī; fī-ndī, „two fall (numbers)", viz twice the number of the ten fingers, fī-nsks, „three fall (numbers)" and so on. — How little Koelle was aware of this simple mode of composition, is sufficiently shown by his pérbágin, „I sweep", „I make clean" i. q. feran-nískin, although he himself writes fárab. See vocabulary p. 106, note 5 and compare his two terms tárégin with my vocabulary p. 106, note 1.

bäre- { ní-skin, „ich mache / dí-skin, „ich thue } Feldbau, bearbeite das Land".

tégeri- { ní-skin, „ich mache / dí-skin, „ich thue } Lohn", d. h. „arbeite für Lohn".

So haben wir auch andere Zusammensetzungen mit dí-skin, die mit denen von ní-skin ganz parallel gehen, obgleich das letztere Hülfszeitwort dabei nicht in Gebrauch ist, so bañkal-dí-skin, wörtlich „ich thue Verstand", d. h. „ich passe auf, bin aufmerksam", lä-dískin (eigentlich libaia [ol bâya] dí-skin), „ich thue Verkauf, verkaufe".

Dagegen hält Koelle nun das so überaus wichtige und ausdrucksvolle Hülfszeitwort ní-skin, das er ņęskin schreibt, für eine blosse Nebenform der Form auf ñgin, ja er erklärt sogar ausdrücklich, dass sie ihm eine blosse Nachahmung der Zeitwörter auf skin zu sein scheine, während es in der That nur mit dessen Hülfe gebildet ist. Wir aber haben hoffentlich die Klasse der ursprünglich aktiven Zeitwörter auf diese Weise in ihrer wahren Gestalt und natürlichen Entwickelung erfasst und gehen nun zu der zweiten Klasse über.

II. Die ursprünglich passiven oder zurückbeziehenden Zeitwörter auf ñgin oder (mit elidirtem n) gin.

Diese Klasse war meiner Ansicht nach ursprünglich sehr beschränkt und begriff nur wenige, von Eigenschaftswörtern in substantivischer oder adjektiver Gestalt, abgeleitete Zeitwörter, wie

söba-ñgin, „ich werde ein Freund, befreundet",
kam-be-ñgin, „ich werde ein freier Mann, werde frei",
kária-ñgin, „ich werde ein Sklave, gerathe in Sklaverei",
malam-gin, „ich werde ein Mállem, ein Gelehrter",
döndí-ñgin, „ich werde krank",
ham-gin, „ich werde kalt, kühle ab",
zem-gin, „ich werde, bin niedergebeugt" (Koelle tsęmgin), die passive, geistige Auffassung von zem-nískin, „ich mache niedrig, nehme herab".

Diese passive Endung auf ñgin (die ganz natürlich aus dem nískin durch Ausstossung des aktiven s sich entwickelte), kann man entfernt mit dem Griechischen γιγν-εσθαι vergleichen, das auch im Sanskrit seinen verwandten Ausdruck hat, während im Hausa, wo die Bildung des Passivums übrigens sehr unvollkommen ist, die Form des Particip. Passiv. mit an, wie áñ-ganí, „gegeben", besonders aber an-yí, „gemacht", von dem auf die Wortbildung so einflussreichen Hülfszeitwort yi, direkter sich anschliesst. Auch im Kanúri, wie das auch im Alt-Egyptischen der Fall ist (nach Bunsen I, S. 354), ist diese passive Form sehr wenig ausgebildet worden, selbst in der ersten unbestimmten Zeit, wo wir nur die erste Person Sing. und die erste Person Plur. auf nyön (anstatt des aktiven níyen) eigenthümlich ausgebildet finden, während die übrigen Personen mit den Formen des aktiven Zeitwortes identisch sind. Auf diese passive Form ist aber auch das nyä, „gemacht, geschehen", zurückzuführen, durch dessen Anhängung an die bestimmte Zeit eine Art von conditionel praeteriti gebildet wird, dessen Entstehung Koelle nach der sehr unbestimmten Weise, wie er sich darüber in §. 230, 2. ausdrückt, nicht erfasst zu haben scheint; und doch nur, wenn man sich diese Bildung vergegenwärtigt und diesen Redetheil von dem vorhergehenden sondert, wird man sich in den Geist der Sprache völlig hineinsetzen können. So ist sein kigañtęnyä nichts Anderes als tëí-kote nyä, „er brachte, das war gethan", d. h. „nachdem er gebracht hatte"; so lögányä, „er ging, das war gethan", d. h. „nachdem er gegangen war".

Aus Allem aber, was ich gesagt habe, erklärt es sich ganz von selbst, weshalb dieses passive Zeitwort auf ñgin nur in der ersten Konjugation gebraucht wird, und wir brauchen das keineswegs mit Koelle §. 64, S. 55 bloss auf den gegenwärtigen Zustand der Sprache zu beschränken, als wenn es die anderen Entwickelungsformen verloren hätte.

bāre- {nī-skin, „I make / dī-skin, „I do} cultivation, I till the ground",

tégeri- {nī-skin, „I make / dī-skin, „I do} hire", i. q. „I work for hire".

Thus we have other composite terms with dī-skin, formed in the same manner as those with nī-skin, although the latter is not used in these instances, such as bañkal-dīskin, verbally „I do intelligence", i. q. „I pay attention", lā-dīskin (properly libain [vel bāye] dī-skin), „I do buying, selling, I sell".

Now, this most important and expressive auxiliary verb nī-skin is pronounced by Rev. Koelle, who writes nęskin, to be a mere secondary form of ṅgin, and a mere imitation of the verbs in skin, while it has only been formed with the aid of the latter termination. As for ourselves, having thus settled to satisfaction, as I hope, the question with regard to the class of active verbs in skin and nī-skin, we now proceed to the second class of verbs.

II. The class of passive or reflective verbs in ṅgin or (in cases where the n is lost) gin.

This class of verbs, according to my opinion, originally was very limited, and only comprised a few verbs, derived from such nouns as describe a quality or character, or from adjectives, such as the following:

sōba-ṅgin, „I become a friend, am befriended",
kam-bō-ṅgin, „I become a free man, get free",
kária-ṅgin, „I become a slave, get into slavery",
malem-gin, „I become a mállem, a learned man",
dōndī-ṅgin, „I become sick",
ham-gin, „I become cold, get cool",
sem-gin (Koelle tsęmgin) properly „I become low", „I am dejected, oppressed", the passive and reflective notion of sem-nīskin, „I make low, take down".

This passive termination in ṅgin we may perhaps compare in some respect with γεγν-ευθαι of the ancient Greek, which is likewise represented in Sanscrit, but with infinitely more reason with the form of the passive participle with au in Hausa, such as gá-gaue, „seen", but especially an-yī, „made, done" from the auxiliary verb yī, which has exercised such a remarkable influence upon the formation of verbs in Kanúri. But we must take into account, that the Hausa-idiom has very little developped the passive mood, as is also the case with the ancient Egyptian (Bunsen I, p. 354), and likewise with the Kanúri, and indeed generally with most of the idioms of semi-barbarous people; thus of the form ṅgin only the corresponding form of the plural nyĕn (instead of the active form nīyen) has been derived, while the forms of the other persons are identical with those of the active mood. But to the passive mood of this verbal form ṅgin we must undoubtedly refer the form nyā, by means of which, namely by joining it to the definite tense of the verb, a sort of conditional of the past tense is formed, the character of which Rev. Koelle, from the indistinct manner in which he speaks of it in §. 230, does not appear to have seized; thus his kigūtónyā is nothing but tšī-kote nyā, „he brought, that was done", i. q. „after he had brought it", lógányā, „he went, that was done", i. q. „after he went". No doubt, only by thus entering into the real character of each part of speech we are enabled to seize the character of a whole language, instead of having before us unintelligible and unnatural forms.

Why this passive verb in ṅgin is only used in what Koelle calls the first conjugation, I think must now be clear to every body from what I have said, and we therefore need not attribute with Koelle §. 64, p. 55 the limited range of this verb to the present state of the language, as if it had lost the other forms.

Es erklärt sich ebenso ganz von selbst, weshalb diese Klasse von Zeitwörtern ursprünglich nicht sehr umfassend sein konnte; allmählich aber scheint sie dadurch weitere Anwendung gefunden zu haben, dass es viele verbale Begriffe gibt, die eine passive Auffassung gestatten, besonders bei geistigen Affectionen. Schon das oben angeführte nemgin bildet eine Art von Übergang dazu; daran schliessen sich andere, wie

{tá-skin, „ich ergreife, fasse, halte",
{tá-ṅgin, „ich halte bei mir fest", besonders in Verbindung mit kéla-n, „im Kopfe", „ich erinnere mich",

{ri-nískin, „ich mache Furcht, furchtsame Bewegung",
{ri-ṅgin, „ich empfinde Furcht, werde furchtsam",

{nō-nískin, „ich mache das Wissen, weiss",
{nō-ṅgin, „fühle das Wissen, bin mir bewusst, weiss",

{yē-nískin *), „ich mache entsprechen, gebe zurück",
{yē-ṅgin, „ich antworte", mit kaiga, „singe einen Wechselgesang",

{nem-nískin, „ich mache Aufenthalt, Ruhe, verweile",
{nem-gin, „ich werde, bleibe ruhig, schweige",

{kāriṅg-nískin, „ich mache nahe, nähere mich",
{kāriṅg-gin, „ich werde nahe, komme nahe, nähere mich",

{sudūd-nískin, „ich mache die Niederwerfung",
{sudū-ṅgin (mit elidirtem d), „ich werfe mich nieder".

Allmählich aber muss die Form auf ṅgin die gebräuchlichere geworden sein und muss selbst da zum Theil die andere verdrängt haben, wo eine passive Auffassung kaum möglich war. Dazu scheint ausser der grösseren Kürze dieser Form auch die negative Form mit bágo das Ihrige beigetragen zu haben. So hörte ich fast nur lé-ṅgin bágo, „ich gehe nicht", während, wenn das Zeitwort allein stand, ich vorwaltend die Form lé-nískin hörte; šī-ni lé-ṅgin, „ich gehe zu Fuss", eigentlich „mit meinem Fuss" erlaubt schon eine zurückbeziehende Auffassung. Aber ich erkläre hier auf das Bestimmteste, dass ich bei den meisten der Zeitwörter, die Koelle's Autorität, 'Ali Eisāmi, auf ṅgin endigen liess, besonders den von Koelle in §. 59. seiner Grammatik verzeichneten, nicht ein einziges Mal diese Form gehört habe, und ich möchte fast glauben, dass er die Form auf nískin oder, wie er schreibt, nęskin, öfter unterdrückt hat; wenigstens sagt er selbst bei dem Paradigma von wūṅgin, eine Form, die ich nicht ein einziges Mal hörte, in der Note, dass die Nebenform wūnęskin existire. So kann ich denn Koelle's Verzeichniss von Zeitwörtern auf ṅgin, ob intransitiv (§. 58) oder transitiv (§. 59), nur zum kleinen Theil anerkennen und ebenso wenig den daraus gezogenen Schluss. Auch gesteht Koelle selbst ein, dass das Kanuri in seiner jetzigen Gestalt (d. h. besonders in den von ihm gebrauchten Formen), in sehr willkürlicher Weise über beide Verbalformen verfüge.

Wenn wir nun die eben gemachten Bemerkungen berücksichtigen, so brauchen wir solche Formen, wie ş-iskin (Koelle gęskin) der relativen Konjugation (Koelle, Grammatik §. 55) und t-iskin (Koelle tęskin) der reflektiven (§. 61), nicht mit Koelle von der Grundform ṅgin durch eine (höchst mysteriöse und unverständliche) Umwandelung abzuleiten, sondern werden sie in organischer Entwickelung mit Sicherheit von der Form skin, ni-skin herleiten, wie ger-ni-skin, ger-gi-skin, ger-ti-skin, ger-te-gi-skin; wū-ni-skin, wū-gi-skin, wū-ti-skin, yi-te-wū-gi-skin. Damit fällt natürlich die von falschen Beispielen abgeleitete, ganz widernatürliche Bemerkung Koelle's §. 53, S. 46, dass

*) Daher transitive Form yē-t-iskin, Vokab. S. 119, „ich mache sich entsprechen, drehe das Thun".

From the same reasons it needs no further explanation, why this class of verbs originally comprised only a very limited number. Gradually, however, the form in ṅgin appears to have been used more generally, as there are many verbal notions, especially such as describe a mental action, which admit of a passive or reflective relation, as even the verb zem-gin, which I have adduced above, forms a sort of natural link between the verbs of an active and those of a passive character, and others follow closely in its track, such as

tá-skin, „I seize, lay hold of",
tá-ṅgin, „I keep with myself" especially in connection with kéla-n („in the head"), the next meaning being „I remember";

rí-nískin, verbally „I make fear, a timorous sensation",
rí-ṅgin, „I become frightened, am afraid";

nó-nískin, „I make knowledge, I know",
nó-ṅgin, „I am conscious, I know";

yē-nískin [1]), „I make correspond",
yē-ṅgin, „I respond, answer", with kaigu, „I sing an alternative song";

nem-nískin, „I make a place, I make a stay, I remain",
nem-gin, „I become quiet, I am silent, I remain";

kāriṅg-nískin, „I make near, I approach",
kāriṅg-gin, „I get near, I approach";

sudžud-nískin, „I perform the prostration",
sudžu-ṅgin, „I prostrate myself".

Thus, this passive and reflective form in ṅgin having once become of more general use, it appears to have crept into the place of the form in ní-skin even in many cases, where a passive or reflective notion was not possible. To this effect, besides the easier and shorter character of the form ṅgin, the negative form of speech, with bāgo, also seems to have contributed. Thus, I almost constantly heard lē-ṅgin bāgo, „I do not go", while without the negation the form lē-nískin was almost exclusively used; as for the phrase šī-ni lē-ṅgin (not lē-nískin), „I walk on foot", it allows of a reflective relation, the proper meaning being „I walk (by) my foot". But I have here to repeat in the most decided manner, that with most of the verbs, which 'Ali Eisāmi, the chief and almost only authority, which Koelle used in laying down his grammatical rules, made terminate in ṅgin, especially those registered in §. 59 of his grammar, I have not heard this form used in a single instance; and I am inclined to think, that in many cases he himself has unconsciously suppressed the form nískin or, as he writes ṇgskin; however, with regard to the verb wúṅgin, a form I never heard, he expressly adds in the footnote, that there is besides another form wúnçskin. Thus, therefore, I can by no means acknowledge the correctness of Koelle's list of verbs in ṅgin, whether intransitive (§. 58), or transitive (§. 59), with the exception of a few cases, and as little, of course, I do subscribe to the conclusion thence drawn by him. And Koelle himself acknowledges, that the Kanúri in its present state (especially in the forms used by himself) disposes of the verbal forms in a most arbitrary manner.

Now, if we take into account what I have said, we need certainly not derive with Koelle such forms as g-iskin (Koelle gęskin) of the relative (Koelle, gr. §. 55), and t-iskin (Koelle tęskin) of the reflective conjugation (§. 61), from the form ṅgin, by means of a certainly most mysterious and unintelligible change, but we may derive them without the slightest hesitation in a natural and organical way of development from the form skin, ni-skin, as for instance gor-ni-skin, gor-gi-skin, gor-ti-skin, gor-te-gi-skin; wū-ni-skin, wū-gi-skin, wū-ti-skin, yi-te-wū-gi-skin. Thus also Koelle's remark in

[1]) Thence the transitive form yē-t-iskin, vocab. p. 118 „I make alternate, cause to alternate, I twist (the rope)".

von den Zeitwörtern auf skin nur eine sehr beschränkte Zahl eine causative Konjugation entwickelt habe, in nichts zusammen.

Ich will hier noch bemerken, dass bei der letzteren Konjugations-Form das ye oder yi von yí-skin, „ich gehe", benutzt ist, wie auch sonst, zur Bildung der causativen Form, z. B. lí-skin, „ich lerne", ye-ke-lí-skin, „ich gehe lernen", d. h. „ich lehre", und hieraus erklärt sich ganz einfach und natürlich, warum diese Form das Objekt im Dativ bei sich hat.

Bei dem Zeitwort lí-skin aber will ich noch einen Augenblick verweilen, da es mit seinen verschiedenen Abwandelungen alle drei Formen auf skin, ní-skin und ñgin auf das Schönste erläutert; lí-skin, „ich bringe hervor", „lerne", lí-nískin, „ich mache ab, ziehe ab" (die Kleider), lí-ñgin, „ich komme hervor" (vom Kraut u. s. w.).

Zum Schluss dieser wenigen Bemerkungen über die Verbalformen will ich noch bemerken, dass fast alle höchst verwickelten und unverständlichen Formen bei Koelle sich in die einfachsten Redetheile auflösen, wie wir das oben S. LIV bei der von ihm Conditionel Präteriti genannten Form mit nyā gesehen haben. Eben dasselbe ist der Fall mit der Form, die er Participial-Präsens nennt, § 212, S. 219, 2. Zur Erklärung derselben löse ich zwei der dort angeführten Phrasen aus seinem Schematismus in meine analytische, die natürlichen Redetheile klar darstellende Schreibweise auf. So gibt denn sein túta mánu kámāntsiye nemétsegnagā ši pántši, in meine Schreibweise aufgelöst:

túta monua kamā-ntsi-ye nemé-tse na-ga ší fan-tsi,
Knabe Wort Geführte sein einer sprach das de er hörte,

d. h. der Knabe hörte das Wort, das einer seiner Geführten sprach; eben so per šírō meíyé tsebátsenārō tsebe löse ich in natürlicher Weise auf in

fir ší-rō mai-ye tsebā-tse na-ro ze-bā,
Pferd ihm ein König schickte das auf stieg er,

d. h. er stieg auf das Pferd, das ihm ein König schickte.

na-gā und na-rō haben nichts in aller Welt mit dem Zeitwort zu schaffen, sondern das erste ist Accusativ, das zweite Dativ von dem Pronomen na, „das".

Um nun einen lebendigen Einblick in die allmähliche Entwickelung des Kanúri zu erleichtern, stelle ich eine alphabetische Liste der mir gegenwärtigen einsilbigen Wurzeln derselben zusammen und werde einige Bemerkungen dazu fügen:

a: ām, „Leute"[1]), am, „empor" (heben);

b: bá, „besteigen", bag, „schlagen", bô, „ganz, frei, edel, sein, existiren", „Regenzeit"[2]), bi, „männlich", bu, „essen", bū, „Blut"[3]), bul, „weiss";

d: da, „Fleisch", dā, „aufrecht", dē, „leer" (saftlos, daher dē-nískin, „ich mache saftlos", „ich koche"), dem, „abweisen", di, „thun"[4]), din, „alt", doi, „schnell", dur, „Stamm", „Familie";

---

[1]) ām ist, wie ich schon oben S. XLVI andeutete, keineswegs eine spätere Entlehnung aus dem Arabischen, sondern ein ursprüngliches Kanúri-Wort, eben so gut wie das entsprechende Tédā-Wort anna; ām scheint einfach das umgekehrte ma, „Person". Vgl. Vokab. S. 2, N. 1.

[2]) bô. Dass dasselbe Wort in Bezug auf den Menschen „frei, edel" und in Beziehung auf die Natur, Jahreszeit, Regenzeit und Existenz im Allgemeinen (mbē-tši, „es ist", S. 179, N. 10) bedeutet, ergibt sich ganz einfach aus der Beschaffenheit der Tropenländer, wo in der Regenzeit die Natur ihre ganze Kraft und Fülle entwickelt. Auch bi, „männlich" hängt mit dieser Grundidee eng zusammen.

[3]) bū, „Blut" im Vergleich zu bu, „essen" deutet wol an, dass die erste Nahrung der Kanúri keineswegs in Feldfrüchten bestand, aber allerdings widerlegt das noch nicht die Ansicht derjenigen, die annehmen, dass im Allgemeinen die erste Nahrung der Naturvölker in Feldfrüchten bestand, da die älteren Sitze der Kanúri in wüstere Gegenden fallen, wo es wenig Kraut gibt. Daher kommt es auch wol, dass die Kanúri gar keine monosyllabe Bezeichnungen für Feldfrüchte haben, während sie deren für „Blut" und „Fleisch" besitzen. Später aber scheint auch der „Fisch", bū-ni ein besonderer Nahrungsartikel geworden zu sein.

[4]) di. Ich habe schon oben S. LII auf die Übereinstimmung mit den Indo-Germanischen Sprachen in diesem Falle hingewiesen. Auch im Wandalá haben wir dē, im Bágrimma da.

§. 53, p. 40, that but a very limited number of the verbs in skin has developed a causative conjugation, dissolves itself in nothing, unnatural as it is and merely based on false instances.

I here will only add with regard to the causative conjugation, that the ye or yi of yi-skin, „I give" has been made use of in order to import to the original root the causative tendency, as for instance li-skin, „I learn", ye-ke-li-skin, „I give to learn", i. q. „I teach", and thus we find a very simple and natural cause, why this verbal form demands the object in the dative case.

But the verb li-skin is important enough to detain us a moment longer, as its various transformations exhibit all the three forms in skin, ni-skin and ṅgin; lí-skin, „I produce", „render" (the thing heard i. q. „I learn"), lí-nfskin, „I take off" (the clothes), li-ṅgin, „I come out, shoot forth" (used of plants).

In conclusion of these few remarks on the verbal forms of the Kanúri-language, which follow the only object of showing the natural development of the language, I must state, that almost all the highly complicated and unintelligible forms as given by Koelle, reduce themselves into the most simple and natural parts of speech, as we have seen already p. LV to be the case with the form nyā. In order to prove this statement by another instance, I here must say a word of what Koelle (§. 212, p. 210. 2) calls „present participial", and in order to explain at once what I mean, I dissolve two of the phrases given by him from his schematizing mode into my own analytical way of writing; thus Koelle's túta mána kámāntsiyē nemétseṇagā ši pāutši, translated into my own writing is:

tāta manna kamā-ntsi-ye nemé-tse na-ga ši fau-tsi,
boy word companions his of one said that (acc.) he heard,

i. q. the boy heard the word which one of his companions said, and his:

peṛ šírō melyē tsebátseṇarō tseba, translated into my own writing is:

fir ši-rō mal-ye tsebā-tse na-ro se-bā,
horse him a king sent on that he mounted,

i. q. he mounted the horse sent him by the king.

Thus, we see, that neither na-gā nor na-rō have any thing to do with the form of the verb, but that the first is the accusative, the second the dative case of the pronoun na, „that".

Now, in order to facilitate a clear insight into the gradual development of the Kanúri-idiom, I here give a short list of the most simple roots, such as they occur to me, in an alphabetical order, adding a few remarks to some of them:

a: ām, „people" [1]), am, „upwards" (raise);

b: bá, „mount", bag, „beat", bō, „entire, free, noble, exist", „rainy season" [2]), bī, „male", bu, „eat", bū, „blood" [3]), bul, „white";

d: da, „meat", dā, „upright", dē, „empty, juiceless" (thence de-nfskin, „I make juiceless", „I boil"), dem, „refuse", di, „do" [4]), diu, „old", doi, „swift", dur, „family", „tribe";

---

[1]) ām, as I stated already p. XLVII, has by no means been simply borrowed from the Arabic, but according to my opinion is an original Kanúri-word as well as the corresponding Tédá-term anna, am being merely the reverse of ma, „Person". On the contrary the singular hám is a later form; see vocab. p. 3, note 1.

[2]) bō: the fact, that the same term means „noble, free", with regard to man, and „rainy season" with regard to nature, as well as „existence" in general (mbō-tši, p. 159, note 10 „it is", „exists"), is easily explained by the character of the Tropical regions, where nature develops her whole power only during the rainy season; also bī, „male" is closely connected with the same idea.

[3]) bū with the meaning of blood, in connection with bu „eat", seems clearly to indicate, that the original food of the Kanúri did by no means consist in vegetable food; for, although this fact does by no means affect the general opinion of those, who suppose that reaping the easy produce of the ground rather constituted the original livelihood of the natives of the Tropical regions than the chase, and the meat of wild beasts, yet it is very important with regard to the question of the original seats of the Kanúri, who, while they possess monosyllabic terms for „meat" and „blood", have not a single monosyllabic term for any of the fruits of the earth. Also „fish", bū-nī must at a later period have constituted a principal article of food.

[4]) di: I have already pointed out p. LIII the general harmony between this term and the corresponding one in the Indo-European languages. In Wándalá also we have dó and in Bágrimma da.

f (p̌): fa, „hören, fühlen", fā, „sich rühren", fa (fato), „Haus", fal, „anderes"[1]), far, „über", fe, „Vieh", fi, „voll, bereit", fir, „Pferd", fog, „zusammen", fu, „Wind, Athem";

g: ga, „folgen", gug, „eingehen", gō, „ergreifen";

dž: dže, „Strick";

h: ham, „kalt";

k: kā (alte Form von kéla), „Kopf", kam, „schneiden", kaw, „Mensch", kau, „Stein, Sonne"[2]), kir, „Sklavin"[3]), kō, „grösser, weiter"[4]);

l: lé, „gehen", len (let), „schlafen", li, „hervor (-bringen, -kommen"), lo (lolo), „zittern", lug, „hinausgehen";

m: ma, „Person", mā, „suchen", mai, „Herr, König";

n: na, „das", nu, „Besitz", nam, „entzwei", nda, „was", ndí, „zwei", ne, ni, „machen", né, „klein" (ne-niskin, neńgin, „klein machen, malen", Koelle nyeńgin), nem, „Platz, Wohnung", ni, „du", nū, „wissen", nu, „sterben";

ńg: ńgā, „lebendig", ńgál, „schön", ńgé, „Topf", ńgim, „Hütte", ńgúm, „Stirne", ńgúr, „Kern", nki, „Wasser"[5]);

r: rā, „fähig", rak, „gerade, lieb", ram, „verbergen", ré, „entzwei", ri, „fürchten", ro, „Leben, fest", ru, „sehen", rúm, „Holzstange, Lanze";

s: sa, „erschüttern, treffen", sum, „versammeln, alles", sam, „teilen", se, sei, „ausser, nur", sā, „Eisen", sum (summo), „Ohr"[6]);

š: ši, „er", šī, „Fuss", šim, „Auge";

t: ta (tata), „Kind", tu, „fassen, halten", ter, „auseinander", tim, „Zahn", tló (ursprüngliche Form von tílo), „eins", tsak, „gerade", tsal, „schneiden", tser, „sehr", tsu, „Name, Wort"[7]), tse und tše, „sprechen"[8]), tšī, „Mund";

u: ū, „ich";

z: zuu, „warm, schwer, schwierig";

y: ya, „trinken", yá, „älterer Verwandte, Mutter"[9]), ye, yi, „geben", yé, „zurückgeben", yim, „Tag", yog, „vorwärts";

w: wu (bu), „nein" (wu-nískin, „ich mache nein", „will nicht"), war, „brennen, schmerzhaft"[10]).

Laute wie diese sind allerdings mehr ein „stridor, non vox" wie Plinius (H. N. l. V, c. 8) sich über die Sprache der im Afrikanischen Binnenlande wohnenden Völker ausdrückt, und

---

[1]) fal. Koelle führt fal oder pal mit der Bedeutung „eins" auf, aber es ist keineswegs gleichbedeutend mit tló, tílō, sondern heisst „ein Anderes". Daher fal-nískin, „ich mache ein Anderes, ich tausche, setze über (einen Fluss)". S. Vokab. S. 97, N. 1.

[2]) kau bedeutet „Sonne" und „Stein", ganz wie fast derselbe identische Ausdruck bei den Wolgaischen Finnen „Mond" und „Stein" bedeutet. Das erklärt sich ganz natürlich aus der Auffassung dieser Planeten als eines feurigen Steins und es ist daher nicht nöthig, dass wir mit Koelle eine Unterscheidung dadurch künstlich erzwingen, indem wir Stein kou schreiben. — kau bezeichnet übrigens eben nur die volle, runde Sonne, während das viel später gebildete Wort kengal, ke-ńgal für die Sonne besonders in ihrem Aufgang und Untergang, wahrscheinlich „das schöne Schauspiel" verherrlicht, von ńgál, ńgála, „schön".

[3]) kir beweist wol zur Genüge, dass die ursprüngliche Form für „Sklave" (kálla) kar war.

[4]) kō, daher kō-niskin, „ich mache grösser", „ich übertreffe"; „ich mache weiter, ich passire, gehe vorbei".

[5]) ńkī. Die Grundbedeutung ist wahrscheinlich wie ńgā, „das sich Bewegende", „Lebendige".

[6]) sum war entschieden die alte Form von summo, entsprechend tim, und wir können mit ziemlicher Sicherheit andere ältere Formen auf dieselbe Weise mit Ausscheidung des Endvokals a oder o auffinden.

[7]) tsu hatte wahrscheinlich die generelle Bedeutung von „Wort", ehe das Fremdwort maana (magana) aus dem Hausa aufgenommen wurde.

[8]) tše. Ich habe schon früher (S. L, N. 1) angedeutet, dass ich es für durchaus zweifelhaft halte, ob diese Form auf ein nískin oder ńgskin zurückzuführen sei, wohin allerdings die Form ge-ne zu gehören scheint.

[9]) yá. Aus dem Grundbegriff „älterer Verwandte" erklärt sich, wie yá zugleich Mutter und den älteren Bruder und die ältere Schwester bezeichnet.

[10]) war heisst daher „Tripper"; auch dua für den späteren Begriff „Syphilis" gehört hierher.

f (p̄): fa, „hear, feel", fā, „stir", fā (fāto), „house, dwelling", fal, „other, some other" [1]), far, „over", fo, „cattle", fi, „ready, full", fir, „horse", fog, „together", fu, „wind", breath";

g: ga, „follow", gag, „enter", gō, „seize";

dž: dže, „rope, cord";

h: ham, „cold";

k: kā (original form of kélā), „head", kam, „cut", kām, „man, person", kan, „stone, sun" [2]), kir, „female, slave" [3]), kō, „greater, wider" [4]);

l: lé, „go", len, lot, „sleep", li, „forth" (produce), lu (lulo), „trouble", lug, „go out";

m: ma, „person", mā, „search", mai, „master, king";

n: na, „that", nā, „possession", nam, „asunder", ndā, „what", ndi, „two", ne, ni, „make", nē, „small" (nē-níkin, nēngin, Koelle nyēngin, „make small", „grind"), num, „place, dwelling", ni, „thou", nō, „know", nu, „die";

ṅg: ṅga, „alive", ṅgál, „fine", ṅgē, „pot", ṅgim, „hut", ṅgum, „front", ṅgur, „stone, kernel", ūkl, „water" [5]);

r: rā, „able", rak, „straight, dear", ram, „hide", „bury", rē, „in-two, divide", ri, „fear", ro, „firm, live", ru, „see", rūm, „pole, spear";

s: sa, „shake, strike", sam, „gather, all", sām, „rub", sē, „only", sū, „iron", sum (summo), „ear" [6]);

š: ši, „he", ši, „foot", šim, „eye";

t: ta (táta), „child", ta, „hold, seize", ter, „asunder", tim, „tooth", tló (original form of tílo), „one", tsak, „straight", tsal, „cut", tser, „very", tsu, „name, word" [7]), tše and tšē, „speak" [8]), tši, „mouth";

u: ū, „I";

z: zau, „warm, heavy, difficult";

y: ya, „drink", yā, „older relation, mother" [9]), ye, yi, „give", yē, „give back", yim, „day", yog, „forward";

w: wa (ba), „no" (thence wa-níkin, „I make no", „dislike"), war, „burn, burning disease" [10]).

Sounds like these, no doubt, are truly to be called „stridor, non vox", as Pliny in his Encyclopaedia of Nature (l. V, ch. 8) expresses himself with regard to the language of the

---

[1]) fal: Koelle gives fal or pal with the notion „one", but it is by no means equivalent with tló, tiló, but rather means „another", thence fal-níkin, „I make another (thing), change, cross from one shore to the other"; see verb. p. 93, note 4.

[2]) kan means „stone" as well as „sun", just as almost the very identical word means „moon" as well as „stone" with the Fine of the Wolga, a fact which is easily explained by means of the conception of the planet as a fiery stone, and it is therefore not necessary, to try to distinguish these two terms by different spelling, as Koelle writes the term meaning stone „kon". — kan, moreover, denotes only the round, full sun, as it appears in the zenith, while the other term kengal means the sun as far as it is rising and setting. Indeed kengál, ke-ngál, which is of much more recent origin, seems to have been understood as „the beautiful spectacle", „what is fine", ngál, ngála.

[3]) kir seems to prove sufficiently, that the original form for „male slave" was kar, later form kárle.

[4]) kō, thence kō-níkin, „I make larger, I surpass"; „I make farther, I pass by".

[5]) ūkl: the original notion of this term is probably identical with that of ṅgā, „what is moving, alive".

[6]) sum was decidedly the original form of summo, corresponding exactly in form with šim. In the same manner we may with a considerable degree of certainty find other original forms by throwing away the final a or o.

[7]) tsu most probably had the original meaning of „word", before the term magan (mágana) was borrowed from the Hausa-language.

[8]) tše: I have already remarked before (p. LI, note 1), that I doubt, whether we have to derive this form which occurs only in the 3rd person sing. from a root níkin or ngakin.

[9]) yā: taking as the original notion of this term the meaning of „older relation", we understand easily, how it happens that the same term means „mother" as well as „elder brother" and „elder sister".

[10]) war; thence also the name for „clap"; we have also to mention here dun, „venereal disease".

sie bildeten nach meiner Ansicht die Hauptelemente der Rede bis in das sechste oder siebente Jahrhundert unserer Zeitrechnung, wo die Kanúri durch die gänzliche Erschütterung der Völkerverhältnisse Nord-Afrika's und die grössere Berührung mit weiter entwickelten Völkern auch ihre Sprache weiter auszubilden anfingen. Das Hausa-Volk ging ihnen in der Entwickelung unfehlbar um einige Schritte voraus. Ich will hier nur bemerken, dass auf diese höchst einfache Weise sich fast alle Afrikanischen Sprachen in ihrem natürlichen Bildungsgange darstellen lassen, fast am deutlichsten die Yolof-Sprache, in deren Geist der Abbé Boilat in seiner weitschichtigen Grammatik (grammaire de la langue Woloffe, 1858) keineswegs so eingedrungen ist, wie das zu wünschen wäre. Seine paradoxe Aussage „les noms et les adjectifs se conjuguent" löst sich in die einfache Erklärung auf, dass die verbale Abwandelung selbst der einfachsten Begriffe vermöge eines dem Grundbegriffe angefügten Hülfszeitwortes geschieht.

Ich will nun noch ein kurzes Verzeichniss derjenigen Ausdrücke geben, die mir im Kanúri und Hausa als übereinstimmend oder einander nahe verwandt erschienen sind und hier werden wir nun finden, dass eine solche Übereinstimmung zwischen diesen keineswegs wortarmen, sondern vielmehr reich entwickelten Sprachen sehr beschränkt ist, zumal, wenn es sich um ursprüngliche Begriffe handelt, woraus wir denn die Bestätigung des oben ausgesprochenen Satzes erlangen, dass der, eben durch meine obige Untersuchung wol ziemlich deutlich bewiesene, Einfluss, den die Hausa-Sprache auf die grammatische, besonders die verbale Ausbildung des Kanúri ausgeübt hat, erst einer bezüglich jungen Zeit zuzuschreiben ist, und dass die Sprachen ihrem Grundelemente nach nicht verwandt sind.

Kanúri.	Hausa.	Deutsch.
agô	abu	Sache, Ding
bug (niskin	(na) bugga	schlage (ich)
bugo [ba ugo] [1]) .	bâbû [ba abu] . .	nichts, nicht
dâma	(na-t da) dâma . .	Bewegung
fiska (Koelle pesga) [2])	fuska	Gesicht, Züge
gode (ñgin [3]) . . .	(na) gôde	danke
fer (skin [4])	ni-)isâ	komme an
ka [kéla] [5])	ka	Kopf

[1]) bâgô. Obgleich der eine, gleichfalls dem Hausa entlehnte, Bestandtheil dieser Zusammensetzung, agô, ein ganz gewöhnliches Kanúri-Wort geworden ist, ist doch bo allein im Kanúri durchaus nicht in Gebrauch, und obgleich Koelle die Entlehnung aus dem Hausa nicht kannte, fiel ihm doch auf, dass dieser negative Partikel nur in ganz besonderen Verhältnissen vorkomme (Gr. §. 48. „a negative not otherwise occurring"). Die Priorität des Hausa-Ausdrucks zeigt sich deutlich in dem Umstande, dass bâba oder bâbo sogar in die Bullý-Sprache, der er der Ableitung nach ganz fremd ist, übergegangen ist. Siehe Hanoteau grammaire Tamachek (l. c. Temâšiy), S. 119, N. 1, verglichen mit meinen Reisen Th. I, S. 258, N.). Ziemlich früh aber muss bâgô in die Kanúri-Sprache eingeführt worden sein und ist darin dermassen einheimisch geworden, dass Koelle sogar ein (mir unbekanntes) Zeitwort bâgângin aufführt mit der Bedeutung „ich sterbe", d. h. „ich werde zu nichts".

[2]) fiska. Darüber, dass dies kein ursprünglicher Kanúri-Ausdruck war und erst später das einheimische peli verdrängte s. an betreffender Stelle des Vokabular's s. v.

[3]) godê(-ñgin. In diesem Falle steht wiederum die Priorität des Hausa-Ausdruckes aus demselben Grunde fest, wie bei bâgô, weil auch die Hausa-Phrase ina gôde in die gewöhnliche Umgangssprache selbst der nördlicheren Mozy-Stämme übergegangen ist, wie z. B. der Isakkamâren, die seit mehreren Jahrhunderten aller Berührung mit den südlicheren Völkern ganz entzogen sind. S. die Phrase nogôndai (d. e. nogôdai) fallo bei Hanoteau Gr. T. S. 227.

[4]) isa-skin. Aus dieser unzweifelhaften Ableitung dieses Zeitwortes aus dem Hausa erklärt es sich, wie es kommt, dass isa-skin, wie schon Koelle auffiel (Gr. §. 24, Nota), das einzige Kanúri-Zeitwort ist, das mit einem i anfängt; ich habe allerdings auch ift-skin, „ich kaufe", das Koelle yaftskin schreibt, aber auch dies Zeitwort scheint, wie wir an anderer Stelle sehen werden, ein Fremdwort zu sein.

[5]) kâ. Dass dies die ursprüngliche Form für kéla ist, kann nicht zweifelhaft sein, da die Kanúri noch jetzt kâ tsî-bo ugun „Kopf des Mundes", d. h. Lippen, und andere derartige Zusammensetzungen. Aber der Ursprung ist nicht sicher, da wir ka auch im Lógone haben. Koelle gibt sonderbarer Weise diesem kâ mit der Bedeutung „Spazierstock", die es erst in Folge mehrerer Combinationen erhält.

people living beyond the Northern coast of Africa, but, nevertheless, I am of opinion, that they formed the chief element of the Kanúri-idiom till about the 6th or 7th century of our era, when these people like their neighbours, especially the Hausa, who were setting them the example, in consequence of the thorough revolution which affected all national relations of Northern Africa, and through the closer connection into which they were brought with people of a higher state of civilization, began to develop their language likewise. I only want to add, that in this simple manner most African languages are easily dissolved into their original elements, and their natural course of development illustrated, and that a very excellent instance of such a structure is the Y-olof-language, the character of which the Abbé Boilat in his voluminous grammar (grammaire de la langue Woloffe, 1858) has not so clearly developed, as we might expect. Thus, his paradox statement „les noms et les adjectifs se conjuguent" means nothing, but that the verbal formation and conjugation even of the most simple notions is achieved by means of an auxiliary verb being added to the root.

I now shall add a short list of those terms in the Kanúri- and Hausa-languages, which I have found identical, or nearly related, when I hope, we may convince ourselves, that such a harmony between those two languages, the development of which is rather considerable, is of a very limited nature, especially as far as regards primitive notions; and thus will be confirmed the statement I have made before p. XXXI, that notwithstanding the remarkable influence, exercised by the Hausa-language upon the grammatical, and particularly the verbal development of the Kanúri, as is shown by my own inquiries, such an influence belongs to a relatively recent period, while the original elements of these two languages are not related.

Kanúri.	Hausa.	English.
agō	abu	thing
bag (niskin	(na) bugga	beat (I)
bägō [ba agō][1]) .	bābu [ba abu] . .	nothing, not
dama	na-i da) dama . .	recovery, doing better
fiska [Koelle pēsga][2])	fuska	face, features
godē (igia[3]) . . .	(na) gode	thank (I)
lee (skin[4])	ni-)isa	arrive (I)
kā [kēla][5])	ka	head

[1]) bägō: although the term agō, one of the two portions of this composite term, which has itself been borrowed from the Hausa-idiom, has become a very common Kanúri-word, the other negative element ba alone is quite foreign to that language, and even Koelle, who was not aware of the origin of the negative particle bägō, was struck by the fact of it occurring only in certain relations (gr. §. 48 „a negative not otherwise occurring"). The priority of the Hausa-term bābu or bābō is clearly shown by the fact, that it has been adopted by the Máziy-tongue, which could only happen in consequence of the intercourse of the Hausa with many sections of this farspread nation. Compare Hanoteau grammaire Tamachek (i. e. Te-mäshiyt), p. 119, note 1, with my Travels and Disc. I, p. 236, note 1. However, the negative particle bägō must have been introduced into the Kanúri-idiom at an early period, and has become so naturalized, that Koelle has even a verb bägōngin with the notion „I shall be no more, I shall die", verbally „I become nothing".

[2]) fiska is not an old Kanúri-term, but has been introduced at a later period, when it took the place of the indigenous Kanúri-word pēli, as I have shown in my vocabulary, s. v.

[3]) godē-ágia: in this case, likewise, the priority of the Hausa-term is well established from the same reason, as in the case with bägō, the Hausa-phrase ina góda having been adopted as a term of daily life even by the most Northern of the Máziy-tribes, such as the Imóshaghen, who have been deprived of all direct intercourse with the Negro-tribes for a very long period. See the phrase negoudai (i. e. negúdeḫ) falls with Hanoteau, gr. T. p. 121.

[4]) lee-skin: the well established circumstance of this verb having been borrowed from the Hausa-idiom explains satisfactorily, how it happens, that lee-skin is (almost) the only Kanúri-verb which begins with an l, a circumstance which attracted the notice of Rev. Koelle (gr. §. 34, note). Certainly, according to my spelling we have besides also the verb lfi-skin, which Koelle writes yeféskin; but this too may be a foreign term.

[5]) kā: there can be scarcely any doubt, that this is the original form of kēla, as the Kanúri still has the term kā tši-be, „head of the mouth", „lips", but the origin is not quite certain, as in Lógone also we have kaa for head.

Kanúri.	Haussa.	Deutsch.
k-ágel . .	m-ákeri	K. Amboss H. Schmied
kam (-nískin[1]) .	(na) kamna	schneide
kirre(-nískin . .	(na) kirra	K. horche H. rufe
koṭ(-iskin . . . . . kuṭ(-skin	(na) kan	bringe
mana[2])	mágana	Wort, Rede
na[3])	nan	dies, das
nda	nda	wer, was
ni(-skin	(i)na	mache, bin thuend
ši[4])	ši	er, es
tamba-skin[5]) . . .	(na) tamma . . . tebba	koste, schmecke
tse[6])	tše	sage
tši	(na-)tši	K. Mund H. esse
wuse -nískin[7] . . . wuse -ñgin . . .	usé	K. begrüsse H. sei gegrüsst
yá[8])	ša	trinke.

Allerdings wird es möglich sein, nach längerem Suchen dieses spärliche Verzeichniss etwas zu vervollständigen, wie selbst im Tédā einige Anklänge zurückgeblieben sind von Wortähnlichkeiten mit dem Haussa, die sich im Kanúri später verloren haben oder von anderen Ausdrücken ersetzt worden sind, ein Verhältniss, das sich vollkommen erklärt aus den früheren Wohnsitzen des Haussa-Stammes, selbst noch vor wenigen Jahrhunderten in der Landschaft Asben, von wo aus sie, besonders wegen der Salzminen von Bilma, mit den Tédā in fortwährender Berührung stehen mussten, zumal in Kauf- und Rechnungsbeziehungen. So haben wir z. B. noch jetzt in beiden Sprachen den in seiner Wurzel vollkommen identischen Ausdruck für „ich zähle", im Tédā kit-erik, im Haussa (na ked-nia, während wir im Kanúri den völlig verschiedenen, nicht ursprünglichen Ausdruck tamisar-niskin haben. Dagegen gehören alle jene, vom Haussa und Kanúri gemeinsam, dem Arabischen entlehnten Ausdrücke nicht hierher und zu ihnen sind viele Redensarten zu rechnen, deren Ursprung nicht gerade auf den ersten Blick deutlich wird.

---

[1]) kam-niskin mit (na kamna verglichen, lässt uns etwas zweifelhaft, ob in diesem Falle niskin das blosse Hülfszeitwort, oder ob kama die Wurzel ist.

[2]) mana ist unzweifelhaft eine Zusammenziehung des Haussa-Wortes mágana, daher meine Schreibweise (mágana, magna, manna), die ganz der Aussprache entnommen ist, Koelle's mána wol vorzuziehen. Dass dass dies ein später eingeführtes Wort ist vergl. taū, S. LX, N. 7.

[3]) na ist später im gewöhnlichen Gebrauch verloren gegangen. Es erscheint noch, ausser in den S. LVIII angeführten Formen, in der Pluralform a-ni, á-ni-ma, „diese".

[4]) ši. Auch hier ist das Haussa wol unzweifelhaft in der Priorität und ist doch wol verwandt mit dem Alt-Ägyptischen si, „Jemand", „ein Gewisser". Bunsen I, S. 345.

[5]) tamba-skin. Auch die Tédā-Form tôb-erik müssen wir hier vergleichen.

[6]) tse ist allerdings 3te Person Präterit., aber ich zweifle daran, ob wir dies mit Koelle auf eine Wurzel niskin (bei ihm ngskin oder ágin) zurückführen dürfen. Die Form ge-nē zeigt wol auf etwas Ähnliches hin; seine Form gám aber bezweifle ich. Siehe S. L, N. 1.

[7]) wusé-niskin ist ein recht lehrreiches Beispiel zu dem, was ich oben S. LII über die Wortbildung mit niskin gesagt habe; wörtlich „ich mache (den Gruss) usé".

[8]) yá ist eine zweifelhafte Verwandtschaft mit šā.

Kanúri.	Hausa.	English.
k-ágel	m-ákeri	K. anvil H. blacksmith
kam (-niskin [1]) . . .	(na) kamnu	cut (I)
kirre(-niskin . . .	(na) kirra	K. hark, listen (I) H. call (I)
kot(-iskin . . . . . ku(-skin	(na) kau	bring (I)
manna [2])	mágana	word, speech
na [3])	nan	this, that
nda	nda	who, which, what
ni(-skin	(i)na	make, am doing (I)
ši [4])	ši	he, it
túmbu-skin [5]) . . .	ina { tamma . . . tebba	taste, try (I)
tše [6])	tše	say (I)
tši	(na-)tši	K. mouth H. eat (I)
wuse { -niskin [7]) . . . ngin	use	K. welcome (I) H. be welcome
yā [8])	ša	drink (I).

No doubt, it may be possible to add one, or another word to this short list, but, in general, it is conclusive as to the rather limited relationship which intercedes between the Kanúri- and Hausa-languages. Even the Tédá-idiom has preserved some vestiges of such a relationship between the Kanúri and the Hausa, while the corresponding terms in the former have been lost, or have made place to another term, such as the Tédá-term kil-erík, which is identical with the Hausa-term i-na ked-nia, „I am counting", while in Kanúri we have the totally different term tamisse-niskin, and such a case is perfectly intelligible, if we take into account the fact, that the seats of the Hausa nation, even so late as a few centuries ago, were in the country of Asben, from whence, especially on account of the saltmines of Bilma, they necessarily had direct commercial intercourse with the Tédá nation. As for the terms borrowed by both languages, the Kanúri as well as the Hausa, from the Arabic, they do not belong hither, and to this class do belong many terms, the origin of which is not clear at first sight.

---

[1]) kam-niskin compared with the Hausa-term ina kamna leaves some doubt, whether niskin in this case be the auxiliary verb, or whether the n belongs to the root.

[2]) manna, beyond a doubt, is a contracted form of the Hausa-word (mágana, magna, manna), and therefore my spelling, which is totally accommodated to the pronunciation of the people, preferable to the mána of Koelle. See, what I have said with regard to the term tsû p. LXI, note 7.

[3]) na in Kanúri is used very rarely, appearing, besides the forms mentioned p. LVIII, in the plural-form á-ni, á-ni-ma, „these".

[4]) ši; this pronoun, if originally identical in both languages, would be a remarkable proof of original relation between them, but such is not the case, the ši being quite foreign to that class of Hausa-pronouns which are identical with those of the Mósly. It may be compared with the old Egyptian si, „somebody". Bunsen I, p. 345.

[5]) túmbu-skin: we must here also take into account the Tédá-form tib-erík.

[6]) tše certainly is 3rd person perf., but I doubt, whether we are right in deriving this form from a form of the present niskin, or as Koelle writes ngin i. q. nyskin, which is never used (see p. LI, note 1). The form gené which is in common use, no doubt, points to such a root, but his form gen is certainly not right.

[7]) wusé-niskin is one of the most instructive instances for illustrating and proving the correctness of what I have said p. LIII with regard to the composition of verbs with niskin.

[8]) yá is a doubtful instance of original relationship between Kanúri and Hausa.

Fünftes Kapitel.

Die Téda-Sprache: modi Téda.

1. Zuerst muss ich ein Wort über den Namen Tédā sagen. Dieser ist die einzige ächt einheimische Namensform. Die Form Tubu oder Tebu rührt von den Kanúri- oder Bornu-Leuten her, welche die zweite Sylbe dā in die ihnen gängliche Pluralform bu umgewandelt haben, und ist dem Stamme selbst ganz fremd. Diese Silbe dā nun bezeichnet nach den deutlichsten Anzeichen die Lokalität — vergleiche do, da, ndi, K. nda, „wo" — oder den Wohnsitz eines Stammes. So haben wir die Stammnamen Kar-dā, Súker-dā, Búlgu-dā, Gou-dā A'rin-dā, Yer-dā und am deutlichsten von allen Elbué-dā, „der in Elbué" und Kirdi-dā, „der in Kirdi wohnende Stamm" (Reisen Th. III, S. 447). Der Name Tú-gu-bá aber, den die Tédā ihren Vettern, den Kanúri geben (s. oben S. XLII), steht wahrscheinlich in Beziehung zu Tubu, der Kanúri-Form ihres eigenen Namens. Tédā ist Singular und Plural, Substantiv und Adjektiv zugleich, wie die Gesammtheit des Volkes als Nation Téda gubri heisst, das Land Iurdo (ein späterer dem Arabischen entlehnter Ausdruck, der den entsprechenden nationalen verdrängt hat) Tédā, das Thal Kauār, das den Mittelpunkt des Téda-Landes bildet, hénderi („das Baumthal") Tédā, die Téda-Sprache mōdi Tédā.

2. Die Tédā sind wol unzweifelhaft dieselben mit den Garamanten der alten Schriftsteller — von Herodot herab bis nahe zur Zeit der Byzantiner — deren Herrschaft sich nach der Andeutung bei Ptolemaeus (L. I, c. 8, S. 27 Wilberg) selbst bis in das eigentliche Negerland (über verwandte Völkerschaften?) hinein erstreckte und die eben da auch als eigentlich äthiopischer Stamm im Gegensatz zu den Libyschen Völkern erscheinen; zur Erklärung des Namens Garamanten, der doch wol mit Ammon in Verbindung steht, werden vielleicht weitere Forschungen auf diesem Gebiete beitragen. Die Garamanten (Tédā) waren also die eingeborene Bevölkerung des ganzen Fezān und beherrschten die grosse Strasse von da nach Bornu. Nun erwähnt der sogenannte Leo Africanus im ersten Viertel des XVIten Jahrhunderts in eben diesen Gegenden einen Stamm, den er als einen der fünf grossen Berberstämme anerkennt und dessen Namen bei ihm bald Berdeoa, bald Berdoa, ja selbst Berdeva und Birdeva geschrieben ist (s. L. VII, c. 57, 68 und 63). Wir würden also über die Form des Namens ganz unsicher sein, wenn nicht schon Makrizi einen Stamm Berdóa in eben diesen Gegenden erwähnt hätte. (S. Reisen Th. II, S. 269). Wir können also wol mit ziemlicher Sicherheit annehmen, dass dies derselbe Stamm ist, und da nun auch Makrizi ihn einen Berberstamm nennt, so haben wir keinen Grund, Leo's wiederholte Angabe (s. L. I, c. 6) in Frage zu ziehen. Wir müssen also annehmen, dass damals wirklich ein Berberstamm diese Gegenden inne hatte und dies erklärt sich leicht aus dem Umstande, dass die Tédā durch die langjährigen Kriege, die sie im XIIIten Jahrhundert mit Dúnama Selmāmi (Reisen Th. II, SS. 275 und 636) geführt hatten, vollkommen geschwächt waren, und dass die hierauf folgende Herrschaft von Kānem oder Bornu, die noch im XIVten Jahrhundert diese ganze ungeheure, aber meist wüste Landschaft umfasste, in dem darauf folgenden Jahrhundert, dem unglücklichsten der ganzen Dauer dieses Reiches, völlig zerfiel. Wir müssen also annehmen, dass in Folge dieser Schwäche Berberstämme, die einzeln schon viel früher nach Fezān eingedrungen waren, diese Landschaften in Besitz nahmen, da sie wegen der Salzmine von Bilma Bedeutung hatten. Sie drängten also offenbar den Téda-Stamm zeitweilig zurück und wir haben keinen Grund anzunehmen, dass Leo die Tédā selbst für Berber hielt, obgleich die zweite Hälfte des von ihm angegebenen Namens, besonders in der Form Berdeva entschieden an die Tebu erinnert und vielleicht auf eine Mischung mit ihnen hinweist. Dagegen erwähnt Leo die Tédā unter dem Namen Gorau oder Gorran als ein ganz barbarisches Volk „una generazione di zingani" von nomadischen Sitten und mit einem vollständig unverständlichen Idiom (L. VII, c. 17), also ganz

Chapter the fifth.

The Téda-language: modi Téda.

1. First I must say a word about the name Tódā. Tódā is the only right indigenous form of what is generally called Tubu or Tobu. The two latter forms belong entirely to the Kanúri- or Bornu-people who have exchanged the second syllable dā against their common plural form bū, which form is quite foreign to the Tédā. As for dū, we have the clearest proofs, that it indicates the locality — compare do, du, ndi, Kanúri ndu, „where" — or the seats of a tribe. Thus, we have the following names with the same termination Kar-dā, Sákor-dā, Búlgu-dā, Gon-dā, A'rin-dū, Yor-dā, and the most instructive of all, Kirdi-dā „(the tribe dwelling) in Kirdi" and Elbnó-dū „(the tribe dwelling) in Elbuó" (Tr. vol. III, p. 496). As for the name Tú-gu-bá, given by the Tédā to their relatives, the Kanúri (p. XLIII, Tr. III, p. 494), most probably it has some relation to the Kanúri form Tubu of their own name. The form Tédā belongs as well to the singular as to the plural, to the substantive as well as to the adjective. Thus, the whole of the Tédā are called Tódā gubri, their country lardo (a later term, borrowed from the Arabic, which has supplanted the original one) Tódā, the valley Kawār which forms the centre of their country is called hónderi („the valley") Tódā, and the Tédā-language mödi Tédā.

2. The Tédā, I have not the slightest doubt, are identical with the nation called Garamantes by the ancients, from Herodotus down to the period of the Byzantines, a name probably of no national origin, but which seems to be connected with the veneration of Ammon, and which may find its true interpretation in the course of future inquiries on this field. The territory of the Garamantes according to Ptolemy (L. 1, ch. 8, p. 27 ed. Wilberg) extended into the very heart of Negroland, probably over related tribes, and they are distinctly designated by him as rather themselves of an Ethiopic (not Libyan) character. The Garamantes (Tédā), therefore, formed the indigenous population of the whole of Fezzān, and dominated entirely the commercial highroad leading thence to Bornu. Now, Leo Africanus (L. VII, ch. 57, 58 and 63), in the first quarter of the XVIth century, mentions in this very same region a tribe which, he designates expressly as one of the five great Berber-tribes, and the name of which in our copies is written sometimes Berdeoa, at others Berdoa, nay even Berdeva and Birdeva (L. I, ch. 6). Thus, we should have remained totally uncertain with regard to the true form of the name, if Makrisi had not mentioned the tribe Berdóa in this neighbourhood (see Tr. vol. II, p. 269). We, therefore, may with certainty place here a tribe of the name Berdóa, and, as Makrisi calls it likewise a Berber-tribe, we have no reason to call into doubt the repeated statement of Leo with regard to its origin. And it is easily to be explained, how a Berber-tribe could have possession of these regions at the end of the XVth, or the beginning of the XVIth century, if we take into account the facts, first, that the Téda had been greatly weakened in consequence of the long and bloody war which in the XIIIth century they had waged with Dúnama Selmāmi, when they were totally conquered (Tr. II, p. 276 and 636), and secondly, that the rule of the Bornu-people, planted upon their destruction, and which during the XIVth century comprised this whole region as far as Wadān, was overthrown in the following century; the XVth century forming the most gloomy period of the history of Bornu. It is, therefore, more than probable, that in consequence of this total overthrow of the former power, Berber-tribes, which already many years ago had begun to settle in Fezān, should take entire possession of these regions which were of great consequence on account of the saltmines of Bilma. These tribes, therefore, would have thrown, and kept back the Tédā-nation, as long as they remained powerful, and till the latter reoccupied their former seats; and thus, we have not the slightest reason to suppose, that Leo thought the Tédā to be Berber. On the contrary, he mentions the Tédā under the name Goran or Gorran

entschieden nicht von Berber-Ursprung. Dass dieser Name Goran, den man früher nicht zu deuten wusste und den Mr. Cooley (Negroland of the Arabs, S. 130, N. 214) fälschlich auf Kordofan bezog, die Téda bezeichnet, ist völlig sicher; die im Sudan angesessenen Araber nennen noch jetzt die Téda nur bei diesem Namen *Gurúân* (Reisen Th. III, S. 194). Allerdings erwähnt Leo diese Goran nur in dem Theil der Wüste, der westlich an Nubien stösst; die Tédâ, von der Westseite und Nordseite damals zurückgedrängt, konnten aber auch eben nur von dieser Seite her ihm bekannt werden, und höchst interessant und lehrreich ist es nun, dass er dieses Reich der Goran — denn als ein Reich bezeichnet er es im ersten Buche (c. 7 am Ende) — genau da angibt, wo die Arabischen Geographen des XIIIten und XIVten Jahrhunderts die Herrschaft der Zoghaua angegeben hatten. Die Zoghaua aber bilden einen mächtigen und hervorragenden Stamm der Tédâ-Nation (Reis. Th. III, S. 506) und *sie eben bezeichnete Leo unzweifelhaft mit seinem Namen Goran.* Wir sehen also hieraus, dass Leo selbst keineswegs die Tédâ oder Tebu als Berber bezeichnet, im Gegentheil hat er sie entschieden als Nicht-Berber bezeichnet. Dennoch aber bezog man, ohne Rücksicht auf die Umwälzungen von Jahrhunderten zu nehmen, ohne Weiteres seinen Namen Berdoa mit sammt seinem Berber-Charakter auf das jetzt in denselben Gegenden lebende Volk der Tebu und erklärte diese demnach für Berber. Dies dauerte bis auf die neueste Zeit und selbst noch jetzt, nachdem ich das Richtige schon vor mehreren Jahren angedeutet und in meinem grösseren Reisewerk, Th. II, S. 299 f., III, S. 441 historisch weiter ausgeführt, gibt es noch immer ausgezeichnete Forscher, die an jener althergebrachten Anschauung festhalten, und ich führe hier nur Vivien St. Martin an, der in einer ganz neuen Abhandlung die Tibbu (Tédâ) für eine ganz entartete Berber-Race erklärt[1]).

3. Ich gehe nun zur Sprache selbst über; die Sprache bietet zur Entscheidung der Frage über Abstammung das sicherste Mittel. Fast keine Sprache aber unter allen denen Inner-Afrika's war den Europäern bisher so unbekannt geblieben, wie die Tédâ-Sprache, obgleich sie von einem Stamme gesprochen wird, der in so geringer Entfernung von der Küste lebt. Aber der Grund hiervon ist die politische Unbedeutendheit des Stammes, und die theilweise Unzugänglichkeit seiner Sitze in einem ungeheuren Wüstengebiet, über das es zerstreut lebt, so wie auch andererseits durch den nicht sehr offenen und mittheilenden Charakter der Leute selbst. Nun brachte allerdings der hochverdiente Kapitän Lyon ein Verzeichniss von 54 Wörtern dieser Sprache zurück[2]), aber bei der damals höchst geringen Bekanntschaft mit den reinen ungemischten Dialekten der Berber-Sprache sowol auf der einen, als mit dem grammatischen Bau der Kanúri-Sprache auf der andern Seite, trugen diese geringen und unzulänglichen Proben nur dazu bei, die frühere Meinung zu bestätigen[3]). So war ich denn der Erste, der, wie oben S. X erwähnt, nach einer damals noch ganz oberflächlichen Bekanntschaft mit der Tédâ-Sprache im Jahre 1852 auf ihre enge Verwandtschaft mit dem Kanúri hinwies.

4. Hier will ich nun diese Behauptung näher im Einzelnen begründen und eine kurze Analyse dieser Sprache versuchen, die besonders zur richtigen historischen Erkenntniss des Kanúri von grösster Bedeutung ist. Allerdings mache ich nach dem, besonders in zusammenhängenden Erzählungen sehr unvollständigen, Material, das mir zu Gebote steht, nicht den

[1]) Vivien St. Martin in der Revue Germanique vol. XI, S. 662 nennt die Tibbus „les plus dégradés de tous les Berbers par le mélange du sang nègre", und S. 669 „la race métisse et tout à fait dégradée des Tibbous".

[2]) Captain Lyon, Narrative of Travels in Northern Africa. Engl. Original-Ausgabe S. 133. — Die hier verzeichneten Wörter weichen mit wenigen Ausnahmen von den entsprechenden in meiner Sammlung nur in der Orthographie ab; zu den Ausnahmen gehört *woogghe* für „Vogel", *badinol*, „Schaf" (vielleicht mein *uddno*, „Gazelle"), *tonggoe*, „die Sonne" (sehr merkwürdig, wenn wirklich, wie ich aber kaum glaube, eine Dialektverschiedenheit), *woo*, „alt", *ragoddi*, „Gesicht", *awana*, „Hand".

[3]) Dr. Latham war es besonders, der einige Zweifel an dem Zusammenhange der Tebu mit der Berber-Race schon im Anfang der fünfziger Jahre aussprach.

as a totally different people of a very peculiar character, „una generazione di zingani", of nomadic habits, and with a totally unintelligible idiom (L. VII, ch. 17), and, therefore, **undoubtedly not of Berber origin**. This name Goran, geographers did not know what to make of, and Mr. Cooley (the Negroland of the Arabs p. 130, note 214) referred it wrongly to Kordofan, but there cannot be the slightest doubt, that it means the Téda, **Guráan** being the common name by which the Téda are called at the present day by the Arabs of Negroland (see Trav. vol. III, p. 494). No doubt, Leo mentions these Goran only in that part of the desert, which borders on Nubia, but **the Téda**, thrown back from the Western, and Northern frontier of their former territory, **could only become known to him on their Eastern border**, and it is a very instructive fact, and corroborative of our view, that he mentions the dominion of the Goran — for in L. I, ch. 7 he expressly describes it as a kingdom or dominion — in the very same place, where the Arab geographers of the XIIIth and XIVth century had described the dominion of the Zoghawa. For the Zoghawa formed at that period a powerful, and distinguished section of the Téda-nation (Tr. III, p. 544); nay, even at the present time they keep almost the same seats, and it was them whom Leo comprised especially under the name Goran. Thus we see, that Leo by no means meant to designate the Téda-nation as belonging to the Berber-race, but that, on the contrary, he noted distinctly their different origin. Nevertheless, without taking the least regard to the revolutions of centuries, the learned have applied his name Berdoa, and the character he gave them, to the Tebu or Téda who at present live in the same regions. Nay, even at the present day, several years after I have pointed out their true connection, there are eminent scholars, who stick to that old prejudice, as an instance of which I here mention Mr. Vivien St. Martin, who in a recent Mémoire calls the Tibbu, as he writes their name, a degraded Berber-race [1]).

3. I now proceed to speak of the language. Language in all the questions of national origin is one of the surest means of inquiry. But of all the languages of the Interior of Africa none has become so little known to Europeans, as the Téda-language, although it is spoken by a tribe, which lives at so short a distance from the coast. But the fact is explained to a certain degree, as well by the little importance the tribe has in a political respect, as by the nature of their seats, scattered as they are over an immense tract of partially impenetrable desert, and finally by their individual character which is by no means very communicative. Now, already Captain Lyon, that energetic officer, who altogether has merited exceedingly well for increasing the knowledge of North-Africa, did bring back a list of 54 words of this language [2]); but in consequence of the very limited acquaintance which people at that time had with the pure unmixed dialects of the Berber-language, on the one, and with the grammatical structure of the Kanúri-language on the other side, these specimens, insufficient as they were in themselves, served only to corroborate the prevailing false opinion [3]). Thus, I myself was the first, who, as mentioned p. XI, after a first, indeed very limited, acquaintance with the Téda-language, pointed out its close relationship with the Kanúri in the year 1852.

4. These Introductory remarks afford the right place for entering more into particulars with regard to a short analytical view of this language, which is of the highest importance for a true historical appreciation of the Kanúri. No doubt, my material being very imperfect, and especially wanting in longer national compositions, although I have a good many phrases

---

[1]) Vivien St. Martin in the Revue Germanique vol. XI, p. 648 calls the „Tibboû" „les plus dégradés de tous les Berbers par le mélange du sang nègre", and p. 649 „la race métisse et tout à fait dégradée des Tibboû.

[2]) Captain Lyon, Narrative of Travels in Northern Africa, p. 232. — The words contained in this list, with but a few exceptions, do not differ from the corresponding terms in my vocabulary, but by orthography; to the exceptional cases belongs his woogghe, „bird", hedinni, „sheep" (perhaps identical with my udĕno, „gazelle"), tooggoo, „ass" (very remarkable, if indeed a real dialectical difference, and not, as I fancy, caused by some misunderstanding), wow, „cold", engaddi, „visage", awana, „hand".

[3]) As an exception I have here to mention Dr. Latham who, guided by his well known acuteness in matters of language, as early as 1850 expressed some doubt as to the connection of the Tebu with the Berber-race.

geringsten Anspruch auf Vollständigkeit, hoffe aber die richtige Grundlage zu weiterem erspriesslichem Forschen auf diesem zur lebendigen Einsicht in das innere Völkerleben auf der Grenzscheide von Asien und Afrika keineswegs unwichtigen Felde legen zu können.

Zuerst will ich bemerken, dass mein Vokabular besonders nach zwei verschiedenen Dialekten aufgeschrieben ist, und zumal nach zwei verschiedenen Personen, von denen der Eine mein in meiner Reisebeschreibung oft genannter Diener Mohammed war, ein Tédā-Mischling aus dem Dorfe Gatrōn im südlichen Theile Fezān's, während der Andere einem in Kānem angesiedelten Stamme angehörte, weshalb ich sie mit N. und S. bezeichnete, mit N. den in den nördlicheren Gegenden, in Bilma und dem Süden Fezān's, mit S. den von den in Kānem angesessenen Tédā-Stämmen gesprochenen Dialekt. Wo nur Ein Ausdruck angegeben ist, da gehört er dem nördlichen Dialekte an, und bin ich ungewiss, ob der südliche einen verschiedenen Ausdruck daneben besitzt; denn während meines Aufenthaltes in Kānem war ich vom Fieber so geschwächt, dass ich nur höchst wenig thun konnte. Aber die Dialekt-Abweichungen, besonders bei den östlichen Stammabtheilungen, sind noch ungemein viel durchgehender, wie wir z. B. bei der Mundart der Teranye bemerkt haben (Reis. Th. III, S. 497), wenn sie anders der Tédā-Sprache angehört. Überhaupt bildet das, was ich gegeben habe, nur schwache Proben. Viele dieser Dialekt-Verschiedenheiten übrigens sind aus Zusammenziehung oder Ausdehnung der Wörter in einer der Mundarten entstanden; so

Gesang	S. d(eb)ōna	. . . .	N. dōna,
Hirte	S. d(ebb)edir	. . .	N. dōdir,
Tochter	S. dōbu	. . . . . .	N. dōū.

Der reinste Dialekt dieser weit ausgebreiteten Sprache wird wol unzweifelhaft in Abō und Tibesti gesprochen und wir müssen von dort eine grosse Bereicherung der Kenntniss dieser Sprache erwarten.

5. In Bezug auf die Orthographie will ich nur bemerken, dass nicht allein in den verschiedenen Dialekten dieser Sprache, sondern sogar in demselben Dialekte, ja bei demselben Worte in verschiedenen Verbindungen die Buchstaben h, f, k stets mit einander wechseln, wie wir das auch in so vielen anderen Sprachen sehen, z. B. im Fūl und in den verschiedenen Kafir-Dialekten; so ákeri, áferi (bei Lyon sogar afhirri), „Schulter"; báfo, „reif"; báhe-ni, „nicht reif"; kusear, fusenr, „Rücken". Ich bin demnach der Ansicht, dass die Namensformen Febābo und Kebābo der Oase im Süden von Audžila wol Dialekt-Verschiedenheiten darstellen, und dass die erstere Form nicht bloss auf einem Missverständniss des Maghrebinischen ق beruht, wie Fresnel meinte.

6. Ich bespreche nun das Pronomen Personale. Dieses ist sehr eigenthümlich gebildet und bietet nur wenige Vergleichspunkte, selbst auch nur mit dem verwandten Kanūri, am meisten noch mit Berberischem und Koptischem, und dient auch dieses wieder zum Beweis, dass dergleichen Redetheile gar nicht aus dem Geiste der einheimischen Sprache weiter gebildet, sondern erst durch Berührung mit anderen weiter vorgeschrittenen Sprachen entwickelt sind.

	Singular.		Plural.
1ste Person	tá-ne oder tá-ni	. .	tin-ta,
2te „	neb-rē	. . . .	nob-ral,
3te „	me-rē	. . . .	me-rā oder ána-ta.

Hierzu will ich nur bemerken, dass n oder ne, verwandt dem entsprechenden Alt-Egyptischen und Makiy, die Wurzel der Form der 1sten Pers. zu sein scheint, daher né-rne die Form des Pronomen Possessivum. Obgleich ta somit ein blosser Vorschlag zu sein scheint — auch das Sonγai-Pronomen hat ein verstärkendes ta — erinnert doch tan, Plur. tin an die Form tan des Pronomen Possessiv. im Alt-Egyptischen. Das t oder ţ, wie es wenigstens in der 1sten Person zur Bildung des Plural gebraucht ist und auch zur Bildung der Plural-Form im Zeitwort dient, erscheint gleichfalls in ähnlicher Bedeutung im Koptischen. — Als einen leichten Versuch, das

with regard to the common daily occurrences of the traveller, I do not make the very least pretension to completeness, but I hope, by what I am able to do to lay the foundation of a deeper and more productive inquiry on this field, which is by no means destitute of a high importance for obtaining a true insight not only into the mental activity, but into the true historical connection of the whole group of nations of North-East Africa.

Before entering into the particulars of the language I must observe, that my glossary was written down especially from the mouth of two persons, one of whom was my servant Mohammed, a native of the village of Gatrōn, in the Southern part of Fezzān, but of Tédā origin, whom I have had frequent opportunity of mentioning in the Narrative of my Travels and Discoveries, and the other an individual belonging to one of the tribes settled in Kānem. The glossaries taken down from these two persons representing two very different dialects, one of which belongs to the Northern, the other to the Southern quarters of the region occupied by the Tédā-nation, I have denoted the different terms by adding N. to those of Mohammed, S. to those of my other authority, while, where there is no divergency, the term belongs to Mohammed, as during my stay in Kānem I was so sick with fever, that I could do but very little. But there are many more dialectical varieties of this farspread idiom and there may be some which vary to a much greater degree, as for instance the Terauye (Tr. III, p. 497), if it belongs at all to this group. However, in our case many of the divergencies of N. and S. are easily explained by a simple contraction of the longer form in the one into a shorter form in the other, or by a contrary process, as for instance

song	S. d(eb)ōna	. . . .	N. dōna,
shepherd	S. d(ibb)edir	. . .	N. dōdir,
daughter	S. dōbu	. . . . .	N. dōō.

The purest dialect of the Tédā-language I suspect to be that spoken by the section of the Abō settled in Tibestī.

5. With regard to orthography I only want to observe, that not only in the different dialects of this language, but even in one and the same dialect, nay even in one and the same word, the letters h, f, k are interchanged, as we are also in so many other languages, such as in Fūl, and in the various Kāfir-dialects; thus áheri, áferi (with Lyon even afhirri), „shoulder"; báfo, „ripe", báke-ni, „not ripe"; hussar, fussar, „back". I am therefore of opinion, that the forms of the name of the oasis to the South of Audžila, which in consequence of Capt. Lyon's researches first became known to Europeans as Febābo, and afterwards through Mr. Fresnel as kebābo, may be dialectical differences, and the f in the former form not merely to be explained from a false reading of the Moghrebine ڧ.

6. I first speak of the personal pronoun. This is formed in a very individual manner and admits only of few points of comparison even with the Kanúri; while the Berber and Coptic seem to be closer related, thus exhibiting another instance of the manner in which parts of speech, like this, are frequently not developed according to the character of the native idiom, but merely by contact with other languages in an advanced state of development.

	Singular.		Plural.
1st person	tá-nē or tá-ni	. .	tin-ta,
2nd „	neb-rē	. . . . . .	neb-ral,
3rd „	mo-rō	. . . .	me-rā or ána-ta.

With regard to the form of the 1st person sing. tá-nē, the form of the possessive pronoun né-rāā which is rather the genitive case, shows evidently, that n or ne is the root, which therefore is nearly related to the ancient Egyptian and Berber; the t is also the characteristic of the plural in the verbal forms just in the same manner as in Coptic, and we, therefore, with regard to the form tan itself, are reminded of the Egyptian possessive pronoun tan, „of us", ours", a view which is confirmed by the form tange, to be mentioned further

neb-ré zu erklären, erinnere ich an das Alt-Egyptische neb, „dominus". Auch me-rā lässt sich wol ähnlich erläutern; was die Plural-Form me-rā betrifft, so ist sie im alltäglichen Gebrauch, wie das so oft auch anderswo geschehen, durch das demonstrative ánu-tu verdrängt worden.

Wie ich es überhaupt zu meinem Grundsatz gemacht habe, nur Sicheres zu geben, so gebe ich auch hier nur die folgenden Formen: Dativ und Accusativ der 1sten Person Sing. tánē-he und ti beide als Präfixe, wie in táne-he tin, „gib mir" (ich bemerke hier im Vorbeigehen, dass auch tin, „gib", von einer in den übrigen Zeiten nicht gebrauchten Wurzel, an das Alt-Egyptische ti erinnert); ánefi ti ke-múk, „Schlaf ergreift mich", ánefi ti ke-mú-en, „Schlaf ergreift mich nicht", d. h. „ich bin wach"[1]), ánu-tu ti ke-bappi, „sie schlagen mich", ánu-tu ti ke-dú-kodé, „sie lieben mich"; in einigen Fällen, besonders, wenn es sich um einen Gegensatz handelt, werden beide Formen verbunden, wie in táne-he ti ke-dū, „mich liebt er", eigentlich „ich zu, mich er liebt".

uns, Accusativ und Dativ { tū als Suffix; „gib uns", tin tu (oder tin nū?), tíuta-he als Präfix;

Accusativ und Dativ von 2ter Person Sing. nebrā-he:

tánē nebra-he dāro oder dā-erík, „ich liebe dich",
táne nebra-he no-rík, „ich gebe dir",
tánē nebra-he girnán-orík, „ich helfe dir";

Accusativ und Dativ von 2ter Person Plur. nebrā-i-hé oder nebrā-ye-hé:

táne nebra-je-hé no-rík, „ich gebe euch";

Accusativ und Dativ von 3ter Person Sing. merā-he:

tánē mera-he dā-erík, „ich liebe ihn",

Accusativ und Dativ von 3ter Person Plur. merā-he: merá-he bū-t-urdé, „(wir) haben sie gegessen, ausgeplündert", mera-he tyen, „gebt ihnen".

7. *Pronomen Possessivum.*

Hier habe ich weit mehr Material, als ich auf S. 2 und 3 des Vokabular's benutzt habe, und das ich demnach hiernach zu berichtigen bitte, ohne dass ich nöthig habe, jedes Einzelne zu besprechen. Für alle hier behandelten Sprachen halte man sich deshalb an die Einleitung.

mein	Kameel	gōni	né-ruā oder nir[2]),
dein			nó-mā, num, num-ma,
sein			hó-nuā,
unser			ínt-eri, int-ir, ánt-era[3]),
euer			timma, autymme[4]),
ihr			hí-ntuā,

statt gōni hí-ntuā sagt man auch weniger grammatisch gōni ánutu, „Kameel, sie", und daher vielleicht auch gōni tá-nē, „Kameel, ich" u. s. w., während man in voller Form sagt „ich, Kameel von mir", táne gōni né-ruā u. s. w.

Im Plural verändert sich das Pronomen Possessivum nicht, also auch gōna né-ruā, „meine Kameele" u. s. w.

a) Neben né-ruā gibt es auch noch eine andere, seltener gebrauchte, direkt von tánē gebildete, und an die oben erwähnte Alt-Egyptische des Pronomen Possessivum eng sich an-

[1]) tia ist S. 40, N. 6 des Vokab. zu lesen. Auch in Note 6 ist ánefi ti statt áne-fitti zu lesen.

[2]) né-ruā. Dieses angehängte ruā, das wir auch im Lógoné und Wándalá finden, werde ich weiter unten noch einmal berücksichtigen. Die Form des Accusativs im Kanúri auf rò hängt vielleicht damit zusammen.

[3]) ínt-eri, ánt-era. Der Anfangs-Vokal wird nach einem vorhergehenden Vokal verschlungen und man sagt: mená (-)ntere, „unser Abendbrod", léma (-)nteri, „unser Zeit".

[4]) antymme ist wol durch Arabischen Einfluss entstanden, eben so wie ántumu zuweilen für „ihr" vorkommt.

on. As an attempt of illustrating neb-rō I mention the Egyptian neb, „dominus". mo-rā, of course, is the original form of the 3rd person plural, but at present it seems very rarely to be used, the demonstrative pronoun ánata having taken its place.

As I make it my principle to give nothing what is not certain, I here mention only the following forms: dative and accusative of 1st person sing. táne-ho and ti, both forms used as prefixes, táne-he tin, „give me" (tin, „give" reminds strongly of the ancient Egyptian ti); dnešī tí ko-múk, „sleep seizes me"[1]); ánešī ti ke-mú-en, „sleep seizes me not", i. e. „I am awake"; ána-ta tí ke-bappi, „they are beating me"; ánata ti ke-dá-kedó, „they do like me"; sometimes, especially where there is a contrast, both forms are joined as in táne-he ti ko-dā, „he likes me", properly „I to, me he likes".

Accusative and dative of 1st person plur. tínta-há and tū: tin tū, „give us";
accusative and dative of 2nd person sing. nebrā-ho:
táno nebrā-he dā-ro or dā-erík, „I like thee",
táne nebrá-he ne-rík, „I give thee",
táne nebrá-he girnáo-erík, „I help thee";
accusative and dative of 2nd person plur. nebrā-i-hé or nebrā-yo-hé:
táne nebra-ye-hé ne-rík, „I give you" (plur.);
accusative and dative of 3rd person sing. mera-he:
táne mera-he dā-erík, „I like him";
accusative and dative of 3rd person plur. mera-ha:
mera-ha bū-t-urdé, „we have eaten, plundered them".
mera-ha iyou, „give them".

7. *The possessive pronoun.*

With regard to the possessive pronoun I have a good deal of material among my phrases, of which I did not make use, when compiling the first pages of my vocabulary, which I beg once for all to correct from what I give in these Introductory Remarks:

my	camel	gōni	né-ruā or nir[2]),
thy			nó-mā, num, num-mo,
his			hó-nuā,
our			ínt-eri, int-er, ánt-era[3]),
your			timmo, antyumme[4]),
their			hí-ntuā, ho-ntū;

instead of gōni hí-ntuā people use also the less grammatical phrase gōni ána-ta, „camel, they", and perhaps even gōni, tá-né, „camel, I" instead of gōni né-rua, while the full phrase of the latter is tá-né gōni né-rua, „I, camel mine".

In the plural number the form of the possessive pronoun is not changed, the people saying, gōna né-rua, „my camels" and so on.

a) Besides né-ruā there is also another form for the 1st person of the possessive pronoun, viz tañge, which has been directly derived from tá-né, but seems to be not so much used;

---

[1]) Thus we have to spell also p. 40, and p. 41, note 6 has to be corrected accordingly.

[2]) né-ruā: the suffix particle ruā, which we find also in the Lógoné- and Wándalá-languages, I shall have to take into account once more farther on. Even rō, the suffix form of the accusative case in Kanúri, may have some connection with the former.

[3]) íntir, ánt-era: the first vowel is thrown off when another vowel precedes, as in masá (-)ntera, „our supper", lēma (-)nteri, „our tent".

[4]) antyumme may be due to Arab influence, just as ántume is sometimes used for „you", plur.

schliessende Form taṅgo oder taṅge; wir haben sie in der Phrase S. 56 des Vokabular andr tánge keau geue, „Herz mein (von mir) süss nicht ist", d. h. „ich bin traurig".

b) num, „dein" ist die populäre Form in Phrasen, wie „dein Name?", kyir-num.

8. *Das Zeitwort.*

Die Konjugations-Formen kann ich nur sehr unvollständig geben, auch glaube ich nicht, dass das Zeitwort in Wirklichkeit einigermassen reich ausgebildet sein wird, da es unter den Tédā an jedem Mittelpunkte solcher Ausbildung fehlt. Dennoch kann eine vollständige Ergründung aller Formen des Zeitwortes zum richtigen Verständniss der Nord-Afrikanischen Sprachen und ihres Verhältnisses zum Alt-Egyptischen von höchster Bedeutung werden. Ich erinnere hier nur an das Alt-Egyptische Hülfszeitwort iri als spätere Bildung (Bunsen I, S. 350, 566 und V, S. 78, vergl. S. 135), das wir vollständig in der 1sten Person des Tédā-Zeitwortes eri-k wiederfinden. Über das k als Bezeichnung der 1sten Person s. Bunsen V, S. 86, so wie über das Alt-Egyptische Zeichen der Verneinung en oder n Bunsen I, S. 35; V, S. 80. Die durchgehend verneinende Konjugation, die wir fast in allen Afrikanischen Sprachen so gut wie in den Turanischen finden, war im Alt-Egyptischen (nach Bunsen) noch nicht ausgebildet, dagegen aber schon im Koptischen.

Ich will hier einfach geben, was ich an sicheren Formen habe. Ich bemerke dabei, dass im gewöhnlichen Leben der gemeine Mann wenigstens für die Form der Gegenwart einfach das Pronomen mit der Infinitiv- oder Imperativ-Form gebraucht, táne ńa-re, „ich will", táne la-re, „ich sehe".

Ich gebe zuerst ein Paradigma von bū, „essen".

Präsens, positiv.

		Singular.		Plural.
1ste	Person	tá-ne bū-(e)rik	. . .	tin-ta bū-t-eri,
2te	„	neb-re ye-bū	. . . .	neb-ral yá-bu-ti,
3te	„	me-rē ke-bū	. . . .	ána-ta kú-bu-ti.

Präsens, negativ.

		Singular.		Plural.
1ste	Person	tá-ne bū-(e)ri-n	. . .	tin-ta bū-t-eri-n,
2te	„	neb-re bū-mo-ni	. .	neb-ral bū-tú-mu-ni,
3te	„	me-re kó-bu-in	. . .	ána-ta kē-bu-te-n.

Präteritum, positive Form.

		Singular.		Plural.
1ste	Person	tá-ne bu-r [bu-rdē?]		tin-ta bū-t-urde,
2te	„	neb-re yá-bu-dé	.	neb-ral bū-t-umi,
3te	„	me-re kyá-bu-dé	.	ána-ta ke-bū-t-umi [ke-bū-t-on?]

Individuelle negative Form nicht gebraucht.

Präteritum von kyöās-orík oder tšoās-orík, „ich verkaufe".

		Singular.		Plural.
1ste	Person	tá-ne kyöās-erdē	.	tin-ta kyöās-át-erde,
2te	„	neb-re kyöās-immi	.	neb-ral kyöās-át-immi,
3te	„	me-rē yo-kyöās-idē		ána-ta yo-kyöās-öā [1].

Imperativ: i-kyöās.

[1] ye-kyöās-öā wol nicht richtig; von yár-erík habe ich 3te Person Plur. ke-yár-ke-dē, das scheint richtig. Aber dagegen habe ich mórk-indé, „es ist verloren", mork-yō, „sie sind verloren", lébkindē, „er ist ermüdet" (von lóbtekin, „ich bin ermüdet"), lobyō, „sie sind ermüdet".

we have an instance of it in the phrase mentioned vocab. p. 56 nuár tánge kése gené, i. q. „heart of me (mine) sweet not is", „my heart is sad".

b) num, „thy" is the popular form in phrases of daily life, such as kyir-num, „(what is) thy name".

6. *The verb.*

The forms of conjugation I am not able to give with some degree of completeness, although I am of opinion, that the verb in the Tédā-language has not been well developed, there being no centre whatever from whence a civilizing influence might have extended. Nevertheless, a complete investigation of the verbal forms of this idiom may possibly lead us a considerable step in advance in the thorough knowledge of this group of languages, and especially as to their relation to the ancient Egyptian. I here call attention to the later auxiliary verb iri in that idiom, such as spoken of by Bunsen (I, p. 350, 566; V, p. 78 compared with p. 138) which we find in the Tédā almost in the same form eri-k, especially if we take into account what Bunsen says vol. V, p. 86, with regard to the k as characteristic of the 1st person sing.; I moreover point out the form en or n as the sign of negation in ancient Egyptian (Bunsen I, p. 35, V, p. 80), while the complete negative form of conjugation, which we find in almost all African languages as well as in the Turanian, was not developed in the ancient Egyptian, but only in the Coptic.

I here intend to communicate only what well established forms I have, prefacing first, that in the vulgar idiom the pronoun is simply joined to the form of the imperative or infinitive in order to denote the present tense, as for instance táné ǹa-re. „I will", táné la-re, „I see, look".

I first give a paradigm of bū, „eat".

Present tense, positive form.

	Singular.	Plural.
1st person	tá-né bū-(e)rik	tin-ta bū-t-eri,
2nd „	neb-ré yo-bū	neb-rat yú-bu-ti,
3rd „	mo-rē ke-bū	ána-ta ká-bu-ti.

Present tense, negative form.

	Singular.	Plural.
1st person	tá-né bū-(e)ri-n . . .	tin-ta bū-t-eri-n,
2nd „	neb-ré bu-mo-ni . .	neb-rat bū-tú-mu-ni,
3rd „	me-ré ké-bu-in . . .	ána-ta ké-bu-te-n.

Past tense, positive form.

	Singular.	Plural.
1st person	tá-né bu-r [bu-rdē?]	tin-ta bū-t-urde,
2nd „	neb-ré yá-bu-dē .	neb-rat bū-t-umi,
3rd „	mo-ré kyá-bu-dē .	ána-ta ko-bū-t-umi [ko-bū-t-on?]

Individual negative form not used.

Preterite tense of kyöās-erík or töōās-erík, „I sell".

	Singular.	Plural.
1st person	tá-né kyōās-erde . .	tin-ta kyöās-át-erde,
2nd „	neb-ré kyōās-immi .	neb-rat kyöās-át-immi,
3rd „	mo-ré ye-kyöās-ide	ána-ta ye-kyöās-öā *).

Imperative: i-kyōās.

*) ye-kyöās-öā is perhaps not right; from yár-erik I have 3rd person plur. ke-yár-kedé, which may be right. But different are the forms merh-yá, „they are lost", singl. mérh-ledé, „it is lost"; lobyé, „they are fatigued" (s. lébtekin, „I am weary"), lébhindē, „he is weary".

Präteritum von yöb-erík, „ich kaufe".

	Singular.	Plural.
1ste Person	tá-ne yöb-erdé . . .	tin-ta yóp-urdé,
2te „	neb-re yöb-immi . .	neb-ral yóp-umí,
3te „	me-re ke-yöb-un . .	ána-ta ke-yöb-un.

Ich gebe hier als Beispiel der Zusammenstellung zweier Zeitwörter das Beispiel kór-n-erík yöb-erík, „ich will ich kaufe", d. h. „ich will kaufen", aber auch umgekehrt kón-erík e-däro, „ich besteige ich will", d. h. „ich will besteigen".

Es gibt sehr viel unregelmässige oder vielmehr unvollständige Zeitwörter, z. B. död-erík, „ich sehe", 1ste Person Plur. tin-ta te-dúr-t-eri, Imp. lan von lán-erík, ein anderes Zeitwort, das viele Formen zu död-erík hergibt; 1ste Person Sing. Präterit. tá-nö durär; „hast du gesehen", durámi; „ich habe nicht gesehen", dulli-n.

Unregelmässig und unsicher ist folgendes Präsens von todödi, „ich gehe".

	Singular.	Plural.
1ste Person	tá-nä todödi.	tin-ta tóteri,
2te „	neb-rä in-tédi	neb-ral ye-terri,
3te „	me-rö ye-tédi	ána-ta terri?

Die Formen des Präteritums dieses Zeitwortes zu unsicher, um herzustellen.

Imperativ, 2te Person Sing. yeaü; 2te Person Plur. sirru?

Ich habe auch Andeutungen eines Conditionnel's, „wenn ich ginge":

	Kandri.	Tódá.
1ste Person Sing.	täö-ní-skin .	táné yér-nor-uö (von yér-n-erík),
2te „ „	täé-ni-mié .	(unsicher),
3te „ „	täé-täi-a . .	meró yér-kenuä,
1ste „ Plur.	täé-ní-ya . .	tinta yer-ínteró,
2te „ „	täé-ni-wi . .	neb-ral yér-intö,
3te „ „	täé-täi-ya .	ána-ta yer-kyö,

verglichen mit der Phrase kun wa pginüö yer-énteri, „wenn die Hitze vorüber ist, brechen wir auf".

yeni = Kandri yaië, „es mag sein", „wenn auch ist", von keni, „es ist", „es macht" (Präterit. kindé).

duski tegáaui úneki ye-ni tikkeri yéko,
Tagemarsch ? warm mag sein macht nichts.

Subjonctif.

föti-a ki-ni kóp-ri-a (von köb-erík),
„Fluss gibt es dass wir passiren", „haben wir einen Fluss zu passiren?";
tíri-a tetéri-a, „der Weg, dass wir gehn";
ndmai téteri tíni-ai, „die Stadt wir gehn, dass wir schlafen".

Participium Passivi.

te-büp-edö, „geschlagen", „verwundet", von büb-erík,
te-kír-kedé, „zerbrochen", von kír-erík, „ich zerbreche",
te-güp-edé, „zerschnitten", von köb-erík, „ich schneide", S. 110, N. 11,
dé-te-de, „gekocht" = Kandri dé-gata von dé-n-erík (K. dé-níakin).

Zur Passiv-Form gehört auch die Redensart yebúr tuggúr-kede S. 96 „der Krieg ist zerstört", von tiggír-erík (ich selbst hörte nur die Form tiggírke), ebenda „ich zerstöre".

Ich stelle hier nun einige Imperative zusammen, so weit sie mir bekannt wurden:

lan (lán-erík), „sieh"; yer (yer-dik *)), „stehe auf"; tobún (tobúa-erík), „bleibe",

*) yer-dik ist eine unregelmässige Verbalform.

Preterite tense of yōb-erík, „I buy".

	Singular.	Plural.
1st person	tá-nō yōb-erdō	tin-ta yóp-erde,
2nd „	neb-rē yōb-immi . . .	neb-rai yóp-umi,
3rd „	mo-rē ke-yōb-un . . .	ána-ta ke-yōb-un.

I here give two instances of two verbs being joined in different ways: kór-n-erík yōb-erík, „I will I buy", i. q. „I will buy"; kón-erík o-dāro, „I mount I will", i. q. „I will mount".

There are a great many irregular, or rather incomplete verbs in the Tédā-idiom, as for instance dōd-erík, „I see, look, regard", 1st person plur. tin-ta te-dúr-t-eri, imp. lan, a form belonging properly to the verb lán-erík; 1st person sing. past tense tá-no durār; „hast thou seen", durúmi; „I have not seen", dulli-n.

Irregular, and not quite certain are the following forms of the present tense of todēdi, „I go".

	Singular.	Plural.
1st person	tá-nō todēdi	tin-ta tóteri,
2nd „	nob-rā in-tódi	nob-rai yo-terri,
3rd „	mo-rō ye-tōdi	ána-ta terri?

The forms I have of the past tense are too uncertain to be given them in this place.

Imperative, 2nd pers. sing. yeuū, 2nd pers. plur. sirru?

I have also some slight indications of a conditional mood, as for instance „if I went":

	Kanúri.	Tédā.
1st person sing.	tēē-ní-skia .	tánō yór-ner-nō (from yár-n-erík),
2nd „ „	tēē-ni-miá .	(uncertain),
3rd „ „	tēē-tēí-a . .	merā yór-kenuā,
1st „ plur.	tēē-ní-ya . .	tinta yer-íuterō,
2nd „ „	tēē-ni-wi . .	nob-rai yér-intā,
3rd „ „	tēē-tēi-ya . .	ána-ta yer-kyā,

compare also the phrase: kun wu pχínōō yer-éuteri, „the heat of the day having passed by, we shall start".

yeni identical with the Kanúri yaiō, „it may be, if it be so", from koni, „it is", „it does" (past tense kindō).

Compare the phrase: duski togánni dueki ye-ai tíkkosi yóko,
march ? warm may be imports not.

Instances of a subjunctive mood.

fōti-a ki-ni kóp-ri-a (from kōb-erík),
„a river is there that we cross (it)", „have we to cross a river";
tíri-a tótori-ā, „the road that (which) we go";
nómai tótori tíei-ai, „the town we go, that we sleep (there).

Participle of the passive mood.

te-bāp-odō, „beaten", „wounded", from bāb-erík,
te-kír-kedō, „broken", from kír-erík, „I break",
te-gúp-odō, „cut", from kōb-erík, „I cut", p. 110, note 11,
de-te-dō, „boiled" = Kanúri dē-gatu, from dē-n-erík (K. dē-nískin).

To the passive mood belongs also the phrase yebúr tuggúr-kedō p. 96 „the war is spoiled", from tiggír-erík (probably the correct form for tiggírke), „I destroy, spoil".

I now give a few forms of the imperative mood, such as have become known to me: lan (lán-erík), „look"; yor (yor-dik[1]), „rise"; sobás (tobás-erík), „remain";

[1]) yer-dik is a very irregular verbal form.

bóbiya (bóbiya-(e)rík), „ruhe aus"; dingir (dáñgerik¹); yer-ô (yár-n-orík), „breche auf"; fau-ó (fán-erík), „steig' ab"; yak (yarik), „lauf"; yosú (tededi), „geh", 2ᵗᵉ Pers. Plur. sirru?; yerdk (rô-erík), „geh' hinaus"; kon-tú, 2ᵗᵉ Person Plur. Imp. von kón-orík, „ich steige zu Pferd"²); derí-terô, 1ˢᵗᵉ Person Plur. Imp. von derí-n-erík, „ich gehe umher, suche".

Unpersönliche Zeitwörter bestehen durchgängig aus einem Substantiv oder Adjektiv mit einem angehängten kent, „es ist", „macht", im Präterit. kinde, auch mit abgeworfenem k. yumár-kent, „er blitzt"; deri-kent, „ist rund"; yü-kinde, „ist geschmolzen"; gibí-kindé, „ist alt geworden"; forrist-indé, „hat sich verändert". Das de am Ende fällt aber oft fort, besonders wenn schon ein anderes de vorhergegangen, wie z. B. tíria-de morkis statt mór-kindé, „er) hat sich vom Wege verirrt".

9. *Das Nennwort.*

Fast alle Nennwörter endigen auf Vokale, vornämlich o, u und i; als Konsonant erscheint in anscheinend einheimischen Wörtern nur r am Ende und auch das nur in zwei oder drei Beispielen, die wol ebenfalls fremden Sprachen entlehnt sind.

Das Geschlecht wird bei Menschen und Thieren ausgedrückt durch den Zusatz von añker, „männlich" und ódi, „weiblich" (von ádi, „die Frau"), wie aski añker, „Hengst", aski ódi, „Stute"; áfandê, „Bräutigam", ádi áfandê, „Braut"; wir finden aber auch eine wirkliche Feminin-Endung, z. B. kóki-ya, „die Henne", von kóki, „der Hahn". Das Geschlecht des Nennwortes, wenn auch bloss durch die Form motivirt, scheint auf das begleitende Adjektiv Einfluss zu haben; so bul, „gross", aber tíria búya, „die grosse Strasse".

Die Endungen des Singulars auf a oder ia scheinen selten zu sein, hingegen ist es die gewöhnlichste Form des Plurals. Ich gebe hier einige Beispiele des letzteren: gôni, Plur. gôa-a, „Kameel"; aski, Plur. áski-a, „Pferd"; kinnir, Plur. kiunir-a, „Garten, Feld"; éskenô, Plur. eskénuâ, „Himmel"; dógeso, Plur. dégosa, „Nacht"; dann auf ai: bô, bi, Plur. bi-ai, „Tag"; mákara, Plur. mákarai(?), „Boot"; auf e: fôeu, Plur. fôse, „Fisch". Als Beispiele ganz unregelmässiger Formation des Plurals führe ich an am, „Mensch", anea, „Leute, Volk"; yébô, „Haus", yérahâ (etwas unsicher) „Häuser".

Die Kasus kann ich wenigstens in einzelnen Fällen klar nachweisen.

Im Nominativ habe ich in einzelnen Beispielen das von Koelle im älteren Kanúri so bestimmt erfasste, aber von mir in der Vulgär-Sprache weniger bezeichnete ye im Tédâ mehrmals aufgefasst, z. B. derdai, „Fürst, Häuptling", dérdaye, „der Fürst, ein Fürst"; jedoch finden wir dieselbe Form auch als eine Art von Genitiv.

Als eine Art regelrechter Bildung des Genitiv's finden wir auch im Tédâ in einzelnen Beispielen das n oder en der Berber- oder Mâšiy-Sprache, aber nicht in der Weise, wie es dort gebraucht ist, sondern so, dass das Objekt vorhergeht und das nachfolgende Subjekt mit Hülfe des n damit verbunden wird, wie in bô-n-torô³), „der Hausherr", d. h. „der Erste (torô) des Hauses" (bô), dann auch in der Weise, dass das en dem nachfolgenden Objekt angehängt wird, wie in keri fôli-en, „das Steilufer des Flusses". Aber wir finden auch Subjekt und Objekt auf beide Arten verbunden mit Voranstellung bald des einen, bald des anderen,

¹) dáñgerik. Wenn dáñgir die Wurzel ist, wird die volle Form der 1sten Pers. Prs. dañgir-erik sein.

²) Danach vielleicht zu verbessern S. 97, N. 6 hórreri (kón-erik?) kon-tú, „steigt auf, ich steige auf", als Befehl des Oberen, statt „macht, steigt auf".

³) bô-n-torô. Eine ähnliche Zusammensetzung finden wir noch in einzelnen Beispielen beim Kanúri, die sich nur von diesem Gesichtspunkte aus erklären lässt.

bóbiya (bóbiya-(e)rík), „rest"; diṅgir (dúṅgerik [1]); yer-ō (yár-n-erík), „start"; fan-ō (fán-orík), „dismount, descend"; yak (yarik probably contracted form of yák-erík), „run"; yeañ (tedédi), „go", 2nd person plur. sirru!; yerúk (rō-orík), „go out"; kon-tū, 2nd person plur. imp. from kón-erík, „I mount on horseback" [2]); derí-torō, 1st person plur. imp. from derí-n-erík, „I walk about, search".

Impersonal verbs generally consist of a substantive or adjective to which the verbal form kent, „it is, makes" (past tense kinde, or, the k thrown off, inde), has been added. yumár-kent, „it lightens", derí-kent, „it is round"; yū-kindé, „it is molten"; gibí-kindé, „has grown old"; forríst-indé, „has become changed". However, the final de is often lost, particularly when another dē is preceding, as, for instance, tíria-dé morkin instead of mór-kindé, „it has strayed from the road".

9. *Nouns.*

All nouns of indigenous origin, with very few exceptions, terminate in a vowel, especially o or u, and i; of consonants terminating nouns of apparently indigenous growth, we have among my list only r, and this but in two, or three instances, so that we may thence conclude, that these very words are borrowed from a foreign language.

The sex with regard to human beings, and animals is expressed by adding añker, „male", and ádi, ódi, „female", as aski añker, „full horse", aski ódi, „mare", áfandē, „bridegroom", ádi áfandē, „bride"; but we find also instances of a real feminine termination, such as kóki-ya, „the hen", koki, „the cock". The sex, even if indicated merely by the form of the noun, seems to exercise some influence upon the form of the adjective by which it is accompanied, as for instance tíria búya, „the high road" from but, „great".

However, the nouns seem to terminate rarely in a or ia in the singular number, while it is a very common form of the plural. I here give a few instances of the formation of the latter: gōni, plur. gōn-a, „camel"; aski, plur. áski-a, „horse"; kinnir, plur. kínnir-a, „garden, field"; ésheno, plur. eshénna, „heaven, sky"; dógeno, plur. dógena, „night"; then in ai: bō, bi, plur. bi-ai, „day"; múkara, plur. múkarai, „boat"; in e: fōsu, plur. fōse, „fish". As instances of a very irregular formation of the plural I give: am, „person", anna, „people"; yébō (a later composite form of the original ye, and bō, „house") plur. yérubū (not quite certain).

As for the cases, I have some material, by means of which to illustrate their use.

Thus, in the nominative termination I have some instances of the yo, which in the related Kanúri-language has been so distinctly brought forward by Rev. Koelle in the older dialect, while I have had only rare opportunity of observing it in the vulgar dialect of that idiom; thus dordai, „chief", dórdayó, „a chief"; but this same termination yo we find also used as a kind of genitive case.

As a regular formation of the genitive we find the n or en of the Máṡiγ- or Berber-idiom, but not in the same manner, in which it is used in the latter, but so that the object precedes the subject, being joined to it by means of the n, as in bō-n-torō, „the landlord", i. q. „the first" (torō) „of the house" (bō [3]) while in other instances the en is attached to the succeeding object, as in keri fáti-en, „the steep bank of the river". But we find even subject and object joined in both manners without adding n, as for instance kómmolo-sorō, „vomitive" from kómmolo, „bitterness", soro, „remedy"; ódi-bō, „landlady" from

[1]) dúṅgerik: if diṅgir be the root, the full form of the 1st person ought to be diṅgir-erik.

[2]) Thence we may perhaps better explain the phrase kérreri kon-in p. 93, note 6 by reading kón-erik kon-in, „mount (you), I (myself) mount", as the form of command of the superior.

[3]) bō-n-torō: a similar mode of composition we find also in some instances in the Kanúri-language.

ohne die Vermittelung von a, wie z. B. kómmolo soró, „Brechmittel“, von kómmolo, „Übelkeit“ und soro, „Heilmittel“; édi-bo, „Hausfrau“, von ádi, édi, „Frau“ und bō, „Haus“ und letzteres Beispiel ist um so interessanter, als es in enger Gleichstellung neben bō-n-torō gebraucht wird. Ganz ebenso ist gebildet némai dirdai, „Residenz, Hauptstadt“, von némni, „Stadt“ und dirdai, „Häuptling“; túgus dirdai, „Palast“, von túgus, „Lehmbau“, dirdai, „Häuptling“; búya dírdaye, „Hofchargen“, von búya, „die Grossen“, dirdai, „Häuptling“; ída léma, „Zeltpflöcke“, von ída, „Hölzer“, léma, „Zelt“.

Nun habe ich auch wenigstens Ein Beispiel einer Genitiv-Form mit Hülfe eines dem Subjekt angehängten ńga, nämlich ēmi dūho-ńga, „der Gipfel (dūho) des Berges“, eigentlich „Berg, Kopf von ihm“, eine Form, die sich der selteneren Form des Pronomen Possessivum tańge, „mein, von mir“ eng anschliesst.

Aber viel gewöhnlicher als diese Form ist die vermittelst der vollen Form des Pronomen Possessivum der 3ten Person, wie bei „Königin Mutter“, dérdayē dé hé-aaá („der Fürst, seine Mutter“); „Baumwollsamen“, kulkutton miga hé-aaá („Baumwolle, ihr Same“); „Aufseher der Sklaven“, agrē but he-ata („die Sklaven, ihr Grosser“); „die flache Hand“, kobē ife hé-asā („Hand, ihr Inneres“), während für „Rückseite der Hand“ der Ausdruck kobē fúkiakat in ganz anderer Weise gebildet ist.

Dativ und Accusativ fallen im Tédā zusammen und werden, wie bei den Pronomina, durch ein angehängtes he ausgedrückt, das auch dem Adjektiv zugefügt werden kann und seinen Vokallaut durch Einfluss des vorhergehenden Vokals verändert.

áski-hé tó-nu-mi, „hast du das Pferd gebunden“?
sirdi ai aski-hé ko-bābi, „dieser Sattel belästigt das Pferd“;
tíria búya-hé téteri, „lasst uns die grosse (búya) Strasse gehn“;
némai torō-he bū-erik, „ich zerstöre eine (torō) Stadt“.

Ablativ oder Kausativ mit a:

kubē-a kyorro, „an, mit der Hand (kubē) sparsam“, d. h. „geizig“.

Lokativ „in“, „auf“, „von her“, dé:

eyi ki-ni tíria-de, „gibt es Wasser auf der Strasse“ (tíria)?;
ábonō dī-de leki, „der Wind kommt von Westen“ (dī);
áski-de te-bā-pedē tobúr, „er fiel verwundet vom Pferde“.

Ein solches lokales „woher“ aber auch kausativ aufgefasst „aus Rücksicht, auf Grund“,

tíria lāmer-de, „auf Grund (lāmer Arab.), aus Rücksicht der Reise“.

In gewöhnlicher Rede wird übrigens das lokative dé oft fortgelassen, obgleich die Beziehung in der folgenden Phrase auch als Genitiv gefasst sein mag.

„Welcher Berg ist der höchste im ganzen Tédā-Lande?“:

lardo Tédā gybei ēmi drgasa nokórde ki ke-dé,
Land Tédā alles Berg hoch (höchst) wo ist denn?

10. *Adjektive und substantive Eigenschaftswörter.*

Die eigentlich nur eine Eigenschaft von einem schon bezeichneten Subjekt angebenden Zusatzwörter werden, wie in fast allen Sprachen, so auch im Tédā in weitester Ausdehnung zu Substantiven. In ihrer Bildung aber müssen wir auch die letzteren als Adjektiva fassen.

Diese Bildung geschieht nun meist, indem eben jenes lokative dē einem Substantiv angehängt wird, das oft höchst bezeichnend und charakteristisch ist. So

áski-de (der Mann) „vom Pferde“, d. h. „der Reiter“;
ába-de (der Mann) „vom Vater“, d. h. „der Onkel väterlicher Seite“;
dā-de (der Mann) „von der Mutter“, d. h. „der Oheim mütterlicher Seite“;

ádi, ódi, „wife", bó, „house", the latter instance being still more remarkable, as it is used side by side with the differently formed bā-u-torō. In the same manner is formed némai dirdai, „residence, capital" from némai, „town", dirdai, „chief"; túgui dirdai, „palace" (túgui, „claybuilding", dirdai, „chief"); búya dírdaye, „courtiers" (búya, „the great men", of „the chief"); ída léma, „pegs" of „the tent".

Now, I have also one instance of a kind of genitive, formed by means of ṅgu being attached to the subject, namely emi dābo-ṅga, „the top (dābo) of the mountain" (emi), verbally „mountain, top of it", a form which approaches quite closely to the rare form of the possessive pronoun tañgo, „mine, of me", which we have had above.

But a much more common way of expressing the genitive is that by means of the possessive pronoun of the 3rd person, as, for instance, „Queen mother", dérdaye de hé-nna („the chief, his mother"); „cottonseed", kulkutton miga hé-nna („cotton, its seed"); „overseer (of the slaves)", agré bui he-stã („the slaves, their great man or master"); „the palm of the hand", koba ife hé-nna („hand, its inside"), while the term for „back of the hand" is formed in a totally different manner kobe ihkinkai.

As for the dative and accusative cases, both of them are expressed in the same manner, as is the case with the pronoun, by adding be, which may also be attached to the adjective, and the vowel of which sometimes is changed according to the nature of the preceding one.

> áski-bé tú-nu-mi, „hast thou bound the horse"?
> sirdi ai áski-bé ke-bābi, „this saddle wounds the horse";
> tíria búya-bé tétorí, „let us follow the great (búya) road";
> némai torō-be bū-crík, „I destroy a (torō) town".

The ablative or causative case is expressed by adding an u:

> kubé-u kyerro, „sparing as for the hand (kube) i. q. niggard.

The locative conveying the meaning of „in", „upon", „from" by dé:

> cyi ki-ni tíria-dé, „is there water on the road" (tíria)?;
> ábonō di-de leki, „the wind comes from the west" (di);
> áski-de te-bap-odé tobúr, „he fell wounded from the horse".

While in the latter phrase the dé has a local meaning, in the following it is to be understood in a spiritual sense, indicating the reason, why

tíria lāmer-de, „on account of", „for the sake (lāmer Arabic) of, the journey".

However, in the vulgar idiom the locative termination dé is often left out, although in the following phrase it might have been understood as a genitive.

> larde Tédā gṇbri emi dryasa nohórdo ki ke-dĕ,
> country Tédā all mountain high where is it then?,

i. q. „what, or where is the highest mountain in the Tebu country?",

10. *Adjectives, and nouns expressing a quality.*

a) Adjectives expressing a certain quality or character of an object, already mentioned, or at least understood, in the Tédā, as in most other languages, are used as substantives to a very wide extent.

However, according to their formation I look upon them as adjectives, although for the greater part they are formed from nouns, by adding the very dé we have just spoken of as designating the locative case. By endeavouring to understand this sort of formation we obtain a highly interesting insight into the origin of many words of this class, although others remain as yet unexplained. Thus we have

> áski-de (the person) „of the horse", i. q. „the horseman";
> ába-de (the person) „of the father", i. q. „the paternal uncle";
> dā-de (the person) „of the mother", i. q. „the maternal uncle";

lúnta-dē (der Mann) „von den Lumpen", d. h. „der Bettler";
téski-dē (der Mann) „von den Sternen", d. h. „der Führer", weil in der Wüste, wo die Téda hausen, man nur nach den Sternen seinen Weg nimmt.

Ganz ebenso bezeichnend wird der Name úfan-dē für „die Braut" sein, obgleich ich das Charakteristische, wonach sie benannt ist, noch nicht erklären kann.

So auch erklären sich nun viele Stammnamen im Munde der Téda, z. B. der mir selbst früher ganz unverständliche Name, mit dem sie den Mâšiy bezeichnen, yébur-dē, d. h. eigentlich „der Mann vom Kriege", „vom Raubzug", also „Freibeuter", weil die Téda mit diesem Stamm fast nur in feindliche Berührung getreten sind und von den unaufhörlichen Raubzügen der Mâšiy schrecklich zu leiden haben. Ja die oben S. LXVI besprochene Endung da, als in Tó-da, ist nichts Anderes als dies dē.

So haben wir nun dýune-dē, „von Kraft", „stark"; tíkke-dē, „von Gewicht", „schwer"; úgon-dē, „vom Leibe", d. h. „schwanger"; bei einigen bin ich noch zweifelhaft, ob das de zur Wurzel gehört, oder dieses lokative Anhängsel ist, wie bei gode, „durstig", während ich es bei kénede, „geduldig" weiterhin (S. XC, N. 2) nachgewiesen habe. Gerade bei diesen beiden Wörtern [1]) aber ist es von der allerhöchsten Bedeutung, diesen Umstand zu ergründen, da dies für das Verhältniss der Kanúri-Sprache, in der wir gúdun, „durstig" und kánadi, „geduldig, Geduld" haben, von wahrhaft entscheidender Bedeutung ist.

b) Neben der Endung mit de haben wir nun aber auch eine andere auf gi, unzweifelhaft = K. gai, „gleich, ähnlich", aber allerdings ist diese Form viel seltener, so z. B.

wóéni-gi, „feuergleich" = K. kannu gai, d. h. „warm", von wóéni, „Feuer".

Dann habe ich auch eine, offenbar mit der oben S. LXXIII, 7, a. angeführten Form des Pronomen Possessivum zusammenhängende, den Besitz bezeichnende Endung onge in

adi-önge, „eine Frau besitzend", d. h. „verheirathet" (vom Manne),

neben dem ich als gleichlautend im N-Dialekt ádi-be-de habe, d. i. wol nichts Anderes als ádi-dē mit einem des Wohllautes halber eingeschalteten be.

c) Anstatt eines eigentlichen Eigenschaftswortes finden wir auch ein blosses Subjekt als Prädikat einem anderen beigesellt,

némai tdgur, „Stadt Lehmmauer", d. h. „ummauerte Stadt".

d) Eine im Deutschen durch „mit" ausgedrückte Eigenschaft wird im Téda vermittelst des Pronomen Possessivum umschrieben, wie

„Dieses Pferd mit der weissen Stirn und den weissen Füssen",

aski ni fómfoni bé-nna kyñ, sé bé-nna kyñ,
Pferd dieses Stirn seine weiss, Fuss sein weiss.

e) Als negative Eigenschaftsform, entsprechend unserem „bar", „un" oder „miss", habe ich tane, tanen, Formen, die mit der Pronominalform tá-ne nichts zu thun haben, so

baarfuss, d. h. „ohne Schuhe" . . .	zini-tánen,
un-fleissig	surri-tánen,
un-geduldig	kénede-tánen.

in adi-dáne, „ohne Frau", „unverheirathet", ist das t wol nur des vorhergehenden d wegen ebenfalls in d übergegangen. Zu dieser negativen Eigenschaftsform gehören auch die Zusammensetzungen mit ge-ne, „was nicht ist", kesn ge-nē, „nicht süss, bitter".

11. *Stellung der sogenannten Präposition.*

Im Téda wird die Partikel dem Nomen stets nachgesetzt (im Kanúri bald voran, bald hinterher) und wird meist in Genitiv-Form damit verbunden; „im Hause", T. ivé féret,

[1]) Interessant ist in Beziehung für die Wortbildung der Téda-Sprache auch der Vergleich von kedē, „warm" mit keri, „kalt".

lánta-dē (the person) „of the rags", i. q. „the beggar";

tóski-dē (the person) „of the stars", i. q. „the guide", a very characteristic name, as people travelling in those desert countries where the Tédā live, cannot make out their direction but by means of the stars;

áfan-dē meaning „the bride", I have no doubt, will be found out to be quite as characteristic, as soon as we shall be able to explain the term áfan.

In this same manner several names designating tribes in the Tédā-language find their explanation, as for instance the name they give to the Mášiy or Tawārek, and which till the present moment has remained unintelligible to myself, I mean yóbur-dē, which means nothing but „(the man) of the war", i. q. „the freebooter", the Tédā having to suffer continually from the predatory excursions of their Western neighbours. Nay, the termination dā, as in Té-da, is nothing else.

Thus we have also dĝnur-dē, „of strength, strong"; tíkhe-dē, „of weight, heavy"; ágon-dē, „of a (large) body", „with child", and a great many other adjectives, although with regard to several I am as yet doubtful, whether dē belongs to the root, or whether it be this particle dē, as, for instance, with regard to the word godé, „thirsty", while with regard to kénede, „patient", I have analysed it fully p. XCI, n. 2; and it is of the very highest importance with regard to the relation of the Tédā- with the Kanúri-language to make sure of the formation of these words[1]), as we have in the latter the closely related terms gúdwa, „thirsty" and kánadi, „patience".

b) Besides this formation of the adjectives by means of dē, we have another one with gi undoubtedly = K. gai, which, however, is not by far so frequent as the former, as for instance

wúēni-gi = K. kannu gai, „like fire", i. q. „warm, hot".

Moreover, I have another adjective termination in ónge, which seems to be connected with the ṅge mentioned above as designating the possession of an object; thus we have

adi-ónge, „possessing a wife", i. q. „married (of the man)",

besides which form I have in the other dialect (N) ádi-be-dē, which seems to be nothing but the form with dē, the be being inserted on euphonical grounds.

c) In some cases we find the character of an object or person designated, instead by an adjective, by merely adding another substantive, as for instance

némai tágal, „town claywall", i. q. „a walled town".

d) A quality described by a substantive and adjective by adding „with" is in Tédā expressed by means of the possessive pronoun, as for instance

„This horse with the white front and the white legs",

aski ai fómfoni hé-naa kyu, so hé-naa kyu,
horse this front his white, legs his white.

e) As a negative form of the adjective, that is to say, a form expressing the want of a quality I have tane, tanen, forms totally distinct from the pronominal form tá-ne, as for instance

barefoot, properly „without shoes" . . . . aini-tánen,
wanting diligence . . . . aurri-tánen,
impatient . . . . kénedi-tánen;

as for adi-dáne, „without a wife", the t seems to have been changed into a d merely from euphonical reasons. Hither belongs likewise ge-nē, „what is not"; thus, krem ge-nē, „not sweet", „bitter".

11. *Position of the so-called prepositions.*

In the Tédā-language the particle is constantly placed after the noun, while in Kanúri it is sometimes placed before, sometimes behind it; thus „inside the house", T. ive férete,

[1]) The comparison of kedē, „warm" and keri, „cold" also is interesting on account of the development of the language.

K. tâfro fâto; „dem Regen zuvor", T. iya bordê. K. delagu-n bargesi „hinter dem Zelte", T. loma-yé fôdi. K. tagâfo-n lôma-bê; „nach dem Regen folgt der Sturm", eyi dâgga-n-dê ôbono loki; némai ai bini, „bis zu dieser Stadt".

12. a) Positive Verbindung „und" („oder", siehe bei dem folgenden Paragraphen), „bringe trockenes Holz und Wasser", ida (a)a kyorra kurtu eyi aa
Holz und trockenes bringe Wasser und.

b) Negative Verbindung „weder" — „noch":
„wir sehen weder Städte, noch Strasse",
némai nê dúr-i-erí-a tíriai nê dúr-i-erí-a.
Stadt weder wir sehen nicht, Strassen noch wir sehen nicht.

13. *Frageformen und Wortstellung.*

a) mit angehängtem ni.
kyi-ni, „ist es, gibt es"? hâñkeri-ni, „finden wir"?
b) ni — yê, ni — nié, „entweder — oder".
dôke-ni yê e-narkai, „(ist es) fern denn oder nah"?;
kyi-ni yê yokô, „gibt es oder gibt es nicht"?, oder in anderer Form kyi ke-ni yokô-nié.

Vergleiche noch folgende Phrase: „Geht die Strasse gerade aus oder wendet sie sich zur Rechten ab oder zur Linken"?,
tíria térize tedi ni yê giui-keni bri-hen (Lokativ s. oben S. LXXX) tedi
Pfad gerade aus geht denn oder wendet sich ab zur Rechten geht
yê ánkia tedi ni?
oder Linke geht denn.

c) Bezeichnend ist folgende Phrase mit yé-yê und kedê und nién:
harda yê anna yê ki kedê yoko nién.
Ortschaft oder Menschen oder gibt es wol gibt nicht oder.

d) in-di, „was" (kuku in-di, „welcher Art", „wie"), in-dukkur, „wie viel".
in-di wird entweder ganz an das Ende der Phrase gestellt oder voran, dann aber mit noch angehängtem ni; „was (welche Waare) geht (hat Cours) auf ihrem Markt"?,
kúsuku hi-unuâ éni tédi in-di.
Markt ihr ?auf geht was;
„was bedürfen wir sonst"?, in-di ni dakkôrua gedi,
was denn bedürfen wir sonst;
„wie gross ist der Preis dieses schwarzen Pferdes"?, temman indûkkur aski ai korê,
Preis wie gross Pferd dieses schwarze.

e) Das Objekt dem Subjekt vorangestellt.
„Während ich schlummere, dringt ein Dieb in das Haus ein",
lâne nêñg-eri ivé borômi tondi,
ich schlummere? Haus Dieb dringt ein.

14. *Die enge Geschwister-Verwandtschaft des Têda mit dem Kanúri.*

Diese Verwandtschaft, von der viele der vorhergehenden grammatischen Bemerkungen sehr sprechende Beweise liefern, wird, hoffe ich, durch die hier folgende Zusammenstellung, mit der man ein genaues Durchgehn meines Vokabular's verbinden kann, wol selbst für den Skeptischsten klar und überzeugend werden [1].

---

[1]) Ich will hier nur den schon oben (S. LXVI) berührten interessanten Umstand noch einmal anführen, dass

K. tšíre fāto; „before the rain", T. ɔya bardē, K. delágu-n bergea: „behind (the tent", T. lēma-yē fūdi, K. lagáfe-n lēma-bē; „after the rain follows the storm", T. eyi dággu-n-dē dbonō loki; K. lagáfe-n úkt (áti-bo) kdrun le-tšin; némai ai bini, „as far as this town". In both these languages these particles are originally substantives.

12, a) Positive conjunction „and" (as for „or", „either — or", see the following paragraph), „bring dry wood and water", ída (a)n kyorra kurtu eyi an.
wood and dry bring water and.

b) Negative conjunction „neither — nor",
„we see neither towns, nor roads",
némai nē dúr-i-erí-n tírini nē dúr-i-erí-n.
town neither we see not, roads nor we see not.

13. *Interrogative form.*

a) by adding ní.
kyi-ní, „is there"? háñkeri-ni, „do we find"?

b) ni — yē, ni — nté, „either, or",
dōke-ní yē e-narkai, „(is it) far or is it near"?;
kyi-ní yē yeko, „is there or is there not"? or in another form kyi ke-ni yeko-nté.

Compare also the phrase: „Does the road follow a straight direction, or does it turn to the right, or to the left"?,
tíria térisó tēdi ní yē giui-kenī bei-hen (locative case, see p. LXXXI)
track straight on does go either or does it turn to the right
tēdi yē ánkin tēdi ni,
does go or left does go either.

c) Characteristic is the following phrase with yē — yē as well, as kedo and nténi
barda yē anna yē ki kedō yeko nté.
Villages either people or are there perhaps are not or.

d) in-di, „what"? (kūka in-di, „in what manner, how") in-dukkur, „how much".
in-di is either placed at the end of the phrase or, if placed at the beginning, a ni is, besides, added to it; „what (kind of merchandize) does go (is marketable) on their market"?,
kásuku bí-niuā éni tedi in-di,
Market their on? does go what;
„what else do we want"?, in-di-ni dakkdruā godi,
what then do we want else;
„what is the price of this black horse"?, temman inddkkur aski ai kore.
price how much horse this black.

e) The object precedes the subject.
„While I am slumbering, the thief enters the house",
táné néñg-eri ivē boromi tozúi,
I slumber house thief enters.

14. *The close relationship between the Tēda- and the Kanúri-language.*

The relationship between these two languages, many proofs of which are contained in the foregoing grammatical Remarks, will I hope, become perfectly clear, and fully demonstrated even to the most sceptical inquirer through the following very imperfect list of the coincidences of the two languages with which an exact investigation of my vocabulary may be connected [1]).

[1]) I here want only to call once more the attention of the reader to the circumstance, that Ptolemy, indi-

Ich will die in beiden Sprachen übereinstimmenden Wörter nach den Anfangsbuchstaben derselben im Tēda alphabetisch einander gegenüberstellen, indem ich diejenigen Wörter, die mir ihres Grundbegriffes halber von besonderer Bedeutung in der Verwandtschafts-Frage zu sein scheinen, mit einem * bezeichne, solche Ausdrücke aber, die beide Sprachen gemeinschaftlich vom Arabischen geborgt haben, möglichst fortlasse.

Tēda.	Kanúri.	Deutsch.
ága / yéga	déka	aussen
agáfir	kabía	Leichnam
ágozo	yasko	drei
ai-te	á-te	dieser
*algi (N. kubu)	k-algū / k-algu	Hemd, Tobe
am, plur. anna[1])	k-ām, Plur. ām	Mensch, Volk
*aṅker[2])	k-éṅgeri / k-éṅgeli	männlich
ánkia	antsa	Gepäck, Werkzeuge
*ásu, ásubu	ŝū	Eisen
*ála-(ye[3])	tála	Kind
ári, éri	džē	Tau, Seil
bab(-erik	bag(-nískin	ich) schlage
bāfe	báfena	reif
baré	baréma	Landmann
berént(-erik	baré(-nískin	ich) säte
barma	baru	Posten
*bolle	birrim	Wassertümpel
*berl	peli	T. Gesicht / K. Wange[4])
*bú-erik	bú-skin	ich) esse
debbo	dabu	Nabel
de-n-erík	de-nískin / dé-ṅgin	ich koche
dúguri	kúrguri	Löwe
dʃonne-dé	dʃnnoa	stark, kräftig
dźére-dé	džirē	wahr
éferi	k-abéllo	Händeklatschen
*égeri, égéli[5])	k-āgil	Amboss

schon Ptolemaeus eine enge Verwandtschaft der Garamanten, d. h. doch wol der nach der Hauptstadt Djerma-Garama benannten Tēda mit dem südlich der Wüste im heutigen Bórnu oder wenigstens Kánem wohnenden Volksstamme anzeigt, der zur Zeit des Julius Maternus mit jenem einen gemeinsamen Häuptling hatte. *Τῶν Γαραμάντων ὄντων τε καὶ αὐτῶν ἤδη μᾶλλον Αἰθιόπων* (also Ptolemaeus rechnete die Garamanten oder Tēdā sicherlich nicht zu den Berber-Stämmen) *καὶ τὸν αὐτὸν ἐχόντων βασιλέα — ἐκτέταται* auf die Bewohner von Agisymba bezogen', einem Lande, das durch die Menge der Rhinocerosse gekennzeichnet wird (Ptolemaeus I, c. 8, p. 27 Wilberg), wenn auch Ptolemaeus die Entfernung von vier Monaten von Garama bezweifelt.

1) am. Nach meiner Ansicht ist dies Wort nicht erst aus dem Arabischen eingeführt, sondern ist ursprünglich.

2) aṅker ist von der grössten Bedeutung und lässt keinen Zweifel darüber, dass kéṅgeri ein mit ka componirtes Wort ist, eigentlich ka-éṅgeri, „mit einem Glied"; éṅgeri noch jetzt gebraucht, Koelle unbekannt.

3) ála-(ye. Das ye ist Nominativ-Endung.

5) égeri ist überaus interessant, nicht allein als das ursprünglichere zu kāgil, wo erst das k eingeschoben, sondern auch im Vergleich zum Hausa-Wort mákeri, Lógonē mágil.

4) pēli. Die Kanúri nämlich haben ihr heutiges Wort fuska erst von den Hausa geborgt (fuska), und pēli hatte wahrscheinlich auch bei ihnen früher die allgemeinere Bedeutung „Gesicht".

I shall arrange the corresponding words in both languages alphabetically according to the first letter, with which each word does begin in the Téda-language, marking out by a * those words, which according to my opinion are of paramount importance in this question, while I do not take into account any of those terms, which each of the two languages has borrowed from the Arabic.

Téda.	Kanúri.	English.
éga . . . . / yéga	déka	outside, out of
agáfir	kabíu	corpse
ágozó	yasko	three
ai-te	á-te	this, this one
*algi (N. kuhu) . .	k-algu . . . . / k-ulgu	shirt, tobe
am, plur. aunu [5]) .	k-âm, plur. âm . .	man, people
*aṅker [6])	k-éṅgeri . . . . / k-éṅgeli	male
áukia	autem	luggage, things
*asu, ásubu . . .	šu	iron
*áta-(ye [7]) . . .	táta	child
ázi, ézi	džé	rope, cord
bäb(-erik	bag-niskin . . .	I) beat
báfo	báfeua	ripe
bare	barema	husbandman
beréul(-erik . . .	bare(-niskin . . .	I) till the ground
barma	baru	small-pox
*belle	birrim	waterpool
*beri	péli	T. face / K. cheek [9])
*bu(-erik	bu(-skin	I) eat
debbo	dabu	navel
dé-u-erik	de-niskin . . . / de-ngin	I cook
dáguri	kúrguri	lion
dgunne-dé	dgnnou	strong
džére-de	džire	true
éferi	k-abéllo	clapping of hands
*égeri, ógeli [8]) . .	k-ägil	anvil

enter a close relationship between the Garamantes (or the Téda-nation, probably called by that name from their capital Djerma or Garama), and the tribes settled south of the Desert, in what at this day constitutes Bórnu, or at least Kánem, stating, that these tribes had at the time of the expedition of Julius Maternus one and the same chief with the former „a Garamantibus quippe qui et ipsi magis iam sunt Aethiopes eandemque quem illi habent regem" (Ptolemy I, ch. 8, p. 27 ed. Wilberg), the „illi" referring to the inhabitants of Agisymba, a country sufficiently marked out by the numbers of rhinoceroses in which it is said to abound.

[5]) am according to my opinion is not borrowed from the Arabic, but belongs originally to both languages.

[6]) aṅker: this term is of great importance in this question and does not leave the slightest doubt, that the Kanúri-term kéngeri is a compound word, originally ke-ingeri, „with a veretrum", the substantive íngeri, although not known to Koelle, being still used.

[7]) áta-(ye: the ye does not belong to the root, but is the mere nominative termination.

[8]) égeri is very interesting, not only as the more original form of the Kanúri k-ägil where the k, ke has been added, but also, if compared with the Hausa-form mákeri, Logoné mágil.

[9]) pêli: this word also in the Kanúri-language, beyond a doubt, originally had the meaning „face", the term fuske which at present is used, being a foreign term, having been borrowed from the Hausa-idiom (fuska).

Tédā.	Kanóri.	Deutsch.
*eyı	ńkı	Wasser
furak	farúg	offen, eben
ferin(-erík	pérríngin [4]	ich ziehe den Faden
*foli	beri	T. Tiggra [7]) / K. Bazin
fulū-n-erík . . .	fulū-nískin . . .	ich ziehe ab
*fū-n-erík	fū-nískin	ich blase
*gai	ńgō	Kochtopf
*gále	ńgala . . . . . / ńgilla	gut, schön
gálu	ńgālu	Bohnen
gám-(erík	gamb(uskin . . .	ich reihe
*genē	geni	nicht seiend, nicht
*gi	gai	ähnlich, gleich
gir-gí-kent [1]) . .	gir-ĭšin	es donnert
girt(-erík . . . . . / gúrd(-erík [2]) . . .	girt(-ískin	ich theile
*godē	gudwa	durstig
gódomo [3])	ńgummo	Kinn
gódu	gádo	Schwein
grábenn	grasán	Faden
gŋb-ri	ngŋbbu	viel, viele
hó-bere / kó-bere	bíggela	Erntezeit
hēde	kádui	Schwanz
helú-n-erík . . .	alū-nískin . . .	ich bezahle
hógodē	wágerū	übermorgen
illi	k-ālu	T. Gras, Kraut / K. Gemüse
in-di	ndá	was
inddkkur	ndāgō [5])	wie viel
ingál-d-erík . . .	gal-ískin [6]) . . .	ich messe (Korn)
insiri	indžeri	Leder
*irdi	k-irdi . . . . . / k-érdi	T. Feind / K. Heide [8])

[1]) gir-gí-kent ist der eigentliche Ausdruck für „es donnert", während der Ausdruck eošénuē kó-yodi (S. 178) wörtlich heisst „der Himmel fällt".

[2]) gúrd-erík wird möglicherweise besser mit einem ŗ geschrieben, aber in der Volks-Sprache habe ich diese Buchstaben nicht unterschieden.

[3]) gódomo ist unzweifelhaft ältere Form als ńgummo, das aus jenem erst durch Kontraktion entstanden ist.

[4]) perlágin ist ein sehr unparteiisches Beispiel der Übereinstimmung zwischen Tédā und Kanóri, als dieser Ausdruck mir selbst unbekannt geblieben, nur von Koelle gegeben ist. Siehe S. 118, N. 4.

[5]) ndāgō ist anscheinend zusammengesetzt aus ndá und āgo, ist also wol zur Hälfte ursprünglich Kanóri. Auch inddkkur scheint zusammengesetzt aus indi und akkur.

[6]) gal-ískin hat mehr den Anschein, vom Arabischen [illegible] abgeleitet zu sein, als das Tédā ingál-d-erík. Ich habe übrigens absichtlich im Tédā vorgezogen, nie ńg zu schreiben, sondern in vor g als eine Silbe zu betrachten.

[7]) foli und beri stehen sich darin in ihrer Bedeutung vollkommen gleich, dass der trockene Teig der Tiggra für den Wüstenbewohner dasselbe ist, was warmer Hirsenpudding dem Bewohner der fruchtbaren Landschaften ist.

[8]) Der Heide ist der natürliche Feind des Moslim und der Begriff von Heide und Feind steht sich noch jetzt ganz gleich. Der Kanóri nennt kirdi auch den Mohammedaner, den er als feindlich [illegible] will.

Tédā.	Kanúri.	English.
*eyi	ńki	water
farak	farág	open, plain
ferin(-erík	pértngin[4]) . . .	I) spin yarn
*foli	beri	T. tiggra[7]) / K. bazeen
fulū-n-erík . . .	fulū-nískin . . .	I withdraw
*fū-n-erík . . .	fū-nískin	I blow
*gai	ńgē	cooking pot
*gále	íngala . . . . . . / íngilla	good, fine
gálu	ńgālu	brass
gám(-erík	gamb(askin	I) rub
*genē	gani	not being, not
gi	gai	like
gir-gé-keni[1]) . .	gir-tšin	it thunders
gíri(-erík . . . . / gúrd(-erík[2]) . . .	giri(-iskin	I) divide
*godē	gudwa	thirsty
gódomo[3])	ńgummo	chin
gōdu	gádó	sow, pig
gráhanu	grasáu	thread
gūb-ri	ngūbbu	much, many
hé-bere / ké-bere	híggela	harvesttime
hōde	kúdui	tail
helū-n-erík . . .	alū-nískin . . .	I pay a debt
hógodē	wágerū	the day after to morrow
illi	k-ālu	T. grass, herb / K. vegetables
in-di	nda	what, which
indukkur	ndágó[5])	how much, how many
ingál-d-erík . .	gal-ískin[6]) . . .	I measure
ínairi	índžeri	leather
irdi	k-irdi . . . . . . / k-érdi	T. enemy / K. pagan[8])

[1]) gir-gé-keni is the proper term for „it thunders", while the term se[illegible] ké-yadi (p. 126) verbally means „the sky is tumbling".

[2]) gúrd-erík: it may be more correct to write this word by a ḍ, but in the popular idiom I have not been able to distinguish these two sounds.

[3]) gódomo, beyond a doubt, is the more ancient form of ńgummo, which has been derived from the former by contraction.

[4]) perfngin, on my side, is a most impartial proof of coincidence between the two languages, as this Kanúri-term, which has remained unknown to myself, is given by Koelle. See p. 119, note 4.

[5]) ndágó seems to be composed of nda and ágo, and thus to be of independent Kanúri-formation; but indukkur also seems to be composed of indi and ukkur.

[6]) gal-iskin as well as the corresponding Tédā-word may possibly be derived from the Arabic [illegible], but the latter, at least, does not look much like it. I here remark, that I advisedly do not use the ńg in the Tédā-language at the commencement of the words, but regard in as a syllable by itself.

[7]) foli and beri are so far totally identical terms as both of them indicate the most common daily food, the dry figures constituting for the inhabitant of the desert the same necessary article, as the common paste of Negro-millet for the inhabitant of the fertile region.

[8]) kirdi: the un converted pagan is the natural enemy of the Moslim and „pagan" and „enemy" are synonymous terms, the Kanúri designating as a kirdi also him whom he is well aware to be a Mohammedan, when he wants to express his hostile feelings towards him.

Têdâ.	Kanúri.	Deutsch.
ingădži	ŭgădži	Gericht aus Sorghum
ingʉbbel	úgʉbbel	Ei
káfaka	kábaga	Spanne
kampoi	kámpoi, Kl. . . . / kámpoë . . . . / kámfoé	leicht, schlank
*kangíe	kantše	Hauch
karro	kerro	Gepäck
kau	kau	T. Fruchtkern, Stein / K. Stein, Fels, Berg
káz-erík [1])	káz-utú	T. ich lache / K. Gelächter
*kéne-dé [2]) . . .	kánadi	T. geduldig / K. Geduld
ke-dä [3])	kí-da	Werk, Arbeit
k-édi [4])	kéri	Hund
keŭgē . . . . . . / gingge	kaŭgē	Fieber
kéki	kókiö	Schopf, Gipfel
kyedö	kergēko	Strauss
kēsu	kerš	süss, angenehm
kindžer	kindžer	Giraffe
kōb-erík	kám-nískin, 3te Pers. Sing. káb-tšin	ich zerbreche, zerschmeisse
koki	koki	Huhn
kōli	kōri	Holzhammer
kóŭg-erik	kóg-niskin . . .	schlage auf (das Zelt)
kón-erík	kō-nískin	T. ich steige auf / K. ich gehe vorbei
kúri-erík	kō-t-iskin [6]) . . .	ich bringe
*konó [5])	kunnó . . . . / kanó	Freude
kulkuttou	kalkutta	Baumwolle

[1]) káz-erík ist hier entschieden das Ältere, da káz-utú im Kanúri unzweifelhaft erst abgeleitet ist von einem Zeitwort káza-niskin, das verloren gegangen.

[2]) kéne-dé ist ohne Zweifel das ursprünglichere und zeigt auf eine Wurzel kéne, wie wir wirklich ein Zeitwort kené-n-erík haben. Dieses ist von ausserordentlichem Interesse. Die Kanúri machten das Adjektiv ganz gegen seine Natur zu einem Substantiv, während die Têdâ dafür kéne-dé sagen. Vergl. S. LXXX.

[3]) ke-dä. In diesem Falle ist wol das Kanúri ki-da, das von der Wurzel di-skin kommt, das Eigenthümliche, während ich das Têdâ-Wort aus sich selbst nicht erklären kann.

[4]) k-édi ganz nahe verwandt dem Ausdruck für „Hund" in der Bełem-Sprache gedeng. (Bei dieser Gelegenheit erlaube ich mir, auf die bis jetzt nur im Manuskript vorhandene kurze Grammatik und Vokabular dieser Sprache von Herrn Werner Munzinger, der nun auf dem Wege nach Wadäï ist, aufmerksam zu machen.) Bei diesem Worte haben wir jedoch ein kultur-historisches Verhältniss, kein sprachliches vor uns und haben so den „Hund" als édi (Temáśiyt), k-édi (Têdâ), gedeng (Bełem), kare, kela (Hausa), kalé (Logone), kré (Wándalá), kéri (Kanúri). Die Bagirmi-Sprache aber hat nicht, wie Koelle's Polyglotta angiebt, ebenfalls kalé, sondern das ganz verschiedene bišì, das sich einer anderen südöstlichen Sprachen-Gruppe anschliesst.

[5]) koné, jetzt mir nur noch im Zeitwort koné-n-erík bekannt. Koelle dagegen hat nicht das Kanúri-Substantiv kunnó oder kanó, sondern ein Zeitwort kánógin, das mir wiederum unbekannt geblieben.

[6]) kō-t-iskin scheint anderer Seits allerdings dem entsprechenden Hausa-Ausdruck (-na) kau näher zu stehn.

Tédā.	Kanúri.	English.
ingāddži.	ńgāddži	dish of sorghum
ingābbel	ńgųbbel	egg
káfaka	kábaga.	span
kampoi	kámpoi, Kl. . . / kámpoē . . . . / kámfoē	slender, light
*kangís.	kaniše	smoke
karro	kerre	luggage
kau	kau	T. kernel, stone / K. stone, rock, mountain
káa-erík[1]) . . .	káa-utū	T. I laugh / K. laughter
*kéne-dē[2]) . . .	kánadi	T. patient / K. patience
ko-dā[3])	kí-da	work, labour
k-édi[4])	kéri	dog
kongo . . . . . / gigge	kańgé	fever
kóki	kókia	tuft, top
kyedō	kergéko	ostrich
kesu	kemši	sweet, agreeable
kindžer	kindžer	camelopard
kōb-erík	kám-nískin, 3ᵈ Pers. Sing. káb-šin .	I break, cut
kokí	kokí	fowl
kōli	kōri	mallet
kóńg-erík . . .	kóg-nískin . . .	I pitch (the tent
kón-erík	kō-nískin	T. I mount / K. I pass by
kúri-erík	kō-t-ískin[6]) . . .	I bring
*konō[5])	kunnō . . . . . / kunō	joy, delight
kulkutton . . .	kalkutta	cotton.

[1]) káa-erík is evidently the elder, and more original of the two terms, the Kanúri-word káa-utū being undoubtedly derived from a verb káan-nískin, which has become obsolete.

[2]) kéne-dē is undoubtedly the more original word of the two, and points to a root kéne, as we have in reality a Tédā-verb kené-n-erík, and we thus see, that what in the Tédā-language was formed regularly according to the laws of that language, was applied in the Kanúri-idiom to another purpose, kána-di being used as a substantive, which in reality it is not.

[3]) ko-dá: here we have the reverse of what I have observed with regard to the preceding word, the Kanúri-term being easily explained and derived from its root di-skin, while in the Tédā-language I have not met with such a verb.

[4]) k-édi is closely related to gedeng, the corresponding term in the Bulom-language, of which there exists a short Mscr. grammar and vocabulary by Mr. Werner Munzinger, who has spent many years in that country, and is now about to penetrate towards Wádāy. With regard to the identity of this term, however, we have not to look for a linguistical connection, but have to explain it from another point of view, the „dog" having been introduced into those Regions from one and the same quarter. Thus, we have édi in the Mābjy, k-édi in Tédā, gedeng in Bulom, kare or kele in Hausa, kalé in Lógoné, krō in Wándalā, kéri in Kanúri. But the Bagrimma-language has not kálé, as Koelle has it in his Polyglotta, but the totally different term bíšī, belonging to another group of languages.

[5]) konō is only known to me in the verb konō-n-erík, while Koelle has not the Kanúri-substantive kunnō or kunō, but only the verb kúndógin, which latter remained unknown to myself.

[6]) kō-t-iskin, on the other hand, may seem to be more closely related to the corresponding Hausa-term (-na) kan.

Tédā.	Kanúri.	Deutsch.
*komögun, kûn [1]) .	kemâun	Elephant
*kuntšu [2])	ûgandži . . . . / ṅgántši, Kl. . .	Brust
*kunū	gana	klein, jung
*kyā, tšá [3]) . . .	kintsā	Nase
*kyī	tsui	reicht hin
*lā	lēma	Zelt
lehilla	rifilla	Silber
māsa	másana	T. Abendbrod / K. Speise im Allgemeinen
mēdo, méti . . .	ki-mínde [7]) . . .	heuer
mós-erík	mús-skin	siehe mich an
mūgo . . . . . / mōka	mūga	stumm, taub
ṅgēle . . . . . / níṅgeli	níṅgeri	Regen / Regenzeit
nós-erík [4]) . . .	nú-skin	ich sterbe
osō, yṳeu	asku	acht
*rō	rōa	T. Seele, Herz / K. Leben
sāga	sāga	Jahr
*se . . . . . . / saye . . . . . / šaye	ši	Fuss
*sau . . . . . / sammo	sim	Auge
*šī . . . . . . / summo	simmo	Ohr
šímberi	kámberi	T. Dorn / K. Blüthe [8])
súnuri [5])	súnuri	Schlächter
*šówoš	sṳbbio	Mark
*ta-rík	tá-skin	ich nehme
*tirbe [6]) . . . . / tirmesu	télam	Zunge

[1]) kûn sieht sehr ursprünglich aus, ist aber doch wol nur zusammengezogene Form von komögun (Hodgson. Notes on Northern Africa p. 108, komokan'; „Elfenbein", Tédā te-kûn, Kanúri timmi komine-hā.

[2]) kuntšu. Das Tédā mit anlautendem k verhält sich zum Kanúri mit dem ṅg ganz wie das (Se)-Súto- zum Kāfir-Idiom. S. Bleek catalogue of S. G. Grey's library I, S. 116. Eben so finden wir ein ganz ähnliches Verhältniss, wie wir es hier im Kanúri sehen, dass so viele Wörter, die im Tédā mit einem Vokal anfangen, ein k vorsetzen, im Kanandīe wieder in seiner Beziehung zur Sprache von Bangwele.

[3]) kyá wieder das ursprüngliche, aber beide von yí, „trinken", abgeleitet. Hodgson's chemmee von شم.

[4]) nós-erík ist auffallend, da im Kanúri wenigstens, wie das Präterit. nu-í zeigt, das s entschieden nicht zur Wurzel gehört; aber im Tédā gehört das s entschieden zur Wurzel, wie nós-edō zeigt.

[5]) súnuri ist möglicherweise von dem Tédā der mehr ausgebildeten Kanúri-Sprache später entborgt, da solche Nomaden-Stämme eigentlich keinen besonderen Schlächter haben, sondern Jeder für sich schlachtet, wie denn bei den Tédā überhaupt die Namen von Handwerkern sehr roh und unausgebildet sind.

[6]) Die ursprüngliche Form war offenbar tir, die auch dem Kanúri-Wort zu Grunde liegt.

[7]) ki-minde. Dem dem Tédā-Wort näher liegenden Worte minde haben die Kanúri die Bedeutung „im vergangenen Jahr" gegeben.

[8]) „Blüthe" nennen die Tédā hōbo. — Ich will hier erwähnen, dass Hodgson's pegedee für „Zelt" falsch ist.

Tédā.	Kanúri.	English.
*homōgun, kūn [1])	kemūun	elephant
*kuntšu [2])	ngandži / ngántši, Kl.	breast
*kunū	ganā	small, young
*kyā, tšā [3])	kintsā	nose
*kyí	tsui	it suffices, is enough
*lā	lōma	tent
lohilla	rifilla	silver
māsa	másana	T. supper / K. food in general
mōdo, mōti	ki-mínde [7])	this year
mōs-erík	mús-skin	I dress
mūge / mōka	mūgu	mute, dumb
ngēle / níngeli	níngeri	rain / rainy season
nōs-erík [4])	nú-skin	I die
osū, yusū	usku	eight
*rō	rōa	T. soul, heart / K. life
sāga	sāga	year
*se / saye / šaye	šī	foot
*sau / sammo	sim	eye
*ši / summo	simmo	ear
šimberi	kámberi	T. thorn / K. blossom, flower [8])
sánuri [5])	sánuri	butcher
*šdwoū	sūbbio	marrow
*ta-rík	tá-skin	I take
*tirhe [6]) / tirmēsu	télam	tongue

[1]) kūn looks very original, but nevertheless may be nothing, but the contracted form of homógun (Hodgson, Notes on Northern Africa p. 106, homohon); „ivory" Tédā te-hún, Kanúri timmi homáun-hé.

[2]) kuntšu: the relation of the k in Tédā to the ng in Kanúri is very much the same as it is in (Se)-Sūto in comparison with the Kafir-idiom. Bleek catalogue of S. G. Grey's library I. p. 116. Likewise we find a very similar relation in the Kosandie with regard to Benguela, as we see here exhibited by the Kanúri, which prefixes a k in many of the words, which in Tédā begin with a vowel.

[3]) kyā again is the original form, kin-tsā (Kl. kéntsā) the later one, both of them being derived from yā, „drink". As for the shemmes of Hodgson, it is nothing but the Arabic شم, „to smell".

[4]) nōs-erík: it is remarkable, that in this Tédā-word the s belongs evidently to the root, as is clearly shown by the forms of the past tense nós-edō, and so on, while the forms of the past tense of the Kanúri-word nu-i, and so on, leave no little doubt, that in the latter the s does not belong to the root.

[5]) sánuri: this term originally may have belonged to the Kanúri-language, and may have thence been borrowed at a later time by the Tédā, with the nomadic tribes each head of a family in general slaughtering his own cattle, as we find also the terms for most of the other kinds of handicraft very little developed in Tédā.

[6]) tirhe: the original form of this word was evidently tir, which is also the fundamental form of the Kanúri-term.

[7]) ki-minde. in this composite form the original notion has been retained, while to the term minde without the addition of ki, the Kanúri have given the notion „last year".

[8]) The term „blossom" is expressed in Tédā by the word hōbu. — For „tent" Hodgson has pogados.

Téda.	Kanúri.	Deutsch.
*tön [1]) . . . . . . / tómai	timmi	Zahn
töb-erik [2]) . . .	támbu-skin . . .	ich schmecke
*torō, trō	tílō	ein
*täúm(-erik . . .	zem(-nískin [4]) . . / tsém(-gin . . .	ich) steige ab
*tšī . . . . / kai	tšī	Mund
*túddrau . . . / túrresiō . . .	tyllur	sieben
*tuggum 1 . . . . / toúgwa 2 . . .	tiggam	Euter T. 1 / Brust T. 2 } K.
túld(-erik	tul(-dskin . . . / túl(-ígin	ich) wasche
tún-erik	tu-g-dskin . . . / túúgin, Kl. . . .	ich lade, befestige
ungo . . . . / úngul	k-úngu	Wunde
wanzäm	wanzemma . . .	Barbier
wasā	wasā-wasā . . .	Bohnengericht
woski	biska'	gestern
*yā(-(e)rik	yā(-skin	ich) trinke
*yár(-n-erik [3]) . . .	arē	ich) komme T. / komme, Imp. K.
yöb-erik	ífi-skin . . . . . / yíbuskin, Kl. . .	ich kaufe

15. Diese Beispiele einer inneren, engen Verwandtschaft zwischen Kanúri und Téda sind so entscheidend, da sie bis in das innerste Wesen der Wortbildung hinabreichen, dass sie allein schon den klaren Beweis liefern, dass die beiden Völkerschaften, wie ich das in meinem Reisewerk auch historisch ausgeführt habe [5]), nur Bruchstücke eines grossen Stammes sind, dessen gemeinsame Sitze wir vorläufig im Nord-Osten von Kánem annehmen können. Wenn diese Verwandtschaften des Glossars, die übrigens bei weiterer Bekanntschaft mit der Téda-Sprache noch zahlreiche Vermehrung erfahren werden, nicht grösser sind, und meist nur die einfachsten Ausdrücke berühren, während ich selbst alles nicht ganz in die Augen Springende absichtlich fortgelassen habe, so ist das durch eine frühere Trennung leicht erklärlich, wo dann die Kanúri mit ganz anderen Stämmen in Verbindung traten und von ihnen, wie ich weiterhin zeigen werde, nicht allein die Ausdrücke für ihre in ihren früheren Wüstensitzen unbekannten Anschauungen oder Beschäftigungen entlehnten, sondern auch manche andere, wofür sie ursprünglich eigene Ausdrücke besassen, wie wir das mit den Worten fiska und peli gesehen haben, und was mit vielen anderen Ausdrücken wahrscheinlich ist.

[1]) Wie sehen aus dem oben S. XCII, N. 1 angeführten Ausdruck te-kōw für „Elfenbein" („Zahn des Elephanten"), dass die ursprüngliche Form für „Zahn" te war.

[2]) töb-erik ist besonders interessant, weil es wiederum auch mit der Hausa-Sprache verwandt ist, wo wir zwei Formen haben, mitten inne zwischen der Téda- und der Kanúri-Form, ina tamma und ina tebba.

[3]) Dieses Wort ist eins der aller bedeutendsten für den Beweis der Verwandtschaft zwischen diesen beiden Stämmen, da alle übrigen Formen von arē im Kanúri verloren gegangen sind (s. Koelle, Grammatik §. 118, 2) und wir nun erst durch das Téda den lebendigen Aufschluss über diese, so wie über so viele andere schwierigen Punkte der Kanúri-Sprache erhalten.

[4]) zem-niskin, vergl. S. 91, N. 2.

[5]) Reisen II, S. 309.

Têda.	Kanúri.	English.
*{tóa[1] {tómmai	timmi	tooth
tōb-erík[2]	támbu-skin	I taste
*torō, tro	tíló	one
*tšám(-erík	{sem(-nískin[4]) {tsém(-gin	I) descend
*{tši {kai	tšī	mouth
*{túdduru {túrrusiō	tulur	seven
*{tuggum 1 {toñgwa 2	tiggam	{udder T. 1 {female breast T. 2} K.
táld(-erík	{tul(-úskin {tul(-ngin	I) wash
tún-erík	{tu-g-úskin {túúgin, Kl.	I load (a gun), fasten
uñgo úñgul	k-uñgu	wound
wanzām	wanzemma	barber
wasā	wasā-wasā	dish of beans
woshi	biska	yesterday
*yá(-(e)rík	yá(-skin	I) drink
*yár-(u-erík[3])	are	{I) come T. {come, imp. K.
yóh-erík	{ífi-skin {yíbuskin, Kl.	I buy

13. These instances of a close relationship between Kanúri and Têda are of such a decisive character, as entering into the very innermost recesses of the formation of the language, that they alone seem sufficient to prove, and to confirm, what from an historical point of view I have made out in the account of my Travels[5]), that the two tribes are merely sections of one large nation. Here we must not forget, that the list of words identical in both languages, such as given by me, will certainly receive many more additions in consequence of a more complete knowledge of the Têda-language, while I have only given what seems to me placed beyond a doubt; and if thus the cases of identity are not more numerous, we must take into account the early separation of the two tribes, in consequence of which the Kanôri became allied with tribes of a different descent, from whom they borrowed not only such terms as designated notions or occupations formerly foreign to them in their desert home, as I am about to show further on, but also such as replaced original terms, which they had possessed themselves, as we have seen to be the case with the terms fiska and pêli.

---

[1]) tóa: from the term to-hûn for „ivory" („tooth of elephant"), mentioned on the preceding page we see, that the original form for „tooth" was to.

[2]) tōb-erík is peculiarly interesting, because on the other side it appears to be connected with the Hausa also, which has two forms ìna somma and ìna ìabba, which appear to stand midway and to form a link between the Têda and the Kanúri-terms.

[3]) yár-u-erík is one of the most important instances for proving the degree of relation between these two languages, all other forms, belonging to the verb arô, having been lost in the course of time (compare Koelle's grammar §. 112, 2), while now the Têda-language throws light also on this point, as on so many others with regard to the Kanúri-language.

[4]) sem-nískin: compare p. 83, note 2.

[5]) Trav. and Disc. II, p. 278.

Allerdings gehen die Pronomina in ihrer jetzigen Form sehr auseinander; nach meiner Ansicht aber ist kein Theil der Grammatik bei diesen Naturvölkern so später Bildung, als dieser, der eine so völlige Abstraktion nöthig macht, und doch ist das charakteristische Zeichen der 2ten Person Sing. und Plur. in beiden Sprachen identisch, nämlich n, und das ist wol das einzig Ursprüngliche bei den Pronomina, nämlich die Bezeichnung der von dem Redenden geschiedenen Person, mag sie nun die angeredete (zweite) oder eine andere (die dritte) Person sein. Wie spät die weitere Entwickelung des Pronomen bei den Kanúri ist, zeigt die ganz klare Bildung des Plurals vermittelst eines angehängten ndi, „zwei". Die Tédā haben ihren Plural der 1sten Person wol erst gebildet, nachdem sie das Zeitwort ausgebildet hatten und nahmen danach das t als Kennzeichen, indem sie von tánē, „ich" tin-t-a, „wir" bildeten; vielleicht war es auch gleichzeitig mit dem Zeitworte.

In den Zahlen stimmen die beiden Sprachen bei 1, 3, 8 und 10 sehr nahe überein, aber auch Tédā kyū (2) steht dem Kanúri ndi nicht fern, so wie Tédā ţozó dem Kanúri dégu; bei 6 folgen beide verschiedenen Anschauungen, die Kanúri nennen es „noch ein Mal, wiederum (re) drei", re-yasko = rasko; das Tédā dise kann ich nicht analysiren.

Sehr natürlich ist nach dem, was ich entwickelt habe, dass, während die Namen für die auch im Bereiche oder am Rande der Wüste vorkommenden wilden Thiere, wie Löwe, Giraffe, Elephant, Strauss, in beiden Sprachen eng verwandt sind, der Unterschied der Ausdrücke zwischen Kanúri und Tédā in Bezug auf die Benennung der Hausthiere ausser Huhn, Hund und Katze sehr gross ist; den allgemeinen Namen dafür kazu scheinen die Kanúri der Bágrimma-Sprache (kátšu) entlehnt zu haben oder beide aus gleicher Quelle; dem Kameel haben sie einen von der bezeichnenden Vorliebe dieses Thieres für die Dornen hergenommenen Namen „Dornenfresser", kárgi-mó gegeben; der Kanúri-Name für „Rind", fe steht dem Tédā fur nicht so ganz fern, ist aber in seiner näheren Form wol mehr durch das fla der Mana-Sprachen bestimmt; am allerverschiedensten ist der Name des weder der Wüste, noch dem Afrikanischen Tropenlande eigenthümlichen Pferdes. Bedeutend ist auch der Unterschied in der Benennung der Gegenstände der Pflanzenwelt, vielleicht aber, dass noch andere Dialekt-Verschiedenheiten im Tédā nähere Beziehungen bieten; das allgemeine Wort für „Baum" im Tédā, akā scheint dem Kanúri-Wort für „Wald", kar-agu (ke-re-aku) zu Grunde zu liegen.

16. Sehen wir nun, was auf der anderen Seite die Tédā-Sprache, so weit sie mir eben bekannt geworden, mit dem Mášiy und anderen benachbarten Sprachen ausser dem Kanúri gemein hat, so ist das äusserst gering. Mit Mášiy und irgend einem der Dialekte der sogenannten Berber-Sprachen, wozu doch noch immer so viele Gelehrte die Tédā-Sprache zu rechnen bestrebt sind, reduciren sich, so viel ich finden konnte, die Gleichheiten oder Ähnlichkeiten von Ausdrücken dieser Sprache auf folgende höchst spärliche, ganz vereinzelte und zur Hälfte aus materiellen Beziehungen des Lebens und Verkehrs mit Sicherheit zu erklärende Fälle:

Tédā.	Mášiy.	Deutsch.
aunr	ul	Herz,
auri	ayōr	Mond,
ánnero	éneli	Hirse,
tiuni	teni	Dattel,
tirko	étterik	Reitsattel zum Kameel.

Die beiden ersten Ähnlichkeiten sind schon sehr zweifelhafter Natur und erklären sich zum Theil durch Einfluss des Koptischen; noch unsicherer wäre es eve, ivuó mit Nebenform yé-bō, im Tédā „Haus", mit ehe im Mášiy zusammenzubringen, oder aski, Tédā „Pferd" mit aïs im Mášiy, ebenso murdo, „zehn" Tédā mit meyau im Mášiy, obgleich die Kanúri-Form megū dem letzteren sich näher anschliesst (vgl. Reis. II, S. 297, N. *). Fest steht

No doubt, the pronouns go very far asunder in those two languages, but, according to my opinion, with those simple people no part of the grammar is of such a late formation as this one, and even here we find in both languages the same characteristic sign for the 2nd person sing. and plur., viz a, and that I think to be the only original part of the pronoun, namely the person distinguished from the speaker, whether it be the person addressed, or a third one. How late the further development of the pronoun in the Kanúri-language is, appears clearly from the formation of the plural by means of ndi, „two", which has been added to the form of the singular. As for the Tédā, they have probably formed their plural of the 1st person, after they had developed the verb, and thence took the t as sign of the plural, forming from the singular tan, táné the plural tin-t-a; may be, that this formation of the pronoun proceeded hand in hand with that of the verb, but certainly it did not precede it.

As for the numbers, the terms for 1, 3, 5 and 10 are nearly the same in both languages, and even those for 2, kyū in Tédā, and ndi in Kanúri are not very different, as little as those for 4, Tédā ţozō, Kanúri dōgu; with regard to 6, each of the two languages seems to follow a different point of view, the Kanúri calling it „once more three", re-yasko = yasko, while I am not yet able, to explain the Tédā-term disú.

After what I have said it is very natural, that, while the names for those wild beasts which are found also along the borders of the desert such as the lion, the giraffe, the elephant, the ostrich, are closely related in both languages, the difference of the terms given to the domestic animals, besides the fowl, the dog, and the cat, is very great. The term kāsu, designating domestic animals in general, seems to have been borrowed by the Kanúri from the Bagirmi language (kūtĕn), or to have been derived by both from the same source, while the Kanúri gave to the camel another name, kárgi-mō taken from the remarkable predilection which this animal has for the thorns. As for the term fe „cattle", it is not so very unlike the Tédā-term for, while its form may have been influenced in some degree by fă, the corresponding term of the Māsa-languages. The greatest difference is observed in the terms given by the two languages to the horse, and this is very natural, as the horse is neither indigenous in the desert, nor in the Tropical Regions of Africa. Very considerable likewise is the difference in the nomenclature of objects of the Vegetable Kingdom, but the generic name for „tree" in Tédā, viz akā, seems to be the root, whence the Kanúri-name kar-āga (ko-ru-aka, „what (of) several trees") meaning „forest" has been derived.

16. If we now see, what are the points of identity, or coincidence between the Tédā-language, as far as I have become acquainted with it, and the Māšiy, or between the former, and other languages of neighbouring tribes, these are very few, and of very little importance indeed. With regard to the Māšiy-idiom, or any of the dialects of the socalled Berber-languages, among which many learned men as yet class the Tédā-idiom, the cases of coincidence of the latter, as is shown in the following list, are quite isolated, and partly are easily, and with perfect certainty explained in consequence of material relations of life and intercourse.

Tédā.	Māšiy.	English.
anar	ul	heart,
auri	ayōr	moon,
ánnere . . .	éneli	millet,
tinni	tēni	date,
tirke	éttcrik	saddle for riding the camel.

The two first instances of coincidence are of rather doubtful character, and even if really identical might be easily explained by means of an influence exercised upon both languages by the Coptic, while it would be quite unwarranted to compare such words as ǝve, ivuā, in another form yé-bō in Tédā („house"), with ēhe in Māšiy, or aski in Tédā („horse") with aïs in Māšiy, or murdō in Tédā („ten") with mcyau in Māšiy, although the form of the

nur die Selbstigkeit der Ausdrücke für „Hirse" und „Kameelsattel", und diese erklärt sich ganz natürlich einerseits aus dem thatsächlichen, durch Naturverhältnisse bedingten Umstande, dass die Tédā fast ihren gesammten Vorrath von Hirse durch die Mášiy-Leute oder Tuarek erhalten, die mit diesem Artikel vornehmlich das Salz von Bilma in so ungeheurer Masse einhandeln (s. Reisen Th. I, S. 504), andererseits darum, dass diese Berber die eigentlichen Kameelzüchter Afrika's vom Anfang unserer Zeitrechnung an waren und auch die eigenthümlichen kleinen Reitsättel für dies Thier erfanden. Auch der Tédā-Name góne für „Kameel" mag mit dem Mášiy-Namen für dieses Thier in seiner früheren ursprünglichen Form einerlei sein, obgleich die jetzt bei den nördlichen Stämmen gebräuchliche Form alyom schon ferner liegt [1]), und obgleich die südlicheren Stämme, mit denen die Tédā im Laufe des letzten Jahrhunderts besonders in Berührung kamen, einen gänzlich verschiedenen Ausdruck für Kameel haben, nämlich ámenia.

Auch die Anklänge des Tédā an andere benachbarte Sprachen zeigen nichts weiter, als dass es mit ihnen Berührungen gehabt habe, so die wenigen meist äusserlichen Übereinstimmungen mit der Hausa-Sprache, und wir können in diesem letzteren Falle wol eines Theils mit voller Berechtigung annehmen, dass das Kanúri die Vermittlerin spielte, indem die im Kanúri entsprechenden Ausdrücke nur verloren gegangen sind, während wir anderer Seits die Örtlichkeit der früheren Sitze des Hausa-Volkes berücksichtigen müssen.

Tédā.	Hausa.	Deutsch.
borómi	barāu	Räuber, Dieb,
borē	baraie [2])	Diener, Taglöhner,
kaši	töchi	Leib,
két-erík	ked-aia	ich zähle,
kyir	kyirra	T. Name, H. rufe, nenne,
kúr-t-erík (K. kö-t-iskin)	(na) kau	ich bringe,
kómmolo	komíllo	Übelkeit.

Vielleicht mag auch der Name éringi, womit die Tédā das „Muschelgeld" bezeichnen, mit dem Namen uri für die „einzelne Muschel" im Hausa zusammenhängen und noch einige andere derartige Berührungen Statt finden; deshalb bleiben die Sprachen doch einander gänzlich fremd.

Mit Lógonē, Wándalā und Bágrimma hat die Tédā-Sprache nach dem mir vorliegenden Material je drei bis vier sehr allgemeine Übereinstimmungen; ganz fest steht hier nur wieder ausser „Baum", im Tédā aka, im Bágrimma kagā, der Ausdruck für „Butter", im Tédā und L. dort empi, impi, hier imbi, aus bestimmten materiellen Lebens-Verhältnissen sich erklärend; mit Máha scheint die Tédā-Sprache einige ähnliche Ausdrücke zu haben, wie für „Sturm", T. ábonō, M. éffolō (W. éffuyā); „Blitz", T. yumár, M. marrā; „Vogel", T. kebri, M. kebél; „Schlacht, Krieg", T. tullo, M. torro; „kalt", T. keri, M. kēra; „Wasserschlauch", T. teri, M. átteri (B. ótili), indem diese Übereinstimmung sich aus materiellen Verhältnissen auf das Einfachste erklärt und endlich „Thalfurche, Fluss", T. föti, M. bötak

---

[1]) Überaus merkwürdig ist, dass der in der Wándalā-Sprache noch jetzt übliche Ausdruck eldegóme oder elgóme dem Mášiy-Worte so viel näher liegt und können wir dies Verhältniss uns nur schwer anders erklären, als dass in alter Zeit die Form des Namens dieses Thieres in der Tédā-Sprache sich gleichfalls jener eng angeschlossen habe, da die Tédā seit alter Zeit mit Wándalā in Handelsverbindung stehen, was von den Mášiy kaum gesagt werden kann. Jedoch ist zu berücksichtigen, dass elyom noch heute in Síwa üblich ist.

[2]) Aus baraie ist erst der in Sókoto übliche Fulfúlde-Ausdruck bareyāro entstanden.

corresponding Kanúri-term megĕ resembles the latter somewhat more closely (see Tr. and Disc. II, p. 271, note 1). Thus, there remain only as undisputable cases of identity the terms for „millet" and „camelsaddle", and the coincidence in these cases is explained very easily, in the one by means of the circumstance based upon natural conditions, that the Tédā receive almost their whole supply of Negro-millet from the hands of the Mášiy-people or Tawárek, who principally by means of this article annually buy such enormous quantities of salt at Bilma (Tr. and Disc. I, p. 504), in the other from the circumstance of these same Mášiy-people having been eminently the camel-breeders of Africa from the very beginning of our Era, and in consequence having also invented the peculiar little saddle used for riding this animal. Even gōnc, the Tédā-name for the camel may be identical with the Mášiy-name of the latter in its original form, although it does not even resemble very closely the form alyom¹), not used at present but by the Northern sections of the Mášiy-nation, including Siwah while the Southern tribes, with whom the Tédā have come especially in contact in the course of the last century, have a totally different term for designating the camel, viz ámenis.

The points of resemblance also which the Tédā-language exhibits with other neighbouring languages prove nothing, but that there have been certain points of contact. Thus, in order to explain the few instances of coincidence with the Hausa-language we are authorized on the one side to look upon the Kanúri as the medium, even in such cases where the corresponding term in that language has at present been lost, while on the other we must take into account the former seats of the Hausa-people.

Tédā.	Hausa.	English.
borōmi	barău	robber, thief,
borê	baraie²) . . .	servant, labourer,
kešī	těckī	body,
kél-orík	ked-aia . . .	I count,
kyir	kyirra	T. name, H. call, name
kúr-t-orík (K. kō-t-iskin) .	(na) kau . . .	I bring
kómmolo	komíllo . . .	bitterness, nausea.

The name érińgi also by means of which the Tédā designate „the cowries", may be connected with the Hausa-term uri, „the single shell", and there may be some few more points of coincidence, or identity between these two languages.

As for the Lógonē-, Wándalā- and Bágrimma-languages, the points of contact between them and the Tédā-language according to the material I have before me, appear to reduce themselves to three or four respectively at the utmost, while only the following few seem to be established beyond a doubt, „tree", akā in Tédā, kagā in Bágrimma; „butter", empī or impī in Tédā, imbī in Lógonē, a point of coincidence easily to be explained from material relations of life and intercourse; with regard to the term for camel in Tédā and Wándalā see the note at the bottom of this page. With Mába also the Tédā-language seems to have a few terms in common, such as „storm", T. ábonō, M. éffolō (W. éffuyā); „lightning", T. yumár, M. marrā; „bird"; T. kebrī, M. kobdī; „cold", T. kerī, M. kera; „battle, war", T. tullo, M. torre; „waterskin", T. teri, M. átteri (B. étili), the latter coincidence being easily explained from material relations; and finally „valley, torrent", T. fōli,

¹) It is very remarkable, that the term aldegéme or algéme used still at the present time in the Wándalā-language bears so much more closer resemblance to the ancient Mášiy-term, than the present form of the corresponding Tédā-term, for, while the Tédā from ancient times keep up a regular intercourse with the Wándalā-people, and supply them with the products of the North, this can scarcely be said of the Mášiy: but we must take into account, that the term alyom is still at the present time in common use in Siwah.

²) From the term baraie the Fulfúlde-term barayêre which is used in Sókoto has been derived.

obgleich die letztere Übereinstimmung sehr zweifelhafter Natur ist, da bêtak vielleicht auf das Arabische '[illegible]' zurückzuführen ist, und einiges Andere, das sich durch die nahe Berührung der beiden Völkerschaften am Saume der Wüste leicht erklärt.

Zum Schluss will ich hier nur noch eine kurze Liste einsilbiger Wörter der Tédâ-Sprache ausser den schon oben als mit den entsprechenden Kanúri-Ausdrücken verwandt aufgeführten, hersetzen: ai, „Vieh"?, be, „nicht", bē, „Tag", bo, „Blüthe" (wo, wahrscheinlich ursprünglich identisch damit, „männliches Glied" als Samenknospel), bu, „genug", dor, „Rind", du, „Getreideschober", fai, „ja", fo, „fünf" („Hand" vgl. afôa, „Hand" im Mâbá), fû (fû-kinde S. 131, N. 9), „mehr, vorwärts", ga, „früher", gir, „brechen", grē, „Blut", lau, „halb", lo, „Thon", loi, „Messer", me, „Enkel", mô (mô-kinde S. 132), „weniger, rückwärts", unk, „hinstellen", uir, „Schildkröte" (sehr gewöhnlich in den günstigeren Distrikten der Wüste), sô, „Dumpalme" (jenen Landstrichen recht eigen und der Hauptbaum), tî, „Hirsebrei", wor, „stark", ye, „Milch", yi, „auslöschen, tödten". Auch will ich noch auf folgende Ausdrücke als mir besonders auffallend scheinend die Aufmerksamkeit der Sprachforscher lenken: ozē, yozē, „Sonne", arē, „Natron", fôsu, „Fisch" (besonders merkwürdig in dieser an Fischen fast baaren Gegend), golfa, „Salz", edi, „Lanze", aňěře, „Baumwollstreifen"; auro, „Schwiegersohn", „birbē, bdruô, „grösserer Handelsherr", erski, „reisender Kaufmann", dirdē, derdai, „Fürst, Häuptling", dé-ningē (bei Hodgson S. 106 dembree i. q. dé-(e)mbri, „männlicher Verwandte"), „Bruder", dé-n-derdo (bei Hodgson dudoboo i. q. dé-dobu, „weibliche Verwandte"), „Schwester".

Somit verlasse ich nun für das Erste die Tédâ-Sprache, die ich des grossen Interesses halber, das sie mir zu verdienen scheint, so wie des ganz neuen Lichtes wegen, das ich über diesen Gegenstand verbreiten zu können mir bewusst war, etwas ausführlicher behandelt habe; aber, was ich gebe ist nur ein Anfang, und nichts wünsche ich sehnlicher, als dass Andere das Angefangene bald weiter führen mögen, und dazu scheint einige Aussicht vorhanden zu sein. Ich will deshalb die übrigen Sprachen mit Ausnahme der schon von anderer Seite her in Angriff genommenen Hausa-Sprache in ähnlich ausführlicher Weise analysiren.

Sechstes Kapitel.

Die Hausa-Sprache: mágana-n Hausa.

In Betreff des Hausa-Volkes selbst will ich hier nur, anknüpfend an das, was ich oben (S. VIII) im Allgemeinen ausgeführt habe, zu dem Umstande der Lokalität der früheren Sitze dieses Volkes, auf einen höchst interessanten, im engen Zusammenhange mit seiner Sprache stehenden Umstand aufmerksam machen.

Der treffliche, lebensfrische Herodot, der dem Forscher mit jedem Schritte, den seine eigenen Studien vorwärts machen, stets lieber und schätzenswerther wird, und dessen Bericht in der reinlichen Bekker'schen Ausgabe mich nicht allein auf meiner ersten mittelländischen, sondern auch auf meiner grossen Binnen-Afrikanischen Reise begleitete, setzt in seiner grossartigen Skizze des Nordens von Afrika, im 184sten Kapitel des vierten Buches 10 Tage W.S.W. von den Sitzen der Garamanten mit den Salzlagern (von Bilma), einen Stamm, den er Atáranten (Ἀτάραντες) nennt; dass dies jedoch kein National-Name war, erklärt er selbst ausdrücklich, indem er sagt, dass dieser Name der Gesammtheit des Volkes (eigentlich „den Versammelten", ἁλέας) zukomme.

Nun heisst târa in der Hausa-Sprache „versammeln", ina târa, „ich versammele", sun-târu, „sie haben sich versammelt" und a-târa ist das Participium Passivi mit der Bedeutung „versammelt". Da nun Herodot's Angabe der Sitze dieses Stammes der Ataranten ihn genau dorthin verlegt, wo wir die früheren Sitze des Hausa-Volkes nach historischen

M. bŏtak, although the latter term may perhaps be more closely related to the Arabic "بطاقة", and a few other terms the identity, or similarity of which is easily explained by the proximity of the seats of these two tribes on the borders of the desert.

Before concluding this chapter I will only add a short list of monosyllables in the Tédā-language besides those already mentioned above as identical with the corresponding terms in Kanúri: ai, „cattle"?, be, „not", bē, „day", bo, „blossom" (wo, „membrum virile", probably originally identical with the latter), bu, „sufficient", dor, „bull", du, „cornstack", fai, „yes, yes", fo, „five", fū, „more, forward" (fū-kíndo, p. 130, n. 9), ga, „formerly", gir, „break", grē, „blood", lau, „half", lo, lu, „clay", loi, „knife", me, „grandchild", mō, „less, backward" (mō-kínde p. 133), nak, „put", nir, „turtle" (an animal very frequent in the more favoured districts of the Desert), sā, „doompalm" likewise very frequent in, and the noblest tree of these regions; ti, „common paste of millet", wor, „strong", ye, „milk", yi, „to kill, extinguish". Besides, I call the attention of the linguist to the following terms, the etymology of which seems to me to be of peculiar importance: ozō, yozē, „sun", arē, „natron" fosu, „fish" (especially remarkable with regard to the desert character of the Tédā-territory), golín, „salt", odi, „spear", sōŏe, „cottonstripes"; anro, „son in law", hirbō, bérue, „wealthy, resident merchant", orski, „travelling merchant", dirdō, derdai, „chief", dé-ningē (with Hodgson p. 106 dembroe i. q. dé-(o)mbri), „brother", dé-n-derdō (with Hodgson dedoboo i. q. dé-dobu), „sister".

After these observations I take leave for the present of the Tédā-language, which as well on account of the great interest that it seemed to deserve to me, as with regard to the totally new light which I was able to shed upon this subject, I have treated at some length, but I am well aware, that what I give is merely a first opening of the question, and I wish nothing more ardently, than that others may soon complete, what I have begun, and there being held out a shade of hope by the Heuglin expedition, that such may soon be the case, I intend analyzing the other languages in the same manner.

Chapter the sixth.

The Hausa-language: mágana-n Hausa.

First I want to make a short remark with regard to the locality of the ancient seats of the Hausa-people in connection with their language, while referring to what I have said in general p. IX.

Herodotus, whose beautiful and graphic description of the ancient world accompanied me on all my Travels even into the far Interior of Africa, places ten days to the W.S.W. of the seats of the Garamantes with the saltlayers of Bilma, a tribe which he calls Atárantes, Ἀτάραντες (book IV, ch. 184). But, while calling them by this name he expressly adds, that such was not their national name, but that it designated them altogether, as a community (ἁλέσι).

Now, the word tāra in the Hausa-language means „to gather", 1st person sing. of the present tense ina tāra (sun-tāra, „they gather") and a-tāra is the participle of the passive mood „gathered, joined"; and this, I have not the slightest doubt, is the real term which Herodotus meant, and whence he formed in true Greek fashion his noun Atāra-s, genitive Atāra-ntos, plur. Atāra-ntes. If this be true as I have not the slightest doubt, it is, we obtain an antiquity of at least 2300 years for the Hausa-people in the very country

Zeugnissen nachgewiesen haben, hege ich nicht den allergeringsten Zweifel, dass die angegebene Verbalform der Hausa-Sprache für „die Gesammtschaft, die Volksgemeinde" der wirkliche Ursprung jenes von Herodot angegebenen Namens ist, indem der Grieche von jener Form a-tāra mit Zufügung eines s einfach den Namen Atāras (ἀτάρας) für ein einzelnes Individuum bildete; da nun die natürliche Genitiv-Form hiervon ἀτάραντος lautet, so konnte er dem Plural nur die Form ἀτάραντες geben. So erlangen wir denn für die Hausa-Nation, und zwar gerade für ihre Sitze im Berglande Asben, wo wir ihnen noch um die Mitte des verflossenen Jahrhunderts begegnen, und wo zwar keine natürlichen Salzlager sich befinden, aber wo durch natürliche Bedingungen die Haupt-Niederlage des Salzes von Bilma von Alters her sich finden musste, ein Alterthum von wenigstens 2300 Jahren.

Dieses Verhältniss ist von ausserordentlicher Wichtigkeit, selbst in linguistischer Beziehung, und erklärt wol am einfachsten einige Berührungspunkte, die die Hausa-Sprache unläugbar mit dem Alt-Egyptischen hat. Ich erwähne hier nur ausser dem persönlichen Fürwort, dessen Übereinstimmung durch das Berberische vermittelt scheinen kann, die drei auf Zahlenverhältnisse bezüglichen Ausdrücke, Hausa sō, das Alt-Egyptische sop, „Mal" („ein Mal" u. s. w.), H. fodū, Alt-Egyptisch ftu, „vier", und das merkwürdigste und sicherste von allen den in alle bei mir vertretenen Central-Afrikanischen Sprachen übergegangenen Ausdruck dubū für die gewiss erst durch grösseren Verkehr benothwendigte Zahl 1000, im Alt-Egyptischen tba. Allerdings mag der letztere Ausdruck durch das in Kultur dem Hausa- wahrscheinlich vorangeschrittene Sonyai-Volk vermittelt sein, was für den die Adansonia digitata bezeichnenden Ausdruck, wo wir die einfache monosyllabe Form kō bei letzterem finden, wol unzweifelhaft ist.

Über den Ursprung des Namens Hausa können wir bis jetzt wenigstens nichts Sicheres angeben und muss ich auf das Wenige verweisen, was ich im Berichte meiner Reisen darüber gesagt habe (Th. II, S. 79). Hier will ich nur auf die höchst charakteristische Namensform des einzelnen Individuums dieses Stammes hinweisen; ein einzelner Hausa-Mann nämlich führt den Namen ba-Hanše [1]), also in sehr ähnlicher Form wie die Volksnamen der Süd-Afrikanischen Familie, und wenn die Plural-Form diesen Vorsatz ganz abwirft und Hansaua lautet, so können wir wol mit Fug annehmen, dass dies nicht die alte, ursprüngliche Form ist.

Über die Hausa-Sprache selbst will ich mich ganz kurz fassen, da sie, wie S. XVI erwähnt, den besonderen Gegenstand schon langjährigen Studiums des Missionars Schön gebildet hat, der hoffentlich bald mit einer neuen, ungleich reicheren grammatischen Bearbeitung dieser Sprache hervortreten wird, als er vor 20 Jahren geliefert hat. Auch habe ich die Hausa-Sprache, insofern es ihre Verwandtschaft mit anderen Sprachen, die in das Bereich meiner Untersuchung fallen, betrifft, eben bei den letzteren berücksichtigt.

Ich bemerke hier nur, dass Schön's Schreibweise von der meinigen bedeutend abweicht, so dass die Selbstheit mancher Worte auf den ersten Blick kaum zu erkennen ist. Diese Erscheinung habe ich schon oben (S. VIII) zum Theil erklärt und will hier noch Folgendes hinzufügen. Meine Schreibweise habe ich genau nach der klaren Aussprache der in den Kernprovinzen der Hausa-Staaten üblichen Volks-Sprache bestimmt und bin fest überzeugt, dass spätere Forscher, denen es gelingt, in jene Länder einzudringen, sich von dem Vorzug meiner Schreibweise vor derjenigen Schön's überzeugen werden. Dazu kömmt, dass Schön, wenigstens in seinen früheren Arbeiten vor 1858, gar keine Accente benutzt, während bei der Hausa-Sprache die Accentuation der Wörter um so wichtiger ist, da mehrere Wörter von ganz verschiedener Bedeutung sich nur auf diese Weise von einander unterscheiden, so gāri,

[1]) Beiläufig will ich hier bemerken, dass Schön nach diesem Vorgange für „den Egypter" die falsche Namensform ban Masare gebildet hat (Exodus II, v. 14) anstatt ba-Māsare oder vielmehr ba Māsare, da das bezeichnende, das Genitiv-Verhältniss zwischen zwei Ausdrücken darstellende n hier gar keine Anwendung findet.

of Asben, where we find them still so late as the middle of the last century. For, although nature did not provide that district with saltmines, at least not very extensive, and important ones, yet from the beginning of human intercourse and commerce it was destined to become the principal deposit of the salt extracted from the mines of Bilma.

This historical relation, and condition is of the very greatest importance even in linguistical respect, and seems to explain in a simple and unsophisticated manner some points of contact which appear to me to intercede between the Hausa-idiom on the one, and the ancient Egyptian on the other side. I here mention besides the forms of the personal pronoun, the harmony of which, as exhibited in both languages, may seem to be mediated through, and based upon the Berber-language, the following three terms relative to numerical notions, viz Hausa sö, the ancient Egyptian sop, „time" (as for instance „three times"), H. fodū, ancient Egyptian ftu, „four", and, the most remarkable, and most unquestionable of them all, the term dubū, „thousand" which has been adopted by all Central-African languages as far as represented in my collection, and which, no doubt, does not at all designate an original idea, but such as is only wanted in consequence of an intercourse on a large scale. Certainly, I deem it most probable, that this term which, I have no doubt, has been derived from the ancient Egyptian tba, may have been first made known to those Central-African nations by means of the Sonyai-people, a circumstance which I think to be placed beyond a doubt also with reference to the term designating the Adansonia digitata for which in the Sonyai-language we find the simple monosyllabic form kō.

As for the origin, and meaning of the name Hausa, I am as yet not able to give a full explanation, and can do nothing but refer the reader to the little which I have said in this respect in my Narrative (Tr. and Disc. II, p. 84). Here I only want to point out the very characteristic form of the name of the single individual of this tribe, viz ba-Haúše, which bears a strong resemblance to the forms of names of the South-African tribes, the plural form Haúsaua which throws off this prefix entirely, not being, as it seems, an original form.

With regard to the Hausa-language itself I can and will be short, as it has formed the object of a particular study of Rev. Mr. Schön for so many years, and, as we may hope, that he may soon publish a full grammatical analysis of this language infinitely more accurate, and complete, than what he has given to the public nearly twenty years ago. Besides, I have repeated occasion of considering this language, as far as regards its relation to other languages, which have fallen under my observation, under the head of each of the latter.

I therefore restrict myself here to stating in general the points of disagreement in spelling between myself and the Rev. Schön, which in some cases is so great as to make it rather difficult to recognise the identity of the word. Referring the reader in this respect to the general observations I have made on a former occasion (p. IX), I here only state, that I have followed the clear mode of pronunciation as is usual in the chief provinces of the Hausa-states, such as Kanō and Kátsena, and I am fully convinced, that succeeding inquirers, who may penetrate into those regions, will have full opportunity of acknowledging the greater exactness of my labours in this respect with reference to those of the Rev. Schön, especially as the latter in his translations before the year 1858 does not make use of accents, while accentuation with regard to this language is the more important, as several words of totally different import are only to be distinguished from each other in this manner, such as gārī, „morning" (compare „the Gospel according to St. Matthew, translated into Hausa by the Rev.

---

*) By the by I will point out here, that the Rev. Schön has wrongly formed after this instance the name ban Masare (Matthew II, v. 14) for designating the Egyptian, instead of ba-Másare, or rather ba-Másare, as the n indicating and representing the genitive relation which obtains between two terms, finds no application whatever in this case.

„Morgen" (woiyewan gari Evang. Matthäi, Übersetzung Schön's 1857, XX, v. 1) und garí, „Stadt"; bâba, „Eunuch" und babá, „gross"; kâka, „Grossvater, Grossmutter" und kaká, „wie"; kôma, „ergreifen" und kamá, „gleichwie" und mehrere andere.

Ein Punkt von geringer Bedeutung berührt die Verdoppelung eines Konsonanten an dem Zusammenstosse zweier Silben und ist es oft schwer zu ermitteln, ob der hier erscheinende Konsonant ein einfacher oder ein gedoppelter ist, besonders wenn der vorhergehende Vokal scharf betont ist. So schreibt Schön gidda statt meines gída, „Haus"; taffi statt meines tafī, „reisen"; sanni statt sáni, „wissen" (o-sán-agh in Mášiy); kamma statt kamá, „gleichwie, ähnlich"; onna statt īna, „wo"; kasea statt kûea, „nahe"; kaššie statt kašē, „tödten"; filta statt fitō, „hinausgehn". Dagegen gebraucht er in ähnlichen Fällen nur einen einzelnen Konsonanten, wo mir eine Verdoppelung Statt zu finden schien, wie er buga schreibt statt meines bugga, „schlagen"; tudu statt tuddu, „Hügel, Berg"; duka statt dukka, „ganz, alles".

Eine andere wichtigere Abweichung zwischen mir und Schön besteht darin, dass er oft einen Konsonanten statt eines anderen verwandten gebraucht, wie er z. B. manchmal s statt z setzt. So schreibt er sa für za, „hinstellen"; samna für zamua, „sitzen"; banen für banze, „umsonst"; yausu für yenzū, „jetzt"; sinaria für zinária, „Gold"; árseki für ázaki, „Macht"; und ein doppeltes ss statt z in dem Worte massa statt mazá, „schnell".

Dagegen gebraucht er z statt s z. B. in dem, mit einer dazutretenden Verwechselung fast aller Vokale kaum wieder zu erkennenden zuriki statt meines sorukko, „Schwiegervater".

š statt ž in ši statt žī, „hören, fühlen"; daši statt dáži, „Wüste"; šia statt žia, „gestern"; šinni statt ženi, „Blut"; rišia statt rížin, „Brunnen"; išia statt ožin „(eine einzelne) Muschel"; Obangiši statt Oba-n-giži, „Gott der Herr". Aber das beste Beispiel, die Wichtigkeit des Unterschiedes zwischen š und ž zu zeigen, ist das Wort ža „(Wasser) schöpfen", das Schön ša schreibt, sogar in folgender Phrase, wo es neben dem wirklichen Zeitwort ša, „trinken" steht, sunzakka sunša rūa (statt sun-zakka sun-žu rūa, „sie kamen und schöpften Wasser") da sunba da ša ga tumakin obansu, „und gaben es zu trinken den Schafen ihres Vater's" (Exodus II, v. 16). Vgl. ebenda v. 19, wo dieselbe Zweideutigkeit noch einmal vorkommt.

ši statt ž gebraucht Schön in den beiden Wörtern šiakai für žakí, „Esel" und šiefa für žéfa, „werfen".

Dann hat Schön gelegentlich die einander nahe verwandten Doppel-Konsonanten verwechselt, wie ds und dz mit ts, tš mit dš, indem er dzayo für tsaia, „stillstehn" schreibt, dzoro für tsoró, „Furcht, furchtsam"; dzakka für tsakka, „mittlere"; altšima für aldšumma, „Freitag". Hier besonders mag viel Dialekt-Unterschied walten.

Was die Vokale anbetrifft, so gebraucht Schön häufig ai, wo ich ein einfaches e habe, vielleicht eine einfache Folge dialektischer Verschiedenheit; so schreibt er daia statt dēa, „ein"; daynwa statt dēwa, „viel"; rairai statt rērē, „Sand"; sai statt sē, „nur, ohne".

Für o gebraucht Schön häufig ein u, indem er tukuna statt tókonā, „noch nicht" schreibt; kuna statt kōne, „verbrennen", wiewohl er in einigen Stellen, wie Exodus III, v. 3, das letztere Wort selbst mit o schreibt.

Die mit u anhebenden Wörter lässt er nach Englischem Gebrauche mit w beginnen, wozu in der Sprache selbst nicht der allergeringste Grund vorhanden ist; so schreibt er denn wuri statt uri, „Ort, Stelle"; wūta statt ūta, „Feuer".

Schön schiebt zuweilen einen Vokal zwischen zwei Konsonanten ein, wo ich keinen habe, wie er denn girima statt meines girma, „Grösse"; sariki statt meines serki, „Herrscher, Häuptling" schreibt und so weiter.

Diese Abweichungen sind für das Ganze ziemlich unwesentlich, wenn wir von einigen wenigen Beispielen absehen, wie das oben angeführte zuriki, das allerdings von meinem

Schön, London 1857, ch. XX, v. 1 wayowan gari) and garí, „town"; babá, „large, great", and bába, „eunuch"; kaká, „how", and káka, „grandfather, grandmother"; kamá, „like as, similar to" and káma, „to seize".

I first mention the slighter cases of discrepancy. Rev. Schön in general redoubles almost all the consonants at the joining of two syllables, writing giddu instead of gída, „house"; sanni instead of sáni, „to know" (o-sán-agh in Mášiy); kamma instead of kamá, „like as, similar"; ennu instead of ina, „where"; kusse instead of kūse, „near"; kaššio instead of kašō, „to kill"; fitta instead of fitō, „to go out". But on the other side in some cases he makes use of a single consonant where to me a reduplication seems to take place, writing buga instead of bugga, „to beat"; tudu instead of tuddu, „hill, mountain"; duka instead of dukka, „whole, entire".

Rev. Schön in many cases puts one consonant instead of another related one, as, for instance, he uses s instead of z: writing sa instead of za, „to place"; samna instead of zamna, „to sit"; banse i. e. banza, „for nothing"; yansu i. e. yenzū, „now"; sinaria i. e. sinária, „gold"; ársoki i. e. árzeki, „power"; and he uses a double ss instead of z in the case of masse instead of mazd, „swift".

On the contrary he uses z instead of s, writing for instance suriki (with a change of nearly all the vowels) instead of serukko, „father in law".

š instead of ž: ši i. e. ži, „to hear, feel"; daši i. e. dáži, „desert"; šia i. e. žia, „yesterday"; šinni i. e. žoni, „blood"; rišia i. e. rížia, „well"; išia i. e. ežia, „(a single) cowry"; Obangiši i. e. Oba-u-giži, „lied", „Lord". The most illustrative instance for showing the importance of distinguishing between š and ž is the word ža, „to draw (water)", written by Schön ša even in the following phrase, where it is placed side by side with the true verb ša, „to drink", sunzakka, suuša rūa (instead of suu-ža rūa, „they drew water"), da sunba da ša ga tumakin obansu, „and they gave to drink their fathers' sheep (Exodus II, v. 16). Compare also v. 19 where the same equivocacy occurs.

ši instead of ž: šiakai i. e. žakí, „donkey"; šiofa i. e. žūfa, „to throw".

Besides, Rev. Schön has occasionally confounded the nearly related double consonants ds and dz with ts; tš with dš, writing dsaye i. e. tsaye, „to stand still"; dsoro i. e. tsorō, „fear, apprehension"; dsakka i. e. tsakka, „middle"; altšima i. e. aldšymma, „Friday".

As for the vowels, Schön frequently has ai, where I have a simple o, a discrepancy which may be attributed to dialectical difference; thus he writes daia i. e. dūn, „one"; dayawa i. e. dēwa, „much, many"; rairai i. e. rērē, „sand"; sai i. e. sē, „without, only".

Instead of o he frequently uses u, writing tukuna i. e. tókonā, „not yet"; kuna i. e. kōna, „to burn", although in other instances, such as Exod. III, v. 3 he himself writes this verb by o.

The words beginning with u he begins by an w after the English fashion, writing wuri i. e. uri, „place"; wūta i. e. ūta, „fire".

Schön sometimes inserts a vowel between two consonants, where I have none, writing girima i. e. girma, „greatness, size"; sariki i. e. serki, „chief" and so on.

These discrepancies, on the whole, are of little importance, if we do not take into account a few instances, such as the above mentioned suriki, which bears very little resemblance

serakke ungemein abweicht, aber ungleich wichtiger ist mein Einwurf gegen Schön's Schreibweise in Bezug auf seine Art, die Wörter abzutheilen und die daraus entstehenden Abweichungen bei uns. Denn, während mein System, die Wörter unter einander und wieder jedes in seinen besonderen Elementen abzusondern, ganz ausschliesslich von einer gewissenhaften Betrachtung der Wurzeln geleitet wurde, so weit es irgend möglich war, scheint Schön solche Rücksicht kaum genommen zu haben. Vergleiche z. B. meine Schreibweise des unbestimmten Pronomen wo-ne mit Schön's wenni, im Vokabular S. 4. So scheint er sich auch zum Grundsatz gemacht zu haben, die verbale Wurzel von dem sie eng gestaltenden pronominalen Hülfszeitwort zu trennen und dagegen mit dem regierten, nur ganz äusserlich mit ihr verbundenen Fürwort zu einem Worte zu verschmelzen, eine Schreibweise, die oft selbst dem der Hausa-Sprache sehr Kundigen das Verständniss einer Phrase äusserst erschwert. So z. B. schreibt er ya saka anstatt ya-sā ka, „er hat dich (ka) hingestellt", von sā, „hinstellen", während saka als selbstständiges Wort im Hausa „weben" bedeutet. Aber ausserdem verbindet und theilt er Wörter ab ohne die allergeringste Rücksicht weder auf ihre Wurzel, noch auf ihre grammatische Form. So schreibt er da Musa ya šidsoro (Exodus III, v. 6) anstatt da Mūsa ya-ži tsorō, „und Moses empfand Furcht", von ina-ži, „ich fühle" und tsorō, „Furcht", und im vorhergehenden Vers schreibt er in völlig unverständlicher Weise ka fitta asda takalmanka anstatt ka-fitās da tákolmí-n-ka von fitás, „ausziehn, abziehn", der transitiven Bedeutung von fitō, „hinausgehn" und der Partikel da, „damit du deinen Schuh ausziehest"; anders schreibt er eben denselben Ausdruck v. 10 und 11 und weiterhin fittasda ka yisn anstatt fitás da ka-yi sū, „dass du ausziehest und hinstellest sie (sū)" (das letztere von ina-yi, „ich stelle hin"). So schreibt er auch dage šangulbi statt daga-tšán gulbi, „von jenseit des Flusses", und so durchgehends ohne alle Rücksicht auf Wortbildung.

Um nun noch klarer und übersichtlicher zu zeigen, in welchen Punkten besonders meine Schreibweise des Hausa von derjenigen Schön's abweicht, lasse ich hier ein Kapitel des neuen Testamentes in drei Kolumnen folgen, deren erste den Griechischen Text gibt, die zweite Schön's und die dritte meine eigene Übersetzung, und damit beschliesse ich dieses Kapitel über die Hausa-Sprache, zu der ich noch einmal zurückkehren werde, wenn ich den von dem Mášiy auf die hier behandelten Sprachen im Allgemeinen ausgeübten Einfluss im Gesammtüberblick betrachte.

indeed to my serukko. But, what I object more against Schön's way of writing, is the manner in which he separates the words. For, while my manner of writing the words and that of separating them into their different elements has been motived entirely by a conscious consideration of their roots, as far as it was possible as, for instance, with regard to the pronoun wo-ne (Schön wouni) and so on, vocabulary p. 4, with Schön such a consideration was quite out of the question. Thus, throughout his writings he constantly separates the verbal root from its pronominal form, which he might well do, but at the same time joins it intimately with the pronoun which is ruled by it, a manner of writing which makes it often very difficult even for a person well versed in the Hausa-language to understand the sense of a phrase. Thus, for instance, he writes ya saka i. e. ya-sā ka, „he has placed thee" from sā, „to place", while saka, thus written conjointly is quite a different term in Hausa meaning „to weave". But, besides this, he separates the words without taking the slightest regard neither to their root nor to the grammatical form. Thus, he writes da Musa ya šidsoro (Exodus III, v. 6) i. e. da Mūsa ya-ži tsorō, verbally „and Moses felt fear", i. q. „became frightened" from ína-ži, „I feel" and tsorō, „fear"; and in the preceding verse ka fitta sada takalmanka i. e. ka-fitás da tákolmí-n-ka from fitás („to draw out, put off" the transitive form from fitō, „to go out") and the particle da, „that thou puts off thy shoes", and v. 10 and 11 he writes the same term twice fittasda, and further on in conjunction with the same particle but with quite a different meaning fittasda ka yieu i. e. fitás da ka-yi sū, „that thou takest off and puts them away" (from ína-yi, „I place"). Thus, he writes also daga šangulbi i. e. daga-tšán gulbi, „from opposite, from the other side of, the river".

In order to show, in what points especially my way of writing the Hausa-language deviates from that of the Reverend Schön's, I here insert a chapter of the New Testament, giving in the first column the Greek text, in the second Schön's, and in the third my own translation, and thus close this chapter on the Hausa-language, having to return to it once more at the end of this whole work, where I shall bring under a general head the influence exercised by the Mášiy upon the languages considered in this vocabulary.

Evangelium Matthaei II (ex rec. Lachmanni 1846).	Schön's Übersetzung. — Schön's translation, 1857.	Meine Übersetzung. — My own translation.
1) *Τοῦ δὲ Ἰησοῦ γεννηθέντος ἐν Βηθλεὲμ τῆς Ἰουδαίας, ἐν ἡμέραις Ἡρῴδου τοῦ βασιλέως, ἰδοὺ μάγοι ἀπὸ ἀνατολῶν παρεγένοντο εἰς Ἱεροσόλυμα*	Amma da Isa akahaifasa tšikin Bethlehem garin Yuda lokatši da Herod sariki ne, duba, masuwayo mutane sun fito gabas ga Yerusalem.	amma Isu da aká-haifa-sa tšikí-n Betláhamu garí-n Yūda lattu-n sorkí-n Horōda dūba mótane mā̈su-wāyo sūna fitō daga gabbas sūna tafía ga Algúddusa.
2) *λέγοντες· Ποῦ ἐστιν ὁ τεχθεὶς βασιλεὺς τῶν Ἰουδαίων; εἴδομεν γὰρ αὐτοῦ τὸν ἀστέρα ἐν τῇ ἀνατολῇ, καὶ ἤλθομεν προσκυνῆσαι αὐτῷ.*	Sun yi tambaya: enna šiko haifaši sabo Sarikin Yahudawa, don mun ganni tamrarunsa daga gabas, mun zakka mu yi addua garesa?	sū-na yi mágana (na ši-kō serkí-n yehudaua wó-no aká-haifa-sá, doṅg mūn-gani temrāro-n-sa daga gabbas da mun-zakka doṅg mu-nyī ma-sá girma (mu-nyī afū garé-sa S. 74, N. 10).
3) *Ἀκούσας δὲ ὁ βασιλεὺς Ἡρῴδης ἐταράχθη, καὶ πᾶσα Ἱεροσόλυμα μετ' αὐτοῦ,*	Herod, sariki, da ya ši wonnan ya ši giatšin sutšia, ši da mutane duka na Yerusalem taro daši.	amma sorkí-n Horōda da ya-ši labāri n wo-nan sū-tšia-n-sa yá-tašo da garí-n Algúddusa dukkan-ta tarō da-ši.
4) *καὶ συναγαγὼν πάντας τοὺς ἀρχιερεῖς καὶ γραμματεῖς τοῦ λαοῦ ἐπυνθάνετο παρ' αὐτῶν ποῦ ὁ χριστὸς γεννᾶται.*	Da ya tara mainya mallamai duka, da marubutan mutane, ya tambayesu: enna wuri za ahaifua Kristu?	da ya-tāra babá-n mallemai da mā̈su-kárātū dukka-nsū da ya-tambēa sū urí-nda Kristu zā a-haifua-sa.
5) *Οἱ δὲ εἶπον αὐτῷ· Ἐν Βηθλεὲμ τῆς Ἰουδαίας· οὕτως γὰρ γέγραπται διὰ τοῦ προφήτου,*	Sunka amsa masa: tšikin Bethlehem, garin Yuda, don anrubutaši daga hanun Anabi,	amma sū sun-ka amsa ma-sá: tšikí-n Betláhamu kása-n Yūda dō, doṅg hákkanan an-rúbutū ši-kē dagá hanú-n Annábi,
6) *καὶ σὺ Βηθλεὲμ γῆ Ἰούδα, οὐδαμῶς ἐλαχίστη εἶ ἐν τοῖς ἡγεμόσιν Ἰούδα· ἐκ σοῦ γὰρ ἐξελεύσεται ἡγούμενος, ὅστις ποιμανεῖ τὸν λαόν μου τὸν Ἰσραήλ.*	Kai Bethlehem garin Yuda, kai ba kankane ba tšikin gunin Yuda, don daga gareka ši fito sariki maikiwon mutane Israel.	da kī Betláhamu tšikí-n kása-n Yūda kī bá káramí ba tsaká-n mā̈su-girma-n Yūda, doṅg dagà garē-ki ši-fitō serkí mai-kīvo-n mótanē-nā, mótane-n Israēla.
7) *Τότε Ἡρῴδης λάθρᾳ καλέσας τοὺς μάγους, ἠκρίβωσεν παρ' αὐτῶν τὸν χρόνον τοῦ φαινομένου ἀστέρος,*	Sannan Herod da ya kirra masuwayo gboye, ya tambayesu kwarei, yaušo sunka ganni tamraru.	sa nan Horōda da ya-kirra mā̈su-wāyo bōya-n mótane ši-na tambēa-sū koró lattu-nda temrāro wó-nan anga-nō-sī.
8) *καὶ πέμψας αὐτοὺς εἰς Βηθλεὲμ εἶπεν· Πορευθέντες ἐξετάσατε ἀκριβῶς περὶ τοῦ παιδίου· ἐπὰν δὲ εὕρητε, ἀπαγγείλατέ μοι, ὅπως κἀγὼ ἐλθὼν προσκυνήσω αὐτῷ.*	Da ya aikesu ga Bethlehem, ya tše, ku taši, ku yi bidda kwarei ga ďariri, en kun gamsa, ku dawoyo, ku kawo mani labari, don en taši, en yi addua garesa.	da ya-aiko sū ulō-n Betláhamu da ya-tšē da-sū kú-taši kū-ko-bidda séggari sà-badan wó-nan ďarili, amma en kun-sāmo ši, ku-kau me-nī labāri-nsa doṅg nī komā nī-taši da i-nyī ma-sá girma.
9) *Οἱ δὲ ἀκούσαντες τοῦ βασιλέως ἐπορεύθησαν. Καὶ ἰδοὺ ὁ ἀστήρ, ὃν εἶδον ἐν*	Amma da sunka ši magnan sariki sun taši, duba, tamraru da suka ganni gabas, ya taši	amma sū da sún-ka-ši mágana-n serkí sún-taši. da sūna tafía dūba temrāro wo-nda

τῇ ἀνατολῇ, προῆγεν αὐτοὺς ἕως ἐλθὼν ἐστάθη ἐπάνω οὗ ἦν τὸ παιδίον·	gabas garesu, har ya zakka, ya dasaya warin da šariri ši ke.	sin-ganó-ai dagá gabbra ši ši-ua talia kabá garó-sū har ši-na zakka sí-na-tanya dagá bisan urí-n-da šarili wo-nan ši-ke.
10) ἰδόντες δὲ τὸν ἀστέρα ἐχάρησαν χαρὰν μεγάλην σφόδρα,	Da sunka ga tamraru sun yi murna da baba murna.	da sū temráro wo-nan an-ganó-ši sun-yi babá n murna kere.
11) καὶ ἐλθόντες εἰς τὴν οἰκίαν, εἶδον τὸ παιδίον μετὰ Μαρίας τῆς μητρὸς αὐτοῦ, καὶ πεσόντες προσεκύνησαν αὐτῷ καὶ ἀνοίξαντες τοὺς θησαυροὺς αὐτῶν προσήνεγκαν αὐτῷ δῶρα, χρυσὸν καὶ λίβανον καὶ σμύρναν.	Da sun šigga gidda, sun ga šariri, da Miriam uwasa, sun rusuna, suna sidoansa, da sunka buda kayansu, sun baši kauta, sinaria da turare da mirma.	da sun-šigga gída da ain-ganó šarili tare da wā-sa Miriám da sun-yi duhaúa da afli garé-sa da an-buda kaya-nsū sun-ba-ši kiautá, sinária da túrare da alwordi.
12) Καὶ χρηματισθέντες κατ' ὄναρ μὴ ἀνακάμψαι πρὸς Ἡρῴδην, δι' ἄλλης ὁδοῦ ἀνεχώρησαν εἰς τὴν χώραν αὐτῶν.	Da sūforosu da mafalki, kada su koma ga Herod sun taš garinsu ga wota hainya.	da an-rike-sū da má-falki hadda sū-kóme uǎó-n Heróda sū-na dauǒo tšikí n garí-n-sū ga wó-ta hana dobám.
13) Ἀναχωρησάντων δὲ αὐτῶν, ἰδοὺ ἄγγελος κυρίου κατ' ὄναρ ἐφάνη τῷ Ἰωσὴφ λέγων Ἐγερθεὶς παράλαβε τὸ παιδίον καὶ τὴν μητέρα αὐτοῦ, καὶ φεῦγε εἰς Αἴγυπτον, καὶ ἴσθι ἐκεῖ ἕως ἂν εἴπω σοι· μέλλει γὰρ Ἡρῴδης ζητεῖν τὸ παιδίον, τοῦ ἀπολέσαι αὐτό.	Amma da sunka taši, duba, Malaikin Alla ya gudda ma Yusufu da mafalki, yatše, taši, dauki šariri da uwasa, ka guddu ga Egipt, ka zamna tšan har enkao labari, don Herod šina nema šariri nan ši kaššioši.	amma da sun-ka taši dūba Malaiki n Alla ya-godda ga Yūsufu da má-falki da ya-tše ma-sá táši kai da káma žarili da wā-sa da ká-gudu uǎó n Mísera da zamna tšan har íno kau ma-ká labāri, dong Heróda ší-na néma žarili ši-na sū ši kašé-ai.
14) ὁ δὲ ἐγερθεὶς παρέλαβε τὸ παιδίον καὶ τὴν μητέρα αὐτοῦ νυκτὸς καὶ ἀνεχώρησεν εἰς Αἴγυπτον,	Amma da ya taši ya dauki šariri da uwansa dadere, ya taš ga Egipt.	amma ši da ya-táši ya-kāma žarili-nsa da wā-sa dá deré da yá-tafi garó Mísera.
15) καὶ ἦν ἐκεῖ ἕως τῆς τελευτῆς Ἡρῴδου, ἵνα πληρωθῇ τὸ ῥηθὲν ὑπὸ κυρίου διὰ τοῦ προφήτου λέγοντος Ἐξ Αἰγύπτου ἐκάλεσα τὸν υἱόν μου.	Nan ya zamna, har mutuan Herod, hakkanan akatšitšika magana Obangiši, da Anabi ya tše: daga Egipt na kirrawo dana.	tšan ya-zamna har lattu-n mútun-n Heróda dong ši-tšika mágana n Olu-n-giži-n Alla da bakí-n Annábi wo-ne ší-na fadda· daga tšikí-n Mísera ni na-kirra da-na.
16) τότε Ἡρῴδης ἰδὼν ὅτι ἐνεπαίχθη ὑπὸ τῶν μάγων, ἐθυμώθη λίαν καὶ ἀποστείλας ἀνεῖλεν πάντας τοὺς παῖδας τοὺς ἐν Βηθλεὲμ καὶ ἐν πᾶσι τοῖς ὁρίοις αὐτῆς ἀπὸ διετοῦς	Nanan Herod da ya ga masuwayo mutane suna yi masa munafutši, ya yi haban fuši, ya aike, ya kaššie yaya duka, woddanda ke tšikin Bethlehem, dian šiekaru biu,	sa nan Heróda da yá-gani másu-wāyo mútane da sun-yi ma-sá munáfetši šina-yi fūši kері da šíma-aiko mútane da ši-na kašé yāya tšikí n Bethlehem da tšikí n kasa-nsa duk-ka wodá-nda sun-tšika šekaru biu da wodá-nde ba sun-

καὶ κατωτέρω, κατὰ τὸν χρόνον ὃν ἠκρίβωσεν παρὰ τῶν μάγων.	da woddanda ba su tšika šiekaru biu ba.	tšīka bá tókonā dukka-nañ da ší-na yī háñhali da lattu n wo-nda ya-tambōs daga māsu-wāyo.
17) *τότε ἐπληρώθη τὸ ῥηθὲν διὰ Ἱερεμίου τοῦ προφήτου λέγοντος*	Sannan akatšika magana wodda akafaddi ga Yeremi anabi, ya tše:	saa nan a-ka-tšīka mágana wo-nda a-ka-faddi bakí-n Yeremia Annábi wó-no ší-na tšē
18) *Φωνὴ ἐν Ῥαμᾶ ἠκούσθη, θρῆνος καὶ κλαυθμὸς καὶ ὀδυρμὸς πολύς, Ῥαχὴλ κλαίουσα τὰ τέκνα αὐτῆς, καὶ οὐκ ἤθελεν παρακληθῆναι, ὅτι οὐκ εἰσίν.*	Tšikiu Rama muria akaši, tausai, da kuka, da luwaye, da baban tukaba: Rahel tana kuka, don yayanta, ta ki hañkuri, don ba su ba.	múria tšikí-n Rama á-kaži da kūka da babá n tukāba(?) Rahel tá-na kūka doñg yāyanta, da tā-ki háñkuri doñg sū sún-mutu.
19) *τελευτήσαντος δὲ τοῦ Ἡρῴδου, ἰδοὺ ἄγγελος κυρίου φαίνεται κατ' ὄναρ τῷ Ἰωσὴφ ἐν Αἰγύπτῳ,*	Amma da Herod ya mutu Malaikin Alla ya gulda ma Yosufu da mafalki tšikin gari Egipt,	amma Herōda da yá-mutu dūba Malaíki n Alla ší-na godda ga Yúsufu da máfalki tšikí n kásan Mímera.
20) *λέγων Ἐγερθεὶς παράλαβε τὸ παιδίον καὶ τὴν μητέρα αὐτοῦ, καὶ πορεύου εἰς γῆν Ἰσραήλ· τεθνήκασιν γὰρ οἱ ζητοῦντες τὴν ψυχὴν τοῦ παιδίου.*	ya tše, taši, dauki yariri, da uwasa, tafi ga gari Israel, don su mutu, woddanda su ke bidda rain yariri.	ší-na faddá ma-sá, tāší da kāma yáro-ñka tare da wā-sa da tafi tšikí-n kāsa n Israéla, doñg sū sán-mutu wo-dá-nda sū-ko bidda sún-kašš yāroñ-ka.
21) *ὁ δὲ ἐγερθεὶς παρέλαβεν τὸ παιδίον καὶ τὴν μητέρα αὐτοῦ, καὶ εἰσῆλθεν εἰς γῆν Ἰσραήλ.*	amma da ya taši, ya dauki yariri, da uwasa, ya zakka gari Israel.	amma šī da ya-tāši yadauki žatlli-nsa tarō da wā-sa, da ya-žigga kāsa-n Israel.
22) *ἀκούσας δὲ ὅτι Ἀρχέλαος βασιλεύει τῆς Ἰουδαίας ἀντὶ τοῦ πατρὸς αὐτοῦ Ἡρῴδου, ἐφοβήθη ἐκεῖ ἀπελθεῖν· χρηματισθεὶς δὲ κατ' ὄναρ ἀνεχώρησεν εἰς τὰ μέρη τῆς Γαλιλαίας,*	amma da ya ši Arkelaus šina tšin sarautu ga Yuda, wurin Herod, ubansa, ya ši dsoro zua wuri nan, amma aiiforwa da mafalki ya širikidda wañion Galili.	amma da ya-žī labāri-n Arkelān da ya-bī Herōda obánsa tšikí a sa-rauta-n Yūda ya-žī tsorō da yāki sūa-n urī nan da an-riko da má falki yá-tai? nšō-n Galili.
23) *καὶ ἐλθὼν κατῴκησεν εἰς πόλιν λεγομένην Ναζαρέθ, ὅπως πληρωθῇ τὸ ῥηθὲν διὰ τῶν προφητῶν, ὅτι Ναζωραῖος κληθήσεται.*	da ya zakka, ya samun gari da akekirra Nazareth; bakkana akatšika, magana Anabi en kirrawoši dan Nazarim.	da ya-zakka, ya-samna garí-n wo-nda sūná-nsa Nazarétha, doñg a-ka-tšīka mágana-n Annabaua sū súna kirra-šī ba-Názare.

Sammlung und Bearbeitung
Central-Afrikanischer Vokabularien

von

Heinrich Barth.

Zweite Abtheilung.

Einleitung, Kap. 7—12. Analyse der Fulfúlde-, Soṅyai-, Lógonē-, Wándalá-, Bágrimma- und Mába-Sprachen.

Collection

of

vocabularies of Central-African languages

compiled and analysed

by

Henry Barth, C. B. D. C. L.

2d part.

Introductory Remarks, chapter 7—12.

Analysis of the Fulfúlde-, Soṅyai-, Lógone-, Wándala-, Bágrimma- and Maba-languages.

Gotha: Justus Perthes.

1863.

Siebentes Kapitel.

Die Pūl- oder Ful-fúl-de-Sprache: bolī-de Ful-fúl-de.

Ich muss vorerst Einiges über den Namen sagen.

Die Grundform ist pūl, p̃ūl, „hellbraun", „roth", im Gegensatz zu olof, „schwarz" (w-olof, y-olof), indem die beiden am Senegal zusammen wohnenden Stämme der Fulbe und Wolof ein gewisses verwandtschaftliches Verhältniss zu einander haben; Sing. pūl-o, d. h. „er Pūl", Plur. pūl-be, p̃ūl-be, d. h. „sie Pūl"; das Adjektiv eigentlich pūl-de oder p̃ūl-de, mit Wiederholung, um den ganzen Eigenschaftscharakter auszudrücken pūl-pūl-de, p̃ūl-p̃ūl-de, ful-fúl-de. — fulah, welche Namensform auffallender Weise selbst der Missionar Reichardt gebraucht und seinen Arbeiten zum Titel gibt, ist die bei den von uns so genannten Mandingo übliche Form des Namens und dem Charakter der Sprache selbst widersprechend. Über die Hausa-Form Féllani und die Kanúri-Form Fellāta brauche ich hier nach dem anderswo Gesagten nichts mehr zu sagen. bolī-de ist der Plural von wolí-nde, „Wort, Idiom".

Über den in meinem Vokabular hauptsächlich vertretenen Dialekt dieser weit verbreiteten und im Glossar je nach den verschiedenen Provinzen sehr abweichenden Sprache habe ich schon hinreichend in einem früheren Kapitel S. XX gesprochen. Hier muss ich nur die in Bezug auf den in Fúmbina oder Adamaua gesprochenen Dialekt S. X gemachte Bemerkung dahin berichtigen, dass doch manche der in den von mir bereisten Landschaften nur dort üblichen Ausdrücke schon nach den wenigen Vergleichungspunkten, die Reichardt's A-B-C-Buch bietet, sich als durchaus nationalen Ursprungs erweisen, so dass doch wol jener Dialekt zur richtigen Erkenntniss dieses ganzen weiten Sprachgebietes eine besondere Berücksichtigung verdienen mag. Hier führe ich folgende Beispiele einer Übereinstimmung zwischen den von mir in der Provinz Fúmbina am Benue niedergeschriebenen und der geringen

Chapter the seventh.

The Pūl- or Ful-fúl-de-language: bolī-de Ful-fúl-de.

I first must make a few remarks with regard to the name.

The root is pūl, p̃ūl, meaning „light-brown", „red" in opposition to the term olof (w-olof, y-olof) which means „black", the two tribes of the Fulbe and Wolof being related to a certain degree. From the root pūl the singular is formed pūl-o, i. q. „he Pūl", and the plural pūl-be, p̃ūl-be, i. q. „they Pūl". The original form of the adjective is pūl-de or p̃ūl-de, from whence by repetition, in order to express the whole character pūl-pūl-de, p̃ūl-p̃ūl-de, ful-fúl-de has been formed. — The name fulah which, to my great astonishment, even the Rev. Reichardt has chosen to prefix as title to his labours, is the form usual with the Mandingoes, and is entirely foreign to the language itself. With regard to the other forms of this name, Féllani which is peculiar to the Hausa, and Fellāta which is peculiar to the Kanúri-language, I need not say here any thing more about them. As for the term bolī-de, it is the plural from wolí-nde, meaning „word, idiom".

This language being spread at present over a vast territory, and the dialects spoken in the different provinces varying greatly, at least with regard to their glossary, I have already pointed out above p. XXI the dialect principally represented in my collection. In this place I have only to correct the observation made p. XI with regard to the dialect spoken in the province of Fúmbina or Adamawa by stating, that several terms not used, and even not known in the other provinces occupied by the Ful-race, except in that of Adamawa, by a closer examination of even the very scanty glossary given in Rev. Reichardt's Primer, turn out to be of totally national make. I therefore recommend an accurate study of the dialect spoken in the province of Fúmbina as being essential to a correct acquaintance with this vast linguistic

territory, and I here adduce the following three instances of a radical relation between my Fúl-terms written down in the province of Fúmbina on the Bénuwe, and those terms given by Reichardt as belonging to the dialect spoken in Fūta-Džālo:

„knee" . .	in Fúmbina	fáfe-ru . .	with Reichardt		kūpe.
„backside" .	„	féru-ru . .	„	„	wōru.
„lithām" .	„	pétalal . .	„	„	mēdelol.

In these instances we find the same root, but a great change produced in consequence of the consonants having been exchanged against others of a related character, and in two cases moreover the termination ru, which we have to subject further on to a more scrupulous consideration, having been added to the root in the dialect spoken in the province of Fúmbina.

As I am just speaking of Reichardt's Primer I will at once make here the remark, that in many cases he exhibits contracted forms where I have the longer ones, thus

„finger"	in my vocabulary	hóhondu,	in Reichardt's Primer	hondu,
„fingers", pl.	„ „	kóholi	„ „	kōli,
„ear" . .	„ „	nófuru	„ „	nōru,
„cutlass" .	„ „	káfohi	„ „	kāfa,
„beard" .	„ „	wáharo	„ „	wāro,
„heart" .	„ „	bérende	„ „	berde.
„scorpion"	„ „	yáharo	„ „	yāro.

In the second instance there is a considerable difference between my own writing and that of Rev. Reichardt's with regard to the dž and tš, he writing generally a dz or dž, where I have tš, as for instance R. dzęlu, I tšōdu, „dry"; R. dzobal, I tšóbal, „bread"; R. daūdi, I tšūdi, plur. of sūdo, „house"; R. bedžo, I hōtšo, „ribs"; R. pudžu, I putšu, „horse"; R. džurki, I tšúrroki, „smoke".

Besides, the Rev. Reichardt often uses the nasal ṅ, where I have m, as, for instance, he writes

landaṅ, „salt", instead of my . . . . . . lamdam,
nebaṅ, „butter" (fresh), instead of my . . nébam,
kainaṅ, „(boiled) butter", instead of my . . kainādam,

the latter instance exhibiting moreover a contracted form.

I also remark, that Rev. Reichardt, and not without some reason, as it would seem, distinguishes between ḍ and d, as, for instance, he writes huḍo instead of my hūdo, „grass"; however in the vulgar idiom of various provinces such a distinction could not be carried through. I will only add, that most of the above mentioned divergencies, as proceeding from dialectical differences, are confirmed by the few specimens given by Rev. Koelle in his Polyglotta, which are likewise taken from the dialect of Fūta Džālo.

I now shall try to reduce to some general principles, and to join under different heads the manifold grammatical features represented by this language, considering, however, only my own material, and not what has been occasionally published elsewhere, the greater part of which is far from being reliable.

I begin with arranging systematically those letters, which in different forms of the same word are interchanged against each other, a change which it is well for any body not to leave out of sight from the first moment when he begins to study this language.

b in w: bodžol, plur. woddžo-re, „hare"; bodō-džo, plur. wodé-bo, „the red (man)";
d in r: débo, plur. rauhe, „woman"; dommó-wo, plur. rem mō-be, „husbandman";
f in p: fa-ndu, plur. pā-li, „watermelon";
g in w: gor-ko, plur. wor-be, „woman"; gā-džo, plur. wuj-be, „thief";
g in y: gimmō-wo, plur. yimmō-be, „drummer";
h in f: ho-ndu, plur. fō-li, „pigeon"; h in g: hite-re, plur. gite, „eye";

h in k: hódo-re, Plur. kōdo, „Stern"; mé-dō hókku, „ich gebe", hokku mā, „gebt uns"; h in tš: mé-dō hebbi, „ich finde", Plur. min-tšebbi, „wir finden";
k in h: kéfer-o, Pl. héfer-be, „Heide"; kā-do, Pl. hā-be; kor-do, hor-be, „Sklavin";
p in f: paš-o, Plur. fam-be, „Jüngling"; pipí-do, Plur. fiff-be, „Schütze";
r in d: mé-dō-rāra, „ich sehe", dār-de, „sehet"; rūl-de, Plur. dūl-e, „Wolke";
s in tš: mé-dō sōdi, „ich kaufe", min-tšōdi, „wir kaufen"; sebā-re: tšebō-dže, „Brunnen";
tš in s: tšūdum, Plur. sūdi, „Leichnam"; tšoi-do, Plur. soi-bo, „Bettler" u. s. w.;
tš in si: tšūto, Plur. siūtu-be, „Zwillinge";
w in b: wam-de, „Berg", Plur. bam-le;
in g: me-wōdi, 2te Pers. Plur. onom gōdi; walādu, Plur. galādi, „Horn"; wúnduwo, „Flusstiefe", Plur. gundúppe;
y in dž: yáha-re, Plur. džébe, „Skorpion"; y in g: yená-ụde, Plur. genā-li, „Grab".

1. *Das persönliche Fürwort.*

	Singular.		Plural.	
1ste Pers.	kurze Form me,	volle Form meñg;	kurze Form min,	volle Form ménoñg*),
2te „	„ „ a	„ „ añg	„ „ ono	„ „ ónoma,
3te „	„ „ o	„ „ kañ-ko	„ „ be	„ „ kam-be.

Ich gehe nun die Abwandelung mit Einschluss des Pronomen Possessivum, das sich eng daran schliesst.

1ste Person Sing., Accusativ mi:
añg á-da-ı mi, „du liebst mich",
kañ-ko o-mo-fiye mi, „er schlägt mich";
1ste Person Sing., Dativ und Genitiv und possessive Form am (á-me):
hokk(u) am, „gib mir", well am, „hilf mir",
añg a-da-ramtšo to am, „du leihest von mir, das Meinige",
me hōre am, „ich (mit) mein(em) Kopf(e)", „ich selbst",
gelōba am, „mein Kameel, gelōdi am, „meine Kameele";
1ste Person Plur., Dativ und Accusativ mā:
hokku mā, „gib uns",
onom odon-gidi mā, „ihr liebt uns",
(Variante mai wol nur in Folge der Aussprache onom on-fiyo mai, „ihr schlagt uns");
1ste Person Plur., Genitiv und possessive Form ammiñg (á-miñg):
kam-be be-dō ramtšo to ammiñg, „sie leihen von uns, das Unsrige",
ménoñg hōre ammiñg, „wir (mit) unseren Köpfen, wir selbst",
gelōba ammiñg, „unser Kameel; gelōdi ammiñg, „unsere Kameele";
2te Person Sing., Dativ, Genitiv, Accusativ und possessive Form mā:
mé-dō hokku ma, „ich gebe dir",
kañ-ko ó-mo-ı ma, „er liebt dich",
mé-dō ramtšo to ma (oder ho-mū), „ich leihe von dir, das Deinige",
añg hōre ma, „du mit dein(em) Kopf, du selbst",
gelōba ma, „dein Kameel"; gelōdi ma (oder mā-da?), „deine Kameele".

Ich hatte lange Zeit das erwähnte mā-da für eine vollere Form der 2ten Person Plur. des Pronomen Possessivum gehalten, aber sie scheint mir sehr zweifelhaft und besteht wol nur aus der der einfachen Form mā angehängten fragenden Partikel da. Vielleicht hat auch das vorhergehende di darauf eingewirkt; jedenfalls hat sie nichts mit dem Plural zu thun.

*) ménoñg. Die Nebenform ónoṅe ist wahrscheinlich später eingeschoben.

h in k: hóde-re, plur. kōde, „star"; „mé-dō hókku. „I give", kokku mē, „give us"; h in tš: mé-dō hobbi, „I find", plur. min-tšebbi, „we find";
k in h: kéfer-o, pl. héfor-be, „pagan"; kā-do, pl. hā-be; kor-do, pl. hor-be, „female slave";
p in f: pañ-o, plur. fam-bo, „youth"; pipí-do, plur. fiff-be, „bowman";
r in d: mé-dō-rāra, „I see", dār-de, „see"; rūl-de, plur. dūl-e, „cloud";
s in tš: mé-dō sōdi, „I buy", plur. min-tšādi; sebō-ro: tšebō-dže, „well";
tš in s: tšādum, plur. sādi, „corpse"; tšoi-do, plur. soi-be, „beggar";
tš in si: tšūto, plur. siūtu-be, „twins";
w in b: wam-de, „mount", plur. bam-le;
in g: me-wōdi, „I do", 2nd person plur. onom gōdi; walādu, „horn", plur. galādi; wúnduwe, „depth of river", plur. gundúppe;
y in dž: yáha-re, plur. džehe, „scorpion"; y in g: yend-ude, „tomb", plur. geuš-li.

1. *The personal pronoun.*

	singular.		plural.	
1st person,	short form me,	full form mońg;	short form min,	full form mónoṅg [1]),
2nd „	„ „ a	„ „ añg	„ „ ono	„ „ ónoma,
3rd „	„ „ o	„ „ kaṅ-ko	„ „ bē	„ „ kam-be.

I now give the cases, with which the forms of the possessive pronoun are intimately related.

1st person sing. accusative case: mi:
 añg á-da-ī mi, „thou lovest me",
 kaṅ-ko o-mo-fīye mi, „he beats me";

1st person sing. dative and genitive case, as well as the form of the possessive pronoun: am (á-mo):
 hokk(u) am, „give me", well am, „help me", „assist me",
 añg a-da-ramtšo to am, „thou lendest from me, lendest (what is) mine",
 me hōro am, „I (by) my head", „I myself",
 gelōba am, „my camel; gelōdi am, „my camels";

1st person plur. dative and accusative case: mē:
 hokku mē, „give us",
 onom odon-gidi mē, „you love us",
 (the form mai in the phrase onom om-fiye mai, „you beat us" is perhaps only a slight change of pronunciation);

1st person plur. genitive case, and possessive pronoun: amming (á-miṅg):
 kam-be bo-dō ramtšo to amming, „they lend from us, what is ours",
 mónong hōro ammiṅg, „we (by) our heads, we ourselves",
 gelōba ammiṅg, „our camel"; gelōdi ammiṅg, „our camels";

2nd person sing. genitive, dative, accusative, as well as possessive form: mā:
 mó-dō hokku mā, „I give thee",
 kaṅ-ko ó-mo-ī ma, „he likes thee",
 mé-dō ramtšo to mā (or ho-mā), „I lend from thee, what is thine",
 ang hōre ma, „thou (by) thy head", „thou thyself",
 gelōba mā, „thy camel"; gelōdi ma (or mā-da?), „thy camels".

With regard to this form mā-da, I have to remark, that it does not appear to be a characteristic form of the plural, but seems to be only called forth by the preceding syllable di in gelōdi, if it is not merely a sign of interrogation, as I shall have occasion to show further on. Thus „thy horses" is simply putši ma.

[1]) The other form ánone which occurs besides mó[illegible]óng, if correct, is evidently of later origin.

2te Person Plur., Dativ yō:

kam-bo kokki yō, „sie haben euch gegeben";

2te Person Plur., Accusativ ong:

kam-bo e-ben-gidi ong, „sie lieben euch",

kam-bo bo-fly(e) ong, „sie schlagen euch";

2te Person Plur., Genitiv und possessive Form me-ong:

ménon mé-dong ramtšo to me-ong, „wir leihen von euch, das Eurige",

ónom(e) höre me-ong, „ihr mit eurem Kopfe, ihr selbst",

golōba me-ong, „euer Kameel"; golōdi me-ong, „eure Kameele";

3te Person Sing., Dativ und Accusativ mō:

hokku mō, „gib ihm, ihr",

mé-dō idi mō, „ich liebe ihn, sie;

3te Person Sing., Genitiv und possessive Form mā-ko:

mé-dō ramtšo ho mā-ko, „ich leihe von ihm, ihr, das seinige, ihrige",

kańko höre mā-ko, „er (sie) mit sein(em) (ihrem) Kopf"; er, sie selbst,

golōba mā-ko, „sein, ihr Kameel", golōdi mā-ko, „seine, ihre Kameele";

3te Person Plur., Dativ dō:

kokkō dō, „gebt ihnen";

3te Person Plur., Accusativ bō:

ménong ménon-gidi bō, „wir lieben sie",

ménong ménon-flyo bō, „wir schlagen sie";

3te Person Plur., Genitiv und possessive Form mā-bō:

onom o-dō ramtšo to mā-bō, „ihr leihet von ihnen, das Ihrige",

golōba mā-bō, „ihr Kameel"; golōdi mā-bō, „ihre Kameele";

kam-bo höre mā-bō, „sie mit ihrem Kopfe, sie selbst".

So gewinnen wir also folgendes Schema des persönlichen Fürwortes:

Singular.

mo, meng, „ich" .	a, ang, „du" . . .	o, kań-ko, „er, sie",
am, „von mir, mein", [meine"	mā, „von dir, dein, deine"	mā-ko, „von ihm, ihr; sein, ihr, seine, ihre",
am, „mir"	mā, „dir"	mō, „ihm, ihr",
mo, „mich"	mā, „dich"	mō, „ihn, sie".

Plural.

min, ménong, „wir"	ono, ónoma, „ihr"	bō, kam-bo, „sie",
amming, „von uns, unser, unsere" . .	me-ong, „von euch, euer, eure" . . .	mā-bō, „von ihnen, ihr, ihre",
mē, „uns"	yō, „euch"	dō, „ihnen",
mē, „uns"	ong, „euch" . . .	bō, „sie".

Für das unbestimmte und demonstrative Fürwort kann ich auf das Wörterverzeichniss S. 6 ff. selbst verweisen; auffallend ist mo vor dum, „dies" in vielen der Phrasen S. 122 f.

2. *Zahlwörter.*

In Betreff der Zahlwörter will ich ausser den einzelnen Punkten, die ich zu den betreffenden Ausdrücken in den Noten berührt habe und was ich am Ende dieses Kapitels über einige verwandtschaftliche Verhältnisse sagen werde, hier nur folgenden Umstand berühren.

gō (ko), „eins" scheint mir die monosyllabe Wurzel von kóheli, „Finger", dšō, „fünf" — die Form dšō-i ist, wie ich weiter unten ausführen werde, verbal — ist unzweifelhaft die Wurzel von dašúgo (d. h. dšū-u-gō, „eine Fünf", d. h. „Hand", Plural oder Dual dšunde).

2nd person plur., dative case: yō:

kam-be kokki yō, „they give you";

2nd person plur., accusative case: oṅg:

kam-be e-ben-gidi oṅg, „they like you",

kam-be be-fly(e) oṅg, „they beat you";

2nd person plur., genitive case as well as possessive form: mo-oṅg:

mónon móduṅg-ramtōo to me-oṅg, „we lend from you, what is yours",

ónom(a) hōro me-oṅg, „you (by) your head, you yourselves",

golōba me-oṅg, „your camel"; golōdi me-oṅg, „your camels";

3rd person sing., dative and accusative case: mō:

hokku mō, „give him, her",

mé-dō idí mō, „I like him, her";

3rd person sing., genitive case and possessive form mā-ko:

mé-dō ramtōo ho mā-ko, „I lend from him, her, what is his, hers",

kaṅko hōro mā-ko, „he (she) by his (her) head",

golōba mā-ko, „his, her camel"; golōdi mā-ko, „his, her camels";

3rd person plur., dative case: dō:

kokkō dō, „give them";

3rd person plur., accusative case: bē:

mónoṅg mónon-gidi bē, „we do like them",

mónoṅg mónon-flye bē, „we do beat them";

3rd person plur., genitive case as well as possessive pronoun mā-bē:

onom o-dō ramtōo to mā-bē, „you lend from them, theirs",

golōba mā-bē, „their camel"; golōdi mā-bē, „their camels",

kam-be hōro mā-bē, „they (by) their head, they themselves".

Thus we obtain the following scheme of the pronominal forms:

Singular.

me, moṅg, „I" . .	a, aṅg, „thou" . .	o, kaṅ-ko, „he, she",
am, „of me, mine" .	mā, „of thee, thine"	mā-ko, „of him, her; his, hers",
am, „me, to me" . .	mā, „thee, to thee"	mō, „him, her, to him, to her",
mo, „me"	mā, „thee"	mō, „him, her".

Plural.

min, mónoṅg, „we"	ono, ónoma, „you"	bō, kam-be, „they",
ammiṅg, „of us, our"	mo-oṅg, „of you, your"	mā-bē, „of them, theirs",
mō, „us, to us" . .	yō, „you, to you" .	dō, „to them",
mē, „us"	oṅg, „you"	bē, „them".

As for the forms of the indefinite and demonstrative pronoun I may refer the reader to the relative pages of the vocabulary (p. 6), as I have not to offer any observation as to the grammatical character of that part of speech. I only point out the mo before dum, „this" p. 122 ff.

2. *Numerals.*

With regard to the numerals, besides the remarks which I shall have to offer in connection with each of the terms concerned, and a few observations at the end of this chapter I here will only point out the following facts.

gō (ko), „one" seems to me to be the original root of the term kóheli, „finger", while dūō, „five" — dūō-i is the verbal form as I shall have occasion to show further on — is beyond the least doubt the root of dūṅgo (i. q. duū-n-gō, „one five (fingers)", „the hand", plur. dūūde, this latter being properly a dual form.

Von „fünf" bis „zehn" gilt das Fünfsystem „fünf und ein" u. s. w. und stimmen sie hierin vollkommen mit den Berbern überein [1]), während fast alle jetzt im Tropischen Afrika sie umgebenden Völkerschaften davon abweichen, mit Ausnahme der verwandten Wolof; für „zehn" aber hat die Sprache den selbstständig gebildeten Ausdruck sappo, und nun finden wir den höchst merkwürdigen Umstand, dass das Fúl für die Zahlen über „zwanzig" die beiden Zählungsweisen nach Zehnern und Zwanzigern hat, z. B. 30 tšappánde (Plur. von sappo) táti, „drei Zehner" und lasso e sappo, „zwanzig und zehn"; von den Vierzigern an aber fand ich in den von mir bereisten ausgedehnten Landschaften des Fúl-Stammes sogar drei Ausdrücke, z. B. 50 tšappánde džo-i, „fünf Zehner", lassō-dži d(di e sappo, „zwei Zwanziger und zehn" und tobō-dži d(di e sappo, gleichfalls bedeutend „zwei Zwanziger und zehn". Die letzte, in Másina gebräuchliche Form ist sehr interessant, da die Bewohner dieses Landes den weiter im Westen üblichen, mir nur durch Reichardt's Angabe bekannt gewordenen Ausdruck tobe, die Einheit von tobō-dži, für 20 selbst, so viel ich erfahren, gar nicht gebrauchen, sondern dafür nogai sagen, eine andere Form des weiter östlich üblichen nogás, das wiederum seinerseits keine Mehrheit zu bilden scheint.

Auch nach meiner bestimmten Ansicht, die ich schon bei Gelegenheit des Hausa-Ausdruckes hauya geäussert habe, ist das Zahlsystem nach Zwanzigern, als Finger und Zehen von Hand und Fuss zusammen begreifend, älter, als das nach Zehnern, eine Ansicht, für die ich auch den dieser Sprachverhältnisse Kundigsten, Herrn Prof. Pott, zum Gewährsmann habe.

temerre, der Ausdruck für 100 im Fúl, ist wahrscheinlich der Wolof-Sprache entlehnt; zombur dagegen, der gewöhnlichste Ausdruck für 1000, ist der Sonyai-Sprache entlehnt.

3. *Das Zeitwort.*

Von der Ausbildung des Zeitwortes im Fúl giebt mein Material nicht eben mannichfaltige Formen an die Hand; neben dem Imperativ und Particip kann ich nur vollständige Paradigmen von einem die dauernde Handlung darstellenden Präsens, so wie von einer Art Aorist geben, beide mit entsprechender negativer Form.

a) Die gegenwärtige Zeit wird gebildet, indem man zwischen das einfache Fürwort und die infinitive Form des Zeitwortes die Hülfszeitform dō einschiebt. Dies verbale dō ist unzweifelhaft dasselbe dō, was das Wort bondō (bo-n-dō, von bo = te, „was", S. CXIV), „das was geschieht", „Ding, Sache" bildet, und das ich noch später in mehreren Beziehungen näher zu berühren haben werde.

So entspricht also die erste Person Sing. dieses Hülfszeitwortes mé-dō, wofür ich in meinem Vokabular weniger richtig mēdo geschrieben habe, da das é in me erst in der Accusativ- und anderen Formen wirklich lang zu werden scheint, wörtlich der Hausa-Form í-na und der Kanúri-Form skin oder ni-skin, nur dass das erste dem Verbalstamm vor-, das letztere nachgesetzt wird, also mé-dō nyāma, „ich esse" oder „bin essend", H. í-na tšī, K. bú-sklin mé-dō ya ha, „ich gehe", H. í-na tafía, K. lé-ngiskin. Allerdings wird diese Form des Hülfszeitwortes in vielen Fällen abgeworfen, besonders in der dritten Person, wo ich es nur ein einziges Mal im Singular, kaṅko o-do-sotta und ein Mal im Plural gefunden habe, eben in dem S. CXIV angeführten kam-bo be-do ramšo.

[1]) In meinem Wörterbuch des Tumálijt habe ich nur die später eingeführten und jetzt üblichen Arabischen Zahlwörter aufgeführt, der alte einheimische Ausdruck für „sechs", „fünf und ein", aber hat sich z. B. noch bei den Beni Mzab erhalten, wie Herr Letourneux zuerst beobachtet und Hanoteau dann bestätigt hat. S. Reinaud's Notice sur le système primitif de la numération chez les peuples de race Berbère, lue à l'académie des inscriptions, le 27 Juillet 1860.

The numerals from „five" to „ten" follow what may be called the quinquarticular system, meaning originally „five and one", and so on, and in this respect the Fúl-language, what is very remarkable, fully harmonizes with the Berber-idiom *), while nearly all the surrounding languages of Tropical Africa with the only exception of the Wolof which, as I have stated above, is somehow related to the Fúl, do not show the slightest influence of this system of reckoning. For „ten", however, the Fúl-language has the independent and original term sappo, and now we find the remarkable circumstance, that for the numerals above „twenty" it possesses both ways of reckoning, as well by tenths as by twentieths, as, for instance, for „thirty" we find two terms tšappándo (plur. of suppo) táti, „three tenths", and lasso e sappo, „twenty and ten"; nay, for the numerals above forty in the extensive provinces occupied by the Fúlbe through which I travelled, I found three different terms to be commonly used, as for „fifty" tšappánde džó-i, „five tenths", lassó-dži dídi e suppo, „two twentieths and ten", and tobé-dži dídi e sappo, all three conveying the same meaning. The latter term which is principally used in the province of Másina between Džinni and Timbúktu is rather interesting, the inhabitants of that country never using, as far as I know, the term tobe, the singular of tobe-dži for twenty, and which I only learnt from Reichardt as being the very term used in Futa Džálo, but using instead nogai, another form of nogás which is used farther to the East; and it is remarkable, that this latter term again does not seem to form any plural. This way of reckoning by twentieths, as comprising the fingers and toes of both hand and foot, according to my opinion also, as I have had already occasion to state, when speaking of the Hausa-term hauya, as well as according to that of the best scholars, is of more ancient origin than that of reckoning by tenths. As for the Fúl-term temerre for „one hundred", it has most probably been borrowed from the Wolof-language, while the term sambar for „one thousand" must have been taken from the Sonyai.

3. *The verb.*

Of the verb in the Fúl-language besides the imperative, and some participial forms, I am only able to give a complete paradigm of the present tense, and of a kind of aorist, both with the corresponding negative forms.

a) The present tense, representing the action in its very development, is formed by inserting the auxiliary verb dō between the simple form of the pronoun, and the infinitive form of the verb. This auxiliary verb dō is undoubtedly the very same dō, by the aid of which the substantive hondō (hu-n-dō, „what [ho = to, see above p. CXV] is doing") meaning „thing, business" has been formed, and which I shall have full opportunity in the course of this inquiry of pointing out in several other relations.

Thus, therefore, mé-dō, as I think it may more correctly be written than médo, the 1st pers. sing. of this auxiliary verb, corresponds exactly with the form (-na in Hausa, and with the Kanúri verbal termination skin or ni-skin, with the only difference, that in Kanúri it is placed after the verbal root, while in Fúl as well as in Hausa it precedes the latter. Thus mé-dō nyāma, „I am eating", or rather „I do eat" is identical with the Hausa (ni) i-na tšī, and with the Kanúri bú-skin; mé-dō yā-ha, „I am going, I do go" with the Hausa i-na tafia and the Kanúri lé-niskin. No doubt, this auxiliary form dō is frequently thrown off, especially in the 3rd person, where I have not found it, but in two instances, viz kañ-ko e-dō-sotte and the kam-be be-dō ramtšo cited p. CXIV.

*) In my vocabulary of the Tamáshyt-language for the numerals above „five" I have only mentioned the terms which are used at present, and which have been derived from the Arabic; but the old original term for six, meaning likewise „five and one", is still preserved with the Beni Mzab, according to the observation of Mr. Letourneux which has been fully confirmed by Mr. Hanoteau. See Brisaud „notice sur le système primitif de la numération chez les peuples de race Berbère, lue à l'académie des Inscriptions le 27 Juillet 1860".

Dieses dō, obgleich es „thun" bezeichnet, hat so sehr den Charakter eines blossen Hülfszeitwortes, dass das selbstständige Thun, Bewerkstelligen in Verbindung mit einem substantivischen Begriff auch im Fulfúlde noch durch ein besonderes Zeitwort wuddi ausgedrückt wird, = yi im Hausa, di im Kanúri, also „ich treibe Handel" im Fulfúlde mé-dō wuddi tŏggu = Hausa ni na-i tšínoki, Kanúri a libaia di-skin.

Durchschnittlich scheint der Verbal-Stamm in dieser Präsens-Form auf a und o auszugehen, das ist aber, wenigstens im Volksgebrauch, keineswegs zum Gesetz geworden und hörte ich neben mé-dō sōd-a eben so oft mé-dō sōd-i und nie mé-dō dān-a, sondern stets nur mé-dō dān-i. Auch mé-dō dill-i kommt vor.

a, α) Die negative Form dieses Präsens wird stets durch ein dem Verbal-Stamm angehängtes ta gebildet, also mé-dō nyāma, „ich esse", mé-dō nyāma-ta, „ich esse nicht" = Hausa ba ni-na tši ba; mé-dō soda oder mé-dō sōdi, „ich kaufe", mé-dō sōda-ta, „ich kaufe nicht" = Hausa ba ni-na sóa ba.

Nur durch Verwechselung der Zeiten scheinen negative Formen wie mé-dō wadd-a, „ich besteige nicht", entstanden zu sein durch die Vermittelung der falschen Form mé-dō wadd-i, während von mé-dō dill-i doch die negative Form mé-dō dílla-ta lautet.

b) Der Aorist oder die unbestimmte Vergangenheit zeigt die Verbalform in ihrer grössten Einfachheit, indem hier der einfachen die Sache ausdrückenden Wurzel, das verbale i, das auch in vielen anderen, theils schon berührten, theils noch zu berührenden Sprach-Verhältnissen die aktive Thätigkeit auszudrücken dient, angehängt und die einfache pronominale Form vorgesetzt wird; so lautet der Aorist von mé-dō nyām-a: me-nyām-i; von mé-dō sōd-a: me-sōd-i; von mé-dō hō-a, „ich gebäre", me-hō-i, „ich gebar"; zuweilen tritt auch eine leichte Veränderung des Vokal-Lautes ein, z. B. mé-dō nann-a, „ich höre", me-nenn-i, „ich hörte".

Dies ist die regelmässige Bildung; in vielen Fällen aber haben die Zeitwörter unregelmässige Präterita oder vielmehr bilden diese mit Hülfe eines ganz verschiedenen Zeitwortes, dessen übrige Formen in einigen Fällen ausser Gebrauch gekommen sind, z. B. hat das in der gegenwärtigen Zeit fast ausschliesslich gebrauchte mé-dō yāha, „ich gehe" kein Präteritum und man gebraucht dafür me-dilli; von mé-dō rāra, „ich sehe" wird das Präteritum von einem anderen Zeitwort yi gebildet, me-yi, „ich sah", und diess ist offenbar die Wurzel von hi-te, gi-te, „Auge".

b, α) Die negative Form dieses Aorist wird gewöhnlich, um bei illiteraten Sprachen nicht den Ausdruck „Regel" zu gebrauchen, durch ein langes ā gebildet, das zwischen der Verbal-Wurzel und der Endung i eingeschaltet wird, also me-nenn-i, „ich hörte", me-nenn-ā-i, „ich hörte nicht"; me-wōd-i, „ich that", me-wōd-ā-i, „ich that nicht"; me-sott-i, „ich kaufte", me-sott-á-i, „ich kaufte nicht". Auch im Präsens mag das eigentliche Zeichen der Negation das a sein und t nur des Wohllautes wegen nach dem vorhergehenden a eingefügt sein. Vergleiche noch die beiden Phrasen o-dill-i kō o-dill-ā-i fū go, „er geht oder er geht nicht, Alles (ist) Eins". So S. 132 bingol leggel ō-béudi, „die Frucht ist reif, reif geworden" und S. 134 bingol leggel bend-ā-i, „ist nicht (noch nicht) reif".

Nun aber findet oft eine Verwechselung beider Formen Statt und neben dieser Form mit eingeschaltetem ā hörte ich fast eben so oft auch hier die auf ta, als me-nénna-ta, „ich hörte nicht", me-sótta-ta, „ich kaufte nicht", obgleich man hierbei nicht vergessen muss, dass das gewöhnliche Volk die Gegenwart und Vergangenheit nicht stets auseinander hält und zumal bei so wenig entwickelten geistigen Beziehungen, wie das bei diesen Sprachen der Fall ist, sich dessen oft wol gar nicht bewusst ist, während auch in der negativen Form des Präsens das dō häufig und bei vielen Zeitwörtern durchschnittlich fortgelassen

However, as for the notion of „performing" in connection with a substantive any business or work denoting, the auxiliary verb dō does not suffice, but another verb, expressing this action, must be added. This verb is waddi, corresponding to the Hausa yi and the Kanúri di, as for instance „I do make commerce", in Fulfúlde mé-dō waddi tšoggu = Hausa ni na-f tšíaeki, Kanúri n libnia él-skin.

The verbal root thus put in motion by means of the auxiliary verb mé-dō, in general terminates in a or e, and may be looked upon as a kind of infinitive; however, in these illiterate languages there are scarcely any fixed laws, and thus, for instance, besides the regular form mé-dō sōd-a I very often heard mé-dō sōd-i, „I am buying", and I never heard mé-dō dān-a, but constantly mé-dō dān-i. Thus we have also mé-dō dill-i.

a, α) The negative of this present tense constantly is formed by adding to the infinitive form of the verbal root the syllable ta corresponding with the Hausa-particle ba, thus: mé-dō nyāma, „I do eat", mé-dō nyāma-ta, „I do not eat" = Hausa ba i-na tši ba; mé-dō sōda (or mé-dō sōdi), „I do buy", mé-dō sōda-ta, „I do not buy".

It seems only to be due to an interchange of the tenses, that are to be reduced negative forms, such as mé-do wadd-a, „I do not mount", caused as it may be through the influence of the positive form mé-do wadd-i, although we have mé-dō dilla-ta as the negative form from mé-dō dill-i.

b) The aorist or indefinite past tense is formed by joining the simple personal pronoun to the verbal root, and adding to the latter i, the general sign of activity, which we have met already in many relations and shall meet as yet in many more, instead of the quiescent vowel a, for instance mé-dō nyām-a, „I do eat", me-nyām-i, „I have eaten"; mé-dō hō-a, „I do bear", „do bring forth", mo-hō-i, „I bore"; mé-dō sōd-a, „I do buy", me-sōd-i, „I bought". Occasionally a slight change of the vowel takes place, as for instance mé-dō nann-a, „I do hear", me-nena-i, „I heard".

This is the regular form of conjugation; in many cases, however, the verbs have irregular forms for the past tense, or rather form the latter from a totally different root, as, for instance, the verb mé-dō yāha, „I do go", which does not form the past tense from the same root, but the totally different verbal form me-dilli is used instead; as for mé-dō rāra, „I do see, look", the past tense is formed from a different root yī, me-yī, or, by repeating the pronominal form, mo me-yī, „I saw".

b, α) The negative form of this kind of aorist, in general (in order not to use the terms „rule" or „regular" with regard to illiterate languages), is formed by inserting a long ā between the verbal root and the final i, as for instance me-nenn-i, „I heard", me-nenn-ā-i, „I did not hear"; me-wōd-i, „I performed", me-wōd-ā-i, „I did not perform"; me-sott-i, „I bought", me-sott-ā-i, „I did not buy". Compare also the two phrases, o-dilli kō o-dill-ā-i fū gō, „(whether) he went or did not go, (is) all the same", and biñgol loggel ō-bénd-i, „the fruit is ripe, has ripened" (p. 132) with biñgol loggel bond-ā-i, „the fruit has not (yet) ripened". As for this characteristic sign of the negation, I deem it very probable, that with regard to the present tense the t has only been added from euphonical reasons; and thus forms, such as mé-dō wadd-a mentioned above, might be easily explained.

Now, however, an interchange of the two forms mentioned very often takes place, and besides the form of the past tense with an ā inserted I heard nearly as often the other form with the termination ta, as, for instance, me-nénna-ta, „I did not hear", me-sōtta-ta, „I did not buy", and we must not forget, that the common people do not constantly distinguish between the present and the past tense, and especially, where the mental powers are so little developed as with these African tribes, do not even become conscious of such a relation. And such an exchange of the two forms is greatly facilitated through the circumstance,

wird. Z. B. hörte ich von mé-dō andi, „ich weiss" nur die negative Form mo-anda, „ich weiss nicht"; von mé-dō idi, „ich will, liebe" nur die contrahirte Form mida d. h. mo-id-a, wo wir also in beiden Formen, der positiven wie der negativen, ein gänzliches Zusammenwerfen der gewöhnlichen Formen für Gegenwart und Vergangenheit sehen.

Zusatz. Nur in einem einzigen Falle habe ich eine negative verbale Form mit la, nämlich negative Form zu wō-di, „es ist", wō-la, „es ist nicht", und nur noch ein einziges Mal kommt diese la in meinen Collektaneen in anderer Stellung als negativ vor, nämlich bei der Bildung einiger negativer Adjektiva, wie mo-la-džendi. S. weiter unten, Bildung der Adjektiva.

N. 1) Was die auf die Verstärkungsformen to und ko, von denen ich weiter unten sprechen werde, ausgehenden Zeitwörter betrifft, so scheint die erste Klasse gar keine besondere negative Form zu besitzen und wird bei der zweiten die Form der Negation ta zwischen der Verbal-Wurzel und dieser Endung eingefügt, jedoch so, dass vielleicht durch Einfluss der anderen auf to ausgehenden Klasse das End-e in o verwandelt wird. Auch wird die Vergangenheit von der Gegenwart höchstens durch Weglassung des do unterschieden, also mé-dō ümmo-to, „ich breche auf", so wie me-ümma-ke, beide in negativer Form, me-umma-ta-ko.

N. 2) In allen Fällen entscheidend als eine Negation enthaltend ist die Endung ai keineswegs anzusehn, wie ich denn folgende auf ai ausgehende positive Verbalformen habe, die ein Mittelding zwischen Präsens und Aorist darzustellen scheinen, me-aillai, „ich mache Wasser", me-fiddai, „ich schiesse (den Pfeil)", me-hai (gädo südo), „ich gehe um die Ecke" (um ein Bedürfniss zu verrichten), me-dōrai, „ich begatte".

Bemerkung über das weibliche Geschlecht. Das weibliche Geschlecht wird in der Fül-Sprache, wie überhaupt nicht, wenigstens in organischer Weise, so auch nicht im Zeitwort unterschieden, doch will ich nicht unterlassen zu bemerken, dass ich trotzdem zuweilen besondere Formen bei letzterem hörte; so habe ich z. B. neben kaṅ-ko wāda-dum, „er macht das" die Form débo) en-hēda-dum, „die Frau macht das", und neben kaṅ-ko sm-o-sōda, „er kauft" die Form débo en-bi-sōda, „die Frau kauft". Jedoch stehen diese Formen ganz vereinzelt und scheinen mir durch ein, vielleicht unbewusstes, Bestreben hervorgerufen zu sein, der Hausa-Sprache nachzuahmen, die die Formen des weiblichen Geschlechts so hervorhebend unterscheidet.

c) Der Imperativ wird von der Stammwurzel des Zeitwortes gebildet, so dass das a gewöhnlich in o, das i in e übergeht und andere Veränderungen der Endsilbe eintreten; also „geh", yaho von mé-dō yaha und dille von der anderen Form für den Aorist me-dilli; „iss" yaṅg, von mé-dō nyāma, indem das Anfangs-n in letzterer Form vielleicht nur aus euphonischen Gründen hinzugefügt ist, das m aber auch sonst in ṅ übergeht.

Auch die negative Form des Imperativs wird vermittelst ta oder to gebildet, jedoch so, dass es der Verbalform, die gewöhnlich an der Verbindung mit dem Fürwort nichts ändert, nicht nach-, sondern vorgesetzt wird, wie z. B. on-dilli, „gehet", ta on-dilli, „gehet (ihr) nicht", ta an-yāṅg, „iss (du) nicht", to on-yāma, „esst (ihr) nicht", ta umma, „stehe nicht auf", to oṅg-ummo, „stehet (ihr) nicht auf". Aus diesen Beispielen ersehen wir zugleich, dass wegen der Anwendung von ta oder to keine feste Regel beobachtet zu werden scheint, sondern dass der Wohlklang allein entscheidet. So ist es auch mit der lokalen, ganz gleichlautenden Partikel ta oder to, z. B. in den eigenthümlichen, noch weiter zu besprechenden Phrasen to a-džā-ta, „wohin gehst du"?, to on-džā-ta, „wohin geht ihr"?

d) Die einfachste Form des Particips wird gebildet mit der Endung o, in die der Grundvokal a, i oder e übergeht, ohne oder mit Veränderung des Anfangsbuchstabens, wie z. B.

that in the negative form of the present tense the auxiliary verb dŏ very frequently is left out; nay, as it would seem, with some verbs this takes place almost constantly. Thus, from mé-dŏ and-i, „I know", I only heard the negative form me-and-a, „I do not know", from mé-dŏ ídi, „I like, love", I did not learn but the contracted form mida (i. q. me-íd-a), these two forms, the positive as well as the negative, exhibiting a total confusion of the common forms of the present and past tense.

Remark. Only one single instance appears in my collectaneous Notes of a negative verbal form with la, namely wō-la, „there is not", the negative form of wō-di, „there is", and besides I have only another instance of la conveying a negative meaning in a few composite adjectives, such as mo-la-dŽendi of which I shall have to speak further on.

N. 1) As for the verbs terminating in the stronger form to and ko, of which I shall have to say more further on, the first class seems to have no particular negative form, while with the second the negative form ta becomes inserted between the root of the verb, and the termination ko, but so, that the final o is exchanged against an o, a change which may be influenced by the other form in to. Thus, from me-ûmma-ko the negative form is me-umma-tă-ko which seems to be likewise the negative form of the verb mé-dŏ ûmmo-to. As for the past tense of these verbal forms, it is at the utmost only distinguished from the present tense by omitting the auxiliary form dŏ.

N. 2) As for the termination ai, I have to remark, that we are not allowed to look upon it as decidedly of a negative character, so that we may conclude a priori, that each verb ending in this termination does convey a negative meaning. For I have the following verbal forms terminating in ai, and nevertheless conveying a positive meaning while they do not represent the full form of the present tense, me-sillai, „I make water", me-fiddai, „I shoot (the arrow)", me-hai (gâdo sūdo), „I retire (behind the wall, in order to ease nature)", me-dōrai, „I lie with (a woman)".

I must here add a remark with regard to the feminine gender: In the Fūl-language the feminine gender, in general, is not distinguished, neither in the other parts of speech, nor in the verb, but I must here state, that nevertheless occasionally I found particular forms to be used, in order to distinguish the latter; thus for „the woman does perform that", I heard the form ďébo) en-hêda-dum, side by side with the form kan-ko wâda-dum for „he does perform that", and for „the woman is buying", ďébo en-hi-sôda, side by side with kan-ko em-o-sôda, „he is buying". But these two instances remain isolated in my experience, and seem to me to be produced by an attempt at imitating the laws of the Hausa-idiom, which distinguish so prominently the forms of the feminine gender.

c) The imperative mood is formed from the very root of the verb, to which e is added when the present tense terminates in a, i when it terminates in e, while in some cases other changes take likewise place; thus from mé-dŏ yâha, „I go", is formed the imperative yâh-e, and from the other form me-dilli, dill-ei from mé-dŏ nyâma, „I do eat", where the u in the beginning has probably been added from euphonical reasons, yañg.

With the negative form of the imperative, the negative ta is not placed after, but before the verb, as for instance on-dilli, „go (you)", ta on-dilli, „do not go (you)", ta an-yâñg, „do not eat (thou)", to on-yâma, „do not eat (you)"; ta umma, „do not rise (thou)", to oñg-ummo, „do not rise (you)". From this, and from other instances we see at the same time, that the vowel of the negative particle ta is sometimes changed into o, but there appears to obtain no fixed rule as to its use. This negative particle has the great inconvenience of being identical as well with the particle to, meaning „if", and forming the conditional mood, as with the local to meaning „where".

d) The most simple form of the participle is produced by changing the final vowel, whether a, i, or whatever it may be, into o, and sometimes changing also the first letter according

nédo yām-e ádune, „ein Mensch die Leute essend" (von mé-dō nyām-a), d. h. „Menschenfresser", nédo g-id-e ádune, „ein Mensch die Leute liebend" (von mé-dō idi), d. h. „ein Menschenfreund". Den ausgedehnten Gebrauch von einer Art Participium activi der Vergangenheit und Gegenwart auf do (e-do, i-do, o-do), selbst mit transitiver Bedeutung, kann ich durch mehrere Beispiele nachweisen, z. B. tel-é-de dum ádune, „dieser die Leute beeinträchtigend", hokk(e) am nédo and-ō-de laucl, „gib mir eine Person wissend" (von mé-dō and-a), „den Weg. die den Weg kennt"; Allāhu dšou-f-de losdo fú-ka, „Gott erleuchtend die ganze Welt" (das letztere nur poetisch); ebenso „du früh aufgebrochen" (d. h. „wenn du früh aufbrichst), kommst du da und dorthin", ang a-finí-de, von mé-dō fini, „ich breche früh auf", wóla džāhe-de, „es gibt nicht den gegangen Seienden", d. h. „Keinen der gegangen wäre", von mé-dō yāha, „ich gehe"; dahin gehören aber auch später zu Substantiven gewordene Ausdrücke, wie mai-de, „der Gestorbene, der Todte, der Leichnam", lámi-de, „Herrscher", bátši-do, „Minister". Andere dagegen wie obi-do, „frei", scheinen eine mehr passive Grundbedeutung zu haben, worüber weiter unten in f, α. Hier will ich nur hinzufügen, dass ich keinen Zweifel habe, dass dieses angehängte do dasselbe ist, mit dessen Hülfe das Präsens gebildet wird.

e) Eine Art Conditionel wird gebildet durch Vorsatz der Partikel to, „wenn" vor der Form der Vergangenheit, wie te mo-dilli, „wenn ich ginge" oder „wenn ich gegangen wäre", to naňgo yauti, „wenn die Sonne sich abwärts neigt" oder „nachdem die Sonne sich abwärts geneigt". Ähnlich wird auch durch Hinzufügung der Phrase „mit dem Willen des Allerhöchsten", yidde Džomirāo oder hobande Džomirāo, die dem Sinne nach ganz zusammenfällt mit der Mohammedanischen Phrase to Alla idi, „so Gott will", vor der Form der Gegenwart oder der Vergangenheit, eine Art Futurum gebildet, wie to Alla idi mé-dō yāha, „so Gott will, gehe ich" oder to Alla idi me-dilli, „so Gott wollte, ginge ich", oder yidde (oder hobande) Džomirāo me-dilli, „mit Gottes Willen, nach Gottes Rathschluss ginge ich" u. s. w. Zahlreiche Optativ-Formen, aber nur in der dritten Person, werde ich am Ende des Vokabular's unter den Phrasen geben.

f) Das Passivum hat, so weit ich selbst im Volksgebrauch zu erkennen Gelegenheit hatte, nur höchst unausgebildete Formen, wie wir das nach ganz natürlichen Gesetzen bei fast allen diesen Sprachen finden. Nur ein Participium kann ich mit bestimmter passiver Form nachweisen, mit der Endung auf āma, 3te Pers. Sing. āmo, mit einer gelegentlichen Pluralform auf e, also von mé-dō nyāma, „ich esse", nyām-ama, „(dies) gegessen"; mé-dō fiddai, „ich schiesse mit dem Pfeil", fidd-ama, „getroffen"; mé-dō lōti, „ich wasche", lōt-áma, „gewaschen"; von mé-dō habba, „ich binde", o-habb-āmo, „(er) gebunden", Plur. mō kabb-āma anstatt bō kabb-āma, „sie gebunden", nédo habb-āmo, „Mensch gebunden, ein Gefangener", von mé-dō wāra, „ich tödte" (me-hobbi nédo) wār-āme „(ich fand einen Menschen) getödtet" (d. h. „der getödtet war"), Plur. (me-hebbi yimbe) bin-bar-āme [bin anstatt bē], „(ich fand Leute) getödtet" (d. h. „die getödtet waren").

Besondere Bemerkung: Dass in diesem letzteren Fall übrigens das e nicht eine wirkliche Pluralform ist, sondern nur durch das vorhergehende e in yimbe bedingt wird, sieht man aus folgendem Beispiel eines Singulars mit e, wo es gleichfalls durch das nachfolgende e bedingt wird, o-yu-āme lobbo é-yeni do putšu, „er getroffen vom Speer fiel vom Pferde".

Ein Beispiel wenigstens habe ich auch von einer Endung auf īmo, o-dall-īma, „(er) freigelassen", von mé-dō dalla, „ich lasse frei".

f, α) Neben dieser passiven Form auf āma, āmo, īmo aber habe ich noch Beispiele einer Participial-Form auf re, wie déffe-ré, „gekocht", von I-na deffa, „ich koche", obgleich

to the laws of the language, as for instance nddo yām-e ádune, „a person eating (from mé-dō nyām-a) the people" i. q. „a cannibal", nédo g-id-e áduno, „a person loving" (from mé-dō idi) the people" i. q. „a philanthropist". Then we have a sort of participle of the active mood, past as well as present tense, terminating in do (e-do, i-do, o-do) which I am able to illustrate by means of several instances, such as the phrase hokk(a) am nédo and-ō-do lanol, „give me a person knowing the road", or „who knows the road", from mé-dō and-a, „I do know"; Allāhu dēen-i-do leado fá-ka, „God illuminating the whole world" (this rather partical), and in the same manner „thou, having started early (shalt arrive in such and such a place)", aṅg a-fini-do from mé-dō fini, „I start early"; „there is none having gone" i. e. „nobody went", wōla (there is not) džāba-do, „he who is gone" from mé-dō yāha, „I go". To this class belong likewise other terms which in the course of time have become substantives, such as bátši-do, „minister", lámi-do, „king, chief", mai-do, „the dead, corpse". Other terms, on the contrary, with the same termination, such as obi-do, „freeman", seem to have had originally a passive signification, and shall be treated lower down under f, α. Here I will only add, that there can scarcely be any doubt, that this terminal do is the same auxiliary form, by the aid of which the present tense has been formed.

e) A kind of conditional mood is formed by prefixing the particle to, „if", to the form representing the past tense, as, for instance, to me-dilli, „if I went", or „if I had gone"; to naṅge yauti, „when the sun is going down" or „after the sun shall have gone down". In the same way by adding to the form of the present or past the phrase, to Alla idi, conveying the common Mohammedan clause „if God approves, if it please God", identical in meaning with another phrase yidde Džomirāo or hobaude Džomirāo, „with the will of the Almighty", a sort of future is formed, as, for instance, in the phrase to Alla idi mé-dō yāha, „if it please God, I (shall) go" and to Alla idi me-dilli, verbally „if it please God, I went", instead of „if it had pleased God, I should have gone". And the very same meaning is conveyed by the other phrase „yidde (or hobaude) Džomirāo me-dilli, „by the will of God I should go". A considerable number of forms of the optative, but only of the third person sing., will be found among the phrases at the end of my vocabulary.

f) The passive mood, as far as I was able to, and had opportunity of, discerning in the idiom of the daily intercourse, is very little developped, just as, according to very natural conditions, we find to be the case with almost all these languages. Thus I am only able to exhibit a decidedly passive form in a participle terminating in āma or āmo with an occasional pluralform in o; thus, from mé-dō nyama, „I do eat", is formed nyam-āma, „eaten"; from mé-dō fiddai, „I let fly (the arrow)", fidd-āma, „struck (by the arrow)"; from mé-dō lōti, „I do wash", lōt-ama, „washed"; from mé-dō habba, „I do bind", o-habb-āmo, „(he) bound", with the corresponding plural form me-kabb-āma instead of be-kabb-āma, „(they) bound"; nddo habb-āmo, „a person bound", „the prisoner"; from mé-dō wāra, „I kill, murder", (mo-hebbi nédo) wār-āmo, „(I found a person) murdered" or „who was murdered", in the plural (mo-hebbi yimbe) bin-bar-ame [bin instead of bō], „(I found people) murdered", or „who were murdered".

Remark: That the final e in this latter case is not a real sign of the plural, but is merely a euphonical change, caused by the preceding e in yimbe, is sufficiently shown by the following instance of a singular, where the same form is produced through the influence of a following e: o-yu-āme lebbe é-yoni do putšu, „he struck by the spear fell from the horse".

One single instance at least of a participle pass. in ime occurs among my phrases, o-dall-īme, „(he) set free", „liberated", from mé-dō dalla, „I set free".

f, α) Besides this passive form, terminating in āma, āmo, and occasionally in ime, as it would seem, I have also a few instances of a participial form terminating in re, such as

es mehr mit adjektiver, als mit participialer Bedeutung gebraucht wird = deffādam, worüber bei den Adjektiv-Formen. Dann habe ich auch manche unzweifelhafte Beispiele der oben angeführten Form auf do mit passiver Bedeutung. So habe ich neben gi-āma, oder yā-ma, (mit einem Vorsatz je nach der Person), „gesehen", von yi, „sehn", ganz in derselben passiven Bedeutung die Form gi-ādo, und von dem oben angeführten mé-dō hobba neben der Form hubb-āmo, „gebunden" auch in ganz derselben Bedeutung die Form hubb-ādo. Auch tšort-ādo, „der Verschnittene" ist unzweifelhaft ein Participium Passivi von mé-dō sort(u), obgleich ich das letztere nicht habe. Eben so rumdia-ādo, „freigelassen" von mo-dímdini-(mo), „ich lasse (ihn) frei", wo ausser dem Übergang des Konsonanten auch noch eine Veränderung des Vokals eingetreten ist.

f, β) Wenn wir schon in dieser Participial-Form auf do ein Zusammenfallen der aktiven und passiven Bedeutung finden, so ist das noch viel mehr der Fall mit den definitiven Zeiten, wo je nach dem Zusammenhang und mit leichtem Unterschied der Betonung dieselbe Form aktive und passive Bedeutung haben kann, so kañ-ko o-fússi, „er zerstört", konno o-fússi, „der Krieg ist zerstört, verloren", mé-dō wódi, „ich thue, mache", (dum) wódi, „das ist", eigentlich „ist gethan", be-delli, „sie lassen los" und „sie sind losgelassen". Ein leichter Unterschied durch ein angefügtes n findet sich vielleicht in folgendem Beispiel mo-yōri, „ich trocknete", nyōri, „es ist trocken".

f, γ) Aber jene Participial-Form wird auch oft statt des definitiven Tempus der Vergangenheit gebraucht; so sagt man mo rimm-āma, „ich geboren" statt „ich bin geboren", to a-rimm-āma, „wo du geboren" statt „wo bist du geboren", hite hubb-āma, S. 140 „das Feuer angezündet" statt „ist angezündet", „brennt", von mé-dō hobba, S. 108 „ich zünde an (das Feuer)".

Zusatz 1. Als Participial-Form müssen wir auch wol ansehn die Form hebóīma oder vielmehr he-bo-īma in der Phrase zemāni he-bō-īma, „in alter Zeit, vor Alters", eigentlich „die Zeit sie die vergangene", vielleicht auch olma, „einst".

Zusatz 2. Eine Doppelform von do (ido) und āmo scheint mir folgendes Beispiel zu enthalten o-nāng-ido-āmo kañ-ko he biko, „es wurde ergriffen er und sein Sohn", doch wol von mé-dō nañge, „ich ergreife". Eine zusammengezogene Form dāma erscheint in folgendem Beispiel džaudi mā-be hor-dāma e hōre mā-be, wörtlich „ihr Vermögen getödtet und ihr Kopf", d. h. „ihr Vermögen (besonders in Sklaven und Viehstand bestehend) ward vernichtet und sie selbst gemordet" von mé-dō wār-a, „ich tödte". Die Erklärung zu diesen passiven Formen mit d gibt wol folgende definitive Form me-dum yam-di, „dieses gegessen", statt nyam-āma von mé-dō nyāma, „ich esse".

Ich gebe nun einige vollständige Paradigmen des Zeitwortes, so weit ich es kennen gelernt.

mé-dō nyāma, „ich esse".

Präsens. Singular.

	affirmativ.	negativ.
1ste Person	mé-dō nyāma	mé-dō nyama-ta,
2te „	añg a-nyāma	añg a-nyāma-ta,
3te „	kañ-ko o-nyāma	kañ-ko o-nyāma-ta.

déffe-ré, „boiled" from í-na deffa, „I boil", although it is rather used as an adjective identical with deffādam, of which I shall have to speak further on, than as a real participle; moreover, I have several well ascertained instances of the form terminating in do, of which I have spoken above, as conveying a passive meaning. Thus, besides the form gi-āma (or yá-ma), „seen", to which a pronominal form is added according to the person, or persons concerned, from me-yi, „I saw", I have the form gi-ade with the very same passive meaning „seen", and from the verb mé-dō babba, besides the form habb-āmo, „bound", and with the very same meaning I have the form kabb-ade. The very same form we have in rumdin-ade, „set free, liberated" from mo-dimdini-(mo), „I set (him) free". In this latter instance, however, we have besides a change of a consonant also the change of the original vowel. tšort-ādo also, meaning „eunuch", is undoubtedly a participial form of the passive mood, and the same appears to be the case with other terms such as powādo, „struck with fever (póo)".

f, β) Already this form of the participle in do affords an instance of how the same form in the Fūl-language may have an active, and a passive meaning, but this is still more the case with the definite tenses, where, besides a slight difference of pronunciation, the context alone must show, whether the word has an active or a passive meaning; thus, the phrase kań-ko o-fúesi means „that person destroys", while on the contrary konno o-fussi means „the war is destroyed, is lost"; thus also mé-dō wōdi, „I do perform", (dum) wōdi, „that is", properly „has been performed"; he-delli, „they let loose", as well as „they have been let loose". Another instance me-yōri, „I dried", compared with nyōri, „it has dried", may perhaps exhibit the difference of an n being added in the passive mood.

f, γ) Now, I have several instances of the participial form in āma being used instead of the definite tense of the past; thus, the Fúl-be say me rimm-āma, „I born" or „me born" instead of „I am born" („in such and such a place"), ta a-rimm-āma, „where thou born" instead of „where art thou born"; hite hubb-āma p. 140 „the fire lighted" instead of „is lighted" from mé-dō hobba or hubba p. 108 „I light the fire".

Additional remark, 1) As a participial form, I think, we must also look upon the form he-bót-ma in the phrase zomāni he-bót-ma (hēbóīma), „in the old time, p. 22, verbally „the time, which has past by", and perhaps even the particle oima, „once".

Additional remark, 2) A form composed of both forms, that terminating in do (ído) as well, as that in āmo seems to be contained in the following instance o-náńgide-āme kań-ko he biko, „he (was) seized, he himself and his son", most probably from mé-dō nańge, „I seize"; for the termination āmo can scarcely have any other meaning. A contracted form of the two in dāma appears in the following instance džaudi mā-bū bor-dāma o hōre mā-bē, meaning verbally „their property (especially „slaves and cattle") killed and their head", i. q. „their property having been destroyed, and they themselves killed" from mé-dō war-a, „I kill". And some sort of explanation of this double form with d may be gleaned, as it seems, from the phrase me-dam yām-di, „this eaten", instead of nyām-āma, from mé-dō nyāma, „I eat", the adding of the me before dum being rather of common occurrence.

I now proceed to give a few perfect paradigms of the verb, as far as the forms have become known to me.

mé-dō nyáma, „I eat".

Present tense, singular.

	affirmative.	negative.
1st person	mé-dō nyāma	mé-dō nyāma-ta,[1]
2nd „	ańg a-nyāma	ańg a-nyāma-ta,
3rd „	kań-ko o-nyāma	kań-ko ó-nyāme-ta.

r

Plural.

	affirmativ.		negativ.
1ste Person	ménon min-nyáma	. . .	ménon min-nyāma-ta,
2te „	onom on-nyáma	. . . .	onom on-nyáma-ta,
3te „	kam-be be-nyáma	. . . .	kam-be be-nyáma-ta.

Aorist, Singular.

	affirmativ.		negativ.
1ste Person	me) me-nyámi	. . . . .	me) me-nyām-ā-i (gädum [1]),
2te „	áńg a-nyámi	. . . . . .	áńg a-nyām-ā-i,
3te „	kań-ko o-nyámi	. . . .	kań-ko o-nyām-ā-i.

Plural.

1ste Person	ménon min-nyāmi	. . .	ménon min-nyām-ā-i,
2te „	onem on-nyāmi	. . . . .	onom on-nyám-ā-i,
3te „	kam-be be-nyāmi	. . . .	kam-be be-nyām-ā-i.

Imperativ, Singular.

	affirmativ.		negativ.
2te Person	yańg	. . . .	ta a-nyáńg.

Plural.

1ste Person	mé-dońg-nyāma	. . . .	
2te „	on-nyāma	. . . .	ta on-nyāma.

Participium Passivi.

dum) nyām-āma, abgekürzt dum) nyāmā.

mé-dö yāba, „ich gebe".

Präsens, Singular.

	affirmativ.		negativ.
1ste Person	mé-dö yāba	. . . .	mé-dö yā (ba)-ta,
2te „	áńg a-yāba	. . . .	áńg a-yā (ba)-ta.
3te „	om o-yāba	. . . .	kań-ko o-yā (ba)-ta.

Plural.

1ste Person	ménon min-džābe	. . .	ménon min-džā (ba)-ta,
2te „	onom on-džābe	. . . . .	onom on-džā (ba)-ta,
3te „	kam-be in-džābe	. . . .	kam-be in-džā (ba)-ta.

Aorist oder Präteritum, Singular.

	affirmativ.		negativ.
1ste Person	me-dilli	. . . .	me-dilla-ta [2],
2te „	áńg a-dilli	. . . . . .	áńg a-dillā-i,
3te „	kań-ko o-dilli	. . . . .	kań-ko o-dilla-ta.

Plural.

1ste Person	min-dilli	. . . .	ménon min-dill-á-i,
2te „	onom on-dilli	. . . . . .	onom on-dill-á-i,
3te „	kam-bo bo-dilli	. . . . .	kam-bo be-dill-á-i.

[1] gädum, „Sache" (von mé-dö wódi), ist eine Verstärkung der Negation, entsprechend unserem „gar nichts".

[2] Ich gebe die Form, wie ich sie im Gebrauch gefunden. me-dill-á-i habe ich nie gehört, aber sie scheint möglich.

Plural.

affirmative. negative.

1st person ménon min-nyáma . . . . ménon min-nyāma-ta.
2nd „ onom on-nyāma . . . . . onom on-nyāma-ta.
3rd „ kam-be be-nyāma . . . . kam-be be-nyāma-ta.

Past tense, singular.

affirmative. negative.

1st person me) mo-nyāmi . . . . . . me) mo-nyam-ā-i (gōdum [1]),
2nd „ aṅg a-nyāmi . . . . . . aṅg a-nyām-ā-i,
3rd „ kaṅ-ko o-nyāmi . . . . kaṅ-ko o-nyām-ā-i.

Plural.

1st person ménon min-nyāmi . . . . ménon min-nyam-ā-i,
2nd „ onom on-nyāmi . . . . . onom on-nyām-ā-i,
3rd „ kam-be be-nyāmi . . . . kam-be be-nyām-ā-i.

Imperative, singular.

affirmative. negative.

2nd person yaṅg . . . . ta a-nyáṅg.

Plural.

1st person mé-doṅg-nyāma . . . . .
2nd „ on-nyāma . . . . te on-nyāma.

Participle of the passive mood.

dum) nyām-āma, abbreviated dum) nyāmā.

mé-dō yāha, „I go".

Present tense, singular.

affirmative. negative.

1st person mé-dō yāha . . . . mé-dō yā (ha)-ta,
2nd „ aṅg a-yāha . . . . aṅg a-yā (ha)-ta,
3rd „ om o-yāha . . . . kaṅ-ko o-yā (ha)-ta.

Plural.

1st person ménon min-džāho . . . . ménon min-džā (ha)-ta,
2nd „ onom on-džāho . . . . . onom on-džā (ha)-ta,
3rd „ kam-be in-džāho . . . . kam-be in-džā (ha)-ta.

Past tense, singular.

affirmative. negative.

1st person me-dílli . . . . me-dílla-ta [2]),
2nd „ aṅg a-dílli . . . . aṅg a-dillā-i,
3rd „ kaṅ-ko o-dílli . . . . . . kaṅ-ko o-dílla-ta.

Plural.

1st person min-dílli . . . . ménon min-dill-ā-i,
2nd „ onom on-dílli . . . . . . onom on-dill-ā-i,
3rd „ kam-be be-dílli . . . . . kam-be be-dill-ā-i.

[1]) gōdum, „thing", „affair" (from mé-dō wōdi), if added to the simple negative form of the verb, corresponds exactly to the English „nothing".

[2]) I give these forms, such as I have found them. For I have never heard a form me-dill-ā-i, but nevertheless it seems possible.

Conditional.

	Singular.		Plural.
1ste Person	tö me-dílli	. . . . . .	tö min-dílli,
2te „	tö a-dílli	. . . .	tö on-dílli,
3te „	tö o-dílli	. . . .	tö be-dílli.

Art Futurum.

	Singular.		Plural.	
1ste P.	tö Alla īdi . . .	me me-dílli	tö Alla īdi . . .	(ménon) min-dílli
2te „	yíde Džomirão .	ańg a-dílli	yíde Džomirão .	(onom) on-dílli
3te „	bobaude Džomirão	kaúko o-dílli	bobaudo Džomirão	(kam-be) be-dílli

Imperativ, Singular.

	affirmativ.		negativ.
2te Person	dillo / yāho	. . . .	tä n-dílle.

Plural.

1ste Person	min-ámma-kö *) min-dílli		
2te „	on-dílli	. . . .	tä on-dílli.

Participium Perfecti.

yāha-dö, „der gegangen ist".

„Es wäre besser gewesen, wir wären gestern gereist":

dšábangel / yādū . . } keñe be-būri, wörtlich „die Reise gestern war besser".

4. *Verstärkende Formen des Zeitwortes.*

a) Die Endung auf kö.

Ich habe viele Zeitwörter mit der Endung auf kö, von denen ich unsicher bin, ob ich sie als selbstständige verstärkte Zeitwörter oder bloss als eine Art Participial-Form ansehen soll, was besonders von denen gilt, von denen auch die einfache Form im Gebrauch ist, während wir andererseits diese doch nicht als eine gewöhnliche Verbalform ansehen können, weil unzählige Zeitwörter sie nicht haben, z. B. yāha oder dílli, „gehen", nyāma, „essen", rāre, „sehn". Auch ist es schwer zu sagen, was die eigentliche Bedeutung dieser Form ist, ausser dass es die Gegenwart der durch das Zeitwort dargestellten Handlung noch plastischer bezeichnet; denn einige Handlungen, die von den Zeitwörtern bezeichnet werden, bei denen diese Form üblich ist, sind so schnell vorübergehender Natur, dass von einer Dauer nicht die Rede sein kann, wie das folgende Verzeichniss zeigen wird. Gewiss ist aber dennoch, dass diese Verbalform auf kö den Übergang bildet von der einfachen Verbalform zu der weiter unten aufzuführenden Form des Substantivs auf kī, z. B. me džōda-kö, „ich bin sitzend", džōdá-kī, „das Sitzen, der Aufenthalt", me-tūra-kö, „ich verbeuge mich im Gebet", tūrá-kī, „die Verbeugung".

Allerdings hörte ich diese Form auf kö auch in Verbindung mit der vollen Pronominal-Form der ersten Person der Gegenwart mé-dö, aber doch nur ganz ausnahmsweise und vielleicht missbräuchlich, und so scheint mir me-džōda-kö z. B. der anderen Form mé-dö džōda mit dö und ohne kö ganz gleichbedeutend zu sein.

Ich gebe hier nun ein Verzeichniss der mir bekannt gewordenen Verbalformen auf kö,

*) min-ámma-kö, „lasst uns aufstehn, aufbrechen" wird in diesem Fall gewöhnlich hinzugesetzt.

Conditional.

	Singular.	Plural.
1st person	tō mo-díllì	tō min-díllì,
2nd „	tō a-díllì	tō on-díllì,
3rd „	tō o-díllì	tō be-díllì.

A kind of future tense.

	Singular.		Plural.	
1st P.	to Alla ìdi . . .	mo mo-díllì	tō Alla ìdi . . .	mónon) min-díllì
2nd „	yído Džomirāo .	aṅg a-díllì	yído Džomirāo .	onom) on-díllì
3rd „	hobaude Džomirāo	kaṅko o-díllì	hobaude Džomirāo	kam-bo) be-díllì

Imperative, singular.

	affirmative.	negative.
2nd person	dillo yāho	tā a-díllo.

plural.

1st person	min-émma-kē [1]) min-díllì .	
2nd „	on-díllì	tā on-díllì.

Participle of past tense.

yāha-dō, „he who has gone, travelled".

„It would have been better we had travelled (started) yesterday":

dzáhaṅgel
yādū . . } koṅa ho-būri, verbally „the journey of yesterday was better".

4. *Intensive forms of the verb.*

a) The termination in kē.

Among my list of verbs appear a good many terminating in kē, with regard to which I am not quite certain, whether they are to be looked upon as an independent class of intensive verbs, or whether the kē is a mere kind of participial form. For, while on the one side this form in kē does not seem to constitute a class of verbs by itself, as of many, which possess this termination, we have also the simple form, on the other side it does not seem to be a mere verbal form, as many verbs such as yāha or díllì, „to go", nyāma, „to eat", and rāra, „to see" do not possess it. It is also difficult to say, what the original meaning of this form may be, except, that it describes in a more intensive and graphic manner the presence of the action represented by the verb; for we dare not say, that the duration of such an act is particularly represented by this form, several of the verbs terminating in kē designating actions of such a transitory character, that they do not allow of such an explanation, as the list which I shall give further on, will serve to show. Be that as it may, thus much is certain, that this verbal form in kē serves as a stage of transition from the simple verbal form to the form of the substantive terminating in ki, of which I shall have to say more further on, as, for instance, mo džōda-kē, „I am sitting", džōdá-ki, „the rest, stay", mo-tūra-kē, „I am bowing (in prayer)", tūrá-ki, „the bow, reverence".

In some instances I heard this form in kē also in connection with the full pronominal form of the 1st person of the present tense mé-dō, but only by way of exception and perhaps not quite correctly. Indeed, the form mo-džōda-kē for instance, seems to be entirely identical with the other form by means of dō and without kē, mé-dō džōda.

I now proceed to give a list of those verbs in kē which have come to my knowledge,

[1]) min-émma-kē, „let us rise", in this case is generally added to the other verb.

mit Weglassung des Fürwortes: höba-kē, „werfe"; kāre-kō, „parire" (Hausa kária); ſiša-kē, „knie nieder zum Schoss"; búda-kē, „nähere mich"; fótta-kō, „rücke näher"; úmma-kē, „breche auf"; ótta-kō, „erreiche"; wódda-kē, „entferne mich"; yimbe) tšenkéte-kē, „(die Leute) gehen auseinander"; džōda-kē, „sitze"; dárra-kō, „stehe aufrecht"; wáha-kō, „lehne mich an"; džíppa-kē, „steige ab"; búkka-kē, „werfe Staub auf mein Haupt"; húnna-kē, „schwöre; ſala-kē, „niese"; fádda-kō, „bin schwindelig, betrunken"; sudžóda-kē oder túra-kē, „verbeuge mich im Gebet". Besonders das su-džóda-kē ist ein belehrendes Beispiel, da wir die Arabische Wurzel deutlich vor Augen haben.

b) Form auf tō.

Ich habe nun auch mehrere Beispiele einer Form auf tō, in einzelnen Fällen neben der auf kō gleichbedeutend hergehend, wie mó-dō džíppo-tō = mo džíppa-kō, mó-dō úmmo-tō = mo úmma-kē. Ausserdem habe ich wur-tō, „kehre zurück"; díllo-tō, „gehe"; wádo-tō, „reite"; fóbbo-tō, „bleibe zurück"; éggo-tō, „gehe zu"; woini-tō, „nehme Abschied"; tórro-tō, „bitte"; dábbi-tō, „bettele"; sūmo-tō, „faste", aber wol stets nur in Verbindung mit der Form der ersten Person mó-dō wádo-tō u. s. w.

Von diesen Zeitwörtern möchten einige, wie besonders wádo-tō, „(zu Pferde) reiten" (wenn man wádo, „aufsteigen [zu Pferde]" vergleicht), den Schluss zu begründen scheinen, dass diese Endung auf tō eine Wiederholung oder Dauer bezeichnet, andere aber lassen eine solche Erklärung nicht wol zu.

c) Verstärkende Form auf ta.

Wir haben früher die Endung ta als die negirende Form des Zeitwortes gehabt, obgleich ich schon Gelegenheit gehabt habe, zu bemerken (S. CXX, b.), dass in vielen Fällen das eigentlich charakteristische Zeichen der Negation a ist, während das t nur aus euphonischen Gründen zugesetzt zu sein scheint, wiewol wir es vor dem Imperativ wenigstens ganz selbstständig finden; nun aber tritt die wirkliche Endung ta auch als eine verstärkende verbale Form auf, wie denn eine solche Bedeutung des ta, hier noch als vereinzelte Partikel aufgefasst, am klarsten aus folgender Phrase als Zusatz hinter dem Fürwort sich ergibt: o-dílli kañ-ko ta, „es ging eben er" (kein Anderer). Ebenso deutlich scheint diese Bedeutung sich aus einigen verbalen Formen zu ergeben, wo ta als enger Anschluss an den Verbalstamm auftritt, so besonders mó-dō) rār-ta, „suche" von mó-dō) rāra, „sehe", wo das ta nicht an die Verbal-Endung, sondern an die reine Stammwurzel angehängt ist; das ta erscheint sogar zweimal wiederholt in der Phrase kō on-dār-ta-ta, „was sucht ihr denn"?, S. 70. Ähnlich ist hō fúlla-ta, „was fürchtest du", von mó-dō hulla, „ich fürchte"; wel-wel-ta, wo die Verstärkung gleichzeitig durch Wiederholung der Verbal-Wurzel ausgedrückt ist, „lustiger Dinge sein", von der Wurzel wel in der Phrase bérende an-wēl-i, „das Herz ist heiter". In anderen Fällen scheint dieses ta dazu zu dienen, die jedesmalige Wiederholung des in dem einfachen Zeitwort enthaltenen Begriffes zu bezeichnen, wie aus den Phrasen deutlich wird duñgu fūda-ta (von fōdi, „fängt an"), duñgu rēa-ta-ta (rēī, „hört auf, ist vorbei"), von dem jedesmaligen jährlichen „Anfangen und Aufhören der Regenzeit" (duñgu).

Eine transitive Beziehung möchte das angehängte ta zu haben scheinen in mó-dō ékke-ta, „ich lehre", verglichen mit mó-dō ékke-to, „ich lerne".

5. *Verbindung zweier Zeitwörter.*

Bei Verbindung zweier Zeitwörter, wo im Deutschen das eine in der bestimmten, das andere in der unbestimmten Zeit steht, wird im Fūl gewöhnlich das zweite gleichfalls mit Wiederholung des einfachen Fürwortes in die bestimmte Zeit gesetzt, wie mó-dō idi mo-

omitting the pronominal form: hūba-kō, „throw"; kāro-kō (in Hausa kária), „parry"; ftōa-kē, „kneel down to fire"; báda-kō, „approach"; fótta-kō, „draw near"; ūmma-kō, „start"; ótta-kō, „reach"; wódda-kō, „withdraw"; yimbe) tšonkóte-kē, „(the people) go asunder"; džōda-kē, „sit"; dárra-kē, „stand upright"; wáha-kē, „lean against"; džíppa-kō, „dismount"; búkka-kē, „throw dust on my head"; hónna-kē, „swear"; isla-kē, „sneeze"; fádda-kē, „am giddy, drunk"; sudžóda-kē or tūra-kō, „make a bow". The term sudžóda-kō as derived from a wellknown Arabic verb is of particular interest.

b) Verbs terminating in tō.

Now, I have also several instances of a form in tō, which in some cases takes place side by side with that of kō, such as mé-dō džíppo-tō besides me-džíppa-kē, mé-dō úmmo-tō = mo-ūmma-kō. Besides, I have the verbal forms wor-tō, „return", dillo-tō, „go"; wádo-tō, „go on horse-back"; fóbbo-tō, „remain behind"; éggo-tō, „go on"; waini-tō, „take leave"; tórro-tō, „beg, pray"; dábbi-tō, „beg (almons)"; sūmo-tō, „fast"; but I have scarcely ever heard these forms, I think, in connection with any other person, but the first, mé-dō wádo-tō and so on.

Some of these verbs, as especially the verb wádo-tō, „go (on horseback)", if we compare the simple form wádo with the meaning of „mounting on horseback", might seem to confirm the conclusion, that the verbs terminating in tō indicate a repetition or duration of the action expressed by the simple form of the verb; but other terms of the same class do not allow of such an explanation.

c) Intensive verbal form in ta.

In a former paragraph we have met with the termination ta, as a negative form of the verb, although I have had already an opportunity of observing p. CXXI, b, that the really characteristic sign of the negation in many cases is the single a, the t seeming to be added from euphonical reasons. But now we have to speak of the real termination ta, as an intensive verbal form. First I will point out a phrase, where it occurs as a particle by itself, in order to strengthen the preceding demonstrative pronoun, o-dilli kań-ko ta. „it was he who went (no body else)". Almost quite as clear is this notion of ta in some of the verbal forms, where it is closely joined to the verbal root, such as especially mé-dō rār-ta, „I do search, look for", from mé-dō rāra, „I do see", where the ta has not merely been subjoined to the verbal termination, but has been brought into intimate connection with the verbal root. Nay, we even find the ta in connection with this verb repeated twice in the phrase explained p. 70 of the vocabulary kō on-dār-ta-ta, „what is it, that you look for"?. Similar is the case with hō fúlla-ta, „what doest thou fear" from mé-dō hulla, „I do fear"; wol-wel-ta, „to be extravagantly merry", where the intensive character of the notion has been expressed moreover by a repetition of the verbal root, the simple wel appearing in the phrase bórende an-wēl-i, „the heart is merry", „I am merry". In some other cases the termination ta seems to have the import of indicating the repeated occurrence of the notion contained in the simple verb, as is clearly shown by the phrase duńgu („the rainy season") fūda-ta (from fūdi, „has begun"), duńgu rēa-ta-ta (from rēï, „has ceased"), used of the annual beginning and ceasing of the rainy season".

Of a totally different character seems to be the notion of the ta in the term mé-dō ókke-ta, „I teach", if compared with mé-dō ókke-ta, „I learn".

5. *The way of joining two verbs.*

When two verbal notions are joined together, where in English the one is placed in the definite, the other in the indefinite tense, in the Fūl-language in general the second likewise is put in the definite tense, while repeating the simple form of the pronoun, without adding dō, as,

sōda, „ich will kaufen"; om-o-nadi om-o-holli am, „er weiss mir zu zeigen" (wörtlich „er weiss, er zeigt mir"); aber dagegen habe ich auch mé-do idi waddo, „ich will besteigen", wo also bei dem zweiten Zeitwort das persönliche Fürwort nicht wiederholt ist; eben so nō n-gida wōdi n-gōdum, „wie willst du das Ding machen", wieder von mé-do idi, „ich will" und mé-do wōdi, „ich mache", wo also das zweite Zeitwort in einer Art von Infinitiv steht.

Interessant ist das Beispiel hokk(u) am ndiam nyēre, „gib mir Wasser zu trinken", von mé-do yāra, „ich trinke", wo nyēro als eine Art Infinitiv erscheint; sicher bin ich nicht, wie ich die Form bezeichnen soll.

In Bezug auf Stellung geht das Zeitwort im Fūl dem Objekte stets vorher.

6. *Nennwörter.*

Ich gehe nun zur Besprechung des an Mannichfaltigkeit und Unregelmässigkeit der Formen überaus reichen Gebietes der Nennwörter in der Fūl-Sprache über; denn es ist für die Geschichte dieser Sprache ein höchst zu beachtender Umstand, dass sie in ihrer jetzigen Entwickelung fast nicht ein einziges Beispiel einer monosyllaben Form eines Nennwortes enthält, während die ursprünglichen Begriffe in der mannichfaltigsten Weise abgewandelt und mit secundären Begriffen verbunden sind. So sehen wir z. B., erst rückwärts gehend von den zusammengesetzten Formen, dass die ursprüngliche Form von biñgel, „Sohn" bi war.

Ich will nun einige Beispiele geben von Ableitung der Nennwörter vom Zeitwort, ohne auch nur den allergeringsten Anspruch an Vollständigkeit zu machen:

a) Ich habe zwei interessante Beispiele der Bildung von Nennwörtern von einfachen verbalen Begriffen, indem die Endung um hierbei das Sachliche „es", vergleiche d-um, die Endung o das Persönliche a, „er" bezeichnet, nämlich das schon mehrfach erwähnte gōd-um, „Sache" von mé-do wōd-i, „ich mache" und gūdž-o, „Dieb" von mé-do ūdž-i, „ich stehle". Was den Übergang des u- oder w-Lautes in den Konsonanten g betrifft, so ist das nach dem oben S. CXIV Gesagten schon an sich deutlich und habe ich mich wol geirrt, wenn ich zuerst in dem g noch ein go, „eins" suchte, so dass gōdum eigentlich go wōd-um wäre „ein Ding", gūdžo: go ūdž-o, „ein Stehlender". Ich führe als Beispiel der Ableitung eines Substantivs von verbaler Wurzel mit blosser Veränderung des Anfangs-Konsonanten an konno, „Krieg" von mé-dō honno, „ich kriege, führe Krieg", während bār-o (in bār(o) ónduno), „der Mörder" von mé-dō wār-a, „ich tödte, morde" mehr dem gūdž-o in seiner Bildung sich annähert.

b) Dann haben wir allem Anscheine nach eine Klasse von verbalen Wurzeln abgeleiteter Substantive, wo an den im Anfangsbuchstaben veränderten oder unveränderten Stamm ein gu (go) angehängt wird, wie z. B. tšoggu (tšod-gu), „Handel, Kauf", ohne Zweifel abgeleitet von sōd-a, „kaufe" (Plur. tšōd-a). So ist auch wol džaggu abgeleitet, und entfernt dahin gehört auch džū-n-go, „Hand", s. oben S. CXVI.

c) Nun habe ich drittens eine ziemliche Anzahl von verbalen Wurzeln abgeleiteter Substantiva mit aktiver sowol, als passiver Bedeutung, die auf ki ausgehn, zuerst einige von einfachen Zeitwörtern abgeleitete, wie fi-ki, „das Schlagen" und „das was geschlagen wird" (musikalisches Instrument) von mé-dō fi-yo, „ich schlage", dann z. B. bad-ír-ki, „Leiter" von mé-dō wád-o, „ich steige", indem das ir zur Bezeichnung der Instrumentalität zwischen Wurzel und Endung eingeschoben ist. Drittens andere von der auf kō ausgehenden intensiven Verbalform, über die ich oben S. CXXX gesprochen habe, abgeleitet, wie z. B. džōdá-ki, „die Ruhe" von mé-dō džōda-kō, „ich ruhe, bleibe" und viele andere.

d) Auf de und ndē auch Eigenschaft und Zweck bezeichnend: yil-do, „Licht" (des Feuers) von yil, yel, „leuchten, scheinen", woher auch das Nennwort yél-o-ma, nyél-o-ma, „Tageslicht" abgeleitet ist, pōf-de, „Lunge" (Ding zum Athmen); nyāma-ndē, „Ding

for instance, mé-dō idi mo-sōda, „I will buy"; om-o-andi om-o-holli am, verbally „he knows, he shows me", i. q. „he knows to show me". But, on the other hand, I have also instances of the pronominal form not being added to the second verb, and the latter, therefore, being used as a sort of infinitive, in the phrases mé-dō idi wádo, „I will mount", and no n-gida wōdi n-gōdum, „how wilt thou arrange this thing", from the same verb mé-dō idi, „I will", and mé-dō wōdi, „I make, arrange".

As for the phrase hokk(u) am ndiam n-yĕre, „give me water to drink" from mé-dō yāra, I think, we must look upon nyere as a sort of infinitive.

As for the place, the verb occupies in a phrase, I have to observe, that it always precedes the object.

6. *Nouns.*

I now proceed to treat of the noun in the Pūl-language, a chapter exceedingly rich on account of the many irregular forms which it contains. For it is very remarkable, that this language in its present state of development scarcely exhibits one single instance of a monosyllabic form of a noun, while the original forms have been combined in the most different manner. Thus, we learn only by going backwards from composite forms, that the monosyllabic root of biṅgel, „son", was bi.

In order to show, how nouns have been formed in this language from verbal notions, I here give a few instances of such a formation, without however making the very slightest attempt at completeness:

a) First I have two interesting instances of how nouns have been derived from the verb by simply changing the first consonant according to the laws registered p. CXV, and forming the termination partly in o, as indicative of the activity of an individual, partly in um, when indicating an inanimate being. One of these instances is gōd-um, „a thing", from mé-dō wōd-i, „I make, perform"; the other gūdž-o, „thieving he" i. q. „the thief" from mé-dō ūdž-i, „I do steal, rob". We have, therefore, scarcely to look upon the first syllable of these nouns as containing go, „one". As instances of such a simple change of the first consonant I mention konno, „war" from mé-dō honno, „I make war", and bār-o (in bār(o) ɗadune), „the murderer", from mé-dō wār-a, „I kill, murder".

b) Then it seems, that there is a class of nouns derived from verbal notions by means of a change of the first consonant, and by adding gu or go at the end, such as tăoggu (tăod-gu), „bargain, trade", most probably derived from (mé-dō) sōd-a, „I buy", (mé-noṅg) tăōd-a, „we buy", as well as dšaggu, „slavery", although I have as yet not been able to make out the verbal root of the latter term. From a certain point of view the term dšū-n-go, „hand", also (p. CXVII) does belong hither.

c) Now, I have a numerous list of nouns derived from verbs, and terminating in ki, first a few derived from simple verbs, such as fi-ki with an active, as well as with a passive meaning, „the beating", and „what is beaten" (musical instrument) from mé-dō fi-yo, „I do beat"; bad-ir-ki, „scale, ladder" from mé-dō wád-o, „I mount", the ir being inserted, as we shall see more clearly further on, in order to designate the instrumentality, by means of which the ascending is made; then others from the intensive verbal form in kĕ, of which I have treated p. CXXXI, such as dšōdá-ki, „the rest, stay", from mé-dō dšōda-kĕ, „I stay, remain", and many others.

d) We have further a class of nouns terminating in de, nde, ndĕ, and indicating a quality or instrumentality, such as yil-de, „the light (of the fire)" from yil, yel, „to light, shine", from whence also the substantive yél-o-ma, nyél-o-ma, „daylight" has been derived; pōf-do, „thing for breathing", „lungs"; nyāma-nde, „a thing to eat", „food" = kō-

zum Essen", Nahrung (identisch mit kō-nyāma-te) und eben daher unzweifelhaft yāme-nde oder yāma-nde, „Erntezeit", besonders interessant durch den Zusatz von gauri und buiri, eigentlich „die Zeit, wo man viel (oder frische) Hirse verzehrt"; ja eben so sicher haben wir von eben dieser Wurzel herzuleiten den Begriff des nur durch leichte Betonung verschiedenen yāmú-nde, „Schuld, Forderung", d. h. „das was aufzehrt"; dā-nde, „Hals"; bérende, wol bér-e-nde, „Herz" (wahrscheinlich mit wār-u, „tödten" zusammenhängend, „wo man getödtet wird, woran man stirbt"); semté-nde, „Schaam"; wolf-nde, „Rede", von me-wól-ai, „ich spreche"; džūl-de, „Gebet", von mé-dō džūl-a, „ich bete"; hȳl-le-nde, „Bosheit", vielleicht mit dem Arabischen حيلة verwandt; bitú-nde, „Jahr" (wolánde bitá-nde, „Neujahrstag", eigentlich „Neujahrs-Nacht"); wolúnde selbst, im Plural bulde scheint nicht hierher zu gehören, da schon das Zeitwort mé-do weldi lautet, 1ste Pers. Plur. mim-boldi; tingú-nde, Kopfkissen" d. h. eigentlich „wo anzulehnen (den Kopf)".

Bemerkung. Während diese Endung de, nde als das Mittel anzeigend, vermöge dessen etwas geschieht, sich an das Zeitwort do anzuschliessen scheint, möchte dagegen dieselbe Endung bei einer anderen Klasse von Substantiven, wie yol-de, balbúl-de, „Hügellandschaft", vielmehr die Örtlichkeit bezeichnen, und diese Ansicht erhält ihre Bestätigung durch solche Ortspartikeln wie badde, „nahe bei"; gudde, „ausserhalb"; hákkunde, „zwischen", „in der Mitte". Was dagegen rug-ór-de, „Fährort", „Punkt, wo man einen Fluss passirt", betrifft, so bin ich ungewiss, ob er zu dieser Klasse oder der nächstfolgenden gehört. Vergleiche dazu bok-ór-de, „Schweif"; sag-ór-de, „Ellbogen".

c) Wir haben nämlich eine andere Reihe von Substantiven, die vor der Endung de noch ein ir aufweist. Da wir nun dieses selbe ir schon oben S. CXXXIV, c. in bud-ír-ki in ähnlicher Bedeutung gefunden haben und noch ferner bei den Adjektiven wiederholt finden werden, ist es mehr als wahrscheinlich, dass die zuweilen vorkommende Form ríde, wie in doffo-ríde, „Küche", wo auch die Rücksicht auf Wohllaut ihren Einfluss übte, nur eine später entstandene Korruption ist. Die Endung ir-de finden wir nun besonders Verbalwurzeln angehängt, wie z. B. džōd-ír-de, „Ort zum Sitzen", „Bank", von mó-dō džōd-a, „ich sitze"; džang-ír-de, „Ort zum Lesen, Schule", von mó-dō džang-a, „ich lese"; foll-ír-de, „Ort der Verbindung, Konfluenz (von Flüssen)". Jedoch scheint sie auch direkt mit Substantiv-Begriffen verbunden zu werden, obgleich wol in den meisten Fällen verbale Wurzeln zu Grunde liegen, aber bat-ír-de, „Versammlungsort zur Unterhaltung" z. B. scheint einfach durch die dem Fremdwort batū, „Rede" angehängte Endung ir-de gebildet zu sein. Eine Art von Verbindungsglied zwischen diesen beiden Kategorien scheint džūl-ír-de, džūld-ír-de, džūd-ír-de zu bilden, von mé-dō džūla, „ich bete"; džūl-de, „das Gebet". Von ram-ír-de, „Tränkstätte (des Viehes)" und lum-ór-de, „Regierungssitz" sind mir keine verbale Wurzeln bekannt, ich zweifle aber kaum, dass solche existiren. Auch bangá-rde, džogá-rde gehören hierher. — Nahe verwandt dieser Klasse Komposita auf ir-de sind die auf ir-dum ausgehenden, wie kopp-ir-dum (lūna, „die Naht (des Bootes)", wahrscheinlich von mó-dō habba, „ich binde"; nang-ir-dum (lídi, „Fisch-) Harpune", von mó-dō nanga, „ich ergreife". Die auf ir-gel ausgehenden werden wir unter g) berücksichtigen.

f) Nun haben wir weiter eine zahlreiche Klasse von Substantiven, die auf ol, gol, ngol; al, gal; ol, ul, gul ausgehen, je nach dem Charakter des Vokal-Lautes der Stammsilbe. Wahrscheinlich sind die hierher gehörigen Substantive insgesammt von verbalen Wurzeln abgeleitet, obgleich ich dieselben erst in wenigen Beispielen nachweisen kann, wie z. B. kabb-ol, „das Band", von mó-dō habb-a, „ich binde"; kira-ol, „die Wunde", „der Schnitt", von mó-dō hira-a, „ich schneide, verwunde"; džāha-ngol, „Marsch, Karawane", von mó-dō yāh-a, „ich marschire, reise". Dass auch lan-ol, „Pfad" so abgeleitet ist, ersehen wir aus dem unter g) anzuführenden lan-ir-gel. Ebenso gebildet sind dimgel, „Dorn", giyel, „Gepäck".

nyāma-te from mó-do nyāma, „I eat", and from the same root, no doubt, the term yāme-nde or yáma-nde, „the harvesttime", properly the time, „where there is much to eat", as is best shewn by the adding of the terms gauri, „millet" and hairi, „Indian corn"; nay, considered from another point of view and with a slight change of accent yamá-nde very naturally conveys the meaning of „debt"; wolí-nde, „word, speech" from me-wól-ai, „I speak"; dŭāl-de, „the prayer", from mó-dō dŭāl-a, „I pray"; bér-e-nde, „heart", most probably with the original meaning „(the spot) where one is killed", „the most vulnerable part" from mó-dō wār-a, „I kill"; then the following terms, the verbal roots of which I am not acquainted with, such as dā-nde, „neck", probably with the original meaning of „supporter" (compare yā-nde, „the eater, glutton"; yaná-nde, „tomb"); semté-nde, „bashfulness"; hájjle-nde, „malice", perhaps derived from an Arabic root; hitá-nde, „year"; wolándo hitá-nde, „(new) year's day", properly „(new) year's night"; wolánde, plur. balde itself not seeming to belong to this class, as the verbal form is mó-do woldi, 1st person plur. mim-beldi, „I pass a night", vocab. p. 40; tingá-nde, „where to lay down (the head)", „cushion". — Rather a locality seems to be implied by the termination de in some other instances, such as yol-de, bulhól-de, „hilly country", and others, this view being confirmed by the form of the local particles such as badde, „close by, near"; hákkunde, „between"; gadde, „outside". As for rag-ér-de, „fording place", and other terms, I am uncertain whether it belongs to this, or rather to the following class of nouns.

e) For we have another class of nouns terminating in de, as clearly indicating a place, locality, and inserting before it the syllable ir, as indicative of the purpose or object of the action. Of this sort of composition we have met already with an instance in the term bad-ír-kí mentioned above, „a thing for mounting, ascending", and which makes it probable, that the form ríde which occurs in some instances instead of írde, such as defto-ríde, „cooking place", in which instance there is moreover a euphonical reason, is nothing but a later form of the same composition. Now, we have as well composite nouns where this termination has been added to a verbal root, as on the other hand such, where it is added to a substantival notion, or at least, where I am not able to make out the verbal root. Thus, for instance, we have the term džōd-ír-de, verbally „where to sit", i. q. „a place for sitting, a seat" from mó-dō džōd-a, „I sit down"; džang-ír-de, „where to read", a school, from mó-dō džang-a, „I do read"; fott-ír-de, „where to join" i. q. „the confluence (of rivers)"; a sort of transition from one of these subdivisions to the other is formed by džūld-ír-de, or in vulgar pronunciation džūd-ír-de, „where to pray" from dŭāl-de, „the prayer" (mó-dō džūl-a, „I pray"). For the terms hat-ír-de, „where to speak" i. q. „the meeting place where people gather for passing the evening"; ram-ír-de, „where to give to drink", „the watering place" and lam-ór-de, „seat of government", I have no verbal roots, but I have no doubt, that for the two latter at least such exist. Nearly related to this class of nouns terminating in ír-de seem to be the few nouns composed with ir-dum, kopp-ir-dum lāna, „the juncture of the boat"; nok-ir-dum ndiam, a. hite; nang-ir-dum lídi, „the fishhook" from mó-dō nang-a, „I seize", and the few in ir-gol such as korb-ir-gol lāna, lau-ir-gol lána, „the rudder, oar" i. q. „the instrument for directing the boat", and the other similar terms which I am going to mention under g).

f) Moreover, we have a very numerous class of nouns, terminating in el, gel, ngel; al, gal; ol, ul, gul according to the character of the vowel which precedes, and probably all of them derived from verbal roots, although only in a few instances I am able as yet to point out those roots: kabb-ol, „the bundle" from mó-dō habb-a, „I bind"; kirs-ol, „the cut, the wound" from mó-dō hirs-a, „I cut, I wound"; lau-ol (compare lau-ir-gol above), „the path"; dimgel, „thorn" and giyol, „luggage", and other similar terms. Then with the termination ngol, as, for instance, džāha-ngol, „the march, caravan" from mó-dō yāh-a, „I go".

X. 1) Ich muss hier jedoch bemerken, dass nicht alle Substantive auf el auf solche Weise von einfachen verbalen Begriffen abzuleiten sind, sondern dass wir zuerst alle die auf diese Form ausgehenden Diminutiva auszunehmen haben, wie sûka-el, „der kleine Knabe", von sûka, „Knabe"; putâ-el, „Füllen", von putšu, „Pferd"; hos-el, „kleiner Felshügel", von hosere, „Fels, Berge"; kaad-el, „Körbchen", von handere, „Korb" und so weiter.

X. 2) Eine weitere Klasse von auf el ausgehenden Substantiven begreift solche, die der Haussa-Sprache entlehnt sind, wie sirkinuel, „Ingenschuo" (H. sirkin), dárto-el, „Feile" (H. darto). Allerdings sind diese Entlehnungen nicht so zahlreich, wie die auf ri ausgehenden.

g) Wir haben nun auch, wie schon unter c) angedeutet, eben diese Endung el, gel, gol u. s. w. in Verbindung mit der Silbe ir, verstümmelt r. Dahin gehören daru-r-gel, „das Instrument (sich) zu sehn", d. h. „der Spiegel", von mé-dô dâra, „ich sehe"; bind-ír-gul, „das Ding zum Schreiben", „die Feder", von mé-dô wind-a, „ich schreibe"; nyo-r-gal, „das Ding zum Nähen", „die Nadel", von mé-dô nyô-a, „ich nähe"; mábu-r-gel, „das Ding zum Schliessen", „das Schloss", von mé-dô mâbi, „ich schliesse"; omt-ír-gel, „das Ding zum Öffnen", „der Schlüssel", von mé-dô omti, „ich öffne"; ja wir haben selbst einen dem letzteren synonymen Ausdruck mubi-t-ír-gel von mé-dô mubi-ta, der negativen Form von mábi. Ganz ähnlich haben wir nun offenbar auch zu erklären korb-ír-gel lânu und lau-ír-gel lânu für „Ruder" und „Steuer", indem das letztere mit lau-el, „Pfad" verglichen, die Grundbedeutung zu haben scheint „das Richtungswerkzeug des Bootes".

h) Ich habe nun eine beschränkte Klasse von auf am ausgehenden Substantiven, die insgesammt etwas Flüssiges bezeichnen, und auf die ich bei den Adjektiven zurückkommen werde. Beispiele sind ndiam, „Wasser"; îyam, „Blut"; kossam, „saure Milch"; kêtšam, „süsse Milch" (kêtšum, „süss"); nebbam, „Butter", nämlich im geschmolzenen Zustande.

i) Wir haben nun hier auch die ursprünglich verbalen Formen zu berücksichtigen, die ich schon oben S. CXXIV erwähnt habe, nämlich die die Eigenschaft oder die Beschäftigung von Menschen bezeichnenden, auf do als ursprüngliche Form des Particips der Vergangenheit, und auf ido, udo als Participial-Form der Gegenwart ausgehenden, die wir auch bei den Adjektiven wiederum zu berücksichtigen haben werden. Dahin gehören als ganz selbstständig gebrauchte Substantiva Formen wie lâm-ido, „Häuptling, Herrscher"; bâtš-ido, „Minister" und höchst wahrscheinlich auch mâtšudo, „Sklave"; tšútudo, „Streithammel".

k) Eben so bilden die mit dem Vorsatz von džom, „Herr, Meister von" gebildeten Charakter-Namen von Menschen, wie džom-tšêde, „Herr der Muscheln", d. h. „reich"; džom-goûga, „Herr der Wahrheit" oder „Wahrheitsfreund", ein Mittelding zwischen Adjektiven und Substantiven und müssen, da sie mehr in ersterer Beziehung gebraucht werden, weiter unten näher berücksichtigt werden.

l) Hier muss ich noch auf die Endung erâ-o, irâ-o hinweisen, die ausschliesslich den verwandtschaftliche Beziehungen der Familie bezeichnenden Wurzelwörtern hinzugefügt wird, wie tan-irâ-o, „der Enkel", obgleich man sagt tan-am, „mein Enkel"; maun-irâ-o, „älterer Bruder" (maun-am, „mein älterer Bruder"); miñ-orâ-o, „jüngerer Bruder" (miñ-am, „mein jüngerer Bruder"); ês-erâ-o, „Schwiegervater" (ês-am, „mein Schwiegervater"). Es ist dieses ein für die Abstammung der Ful überaus wichtiges Verhältniss, auf das ich zurückkomme.

m) Das Geschlecht wird im Ful durch die Endung fast gar nicht angedeutet — eine Ausnahme macht mollu, „männliches", mollil, „weibliches Füllen" — und übt überhaupt wenig Einfluss, da das Zeitwort keine besonderen Formen für das Geschlecht hat. Bei Menschen wird das weibliche Geschlecht durch den Zusatz von débo, „Frau", Plur. rewbe, bei Thieren durch dôu oder rêo-ru bezeichnet, bei dem männlichen wird selten gorko, „Mann" hinzugesetzt, mâmu gorko, „Grossvater"; mâmu débo, „Grossmutter"; putšu, „Pferd"; putšu dôu, „Stute". Diese substantive Beifügung ist für unser Gefühl etwas auffallend, da von gorko und débo Adjektiv-Formen existiren, gorâku, „männlich" und dewâku, „weiblich".

N. 1) I must here, however, add, that not all the nouns terminating in **el** are formed in this manner, but that we must first exterminate from this class all the diminutives formed in this way, such as **suka-el**, „the young boy" from **sūka**, „boy"; **putš-el**, „the foal" from **putšu**, „the horse"; **dek-el** from **deko**, „youth"; **kos-ël**, „the small rock", „hill" from **hosere**, „the rock", „mountain"; **kaud-ël**, „a small basket" from **handëro**, „basket", and so on.

N. 2) Another class of nouns terminating in **el** comprises such terms, as have been borrowed from the Hausa, such as **sirkiauel**, „string of bow" (H. **sirkin**); **dúrto-el**, „file" (H. **durto**). This class of borrowed terms, however, is not by far so numerous as that terminating in **ri**, as for instance **gerö-ri** (H. **gérö**), „Negro-millet".

g) We have now another class of nouns inserting before the termination **gel**, and so on, the above mentioned **ir**, abbreviated **r**, in order to indicate the purpose, for which the instrument is used, as, for instance, **dura-r-gol**, „the instrument for seeing (one's self), the mirror", from **mé-dō dārа**, „I see, look"; **nyo-r-gal**, „the instrument for sewing, the needle" from **mé-dō nyō-u**, „I do sew"; **bind-ir-gul**, „the instrument for writing, the pen" from **mé-dō wind-a**, „I write"; **mábu-r-gol**, „the thing for closing, shutting, the lock" from **mé-dō mábi**, „I shut"; **omt-ir-gel**, „the thing for opening, the key" from **mé-dō omti**, „I open"; nay, we have even another term with the same meaning, viz **mábi-t-ir-gel** formed from **mábi-ta**, the negative form of **mábi**, and meaning „not to shut, let open, to open".

h) We have now another class of nouns terminating in **am**, and all of them indicating, as it seems, a fluid substance, although only in a few cases I am enabled to point out the root, as, for instance, **ndiam**, „water"; **ïyam**, „blood"; **kossam**, „(sour) milk"; **kétšam**, „sweet, fresh milk" from **kétšum**, „sweet"; **nebbam**, „butter" (in a fluid state).

i) I now proceed to point out those nouns which indicate individual characters of man, terminating in the form **ido**, which is evidently a kind of participle of the present tense (see above p. CXXV), and in **udo**, as well as in **do**, the latter form being originally a kind of participle of the past tense, such as **lám-ido**, „ruler, chief"; **bátš-ido**, „minister"; **mátšudo**, „slave". Such forms, however, being more frequently used as adjectives, especially those terminating in **do**, I have once more to return to this question under the relative head.

k) In a similar manner the terms denoting individualities or occupations of man, and composed with **džom** meaning „master of, possessing", such as **džom-tšédo**, „master of (many) cowries", „rich"; **džom-gonga**, „master of truth", „sincere", form a kind of intermediate class between adjectives and substantives, and have to be considered once more when treating of the formation of the former.

l) Finally, I have still to point out the very remarkable termination **erā-o**, **irā-o**, which is exclusively added to the roots of nouns signifying degrees of relationship, such as **tan-irā-o**, „the grandson", while the Fulbe say **tan-am**, „my grandson", the root therefore being **tan**; **maun-irā-o**, „elder brother" (**maun-am**, „my elder brother"); **miñ-erā-o**, „younger brother" (**miñ-am**); **ös-erāo**, „father in law" (**ös-am**, „my father in law").

m) As for **the gender**, as far as I am aware, it is not indicated in the Fūl-idiom by the termination, and in general exercises very little influence upon the whole of the grammar, the verb possessing no individual forms of distinction between the two genders. In order to indicate the female sex, therefore, the term **débo**, „woman", plur. **rauhe** is added, when human beings are concerned, while with regard to animals the female sex is indicated by adding **dêu** or **rëo-ru**; the male sex in general being understood, where nothing is added, only in a few cases, where the notion might be equivocal, **gorko**, „man" is added with regard to human beings. Thus, I have **mâma gorko**, „grandfather"; **mâma débo**, „grandmother"; **putšu**, „horse"; **putšu dêu**, „mare". The Fūl-language, however, possesses a full adjective form derived from these nouns, viz **gorâku**, „male", and **deváku**, „female". An isolated instance of a peculiar formation distinguishing the gender is **mollu**, „colt", **mollil**, „filly".

7. *Verbindung, Abwandelung und Pluralbildung der Nennwörter.*

a) Von Abwandelung der Kasus im Ful habe ich nur in sehr seltenen Fällen Beispiele gefunden. So wird auch Subjekt und Objekt ohne Binde-Partikel oder Kasus-Veränderung an einander gefügt, umgekehrt als im Deutschen, indem jenes dem letzteren nicht nach-, sondern vorgesetzt wird; so sagt man im Ful anstatt „Ohr-loch", bude hinnere („Loch-ohr"); „Grundtaxe" („Feld-erde"), lede leadi; „Sitz des Fürsten", gellure lámido; „Hauswirth", „Hausherr", džom-sudo („Herr-Haus"); „Hauswirthin", inna suro („Mutter-Haus"), und so weiter die zahlreichen mit džom zusammengesetzten Begriffe; so auch in Verbindung mit dem Zeitwort, wie bâba sûka o-mai, „(der) Vater (des) Kind(es) ist gestorben".

Die wenigen Beispiele, wo ich bei den in den Haussa-Staaten angesiedelten Fulbe ein n als Bindeglied zwischen Subjekt und Objekt eingefügt fand, sind offenbar eben auf Einfluss der Haussa-Sprache zurückzuführen, wie džungo-n toggóre, „Ärmel vom Hemd"; bi-n džinnu, bi-n džâlu, „Sohn der Hure", „Hurensohn".

Eine Art Ablativ mit einem angehängten go habe ich bei Eigenschaftswörtern mit substantivischem Begriff gefunden, wie bûri dâûtu-go, „es übertrifft an Länge, ist länger"; bûri dudo-go, „übertrifft an Vielheit, ist zahlreicher". Und dasselbe go finden wir selbst der lokalen Partikel to, „wo", angefügt in der Form to-go.

b) Ich will gleich hier die Stellung der Präpositionen in Bezug auf das Substantiv erwähnen; „auf", „über", dô; „unter", les; „in", der; „zwischen", húkkunde; „mit", „für", be u. s. w. werden dem Substantiv, worauf sie Bezug haben, vorgesetzt, wie dô tondi, „auf den Berg, auf dem Berge"; les dâgo, „unter die Matte, unter der Matte"; der mâyo, „in den, in dem Fluss"; húkkunde gellâdže, „zwischen den Stühlen"; be lana, „mit dem Boote, für das Boot" u. s. w.

c) Ich gehe nun zur Bildung der Mehrheit des Substantivs über, die einen der reichsten und mannichfachsten Abschnitte der Ful-Sprache bildet, und die ich deshalb bis zum Ende dieses Paragraphen gelassen habe. Ich werde hier in alphabetischer Ordnung ein vollständiges Verzeichniss der mir bekannt gewordenen Abwandlungen der Endungen geben, wobei ich bemerke, dass die dadurch in vielen Fällen motivirte Umwandlung der Anfangsbuchstaben des Wortes nach den S. CXII aufgestellten Grundsätzen nicht näher in Betracht gezogen ist. Ich gebe stets die Bedeutung im Deutschen dabei, weil, wie man sich leicht überzeugen wird, die Abwandlungen sich in vielen Fällen auf Klassenbegriffe zurückführen lassen, wie wir das mit den Endungen erâ-o und am schon gesehen haben.

Sing. a Plur. e (sehr selten): gess-a, gess-e, „Felder, Feldgärten";
 „ a Plur. i: edd-a, edd-i, „wilde Büffel"; mbann-a, baun-i (anderer Ausdruck), „wilde Büffel"; kob-a, kob-i, „Antilopen";
 „ a Plur. abe: sûk-a, sûk-âbe, „Knaben";
 „ a Plur. erâ-be: bâb-a, bâb-erâ-be, „Väter"; inn-a, inn-erâ-be, „Mütter"; mâm-a, mam-erâ-be, „Grosseltern"; maun-a, maun-erâ-be, „ältere Brüder"; miñ-a, miñ-erâ-be, „jüngere Brüder". S. die Bemerkung oben S. CXXXVIII, 1; aber von bâba und inna sind keine Nebenformen auf erâ-o vorhanden;
 „ aa Plur. ebbi: daa, debbi, „Strausse";
 „ ao Plur. aiwerrâbe: ka-o, ka-iwerrâbe, „Oheime"; s. S. CXXXVIII, 1;
 „ aua Plur. âdže: harag-aua, harag-âdže, „Art von Bettstelle";
 „ auel Plur. âdže: džig-auel, džig-âdže, „Adler"; ruggum-auel, ruggum-âdže, „Glöckchen";
 „ auel Plur. âdži: debb-auel, debb-âdži, „Vieh";

7. *The manner of declining the nouns, and the manifold ways of forming their plural.*

a) As for the declension of the noun, very rarely I have found an instance of case. Thus, even the subject and object are joined together without the slightest change, but in the inverse way as is the case in German and English. Thus, in the Fûl-idiom instead of „ear-hole" they say verbally „hole-ear", bude hiunero; instead of „ground-rent", „money-ground", tâôdo lesdi; thus, they say also for „residence, capital", gellûre lâmido („town-prince"); for „landlady", inna ûro („mother-house"); for „landlord", džom-sûdo („master-house"), and in the same manner all the terms with džom, „master", are composed. The same construction is observed also in connection with the verb, as, for instance, bâba sûka o-mai, „(the) father (of the) child died".

The rare instances, where I have found an n inserted between subject and object, all regard terms employed by the Fúlbe, settled in provinces formerly occupied by the Hausa-race, and where the Fûl-idiom in consequence has lost much of its original purity, as for instance džûúgo-n toggôre, „the sleeve", properly „hand of shirt"; bi-n džinu, bi-n džâlu, „son of whore", „whoreson".

Of a sort of ablative case by adding go I have found instances in connection with adjectives, when used like substantives, as, for instance, bûri džûtu-go, „it surpasses in length, is longer"; bûri dûdo-go, „it surpasses in multitude", „is more numerous". The same go we find also added to the local particle to meaning „where" in the form to-go.

b) I think this a fit place for speaking of the position which is assigned to prepositions in connection with substantives, such as dô, „on, upon",; les, „under"; der, „in"; hákkundo, „between"; he, „with, by", and so on, all of them preceding the object. Thus they say dô tondi, „on the mountain"; les dâgo, „under the mat"; der mayo, „in the river"; hákkundo gellûdže, „between the towns"; he lâna, „by (the) boat".

c) I now proceed to treat of a very important subject which, on this very account, I have left to the end of this paragraph, I mean the forms of the plural number, of which I shall here endeavour to give a complete list in an alphabetical order, as far as they have become known to me, taking as little regard as possible to the change of the beginning vowel or consonant, which takes place according to the laws developed above p. CXIII. However, it is very essential to add always the meaning of each word in English, the notion of many of these terms importance exercising a great influence upon the termination, as in certain cases there is evidently a common law which rules the formation of the terms of a similar notion, as we have already seen to be the case with erâ-o and am.

sing. a plur. e (very rare): gesa-a, gese-e, „fields";

„ a plur. i: edd-a, edd-i, „wild buffaloes"; mbanu-a, bann-i, „wild buffaloes" (other term); kôb-a, kôb-i, „antelopes";

„ a plur. âbe: sûk-a, sûk-âbe, „boys";

„ a plur. erâ-be: bâb-a, bâb-erâ-be, „fathers"; inu-a, inn-erâ-be, „mothers"; mâm-a, mam-erâ-be, „grandfathers"; mann-a, mann-erâ-be, „elder brethren"; miñ-a, miñ-erâ-be, „younger brethren". See however, the remark above p. CXXXIX, I, with regard to the termination erâ-o, irâ-o, although of bâba, and inna there is no other form for the singular;

„ au plur. ebbi: dau, debbi, „ostriches";

„ ao plur. aiwerâbe: ka-o, ka-iwerâbe, „uncles", see p. CXXXIX, I;

„ aaa plur. âdže: harag-aaa, harag-âdže, „a kind of bedstead";

„ auel plur. âdže: dâig-auel, dâig-âdže, „eagles"; ruggum-auel, ruggum-âdže, „small bells";

„ auel plur. âdži: debb-auel, debb-âdži, „milk";

Sing. aau Plur. adže: wall-aau, ball-ādže (H. balawal), „Schultern";
„ aure Plur. wāi: ho-aure, Plur. ko-wōi, „Mistkäfer";
„ al Plur. e: gerl-al, Plur. gerl-e, „Rebhühner"; dūt-al, dūt-e, „Pfade, Wege";
„ ambe Plur. ande [?mbe Plur. nde]: džau-ámbe, džau-úndo, „Leute aus dem, Reisen IV, S. 147, erwähnten Stamm";
„ ādže Plur. be: tiggar-ādže, tiggár-be, „reisende Kaufleute";
„ ādžo Plur. oë: bar-ādžo, bár-oë, „Diener";
„ áñkol Plur. idē: temb-áñkol, témb-idē, „die Arme".

„ ba Plur. di: gelō-ba, gelō-di, „Kamele"; bab-ba, bam-di (statt bab-di), „Esel";
„ be, „sie", zur Bezeichnung des Plurals hinzugefügt, džom, džom-be, „Herren von", „im Besitz von", s. oben S. CX;
„ be Plur. be [o Plur. e]: módibo, módibe, „Gelehrte".

„ da Plur. rādži: mbā-da, mba-rādži, „Antilope Soemmeringii";
„ dal Plur. le: tšō-dal, tšō-le (contrahirt von tšōdale?), „eine Art Vogel";
„ de Plur. e: kūl-de, kūl-e, „Klafter";
„ de Plur. le: wam-de, bam-le, „Berge";
„ débo Plur. rawbe, „Frauen";
„ di Plur. le: dō-di, dō-le, „Schatten";
„ di Plur. lle: bó-di, bo-lle, „Schlangen"; bú-di, ba-lle, „Geschwüre";
„ do Plur. lbe: dū-do, dū-lbe (neben der Form dū-di), „viele";
„ do Plur. be: bí-do, bí-be, „Söhne"; džūl-do, džūl-be, „Moslemin"; hodé-do, fodé-be, „Plänkler"; hā-do, hā-be, „Neger"; góddu-do, wóddu-be, adjekt. „ferne"; kod-do, hob-be, „Gäste"; hob-bo wóddu-be, „weithergekommene Gäste"; kor-do, hor-be, „Ehefrauen freien Geblütes"; lillā-do, lillū-be, „Boten"; mátšu-do, mátšu-be, „Sklaven"; nilā-do, nilā-be, „Adjudanten"; pipí-do, fifí-be, „Schützen"; tšautšán-do, sausám-be, „Weber"; tšoi-do, soi-be, „Bettler"; džëotó-do, džootó-be, „Trommler"; džan-do, yan-bo, adj. „hitzig, Hitzköpfe";
„ do Plur. lli: fé-do, pelli, „Tuareg".

„ e Plur. ēdži: bill-e, bill-ēdži, „Stühle"; yatim-e, yatim-ēdži, „Waisen";
„ ēdžo Plur. ai: berber-ēdžo, bérber-ai, „Bororo-Leute";
„ egge Plur. ai: negge, nai, „Kühe";
„ ebi Plur. ēdži, s. weiter unten bei Plur. dži;
„ el Plur. de: nyal-el, nyal-de, „Viehhüter";
„ el Plur. e (l abgeworfen): giy-el, giy-e, „Dorne"; komb-el, komb-e, „Röhre"; lū-ol, lū-e, „Hörner"; tubb-el, tubb-e;
„ el Plur. le: dong-el (lingo, dong-le (lidi, „Fischgräten";
„ ēo Plur. eyēbe: gēo, geyēbe, „Kräuter";
„ ēu Plur. ēdži: dau-ēu, dau-ēdži, „Art Erdfrucht";
„ ēul Plur. ēdži: lill-ēul, lill-ēdži, „Flügel";
„ edōrl Plur. tšēde, „Muscheln".

„ fu-ru Plur. pi [fu Plur. pi, s. S. CXII]: nó-fu-ru, nó-pi, „Ohren".

„ gel Plur. de: leg-gel, led-de (leg-de), „Bäume"; dámbo-gel, dámbo-de, „Thüren"; kathán-gel, hathán-do, „Lebern";

sing. aua plur. ádže: wall-auu, ball-ádže (H. balawul), „shoulders";
„ aure plur. wõi: ho-auro, plur. ko-wõi, „dung-beetles";
„ al plur. e: gerl-al, plur. gerl-e, „partridges"; dũl-al, dũl-e, „paths, tracks";
„ ambe plur. aade [ĩmbe plur. ude]: džau-ámbe, džau-áade, „individuals belonging to the tribe mentioned" Tr. and Disc. IV, p. 140;
„ ádže plur. be: tiggar-ádže, tiggár-be, „travelling merchants";
„ ádže plur. oë: bar-ádže, bár-oë, „servants, labourers";
„ áñkel plur. idë: tomb-áñkel, témb-idë, „arms".

„ ba plur. di: gelõ-ba, gelõ-di, „camels"; bab-ba, bam-di (instead bab-di), „asses";
„ be, „ibry" added to the root, in order to designate the plural form: džom, džom-be, „masters of", „possessing", see above p. CXI;
„ bo plur. be [o plur. o]: móddibo, móddibe, „learned men".

„ da plur. rádži: mbá-da, mba-rádži, „antilope Soemmeringii";
„ dal plur. le: tšõ-dal, tšõ-le (contracted from tšódale?), „some kind of bird";
„ de plur. e: hũl-de, kũl-e, „fathoms";
„ de plur. le: wam-de, bam-le, „mountains";
„ débo plur. rabbe, „women";
„ di plur. le: dõ-di, dõ-le, „shades, shadows";
„ di plur. lle: bó-di, bo-lle, „serpents"; bú-di, bu-lle, „sores, ulcers";
„ do plur. ībe: dũ-do, dũ-ībe (besides the form du-dĭ), „many";
„ do plur. be: bí-do, bí-be, „sons, children"; džul-do, džũl-be, „Mohammedans"; hodé-do, fodé-be, „skirmishers"; kã-do, hã-be, „negroes"; góddu-do, wóddu-be adj. „distant"; hod-do, hob-be, „guests" (hob-be wóddu-be, „guests from afar"); kor-do, hor-be, „wives of free descent"; lillã-do, lillã-be, „messengers"; mátšu-do, mátšu-be, „slaves"; nilã-do, nilã-be, „aides de camp"; pipí-do, fifí-be, „bowmen"; tšantšán-do, sausám-be, „weavers"; tšoi-do, soi-be, „beggars"; džëotõ-do, džeoto-be, „drummers"; džau-do, yau-be, adj. „hotspurs";
„ do plur. lli: fó-do, polli, „Tuwárek".

„ e plur. ëdži: bill-e, bill-ëdži, „towns"; yalím-e, yalím-ëdži, „orphans";
„ ëdže plur. ai: berber-ëdže, bérber-ai, „Bornu-men";
„ egge plur. ai: negge, nai, „cows";
„ ehi plur. ëdži, see further on hi plur. dži;
„ el plur. de: nyal-el, nyal-de, „cattlebreeders";
„ el plur. e (l thrown off): gíy-el, gíy-e, „thorns"; homb-el, komb-e, „reeds"; lũ-el, lũ-e, „horns"; tubb-el, tubb-e;
„ el plur. le: doñg-el (liñgo, doñg-le (lídi, „fishbones";
„ ëo plur. eyëbe: gëo, geyëbe, „fripperers";
„ ëu plur. ëdži: dau-ëu, dau-ëdži, „kind of yams";
„ ëul plur. ëdži: lill-ëul, lill-ëdži, „wings";
„ edárl plur. tšëde, „cowries".

„ fu-ru plur. pi [fu plur. pi, see p. CXIII]: nó-fu-ru, nó-pi, „ears".

„ gel plur. de: leg-gel, led-de (leg-de), „trees"; dámbo-gel, dámbo-de, „doors"; hathán-gel, hathán-de, „livers";

Sing. gel Plur. di: donyúr-gel, donyúr-di, „Jungfrauen";
„ gel Plur. bakki: lō-gel, lō-bákki, „Jäger";
„ gel Plur. le: té-gel, té-le (contrahirt aus tégele!), „Hochzeiten"; kō-gel, kō-le, „Hochzeiten" (anderer Ausdruck);
„ gel Plur. dži: bi-gel, bi-dži, „Kälber";
„ go Plur. de: džūṅ-go, džūn-de, „Hände" (vgl. S. CXVI; jedoch džū-de richtiger);
„ gel Plur. di: džuréu-gel, džuréu-di, „Sandhügel";
„ gu Plur. di: ten-gu, ten-di, „Flöhe";
„ ṅgal Plur. li: ássa-ṅgal, ássa-li, „Hüften";
„ ṅgel Plur. be: bi-ṅgel, bí-be, „Kinder";
„ ṅgel Plur. de: koi-ṅgel, koi-de, „Beine";
„ ṅgel Plur. ki: kállu-ṅgel, kállu-ki, adj. „schlechte";
„ ṅgel Plur. ko: bi-ṅgel, bí-ko, „Söhne, Kinder";
„ ṅgel Plur. le: kúddu-ṅgel, kúddu-le, „Kleidungsstücke"; dau-ṅgel, dau-le, „Krähen"; džau-ṅgel, džau-le, „Perlhühner";
„ ṅgo Plur. de: džū-ṅgo, džū-de (diess ist die richtigere Form als džūnde), „Hände";
„ ṅgo Plur. di: lí-ṅgo, lí-di, „Fische";
„ ṅgo Plur. li: falmá-ṅgo, palmá-li, „Donnerschläge"; fedé-ṅgo, fedé-li, „Fingernägel";
„ ṅgel Plur. li: dže-ṅgel, dže-li, „Lichter";
„ ṅgo Plur. bi: du-ṅgo, dū-bi, „Jahre";
„ ṅgo Plur. di: bo-ṅgo, bō-di, „Mücken"; tšúddu-ṅgo, tšúddu-di, „gespornte Reiter";
„ ṅgu Plur. ye: gil-ṅgu, gil-ye, „Würmer";
„ džo Plur. be: bode-džo, wode-be, „rothe"; kilā-džo, kilā-be, „Schmiede";
„ džo Plur. ibe: bu-džo, bu-ibe, „erste Eunuchen"; gū-džo, wu-ibe, „Diebe";
„ džō Plur. de: torō-džo, torō-de, „Leute aus dem Stamme der Toro";
„ džo Plur. in: fattaké-džo, fattake-in, „reisende Kaufleute"; sōbá-džo, sōbu-in, „Freunde"; talké-džo, tálke-in, „Clienten"; tūru-džo, tūra-in, „Araber"¹);
„ džo Plur. ye: abí-džo, abí-ye, „fahrende Schüler".

„ he Plur. dži: sálekō-he, sálekō-dži, „Mähnen";
„ hi Plur. dži: káre-hi, karé-dži; gélle-hi, gellé-dži; búmme-hi, bummé-dži; kúrne-hi, kurné-dži; insgesammt Baumarten; dúgor-kulé-hi, dúgor-kulé-dži, „Antilope leucoryx".

„ i Plur. e: dugb-i, dugb-e, „Delebpalmen"; gauār-e, gauār-i, „Talha-Bäume"; tunn-i, taun-e, „Balanites Aegyptiacus"; folánd-i, folánd-e, „Kichebsen";
„ i Plur. idžidži (džidži angehängt): fi, fidžidži, „Sachen";
„ ido Plur. be: lám-ido, la-lám-be, „Fürsten, Häuptlinge". (Das erste la ist Vorsatz durch Reduplikation). (Von bátš-ido kenne ich leider den Plural nicht);
„ io Plur. idži: bir-io, bir-idži, „Erdmandeln";
„ io Plur. ūbe: džio, džūbe, „heirathsfähige Jungfrauen".

„ ka Plur. de: gas-ka, gas-de, „Löcher";
„ ki Plur. de: bel-ki, bel-de, „(Messer-)Scheiden"; fóndu-ki, fóndu-de, „Klafter";
„ kki Plur. dodže: bo-kki, bo-dōdže, „Adansonia digitata";

¹) Alle diese Wörter sind Fremdwörter, der Haussa- oder Kanúri-Sprache (sōba K. „Freund") entlehnt und die Singular-Form ist offenbar das Spätere, durch den Zusatz des erweichten go, „einer" entstanden.

sing. gel plur. di: donyúr-gel, donyúr-di, „virgins";
„ gel plur. hukki: lō-gel, lō-húkki, „sportsmen";
„ gel plur. le: tō-gel, tō-le (contracted from tógele?), „marriages"; kō-gel, kō-le, „marriages" (other term);
„ gel plur. dži: bī-gel, bī-dži, „calves";
„ ge plur. de: džūń-ge, džuu-de, „hands" (compare p. CXVII; better form džū-de);
„ gol plur. di: džaróu-gol, džaróu-di, „sanddowns";
„ gu plur. di: ten-gu, ten-di, „fleas";
„ ṅgal plur. li: dasa-ṅgal, dasa-li, „haunches";
„ ṅgel plur. be: bi-ṅgel, bí-be, „children";
„ ṅgel plur. de: koi-ṅgel, koi-de, „legs";
„ ṅgel plur. ki: kállu-ṅgel, kállu-ki, adj. „bad ones";
„ ṅgel plur. ko: bi-ṅgel, bí-ko, „sons, children";
„ ṅgel plur. le: káddu-ṅgel, káddu-le, „articles of dress"; duu-ṅgel, duu-le, „crows"; džau-ṅgel, džau-le, „guinea-fowls";
„ ṅge plur. de: džū-ṅge, džū-de, „hands" (this is the more correct form);
„ ṅge plur. di: lí-ṅge, lí-di, „fish";
„ ṅge plur. li: falmá-ṅge, palmā-li, „thunderstrokes"; feddé-ṅge, feddē-li, „nails (of the fingers)";
„ ṅgel plur. li: džo-ṅgel, džō-li, „lights";
„ ṅgu plur. bi: du-ṅgu, dū-bi, „years";
„ ṅgu plur. di: bo-ṅgu, bō-di, „mosquitoes"; tšúddu-ṅgu, tšúddu-di, „heavy horsemen";
„ ṅgu plur. ye: gil-ṅgu, gil-ye, „worms";
„ džo plur. be: bodē-džo, wodé-be, „red ones"; kilā-džo, kilā-be, „blacksmiths";
„ džo plur. ībe: bū-džo, bu-ībe, „chief eunuchs"; gū-džo, wu-ībe, „thiefs";
„ džō plur. de: torō-džo, torō-de, „people from the tribe of the Toro";
„ džo plur. in: fattāké-džo, fattāke-in, „travelling merchants"; sōbá-džo, sōba-in, „friends"; talké-džo, tálke-in, „clients"; tūra-džo, tūra-in, „Arabs"[1]);
„ džo plur. ye: ahí-džo, ahí-ye, „travelling scholars".

„ he plur. dži: sálekō-he, sálekō-dži, „manes";
„ hi plur. dži: káre-hi, karē-dži; géllo-hi, gellō-dži; búmme-hi, bumme-dži; kúrue-hi, kuruē-dži, „all of them species of trees";; dáger-kule-hi, dáger-kulé-dži, „antilope leucoryx".

„ i plur. e: dugb-i, dugb-o, „delebpalms"; gaudr-o, gaudr-i, „talha-trees"; tann-i, tann-e, „Balanites Aegyptiacus"; folúnd-i, folúnd-e, „lizards";
„ i plur. idžidži (džidži added): fi, fidžidži, „things";
„ ido plur. be: lám-ido, la-lám-be, „kings, chiefs". (The first syllable la has arisen from reduplication);
„ io plur. idži: bīr-io, bir-idži, „groundnuts";
„ io plur. ūbe: džio, džūbe, „girls fit for marriage".

„ ka plur. de: gas-ka, gas-de, „holes";
„ ki plur. de: bel-ki, bel-de, „edges" of knife; fóndu-ki, fóndu-de, „fathoms";
„ kki plur. dedže: bo-kki, bo-dodžo, „Adansonia digitata";

---

[1]) None of these terms is indigenous, but all have been borrowed either from the Hausa- or the Kanúri-language (sōba meaning „friend" in Kanúri), the plural exhibiting the original form to which džo, a softer form of go, „one" seems to be added in the singular.

Sing. ko Plur. be: gor-ko, wor-be, „Frauen"; dō-ko, dō-be, „junge Leute"; gainā-ko, wainā-be, „Hirten".

l im Plural abgeworfen: glyo-l, glye, „Dorne", s. oben el Plur. e;
„ l Plur. di: kongo-l, kóngo-di, „Rufe";
„ l Plur. re: bōdžo-l, wóddže-re, „Hasen";
„ lde Plur. di: wu-lde, bā-di, „Ameisenhügel";
„ lde Plur. nde: borrendó-lde, korrendó-nde, „Ameisen";
„ ldo Plur. be: kungá-ldo, hangá-be;
„ lel Plur. lli (el Plur. li): lelel, lelli, „Gazellen";
„ lo Plur. be: bahíl-lo, bahíl-be, „Schmiede"; wol richtiger o Plur. be: bahíl-o, bahíl-be.

„ m Plur. mbe, s. oben be angehängt.

„ nde Plur. de: wolí-nde, bolí-de, „Wörter, Sprache";
„ nde Plur. le: yenū-nde, genū-le, „Grillen";
„ ndi Plur. li: dā-ndi, dā-li, „Lastochsen";
„ ndu Plur. di: wa-ndu, bā-di, „Affen"; rauá-ndu, dauá-di, „Hunde";
„ ndu Plur. li: butá-ndu, búta-li, „Kornähren"; hóhe-ndu, kóhe-li, „Finger"; ho-ndu, fō-li, „Turteltauben"; fu-ndu, pū-li, „Melonen"; we-ndu, be-li, „Brunnen"; sú-wu-ndu, sū-li, „ein wildes Thier";
„ ndu Plur. lli: so-ndu, tšo-lli, „Vögel";
„ ñédo Plur. yimbe, „Leute, Individuen";
„ nyu, ñu Plur. di: nyú-nyu (ñú-ñu), nyū-di (ñū-di), „schwarze Ameisen";
„ nyo, ño Plur. mbe: pa-nyo (pa-ño), fa-mbo, „Jünglinge". (Vielleicht richtiger yo Plur. be, oder selbst o Plur. be, s. S. CXIV).

„ o Plur. ande: sapp-o (sáp-o), tšapp-ándo (tšap-ánde), „Zehner";
„ o Plur. be: pūl-o, fūl-be; kófer-o, húfer-be, „Heiden"; bangár-o, wangár-be, „Barbiere". Hierzu gehören auch die oben S. CXL unter a: erā-be erwähnten Nebenformen mann-erā-o, mann-erā-be; miñ-erā-o, miñ-erā-be;
„ o Plur. erā-be: ás-o (?es-erā-o), es-erā-be, „Schwiegerväter"; gogg-o, gogg-erā-be, „jüngere Tanten". Siehe oben zu a: erā-be;
„ o Plur. i: mōy-o, mōy-i, „termites fatales"; ṅgabb-o, ṅgabb-i, „Nilpferde";
„ o Plur. idži: diūr-o (džūr-o), diūr-idži (džūr-idži), „Hyänen";
„ o Plur. ōdži: fidž-o, fidž-ōdži, „Spiele, Tänze"; samg-o, samg-ōdži, „Galoppreitereien, Angriffe"; hóg-o, hog-ōdži, „rauhe Felspassage";
„ o Plur. ōbe: dor-ō, dor-ōbe, „Rinderhirten";
„ o Plur. terābe: híg-o, híg-oterābe, „Freunde". Offenbar hat auch hier das oben besprochene, verwandtschaftliche, geistige Verhältniss seinen Einfluss auf die Form geübt. Eine Form híg-oterāo für den Singular fand ich nicht in Gebrauch;
„ o Plur. ube: tšūt-o, siūt-ube, „Zwillinge";
„ o Plur. yébe: gé-o, ge-yébe, „Krämer";
„ ōde Plur. erēde: bort-ōde, bort-erēde, „enge Hemden";
„ ol Plur. i: lepp-ol, lepp-i, „Baumwollstreifen";
„ ol Pl. dže: gáru-ol, gará-dže, „ummauerte Städte"; danné-ol, danne-dže, „weiss";
„ ol Plur. ōdže: saff-ol, saff-ōdže, „Schiffe (der Muselmen)";
„ oru Plur. urri: ingdru, ingurri, „gegerbte Rindshäute";
„ oul Plur. ēdže: kéb-oul, kéb-ēdže, „Steigbügel".

sing. ko plur. be: gor-ko, wor-bo, „women"; dō-ko, dō-be, „young man"; guinā-ko, wainā-be, „shepherds".

l thrown off in the plural number: gīyo-l, gīy-o, „thorns"; see above ol plur. e;
„ l plur. di: kengo-l, kóṅgo-di, „clamours";
„ l plur. re: bēdžo-l, wódžo-re, „hares";
„ lde plur. di: wa-lde, bā-di, „anthills";
„ lde plur. nde: borrendd-lde, korrendó-ndo, „ants";
„ ldo plur. be: kangá-ldo, haagā-bo;
„ lel plur. lli (ol plur. li): lolel, lolli, „ghazelles";
„ lo plur. be: bahíl-lo, bahíl-be, „blacksmiths"; perhaps more correct, o plur. be: bahíl-o, bahíl-be.

„ m plur. mbe, see above be added as a sign of the plural.

„ nde plur. de: wolí-nde, boll-de, „words, language";
„ nde plur. le: yenā-nde, genā-le, „tombs";
„ ndi plur. li: dā-ndi, dā-li, „oxen of burden";
„ ndu plur. di: wa-ndu, bā-di, „monkeys"; rawá-ndu, dawā-di, „dogs";
„ ndu plur. li: butá-ndu, búta-li, „ears of corn"; hóbe-ndu, kóbe-li, „fingers"; bo-ndu, fō-li, „turtledoves"; fa-ndu, pā-li, „melons"; wo-ndu, bó-li, „wells"; sú-wu-ndu, sū-li, „a kind of wild beast";
„ ndu plur. lli: so-ndu, tšo-lli, „birds";
„ nédo plur. yimbe, „people";
„ nyu, ñu plur. di: nyú-nyu (ñú-ñu), nyū-di (ñū-di), „black ants";
„ nyo, ño plur. mbe: pa-nyo (pa-ño), fa-mbe, „youths"; perhaps more correctly to be considered as yo plur. be, or perhaps even as o plur. be (see p. CXV).

„ o plur. ande: sapp-o (sáp-o), tšapp-ánde (tšap-ánde), „tenths";
„ o plur. be: pūl-o, fūl-bo; kéfor-o plur. héfer-bo, „pagans"; baṅgār-o, waṅgár-be, „barbers"; to this class belong likewise the byforms in a: urā-be, mentioned above p. CXLI, such as maun-orā-o, mauu-orā-bo; miñ-erā-o, miñ-erā-bo;
„ o plur. erā-be: ás-o (?us-erā-o), os-orā-be, „fathers in law"; gogg-o, gogg-orā-bo, „younger aunt"; see above the remark with regard to a: erā-be;
„ o plur. i: mōy-o, mōy-i, „termites fatales"; ṅgabb-o, ṅgabb-i, „riverhorses";
„ o plur. idži: diūr-o (džūr-o), diūr-idži (džūr-idži), „hymns";
„ o plur. ōdži: fídž-o, fídž-ōdži, „plays, dances"; samg-o, samg-ōdži, „cavalcades, assaults"; hóg-o, hog-ōdži, „rough passages";
„ o plur. ōbe: dor-ō, dor-ōbe, „neatherds";
„ o plur. terābe: híg-o, híg-oterābe, „friends". Evidently also in this case the cause of kindred and relationship, at least from a mental point of view, has exercised its influence upon the formation of the plural; I never heard híg-oterāo;
„ o plur. ube: iššūt-o, siūt-ube, „twins";
„ o plur. yēbe: gē-o, ge-yēbo, „fripperers, small trades men";
„ ode plur. erēde: bort-ōde, bort-erēde, „tight shirts";
„ ol plur. i: lepp-ol, lepp-i, „cottonstripes";
„ ol plur. dže: gárn-ol, garū-dže, „walled towns"; danné-ol, danne-dže, „white";
„ ol plur. adže: saff-ol, saff-ādže, „naves (of the mosque);
„ oru plur. erri: ingóru, ingurri, „tanned bullox-hides";
„ oul plur. ēdže: kéb-oul, kéb-ēdžo, „stirrups".

re im Plural abgeworfen: hínne-re, kinne, „Ohren"; hódo-re, kōdo, „Sterne"; húfund-re, kúfune, „Mützen"; lógge-re, loggo, „Thäler"; nyébbe-re, nyebbe, „Bohnen"; dšágge-re, dšaggo, „Löwen"; úde-re, gúde, „Frauenkleider"; holeé-re, kol-tše, „Erdmandeln";

Sing. re Plur. dže: gellā-re, gellā-dže, „Städte"; toggō-re, toggō-dže, „Hemden"; hosē-re, kosé-dže, „Felsen"; sobō-re, tšobō-dže, „Brunnen"; sotō-re, sotō-dže, „Schalen"; dagguwī-re, dugguwī-dže, „Antilope oryx"; hai-re, kā-dže, „Steine" gehört auch hierher, obgleich ausser der Veränderung des Anfangskonsonanten auch noch das i im Plural ausgefallen ist;

„ re Plur. dži: humné-re, kumnē-dži, „Mützen"; toggō-re, toggō-dži (andere Form), „Hemden"; ballē-re (andere Form ballē-dže), ballē-dži, adj. „schwarze";

„ re Plur. ye: tšī-re, tšī-ye, „Dörfer";

ri im Plural abgeworfen: dšáudi-ri, džaudi, Hammel"; dámdi-ri, damdi, „Ziegenböcke";

„ ri Plur. dži: olō-ri, olō-dži, „Ziegenböcke"; sákarā-ri, sákarā-dži, „Hähne";

„ ro Plur. dži: logō-ro, logō-dži, „Taubstumme"; tami-ro, tami-dži, „Schlafgemächer";

„ ru Plur. bi: bō-ru, bō-bi, „Männer";

„ ru Plur. di: musū-ru, musū-di, „Katzen";

„ ru Plur. e: busú-ru, busú-e, „Zwitter von freier Tarki-Frau mit einem Sklaven";

„ ru Plur. hul: dondō-ru, dondō-hul, „Leoparde";

„ ru Plur. i: fāb-ru, fāb-i, „Frösche";

„ ru Plur. dže: katō-ru, katō-dže, „bärtige Männer";

„ ru Plur. dži: layā-ru, layā-dži, „kleine Täschchen für Amulette"; musū-ru, musū-dži (andere Form des oben erwähnten Plurals in di), „Leoparden"; tantabarā-ru, tantabarā-dži, „zahme Tauben"; yibki-ru, yibki-dži, „Affen-Art"; džíndžimi-ru, daindžimi-dži, „Papageien";

ru aus der Mitte ausgeworfen: áu-ru-de, au-do, „Samen".

„ se Plur. tše: lē-se, lē-tše, „Schweine";

„ sei Plur. tše: lō-sei, lō-tše, „Peitschen";

„ sul Plur. tši: lō-sul, lō-tši, „Zweige". Wahrscheinlich ist dieser Ausdruck mit dem vorhergehenden ursprünglich identisch, da Zweige natürliche Peitschen sind.

„ to Plur. be: tšapā-to, sapā-be, „ein Spottname der Tuareg";

„ tšiči Plur. tidži: ako-tšiči, ako-tidži, „Pistolen".

„ u Plur. e: baild-u, baild-e;

„ u Plur. i: bāl-u, bāl-i, „Schaafe"; būb-u, būb-i, „Fliegen"; babatt-u, babatt-i, „Heuschrecken"; metoll-u, metoll-i, „Ameisen"; tond-u, tond-i, „Lippen", „Berge"; walād-u, galād-i, „Hörner"; putš-u, putš-i, „Pferde";

„ u Plur. edže: kūdž-u, kūdž-edže, „Sachen" = fi-dšidži oben;

„ u Plur. edži: putš-u, putš-edži (andere Form), „Pferde";

„ ul Plur. i; batš-ul, batš-i, „Deleb-Schössling"; dadd-ul, dadd-i, „Nerven";

„ ul Plur. edži: gēb-ul, gēb-edži, „Thäler";

„ ul Plur. idži: dadd-ul, dadd-idži, „Wurzeln" von Bäumen;

„ um Plur. i: tšād-um, sād-i, „Leichname";

„ uru Plur. bbi: lō-uru, lebbi, „Monde, Monate";

„ uru Plur. el: tšifátt-uru, tšifátt-el.

re thrown off in the plural number: hínne-re, kinne, „ears"; hóde-re, kōde, „stars"; húfuné-ro, kúfune, „caps"; lúgge-re, lugge, „valleys"; nyébbe-re, nyebbe, „beans"; džágge-re, džaggo, „lions"; úde-ro, gúde, „female dresses"; bolsó-re, kol-tšo, „groundnuts";

sing. re plur. dže: gollū-re, gollū-džo, „towns"; toggō-re, toggō-džo, „shirts"; kosē-re, kosē-dže, „rocks"; sebō-re, tšebō-džo, „walls"; sotō-re, sotō-džo; dugguwī-re, dugguwī-džo, „antilope oryx"; also bai-re, kā-dže, „stones" does belong hither, the i being thrown off in the plural;

„ re plur. dži: kumné-re, kumné-dži, „caps"; toggō-re, toggō-dži (other form), „shirts"; ballē-re (other form ballē-dže), ballē-dži, adj. „black ones";

„ re plur. ye: tšī-re, tšī-ye, „villages";

ri thrown off in the plural number: džáudi-ri, džaudi, „rams"; dámdi-ri, damdi, „goats";

„ ri plur. dži: elō-ri, elō-dži, „goats"; adkarā-ri, adkarā-dži, „cocks";

„ re plur. dži: logō-re, logō-dži, „the deaf and dumb"; tamī-re, tamī-dži, „bedrooms";

„ ru plur. bi: bō-ru, bō-bi, „mortars";

„ ru plur. di: musū-ru, musū-di, „cats";

„ ru plur. e: busú-ru, busu-e, „bastards from a Tarki mother with a slave";

„ ru plur. hul: dondō-ru, dondō-hul, „leopards";

„ ru plur. i: fāb-ru, fāb-i, „frogs";

„ ru plur. dže: katō-ru, katō-dže, „bearded men";

„ ru plur. dži: layā-ru, laya-dži, „small pockets for talismans"; musū-ru, musū-dži (another form of the plural in di), „leopards"; tantabarū-ru, tantabarā-dži, „tame pigeons"; yibkī-ru, yibkī-dži, „a species of monkeys"; džindžimī-ru, džindžimī-dži, „parrots";

ru thrown off in the midst of the word: áu-ru-de, au-de, „seeds".

„ se plur. tše: lē-se, lē-tše, „hogs";

„ sel plur. tše: lō-sel, lō-tše, „whips";

„ sel plur. tši. „twigs". Probably the latter term originally has been identical with the preceding one.

„ to plur. be: tšapū-to, sapū-be, „a nickname of the Tawárek people";

„ tšiři plur. tiadži: ako-tšiři, ako-tiādži, „pistols".

„ u plur. e: baild-u, baild-e;

„ u plur. i: bāl-u, bāl-i, „sheep"; būb-u, būb-i, „flies"; babatt-u, babatt-i, „locusts"; metoll-u, metoll-i, „ants"; tond-u, tond-i, „lips", „mountains"; walād-u, galād-i, „horns"; putā-u, putā-i, „horses";

„ u plur. ědže: kūdž-u, kūdž-ědže, „things" = fi-dżīdži above;

„ u plur. ědži, putā-u, putā-ědži (another form), „horses";

„ ul plur. i: batā-ul, batā-i, „shoots of delēbpalms"; dadd-ul, dadd-i, „nerves";

„ ul plur. ědži: gōb-ul, gōb-ědži, „valleys";

„ ul plur. īdži: dadd-ul, dadd-īdži, „roots" of trees;

„ um plur. i: tšād-um, sād-i, „corpses";

„ uru plur. bbi: lé-uru, lebbi, „moons", „months";

„ uru plur. ei: tšifátt-uru, tšifátt-ei.

Sing. wa Plur. bi: nyi-wa, nyi-bi, „Elephanten"; dé-wa, dé-bi, adj. „weibliche";
„ wa Plur. dži: beē-wa, beē-dži, „Ziegen";
„ we Plur. ppe: wdudu-we, gunddū-ppe, „Flussliefen";
„ wo Pl. be: Alle Adjektiva und derartigen adjektivischen Charakterbezeichnungen auf wo: demmō-wo, remmō-be, „Ackerbauer"; gimmō-wo, yimmō-be, „Musikanten"; džoho-wo, džehō-be, „reisende Kaufleute"; pombo-wo, fembō-be, „Barbiere".
„ yo Plur. dže: mā-yo, mā-dže, „Flüsse";
„ yābare Plur. džēbe, „Skorpione".

In keiner Sprache gibt es wol eine reichere Liste mannichfaltiger Abweichungen, obgleich man manche derselben auf einfachere, allgemeiner angewandte Gesetze zurückführen kann, wie sich die Endungen des Singulars auf go, ro, ru, vielleicht auch re und džo, unzweifelhaft auf „ein" zurückführen lassen, woraus sich das Fortfallen dieser Silbe im Plural, zuweilen in Verbindung mit einer Veränderung des Anfangskonsonanten ganz von selbst erklärt. Nur muss man auf der anderen Seite bedenken, wie unvollständig mein Material ist und wie manche neue Formen, zumal aus anderen Dialekten, noch hinzukommen werden.

8. *Eigenschaftswörter.*

Die Eigenschaftswörter im Fūl sind nach meinen Erfahrungen zum grössten Theil von Zeitwörtern abgeleitet und können daher auch als ursprüngliche Participial-Formen angesehen werden. Da sie jedoch in der weiteren Ausbildung und Fortbildung der Sprache eine ganz selbstständige Stellung erlangt haben und nicht allein dem Substantiv beigeordnet werden, um den Charakter desselben näher zu bestimmen, sondern dasselbe mit diesem Charakter auch eben vollständig vertreten, werden sie füglich für sich betrachtet. Ich werde daher auch hier nun noch wiederum ausführlicher einzelne Formen betrachten müssen, die ich im Allgemeinen schon oben bei dem Substantiv berücksichtigt habe.

Zuerst habe ich als charakteristisch für die Fūl-Sprache zu bemerken, dass ein Unterschied zwischen denjenigen Eigenschaftswörtern, welche die Eigenschaften von Menschen, und denjenigen, welche die von Thieren bezeichnen, sich in den Endungen nachweisen lässt und das bezieht sich nicht allein darauf, dass die erstere Klasse vornehmlich vom Zeitwort direkt abgeleitete participiale Formen darstellt. Dies sind die beiden Adjektiv-Endungen a) auf ōwo oder wōo und b) auf do (i-do, o-do, u-do). Denn ausserdem enthält diese auf menschliche Eigenschaften vorzüglich angewandte Klasse c) die einem nicht verbalen Begriff angehängte Endung ēdžo und d) die einem Substantiv vorgesetzte Silbe džom oder e) die einem umfassenderen Begriff vorgesetzte Silbe mo.

Der zweiten Klasse von Eigenschaftswörtern, die ausschliesslich, wie es scheint, von Thieren oder leblosen Dingen gebraucht wird, gehört zuerst an f) die der unter c erwähnten Form genau entsprechende Adjektiv-Bildung mit einem vorgesetzten gu an; dann g) eine ganz der Endung do der ersten Klasse entsprechende Form mit den Endungen go, ṅgo; gu, ṅgu; ge, ṅge, woran die auf gel endende sich anschliesst und endlich h) ausser wenigen vereinzelten anderen Bildungen eine zahlreiche Abtheilung mit der Endung am, dam.

1) Erste Klasse: Von Menschen gebrauchte Eigenschaftswörter.

a) Eigenschaftswörter mit der Endung ōwo oder wōo.

Wie schon angegeben, betrachte ich diese Formen als ursprünglich einer Participial-Form des Zeitwortes angehörig, selbst in solchen Fällen, wo wir jetzt keine Verbalform mehr besitzen, wenigstens wo eine solche mir unbekannt geblieben ist. Dies Letztere ist z. B. der Fall mit dem Adjektiv džēnū-ōwo, „Ehebruch treibend", „ehebrecherisch", „unkeusch", „die Hure", wozu ich jetzt nur ein Nennwort džena, zena, „Ehebruch" und kein dem Arabischen, von dem es abgeleitet ist, entsprechendes Zeitwort im Gebrauch fand. Desgleichen weist mein Wortverzeichniss zur Erklärung des Eigenschaftswortes tāemt-ōwo, „sich schä-

sing. wa plur. bi: nyí-wa, nyí-bi, „elephants"; dó-wa, dó-bi, adj. „females";
„ wa plur. dži: beē-wa, beē-dži, „she-goats";
„ we plur. ppe: wándu-we, gundú-ppe, „deep places of river";
„ wo plur. be: all the terms terminating in wo which originally have been adjectives, such as demmō-wo, remmō-be, „husbandmen"; gimmō-wo, yimmō-be, „musicians"; džehō-wo, džehō-be, „travelling merchants"; pombō-wo, fembē-be, „barbers".
„ yo plur. dže: mā-yo, mā-dže, „rivers";
„ yábare plur. džēbe, „scorpions".

This is the list of plural forms which I am able to give from my incomplete materials, and I think, there will scarcely be found another idiom exhibiting a greater variety of forms. However, I am sure, that several of these varieties may be reduced to more simple and general principles; thus, for instance, I have no doubt, that the termination of the singular in go, ro, ru, perhaps also re and džo must be reduced to the numeral go meaning „one", it being thus at the same time easily explained, how it happens, that this termination is lost in the plural number, the latter, as indicating the object in general, having been the original form.

6. *Adjectives.*

Most of the adjectives in the Fúl-language, according to my researches, have been derived from verbs, and may, therefore, be looked upon as being originally participial forms. But, as in the further development, and formation of the language these verbal forms have acquired an entirely independent character, so that they are not only joined to the substantive, in order to describe more fully the character of the latter, but even take its very place, we do well to consider these forms by themselves in a separate chapter. I, therefore, have here to consider more fully some of those very forms which I have already slightly touched upon in the chapter treating of the noun.

First, I have to point out as a characteristic feature of the Fúl-language the circumstance of a distinction being made in the terminations of the adjectives between those which are applied to man, and those which are applied to animals or inanimate beings; such an almost exclusive use not only referring to that class of adjectives which comprises participial forms directly derived from a verbal root, and comprising the two terminations a) in ōwo or wōo, and b) in do (i-do, o-do, u-do), but even such adjectives as are composed c) by adding the termination ēdžo to a root which is not of a verbal character, or d) by prefixing the term džom meaning „master of", „possessing", to a noun, and e) by the prefixing of the syllable mō to a more general or comprehensive notion.

To the second class of adjectives, which, as it seems, are exclusively used of animals, and inanimate beings, belong f) those adjectives which are formed by the prefixing of the syllable gu before a simple or composite notion, and which correspond exactly with the subdivision e; further g) the adjectives terminating in go, ṅgo; gu, ṅgu; ge, ṅge, to which the termination gel is intimately allied, and which correspond exactly with the adjectives terminating in do of the first class, and finally h), besides a few isolated specimens of a different formation, a numerous list of adjectives terminating in am, dam.

1) First class, adjectives used of man.

a) The adjectives with the termination ōwo or wōo. As I have stated before, I look upon these forms as originally those of a participle of the verb, even in cases, where we have now no such verbal root, at least where such has not become known to me. This, for instance, is the case in a certain degree with džen-ōwo, „adulterous", „whoresome", „the whore", as the verbal form of zena, džena, „adultery" is not used, as far as I know. Thus, for illustrating the formation of tšemt-ōwo, „bashful", I have only the substantive

men", „schamhaft" nur das Nennwort semt-ōndo auf, und doch kann es nicht zweifelhaft sein, dass beide Formen von einem Zeitwort semt(-), „sich schämen" abgeleitet sind. Dies stellt sich klar heraus durch Vergleichung der langen Liste von adjektiven und substantivisch gebrauchten Eigenschaftswörtern mit dieser Endung mit den entsprechenden Verbalformen, wie

nyō-wōo, „nähend", „der Nähter", „die Nähterin", von mé-dō nyōa, „ich nähe";

moll-ōwo, „den Faden ziehend", „der Fadenzieher", von mé-dō motta, „ich ziehe den Faden";

māh-ōwo, „bauend", „der Baumeister", von mé-dō māha, „ich baue (ein Haus)";

pemb-ōwo, „rasirend", „der Barbier", von mé-dō fembo, „ich rasire";

pi-ōwo, „schlagend" in den verschiedensten Beziehungen (die Trommel) „der Trommler", (die Cither) „der Citherspieler", (das Hemd) „Glätter", von mé-dō fi-yo, „ich schlage";

dšeh-ōwo, „reisend", „der Reisende", von mé-dō yāha, „ich reise";

konn-ōwo, „Krieg führend, kriegerisch, der Krieger", von mé-dō honno, „ich mache Krieg" (konno);

dugg-ōwo, „laufend, schnell, der Läufer", von mé-dō dugga, „ich laufe";

gimm-ōwo, „singend", „der Sänger", von mé-dō yimma, „ich singe".

In Anbetracht dieser, die Entwickelung deutlich darstellenden Beispiele habe ich keinen Zweifel, dass auch alle übrigen Adjektiva und Substantiva mit dieser Endung, wie z. B. nokk-ōwo, „der Töpfer"; kutt-ōwo, „der Schlächter"; tšin-ōwo, „der Färber" in derselben Weise gebildet sind. Das letzterwähnte Wort ist von besonderem Interesse, da es allem Anscheine nach mit dem Sonyai-Ausdruck šini für „Indigo" zusammenhängt, von welcher Wurzel höchst wahrscheinlich ein Zeitwort in der Fül-Sprache vorhanden war oder noch ist, indem das höchst auffällig gebildete Zeitwort mé-dō b-alfnna, das mein Wortverzeichniss S. 118 aufweist, nicht ursprünglich ist; alfn heisst „Indigo", aber nicht im Fül.

a, α) Erwähnen muss ich hier als Ausnahme von der ausschliesslichen Anwendung dieser Form auf Menschen, dass ich einmal die Form dugg-ōwo, „schnell" vom Pferde, putšu, gebraucht fand.

b) Ich komme jetzt zu den Eigenschafts- und Nennwörtern mit der Endung do, und auch in Bezug auf sie bin ich der Ansicht, dass sie ursprünglich verbale Formen sind, wie ich das schon oben S. CXXIV, d) ausgeführt habe, obgleich die Formen hier vielfältiger zusammengesetzt sind, so dass ich noch nicht mit voller Klarheit über alle dahin einschlagenden Punkte zu reden im Stande bin. Zuerst gebe ich also diejenigen Beispiele dieser Form, die ich mit Sicherheit von verbalen Wurzeln ableiten kann und die doch adjektivisch gebraucht werden, wie

džāñg-udo, „der (viel) gelesen hat, belesen, Gelehrte", von mé-dō džañga, „ich lese";

fūd-udo, „der angefangen hat", „der Anfänger", von mé-dō fūdi, „ich fange an", daher fūd-udo dum hōre mō, „der selbst (eigentlich, mit seinem Kopfe) angefangen hat", „der Parvenu";

džámd-udo, „gesund seiend, wohl", „der Kräftige", von mé-dō džam-di, „ich bin wohl", und eben so sind unzweifelhaft gebildet ońá-udo, „krank"; džá-udo, „heissen Temperaments"; bá-udo, „aufgeweckt"; háll-udo, „böswillig"; tšatt-udo, „streitsüchtig" und viele andere. Ein belehrendes Beispiel dieser Adjektiv-Bildung mit der Endung ōdo ist auch gōd-ōdo yuñki, Plur. wōd-ōbe yuñki, „am Leben seiend", „lebendig", von me-wōdi yuñki, „ich bin am Leben".

Denselben Charakter scheinen die Eigenschaftswörter zu haben, die auf ído ausgehen und die entweder eine geistige Fähigkeit oder eine körperliche Beschaffenheit des Menschen bezeichnen, wie o-mótχ-ido, „freigebig"; suli-ído oder o-tšāh-ído, „grausamüthig"; tšo-ído, „arm"; nebbot-ído, „geschickt"; monot-ído, „hartnäckig"; džaun-ído, „demüthig, unterwürfig" und die folgenden Ausdrücke, die insgesammt eine Krankheit oder einen gewissen Zustand des Körpers anzeigen, wie fort-ído, tenn-ído, wuli-ído, nyobb-

somt-onde, both evidently derived from a verbal root somt(-), though I have not taken it down. For we have now a long list of adjectives and adjectival substantives with this termination, the corresponding verbs of which I have still found in use, and which make it more than probable, that the others have been formed in the same way. These instances are

nyō-wōo, „sewing", „the seamer", „the seamstress", from mó-dō nyōa, „I sew";
mott-ōwo, „twining the thread", „the twister", from mó-dō motta, „I twine thread";
māh-ōwo, „building", „the architect", from mó-dō māha, „I build (a house)";
pomb-ōwo, „shaving", „the barber", from mó-dō fomho, „I shave";
pi-ōwo, „beating" in various relations, „beating the drum", „the drummer", „striking the guitar", „the musician", „beating (giving lustre to) the shirt" from mó-do fi-yo, „I strike, beat";
džoh-ōwo, „travelling man", „the traveller", from mó-dō yāha, „I travel";
konn-ōwo, „making war, warlike, warrior", from mé-dō honno, „I make war" (konno);
dugg-ōwo, „running", „swift", „the runner", from mó-dō dugga, „I run";
gimm-ōwo, „singing man", „the singer", from mó-dō yimma, „I sing".

Thus, therefore, I have no doubt, that also all the other adjectives and substantives with this termination, such as nokk-ōwo, „the potter"; kutt-ōwo, „the butcher"; tšin-owo, „the dyer", have been derived in the same manner. The latter term is especially interesting, as it appears to be connected with the Soñyai-term šini for „indigo", from which root there must have been formed a verb in Fūl, instead of which I have the awkward term mó-dō b-alīnna p. 118 of my vocabulary, which is certainly not original, and may be wrong; alīn meaning „indigo", but not in Fūl, as it seems.

n, a) With regard to what I have said before (p. CLI), however, as for the almost exclusive use of these forms of adjectives in relation to human beings, I must not omit to state, that I have heard once the form dugg-ōwo, „swift" applied to the horse, putšu.

b) I now proceed to speak of the adjectives and substantives with the termination do, which I likewise take to have been originally verbal forms, as I have already stated to be my opinion on a former occasion p. CXXV, d), although the forms are here more complicated, so that I am not as yet able to speak clearly of all points. I first give those instances of this form, which I can with surity derive from verbal roots, and which are really used as adjectives.

džáñg-udo, „who has read a great deal, learned man" from mó-dō džañga, „I read";
fūd-udo, „who has begun, beginner", fūd-udo dum hōro mō, „he who has begun by (his own head) himself", „a parvenu" from mó-dō fūdi, „I begin";
džámd-udo, „being well, healthy": mó-dō džam-di, „I am well". In the same manner, no doubt, have been formed oñá-udo, „sick"; dūá-udo, „of hot temperament", „hotspur"; bá-udo, „clever"; káll-udo, „mischievous"; tšáll-udo, „quarrelsome person, wrangler", and many others. An interesting instance of this formation is also gōd-ōdo yuñki, plur. wōd-ōbe yuñki, „being alive" from mo-wōdi yuñki properly „I do, achieve live" i. q. „am alive".

Of the same character seem to be the adjectives terminating in ido, and indicating either a mental or bodily quality of man, such as o-móiχ-ido, „liberal"; tšo-ído, „poor"; sah-ído or o-tšah-ído, „openhanded"; nobbot-ído, „clever"; monet-ído, „obstinate"; džaun-ído, „humble, submissive", as well as the following terms, all indicating sickness, or a certain position of the body, such as fort-ído, tenn-ído, wah-ído, nyobh-ído, džimmen-ído. The verbal character of these forms seems to be indicated by the prono-

ído, džimmen-ído. Der verbale Charakter dieser Adjektiva wird gewissermassen angedeutet durch das ihnen zuweilen vorgesetzte pronominale o, das allerdings in gewissen Fällen auch bei dem Substantiv erscheint, wie in der Phrase o-nédo kirke, „er Mensch tüchtig", und noch lebendiger durch die, manchen dieser Formen in ganz verbaler Bildung entsprechenden, negativen Formen wie pê-ído, „mager seiend"; pâ-ído, „nicht mager, fett".

Dagegen scheint g-ido, „liebend, Freund von", das ein sehr wichtiges Element für Zusammensetzungen ist, wie in den Ausdrücken g-ido ádune, „die Menschen liebend", „menschenfreundlich"; g-ido džandi, „Reichthum liebend", „habgierig"; g-ido kugel, „Arbeit liebend", „fleissig"; g-ido raube, „Frauen liebend", „verliebt", nur uneigentlich hierher zu gehören, da das d schon der Wurzel angehört, mé-dô idi, „ich liebe".

b, α) Als Beispiel eines Eigenschaftswortes in do, das wahrscheinlich von einem Nennwort abgeleitet ist, gebe ich wêl(o)-ôdo, „hungrig", von wêlo, „der Hunger", da ich für den verbalen Begriff „ich bin hungrig, leide Hunger" keinen andren Ausdruck habe, als den zusammengesetzten mé-dô nanna wêlo, „ich empfinde Hunger".

b, β) Dagegen scheint mir dšû-do, dšu-tó-do, „hoch" von einem adverbialen Begriff dšû, „über, oberhalb" herzukommen, von dem auch das zuweilen als Eigenschaftswort gebrauchte Nennwort dšû-ude, „Höhe", so wie die Form dšû-tó-ki gebildet ist.

b, γ) Als allgemeine Beispiele dieser adjektiven Endung in do, ohne im Stande zu sein, die Wurzeln anzugeben, führe ich an mándudo, „gelehrt"; góddudo, „entfernt"; tšorrádo, „siegreich"; o-bûmdo, „blind"; boedo, „taub"; tšamdo, „behende"; bado (fadde), „Schuhmacher"; semotôdo (gûri), „Gärber"; láfudo, „Bettler"; bambâdo, „Sänger"; džonnaido datti oder passotôdo datti, „Strassenräuber" (wörtlich „Zerschneider des Weges") und ich könnte deren mehr angeben.

b, δ) Es ist sehr bemerkenswerth, dass ich nicht Ein sicheres Beispiel weiss, wo diese Adjektiv-Form auf do von einem Thier oder leblosen Wesen gebraucht wird, es sei denn das Adjektiv gurído, „rund", über dessen Ableitung ich unsicher bin, obgleich es mir von gu und einem Worte wie redu, „Leib" zusammengesetzt zu sein scheint. Dagegen werden wir weiter unten bei Besprechung der zweiten Klasse die Wurzelstämme mehrerer dieser Eigenschaftswörter mit verschiedener Endung finden, wenn von Thieren oder leblosen Wesen gebraucht. Denselben Charakter hat aber keineswegs die Endung auf du, obgleich sie nur eine kleine Variation von do zu sein scheint. So habe ich ték-udu, „breiartig"; lém-udu, „sauer"; lúr-udu, „eckig"; di-udu, „halb"; heedu, „mehr", obgleich das Letztere, das entschieden in enger Beziehung zu bustu, „weniger" steht, vielleicht eine andere Erklärung zulässt.

c) Ich will nun diejenige Form der Eigenschaftswörter erwähnen, die mit Hülfe von édžo gebildet wird, das im Allgemeinen Nennwörtern angehängt zu sein scheint. So haben wir

von bérendo, „Herz", bérend(o)-édžo, „herzhaft, grossherzig";
von hakkíllo, „Verstand" (aus dem Arabischen) hakkill(o)-édžo, „verständig";
von konno, „Krieg" mit Einschiebung von nk: konno-nk-edžo, „kriegerisch";
von ne, nai, „Alter", ne-édžo, „alt";
von rédu, „Mutterleib", rédú-(e)džo, „mit Mutterleib", d. h. „schwanger";

dasselbe mit geringer Veränderung des Sinnes in umschreibender Weise dóbo) rédu ma-ko nonnero, „Frau, Leib ihr voll". — Dieses édžo zeigt entschieden Reichthum, Fülle an.

d) Ich komme jetzt zu derjenigen Abtheilung der von menschlichen Charakteren gebrauchten Eigenschaftswörter, welche dadurch gebildet werden, dass das Wort džom, „Herr (von)", d. h. „besitzend (das und das)" einem anderen, substantivisch ausgedrückten, Begriff vorgesetzt wird, wie z. B.

gonga, „wahr, Wahrheit", džom-gonga, „Herr der Wahrheit, aufrichtig";
ganándi, „Hass, Neid", džom-ganándi, „neidisch";

minal o prefixed to some of these forms, although, no doubt, I have also instances where the same o is prefixed to substantives, as in the phrase o-nédo kirko, „he man excellent". But of greater consequence are some very interesting instances of such adjective formation where a negative form corresponds to the positive one, as, for instance, „meagre", „lean", pă-ído; „not lean", „fat", pă-ído, the latter adjective having invested the negative verbal form.

As for g-ido, „loving", „fond of", which is a most important word for compositions, as, for instance, g-ido ádune, „fond of people"; g-ido džaudi, „fond of wealth, avaricious"; g-ido kăgol, „fond of work, industrious"; g-ido raube, „fond of women, amorous (of man)"; g-ido worbe, „fond of men, amorous (of woman)", it does not so much belong hither, as the verbal root is mó-dō idi, „I like".

b, α) As an instance of an adjective terminating in do, and most probably derived from a substantive, I give wōl(e)-ōdo, „hungry" from wōlo, „hunger", as I have no other verbal form for „I am hungry" but the composite one mó-dō nanna wōlo, „I feel hunger".

b, β) As an instance of an adjective with this form derived from an adverbial notion I mention dšū-do, dšū-id-do, „high", from dšū, „above, over", substantive dšū-ado (used also as an adjective), and dšū-ió-ki.

b, γ) As general instances of this adjective termination in do, without being sure of the root, I mention mándudo, „learned"; góddudo, „distant"; išorrádo, „victorious"; o-búmdo, „blind"; bosdo, „deaf"; išomdo, „swift, agile"; bădo (ſadde), „shoemaker"; sumotōdo (gūri), „leather-dresser"; láfudo, „beggar"; bambădo, „singing man"; džennaido datti or passotōdo dutti, „high way robber" (verbally „cutter of roads"), and I might mention many more.

b, δ) It is very remarkable, that there is scarcely a single instance of these two classes of adjective forms in ōwo and do being used of inanimate beings, but guríďo, „round", which itself may be composed in a totally different manner, viz from gu and rōdu, „body"; and I shall have occasion further on for citing several of these same adjectives with a different termination, when used of animals or inanimate beings. But the same is not to be said of the termination du, probably only a slight variation of do, as I have several adjectives with this termination used of inanimate substances, such as tók-udu, „clammy"; lém-udu, „sour"; lúr-udu, „angular"; di-udu, „half"; as for bosdu, „more", I will not include it in this category, as it seems to stand in close relation to busia, „love".

c) I will here mention the adjective form terminating in ōdžo, which termination in general seems to be added to substantives, and is evidently connected with the plural form in ōdži mentioned above; thus,

from bérendo, „heart" we have bérond(e)-ōdžo, „having a (big) heart";
from hakkíllo, „intelligence" (Arabic) hakkill(o)-ōdžo, „intelligent";
from konno, „war", by inserting nk, konno-nk-ōdžo, „having love of war, warlike";
from ne, nal, „age", ne-ōdžo, „old";
from rédu, „womb", redú-(o)džo, „having a womb, being with child";

for redú-(e)džo I have a circumscribing term débo) rēdu mă-ko nonnēro, „woman, belly her full".

d) I now, in order to absolve this list of forms of adjectives used of human beings, have first to mention the adjectives formed by the prefixing of the term džom, „master", before another notion, expressed by a substantive, as for instance:

goṅga, „true", „the truth", džom-goṅga, „master of truth", „sincere";
ganándi, „envy", džom-ganándi, „envious";

tšede, „Muscheln", džom-tšede, „Herr von (vielen) Muscheln", „reich";
džaudi, „Reichthum", džom-džaudi, „wohlhabend",

und so viele andere. Diese Zusammensetzung also stimmt genau überein mit der Art der Zusammensetzung in der Hausa-Sprache vermittelst mai, mit dem Unterschiede jedoch, dass das Letztere zuweilen auch mit verbalen Begriffen zusammengesetzt wird, was bei Ersterem nicht der Fall zu sein scheint.

e) Wir kommen jetzt zu der Bildung von Eigenschaftswörtern durch den Vorsatz der Silbe mo (wahrscheinlich entstanden aus mo-wo, dem wo in wo-di, „wer" oder „was thut") vor verbalen oder zusammengesetzten substantivischen Begriffen, wie folgende Beispiele zeigen:

mo-kullul, „furchtsam", von mé-do hulla, „ich fürchte";
mo-donka, „durstig", von donka, „Durst";
mo-ae, „listig, schlau"; mo-indo, „aufmerksam, sorgsam"; Wurzeln von ae („alt, allerfahren"?) und indo mir ungewiss;
mo-bûte, „von nichts" (bûte), d. h. „arm, zerlumpt";
mo-džam, „gutmüthig, friedfertig", von džam, „gut", „Friede";
mo-dudi bolide, „von vielen (dudi) Worten (bolide)", „schwatzhaft";
mo-bérende maududé, „von grossem (maundu) Herzen" (bérende), „grossherzig";
mo-bérende tokoire, „von kleinem Herzen", „engherzig".

Aber die interessantesten Beispiele dieser Art der Zusammensetzung sind diejenigen, welche einen negativen Sinn haben,

débo mo-rimma-ta, „die Frau von (sie) gebärt nicht", d. h. „die unfruchtbare Frau";
nédo mo-id-a ádune, „eine Person von (sie) liebt nicht Leute", d. h. „der Menschenfeind" das Gegentheil von dem oben erwähnten g-id-o ádune, „menschenfreundlich".

Vielleicht noch merkwürdiger, als diese Zusammensetzung mit verbaler Negation ist folgendes Beispiel eines negativen Eigenschaftswortes mit substantiver Verbindung, débo mo-la yendi, wörtlich „eine Frau von nicht Brüsten", d. h. „eine Frau von trockener Brust", der Gegensatz von mo-yendi und ausser der oben S. XL erwähnten, negativ verbalen Form wo-la, „es ist nicht", mit der es aber nach dem oben von mo Gesagten zusammenfällt, das einzige Beispiel, das ich von einem Gebrauch der negativen Partikel la gehört habe, die in den Westlichen Provinzen ein völlig integrirender Theil der negativen Konjugation sein soll.

2) Zweite Klasse der Eigenschaftswörter.

f) Ich komme nun also zu denjenigen Formen der Eigenschaftswörter, welche gewöhnlich, wenn nicht ausschliesslich, von Thieren und leblosen Dingen gebraucht werden, und um diese zweite Klasse eben da anzufangen, wo ich die erste verlassen habe, die von menschlichen Eigenschaften gebraucht wird, bespreche ich zuerst diejenigen Eigenschaftswörter, die dadurch gebildet werden, dass man die Silbe gu, vollkommen entsprechend dem mo der Eigenschaftswörter der ersten Klasse, einem einfachen oder zusammengesetzten Ausdruck vorsetzt, wie z. B.

putšu) gu-koide tšoide, „ein schnellfüssiges Pferd", wörtlich „ein Pferd von leichten Füssen";
putšu) gu-gitte naudé, „ein krankäugiges Pferd", wörtlich „ein Pferd von kranken Augen";
putšu) gu-gesádži danedži, „ein Pferd von (mit) weissen Mähnen",

und nun wieder ein Beispiel einer negativ verbalen Zusammensetzung auch mit dieser Vorsatz-Silbe und das uns zugleich einen deutlichen Beweis davon gibt, dass diese Art von Zusammensetzungen wirklich als Eigenschaftswörter aufzufassen sind,

putšu gu-nánna-la langábi, „ein ungezähmtes, wildes Pferd", wörtlich „ein Pferd von nicht kennt (es) die Zügel".

g) Eine sehr gewöhnliche Form von Eigenschaftswörtern dieser Klasse, die den auf owo und ido endigenden der ersten Klasse entsprechen, ist die auf die Endung go, gu; ngo, ngu; ge, nge ausgehende Form mit einer Art von Diminutiv-Endung gel, ngel.

tšōdo, „cowries", džom-tšōde, „master of (many) cowries", „rich";

džandi, „wealth", džom-džaudi, „wealthy",

and many others. This kind of composition, therefore, corresponds exactly with the composition in the Hausa-language by means of mai, with the only difference, that džom seems never to be joined to verbal notions, which, as far as it seems, is sometimes the case with mai in Hausa.

e) I now come to speak of the forming of adjectives by prefixing mō (probably contracted form of mo-wō instead of mo-wō-di, „he who does, has") to all sorts of verbal or composite substantive notions, as for instance:

mō-kūllul, „timid" from mé-dō hulla, „I fear";

mō-ddṅka, „thirsty" from doṅka, „thirst";

mō-ne, „crafty, cunning"; mō-ĩndo, „careful, attentive"; roots ne (perhaps „old", therefore „experienced"), and indo uncertain;

mō-būte, „of nothing" (būte) i. q. „ragged, poor";

mō-džam, „peaceful" from džam, „good, peace";

mō-dūdi bolĩdo, „of many (dūdi) words (bolĩde)", „talkative";

mō-béronde maúndudē, „of a big (maundo) heart (bérende)";

mō-bérende tokoiro, „of a small heart", „narrow-hearted".

But the most remarkable instances of this sort of composition are those which imply a negative sense, such as

débo mō-rímma-ta, „the woman of not bearing" i. q. „the sterile woman";

nédo mō-ĩd-a áduno, „a person of not liking the people" i. q. „the misanthrope", and the reverse of g-ĩd-e áduno, „liking the people", which I have mentioned above p. CLV, b.

A very remarkable instance of such a complicated negative form of an adjective is also the composite term débo mō-la-yendi verbally „a woman of not breasts" i. q. „a woman with a dry breast", the negative form of mō-yendi, and the only instance besides the negative verbal form wō-la mentioned above p. XLI, where I have met with the negative particle la, which in the Western provinces is said to be the chief integrant part of the negative conjugation; but, if, what I have said above with regard to the origin of mō, is correct, as I have no doubt, it is, we have in this case to acknowledge the very identical form wō-la; mō-la being nothing but mo wō-la, „what" or „who is not".

2) Second class of adjectives, or such as are used of animals, or inanimate beings.

f) I now proceed to those forms of adjectives which are generally, if not exclusively, used of animals, and inanimate beings, and in order to begin this class, where I left the other, which comprises the adjectives used of human beings, I begin with the adjectives formed by prefixing the syllable ga before another simple or composed term, and corresponding exactly with the prefix mō, just spoken of as used of human beings, as for instance

putšu) ga-koide tšoido, „a horse of light feet (koide)", „a swift horse";

putšu) ga-gitte nanéde, „a horse of sore eyes (gitte)";

putšu) ga-gosādži danaōdži, „a horse of (with) a white mane",

and now an instance of another curious sort of composition

putšu ga-nánna-ta laṅgābi, „a horse of not knowing the bridle" i. q. „an unmanageable horse".

From these instances we see, that these compositions are really to be understood as a kind of adjective.

g) A very common form of adjectives applied to animals or inanimate beings is that which terminates in go, gu; ṅgo, ṅgu; ge, ṅge, and, with a sort of diminutive change, in gel or ṅgel.

So haben wir eine Form tšoṅ-gu (eigentlich tšom-gu), die genau der oben unter b) erwähnten Form tšom-de entspricht, also putšu tšoṅ-gu, „das schnelle Pferd", aber nédo tšom-de, „der lebende Mensch"; ebenso tšembí-ṅge, „stark" von Thieren = tšómbi-de von Menschen; yadžú-ṅge, „geräumig, gross" von leblosen Dingen = yádžu-de, „gross" von Menschen. In der That scheint die Endsilbe gu in gewisser Beziehung mit der vorgesetzten Silbe gu, die wir unter f) behandelt haben, identisch zu sein. So haben wir viele andere Eigenschaftswörter mit dieser Endung, wie yeltíṅgo, „wild"; fafáṅge, „schwach" und andere.

Ich muss jedoch erwähnen, dass ich auch eine Form mit da, uda habe, dúggu-da mit der Bedeutung „schnell", von Pferden gebraucht, die der von Personen gebrauchten Form dugg-ewe entspricht, und dass ich, wie oben S. CLII, a, α) angegeben, diese letztere Form selbst einmal vom Pferde gebraucht gefunden habe.

g, β) Einige Adjektiv-Formen in ṅgo und ṅgel scheinen eine passive Bedeutung zu haben, wie z. B. džudá-ṅgo, „geröstet", von mé-dŏ džudo, „ich röste"; dirá-ṅgel, „getrocknet" (besonders in Verbindung mit „Fleisch", kasil), vielleicht verwandt mit mé-dŏ yŏri, „ich trockene".

Als Beispiele der Endung ge, ṅge erwähne ich billáṅge, „fruchtbar"; biretíṅge, „Milch gebend", in Verbindung mit neggo, „Kuh", „die Milch-Kuh" (vergleiche birádam, „Milch"), ebenso wie fodíṅgo in derselben Verbindung „unfruchtbar".

Von der Endung gel oder ṅgel erwähne ich noch die Adjektiva kesuṅgel, „voll" und démmogel, „kurz".

g, γ) Als eine der sehr wenigen Beispiele mit der einfachen Endung el führe ich an tókotšel, „klein", wahrscheinlich eine Diminutiv-Form von tokoi-re, wenn man vergleicht, was ich S. CXXXVIII gesagt habe. Um die vereinzelten Formen abzumachen und von der nächsten, umfassenderen und wichtigeren Form gleich einen Übergang zu einer anderen mit diesem Gegenstande eng zusammenhängenden Frage zu gewinnen, erwähne ich hier noch zwei vereinzelte Beispiele einer Endung auf irka, die wahrscheinlich wieder an das S. CXXXVI bei den Nennwörtern besprochene ir anknüpft, nämlich lamm-írka, „salzig" und kad-írka, „sauer". Von kad-írka habe ich auch eine einfache Form hadi; die Wurzel von lamm-írka aber ist unzweifelhaft lamd, da die Endung am in lamd-am gleich erklärt werden soll.

h) Ich gehe nun zu denjenigen Eigenschaftswörtern über, welche auf am und dam ausgehn und deren Anzahl sehr bedeutend ist, obgleich sie mit einer oder zwei Ausnahmen ausschliesslich Flüssigkeiten anzuzeigen scheinen. Auch die Nennwörter mit dieser Endung (s. S. CXXXVIII, h) gehören augenscheinlich hierher. Da das Prinzip solcher Formationen nach Begriffen am anschaulichsten die Entwickelung einer Sprache erklärt, will ich, um die Bedeutung dieser Endung zu veranschaulichen, ein möglichst vollständiges Verzeichniss aller Nenn- und Eigenschaftswörter mit dieser Endung hier geben: ndlam, „Wasser"; iyam, „Blut"; nyékam, „Brühe"; tšútam, „Hirsenaufguss"; tšimtinádam, „eine Art berauschenden Getränks"; dann alle die verschiedenen Ausdrücke für „Milch" und „Butter", wie kotšam, „süsse Milch" (von kotšum, „süss"); birádam, kosam, danidam, féndidam, bakham, burnádam; belinádam, kuinádam, deffádam, das Letztere mit einer entschieden passiven Bedeutung „gekochte (Butter") und identisch mit déffe-re; denn hier nun wieder ist es so höchst charakteristisch für die Frage, die wir behandeln, dass eben diese Form déffe-re gewöhnlich gebraucht wird, wenn es sich um etwas Trockenes, wie z. B. „Fleisch" handelt. So gibt es selbst besondere Ausdrücke für die Begriffe „warm", guldam und „kalt" féndam, mit eben dieser Endung, wenn sie sich auf „Wasser" beziehen. Allerdings müssen wir, ehe wir einen bestimmteren Schluss aus dieser Form ziehen, gewissenhaft berücksichtigen, was ich in Bezug auf die allgewaltigen Gesetze des Wohlklangs, die in weiter Ausdehnung die Endungsformen der Eigenschaftswörter bestimmen, im folgenden Abschnitt sagen werde; aber

Thus, we have a form **tšoṅ-gu** (properly **tšom-gu**), corresponding exactly with the form **tšom-do** mentioned above under b as applied to men, as, for instance, **patša tšoṅ-gu**, „the swift horse" corresponding with **nédo tšom-do**, „the swift, agile person"; **tšembi-ṅge**, „strong", used of animals, corresponding with **tšémbi-do** used of men; **yadžú-ṅge**, „spacious", used of things, being = **yádžu-do**, „big" used of men. Indeed, the termination **gu** in a certain respect seems to be identical with the prefix **gu** which we have treated under f. Thus, we have many other adjectives, as **yollíṅgo**, „wild"; **fafúṅgo**, „weak", and so on, which seem to be exclusively used in the above said manner.

I must, however, mention that I have, besides, a form with **da**, **uda**, as, for instance, **dúggu-da**, „swift", used of horses, corresponding with the form **dugg-ðuo** used of men, and that, moreover, as I have already mentioned p. CLIII, a, α, I have in one instance found the very form **dugg-ðuo** used of horses.

g, β) Some adjective forms terminating in **ṅgo** and **ṅgel** seem to convey a passive meaning, such as **džūdá-ṅgo**, „fried" from **mé-dō džūda**, „I fry"; **dirú-ṅgel**, „dried" („sasal", **kūsil**), perhaps from **mé-dō yōri**, „I dry".

As instances of the form in **ge**, **ṅgo** I mention the following terms, the roots of which I am partly not acquainted with, **billáṅge**, „prolific"; **biretíṅge**, „giving milk" (in connection with **negge**, „cow", „a milkcow"; compare **bir-ādam**, „milk"), and **fodíṅge**, likewise used of a cow, „barren".

Of the form in **gel**, or **ṅgel** I mention, besides, the adjectives **keauṅgel**, „full" and **démmogol**, „short".

g, γ) As one of the very rare instances of the simple termination in **el** I mention **tókotšel**, „small" which is evidently a diminutive form of **tokoi-re**, the import of **el** in this respect having been explained above (p. CXXXIX). In order to do at once with the other isolated forms, I here mention likewise the termination **irka** of which I have only two instances, viz **lamm-írka**, „saltish" and **kad-írka**, „sour", it appearing to be connected with what I have said p. CXXXVII with regard to the **ir** in the formation of nouns. For, while of the latter term I have also the simple form **hadi**, the form **lamm-írka** is beyond the slightest doubt to be derived from the root **lamd** in **lamd-am**, „salt", I going to explain the termination **am** in the following paragraph h).

h) For I now, following up the remark made above (p. CXXXIX, h) with regard to the substantives terminating in **am**, proceed to treat of the adjectives terminating in this form, and in **dam**, which constitute a rather numerous list, although they appear to be applied exclusively to fluids. In order to prove what I have said, I shall give as complete a list as possible of nouns and adjectives with this termination, as the idea of such classes of forms best serves to illustrate the principle on which the different parts of speech have been developed: **ndiam**, „water"; **iyam**, „blood"; **nyékam**, „broth, gravy"; **tšūtam**, „ghussubwater"; **tšimtinādam**, „a kind of intoxicating drink"; thus all the various terms designating milk and butter, such as **kotšam**, „sweet milk" (from **kotšum**, „sweet"); **birādam**, **kosaam**, **dunidam**, **féndidam**, **bakkam**, **burnādam**; **bolinādam**, **kainādam**, **doffādam**, this latter form having an entirely passive meaning „boiled", and being identical with **dóffe-re**, which is constantly used, when the question is of a dry substance, such as meat. Thus, there are also peculiar terms for „warm", **guldam**, and „cold", **féndam**, ending in this form when in connection with „water". No doubt, what I have to say further on with regard to the laws of euphony as influencing, and changing to a great degree, the

v

dennoch scheint der diese Form bestimmende Grundsatz unzweifelhaft zu sein und gerade der einzige Ausnahmefall von dieser Regel, der mir bekannt ist und der völlig isolirt dasteht, scheint vielmehr zu bestätigen, was ich gesagt habe.

Diese scheinbare Ausnahme ist lamdam, „Salz". Das scheint nun nicht flüssig, aber das Wort hängt augenscheinlich zusammen mit lamde mit der Bedeutung „Silber"; ja es bedeutete ursprünglich wahrscheinlich nichts Anderes als „flüssiges Silber", nicht allein aus dem Grunde, weil Salz sich in Wasser auflöst, sondern weil es, wie in vielen Afrikanischen Minen, z. B. in Bilma der Fall ist, in einem flüssigen Zustand gewonnen und geformt wird.

Andere Ausnahmen von dieser Regel sind einzig und allein eben wieder veranlasst durch die euphonischen Gesetze, welche, wie gesagt, in der Fûl-Sprache einen grossen Einfluss ausüben und von denen ich jetzt zu sprechen habe.

f) Die Übereinstimmung der Endung des Nennwortes mit der des Eigenschaftswortes.

Der Einfluss, den die Endung des Nennwortes auf die Endung des das erstere begleitenden und kennzeichnenden Eigenschaftswortes ausübt, ist eine Frage, die auf das Engste mit der Betrachtung des Geschlechts und der Pluralform des letzteren zusammenhängt. Denn wir haben augenscheinliche Beweise des Überganges der Endsilbe des Eigenschaftswortes in Verbindung mit dem Nennworte, aber bei jedem einzelnen Beispiel ist es schwer zu sagen, ob die Veränderung ihren Grund hat in blosser Rücksicht auf Wohlklang oder ob sie durch ein grammatisches Gesetz bestimmt wird, und ich ziehe daher vor, einfach die Beispiele einer solchen Veränderung anzugeben, ohne die eben gestellte Frage zu beantworten.

So habe ich für „gross" folgende abweichende Formen je nach der Form des Nennwortes, dem es beigegeben ist, wie z. B. mâyo mañge, „der grosse Fluss", korga mañga, „die Hauptsklavin" (dieses Beispiel im höchsten Grade merkwürdig, weil die einfache Form für „Sklavin" kordo ist und wir hier also auch eine Rückwirkung des Adjektivs auf das Substantiv haben), lâna makka, „grosses Boot", lekki makki, „grosse Holzkloben", nédo maundo neben dem unten zu besprechenden o-nédo ho-maune, „grosser Mann", kóñgodi maundi, „grosse Ausrufe, grosses Geschrei", bérnde maundere, „grosses Herz".

Hier also haben wir eine vollkommene Übereinstimmung zwischen der Endung und den Hauptcharakteren des Nennwortes mit denjenigen des Eigenschaftswortes; aber, wie zumal das Beispiel von korga mañga zu zeigen scheint, hat sie einen mehr euphonischen, als grammatischen Charakter.

Ich gebe nun weitere Beispiele: yâho yau-ma, „eine warme (d. h. ermüdende) Reise", nédo yau-de, „ein warmer, hitziger Mensch", himbo yau-be, „warme Leute"; nédo fêu-de, „ein kalter Mensch", himbo fêu-be, „kalte Menschen", ndiam fêu-dam, „kaltes Wasser"; nédo kállu-do, „ein schlechter Mensch", bérnde kállu-nde, „schlechtes Herz", dum kállu-dum, „dies (ist) schlecht", fdituki kállu-ki, „schlechte Begebenheiten, Unglücksfälle"; putšu bodedže, „rothes, braunes Pferd", putši bodedži, „braune Pferde", nebbam bodedžam, „rothe Butter"; putšu buldu, „ein Pferd mit weissen Füssen", putši bul-ždži, „weissfüssige Pferde"; dum keñ-am, „dies (ist) reif", bîbe lodde kêtšu-de, „reife Baumfrüchte". Dieses letztere Beispiel zeigt wiederum recht klar, dass die Endung keine auf inneren Gesetzen beruhende Umwandelung, sondern eine bloss ganz äusserliche, harmonische Veränderung ist.

Als ein höchst merkwürdiges Beispiel der Form des Eigenschaftswortes in am oben mit Bezug auf Salz habe ich zu erwähnen lamdam Balmâdžam, „Salz von Bilma".

Aber der Einfluss, den eine solche Silbe wie am ausübt, ist so gross, dass sie, selbst als Bestandtheil eines Wortes, die letzte Silbe des vorhergehenden Wortes sich assimilirt, und so haben wir denn z. B. nañgirdam džamdi anstatt nañgirde džamdi, „Hammer von Eisen".

Aus allen diesen Gründen nun ist es fast unmöglich, ein selbstständiges Verzeichniss der Pluralformen der Eigenschaftswörter zu geben, obgleich, wenn sie in unabhängiger Stellung

terminating forms of the adjectives, exercises a great influence upon this question, but, nevertheless, the very exception to this rule of which I know of, and which is totally isolated, serves rather to confirm what I have said.

What seems to be an exception to this rule spoken of is **lamdam**. But this term, meaning „salt" has evidently been derived from **lamde**, meaning „silver", and probably originally meant „*fluid silver*", not only because salt, a substance likening silver in whiteness dissolves in water, but on account of its being obtained in a fluid state in several mines, as is especially the case in Bilma.

Other exceptions to this rule find their simple explanation in the very laws of euphony, which exercise such a remarkable influence in the Fúl-language, and of which I am going to speak in the following paragraph.

i) The corresponding of the termination of the substantive with that of the adjective. The influence which the termination of the substantive exercises upon that of the adjective by which it is accompanied, is a question intimately allied with the consideration of the gender, and of the plural form of the latter. For, we have evident instances of the change of the terminating syllable of the adjective in connection with the substantive, but in each single case it is difficult to say, whether the change be occasioned by a mere regard to euphony, or by a grammatical rule; and I, therefore, prefer giving simply the instances of such a change, without answering the former question.

Thus, for „large", „great" I have the following variety of forms in connection with the form of the noun which it serves to characterize: **mâyo mange**, „the large river"; **korga manga**, „the great, chief female slave" (the simple form of **korga** being **kordo**, we have here, moreover, an instance of an evident influence exercised by the adjective upon the substantive); **lâna makka**, „large boat"; **lokki makki**, „large piece of wood"; **nédo manndo** (besides the form **o-nédo ho-manne** which we have to consider under k, α), „great man"; **kóngodi maundi**, „great clamours"; **bérende maundude**, „big heart".

Here, therefore, we find a perfect harmony between the termination, and the principal character of the adjective on the one, and that of the substantive on the other hand; but, as the instance of **korga manga** seems clearly to show, it is more of a euphonical, than of a grammatical character.

I now give some other instances: **yĕho jau-ma**, „a warm, fatiguing journey", **nédo jau-do**, „a (warm) man, a man of hot temperament", **himbe jau-be**, „people of hot temperament"; **nédo fêu-do**, „a cold person", **himbe fêu-be**, „cold people", **ndiam fêu-dam**, „cold water"; **nédo kállu-do**, „a bad person", **bérende kállu-nde**, „a bad heart", **dum kállu-dam**, „this (is) bad", **féttuki kállu-ki**, „bad events, mishaps"; **putšu bodĕdže**, „a brown horse", **putši bodĕdži**, „brown horses", **nebbam bodĕdž-am**, „red butter"; **putšu bulde**, „a horse with white feet", **putši bul-ĕdži**, „horses with white feet"; **dum ketš-am**, „this (is) ripe"; **bíbe leddo kétšu-de**, „ripe fruits". The latter form especially can by no means be the simple form of a plural, but is merely dependent on the termination **de** of the preceding noun.

As a very curious instance of the adjective form in **am**, in connection with the very term „salt", spoken of before, I have to mention **lamdam Balmâdžam**, „salt from Bilma".

The influence of euphony is even so great, that a syllable like **am**, even if not terminating a word, but forming its first syllable, may change the last syllable of the word which precedes; and thus we have **nangírdam džamdi** instead of **nangírde džamdi**, „an iron hammer".

From all these reasons it is almost impossible to give a list of the plural forms of the adjectives; but, if they are used independently, the change is the same as with the substan-

gebraucht werden, die Veränderung der Endsilbe im Allgemeinen dieselbe ist, wie bei dem Nennwort mit der gleichen Endung. Solche Beispiele, wie bolɨ-de dūdi, „viele Worte"; himbe dūdi, „viele Leute", wo die Plural-Endung des Eigenschaftswortes von derjenigen des begleitenden Nennwortes abweicht, möchten zu zeigen scheinen, dass es doch eine bestimmte Regel für jenes gibt, unabhängig von letzterem; aber der folgende Paragraph wird zeigen, dass diess irrthümlich ist und neben der Form himbe dūdi habe ich auch himbe dulbe.

k) Nun kommt eben ein sehr beachtenswerther Umstand hinzu, der die Schwierigkeit dieser Frage bedeutend erhöht. Denn ich habe zahlreiche Beispiele, wo das Eigenschaftswort als Prädikat gefasst und in eine verbale Form verwandelt ist. Diess geschieht auf zwei verschiedenen Wegen; erstlich einfach dadurch, dass man den Endvokal des Eigenschaftswortes o oder a in i verwandelt, wie z. B. dum weld-i, „diess ist süss" ganz identisch ist mit dum beld-am, „diess süsse". So haben wir denn auch die ganz verbale Form dum sadd-i, „diess ist schwer" mit der entsprechenden negativen dum sadd-a, „diess ist nicht schwierig, ist leicht"; dum tedd-i, „diess ist schwer" (von Gewicht) mit der negativen Form dum tedd-a, „diess ist nicht schwer". Ebenso haben wir dum yair-i, „diess ist theuer"; dum hō-i, „diess ist billig".

Den Charakter dieses angehängten verbalen i lernen wir noch besser kennen durch diejenigen Beispiele, wo wir es pronominalen Formen angehängt finden, wie z. B. von mō, „wer", dum mō-i, „wer ist das", wörtlich „diess wer ist"?; von tō, „wo", tō-i, „wo ist (es)"?; von nō, „wie viel, wie viele", dum nō-i, „wie viel ist diess". Nun aber ist es höchst auffallend, dass wir dasselbe i selbst der zweiten Person des Singular hinzugefügt finden in der Phrase ang a-mō-i, „wer bist du"?, und wir werden es selbst im Plural finden.

Hier komme ich nun auf die eben erwähnte Form dūd-i zurück, von der ich schon andeutete, dass sie gar nicht für eine regelmässige Pluralform gelten kann, und führe in Bezug auf sie an, dass, wie von anderen verbalen Adjektivformen ganz nach Art des Zeitwortes negative Formen gebildet werden, ebenso auch von dieser verbalen Form dūd-i („ist zahlreich, sind viele") die negative Form dūd-a („ist nicht zahlreich, sind nicht viele"), die ganz allgemein in Gebrauch ist, z. B. in der Phrase himbe ben dūd-a, „Leute sie sind nicht zahlreich", d. h. „wenige Leute".

k, a) Die zweite Art, dem Eigenschaftswort eine verbale Form zu geben, besteht darin, dass man die Silbe he oder hi der Wurzel desselben vorstellt, wie z. B. in der Phrase o-nēdo he-maune, „dieser Mensch ist gross" (hier der verbale Charakter noch durch das dem Substantiv vorangestellte pronominale o näher bezeichnet); henni hi-pōol, „die Luft ist kalt". In diesen beiden Beispielen haben wir in maune sowol, wie in pōol (mit Nebenform pōore) unveränderte adjektive Formen; dagegen hat in den folgenden Beispielen das Eigenschaftswort selbst eine verbale Form und wir können über seinen eigentlichen Charakter zweifelhaft sein, wie z. B. he-wal-i, „es ist warm"; he-nand-i, „es ist gleich"; māyo he-lugg-i „der Fluss ist tief"; sādo hi-hab-i, „das Gemach ist hell". Dann aber haben wir Beispiele, wo dieses selbige he unzweifelhaften, nicht adjektivischen, sondern an sich schon selbstständigen, verbalen Formen vorgesetzt wird, wie z. B. in der Phrase dādhañgel keña he-būri, „die Reise (von) gestern ist (oder war) besser", d. h. „es wäre besser gewesen, gestern zu reisen", wo būri schon an sich eine vollständige Verbalform ist. Eben so lodde hi-ñgode do wamde de, „gibt es Bäume auf diesem Berge"?, wofür wir eben so correkt sagen könnten ñādi ledde do wamde de. Es kann kaum zweifelhaft sein, dass wir die Form hi-ñgode wie eine Art von Particip anzusehen haben und ich bin überzeugt, dass derselbe Charakter auch der Phrase eigenthümlich ist be hi-džōdi be hi-dilli, „die Einen geblieben, die Anderen gegangen". — So sind auch on-hōda-dum und on-hi-sōda S. CXXII zu verstehen.

In welcher Grundbeziehung dieses, schon an sich verbalen oder adjektiven Formen hinzugefügte, he oder hi zu der Partikel he, „mit, auf, in, zu" steht, lässt sich eher fühlen als

tives of a corresponding termination. Instances such as boli-de dūdi, „many words", himbo dūdi, „many people", where the plural form of the adjective does not harmonise with, but differs from, that of the accompanying substantive, might seem to show, that there is some fixed rule for the plural change of the adjective, independent from that of the latter. But this is erroneous, as the following paragraph will, I hope, not fail to show; and moreover, besides the form mentioned in the latter instance, I have also himbo dulbe.

k) But now we come to a very remarkable circumstance, which tends greatly to increase the difficulty of this question. For I have numerous instances of the adjective, when used as a predicament, being changed into a verbal form in two different ways, first by changing the final vowel o or a, into i, as, for instance, dum weld-i, „this is sweet", which is identical with dum beld-am, „this (is) sweet". In the same manner I have dum sadd-i, „this is difficult", with the corresponding negative form dum sadd-a, „this is not difficult"; dum tedd-i, „this is heavy", with the negative form dum tedd-a, „this is not heavy"; and thus I have also dum yair-i, „this is dear"; dum hō-i, „this is cheap", and many others.

Now, this very same final i we find even added to pronominal forms, such as to mō, „who" in dum mō-i, verbally „this who is", „who is this"?; and to tō, „where", tō-i, „where is (it)"; to nō, „how much, how many", dum nō-i, „how much is this". But, what is very remarkable, we find the very same i even added to the second person of the singular in the phrase añg a-mō-i, „who art thou"?, and we are to meet with it even in the plural number.

After these remarks I may return once more to the form dūd-i, of which I observed a short time ago, that it is not to be looked upon as a regular plural, but rather as a verbal form, and in this respect I argue the case, that from this adjective likewise in the same manner as from the other adjectives mentioned above, a negative verbal form has been derived, dūd-i meaning „(is) much, (are) many", dūd-a, „not many" which is in common use, as for instance in the phrase himbo ben dūd-a, „people, they are not many, not numerous", i. q. „few people".

k, a) The second mode of changing the adjective into a verbal form consists in prefixing the syllable he or hi before the root, as, for instance, o-ndde he-mauno, „this man is great" (the verbal character of the phrase in this instance being, moreover, indicated by the o prefixed to the substantive); benni hi-péol, „the atmosphere is cold". In these two instances mauno as well as péol (with the byform péore) are pure adjective forms, while in the following instances the adjective has invested an entirely verbal character, as in he-wul-i, „it is warm"; he-nand-i, „it is similar"; māyo he-jugg-i, „the river is deep"; sūdo hi-hāb-i, „the apartment is light". But now we have also instances, where this same he or hi has been added not to adjectives, but to perfect verbal forms, as, for instance, in the phrase džáhañgol keña he-būri, „the journey of yesterday is (or „was") better" i. q. „it would have been better to travel yesterday", where būri is a perfect verbal form by itself. The same is the case with the phrase leddo hi-ñgōdo dō wamdo dē, „are there trees on this mountain"?, while we may say quite as correctly wōdi ledde dō wamdo de; and there can scarcely be any doubt, that we have to look upon this form hi-ñgōde, as a sort of participle. Thus, I am sure, we have likewise to explain the phrase bē hi-džādi bē hi-dilli, „some of them remaining, some of them gone", i. q. „some of them went away, others remained behind".

What the relation of this he or hi, which is prefixed to adjective or verbal forms, may be with regard to the preposition he or hi, „with, by, in", as, for instance he lāna, „by

definiren; so haben wir be lāna, „zu Boot"; be džam, „in Wohlsein"; be laual, „auf dem Wege"; be džippáko, „zum Absteigen". Ein Übergang von der Beziehung der einfachen Partikel zu der adjektivisch verbalen scheint mir in folgenden drei Phrasen zu liegen, die insgesammt den Ausdruck wiedergeben „jede Stadt hat ihre Sitten", wörtlich „jede Stadt mit, oder zu, ihren Gewohnheiten, mit ihrem Charakter, zu ihrem Werk", gari fū bi gikā-mō; gari fū be tabīn-mō; gari fū be kūgel-mō.

l) In Betreff der Stellung des Eigenschaftswortes, dass es nämlich dem Subjekt, worauf es sich bezieht, gewöhnlich nachfolgt, brauche ich keine weiteren Beispiele hier anzuführen, da die unter g) und h) angeführten auch diesen Satz hinlänglich erläutern. Jedoch gibt es von der allgemeinen Regel zahlreiche Ausnahmen, besonders in solchen Fällen, wo das Eigenschaftswort in enger Beziehung zu einem Objekte steht, wo dann sonderbarer Weise das Subjekt zwischen beide in die Mitte gestellt wird, wie z. B. džella nédo ádune, „verspottend ein Mensch die Leute", d. h. „maliciös", „der Spötter"; gaña nédo ádune, „betrügend ein Mensch die Leute", d. h. „betrügerisch", „der Betrüger".

m) Was den Komparativ und Superlativ anbetrifft, so werden beide in der Fūl-Sprache vermittelst des verbalen būri, „es übertrifft, ist besser" gebildet, so jedoch, dass der Superlativ nur sehr ungenügend ausgedrückt werden kann, entweder im engen Anschluss an den Komparativ oder durch Angabe des Objektes, unter dem dieses das hervorragendste ist, wie „alle". So habe ich z. B. die Phrase ka lāna būri mañgo ka lāna būri ka, „dieses Boot übertrifft an Grösse" (eigentlich „gross"), „dieses Boot übertrifft noch mehr", d. h. „ist grösser als eben dieses", also „ist das grösste von allen". Nur hat diese Phrase den Nachtheil, die Partikel ka in zwei verschiedenen Bedeutungen aufzuweisen, einmal als eine Art demonstrativen Fürwortes und das zweite Mal in der hier berührten Bedeutung; ausserdem hat die Adjektivform mañgo für „gross", der wir auch sonst begegnen, nicht deutlich erkennen lassen, ob mit der einfachen Form des Eigenschaftswortes eine Veränderung vorgegangen ist oder nicht. Wie sich aber aus anderen Beispielen zu ergeben scheint, bildet die Endung go einen wesentlichen Bestandtheil dieser Phrasen und hat allem Anschein nach die Bedeutung eines Ablativs, wie z. B. in der Phrase būri džūtu-go, „es übertrifft an Länge, ist länger", von der einfachen Form džūtu, „lang"; dum būri dūdo-go, „dieses übertrifft an Vielheit, Anzahl", „ist zahlreicher", von dūdo, „viel".

n) Nachdem ich nun so nach besten Kräften die Hauptbestandtheile der Sprache, wie das Fürwort, zumal das persönliche, das Zeitwort, das Nennwort und das Eigenschaftswort besprochen habe, und da das Beiwort oder Adverb keine besondere Besprechung erfordert, sondern mit dem letzteren fast durchgängig übereinstimmt, kann ich hiermit die Besprechung des Fūl an sich vorläufig beschliessen, indem ich mir die Erwägung einiger die Syntax betreffender Fragen bis zur Behandlung meiner Phrasen am Ende des Vokabulars aufspare.

Nur will ich hier noch auf eine bemerkenswerthe Eigenthümlichkeit in der Bildung einiger Zeitpartikeln hinweisen, wie rad-ani, rad-i-ani, rad-ti-t-ónni, „im vergangenen Jahre", „vor zwei Jahren", „vor drei Jahren"; fābi, fābi-ti, fābí-ti-ti, „übermorgen", „in zwei Tagen", „in drei Tagen". (Vokab. S. 24, N. 11.)

8. *Die Verwandtschaft des Fūl mit anderen Sprachen.*

In Bezug auf diese Verwandtschaft will ich hier nur einige vorläufige Andeutungen machen, da ich auf diesen Gegenstand zurückkommen werde.

a) Im Allgemeinen sind die Berührungen des Fūl mit anderen in meinen Wörtersammlungen vertretenen Sprachen überaus gering; nur mit der Hausa-Sprache hat sie deren in ansehnlicher Menge, aber, wenn näher betrachtet, erweisen sich diese fast insgesammt als spätere Adoptionen, die, wie ich nicht den geringsten Zweifel habe, ausschliesslich den auf früherem Hausa-Gebiet gesprochenen Dialekten dieser Sprache angehören, weshalb sie eben

boat"; he dĳam, „in well being, in (good) health"; he lauol, „on the road"; he dželppáko, „to, with regard to the dismounting", it is difficult to say; but, nevertheless, a certain relation between the two forms, and a sort of transition from one notion to the other, seems to be indicated by the following three phrases, each of which expresses the meaning „every town has its own customs", garí fū hi gikū-mō; garí fū he tabía-mō; garí fū he kūgel-mō.

l) As for the general position of the adjective, namely, that it follows the substantive, I need not further speak, as the very same instances, which I have adduced under g) and h), serve to illustrate this rule. However, there occur numerous exceptions to the latter, especially in such cases, where the adjective is intimately related to an object, which it rules, when the subject, if added, is often, if not generally, placed in the midst between the adjective and the object, as for instance džella nédo ádune, „abusing a man the people" i. q. „the jester"; gaña nédo ádune, „cheating a man the people" i. q. „the impostor".

m) As for the comparative, and superlative, they are both expressed in the Fūl-language by means of the verbal form būri, „it is better, exceeds", the superlative being only capable of being expressed either in close connection with the comparative, or by adding the term „all", or something similar, as, for instance ka lāna būri mango ka lāna būri ka, „this boat exceeds in size, (and) this boat exceeds that one" i. q. „this boat is larger (than the others), and this one is the largest of all". But this phrase has the inconvenience, that, besides that the particle ka occurs here twice as a sort of demonstrative pronoun, mango is a form of the adjective meaning „large, big", which occurs also in other connections besides this one, and which does not give us the opportunity of deciding whether the original form of the adjective has undergone any change or not; but we see from other instances, that the termination go forms an essential part of these phrases, and according to all appearances has the character of an ablative form, as for instance būri džūtu-go, „it exceeds in length", „is longer", from the adjective džūtu, „long"; dum būri dūdo-go, „this exceeds in number" i. q. „is more numerous" from dūdo, „much, many".

n) Having explained the chief parts of speech to the best of my ability, such as the pronoun, the verb, the substantive, and the adjective, and there being no regular formation of the adverb, I may herewith consider my purpose of solving the general questions in connection with my vocabulary of the Fūl-language as accomplished, referring as for the rest to the vocabulary itself, at the end of which I intend to settle a few questions regarding the syntax, when analyzing my collection of phrases.

I here want still to point out the remarkable gradation of the particles indicating time, such as raú-ani, rad-t-ani, rad-ti-t-ćuni, „last year", „the year before last" („two years ago"), „three years ago"; fābi, fābi-ti, fabí-ti-ti, „the day after to morrow", „in two days", „in three days". (Vocab. p. 25, note 11.)

6. *The relationship of the Fūl with other languages.*

With regard to this point I here want only to make a few precursory remarks, being obliged to return once more to this question.

a) In general I have to remark, that the points wherein this language is allied to others represented in my collection, are very scanty indeed; only with the Hausa language there are some more points of contact, but of such a character, that, when considered more closely, all the terms are shown to be borrowed from the Hausa idiom at a recent period by that dialect of the Fūl which is spoken in the former Hausa territories, which is the reason, why they

den westlicheren Dialekten, wo solche Berührung mit dem Hausa-Volk nicht Statt fand, ganz unbekannt sind. So haben wir als dieser Klasse entschieden angehörig die Namen mehrerer nützlicher Pflanzen, geróri, „Neger-Hirse" (H. géro); maiwári, „Sorghum" (H. maiwa); takautadžo, „Sorghum saccharatum" (H. takauta); saidádži, „Arthatoron pungens" (H. saida) und viele ähnliche Pflanzennamen mit der Endung dže oder dži; auch mit anderer Endung, wie babáho, „Indigo" (H. bába). Dann andere Ausdrücke, wo sich das Fremdwort durch irgend welche Beziehung besonders empfahl, wie bíñgiri, „männlicher Esel" (H. biñgi); gándus, „Sklaventrupp" (H. gando); gommel, „kleiner Bündel" (H. gomma); selbst Ausdrücke der allergewöhnlichsten täglichen Rede, wie bantai, „Morgen", der in diesen Provinzen den eigenthümlichen Fül-Ausdruck zurückgedrängt hat und tšakka, „mittlere" (H. tsakka), auch Präpositionen wie daga, „von" und die damit zusammengesetzten; ja, sogar Partikeln wie só, „nur" gehören zu dieser Klasse.

a, α) Trotz des Vorwiegens solcher, in späterer Zeit und nur ganz äusserlich, adoptirter Ausdrücke bleiben aber immer Übereinstimmungen in einzelnen Ausdrücken zwischen der Fül- und Hausa-Sprache übrig, die Beachtung verdienen und jedenfalls auf ein früheres Alter zurückgehen, wohin nicht allein der auch bei Reichardt, also im westlichsten, dem Gebiete der Hausa-Sprache so fern liegenden, Dialekt von Füta-Džálo erscheinende Ausdruck báo (H. bayo), „Rücken", sondern auch einige Namen durch die ganze Tropengegend Afrika's verbreiteter Thiere gehören, wie z. B. der Name für „Elephant", F. nyíwa, sogar im Dialekt des westlich fernsten Salum, nach Koelle's Polyglotta, níwa, H. gíwa; „Waldbüffel", F. mbanna, H. bauna; ein anderes wiederkäuendes Thier F. ndérrua, H. derri.

b) Mit dem Kanúri sind die Berührungen des Fül noch geringer; auffallend ist der gerade bei Reichardt erscheinende Ausdruck dandúru für „Hauptpromenade", K. dendal. Der in Fúmbina übliche Ausdruck sobá-džo, „Freund" (K. sóba) erklärt sich eben einfach durch die nahe Berührung der Landschaften und durch die zahlreiche Ansiedelung von Bornu-Leuten in Adamaua.

c) Mit dem Soñyai mag das Fül vielleicht eine leichte Berührung haben in dem Ausdrucke für „heute", hande, han-dé, „diesen Tag" (hau, „Tag" im S.) verglichen banki, han-ki für „gestern", noch erhalten in dem Fül-Ausdrucke hanki džemma, „gestern Nacht", während für das einfache „gestern" der Ausdruck kenyo gewöhnlicher wurde. Daneben gehören entschieden hierher die Benennungen von Sprachen mit der Endung tši, dži = Soñyai ki, „Sprache", von denen ich bei Gelegenheit der Beschreibung von Adamaua so zahlreiche Beispiele aufgezählt habe, wie Bátta-u-tši, Búma-n-tši, Dáma-n-tši u. s. w. (Reis. Th. II, S. 617); aber ebenso wenig hege ich einen Zweifel, dass diess eine blosse Entlehnung ist, welche die Fül der Soñyai-Sprache entnommen haben.

d) Unzweifelhafte Berührungen aber hat das Fül, ausser der schon S. CX angedeuteten Beziehung zum Yolof, mit dem Kadžága nach den wenigen, in Koelle's Polyglotta gegebenen, Proben und auch nach Andeutungen in meinem kurzen Azër-Vokabular. Denn, wie ich ausführlicher in der Einleitung zu meinen kleinen Vokabularien nachweisen werde, war Kadžága die Sprache des alten weitumfassenden Reiches Ghánata und begriff daher auch das Azër, d. h. die Dialekte von Wádân und Tíšît. Was ich, bevor ich die linguistischen Fragen ergründet hatte, in dem Berichte meiner Reisen wiederholentlich gesagt habe, dass das Mandingo oder ein Dialekt desselben die Sprache von Ghánata gewesen sei, ist darnach zu berichtigen. Aus jener Übereinstimmung sehen wir ganz klar, dass die Fúlbe nicht allein die Kultur der „Baumwolle", F. póttolo, K. kotóle und des „Reises", F. maróri, K. maro von jenem allen anderen Afrikanischen Stämmen in gewisser Macht und Bildung weit vorangeschrittenen Stamme erhielt, wenn auch in Bezug auf Reiskultur die Soñyai („Reis", mo, s. oben S. XXXII) den Kadžága noch voran gingen; sondern selbst die Rinderzucht, die sie selbst erst bei den meisten

are not used in those dialects of the Fūl-language which are spoken in the Western provinces. Thus, we have as decidedly belonging to this class the terms denoting useful plants, such as „Negromillet", gerōri (H. gèro); „sorghum", maiwāri (H. maiwa); „sorghum saccharatum", takantādže (H. takanta); „arthraterum pungens", saidādži (H. saida), and many other similar names to which the Fūl have appended the termination džo or dži: then, with other terminations, such as bubāho (H. bābu), „indigo". We have also terms belonging to other classes, as, for instance, bíṅgiri (H. biṅgi), „male ass"; gándua (H. gando), „troop of slaves"; gommel (H. gomma), „small bundle, parcel". Nay, even terms belonging to the most common daily phraseology, such as hantsi, „morning", have been borrowed by the Fūl of Sókoto from the Hausa, and have taken the place of the corresponding national terms; even the adjective tākka (H. tsakka), „middle", and prepositions, such as daga, „from, from out", and the terms composed by means of the latter belong to this class, as well as the particle sé, „only, with the exception of".

a, α) But notwithstanding all, what I have said, a few cases of close relationship between the Fūl- and Hausa-language remain, which are well worth attention, as going back to an early age; and to this class belongs, for instance, the term bāo (H. buyo), „back", which is found also in the short glossary of Rev. Reichardt, as belonging to the Westernmost dialect of the Fūl-language, viz that of Fūta-Džālo, which is, no doubt, placed beyond any influence of the Hausa-language, and, besides, some names given to wild beasts spread through the whole of the Tropical regions of Africa, as for instance F. nyíwa (appearing even in the dialect of the most Westerly and isolated province of Salum in the form níwa, according to Koelle's Polyglotta) H. gíwa, „elephant"; mbanna, H. bauna, „buffalo"; ndárrua, H. derri, another beast of prey.

b) As for the Kanūri, the cases of relationship with the Fūl-language are almost none; as a curious instance of coincidence, however, I will mention the term dandūru, appearing in Rev. Reichardt's Primer and being identical with the Kanūri dendal, „chief street, square".

c) With the Soṅyai, the Fūl may have some slight sort of coincidence in the term meaning „to day", hande (han-dé, „this day", han meaning „day" in Soṅyai), compared with hanki (han-ki, „the day past") meaning „yesterday", and preserved in the composite term hanki džemma, „last night", while in cases where the term „yesterday" is used independently the native kenya is generally used. Besides, I am sure, we have to mention under this head the terms of languages with the termination tši (dži) of which, in describing the province of Adamawa, I have given such a long list (Tr. II, p. 513 f.), as for instance Bátta-n-tši, Fála-n-tši, Būma-n-tši, and so on; and I have not the least doubt, that this form has been simply borrowed by the Fūl from their Western neighbours, the Soṅyai.

d) On the other hand the Fūl-idiom, besides its relation to the Yolof, which I have pointed out p. CXI, has some undoubted points of contact of a great historical interest with the language of Kadžāga, as will be seen as well from the specimens under this head given in Koelle's Polyglotta, as from my own short glossary of the Azēr-language. For, as I shall have occasion to show when treating of the latter, the Kadžaga was the idiom spoken in the empire of Ghánata, and, therefore, comprises the Azēr-dialects spoken in the towns of Tīšīt and Wádān. What I have said in this respect in my Narrative of a dialect of the Mandingo having been the idiom of Ghánata, is a mistake and has to be modified accordingly. The points of coincidence mentioned, however, are rather of a material, than of a linguistic character, it appearing from them, that the Fūl have adopted from the Kadžāga the cultivation of „cotton" (F. póttolo, Kadžāga kotólo), as well as that of „rice" (F. marōri, Kadžāga maro), even if the Kadžāga-people, as most probably they do, owe to the Soṅyai the precedence with regard to the latter article (S. „rice", mo, compared with what I have said p. XXXIII). The Fūl even

östlichen Stämmen bis zum Tsâd-See auf ihren östlichen Wanderungen einführten, haben die Fül wahrscheinlich von den Kadžāga angenommen; denn das Kadžāga-Wort nde für „Kuh" ist offenbar die ursprüngliche Form des Fül-Wortes nage, negge, d. i. na go, „eine Kuh", Plur. nai, na-i.

Erwähnen will ich bei dieser Gelegenheit als einen sehr merkwürdigen Wink enthaltend für die Kulturgeschichte jener Gegenden den Umstand, dass der Haussa-Name tōro, F. torōri für den ungewöhnlich grossen Elephanten augenscheinlich mit dem entsprechenden Namen tūre, Plur. tūru der Kadžāga-Sprache zusammenhängt, und dass dies vielleicht ursprünglich der Name für den gezähmten Elephanten war; denn, wie die alten Karthager, wenn nicht ausschliesslich, so doch besonders eben den Afrikanischen Elephanten zu dem Roll- und Schreckwerk ihrer Heere gebrauchten, da die Münzen auf die entschiedenste und klarste Weise eben den Afrikanischen Typus dieser Thiere darstellen, so kannte man noch im Reiche Ghánata die jetzt in Binnen-Afrika, selbst bis auf die Erinnerung, völlig verloren gegangene Kunst des Zähmens dieses merkwürdigsten aller Thiere der Wildniss.

c) Die Übereinstimmung einiger Zahlwörter der Fül-Sprache mit den entsprechenden einiger Süd-Afrikanischen Sprachen, wie besonders tāti, „drei"; nai, „vier" ist schon Anderen aufgefallen und hat zu allerlei verfänglichen Schlüssen geführt, seitdem besonders Richard Lander diesen Stamm in vielen Punkten mit den Kafirn Süd-Afrika's übereinstimmend fand. Aber, obgleich ich noch zwei oder drei weitere Berührungspunkte hinzuzufügen habe, halte ich diese Ähnlichkeiten, wenigstens zum Schluss auf örtliche Berührung dieser Stämme doch für durchaus der Gültigkeit derjenigen nachstehend, die den entschiedenen Gang der Wanderungen der Fül-Nation in historischer Zeit von Westen nach Osten darstellen; da aber dieser merkwürdige Stamm in seinen westlichen Sitzen am Senegal nicht einheimisch und noch im 7ten Jahrhundert unserer Zeitrechnung, zum Theil wenigstens, in den südlichen Oasen von Marocco und in Tuat angesessen war und da er wol entschieden einmal aus dem Osten gekommen sein muss, so mögen diese Berührungen mit den Süd-Afrikanischen Stämmen in die graue Vorzeit zurück reichen; jedenfalls sind sie älter als die Ansiedelung des Māšiγ-Stammes in Nord-Afrika, der dieser Wanderung den Weg abgeschnitten hätte. Die Ähnlichkeiten, die ich anzuführen weiss, sind wenige, aber nicht unbedeutend, „Sonne", F. nañge, in der Kōsa-Sprache ilāñga; „Fluss", F. māyo, Plur. mādži, „Wasser", in Kōsa māsi. Dann wüsste ich als merkwürdig nur anzuführen den Ausdruck für „Negerhirse", F. mohūri, in Meto (Koelle's Polyglotta, d. h. der Makua-Sprache) mahele.

Achtes Kapitel.

Die Sonγai-Sprache: Sonγai ki-ni.

Über den Namen Sonγai kann ich nichts zur Erklärung beibringen. Jedenfalls ist er bezüglich alten Ursprunges, obgleich er von El Bekri, dem berühmten und hoch verdienten Andalusischen Geographen des XIten Jahrhunderts, der uns über die Sitze dieses Stammes am mittleren Niger die ersten Nachrichten überliefert hat, noch nicht erwähnt wird und zum ersten Mal bei Leo Africanus erscheint, in der allbekannten Beschreibung Binnen-Afrika's, in der Form Sungai. Obgleich nun der Letztere, ein Mann, der seinen Arabischen Charakter und sein Arabisches Wissen gegen die Romanische Bildung des südlichen Europa's eingebüsst hatte, das γ in diesem Namen entschieden als einen g-Laut aufgefasst hat, hat es doch so sehr den Charakter eines Moghrebinischen γ, dass Manche den Laut für ein r angesehen haben; und nur so allein lässt sich, wie ich anderswo gezeigt (Reis. IV, S. 321), das Missverständniss Caillié's erklären, der den Volksnamen, wenigstens für Timbuktu selbst, in der

appear to have learnt from the Kadžāga the breeding of cattle which they themselves in their turn, while migrating Eastward, have communicated with the other tribes of Central-Negroland settled more to the East as far as the Tsād; for the Kadžāga-term nā, meaning „cow" is evidently the original form of the Fūl-term nage, negge (i. q. na go, „one cow"), plur. nai, na-i.

On this occasion I will also mention a circumstance containing, as I fancy, an interesting hint as to the history of civilisation of those Regions, namely that the Hausa-name tōro, F. torori, denoting an elephant of unusual size, is evidently connected with the corresponding name tūre, plur. tūru of the Kadžāga-idiom, and I am of opinion, that this term originally designated the tamed elephant; for the inhabitants of Ghánata were as yet acquainted with the art of taming that most remarkable of all beasts of the forest, an art which has since been lost entirely by the tribes of Negroland.

e) As for the relation of a few of the numerals of the Fūl-language with the corresponding ones of some of the dialects of the South African group, such as especially táti, „three", nai, „four", it has already been argued by some writers on this subject, and has led to all sorts of captious conclusions, especially since the time when Richard Lander thought, he found points of similarity between this tribe and the Kafirs of South-Africa. But, although I have to add two or three instances of coincidence more, nevertheless I am convinced, that these cases are of a totally subordinate character, when compared with those which indicate the direction of the wanderings of the Fūl-nation in the historical period from West to East. However, as a portion of this remarkable tribe was most probably as yet settled in the Southern part of Morocco and Tawāt in the VIIth century of our era, and must once have come from the East, these points of linguistical contact with the South-African tribes may reach back into the time of yore, when the Fūl and South-African tribes were settled somewhere close together; but they may also be quite accidental, although the circumstance that two succeeding numerals „three", „four" in both languages are identical, is, no doubt, of very considerable importance. At all events, such a migration of the Fūl from the Eastward towards the West must have happened before the time when the Mašiγ-race occupied the whole of North Africa, as these latter would most probably have obstructed the march of the former. The cases of probable identity between the Fūl and the Kāfir-idioms which I have still to adduce, are „sun", F. naňge, in the Kosa-language ilánga; „river" in F. māyo, plur. madži, „water" in Kosa mási. There may be some other cases of similarity, but I can only point out as another remarkable instance the term for „negro-millet", F. mohūri, in Méto i. q. the Mukwa-language (Koelle Polyglotta) mahēlo.

Chapter the eighth.

The Soṅγai-language: Soṅγai ki-ni.

With regard to the name Soṅγai I am not yet able to explain it or to illustrate its origin. I have not the slightest doubt, however, that it is by no means of such a recent date, although it has not been mentioned by El Bekri, the celebrated and highly meritorious Andalusian geographer of the eleventh century, to whom we are indebted for the first account of that Region, viz the middle course of the Niger, and its inhabitants. Indeed, I look upon it as merely accidental, that the name appears for the first time in the well known account of Leo Africanus, where Sungai is represented as one of the great divisions of Northern Central Africa as well in political, as in linguistical respect. But, although that form of the name shows, that Leo, a person who had exchanged his Arabic character, and learning for that of the Romanesque population of Southern Europe, understood and caught the γ as a g sound, nevertheless it has so entirely the character of the African γ, that many a person

Form Cissour, d. h. Kissur gab; nämlich entstanden aus ki Sōγi, dem Namen der Sprache in etwas veränderter, umgestellter und abgekürzter Form, statt der vollen Form Soṅγai ki-ni, wie man das unter dem Einflusse des Arabischen häufig hört. So habe ich denn keinen Zweifel, dass die eigentliche Wurzel dieses Namens in zwei Buchstaben besteht, s und dem vieldeutigen nasalen γ.

Über die wahrscheinlichen Ursitze des Volkes, so weit irgend welcher geschichtliche Anhalt zurückreicht, habe ich ebenfalls in meinem Reisebericht gesprochen (Th. IV, S. 418); hier will ich nur noch besonders darauf hinweisen, dass in Folge der ungemein ausgedehnten Eroberungen der Soṅγai-Herrscher am Ende des XVten und im Anfange des XVIten Jahrhunderts das von Leo der Sungai-Sprache angewiesene Gebiet ein in vielen Beziehungen verkehrtes und nur beziehungsweise wahres ist, indem er zu ihm ausser Anderem schon Wálāta hinzurechnet, obgleich die Sprache der Eingeborenen jener Stadt eine grundverschiedene war und das Soṅγai nur als Sprache des herrschenden Stammes und vielleicht in Folge einer Kolonisation daselbst im öffentlichen Leben vorwiegen konnte¹). In Betreff derselben Erscheinung in Bezug auf A'gades und anderer benachbarter Punkte habe ich schon im zweiten Kapitel S. XVIII das Bezügliche beigebracht.

In Bezug nun auf Verwandtschaft mit anderen Afrikanischen oder sonstigen Sprachen steht das Soṅγai für mich wenigstens bis jetzt sehr vereinzelt da, obgleich ich nach einzelnen, weiter unten zu berührenden Anzeichen nicht zweifle, dass gerade diese Sprache mit dem Fortschritt des vergleichenden linguistischen Studiums, gestützt auf noch umfassendere Wörtersammlungen als die meinige, einen merkwürdigen Aufschluss über die geschichtliche Entwickelung dieser ganzen Gruppe der Afrikanischen Sprachen geben wird.

Wir betrachten nun in kurzer Übersicht die einzelnen Redetheile.

1. *Das persönliche Fürwort.*

	Singular. präfix.	suffix.	Plural. präfix.	suffix.
1ste Person .	a, ai, ai-ta;	— i . . .	yer, yiri, yer-ta;	— yer;
2te „ .	ni, ni-ta;	— ni . .	war, wiri, war-ta;	— war;
3te „ .	ṅga, aṅga, áṅga-ta;	— ga . .	ṅgi, iṅgi, íṅgi-ta;	— gi.

Wir haben also für die erste Person Sing. einen Vokal, der zwischen a, dem Alt-Egyptischen (nach Bunsen I, S. 557) entsprechend, und zwischen i schwankt, und dann den diese beiden Laute vereinigenden Diphtong ai.

Für die zweite Person haben wir ein dem Kanúri vollkommen identisches Zeichen ni.

Für die dritte Person haben wir das dem Lógone, wie wir sehen werden, entsprechende ṅga.

Die erste Person des Plural ist von dem i-Laut der entsprechenden Form des Singular durch ein angesetztes er gebildet.

¹) Ich gebe hier die ganze Stelle Leo's, Buch I, c. 11: „Nelle Terrenegre favellasi in diverse lingue, una delle quali è da lor detta sungai: e questa serve a molte regioni, come è in Gualata, in Tombutto, in Ghinea, in Melli e in Gago". In Melli, dem Mandingo-Reiche, war diese Sprache natürlich ursprünglich noch weniger heimisch als in Wálāta, aber das Reich wurde eben von den Soṅγai-Herrschern zertrümmert und die öffentliche Sprache wurde die der Eroberer, so lange es eben dauerte, und hat sich dort jetzt nicht die geringste Spur der Anwendung des Soṅγai erhalten. Dazu kommt aber nun, dass jene wirkliche Eroberung Melle's bedeutend nach der Zeit eintrat, wo Leo schrieb und er muss also in diesem Falle eines entschiedenen Irrthums beschuldigt werden, wenn ihn oder seine Berichterstatter, da er Melle nicht selbst besucht hat, nur die vereinzelte weitere Anwendung des Soṅγai selbst in jenem Lande veranlasste. Wegen Ghanata's, von Leo Ghinea genannt, kann man zweifelhaft sein.

has misunderstood it for an r, and from this point of view alone, as I have had opportunity of developing in another place (Tr. and Disc. vol. IV, p. 316), we are enabled to explain, how the traveller Réné Caillié came to his error in giving the name of Cissour i. q. Kisour to the inhabitants of the town of Timbuktu, this wrong form originating in the two words ki, „language, idiom", and Soy and Sŏyi instead of the full form Soṅyai, the whole term ki Soy being an abbreviated and corrupted form instead of the full and correct form Sonyai ki-ni.

As for the probable quarter of the original seats of the Soṅyai-nation, as far as any historical records allow to go back, I have likewise stated my opinion in my Narrative (see vol. IV, p. 410; vol. V, p. 470); here I want only to point out in particular the circumstance, that in consequence of the vast conquests made by the kings of Soṅyai towards the close of the XVth, and in the beginning of the XVIth century the limits assigned by Leo to the dominion of the Soṅyai-language about that very period, are wrong in general and only correct from a certain point of view. Thus, for instance, he includes Wálata in that category, although the idiom spoken by the inhabitants of that place was, and still is, a totally distinct one, allied to the Azér and the Kanḗri, while the Soṅyai-language could only prevail there for a certain period, as the idiom spoken by the ruling tribe, and perhaps also in consequence of a colony of Soṅyai-people having been settled there *), in the same manner as has been the case with A'gades, and other places, with regard to which circumstance I have already stated my opinion in the second chapter p. XIX.

As for relationship with other African languages, or with idioms of another origin, the Soṅyai-idiom, as yet, has not disclosed to me many points of reference, although according to certain indications which I shall dwell upon further on, I have not the slightest doubt, that, as the study of comparative philology advances, this very idiom will serve to spread a great deal of information upon the question of the historical development of this group of African languages.

We now proceed to consider the single parts of speech.

1. *The personal pronoun.*

	singular. prefix.	suffix.	plural. prefix.	suffix.
1st person .	a, ai, ai-ta;	— i . . .	yer, yiri, yer-ta;	— yer;
2nd „ .	ni, ni-ta;	— ni . . .	war, wiri, war-ta;	— war;
3rd „ .	ṅga, aṅga, áṅga-ta;	— ga . .	ṅgi, iṅgi, íṅgi-ta;	— gi.

Thus, we have as the sign for the 1st person of the singular a vowel, fluctuating between an a (identical with the corresponding vowel in the ancient Egyptian, if Bunsen vol. I, p. 557 is right) and an i, and secondly a diphtong composed of these two vowels.

For the 2nd person we have ni, perfectly identical with the corresponding form in the Kanúri-language.

For the 3rd person we have ṅga, identical, as we shall see further on, with the corresponding term in Lógone.

The 1st person of the plural has been derived from the corresponding i of the singular by adding the syllable er, which I hope, I may be able to explain further on.

*) I here give the whole passage of Leo, book I, ch. 11: „Nella Terranegra favellano in diverse lingue, una delle quali è da lor detta sungai; e questa corre in molte regioni, come è in Gualata, in Tombutto, in Ghinea, in Melli e in Gago". In Melli, the great and once powerful Mendingo empire, the Soṅyai-language, of course, was still less indigenous, than in Wálata, and not the slightest trace of it has been preserved to the present day, but that empire having been overthrown by the Soṅyai-kings, the idiom of the conquerors became for a short time the ruling language of the higher classes. But that having happened after the time when Leo wrote, and published his account of Africa, we must look upon this statement of his as wrong in every respect. As for Dḗnni, here called Ghinea, we may hesitate as yet as for the idiom originally spoken in that province.

Die zweite Person Plur. ist ähnlich abgeleitet, nur dass der Anfangslaut fast auf ein ursprüngliches u in der entsprechenden Person des Singular schliessen lässt.

Die dritte Person Plur. ist einfach von derjenigen des Singulars abgeleitet durch Veränderung des schliessenden a in i.

Das in der verstärkten Form angehängte ta kann ich nur durch einen Vergleich mit dem ta in der Ful-Sprache, wie in hañko ta S. CXXXII, einigermaassen erklären.

Die oben angeführten Suffix-Formen vertreten im Allgemeinen die Accusativ-Beziehungen des persönlichen Fürwortes, für den Dativ werden mannichfache andere Abwandelungen derselben gebraucht:

„mich" (Accus.) i: „du liebst mich" („lieben", bā), ni-ta ní-ga bá i; „er schlägt mich" („schlagen", kar), áñga-ta á-ga kár i;

„mir" (Dativ): für „gib (nō) mir" habe ich vier oder vielmehr fünf verschiedene Formen: nō i, no ye, no re und é nō, í nō, die beiden letzteren besonders auffallend.

In der Phrase kóbbere se fondo, „zeige mir den Weg", ist wahrscheinlich abzutheilen kóbber(e) é-sē oder í-sē fondo, Vokab. S. 71.

„dich" (Accus.) ni: „er liebt dich", áñga-ta á-ga bā ni;

„dir" (Dativ) ni, ni-sé: „ich gebe dir (Etwas)" { é-ga nō ni; é-ga ni nō; é-ga nō ni-sē;

„ihn, es" (Accus.) ga, ñga: „ich liebe ihn", ai-ta é-ga bā ga[1]; „ich habe ihn nicht getroffen", ai-ta é-sa harta ñga; „hebe es empor", zau ñga bóne;

„ihm" (Dativ): ich habe nur ein Beispiel der verstärkten Form áñga-ta-sé, wahrscheinlich um das Objekt dem Subjekt mit mehr Nachdruck entgegenzustellen, so dass die einfache Form wäre ga-sé;

„uns" (Accus.) yer: „ihr liebt uns", war-ta war-ga bā yer;

„uns" (Dativ) yere, yer-sé: „gib uns", nō yerē; yer-sé: „es wäre besser für uns, wir wären gestern gegangen", a-bíssa yer-sē yer-koi bi;

„euch" (Accus.) war: „sie lieben euch", íñgi-ta í-ga bā war;

„euch" (Dativ) war-sé: „sie haben euch gegeben", íñgi-ta í-nō war-sē;

„sie" (Accus.) gi: „wir lieben sie", yer-ta er-ga bā gi;

„ihnen" (Dativ) gi-sé: „gib ihnen", nō gi-sē; auch íñgi-ta-se scheint unter gewissen Verhältnissen gebraucht zu werden, ganz entsprechend dem áñga-ta-sé des Singular.

2. *Genitiv und Pronomen Possessivum.*

a) Der Besitz oder die Beziehung einer Sache oder einer Person zu einer anderen wird durch di ausgedrückt, das dem Subjekte angefügt wird, wie in der Phrase idžo wo bába di a-bū, wörtlich „Kind dies Vater von (sein) starb", d. h. „der Vater dieses Kindes ist gestorben"; also erhalten wir in Bezug auf das Pronomen, das hier als Subjekt in einfacher Form vor dem Objekt steht, folgendes Schema:

Singular.	Plural.
a — di, „ich — von", d. h. „mein"	yir — di, „wir — von", d. h. „unser",
ni — di, „du — von", d. h. „dein"	war — di, „ihr — von", d. h. „euer",
áñga / ñga } — di, „er — von", d. h. „sein"	íñgi — di, „sie — von", d. h. „ihr".

[1] é-ga bā ga. Dieses angehängte, sich auf ein allgemeines Objekt beziehende ga müssen wir bei vielen Zeitwörtern ablösen, um die Wurzel zu erhalten, so S. 105 hauga, „binden", S. 114 forga, S. 110 téga und viele andere. Aber, wenn wir den Imperativ ai-ba-ra, „ich will", vergleichen mit é-ga bá ga, so möchte es fast scheinen, als wenn wir auch hier ein g hätten.

The 2nd person of the plural has a similar termination, while the root, from whence it has been derived, is totally different from that used in the singular, and looks as if there had been u.

As for the 3rd person of the plural, it has been simply derived from the corresponding form of the singular by changing the final a into i.

As for the ta added to the stronger form, I have nothing to illustrate it, if not by comparing it with the identical ta added in the Fûl-language, not only at the end of a verbal form, but also after the pronoun, as for instance kañko ta p. CXXXIII.

The simple form of the suffix is used to express the accusative case, while for the dative there are, besides, various other modes of changing the pronominal form, as the following instances will serve to show:

„me" (accus.): „thou lovest me" („love", bā), ni-ta ní-ga bā i; „he beats me" („beat", kar): añga-ta á-ga kár i;

„me" (dative): for „give me" („give", nō) I have the four, or rather five following forms: nō i, nō ye, nō re, é nō, and í nō, the two latter of which are especially remarkable.

Besides these different forms for the dative case we have probably to register another form é-sé or í-sé, and have to spell kóbber(e) é-sē (or í-sē) fondo instead of kóbbere sē fondo, „show me the way", vocabulary p. 71.

„thee" (accus.) ni: „he likes thee", añga-ta á-ga bā ni;

„thee" (dative) ni, ni-sē: „I give thee (something)" { é-ga nō ni; é-ga ni no; é-ga nō ni-sē;

„him", „it" (accus.) ga, ñga: „I love him", ai-ta é-ga bā ga*); „I have not met him", ai-ta é-sa haria ñga; „raise, lift it", saa ñga bene;

„him" (dative): I have only one instance of the stronger form añga-ta-se, the ta having been added to this form, probably in order to oppose more strongly the object to the subject, in which case the simple form would be ga-sé;

„us" (accus.), yer: „you love us", war-ta war-ga bā yer;

„us" (dative), yere, yer-sē: „give us", nō yerē; „it would have been better for us, we went yesterday", a-bísaa yer-sē yer-koi bi;

„you" (accus.), war: „they like you", íñgi-ta í-ga bā war;

„you" (dative), war-sē: „they have given you (something)", íñgi-ta í-sō war-sē;

„them" (accus.), gi: „we like them", yer-ta er-ga bā gi;

„them" (dative), gi-sē: „give them", nō gi-sē. Under certain circumstances also the stronger form íñgi-ta-sē seems to be used.

2. *The genitive case and possessive pronoun.*

a) The possessing, or the relation of an object to a subject being indicated in Soñyai by adding the particle di to the subject which follows the object, as, for instance, in the phrase: idže wo bába di a-bū verbally „child this father of (i. q. „his") died" i. q. „the father of this child died", the same is the way of forming a sort of possessive pronoun, thus:

singular.	plural.
a — di, „I — of" i. q. „mine"	yir — di, „we — of" i. q. „our",
ni — di, „thou — of" i. q. „thine"	war — di, „you — of" i. q. „your",
añga / añga — di, „he — of" i. q. „his"	íñgi — di, „they — of" i. q. „their".

*) é-ga bá ga: this ga which relates to an object in general, is very often so closely united with a verb, that in certain cases we may hesitate, whether it belongs to the root or not. See, for instance, vocab. p. 100 haaga, „blind", p. 118 forga, p. 119 tága, and many others. However, I have to observe, that the g in é-ga ba ga resembles rather an y, especially, if we compare with it the ai-ba-ra, „I will" of the Hombori dialect.

Also mit „Kameel", yo, Plur. yöëo erhalten wir folgendes Paradigma des possessiven Fürwortes:

		Singular.			Plural.
mein	Kameel	a yo di	meine	Kameele	a yöëo di,
dein		ni yo di . . .	deine		ni yöëo di,
sein		ènga yo di . .	seine		ènga yöëo di,
unser		yer yo di . . .	unsere		yer yöëo di,
euer		war yo di . . .	eure		war yöëo di,
ihr		ingi yo di . . .	ihre		ingi yöëo di.

Mit Hülfe dieses di ist auch wol das afö-di S. 5 zu erklären, nämlich nur in Bezug auf eine hinzu gedachte Menge, „die Einen, Einige von ihnen". Dann haben wir di pleonastisch S. 111 zweimal und als eine Art Accusativ S. 113 vier Mal, 117, 119. Über einen anderen Gebrauch des beziehungsreichen di als verbindendes Glied der Redetheile siehe weiter unten.

b) Nun aber finden wir ganz in derselben Beziehung, sowol zum Pronomen wie zu Substantiven, eine Endung ni statt di hinzugefügt, wie in der Phrase

„Welcher Art ist die Sprache der Leute dieses Landes"?,

gande wo borëo mésofo ingi ki-ni, wörtlich „Land dies Leute welcher Art, sie, Sprache von (ihnen", d. h. „ihre Sprache". Ganz ebenso ist der oben angeführte Name der Soñyai-Sprache, Soñyai ki-ni, „Soñyai, seine Sprache", aufzufassen. Unzweifelhaft sind so auch zu erklären die Formen für „dies ist mein" u. s. w., wörtlich „dies ich, dies von", die ich nicht richtig verstand, als ich auf dem ersten Bogen des Vokabulars (S. 5) die Pronomina abhandelte und die ich hiernach zu berichtigen bitte.

„dies ist mein, gehört mir" . . . . . . woki ī wo-ni,
„dies ist dein, gehört dir" . . . . . . woki ni wo-ni,
„dies ist sein, gehört ihm" . . . . . . woki a(ñga) wo-ni,
„dies ist unser, gehört uns" . . . . . . woki yiri wo-ni,
„dies ist euer, gehört euch" . . . . . . woki war wo-ni,
„dies ist ihr, gehört ihnen" . . . . . . woki ingi wo-ni.

Da die angeführten Beispiele das ni nur in Verbindung mit einem vorhergehenden k zeigen, so können wir es wol als eine durch blosse euphonische Rücksichten hervorgebrachte Umwandelung von di ansehn. Diese Ansicht würde selbst stichhaltig sein, auch wenn gorai tšini (i. e. kši-ni) S. 23 „in alter Zeit" hierher gehörte, da tš nur ein erweichtes k ist.

c) Beide, di sowol wie ni werden auch oft fortgelassen, besonders bei Substantiven, wozu wir auch wol die beiden Ausdrücke ni me böre, „mein älterer Bruder" und ni me kaine, „mein jüngerer Bruder" zu rechnen haben; me, mö kommt mehrfach für „besitzen" vor. Hierher gehört jedoch nach meiner Meinung keineswegs der Ausdruck ni-ta näti (nä-ti?), Vokabular S. 2 u. s. w. für „ich selbst", da hier das ti vielleicht nur veränderte Form des di ist.

3. Unter den Zahlwörtern stehen 2 und 3; 5, 6 und 7; 8 und 9 in augenscheinlich enger Beziehung der Bildung und Bedeutung. Höchst auffallend ist es, dass, obgleich die Sprache anscheinend gleich bis „zehn" zählt und dafür einheimische kurze Ausdrücke hat, diese in den östlichen Landschaften des Songhai-Reiches, wie in A'gades, von 5 an von den Arabischen Zahlwörtern verdrängt sind, S. 9, Note 10. In Bezug auf einzelne Punkte verweise ich auf die Noten zu den einzelnen Formen, besonders auf Note 9, S. 9 des Vokabulars.

4. *Das Zeitwort.*

Das Zeitwort wird in ähnlicher Weise gebildet wie im Hausa, nur dass im Soñyai ga, go mit dem Vorsatz des entsprechenden Fürwortes die Stelle des na im Hausa vertritt und hier den Charakter des Hülfszeitwortes bestimmter beibehalten hat. Allerdings kann auch

Thus, in connection with the term „camel", yō, plur. yōëo, we obtain the following paradigm of the possessive pronoun:

		singular.			plural.
my	camel	a yō di	my	camels	a yōëo di,
thy		ni yō di	thy		ni yōëo di,
his		ńga yō di . . .	his		ńga yōëo di,
our		yer yō di	our		yer yōëo di,
your		war yō di	your		war yōëo di,
their		ingi yō di	their		ingi yōëo di.

From this same point of view we have also to explain, I think, afō-di p. 6, „some of (them", with regard to the whole number, to which it is referred). But this particle di has a most comprehensive meaning, indicating every kind of relation between two notions, which is the reason why we shall have frequent opportunity of returning to it; for it not only serves to express the genitive relation between a subject and an object, even in connection with prepositions, but also the accusative relation between a verb and an object, as for instance p. 113, 117 and 119; nay, it even serves as a kind of conjunction between entire phrases.

b) Instead of this di we find also ni in exactly the same position, as well in connection with the pronoun, as with the substantive, as for instance in the phrase:

gande wō bórüō mésofō ingi ki-ni,

verbally „country this people what them language of" (or „their") i. q. „what is the language of the people of this country"?, and, exactly as we have here ingi ki-ni, „their language", we have to look upon the term Soṅyai ki-ni, „language of Soṅyai" or „the Soṅyai-language". And from the same point of view, no doubt, we have to explain the phrase wōki a wō-ni, „this is mine", which I did not seize well, when on the very first sheet of my vocabulary I treated the pronoun, and therefore beg to correct p. 5 accordingly

„this is mine, belongs to me"	wōki a wō-ni,
„this is thine, belongs to thee" . . .	wōki ni wō-ni,
„this is his, belongs to him"	wōki a(ńga) wō-ni,
„this is ours, belongs to us"	wōki yiri wō-ni,
„this is yours, belongs to you"	wōki war wō-ni,
„this is theirs, belongs to them" . . .	wōki ingi wō-ni.

But, as all these instances exhibit the form ni only in connection with a preceding k, we may with some reason look upon it as a mere euphonical change of di. This would even be the case, if we had to explain from the same point of view the term gōrai tāni (tāi-nif) p. 23, „in old time", the tā being nothing but a softened k.

c) I have to remark, however, that di as well as ni are often left out, and thus, I think, we have to explain the terms ai me bēre, „my elder brother", and ai me keine, „my younger brother", me, mē recurring repeatedly in my phrases with the notion „to possess". But this, I think, does not regard the term ai-ta eāti (eā-ti), vocab. p. 8, and so on, „I myself etc.", the ti being probably nothing but a slight euphonical change of di.

3. Of the numerals I will only state here, that 2 and 3; 5, 6 and 7; 8 and 9 are evidently closely related amongst each other, while with regard to a few other particulars I may refer the reader to the foot notes of that portion of my vocabulary, especially to note 9 on p. 9. It is very remarkable, that, although the Soṅyai numerals appear to follow an uninterrupted system as far as ten by simple and original terms, the latter from five upwards have been superseded by the corresponding Arab terms in the Eastern provinces (note 10 ibid.).

4. *The verb.*

I now proceed to make a few remarks with regard to the verb in the Soṅyai-language. In general, verbs are conjugated in this language in a similar manner as in the Hausa-idiom,

im Hausa die 3te Person Sing. ii-na selbstständig gebraucht werden, aber nur in Verbindung mit örtlichen Partikeln, wie ina, „wo", und doch hat diese Sprache für den bestimmteren Ausdruck „es gibt" einen ganz anderen, eigenthümlichen Terminus, nämlich á-koi, einen Ausdruck, der in der Hausa-Sprache gar keine Wurzel hat und keine Erklärung findet; auch ist er, wie ich nicht den geringsten Zweifel hege, eben der Sonyai-Sprache entlehnt und zwar nichts Anderes als unser á-go. Das Letztere nämlich wird ganz entschieden in diesem selbstständigen Sinne gebraucht, ja sogar die entsprechende negative Form á-si für „es gibt nicht", z. B. „gibt es Bäume auf diesem Berge oder nicht", túri á-ge tondi bêne, olla á-si bêne; „gibt es Wasser auf der Strasse" (H. á-koi rúa tšikí-n hañá) bári á-ga fonda. Daher kann á-go auch ganz einfach mit Substantiven verbunden werden, wie bãna, „Regen", á-go bãna, „es regnet". Allerdings gibt es neben á-go im Sonyai eine vollere Form a-gá kunu mit der negativen Form a-sá kunu, wo das kunu eine Art Participium zu sein scheint; aber das Andere ist das Gewöhnlichere.

b) Schon von diesem Gesichtspunkte aus erklärt es sich, wie es kommt, dass im Sonyai das Hülfszeitwort vom Verbalstamme getrennt werden kann, was im Hausa mit na nicht der Fall ist, so „ich thue dir geben", é-ga ni nõ, im Hausa ni í-na bã ka; „ich thue etwas zeigen dir", é-ga hayã kóbbere ní-nõ, im Hausa ni í-na nũna ma-ká abũ. Ja, es scheint sogar, als ob die einfache Pronominalform von dem ga getrennt werden könnte, und erkläre ich jetzt mit Sicherheit die zur Zeit mir unverständlich gebliebene Phrase ébena gakáu S. 55 é bina ga kán, „ich im Herzen (bina) thue freuen (mich)", d. h. „ich bin froh".

c) Indem ich nun auf eine genauere Betrachtung dieser verbalen Hülfszeitform eingehe, bemerke ich zuerst, dass der Vokallaut dieser Verbalform nicht ganz sicher ist und zwischen o und a schwankt; so geht in dieser Hülfssilbe ga das a vor einem in der Wurzel des Zeitwortes selbst erscheinenden o gewöhnlich in o über, wo dann für das Fürwort selbst das a vorwiegt, also á-go koi, obgleich man auch é-ga koi sagt. Aber umgekehrt wird wol Niemand á-ga gnã, „ich esse" sagen, sondern allgemein scheint die Form é-ga gnã zu sein. Eben so ist es mit der negativen Form, wo in vielen Fällen und, wie es fast scheint, ganz nach Belieben, für á-si die Form é-sa gebraucht wird, so é-sa bõ, Vokab. S. 55; é-sa bã S. 63; é-sa kóbbere S. 71, ja, selbst é-sa koi S. 65 für die gewöhnlichere Form á-si koi.

d) Im Präteritum oder Aorist fällt das Hülfsverbum im Sonyai ganz weg, was im Hausa nicht der Fall ist, wo der Wurzel-Konsonant von na, n auch in den Formen des Präteritums bleibt. Doch haben wir im Sonyai eine ausgebildete verneinende Form, wie im Präsens mit si, so im Präteritum mit na oder no. Diese Form hängt sicherlich mit der verneinenden Partikel no zusammen, woraus sich auch erklärt, wie sie in gewissen Fällen dem Verbalstamm nachgewiesen werden kann; auch in anderen Fällen ist das o ganz deutlich, wie ich oft ai-ta ai-no koi statt é-na koi hörte; so auch bóro fõ na koi, „ein Mensch ist nicht gegangen", d. h. „Niemand ist gegangen".

e) Ich gebe nun ein Paradigma von koi, „gehn", indem ich nur noch bemerke, dass bei diesen Verbalformen die volle Pronominalform ai-ta gewöhnlich gebraucht wird; sogar die Form ai-ga, die doch schon das Hülfszeitwort ga enthält, wird nicht selten vor der vollen Verbalform gebraucht, wie z. B. ai-ga á-go koi, ai-ga á-ga gunna.

Präsens.

positiv.	negativ.
ai-ta á-go koi	ai-ta á-si koi,
ni-ta ní-ga koi	ni-ta ní-si koi,
ánga-ta á-go koi	ánga-ta á-si koi,
yer-ta (y)er-ga koi . . .	yer-ta yer-si koi,
war-ta war-ga koi . . .	war-ta war-si koi,
ífigi-ta í-ge koi	ífigi-ta í-si koi.

by prefixing to the verbal root the auxiliary form ga, go added to the corresponding form of the pronoun, just as is the case with the Hausa form na; nay, the Sonyai ga has retained the character of an independent verbal form much more clearly than the latter. For, while in Hausa ší-na, the 3rd person of this auxiliary verb, is only used in an independent position in connection with the local particles, as, for instance ší-na nan, „he is here", the proper notion „there is" being expressed in the Hausa-idiom by a totally different term, viz. á-koi, a term which has no original root in that language, and which has evidently been borrowed from the very Sonyai, in the latter idiom á-go, besides the fuller form a-gá-kuna, neg. a-sá-kunu, is decidedly used in such an independent position; nay, we even find there the corresponding negative form á-si, „there is not", as, for instance in the phrase „are there trees or not on this mountain"?, tūri á-go tondi bēno, olla á-si bēne; „is there water on the road"? (H. a-kai rua tšikí-n hañn) hári á-go fondo.

b) From the same point of view we can easily understand, how it happens, that in Sonyai this auxiliary verb may be separated from the root, which is not the case with the na in Hausa, as, for instance, in the phrase ó-ga ai nō, verbally „I do thee give", in Hausa ni í-na bā kai ó-ga hajā kǫbbore ní-sō, „I do something show thee", in Hausa ni í-na nūna ma-ká abū. Nay, it even seems, as if in Sonyai the simple pronominal form in some cases may be separated from this auxiliary verbal form ga; and thus, no doubt, we have to explain the phrase óbena gakán (p. 55 vocab.) by writing ó bina ga kán, „I in (my) heart (bina) do rejoice".

c) Entering now upon a closer inspection of this auxiliary verbal form, I have first to observe, that the vowel is rather of an uncertain character, fluctuating between a and o; thus, if the root itself contains an o, the vowel of the auxiliary form is likewise changed into o, while the pronominal sign in this case becomes an a. The common form, therefore, for „I do go" is á-go koi, without however forming the rule, as I have heard as well the form ó-ga koi. But, on the other hand, no body, I think, would say á-go gnā, „I do eat", but the only true form, such as required by the laws of euphony, seems to be ó-ga gnā. Just the same uncertainty prevails with regard to the vowel of the negative form, which in general may be said to be á-si, but instead of which we very often meet also with the form é-sa, as for instance ó-sa bó, vocab. p. 55; ó-sa bā p. 63; ó-sa kǫbbore p. 71; nay, we even have ó-sa koi p. 83 instead of the more common form á-si koi.

d) In the past tense the auxiliary verbal form ga is lost, and the simple pronominal form is directly joined to the root, such as ai-ta ó-koi, „I went", while in the negative form of the past no or na takes the place of si or sa of the present tense, as for instance ai-ta ó-ne koi, as well as ni-ta ai-ne koi, „I did not go". Thus also, bóro fō ne koi, „no body went". This negative auxiliary form of the past, which may be derived with certainty from the negative particle no, in certain cases seems to follow the root instead of preceding it.

e) I now proceed to give a paradigm of the verb koi, „go"; I first remark, that in these verbal forms the full form of the pronoun is generally used, nay, even the composite form ai-ga is employed instead of ai-ta, although the former contains already the auxiliary verb ga; thus, I have ai-ga á-go koi, ai-ga á-go gnana.

Present tense.

positive.		negative.
ai-ta á-go koi	. . . . .	ai-ta á-si koi,
ni-ta ní-ga koi	. . . . .	ni-ta ní-si koi,
ángu-ta á-ga koi	. . . .	ánga-ta á-si koi,
yer-ta (y)or-ga koi	. . .	yer-ta yer-si koi,
war-ta war-ga koi	. . .	war-ta war-si koi,
íngi-ta í-go koi	. . . .	íngi-ta í-si koi.

Aorist.

positiv.	negativ.
ai-ta é-koi	ai-ta é-na koi,
ni-ta ní-koi	ni-ta má-na koi [1]),
áñga-ta á-koi	áñga-ta á-na koi,
yor-ta y)ór-koi	yer-ta { ór-na / én-na } koi,
war-ta wár-koi	war-ta { wár-na / wán-na } koi,
íñgi-ta í-koi	íñgi-ta í-na koi.

Imperativ.

2te Pers. Sing. koi	má-si koi,
1ste Pers. Plur. yer ma koi .	yer má-si koi,
2te Pers. Sing. k)okoi [2]) . . .	war má-si koi.

Ganz ebenso werden conjugirt dē, „kaufen"; ñáá, „essen"; gunna oder góna, „sehn"; hau, „binden"; mō, „hören"; tun, „aufbrechen", kurz, alle Zeitwörter, mit deren Abwandelung ich näher bekannt geworden. Ganz vereinzelt ist das dō, „thut, macht, findet", in den Phrasen bóri dō džañga, „das Pferd wiehert", hanši dō sū, „der Hund bellt", hanši dō nam, „der Hund beisst", Vokab. S. 137; hier scheint die Verbalwurzel ganz ohne persönliche Abwandelung gebraucht zu sein. Dagegen habe ich S. 95 wongo a-dō, „der Krieg findet".

f) Nun wird auch ein Conditionel gebildet vermittelst einer den Formen des Präteritums vorgesetzten Redeform indakar oder indagar, die wol unzweifelhaft mit dem vieldeutigen Zeitwort kar [3]), „behandeln, finden" zusammenhängt und also ind(a) a-kár oder ind(a) a-gár zu schreiben ist, und eigentlich bedeutet „wenn es sich gefunden hätte" (dass ich das und das gethan hätte). So habe ich „wenn ich gegangen wäre", ind(a) a-gár é-koi, das ohne jede Veränderung des ind(a) a-gár folgendermassen abgewandelt wird.

	Singular.	Plural.
1ste Person	ind(a) a-gár é-koi .	ind(a) a-gár yór-koi,
2te „	ind(a) a-gár ní-koi	ind(a) a-gár wár-koi,
3te „	ind(a) a-gár á-koi .	ind(a) a-gár í-koi;

ebenso ind(a) a-gár é-gúnna, „wenn ich gesehn hätte"; ind(a) a-gár é-tún, „wenn ich aufgebrochen wäre". Man kann auch, wenn man die Person mit mehr Nachdruck bezeichnen will, das jedesmalige volle Fürwort zwischen ind(a) a-gár und der Verbalform einschieben, wie ind(a) a-gár ai-ta é-koi.

g) Von einer Participialform auf ndo habe ich mehrere Beispiele und werde bei den Nennwörtern (5, a), so wie bei den Eigenschaftswörtern (8, g) auf diese Form zurückkommen. Hier führe ich nur an die wirklich participiale Phrase é-nō-ndo tilis é-na bā ga, wörtlich „ich geb-end unfreiwillig ich nicht wollte es", d. h. „ich gab es aus Zwang und wider meinen Willen". Gewöhnlich aber wird diese Form nur angewandt, um Gegenwärtigkeit oder

[1]) má-na koi statt ní-na koi ist auffallend, aber ganz sicher bewährt durch viele andere Beispiele, so „du hast dieses nicht gut gemacht", ni-ta má-na hinza ge gamme; „du hast nicht gegessen", ni-ta má-na gaš; „du hast nicht gesehn", ni-ta má-na gunna. Dieses ma scheint mir aus der Form des negirenden Imperativs hineingekommen zu sein, aber wir finden es auch sonst.

[2]) k)okoi. Ich bin etwas unsicher, ob das erste k dazu gehört, da ich nur die Phrase hein tan kokoi, „steht auf (und) geht".

[3]) Eben dieses Zeitwort kar ist eins der sprechendsten Beispiele der ausserordentlichen Armuth der Songai-Sprache, da es nach dem jedesmaligen Begriff, mit dem es verbunden wird, die mannichfachste Bedeutung erhält, so é-ga kár béri, „ich behandle", d. h. „besteige ein Pferd", „reite"; é-ga kár kórai, „ich behandle", d. h. „schlage den Schild"; é-ga kár melfa, „ich behandle das Gewehr", d. h. „feuere ab, schiesse". Ja sogar hanši á-ga kár špadára, „der Hund wedelt mit dem Schwanz".

Aorist.

positive.	negative.
ai-ta ó-kol	ai-ta ó-na kol,
ni-ta ní-kol	ni-ta má-na kol [1]),
áñgu-ta á-kol	áñgu-ta á-na kol,
yer-ta y)ór-kol	yer-ta { ór-na / ón-na } kol,
war-ta wár-kol	war-ta { wár-na / wán-na } kol,
íñgi-ta í-kol	íñgi-ta í-na kol.

Imperative.

2nd pers. sing. kol	má-si kol,
1st pers. plur. yor ma kol . .	yor má-si kol,
2nd pers. plur. k)okol [2]) . . .	war má-si kol.

In the very same manner are conjugated the verbs gúá, „eat"; guuna or góna, „see"; han, „tie"; mö, „hear"; tun, „rise"; in short, all the verbs with the conjugation of which I have become more intimately acquainted. As for the phrases bóri dö dŝañga, „the horse is neighing", and so on vocab. p. 137, the verbal root dö has been left unchanged.

f) Now, besides the tenses mentioned, a sort of conditional mood is formed by means of prefixing indakar or indagar before the form of the aorist, a turn of expression which, I have no doubt, is to be derived from the verb kar which implies the greatest variety of notions [3]), and in this connection is to be understood as „happen", inda kár or ind(a) a-kár, as, I think, we have to write this form, meaning „if it happened" (that I did so and so). Thus, we have for „if I had gone", ind(a) a-gár é-kol which is conjugated in the following manner, the ind(a) a-gár remaining unchanged.

	singular.	plural.
1st person	ind(a) a-gár ó-kol .	ind(a) a-gár yór-kol,
2nd „	ind(a) a-gár ní-kol .	ind(a) a-gár wár-kol,
3rd „	ind(a) a-gár á-kol .	ind(a) a-gár í-kol;

and in the same way we have ind(a) a-gár ó-gúuna, „if I had seen"; ind(a) a-gár ó-tún, „if I had started", and so on. But, if the person is to be distinguished with more emphasis, the full form of the pronoun may be inserted between the prefix ind(a) a-gár and the verbal form, as for instance ind(a) a-gár ai-ta ó-kol.

g) I have also various instances of a participial form terminating in nde, to which I shall have to return when treating the forming of nouns under 5, a, as well as with regard to the forming of the adjectives under 8, g. In this place I only mention the truly participial phrase ó-nö-nde illis ó-na bä ga meaning verbally „I giv-ing by force I did not wish it", i. q. „I gave it by force, and not from my own free will". In general, however, this form is only used in order to put forth with more emphasis the present and lasting state of an action as, for instance, ó-ga dö-nde (p. 80, note 14), „I do" or „I am reach-ing" i. q.

---

[1]) má-na kol instead of ní-na kol is a remarkable exception, but is placed beyond a doubt by other instances, such as ní-ta má-na hiese ga gumme, „thou hast not made this well"; ni-ta má-na gúá, „thou hast not eaten"; ni-ta má-na guuna, „thou hast not seen". I myself am inclined to look upon this ma as having crept into this tense from the negative form of the imperative.

[2]) k)okol: I am rather uncertain, whether the first k belongs to this form or not, as I have it only in connection with tun, tun kokol meaning „rise (and) go". But I have scarcely any doubt, that it does not belong to the true verbal form.

[3]) This very same verb kar is one of the most instructive instances for illustrating the extraordinary poverty of the Sciyal-idiom, implying as it does a great variety of different meanings according to the connection in which it is placed, as, for instance é-ga *kár* héri, „I treat a horse" i. q. „mount, go on horseback"; é-ga *kár* kórai, „I treat" i. q. „I beat the shield"; é-ga *kár* melfa, „I treat, fire the gun", nay we have even beeli é-ga *kár* ngadáre, „the dog treats the tail" i. q. „wags with the tail".

Dauer kräftiger zu bezeichnen, wie in é-ga dō-ade (Note 14, S. 86), „ich thue, bin eintreffen-d", d. h. „ich bin da". So auch é-ga sġrre-ade béri, „ich antreiben-d das Pferd", d. h. „ich galoppire" und é-go-ade hayō u. s. w. „ich besitze-nd, habe, besitze" S. 63.

h) Sehr unvollständig, wie in fast allen diesen Sprachen scheint das Passivum ausgebildet zu sein, indem die äussere Form desselben derjenigen des Aktiv gleich ist und nur einigermassen durch Betonung oder Stellung unterschieden wird. So haben wir S. 35 aí-haí, „ich gebäre", ai-haī, „ich bin geboren"; á-ga hau, „er bindet", a-ga haū, „er ist gebunden" („ist er gebunden oder nicht"?, a-ga haū woll(a) a-si haū); í-ga hau, „sie binden", i-go haū, „sie sind gebunden"; ja, bei den meisten Formen lässt es sich kaum einmal durch den Ton unterscheiden, so á-ga góna, „er sieht" und a-ga góna, „er wird gesehn"; á-si góna, „er sieht nicht" und a-si góna, „er wird nicht gesehn". Einen Versuch der Aushülfe einer passiven oder medialen Form vermittelst das oben S. CLXXII, 2 besprochenen, beziehungsreichen di glaube ich in der Form a-ga dō-di bemerkt zu haben „es thut finden sich", „wird gefunden", von dō, „finden".

i) Da das Passiv schon im Allgemeinen so ungenügend vertreten ist, kann natürlicher Weise von einer wohl entwickelten Form des Particips dieses Modus keine Rede sein. So finden wir denn auch das letztere durch die einfache Wurzel des Zeitwortes ausgedrückt, wie z. B. duṅgu, „geschnitten", von é-ga duṅgu, „ich schneide". Gewöhnlich jedoch wird das Participium umschrieben, so „ich habe einen Menschen ermordet gefunden", ni-gár bóro fō a-wiga („er war getödtet"); „ich habe Menschen ermordet gefunden", ni-gár bórōō i-ga wiga oder i-wiga, „sie sind oder sie waren getödtet".

Aber doch habe ich zwei Fälle von eigenthümlichen Formen des Particips Passivi, die ich anführen muss; der eine dieser beiden Fälle ist birtšin in dem Kompositum tam birtšin, „befreiter Sklave", zu dessen Erklärung ich nichts beibringen kann, der andere augleich wichtigere ist himni-adi, „gewaschen" (S. 109), von á-go himai, „ich wasche", wo wir in dem adi vielleicht eine Verbindung der aktiven Participialform ade mit dem unter h) angedeuteten zurückbeziehenden, medialen oder passiven di zu erkennen haben. Diese passive Participialform erhält dadurch ihre Bestätigung, dass wir auch bei der Bildung der Nennwörter mit passiver Bedeutung dieselbe Form wiederfinden werden.

k) Über die Art der Verbindung zweier Zeitwörter, von denen das eine das andere regiert, kann ich nichts Bestimmtes angeben und führe nur folgende zwei Beispiele an: „ich will verkaufen", é-ga bā ta de; de, „verkaufen", also das ta doch wol dasselbe, was in der vollen Form dem Fürwort angehängt wird, ai-ta. Auffällig ist zumal ein me in Verbindung mit der einfachen Pronominal-Form bei dem zweiten regierten Zeitwort in der Negation „ich will das nicht thun", ni-ta á-si bā ai-me hinsa ga; á-si-bā, „ich will nicht"; hinsa, „thun". Zu dem me vergleiche die Form a-go mē-ri weiter unten S. CLXXXVIII, f.

b. *Nennwörter.*

a) Im Soṅyai begegnen wir fast mehr als in irgend einer anderen der von mir behandelten Sprachen monosyllaben Nennwörtern, was wol besonders daher kommt, dass sich in dieser Sprache, der es an einer reichen Weiterbildung und Vervollkommnung fehlte, die ursprünglichen Formen in ausgedehnterer Weise erhalten haben. Eben deshalb aber hat das Soṅyai zur Erforschung der sprachlichen Verwandtschafts-Verhältnisse grosse Bedeutung. Ein lehrreiches Beispiel ist ma, „Name" in Beziehung zu ma, „verstehn".

„I am just arriving", „me voila". Thus, my vocabulary has also the phrase é-ga aŭ̈rre-ade béri, „I driv-ing on the horse", i. q. „I am going at a galop", and ó-go-ade hayō and so on „I am possess-ing", „do possess".

h) As for the passive mood, also in the Sońyai-idiom, as in most of those languages, it seems to be very little developed, the form of the passive mood resembling entirely that of the active, and being only distinguished from the latter by some slight difference of accentuation or of position. Thus p. 35 we have aí-hai, „I bear, bring forth", ai-hai, „I am born"; á-ga hau, „he ties", a-ga hau, „he is tied, emprisoned" (thus, „is he bound or not"?, a-ga hau woll(a) a-si hau); í-ga hau, „they tie", i-ga hau, „they are tied". Nay, with most of the verbal forms the active and passive moods are not even to be distinguished by such a slight difference of accentuation, such as á-ga góna, „he does see"; a-ga góna, „he is seen"; á-si góna, „he does not see" and a-si góna, „he is not seen". As an attempt of forming a passive or medial mood by means of the expressive and significant termination di, which we have treated above p. CLXXIII, 2, I have to point out, I think, the form a-ga dō-di verbally „it does find of (itself" i. q. „it is found", „it exists" from the verb dō, „find".

i) The passive mood, in general, being thus insufficiently represented, of course there can be no question of a perfect and independent form of the participle of that mood. Thus, we find the latter expressed by the simple root of the verb, as is also the case with many English verbs, as, for instance, dońgu, „cut" (pass.) from é-ga dońgu, „I cut". However, this participle is very rarely used, and more frequently it is circumscribed by the definite passive mood, which certainly is not different from the active form; thus, I have the phrase ai-gár bóro fō a-wiga, „I found a man (he) was murdered" instead of „I found a man murdered", and in the plural ni-gár bórēō i-ga wiga or i-wiga, „I found men, they are killed" or „they were killed".

But, besides, I have two instances of an individual form of a participle of the passive mood which I must point out; one of these instances is the form birtšin in the term tam birtšin, „the freed slave", which I cannot explain, while the other much more remarkable one is himai-adi, „washed", vocab. p. 109 from á-go hímai, „I do wash". For I presume, that we have to recognise in this form adi a joining of the form ade representing the active participle, and of the very di which I have characterized under h) as conveying a medial or passive meaning, a composite passive form which we are to meet also among the nouns.

k) When two verbs are joined, one of which rules the other, the way of joining them is various, as, for instance „I will buy", é-ga bā ta dō, where dō meaning „buy", the ta seems to be identical with the ta of the full pronominal form ai-ta. And that the pronominal form is really expressed a second time in connection with the second verb we see from the following instance in a negative case „I do not like to do that", ai-ta á-si bā al-me hinsa ga, meaning verbally „I do not like I (that) not do this", the negative or preventive me finding its explanation in the verbal form a-go mē-ri to be mentioned p. CLXXXIX, f.

5. *Nouns.*

a) With regard to the chapter of nouns, the Sońyai-language seems to me to claim considerable interest, as possessing a greater number of monosyllabic terms, than almost any other of the languages here treated, and the reason hereof seems to be, that this idiom, wanting as it was in a free development, preserved the original forms to a greater extent, than the other languages. It is on this account, that the study of the Sońyai-idiom is of more than common importance for investigating the cause of linguistic relationship. As an instance of perfect identity of the form of the noun with that of the corresponding verb I mention ma, „name" with reference to the verb ma, „understand".

Andere Nennwörter dieser Sprache, jedoch in sehr geringer Anzahl, sind, wie deutlich nachzuweisen, um eine Art passiver Beziehung hineinzutragen, mit Veränderung des Vokallautes, von Zeitwörtern abgeleitet, wie fári, „Acker, Garten", von (é-ga) féri, „(ich) gäte, bearbeite (den Boden)". Ähnlich ist vielleicht béri, „Pferd" abgeleitet. Eine etwas zahlreichere Klasse von verbalen Begriffen abgeleiteter Nennwörter finden wir vermittelst der Endungen nde und ndi gebildet und haben in ihnen, zum Theil wenigstens, unzweifelhaft die oben besprochenen identischen Participialformen zu erkennen. So haben wir dži-nde (eigentlich tši-nde), „Sprache (ki, tši, dži) machend", „reden-d", „Werkzeug der Sprache", „Stimme"; hu-nde, „athmen-d, Athemwerkzeug, Lunge", von einer Wurzel hu, fu, die entschieden an die entsprechenden Kanúri- (fu) und Hausa-Ausdrücke (fu-fo), Fúl (pöf-de) und anderen Völkern gemeinsame Grundbegriffe anknüpft; ga-nde, „Wohnort bildend (ga, „Lagerdorf", ko, „Stadt"), „Land", also nicht, wie es scheinen könnte, verwandt mit dem Malaiischen χanda. Ähnlich sind auch wol gebildet die mir in ihrer Ableitung weniger sicheren Ausdrücke tárkó-nde, „Elephant"; azohú-nde, „Mörder" (a-zö-hú-nde, „er Leben bekämpfend"?, von zö, „bekämpfen"); lobti-nde, „Melone"; dann als passive Formationen mit ndi: lu-ndi, „Mark"; ti-ndi, „Stampfgefäss", „Mörser"; do-ndi, „Pfeffer", und vielleicht auch iadi (in-ndi?), „Ruder".

Einen wirklichen Übergang von der verbalen Bedeutung dieser Endung nde zu der Bildung des Nennwortes und die Ableitung von a-zö-hú-nde völlig rechtfertigend haben wir in der Phrase á-ga mai wa-nde, „habend eine Frau", wo diese participiale Endung nicht dem Zeitwort, mai, „besitzen, haben", sondern dem Nennwort, wai, „Frau", angefügt ist.

b) Sonst ist die Sonyai-Sprache überaus arm an abgeleiteten und weiter ausgebildeten Begriffen. Dagegen werden äusserlich zusammengereihte Begriffe ähnlich wie im Deutschen gebildet durch Voransetzung des allgemeineren Begriffes als Objekt und Anfügung des engeren als Subjekt; so von kóru, „Feuer", dëne, „Zunge" wird der zusammengesetzte Begriff kóru-dëne, „Feuerzunge", d. h. „Flamme" gebildet; von hári, „Wasser", mö, „Auge", hári-mö, „Wasser-Auge", d. h. „Quelle"; von eben diesem hári und ham, „Fleisch", hári-ham, „Wasser-Fleisch", d. h. „Fisch". Eben so gebildet sind túguri-iddžo, „Baum-Kind", d. h. „Frucht"; túguri-kamba, „Baum-Hand", d. h. „Zweig"; tšipsi-handu, „Wallfahrts-Monat"; ganda-korfu, „Erd-Strick", d. h. „Schlange", dieser letztere Ausdruck besonders belehrend durch den Vergleich mit dem entsprechenden und ganz aus denselben Elementen bestehenden Fúl-Ausdruck bókul lédi, wo aber das Subjekt „Strick" dem Objekt „Erde" vorhergeht. Ausnahme von dieser Zusammensetzung mit vorangehendem Objekt scheint im Sonyai nime (ni-mo? mé, „Mund"), „Lippe" zu sein. Nur selten habe ich ein Beispiel gefunden, dass das oben erwähnte beziehende di zur Vermittelung solcher Zusammensetzungen benutzt ist, wie ich neben hógu-mö, „Haus-Mund", d. h. „Thür", auch die Form hö-di mö gehört habe (hö die einfache, ältere Form von hógu, „Haus"), und eben so für „Furt", isa-di dži ödi, „Flusspassirung", von isa, „Fluss" und dzödi, „passiren". Ganz vereinzelt habe ich übrigens auch hier das berberische n als Verbindungsglied gefunden, wie ich einmal neben kóru-dëne die Form kóru-n dëne hörte und im Emgeddesi ist das gewöhnlich.

c) In ganz ähnlicher Weise sind nun auch die zahlreichen Composita gebildet, welche Charaktere und Beschäftigungen von Menschen bezeichnen, alle mit Hintansetzung von koi, „Herr" hinter ein Objekt, wie hio-koi, „Boot-Herr", d. h. „Bootsmann"; kur-koi, „Heerden-Herr", d. h. „Hirte"; béri-koi, „Pferd-Herr", d. h. „Reiter"; bon-koi, „Todes-Herr", d. h. „Leichnam"; aber das koi wird, wie schon in letzterem Beispiele angedeutet, nicht allein mit Nennwörtern, sondern auch mit einfach verbalen Begriffen verbunden, wie z. B. dé-koi, „Verkaufs-Herr", d. h. „Kaufmann", von dé, „verkaufen", ta-koi, „Näher, Schneider", von ta, „nähen". Ja, es werden auf diese Weise auch Zusammensetzungen gebildet aus einem Nennwort als Objekt, daran das bezügliche Zeitwort und koi als Subjekt dem Zeitwort angefügt,

Other substantives, but of rather a limited number, can be clearly shown to have been derived from verbal notions through a simple change of the vowel, in order to give to the term a passive meaning, such as, for instance, fári, „garden, field" from (é-ga) féri, „I) till (the ground)"; and other terms, such as bóri, „horse", may be derived in a similar manner. A rather more numerous class of nouns has been derived from verbal notions by means of the termination nde and ndi, and part of them, at least, seem to belong originally to that category of participial forms which I have spoken of under i. Thus, for instance, we have dži-nde (properly tši-nde), „making words, speech" (ki, tši, dži) i. q. „instrument of language", „voice"; hu-nde, „instrument for breathing, lungs" from a root hu, fu, which is common to the Kanúri (fū-ńfskin), Hausa (fo-fo), Fúl (pōf-de) and many other languages; and most probably the following terms are formed in a similar manner ga-nde, „forming encampments" i. q. „country" from gu, „encampment" (ko, „village", „town"); tarkó-nde, „elephant"; azobú-nde, „murderer" (a-zō-bú-nde, „he waging war against life" from the verb zō and the very bu mentioned shortly before); lebtí-nde, „melon". As similar formations terminating in ndi, but conveying a passive meaning, I mention lu-ndi, „marrow"; ti-ndi, „mortar"; de-ndi, „pepper" and as a doubtful instance in-di (un-nde?), „ear".

As an instance of a real transition from the verbal notion of the termination nde to the formation of this class of substantives I here mention the remarkable phrase á-ga mai wu-nde, „possessing a wife", „married", where the participial form has not been added to the verb mai, „possess, have", but to the substantive wai, „woman".

b) In general, however, the Soñyai-language is extremely poor in such terms as have been developed from a grammatical point of view, while composite terms are formed in tolerable number and in the same manner, as is constantly done in German, and in many instances in English too, by prefixing as the object the general notion, and suffixing as subject the narrower notion dependent on the former; thus, from kōru, „fire" and dene, „tongue" is formed the composite term kōru-dene, „fire-tongue" i. q. „flame"; from hári, „water" and mō, „eye", hári-mō, „water-eye" i. q. „fountain, source"; from the same hári and from ham, „meat", hári-ham, „water-meat" i. q. „fish". As composite terms of the same character we have, besides, tóguri-iddže, „tree-child" i. q. „fruit"; tóguri-kambu, „tree-hand" i. q. „branch"; tšipsi-handu, „pilgrimage-month" i. q. „Dhu el hádži"; but of especial interest is the term gandu-korfu, „ground-rope" i. q. „snake", if compared with the corresponding, and totally identical term of the Fúl-language bókul ledi from bókul, „rope" and ledi, „ground", the subject preceding the object. An exception to the rule of the object preceding the subject in composite terms of the Soñyai seems to be alme, „lip", if we are right in deriving it from mō, „mouth". All the instances mentioned exhibit the subject and object joined together without any outward connection, and I have found only rare instances, where the di mentioned above, as forming the genitive or possessive case, has been used as the means of such a composition; as one of these cases I have to mention the form hó-di mē side by side with hōgu-mē, „the door, gateway" (verbally „house-mouth"), from the simple and older form hō for hōgu, „house", and mē, „mouth"; and in the same manner isa-di džiōdi, „ford", from isa, „river", and džōdi, „to pass, cross over".

c) Exactly in the same manner also the numerous terms are formed in the Soñyai-language, which indicate characters or occupations of men, all being formed by adding the monosyllabous term koi, „making", „master", behind the relative object, such as hīo-koi, verbally „boats-man", „boat-swain"; kur-koi, „sheep-herd"; béri-koi, „horse-man"; bun-koi, „death's-master" i. q. „corpse". This same koi, however, is not only joined to nouns, but also to simple verbal notions, as, for instance dē-koi, „selling-master" i. q. „merchant", from dē, „sell". Nay, in the very same manner terms are composed by adding koi to a verb which rules an object, such as, for instance, fond(o)-a-bé-koi, verbally „way-he-shows-

wie fond(o)-a-bē-koi, „Weg-er-weiss-Herr", d. h. „Führer"; fondo-dumbu-koi, „Weg-abschneider", d. h. „Räuber". Ähnlich werden auch andere Kompositionen gebildet, wie subu-dumbu-hōri, wörtlich „Kraut-schneide-messer". Durch diese Art der Zusammensetzung unterscheidet sich das Sonyai von allen umgebenden Sprachen und nähert sich anderen fernliegenden Gruppen, wie auch nach vielen anderen Anzeichen die Sonyai am Niger oder Isa keineswegs alteinheimisch waren. Allein das ungeschickte Kompositum „Wasser-fleisch" für „Fisch" würde das zeigen; aber ich hoffe noch, ihre Wanderung vom Norden sicherer nachweisen zu können.

d) Der Plural wird im Allgemeinen durch Anfügung eines ō (wol = hō, „mehrere, viele") gebildet, in gewissen Fällen durch Vermittelung eines i oder y-Lautes, hau Plur. hau-ō, „Kühe"; hiñe Plur. híñe-ō, „Zähne"; derbe Plur. dérbe-ō, „Kleidungsstücke"; kari Plur. kári-ō, „Zwillinge"; bóri Plur. béri-ō, „Pferde"; farka Plur. fárka-yō, „Esel"; kaga Plur. kága-yō, „Grossväter"; faffa Plur. fáffa-yō oder, mit einem auch sonst vorkommenden Vokalvorschlag, i-fáffa-yō, „Brüste". Anstatt wai-yō Plur. von wai, „Frau", hörte ich wai-dio; eine solche Einschaltung eines d-Lautes in diesem einzelnen Falle erklärt sich jedoch leicht auf Grund des Wohllauts.

d, α) Neben dieser regulären Form auf ō giebt es aber in einigen Fällen eine Nebenform auf e, das nicht bloss dem Endvokal der Singularform angehängt wird, sondern ihn verschlingt, und diese Form hat zuweilen die andere ganz verdrängt; so hat man neben fári-ō von fári, „Garten, Feld" die Form farē und von kamba, „Hand" hörte ich nur die Pluralform kambe. Die Form tūri, die in der allgemeinen Bezeichnung von „Bäumen, Wald, Holz" gebraucht wird, scheint eigentlich nicht als Pluralform von túguri anzusehn zu sein, sondern als populär contrahirte Form mit genereller Bedeutung. Allerdings haben wir auch das Eigenschaftswort dazu in scheinbarer Pluralform, tūri bēri, „grosse Bäume", von bēre, „gross".

e) Das Geschlecht scheint in der Sonyai-Sprache nur bei Menschen und Thieren unterschieden zu werden und zwar durch den einfachen Zusatz von har, „Mann" oder wai, „Frau", obgleich das männliche Geschlecht meist nicht besonders ausgedrückt wird, sondern nur da, wo ein Gegensatz auftritt; kaga har, „Grossvater", kaga wai, „Grossmutter"; yō allein, oder yō har, „Kameel", yō wai, „Kameelin". Dagegen finden wir für „Stute" den besonderen Namen tēfe oder auch das letztere adjektivisch gebraucht bēri tēfe und für „Ziege" habe ich, im Gegensatz zu hantši har, „Ziegenbock", hantši ñē. Dass die Sonyai einen besonderen Namen für „Stute" haben, ist wieder für ihre früheren Wohnsitze bedeutend. Diese Geschlechtsbezeichnung wird hinter dem Adjektiv angehängt, wenn dieses letztere mit dem Nennwort zu Einem Begriff verschmolzen ist, wie ai bēre wai, „die ältere Schwester", wörtlich „Verwandte gross Frau"; ai kaino wai, „jüngere Schwester", wörtlich „Verwandte klein Frau".

f) Von regelmässiger Entwickelung der Kasus scheint nicht die Rede zu sein. Eine gewisse Vertretung des Genitivs bildet das oben S. CLXXIV besprochene, angehängte di, das jedoch auch, wie ebenda gesagt, zur Bezeichnung des Accusativs vorkommt. Ausserdem finden wir ein uda, um das Mittel auszudrücken oder eine Art Causativ zu bilden, auch uda in Verbindung mit di. So sagt man é-ga hau ga uda korfo, „ich binde ihn mit einem Strick"; é-ga kukúr ga uda nūne-di, „ich zerstöre es vermittelst Feuer-s", von nūne, „Feuer". Auch haben wir auffallender Weise eine Art Ablativ oder Lokativ mit angehängtem ga, wie z. B. „ich erhob mich vom Schlaf", á-tun dširhi-ga. Das S. CLXXII bei der Bildung der Fürwörter erwähnte angehängte se zur Darstellung des Dativs habe ich bei den Nennwörtern nur ganz ausnahmsweise angetroffen, und dieses zeigt am besten, wie wenig diese zuweilen angewandten äusseren Hülfsformen in den Geist der Sprache übergegangen sind.

g) Diese Betrachtung führt uns zu der Erwägung dessen, was man gewöhnlich Präpositionen nennt und was in der That nur Ergänzungsformen der Beziehungen des Nennwortes

master" i. q. „guide"; fondo-dumbu-koi, „road-cutting-master" i. q. „highway-robber". In a similar manner other composite terms are formed, as, for instance, sūbu-dumbu-hōri, „herb-cutting-knife" i. q. „sickle". It is this peculiar mode of composition, which distinguishes the Soñyai-language from all surrounding idioms, assimilating it to other rather distant clusters of languages, as we see also from several other arguments that the Soñyai-nation did not have its original seats on the Niger or Isa; a conclusion the correctness of which the composite term „water-meat" for „fish" alone is fully able to prove.

d) As for the plural, in general it is formed by adding ō to the root, either directly or by means of an intermediate i or y, such as hau plur. hau-ō, „cows"; biñe plur. híñe-ō, „teeth"; dorbe plur. dórbe-ō, „clothes"; kari plur. kári-ō, „twins"; béri plur. béri-ō, „houses"; kaga plur. kága-yō, „grandfathers"; faffa plur. fáffa-yō or i-fáffa-yō, „breasts". In the isolated instance wai-dio, „women", the plural form of wai, instead of wai-yō, the inserting of d between the two vowels is easily explained.

d, a) Besides this regular form in ō, however, in some instances we have a secondary form terminating in e, the e not being appended to the final vowel of the singular, but rather absorbing the latter; a form which, in some cases has entirely expelled the other one in ō; thus, for instance, besides fári-ō plur. of fári, „garden, field", I have the form fare, and of kumba, „hand" I heard the form kambe. As for the form tūri, meaning „trees, forest, wood" in general, I doubt, whether it is to be looked upon as a plural, and not rather as a contracted form of the singular túgari; the circumstance, however, of the accompanying adjective being also placed in the plural, as in the phrase tūri bēri, „large trees", from bēro, „large", favours the former assumption.

e) As for the gender in the Soñyai-language, it does not seem to be distinguished but in connection with human beings and animals, and in these cases by simply adding the terms har, „man", or wai, „woman", although the masculine is only distinctly expressed in such cases, where it is opposed to the feminine gender. Thus, for instance, I have kaga har, „grandfather", kaga wai, „grandmother"; yō alone as well as yō har, „male camel", yō wai, „she camel". As exceptions to this rule I have to mention tōfo meaning „mare", or used as an adjective, bóri tōfo, and the term hantšī ñē for „she-goat" as opposed to hantšī har, „he goat". The term indicating the gender generally follows the adjective, at least in such cases, where the latter is intimately connected with the notion indicated by the noun, such as ai bēro wai, „the elder sister", properly „relation great female", and ai kaine wai, „younger sister", „relation small female".

f) Of a regular declination of the nouns there cannot be the question. A certain representation of the genitive case is formed by means of the termination di, of which I have spoken p. CLXXV, being added to the noun, although it is also employed to indicate a sort of accusative relation; besides, we find nda employed in order to indicate the means by which something is done, or to form a sort of causative; nay, we even find nda in connection with di. Thus, the Soñyai say é-ga hau ga nda korfo, „I tie it with a rope"; é-ga kuhár ga nda nūne-di, „I destroy it by means of fire", from nūne, „fire". Besides, we have a sort of ablative or locative, formed by adding the particle ga which, of course, must be of quite a different origin from the identical form of the accusative of the personal pronoun, as, for instance „I arose from sleep", á-tun dáirbi-ga. How very little these forms have become integrant portions of a grammatical rule, is evident from the fact, that the termination se which, as I have shown above p. CLXXIII, is used to form the dative case of the personal pronoun, is, as far as I am aware, scarcely ever used in connection with the noun.

g) This consideration leads us in a natural course of development to those terms which we call generally prepositions, and among which already nda may be classed. These forms

sind, wie das schon der Fall mit uda ist. Auch werden diese Partikeln im Soñyai in der That zu Postpositionen, indem sie dem Nennwort, auf das sie sich beziehen, nachgesetzt und, da sie ursprünglich selbstständige, zum Theil substantivische, Begriffe sind, in Genitivform mit ihm in Verbindung gesetzt werden, wie z. B. „aus dem Brunnen", „bañgo-di koná (bañgo, „Brunnen"); „innerhalb, inmitten der Stadt", koire-di di-mās („Stadt", koire); „diesseit des Flusses", (sa-di néda hére, wörtlich „Fluss- von hier Seite".

6. *Eigenschaftswörter in Verbindung mit Nennwörtern und Zeitwörtern.*

Über die Bildung von Eigenschaftswörtern im Soñyai kann ich mehrfachen Aufschluss geben.

a) Einfache Ableitungen von einem einigen selbstständigen Begriff geschehen durch Anfügung von na, no; re, ri an die Wurzel. So haben wir vom Grundbegriff bā, „gut, angenehm sein", bā-na (wā bā-na, „süsse Milch"); von hor, „scharf", hári hor-no, „salziges Wasser". Eben so gebildet scheinen bé-re, „gross" und bō-ri, „viel, tüchtig", obgleich ich das letztere nicht rein adjektivisch gebraucht gefunden habe. Ich habe aber ein interessantes Beispiel einer solchen Adjektivbildung auf ri und zwar abgeleitet von einem Substantiv, nämlich hau wā-ri, „die Milchkuh", von hau, „Kuh" und wā, „Milch". Hier hat wā-ri den Charakter eines wahren Adjektivs, obgleich dies unzweifelhaft dasselbe ri ist, was wir auch als Bildungs-Element von Nennwörtern finden, wie z. B. tā-ri, „Gewebtes, Baumwollstreifen", von ta, „weben, nähen"; es ist wol eigentlich verbal aufzufassen. Daran schliessen sich auch Beispiele einer umschreibenden Formel des Adjektivs, nämlich (ā) a-gá-ra, wörtlich „Schüssel) es thut seiend", d. h. „eine Schüssel, worin etwas ist" und der Gegensatz (ā) a-sá-ra, „Schüssel) worin nichts ist"; eben so áraska a-sá-ra, „wo kein Glück ist", d. h. „unglücklich". Diese Form scheint mir einigermassen den häufigen Gebrauch des ro im Emgédesi zu erklären, wie z. B. hum ra bére, „Fleisch (Thier) seiend gross", oder „Thier was gross", d. h. „Elephant".

b) Während diese Ableitungen einen versteckten verbalen Charakter zu haben scheinen, sind andere dagegen offen verbaler Natur. Wir finden nämlich zuerst so die oben S. CLXXX. i) besprochene Participialform auf ude gebraucht, wie z. B. bóro) a-gó-ude bine, „Mensch er sei-end von Herz" oder „hab-end ein Herz", d. h. „herzhafter Mensch"; bóro) a-gó-ude sāhu, „Person er sei-end von" oder „hab-end Gesundheit", d. h. „gesunder Mensch"; wai) a-gó-ude gunde, „Frau sie sei-end von Leib" oder „hab-end einen Leib", d. h. „schwangere Frau"; bóro a-gó-ude tšermai, „Mensch er hab-end List", d. h. „betrügerischer Mensch, Betrüger"; bóro a-gó-ude lakkal, „Mensch er hab-end Verstand", d. h. „kluger Mensch", mit der ganz eben so gebildeten negativen Form bóro a-sí-ude lakkal, „Mensch er nicht hab-end Verstand", d. h. „Narr". Wie wir nun diese selbe ude schon bei der Bildung von abgeleiteten Nennwörtern gefunden haben, S. CLXXXII. a), so finden wir es auch hier zur Bildung einer Art zusammengesetzten Adjektivs dem Substantiv angefügt, z. B. ho-ude bóro, „schlau", wahrscheinlich „von grosser Verschlagenheit".

c) Als eine andere Art verbaler Adjektiv-Bildung erwähne ich die Endung kona, z. B. nō-kona, „freigebig", von nō, „geben", é-ga nō, „er thut geben", „gibt", und am deutlichsten dargestellt in der sonderbar construirten Phrase derbe el-hari gá-kona, wörtlich „Hemd Seide thut (oder „ist"), seiend", d. h. „ein mit Seide gesticktes Hemd". Dieses kona haben wir wol als Art Participium von kunu in a-gá kunu, der längeren, ausdrücklicheren Form für „es ist" anzusehen, woran das gá-kona der zuletzt erwähnten Phrase kaum einen Zweifel lässt. Die Präposition koná, „aus, heraus" scheint davon ganz verschieden zu sein.

d) Als ein allerdings vereinzeltes, aber in mehreren Beziehungen sehr merkwürdiges Beispiel einer verbalen Adjektiv-Bildung habe ich noch anzuführen mai-lakkal, „habend Verstand", „verständig", also dem Sinne nach ganz gleichbedeutend mit dem obigen a-gó-ude lakkal und in Form so wie Bedeutung völlig identisch mit dem Hausa-Ausdruck mai-hánkali. Dieses mai scheint im Hausa, wo es eine so unzählig wiederkehrende Bedeutung

which, for the greater part, are originally independent substantive notions, in the Soṅyai-language become postpositions, being postponed to the noun to which they relate, the latter being generally placed in the genitive case, as, for instance „out of the well", bañgo-di koná; „inside the town", koire-di di-màso, where the di has been repeated; íssa-di ńédo here, „on this side of the river".

6. *Adjectives in connection with nouns and verbs.*

With regard to the formation of adjectives in Soṅyai I am able to give a few valuable hints.

a) Adjective forms from simple notions are derived by adding to the root the termination na, no; re, ri. Thus we have bā-na from the original notion bā, „being good, sweet", wā bā-na, „sweet milk"; hor-no from hor, hári hor-no, „saltish water". In the same manner seem to be formed the adjectives bē-re, „great, large" and bū-ri, „much, fine, excellent", although I have not found the latter used as an independent form of an adjective, but rather as a verbal form. But I have another very interesting instance of such a form being derived from a substantive, viz hau wā-ri, „milk-cow" from hau, „cow" and wā, „milk", where wā-ri bears the character of a real adjective, although this is evidently the very same termination ri which we find also as an integrant element in the formation of nouns, as for instance tā-ri, „cottonstripes", „what is woven" or „sewn", from ta, „weave, sew"; from this I conclude, that we may look upon it as an originally verbal form, in connection with which I will adduce here a curious instance of a circumscribing form of an adjective notion, viz tā) a-gá-ra, „a dish wherein there is something", „full" from á-go, „it is", and the opposite tā) a-sá-ra, „a dish) where there is nothing", „empty"; just the same case we have in árzaka a-sá-ra, „where no profit is", „unprofitable". This form ri, ra seems to explain to me in a certain respect the frequent use of the ro in Emgédesi as a mode of conjunction between subject and adjective, as for instance ham ro bére, meaning verbally „meat (beast) being big" i. q. „the big beast", „elephant".

b) While formations like these bear the verbal character less prominently, others are decidedly of such a nature. For, first, we meet also here with the participial termination nde, as, for instance, bóro a-gó-nde bína, „person he be-ing of heart", or „he hav-ing a heart" i. q. „a courageous person"; bóro a-gó-nde sāha, „person he be-ing of" (or „hav-ing") health" i. q. „healthy person"; wai) a-gó-nde gundo, „woman she be-ing of" (or „hav-ing") a womb" i. q. „pregnant (woman"; hóro a-gó-nde tšermai, „person) he hav-ing shrewdness" i. q. „cheating (person"; bóro a-gó-nde lakkal, „person he hav-ing intelligence" i. q. „intelligent (person)", with the corresponding negative form bóro a-sí-nde lakkal, „person he not hav-ing intelligence" i. q. „foolish (person". And now, as we have found p. CLXXXIII, a) this termination nde forming an integrant portion of a class of substantives, thus we meet with it here in a similar position, as circumscribing the notion of an adjective auxiliary verb, for instance ho-nde bōro, „of great shrewdness".

c) As another class of verbal adjectives I mention those terminating in the form kona, as f. i. no-kona, „liberal, generous" from nō, „give", á-ga nō, „he does give"; and, as yet more illustrative, the phrase derbo el-harī gá-kona meaning verbally „shirt silk does being" i. q. „a shirt embroidered with silk". This form kona, I think, we have to look upon as a sort of participle from kunu in the form a-gá kunu, „it does exist", of which the phrase mentioned in the last place does scarcely leave a doubt.

d) As a rather isolated, but in several respects remarkable instance of a peculiar verbal form of an adjective I mention mai-lakkal, „possessing intelligence", „intelligent", identical in meaning with a-gó-nde lakkal mentioned above, and perfectly identical in meaning as well as in form with the Hausa-term mai-háṅkali. This term mai, although it forms a so frequently recurring ingredient in the formation of Hausa adjectives, yet appears to have no root

zur Bildung der Adjektiva hat, keine Wurzel zu haben, so wenig wie das oben S. CLXXVI besprochene a-koi; dagegen gehört es dem Soñyai lebendig an von mō, mai, „besitzen"; „er besitzt", á-go mō, á-go mai. Von eben dieser schon mehrfach betrachteten und weiter zu berücksichtigenden Wurzel habe ich nun auch ein höchst merkwürdiges, adjektives Kompositum, welches das Haben, Besitzen stärker ausdrückt als das oben erwähnte a-gó-nde, nämlich mē-gó-nde.

e) Schon aus dem hier Entwickelten ergibt sich, dass diese Adjektiva dem Nennwort, das sie charakterisiren, nachgestellt werden, aber dass sie nur in wenigen Fällen in der Endung mit ihm harmoniren können. So habe ich zwar in zufälliger Übereinstimmung hári bibi, „dunkles, offenes Wasser", da das i in bibi, einer blossen Verdoppelung von bi, schon ursprünglich erscheint, aber daneben habe ich hári horne, „salziges Wasser", und neben wā bāna, „süsse Milch", wā mōre, „saure Milch". So bin ich denn auch mit Bezug auf die Form von tūri (s. oben S. CLXXXIII, d, α) ungewiss, ob ich tūri beri als wirkliche Pluralform anzusehen habe, obgleich ich für „gross" im Einzelfall sonst entschieden nur die Form bére gefunden habe.

f) Übrigens wendet das Soñyai, wie alle diese Sprachen, viel seltener eigentliche Eigenschaftswörter an, als stellvertretende verbale Formen, wie ja auch die mit a-gó-nde zusammengesetzten nur sehr uneigentlich als wirkliche Eigenschaftswörter angesehen werden können. So werden denn Eigenschaften gewöhnlich in bestimmter verbaler Form dem Nennwort beigefügt, bei positiven Fällen mit á-go, bei negativen mit á-si. So sagt man statt „ein guter Mensch", „Mensch er ist gut", bóro á-ga bōri; statt „schlechter Mensch", „Mensch, er ist nicht gut", bóro á-si bōri; statt „hübscher Mensch", „Mensch (im) Antlitz er ist gut", bóro nine a-bōri oder á-ga bōri; statt „hässlicher Mensch", „Mensch (im) Antlitz er ist nicht gut", bóro nine á-si bōri. So habe ich auch für „viele Leute" die verbale Form bóro-ō á-ga bō, wörtlich „Leute es gibt viel", nicht í-ga bō, „sie sind viel". Als ein Beispiel einer wunderbar componirten, halb verbalen, halb adjektivischen und scheinbar negativen Form eines derartigen Adjektivs habe ich zu erwähnen á-go-mē-ri in einer, mit der letztangeführten identischen Phrase für „hässlich", bóro dūmo á-go-mē-ri, wo das negative mē nichts mit dem Zeitwort mō, „besitzen" zu thun hat, sondern sich an die oben S. CLXXX angeführten Beispiele anschliesst, während das angefügte ri trotz des vorhergehenden definitiven á-go der ganzen Form den Charakter einer Participialform gibt.

g) Was die Vergleichungsgrade der Eigenschaftswörter betrifft, so findet solche Vergleichung meist gleichfalls in völlig verbaler Weise Statt durch das impersonelle a-bíssa oder bissa, „es übertrifft", wie z. B. wō bi(a)bissa á-ga bére, wörtlich „dieses Boot übertrifft, es ist gross", d. h. „übertrifft an Grösse, ist grösser". Wir finden aber auch eine eigenthümliche Bildung mit nda und nde, wie z. B. wō bōre nda wō, „dieses ist grösser als das"; wō bā nde wō, „dieses ist mehr als dieses"; wō katšá nde wō, „dieses ist weniger als dieses", wo ich in der Form nda, nde von einer wirklichen Steigerung nichts entdecken kann und über seine ursprüngliche Bedeutung ungewiss bin, obgleich nda sich dem oben S. CLXXXIV, f) bei dem Causativ oder Ablativ des Substantivs erwähnten identischen nda eng anzuschliessen scheint. katšá-nde und bā-nde kommen aber auch alleinstehend ganz gewöhnlich mit der Bedeutung „mehr" und „weniger" vor und hiervon hat das einfache katšá ganz entschieden die Bedeutung „klein" = kaina, während wir bā als Wurzel gleichfalls mit der Bedeutung „viel, gut" haben.

Ein eigenthümliches Zusammentreffen von Nennwort, Adjektiv und Adverb finden wir in den Worten bene, „Himmel", „obere", „oben" und ganda, „Erde", „untere", „unten".

Um nun eine gründliche Analyse der Soñyai-Sprache, die noch reicheren ferneren Aufschluss verspricht, noch weiter anzubahnen, gebe ich hier ein Verzeichniss der bei mir vorkommenden einsilbigen Wörter, indem einige Fragen der Syntax sich noch in den allerdings gerade in dieser Sprache wenig zahlreichen Phrasen am Ende des Vokabular's erledigen werden.

in the Hausa-language, as little as the common verbal form a-kol; on the contrary it belongs organically to the Sonyai-idiom, where mó, mai is a common term for „possess, have", á-go mó, á-go mai, „he does possess". From this very root, which we have to meet also further on, in connection with go I have a curious form of verbal adjective, expressing the possessing in a stronger manner than the simple a-gó-nde, vis mĕ-gó-nde.

e) Already from what I have said we may draw the conclusion, that these adjective forms are placed behind the subject which they are destined to characterise, but that their termination can harmonize with that of the latter only in a few cases. Thus, in the case of hári bibi, „black, open water, sea", the harmony of the termination is quite accidental, bibi being a mere reiteration of bi, „dark, darkness", and side by side with it I have hári horne, „saltish water", just as together with wā bāua, „sweet milk" I have wā mōra, „sour milk". Thus, also with regard to the phrase tūri bēri, taken into account what I have said p. CLXXXIV, d, a) on the subject of the form tūri, I am not certain whether we have to look on the termination i as a sign of the plural, or not, although in the singular I have certainly bōre for „big, large".

f) However the Sonyai, as most of these languages do, employs really adjective forms rather rarely, but generally substitutes in their case verbal forms, as we have already seen, that a-gó-ndo is rather improperly to be termed an adjective; thus, qualities characterising the subject are expressed by definite verbal forms, in positive cases by means of á-go, in negative ones by means of á-si. Thus, instead of „a good person" the Sonyai say „person he is good", bóro á-ga bōri; instead of „bad person", person he is not good", bóro á-si bōri; instead of „handsome person", „person (in) face he is good", bóro nine a-bōri or á-ga bōri and instead of „ugly person", „person (in) face he is not good", bóro nine á-si bōri. Thus, I have also for „many people", „a numerous congregation" the remarkable verbal form bóre-ō á-ga bō, „people it is much", not í-ga bō, „they are many" i. q. „many people". As an instance of a very remarkable composite form, half verbal, half adjective, with a doubtful negative meaning, I mention á-ge mē-ri in a phrase identical in meaning with the one mentioned before for „ugly", vis bóro dúmo á-ge-mē-ri, where mē seems to convey a negative meaning in confirmation of what I have said above p. CLXXXI.

g) As for the degrees of comparison of the adjectives, such a comparison, in general, likewise takes place by means of the verbal form a-bíssa, „it exceeds, excels", as, for instance, wō hi (a)bissa á-ga bēre meaning verbally „this boat excels it is great" i. q. „excels in size, is larger". But we find also a very peculiar construction by means of the forms nda, nde, as, for instance wō bēre nda wō, „this is larger than this"; wō bā nde wō, „this is more than that"; wō katšá nde wō, „this is less than that", where I do not know how to explain the form nde, which seems to have no relation whatever to the following wō, but to be nothing but the participial form explained p. CLXXX, i, the very same forms bā-nde, katšá-nde being also used when standing quite alone, and meaning in general „more" and „less", although bā means only „much, good", while katšá, another form for kaina, means „little". The comparison, therefore, appears not to be expressed by form, but to be merely understood. As for nda, it reminds of the ablative case p. CLXXXV, f.

I will here also mention, that we find a curious instance of coincidence of the noun, the adjective and adverb in the Sonyai-terms bēno meaning „sky", as well as „upper" and „over", and ganda meaning „earth, ground", as well as „lower", and „under, below".

Leaving a few questions of syntax to the explanation of the phrases at the end of the vocabulary, in order to take a further step towards analyzing this language, which as yet holds forth the hope of much further information with regard to many ethnological questions of the highest interest, I here give a list of the monosyllabous terms which appear in my Notes.

7. *Verzeichnis einiger monosyllaben Wörter des Sonrhai.*

a: ai, „ich"; wegen der Bedeutung „Verwandter, Bruder" u. s. w. bin ich etwas zweifelhaft.

b: ba, „zerbrechen"; ba, „wollen, lieben"; bà, bō, „viel, gut"; ban, „genesen"; bār, „wechseln"; be, „wissen"; ben, bin, „aufhören"; bi, „dunkel, schwarz"; bī, „spinnen"; bo, „zerstören"; boṅg, „Kopf"; bor, „Sterblicher, Mensch"; bu, „zerstört werden", „sterben", „stumpf sein"; bun, „Tal"; bur, „wohlthun".

d: da, dam, dan, „zeugen, machen, betreiben"; daṅg (fa, „Fluss bearbeiten, passiren"; de, „erfassen" (handgreiflich), „erfassen" (geistig), „lernen"; dé, „kaufen, verkaufen"; dê, „voll, vollständig"; dem, „anziehen"; di, „machen"; di, „von, zu"; dī, der im Hause inkkurdu genannte Baum; dō, „finden, thun"; dā, „Sand, Boden"; don, „zart, weich, lustig, Gesang, lässig" (daher „spät"); dōr, „böse, krank"; dum, „helfen" (daher auch „verbürgen"), „begleiten"; dur, „stampfen".

f: fan, „hinstellen"; far, „scharf machen, schleifen"; fār, „scharf, durstig sein, Durst"; fer, „öffnen"[1]; for, „das Fell abziehen, schinden"; fō, „ein, eins"; fō, „danken"; foi (hoi), „Blatt"; fu (hu), „blasen (fu-nau, „anblasen"), athmen, leben"; fūs, „Geschwür".

g[2]: gō, go, „thun, sein"; ga, „ihn, sie, es"; ga, „Lagerdorf"; gā, „Leib"; gab, „Aasgeier"; gai, „hell, Licht"; gau, „tanzen"; (gar, Zeitwort, siehe kar); gar, „Thonhaus"; ger, „begegnen"; goi, „thätig sein, thun"; gu[3]), „(grosses, schönes) Pferd"; gum, „daniederliegen"; gum, „Dunkelheit"; guu, „wildes Thier, Löwe".

h: ha, hai, „gebären, zeugen", „geboren werden, nachkommen, folgen"; hai, „Sache, Ding"; ham, „helfen"; ham, „Fleisch"[4]); hau, „fragen" (sich belehren); hau, „Tag" als Zeitmass; haṅg, „trinken"; har, „sagen"; har, „Mann, männlich"; har, „bis"; hau, „binden, gebunden sein", „zur Enthaltsamkeit gebunden sein", d. i. „fasten", „kränken, beschimpfen"; hau, „Rind"; hè, „weinen (schreien)"; heṅg, „schreien"; hi, „Boot"; hin, „machen, begehen" (einen Fehler); ho, „Verstand"; hō[5]), „Haus"; hoṅg, „heute"; hor, „scharf" (von Geschmack), „warm" (vielleicht Arab.); hoi, „zu Fuss gehn"; hu (s. fu), „athmen"; hū, „suchen"; hun, „herauskommen"; hur, „hineingehn".

i: in (ursprünglich wol un, „rudern", daher in-de, un-de, „Ruder"); idā, „sieben"[6]).

k: ka, „alle", „ruhig"; ka, „kommen"; kai, „stillstehn, weit, geräumig"; koi, „gehn"; kam, kaṅg, „fallen", „untergehn"; kau, „liegen, ruhig sein, zufrieden sein[7])"; kau, „machen, zubereiten, zubereitet sein, scharf sein"; kar (gar), „berühren, bearbeiten" in allen Beziehungen, daher „begegnen, antreffen, besteigen, angreifen, schlagen, strafen", passivisch

---

[1]) fer und far gehen offenbar auf dieselbe Grundbedeutung zurück; daher auch fēri, „öffne den Boden, bebaue das Land"; fēri, „Acker"; far-ru, „offene, kahle Ebene"; far-ss, analog gebildet wie fa-nau, „spalte, theile"; far-ta, „sich öffnen, hervorkommen"; auch fār, „durstig sein" kommt auf die Grundbedeutung zurück, ebenso fōr, „das Fell öffnen, schinden".

[2]) Zu g muss ich bemerken, dass mehrere der unter diesem Buchstaben angeführten Wörter möglicherweise mit γ anfangen mögen. Vielleicht gilt dies auch von dem in meinem Emghedesi-Wörterbuch so oft wiederkehrenden beziehenden Pronomen γo, „welcher, was", und wenn dieses mit ga, go zusammenhängt, so hätten wir das auch γa, γo zu schreiben. Doch s. oben S. CLXXXVII, a.

[3]) Mit gu muss es eine besondere Bewandtniss haben; gau für das „stattliche" Thier der Wildnis scheint damit zusammenzuhängen.

[4]) ham kann kaum dem Arabischen entlehnt sein, obgleich es dem lham so ähnlich sieht.

[5]) hō könnte allerdings Manchem nicht als ursprünglich monosyllabe, sondern als contrahirte Form von hōgu erscheinen. Wenn man das letztere mit hur, „hineingehn" vergleicht, möchte man beide Wörter mit γ schreiben.

[6]) idā, „sieben". Schon oben S. CLXXIV, 3. habe ich angegeben, dass die Ausdrücke für „fünf" und „sechs" entschieden mit dem für „sieben" in Verbindung stehen und die ersteren gehören nur zufällig wegen der später angefügten Vokal-Endung nicht hierher. Durch diesen inneren Zusammenhang der drei genannten Zahlwörter allein erklärt sich auch das sonst ganz unbegreifliche, auch schon oben bezeichnete Faktum, dass man in den östlichen Provinzen von Sonrhai schon mit der Zahl „fünf" und nicht mit „sechs" an die Arabischen Ausdrücke anfing. Vielleicht hängt idā mit idie, „Kind, Sohn" zusammen.

[7]) kau. So erklärt sich der Ausdruck ó bina ga kau, „ich im Herzen bin ruhig, zufrieden". S. 65 des Vokabular's vergl. mit S. CLXXVI, b) der Einleitung.

7. *List of monosyllabous words of the Kanyai-language.*

a: ai, „I"; as for the meaning „relation, kinsman, brother" I want as yet further confirmation.

b: ba, „break"; bâ, „like, wish"; bā, bō, „good, many"; bai, „be good, be better"; ban, „become well, recover"; bār, „change"; bê, „know"; bea, bin, „cease"; bi, „dark, black"; bi, „spin"; bo, „destroy"; bong, „head, chief"; bu, „become destroyed, die, be blunt"; bor, „mortal, human being"; bun, „death"; bar, „do well".

d: da, dam, dan, „agitate, procreate, beget"; dang (fea, „work a river, cross"; de, „seize" (actually „lay hold of"), from a mental point of view „learn"; de, „lay, sell"; de, „complete, full"; dem, „dress"; di, „make, perform"; di, „of, belonging to"; di the tree called tukkurda in Hausa, „pole, perch"; dō, „find, meet, do"; dè, „sand, soil"; don, „tender, soft, sweet, song, lazy, late"; dōr, „bad, sick"; dum, „assist" (thence also „stand security, warrant"), „accompany"; dur, „to pound".

f: fan, „put down, place"; far, „make sharp, wet"; fār, „be thirsty, thirst"; fer, „open"[1]; fer, „draw off the skin, flay"; fō, „one"; fō, „thank, render thanks"; foi (hoi), „leave, foliage"; fu (hu), „respire, live"; fūs, „ulcer".

g[2]: ga, go, „do, be, exist"; ga, „him, her, it"; gu, „body, herd, encampment"; gab, „vulture"; gai, „clear, light"; gan, „dance"; verb gur see kar; gur, „clayhouse"; gor, „meet"; goi, „be active, achieve"; gu[3], „(large, fine) horse"; gum, „be sick mind", „darkness"; gun, „wild beast, lion".

h: ha, hai, „beget, procreate, bear, be born, follow"; hai, „thing, business"; ham, „assist, help"; ham, „meat"[4]; han, „ask, inform one's self"; han, „day"; hang, „drink"; har, „speak, relate"; har, „man, male"; har, „as far as, until"; hau, „tie, be tied", „be bound to abstinence", i. q. „fast; offend, insult"; hau, „cattle"; he, „weep" (cry); heng, „cry"; hi, „boat"; hin, „make, commit (a mistake)"; ho, „understanding"; hō[5], „house"; hoi, „walk on foot"; hong, „to day"; hor, „strong (to the taste), warm" [perhaps Arabic]; hu (see fu), „respire, live"; „hu, „seek, search"; hun, „come out"; hur, „go in, enter".

i: in (un), „row" (with the oar); idž, „seven"[6].

k: ka, „sweet, quiet"; ka, „come"; kai, „make stop, arrest; stop, stand still; spacious"; kai, „go"; kam, kang, „fall, lie quiet, be content"[7]; kan, „make, prepare; be prepared, be sharp"; kar (gar), „touch, deal with (in all sorts of meanings), meet, mount, attack, beat, punish"; (in a passive sense) „happen", and so on; ki, „language, idiom";

[1] fer as well as far evidently belong to the same original notion, whence fêri, „open, cultivate the ground"; fāri, „field"; far-ra, „open, treeless plain"; far-ea, „divide, split"; fer-ra, „open itself, come forth (these two verbal forms we have to add to the chapter treating the verb); fer, „open the skin, flay"; may, even fār, „be thirsty" appears to proceed from the same idea.

[2] With regard to the g I have to remark, that several of the terms adduced under this head may possibly begin rather with a y. At any rate, this seems to be the case with the relative pronoun ro, which recurs so repeatedly in my Kugiddei-vocabulary, and which seems to be related to the auxiliary verb ro, ga, in which case we ought to write the latter likewise by a y: but see, what I have said p. CLXXXIX. f).

[3] There seems to have been a particular reason, why the term gu settled on a fine horse, the term for „lion" appearing to be closely related to it.

[4] ham can scarcely be borrowed from the Arabic, although it bears so great a resemblance to lham.

[5] hō: the fuller form being hōgu it may be doubtful, whether we have to look upon hō as an originally monosyllabic, or rather as a contracted form. As for hōgu itself, I do not know, whether it has any etymological connection with the verb hur, „enter": if it has, we ought to write hoyu as well as huy.

[6] idž, „seven". Already above p. CLXXV. 3. I have mentioned, that the terms for 5 and 6 are etymologically connected with that for 7, and it is merely accidental, that the former do not belong to our list of monosyllables on account of a vowel being added at the end. This apparent connection of the numerals 5, 6 and 7 serves also to explain the remarkable fact, why in the Eastern dialect the original term for five has not been preserved, but has been lost together with the following numerals. — As for idž it may be connected with idie, „child".

[7] kan: thus the term ŧ bien ga kan p. 55 of the vocabulary is easily explained, meaning verbally „I (in) heart do repose", „am content, glad"; compare p. CLXXVII, b) of the Introductory Remarks.

„sich ereignen" u. s. w.; ki, „Sprache"; kò, „herausziehn, abziehn, schöpfen", passivisch „herausgezogen, ausgeschöpft werden", daher „austrocknen" [1]); ko [2]), „Stadt"; koi, „Herr"; koṅg, „Blatt der Dumpalme"; kor, „kochen, schmoren"; ku, „hoch"; [kul, „jeder, alles", Arab.]; kur, „weiden", „Heerde"; kyau, „lesen".

k, tš [3]): tšau = kyau; tše, „Bein, Fuss"; tši, „Sprache", „Befinden, Zustand" (Dialekt-Verschiedenheit von ki); tšen, „aufschlagen, errichten" [4]).

l: lo, „Gastgabe, Geschenk".

m: ma, „verstehn, Name"; me, „was"; ma, me, „dass nicht, nicht" [5]); mau, „nahe"; mar, „Leopard"; mai, me, „besitzen, haben"; mo, „Mund"; mó, „Auge"; mò, „Reis"; mon, „hören"; mun, „überlaufen".

n: na, „thun, begehen, bearbeiten"; nam, „beissen, Biss"; naṅg, „lassen"; ni, „du"; no, „nein, nicht"; nō, „geben"; nya, „Mutter"; nyin, „trinken".

r: re, „zurückweisen".

s: sai, „Fluss"; so, „zu" (Beziehung des Dativs); sò, „trennen"; som, „loslassen"; si, „nicht, später" [6]); sō, „Gaumen"; su, „Laut, Rellen"; sum, „spenden (Segen)".

t: ta, „entsprechen machen, erwidern", daher „flechten, nähen" [7]); tui, „trocken, hart sein"; tum, „fischen, fangen"; „Gefangener, Sklave"; ti, „Mal" („ein Mal", ti fo, „zwei Mal", ti ahiṅka u. s. w. S. 21 hinzuzufügen); tiṅg, „schwer"; ton, „voll, hinreichend"; tō, „Schüssel"; tun, „aufstehn".

w: wa, „Milch"; wai, „Frau"; war, „ihr" (Plur.); war, „Zehner" [8]); wir, „suchen"; wō, „diese".

y: yā, „fern"; ye, „loslassen, entlassen"; ye, „trocken"; yē, „Scheibe, Apfel" (mó-yē, „Aug-apfel", zári-ye, „Tages-Scheibe, Tagesanbruch"); yer, „wir"; yī, „Butter"; yō, „Fremdling, Kameel" [9]); yū, „Honig".

dž [10]): dža, „zögern, lange währen"; džen, „dauernd, alt"; džo, „Gepäck".

z: zan, „emporheben"; ze, „Kern, Fruchtstein"; zem, „Schmied"; zó, zū, „bekämpfen, zerstören"; zur, „fliehen"; zur, „Mitleid".

6. *Verwandtschaftliche Beziehungen des Soṅyai mit anderen Afrikanischen Sprachen.*

Wie wohlbegründet die oben gemachte Bemerkung ist in Betreff der Bedeutung des Soṅyai wegen seiner bewahrten monosyllaben Wörter im Vergleich zu den meisten anderen hier behandelten Sprachen werden folgende Beispiele klar machen:

„Kameel" . . . . . . Soṅyai yó, im Tédā . . . . gōne;
„Adansonia digitata" „ kó, in fast allen anderen Central-Afrikan. Sprachen kuka;

---

[1]) Vielleicht ist daraus auch wieder eine transitive Form kok gebildet, Vokab. S. 109, „trocknen"; aber fast möchte ich glauben, dass das End-k nichts ist als ein halb verschlungenes go, „es".

[2]) Daher ka-ko, Gogo der Name der Hauptstadt; ko in späterer, längerer, wol verbaler Form koira.

[3]) Der tš-Laut schliesst sich in vielen Sprachen und ganz besonders im Soṅyai dem k eng an, indem den Übergang dazu das erweichte k oder ky macht, wie etwa in kyau, „lesen". S. Einleitung S. XXXVIII.

[4]) tše, tšen verhalten sich genau ebenso und zeigen dieselbe organische Entwickelung wie das weiter unten erwähnte dže, džen.

[5]) ma. Auch die Form man kommt vor, besonders in Verbindung mit dem dem Arabischen entlehnten ábadan, „niemals", wie z. B. man a-kai ábadan, „er ging niemals".

[6]) si. Die Bedeutung „später" ist erst nachträglich, wie in subba-si, „morgen nicht", d. h. „übermorgen".

[7]) ta. Durch diese einfache Deduktion des Begriffes erklärt sich Alles auf das schönste. Daher tà-ri, „Geflochtenes, Matte", tà-ri oder tà-ra, „Gewebtes, Baumwollstreifen".

[8]) war, „Zehner" erscheint als Einheit ganz deutlich in dem Kompositum war-inka, „zwei Zehner" u. s. w.; iwaui, „zehn" dagegen ist keine ursprüngliche Form.

[9]) Die Homonymie des Namens für „Fremdling" und „Kameel" ist auffallend und bemerkenswerth; sie wird auf natürlichen Bedingungen beruhen. Das Kameel ist eben ein Fremdling in Afrika.

[10]) dž schliesst sich im Soṅyai an y eng an und habe ich es deshalb hier eingereiht, obgleich doch auch ein Paar Beispiele einer Verwechselung des dž mit tš vorkommen.

kō, „draw out, take away", thence in a passive sense „become exhausted, dry up"[1]; ko, „town"[2]; koi, „master"; koṅg, „leave of doompalm"; kor, „cook, fry"; kū, „high"; [kul, „every one, all" is Arabic]; kur, „tend (a flock)", subst. „herd"; kyan, „read".

k, tš[3]): tšan = kyan; tše, „leg, foot"; tšen, „(give a foot), pitch (a tent)[4]"; tši = ki, „word, language; condition, health".

l: lō, „hospitable gift, present".

m: ma, „understand, name"; me, „what"; ma, me, „that not, not"[5]); mar, „leopard"; mai, mō, „possess, have"; me, „mouth"; mō, „eye"; mo, „rice"; mon, „hear"; mun, „run over, spill".

n: na, „do, commit"; nam, „bite"; naṅg, „let, leave"; ni, „thou"; no, „no, not"; nō, „give"; nya, „mother"; nyin, „give to drink".

r: re, „refuse".

s: sai, „river"; se, „to" (relation of dative case); sē, „separate"; som, „let go"; si, „not, later"[6]); su, „sound, barking"; sum, „bestow (a blessing)".

t: ta, „make correspond", „plait, sew"; „respond"[7]); tai, „be dry, hard"; tam, „catch, fish" (verb); „caught, slave"; ti, „time" („one time, once", ti fō; „two times", ti ahíṅka; and so on, to be added vocals p. 21); ting, „heavy"; ton, „full, sufficient"; tū, „dish, bowl"; tun, „rise".

w: wā, „milk"; wai, „woman"; war, „you" (plur.); war, „tenth"[8]); wir, „search"; woo „this".

y: yā, „far, distant"; ye, „let loose, dismiss"; ye, „dry"; yē, „orb" (mō-ye, „eye-ball, pupil", zāri-ye, „orb of daylight", „day-break"; yer, „we"; yī, „butter"; yō, „stranger, camel"[9]); yū, „honey".

dš[10]): dše, „last long, tarry"; dšen, „lasting, old"; dšo, „luggage".

z: zau, „raise, lift"; zē, „kernel, stone"; zem, „blacksmith"; zo, zū, „fight, destroy"; zur, „run away, fly"; zur, „pity".

8. *Affinity of the Soṅγai-idiom with other Central-African languages.*

How well founded the remark is, which I have made above as to the importance of the Soṅγai-language on account of the monosyllabic terms, which it has preserved, when compared with most of the other surrounding languages, the following instances of some of the most common terms may serve to show:

„camel" . . . . . Soṅγai yō, Téda . . . . gōne;
„Adansonia digitata" „ kō, in almost all the other C.-African languages kuka;

— .

[1] kō: perhaps from this root another form koh has been derived, conveying the transitive meaning „dry, make dry" p. 109; but I almost think, that the final h in this instance is nothing but gu (it) half swallowed.

[2] ko: thence the name of the Soṅγai capital ko-ko, Gogo; the later fuller and verbal form of ko is koira.

[3] tš in Soṅγai, more than in any of the languages here treated (s. Intr. Remarks p. XXXIX), is closely allied to the k sound, the link between both being formed by ky, k, as, for instance, in the term kyan, „read".

[4] tše, tšen exhibit the very same trace of organic development, as dše, dšen to be mentioned further on.

[5] ma: the form man also occurs, especially in connection with ábadan which has been borrowed from the Arabic, meaning „never", as, for instance, man a-koi ábadan, „he went never".

[6] si originally seems to mean nothing but „not", the meaning „later" being merely implied a posteriori, as, for instance, súbba-si, „to morrow not", i. q. „the day after to morrow".

[7] ta: this simple deduction of the original notion explains every thing: thence tā-ri, „what is plaited, mat", tā-ri or ta-ya, „what is woven, cotton-stripes".

[8] war, „tenth" appears very distinctly as a unit in the composite terms war-ìika, war-ínza, „one tenth, two tenths", and so on, while áwaal, „ten" is not an original form.

[9] yō: the identity of the term for „stranger" and „camel" is remarkable, but placed beyond a doubt, and may be based on natural conditions, the camel not being indigenous in these Regions, and not being introduced into them but some time after the beginning of our Era.

[10] dš in Soṅγai is closely allied to y, which is the reason why I have assigned to it this place, although there occur also a few instances of dš and tš being interchanged.

„Reis" [1]	Soṅγai mō, Mandi-Dialekte	māro, māro, mālo, māyo;
„Butter"	„ yī, Lógonē	ȷimbi;
„Honig"	„ yū, Hausa	zúmua;
„gehören"	„ hai, Hausa	haifo.

und manche andere. Das letztangeführte Wort würde ich nicht benutzt haben, wenn sich nicht auf das Klarste herausstellte, wie unendlich viel die Hausa-Sprache vom Soṅγai in sehr alter Zeit entlehnt hat.

Dieses Ergebniss wird sich, hoffe ich, aus folgender Liste übereinstimmender Ausdrücke in der Soṅγai- und anderen Nord-Afrikanischen Sprachen klar herausstellen.

„aufstehn"	Soṅγai tun, Alt-Egyptisch (Bunsen I, S. 590)	tun;
„augenblicklich"	„ amoreder, Mūšiγ	amurādar;
„Capparis sodata"	„ tēšak, Mūšiγ	tēšak;
„Gold" (lat. aurum)	„ ūray, Mūšiγ	úray;
„Silber"	„ indžorfu, Mūšiγ	ázeref;
„Schwert"	„ tákoba, Mūšiγ	tákoba;
„Haus"	„ hō, Dahōme, Māhi (Koelle Polyglotta)	ḫo;
„Kind"	„ idžo, Wándalā	edza;
„Blitz"	„ mellu, Māba	moldek;
8 „Krokodil"	„ ákarai, Yóruba	agelliti [2];
„Stute"	„ tefe, Fūl	teffe;
„Thon"	„ lābo, Fūl	lōfe;
„Maulthier"	„ lumbāna, Fūl-Dialekt von Másina	lambāna;
„Medicin"	„ séfori, Fūl	safáre;
„Einschnitte, Tättowiren"	„ siri, Fūl	yeri;
„Haut"	„ gūru, Fūl	kūru;
„Kopftuch"	„ fátala, Fūl	pétalol;
„ich glaube"	„ é-(gu) yāfa, Fūl	mé-(do) yāfa;
„dieser"	„ wō, Hausa	wó-ne;
„was"	„ me, Hausa	me;
„was, weshalb"	„ me-nin / me-nenne Hausa	me-né-ne;
„hundert"	„ zaṅgo, Hausa (neben durf)	zaṅgo;
„tausend"	„ zambar, Hausa (neben deba)	zambar;
„bis"	„ har, Hausa	har;
„in drei Tagen"	„ gatta, Hausa, nordwestl. Provinzen	gatta;
„in vier Tagen"	„ tšitta, „ „ „	tšitta;
„er ist, er gilt"	„ á-go, Hausa	á-koi;
„ist reif, gar"	„ ú-nin, Hausa	ánona;
„ist nicht reif"	„ n-nú-nin, Hausa	aṅánina;
„besitzend, Herr von"	„ mai, Hausa	mai;
„heirathen"	„ umbék, Hausa	amre;
S. „zeugen", H. „Erzeugtes, Kind", da, Hausa		da;

[1] Hierzu erwäge man, dass eben dieser ursprüngliche monosyllabe Ausdruck mō für „Reis" sich noch bis heute im Yóruba und bei anderen Stämmen, wie den Bini und Dëwoi bis an das Gestade des Oceans erhalten hat und man vergleiche man an dieser sprachlichen Eigenthümlichkeit das von mir in meinem Reisebericht berührte sachliche Verhältniss wegen des Anfanges der Reiskultur am Niger, Th. V, S. 185.

[2] agelliti nach dem vortrefflichen Crowther's Yóruba-Vokabular ist nicht das eigentliche Krokodil, sondern der sangaal (Reisen V, S. 141), oder wie er dieses naturwissenschaftlich noch nicht beschriebene Thier mit dem Amerikanischen Namen nennt, guana.

„rice" ¹) . . . . Soñyai mō, in the several Mandi-dialects mŏro, mălo, mălo, măyo;
„butter" . . . . „ yi, Lógone . . . . ylmbi;
„honey" . . . . „ yū, Hausa . . . . zúmua;
„to bear, bring forth" . . „ hai, Hausa . . . . haïfo;

and several others may be added to this list. I should not have introduced into it the latter instance, if it did not appear, that the Hausa-language has really borrowed extensively from the Soñyai at a very early period.

This will, I think, be fully demonstrated by the following list of corresponding terms in the Soñyai- and other North-African languages.

„rise" . . . . Soñyai tun, ancient Egyptian (Bunsen I, p. 590) tun;
„instantly" . . . . . „ amorēder, Mā̆šiy . . . . amarădar;
„Capparis sodata" . . . „ tésak, Mā̆šiy . . . . teššak;
„gold" (Lat. aurum) . . „ ūray, Mā̆šiy . . . . úray;
„silver" . . . . „ indžorfu, Mā̆šiy . . . . ázeref;
„sword" . . . . „ tákoba, Mā̆šiy . . . . tákoba;
„house" . . . . „ hō, Dahóme, Māhi (Koelle Polyglotta) . . ḥo;
„child" . . . . „ idžo, Wándalā . . . . odza;
„lightning" . . . . . . „ mella, Māba . . . . meldek;
„crocodile" . . . . . . „ ákarai, Yóruba . . . . agiliti²);
„mare" . . . . „ téfo, Fūl . . . . teffe;
„clay" . . . . „ lābo, Fūl . . . . lōfu;
„mule" . . . . „ lumbāna, Fūl-dialect of Másina . . . lambāna;
„medecine" . . . . . . „ sóferi, Fūl . . . . safāro;
„tattooings" . . . . . . „ siri, Fūl . . . . yōri;
„skin" . . . . „ gūru, Fūl . . . . kūru;
„turban, litham" . . . „ fátala, Fūl . . . . pétalul;
„I believe" . . . . . . „ ó-ga) yă̄fa, Fūl . . . . mé-dō) yăfa;
„this" . . . . „ wō, Hausa . . . . wó-ne;
„what" . . . . „ mo, Hausa . . . . me;
„what, why" . . . . . „ {mo-nin / me-ornne} Hausa . . . . mo-nū-ne;
„hundred" . . . . . . „ zañgo, Hausa (besides darī) . . . . . sañgo;
„thousand" . . . . . . „ zambar, Hausa (besides dubū) . . . . zambar;
„till, until" . . . . . . „ har, Hausa . . . . har;
„in three days" . . . . „ gatta, Hausa, North-Western provinces . gatta;
„in four days" . . . . „ tšitta, Hausa, „ „ . . . tšitta;
„there is, it obtains" . . „ á-go, Hausa . . . . á-kol;
„is ripe, well boiled" . . „ á-nin, Hausa . . . . ánona;
„is not ripe, crude" . . „ a-ná-nin, Hausa . . . . añáninn;
„possessing, master of" . „ mai, Hausa . . . . mai;
„marry" . . . . „ ambók, Hausa . . . . amré;
S. „procreate", H. „son, child", da, Hausa . . . . da;

---

¹) If we now take into account, that this very same original monosyllabic form mō of the name for „rice" is as yet preserved in the idiom of Yóruba, and with the Bása and Déwoi to the very shores of the Atlantic, the remarks I have made in my Narrative (Tr. vol. V, p. 194) quite independently of this circumstance, with regard to the priority of the cultivation of rice along the middle course of the Niger, claim a by far greater importance.

²) agiliti, I have to observe, according to Rev. Crowther in his Yóruba-vocabulary, does not mean the crocodile, but what he calls wrongly guana, that is the animal called sangwai by the Soñyai, Tr. vol. V, p. 146.

„sehen" . . . . Soñyai góna, Hausa . . . . ganí;
„schnarchen" . . . . „ hánsora, Hausa . . . . hánsari;
„es ist zerbrochen" . „ a-kairi, Hausa . . . . yá-kare;
„Manatus" . . . . . „ ayū, Hausa . . . . ayū;
„Schildkröte" . . . . „ kóógura, Hausa . . . . kúńkuru;
„zahme Taube" . . . „ téddaber, Hausa . . . . tautábora ¹);
„Grossvater" . . . . „ kága, Hausa . . . . káka ²);
„jüngerer (Bruder)" . „ kaina, Hausa . . . . kané;
„Freund" . . . . . „ abakkoi, Hausa . . . . áboki;
„Krätze, Ausschlag" „ kasūma, Hausa . . . . kásua;
„Pocken" . . . . . „ mása-mása, Hausa . . . . maadsera;
„Berg, Hügel" . . . „ toudi, Hausa . . . . tuddu;
„Rohr" . . . . . . „ kāri, Hausa . . . . kará;
„Löffel" . . . . . . „ sókol, Hausa . . . . tūdkali;
„Flöte" . . . . . . „ algaita, Hausa . . . . olgaita;
„Thonhaus" S., „Thonstadt" H., gar, Hausa . . . . garí;
„Miethe, Lohn" . . Soñyai sūfuri, Hausa . . . . súfuri;
„Silber" . . . . . . „ indžorfa, Hausa . . . . ázerfa;
„Kolanuss" . . . . . „ huóro, Hausa . . . . gūro;
„schwarzes Baumwollgewand", turki (gen. túrki-di), Hausa . . . . túrkedi;
„stumm" . . . . . Soñyai bēbe, Hausa . . . . bēbe;
„arm, schutzbefohlen" „ talkan, Hausa . . . . talakka.

So sehen wir also, dass das Soñyai im Ganzen wenige Übereinstimmungen in seinem Glossar mit den benachbarten Sprachen hat, ausgenommen allein mit dem Hausa, und es ist mir nicht im Allergeringsten zweifelhaft, dass in Bezug auf die letzteren Übereinstimmungen das Hausa-Volk von seinem ihm an Bildung wie an politischer Entwickelung in der Zeit weit vorangegangenen nord-westlichen Nachbar entlehnt hat, nicht dieser von jenem. Dies ergiebt sich auf das Allerklarste aus Verbalformen wie ákoi, daona und ganz besonders der negativen Form sāánius, die durchaus keine Wurzel in der Hausa-Sprache haben, während sie im Soñyai ihre organische Erklärung finden. Auch die Erscheinung, dass die bedeutendsten Artikel des Handels und der Industrie, schwarze Baumwollwaaren und Kolanüsse und in Folge dessen Zahlausdrücke u. s. w. von den Soñyai zu den Hausa gekommen sind, reiht sich dem ganzen Gang der Entwickelung dieser Negerstaaten auf das Lebendigste ein. Ob wir weiteren Aufschluss über den merkwürdigen Stamm der Soñyai erhalten sollen, wird die Zeit lehren. Ich brauche nur noch hinzuzufügen, dass, wie ich das schon anderswo angedeutet, das Aruma Raffenel's (nouveau voyage dans le pays des Nègres II, S. 402 ff.) nichts ist als ein im Munde der Ruma, d. h. der von Mólai Hamed el Dhéhebi, dem Eroberer Soñyai's (Reis. und Entd. IV, S. 430, 440, 663) in den dortigen Städten zurückgelassenen Garnison fast rein bewahrter Dialekt eben des Soñyai. Sein alter Dollmetscher selbst, von dem er diese interessanten Sprachproben erhielt, bezeichnete sie als ursprünglich die Sprache der Diriman („la langue des Dirimans" ibid. p. 419 vergl. mit p. 351), die eben nach meinen Untersuchungen die älteste und ursprünglichste Abtheilung der Soñyai sind (Reis. und Entd. IV, S. 429).

¹) Auch diese Taubenzucht ist ein entschieden Egyptisches Produkt, das durch die Soñyai nach Binnen-Afrika eingeführt wurde. Dazu vergl. Reisen V, S. 3.

²) Auch der in der Hausa-Sprache gar nicht wurzelnde Ausdruck layê für „Verwandte" im Allgemeinen ist wol von dem gleichbedeutigen Soñyai-Wort al abgeleitet.

„see, look" . . . . Soṅyai	góun, Hausa	ganí;
„snore" . . . . . . „	hánzuru, Hausa	hánsuri;
„it is broken" . . . . „	u-kairi, Hausa	yá-kare;
„Manatus" . . . . . „	uyu, Hausa	ayú;
„turtle" . . . . . . „	kóṅgura, Hausa	kúṅkuru;
„tame pigeon" . . . . „	tódduber, Hausa	tantúburu[1]);
„grandfather" . . . . „	kága, Hausa	káka[2]);
„younger (brother)" . . „	kaina, Hausa	kané;
„friend" . . . . . . „	abokkoi, Hausa	áboki;
„itch" . . . . „	kaáñan, Hausa	kásun;
„small-pox" . . . . . „	mása-mása, Hausa	musásera;
„hill, mountain" . . . „	tondi, Hausa	tudda;
„reed, stalk" . . . . „	kári, Hausa	kará;
„spoon" . . . . „	sókol, Hausa	tšókali;
„flute" . . . . „	algaita, Hausa	algaita;
„clayhouse" S., „claytown" H.	gar, Hausa	garí;
„hire, rent" . . . . Soṅyai	sáfari, Hausa	sáfari;
„silver" . . . . „	indžorfu, Hausa	ázurfa;
„kolanut" . . . . . . „	guóro, Hausa	góro;
„black cotton-cloth" . . „	turki (gen. túrki-di), Hausa	túrkedi;
„dumb" . . . . „	bebo, Hausa	bébe;
„poor, client" . . . . „	talkan, Hausa	talakka.

Thus we see, that the Soṅyai glossary contains exceedingly few cases of identity or coincidence with the neighbouring languages, with the only exception of the Hausa; and I do not doubt, that with regard to this latter relationship the Hausa people have borrowed from their North-Western neighbours, who had the start before them as well in political development, as in a certain degree of civilization. This result is placed beyond a doubt by verbal forms, such as ákoi, ánona, and especially the negative form abúnina which have no root in, and find no explanation whatever from the character of the Hausa-language, while in Soṅyai they are organically developed according to the laws of that language. The fact also of the most common and important articles of commerce and industry, such as cottoncloth, and especially died cottoncloth, and colanuts having come to the Hausa-people from the Soṅyai, and in consequence also various other terms having been imported to the former from the same quarter is in perfect harmony with the whole history of civilization of Negroland. I thus take leave of the Soṅyai, hoping that time may bring as well new linguistical materials as some further information with regard to the more ancient seats of this tribe which is of paramount importance for understanding the whole development of this cluster of races and languages; and I only add the remark, that, as I have already indicated elsewhere, the Arama of Raffenel (nouveau voyage dans le pays des Nègres II, p. 403 ff.) is nothing but a dialect of the Soṅyai as spoken by the Ruma, the garrison left by the conqueror Múlái Hámed el Dhéhebi in the conquered kingdom of Soṅyai (Tr. and Disc. vol. IV, p. 431 and p. 624).

---

[1]) Also the breed of pigeons was a branch of industry introduced into the Soṅyai country from Egypt; compare with this linguistical fact what I have said in my Narrative vol. IV, p. 443.

[2]) Also the Hausa-term iayé meaning „relatives", „kindred" in general, and which has no root in that idiom whatever has probably been borrowed from the Soṅyai, where ai indicates every degree of kindred and relationship.

Neuntes Kapitel.

Die Lógonē-Sprache: kélakū na Lógonē.

Ich gehe nun zur Analyse der Lógone-Sprache über, der Sprache des kleinen, zwischen den beiden Armen des Shari gelegenen Ländchens, die ich bei den kurzen Vokabularien in Bezug auf einige andere Zweige der Mása-Gruppe noch weiter berücksichtigen muss. Hier will ich vorläufig nur auf dasjenige, was ich über diese Frage und über das alte Reich Kótoko in meinem Reisebericht Th. III, S. 216 gesagt habe, hinweisen. In dieser Vokabularien-Sammlung würde ich die Lógonē-Sprache gleich neben dem Hausa gruppirt haben, wenn es mir nicht erwünscht gewesen wäre, dem letzteren erst das Fulfúlde folgen zu lassen, da das letztere in dem Dialekte von Sókoto so viele Ausdrücke vom ersteren geborgt hat, und da liess ich denn vom historisch-geographischen Standpunkt dem Fulfúlde wiederum das Sonyai folgen, weil das geographische Gebiet dieser beiden Sprachen so gänzlich durch und über einander geschoben ist. Hier in unserer analytischen Betrachtung aber müssen wir das Lógonē dem Hausa mehr annähern, weil diese beiden Sprachen einige viel nähere Berührungspunkte haben, als das Sonyai und Hausa, und von so intimer Art, dass es deutlich einleuchtet, dass die beiden Völkerstämme einst nahe bei einander angesessen gewesen sein mussten oder wenigstens engsten geistigen Verkehr unter einander hatten. Und nun ist es überaus interessant, dass wir auch einige Beweise einer nahen Berührung zwischen der Lógone- und Galla-Sprache finden und zwar selbst in solchen Fällen, wo das letztere nicht mehr mit dem Hausa übereinstimmt.

Dieses aus meiner Wörtersammlung sich ergebende verwandtschaftliche Verhältniss zwischen dem Lógonē und Hausa ist um so bedeutender, da ich bei dem Niederschreiben des Ersteren nicht die Hausa-Sprache als Vermittlerin benutzte, sondern da, wie oben angeführt (S. XIV), das Kanúri in diesem Falle mein ausschliessliches Verkehrsmittel bildete, während das Hausa meinen Lehrern ganz unbekannt war. So haben wir denn Aussicht, auch wieder aus dieser Quelle viel neue und werthvolle Belehrung in Betreff der historischen Entwickelung der verschiedenen Sprachgruppen dieser Landschaften Inner-Afrika's zu schöpfen.

In Bezug auf dieser Sprache eigenthümliche Punkte der Rechtschreibung will ich nur andeuten, dass sie ausgedehnten Gebrauch macht von ð, χ, ɣ und θ und schwer auszusprechende Worte in Menge hat, wie z. B. pχum, sχrd, χsn. Auch in ihr gehen r und l ganz gewöhnlich in einander über, wie denn roáde und lóde beides regelrechte Formen für „Erde" sind.

1) Wenn ich nun zuerst das Fürwort betrachte, so muss ich hier meine Überzeugung dahin abgeben, dass die von mir im Vokabular S. 3 gegebenen Formen des persönlichen Fürwortes, nämlich

	Singular.	Plural.
1ste Person	indo	mé;
2te „	kan	wūni;
	kin	oué;
3te „	ni	lē; lē-li,

nicht insgesammt die ursprünglichen Formen des Fürwortes sind, indem nur die Formen für die 3te Person Sing. ni und die 1ste und 3te Person Plur. mé und le sich den ursprünglichen Formen nähern, die übrigen dagegen nur durch eine Verschmelzung mit den verbalen Formen veranlasst sind, indem die ursprüngliche Form der ersten Person, eben wie das im Hausa wahrscheinlich ist, der einfache Vokal u war, die der zweiten Sing. ka und die der zweiten Plur. ku. Ausser im Hausa ist auch in den Kafir-Sprachen ka Zeichen der zweiten Person Sing. und als Suffix k auch im alten Egyptischen, Bunsen V, S. 87. Über die vielmehr verbale Form indo in's Besondere werde ich noch Einiges beibringen, wenn ich vom Zeitwort spreche.

Chapter the ninth.

The Lógonē-language: kélakū na Lógonē.

I now proceed to treat of the idiom of the small and narrow province of Lógonē, situated between the two branches of the Shāri, which I shall have to consider once more in its connection with other branches of the Māsa-group. Here I will only refer the reader to what I have said in my Narrative vol. III, p. 303 in this respect, and with regard to the ancient kingdom of Kótoko. In this collection of vocabularies I should have arranged the Lógonē-idiom in the column next to the Hausa, if I had not preferred placing side by side with the latter language the Fūl, as spoken in Sókoto, on account of the many terms borrowed by the latter from the former; which arrangement once decided upon I thought proper to place the Sonyai next to the Fūl, a great portion of the territory of these two languages, geographically speaking, being one and the same. For, on the other hand, there cannot be the slightest doubt, that there are many points of contact of the most intimate character between the Hausa- and the Lógonē-language, and of such a nature, that they evidently prove, that there must have been a time when both tribes, to say the least, were settled close together, or had the most intimate mental intercourse amongst each other; and, what is highly interesting, we find also proofs of a close contact between the Lógone- and the Galla-language, the relationship of which latter idiom with the Hausa has long been remarked upon, and even in such cases where the Galla does not now harmonize with the Hausa.

And this relationship between the Lógone- and the Hausa-language, as it appears from my vocabulary, is the more important as, for writing it down, I did not make use at all of the latter language, but, as I have stated before p. XV, Kanūri formed my only means of interpretation in this case. Thus, therefore, we have full reason to hope, that in the course of time we may derive much valuable and new information with regard to the historical development of the various linguistic clusters of those Regions of Inner Africa, even from this source which at first sight looks so poor and scanty.

As for matters of orthography peculiar to the Lógoné, I have only to point out, that it makes a most extensive use of γ, δ, θ and χ, forming through the collision of these consonants with other ones words very difficult to be pronounced; besides, r and l are frequently interchanged, almost as frequently as is the case in Hausa, as, for instance, roāde as well as lōde are both correct forms for „earth". The adding of an n before k, γ, θ, and of m, before b and w, is very frequent.

1) Now, when considering first the pronoun, I must state my opinion, that the forms of the personal pronoun, such as given in my vocabulary, as

	singular.	plural.
1st person	indo	mθ;
2nd „	kan	wθni;
	kin	onθ;
3rd „	ni	tē; / tθ-ti,

do not all of them represent the original forms, but that several of these have been produced by a combination with the relative verbal forms, only ui, mθ, and tθ approaching somehow the original forms, while the original form of the 1st person sing. was probably the simple vowel u, that of the second person sing. ka like the corresponding Hausa-form (in the Kafir-languages also k is the characteristic sign of the 2nd person sing., while it is the sign of the suffix also in the ancient Egyptian, Bunsen V, p. 87), the form of the 2nd person plur. being wu, or rather ku. Of the form indo I shall say something more, when treating of the verb.

Was ich hier aufstelle, ist nicht eine blosse Vermuthung, sondern ergibt sich mit Sicherheit, wenn wir die Formen des possessiven Fürwortes (Vokab. S. 5) vergleichen:

	Singular.	Plural.
1ste Person	na-ĩ	na-mũ;
2te „	na-kó	na-kũ, na-kún;
3te „	na-ni	na-tén.

In einigen dieser Formen scheint der Vokallaut u nicht ursprünglich zu sein; die ursprüngliche Form der 2ten Person Sing. ist wol na-ka. Für die eigentliche Form der ersten Person des persönlichen Fürworts ist es interessant, dass ich mehrere Beispiele habe, wo sie ausschliesslich durch das einfache u vertreten wird, z. B. u wā ku, „ich gebe Dir"; obgleich ich gewöhnlich wu, ja, je nach dem nachfolgenden Vokallaut wa und wo gehört habe.

Diese Bemerkungen finden weitere Bestätigung in den angehängten Formen des Fürwortes. Da haben wir als Formen des Accusativ und Dativ der ersten Person Sing. an und in:

„gib mir", wā an; „du liebst mich", kan ke-gém in.

Als Accusativ und Dativ der 1sten Person Plur. mū, mō:

„gib uns", wā mū; „ihr liebt uns", wū-ni ne-gám mū.

Daneben jedoch habe ich auch eine Form nin, nen oder nun, wie die Beispiele zeigen wā nin, „gib uns"; wū-ni na-θā nen, „ihr schlagt uns" — und tō ya-θō nen, „sie schlagen uns".

Als Accusativ und Dativ der 2ten Person Sing. habe ich ku:

„ich gebe dir", u wā ku; „er liebt dich", ni a-gím ka.

Accusativ und Dativ der 2ten Person Plur. kun:

„ich gebe euch" (Plur.), „u wā kun; „wir helfen euch", mō mí-sumíd go kun.

Accusativ und Dativ der 3ten Person Sing. ni:

„gib ihm", wā ni; „ich liebe ihn", indo wu-gám̧ ni; „ich schlage ihn", indo wu-θā ni.

Accusativ und Dativ der 3ten Person Plur. tan, in einigen Fällen tan-na:

„gib ihnen", wā tan; „wir lieben sie", mō-me me-gím tan; „wir schlagen sie", mō ma-θā tan; „ich verfolge sie", wá-γala (wú-γala) tan-na.

Was nun den Genitiv anbetrifft, so fällt der, wie in diesen Sprachen gewöhnlich, zusammen mit dem Pronomen Possessivum, und von der vollen Form des letzteren mit Hülfe des Berberischen n haben wir schon auf der vorhergehenden Seite ein Beispiel gesehen; vergleiche hierzu, was ich S. XLVI über dasselbe Verhältniss in der Kanúri-Sprache gesagt habe.

Neben dem S. 3 des Vokabular's gegebenen Beispiel indo) húmwusi na-ĩ, „ich Geist von mir", d. h. „ich selbst", gebe ich hier nun noch ein anderes Beispiel von dieser Form:

mein	Kameel — kurgúmma	na-ĩ . .	unser	Kameel — kurgúmma	na-mũ,
dein		na-kó .	euer		na-kún,
sein		na-ni . .	ihr		na-tén, na-tén.

Dies besitzende Fürwort erleidet offenbar in der Mehrheit keine Veränderung, ausgenommen in einigen besonderen Fällen durch den Einfluss der verbalen Form, wenn es der letzteren vorangeht, wie z. B.

meine	Kameele haben sich verlaufen	kurgúmme	ya-ĩ	yévtia.
deine			ya-kó . . .	
seine			ya-ni	
unsere			ya-mũ . . .	
eure			ya-kún . . .	
ihre			ya-tén . . .	

Dass die Umwandelung der pronominalen Form in dieser Phrase durch Übergang des n in y nur eine ganz äusserliche und euphonistische ist, veranlasst durch das y der folgenden

This is not a mere conjecture, but appears to be a well established fact, if we compare the forms of the possessive pronoun, vocab. p. 5

	singular.		plural.
1st	person na-ā	. . . .	na-mā;
2nd	„ na-ké	. . . .	na-kā, na-kān;
3rd	„ na-ní	. . . .	na-tán.

Even in my list of verbs the real form of the first person of the pronoun generally appears behind the verbal form indo, and in a few cases it is met even alone, as, for instance, in a wā ku, „I give you", although, in general, I have the form wu, and even wa and wo according to the character of the succeeding vowel. As for the form of the 2nd person sing., it may originally have been na-ka.

These remarks find further confirmation through the suffix forms of the pronoun.

Accusative and dative case of 1st person sing. an and in:

„give me", wā an; „thou likest me", kan ko-góm in.

Accusative and dative case of 1st person plur. mū, mō:

„give us", wā mā; „you like us", wū-ni no-gám mō.

Besides this mū, or mō, however, I have also instances of the forms non, nin or nun, wā nin. „give us", wū-ni na-ßā nen, „you beat us", and tō ya-ßō nen, „they beat us".

Accusative and dative case of 2nd person sing. ku:

„I give thee", u wā ku; „he likes thee", nī a-gím ku.

Accusative and dative case of 2nd person plur. kun:

„I give you (plur.), u wā kun; „we assist you", mō mí-sumíd go kun.

Accusative and dative case of 3rd person sing. ni:

„give him", wā ni; „I like him", indo wu-gám ni; „I beat him", indo wu-ßā ni.

Accusative and dative case of 3rd person plur. tan, in some cases tan-na:

„give them", wā tan; „we like them", mō-mo me-gím tan; „we beat them", mō ma-ßā tan; „I pursue them", wá-yala (wú-yala) tan-na.

As for the genitive case, it is identical with the possessive pronoun, and of the full form of the latter by means of the Berber-element n or na I have given a paradigm on the preceding page; the reader may compare what I have said p. XLVII with regard to the same case in the Kanúri-language.

Besides the instance indo) húmwusi na-ā etc. adduced p. 3 „I, spirit of me" i. q. „I myself", I here give another paradigm of this form of the pronoun

my	camel — kurgúmma	na-ā . . .	our	camel — kurgúmma	na-mā,
thy		na-ké . .	your		na-kān,
his		na-ní . . .	their		na-tán, na-tán.

These pronominal forms do not appear to be changed in the plural number, except in some cases, through the influence of the verbal form, when the latter follows, as, for instance

my	camels have strayed . . .	kurgúmma	ya-ā	yávtia.
thy			ya-kó . . .	
his			ya-ní . . .	
our			ya-mū . . .	
your			ya-kún . . .	
their			ya-tán . . .	

This change of the n of the pronominal form into y has evidently not been produced but by the y of the following yávtia, the plural of dúvtia, as is shown by other instances,

as *

vorleren Form, jávtia Plural von dávtia, erkennen wir aus anderen Beispielen, wo die pronominale Form im Plural nicht die geringste Veränderung erleidet, wie z. B. ind(o) u-yol básakwă aa-ă. „ich verkaufe meine Pferde", Plur. von ind(o) u-yol byakwán aa-ă.

Dass jedoch das a oder aa, mit dessen Hülfe diese Pronominalform gebildet wird, nur das die Beziehung oder den Besitz anzeigende Zeichen ist, wird klar bewiesen durch den für den Ausdruck „ich habe", „du hast" üblichen Terminus nág-a-ă, núg-a-hé u. s. w. S. 64, wo keine weitere Anzeige eines solchen Verhältnisses nöthig ist, da nag die besitzende Beziehung, den „Besitz" anzeigt und da die ursprüngliche Bedeutung von nág-a-a ist „mein Besitz, meine Sache". Aber auch sonst habe ich einige Beispiele dieser einfacheren Form des possessiven Fürwortes, wie z. B. nif-a-ă, nif-a-af, „meine, seine Seele"; lem(a) a-mé, „unsere Zeit"; imtsăl(e) a-tán, „ihr Haar". In manchen Fällen, besonders nach einem, das vorausgehende Substantiv abschliessenden n, bin ich über die Form unsicher gewesen.

Ich beschliesse diese kurze Analyse des persönlichen und besitzenden Fürwortes mit der Bemerkung, dass ein Jeder sich von der fast vollkommenen Einerleiheit der entsprechenden Formen im Lógoné und Hausa überzeugen kann, wenn er die beiden betreffenden Kolumnen auf S. 5 des Vokabular's mit einander vergleicht.

Von den anderen Formen des Fürwortes will ich hier nicht sprechen und will nur die gewöhnliche suffixe Form des unbestimmten Pronomens „es", gi, ge oder ńgo anführen, wie z. B. „hebe es empor", sí gi; „leihe es mir", inta an ge.

2. Ich will jetzt einige Bemerkungen zu den Zahlwörtern machen. Die Zählungsweise im Lógoné ist entschieden auf einem quinalen Prinzip begründet und „fünf" war die ursprünglich höchste Zahl, indem sési wahrscheinlich eine dieser Beziehung entsprechende Bedeutung hat, „Figur" oder so etwas (vergl. uχse, „Inneres"; óχ-sesl, „Schatten"). Der Ausdruck für „sechs", vondχkir ist einfach gebildet aus „zweimal drei"; der für „acht" aus „zweimal vier", während man für „sieben" und „neun" besondere Ausdrücke bildete. Was die Ausdrücke für „zehn" und „zwanzig" betrifft, so müssen sie offenbar auf ein anderes Prinzip zurückgeführt werden, aber es scheint nicht, dass der letztere von ersterem abgeleitet ist, so dass wir ein unabhängiges Zählungssystem nach „zwanzig" haben*). So bildet denn auch thám noch heut zu Tage die höchste Zahl in den Beziehungen des täglichen Lebens, gerade wie dasselbe der Fall im Hausa ist mit dem Ausdruck hauya, indem man statt „vierzig" sagt „zwei Zwanziger", statt „fünfzig" „zwei Zwanziger und zehn" und so weiter, wie wir das, ausser im Hausa, auch in anderen Sprachen haben. Das Lógoné hat aber keinen nationalen Ausdruck für „hundert", sondern eben nur das Arabische mia. Über Ordinalformen s. S. CCXIV, f.

3. Ich gehe jetzt zum Zeitwort über.

Die verbalen Formen im Lógoné sind mannichfach verschiedener Art, die ich nur durch einzelne Beispiele erklären kann, da es meiner Ansicht gemäss unrichtig sein würde, schon von diesem Wenigen bestimmte, allgemein gültige Regeln abzuleiten.

a) Ich muss zuerst ein Wort in Bezug auf die volle Form der ersten Person Sing. der gegenwärtigen oder unbestimmten Zeit sagen. Ich bin nämlich, wie schon oben S. CXCVIII angedeutet, der Ansicht, dass das S. 5 des Vokabular's aufgeführte indo als Form der ersten Person des persönlichen Fürwortes nur eine in Verbindung mit dem Zeitwort geschaffene und deshalb vielmehr als verbal anzusehende Form ist. Allerdings findet sich diese Form im Allgemeinen eben nur in Verbindung mit der ersten Person des Zeitwortes und entspricht also genau der Form mé-dö in der Fül-Sprache, doch habe ich ein etwas zweifelhaftes Beispiel, wo eben dieses do auch in Verbindung mit der zweiten Person des Zeitwortes erscheint.

*) Was den Ausdruck thám anbetrifft, so habe ich in der demselben angefügten Note S. 12, N. 4 einen wunderbaren Irrthum begangen, indem ich thám von χhán, „zehn" und tekó ableitete, da ich den Augenblick stillschweigend annahm, dass tekó, „zwei" bedeute, während es in Wirklichkeit „eins" bedeutet.

where the pronominal form does not undergo the slightest change, such as ind(o) u-ẏol bázakwā aa-ā, „I sell my horses", the plural form of ind(o) u-yol byskwán aa-ā, „I sell my horse".

That the a or aa, however, which is used for forming this pronoun, is simply the sign indicating the relation or possession, is most clearly demonstrated by the term for „I have", „thou hast" etc. nág-a-ā, nág-a-kú etc. p. 64, no further indication of such a relation being necessary in this case, as nag itself means „possession", the proper meaning of nág-a-ā being „my possession, my property". But, besides this, I have also a few other instances of this simple form of the possessive pronoun, as, for instance, níf-a-ā, níf-a-ni, „my, his soul"; lém(a) a-mé, „our tent"; imtsāl(e) a-téa, „their hair". In other cases, where the preceding substantive is terminating in n, I was rather uncertain as for the form of the pronoun.

I conclude this analysis of the personal, and possessive pronoun in Lógone with the remark, that any body by simply comparing these forms with the corresponding ones in the Hausa-language in the relative columns vocab. p. 5, may convince himself, that they are almost identical.

Of the of the demonstrative pronoun I shall not speak here; I merely want to indicate the common suffix for „it", gi, ge or ñge, as, for instance, „raise it", sí gi; „lend it me", inte an ge.

2. I now proceed to say a word of the numerals.

The system of counting in Lógone originally appears to have been quinal, and „five" to have been the highest original number, the term sēsi probably conveying a meaning corresponding to this notion, such as „figure" (dχ-sosi, „son, child of figure", i. q. „shadow"); the term vondχhir for „six" was simply formed from „twice three", „eight" from „twice four", while for 7 and 9 peculiar terms were formed; as for χkán, „ten", and tkám, „twenty", they are evidently to be reduced to some other notion of unity, but it does not seem, that the latter has been derived from the former [*]. Thus, tkám still at the present day forms the highest number in transactions of daily life, just as is the case in Hausa with the term hauya, the people saying „two twenties" instead of „forty", „two twenties and ten" instead of „fifty", and so on, just as is the case in Hausa, and in many other languages. Nay, the Lógone-idiom, at least in its present state of development, has no proper term for „hundred", and uses instead the Arabic term mia. As for some terms of ordinals see what I shall say further on p. CCXV, f.

3. I now proceed to speak of the verb.

The verbal forms in Lógone, as far as I have written them down, present a considerable variety, which I can only illustrate by giving instances of single cases, as they are too scanty according to my opinion to deduce from them certain grammatical rules.

a) I first must say a word with regard to the full form of the 1st person sing. of the present tense, having already stated my opinion, that the form indo of the 1st person sing. of the personal pronoun has only been caused in connection with the active form of the verb, and, although this pronominal form with do, in general, is not but found in the 1st person of the present tense, and thus corresponds exactly with the form mó-dō in the Fūl-language, yet I have also one instance of this same do appearing in connection with the second person in the remarkable, although not quite unobjectionable phrase ké-na wa-de gun, „thou doest assist me" from the verb gun, „assist". That this form indo serves to indicate the

[*] As for tkám, in a foot-note appended to that term in my vocabulary p. 13, note 8 I have committed a most awkward mistake, deriving tkám from χkan, „ten" and tekā, the latter meaning „one", and not „two", as I supposed at the time.

nämlich kó-na wa-de gun, „du hilfst mir", vom Zeitwort gun, „helfen". Was das indo eigentlich bedeutet, scheint die S. CCIV, c) anzuführende Phrase indo ind(o) ăli auszudeuten. Vielleicht einem Einflusse des Kanúri ist zuzuschreiben, wenn den Pronominalformen bisweilen noch ein ma angefügt wird, indo-ma, nĭ-ma; aber ich finde das ma selbst dem negativen să angehängt in der Phrase mĭ mu-ñgo nĭ să mă, „wir sehen ihn nicht".

b) Als Beispiel regelmässiger Präsensbildung gebe ich indo n-súm, kó-na ka-súm, nĭ na-súm, mĭ ma-súm, wū-ni na-súm, tó-ti a-súm, „ich esse" u. s. w., dann will ich von einem anderen Zeitwort ein Paradigma der gegenwärtigen Zeit geben, als ein Beispiel, wie in gewissen Fällen der Vokal der Verbalwurzel selbst umgewandelt wird in Gemässheit und Übereinstimmung mit dem Charakter des Fürwortes.

	Singular.	Plural.
1ste Prs.	indo wo-gím nĭ, „ich liebe ihn",	mō-mi me-gím tan, „wir lieben sie",
2te „	kan ko-gém lu, „du liebst mich",	wū-ui ne-gám mo, „ihr liebt uns",
3te „	nĭ a-gím ku, „er liebt dich",	to-ti yo-gím kun, „sie lieben euch".

Hierauf lasse ich nun ein Paradigma der gegenwärtigen Zeit eines anderen Zeitwortes „ich sehe (ihn)" folgen, sowol positive als negative Form, zusammen mit einer Art von Conditional:

Gegenwärtige Zeit, affirmativ.

	Singular.	Plural.
1ste Person	indo wó-ñgo nĭ.	mō-mi mú-ñgo nĭ,
2te „	kó-na kó-ñgo nĭ	wū-ni nú-ñgo nĭ,
3te „	nĭ-n(a) á-ñgo nĭ	tó-ti á-ñgo nĭ.

Gegenwärtige Zeit, negativ.

	Singular.	Plural.
1ste Person	indo wó-ñgo nĭ să . . .	mō-mi mú-ñgo nĭ să,
2te „	kó-na kó-ñgo nĭ să . . .	wū-ni nú-ñgo nĭ să,
3te „	nĭ-n(a) á-ñgo nĭ să	tó-ti á-ñgo nĭ să.

Conditional.

	Singular.	Plural.
1ste Person	indo wó-ñgo nĭ ya . . .	mō-mi mú-ñgo nĭ ya,
2te „	kó-na kó-ñgo nĭ ya . . .	wū-ni nú-ñgo nĭ ya,
3te „	nĭ-n(a) á-ñgo nĭ ya . . .	tó-ti yá-ñgo nĭ ya.

Gerade wie wir hier in der 3ten Person Plur. sehen, so habe ich auch einige Beispiele, dass auch in der 3ten Person Sing., wenn die einfache pronominale Form nĭ gebraucht wird, ein y, als Auslaut des vorhergehenden i, der verbalen Wurzel vorgesetzt wird, wie z. B. von wa-dō, „ich bringe", 3te Person Sing. nĭ ya-dō; von wú-mala, „ich lasse", 3te P. S. nĭ yú-mala. Dass die reine pronominale Form von der verbalen getrennt werden kann, sehen wir aus dem Beispiel mĭ kylli mú-mberiă, „wir Alle sind ermüdet". Als ein anderes Beispiel einer conditionellen Form führe ich hier an wá-ŋa ya, „wenn, im Falle ich aufbräche", ganz entsprechend der Kanúri-Form tĭl-nĭski-a, vom Zeitwort indo wa-ŋá, „ich breche auf". Jedoch scheint diese Form in manchen Fällen mit der der Vergangenheit zusammenzufallen und hat in anderen mehr die Bedeutung eines Particips, weshalb ich weiterhin noch einmal darauf zurückkommen muss. Auch habe ich neben dieser Form ya Beispiele anderer Formen des Conditional des Präsens mit na, wie wa-yán-na, „wenn ich thäte"; ma-yán-na, „wenn wir thäten", und selbst mit einem dem ya angehängten ka, wie ich in der 2ten und 3ten Pers. von eben jener Form wa-ŋa-ya habe ka-ŋá-ya-ka, a-ŋá-ya-ka.

b) Hier will ich nun gleich die Besprechung des Futurums anreihen. Ich war nämlich lange unsicher, ob ein, in vielen Verbalformen entweder die Pronominalform umwandelndes, oder zwischen ihr und der Verbalwurzel eingeschobenes, o nicht bloss eine nur äusserliche Einwirkung des nachfolgenden negativen să sei; zuerst beachtete ich es auch nur bei negativen Formen, wie z. B. indo so-yán să von indo wo-yá oder wo-yán, „ich thue"; indo

presence of the action, the phrase indo ind(o) ăli, „I bring present, in my presence" to be mentioned p. CCV, c) seems to indicate, while the adding of the termination ma to this form (indo-ma, ni-ma) may be due to an influence exercised by the Kandri, although in one instance I have even found it added to the negative verbal forms by means of sa, mi mu-ńgo ni sẵ ma, „we do not see him".

b) As an instance of a regular formation of the present tense I give indo u-súm, kó-na ka-súm, ni na-zúm, mi ma-zúm, wū-ni na-súm, tō-ti a-zúm, „I eat, thou eatest", and so on; further, as an instance, how the vowel of the verbal root itself is changed according to, and in harmony with, the character of the pronoun I give the following instance.

	singular.	plural.
1st pers.	indo wo-gém ni, „I like him" .	mō-mi me-gím tan, „we do like them",
2nd „	kan ke-gém in, „thou dost like me"	wū-ni ne-gám mō, „you do like us",
3rd „	ni a-gím ku, „he does like thee"	tō-ti ye-gím kun, „they do like you".

I now give a complete paradigm of the present tense of another verb „I see (him)", together with the negative form, and that of a kind of conditional mood:

Present tense, affirmative form.

	singular.	plural.
1st person	indo wó-ńge ni	mō-mi mú-ńge ni,
2nd „	kó-na kó-ńge ni	wū-ni nú-ńge ni,
3rd „	ni-n(a) á-ńge ni	tō-ti ú-ńge ni.

Present tense, negative form.

1st person	indo wó-ńge ni sa . . .	mō-mi mú-ńge ni sẵ.
2nd „	kó-na kó-ńge ni sa . . .	wū-ni nú-ńge ni sẵ.
3rd „	ni-n(a) á-ńge ni sa . . .	tō-ti ú-ńge ni sẵ.

Conditional mood.

1st person	indo wó-ńge ni ya	mō-mi má-ńge ni ya.
2nd „	ká-na kó-ńge ni ya . . .	wū-ni nú-ńge ni ya.
3rd „	ni-n(a) á-ńge ni ya . . .	tō-ti yá-ńge ni ya.

Just, as we see here in the 3rd person plur., thus likewise in the 3rd person sing., if the simple form ni is used, the preceding i frequently causes the prefixing of a y before the verbal root, as, for instance from wa-dō, „I bring", I have in the 3rd person sing. ni ya-dō, from wú-mala, „I let, dismiss", ni yú-mala. The pronoun may be separated from the verbal form, as in mō kytti má-mberiă, „all of us are tired". As another instance of the conditional form in ya I here adduce wá-θa-ya, „if I started" corresponding entirely with the Kandri-form tĭl-níaki-a, from the verb indo wu-θá, „I start". But, no doubt, this form terminating in ya in some cases seems to represent the past tense, while in others it appears to convey rather the notion of a participle, which is the reason, why I have to return to it once more further on. Moreover, besides this conditional form in ya I have instances of another one in na, such as wa-yán-na, „if I did"; ma-yán-na, „if we did", and so on, and even of ka being added to the ya, as of the 2nd and 3rd person of the very form wa-θa-ya I have the forms ka-θá-ya-ka, a-θá-ya-ka.

b) Here I now subjoin the future tense. With regard to this tense I was long doubtful, whether an s appearing in many verbal forms, and either changing the pronoun itself, or inserted between it and the verbal root, was not rather produced through the influence of the following negative sẵ, as indeed I first observed it only in connection with negative forms, as, for instance indo so-yán sẵ from indo wo-yá or wo-yán, „I do"; indo su-gár-sẵ from indo wu-gár, „I go"; sí-mala-sẵ from wú-mala, „I show". But

su-gúr sa von indo wu-gúr, „ich gehe"; sí-mala sa von wú-maln, „ich zeige". Bald aber bemerkte ich, dass, während einerseits einige negative Formen solche Umwandelung nicht aufwiesen, ein solches s andrerseits auch in positiven Formen erscheine, wie z. B. ni-na se-gír statt ni-na ne-gír, „er geht", und mehrere Mal in der 3ten Person Plur. tē se-gír; so habe ich es auch in der Phrase se gi[1]) am sé von wu-sé am, „ich trinke Wasser". Dass in jenen Negativformen eine doppelte Negation enthalten sein kann, zeigt mē sā me-gír-sa, „wir nicht, wir gingen nicht"; hill(e) a-sa-m(a) u-gír-sā, „Person keine ging nicht", d. h. „Niemand ging". Die negative Form sā ist eben eine selbstständige Partikel, wie folgendes Beispiel zeigt, mu-ñgo zįbbelo sā fo, mu-ñgo rō sā fo, „wir sehen Weg nicht entweder, wir sehen Stadt nicht noch", d. h. „wir sehen weder Weg noch Stadt". Trotz dieses redundirenden s bei negativen Formen überzeugte ich mich aber, dass das s oder se in positiven Formen eine Art von Futurum bezeichnet, wofür folgende beide Phrasen massgebend schienen, se me-θā θintá, „wann werden wir aufbrechen"?, me-θā, „wir brechen auf", θintá, „wann"; wolla se me-θā amdi wolla se me-θā diāsun, „werden wir heute (amdi) reisen oder werden wir morgen (diāsun) reisen"?.

c) Nach dieser, durch die negative Form mit sā veranlassten, Digression muss ich zuerst Einiges beibringen in Bezug auf eine vollere Form der gegenwärtigen Zeit durch Einschiebung der Sylbe al zwischen dem Fürwort und der verbalen Wurzel, wie z. B. ind(o) al u-gúr, „ich bin gehend", wo zugleich in Folge dieser Form der w-Laut vor der verbalen Wurzel fortgefallen ist (vgl. oben wu-gúr), n-āl á-kulá halgē, „er ist singend", von wú-kulá halgē, „ich singe". So müssen wir auch die Form n-al su (sic) augóñgibā, S. 75, N. 18 auffassen als 3te Pers. Sing. „er ist mir gehorsam, folgsam"; dagegen möchte ich anstatt ka θonālla da, „hörst du"?, Vokab. S. 10 lieber ka-θenā-ni-a da schreiben „hast du es gehört". Von der vollen Form ālo habe ich die folgenden Beispiele, zuerst ein sehr entschiedenes, klares ind(o) ālo wiran, „ich bin schlafend" oder „während ich schlafe", in der Phrase ind(o) alo wiran muoχoi u-sa rā, „ich seiend schlafend, Dieb dringt ein (in das) Haus" (u-sa von wu-sa, „ich gehe ein"). So ist unzweifelhaft auch die Form indo ind(o) āli zu erklären „ich anwesend seiend" d. h. „in meiner Anwesenheit", der Gegensatz von indo-ma ōēn, „ich nicht seiend" d. h. „in meiner Abwesenheit". Ja, ich glaube wir haben den Ausdruck hanno lē-sā S. 31 als eine negative Form derselben Art anzusehn mit der Bedeutung „dieses ist nicht", d. h. „nein, Ihr irrt euch" und mit Hülfe dieses selben ālo haben wir wahrscheinlich die Phrase S. 87 wálone sio zu erklären und anstatt dessen w(n) ālo ne sio zu schreiben. Unzweifelhaft haben wir eben hierher den verbalen Ausdruck nāli, ne-āli, zu rechnen „es ist, es gibt", ebenso wol wie belín, „es mag sein" als eine Art von Conditionel, wie wir deutlich aus der Phrase sehen θinta belin N. 23, die völlig identisch ist mit der Kanúri-Phrase yimbi ṭalē, „wann immer es sein mag", d. h. „beständig, fortwährend".

d) Jetzt müsste ich die Form der Vergangenheit behandeln, aber hier bin ich sehr unsicher. Auch hier habe ich in vielen Fällen ein angehängtes na, wie indo u-yán-na, „ich that"; indo wa-zǵm-na, „ich ass", in anderen Fällen erscheint das Wurzelwort in der Vergangenheit in kürzester, im Vokallaut veränderter Gestalt mit einfacher Pronominalform. So habe ich wa-gír als 1te Person der vergangenen Zeit von wu-gúr und habe als weitere sichere Formen davon 2te Person ka ku-gír, 3te Person ni na-gír, 1ste Person Plur. mē mim-gír. Daran anschliessend will ich hier eine von eben dieser Form abgeleitete Art von Conditionel „wenn ich gegangen wäre" geben, die gebildet wird durch Anhängung von ṭa oder da, indem jedoch in meinem Paradigma die 2te Person Sing. von dieser Regel abweicht, indem sie mit nó gebildet ist, in folgender Weise:

[1]) Wegen der Beschaffenheit und Bedeutung dieses ge bin ich nicht ganz sicher; ganz ähnlich habe ich es, auch in Verbindung mit s, in ni ge dim, „er schmeckt", wo das Objekt sonst nicht ausgedrückt ist und ge also „es" bedeuten kann; auffallender ist hinne ge na-ni, „ist dieses sein", „gehört es ihm"?; hinne, „dies".

I soon observed, that, while some negative forms did not exhibit the very slightest sign of such a change, on the other hand the very same s appeared in certain positive forms, such as, ni-na se-gír instead of ni-na ne-gír, „he does go", and repeated instances of té se-gír in the 3rd person plur. Thus, it appeared also in the phrase se gi*) am sé, 3rd person sing. of wa-sé am, „I drink water". As for the first class of cases, I certainly convinced myself, that the negative form might be represented twice in the same phrase, as I have mö sã mo-gír sã, „we not did not go", and bill(e) a-sí-m(a) a-gír sã, „person none went not" i. q. „no body went", for, sã is an independent negative particle, which may be wholly separated from the verb, as the following instance fully tends to show mu-ñgo züʼbbele sã fo, mu-ñgo rö sã fo, „we see track not either, we see town not either" i. q. „we see neither track nor town". But, as for the class of positive forms, I arrived at the conclusion, that s or se indicates a kind of future, a result about which the two following phrases seemed to leave but little doubt se mo-θã θinté, „when shall we start", mo-θã meaning „we start" and θinté, „when", and wolla se mo-θã amdi wolla se mo-θã diãsun, „are we to start to day (amdi), or are we to start to morrow (diãsun).

c) After this digression caused by the negative form with sã, I must first say a word with regard to a fuller form of the present tense by means of the syllable al, full form ãlo, being inserted between the pronoun and the verbal root, as, for instance, ind(o) al a-gúr, „I am walking", where the w-sound before the verbal form has been lost, n-ãl á-kulé halgé, „he is singing" from wú-kulé halgé. Thus is also to be explained the 3rd person sing. n-ãl au (sic) angóñgibã, „he is following me, is obedient to me", from wa-angóñgibã p. 75, note 18, but as for the form ka-θonálla-da, „dost thou hear", p. 49 I prefer writing ga θonã-al-a da, „hast thou heard it". Of the full form ãlo I have the following instances, first a very decisive one ind(o) ãlo wisan, „I being asleep, while I am sleeping" in the phrase ind(o) ãlo wisan musχoi a-sa rã, „while I am (was) sleeping, the thief entered the house" (a-sa from wa-sa, „I enter"). Thus, we have also the form indo ind(o) ãli, „I being present, in my presence", the opposite of indo-ma lẽa, „in my absence". Nay, I think, we have to look upon the term haune lẽ-sa p. 31, „this is not", „no, you are wrong", as a negative form of this same root, and by means of this ãlo we have probably also to explain the phrase wálone zió contained in the vocab. p. 87, and have to write instead w(a) ãlo ne-zió. To this same verbal form we have undoubtedly to reckon the term nãli (ne-ãli), „there is", as well as belfa, „it may be", the latter being a kind of subjunctive, as is seen from the particle θinta belfa, vocab. p. 23, being verbally identical with the Kanúri yimbi ralẽ, „whenever it may be" i. q. „always, constantly".

d) I now must say a word of the form of the past tense, although, what I can give with some degree of certainty with regard to this form, is rather scanty. Also here in several cases I have na added to the root, as, for instance, indo u-yán-na, „I did"; indo wa-zím-na, „I did eat", while in other cases the form of the root is shortened. Thus, I have wa-gír, „I went", from the present tense indo wa-gúr, and have also the other persons regularly derived from the same form, 2nd person ka ka-gír, 3rd person ni na-gír, 1st person plur. mé mim-gír. To this form of the past tense I will also subjoin a sort of conditional mood „if I had gone", derived from this same form by means of ta, da, from which, however, the form of the 2nd person sing. seems to deviate, being composed with nẽ, thus:

---

*) As for the gi in this instance I am not quite sure; however it may, I think, be the same, as the ge in the two phrases hinne ge na-ni, „is this him"?, and ni-ge-dim, „he tastes" from wa-dim, „I taste".

	Singular.	Plural.
1ste Person	indo wa-gír-ṭa	mi-mo ma-gír-ṭa,
2te „	kä-nu ka-gír-ṭa	wü-ni na-gír-ṭa,
3te „	ni-u(a) a-gír-ṭa	tö-ti a-gír-ṭa.

Dieses zur Bildung des Conditionels der Form der Vergangenheit angehängte ṭa würde also dem derselben Form vorgesetzten tö im Fül entsprechen S. CXXIV, e).

e) Was den Imperativ anbelangt, so scheinen meine Beispiele ausreichend zu zeigen, dass die 2te Person Sing. durch die einfache Verbalwurzel vertreten wird, wie von θu, „gehn", θa wäton, „geh' nieder, steig' ab"; dö, „bringe"; si, „nimm"; bä, wä, „gib"; dukal, „warte". Von wu-gúr, „ich gehe" habe ich als Form des Imperativs gulu S. 85, und das wird durch eine andere Form der bestimmten Zeit, kö-nu gulu, bestätigt.

Von der ersten Person Plur. des Imperativs habe ich zwei Beispiele, nämlich mo-yá, „lasst uns thun, machen", von wo-yá, „ich thue" und mú-wahe, „lasst uns die Hitze passiren", von indo wahö, aber von θa, „aufbrechen" habe ich die unsichere Form θa-né-muå, „lasst uns aufbrechen".

f) Oben S. CCIV, a) habe ich die Form mit der Endung ya als eine Art von Conditionel betrachtet, doch habe ich mehrere Beispiele, wo solche Formen mehr die Bedeutung von Participien zu haben scheinen und man kann sich wol erklären, wie eine solche dauernde Handlung als Folge einer einmalig bedingungsweise gestellten Handlung betrachtet werden kann; so habe ich wágria von wu-gúr, „ich gehe", mit der Participialbedeutung „gehend", und ebenso wu kág-aya, „ich rückkehrend, auf der Rückkehr", von der Wurzel kag, kog. Solche Formen können leicht erklärlicher Weise selbst substantive Bedeutung erhalten, wie z. B. a-son ṣubbel-aya, „der den Weg Wissende, der Führer", wiewol hier das aya dem Substantiv ṣubbel und nicht dem Zeitwort son angehängt ist.

Dagegen betrachte ich als wirklich echte Participialform des Aktivs die auf en ausgehenden Eigenschaftswörter, von denen ich weiterhin zu sprechen habe. Hier will ich von ihnen nur zwei Beispiele erwähnen, welche die Participialform recht klar und bündig darstellen, nämlich bille gem-en θa, „Person hütend das Vieh", d. h. „der Rinderhirte" und bille gurau-en, „Person landbauend", „Landmann".

g) Ich will jetzt einige Bemerkungen in Betreff des Passivs machen, obgleich ich wenig Bestimmtes darüber zu sagen habe, da, wie bei allen diesen Sprachen, so auch bei dem Lógonē dieser Modus sehr wenig entwickelt ist. So kann ich denn mit Sicherheit nur wenige Beispiele eines Participiums Passivi angeben, welche zeigen, dass er gebildet wird, indem man d der Verbalwurzel vorsetzt und die Endung ēa anfügt, wo solche nicht schon in dem Stamme enthalten ist. So habe ich d-äg-ēa, „zerbrochen" von w(a)-äg-a, „ich zerbreche" und d-áp-ēa, „geschnitten" von w(a) áf-ēa, „ich schneide", wo jedoch das d verloren zu gehn scheint, wenn dieses Particip als Eigenschaftswort einem Substantiv beigeordnet wird, wie in bụskwán áp-ēa rúmmia, „Wallach", wörtlich „ein Pferd ausgeschnitten die Hoden"; vergleiche wárrina anniasi á-kaba nakál bụskwán, „nachdem er verwundet worden war, fiel er vom Pferde".

h) Ich will hier noch Einiges über die einheimische Umwandelung der dem Arabischen entborgten Zeitwörter sagen. Dies geschicht im Lógonē auf ähnliche Weise wie im Kanúri, indem man der Arabischen Verbalform oder dem daraus abgeleiteten substantiven Begriff das Hülfszeitwort wo-yá, wo-yán, „ich mache, thue" hinzufügt; z. B. entspricht wo-yán ku gadér, „ich verrathe dich" wörtlich der Kanúri-Phrase uí-ga gadér-niskin, vom Arabischen Zeitwort غدر, „prodidit, perfidus fuit", n. a. غدر, „perfidia"; ebenso wo-yán ku gráffera, „ich verzeihe dir", vom Zeitwort غفر, „condonavit peccatum", n. a. غفر, und ähnlich wo-yán ku dauu, „ich leiste dir Hülfe", S. 76, verglichen Note 17 daselbst.

3. Ich gehe nun zu einer kurzen Betrachtung des Substantivs in der Lógonē-Sprache über.

	singular.		plural.
1st person	indo wa-gír-ṭa	. . . . . .	mi-mo ma-gír-ṭa,
2nd „	ká-na ka-gír-ṭa	. . . . . .	wū-ni na-gír-ṭa,
3rd „	ni-n(e) a-gír-ṭa	. . . . . .	té-ti a-gír-ṭa.

If this ṭa joined to the form of the past tense really represents, as it seems, a kind of conditional mood, it corresponds with the Fūl tō, which I have considered p. CXXV, e).

e) As for the imperative, the instances I have collected seem fully to prove, that the 2nd person sing. is represented by the simple verbal root, as, for instance θa, „go"; θa wāten, „go down" i. q. „dismount"; dō, „bring"; ei, „take"; bā, wā, „give"; dakal, „wait". From wu-gúr, „I go", I have the 2nd person sing. of the imperative gúlū p. 85, and this is confirmed by the corresponding form of the definite tense ké-na gulū.

Of the 1st pers. plur. of the imperative I have two instances, viz mo-yá, „let us make" from wo-yá, „I make, do", and mū-wahō, „let us pass the heat of the day" from indo wahō; but from θa, „go, start" I have the rather doubtful form θu-né-muā, „let us start".

f) On a former occasion, p. CCV, a) I have mentioned the verbal form terminating in ya as a sort of conditional mood, but I have several instances of such forms, where they appear to have rather the meaning and bearing of participles, and it does not seem to be so difficult to explain, how an action being once considered conditionally may be subsequently considered as a continuing and permanent one; thus I have wágria from wu-gúr, „I go" with the participial notion „going", as well as the form wu kág-aya, „I returning, on the return", from the root kag, kog. A very curious instance of this formation appears to be the composite term a-sen-ṣgbbel-aya, „he-knows-track-if (or „whenever")", „guide", where the conditional form has been added to the substantive ṣgbbel, and not to the verb sen.

As for participial forms of the active mood I am of opinion, that we have to reckon to this class the adjective forms terminating in en of which I shall speak further on. Here I will only adduce two instances which seem to exhibit the participial form most clearly, bille gem-ea úa, „person pasturing cattle" i. e. „neat-herd", bille gurnu-ea, „husband-man".

g) I now proceed to make a few observations with regard to the passive voice.

Of the passive voice very little is to be said, as we have already seen, that the languages here treated, in general, have this mood but very little developed. Thus, I can give with certainty only two instances of a participle of the passive voice, which show it to be formed by prefixing d before the root while adding the termination ēa, if such a one does not already exist. Thus, I have d-āg-ēa, „broken" from w(a)-āg-n, „I break", and d-áp-ēa, „cut" from w(a) áf-ēa, „I cut"; but in the latter instance, at least, the d seems to be dropped under certain circumstances, as I have „gelding" expressed by bụskwán áp-ēa rúmmia, verbally „horse cut the testicles". Compare also the phrase wárrina nanisel á-knha nakál bụskwán, „having been wounded he fell from the horse".

h) As for verbal notions borrowed from the Arabic, the Lógonē-idiom exhibits the same feature which we have already observed in Kanúri, namely that these notions have been formed by adding the indigenous auxiliary verb „I make" (wo-yá), to the substantive form of the Arabic term; thus, for instance, I have wa-yáa ku gadér, „I betray thee", verbally identical with the Kanúri ní-ga gadér-nískin, from the Arabic غدر n. a. غَدْر, „prodidit, perfidus fuit, perfidia"; wa-yáa ku gráffera, „I do thee pardon, I pardon thee" from the verb غفر n. a. غَفْر, condonavit peccatum", and in a similar manner we have to explain wa-yáa ku dana p. 77, „I render thee assistance". See note 17.

3. I now proceed to make a few observations with regard to the noun in the Lógonē-language.

a) Da ich die monosyllaben und ursprünglich einfachsten Ausdrücke am Ende dieses Kapitels in alphabetischer Ordnung gebe, will ich hier nur die Bildungsweise der abgeleiteten und zusammengesetzten Ausdrücke berücksichtigen, obgleich das, was ich in dieser Beziehung zu geben im Stande bin, sehr beschränkt ist. Als deutliche Beispiele der Ableitung des Substantivs von einem verbalen Begriff erwähne ich sĕ-gi-ya, „berauschendes Getränk", von sé, sĕ, „trinken"; ſ-pla, „Wunde", von ſla, „schlage, verwunde" und θi-ma, „Zeit zum Schneiden des Korns", von wu-θĕ, „ich schneide Korn"; gi-wel, „das Rasiren", von gi.

b) Als Beispiele von Substantiven, die von einem verbalen Begriff vermittelst des allgemein sächlichen wa abgeleitet und mit mannichfaltiger Endung gebildet sind, erwähne ich das Wort wa-i-sŋ̈m-mi, „was zu essen", d. h. „Nahrung, Lebensmittel", von indo) u-sám oder u-sŋ̈m, „ich esse" und wa-i-sĕ-wel, „was zu trinken", d. h. „Getränk", von wu-sĕ, wu-sé, „ich trinke". Auch werde ich weiterhin noch andere zusammengesetzte Ausdrücke mit wa zu erwähnen haben.

c) Als Beispiele vermittelst der Partikel ne, „was", zusammengesetzter Ausdrücke erwähne ich ne-fü, „was zum Athmen", d. h. „Lunge"; ne-mfaral, „was vom oder zum König", d. h. „Thronbesteigung"; wahrscheinlich ähnliche Bildung ist nĕ-ŝantſn, „Eingeweide".

d) Nun gehe ich zu solchen substantiven Ausdrücken über, die wieder ihrerseits aus zwei anderen Substantiven zusammengesetzt sind. Eine derartige Zusammensetzung wird in der Lógoné-Sprache auf dreifach verschiedene Weise zu Wege gebracht, entweder so, dass α) das Subjekt einfach ohne weitere äussere Verbindung dem Objekt vorgesetzt wird, oder dass sie β) in dieser Ordnung vermittelst der Partikel na mit einander verbunden werden oder endlich dass γ) das Objekt dem Subjekt vorangeht.

α) Beispiele, wie zwei Substantiva auf solche Weise mit einander verbunden werden, dass das Subjekt dem Objekt einfach vorgesetzt wird, sind folgende: inθe-fü, „Feuerzunge", d. h. „Flamme", von inθe, „Zunge" und fü, „Feuer" und in derselben Weise dünal-fü, „Rauch", θinne-fü, „Feuerkohlen"; auch ul-byskwán, „Junges vom Pferd"; skōol-θĕ, „Speisetopf", von skōol, „Topf" und θă, „Speise"; ebenso skōol-éman, „Honigtopf" (éman, „Honig"); skōol-tăba, „Tabakstopf", d. h. „Pfeifenkopf"; beune-rö, „Stadtmauer", von benne, „Mauer" und rö, „Stadt"; túhe-am, „Wasserloch", von tùhe, „Loch" und am, „Wasser"; wa-mfarĕ, „Sache des Königs", d. h. „Tribut", von wa, „Ding" und mfarĕ, „König"; χsé-mii, „Leichengesang", von χsé, „Gesang" und mii, „der Todte". Zu dieser Klasse zusammengesetzter Nomina gehören auch die mit bille, „Mensch, Person" zusammengesetzten Ausdrücke, die ich, weil sie meist adjektivische Bedeutung bekommen, weiter unten betrachten werde.

α, a) Was dagegen die Formen úl-e-máe, „Sohn der Mutter", d. h. „jüngerer Bruder" und ŋ̈χi-e-máe, „Tochter der Mutter", d. h. „jüngere Schwester" betrifft, so scheint der Vokal e vielmehr aus euphonischen Gründen eingeschaltet zu sein, als ein besonderes Bindeglied für sich zu bilden, wie das auch der Fall zu sein scheint mit dem Ausdrucke gendm-e-zauar, „Weib des Ehebruchs", d. h. „die Hure".

β) Beispiele einer Vereinigung zweier Nomina mit Voranstellung des Subjekts und mit Einschiebung eines a oder na zwischen ihm und dem Objekt sind: erstlich der Name der Sprache selbst kélakü na Lógoné, „die Sprache von Lógoné"; ul-a-rai, „Sohn des Königs, Prinz"; θü-a-kólkoldo, „ein Gericht von Reis"; θă na γólimazĕ, „Speise der oder für die Sklaven"; gŭgu-a-Masr, „Taube von oder aus Egypten"; kabo-a-θa, „Hufe des Viehes"; wubán na γóla, „eine Axt der oder für die Hirse" und viele andere mehr.

β, a) Ich habe auch Beispiele solcher Zusammensetzungen, wo al oder el zwischen Subjekt und Objekt eingeschoben ist; da das jedoch gewöhnlich nur solche Fälle berührt, wo das erstere selbst in al oder el ausgeht, so weiss ich nicht, ob es ausschliesslich Arabischem Einfluss zuzuschreiben ist; so habe ich sintel el am, „kleines Gefäss für Wasser"; bel el gi-wel, „Messer zum Rasiren", „Rasirmesser"; kötal al byskwán, „Mähne des Pferdes", aber

a) As for the monosyllabic and original terms, I shall give a list of them at the end of this chapter; here I will only point out the formation of the derivative and composite terms, although, what I am able to give in this respect is very limited. As evident instances of the derivation of the noun from a verbal notion I mention sä-gi-ya, „intoxicating drink" from sö, sä, „drink"; i-pla, „wound" from ila, „beat, wound", and θi-ma, „harvest time, time for cutting the corn" from wu-θö, „I cut corn"; gi-wel, „the shaving" from gi, „shave".

b) As instances of nouns derived from a verbal notion by means of wa, „thing, object", the termination being of varied composition I mention wa-i-zŋ̇m-mi, „what to eat", „food", from indo) u-zám or u-zŋ̇m, „I eat" and wa-i-sä-wel, „what to drink", „beverage" from wa-sä, wu-sö, „I drink". Further on I shall have occasion to mention a few other composite terms by means of wa.

c) As instances of composite terms by means of ne, „what" I mention ne-fū, „a thing for breathing", „lung"; ne-mfaraI, „what of king", „ascent of the throne", „installation", and probably we have to explain on the same principle the term né-šantin, „bowels".

d) I now proceed to give some instances of nouns composed of two other nouns. Such a composition in the Lógonē-language is achieved in three different ways; either α) the subject is simply placed before the object without the use of any outward link, or β) they are joined by means of na, or finally γ) the object precedes the subject.

α) Instances of how two nouns are joined together, the subject simply preceding the object, are the following: inθe-fū, „fire tongue" i. q. „flame", from inθe, „tongue" and fū, „fire", in the same manner being composed the terms dūual-fū, „smoke" and θinne-fū, „firecoals"; ni-byəkwán, „young of horse"; skȫol-θä, „cooking-pot" from skȫol, „pot" and θä, „food", and in the very same manner skȫol-éman, „honey-pot" (éman, „honey"); skȫol-tāba, „tobacco-pot" i. q. „pipe"; benne-rö, „city-wall" from benne, „wall", and rö, „town"; táhe-am, „water-hole" from táhe, „hole", and am, „water"; wa-mfarē, „what of the king" i. q. „tribute" from wa (see above) and mfarē, „king"; χsē-mii, „song of the dead", „funeral song" from χsē, „song" and mii, „the dead", and many more. To this class of composite nouns belong also all the terms composed with billo, „man, person", of which I shall speak lower down, as for the greater part they are used as adjectives.

α, a) As for the composite terms úi-e-más, „son of mother" i. q. „younger brother", and úχi-e-más, „daughter of mother" i. q. „younger sister", the vowel e seems not to be appended to the subject, ui, uχi, but seems rather to be added from mere euphonical reasons, just as is the case with the term gendm-e-zauar, „the woman of adultery", i. q. „the whore".

β) Instances of a combination of two nouns with precedence of the subject, and by inserting n or na between subject and object, are first the name of the language itself, kélakū na Lógonē, „the language of Lógonē"; further, ni-n-rai, „son of king", „Prince"; θä-n-kálkoldo, „a dish of rice"; θä na γólimaaē, „a dish of, or for slaves"; gūgu-n-Masr, „pigeon from Egypt"; kabe-n-θa, „hoof of cattle"; wubúu na vyéla, „an axe of (for cutting) Negro-corn", and many others.

β, a) I have also instances of such a composition, where al or el is inserted between the subject and the object, but generally only in such cases where the former itself terminates in al or el, and therefore not, as it seems, exclusively through the influence of the Arabic; thus, I have sintel el am, „vessel of (or „for") water"; bel el gi-wel, „knife for shaving", „razor"; kötal al byəkwán, „mane of horse", but I have also geuém al idda,

dagegen habe ich auch genóm ai idda, „Frau der gebotenen Wartezeit", d. h. „Wittwe" und sogar unku-n el ásc, „Leib, Rückseite des Fusses". Auffallend wäre auch sintel e ealla, wenn da das l hinter e, wie im Arabischen, durch Einfluss des folgenden s abgeworfen wäre; es könnte aber auch das oben (unter u, a) besprochene euphonische e sein.

β, β) Ich habe auch ein etwas vereinzeltes Beispiel, wo bei Voranstellung des Subjekts das Genitiv-Verhältniss durch ein dem Objekt angehängtes si ausgedrückt ist, nämlich uχso lebú-si, „der Ärmel des Hemdes", von lebú, „Hemd".

γ) Jedoch ganz so sicher durch Beispiele belegt, wie diese Art der Verbindung, wo das Subjekt dem Objekt vorhergeht, ist die andere, wo es dem Objekt nachgestellt wird, wie z. B. gé-kaa, wörtlich „Bett-kopf", d. h. „der Platz an dem oberen Ende des Bettes"; gō-áse, „Bettfuss", d. h. „der Platz am unteren Ende des Bettes"; gonfm-dobi, „Frauen-Leib", d. h. „Gebärmutter" (dies besonders merkwürdig, da ich auch dieselbe Form mit der umgekehrten Bedeutung habe, „eine Frau mit einem Leib", d. h. „schwangere Frau"); genfm-dákifuē, „Frauen-Blut", d. h. „Regel"; vydla-bunhē, wörtlich „(Neger-)Korn-Bündel"; ūlomasē-aχē, „Sklaven-Aufseher".

γ, a) Nun ist es sehr merkwürdig, dass ich einige Beispiele habe, wo selbst bei dieser Weise der Verbindung, wenn das Objekt dem Subjekt vorangeht, dasselbe n, ja selbst die volle Form na zu energischerem Ausdruck der Beziehung benutzt wird, das wir oben bei der umgekehrten Verbindung fanden, wie z. B. kuskú-n tábu, „Huhn von, Junges" statt „das Junge des Huhns", „das Küchlein"; sági-n tábu, „Dolch von, Kleines", d. h. „das Kind des Dolches", „das Messer"; wuhán-na dzellen, „Axt von, Handgriff", d. h. „die Handhabe der Axt".

e) Diese grosse und auffallende Mannichfaltigkeit der Arten der Zusammensetzung von Substantiven, die im Allgemeinen nicht einer und derselben, sondern mehreren Sprachen eigen sind, kann ich mir nur vermöge des Umstandes erklären, dass die Bewohner von Lógonē in enge Berührung mit mehreren verschieden organisirten Stämmen gekommen und von ihnen Sprachformen angenommen haben, wie wir das auch mit anderen Gebieten der Sprache wahrnehmen.

f) Was nun die Ausdrücke betrifft, welche Beschäftigungen und Charaktere von Menschen anzeigen, so werden sie vorzugsweise auf zwiefach verschiedene Weise zusammengesetzt, entweder, indem man den Ausdruck bille, „Person, Mensch" dem anderen Worte, das den bezüglichen Gegenstand anzeigt, voranstellt, oder vermöge des monosyllaben me, mi. Die der ersten Klasse angehörigen Ausdrücke gehören, wie schon angedeutet, der unter a) besprochenen Art der Zusammensetzung an, wie z. B. bille bŋskwán, „die Person vom Pferde", d. h. „der Reiter"; bille gañga, „die Person der Trommel", d. h. „der Trommler"; bille mōn (mógone), „die Person vom Indigo", d. h. „der Färber" und in derselben Weise viele andere, welche man in der betreffenden Abtheilung meines Vokabulars nachsehen mag.

f, a) Einige mit Hülfe von bille zusammengesetzte derartige Ausdrücke enthalten zugleich den verbalen Begriff und gehören deshalb nicht ganz in dieselbe Kategorie, wie z. B. der Ausdruck bill(e) ubú-lebú, „Person vom Nähen der Hemden", d. h. „der Schneider" und andere. Ob auch der den „Jäger" bezeichnende Ausdruck bille gōl ol kille hierher gehört oder vielmehr nach der oben S. VII erwähnten Rubrik, kann ich nicht sagen. bille gem-en θa, „Person weidend das Vieh" habe ich oben (S. CCVIII, f) als Participialform angesehen.

f, β) Als Beispiele von Ausdrücken, die mit me, mi zusammengesetzt sind, erwähne ich zuerst mí-n-rai, „der König", eigentlich „er der König ist", da rai allein schon „König" bedeutet, wie wir z. B. aus dem Ausdruck ui-n-rai sehen, „Königsohn" und aus mehreren anderen. Auch mi-sāti, „Fusssoldat" ist augenscheinlich so gebildet, dass man das mi dem Arabischen Worte sāti vorgesetzt hat, das an und für sich schon dieselbe Bedeutung hatte. Dann gebe ich mí-patkē als ein Beispiel einer Zusammensetzung von mi mit dem sachlichen Objekt, indem patkē allein nicht „Trödeler", sondern „das Trödelgeschäft, den Trödel" be-

„woman of the side" i. q. „widow"; nay, I have even unku-n el ŝao, „back of foot". As for the term sintel e salle, I am rather doubtful, whether we have to look upon the e as the same el, the l being merely thrown off as in Arabic through the influence of the following s, or whether we have to look upon it as a mere euphonical medium of composition, and have to range it accordingly under a, a.

β, β) I have also one rather isolated instance where, the subject preceding, the termination si has been added to the object, viz uχse lobú-si, „the sleeve of the shirt" (lebú).

γ) But, as well established as are these two ways of composition with the subject preceding the object, the third one, where the object precedes the subject, is not less common, as for instance gé-kaa, verbally „bed-head", „the place at the head of the bed"; gé-ŝse, „bed-foot", „the place at the end of the bed"; genim-dehi, „woman-body", i. q. „vulva", this instance being of more than common interest, as I have also the opposite genim-dohi or dohé, „woman of a belly" i. q. „pregnant"; genim-dákifnó, „woman-blood" i. q. „menstruation"; vyóla-bunhé, „corn-bundle", „bushel"; úlomazé-sχé, „slaves-overseer".

γ, a) Now, what is very remarkable, I have some instances of the same n, and even the full form na, which we have just found employed in cases where the subject precedes the object, being inserted between the two nouns in this other case too as, for instance, kusku-n tábu, verbally „the fowl of, young" i. q. „the young of the fowl", „chicken"; sägi-n tábu, „the dagger of, young" i. q. „the young of the dagger", „knife"; wuhán-na daellon, „the axe of, handle" i. q. „the handle of the axe".

e) This great and remarkable variety of ways of composition, which in general are not proper to one and the same language, I can only explain by supposing, that the Lógoné-people have come into close contact with various tribes of different mental organization as represented in their languages, a fact which is confirmed by other peculiarities of this language.

f) As for the terms denoting occupations and characters of man, they are especially composed in two different ways, either by prefixing the term bille, „person" to the term denoting the object, or by means of me, mi. The former terms, as I have already indicated, belong to that class of composition which I have illustrated under a) as, for instance, bille bgskwán, „the person of the horse" i. q. „horseman"; bille gaúga, „the person of the drum" i. q. „the drummer"; bille mén (médgone), „the person of indigo" i. q. „the dyer"; and in the same manner many others are composed, which may be looked after in the corresponding section of my vocabulary.

f, a) As for some terms composed with bille, they contain likewise the verbal notion, and do not, therefore, belong exactly to the same category, as, for instance, the term bill(e) nabá-lebú, „person of sewing the shirt" i. q. „the tailor", and others. Whether the term bille gél el kille, „huntsman" belongs to the same class as the latter I am not quite certain. As for the term bille gem-en ŝa, „person pasturing the cattle", on the contrary, I have explained it above (p. CCIX, f) from another point of view, considering gem-en as a participial form.

f, β) As instances of terms composed with me, mi I mention mí-a-ral, „the king", properly „he) who is king", ral itself meaning „king", as we see from the term ul-n-ral, „son of king" and several others. As, for mi-säti also, it has been evidently formed by prefixing this same mi before the Arabic term säti which by itself means „footsoldier"; mí-patké, „the fripperer", on the contrary, which corresponds exactly to the Kanúri-term fátko-ma, seems to be composed in a different manner, patke alone not meaning fripperer, but „frippery", „lumber". Further, I have at least one instance of this kind of composition by means of

zeichnet und demnach mí-patké ganz wörtlich dem Kundri-Ausdruck fétke-ma entspricht. Ich habe nun aber auch wenigstens ein vereinzeltes Beispiel dieser Art von Zusammensetzung, wo die Partikel ne zwischen me und dem Objekte eingeschoben ist, nämlich me-ne-zauar, „die Hure", ein Synonym des oben angeführten geném-e-zauar. — me-a-rō-ue, „Leute der Stadt (rō), Städter" ist wol unzweifelhaft eine Pluralform einer Zusammensetzung mit demselben me. Wahrscheinlich sind auch andere Ausdrücke, wie z. B. musχei, „Dieb"; masku, „Bogenschütze" vermittelst dieses selben me gebildet. Dieses selbe me oder mi ferner finden wir als einen integrirenden Theil bei der Bildung der Ordinalien, z. B. mí-disχién, „der Neunte"; mi-warínka, „der Zwanzigste", während in anderen Fällen die verbale Form alé, „seiend" hinzugefügt ist, mi-χkún-alé, „wer zehn seiend", d. h. „der Zehnte"; mi-χkun-ká-tekū-ale, „der Eilfte" und so weiter.

Was die andere Art der Bildung der Ordinalien vermittelst mal betrifft, mal-sési-ně, mal-vendχhir-ně, so scheint das vorgesetzte mal substantivisch zu sein und dem mala, „Herr (von)" im Bágrimma zu entsprechen, also „Herr von fünf (seiend?)", d. h. „der Fünfte"; „Herr von sechs (seiend?)", d. h. „der Sechste".

g) Abwandelung der Nomina. Die angeführten Formen der Zusammenreihung zweier Substantiv-Begriffe geben schon Beispiele einer Art von Genitivbildung. Sonst ist von Flexion in der Lógone-Sprache nach dem mir vorliegenden Material wenig zu sagen, und es scheint fast, als wenn dasselbe n, ne, na, was wir zur Bezeichnung des Genitiv-Verhältnisses gefunden haben, in etwas veränderter Form auch benutzt wird, um eine Art Causativ zu bezeichnen, oder das Mittel auszudrücken, wodurch etwas geschieht, wie das S. 97 angeführte Beispiel zeigt wo-ftya ní en mávorám, „ich schlage ihn mit dem Schwerte", wenn en ein umgekehrtes ne ist. Wir haben ein sehr deutliches Beispiel der überaus ungenügenden Weise, ein solches Flexionsverhältniss auszudrücken in der Komposition bille gením, „eine Person mit einer Frau", d. h. „ein verheiratheter Mann", ganz entsprechend dem schon früher angeführten Beispiel gením dehé, „eine Frau mit einem Leib", d. h. „eine schwangere Frau".

h) Zur Unterscheidung des Geschlechts wird denjenigen Substantiven, die Individuen weiblichen Geschlechts bezeichnen, seien es menschliche Wesen oder Thiere, der Ausdruck für „Weib", gením, genóm, ganám beigegeben, und zwar geschieht diess so, dass letzterer Ausdruck dem zu unterscheidenden Begriffe nach Belieben vor- oder nachgesetzt wird, wobei jedoch in beiden Fällen fast beständig das schon oben S. CCX, β, a) erwähnte eigenthümliche el zwischen den beiden Substantiven eingeschoben wird, wie z. B. ul ganám, „Kind-Weib", d. h. „weibliches Kind, Tochter"; bχskwán el genám, „Pferd das Weib", d. h. „Stute"; būri (e)l geném, „Esel das Weib", d. h. „Eselin"; ntē (e)l gením, „Rind das Weib", d. h. „Kuh"; genóm el lardesa, „Brust". Jedoch muss ich bemerken, dass der letztere Ausdruck als Genitivbeziehung gefasst werden kann, „Frau der Heirath", ganz wie oben genóm al idda, „Frau der viermonatlichen Strohzeit".

Dagegen wird das männliche Geschlecht gewöhnlich nicht besonders ausgedrückt, als nur in solchen Fällen, wo eine Zweideutigkeit Statt finden könnte, in welchen Fällen dann mēni hinzugefügt wird, wie z. B. ul-e meni (über das e s. oben S. CCX, a, a), „Kind männlich", d. h. „Knabe".

i) Auch für die Pluralbildung habe ich nur Weniges beizubringen, und scheint in den meisten Fällen das Substantiv in der Form der Mehrheit keine Umwandelung zu erleiden, wie ich z. B. die Form kurgumma für „Kameel" auch im Plural gewöhnlicher als kurgumme habe. Dagegen habe ich von bχskwáu, „Pferd" in der Mehrheit bdsakwā, „Pferde".

4. *Das Eigenschaftswort.*

a) Hier habe ich zuerst solche Ausdrücke zu erwähnen, die sowol wie selbstständige Substantiva, als auch als Substantiven beigefügte Eigenschaftswörter gebraucht werden, wie z. B.

inserting the particle ne between me and the object, viz me-ne-zauar meaning „the person of adultery" i. q. „the harlot", a synonym of the above mentioned geném-n-zauar. Probably other terms also, such as musχoi, „thief"; musku, „archer", have been formed by means of this same me, and me-n-rō-ne, „people of town (rō), town's people", probably is a plural form derived from this same me. This same me or mi, further, we find used in order to form the ordinal numbers, such as mí-disχión, „the ninth"; mi-wnrfňku, „the twentieth", while in other instances the verbal form aló, „being", is besides added, as, for instance, mi-χkán-aló, verbally „who ten being" i. q. „the tenth"; mi-χkau-kā-tekū-aló, „the eleventh", and so on.

As for the other mode of composition of some ordinals by means of mal, this latter term seems to be identical with the Bágrimma mala, „master", so that mal-sési-ne would originally mean „master of five (being?)" i. q. „the fifth"; mal-venáχkir-ne, „master of six (being?)" i. q. „the sixth".

g) As for deflecting the noun, the Lógoné-idiom seems to be very poorly developed; for, besides a sort of genitive being formed by means of n, na, ne of which I have already spoken shortly before, when explaining the mode of compound terms, I have no other instances of cases. As an example of the imperfect mode of expressing the various relations between two nouns, I will mention bille gením meaning „a person (with) a wife", „a bewifed, married person", just in the same manner as gením debe, „a woman (with) a belly" means „a woman with child". On the other hand we see the use of prepositions, as in the instance adduced vocab. p. 97 wo-fiyn-ni en máverim, „I beat, wound him with the sword", this en being probably nothing but an inverted ne.

h) As for gender, the term gením, gondm, gnnám, „woman, female", is generally added to nouns indicating individuals of female sex, whether of human beings, or of animals; this is done in two different ways, the term genám either preceding, or following the other term, but in both cases the remarkable el of which I have already spoken p. CCXI. β, a), when treating of the genitive case, being almost constantly inserted between the two words, as, for instance, ul gandm, „child female, daughter"; bŋnkwán el gunúm, „mare"; būri (e)l gondm, „she-ass"; ua (e)l gením. „cow"; genám el laruasu, „bride". However, I have to remark, that the latter term may be understood as indicating a genitive relation, „woman of marriage", just as we have had above genám ul iddu i. q. „widow", „woman of the period of four month's waiting".

As for the male sex, it is generally understood without being distinctly indicated, although in such cases where the sense may be ambiguous, meni is added, as in ul-e mēni, „male child, son"; as for the inserting of the e, see above p. CCXI, a, a.

i). As for the plural number, only in a few cases of nouns I am able to give a different form from that of the singular, as, for instance, bŋnkwán, plur. bandkwā, „horses". Of kurgumma, „camel", on the contrary, I have heard the identical plural form more frequently, than the other one by means of a slight change of the final vowel, kargumme.

4. *The adjective.*

a) I have first to mention those terms, which are used as well as independent nouns, as as adjectives added to a noun, as, for instance, tū, „black", „darkness"; tšhu, „young",

tū, „schwarz, Dunkelheit"; tābn, „jung, Kind"; kánadī (ein fremder, eingeführter Ausdruck, s. oben S. LXXXII, a), „geduldig, Geduld"; añkal, „verständig, Verstand", und manche andere. So geschieht es denn, dass in vielen Fällen, wo dergleichen Wörter in Verbindung mit bille, „Person" gebraucht sind, man nicht zu unterscheiden vermag, ob sie als Substantiva (z. B. „Person von Geduld, von Verstand") oder als Eigenschaftswörter zu verstehen sind. Jedoch dient das in vielen Fällen, wo eine Eigenschaft urgirt werden soll, zu diesem Zwecke dem Worte hinzugefügte sā, das sonst nur die negative Form des Zeitwortes bildet, wol dazu, anzuzeigen, dass wir an ein abhängiges Eigenschafts-, und nicht an ein selbstständiges Nennwort zu denken haben. Allerdings wird auch diese Ansicht wieder zweifelhaft, wenn wir das negative Eigenschaftswort kélakū-sa, „schweigend, ernst", berücksichtigen, da ich das positive kélakū nur als Substantiv kenne mit der Bedeutung „Rede, Sprache"; añkal-sā, „unverständig" sieht ähnlich aus, obgleich ich das positive añkal, das doch das Arabische عاقل ist, auch adjektivisch habe. Mehr adjektivischen Charakter haben delū-sā, „nicht süss", „bitter" (delū, „süss"); ṅgā-sā (negative Form des dem Kanuri entborgten ṅgā, „lebendig, wohl"), „nicht wohl, krank".

a, α) Dagegen ist sehr uneigentlich als negative Form des Eigenschaftsworts anzusehn die Form mit šōn, die eben nichts ist, als das verbale S. 125 des Vokabulars aufgeführte šēn, „es ist nicht, fehlt", also bille gonóm šōn, „ein Mensch, Frau fehlt (ihm)", d. h. „ein Mann ohne Frau", „ein unverheiratheter Mann"; bille kánadī šēu, „Mensch, Geduld fehlt (ihm)", d. h. „Mensch ohne Geduld, ungeduldiger Mensch". Diese Art der Wortbildung ist sehr klar belegt durch die merkwürdige Zeitpartikel θinta-ma šēn-an, „niemals", deren eigenthümliche Zusammensetzung ich, als ich sie S. 25 des Vokabular's verzeichnete, noch nicht verstand, aber es kann nicht der geringste Zweifel sein, dass die reich componirte Form eigentlich heisst „nicht seiend (šōn-an) wann (θinta)", d. h. die volle Negation des „wann", also „niemals".

b) Ich erwähne jetzt einige andere Formen von Adjektiven. So habe ich ein vom Substantiv fū, „Feuer" abgeleitetes Adjektiv e-fū, „warm", vom Wasser gebraucht und mui-fū (wahrscheinlich zusammengezogen aus me-ui-fū), „warm", von der Luft.

Eine andere abgeleitete Form scheint mir bei den Eigenschaftswörtern iñkál-fi, „lahm" und buχ-fi, „blind" zu beachten zu sein.

Dann haben wir auch als Eigenschaftswörter anzusehn einige der Zusammensetzungen mit dem oben erwähnten me, wie z. B. me-rásχa-nū, „blutdürstig, grausam".

c) Als vom Zeitwort abgeleitete und zwar zunächst mit der bestimmten verbalen Form in al, la, li eng zusammenhängende Eigenschaftswörter betrachte ich die auf lan (la-en?) ausgehenden, wie hosámdir-lan, „hungrig" (zam, „essen"); amiy-lán, „durstig"; saniy-lán, „schläfrig". Daran schliessen sich als entschiednere Participialformen die bestimmt auf en ausgehenden Eigenschaftswörter, wohin auch die oben S. CCVI angeführten substantivisch gebrauchten Ausdrücke bille ŋarau-en, „Landmann"; bille gom-en θā, „Rinderhirte" in gewissem Sinne gehören und zu dieser Klasse zähle ich ebenfalls die auf diese Endung ausgehenden Benennungen von angerichteten Speisen, die ich an der betreffenden Stelle meines Vokabular's zu erklären haben werde, wie θā wa-(a)l-pau-en, θā wa-sa-(a)l-pau-en (von der einfachen Form pau, „weiss"); θūe radau-en, θūe hillu-en, θūe bakkau-en. Auch gonóm muskau-en, „Hurenweib" gehört hierher. Ein sehr belehrendes Beispiel dieser Formation scheint mir der Ausdruck doθanen zu sein, „Angriffswaffen", da er, wie ich nicht zweifle, von dem Zeitwort θa, „schlagen, stossen" abgeleitet ist.

d) Ich erwähne jetzt einige Beispiele, wo die Eigenschaft einer Person oder Sache durch Umschreibung ausgedrückt ist, wie z. B. bille nofā-ni ambai, „Mensch, Herz sein schlecht", d. h. „böswilliger Mensch"; bille lemán fiya, „Person (von, mit) vielem Vermögen", d. h. „reicher Mann"; loādo inkónhe fiya, „Land (mit) vielen Bergen", d. h. „gebirgiges Land".

„child"; kánadī (a foreign term, see p. LXXXIII, a), „patient, patience"; áṅkal, „intelligent, intelligence", and many others, the consequence being, that, wherever these terms are used in connection with bille „person", it cannot always be determined, whether they are to be understood as nouns („a person of patience, intelligence"), or as adjectives. That in many cases, however, they are really to be considered as adjectives, would seem to appear from the negative form which they adopt, by means of the very same sǎ, which serves to constitute the negative forms of the verb. Thus, we have also áṅkal-sǎ, „imprudent", just as we have ṅgā-sǎ, „not well, sick" (from ṅgā, an originally Kanúri term „well, alive"); dole-sǎ, „not sweet, bitter" (dolo, „sweet"); but, on the other hand, I have even a negative adjective form kólakū-sǎ, „silent, serious", although the term kólakū alone in my material does not appear but with the power of a substantive, meaning „speech".

a, α) We have also another negative form of adjective notions by means of šēn, which is undoubtedly connected with substantives, as, for instance bille gonóm šēn, „a man who has no wife" (gonóm), „an unmarried man" and in the same manner kánadī šēn, „having no patience, impatient". This šēn, no doubt, is the very same šēn, which occurs in my vocabulary p. 125 with the notion „there is not, is wanting", the original meaning, therefore, of bille gonóm šēn being „a person, woman is wanting (to him)". This is very clearly illustrated by a very remarkable adverbial composition by means of this same šēn, namely the term θinta-ma šēa-sa adduced in my vocabulary p. 25, when I was not yet sure of its composition; but there cannot be the slightest doubt that it means originally „there not being (šēn-an), when" (θinta), consequently „never".

b) I now mention some other, rather isolated, forms of adjectives; thus, from fū, „fire" I have e-fū, „warm", used of water, and mut-fū (me-ut-fū), „warm", used of the air; but, as for e-fū, it may rather be originally a verbal form.

The adjectives iṅkál-fí, „lame" and buχ-fí, „blind" also seem to be simple derivations of another kind.

Then we have also to consider as adjectives some of the compositions with me, spoken of before p. CCXIV, f), such as me-rásχa-nē, „blood-thirsty, sanguinary", while also the Ordinals there mentioned, properly speaking, belong to this class.

c) As adjectives derived from verbal forms, and connected with the definite verbal form in al, la, li mentioned above, I look upon those terminating in lan (la-en?), as hosūmdir-lan, „hungry" (sum, „eat"); amiy-lán, „thirsty"; saniy-lán, „sleepy", and more distinctly those terminating in es, whereto belong also in a certain respect the two terms cited above p. CCVII bille gurau-es, „husbandman" and bille gozw-es θa, „neat-herd", verbally „person pastur-ing cattle"; and to this class I reckon, moreover, all those terms of dishes with this termination, which I shall have to explain in my vocabulary, such as θā wa-(a)l-pan-es, θā wa-sa-(a)l-pan-es (pan, „white"); θūe radau-es, θūe hilin-es, θao bukkan-es. Also genḗm muskan-es, „harlot", appears to be an instance of this form. A very illustrative instance of this formation seems to me to be the term dotauce, „aggressive weapons", which, I have no doubt, is to be derived from θa, „beat, strike".

d) I now mention a few instances, where the adjective notion is circumscribed, as bille nefā-ni ambai, meaning verbally „person, his heart bad" i. q. „a malicious person"; bille lomán fiya, verbally „a person (of) much property" i. q. „a wealthy person"; loāde inkónho fiya, „a country (with) many mountains" i. q. „a mountainous country".

e) Von einem Vergleichungsgrad des Eigenschaftswortes habe ich nur Ein vereinzeltes und mir nicht ganz klares Beispiel, nämlich bau-uo doma — diffle ban kanē, das heissen soll „dieses ist gross" — „jenes ist grösser", wörtlich vielleicht „übertrifft jenes noch".

f) Schon oben S. CCXIV, 4, a) habe ich angegeben, dass es bei vielen Beispielen schwierig ist zu entscheiden, ob das, was wir vor uns haben, ein Nenn- oder ein Eigenschaftswort sei, und diese Ungewissheit wird noch dadurch vergrössert, dass n, das Zeichen der Beziehung, allem Anschein nach selbst zwischen Substantiv und Adjektiv eingeschoben wird, wie z. B. lebá n tū, „schwarzes Hemd" (lebá, „Hemd"); lebá n pan, „weisses Hemd". Ja, von diesem Gesichtspunkte aus bin ich in der That in Zweifel, ob wir nicht auch so die S. CCXII, γ, α) erwähnten Ausdrücke kuku n tābu, sāgi n tābu und andere ähnliche zu betrachten haben, so dass sie also bedeuteten „junges Huhn", nicht „Junges vom Huhn", „kleiner Dolch" und so weiter, also nicht als zusammengesetzte substantivische Ausdrücke zu betrachten seien.

Aus solchem unsicheren Verhältniss erklärt es sich schon von selbst, besonders da mein Material nicht sehr reich ist, weshalb ich nicht mit Sicherheit über die Anpassung des Adjektivs an das Substantiv in Endung oder Geschlecht sprechen kann.

5. Aus eben diesem Grunde, weil mein Material des Lógonē im Einzelnen so Manches zu wünschen übrig lässt, will ich schon hier einige meiner in dieser Sprache niedergeschriebenen Phrasen heranziehen, während ich im Allgemeinen meine Phrasen in den verschiedenen, hier behandelten Sprachen bis zum Schluss lasse.

So will ich hier zuerst die Frageform vermittelst da beleuchten, besonders da sie mich in meinem Vokabular zu wiederholten Irrthümern veranlasst hat, zumal bei den Zeitpartikeln; auch uāli dā (ne-āli dā) S. 123 ist nur die Frageform, wie wir deutlich erkennen aus der Phrase „giebt es Wasser auf dieser Strasse"?, ugffel dlo am nāli dā (wörtlich „Weg dieser, Wasser ist da denn"?); „wann werden wir diese Stadt betreten"?, slea rō-ne lugt(e) ńrni dā (wörtlich „wir betreten Stadt diese Zeit welche denn"?); „wann dreschen sie ihr Korn aus"?, šitu χan θinta da (wörtlich „wann denn"?). Jedoch wird dies dā nicht immer, wie das in diesen beiden Phrasen der Fall ist, noch denjenigen fragenden lokalen oder Zeitpartikeln hinzugefügt, die schon die Frage enthalten, wie das z. B. mit der Phrase der Fall ist, die sich dem materiellen Zusammenhang nach an die vorhergehende eng anschliesst „wann reinigen, oder harken, diese Leute ihre Felder"?, šita χ(a)dle eχré θintá,

reinigen diese Gärten wann?.

„Wann fängt die Regenzeit in diesem Lande an, wann hört sie auf"?,

loād(e) ále déman säge θintá sádego θintá,

Land dies Regenzeit fängt an wann, hört auf wann?.

„Gibt es Städte auf diesem Wege oder ist (Alles) Wald"?,

bá-no rō nāli dā gá-u gómi é dā,

Ort dieser Stadt ist da denn oder Wald ist denn?.

„Welcher Art ist ihr Korn, ist es Negerhirse oder Sorghum"?,

rγóla na-tdu úle (nāli) zelfnta dā wiyo andi ga mákala,

Saat von ihnen dies ist welcher Art denn Hirse ist es oder Sorghum?.

„Welche Art von Besitzthum haben sie, mehr Rindvieh oder Ziegen"?,

lemúa na-tón zelfnta, mē-ne flyn dā nθá andi gá-u fe dā,

Besitzthum von ihnen welche Art, was viel denn Rindvieh ist es oder Ziegen denn?.

„Gibt es viele Fische in diesem Fluss oder gibt es keine"?,

lúyam ále kii fly(a) andi ga kii šēn dā,

Fluss dieser Fische viel gibt es oder Fisch gibt es nicht denn"?.

„Sind es insgesammt Thonhäuser oder gibt es auch Hütten"?,

wēni kytti andi dā ga maχé dā,

Thonhäuser alle gibt es denn oder Hütten denn?.

e) Of a sort of **comparative** I have only one isolated instance, viz **han-ne domá — diffin han kanĕ** understood to mean „this is great — that is greater", where **diffin** seems to be a verbal form meaning „it exceeds, while **kanŏ** may mean „yet", or something similar.

f) Already above, p. CCXV, 4, a) I have indicated, that in several instances it is difficult to decide, whether it be a substantive or an adjective what we have before us, and this uncertainty is increased by the conjunctional sign n, according to all appearance, being inserted even between the substantive and the adjective, as, for instance, **lebú n tū**, „black shirt" (**lebú**, „shirt"); **lebú m pau**, „white shirt". And seen from this point of view, I doubt, whether we may not have to look upon the terms **kusku n tābu**, **sāgi n tābu**, and similar ones, mentioned above, p. CCXIII, *γ*, *a*) rather as adjectives, and not as composite substantive terms, and, accordingly, meaning „young chicken" (not „young of chicken"), „small dagger", not „young of dagger", and so on.

Such being the uncertainty with regard to the character of the adjective, I am not able to decide, whether at all, or the manner in which the adjective be accommodated to the substantive in gender or termination.

5. My material of the Lógonē-idiom being so scanty, I prefer giving already in this place a few phrases written down in that language, while, in general, I have left my collection of phrases in the various languages here treated for the end of the vocabulary itself. The phrases here given will serve especially to illustrate the form of asking by means of **dā** (a form which I took not into account, while giving in my vocabulary the particles representing time); thus, also the form **nāli dā** (n(e)-āli dā), mentioned vocab. p. 123, is nothing but the interrogative form, as is best shown by the phrase **gŭffel ále am nāli da**, „is there water on this road"? (verbally „road this water is there"?); **sian rō-ne luχt(o) ávai da**, „when shall we enter that town"? (verbally „we enter town this time what"?); **šitu χsa θinta da**, „when, at what season, do they thrash out their corn"?; although this **dā** is not constantly added to the interrogative particle, as is shown by the following phrase **šita χ(a)ále sχrō θintá**, „when do these people cleanse their fields"? (verbally „cleanse these field when"?).

I further give the following phrases:

„When does the rainy season begin in this country, when does it cease"?,
loād(e) ále déman sāge θintá sádege θintá,
country this rainy season begins when ceases when?.

„Are there towns on this track or is (all) forest"?,
bá-ne rō nāli dā gá-n gémi ó dā,
track this town is there then or forest is then?.

„Of what kind is their corn, is it Negro-millet or sorghum"?,
vyála na-tán ále (nāli?) aelínta dā wiyo andi ga mákala,
corn of them this (is there?) of what kind then? millet is it or sorghum?.

„What kind of property have they, have they more cattle or goats"?,
lemán na-tán aelínta, mō-ne fīya dā nθá andi gá-n foda,
property of them what kind what much then? cattle is it or goats?.

„Is there plenty of fish in this river or is there no fish"?,
láyam ále kii fīy(a) andi ga kii šou dā,
river this fish many is or fish is not then?.

„Are all clayhouses or are there (also) cottages"?,
wōni kutti ándi dā ga maχó dā,
clayhouses all are then? or cottages then?

Ich theile hier auch eine Phrase mit, die uns den betreffenden Ausdruck fa für die Partikel „nur, mit Ausnahme von, ausgenommen (das und das)" gibt, den ich S. 7 des Vokabular's übersehen habe:

„Die Bewohner dieser Stadt haben nur Fische zur Nahrung",

me-a rō-ne sųmmi-tan šēn kii fa.

sie welche Stadt dieser Nahrung ihre ist nicht Fische ausgenommen.

6. Ich gebe nun einige monosyllabe Ausdrücke der Lógoné-Sprache, die mir in meiner Sammlung aufgestossen sind.

a: al, āl, „sein"; am, „Wasser".

b: ba, „Ort"; bā (wā), „geben"; bā, „Vater"; bē, „Stimme"(?); bel, „Einschnitte".

d: dā, Fragepartikel; dem, „können"; dim, „schmecken"; dil, „Mütze"; dir, „Deckel"; dō, „bringen"; dū, „Dorn".

e: en, „mit, vermittelst".

f: fa, „nur, allein"; fir, „zur Ader lassen"; fō, „entweder, oder"; fū, „Feuer".

g: ga, „sehn"; gam, „Hacke"; ge, „Lager, Bett"; gem, „Rohr"; gil, „Melone"; gir, „gehn"; grem, „Frucht der Hadjilidj"; gem, gum, „lieben, zufrieden"; guχ, „alt".

γ: γa, γan, „thun, machen"; γa, γan, „Haus".

h: hi, „lassen".

χ: χa, „Person"; χkán, „zwanzig"; χsē, „Frohsinn, Gesang"; χai, „Blut".

k: ka, „du"; kā, „sagen"; kā (kaa), „Kopf"; kas, „Preis"; kī (kii), „Fisch"; kse, ksen, „fragen"; ksdē, „zwei"; kū, „ihr".

l: la, le, „sein, existiren"; lu, „marschiren"; luo, „Preis, Waare".

m: mal, „Herr"; mas, „Mutter"; me, „wir"; me, mi, „wer, was"; mū, „Thau".

n: n, na Beziehungspartikel; na, „wo"; ne, „dieser"; ṅgā, „lebendig"; nθa (θa), „Vieh"; nθī, „Zunge".

p: pam, „weit, geräumig"; pal, „sehr"; pau, „weiss"; pχam, „hell, licht".

r: re, „nennen"; rō, „Stadt".

s: sā, „nicht"; sū, sē, „trinken"; sā, „(berauschendes) Getränk"; sai, „roth"; sel, „Tag"; seu, „wissen"; si, „nehmen"; sī, „Auge"; ske, „loslassen"; sum, „Schlag"; sχē, „Aufseher"; sχrē, „Feld, Garten".

š: šēn, „ist nicht".

t, ṭ: tai, „Stampfer"; tkám, „zehn"; tkū, „ein"; tχúm, „Damm, Deich"; tū, „dunkel, schwarz"; ṭųm (dųm), „verehren".

θ: θa, „Rind"; θā, „Nahrung"; θan, „Zahn"; θa, „aufstehn, aufbrechen, gehn, besteigen, schlagen"; θē, „finden, erlangen"; θū, „Fleisch".

u: ū, „ich"; ul, „Sohn, Kind".

w: wa, „heben, legen"; wa, „Jahr" (wa-n, „heuer"); wā, „geben" (s. bā), „fliessen".

z: zim, „Frucht der Balanites Aegyptiaca"; zū, „Fliege"; zųm, „essen".

7. Ich gehe jetzt zu einer Besprechung der Verwandtschaft über, wie sie zwischen der Lógoné- und anderen Sprachen meiner Sammlung besteht, indem ich jedoch von vornherein jene Verwandtschaftsbeziehungen hier unberücksichtigt lasse, welche das Lógoné mit anderen Idiomen der grossen Masa-Gruppe gemeinsam hat, da ich diese besonders behandeln werde im Zusammenhang mit den kleineren Vokabularien meiner Sammlung.

Jene übrigen Verwandtschaftsgrade betreffen in Besonderheit und fast ausschliesslich die Kanuri- und die Hausa-Sprache, und werde ich die verwandtschaftlichen Ausdrücke mit jener zuerst zusammenstellen, jedoch nicht, wie ich das sonst thue, alphabetisch, sondern nach sachlichen Beziehungen geordnet, da die Ausdrücke zum grösseren Theil nicht ursprüngliche Begriffe, sondern äussere Lebensbeziehungen betreffen. Zuerst jedoch werde ich die ursprünglicheren geben.

I here also adduce a phrase, which serves to supply the notion fa for „but, with the exception of", which I left void, vocab. p. 7:

„The people of this town have no food but fish",

mc-a rō-no χgmmi-tan šōn kil fa,

they of town this food of them not is fish except.

6. I now proceed to give a short list of monosyllabic terms of the Lógonē-language, such as they occur in my Notes.

a: al, āl, „exist, be"; am, „water".

b: ba, „place, locality"; bā (wā), „give"; bā, „father"; bē, „voice"(?); bol, „tattooings".

d: dā interrogative sign; dem, „can, be able"; dim, „taste"; dil, „cup"; dir, „cover"; dō, „bring"; dū, „thorn".

e: en, „with, by, by means of".

f: fa, „except, not-but"; fir, „draw blood"; fō, „either, or"; fū, „fire".

g: ga, „see, look"; gum, „hoe"; gē, „couch, bed"; gom, „reed"; gil, „gourd, pumpkin"; gir, „go"; grom, „stone of fruit, kernel"; gom, gum, „love, content"; guχ, „old".

γ: γa, γan, „do, make"; γa, γau, „house".

h: hi, „let, leave".

χ: χe, „person"; χkán, „twenty"; χsē, „mirth, song"; χal, „blood".

k: ka, „thou"; kā, „say, tell"; kā (kaa), „head"; kae, „price"; ki (kli), „fish"; kae, kaen, „ask"; kadē, „two"; kū, „you" (plur.).

l: la, le, „be, exist"; lu, „march"; lua, „price, merchandise".

m: mal, „master"; mae, „mother"; mo, „we"; mo, mi, „who, what"; mū, „dew".

n: n, na particle of relation; na, „where"; ne, „this"; ṅgā, „alive"; nθa (θa), „cattle"; nθi, „tongue".

p: pam, „wide, spacious"; pal, „very"; pau, „white"; pχam, „clear, light".

r: ro, „call, name"; rō, „town".

s: sā, „not"; sā, sē, „drink"; sā, „(intoxicating) drink"; sai, „red"; sel, „day"; sen, „know"; si, „take"; si, „eye"; ske, „let loose, give forth"; sum, „blow"; sχē, „overseer"; sχrē, „field, garden".

š: šōn, „is not".

t, ṭ: tai, „pounder"; tkám, „ten"; tkū, „one"; tχúm, „dam, dike"; tū, „darkness, black"; ṭum (dum), „venerate, worship".

θ: θa, „cattle"; θā, „food"; θan, „tooth"; θa, „rise, start, go, mount, beat"; θē, „find, obtain"; θū, „meat".

u: ū, „I"; ul, „son, child".

w: wa, „raise, put"; wa, „year" (wa-n, wa-ne, „this year"); wā, „give" (see bā), „flow".

z: zim, „fruit of balanites Aegyptiaca"; zū, „fly" (the); zum, „cat".

7. I now proceed to treat of the degree of relation, which intercedes between the Lógonē-idiom and other African languages, as far as they fell under my observation, excluding however those points of relation, which it has with other dialects of the Mūsa-group, which I shall have to treat in connection with the shorter vocabularies of my other collection.

These other points of relationship particularly, and almost exclusively, regarding the Kanūri- and Hausa-languages, I, in the first place shall give a list of the terms of the former class, but, as almost the whole of them do not regard original notions, but such as belong to a certain state of development of human society, I do not arrange them in an alphabetical order, but rather according to their meaning, giving first, however the more original ones.

Lógoné.	Kanúri.	Deutsch.
si	sim	Auge
sumi	simmo	Ohr
koki	kogō	Stimme
ṅgä	ṅgu	lebend, wohl
dųnuo	dųnno	stark, Stärke
bel	béli	Einschnitte
kánadī	kánadi	Geduld
bálaka	yála	Norden
zųffulo, zųbbel	dibbol	Pfad, Weg
wamberia	tšimbariskin	bin ermüdet
wu-luχse	lug-óskin	(L. ich) lege ab (Kleider (K. ich) gehe hinaus
ingūbri, ṅgūbri	gúmmeri	Festung
láfandīn	láfandín	Turban
sórabúl	zárabún	Stiefel
kápi	kābi	Bogen
sógu	sógo	Köcher
sánteram	sáltorum	kleine Axt
kúteram	kúteram	Spiegel
korfe	karbe	Rührlöffel
kendal	kendé	Rohruntersatz unter Schüssel
kille	fille	Rohrdeckel
sambo	sambo	Lederbüchse
marta	murta	andere Büchse
kaskū	kásukū	Markt
gábaga	gábaga	Vierspannmaass
laúsni	laúsni	Zweispannmaass
darám	dáran	Viereckenmaass
má-fatké	fátke-ma	Trödler
satki	sakti	Wasserschlauch
karábka	karábka	Karawane
gaúga	gaúga	Trommel
gánaro	gonāri	andere Art Trommel
gango) dųnnu	dunū	andere Trommel
dńgulo	ingúllo (katī-be)	Thontrommel
mońgolo	mońgolo	Taschenspieler
šila	šeláñolá	besondere Art Flöte
bandíl	bantíl	Art Trompete
kūku	kugu	Art Guitarre

Diesem Verzeichniss ähnlicher oder identischer Ausdrücke in beiden Sprachen will ich nur einige wenige Bemerkungen hinzufügen.

Ein Jeder wird sich bei dem ersten Überblick desselben überzeugen, dass die Ausdrücke fast insgesammt nicht ursprüngliche Begriffe bezeichnen, sondern mit einem gewissen Grad von Bildung verbundene Gegenstände. Die einzige Ausnahme bilden eben jene fünf oder sechs Wörter, die ich am Anfang des Verzeichnisses aufgeführt habe.

Was nun die beiden ersten Ausdrücke für „Auge" und „Ohr" betrifft, so ist die Ähnlichkeit der in beiden Sprachen dafür vorhandenen Ausdrücke gewiss auffallend, und ebenso auffallend ist nga, ṅgä, da wir anderweitige Belege dafür haben, dass es beiden

Lógone.	Kanúri.	English.
si	sim	eye
semi	simmo	ear
koki	kogō	voice
ṅgā	ṅga	alive, well
dŋuno	dŋuno	strong, strength
bel	béli	tattooings
kánadi	kánadi	patience
hálaka	yála	North
zǒffulo, zŋbhel .	dibbel	path, track
wamberia . . .	tšimbarískin . .	I) am fatigued
wu-luχse	lug-ūskin . . .	L. I) put off clothes K. I) go out
ingūbri, ṅgūbri .	gámmeri	holiday
láfandia	láfandia	turban
sérabdi	sárabún	boots
kāpi	kābi	bow
zōgu	zōgo	quiver
sánteram	sálteram	small axe
kúteram	kúteram	mirror
korfe	karbe	spoon for stirring soup
kendal	konde	basket-stand of dish
kille	fille	reed-cover of dish
sambo	sambo	leather-box
marta	martu	other box
kaskū	kásukū	market
gábaga	gábaga	measure of four spans' length
ladáni	ladáni	measure of two spans' length
darám	dāran	measure of four zekka
mé-fatkē, mí-patké	fátkē-ma	fripperer
satki	sakti	waterskin
karábka	karábka	caravan
gañga	gañga	drum
gúnare	gonāri	other sort of drum
gañge) dŋunu . .	duna	other sort of drum
úñgulo	ingúllo (kaff-be) .	drum of clay
móñgolo	móñgolo	juggler
šila	šulášela	peculiar kind of flute
bandíl	banfíl	kind of trumpet
kūku	kūgu	peculiar kind of guitar

I shall now offer but a few remarks with regard to this list of similar, or identical terms in the Kanúri- and Lógonē-languages.

Every body at a first glance over the columns will convince himself, that almost the whole of them do not designate original notions, but, on the contrary, such as regard a certain degree of civilization. The only exception regards those few terms, which I have placed at the head of the list.

Now, as for ṅga, ṅgā, we have a very remarkable proof, that it is not a foreign term, or at least not introduced into the Lógonē-language at a recent period, but, on the contrary, that it is so very adequate to the whole character of that language, that it has formed even the negative

Sprachen eigenthümlich ist. Auf der einen Seite nämlich muss es wenigstens seit sehr alter Zeit dem Lógoné eigen sein und dem ganzen Charakter der Sprache dermassen angemessen, dass wir sogar eine negative Form davon haben ṅgā-sā, „nicht lebendig, nicht wohl, krank", während wir auf der anderen Seite anerkennen müssen, dass das Wort ṅga ganz eben so berechtigt dem gesammten Charakter der Kanúri-Sprache angehört; denn, wie ich S. LX, N. 5 bemerkt habe, scheint der Ausdruck nki für „Wasser" auf's Engste aus demselben Grundbegriff hervorgegangen zu sein. Diess sind immerhin interessante Fälle verwandtschaftlicher Beziehungen und ich glaube, wir haben ihnen noch einen anderen hinzuzufügen, nämlich den Ausdruck díbi, der beiden Sprachen angehört, aber allerdings in der einen das gerade Gegentheil dessen bezeichnet, was er in der anderen ausdrückt, nämlich im Kanúri „schlecht", im Lógoné „gut"; denn solche Verdrehungen des Grundbegriffs eines gemeinsamen Wortes finden wir auch bei anderen verwandten Sprachen. Was dagegen den Ausdruck für „Einschnitte" oder „Tättowirungsmarken" betrifft, so bleibt nach dem, was ich gleich weiter zu entwickeln habe, kaum ein Zweifel übrig, dass die Kanúri die Sitte, sich zu tättowiren, von den Lógoné-Leuten oder wenigstens den Mása annahmen, da sie dieselbe in ihren ursprünglichen, nördlicher gelegenen Sitzen nicht geübt zu haben scheinen. Diess gibt uns Anlass, zu der Frage überzugehn, welcher der beiden Nationen die Priorität der in der Liste nachfolgenden Ausdrücke zukommt. Für alle Fälle ist diess bis jetzt noch nicht möglich, jedoch habe ich hinreichendes Material, um zu zeigen, dass unzweifelhaft die Kanúri viele von ihnen den benachbarten, in der Kultur ihnen weit vorangeschrittenen Bewohnern des in frühere Zeiten zurückreichenden Reiches Kótoko entlehnt haben; und so wird es denn von den übrigen auch wahrscheinlich. So haben wir z. B. in der Lógoné-Sprache neben dem Ausdruck sambo auch einen anderen, abgeleiteten Ausdruck sámbo-dē, „Löffel", der durchaus den Charakter einheimisch originaler Bildung hat, und durch solche Annahme einer Priorität des Ausdruckes sambo in der Lógoné-Sprache erklärt es sich einfach, wie es kommt, dass die Wándalā-Sprache ganz denselben Ausdruck hat und dasselbe ist der Fall mit den Ausdrücken marta und kendal, woraus wir denn sehen, wie die Lógoné in einem gewissen häuslichen Komfort den Kanúri in der Zeit vorangingen. Und so können wir mit mehr als Wahrscheinlichkeit annehmen, dass das auch der Fall ist mit denjenigen Ausdrücken, welche Kleider, Waffen, musikalische Instrumente und Handelsbezeichnungen bezeichnen. So wird der einfache Ausdruck fatke oder patkē, der „Trödel, Kleinwaaren" bezeichnet, und von dem das Kanúri fátko-ma, so wie das Lógoné mí-patkē und das Hausa maī-fatki, maī-fatki erst abgeleitet ist, im Kanúri und Hausa so gut wie nie gebraucht, während es im Lógoné ganz gewöhnlich ist. Die im Hausa erscheinende Pluralform fatāki von eben dem Singular maī-fatki darf dabei nicht verwundern. Ähnlich ist das Verhältniss des Lógoné-Ausdruckes kaskū, der sich aus der Sprache selbst auf das Schönste erklärt (kas, „Preis"; kū Endung, vgl. kóla-kū), während káskū im Kanúri keine solche nationale Erklärung erlaubt, und während zu gleicher Zeit das Hausa eine mit beiden offenbar verwandte Form káswa bietet. Ebenso ist die Lógoné-Form šila ohne Zweifel ursprünglicher als die Kanúri-Form šelá-šelá, und für diese ganze Frage von der Herleitung dieser und ähnlicher Ausdrücke in den verschiedenen Sprachen ist es nun von grösstem Interesse und von höchster Bedeutung, dass auch der dem Lógoné und Kanúri zugleich gehörige Ausdruck móṅgolo ganz augenscheinlich der ersteren Sprache angehört, wo er sich auf das Einfachste aus zwei vollkommen festgestellten Elementen erklärt, wovon das eine dúṅgulo ist, einer jener, beiden Sprachen gemeinsamen, Namen für ein Instrument, das andere das oben bei der Zusammensetzung der Nomina besprochene me, also móṅgolo oder múṅgulo eigentlich me-dúṅgulo, „der zu dem dúṅgulo Tanzende", während in der Kanúri-Sprache dieser Ausdruck gar keine organische Erklärung zulässt; denn, wäre es nach den Regeln der letzteren gebildet, so würde es dúṅguló-ma, iṅgulló-ma heissen müssen.

Dagegen sind allem Anscheine nach die beiden Ausdrücke sálteram und kúteram

ṅgā-sā, „not alive, not well" i. q. „sick". But, on the other hand, we must also acknowledge, that the word seems to be quite as much belonging to the whole character of the Kanúri-language, for, as I have remarked p. LXI, note 5, the term ńkī, meaning „water", seems to be intimately related to it. The rather close similarity also of the terms for „eye" and „ear" in both languages is remarkable. Nay, I even think, we have to add one more instance to these terms, viz díbi belonging to both languages, but at present meaning „bad" in the Kanúri, „good" in the Lógonē, such changes of the original notion of a word being common to other languages likewise. But these more original coincidences are the exception. As for the term for „tattooings", it serves to show, if we take into account what I have next to say, that the Kanúri-people adopted from the Lógonē, or at least from the Mása, the custom of tattooing themselves, which they did not practice in their original seats in a more Northerly Region. That this was the case, is more than probable from the fact of all the Northern tribes of the Tédā-nation, and those which have less been affected by introduction of Negro-blood or Negro-customs, even at the present day not practising that custom, the Tédā being, as I hope to have shown, the near relations of the Kanúri, and those who have preserved the older type and character of that nation. After these remarks it will be easy to decide, to which of the two nations, the Kanúri or the Lógonē, belongs the priority of the terms next following in the list. In each single case this is as yet impossible, but I am fully able to show, that many of them certainly were borrowed by the Kanúri from the Lógonē, or Mása, a people settled in the most favorable locality on the point of junction of two navigable rivers, and on the highroad between extensive Regions, which was the reason of the relative antiquity and early civilization of the kingdom of Kótoko; and the priority of the Lógonē-idiom once firmly established in some cases, it becomes highly probable, that it has the same claim in the others. Thus, besides the term sambo we have in Lógonē another composite term sámbo-dē meaning „spoon", which is evidently derived from the former, and shows it to be indigenous. Thus also, it is easily explained, how it happens, that the Wándalā-language has the same term sambo, and the same is the case with the terms marta and hendal, showing evidently, that the Lógonē-people had the precedence and start before the Kanúri with regard to a certain comfort of human life. But, moreover, it clearly appears, that also with regard to the terms designating clothes, weapons, musical instruments, commerce, and so on, the Lógonē-language claims the priority. Thus, the simple term fatke or patke, from which fátke-ma in Kanúri, as well as mí-patkē in Lógone has been derived, is so rarely used in Kanúri, that I never heard it, while in Lógonē the term seems to be very generally used; and here we have a similar term in the Hausa-language too, viz maí-fatki, maí-falki with the irregular pluralform fatāki, „(travelling) fripperers" or „merchants". Just in the same manner kaskū in Lógonē appears to be derived from the term kas, „price", kū being the common termination (compare kóla-kū), while the Kanúri-term kásukū allows of no explanation in that language, both terms being again connected in a certain degree with the Hausa-term kásuwa. The simple Lógonē-term šila, likewise, no doubt is more original than the Kanúri-form šelá-šolá, and what is highly interesting and important for deciding this whole question, the term móṅgulo, móṅgolo is evidently of Lógone origin, meaning nothing else but the person of the áṅgulo, he who is dancing to the sounds of the áṅgulo, me-áṅgulo (see the paragraph illustrating this kind of composition above p. CCXIII) that is „the juggler", while the form of that term cannot be explained from the elements of the Kanúri-language; on the contrary, according to the laws of the latter language it ought to be áṅguló-ma or iṅgulló-ma.

While thus, I hope, we have convinced ourselves of the priority of the Lógonē-language with regard to the greater portion of the terms adduced, the two terms sálteram and kúteram, on the contrary, appear to be borrowed by the Lógonē-language from the Kanúri,

von der Lógoné-Sprache dem Kanúri entborgt, da sie sich nur in letzterer Sprache organisch entwickeln lassen, während dem Lógoné sowol die Elemente, als die Form in ram, fremd sind.

Was gañga betrifft, so scheinen beide Sprachen, Kanúri und Lógoné, diesen Ausdruck der Hausa-Sprache entlehnt zu haben, wie sie denn auch gemeinsam gar manche Ausdrücke dem Arabischen entlehnt haben, deren Berücksichtigung ich hier natürlich ausschliesse.

Ich gebe nun ein Verzeichniss der in der Lógoné- und Hausa-Sprache übereinstimmenden Ausdrücke, und ein Jeder wird beim ersten Blick erkennen, dass diese, so spärlich sie auch sind, zum grösseren Theil nicht spätentlehnte, sondern ursprüngliche Redetheile sind.

Lógoné.	Hausa.	Deutsch.
ka	kai	du
ku (suffix)	ka (suffix)	dich
me	mu	wir
mo (suffix)	mu (suffix)	uns
wa	ku	ihr
kun (suffix) . . .	ku (suffix)	euch
me	me	was
me-ni	me-ne-ne	was (das)?
na*)	i-na	wo
amti	mutu	sterben
mott	mútua	Tod
bā, wā	bā	geben
ñge	ga, gani	sehn
sana	sani	wissen
sa, se	sā	trinken
ba	ba	Person, Mensch
ka, kaa	ka	Kopf
ki, kli	kifi	Fisch
kókua, akúkua	kakā	Erntezeit
déman	dámana	Regenzeit
ša	sa	Vieh
meyel	mákeri	Grobschmied
moyúa	mágani	Heilmittel
gálakō	gerkwa	Schild
rāga	rāga	Matte
būtu	būtu	leer.

Allerdings ist dieses Verzeichniss übereinstimmender und verwandter Wörter in der Lógone- und Hausa-Sprache noch kürzer, als das solcher Beziehungen zwischen der Lógoné- und Kanúri-Sprache, aber doch wird ein Jeder, der mit sprachlichen Forschungen einigermassen vertraut ist, leicht sich überzeugen, dass, während die letzteren mit wenigen Ausnahmen ganz äusserlich entlehnte Ausdrücke sind, die ersteren Beziehungen vorzugsweise solche Redetheile oder solche verbale und substantivische Ausdrücke betreffen, die ursprüngliche und alltägliche Anschauungen begreifen, und ein weiteres Eindringen in die Lógoné-Sprache wird wahrschein-

*) na im Lógoné scheint die allgemeine, Art und Zeit anzeigende Partikel zu sein, und wir haben sie als integrirenden Theil aller S. 27 und 29 des Vokabular's angeführten Zeitpartikeln.

to which latter the verbal roots, from which they have been derived, as well as the termination ram are original, while to the former such a termination seems to be foreign.

As for ganga, both languages seem to have borrowed this term from the Hausa; and in a similar manner both have many terms in common, which both of them have borrowed from the Arabic, which therefore we need not here consider.

I now proceed to give a list of those terms which are identical in the Lógone- and Hausa-languages, and most of which bear quite a different character of originality, than the coincidences between the former and the Kanúri-language.

Lógoné.	Hausa.	English.
ka	kai	thou
ku (suffix)	ka (suffix)	thee
mo	mu	we
mo (suffix)	mu (suffix)	us
wu	ku	you
kun (suffix)	ku (suffix)	you (accus.)
mo, me-ni	mo-né-ne	what
na *)	i-na	there, where
amti	mutu	die
moti	mútua	death
bā, wā	bā	give
ṅgo	ga, gani	look, see
sana	sani	know
sa, se	ṡā	drink
ba	ba	person
ka, kaa	ka	head
ki, kii	kifi	fish
kókua, akúkua	kakā	harvest
déman	dámana	rainy season
ṅa	sa	cattle
megel	mákeri	blacksmith
moyán	mágani	remedy, medecine
gálake	gerkwa	shield
rāga	rāga	mat
búta	hutu	empty, devoid of.

This list of identical or related terms in the Lógone- and Hausa-languages, although somewhat shorter, than the preceding one representing such cases of relationship between the Lógone- and Kanúri-languages, will, I hope, convince every body, conversant with the spirit of linguistic matters, that the relation between Lógone and Hausa is much closer, than that between Lógone and Kanúri, most of the terms here adduced being such as regard a primitive state of being and thinking, and not a certain degree of civilization, which is the case with most of the

---

*) na in Lógoné seems to be the general particle indicating place and time, and we find it as an integrant portion of all the terms mentioned p. 77 and 79.

lich die Zahl solcher Beziehungen noch bedeutend vermehren. Wir haben also wol einigen Grund zu dem Schluss, dass es eine Zeit gab, wo die Lógonē oder vielleicht der ganze Mása-Stamm, von dem die Lógonē eben nur eine später ausgesonderte politische Gruppe bilden, einst in naher Berührung mit den Hausa lebten und zwar selbst noch in der Tropischen Zone. Vergleiche dazu, was ich S. XVI gesagt habe.

Was nun die Berührungen des Lógonē mit anderen Sprachen betrifft, so scheinen die sehr sparsam, mit Ausnahme der bei Gelegenheit der kleinen Vokabularien zu besprechenden Verwandtschaftsbeziehungen mit den anderen Idiomen der Mása-Gruppe. Ausnehmen müssen wir auch noch das Galla, obgleich die Berührungen des Lógonē- mit letzterer Sprache meist durch das Hausa vermittelt werden, wie z. B. G. sā, „Kuh", L. ša, vermittelt durch H. sa; jedoch finden wir auch einige in den beiden ersteren Sprachen übereinstimmende Ausdrücke, die in letzterer, wenigstens in ihrer heutigen Gestalt, keine Vermittelung finden, wie z. B. der Galla-Ausdruck laga für „Fluss" dem Lógonē layam sehr nahe verwandt ist, zumal wenn wir bedenken, dass am in letzterer Sprache „Wasser" bedeutet, also die Endung völlig erklärt, während das Hausa jetzt den ganz fremden Ausdruck gulbi hat; ferner L. tekū, „einer" (allerdings auch im Mába tek), G. toko; dann entfernter verwandt L. χkán, „zehn", G. kudán.

Was nun die ziemlich zahlreichen Ausdrücke betrifft, die Gegenstände eines gewissen Grades geselliger Bildung bezeichnen, welche dem Lógonē mit den benachbarten Sprachen Wándalā und Bágrimma gemeinsam sind, so habe ich schon früher die Bemerkung gemacht, dass diese Ausdrücke höchst wahrscheinlich von den anderen Sprachen dem Lógonē entborgt sind, da die Bewohner dieses kleinen, höchst günstig gelegenen Ländchens ihren Nachbarn in Industrie und Civilisation offenbar weit vorangeschritten waren. Nur mit der Wándalā-Sprache möchte es scheinen, dass das Lógonē etwas nähere verwandtschaftliche Beziehung haben könnte, worüber ich im folgenden Kapitel einiges Weitere beizubringen Gelegenheit haben werde.

Zehntes Kapitel.

Die Wándalā-Sprache: ára Wándalā.

In Bezug auf Abstammung und nationale Verwandtschaft des Wándalā-Völkchens, das jetzt das kleine, durch Kapitän Denham zuerst bekannt gewordene, immer mehr eingeschränkte, Bergländchen, das er in der Kanúri-Form Mándara genannt hat, bewohnt, werde ich einiges Weitere in der Einleitung zu meiner Sammlung der kürzeren Vokabularien beibringen. Hier will ich nur von der Sprache selbst reden; denn, obgleich ich die Wörter- und Phrasensammlung derselben bloss äusserlich niederschrieb, wie oben S. XII f. angegeben, und niemals auch nur den Versuch machte, sie zu bemeistern, ist doch mein Material reich und zuverlässig genug, um vorläufig in eine leidlich vollständige Analyse der Sprache einzugehen.

1. In Bezug auf Orthographie will ich nur bemerken, dass die Verwechselung verwandter Laute auch hier ziemlich häufig ist, wie das bei durch Schrift nicht fixirten und schwer aufzufassenden Sprachen sich gar leicht erklärt. Dazu kommt, dass auch das Wándalā Ueberfluss an Kehl- und Zungenlauten hat. So finden wir denn in meinem Material eine mehrfache Verwechselung zwischen s, š und θ auf der einen und θ und χ, sowie f und χ auf der anderen Seite, wie z. B. ich für „Ohr" allein deutlich šoma hörte, mit š, während ich den aus demselben Wort durch Zusammensetzung entstandenen Ausdruck wa-θema mit θ schrieb. So habe ich denn auch für das Nennwort „Kälte" die Form ikθe, während ich das Eigenschaftswort „kalt" éχχio geschrieben habe. So habe ich gleichfalls die verschiedenen Formen kóhie, katχio, koltχe für „viel" und so sind auch das weiche d (δ) und z leicht verwechselt, wie z. B. yedo und yeze, „ich komme".

terms related amongst each other in the Lógone- and Kanúri-languages; and, no doubt, we may thence conclude with some degree of certainty, that there was a time, when the Lógone- and Hausa-people lived close together, keeping up an intimate intercourse amongst each other, and as it seems in the Tropical Region. Compare what I have said in this respect p. XVII.

As for points of contact of the Lógone-idiom with other languages, they seem to be very scanty indeed, with the exception of the points of relationship which intercede between it and the other languages of the Mása-group; we have, moreover, to exclude from this remark the Galla, although the greater portion of the points of contact which intercede between the latter and the Lógone, find their explanation by means of the Hausa, such as the relationship of the Galla-term sá, „cow" with the Lógone θa is explained through the Hausa-term sa; but there are also some cases of relationship between the Galla and the Lógone quite independent from the latter language, such as Lógone layam, „river", Galla laga (where we have to remark, that the termination am in the former word may have some relation to am, „water"); L. tekū, „one" (also in Múba tok), G. toko; L. χkán, „ten"; G. kudán.

As for several terms indicating objects of a certain degree of civilization, which are common to the Lógone with the neighbouring languages of the Wándalā and Bágrimma, I have already remarked above, that they have most probably been borrowed by those other idioms from the Lógone, the latter people in consequence of their own cleverness and the favourable situation of their country having been evidently far in advance of their neighbours, as well those to the East as those to the West and South, in industry and civilization. Only with the Wándalā-language there may seem to intercede some closer relation, of which I shall have opportunity to speak in the following chapter.

Chapter the tenth.

The Wándalā-language: óra Wándalá.

With regard to the origin and national connection of the Wándalā-people, who inhabit the small Alpine country, which in consequence of Captain Denham's adventurous journey has become known to Europeans under the form Mándara, I shall say something more in the Introductory Remarks to my collection of shorter vocabularies; here I shall only speak of the language itself, of which, although I wrote it merely down from the mouth of a native of that country, as stated before p. XIII f., and never even attempted to speak it, my materials are rich and accurate enough to give a somewhat complete analysis. And the Wándalā-idiom claims a particular interest on account of being the most Southern language among my whole collection of larger vocabularies.

1. I first must make a few remarks with regard to the orthography of this language in particular. In the Wándalā we have likewise, as in the Lógone-language, an abundance of harsh guttural and sibilating sounds, while closely related letters are apt to be confounded amongst each other. This is especially the case with the letters s, š and θ on the one and θ and χ, as well as f and χ on the other hand, as, for instance, the term for „ear" I caught with the š sound, writing šema, while the composite term wa-θema I wrote by a θ. Thus I have also the term ikθe, „cold" subst., ékχie, „cold" adj. Thus, also I have the various forms hókio, hóťχio, kóltχe meaning „much, many". Thus also the soft d (đ) and z are easily confounded, as, for instance, yodo and yozo, „I came". Further inquiries in this field will remove uncertainties like those here pointed out.

2. Ich gehe nun zur Besprechung des persönlichen Fürwortes über. Die Bildung dieses Fürwortes scheint mir ziemlich deutlich zu sein und gebe ich, um mich besser verständlich zu machen, zuerst ein vollständiges Paradigma seiner Formen, wie sie mir vorkamen.

	Singular.		Plural.
1ste Person	bá-ja	. . . .	bá-ñga-rê.
2te „	bá-ka	. . . .	wó-ko-rê.
3te „	bá-ñga-nê	. .	bé-te-rê.

Bei näherer Betrachtung dieser Formen sehen wir zuerst, dass dem wirklichen, die bestimmte Person bezeichnenden Ausdruck ba vorgesetzt ist, das unzweifelhaft dem ganz ähnlich lautenden Hausa-Wort ba, „Person", das nationalen Benennungen vorgesetzt wird, entspricht, ganz wie ma im Kanúri der vollen Form des persönlichen Fürwortes in jener Sprache nachgesetzt wird, wie z. B. ñ-ma, ni-ma u. s. w.; jedoch scheint der Unterschied zu bestehn, dass im Kanúri die einfache Pronominalform sehr häufig gebraucht wird, während im Lógonē das ba niemals davon getrennt zu werden scheint, ausgenommen in solchen Fällen, wo das Fürwort mit dem Zeitwort eng verschmolzen oder als Suffix gebraucht ist. Den Charakter dieses ba in der Bedeutung „Individuum" verstehen wir besser, wenn wir berücksichtigen, dass es häufig selbst in Verbindung mit Eigenschaftswörtern gebraucht wird. Es schliesst sich also der Batta-Sprache an.

So behalten wir also ya und ka für den Singular der ersten und zweiten Person des persönlichen Fürwortes, während ga-ne, das für die 3te Person übrig bleibt, wahrscheinlich aus demselben ka besteht, das die 2te Person bezeichnet, mit einem hinzugefügten, wol lokalen, ne, mit der Bedeutung „da da", d. h. „der, er". Dass diess die richtige Ableitung ist, sehen wir, abgesehen davon, dass ñga schon die possessive Form für den Singular der 3ten Person geworden ist, deutlich aus der Pluralform der 2ten Person bá-ko-ré oder wó-ko-ré, wo ba in wo verwandelt und rê das Zeichen des Plurals ist, also ein einfaches ko übrig bleibt. Nur müssen wir uns nicht dadurch stören lassen, dass auch die Pluralform der ersten Person bá-ñga-re ein ga enthält, denn dieses ga, ñga erweist sich als eine Verwandlung der Singularform ya. Was die Pluralform der 3ten Person bé-te-ré betrifft, so scheint hier das ka der Singularform ganz fortgefallen und das näher bezeichnende ne der 3ten Person in te übergegangen zu sein, während das personelle Zeichen ba in be verwandelt ist. Wichtig für die richtige Beurtheilung dieser Formen des persönlichen Fürwortes ist die einfache Form der ersten Person Plur. añge in Zusammenhang mit bédeme, eigentlich bé-deme, da das letztere schon das allgemeine, „Person" bezeichnende, ba, be enthält; so bédem(e) añge, „Alle wir, wir Alle". Von añge werden wir auch eine possessive Form finden.

So behalten wir denn als wirklich charakteristische Zeichen, für die erste Person i, für die zweite k und für die dritte n (vielleicht auch s), indem zu diesem Zeichen im Plural rê hinzugefügt ist, dasselbe re, worüber ich im Verlauf dieser Betrachtung noch ein Weiteres zu sagen haben werde; vergleiche auch ro im Kanúri „noch einmal".

2, a) In Bezug auf die Abwandlung dieser pronominalen Formen und das eng damit zusammenhängende possessive Fürwort kann ich leider nicht völlig Sicheres geben und will deshalb lieber einige diese Beziehungen vertretenden Phrasen hierhersetzen.

1ste Person Sing. Accusativ und Dativ (sehr unsicher):

„du liebst mich", wu ki we bá-ku (we, „lieben", bá-ka, „du");

„gib mir", wil te wa (wil, „geben").

Genitiv und possessive Form:

„Sache von mir, mir gehörig" (S. 5) sa- {raä / ruaä} (sehr an Baskisch erinnernd);

„mein Kameel", lúgume raä;

„meine Kameele", lúgumé-ha raä;

„mein Pferd", bólisse raä;

„meine Pferde", bolissé-ha raä.

2. I now proceed to speak of the personal pronoun.

The formation of the pronoun seems to me to be perfectly clear, and in order to make me better understood, I first give a perfect paradigm of its forms, such as they are now generally used.

	singular.		plural.
1st person	bá-ya	. . . . . .	bá-ṅga-rē.
2nd „	bá-ka	. . . . . .	wó-ke-rē.
3rd „	bá-ṅga-nē	. . .	bé-te-rē.

When subjecting these forms to a closer inspection, we soon become aware, that to the real characteristic sign designating the distinct person in question, the syllable ba meaning „individual" has been prefixed, identical as it appears with the Hausa-term ba prefixed to national terms, such as ba-Haushe, ba-Fullantši, just as we have seen, that in Kanúri ma is added to the full pronominal form, as, for instance, ū-ma, ni-ma, and so on; but the difference is, that the simple pronominal form in the latter language is frequently used, while in Lógonē the ba does not seem to be separated from the pronominal form, except when the pronoun is closely joined to the verb, or is used as a suffix. The true nature of this prefix ba will be better understood, when we take into account, that it is frequently added to adjectives, nay even to particles. Thus, it seems to form a link with the Bati-language.

We, therefore, have ya and ka for the singular forms of the 1st and 2nd person, while ga-nē, which remains to represent the 3rd person, is most probably composed of the same ka representing the 2nd person with an additional nē, meaning „thou there" i. q. „that one, he". That such has been the way of formation, is clearly seen as well from the case, that ṅga has become the form of the 2nd person in the possessive pronoun, as from the plural form of the 2nd person, where rē has simply been added to the form of the singular, the true characteristic sign of the 2nd person plur. being ke, while the first syllable wo is nothing but a slight change of ba, bo. For we must not be puzzled by the fact, that there appears a ga, ṅga also in the 1st pers. plur., this latter ga being nothing but a slight change of ya of the form of the singular. As for the 3rd person plur. bé-te-rē, the ka, ga of the corresponding form of the singular appears to have been entirely thrown off, while n has been changed into t, and the preceding ba has been changed into be. The character of the ba added to these pronominal forms is most clearly illustrated by those cases, where the pronoun is joined to the adjective bédeme (bé-demē), the latter containing already the ba, which on that account is not repeated; thus, we have bédeme aṅge, „we all, all of us".

Thus, there remain as really characteristic signs, of the 1st person i, of the 2nd k, and of the 3rd n (and a), to which signs in the plural number the termination rē, which we find in the very same position in the Tamul- and Telingu-languages, has been added.

2, a) With regard to the declension of these pronominal forms, as well as the possessive pronoun, I prefer likewise giving merely the phrases and instances I have, without abstracting from them positive rules.

1st person sing. accusative (not quite clear) and dative case:

„thou likest me", we ki wo bá-ka (wo, „to like", bá-ka, „thou");

„give me", wil te wa (wil, „give"); „lead me", kaé te kad.

Genitive case and possessive form:

Of me, mine: „thing of me, my property" (p. 5), zá { raē / raaē

„my camel", ldguma raē;

„my camels", ldgumá-ha raē;

„my horse", bélissa raē;

„my horses", bélissá-ha raē.

1ste Person Plur., Accusativ und Dativ:

„ihr helft uns", kú-ma-lá ṅkerẽ wó-kerẽ } (2te anstatt der 1sten Pers. Plur.?);
„sie helfen uns", té-ma-lá ṅkerẽ bé-terẽ }
„gebt uns", wa ṅger-te wila; „rührt uns nicht", vrenga ṅgir ka;
„ihr liebt uns", we ṅkur gur wũea (wũea populär statt wó-kerẽ);
„sie schlagen uns", ta-dže me bé-terẽ;
„ihr schlagt uns", ku-dže ṅga wókerẽ.

1ste Person Plur., Genitiv und possessive Form:

„Sache von uns", „unser Eigenthum", a-zá- { mia (ámaya?), ṅgrena (cf. Baskimb gu-ria);
„unser Kameel", lúgumá ṅgaré;
„unsere Kameele", lúguma-há ṅgare;
„unser Pferd", bélisá ṅgarẽ;
„unsere Pferde", bélisa-há ṅgare;
„unsere Provision", kãši ámaya.

2te Person Sing., Accusativ und Dativ:

„er liebt dich", we wo ṅga né (?we wo ṅga bá-ṅga-né);
„ich gebe dir", yo wa à-te wila;
„ich helfe dir", yé-ma-lá kĩ bá-ya (? „ich helfe euch");

2te Person Sing., Genitiv und possessive Form:

„Sache von dir, dein Eigenthum", zá- { ṅga, ṅgena;
„dein Kameel", lúguma ṅga;
„deine Kameele", lúgumá-ha ṅga;
„dein Pferd", bélisa ṅga;
„deine Pferde", bélisá-ha ṅga.

2te Person Plur. Accusativ und Dativ:

„wir helfen euch", gá-ma-lá ṅkerẽ há-ṅgare;
„sie lieben euch", we ṅkur gur we bé-terẽ;
„ich gebe euch", yo wo ker-te wil wé-kerẽ;

2te Person Plur. Genitiv und possessive Form:

„Sache von euch, euer Eigenthum", a-zá- { kerẽ; ṅgre (zusammengezogene Form);
„euer Kameel", lúgumá (wé)kerẽ } (die einfache Form des persönlichen Fürwortes dem Subjekt angefügt).
„eure Kameele", lúgumá-ha wé-kerẽ }
„euer Pferd", bélisa wé-kerẽ }
„eure Pferde", bélisá-ha wé-kerẽ }

3te Person Sing., Accusativ und Dativ:

„ich liebe ihn, sie", wo a wo bá-ya;
„gieb ihm", wa a-te wilá ṅga-né (?die dritte Person zweimal ausgedrückt);
„er hilft ihm", á-ma-la é-se-rẽ bá-ṅga-né (é-se-rẽ zweifelhaft).

3te Person Sing., Genitiv und possessive Form:

„Sache von ihm, sein Eigenthum", zá a-rã; zá ta-rẽ S. 5 zweifelhaft; Plur.?
„sein Kameel", lúgumá a-ra;
„seine Kameele", lúgumá-ha a-rá;
„sein Pferd", bélisá a-ra;
„seine Pferde", bélisá-ha a-ra.

3te Person Plur., Dativ:

„gib ihnen", wa ter-te wila.

1st person plur., accusative and dative case:

„you assist us", kú-ma-lá ṅkerē wó-korē } (2nd instead of 1st pers. plur.?);
„they assist us", tó-ma-lá ṅkerō bó-terō }

„give us", wa ṅger-te wíla; „do not be angry with us", vroṅga ṅgír ka;

„you like us", we ṅhar gur wũca (wũca popular form of wó-korē);

„they beat us", ta-dže me bó-terē;

„you beat us", ku-dže ṅga wó-korē.

1st person plur., genitive case and possessive form:

„thing of us, our property", a-zá { mia (ámaya?), ṅgreaa (comp. Bask. gu-ria);

of us, our: „our camel", lúgumá ṅgarē;
„our camels", lúguma-há ṅgarē;
„our horse", bólissá ṅgarē;
„our horses", bólissa-há ṅgarē;
„our provisions", kaži ámaya.

2nd person sing., accusative and dative case:

„he likes thee", we wo ṅga nē (?we we ṅga bá-ṅga-nē?);

„I give thee", yo wa k-te wila;

„I assist thee", yé-ma-lá hē bá-ya (?I assist you plur.);

2nd person sing., genitive case and possessive form:

„thing of thee, thy property", zá- { ṅga, ṅgaaa;

„thy camel", lúguma ṅga;
„thy camels", lúgumá-ha ṅga;
„thy horse", bólissa ṅga;
„thy horses", bólissá-ha ṅga.

2nd person plur., accusative and dative case:

„we assist you", gá-ma-lá ṅkerē bá-ṅgarē;

„they like you", we ṅhar gur we bó-terē;

„I give you", yo we ker-te wil wé-korē;

2nd person plur., genitive case and possessive form:

„thing of you, your property", a-zá- { korē; ṅgre (contracted form);

„your camel", lúgumá (we)korē }
„your camels", lúgumá-ha wé-korē } (the simple form of the personal pro-
„your horse", bólissa wé-korē } noun added to the subject).
„your horses", bólissá-ha wé-korē }

3rd person sing., accusative and dative case:

„I like him, her", wo a we bá-ya;

„give him", wa a-te wilá ṅga-nē (?the 3rd person represented a second time);

„he does assist him", á-ma-la á-se-rē bá-ṅga-nē (á-se-rē doubtful).

3rd person sing., genitive case and possessive form:

„thing of him, his property", zá a-rā; zá ta-rē p. 6 probably plural form;

of him, his: „his camel", lúgumá a-rā;
„his camels", lúgumá-ha a-rā;
„his horse", bólissá a-rā;
„his horses", bólissá-ha a-rā.

3rd person plur., dative case:

„give them", wa ter-te wila.

3te Person Plur., Accusativ:

„wir schlagen sie", ánge dźé-na bá-ngare gé-terĕ } (b in g verwandelt).
„wir lieben sie", we ángye-we rēa bá-ngare gé-terĕ }

3te Person Plur., Genitiv und possessive Form:

„Kameel von ihnen, ihr Kameel", lúgum(a) á-terĕ;
„Kameele von ihnen, ihre Kameele", lúgumá-ha ámdna;
„Pferd von ihnen, ihr Pferd", bélissa gé-terĕ;
„Pferde von ihnen, ihre Pferde", bélissá-h(a) á-terĕ;
„ihre Sache, ihr Eigenthum", a-zá- {har / hár-ena} beide Formen wol 2te Pers. Plur.

In diesen Beispielen bleibt nur Weniges unsicher, doch ist die Mannichfaltigkeit der Formen sehr gross, besonders veranlasst durch die Umwandelung ganzer Silben durch nachfolgende. Charakteristisch ist das völlig überflüssig erscheinende, den Phrasen meist vorgesetzte we, wa (gewiss nichts Anderes als das oben besprochene ba), besonders verfänglich in den Phrasen, wo das Zeitwort selbst we ist „lieben". Das den Besitz bezeichnende rĕ oder rā erkennen wir klar aus der Frageform a-zá-n-rĕ, „wessen (Eigenthum) ist das"?; in vielen anderen Fällen dagegen bleibt es zweifelhaft und ist von der einfachen Pluralform des Pronomens kaum zu unterscheiden. me, „uns", hängt mit mia, ámaya, „unser", entschieden zusammen. ámdna für die besitzende Form der 3ten Pers. Plur. wird durch amdo, „sie, die Leute", erklärt.

3. In Betreff der Zahlen habe ich hier keine besondere Bemerkung zu machen, ausser dass die Wándalā-Sprache entschiedener Massen das Decimal-System befolgt; so haben wir denn kel-ana, „zehn"; kal-bua (mit Verwandelung des Vokals), „zwei Zehner", d. h. „zwanzig". Auch habe ich hier im Allgemeinen anzuführen, dass, obgleich dies System so grundverschieden ist von dem in der Hausa-Sprache gebrauchten, dennoch die Ausdrücke für 2, 3, 4 und 7 in beiden Sprachen einige Spuren von verwandtschaftlichen Beziehungen zeigen, wie wir in dem betreffenden Schlussparagraphen sehen werden. Dagegen haben die Kanúri den Ausdruck fal neben tilō für „eins" von den Wándalā nur äusserlich entlehnt.

4. *Das Zeitwort.*

Ich ziehe auch in diesem Falle wieder vor, einige Beispiele zusammenzustellen, bevor ich daraus allgemeinere Schlüsse ziehe. Das sicherste Paradigma, das ich habe, scheint zu sein ye nó-na (ye uá-na) (Wurzel na), „ich sehe".

Gegenwärtige Zeit, positive Form.

	Singular.	Plural.
1ste Person	ye-nó-na bá-ya	ga-uá-na bá-ngarĕ,
2te „	ka-ná-na bá-ka	ko-ná-na wó-korĕ,
3te „	a-ná-na bá-ngané	ta-ná-ne bó-terĕ.

Gegenwärtige Zeit, negative Form.

	Singular.	Plural.
1ste Person	ye-nán ka bá-ya	ga-uán ka bá-ngarĕ,
2te „	ka-nán ka bá-ka	ko-nán ka wó-korĕ,
3te „	a-uán ka bá-ngané . . .	ta-nán ka bó-terĕ.

Aorist, positive Form.

	Singular.	Plural.
1ste Person	ye-nā bá-ya	ga-nā bá-ngarĕ,
2te „	ka-nā bá-ka	ko-nā wó-korĕ,
3te „	a-nā bá-ngané	te-nā bó-terĕ.

Aorist, negative Form.

	Singular.	Plural.
1ste Person	yo-nā ka bá-ya	ga-nā ka bá-ngarĕ,
2te „	ka-nā ka bá-ka	ko-nā ka wó-korĕ,
3te „	a-nā ka bá-ngané . . .	te-nā ka bó-terĕ.

3rd person plur., accusative case:

„we beat them", añga džé-na bá-ñgare gé-terē } (b changed into g).
„we like them", wo añgyo-we rēa bá-ñgarē gé-terē }

3rd person plur., genitive case and possessive form:

of them, their: „their camel", lúgum(a) á-terē;
„their camels", lúgumá-ha ámdna;
„their horse", bélissa yé-terē;
„their horses", bélissá-ha á-terē;

„thing of them, their property", a-zá- { kar / kár-sua } both forms may rather belong to the 2nd pers. plur.

In these phrases there seems to remain very little, that is uncertain although the variety of forms is rather great, caused especially by the change of syllables, as affected by the form of following ones. Characteristic is the apparently redundant we or wa (the very same ba spoken of before) and is puzzling in such phrases where the verb itself is wo, „to like"; and this again reminds one of the forms of speech occurring in the Ba-languages. Some degree of uncertainty is caused by the double character certain forms bear, such as rē, rā, which, while it is an essential part of the forms of the plural number, serves to indicate likewise possession or property, as appears most clearly from the interrogative phrase a-zá-u-rē, „whose (property) is it"?. As for the form ámdna representing the possessive form of the 3rd person plur., it may be illustrated by comparing amde, „they, these people", occurring among my phrases.

3. As for the numerals, I have no particular remarks to offer, except that the Wándalā-language follows decidedly the decimal system of numeration, hel-aua, „ten", hal-bás (with a change of the vowel), „two tenths" i. q. „twenty". I have also to state, that, although this system is so totally different from that used in the Hausa-language, nevertheless the terms for 2, 3, 4 and 7 in both languages exhibit evident traces of relationship. But on the other hand there cannot be the slightest doubt, but that the Kanúri have merely borrowed from the Wándalā-language the term fal, used in certain cases instead of tílo for „one".

4. *The verb.*

I have likewise prefer first giving some paradigms, before drawing thence a few general conclusions. The best of my specimens seems to be ye né-na (ye ná-na), „I see" (root na).

Present tense, positive form.

	singular.	plural.
1st person	ye-né-na bé-ya	ga-né-na bá-ñgarē,
2nd „	ka-ná-na bá-ka	ko-ná-na wó-korē,
3rd „	a-ná-na bá-ñganē	ta-ná-no bé-torē.

Present tense, negative form.

	singular.	plural.
1st person	ye-nán ka bá-ya	ga-nán ka bá-ñgarē,
2nd „	ka-nán ka bá-ka	ko-nán ka wó-korē,
3rd „	a-nán ka bá-ñganē . . .	ta-nán ka bé-torē.

Aorist, positive form.

	singular.	plural.
1st person	ye-nā bá-ya	ga-nā bá-ñgarē,
2nd „	ka-nā bá-ka	ko-nā wó-korē,
3rd „	a-nā bá-ñganē	te-nā bé-torē.

Aorist, negative form.

	singular.	plural.
1st person	ye-nā ka bá-ya	ga-nā ka bá-ñgarē,
2nd „	ka-nā ka bá-ka	ko-nā ka wó-korē,
3rd „	a-nā ka bá-ñganē	te-nā ka bé-torē.

Der Conditionell ist sehr unsicher und gebe ich die regelmässig richtigen Formen, wie sie mir jetzt wahrscheinlich scheinen, in Parenthese neben solchen, wie ich sie niederschrieb:

Singular.

1ste Person me nónnëa (me yo-nán-ëa),
2te „ manna kánnaka (ma ka-nán-ëa),
3te „ maninna bá-ṅganë (m(e) a-nán-ëa bá-ṅganë).

Plural.

1ste Person manangṅenna baṅgórkent (ma ga-nán-ëa ba-ṅgár-kent),
2te „ mennekorenna dokárkent (ma ko-nán-ëa wo-kár-kent),
3te „ menna renna betórkent (me te-nán-ëa be-tór-kent).

Ich gebe nun erst ein Paradigma von yó-do, „ich gehe" (Wurzel do, do, so), obgleich einige Formen mir nicht ganz sicher zu sein scheinen.

Gegenwärtige Zeit, positive Form.

	Singular.	Plural.
1ste Person	ííl-do [1]) bá-ya	ná-do bá-ṅgarë,
2te „	ká-do bá-ka	kó-dol wó-korë,
3te „	á-do bá-ṅganë	tá-do bé-terë.

Gegenwärtige Zeit, negative Form.

Singular.

1ste Person yó-do k-ëa, contrahirt aus yé-do ka bá-ya,
2te „ ká-do ka-ka „ „ ká-do ka bá-ka,
3te „ á-do ka-ṅgne „ „ á-do ka bá-ṅganë.

Plural.

1ste Person ga-n-do k-áṅgarë, regelmässig gá-do ka bá-ṅgarë,
2te „ kó-do k-ókorë, „ kó-do ka wó-korë,
3te „ tá-do k-óterë, „ tá-do ka bé-terë.

Aorist, positive Form.

	Singular.	Plural.
1ste Person	ye-dö bá-ya	mo-zól bá-ṅgarë,
2te „	ka-dö bá-ka	ko-zól wó-korë,
3te „	a-dö bá-ṅganë	ta-zól bé-terë.

Aorist, negative Form.

	Singular.	Plural.
1ste Person	yo-dón ka bá-ya	den-ger k(a b)á-ṅgarë,
2te „	ka-dón ka bá-ka	ko-zól ka wó-korë,
3te „	a-dón ka bá-ṅganë . . .	ta-zól ka bé-terë.

Conditionell (vulgäre, besonders durch Wiederholung der Stammsilbe veränderte Formen).

	Singular.	Plural.
1ste Person	ma den dó-ëa	ma den-ger dá-ṅgarë,
2te „	ma den ká-ka	ma zól-ko-zól kó-rua,
3te „	ma da ká-ṅganë	ma zel-zel e-tó-rua.

Die meisten meiner übrigen Paradigmen sind zu unsicherer Natur, um hier einen Platz zu finden, und will ich deshalb nur die Gegenwart und unbestimmte Vergangenheit von ye-zó-na hersetzen, eigentlich ye-zá-na, „ich esse". Denn das ist offenbar die eigentliche

---

[1]) Die Form ííl-do, so auffallend sie auch auf den ersten Blick scheint, ist doch unzweifelhaft richtig, da ich sie zu wiederholten Malen hörte; ursprünglich mag es ye-el-do sein. Auch das l am Ende der Form kodól scheint seine innere Begründung zu haben, da das Neuwort dale lautet.

The forms of the Conditional mood are very uncertain, and I therefore give here side by side what I actually wrote down with what I now consider to be the right forms, including the latter in a parenthesis.

singular.

1st person me nénnëa (me yo-nén-ëa),

2nd „ manna kánnaka (ma ka-nán-ëa),

3rd „ maninna bá-ngané (m(e) a-nán-ëa bá-ngané).

plural.

1st person manangùonea bangérkent (ma ga-nán-ëa ba-ngár-kent),

2nd „ mennekoreuna dokúrkent (ma ko-nán-ëa wo-kór-kent),

3rd „ menna ronna betórkent (me te-nán-ëa be-tór-kent).

I now give a paradigm of yé-do, „I go" (root do, đo, so), although some of the forms appear to me to be less certain.

Present tense, positive form.

	singular.	plural.
1st person	lil-do[*]) bá-ya	ná-do bá-ngare,
2nd „	ká-do bá-ka	kó-del wó-koré,
3rd „	á-do bá-ngané	tá-do bé-tore.

Present tense, negative form.

singular.

1st person yó-do k-ëa, contracted from yó-do ka bá-ya,

2nd „ ká-do ka-ka „ „ ká-do ka bá-ka,

3rd „ á-do ka-ngne „ „ á-do ka bá-ngané.

plural.

1st person ga-n do k-ángaré (gá-do ka bá-ngaré),

2nd „ kó-do k-ókore (kó-do ka wókoré),

3rd „ tá-do k-étere (tá-do ka bé-teré).

Aorist, positive form.

	singular.	plural.
1st person	ye-dō bá-ya	me-zél bá-ngaré,
2nd „	ka-dō bá-ka	ko-zél wó-koré,
3rd „	a-dō bá-ngané	ta-zél bé-teré.

Aorist, negative form.

	singular.	plural.
1st person	yo-dén ka bá-ya	den-ger k(a b)á-ngaré,
2nd „	ka-dén ka bá-ka	ko-zél ka wó-koré,
3rd „	a-dén ka bá-ngané . . .	ta-zél ka bé-teré.

Conditional, rather corrupted forms.

	singular.	plural.
1st person	ma don dó-ëa	ma don-ger dá-ngaré,
2nd „	ma don ká-ka	ma zél-ko-zél kó-rua,
3rd „	ma de ká-ngané	ma zel-zel o-té-rua.

Most of my other paradigms are too uncertain to find a place here, and I, therefore, give only the present and aorist tense of ye-zé-na, properly ye-zá-na, „I eat"; for that,

---

[*]) This form lil-do is evidently correct, as I have it several times; properly it may be ye-el-do. The l at the end of the form kodél also seems to belong to a fuller form of the root, the substantive being dale.

Form der Gegenwart, und ye-sä, das ich im Vokabular (S. 87) gegeben habe, ist vielmehr eine Form der Vergangenheit. Daneben habe ich allerdings noch yo-zé-n a-sõ, wol „ich habe zu essen aufgehört", wie ich auch von ye-tse, „ich breche auf" habe ye-tse sõ-n, „ich bin aufgebrochen", falls dies nicht eine blos vulgäre Wiederholung der Wurzel ist. In den folgenden Beispielen lasse ich die volle Pronominalform bá-ya u. s. w. fort.

Gegenwart.			Aorist.		
	Singular.	Plural.		Singular.	Plural.
1ste Person	yo-sé-na . .	ma-sé-na,	1ste Person	yo-zõ	ma-sõ,
2te „	ka-sé-na . .	ko-zé-na,	2te „	ka-sõ	ko-zõ,
3te „	a-zé-na . .	te-zé-na.	3te „	a-zõ	to-zõ.

Die ganz unsicheren Daten der negativen Form der Vergangenheit gebe ich in der Note[1].

Nun gebe ich die gegenwärtige Zeit von yé-šokó-na, „ich kaufe", Imp. šokó.

	Singular.	Plural.
1ste Person	yé-šokó-na bá-ya . . .	mé-šoká-na bá-ńgare,
2te „	ké-šoká-na bá-ke . . .	ké-šokó-no wó-korõ,
3te „	á-šoká-na bá-ńganẽ . .	té-šokó-n(e) (b)é-terõ.

Conditionell, populär corrumpirte Formen[2].

	Singular.	Plural.
1ste Person	mi šokdn šok-woi yá-na .	mi šokdn báńgare (bá-ńga-ruá?),
2te „	mi šokdb šok-wẽ ká-na .	mi šokób šok-wẽ kó-ruá,
3te „	mi šokdb šok-án gán-na .	mi šokób šok-wẽ té-ruá.

Ich gebe nun ein anderes Beispiel des Conditionell's, „wenn ich thäte", oder „wenn ich gethan hätte", das uns in deutlicherer Weise darstellt, wie ausser der Veränderung der verbalen Form auch die Endung des Fürwortes eine Umwandelung betroffen hat.

	Singular.	Plural.
1ste Person	me yé-magá bá-yua . . .	ma gá-magá bá-ńga-ruá,
2te „	ma ká-magá bá-kua . . .	mo kó-magá bó-ko-ruá,
3te „	m(a) á-magá bá-ńga-nuá .	ma té-magá bé-te-ruá.

Als ein bemerkenswerthes Beispiel des Conditionell's haben wir unzweifelhaft auch anzusehn die Phrase ma dãir(e)-li, „wenn es (auch) wahr ist" oder „es mag wahr sein", entsprechend dem Kanúri širó yaié.

Als Beispiel eines Subjunktivs theile ich die Phrase mit „ist die Stadt, wohin wir gehn zu schlafen (übernachten), nah oder fern"?,

eks(e) ímmi-dá horúm-kua yeyẽ imtü fírdẽs-hẽ,
Stadt wohin gehn? schlafen dass wir weit oder nahe oder,

wenn wir die Form horúm-kna mit me-häram, „wir schlafen" vergleichen.

Was die Bildung der negativen Form betrifft, so erwähne ich hier noch ye-wíl-ka S. 67, N. 20 von der positiven Form ye-wíla, „ich gebe nicht"; ye-muń-ka, negative Form der 1sten Person Sing. der Gegenwart und meǵín-ka, negative Form der 1sten Person Plur. des Aorists von yé-magá, „ich thue".

---

[1]

	Singular.	Plural.
1ste Person	ne-né-hẽa (yo-sã ka ba-ya)	ne-ágar ká-dame („alle") bá-ágará,
2te „	ne-ba bá-ka	ne-gar ka dé-demi (wó)korõ,
3te „	ne-ké-de bá-ńgené . . .	ne-re ka damé-terõ.

[2] Wenn ich diese Formen populär corrumpirt nenne, so bestreite ich damit keineswegs ihre Richtigkeit; im Gegentheil scheinen sie mir völlig richtig. Die ungewissen Formen des Aorist dagegen ziehe ich vor, ganz wie ich sie niedergeschrieben, hier in der Note mitzutheilen:

	Singular.	Plural.
1ste Person	ye šekonna šekné	mé šekón bá-ngaré,
2te „	me šekóbše kekaua	ká šewók wó-korõ,
3te „	šekóbše kébgené	té šikó yé-tere.

no doubt, is the form of the present tense, while ye-sā, what I have given in my vocabulary p. 37, is rather a form of the past, side by side with which I have another form ye-só-n u-sā which probably means originally „I have finished eating", just as from yo-tse, „I start", I have a past tense ye-tse sē-a, „I have started", although possibly we may have here a mere repetition of the verbal root.

present tense.			aorist tense.		
	singular.	plural.		singular.	plural.
1st person	yo-só-na . .	ma-zé-na,	1st person	yo-sā	ma-zō,
2nd „	ka-zé-na . .	ko-zé-na,	2nd „	ka-sō	ko-zā,
3rd „	u-sé-na . .	to-zé-na.	3rd „	a-zō	ta-sā.

As for my rather uncertain data of the negative forms of the aorist, I prefer giving them in the note [1].

I now give the present tense of yó-šekó-na, „I buy", imp. šekó.

	singular.	plural.
1st person	yó-šekó-na bá-ya	mó-šeká-na bá-ṅgaré,
2nd „	kó-šeká-na bá-ka	kó-šekó-no wó-koré,
3rd „	ó-šeká-na bá-ṅganē . . .	tó-šekó-n(e) (b)ó-toré.

Conditional mood „if I bought", popularly corrupted [2]) forms.

	singular.	plural.
1st person	mi šekón šek-wo yá-na .	mi šekón báṅgare (bá-ṅga-ruá?),
2nd „	mi šekób šek-wē ká-na .	mi šekób šek-wē kó-ruá,
3rd „	mi šekób šek-án gán-na .	mi šekób šek-wō té-ruá.

I now give another instance of the conditional mood „if I did", or „if I had done", where we get a clearer insight into the way, how besides the change of the verbal form the termination of the pronoun has likewise been changed.

	singular.	plural.
1st person	mo yó-magá bá-yua . . .	ma gá-magá bá-ṅga-ruá,
2nd „	ma ká-magá bá-kua . . .	mo kó-magá bó-ko-ruá,
3rd „	m(a) á-magá bá-ṅga-nuá .	ma tó-magá bó-te-ruá.

As a remarkable form of the conditional mood we have also, no doubt, to look upon the phrase ma dair(e)-li, „it may be true" or „even if it be true" = Kanúri žiró yaie.

As an instance of a subjunctive mood I give the phrase „is the town where we go to pass the night there still far, or is it near"?,

oks(e) immi-da herúm-kua yeyō imtū firdža-hē,
town where we go we sleep that far either near or,

herúm-kua compared with mo-háram, „we sleep".

As instances of the formation of the negative form I still mention ye-wil-ka p. 67, note 20, from the positive form yo-wila, „I do not give"; yo-muṅ-ka, „I do not", negative form of the present, and magín-ka, „we did not", negative form of the aorist, from yó-magá, „I do".

---

[1])

	singular.	plural.
1st person	ne-nó-kře (ye-sé ka bá-ya)	na-águr ké-dama („alle") bá-ágeré,
2nd „	ne-ka bá-ka	ou-gár ka dó-damé (wá)koro,
3rd „	ne-kó-da bá-ṅgané . . .	su-re kada bé-teré.

[2]) More uncertain yet are the forms of the aorist, such as I have written down, and which I therefore prefer giving here in the note unchanged, as follows:

	singular.	plural.
1st person	yešekonne šekoē	mé šekón bá-ágeré,
2nd „	mo šekóbša kekone	kó šewók wó-koré,
3rd „	šekóbšo kóbgenē	té šikó yé-tere.

b) Als Formen des Imperativs gebe ich ilda, lada, „gehe", 1ste Person Plur. ingáld-ua, „lasst uns gehn"; gé-tškua, „lasst uns absteigen", von yé-tšokua; tsi-tse, „stehe auf", 1ste Person Plur. gna-tsē von ye-tsē; fo-fō, „stelle hin", 1ste Person Plur. mo-fang-fa von yé-fo-fā und wil, „gib", 2te Person Plur. willa von ye-wil, ye-wila. Als Beispiele negativer Formen des Imperativs gebe ich yē ngir ka, „verlass uns nicht", und trenga ngir ka, „stürme uns nicht".

c) Als eine Art von Participialbildung des Aktivs betrachte ich das géreg-ea in dem zusammengesetzten Ausdruck tšoi géreg-ea áma, „Insekt machend Honig", d. h. „die Biene", ferner solche Formen, wie an-ból (bode), „liegend (auf dem Leib)", dann mit der Hinzufügung von dē, das wol als Präposition zu fassen und mit dem Subjekt zu verbinden ist, an-kál dē orwā, „gekreuzt mit den Armen"; an-kál dē serā, „die Beine) gekreuzt".

d) Was passive Formen anbetrifft, so habe ich einige wenige Beispiele eines Particips Passivi, wie z. B. wó-raa a ūpa, „verwundet mit dem Speer", von yé-wa a ūpa, „ich verwunde mit dem Speer". Während wir in diesem Beispiel die oben angeführte Form des Conditionell's wiederfinden, ist dagegen ganz verschieden gebildet, mit Hinzufügung der Silbe hen vor der Wurzel, die Participialform hén-gia, „gekocht", von yé-gia, „(ich) koche". Anders wiederum ist a-ngdo, „gebunden", von yo-ngdo, „ich binde", eine der 3ten Person Sing. des Aorist Activi ganz entsprechende Form, nur durch Intonation leicht unterschieden. yēyim oder yirgim háya, „ich bin geboren", von ya, „gebären", scheint vollkommen richtig.

e) Indem ich nun diesen Paragraphen über das Zeitwort abschliesse, will ich nur noch die Bemerkung machen, dass die das Präsens auszeichnende, der Verbalwurzel angehängte Endung aa in manchen Fällen mit einiger Schwierigkeit zu unterscheiden ist, zumal wenn der Vokal verloren geht und ein Nennwort davon abhängt, wie z. B. in der Phrase yé-mebá-a kára, „ich facke das Feuer an"; ye-dšá-a kárā, „ich mache das Feuer aus", wo man wol Zweifel hegen kann, ob das a das dem Verbalstamm angehängte aa vertritt oder ob es die Beziehung zwischen dem Zeit- und dem Nennwort ausdrückt.

4. *Das Nennwort.*

Die Wándala-Sprache besitzt eine leidliche Anzahl einsilbiger Wörter, von denen ich, so weit sie mir bekannt geworden, in dem Schlussparagraphen dieses Kapitels ein Verzeichniss geben werde.

Was die Bildung und Zusammensetzung der anderen Nennwörter betrifft und die Weise ihrer Ableitung von verbalen Begriffen, so ist mein Material zu karg, um daraus weittragende allgemeine Schlussfolgerungen zu ziehn. Daher bitte ich denn die folgenden Bemerkungen als einen blossen Versuch anzusehn.

a) Von grossem Einfluss bei dieser Bildung erscheint die einfache Wurzel rā mit der Bedeutung „Mittel, Eigenthum", die unzweifelhaft auch den Kern des besitzanzeigenden Fürwortes der 1sten Person Sing. rua bildet, so wie der 3ten Person Sing. a-rā. Dieses selbige rā nun bildet einen integrirenden Bestandtheil mehrerer zusammengesetzten Nennwörter, wie z. B. ðe-rā mit der Bedeutung „Handwerk, Geschäft", vom Zeitwort ðe, welches wir noch weiterhin auch in vielen anderen zusammengesetzten Ausdrücken finden werden, welche die verschiedenen Beschäftigungen des Menschen bezeichnen; zo-rā, ao-rā, „Fuss", eigentlich wol „Werkzeug zum Gehn", zo, de. Diesem rā eng verwandt ist nach meiner Meinung die Endung rē, irē, die eine Eigenschaft oder einen Zustand anzeigt, wie z. B. téka-irē, „die Einsetzung des Königs" (tokae); maazau-irē, „Schlechtigkeit"; ðimbád-irē, „Bosheit"; ydk-irē, „Grösse", Hoheit".

b) Nun habe ich auch mehrere Beispiele von Zusammensetzung vermittelst wa gefunden, wahrscheinlich nur eine Abwandelung des oben bei den Pronomina erwähnten ganz generellen ba, wie auch in den Papua-Sprachen ein solches wa (oua) den Pronominalformen vorgesetzt wird, aber auch mit der besonderen Bedeutung „Körper, Mund, Hand". So habe ich wá-tšia,

b) As forms of the imperative I give ilda or lada, „go", 1st person plur. ing-álda-ua, „let us go"; gé-tškua, „let us dismount", from yó-tšokua; tal-tse, „rise", 1st pers. plur. gua-tsĕ from yo-tsĕ; fo-fŏ, „place, put", 1st person plur. mo-fúng-fa from yó-fo-fă, and wil, „give", 2nd pers. plur. willa from yo-wíl, yo-wíla. As instances of negative forms of the imperative I further give yé ńgir ka, „do not forsake us"; vreúga ńgir ka, „do not be angry with us".

c) As a kind of participle of the active voice I look upon the form górcg-eă in the composite term tšoi góreg-eă áma, „insect mak-ing honey" i. q. „bee", and moreover upon forms, such as an-ból (bodu), „lying (on the belly)", au-kál do orwă, „with crossed arms"; an-kál dĕ soră, „with crossed legs", in which latter instances I am not quite sure, whether we have to look upon the dĕ as part of the verbal form, or rather as a preposition to be connected with the object.

d) As for forms of the passive voice, my material is rather poor, but nevertheless I have a few instances of such a formation, as, for instance wó-rua n ŭpa, „wounded by the spear", from yó-wa n ŭpa, „I wound with the spear". While in this instance we may clearly recognize the above mentioned form of the conditional mood, quite a different form, by adding the syllable hen before the root, is exhibited by hén-gia, „boiled", from yó-gia, „I boil". As for a-ńgdo with the meaning „bound, tied" from yo-ńgdu, „I tie", it is perfectly identical with the form of the 3rd person sing. of the aorist, and only distinguished from the latter by a slight change of intonation. yĕ-yim báya, „I am born", may be right.

e) While thus closing this paragraph illustrative of the verbal forms, I will only add, that the termination na which being added to the verbal root characterizes the present tense, in many cases cannot but with difficulty be distinguished, especially in such cases where it rules a substantive, as, for instance, in the phrase yó-mebá-n kără, „I kindle the fire"; ye-džá-n kără, „I extinguish the fire", in which cases a scrupulous person may well entertain some doubt, whether the n represents the verbal termination na, or whether it indicates merely the relation obtaining between the verb and the substantive.

4. *The noun.*

The Wándală-language contains a tolerable number of monosyllabic nouns of which, as far as they have become known to me, I shall give a list in the concluding paragraph of this chapter.

As for the formation and composition of the other nouns, and the mode of deriving them from verbal notions, my material is too scanty to draw thence many positive conclusions; as an attempt, however, in this direction I give the following remarks.

a) The Wándală-idiom evidently possesses a simple root ră indicating „nature, possession", which, there can be no doubt, has been made use of for forming the possessive pronoun ruă, and is most clearly preserved in the form a-ră of the 3rd person sing. Now, this same ră forms an integrant part of several composite nouns, as, for instance θe-ră meaning „handicraft, business", from the verb θe, „make, do" which we are to find further on in many composite terms describing the various occupations of man; thus, likewise, so-ră, se-ră, „foot", properly „instrument for walking", from the verb se, &c. Closely related to this ră is, I think, the termination ré, irĕ indicating a character or quality, as, for instance in tékai-ré, „the installation of a king" (tekse); manzau-irĕ, „wickedness"; θimbád-irĕ, „malice"; yék-irĕ, „greatness".

b) I moreover think, I have found various compositions by means of the simple monosyllabic wa, a term obtaining the most manifold meanings, „mouth, outside, body", as I shall illustrate further on, but originally according to all appearance nothing else, but the above mentioned ba, which plays such a conspicuous part in the pronominal forms, and which even in those

„die Sonne", ursprünglich wol bedeutend „der sich bewegende, aufsteigende (Körper)", vom Zeitwort tse, tšé, das auch einen integrirenden Theil von déb-tšia, „Asche" und anderer Ausdrücke bildet. Der Gegensatz zu diesem wé-tšia, „Sonne", ist wá-gia, „Nacht". Auf dieses wa werde ich unter b, a) und bei Besprechung der Monosyllaben in der Wándalā-Sprache zurückkommen.

Als ein kurzes Beispiel der einfachen Ableitung eines Nennwortes von einer verbalen Form erwähne ich ó-faya, „Wind", von ye-féng, „ich blase".

c) Nun gebe ich einige der zahlreichen Zusammensetzungen vermittelst θe, welche die verschiedenen Beschäftigungen des Menschen bezeichnen,

c, a) solche, bei welchen θe mit anderen Nennwörtern einfach zusammengereiht ist, wie z. B. θ(e)-egda, „der Mann vom Amboss (egda)"; θ(e)-dúgole, „der Mann vom Wege (dúgole)", „der Führer"; θ(e)-iggete, „der Freund"; θe-šódane, „der Mann des Teufels", „der Bösewicht". Hierher gehören auch die meisten Namen der Hofchargen im kleinen Wándalā.

c, b) solche, welche vermittelst θe und eines Zeitwortes zusammengesetzt sind, indem in einigen Fällen das letztere wiederum ein substantives Objekt regiert, wie z. B. θe-šē-kalá, eigentlich θé-šekó-kalá, „der Mann (vom) kaufen" (šekó) Waaren (kalá), auch θe-gágánē, „Mann (vom) machen Handel", „der Kaufmann"; θe-nd(a)-akri, „Mann (vom) nehmen Lohn", d. h. „der Miethsarbeiter"; θé-magá, „der Arbeiter"; θé-magá-lipre, „Mann (vom) arbeiten (mit) Nadel", d. h. „der Schneider"; θé-magá-n-átsiri, „Mann vom arbeiten in Leder", d. h. „der Sattler"; θe-gá-n-afā, „Mann vom arbeiten in Holz", d. h. „der Tischler".

d) Diese halte ich auch für den geeigneten Platz, um anzubringen, was ich über die Art und Weise, zwei Nennwörter zu Einem Begriffe zu verbinden, zu sagen habe, obgleich diese Frage eigentlich schon in die Besprechung der Abwandelung des Nennwortes einschlägt, worüber ich aber so gut wie nichts zu sagen habe. Solche Verbindung nun geschieht in verschiedenster Weise,

α) indem man einfach die Ausdrücke neben einanderstellt mit Voranstellung des Subjekts vor dem Objekt, wie z. B. er-wá, „Ende des Armes", d. h. „Hand"; wé-θemā, „Äusseres des Ohres", d. h. „Ohrlappen"; wa-gwē, „Rand des Flusses"; wa-kárā, „Äusseres, Mund des Feuers", d. h. „Flamme"; kárā-džānem, „Feuer der Hölle"; bík-tarē, „Knochen der Nase", d. h. „Nasenbein"; ugž-yire, „Haar des Kopfes", „Kopfhaar"; hā-tekse, „Haus des Häuptlings"; hā-gaye, „Haus des Vogels", d. h. „Nest"; bélissa dúgule, „Pferd (zur) Reise".

α, a) Auch zusammengezogene Formen wie χaχdudalā für χaχa Wándalā, „Land Mandara" gehören hierher, sowie solche Zusammensetzungen, wo ein Vokal eines der beiden Wörter eine leichte Veränderung erleidet, wie z. B. edze akse, „Kind der Stadt" (ekse), d. h. „Landsmann"; eksá tekse, „Stadt (ekse) des Häuptlings", d. h. „Residenz, Hauptstadt".

β) Indem man ein n oder na zwischen Subjekt und Objekt einschiebt, wie z. B. edza-n-afā, „Kind vom Baum", d. h. „Frucht"; edza-n-bélissa, „Kind vom Pferd", d. h. „Füllen"; ábbené-n-afā, „Blume vom Baum", d. h. „Blüthe"; átirā-n-afā, „Krone vom Baum"; ir-a-nfā, „Kopf, Bündel von Holz"; kurgún na bodē, „Arznei vom Leib", d. h. „Abführungsmittel".

γ) Als ein Beispiel des Überganges zur Zusammensetzung von Subjekt und Objekt vermittelst einer Präposition führe ich zuerst die Zusammensetzung mit dā an, das wir auch in anderen Verbindungen als einen bedeutenden Redetheil finden, und schon bei den §. CCXL, c) aufgeführten Participialformen gefunden zu haben glauben, also dúgule dā (e)kse, „Weg zur Stadt" in einer Phrase, die ich weiterhin noch einmal von einem anderen Gesichtspunkte aus zu erwähnen haben werde.

Als entschiedenere Beispiele von der Verbindung von Subjekt und Objekt vermittelst einer Präposition erwähne ich dann kalá dańga gáne, „Dinge zum Handel", d. h. „Waaren"; kalá dańga futē, „Dinge, Waaren vom Westen".

instances frequently is spelt by a w. Thus, I have wé-tšia, „the sun" originally meaning „the moving, rising body" from the verb ye-tsé, ye-tšě, which seems also to form an integrant part of dób-tšin, „ashes"; and of other terms. The opposite of wé-tšia „sun" is wá-gia, „night". To this wa I shall have to return once more under b, α) and in the list of monosyllables.

As clear instance of the simple derivation of a substantive from a verbal notion I mention á-fuyā, „wind" from ye-fúng, „I blow".

c) I now give some of the numerous compositions by means of θe describing the various occupations of man,

c, a) those composed with simple substantives, such as θ(e)-egda, „the person of the anvil (egda)"; θ(e)-úngole, „the person of the road (úngole), „the guide"; θ(e)-iggele, „the friend"; θe-šédane, „the person of the devil", „the mischievous person"; and hither belong most of the titles of the officers of the court of the petty kingdom of Wándalā, to be enumerated in my vocabulary.

c, b) terms composed of θe and a verb, to which in many cases a substantive is still added, as, for instance θé-magá, „he who works", „the workman"; θe-sé-kalá, properly θé-šeké-kalá, „he who buys merchandize", from ye-šoké, „I buy", and kalá, „things", merchandize", „the merchant" and synonymous with θe-gá-gánē, „he who makes commerce"; θe-nd(a)-akri, „he who takes hire", „the hired labourer"; θé-magá-lipre, „he who works with the needle", „the tailor"; θé-magá-n-ántsiri, „he who works in leather", „the saddler"; θe-gá-n-afā, „he who works in wood", „the carpenter".

d) This I think a fit place for adding at once what I have to say with regard to the way of joining two nouns in one composite term, although this question belongs in a certain respect to the consideration of the declension of the noun, but of which I have only very little to say. Nouns are joined in various ways,

α) by simply placing the terms side by side, the subject preceding the object, as, for instance er-wá, „extremity of arm" i. q. „hand"; wá-θemā, „border of ear", „earflap"; wa-gwō, „border (of) river"; wa-kárā, „border, mouth (of) fire", i. q. „flame"; kárā-dānom, „fire (of) hell"; hík-tare, „bone (of) nose", „bridge of the nose"; ugž-yire, „hair (of) head"; hā-tokse, „house (of) chief", „palace"; bélissa úngule, „horse (for the) road", and many others.

α, α) Also those composite terms belong hither, in which one of the vowels of the two words has undergone a slight change which seems to be merely due to euphonical reasons, as, for instance, odze akse, „child (of) town" (okse), i. q. „countryman"; eksá tokse, „town (of) king", i. q. „residence". As a merely contracted form we have to look upon the name of the Wándalā-country χaχándalā = χaχa Wándala.

β) by inserting an a or na between subject and object: edza-a-afā, „child of tree" i. q. „fruit"; edza-a-bdlissa, „child of mare" i. q. „colt"; úbbenē-a-afā, „flower of tree", „blossom"; átirā-a-afa, „crown of tree"; ir-a-afā, „head, bundle of wood"; kurgún na bodē, „medicine of (for) body" i. q. „purgative".

γ) As an instance of the two elements of a composite term being joined together by means of the very dé which in other connections also we find as an important particle of speech, and which we think we have recognized p. CCXL in connection with some participial forms, I mention úngule dē (e)kse, „road (to) of town" in a phrase which I shall have to mention further on from a different point of view.

As other more expressive instances of the subject and object being joined by means of a preposition I further mention kalá danga gánē, „things for commerce" i. q. „merchandise"; kalá danga futē, „things, merchandise from the West".

e) Abgesehen von der unter d, β) erwähnten Art der Zusammensetzung habe ich kaum ein einziges Beispiel von regelmässiger Abwandelung des Nennwortes. Jedoch muss ich als Ausnahme erwähnen eine Art von Accusativ in der Phrase ye-adžě kámbi-ga, „ich lasse frei, lasse als freie Person", obgleich eben dieses Beispiel wieder eine Ausnahme in anderer Beziehung ist, da kambe nicht ein eingeborenes Wándalá-Wort, sondern ein fremder, dem Kanúri erborgter, Ausdruck für das einheimische edze džile, „Kind eines (freien) Mannes" ist.

f) Was die regelmässige Bildung des Plurals vermittelst ha betrifft, so habe ich davon schon oben S. CCXXXII bélissá-ha und lúgumá-ha als Beispiele angeführt, dagegen erwähne ich hier nur als Beispiele einer unregelmässigen Pluralbildung džil, džíla, „Person", Pl. yimde, „Leute", wozu jedoch ein Singular omda sich zu finden scheint; dwe, „Sklave", Plur. wawě(?)

g) In Betreff des Geschlechts scheint das Genus masculini nicht besonders ausgedrückt zu werden, während das weibliche Geschlecht auf zwiefache Weise unterschieden werden kann, nicht allein durch Hinzufügung des in diesen Fällen gewöhnlichen Ausdruckes „Frau", mukse, muksa, sondern auch des ungewöhnlichen „Mutter", úma, vielleicht allerdings nur in Beziehung auf Züchtung, indem hier noch die Besonderheit eintritt, dass diese Bezeichnungen dem Ausdrucke, dessen Natur sie näher charakterisiren sollen, nicht nach-, sondern vorgesetzt werden, wie z. B. muksa algome, „weibliches Kameel", eigentlich „Weib-Kameel"; muksa θa, „Kuh", eigentlich „Weib-Rind"; úma bélissa, „Stute", wörtlich „Mutter-Pferd"; ebenso úma (s)aungá, „Mutter-Esel", „Eselin". So wird das unterscheidende muksa selbst vorangesetzt in Verbindung mit dem persönlichen Fürwort, wie z. B. muksa dé rua, „meine Tante"; muksa edze de rua, „meine Nichte", wörtlich „Weib Kind (von) Onkel von mir".

h) Was nun die Stellung des Nennwortes in Bezug auf das Zeitwort betrifft, so können wir es als Regel ansehen, dass das Zeitwort vorhergeht, selbst in solchen Fällen, wo das begleitende Substantiv das Subjekt und nicht das Objekt bildet, während in den wenigen Fällen, wo das Substantiv vorhergeht, die Form des Zeitwortes einer vollständigen Veränderung unterworfen zu sein scheint, wie z. B. a-χě yöě, „fällt das Wasser" und yöě χě-via, „das Wasser fällt, ist fallend". Dass aber die erste Konstruktion die bei weitem gewöhnlichere ist, ersehen wir aus zahlreichen Beispielen, wie z. B. nátlna (eine unregelmässige Verbalform) gwö, „ist voll der Fluss"; setsa gwö, „steigt der Fluss"; agža hǫde rua, „läuft mein Leib"; kelá-kelá lúguma rua, „verloren ist mein Kameel".

Zum Schluss dieses Paragraphen führe ich im Anschluss an das S. CCXL Gegebene ein Beispiel von einem Nennworte an, das in enge Verbindung mit einer Art Participialform des Zeitworts gesetzt ist, nämlich hurgún a-baz-dwa, „Arzenei zum Brechen", von yé-beza, „ich breche".

5. *Das Eigenschaftswort.*

Ich gehe nun zum Eigenschaftswort über und bin ungeachtet meines sehr unvollständigen Materials doch im Stande, verschiedene Bildungsarten desselben nachzuweisen.

a) Zuerst habe ich zu bemerken, dass sie fast alle, soweit sie wirklich den Charakter von Eigenschaftswörtern haben, auf ě ausgehen, wie z. B. dzeyě, „weiss"; dlěkě, „alt"; deyě, „eng"; dongě, „schwarz"; ulfě, „blind"; pitkě, „nackt". Was die bei Eigenschaftswörtern häufig vorkommende Endung dě, dă betrifft, so bin ich der Ansicht, dass sie eine besondere Bedeutung als Angabe der Eigenschaft enthält, obgleich es in einigen Fällen zweifelhaft sein muss, ob das d zur Wurzel gehört, wie z. B. badě, „leer"; gedě, „sauer"; zíunidă, „kräftig". Dieses selbe dě war ich zuerst geneigt, bei den oben S. CCXL, e) erwähnten Participialformen wiederzuerkennen, indem ich es mit der Verbalform eng verband.

b) Nun habe ich solche Eigenschaftswörter, die einen Besitz anzeigen und vermittelst eines dem Nennworte vorangestellten a gebildet sind, wahrscheinlich das a der 3ten Pers. Sing., indem dieses letztere entweder allein steht oder durch ein die Beziehung anzeigendes n mit

e) Besides the mode of composition illustrated under d, β) I have scarcely one single instance of regular cases of the noun. As an exception, however, I have to mention a sort of accusative case in the phrase ye-ndžč kámbi-ga, „I let free, let as a free man", although this instance is itself an exception in another way, kambe being not at all an indigenous Wándalā-word, but a foreign term used instead of the indigenous one edze džile, properly meaning „son of person".

f) As instances of the regular and most common formation of the plural by means of adding ha to the form of the singular, may serve the forms bélissá-ha, lúgumá-ha given above p. CCXXXIII. As instances of an irregular formation of the plural I further mention džil, džíla, „person", plur. yimdo, „people", although the latter seems to be derived in a regular way from another singular term omda; ówe, „slave", plur. (rather a little uncertain) wawē.

g) As for the gender, the masculine does not seem to be distinctly expressed, while there are two modes of distinguishing the feminine gender, not only by adding mukse, muksa, „woman", but also úma, „mother", these characterizing terms moreover, what is very remarkable, preceding the term which they are destined to characterize, just as is the case in English, as, for instance, muksa algúme, „female camel, she camel"; muksa θa, „cow"; úma bélissa, „mare", verbally „mother horse"; úma (r)sungā, „she ass". With regard to the term úma, however, I have to observe, that it may be used of female animals only with reference to the breeding of young ones. The position, those additional terms occupy, is particularly remarkable when they are joined to the possessive pronoun; muksa dē ruā, „my aunt", verbally „woman uncle of mine"; muksa edze dē ruā, „my niece", verbally „woman child (of) uncle of mine".

h) As for the position of the substantive with regard to the verb, we may regard it as a rule, that the verb precedes, even in such cases, where the accompanying substantive forms the subject, and not the object, while in those few cases, where the substantive precedes, the form of the verb seems to become totally changed, as, for instance a-χē yōē, „falls the water", and yōē χē-via, „the water is falling"; but the former construction seems to be the more common one, as is shown by numerous instances, such as sátina (an irregular verbal form) gwō, „is full the river"; setsa gwō, „rises the river"; egža hōda ruā, „run my bowels"; helá-helá lúguma ruā, „lost is my camel".

I here also, in addition to what I have said p. CCXLI with regard to the participial form of the verb, adduce an instance of a substantive being joined to a sort of participle, viz kurgún a-bes-éwa, „a medicine for vomiting" from yé-besa, „I vomit".

5. *The adjective.*

Notwithstanding my rather scanty material I am enabled to illustrate various ways of forming the adjective.

a) First I have to state, that almost all these terms, as far as they bear really the character of adjectives, terminate in ē, such as dzoyē, „white"; džekē, „old"; deyē, „narrow"; dongē, „black"; ulfē, „blind"; pitkē, „naked", and so on. As for the termination dē, which is likewise very common, I am of opinion, that it is very expressive of the adjective quality, although in some cases it is doubtful, whether the d may not rather belong to the root itself, as, for instance badē, „empty"; gedē, „acid"; sinzidē, „powerful"; and this same dē I was inclined at first to recognise in connection with the participial forms mentioned above p. CCXLI, as I supposed the dē closely to belong to the verbal form.

b) Now, I have some adjectives indicating a possession, and formed by means of a simple a, the characteristic sign of the 3rd person sing., being placed before a substantive either alone, or by adding the n indicating the relation, as, for instance á-hodē, „with a (big) belly" i. q.

dem ersteren vermittelt ist, wie z. B. á-hodé, „mit einem Leibe", d. h. „schwanger"; á-n-θaré, „mit einer Schneide", d. h. „scharf"; á-n-takaí, „mit Flüssigkeit", d. h. „süss"; so wol auch a-n-ūra, „mit einem Mann", d. h. „verheirathet", von der Frau.

c) Eigenschaftswörter, die eine in sich abgeschlossene Eigenschaft anzeigen, werden zahlreich von einem einfachen substantivischen Begriff durch Verdoppelung abgeleitet, wie z. B. tséb-tsafē, „leicht"; tsék-tsakā, „lose"; dém-domē, „schwerfällig", von domā, „gross"; ném-nemē, „schwer (von Gewicht)". Ähnlich ist auch kíl-galā, „fett", von gíla, „Fett"; sín-zidā, „stark", von sida, „Stärke"; díg-degē, „eng zusammengepresst", von degē, „eng". Ganz dieselbe Reduplication finden wir auch in den Süd-Afrikanischen Sprachen.

d) Eigenschaftswörter, die eine Begierde oder einen Wunsch nach Etwas anzeigen, scheinen mit av zusammengesetzt zu werden, vom Zeitwort ávēn, „begehren", wie z. B. av-yendrā, „begierig nach Nahrung", d. h. „hungrig"; av-yōē-a, „begierig nach Wasser", d. h. „durstig"; av-oná-hare dagegen scheint nicht adjektive, sondern verbale Form zu sein, „er begehrt Schlaf, ist schläfrig".

e) Menschliche Eigenschaften, so weit sie etwas aktiv Thätiges bezeichnen, werden meist ausgedrückt durch die Verbindung des oben S. CCXLII, b) bei Gelegenheit der Bildung von Substantiven besprochenen θe, das dem die Sache ausdrückenden Objekt vorgesetzt wird, wie z. B. θe-yana, „eig. furchtsam"; tí-θerā (θé-θorā), „arbeitsam, fleissig"; θe-dáávro, „blutig, grausam" und alle ähnlich zusammengesetzten Ausdrücke, indem selbst die oben als Nennwörter bezeichneten auch als Eigenschaftswörter angesehen werden können.

f) Nun führe ich noch negative Formen von Eigenschaftswörtern an, die den Mangel einer Eigenschaft anzeigen und auf verschiedene Weise zusammengesetzt scheinen, wie z. B. me-ts-ā-ka, „nicht süss, sauer, unangenehm", das Gegentheil von á-n-ta-kaí; se-hengo-sā, „nicht gekocht, roh", das Gegentheil von héngia (scheint mir jetzt zweifelhaft). Dann gibt es eine rohe Art negativer Eigenschaftswörter, nur äusserlich zusammengereiht aus einem Nennwort und der impersonalen Verbalform bāka (bá-ka, offenbar aus dem oben besprochenen ba und dem negativen ka zusammengesetzt), „es gibt nicht", wie z. B. bāka θaré, „da ist keine Schneide", d. h. in Bezug auf ein Messer „stumpf"; bāka tré, „da ist kein Mondschein", d. h. in Bezug auf die Nacht „dunkel"; bāk(a) odúkge, „da ist keine Fröhlichkeit", d. h. „ernst".

g) Endlich können wir als Eigenschaftswörter im uneigentlichen Sinne bezeichnen die Umschreibungen einer solchen Eigenschaft durch eine längere oder kürzere Phrase, wie z. B. „bösartig", manso crwangd(e) á-ra, wörtlich „schlecht Herz sein"; bn) parúk efk(e)-á-ra, „eine Person (s. oben S. CCXXX) offen Antlitz ihr", d. h. „offenherzig", der Gegensatz von aahungdofke, d. h. an-húng dó efke, „verschlossen an der Stirn", ein Adjektiv, das in der oben S. CCXL, e) angegebenen verbalen Weise gebildet ist. So habe ich denn auch die theils hierher, theils zu f) gehörige Adjektivform bāka a zid(a) á-rā, „da ist nicht Stärke sein", d. h. in Bezug auf einen Menschen „schwach", als negative Form des oben angegebenen sínsidā.

h) Was die Endung und gewissermassen das Geschlecht der Eigenschaftswörter betrifft, so habe ich einige Beispiele von Übereinstimmung zwischen ihnen und dem Nennwort, dem sie zur Charakterisirung beigegeben sind, wie ich z. B. von túúko, „klein" die Form túúkwa habe in Bezug auf ähnlich ausgehende Nennwörter, und ebenso die Endungen der Eigenschaftswörter des Pferdes (bélissa), also bélissa džilua, bélissa bíua. Aber, so wie dieses mehr eine äusserliche Accommodation der Endung ist und nicht eine innere Übereinstimmung des Geschlechts, so habe ich auch keine deutlichen Beispiele einer wirklichen Pluralform des Adjektivs.

i) Was die Vergleichungsformen des Adjektivs betrifft, so habe ich einige wenige Beispiele, die auf verschiedene Weise den Versuch machen, ein solches Verhältniss darzustellen. So habe ich die Form iugél mā(na, die dem Kanúri-Komparativ ngdl-kā, „besser, ist besser", auffallend entspricht. Uneigentlicher Weise scheint bamba yokó, „grösser, dicker" eine Art Komparativ von yoke, „gross" zu bilden, obgleich bamba für sich „Leben, lebendig" heisst.

„pregnant, with child"; á-e-θarē, „with, possessing an edge", i. q. „sharp"; á-n-takal, „having sweetness", „sweet"; perhaps also a-n-ūra, „who has a husband", i. q. „married", used of women.

c) Adjectives indicating a quality, are formed from a simple notion by reduplication, as, for instance, taób-tanfē, „easy"; taók-tankā, „loose"; dém-demē, „clumsy" from demā, „great"; ném-nemé, „heavy"; kíl-galā, „fat" (adj.), from gila, „fat" (subst.); zín-zidā, „strong" from zida, „strength"; díg-degē, „close, narrow", from degē. And here I have to observe, that reduplication, in general, is quite as common in the Wándalā-language, as it is in the South-African idioms.

d) Adjectives indicating an appetite, a greediness for something, are composed with av, the root of the verb ávēa, „to wish for", as, for instance, av-yondrā, „greedy for food", i. q. „hungry"; av-yōó-a, „greedy for water" i. q. „thirsty". — av-roá-hare, on the contrary, seems rather to be the verbal form, „he is greedy for sleep" i. q. „sleepy", than a real adjective.

e) As for the qualities of man, as far as they indicate an active agency, most of them are expressed by means of the same θe of which I have spoken above p. CCXLIII, b) as being a most important element in forming composite substantives, as, for instance, θe-yáwa, „cowardly"; tí-θora (θé-θerā), „doing work", „diligent"; θe-džávro, „savage, bloody"; besides, all the terms composed in this manner, which I have mentioned above as substantives, may be considered also, and used, as adjectives.

f) Negative adjectives, indicating the want of a quality, are composed in different ways, as, for instance, me-ta-n-ka, „not sweet, disagreeable", the reverse of á-n-ta-kal, „sweet"; se-hebgo-sē, „not boiled, crude", the reverse of héṅgia, „boiled" (rather doubtful). Then, there is a sort of negative adjective, composed in a rough manner of a substantive and the impersonal verbal form bāka or bá-ka p. 125 (the common ba, of which I have spoken repeatedly, joined to the negative particle ka), „there is not", as, for instance, bāka θarē, „there is no edge", i. q. „blunt", with regard to a knife; bāka trē, „there is no moonlight", i. q. „obscure", with regard to the night; bak(a) odákge, „there is no mirth", i. q. „serious", with regard to man.

g) The quality to be indicated of a person, or a thing, is very often circumscribed by means of a whole phrase, such as manzo erwańgd(e) á-rā, meaning verbally „bad heart his", „malicious"; ba) paráh ofk(o)-á-rā, „person, individual, open his face", i. q. „openhearted", the opposition of anbuṅgdofko i. e. an-háṅg dē ofke, „shut in at the front", an adjective formed in the way indicated p. CCXL, c); thus, I have also the composite adjective form bāka n zid(a) á-rā, „there is no strength of his" i. q. „weak", this being the negative form of the above mentioned zínzida.

h) As for the termination, and gender of the adjectives, I have a few instances, where the latter correspond with the accompanying substantive, as, for instance, from těáko, „little" I have the form tăúkwa in correspondence with a similar termination of the accompanying noun; and thus, I have also the adjectives expressive of the qualities of the horse, corresponding with the form of the name, the latter bears in Wándalā, as, for instance, bólissa dāilwa, bélissa bíra. However, as these cases seem to argue a mere outward correspondence of form, thus neither have I met with any instance of a real plural form of the adjective.

i) As for the forms of comparison of the adjectives, I have a few instances of an attempt at expressing such a relation. Thus, I have the form ingél mā(no, corresponding exactly with the Kanúri ṅgél-kō, „better, it is better"; nay, even bamba yokē, „greater, larger", seems to form a sort of comparative of yokē, „great, large", although bamba, if used alone, means „life, alive".

Im Allgemeinen jedoch werden die komparativen und superlativen Formen des Adjektivs nur durch eine den Gesammtcharakter der Phrase betreffende Umwandelung angedeutet, wie z. B. in der Phrase „was von Beiden ist zahlreicher, Rindvieh oder Ziegen"?,

kótχia ur á-terē mi teré, kótχia θa imtū kótχia n awe,
zahlreich jedes von ihnen was sie, zahlreich Vieh denn zahlreich oder Ziegen.

k) Ehe ich nun dazu übergehe, einige Beispiele der Syntax zu geben, will ich nur noch in Betreff der Stellung des Eigenschaftswortes bemerken, dass es dem Nennworte stets nachgesetzt wird, wie z. B. guláka dolé, guláka ambuma, guláka šíšidē, die verschiedenen Arten des Schildes (guláka).

6. *Einige Beispiele der Syntax und der Frageform.*

Obgleich ich alle Phrasen, welche ich in den neun verschiedenen, hier betrachteten, Sprachen niedergeschrieben habe, am Ende des Vokabulars in vollständiger Parallelstellung geben werde, will ich doch hier einige wenige derselben, gewisse Formen der Wándalá-Sprache betreffende, herausnehmen und im Einzelnen erklären.

„Wir Alle sind ermüdet, auch die Kameele sind ermüdet; lasst uns einen guten Schatten suchen, lasst uns absteigen und ausruhen während der Tageshitze und, wenn die Sonne zu sinken beginnt, lasst uns den Marsch fortsetzen".

bé-dem(e) ańge hod(e)áńgare kodē, kodē a-kód eldegóme, íńgaši hádo-
allo von uns ergriff uns Ermüdung, Ermüdung ergriff die Kameele, Schatten nehmen
kol mogoi, gétš-kua and-kua m-ókeeθē .
lasst uns guten, absteigen lasst uns die Hitze zubringen lasst uns, wenn geneigt sich hat
wétšia iňg-áldua,
die Sonne lasst uns marschiren.

Nun gebe ich eine einfache Frageform: „gibt es Kraut in dieser Stadt"?,

ańk(a) imtū mása ekse na,
gibt es denn Kraut Stadt diese?.

Zweigegliederte Frageform mit „entweder" — „oder":

„Was ist ihre gangbare Münze, Glasperlen oder Baumwollstreifen"?,
ésterc géná (á'teré, ábreθ(e) imtū gébbega í dā.
was Waare ihre, Glasperlen entweder Baumwollstreifen oder.

„Reichen unsere Vorräthe aus oder nicht"?,
káši ámaya a-št-be-ši imtū dā sūla,
Proviant unser reicht aus entweder oder geht aus?.

„Ist diese Stadt nah oder ist sie noch fern"?,
ekse na yeyē imtū fírža í,
Stadt diese nahe entweder fern oder?.

„Brechen wir heute auf oder morgen"?,
mise wá-tenuā dē imtū ma mukaralla í.
wir brechen auf heute ? entweder wir morgen oder?.

„Geht der Pfad gerade aus, oder führt er zur Rechten oder zur Linken"?,
úńgule ba-frát imtū erwe-ue ádafā imtū fnte-n(e) ádawā í.
Weg gerade aus oder Hand zu rechte entweder Seite zu linke oder.

Negative Gegenüberstellung „weder — noch":

„ich liebe nicht nächtlichen Marsch, wir sehen weder Städte, noch den Pfad",
ye-wil-ka dalā wá-gia ikse ke-a ga-né-a-ka úńgule ke-a ga-né-a-ka.
ich mag nicht Marsch Nachtzeit Städte nicht wir sehen nicht Weg nicht wir sehen nicht.

7. Ich werde nun ein alphabetisch geordnetes Verzeichniss monosyllaber Ausdrücke der Wándalá-Sprache geben und will dann dieses Kapitel beschliessen mit Zusammenstellung der mir aufgestossenen Beispiele verwandtschaftlicher Beziehung zwischen dieser und anderen benachbarten Sprachen.

In general, however, the comparative as well as the superlative are merely expressed by a change, involving the whole character of the phrase, as, for instance, „which of both (articles) is more numerous, cattle or goats"?,

kótχia ur á-toré mi toré, kótχia θa imin kótχia n awe,
numerous each of them what them, numerous cattle either numerous or goats.

k) I now want only to observe with regard to the position assigned to the adjective, that it constantly is placed behind the substantive which it serves to characterize, as, for instance, gulāka dolō, gulāka ambūma, gulāka šīšidō, the terms describing the various qualities of the shield (gulāka).

6. *A few instances of syntax, and of the interrogative form of speech.*

Although I shall give at the end of the vocabulary all the phrases I have in the nine different languages represented in my collection, yet I here choose to give a few of them in the Wándala-language, as illustrative of certain forms of speech. I first give the phrase:

„All of us are fatigued, the camels too are exhausted, let us look for a good shade, let us dismount and rest during the heat of the day, and when the sun begins to decline let us (continue our) march",

bé-dem(e) ańge hod(-)áńgare kodē, kodē a-kód eldogome, íńgaši hādo-
all of us seized us fatigue, fatigue seized the camels, shade take
kot mogoi, gótš-kwa awá-kwa m-ókseθō wétšia ińg-áldua,
let us good, descend let us pass the heat let us, when has declined sun march let us.

Form of simple interrogation: „is there herbage in this place"?,

ańk(a) imtā māsa okse na,
is then herbage town this.

Composite form of interrogation „either" — „or":

„What is their currency, glassbeads or cottonstripes"?,
átere góna (á)tere, ábreθ(e) imtā gébbega í dā.
what merchandise of them, glassbeads either cottonstripes or.

„Are our provisions sufficient, or do they not reach"?,
kāši ámaya a-ši-bo-ši imtā dá súla,
provisions our they suffice either or go out.

„Is this town near, or is it still far off"?,
okse na yeyē imtā fírža i,
town this near either distant or.

„Do we start to day, or to morrow"?,
miāo wá-tonuā dē imtā ma mukaralle í,
we start to day ? either we to morrow or?.

„Does the path lead straight on, or does it go to the Right or to the Left"?,
ángulo ba-frát imtā orwe-no ádafa imtā ínte-n(e) ádawā í,
path straight either hand to Right either part to Left or.

Negative opposition „neither" — „nor".

„I do not like travelling by night, we see neither towns, nor the track",
ye-wil-ka dalā wá-gia ikse ke-a ga-nú-a-ka ángulo ke-a ga-nú-a-ka.
I like not march time night towns not we see not, track not we see not.

7. I now shall give an alphabetical list of monosyllabic terms of the Wándala-idiom, and shall then conclude this chapter by giving a few instances of relation between this and other neighbouring languages:

a: a, „er, sie"; ar (dra), „Wort"; av, „begehren".
b: ba, „Person, Individuum"; bir, „Kopfkissen"; bre, „Hutte"; bya, „klein".
d: dā, „rufen, nennen"; dā, „entweder, oder"; dē, „Onkel"; deb, „wollen, gehorchen".
ð: ðo, „kommen".
e: eg, „Rücken, Rückseite".
f: fa, „theilen", S. 97; fak, „einstecken"; fe, „Feld"; foṅg, for, „blasen"; frat, „gerade".
g, ṅg: ga, „machen"; gwo, „Fluss"; ṅga, „er"; ṅgdō, „binden".
h: ha, „Haus"; har (Arb.?), „Tag".
i: ig, ir, „Oberfläche, Kopf"; itš, „Auge".
k: ka, „du"; ka (kā?), „nicht"; ke, „erheben"; ki, „Antilope" (?); ko, ku, „ihr"; krē, „Hund"; kse, „werfen".
m: ma, „von dir, dein"; mo, „wir"; mi, „was"?; mtse, „sterben"; mtsá, „Leichnam".
n: na, ne, „dieser"; na, no (nā, nō), „sehn" *).
p: pa, „fühlen"; pon, „ziehen" (das Schwert); pyo, „werfen" (den Speer).
r: rā, „Besitz, Eigenthum".
s: sa, „ziehen" (Blut); se, „Striemen"; so, „rund", „Kugel"; sō, sā, „geben"; swa, „reiben, pressen".
š: šo, „trinken" *); ši, „hinreichen".
t: tir, tre, „Mond, Monat"; tsu, „fasten"? S. 61; tše, „hören"; tšó, („wach sein"?), „aufrecht", „aufrecht stehn".
u: ur, „Individuum", „ein Jeder".
w: wa, ein Ausdruck mit der allerweitesten Bedeutung „Ding, Sache (s. S. CCXL, 4, b), und der ursprünglich mit ba, „Individuum, Person" eng verwandt sein mag; we, „abfeuern" (ein Gewehr); wēe, „Butter", doch eigentlich monosyllabisch anzusehn; wil, „wollen, lieben"; wó, wuo, „Mund".
z: za, „Sache, Besitz"; zā, „essen, zerstören"; ze, „weiss; zel, „schwören" (?) S. 61; zou, „Hemd"; zó, ðō, „gehn, kommen".
dž: dža, „Ruhe"; dža, ndža, „(ruhig) sitzen"; džā, „tödten" (ruhig machen?); džē, „auslöschen"; džil, „Sterblicher?, Mensch"; džó, „schlagen".
y: ya, „Äusserung, Stimme, Laut"; ya (als erster Laut?) Bezeichnung der redenden Person, mit dem Vorsatz des allgemeinen ba, bá-ya, „ich"; yā, „hervorbringen"; ye, „Nacken"; yir (vielleicht zusammengesetzt aus ye und ir), „Kopf"; yo, „Wasser".
θ: θa, „Vieh"; θo, „er der thut, der Arbeiter".
χ: χa, „theilen (Beute)", „anordnen"; χaχ, „Antheil?, Land"; χe, „anfangen".

8. *Einige Beispiele von Verwandtschaft des Wándalā mit anderen Sprachen.*

a) Mit dem Kandri.

Wándalā.	Kandri.	Deutsch.
θema . . . . / šema	sema	Ohr
gegl	gigi	Backenbart
gólondo	gólondo	Finger, Zehe
kumma	ṅgummo	Kinn
máva, másane .	másanu	Nahrung
baru (džengē .	baru	Pocken
uešin-(kasko) .	ká-nasin	Traum

*) Dies ist die richtige Form des Zeitworts und ist danach S. 47 des Vokabular's ye-ne-ne zu verbessern.

*) Auch hier und in anderen Fällen ist die Endung des Präsens ne, na im Vokabular S. 39 u. s. w. von der Wurzel abzuscheiden.

a: a, „he, she"; ar (árа), „word, idiom"; av, „wish for".
b: ba, „person, individual"; bir, „cushion"; bre, „cottage"; bya, „small".
d: dă, „call"; dă, „either, or"; dē, „uncle"; deb, „will, obey".
đ: đō, „come".
e: eg, „back, backside".
f: fa, „divide", p. 97; fak, „put in"; fo, „field"; foṅg, for, „blow"; frat, „straight".
g, ṅg: ga, „make"; gwo, „river"; ṅga, „he"; ṅgdō, „bind, tie".
h: ha, „house"; har (Arb.?), „day".
i: ig, ir, „surface, head"; ită, „eye".
k: ka, „thou"; ka (ká?), „not"; ke, „raise"; ki, „antelope"(?); ko, ku, „you"; kre, „dog"; kse, „throw".
m: ma, „of thee, thine"; mo, „we"; mi, „what"; mtsa, „die"; mtsà, „corpse".
n: na, ne, „this"; na, ne (nă, ne), „see, look" [1]).
p: pa, „feel"; pon, „draw" (the sword); pyo, „throw" (the spear).
r: ră, „possession, property".
s: sa, „draw" (blood); se, „throng"; so, „ball, round"; só, să, „give"; swa, „rub, press".
š: šo, „drink" [2]); ši, „suffice, reach".
t: tir, trē, „moon, month"; tsu, „to fast"(?) p. 61; tăr, „hour"; tšo, („be awake"?), „upright, stand upright".
u: ur, „an individual, every one".
w: wa, a term conveying the most comprehensive meaning „thing, object" (s. p. CCXLI, 4, b), and which originally may intimately be allied with ba, „person"; we, „fire" (a gun); wšo, „butter"; wil, „will, like"; wé, wué, „mouth".
z: za, „thing, property"; ză, „eat, destroy"; ze, „white"; zel, „swear"(?) p. 61; zen, „shirt"; zō, đō, „go, come".
dž: dža, „repose"; dža, ndža, „remain (quietly)"; dză, „kill" (make silent?); džé, „extinguish"; džil, „mortal(?), human being"; džō, „beat".
y: ya, „uttering, voice", and consequently, as meaning voice in general, the person who is speaking „I", more fully bá-ya; yă, „bring forth"; yo, „neck"; yir, possibly a composite term from yo and ir „head"; yó, „water".
θ: θa, „cattle"; θe, „he who works, performs".
χ: χa, „divide (the booty)", „arrange"; χaχ, „portion (of booty), country"; χo, „begin, commence".

8. *Instances of relationship of the Wándalá with other languages.*

a) With the Kanúri.

Wándalá.	Kanúri.	English.
θoma . . . / šema . . .	sema	ear
gegi	gigi	whiskers
gólondō . . .	góloudō	finger, toe
kumma	ṅgummo	chin
mása, másane .	másana	food
bāru (džeṅge .	bāru	small-pox
nešín-(kasko) .	ká-našín	dream

[1]) na, ne is the real root of the verb, and the first person of the present tense (vocabulary p. 47) has therefore to be written ye-ne-na.

[2]) Also in this, as in the other cases, the termination na, ne of the present tense has to be separated from the root.

Wándalá.	Kanúri.	Deutsch.
sibbe	sgbbio	Mark
süa	süa	Brunnen
butši	butši	Matte
ye-fóng	fū-níškin	ich) blase
ye-dža	ye-dží-škin, 3te Pers. Sing. tše-tšin	ich) tödte
yé-kela	kelug-(níškin	ich) beschlafe
yé-tapá	tambu-(škin	ich) schmecke
bálimi	bálimi	Angriffswaffen
dágali	dágali	Thonbett
kásare	kasár	Mattenthür
lipála	rifilla	Silber, blau
sókwa	zoho	Korb
züri	züri	Handvoll
džani	dženi	Löffel.

Aus diesem Verzeichnisse wird man leicht ersehen, dass es nur wenige Fälle ursprünglicher Berührung zwischen der Wándalá- und Kanúri-Sprache gibt, ganz abgesehen davon, dass meine Autorität, die ich nur ganz äusserlich mit Hülfe des Kanúri abfragen konnte, sich vielleicht in mehr als einem Falle in der Noth des Augenblicks mit einem ähnlich klingenden Worte ausgeholfen hat; zu den übrigen, erst später durch den Verkehr hervorgerufenen, Übereinstimmungen müssen wir aber noch jene Ausdrücke hinzufügen, die nicht allein der Wándalá- und Kanúri-, sondern auch der Lógoné- und Bágrimma-Sprache gemeinsam sind, wie z. B. bir, „Kissen"; kúteram, „Spiegel"; gébboga, láuani, düram und andere Ausdrücke, die sich auf Maass und Gewicht beziehen. Auch das Wort bálimi findet sich in der Bágrimma-Sprache, so wie auch die Namen für verschiedene Arten von Trommel der Lógoné-, Wándalá- und Bágrimma-Sprache gemeinsam sind, und dennoch scheint das Bágrimma mit Bezug auf ursprüngliche Begriffe durchaus keine Gemeinschaft mit dem Wándalá zu haben.

b) Berührungspunkte zwischen der Wándalá- und Haussa-Sprache.

Wándalá.	Haussa.	Deutsch.
bda	biu	zwei
koyé	okū	drei
úfadé	fedū	vier
wüye	bákoi	sieben
mi	me	was?
ka	kai	du
ba	ba[1]	Person, Individuum
uske	fuska	W. Wange; H. Antlitz
kilfé	kifi	Fisch
guwé	giwa	Elephant
ŝe	ŝa	trinken
tšo[2]	ŝi	hören
za	tši	essen.

Allerdings ist diess Verzeichniss kurz, aber dagegen enthält es auch mehrere, von ur-

[1] Dieses ba wird in der schon früher (S. CII) berührten Weise im Haussa bei den ein einzelnes Individuum bezeichnenden Volksnamen, wie ba-Haúsi, ba-Fellantši, ba-Bérbere ganz genau in derselben Weise gebraucht, wie das ba im Lógoné den einfachen pronominalen Wurzeln vorgesetzt wird.

[2] Die Form der Gegenwart von tšo ist ye-tšé-na und daraus ist durch Wiederholung der Stammsilbe entstanden die Form yé-tšo-sén-tše-ná, S. 49 des Vokabular.

Wándalā.	Kanúri.	English.
sibba	sybbio	marrow
sūa	sūa	well (the)
būtši	būtši	mat
ye-fóṅg	fū-nískin	I) blow
ye-dšā	ye-dží-skin, 3rd pers. sing. tšē-tšin	I) kill
yé-kola	kelag-ṭuískin	I) cohabit
yé-tapá	tambu-skin	I) taste
bálimi	bálimi	weapons of attack
dágali	dágali	clay-bed
kásare	kasár	matting-door
lipála	rifilla	silver, blue, azure
sókwa	sōko	basket
zūri	zūri	handfull
džanī	džonī	spoon.

From this list it is easily seen, that there are very few coincidences of an original character between the Wándalā- and Kanúri-languages, even if we do not take into account, that the Kanúri-idiom, being the medium of my conversing with my only authority for learning the corresponding Wándalā-terms, it is more than probable, that in a few instances there are other original terms which at the time did not occur to the person; certainly to the other terms we have to add those, which are common not only to the Wándalā and Kanúri, but also to the Lógonē- and Bágrimma-languages, such as bir, „cushion"; kúteram, „mirror"; gébbega, láuani, dáram, and other terms representing measures. The term bálimi also is found in the latter idiom, just as the names for several kinds of drum also are common to the Lógonē-, Wándalā- and Bágrimma-languages, while with regard to more original terms the latter language seems to have nothing at all in common with the Wándalā.

b) Instances of harmony between the Wándalā- and Hausa-languages.

Wándalā.	Hausa.	English.
búa	biu	two
keyē	okū	three
ūfade	fodū	four
wūye	bókoi	seven
mi	me	what?
ka	kai	thou
ba	ba[1])	person, individual
uske	fuska	W. cheek H. face
kilfa	kifi	fish
guwē	giwa	elephant
šo	ša	drink
tše[2])	ží	bear
sā	tšī	eat.

Among this rather short list, there can be no doubt, that there are several terms of a very

[1]) ba. this ba in the Hausa-terms ba-Haúše, ba-Felláncī, ba-Bérbere, meaning „an individual" of that or that tribe, is used exactly in the very same manner, as in Lógonē the ba is prefixed to the simple pronominal forms.

[2]) The form of the present tense of tše is ye-tšé-na, and the reduplicated form of the latter is the form yé-tše-nén-tše-ná adduced in the vocabulary p. 43.

sprünglichen Begriffen hergenommene Ausdrücke, die klar und deutlich zu zeigen scheinen, dass in bezüglich früher Zeit wenigstens ein enger Verkehr zwischen der Wándalá- und Hausa-Nation obwaltete.

Was nun die Übereinstimmung der Wándalá-Sprache mit anderen Sprachen meiner Sammlung betrifft, so sind dergleichen Fälle sehr wenig zahlreich; ich will jedoch die folgenden erwähnen: „Ohr", das ja eben auch mit dem entsprechenden Ausdrucke im Kanúri verwandt ist, W. semá, L. šémayé; „Regenwetter", W. samá, L. sémade; „Rind", W. θn, L. inθā; „Haus", W. hā, L. yaa; „Frau", W. muksa, M. mušdúg; „Kind", W. edza, S. idze; „Freund", W. θo-iggete, F. higo, Plur. higoterábe. Dann mit anderen Afrikanischen Sprachen erwähne ich im Vorbeigehn folgende Berührungspunkte, „Kopf", W. yiro, Kasm (Koelle Polygl.) yiru; „Auge", W. itā, itāe, im Afúdu und anderen Aku-Dialekten ędzi.

Als ein eigenthümliches Beispiel von Übereinstimmung will ich hier auch den W.-Ausdruck olgom, eldegóme für „Kameel" erwähnen, da er in Verbindung mit den eben gegebenen Beweisen einer nahen Berührung zwischen der Wándalá- und Hausa-Nation einiges Gewicht zu haben scheint, um die früheren Sitze der Wándalá weiter im N. wahrscheinlich zu machen. Denn, wie schon oben S. XCVIII angedeutet, ist dieser Ausdruck wahrscheinlich in früher Zeit von den nördlichen Abtheilungen der Mašiy-Nation entlehnt worden, da die südlichen Stämme derselben gegenwärtig den grundverschiedenen Ausdruck ámenis gebrauchen.

Elftes Kapitel.

Die Bágrimma-Sprache: tar Bágrimma.

Die Bágrimma-Sprache ist von sehr grosser Bedeutung zum vollen Verständniss dieser gesammten Gruppe Central-Afrikanischer Sprachen und gewährt einen so klaren historischen Einblick in ihren Zusammenhang, wie kaum irgend eine andere der hier behandelten Sprachen, eine Behauptung, die ich durch eine kurze Analyse meines allerdings unvollständigen Materials völlig zu begründen hoffe.

Ich betrachte zuerst

1. *Das persönliche Fürwort.*

	Singular.		Plural.
1ste Person	m — ma	. . . .	dž — dže,
2te „	i — yi (ka)	. . . . . .	s — se,
3te „	n — ne	. . . .	dž — dži, dží-gi.

1ste Person Sing. Accusativ und Dativ mā:
„du liebst mich", in-gé mā; „gib mir", áde ma; „hilf mir", ma mā S. 77; „leihe mir", tílka-m-dže, von ma tílka-dže, „ich leihe".

1ste Pers. Sing. Genitiv und possessive Form á-ma[1], á-ma-ne (ne, „dieser"): éna á-ma, „das (ist) mein"; á-ma ētu, „mein ist es, mir gehört es"; mak-ſudši god bab(a) á-ma (S. 85), „ich sitze auf dem Throne meines Vaters"; béle á-ma-ne, „mein Messer"; sinda á-ma-ne, „mein Pferd"; lúguma á-ma-ne, „mein Kameel"; lugúmage a-má-ge-ne, „meine Kameele".

1ste Person Plur. Accusativ und Dativ džē:
so ké-ge-di džē, „ihr liebt uns"; áde-m-džē[2], „gib uns".

[1] á-ma. Ich habe auch ein Beispiel der abgekürzten Form em in agás-em, S. 57, „meine Sache".

[2] áde-m-džē. Die Einfügung des m ist auffallend. adí-m-džē S. 67 ist eine andere Form dafür und bedeutet gleichfalls „gib uns", nicht „gib mir", wie dort irrig angegeben.

original character, which appear to indicate, that at an early period there intercceded at least a close intercourse between the Wándalā- and the Hausa-tribe.

As for instances of relationship of the Wándalā-idiom with other languages of my Collection, as far as they have occurred to me, they are rather scanty; I mention, however, „ear", which, as we have just seen, in Kanúri also is designated by the same term as in Wándala, W. semá, L. šómayē; „rain, tornado", W. samá, L. sémade; „cattle", W. θa, L. inθā; „house", W. hā, L. yaa; „woman, wife", W. mukṡa, M. mušóṅg; „child", W. edza, S. idze; „friend", W. θe-iggete, F. higo, plur. higoturābe. Further, in passing by, I will just mention the two following points of contact between the Wándala, and some other languages not represented in my Collection, „head", W. yire, Kasm (Koelle Polygl.) yiru; „eye", W. itā, itše, in Afúdu, and some other Aku-dialects ẹdzi.

As another interesting instance of coincidence, and which, in connection with the other proofs of a close contact of the Wándalā with the Hausa-nation, which I have just adduced, may well serve to give some probability to the former seats of the Wándala-people having to be looked for much farther to the North, I here mention the term elgom, eldegōme for „camel", which, it is more than probable, has been borrowed from the Māšiγ, and at a very early period, the Southern tribes of that great nation, at the present time, using the totally different term ámenis; compare, what I have said in this respect p. XCIX.

Chapter the eleventh.

The Bágrimma-language: tar Bágrimma.

The Bágrimma-language is of very great importance for correctly understanding this whole group of Central-African languages, and exhibits such a clear historical insight into their character, as scarcely any other of the idioms here treated of. This statement I hope fully to bear out by the following short analysis of my materials, although they are far from being complete.

1. *The personal pronouns.*

	singular.		plural.
1st person	m — ma	. . . . . .	dž — dže,
2nd „	i — yi (ka)	. . . . . .	s — se,
3rd „	n — ne	. . . . . .	dž — dži, dží-gi.

1st person sing. accusative, and dative case: mā:
„thou lovest me", in-gé mā; „give me", áde mā: ma má, „help me" p. 77; „lend me", tílka-m-dže from ma tílka-dže, „I lend".

1st pers. sing. genitive case, and possessive form á-ma[1]), á-ma-ne (ne, „this"): „that is (of me, is) mine, belongs to me", éna á-mai á-ma étu, „it belongs to me, is mine"; mak-ṅdži god bāb(a) á-ma p. 85, „I sit on the throne of my father"; lúgnma á-ma-ne, „my camel"; béla á-ma-ne, „my knife"; sinda á-ma-ne, „my horse"; lúgnmago a-má-ge-ne, „my camels".

1st person plur. accusative, and dative case: džē:
„you love us", se hé-ge-di džē; „give us", áde-m džē[2]).

[1]) I have also an instance of the abbreviated form em instead of á-ma in ágāe-em p. 87 „my business".

[2]) áde-m džē: the inserting of the m is remarkable; adi-m džō p. 67 seems to be another form of this one, and not to mean „give me", as interpreted there erroneously, but rather „give us".

1ste Person Plur. Genitiv und possessive Form á-dže, á-dže-na:
óna á-dže, „das ist unser, gehört uns";
lúguma á-dže-na, „unser Kameel"; lúguma-ge á-dže-na, „unsere Kameele";
sinda á-dže-na, „unser Pferd"; sinda-ge á-dže-na, „unsere Pferde".

2te Person Sing. Accusativ und Dativ ï:
n-in-gé ï, „er liebt dich"; mam-gé ï li[1]), „ich liebe dich nicht";
m-ák-ad ï, „ich gebe dir"; ma m-áko-mä ï, „ich helfe dir";
ma-tad ï mislim, „ich mache dich zu einem Muslim, bekehre dich zum Islam";
ï mam-dóga, „ich antworte dir"; ma ma-tád ï gábraga, „ich verzeihe dir".

2te Person Sing. Genitiv und possessive Form a-yï, a-yï-na[2]):
ó-na a-yï, „das ist dein, gehört dir";
lúguma a-yï-na, „dein Kameel"; lúguma-ge a-yï-na, „deine Kameele";
sinda a-yï-na, „dein Pferd"; sinda a-yï-ge-na, „deine Pferde".

2te Person Plur. Accusativ und Dativ sé, sé-se:
džo dže-gé sé-se, „sie lieben euch".

2te Person Plur. Genitiv und possessive Form á-se, á-se-na:
ó-na á-se, „das ist euer, gehört euch";
lúguma á-se-na, „euer Kameel"; lúguma-ge á-se-na, „eure Kameele";
sinda á-se-na, „euer Pferd"; sinda a-sé-ge-na, „eure Pferde".

3te Person Sing. Accusativ und Dativ aya und lë(?):
mam-gé aya, „ich liebe ihn"; adí aya, „gib ihm";
ne bi kö-ga lë, „er, Schlaf ergriff ihn"; wö-ga lë, „hörst du es"; sel-ga lë, „es genügt ihm".

Dieses aya ist immer von der Verbalwurzel abzusondern, auch in Fällen, wo ich es im Vokabular noch damit verbunden habe, wie z. B. mam-dosí aya S. 69.

3te Person Sing. Genitiv und possessive Form a-nyï, a-nyï-na:
ó-na a-ayï, „das ist sein, gehört ihm";
lúguma a-ayï, „sein Kameel"; lúguma-ge a-ayï-na, „seine Kameele";
sinda a-ayï-na, „sein Pferd"; sinda a-ayï-na-ge, „seine Pferde".

3te Person Plur. Accusativ (und Dativ?) yï:
džo džo-gé yï, „wir lieben sie"[3]).

3te Prs. Pl. Genitiv und possessive Form á-dže, á-dže-na; á-dži-gi, a-džé-ge-na:
ó-na á-dži-gi, „das ist ihr (Plural), gehört ihnen";
lúguma á-dže-na, „ihr Kameel"; lúguma-ge a-džé-ge-na, „ihre Kameele".
sinda á-dže-na, „ihr Pferd"; sinda a-džé-ge-na, „ihre Pferde".

An diesen Beispielen erkennen wir, dass das Zeichen des Plurals nicht regelmässig in der Pronominalform ausgedrückt wird, indem man das charakteristische ge in den Fällen, wo es beim Nennwort schon ausgedrückt ist, bei der Pronominalform, ausgenommen der der 3ten Person Plur., fast stets fortzulassen scheint.

Mit Bezug auf das demonstrative Fürwort ó-na (vielleicht auch í-na) habe ich hier

[1]) mam-gé ï li: so haben wir ebentheilen S. 63. Auffallend als Ausnahme von dieser pronominalen Form wäre mam on dila, „ich lehre dich", wenn das on nicht eine Verbalform zu sein schiene.

[2]) Ich habe übrigens wenigstens ein Beispiel einer ganz verschiedenen, an ka, ku für die persönliche Form der 2ten Person sich anschliessende Form für das possessive Fürwort der 2ten Person, nämlich na-kó, vielleicht Plural, in dem Vaterunser hermel ásamma na-kó, hermel arda na-kó, „die Herrschaft des Himmels ist dein (Euer), die Herrschaft der Erde ist dein". Ein anderes, scheinbares Beispiel yï mága, „dein Name", „wie heisst du"?, will ich nicht als Beispiel anführen, da mága, „welcher, was" heisst, also hier wol nichts mit dem persönlichen Fürwort zu thun hat. Dass aber das k die 2te Person charakterisirt, zeigen auf das Unzweideutigste die Verbalformen ï k-ak-abé, se k-ak-abé-ki u. s. w.

[3]) Die Form adí-se ge, die ich für „gib ihnen" habe, mag in Richtigkeit sein, wenn man berücksichtigt, dass die Partikel ge das allgemeine Zeichen des Plural ist, wie das in anderen Sprachen dieser Sammlung oft der Fall ist.

1st person plur. genitive case, and possessive form: á-dže, á-dže-na:
„that belongs to us, is ours", dna á-dže;
„our camel", lúguma á-dže-na; „our camels", lúguma-go á-dže-na;
„our horse", sinda á-dže-na; our horses", sinda-go á-dže-na.

2nd person sing. accusative, and dative case: ī:
„he likes thee", n-in-gé ī; „I do not like thee", mam-gé ī lī[1]);
„I give thee", m-ák-ad ī; „I assist, help thee", ma m-áke-ma ī;
„I make thee a Mahomedan", ma-tad ī mislim;
„I answer thee", ī mam-dóga; „I pardon thee", ma ma-tád ī gábraga.

2nd person sing. genitive case, and possessive form: a-yī, a-yī-na[2]):
„that belongs to thee, is thine", ó-na a-yī;
„thy camel", lúguma a-yī-na; „thy camels", lúguma-ge a-yī-na;
„thy horse", sinda a-yī-na; „thy horses", sinda a-yī-ge-na.

2nd person plur. accusative, and dative case: sé, sé-se:
„they like you", dže dže-gé sē-se.

2nd person plur. genitive case, and possessive form: á-se, á-se-na:
„that is yours, belongs to you", ó-na á-se;
„your camel", lúguma á-se-na; „your camels", lúguma-go á-se-na;
„your horse", sinda á-se-na; „your horses", sinda a-sé-ge-na.

3rd person sing. accusative, and dative case nya, and lō(?):
„I like him", mam-gé nya; „give him", adī nya;
„he, sleep seized him", no bī kō-ga lē; „hast thou heard it"; wō-ga lē;
„it suffices him", a-sī-ga lē.

This nya is constantly to be separated from the verbal root, even where in the vocabulary it has been connected with the latter, as, for instance, p. 69 we have to write mam deaī-nya.

3rd person sing. genitive case, and possessive form: a-nyī, a-nyī-na:
„that is of him (belongs to him), is his", ó-na a-nyī;
„his camel", lúguma a-nyī; „his camels", lúguma-go a-nyī-na;
„his horse", sinda a-nyī-na; „his horses", sinda a-nyī-na-ge.

3rd person plur. accusative (and dative?) case: yī:
„we like them", dže dže-gé yī[3]).

3rd person plur. genitive case, and possessive form: á-dže, á-dže-na; á-dži-gi, a-džé-ge-na:
„that is of them (belongs to them), is theirs", ó-na á-dži-gi;
„their camel", lúguma á-dže-na; „their camels", lúguma-go a-džé-ge-na;
„their horse", sinda á-dže-na; „their horses", sinda a-džé-ge-na.

From these instances we see, that the sign of the plural number is not regularly expressed in the form of the possessive pronoun, the characteristic ge being sometimes added to the substantive, at others to the pronoun, and, if once added to the former, scarcely ever being again expressed in the latter, with the exception of the 3rd person plur., where a repetition of this kind is of more frequent occurrence.

[1]) Thus we have to read p. 63. — As to mam na dīna, „I teach thee", I doubt, whether na be the pronoun.

[2]) I have, however, at least one instance of a totally different form for the 2nd person of the possessive pronoun, which distinctly points out a form ka, ku for the corresponding person of the personal pronoun; this is the form na-kū, occurring twice in my translation of the Lord's Prayer harmel Assama na-kū, harmel erde na-kū, „the rule of the heaven is thine (yours), the rule of the earth is thine" (yours). Another, rather uncertain, instance of the form nsága is the common phrase yī nsága, „what is thy name", I will not adduce, as nsága generally means „which, what", and, therefore, in this instance also, may have nothing to do with the pronoun. But the verbal forms ī ā-nk-nhō, nu ā-nk-nhō-kī do not leave the slightest doubt, that k, besides ī, is a characteristic sign of the 2nd person of the personal pronoun.

[3]) For „give them", I have the form adī-m ge, which may be right, considered that the form ge is the general sign of the plural, just as is the case with be in some other languages of this Collection.

hinzuzufügen, dass es häufig in der, dem gleichbedeutenden llane ganz entsprechenden, Form eines Suffix nen gebraucht wird. Hiermit nehme ich vom Fürwort Abschied.

2. *Die Zahlwörter.*

In Bezug auf die Zahlwörter in der Bágrimma-Sprache habe ich nur sehr wenige Bemerkungen zu machen. Sie befolgen in den höheren Zahlen auf das Entschiedenste ein Zehner-System, duk-kemo (eigentlich wol duk-kēde), „ein Zehner"; duk-sáb, „zwei Zehner", und so weiter. Dagegen ist in den niedrigeren Zahlen „fünf" die Einheit; denn mi-gā, „sechs" steht im engsten Zusammenhang mit mi, „fünf"; do-sō, „neun", scheint sich, nur in anderer Bildungsweise, an eben dieselbe Einheit anzulehnen, indem es heisst „(fünf) und vier" (mi) dō sō, während wiederum marta, „acht" nichts anderes zu bedeuten scheint, als („fünf" und) „drei" (mutá). Dagegen finden wir auch im Bágrimma, wie in mehreren dieser Sprachen, für „sieben" einen besondern, unabhängig gebildeten, Ausdruck tšili, der seine Erklärung in einem eigenthümlichen, mir nicht klaren Umstand finden muss.

kēde, der Ausdruck für „ein", wird auch als unbestimmtes Fürwort „Jemand" gebraucht, und davon wird, gleichwie in anderen Sprachen, in regelmässiger Weise der Plural kēde-ge gebildet, mit der Bedeutung „Einige".

Die Ordinalien werden gebildet, indem man dem entsprechenden Cardinal-Ausdruck ein na-ki ansetzt, wol entstanden aus na, „von" und ki wol = yi, „ihnen", „der Fünfte von ihnen" u. s. w.

3. *Das Zeitwort.*

a) In Berücksichtigung des Ungewissen und Schwankenden des Gegenstandes will ich diesen Paragraphen mit einem möglichst vollständigen Paradigma aller, mir in der Bágrimma-Sprache bekannt gewordenen, verbalen Formen anfangen, und zu diesem Zwecke wähle ich die Zeitwörter ab, abē, „gehen"; sā, esā, „essen" und kā, gā, akā, „sehen".

(ma) m-ák-abē, „ich gehe".

Gegenwärtige Zeit.

	Positive Form. Singular.	Plural.	Negative Form. Singular.	Plural.
1ste Ps.	ma m-ák-abē	džo dž-ák-abē . .	ma m-ak-abē-li	. džo dž-ak-abē-li,
2te „	i k-ák-abē	. se k-ák-abē-ki .	i k-ak-abē-li .	. se k-ak-abē-li,
3te „	no n-ák-abē	džo dž-ák-abē .	no n-ak-abē-li	. džo dž-ak-abē-li.

Aorist.

	Positive Form. Singular.	Plural.	Negative Form. Singular.	Plural.
1ste Ps.	ma m-ab-džō	džo dž-ab-džō . .	ma m-ab-džō-li	. džo dž-ab-džō-li oder džo dž-abē-li,
2te „	i k-ab-džō	. se k-ab-ki-džō . .	i k-ab-džō-li oder i k-abē-li . . .	se k-ab-ku-džō-li oder se k-ab-ki-li,
3te „	no n-ab-džō	džo dž-ab-džō . .	no n-ab-džō-li oder no n-abē-li	džo dž-ab-džō-li.

Conditionell.

	Singular.	Plural.
1ste Pers.	ma m-ak-áb-gona	džo dž-áb-gona,
2te „	i k-áb-gona . .	se k-ab-kí-gona,
3te „	no n-áb-gona . .	džo dž-áb-gona.

Imperativ.

2te Person Sing. abē [1]),
2te „ Plur. ab-ki,
1ste „ Plur. džo-k-áb [2]).

[1]) abē. Die Imperativ-Form abdžē, die ich S. 67 habe, ist unzweifelhaft von der Nebenform abgeleitet, worüber S. CCLXII, d.

[2]) džo-k-áb. Anstatt dessen habe ich einmal die Form nanga ab-ki, also die Form für die 2te Person Plur. mit dem Vorsatz nange, und bin über deren Richtigkeit mehr als zweifelhaft.

With regard to the demonstrative pronoun é-na (perhaps also í-na) I have to add, that it is also used as a suffix in the form nan, identical with the corresponding Hausa one.

2. *The Numerals.*

As for the Numerals, I have only to offer very few observations. The Bágrimma-language in the higher Numerals follows decidedly a decimal system, saying duk-kome (kédo), „one tenth"; duk-sáb, „two tenths", and so on; originally, however, like most of these languages, it appears to have counted by fifths, mi-gá the term for „six" bearing a very close relation to mi, „five", while do-sō, „nine", beyond a doubt, is nothing but an abbreviation from mi), dū sō, „five") and „four", and in a similar manner marta, „eight", seems to mean nothing but „five and) three" (mutá), while for „seven", in this language as in most of the others represented in this Collection, we find a peculiar term which must have its explanation in some peculiar circumstance, unknown to me.

kōdo, the term for „one", is used also as the indefinite pronoun „some body", and thence the regular plural form kōde-go, „some" has been derived.

The ordinals are formed by adding to the corresponding term of the cardinals the termination na-kí which, no doubt, is composed of the relative particle na, „of", and a pronominal form kí, probably identical with yí, „them", so that the whole means „the fifth of them", and so on.

3. *The verb.*

a) I prefer commencing this paragraph by giving a paradigm as complete as possible of all the verbal forms which have come to my knowledge, and for this purpose I choose the verbs ab, abō, „go"; eā, esā, „eat", and kā, gā, akā, „see".

(ma) m-ák-abō, „I do go".

Present tense.

	positive form. singular.	plural.	negative form. singular.	plural.
1st ps.	ma m-ák-abē	dže dž-ák-abē . .	ma m-ak-abē-li	. dže dž-ak-abē-li,
2nd „	i k-ák-abē	. se k-ák-abē-ki .	i k-ak-abē-li .	. se k-ak-abe-li,
3rd „	ne n-ák-abē	dže dž-ák-abē . .	ne n-ak-abē-li	. dže dž-ak-abē-li.

Aorist or Past tense.

	positive form. singular.	plural.	negative form. singular.	plural.
1st ps.	ma m-ab-džō	dže dž-ab-džō . .	ma m-ab-džō-li	. dže dž-ab-džō-li or dže dž-abē-li,
2nd „	i k-ab-džō	. se k-ab-ki-džō .	i k-ab-džō-li or i k-abē-li . . .	se k-ab-ku-džō-li or se k-ab-ki-li,
3rd „	ne n-ab-džō	dže dž-ab-džō . .	ne n-ab-džō-li or ne n-abē-li	dže dž-ab-džō-li.

Conditional.

	singular.	plural.
1st pers.	ma m-ak-áb-gona	dže dž-áb-gena,
2nd „	i k-áb-gena . .	se k-ab-kí-gena,
3rd „	ne n-áb gena . .	dže dž-áb-gena.

Imperative.

2nd person sing. abē [1]),
2nd „ plur. ab-ki,
1st „ plur. dže-k-áb [2]).

[1]) abē: The form of the Imperative abdžō p. 87 „come" appears to be derived from the secondary form, as I shall endeavour to show further on (p. CCLXIII, d).

[2]) dže-k-áb: As for the form naga ab-ki, which I have in one instance to represent the 1st person plur., I am doubtful, whether it be right, as it is nothing but the form for the 2nd person plur. with an additional naga.

In dem Falle von dšo-k-áb, wie in vielen anderen, ist die 1ste und die 2te Person Plur. nicht zu unterscheiden, und eine solche Unterscheidung findet nur Statt, wenn der letzteren ein ge, gi hinzugefügt wird, wie in dži-gi sá-li.

(ma) m-ák-esá, „ich esse".

Gegenwärtige Zeit.

	Positive Form. Singular.	Plural.	Negative Form. Singular.	Plural.
1ste Ps.	ma m-ák-esa	dže dž-ák-esá . .	ma m-ák-esá-li	. dže dž-ák-esa-li,
2te „	i k-ák-esa	. se k-ák-(e)sá-ki[1])	i k-ák-esa-li . .	. se s-ák-esá-(ki)-li,
3te „	ne n-ák-esa	dže dž-ák-esa . .	ne n-ák-esá-li .	. džo dž-ák-esá-li.

Aorist.

	Positive Form. Singular.	Plural.	Negative Form. Singular.	Plural.
1ste Ps.	ma-m sá-ga	dže dži-sá-ga . .	ma-m sá-(ge)-li	. dže dži-sá-(ge)-li,
2te „	i sá-ga . .	se sá-ki	i sá-(ge)-li . .	. se sa-ki-li,
3te „	ne-n sá-ga,	dže dži-sá-ga . .	ne-n sa-(ge)-li .	. dží-gi sá-(ge)-li.

Conditionell.

	Singular.	Plural
1ste Pers.	ma-m sá-ge-na .	dže dži-sá-ge-na,
2te „	i sá-ge-na . . .	se sá-ge-na,
3te „	ne-n sá-ge-na . .	dže dži-sá-ge-na.

Imperativ.

2te Person Sing. sá.

(ma) m-ák-aká, „ich sehe".

Gegenwärtige Zeit.

	Positive Form. Singular.	Plural.	Negative Form. Singular.	Plural.
1ste Ps.	ma m-ák-aká	dže dž-ák-akē . .	ma m-ak-akē-li	. dže dž-ak-akē-li,
2te „	i k-ák-aka	. se k-ák-aki . . .	i k-ak-akē-li .	. se k-ak-akē-li,
3te „	ne n-ák-aká[2])	dže dž-ák-aká . .	ne n-ak-akē-li	. dže dž-ak-akē-li.

Aorist.

	Positive Form. Singular.	Plural.	Negative Form. Singular.	Plural.
1ste Ps.	ma m-ak-ga[3])	dže dž-ak-ga . .	ma m-ák-ge-li .	. dže dž-ák-ge-li,
2te „	i k-ak-ga	. se k-ak-kí-ga . .	i k-ák-ge-li . .	. se k-ak-kí-ge-li,
3te „	ne n-ak-ga	. dže dž-ak-ga . .	ne n-ák-ge-li .	. dže dž-ák-ge-li.

Conditionell.

	Singular.	Plural.
1ste Pers.	ma m-ák-ge-na .	dže dž-ák-ge-na,
2te „	i k-ák-ge-na . .	se k-ak-ki-ge-na,
3te „	ne n-ák-ge-na .	dže dž-ák-ge-na.

Imperativ.

2te Person Sing. aká.

Ähnlich ist m-ak-al, „ich besteige", Imperativ ála.

b) Die hier aufgeführten Beispiele bieten, mit nur geringen Abweichungen, dieselben Konjugations-Formen, indem der Hauptgrund des Unterschiedes darin liegt, dass die drei angeführten Zeitwörter verschiedentlich den der eigentlichen Wurzel vorgesetzten oder angehängten Vokal abwerfen und dadurch abweichende Formen erzeugen, indem ab die Wurzel von abē, sá die Wurzel von esá, ak die von aká ist.

[1]) Anstatt se k-ak-esá-ki hörte ich zuweilen se s-ak-esá-ki, und eben so die negative Form se s-ak-esá-li.

[2]) In Bezug auf die höchst charakteristischen und wichtigen Nebenformen mit at, wie z. B. ne n-át-kaká, se át-kaki, dže dž-át-kaká, i át-kakē-li, ne n-át-kakē-li, s. weiter unten, CCLXIV. f.

[3]) m-ak-ga. Hiernach hat man die Form m-áka S. 47 zu verbessern, wenn dies nicht eine abgekürzte Form des Präsens ist.

In the case of džo-k-áb, as in many others, the 1st and the 3rd person plur. are not to be distinguished, and such a distinction is only possible by adding to the latter the characteristic ge, gi of the plural form, which seems to be never added to the 1st person plur.

(ma) m-ák-esă, „I do eat".

Present tense.

	positive form. singular.	plural.	negative form. singular.	plural.
1st ps.	ma m-ák-esă	dže dž-ák-esă . .	ma m-ák-esă-li	. dže dž-ák-esă-li,
2nd „	i k-ák-esă	. se k-ák-(e)să-ki[1]	i k-ák-esă-li	. . se s-ák-esă-(ki)-li,
3rd „	ne n-ák-esă	dže dž-ák-esă . .	ne n-ák-esă-li	. dže dž-ák-esă-li.

Aorist, and Past tense.

	positive form. singular.	plural.	negative form. singular.	plural.
1st ps.	ma-m să-ga	dže dži-să-ga . .	m-am să-(ge)-li	. dže dži-să-(ge)-li,
2nd „	i să-ga . .	se să-ki	i să-(ge)-li . .	. se să-ki-li,
3rd „	ne-n să-ga .	dže dži-să-ga . .	ne-n să-(ge)-li .	. dže-gi să-(ge)-li.

Conditional.

	singular.	plural.	Imperative.
1st pers.	ma-m să-ge-na .	dže dži-să-ge-na,	
2nd „	i să-ge-na . . .	se să-ge-na,	2nd person sing. să.
3rd „	ne-n să-ge-na . .	dže dži-să-ge-na.	

(ma) m-ák-akă, „I do see".

Present tense.

	positive form. singular.	plural.	negative form. singular.	plural.
1st ps.	ma m-ák-akă	dže dž-ák-akē . .	ma m-ak-akē-li	. dže dž-ak-akē-li,
2nd „	i k-ák-akă .	se k-ák-akī . . .	i k-ak-akē-li .	. se k-ak-akē-li,
3rd „	ne n-ák-akă[2])	dže dž-ák-akă . .	ne n-ak-akē-li	. dže dž-ak-akē-li.

Past tense.

	positive form. singular.	plural.	negative form. singular.	plural.
1st ps.	ma m-ak-ga[3])	dže dž-ak-ga . .	ma m-ák-ge-li	. dže dž-ák-ge-li,
2nd „	i k-ak-ga	. se k-ak-kí-ga . .	i k-ák-ge-li .	. . se k-ak-kí-ge-li,
3rd „	ne n-ak-ga .	dže dž-ak-ga . .	ne n-ák-ge-li .	. dže dž-ák-ge-li.

Conditional.

	singular.	plural.	Imperative.
1st pers.	ma m-ák-ge-na .	dže dž-ák-ge-na,	
2nd „	i k-ák-ge-na . .	se k-ak-kí-ge-na,	2nd person sing. akă.
3rd „	ne n-ák-ge-na . .	dže dž-ák-ge-na.	

Just in the same way we have mak-al, „I mount", imperative ála.

b) The paradigms which I have heretofore compared, exhibit all, more or less, the same forms of conjugation, the principal reason of difference being based on the circumstance of the root of some of the verbs beginning with a vowel, and that of others with a consonant, a b being the original root of abē, ak of akă, and să of esă, and thus a change being produced.

[1]) Instead of se kak-esă-ki I heard sometimes the form se sak-esă-ki, as well as the corresponding negative form se s-ak-esă-li.

[2]) With regard to the very characteristic, and important forms with ét, such as ne n-ét-kakă, se ét-kakī, dže dž-ét-kakă, i ét-kakē-li, ne n-ét-kakē-li, I shall offer a few observations p. CCLXV, f.

[3]) We have to correct, accordingly, the form m-ákă p. 47 which either must be a contracted form of the present tense, or ought to be written m-ak-ga.

Wir haben also hier in der drastischen Form dieser verschiedenen Zeitwörter ein Hülfszeitwort ak, das der Wurzel vorgesetzt wird. Besonders ist dies eigenthümlich bei dem fast ganz gleich lautenden Zeitwort aka, „sehn", und ich bin der Ansicht, dass die Übereinstimmung jener Hülfszeitform mit diesem Zeitwort keineswegs bloss zufällig ist, wie wir denn aus der Form des Aoristes deutlich erkennen, dass die Wurzel des letzteren eben auch ak ist, so dass es wol scheinen mag, als wenn „sehn" dadurch zu dieser Bezeichnung gekommen ist, dass es als die eigenthümlichste und einfachste Thätigkeit des Menschen angesehen wurde. Denn dass aka wirklich „thun, machen" bedeutet, wörtlich entsprechend dem Englischen do und gleichbedeutend dem identischen dó im Fulfúlde, yi im Hausa, ne im Wándalä,, das erkennen wir deutlich aus der Phrase m-ak-a wáya S. 95, „ich mache Krieg, gehe in den Krieg", wo es nicht eine blosse Hülfszeitform ist; und zwar haben wir hier abermals dieselbe kurze unvermittelte Form, wie die, S. 47 des Vokabular, von „sehn" angeführte. Ganz ähnlich sind ma m-ak idži, „ich mache Wasser, ich harne"; ma m-ak-i ñi (so zu schreiben S. 41 statt mam akiñi), „ich mache Traum, ich träume", von ni, „Traum". Noch deutlicher fast zur Erkennung der im Hülfszeitwort ak enthaltenen selbstständigen Thätigkeit ist das Beispiel von m-ak-bó, wörtlich „ich mache nahe", d. h. „ich vereine, verbinde". So haben wir offenbar auch die Verbalform mam-ók-oro, „ich werde müde" zu verstehen, indem hier das a der Hülfszeitform ak in ein o verwandelt ist durch Einwirkung des folgenden o, daher denn im Aorist mam-or-ga; ähnlich ist der Übergang des a in o zu erklären in den Verbalformen mokod (eigentlich ma m-ak-od), mokol (ma m-ak-ol, ma m-ak-ol), mokus (ma m-ak-us). Die deutliche Einsicht in diese Formen wurde durch derartige Veränderungen ausserordentlich erschwert und ist das Einzelne der in meinem Vokabular gegebenen Formen nach den hier nach langer Überlegung gemachten Bemerkungen zu verbessern.

b, a) Diese Hülfszeitform ak also wird im Präsens zwischen dem Pronomen und der Verbalwurzel eingefügt, indem der Vokal des Pronomens vor dem a des Hülfszeitwortes elidirt wird, also ma ak-abé, m-ak-abé u. s. w., aber wie das in fast allen diesen Sprachen geschieht, wo die Abwandelung vermittelst eines Präfixes Statt findet, wird das persönliche Fürwort in der vollen Form zweimal ausgedrückt, also ma m-ak-abé u. s. w. (wegen des i k-ak-abé s. S. CCLVI, N. 2). Diese doppelte Wiederholung scheint mit Ausnahme der 2ten Person selbst im Aorist gewöhnlich Statt zu finden und hier wurde ich nun unsicher, ob ich das zweite pronominale Zeichen mit der Verbalform oder mit der vorhergehenden vollen Pronominalform verbinden sollte, besonders in Fällen, wo es vor einem Konsonanten erscheint, wie in ma m sá-ga, se s sá-ga. Jedoch wird in gewöhnlicher Rede im Aorist besonders die erste volle Pronominalform ganz fortgelassen und gebraucht man, abgesehen von der gleich zu besprechenden Endung ga, die einfache Form m-od, „ich zog an", von ma m-ak-od; m-us, „ich zog aus", von ma m-ak-us; m-ad, „ich gab", von ma m-ak-ad.

c) Diese Hülfsform aka, ak fällt bei der Bezeichnung der vergangenen Zeit oder des Aoristes fort, oder vielmehr scheint es in diesem Falle dann als ka, ga der verbalen Wurzel angehängt zu werden *), anstatt als wie in der gegenwärtigen Zeit ihr vorgesetzt zu sein, also ma m-ak-esä, ma m sá-ga. Nur ein scheinbares Beispiel der Abweichung von dieser Form ist die Endung džö in dem oben gegebenen ma m-ab-džö, „ich ging" von abé.

*) Dieser Regel scheint die Form m-ak-oi-ga, „ich sterbe", oder vielmehr „ich bin gestorben", zu widersprechen, wo wir die charakteristischen Formen des Präsens und des Aorists zu gleicher Zeit haben. In Betreff dieses Beispiels halte ich es für wahrscheinlich, anzunehmen, dass meine Autorität von diesem Zeitwort, das natürlicher Weise sehr selten in der 1ten Person der gegenwärtigen Zeit gebraucht wird, für meinen grammatischen Bedarf eine solche Präsensform gebildet hat. Denn in der 3ten Person des Aorists habe ich a(a) oi-ga ganz richtig und für „ich bin dem Sterben nahe, sterbe fast" habe ich mak-oi boi, ohne ga.

We have, therefore, throughout the present tense, an auxiliary verbal form **ak**, prefixed to the verbal root. This form is especially remarkable in connection with the almost identical verb **aka**, „see, look", the root of which latter verb is likewise **ak**, as I am of opinion, that this coincidence is not at all purely accidental, it being not unlikely, that the notion „to see, look", has been expressed by this form, as exhibiting one of the most simple and original actions of man. For, there cannot obtain the slightest doubt, but that the auxiliary verb **ak** actually and originally was an independent verb meaning „do", „perform", corresponding to the auxiliary verb **dō** in Fulfúlde, **yi** in Hausa, **ne** in Wándalá, as is distinctly shewn in the phrase **m-ak-a wāya** p. 95, „I make war, go to war"; and in this instance we have the very same form, which p. 129 we have of the verb „I see, look". The very same character is exhibited by the composite verbs **ma m-ak tdŝi**, „I make water"; **ma m-ak-i ñi** (thus to be written vocab. p. 41), „I make dream, I do dream", from **ni**, „the dream". Thus, no doubt, we have also to understand the verbal form **mam-ók-oro**, „I become tired, weary", the a of the auxiliary form **ak** having been changed into o through the influence of the following o, **or** being the only verbal root, whence the form of the 1st person of the aorist **mam-or-ga** is fully explained, the auxiliary syllable having again been lost; and of the same character is the change of a into o in the verbal forms **mokod** (properly **ma m-ak-od**), **mokol**, **mokul** (**ma m-ak-ol**, **ma m-ak-ul**), **mokus** (**mam-ak-us**), and so on. These contracted forms, which in common conversation occur most frequently, have caused me great embarrassment in the beginning, and have been the chief reason, why in my vocabulary I did not choose to reduce the verbal forms in this language to a more regular principle, which I was only able to apply in this place after a long, and scrupulous investigation. But this character of the auxiliary verb **ak** is perhaps yet more distinctly exhibited in the composite term **m-ak-bō**, meaning verbally „I make near, close", i. q. „I join, unite".

b, a) This auxiliary verbal form **ak**, therefore, in the present tense is inserted between the personal pronoun and the verbal root, the a of the pronominal form being ejected before the a of the auxiliary verb, **ma ák-abe** becoming **m-ák-abe**, and so on; but, as is the case in most of these languages, where conjugation takes place by means of a prefix, the personal pronoun is expressed twice in the full form, and thus we get **ma m-ák-abe**, and so on (as for the **l k-ák-abē** see p. CCLVI, note 2). This reiteration of the pronominal form, in general, seems to take place even in the aorist, with the exception of the 2nd person, and here I was uncertain, whether I was to join the second pronominal sign to the preceding first one, or rather with the succeeding verbal form, especially in such cases, where it precedes a consonant, as, for instance, in **ma m sā-ga**, **ne n sā-ga**. In the vulgar idiom, however, the first full pronominal form is generally left away, and, if we take no regard to the termination **ga**, which will be treated of immediately, the simple forms are used, such as **m-od**, „I dressed", from **ma m-ak-od**; **m-us**, „I undressed", from **ma m-ak-us**; **m-ad**, „I gave", from **ma m-ak-ad**.

c) As stated above, the auxiliary form **aka**, **ak** is thrown off in the aorist — at least such I have found to be the case with one single exception which I shall take into account in the Note*) —, and instead of that form in the latter tense we find **ga** added to the root, which we may with some reason suppose to be the same **ak** in an inverted form, **ka**, **ga**. As a remarkable instance of deviation from this form, I have to mention the form **ma-m ab-dŝŝ**,

*) The exception spoken of in the text regards the form **mak-oi-ga**, „I die, am dying", or rather „I am dead" p. 37, where we have the auxiliary form **ak** of the present tense together with the **ga** of the aorist, the root of the verb being evidently **oi**, whence the substantive **yā**, „death"; but we must take into account, that this term, which is never used in the first person, forms quite an exceptional case, and that my informant was probably puzzled in forming it himself, while there is no doubt, that **a(o) oi-ga**, without an **ak**, is the correct form of the 3rd person sing. of the past tense or aorist and while for the term „I am nearly dying" I have the correct form **m-ak-oi boi**, without **ga**.

„gehn", indem wir hier in Betracht ziehn müssen, erstlich, dass džō eine öfter vorkommende transitive Verstärkungsform ist, zweitens, dass selbst bei dieser Form die Endung ga vorkommt, also ma m-ab-džō-ga, se ab-ki-džō-ga, woraus wir dann, mit Heranziehung der oben (S. CCLVIII, N. 1) erwähnten Imperativform abdžō, schliessen können, dass es neben abē eine Nebenform abdžō gibt.

Zu dieser Form der Vergangenheit, vermittelst ga, nun gehören alle jene von mir S. 125 ff. erwähnten Beispiele von unpersönlichen Verbalformen, wie tadž-ga, indžûm-ga, hol-ga, tog-ga; so heisst góto, „es ist nicht, es fehlt", góto-ga, „es ist zu nichts geworden, ist zu Ende". Auch mam tdd-ga S. 41 ist der Form nach Aorist, nicht Präsens, eigentlich „ich habe mich hingelegt", und ebenso liegt bei anderen Verbalformen wie deb-go šid-ga, „die Leute trennen sich", mab-ga, „hin satt" der Grundbegriff doch ebenfalls in der Vergangenheit.

d) Nun aber scheint bei einer grossen Anzahl von Zeitwörtern die gegenwärtige oder drastische Form vermittelst des Hülfszeitwortes ak nicht üblich zu sein, sondern das Pronomen scheint hier ganz einfach der Verbalwurzel mit hinzugefügtem Vokal-Auslaut vorgesetzt zu werden, und zwar in der ersten Person in der vollen Form ma-m, wie ma-m déga, „ich sage", Imp. degō; ma-m džolle, „ich weiss"; ma-m kolle, „ich zürne"; ma-m hōlo, „ich fürchte", und unzählige andere. Aber auch diese Klasse von Zeitwörtern bildet den Aorist mit Hülfe eines der Verbalwurzel angehängten ga, das doch wol eben jene umgekehrte Hülfszeitform ak ist.

Als Paradigma zu dieser Klasse von Zeitwörtern gebe ich das Zeitwort má tad-a oder má-m tad-a, „ich mache", da dieses in verschiedenen Beziehungen besondere Bedeutung hat, besonders auch deshalb, weil es selbst wieder als Hülfszeitwort gebraucht ist = dem Kanúri ní-skin oder dí-skin, wie z. B. bei den Verbalformen ma tad ir-ga (S. 41 so zu schreiben) „ich mache das Geräusch des Schnarchen's, ich schnarche", ma tad asám-ga (sic), „ich mache das Gähnen, ich gähne"; ma tad šeg-ga, „ich mache Zweifel (شكّ), zweifle"; ma-m tad gáda-ga, „ich mache Alter, werde alt". Besonders belehrend aber sind diejenigen derartig gebildeten Phrasen, die wir mit den ähnlich gebildeten der Kanúri-Sprache zusammenstellen können, wie ma-tad boi-ga, „ich mache nahe", K. káriṅg ní-skin; ma-tad ṅgilla-ga, „ich thue wohl", K. ṅgilla dí-skin; ma-tad gádari, „ich mache Verläumdung, verläumde", K. gader ní-skin. Das in diesen Beispielen den Adjektiven oder Substantiven angehängte ga soll bei dem Substantiv besprochen werden, da es eine Art von Accusativ ist; mit dem Zeitwort scheint dieses ga nichts zu thun zu haben.

e) Eben dieses Zeitwort tad aber scheint mir den Schlüssel zum Verständniss einer anderen Klasse von Zeitwörtern zu liefern, die mir, so wie dieses Zeitwort selbst, lange Zeit grosse Noth bereitet haben. Ich habe nämlich mehrere Zeitwörter, die, anstatt mit einem k oder ak, in der drastischen Form mit einem t gebildet sind, und zwar zweierlei Gattung; erstlich solche, wo dieses t (et, at) die ganze Verbalhandlung ausdrückt, dann solche, wo es nur eine Verstärkung der schon hinlänglich ausgedrückten verbalen Thätigkeit zu sein scheint. Als besonders klare Beispiele der ersten Klasse führe ich an mat-ákri, „ich miethe" und mat-mán, „ich tränke, gebe Wasser", da akri, „Lohn", sowol wie man, „Wasser", rein substantive Begriffe sind und die ganze Verbalhandlung in mat ihren alleinigen Ausdruck findet; — dies, so wie die Richtigkeit des t, wird am Anschaulichsten durch die Form des Imperativs in der Phrase et man sinda na-ki, „gib Wasser dem Pferde". Als Beispiele der zweiten Klasse führe ich an die Zeitwörter ma-ét-kogō, ma-ét-uabō*) (S. 115) und

---

*) ma-ét etšidda S. 115 ist wahrscheinlich falsch und sollte heissen ma tad šidda, indem die ursprünglich von mir niedergeschriebene Form lautet ma ta šidda. — ma-é-hed manê in Beziehung zu mohed el-na scheint mir unsicher.

„I went" from abĕ, „go" (see the paradigm); but this irregularity is of no consequence, if we take into account the frequent occurrence of the transitive verbal form in džō, and the forms ma m-ab-džō-ga, so ab-ki-džō-ga. from which, if we compare the form abdžō of the imperative, we see, that besides abĕ there is another form abdžō; whence it appears that džō does by no means take the place of the termination ga, but that the latter has been thrown off.

To this form of the aorist, by means of ga, do belong all those instances of impersonal verbs which I have adduced p. 125 ff., such as tadž-ga, indžúm-ga, bol-ga, teg-ga, and so on; a very instructive instance of this sort of formation being góto-ga, „it has become nothing, is at an end", from góto, „it is not, there is wanting", and in a similar manner several terms of this kind are to be reduced to the original meaning of a past action, although the result of their action seems to be placed in the present tense, such as dob-go šid-ga, „the people are gone asunder, are separating"; mab-ga, „I have eaten enough, am satiated"; mam tód-ga, „I have lain down, am sleeping".

d) But now I must remark, that a great number of verbs do not seem to form the present tense by means of the auxiliary verb ak, but rather simply prefix the pronoun to the verbal root, in the 1st person in the full form ma-m, as, for instance ma-m dóga, „I say", imp. dogó; ma-m dželle, „I know"; ma-m kolle, „I am angry"; ma-m bólo „I fear", and many others. But even this class of verbs, as far as I am aware, form their aorist by means of the termination ga added to the verbal root.

As a paradigm of this formation I give the verb má tad-a or má-m tad-a, „I make, do, perform", this verb being of considerable importance in various respects, especially as it is used in a very extensive way as an auxiliary verb, corresponding to the Kanúri ní-skin or dí-skin, as, for instance, in the phrases ma tad ir-ga (thus to be written p. 41), „I make (the noise of) snoring", „I am snoring"; ma tad asúm-ga ibid. „I make, I am yawning"; ma tad šog-ga, „I make doubt" (شكّ) i. q. „am doubting"; ma-m tad gáda-ga, „I make age", „grow old". But particularly instructive are the terms formed in such a manner, which we are able to compare with the corresponding phrases in the Kanúri-language, such as ma-tad boi-ga, „I make near" = Kanúri kariñ ní-skin; ma-tad ṅgilla-ga, „I do well" = K. ṅgilla dí-skin; ma-tad gádari, „I make calumny, calumniate" = K. gader ní-skin. As for the termination ga, which in these instances we find added to the substantive or adjective, it has nothing to do with the verbal termination of the aorist, but shall be treated in connection with the noun, as it appears rather to be considered as a sort of accusative.

e) This very verb tad seems to me to be the key for fully understanding another class of verbs, which as well as the verb tad itself, for a long time has caused me a great deal of vexation and uncertainty. For I have a number of verbs, which form the present tense by means of a t instead of k or ak, and which may be reduced to two different categories, first such, where the t (et, at) serves to represent the whole verbal action, and secondly such, where it seems to give only more strength to the verbal action, already fully expressed. As clear instances of the first class, I here adduce the verbs mat-ákri, „I hire", and mat-mán, „I give water, I water (the horse)", akri, „salary, hire", as well as man, „water", being a simple substantive, and the whole verbal action being expressed by means of et, at (mat and so on), a fact which is placed beyond a doubt by the forms of the imperative, such as et man sinda na-ki, „give water to the horse". As instances of the second category, I mention the verbs ma-ét-kogō, ma-ét-nabō*) (both verbs being adduced

*) As for ma-ét atšidda which I have given p. 118, it may be wrong, and ma tad šidda may be the correct form, my collectaneous Notes exhibiting clearly the form ma ta tšidda.

ma-m-ét-kadžá kaga (S. 121); nun ist es aber bemerkenswerth, dass alle diese Zeitwörter eine eng verwandte Art der Handlung bezeichnen, indem sie in der Reihe, wie ich sie aufgeführt habe, bedeuten „ich pflanze", „ich gäte", „ich fälle Holz", und besonders belehrend unter ihnen ist das ma-m-ét-kadžá, da ich auch die einfache Form má kadža für „ich haue ab" habe, und so habe ich bei einem anderen der oben erwähnten Zeitwörter, nämlich ma ét-kogō, „ich säe", ein sicheres Beispiel, dass das et in anderen Personen verloren geht, wie ya-kók, „sie säen" (in den Phrasen). Nun ist das Zeitwort tad nach meiner Ansicht ganz in ähnlicher Weise zusammengesetzt aus eben diesem t (et, at) und dem in den verschiedensten Verbindungen vorkommenden Zeitworte ad, „geben", und eben diese augenscheinliche Zusammensetzung machte mich in der Schreibung dieses Zeitwortes unsicher, indem ich das t bald zu ma, bald zu ad zog (= ma t-ad S. 41, ma-tad S. 53 des Vokab.). Nun haben wir aber auch eben dieses et in einer ansehnlichen Anzahl unpersönlicher Zeitwörter, wie man ét-kedē, „das Wasser fliesst"; bisc no et-kauge, „der Hund, er bellt"; et-nō, „(das Thier) schreit, brüllt", und manche andere. Hier scheint mir also ein klarer Zusammenhang zwischen diesen beiden Formen obzuwalten; denn das et ist offenbar ein Übergang zur Adjektivform und findet sich auch bei (verbalen) Adverbien, wie et-nu, „(ist) oben", ét-gadō, „(ist) hinter". Genau betrachtet, ist das Letztere aber wol nichts als ein verkürztes étu, „es ist", und die beiden Formen, die aktive wie die passive, entsprechen vollkommen dem wōdi im Fūl, me-wōdi, „ich mache" und wōdi, „es ist".

f) Nach diesen Vorbemerkungen und Aufklärungen gebe ich das besagte Paradigma von má-tad-a, „ich thue, mache", Imp. tad.

Präsens.

	Positiv. Singular.	Positiv. Plural.	Negativ. Singular.	Negativ. Plural.
1ste Pers.	má tad-a / má-m tad-a	dže dže-tad-a	ma tad-é-li / ma-m tad-é-li	dže tad-é-li,
2te Pers.	í tad-a	se tar-ki*)	i tad-é-li	se tar-kí-li,
3te „	ne ná-tad-a	dže dží-tad-a	ne tad-é-li	dže dži-tad-é-li.

Aorist.

	Affirmativ. Singular.	Affirmativ. Plural.	Negativ. Singular.	Negativ. Plural.
1ste Pers.	ma-m tad-ga	dže dži-tad-ga	ma-m tád-go-li	dže dži-tád-go-li,
2te „	i tad-ga	se tar-ki?	i tád-go-li	se tár-ki-li,
3te „	ne tad-ga	dže dži-tad-ga	ne tád-go-li	dže dži-tád-go-li.

Conditionell.

	Singular.	Plural.
1ste Person	ma-m tád-ge-na	dže dže-tád-ge-na,
2te „	i túd-ge-na	se tad-kí-ge-na,
3te „	ne no-túd-ge-na	dže dži-tád-ge-na.

g) Ich gebe nun als Beispiel einer anderen Klasse von Zeitwörtern einige Formen von m-án-dugo, ma m-án-dugo (S. 66, N. 21), „ich kaufe", Imp. ná-dugo.

Präsens.

	Singular.	Plural.
1ste Person	ma m-án-dugo	dže dž(e)-án-dugo,
2te „	i í-(a)n-dugo	se sé-(a)n-dugo,
3te „	ne n-án-dugo	dže dž(e)-án-dugo.

*) se tar-ki. In den meisten der Formen der 2ten Person Plur. scheint das d der Wurzel entschieden in r übergegangen zu sein, wogegen tad-ki-ge-na im Conditionell das d unverändert erscheint.

p. 115) and ma-m-ét-kadžá (p. 191). Now, it is very remarkable, that all three, or four verbs indicate one and the same kind of activity, namely the cultivating of the ground, they meaning „planting, weeding, and cutting wood"; and one of them, ma-m-ét-kadžá, deserves the more attention, as I have also the simple form má kadža, „I cut". Now, the verb tad, according to my opinion, has been composed in the very same manner of t (et, at) and the verb ad, „give", and this evident character of its composition may excuse my uncertainty in sometimes joining the t to the pronoun, at others to the verb (mat-ad p. 41, ma-tad p. 53 of the vcblry.), the best way of writing it being probably ma-t-ad. Moreover, the very same verbal form et appears also in several impersonal verbs, where it seems to bear a sort of intermedial character between a really verbal, and a mere auxiliary form, such as man ét-kedd, „the water runs"; bise ae et-kaṅgo, „the dog barks", and et-nó, „makes a sound", meaning the roaring, and crying of animals. I, therefore, conclude that in these instances we have a very similar case, as we have seen with wódi in Fulfúlde, me-wódi meaning „I make, achieve", and wódi, „it is", our et being intimately connected with étu, „it is", this being the very reason, why we find it also in connection with adverbial forms, as for instance et-nu, „is) above"; ét-gadó, „is) behind"; and we are to find it likewise in adjectives. — The et not being absolutely essential in these instances, it is easily explained, how it happens that it be lost in connection with other personal forms; at least among my phrases I have the form ya-kók (dža-kók), „they sow" from the very verb ma-ét-koga.

f) After these Introductory Remarks I give the paradigm of má-tad-a, „I do, perform", imp. tad.

Present tense.

	affirmative form. singular.	plural.	negative form. singular.	plural.
1st pers.	má tad-a / má-m tad-a	dže džé-tad-a	ma tad-é-li / ma-m tad-é-li	dže tad-é-li,
2nd prs.	tad-a	se tar-ki*)	i tad-é-li	se tar-kí-li,
3rd „	ne ná-tad-a	dže dží-tad-a	ne tad-é-li	dže dži-tad-é-li.

Aorist.

	affirmative form. singular.	plural.	negative form. singular.	plural.
1st prs.	ma-m tad-ga	dže dži-tad-ga	ma-m tád-ge-li	dže dži-tád-ge-li,
2nd „	i tad-ga	se tar-ki?	i tád-ge-li	se tár-ki-li,
3rd „	ne tad-ga	dže dži-tad-ga	ne tád-ge-li	dže dži-tád-ge-li.

Conditional.

	singular.	plural.
1st person	ma-m tád-ge-na	dže dže-tád-ge-na,
2nd „	i tád-ge-na	se tad-kí-ge-na,
3rd „	ne ne-tád-ge-na	dže dži-tád-ge-na.

g) I now give a few forms of m-án-dugo, ma m-án-dugo (p. 67, note 21), „I buy", imp. ná-dugo, as instances of another class of verbs.

Present tense.

	singular.	plural.
1st person	ma m-án-dugo	dže dž(e)-án-dugo,
2nd „	i í-(a)n-dugo	se sé-(a)n-dugo,
3rd „	ne n-án-dugo	dže dž(e)-án-dugo.

*) In most of the forms of the 2nd person plur. the d of the root seems to be exchanged against an r, while tad-kí-ge-na exhibits the d unchanged.

Negative Form ma m(a)-án-dugé-li.

Aorist.

Affirmative Form.		Negative Form.
ma m-án-dugé-ga	. . . .	ma m-án-dugé-ga-li.

Conditionell: ma m-án-dugé-ge-na.

Ganz ähnlich gebildet sind die Zeitwörter m-án-dżude, „ich koche"; m-án-dżngo, „ich wasche"; m-an-nö, ma m-an-nö, „ich weine"; m-án-dżabí-(nya, „ich brenne, röste".

h) Über die negativen Formen des Zeitwortes brauche ich nicht viel zu sagen, da sich aus den angeführten Beispielen deutlich ergibt, dass sie auf höchst einfache Weise durch Anfügung der negativen Partikel li an die entsprechende positive Form gebildet werden. Dieses li kann wol noch sonst woher seine Erklärung finden, wie es entschieden an die negative verbale Form la im Ful erinnert, und werde ich zu ihm zurückkehren, um über seine Anhängung an adjektive und substantive Begriffe noch etwas Weiteres zu sagen.

i) Der Conditionell scheint gebildet zu werden, indem man an die Form des Aoristes, mit Veränderung des a in e, ein na anhängt, wol mit der Bedeutung „wenn". Jedoch, obgleich an dieser engen Verknüpfung des Conditionell's mit dem Aorist wol nicht zu zweifeln ist, kommen doch Fälle vor, wo die Hülfszeitform ak, die doch eigentlich nur bei der Form des Präsens einen integrirenden Theil bildet, auch in der Form des Conditionells sich findet, wie z. B. in m-ak-áb-gena, der ersten Person Sing. des Conditionell's von m-ák-abé, „ich gehe", und, obgleich in diesem Falle in meinem Paradigma das ak in den Formen der übrigen Personen fehlt, habe ich es in einem anderen Beispiele durch alle Personen durchgehend. Dies ist der Conditionell von m-ak-íngi, „ich breche auf", Aorist má m-ínga, Imp. 2te Person Sing. íngi, 1ste Person Plur. dže-k-íngi, Conditionell „wenn ich aufbräche" oder „aufgebrochen wäre", ma m-ak-íngena (absichtlich theile ich in der letzten Form nicht ab).

	Singular.		Plural.
1ste Person	ma m-ak-íngena	. . .	dže dž-ak-íngena,
2te „	ı k-ak-íngena	. . . .	se inkí-gena,
3te „	no n-ak-íngena	. . . .	dže dže-k-íngena.

Dies ist aber jedenfalls ein ganz besonderer Fall, indem diese Ausnahme, wie es mir scheint, sehr natürlich und vielmehr in Bestätigung dessen, was ich oben gesagt habe, dass das ga oder ka des Aorist's nur die äusserlich umgekehrte Hülfszeitform des Präsens sei, darin ihre Erklärung findet, dass in der Stammwurzel dieses Zeitwortes ein ga, ge schon enthalten ist, so dass ihm, mit Fortlassung des charakteristischen ga des Aorist's, das blosse na als Zeichen des Conditionell's angehängt, dafür jedoch die Form des Präsens beibehalten ist; und doch erkennen wir aus der Form der 2ten Person des Plural in-kí-gena, wo das ak wieder abgeworfen ist, dass auch hier das gena wirklich die gewöhnliche charakteristische Form des Conditionell's ist.

k) Nun aber habe ich zu bemerken, dass diese Verbalform auf gena nicht allein die gestellte Bedingung einer Handlung, sondern auch den Zweck derselben anzeigt, also eine Art von Subjunktiv bildet; und als solche abhängige Form, und nicht als directe Aussage haben wir nach meiner jetzigen Überzeugung auch die S. 41 angeführte Phrase éda tód-gena zu betrachten mit der Bedeutung nicht „wo werden wir schlafen", sondern „der Ort), wo wir schlafen werden". Zur Bestätigung dieser Behauptung führe ich als Erklärung einige andere Phrasen an, zuerst „die Stadt, wohin wir gehen, um dort zu schlafen", bé-ne dže-k-áb tód-gena, wo wir also eben dieselbe Form haben von dem oben angeführten Zeitwort mam tod-ga; dann die längere Phrase „lasst uns einen guten Schatten suchen, dass wir dort absteigen und, wenn es kühl geworden ist, unseren Marsch fortsetzen",

Negative form of present tense ma m(a)-án-dugó-li.

Aorist.

affirmative form.		negative form.
ma m-áo-dugó-ga	. . . .	ma m-án-dugó-ga-li.

Conditional: ma m-án-dugó-ge-na.

In the very same manner are conjugated the verbs m-án-dẑndo, „I cook"; m-án-dẑugo, „I wash"; m-an-nô, ma m-an-nô, „I weep"; m-án-dẑabí-(nya, „I broil, roast".

h) With regard to the negative forms I need not say much, as from the instances adduced it clearly appears, that they have been developed in a most simple manner by adding the negative particle li to the corresponding positive form. This li, which reminds one of the negative verbal form la in the Fül-language, will, I hope, be explained from some other point of view, when I shall have to return to it in another chapter with regard to its being joined to adjective and substantive notions.

i) As for the conditional mood, on the other hand, it appears to be formed by adding na, „if" to the form of the aorist, while changing the a of the characteristic termination of the latter into e. But, nothwithstanding such a close connection of this form with that of the aorist, some instances occur, where the auxiliary form ak, which scarcely ever is combined with the latter, but almost exclusively with that of the present tense, is also found forming an integrant part of the conditional, as we have an instance of such a case in the form m-ak-áb-gena registered above as the conditional of m-ák-abô, „I go"; and, although in this case my paradigm does not exhibit the syllable ak in the forms of the other persons, in another instance I have this very form throughout all the different persons of the tense. This is the conditional of m-ak-fûgi, „I start", aorist má m-íñga, 2nd person sing. of imp. iñgi, 1st person plur. dẑo-k-íñgi, conditional „if I had started", or „if I did start", ma m-ak-íñgena (it is on purpose, that I do not separate the last portion of the form).

	singular.		plural.
1st person	ma m-ak-íñgena	. . . .	dẑo dẑ-ak-íñgena,
2nd „	i k-ak-íñgena	. . . . .	se iñkí-gena,
3rd „	ne n-ak-íñgena	. . . .	dẑe dẑo-k-íñgena.

This is certainly an exceptional case, the exception, as it seems to me, being, however, very natural, and not at all refuting what I have said before, with regard to the ka or ga of the aorist being nothing but the inverted auxiliary form of the present tense; for, the verbal root of m-ak-íñgi itself containing already a gi, ge, this syllable could not well be added a second time, instead of which the form of the present tense, by means of ak, has been introduced in this case, while the form of the 2nd person of the plural iñ-kí-ge-na, where the ak, which has been made use of in the other persons, has again been thrown off, clearly exhibits the regular form of the conditional mood, gena.

k) But now I have to remark, that this termination gena does not only indicate the condition, but also the purpose of an action, and therefore serves to form a kind of subjunctive. As such a mood we have to understand the phrase ôda tód-gena mentioned, p. 41, which, I feel convinced, is not an independent form by itself, but merely the relative concluding portion of a phrase, „where we may sleep" or „pass the night". In order to prove the correctness of this statement, I here adduce a few other phrases, first „the town, where we go to", or „in order to" or „that we may pass the night there", bé-ne dẑe-k-áb tód-gena, where we meet with the very same verbal form of the verb mam tod-ga, which we have had above; further, the phrase „let us look for a good shade, in order to dismount there"

dž-ambol džil-i ṅgilla da-dis-gena džá-wēā girgilla
lasst uns suchen Schatten gut (K.) dass wir absteigen wir bringen die Mittagshitze zu
džil-na úl-gena (von úlu, „es wird kühl") dž-ák-abé;
Schatten in, wenn es kühl geworden lasst uns gehn;

also die Endung gena ein Mal als Subjunktiv, das andere Mal als Conditionell.

Ganz besonders und eigenthümlich dagegen haben wir, wie ich glaube, das gena in der folgenden Phrase aufzufassen, wo es gar nicht einer Verbalform, sondern einer lokalen Partikel hinzugefügt ist, „lasst uns hinausgehn und unser Zelt aufschlagen",

dže-káb aglá-gena dža-ták lema-na,
lasst uns gehn hinaus lasst uns schlagen das Zelt.

In diesem Falle könnte man vielleicht die einer lokalen Partikel (aglá) angehängte Subjunktivform mit einer Art von Accusativ-Endung vergleichen; doch siehe weiter unten.

l) Von einer **Participialform des Aktivs** habe ich kein entschiedenes Beispiel; aber in gewissen Fällen scheint die einfache Wurzel zur Angabe eines derartigen Verhältnisses gebraucht zu werden, wie z. B. deb tad ṅgilla-ga oder deb tad ṅgā-ga, „eine Person machend oder thuend wohl", d. h. in der Besserung befindlich. Ja, daraus dass diese ursprünglich participiale Verbalform wie ein einziger Begriff angesehen wurde, haben wir die S. 83 angeführte Phrase zu erklären ma ma-tad i kurgún tad ṅgā-ga, „ich mache dir eine Arzenei zum Besserwerden", d. h. „ich heile dich". Ebenso haben wir auch zu erklären die zusammengesetzte Adjektivform tad áṅkali, „machend Verstand", d. h. „klug, einsichtsvoll". Zuweilen scheint auch die Endung ga so gebraucht zu werden, wie in tod-ga, „schlafend" = bo-ga-ta im Kanúri, und müssen wir so wol die Verbal-Endung ṅga, ṅge ansehn in den Formen ma dise-na-ṅge, „ich bin im Absteigen begriffen", ma-m dug-na-ṅga, „ich mache meine Verbeugung".

m) Vom **Passivum** habe ich keine einzige, ganz sichere, Form; allerdings habe ich einige Beispiele eines Particips Passivi, aber doch auch diese höchst unsicher. So scheinen allerdings die Formen dže-džok-iṅga, „gebunden", von ma-džok (nya, und dži-ti-ṅga, „gelöst", von ma-tie (nya (S. 129), Participialformen des Passivs; aber unerklärlich ist es mir, wie gerade bei diesen Formen, die in bestimmter Beziehung zu einem Singular stehn (nap. „Mond"), die Pluralform des Pronomens „wir" oder „sie", dže, dži, eine Rolle spielen kann.

4. *Das Nennwort.*

Ich wende mich nun zur Besprechung des Nennwortes in der Bágrimma-Sprache.

a) Zuerst führe ich als Beispiel wahrscheinlicher Ableitung des Nennwortes von der Verbalwurzel an das Wort yō, „Tod", gō, „Leichnam, Todter", von oi, „sterben", dagegen als entschiedenes Beispiel der Priorität eines substantiven (monosyllaben) Begriffes führe ich an die Verbalform mah-i-ñi, „ich träume", im Vergleich mit dem einfachen Nennwort ni, „Traum"; m-ét-a-kā, „ich singe", von kā, „Gesang"; ähnlich sind m-án-dugo und die zu dieser Klasse gehörenden, da dugo, „Kauf, Bezahlung" bedeutet. So habe ich auch andere Beispiele der wahrscheinlichen Priorität substantiver Begriffe, wie mam-bōlo, „ich fürchte" wol unzweifelhaft von bōlo, „Sklavin" abzuleiten ist, mit der Grundbedeutung „ich betrage mich wie eine Sklavin". In Betreff anderer Beispiele bin ich unsicher; so weiss ich nicht, ob der verbale Begriff von mam kollo, „ich zürne" dem Substantiv-Begriff kollo, „Zorn" vorhergeht oder umgekehrt; doch ist das Letztere das Wahrscheinliche, da das Bild vom „Kochtopf" (kolle) hergenommen ist.

b) Die Bágrimma-Sprache aber hat eine sehr gewöhnliche Art, Nennwörter zu bilden, nämlich durch Vorsatz eines k, ke vor einer verbalen Wurzel, eine Bildungsweise, die wir auch im Kanúri an so vielen Beispielen kennen gelernt haben (s. SS. XLVI, LXXXVI ff.), die

dĭ-ambol džil-i ṅgilla da-dís-gena džá-wĕa girgilla džil-na
let us search shade good dismount that we may pass the heat shade (in)
di-gena (from dlu, „it becomes cool") dž-áh-abe;
cool when it has become let us go;

the gena, therefore, in this phrase, appearing in both characters, in the first place as the termination of the subjunctive, and the second time as that of the conditional.

Rather remarkable, but very instructive for understanding the original character and meaning of this form gena, in connection with what I shall have to say further on, is the following phrase, where we find it joined to a local particle „let us go outside (aglá) and pitch our tent",

džr-káb aglá-gena dža-túk léma-na,
let us go outside let us pitch tent (acc.).

l) I have no distinct instance of a participial form of the active voice, but it seems, as if in certain cases the simple root were used for expressing such a relation, as, for instance, dab tad ṅgilla-ga or dob tad ṅgă-ga, verbally „a person making (doing) well", i. q. „recovering". This, originally composite, participial form having become one simple adjective notion, we have thence to explain the phrase adduced p. 83 ma ma-tad i kurgán tad ṅgă-ga, „I make thee a medicine for doing well, or recovering". From the same point of view we have to look upon the composite adjective form tad súkali, „making, having intelligence", i. q. „intelligent, clever". Sometimes the termination ga seems to be used as a participial form, as I have tod-ga, „sleeping", corresponding to the Kanúri-form hó-ga-ta, and I think, we have to look from this point of view upon such forms as ma disc-na-úge, „I am dismount-ing", ma-m dug-nu-ṅga, „I am mak-ing my reverence".

m) Of the Passive voice I have not a single reliable, and unquestionable form, although there occur in my collection a few instances of a participle of that voice; but even these are rather uncertain. Thus, I have the forms dže-džok-inga, „tied", from ma-džokí (nya, and dži-tí-ṅga, „untied, loosened", from ma-tie (nya, p. 129, which appear after all to be understood as participial forms of the passive voice; but, as these instances are distinctly referred to a singular (nap, „moon"), I am unable to explain the plural form of the personal pronoun dže, referring either to the first or to the third person plural, being added to these participial forms.

4. *The noun.*

I now proceed to treat of the noun in the Bágrimma-language.

a) I first mention the substantives yo, „death", go, „corpse", from the verb oi, „to die", as instances of the most simple derivation of the noun from the verbal root; on the other hand I have to mention as instances of the priority of the noun the verb mak-i-ŭi, „I dream", compared with the simple form of the noun ui, „dream", as well as m-ĕt-a-kă, „I am singing", from kă, „song"; a similar instance is m-ŭn-dugo and the other verbs of this class, dugo being a substantive, meaning „payment". Thus, I have also other instances of a probable priority of substantive terms, as, for instance, mam-bólo, „I fear", which, there can be but little doubt, has been derived from the term bólo, „female slave", conveying the original notion, „I behave like a female slave". With regard to other instances, I am uncertain, as, for instance, the verb mam kollo, „I am angry", which, however, I think, has likewise been derived from the nominal term kolle, first meaning „cooking pot", then, in a metaphorical sense, „anger, wrath".

b) Secondly, the Bágrimma-language has a very common mode of forming nouns, by prefixing h. ke to a verbal root, in a very similar manner, as we have seen to be the case with the Kanúri-language (pp. XLVII, LXXXVII ff.), but which in the language of which

aber im Bágrimma durch ihre enge Beziehung zu der verbalen Hülfszeitform der gegenwärtigen Zeit ak ihre viel lebendigere und natürlichere Erklärung erhält. So haben wir von m-ák-abé, „ich gehe", k-abé, „der Marsch"; von m-ák-esä, „ich esse", k-esä oder ke-sä, „Speise, Nahrung" = kumbū (ke-n-bū) im Kanúri von bú-skin; von m-ák-odžo, „ich gebäre", k-odžo, „Geburt".

Diess sind die einfachsten und am klarsten nachzuweisenden Beispiele solcher Bildung, obgleich viele andere aller Wahrscheinlichkeit nach eben so gebildet sind, z. B. ká-dža, „Sonne", „das was Licht gibt, den Tag macht", da dža, wol vom entsprechenden Verbalbegriffe abgeleitet, „Tag" bedeutet, und ähnlich k-oška, „Leben". Was ke-yō betrifft „das Getränk" (auch in Verbindung mit ñgas, „Sache", „die Sache zum Trinken"), ganz entsprechend dem Kanúri ke-u-tsā, von yā, „trinken", so konnte ich es deshalb nicht gleich den unter a) angeführten Beispielen einreihen, da die verbale Wurzel eine Umwandelung erlitten zu haben scheint, indem ich nur mak-ai für „ich trinke" habe, aber vielleicht ist die richtigere Form mák-e-yi. Was ein anderes Beispiel dieser Bildung, k-am-gā, anbetrifft, „der Wille", von der verbalen Wurzel ge, so scheint hier das beziehende n zur Verbindung zwischen beiden Redetheilen gebraucht zu sein, da doch die ursprüngliche Form ko-n-gā zu sein scheint, genau entsprechend dem gleichbedeutenden Kanúri-Nennwort kerrāgo (ke-n-rāgo), obgleich es allerdings auch ke-an-gā sein könnte, mit Benutzung der auch sonst bei mir vorkommenden verbalen Hülfszeitform an.

c) Was zusammengesetzte Nennwörter betrifft, so sind sie gewöhnlich derartig gebildet, dass das Subjekt dem Objekt vorangeht, indem beide ohne Bindepartikel aneinander gefügt sind, wie z. B. man-dža, „Wasser (vom) Fleisch", d. h. „Fleischbrühe"; ká-kesé, „Holz (vom) Pfeil", d. h. „Bogen"; túr-imbi, „Lippe (vom) Ohr", d. h. „Ohrlappen"; mus-né, „Blut (von) Frau", d. h. „Menstruation"; on-mañga, „Junges (von) Kuh", d. h. „Kalb"; kád-mane, „Schöpflöffel (zum) Wasser", und viele andere.

d) Nun habe ich auch einige Beispiele anderer Arten von Zusammensetzung der Nennwörter, z. B. durch Einschiebung eines n zwischen Subjekt und Objekt, als in bé-n báñgena, „Stadt des Häuptlings", wo wir ausserdem noch eine dem Objekt angehängte Beziehungsform haben, wofür ich auch die letztere Form allein, ohne vermittelndes n habe, bé báñgena; und hierzu geselle ich gleich die ähnliche Form gon manda-ïna, „Brust vom Mädchen" (mandu). Diese Anhängungsformen ena, an und andere ihnen ähnliche lassen sich oft schwer von den ihnen fast gleichen Formen des demonstrativen Fürwortes, wie éna, ína, nn, ne unterscheiden, da diese dem Substantiv angehängt werden, wie z. B. in der Phrase mal dób-ge-ne fet-ne oi-ga, „das ganze Eigenthum dieser Leute ist verloren". Hier will ich nun mit einem Mal auch andere dergleichen Verbindungsweisen berücksichtigen. Dem Objekte werden nämlich auch noch andere Endungen angehängt, wie z. B. in der Form dugune lókumá-ade, „Junges vom Kameel"; gon déi-gi, „Kind von Hand", d. h. „Finger". Auch kib-džo-ae, „Marsch zur Nacht" ist wol so zu fassen.

e) Nun habe ich ferner zu bemerken, dass die gewöhnliche Regel wegen Voranstellung des Subjektes vor dem Objekte in gewissen Fällen umgekehrt wird. Anders ist es, was ich hier gleich erwähnen will, wenn die Phrase in Frageform gestellt wird, wie z. B. „was ist die Sprache dieser Stadt"?,

bē nan džyllo džínnodi,
Stadt diese Sprache Art welcher?.

Ein eigenthümliches Beispiel einer Zusammensetzung solcher Art ist der Ausdruck bañg džokíñge, „des Königs Gefangener", indem džokíñge die Participialform des Passivums zu sein scheint (S. CCLXX, n), wenn wir nicht annehmen, dass diese durch die einfache Wurzel džokí ausgedrückt ist, und dass die Endsilbe ñge das a-nyi des persönlichen Fürwortes vertritt. S. oben S. CCLVI. Denn sonst wird allerdings in positiver Rede das

we are now treating is by far more easily explained by means of the close reference it bears to the auxiliary verb ak. Thus, we have the substantive k-abé, „march, journey", from m-ák-abê, „I do march"; k-esâ or ko-sâ, „what to eat", „food", from m(a)-ák-esâ, „I do eat", exactly corresponding to the Kanúri term kumbu (ke-n-bû), from bû-skin; k-odžo, „birth", from má-k-odžo, „I do bear, bring forth".

These are the most simple, and clear instances of this mode of formation which I have, although several others most probably have been formed in the same manner, such as k-otška, „life"; even the term ká-dža, „sun" seems to be formed in the same manner, meaning originally „what gives light, makes the day", dža by itself meaning „day". As for ke-yo, „what to drink, the drink", or in conjunction with ṅgas, ṅgas ke-yô, „something to drink", corresponding exactly to the Kanúri ke-n-tsâ from yu, „to drink", I was not able to place it side by side with ke-sâ (or ṅgás ke-sâ), „food", the verbal form seeming to have undergone a slight change, as I have only mak-ai for „I drink"; but perhaps it ought to be spelt mák-eyi. As for another instance of such a derivation of the noun, viz k-am-ga, „the will", from the verbal root ge, corresponding exactly to the Kanúri kerrago (ke-n-rago), we have a case where also in Bágrimma a combination with the relative n, as it seems, has been made use of, in order to join the ko to the verb, the original form of the word seeming to be ke-n-ga, although it may possibly be ko-an-ga, by means of the auxiliary verbal form an, of which I have a few other instances.

c) As for composite nouns, they are generally formed in such a way, that the subject precedes the object, both being joined together without any kind of copula, as, for instance, mao-džâ, „water (of) meat", i. q. „broth"; ká-kosé, „wood (of) arrow", i. q. „bow"; tár-imbī, „lip (of) ear", i. q. „earlap"; mus-nê, „blood (of) female", i. q. „menstruation"; on-mañga, „young (of) cow", i. q. „calf"; kád-manê, „scooping vessel (for) water", i. q. „vessel for scooping water", and many others.

d) But I have also a few instances of other modes of composition, as, for instance, by inserting an n between subject and object, as in bo-n báṅg-ena, „town of the chief" where, besides this way of joining by means of a copulative n, we have, moreover, a relative particle added to the object, instead of which I have an instance of the same composite term with only the latter form, viz bó báṅg-ena; and to this I join here at once gan manda-ïna, „breast of girl" (manda), as an instance of the similar termination ïna, added to the object. Thus I have also mal wai-na, „the property of war", i. q. „the booty". These suffix relative particles ena, na, and others of a similar kind, often are rather with difficulty distinguished from similar forms of the demonstrative pronoun, such as éna, ïna, na, ne, especially as the latter are likewise affixed to the substantives, as, for instance, in the phrase mal dób-ge-ne fet-ne oi-ga, „all the property of these people has been lost". As instances of other forms I mention ángunu lúkumá-ada, „young of camel"; gon dži-ai, „son of hand", i. q. „finger". Also kdb-džo-ne, „march of, at night", „night's march" does belong hither.

e) Now, I have farther to remark, that the general rule, with regard to the subject preceding the object, is inverted in certain cases. The case is a different one, when the phrase is put in the form of a question, as, for instance „what is the idiom of this town"?,

bó nan diglio dží̈unodi,
town this language of what kind.

A very remarkable instance of such a composition is the term baṅg dšokíṅge, „the king's prisoner", if we take dšokíṅge to be the participial form of the passive mood (compare p. CCLXXI, a), although we may possibly have to look upon the simple root dšokí as that verbal form, while the final syllable ṅge may represent the a-nyi of the possessive pronoun

Objekt dem Subjekt nur in solchen Fällen vorangesetzt, wo das possessive Fürwort die Vermittelung bildet, wie in der Phrase

dób-ge-ne ko-sá á-dže-na kandže gas kwi góto,
Leute diese Speise ihre Fisch, Sache sonst nicht ist.

f) Ich gebe nun solche zusammengesetzte Ausdrücke, welche Beschäftigungen des Menschen bezeichnen. Diese sind in doppelt verschiedener Weise zusammengesetzt, einmal indem man die Silbe kot, kotă, für die ich zuweilen auch die Form kotta habe, wie in kotta-sirde, „Sattler", und das andere Mal, indem man den Ausdruck mala, dem Gegenstand der Beschäftigung (eigentlich des Besitzes) vorsetzt. Die erste Vorsatzsilbe betrachte ich als aus ke und at, ot entstanden, „er der macht, bearbeitet" (in Verbindung mit dem oben S. CCLXIV, f) besprochenen et); mala heisst „Herr". So habe ich also die Ausdrücke kót-gańga, „Trommler"; kót-kurū, „Schäfer"; kótă-mogo, „Schmied"; kotă-totăa, „Tischler"; kotă-álini, „Färber", und andere mehr. Wir können also diese Form der Komposition als verbal ansehen; dagegen ist die andere mit mala substantivisch, indem das Objekt als Art Genitiv diesem regierenden Subjekt hinzugefügt ist, weshalb wir diese Art Komposita zu der auf der vorhergehenden Seite, c) besprochenen Kategorie rechnen müssen. Als Beispiele führe ich hier an mala-sinda, „Herr des Pferdes", d. h. „Reitersmann"; mala-díbu, „Herr des Weges", d. h. „Führer"; mala-kandže, „Herr der Fische", d. h. „Fischer". In einigen Fällen ist auch ein Eigenschaftswort noch hinzugefügt, wie z. B. in mala-tĭída késo, „Herr der schlechten (koso) That", d. h. „der Übelthäter". Ich habe jedoch auch Beispiele, wo das mala nicht mit einem anderen Substantiv, sondern mit einem Verbalbegriff verbunden ist, wie z. B. mala-dissa, „Herr des Rasirens", d. h. „Barbier". Nun kann aber auch einem solchen Zeitwort noch wiederum ein Objekt hinzugefügt werden, wie z. B. mala-tad-kūdži, „Herr des Hütten-Bauens", d. h. „Baumeister". Auch habe ich nun noch zum Überfluss ein Beispiel, wo beide Ausdrücke, sowol mala wie kotă, gemeinsam in obiger Weise verbunden sind und dermassen bestätigen, was ich früher gesagt habe, dass wir nämlich kotă als eine verbale Form anzusehen haben, also mala-kotă-egorra, wörtlich „Meister der bearbeitet Thon", d. h. „der Töpfer".

g) Wenn wir nun die Flexion des Nennwortes in Betracht ziehen, so zeigen schon viele der erwähnten zusammengesetzten Ausdrücke, dass der Genitiv in der Bágrimma-Sprache sehr ungenügend zur Vertretung kommt, und dasselbe gilt in noch stärkerem Grade von den anderen Kasus mit Ausnahme des Accusativ. Denn der Accusativ findet in den meisten Redensarten, die ich lernte, eine bestimmte Vertretung, indem man dem Stamme des Nennwortes ein na hinzufügt, so dass der Ausgangsvokal des Nominativs in vielen Fällen verloren geht, wie z. B. ma-tuk pod-na, „ich zünde an Feuer" (pod-u); ma-tuk si-na, „ich rühre um Milch" (si); ma-tuk lema-na, „ich schlage das Zelt"; ma-sum dži-na, „ich küsse die Hand"; ma ma-túr sínda-na, „ich treibe an das Pferd"; dže dže-kă teńg-na, „sie schneiden Hirsekorn" (teńg-u); yásere báya-na, „sie bebauen das Feld"; indădžum dib-na, „zeige den Weg" (dib-u); ne ne-mā deb-na, „er unterstützt den Mann" (deb-e). Diese Endung na wird selbst dem possessiven Fürworte angefügt, wie folgendes Beispiel zeigt, ma-díssa dāl(a)-am-na, „ich rasire meinen (am) Kopf". Übrigens bin ich überzeugt, dass dieses na ganz dasselbe ist, welches wir oben bei der Zusammensetzung zweier Substantiven fanden, also auch zur Bezeichnung einer Art von Genitiv-Verhältniss dient. Eine Art von Mittelding zwischen beiden Beziehungen, der des Genitiv's und des Accusativ's, finden wir in der Phrase mok-on sinda dib-na, „ich suche ein Pferd für den Weg oder „zu der Reise". Ja, wir werden unter den Phrasen dib-na ganz lokativisch haben mit der Bedeutung „auf dem Wege".

g, α) Dagegen haben wir als verschiedene Accusativform ga in der Phrase mut kákará-ga, „ich zog das Schwert", während in der gleich darauf folgenden mus kákara be-nyi-ga, „ich steckte das Schwert in seine Scheide" die Beziehung eine mehr lokative

(p. CCLVII). For, in general, in such cases, where the object precedes the subject, the possessive pronoun forms the intermediate member of speech, as, for instance, in the phrase

déh-go-no ko-nã á-dže-na kandže gas kwi góto,
people these food of them fish, thing else there is none.

f) I now give such composite terms, as designate the various kinds of human occupation. These are composed in two different ways, one by means of prefixing the terms kot or kotš, or even kotta, as in kotta-sirde, „the saddler", the other by prefixing the term mala, before the object indicated. The first term I look upon as a verbal composition, consisting of ko and the verbal form at, ot intimately connected with the et spoken of before (p. CCLXV, f), and meaning „he who makes, works in", while the second term mala means originally „master (of)", therefore „possessing". Thus, I have the terms kót-gaňga, „the drummer"; kót-kurù, „the shepherd"; kótš-mogo, „the blacksmith"; kotš-totšo, „the carpenter"; kotš-álini, „the dyer", and others. The other mode of forming these terms, that by means of mala, is of a substantival kind, and belongs rather to the class of compositions treated under e), the object being joined to the subject as a sort of genitive case. As a few instances of this very common way of composition I here give mala-sinda, „master of the horse", i. q. „horseman"; mala-dǐbu, „master of the track", i. q. „guide"; mala-kandže, „master of the fish", i. q. „fisherman"; in some cases the character of the object is further indicated by adding to it an adjective, as, for instance, mala-tšǐda késu, „master of a bad (késu) deed", i. q. „the evildoer". But I have also instances where this term mala is not joined to another substantive, but to a verbal notion, as, for instance, mala-dissa, „the master of shaving", i. q. „the barber". I have also an instance of a substantive in the latter case being joined as object to the verb, viz mala-tad-kùdži, „master of making cottages", i. q. „a builder, architect", and now I have also one isolated instance, where both terms, mala as well as kotš, are joined together just in the same manner, confirming what I have said before, viz that we have to look upon kotš as a verbal form, this composite term being mala-kotš-egerra, verbally „master who works in clay", i. q. „claybuilder".

g) If we now consider the declension of the noun, the composite terms registered above serve to show, that not even the genitive case is expressed in a regular manner; and the same is to be said of the other cases with even better reason. No doubt, we find vestiges of such an attempt being made, but without any clear insight into the different character of the relation to be expressed. Thus, we meet with the very same na which we have found used in many instances, in order to express the genitive case, as a very common form of a sort of accusative, as, for instance, in the phrase ma-tuk si-na, „I stir the milk"; ma-sum dǎi-na, „I kiss the hand"; ma-tuk lema-na, „I pitch the tent"; ma ma-túr sínda-na, „I drive on the horse"; yásoro bdya-na, „they cultivate the field"; džu dže-ka teňg-na, „they cut the corn" (teňg-o); ma-tuk pod-na, „I light the fire", from pod-u, „the fire"; indǎdžum dib-na, „show the track" (dib-u); ue ne-ma deb-na, „he assists the man" (deb-e). A sort of intermediate relation between a genitive, and an accusative case I suppose the na to have in the following phrase mok-on sinda dib-na, „I search a horse for the road, for travelling", the simple accusative case in the other noun sinda not being expressed. But among my phrases we even meet with the form dib-na with the meaning „on the road". This termination na is even added to the form of the possessive pronoun, as, for instance, ma-dissa dǎl(a)-um-na, „I shave my (am) head".

g, α) But instead of na I find also ga used, in order to indicate an accusative case, as, for instance, in the phrase mat káskurú-ga, „I drew the sword", while the related phrase mus káskara hé-nyi-ga, „I put the sword into the sheet", rather exhibits the same form with a local meaning. But a very clear instance of the accusative notion of ga is the

ist. S. auch die oben S. CCLXIV, e angeführten Beispiele und füge hinzu gan man-ga (so zu verbessern S. 127), „es wird zu Wasser", d. h. „schmilzt". Als eine Zusammensetzung von ga und na könnte man vielleicht das oben S. CCLXVIII, 1 bei der Besprechung des Conditionell's angeführte gend hinter ogla, „hinaus" erklären.

g, β) Neben dem Accusativ scheint jedoch auch eine Ablativ-Beziehung gelegentlichen Ausdruck zu finden, indem man dem Nennworte ein rä anfügt, dasselbe rä unzweifelhaft, was ich unter den Partikeln S. 29 mit der Bedeutung „nieder, zur Erde", aufgeführt habe, also z. B. mak-um sínda-rä S. 93, „ich steige ab vom Pferde".

g, γ) Wie wir ein angehängtes ki zu fassen haben, bin ich etwas unsicher; es scheint mir jedoch ganz lokal zu sein und daher auch einen integrirenden Bestandtheil der Präposition ná-ki-na zu bilden „innerhalb, in". Allein habe ich es in der Phrase uske-dšö bö kode-ki „dass er uns einquartiere in einem (kode) Hause" (bö). Aber mit dem beziehenden na zusammen vertritt es eine Art von Dativ in der Phrase et man sinda-na-ki, „gib dem Pferde Wasser", wogegen es in der Phrase ongal nang na-ki, „gehe in die Stadt", der Bedeutung der Präposition oder vielmehr Postposition ná-ki-na, die auch nachgestellt wird, mit accusativer Nebenbedeutung „hinein", ganz nahe kommt.

g, δ) Als ein Beispiel des Gebrauchs von Präpositionen, um die Instrumentalität anzuzeigen, entsprechend unserem „vermittelst, mit", erwähne ich die Phrase mak-ub se indž(a)-umä, „ich gehe mit meinem, vermittelst meines Fusses", und dieses se findet wahrscheinlich allgemeinere Anwendung.

h) Was nun die Mehrheitsform des Nennwortes betrifft, so besteht die gewöhnlichste Veränderung, welche es im Plural erleidet, in der Anfügung eines go an den Stamm, ganz in derselben Weise, wie wir das schon bei dem persönlichen Fürwort gesehen haben. So wird von deb, debe, „Person, Mensch" der Plural deb-ge, „Leute", gebildet; von nö, „Frau", né-ge; von lúguma, „Kameel", lúguma-ge; ja selbst von kede, „ein, einer" wird ein Plural kéde-ge gebildet mit der Bedeutung „Einige". Jedoch, wenn die Form des Plurals schon beim persönlichen Fürwort bezeichnet ist, wird sie gewöhnlich bei dem Nennwort nicht noch einmal angegeben; so habe ich neben der Form lúguma-ge a-má-ge-ne éga, „meine Kameele haben sich verlaufen" die Phrase ma sinda a-má-ge-na m-án-dugó korö, „ich habe meine Pferde verkauft", und neben sínda-ge á-dšo-na dše dš-én-dugó korö, „wir haben unsere Pferde verkauft" die andere Form sinda n-só-ge-na se só-ndugó korö, „ihr habt eure Pferde verkauft".

h, α) Diese Pluralform in ge scheint selbst eine Accusativform zu haben auf ne, indem das n der entsprechenden Form des Singular in ein e verwandelt wird, wie z. B. dšo dšó-tuki déb-ge-ne, „wir schlagen die Leute", wenn nicht anders, was ich jedoch nicht glaube, dieses ne vielleicht der Plural von na, „dieser" ist.

Jedoch habe ich auch neben der gewöhnlichsten Pluralform auf ge Beispiele anderer Formen, erstlich eben das erwähnte ne, wie z. B. bé-ne von be, „Stadt" (bé-ne kando, „wie viele Städte"?); dann an, ena in tóge-na von tokö, „Boot", wenn anders das na bei letzterem Beispiel wirklich den einfachen Plural darstellt. Denn hier tritt wieder der schon oben berührte Umstand ein, dass es kaum möglich ist, diese Endung von dem demonstrativen Fürwort zu unterscheiden.

h, β) Als ein Beispiel einer im Plural unverändert bleibenden Singularform erwähne ich lua, „Jahr", in der Mehrheit gleichfalls lua.

i) Was das Geschlecht betrifft, so wird das männliche, wenn es erforderlich ist, es besonders auszuzeichnen, durch den Zusatz von gäbn, „Mann", hervorgehoben, das weibliche durch den Beisatz von né, „Frau", und zwar sowohl bei menschlichen Wesen, als auch bei Thieren. So z. B. sagt man mon gäbn, „Kind Mann", „männliches Kind", „Knabe"; mon né, „weibliches Kind", „Mädchen"; lókuma, „Kameel", lókuma nö, „weibliches Kameel,

form gaa man-ga (sie p. 127), „it turns (to), becomes water", i. q. „it is melting". As a composite form of ga and na we may perhaps look upon gená which I have adduced above p. CCLXIX,), when speaking of the forms of the conditional as being joined to the local particle agia.

g, β) Besides these forms, representing a kind of accusative case, the ablative relation also is occasionally expressed by means of rā added to the noun, the same rā, I think, which I have put down among the particles (vcblry p. 29) with the meaning „below, on the ground", as, for instance, in the phrase mak-um sínda-rī p. 93, „I dismount from the horse".

g, γ) Now, we meet also with a ki added to the noun, but the relation which it does express, seems rather to fluctuate between a dative and an ablative case. In the latter sense it is certainly to be understood in the phrase uako-dăč bé kōde-ki, „that he may quarter us in some (kōde) house" (bé); but in connection with na it seems as decidedly to indicate a dative relation in the following phrase ci mau sínda-na-kí, „give water to the horse", while the same na-kí has again a locative meaning in the phrase ungal nuñ na-kí, „go into the town", and thus the form nà-ki-na by adding one more na has become the common preposition or rather postposition with the meaning „in, inside".

g, δ) As an instance of the use of a preposition, in order to indicate the instrumentality, by means of which something is done, I mention se corresponding to the English „by", in the phrase mak-ab se indž(n)-amā, „I go by my foot", „walk on foot".

h) As for the plural, the most common change which the noun does undergo in that form is by adding ge at the end, in the same manner as we have already seen to be the case with the personal pronoun; thus, from deb, debe, „person", is formed deb-ge, „people"; from né, „woman", nè-ge, „women"; from lúguma, „camel", lúguma-ge; nay, even kōde, „one" forms a plural kōde-ge, „some". However, when the plural form is already otherwise expressed, as, for instance, by the accompanying pronoun, it is not generally indicated by the form of the noun; thus, while I have ma sinda a-mā-ge-na m-ón-dugó korō, „I have sold my horses", I have lúguma-ge u-mā-ge-ne éga, „my camels have strayed", and side by side with the phrase sínda-ge á-dže-na dže dž-éndugó korō, „we have sold our horses", where the plural form is only expressed by the noun, I have the other phrase sinda a-sé-ge-na se sé-udugó korō, „you have sold your horses", where it is not expressed, but by the pronoun.

h, α) This plural form in ge seems even to have an accusative form in ne, the a of the corresponding form of the singular being changed into an e, as, for instance, dže dže-tuki déb-ge-ne, „we beat the people", although I am not quite certain of the import of this form.

For, besides the form of the plural in ge, I have also instances of other forms, and first, combined with this very ne, which, therefore, might seem to be a merely intensive form of the plural number; thus, I have bé-ne from bé, „town"; (bé-ne kaudo, „how many towns"?), and tógo-na from tokō, „boat", if the na in the latter instance really belongs to the plural form. For here again occurs the same difficulty, to which I have already adverted before, viz that of distinguishing these forms from the demonstrative pronoun.

h, β) As an instance of a noun not being changed in the plural number I mention lōa, „year", plur. likewise lōa.

i) As for the gender, the male sex, if necessary to be distinctly expressed, is indicated by adding gāba, „man", the feminine by adding né, „woman", as well with regard to human beings as to animals, as, for instance, mon gāba, „male child", „boy"; mon nē, „female child", „girl"; lúkuma, „camel", lúkuma nē, „she camel"; maṅgo, „bull",

Kameelin"; mango, „Rind, Stier", mang-nē, „Kuh"; bisi, „Hund", bisi nē, „Hündin". Jedoch habe ich auch einige wenige Beispiele von besonderen, das weibliche Geschlecht bezeichnenden, Formen, wie z. B. béli, „Sklave"; bōlo, „Sklavin".

k) Was die Stellung des Nennwortes in Bezug auf das Zeitwort betrifft, so scheint die allgemeine Regel zu sein, dass das erstere dem Zeitwort folgt, von dem es regiert wird, wenn es mit ihm zusammen Einen Begriff ausdrückt, wie die oben S. CCLXIV, e angeführten Beispiele zeigen: jedoch habe ich auch mehrere Beispiele, in denen das selbstständige Objekt dem Zeitwort vorangeht, z. B., ausser den unter h' angeführten, adū-na mam-kelōnga, „ich werfe den Feind zurück"; bē ne má-seti-nya, „ich zerstöre diese Stadt". Das letztere Beispiel ist besonders interessant, indem wir in nya den Accusativ des Fürwortes haben, während bē no der Nominativ zu sein scheint, obgleich gerade hier die oben berührte Unsicherheit wegen ne sich besonders geltend macht.

5. *Eigenschaftswörter.*

a) In Bezug auf das Eigenschaftswort habe ich nach der Unvollständigkeit meines Materials nur wenig zu sagen. Eine grosse Menge derselben gehen auf o aus und diese scheint die einfachste Bildungsweise derselben zu sein, wie ich denn von der ursprünglichen adverbialen Grundform au, „weit", die adjektive Form au-o habe „entfernt". Jedoch habe ich auch viele Adjektiva mit der Endung auf a, i und so weiter. Diese Ausgangsform des Adjektivs stimmt auch keineswegs immer überein mit der Endung des von ihr charakterisirten Nennwortes, welches letztere stets vorangeht, wie ich denn z. B. neben nappe dāppe, „Neumond", wo eine solche Accommodation offenbar vor sich gegangen ist, lele nokka habe „viel" oder „heftiger Wind", wo das n wol nur aus euphonischen Gründen zwischen Substantiv und Adjektiv eingeschoben ist; kadž sungo, „heisse Sonne". Was dagegen die Ausdrücke gal kádžn, „Mittag" und gal o džō, „Mitternacht" betrifft, so ist in diesen Beispielen das gal nicht Adjektiv, sondern Substantiv, wie wir deutlich aus der Phrase erkennen mák-ad-ó gal e-nyá, wo das Pronomen im Genitiv dabei steht, „ich gebe die Hälfte davon".

Als ein Beispiel jedoch, wie die Form des Eigenschaftswortes in einigen Fällen derjenigen des Nennwortes angepasst wird, erwähne ich hier die Phrase dib-ne ingol-no džákuna, „den Weg, den grossen verfolgen wir".

b) Negative Formen von Eigenschaftswörtern werden gewöhnlich gebildet dadurch, dass man der positiven Form die oben S. CCLXVI, i) besprochene verbale Endung li anhängt, wie z. B. die negative Form von áso, „scharf", áso-li lautet, „nicht scharf, stumpf", indem zuweilen noch der Vokal eine Veränderung erleidet, wie z. B. džádu, „gekocht"; džédo-li, „nicht gekocht, roh".

c) Als Eigenthümlichkeit muss ich noch die Verbindungsweise vermittelst al aufführen, naf al kigge, „Neumond"; man al kéde, „Tropfen", wörtlich „Wasser zu eins".

d) Die beiden Vergleichungsgrade, Komparativ sowol wie Superlativ, können nur leicht und in ganz äusserlicher Weise angedeutet werden, indem man der einfachen Form des Adjektivs das demonstrative Pronomen ne hinzufügt und es durch den Ton unterscheidet, wie z. B. ne ingōlo, „dieses ist gross", d. h. „grösser als das" oder auch „das grösste von allen". Allerdings hat die Sprache die Kanúri-Form ngel-kō für „besser" in der Form golko aufgenommen; das ist aber der Sprache ganz fremd.

6. Ich gebe nun noch einige Redensarten, um die Weise zu zeigen, wie im Bágrimma sowol positive, wie negative Redetheile neben einander gereiht werden, besonders da die S. 9 angegebenen Formen nicht ganz richtig sind.

a) „entweder" — „oder":

„ist diese Stadt nahe oder fern", bé ne boi lebá auo;

mang-ne, „cow"; bisi, „dog", bisi ne, „bitch". However, I have also a few instances of peculiar forms of the feminine gender, as, for instance, bāli, „slave", bōlo, „female slave", from which latter form the verb ma-m bōlo, as before stated, seems to be derived.

k) As for the position of the noun with regard to the verb, the general rule seems to be, that the noun follows the verb by which it is ruled, if both together serve to express one idea, as the instances adduced above p. CCLXV, e) seem to show; but I have several instances of the object preceding the verb, in the case of the chief stress being laid on the former, viz adā-as mam-kuléṅga, „I throw back the enemy"; bē ne má-seti-nya, „I destroy this town". The latter instance, however, deserves our attention from various points of view, the accusative of the pronoun nya, „it" being added after the verb, while bē ne seems to be the nominative case, although the various notions of ne, as stated above, do not fail to cause a little uncertainty in this respect.

b. *Adjectives.*

a) As for the adjective, I have only very little to say. A great many of them terminate in o, and this seems to be the most simple formation, as from the original adverbial notion au, „far", I have the adjective form au-o, „distant"; but I have also many adjectives terminating in a, i, and so on. The termination of the adjective does, moreover, not generally correspond with that of the accompanying noun, the latter always preceding; thus, for instance, side by side with nappe džappe, „new moon", which exhibits an instance of such an accommodation, I have lēle nokka, „much", or „heavy wind" (the n in this latter instance being inserted between the substantive and the adjective, from euphonical reasons), kadž suṅgo, „hot sun". As for gal kádža, „mid-day" and gal n džō, „mid-night", gal in these cases is not an adjective, but a substantive, as is clearly shewn by the phrase mák-ad-á gal e-nyá, „I give its half", or „half of it".

As a somewhat doubtful instance of how the form of the adjective is sometimes accommodated to that of the substantive, I mention the phrase dib-ne ingol-ne džákuaē, „are we to follow this large track"?, the character of the ne, in this instance again, unfortunately, not being quite certain.

b) Negative forms of adjectives are generally formed by adding to the positive form the verbal negative particle li, of which we have spoken p. CCLXVII, l), as, for instance, ása, „sharp", áso-li, „not sharp, blunt"; sometimes with a change of the vowel, as, for instance, džádu, „boiled"; džédo-li, „not boiled, crude".

c) As a peculiarity, I have still to mention the way of composition by means of al, naf al kigge, „new moon"; man al kóde, „drop", verbally „water at one" („one by one").

d) The comparative, as well as the superlative, cannot but be slightly indicated by adding ne, „this" to the simple adjective, and distinguishing it by intonation, as, for instance ne ingōlo, „this is great", i. q. „this is larger than that", or even „the largest of all". The Kanúri-form ṅgol-kō, „better", which the Bágrimma-language has borrowed under the form golko, does not touch the spirit of the language, to which it is foreign.

6. I now give a few phrases illustrative of the positive, as well as of the negative coordination of phrases, especially as, what I have given p. 9, is less correct.

a) „either" — „or":

„is this town near or far", bē ne boi lebā ano;

„reichen unsere Vorräthe oder reichen sie nicht"?,
gäd á-dže-na džo-kábse lebä dže-kábse-li;
„ist da Wasser oder nicht"?, bä ḗtu lebā gdto;
„ist ein Berg auf dem Weg oder nicht", d. h. „ist das Land flach oder gebirgig"?,
dib-na tod gdto lebā tod étu,
(Pfad auf Berg nicht ist oder Berg ist);
„reisen wir morgen oder übermorgen"?,
dže-kíṅg džénibi, džo-kíṅg biśerí ba;
„welcher Art ist ihre Kleidung oder haben sie gar keine Kleidung"?,
bol dže-na džil-e džín-odí bol got fū li.
(Kleidung sie von Art welcher, Kleidung ist nicht ganz nicht).

b) „weder" — „noch":
„wir sehen weder Städte, noch Wege",
bö-li dža-kíṅg-ne[1])-li díb-o-li dža-kíṅg-no-li.
(Stadt nicht wir sehen nicht Pfad nicht wir sehen nicht).

c) Ich will hier noch ein Beispiel aus der Übersetzung des Vater-Unsers geben, wie die negative Partikel li auch ausser solcher Doppelstellung wiederholt wird,
anya dän adžé-li dži šitane li džintá-me-li,
verlasst uns ? nicht Hand Satan nicht ergreife uns (mich?) nicht.

7. *Einsilbige Wurzelwörter.*

Ich gebe hier nur, was sicher ist, und suche das Material nicht durch Muthmassungen zu vermehren, besonders in Betreff vieler einsilbiger Wurzeln von Zeitwörtern.

a: ab, „geben"; ai, „trinken"; ak, „thun, sehn"; al, „aufsteigen"; an, „machen"; au, „fern"; aw, „bewahren" (?).

b: ba Frageform; bä, „Gewässer, Fluss"; bar, „Art Sorghum"; bat, „nicht wollen, widerstreben"; bau, „Dach"; bö, „Haus, Stadt"; bi, „Haar, Feder"; bī, „schlafen"; bo, „Art von cucurbita"; bō, „hungrig"; boi, „nahe"; bol, „Hemd"; bū, „Strauss".

d: dä, „zeigen, darstellen"; dar, „aufhören"; dó, „anfangen"; deb, „Person"; der, „Herz"; dib, „Weg"; dis, „herabnehmen"; dō, „arm"; dos, „Flöse"; dū, „Augenübel"; duk, „sehn".

e: el, „Vogel"; ep, „Netz"; et, „sein".

f: fet (pet), „alle"; fod s. pod; fū, „ganz".

g: ga, „Krähe"; gä, gé, „wollen"; gab, „Mann"; gak, „reiben"; gal, „halb, Hälfte"; gas (ṅgas), „Ding, Gegenstand"; gö, „Leichnam"; gos, „Blase-Instrument"; gu, „gleich".

dž: dža, „Tag"; džū, „Fleisch"; džo, „wir, sie"; džē, „Kraut"; džel, „wissen"; džī, „Hand"; džil, „Schatten"; džö, „Nacht"; džok, „binden"; džoṅg, „Excrement".

i, yi: i, yi, „du"; il, „schwarz"; ir, „satt sein".

k: kā, „Gesang"; kag, „Baum"; kau, „Dämon"; ko, „ergreifen"; kod, „pflücken, hervorziehn"; kol, „schneiden"; kos, „stossen, verwunden"; kuā, „Mutter".

l: lel, „Wind"; li, „nicht"; lö, „nehmen, fortführen".

m: ma, „ich"; man (mané), „Wasser"; mas, „Tamarinde"; mi, „fünf"; mo, „unter"; mon, „Kind"; mū, „Gras"; mudž, „Bruder".

n, ṅ: naf, nap, „Mond"; ne, „er"; nė, „Frau"; nel, „innerhalb"; nī, „Traum"; nö, „schreien, weinen"; nya, „ihn, sie, es"; nyo, ṅo, „Erdameise"; ṅö, „Korn"; nu, „über, oben".

---

[1]) Das ne in dieser Form ist mir bemerkenswerth.

„do our provisions reach, or do they not reach"?,
sād á-dže-na džo-kábse lebā džo-kábse-li;
„is there water or not", bā étu lebā góto;
„is there a mountain on the track, or is there not"?,
dib-na tod góto lebā tod étu,
(track on mountain is not, or mountain is);
„do we travel to morrow, or the day after to morrow"?,
dže-kíṅg dždnihi, dže-kíṅg bíňorí ba;
„of what kind is their dress, or have they no dress at all"?,
bol dže-na džil-e dšín-edí bol got fu li,
(dress them of kind which dress is not all not).

b) „neither" — „nor":
„we see neither towns, nor roads",
be-li dža-kíṅg-ue[*])-li dib-e-li dža-kíṅg-ne-li,
(town not we see not road not we see not).

c) The following phrase, in my translation of Our Lord's Prayer, will serve to show, that the reiteration of the negative particle li takes even place under other circumstances,
anya dža adže-li dši šitāne li džintá-me-li,
forsake us ? not hand devil not seize us (me?) not.

7. *Monosyllabic roots.*

I only give what is certain, without multiplying the material by means of conjectures, and I therefore leave out many verbal roots, with regard to which I am not quite certain.

a: ab, „go"; ai, „drink"; ak, „do, see"; al, „mount"; an, „make"; au, „far"; aw, „preserve" (?).
b: ba form of interrogation; bā, „pool, river"; bar, „species of sorghum"; bat, „do not like, am against"; bau, „roof"; bē, „house, town"; bi, „feather, hair"; bī, „sleep"; bo, „a species of cucurbita"; bō, „hungry"; boi, „near"; bol, „shirt"; bū, „ostrich".
d: dā, „show, exhibit"; dar, „vanish, cease"; dó, „begin"; dob, „person"; der, „heart"; dib, „track"; dis, „take down"; dō, „poor"; dos, „salt"; dū, „soreness of eye"; duk, „ten".
e: el, „bird"; ép, „net"; et, „(to) be".
f: fet (pet), „all"; fod, see pod; fū, „whole".
g: ga, „crow"; „gā, gó, „will, wish"; gab, „man"; gak, „rub"; gal, „half"; gas (ṅgas), „thing, object"; gō, „corpse"; gos, „musical instrument"; gu, „alike".
dž: dža, „day"; džā, „meat"; dže, „we, they"; džē, „heritage"; džel, „know"; dži, „hand"; džil, „shade, shadow"; džō, „night"; džok, „lie"; džoṅg, „excrement".
i, yi: i, yi, „thou"; il, „black"; ir, „be satiated".
k: kā, „song"; kag, „tree"; kau, „demon"; ko, „seize, attack"; kod, „pluck, draw forth"; kol, „cut"; kos, „hurt, wound"; kuñ, „mother".
l: lel, „wind"; li, „not"; lō, „take, drive away".
m: ma, „I"; man (manē), „water"; mas, „tamarind"; mi, „five"; mo, „under"; mon, „child"; mū, „grass"; madā, „brother".
n, ñ: naf, nap, „moon"; ne, „he"; né, „woman"; net, „inside"; nī, „dream"; nó, „weep, cry"; nya, „him, her, it"; nyo, ño, „termite"; ñō, „corn"; nu, „above".

*) The ue in this form is very remarkable.

o: od, „herausziehen, erwarten"; oi, „sterben"; ol, „abkühlen"; on (mon, gon), „Kind"; or, „ermüden"; os, „Geruch".

p: pod (podu, fodu), „Feuer".

r: rā, „herab, hinab", „Süden"; ri, „Name".

s: sa, „folgen, sich zuhalten"; sa, „Ende"; sa, „Schuhe"; sā, „essen"; sab, „zwei"; se, „ihr"; seb, „klein machen, stampfen"; si, „Milch"; só, „vier"; sum, „küssen".

š: šid, „entzwei, trennen".

t: tad, „machen, thun"; tadž, „brechen"; tar, „Mund, Sprache"; teg, „hervorkommen"; teńg (tšońg), „Negerhirse"; tib, „Wachs"; tod, „liegen, schlafen"; tu, „abfeuern"; tur, „antreiben".

u: ub, „blasen"; um, „absteigen"; un, „nehmen"; us, „einziehen"; ūs, „Binde"(?).

w: wa, „Sorghum"; wai, „Krieg"; wi, „Art Krankheit"; wo, „horchen".

y: yo, „sie" (Accus.); yū, „Tod".

8. Ich gehe nun dazu über, die Fälle von innerer und äusserer Übereinstimmung zwischen der Bágrimma- und anderen benachbarten Sprachen dieser Sammlung aufzuführen, die uns wol überzeugen werden, dass sie weder zahlreich, noch eigenthümlich sind. Dagegen werden wir finden, dass die Berührungspunkte des Bágrimma mit einer anderen, im Süd-Osten weit entfernten Sprache diese beiden Eigenschaften darbieten, besonders, wenn wir in Betracht ziehen, wie wenig wir von der letzteren wissen.

a) Zuerst erwähne ich die Übereinstimmungen zwischen Bágrimma und Kanúri. Einige dieser Übereinstimmungen, so fern es ganz äussere Entlehnungen sind, besonders in technischen Ausdrücken, habe ich schon früher bei Besprechung des Wándala S. CCLII berührt und werde sie deshalb hier nicht wieder aufführen. In Betreff der hier aufgeführten Ausdrücke scheint es bei manchen jetzt noch sehr schwer, zu entscheiden, welcher Sprache die Priorität gebührt. So möchte es Manchem kaum zweifelhaft scheinen, dass die Bágrimma die ersten drei Ausdrücke der folgenden Liste von ihren westlichen Nachbarn entlehnten, da sie vor der Zeit keinen Ackerbau betrieben hätten. Auffallend bleibt es dabei aber doch, dass das Bágrimma zu bárua, „Regenzeit", den ganz entsprechend gebildeten Ausdruck kírui für „trockene Jahreszeit" hat. Bei bāre-ma hat das Kanúri entschieden die Priorität.

Bágrimma.	Kanúri.	Deutsch.
bárua	bārē	B. Regenzeit K. Landbau (eben zur selben Jahreszeit)
bárē-ma . . .	bārē-ma . . .	Ackerbauer
bíggela	bíggela	Erntezeit
bíggea	bigū	Fehler, Versehn
bútutū	bántenē . . .	Nebel
dolē	delāgo	B. Sturmwolke K. Regen
ímboli	kámboli . . .	reisender Kaufmann
kańgaia . . .	kańgē	Fieber
kasē	kásagē . . .	Husten
kātšū	kāzu	Vieh
kadži	ńgandži . . .	Brust
kirna	kirna	Kalb
kińgar	kingar	Mimosa Nilotica
kolo	kóloram . . .	Klaue
korē	korē	Esel
kusta	kusta	Füllen
mala) gōdo . .	godē-ma . . .	Bettler
sungo	zuńgwa . . .	warm

o: od, „draw out, wait for"; oi, „die"; ol, „get cool"; on (mon, gon), „child"; or, „get tired"; os, „odour".

p: pod (podu, fodu), „fire".

r: rā, „from of, down", „south"; ri, „name".

s: sa, „follow, keep close to"; sa, „end"; su, „show"; sā, „eat"; sab, „two"; se, „you", plur.; seb, „pound"; sī, „milk"; sō, „four"; sum, „kiss".

š: šid, „sunder, separate".

t: tad, „make, do"; tādž, „break"; tar, „mouth, idiom"; teg, „come forth"; teńg (tšeńg), „negro-millet"; tib, „wax"; tod, „lie down, sleep"; tu, „fire (a gun)"; tur, „drive on".

u: ub, „blow"; um, „descend"; un, „take"; us, „draw in"; us, „shawl" (?).

w: wa, „sorghum"; wal, „war"; wi, „kind of disease"; wo, „hearken".

y: yo, „them" (accus.); yō, „death".

8. I now proceed to register the cases of kindred and relationship, or coincidence between the Bágrimma and other neighbouring languages of this Collection, which, I trust, we shall convince ourselves, are neither numerous, nor original, while, on the contrary, the cases of relationship with another rather distant language towards the Nilotic basin in the far South-East, exhibit both these qualities, if we take into regard the little we know of the latter.

a) I first mention the cases of relationship which intercede between the Bágrimma- and the Kanúri-languages. A few of such identical terms, such as are of a distinct technical character, and have, beyond a doubt, been borrowed from the language of that people which was further advanced in a certain degree of civilization, I have already mentioned p. CCLIII, when treating of the Wándalá-idiom. These, therefore, I shall not repeat here. But, with regard to several terms of the following list, we may as yet doubt, to which of the two languages the priority belongs. Thus, while some body may not entertain the least doubt, that the Bágrimma-people have borrowed the three first terms of their Western neighbours, we have to take into consideration, that the Bágrimma does possess the term kírui for „dry season", which seems to be formed analogically with the opposite term bárua, meaning „rainy season". But, as for bāró-ma, the priority does belong most decidedly to the Kanúri-idiom.

Bágrimma.	Kanúri.	English.
bárua	bāré	B. rainy season K. tilling the ground (at that very season)
báré-ma . . .	bāré-ma . . .	husband-man
bíggola . . .	bíggola . . .	harvest
bíggea	bigu	mistake, fault
bútutū	bántonō . . .	fog
dolō	dolago	B. stormcloud K. rain
(mboli	kámboli . . .	travelling merchant
kańgaia . . .	kańgo	fever
kasé	kásagō	cough
katšu	kāsu	cattle
kadži	ńgaudži . . .	breast
kirna	kirna	calf
kińgar	kingar	Mimosa Nilotica
kolo	kóloram . . .	claw
korō	korō	ass
kusia	kusia	colt
mala) gádo . .	godó-ma . . .	beggar
suńgo	suńgwa . . .	warm

Bágrimma.	Kanúri.	Deutsch.
šuffo	sġbbio	Mark
sáni	sāni	Hirte
túnu ĝo	tunū.	Geschwür.

Ich habe also dieser Liste diejenigen Ausdrücke nicht eingereiht, welche den meisten Stämmen dieser Gruppe eigen sind, wie die Namen einiger anderen Arten Bäume, z. B. die Adansonia und die kirua oder korna, dann musikalische Instrumente und einige, auf einem gewissen Grad civilisirten Lebens beruhende, Ausdrücke, z. B. kánadi, „Geduld", den die Kanúri allem Anscheine nach von den Tédā geborgt haben, und den andere benachbarte Sprachen wiederum von letzteren entnommen haben. Auch den Ausdruck kīda für „Arbeit" haben die höheren Klassen des Bágrimma-Volkes zu ihrem eigenthümlichen Ausdruck daua hinzugeborgt, und selbst für „gut" hörte ich keinen anderen Ausdruck in Bagirmi, als das Kanúri-Wort ngilla, ganz wie das französische bon, bien früher unser eigenes gutes Deutsch ganz verdrängt hatte.

Viel wichtiger, als diese späten und bloss äusserlichen Entlehnungen sind die (S. CCLXX, 4, b, vgl. das S. XLVI über kagúlā Gesagte) angeführten Beispiele einer, beiden Sprachen eigenen, ähnlichen Bildung einer Klasse von Nennwörtern vermittelst eines vorgesetzten k.

b) Mit der Tédā-Sprache hat das Bágrimma kaum einen einzigen Berührungspunkt; denn die Verwandtschaft der, in beiden Sprachen den Baum bezeichnenden, Ausdrücke B. kagā, T. akā ist zum wenigsten zweifelhaft. Jedoch sehen wir und können uns leicht erklären, dass die Bágrimma von ihren nördlichen Nachbarn, den Bewohnern der Wüste, den Ausdruck für „Jäger" erborgten, T. kódedā, dem die Bretoren sogar noch den Namen jenes Stammes selbst beifügten und so tebo kóddada daraus machten.

c) Auch von den anderen Sprachen meiner Sammlung scheint kaum die eine oder die andere ursprüngliche Berührung mit dem Bágrimma zu haben, wenn wir absehen von der Lógonē-Sprache. Denn in letzterer mag fū, „Feuer", allerdings verwandt sein mit B. podu, fodu, dessen ursprüngliche Form fod, pod war; B. sözo mag mit L. yoyo (K. dundus) nahe verwandt scheinen und B. mábala, „Welle" mit L. mabelévia. Andere, in beiden Sprachen übereinstimmende, Ausdrücke dagegen erklären sich einfach daraus, dass die Bágrimma dieselben von ihren westlichen, in diesen Industriezweigen vorgeschrittenen, Nachbarn entlehnten, wie z. B. tibi, „Wachs", rāga, „Matte" und andere. — Als Berührungspunkte mit der Hausa-Sprache kann ich nur die Ausdrücke für „Kameel" anführen, B. lúkuma, H. rákomi. — Als zweifelhafte Beispiele der Berührung der Bágrimma- mit der Wándalā-Sprache erwähne ich B. lele, Wind", W. we-lēle; kelā, „laufen" in beiden Sprachen; B. otšo, „viel", W. kdtχia. — Mit der Māba-Sprache mag z. B. der Ausdruck für „Schatten", B. dšili, ndšili, M. andšylók näher verwandt sein. — Dann, was andere Afrikanische Sprachen angeht, ist manē, „Wasser" sehr ähnlich dem entsprechenden Ausdruck im Mampūa oder der Sprache von Sherbro, dem Gura, Akurakura, Penin und anderen, während baṅga, „König", in Koelle's Polyglotta mbaṅ geschrieben, dem entsprechenden Ausdruck in den Móko-Sprachen, deren Gebiet gerade im S. von Bagirmi liegt, sehr ähnlich sieht. Mit der Sprache Fūr's hat das Bágrimma ohne Zweifel den Ausdruck für „Baumwolle" gemein, B. nyeri, F. ndšerē; dann „Ball", B. maṅgo, F. mundšo. Die Ausdrücke B. fodu und F. otū, „Feuer" dagegen können wir nur als sehr zweifelhafte Beispiele von Verwandtschaft oder Übereinstimmung anführen, da das f, p im Bágrimma schon in frühester Zeit zum Stamme dieses Wortes gehört zu haben scheint.

d) Alle diese Beispiele von Verwandtschaft unserer Sprache sind vereinzelt und von wenig Bedeutung; aber dagegen öffnet sich uns nun ein weites Feld der Spekulation durch die augenscheinlichen, schon bei beschränktem Material zahlreichen Punkte ursprünglicher Berührung unserer Sprache mit einer anderen, recht entfernten, nämlich der Sprache der Dōr am westlichen grossen Zufluss des oberen Nil, etwa in 5° N. Br. und 27° Ö. L. Gr. Allerdings ist die letztere nur durch den, in anderen Beziehungen höchst unzuverlässigen, Berichterstatter Petherick (Egypt, the Soudan and Central-Africa, appendix p. 481), etwas bekannt geworden, aber verdient

Bágrimma.	Kanúri.	English.
šuffo	sýbbio	marrow
súni	sũni	herdsman
túan (go	lunũ	ulcer.

This list, as before stated, does not comprise some other terms, which are common to most tribes belonging to this group, as the terms for a few kinds of trees, as, for instance, the Adansonia and the kirna or korna, instruments of music, and some other terms relating to a certain degree of civilised life, as, for instance, the term kánadı, „pastimes", borrowed, as we have seen p. XCI, by the Kanúri from the Tédã, and from the former again having been received by the neighbouring languages; the term kídn, „work" also, which is in use besides the indigenous term dana, I have no doubt, is simply borrowed in this way, as the Bágrimma-people, at least those of the upper classes, have even adopted the Kanúri-term ñgilla for „good"; the corresponding indigenous term not having become known to me at all during my stay in the country.

Of a somewhat greater importance, than the identity of these terms, which have been merely borrowed by one language from the other, are those few instances of a similar formation of the noun by means of k, ko of which I have spoken p. CCLXXI, 4, b, compared with what I have said p. XLVII with regard to the term kagála.

b) With the Tédã-language the Bágrimma has scarcely any point of contact, the identity of the term for „tree", B. kaga, T. akã being at least doubtful. But we see clearly, that, and can as easily explain, why the Bágrimma-people borrowed from their Northern neighbours, the inhabitants of the Desert, the term for „huntsman", T. kédodã, adding to the term even the name of that tribe itself, and forming thence the name tebo kóddoda.

c) Even between the other languages of my Collection and the Bágrimma there seems to be scarcely one single instance of original correspondence. Perhaps B. fodu, podu may be connected with the Lógonē-term fù; B. soso with L. yoyo, „swift"; B. mábala, „wave" with L. mabelóvia, but several other terms, such as tibi, „wax", raga, „mat", and others, have simply been borrowed by the Bágrimma from their Western neighbours who were more advanced in civilisation. — With the Hausa-language the Bágrimma seems to have in common the same term for „camel", B. lúkoma, H. rákomi. — As partly doubtful instances of contact with the Wándalã-language I mention B. lele, „wind", W. wo-lelo; the term kelã, „to run" in both idioms; B. otšo, „much, many", W. kótχia. — With the Mábalanguage the Bágrimma-term for „shadow" seems to be identical, B. ndžíli, M. ándžylúk. — As for points of contact with other African languages, not represented in this Collection, the term manũ, „water" is very similar to the corresponding term in several other African languages, such as the Mampũa-idiom of Serbro, the Gura, Akurakura, Penin and others, while the term bañga, „king", written mbañ in Koelle's Polyglotta, looks like the corresponding term in the Móko-languages, the territory of which stretches a few degrees to the South of Bagirmi. With the language of Fūr the Bágrimma has, no doubt, the term for „cotton" in common, B. nyeri, F. ndžerē; and, besides, that for „bull", B. mañge, F. mundžo, seems to be identical; but, as for the terms B. fodu and F. otó, they are rather doubtful cases of harmony, as the f, or p appears to have formed part of the Bágrimma-term from very ancient times.

d) All these instances of relationship, if such they be, are isolated, and of little importance, while there opens up a wide field of speculation in consequence of the evident and original points of contact which the Bágrimma-idiom proves to have with another rather distant language, the Dōr, on the Westernmost tributary of the Upper Nile, in about 5° N. L. and 27 E. L. Gr., specimens of which have only recently been made known by Mr. Petherick (Egypt, the Soudan and Central-Africa, appendix p. 481). Among the terms adduced in that list, bein one

doch die höchste Aufmerksamkeit. Unter den dort angeführten hundert und vierzehn Wörtern sind etwa dreissig entweder ganz identisch mit den entsprechenden meines Bágrimma-Vokabular's oder können vermittelst desselben leicht und natürlich erklärt werden, während unter der übrigen Anzahl bei Petherick manche augenscheinliche Versehen sind[1], wie das gar nicht ausbleiben kann, wenn auf diese Weise von einem keineswegs sprachgelehrten Manne ein Paar Ausdrücke einer wildfremden Sprache aufgegriffen werden und nun noch dazu, wenn er sich selbst die Sache dermaassen mit Durcheinanderwerfen der verschiedensten Begriffe erschwert, wie das hier geschehen ist.

Ich gebe hier nun ein Verzeichniss der im Bágrimma und Dōr nach dem augenblicklichen Stande der Kenntniss beider Sprachen vorliegenden übereinstimmenden Ausdrücke, die ich nach Begriffen etwas systematischer zusammenzustellen suche.

Bágrimma.	Dōr (nach Petherick's Schreibw.).	Dōr (nach meiner Schreibweise).	Deutsch.
kádža	kade	kade	Sonne
manō	mini	mini	Wasser
fodu	fudoo	fudu	Feuer
bogo	boogo	bugo	Dieb
kámi / kámo[2]	komo	komo	Auge
bi-kámo	hickomoo	hi-komo	Vorkopf[3]
tari	taragi	tara-(gi (Genitiv)	Lippe
bí-tari	betara	bí-tara	Schnurrbart (Mundhaar)
bi-džidžoi	biddoo	bi-dū	Kopfhaar
kam-dži	groji	gi-dži	Arm
ōmi	homogi	homo-(gi (Genitiv)	Nase
deb-dži	hegigee	hi-dži-gi[4]	ein Theil der Hand
bē	bee	be	Dorf
kado	kato / kootoo	kate[5] / kutu	Topf, Gefäss
kesé	kirré	kiré	Pfeil
mondžo	jamunjoo	džaʾ muudžu[6]	Bohnen
kagā	cugga	koga	Baum
bisi	beehee	bihi	Hund[7]
biša	binja	bindša	Ziege
kária	karia	káriu	Antilope
korlo	koolyri	k(l)yri	Giraffe
kēdži	keedi	kēdi	Elephant
kaga	kogoo	kogu	Panther
aña	uñga	uñga	lauf (Imp.).

[1] Ein schon jetzt recht deutliches Beispiel eines solchen wahrscheinlichen Versehens und Missverständnisses von Seiten Petherick's ist der Ausdruck amberoom für „Vogel", der in der Form amhoora noch einmal erscheint für „Perlen"; denn das gründet sich wahrscheinlich nur auf die verschiedene Bedeutung, die im vulgären Arabisch dem Ausdruck [illegible] gegeben wird.

[2] kámo. Zwar habe ich für „Auge" allein die Form kámi, aber für „Augenbrauen" („Haar, bi, des Auges") habe ich bi-kámo.

[3] bi-komo heisst ganz einfach „das, was über dem Auge ist". Vergleiche dazu auch Petherick's bitere (bi-tere), „Himmel", wahrscheinlich „das, was über der Erde ist", vgl. zum letzten Theil des Wortes den Bágrimma-Ausdruck ti-tera, „an dieser Stelle".

[4] hi-dži-gi heisst „das Obere der Hand", ist also das Gegentheil von der ihm von Petherick gegebenen Bedeutung. — Zu der höchst wichtigen, grammatischen Bedeutung des gi in beiden Sprachen vgl. gon-dži-gi S. CCLXXII. d).

[5] Die Form kootoo erscheint in Petherick's Liste in dem Ausdrucke kootoo taeh, „Pfeifenkopf"; taeh, tāb heisst „Tabak".

[6] Das Hinzufügen von ja, dža bei diesem Worte ist leicht und natürlich zu erklären, da ja auch Petherick selbst „Korn" (grain) bedeutet.

[7] Vergl. hierzu das, was ich oben gesagt habe S. XC, N. 4, und den entsprechenden Ausdruck bēše in Harrar.

hundred and fourteen in number, nearly thirty are either identical with the corresponding ones in my vocabulary of the Bágrimma-language, or may thence be easily and organically explained, while even among the rest there are several cases, where the discrepancy is not but due to evident mistakes on the part of the collector [1]), as cannot otherwise be the case, where a few terms of a totally unknown language are thus hastily picked up or written down from memory, as Mr. Petherick expressly states (p. 481) to be the case with this list.

I here insert a list of the terms corresponding with each other in both languages, the **Bágrimma and the Dōr**, arranged systematically according to the class of objects meant, giving warning at the same time, that the knowledge of the latter idiom, is as yet in its infancy, and leaving away all what is not quite certain.

Bágrimma.	Dōr (Petherick's spelling).	Dōr (my spelling).	English.
kádža	kade	kade	sun
manē	mini	mini	water
fodu	fudoo	fudu	fire
bogo	boogo	bugo	thief
kámi / kámo [2])	komo	komo	eye
bi-kámo	bickomoo	bi-komo	forehead [3])
tari	taragi	tara-(gi (gen. case)	lip
bí-tari	betara	bí-tara	whiskers (hair of lips)
bi-džidžoi	biddoo	bi-dū	hair of head
ham-dži	geeji	gi-dži	arm
ēmi	homogi	homo-(gi (gen. case)	nose
deb-dži	hogigee	hi-dži-gi [4])	part of hand
bē	boc	bē	village
kado	kate / kootoo	kato [5]) / kutu	pot, vessel
kesē	kirré	kirē	arrow
mondžo	jamunjoo	dža) mundžu [6])	beans
kaga	ougga	kuga	tree
bisi	brchee	bihi	dog [7])
biña	binja	bindža	goat
kária	karia	kária	antilope
korlo	koolyri	kilyri	giraffe
kēdži	keedi	kēdi	elephant
kaga	kogoo	kogu	panther
uña	uñga	uñga	run (imp.).

[1]) An almost evident instance of such a mistake on the part of Mr. Petherick is the term umbareem for „bird", while it appears once more in the form of umboore for „smallpox", the mistake being explained by the double meaning given to the term جُدَرِي in vulgar Arabic.

[2]) kámo: No doubt, for „eye" alone I have the form kámi, but for „eyebrows" („hair" bi, of the „eye") I have the termination in o, bi-kámo.

[3]) bi-komo, „what is) above the eye". Compare Petherick's bitere (bi-tere), „sky", probably „that which is) above the earth", the latter term being likewise explained through the Bágrimma-term ti-tera, „in this place".

[4]) bi-dži-gi, after what I have said of the meaning of bi in the preceding note, means „the upper part of the hand", and not „palm of hand", as Petherick gives it. But, besides, we have here an evident instance of perfect grammatical analogy between the two languages, the gi appearing in Bágrimma exactly in the same position, as, for instance, in the case of gon-dži-or, „child of hand", i. e. „finger".

[5]) kootoo appears in Petherick's list in the term kootoo tash, „head of pipe", tash meaning „tobacco".

[6]) The adding of dža to the term mundžu is most easily and naturally explained, it meaning „grain" according to Mr. Petherick's own list.

[7]) See with regard to this term for „dog" what I have said p. XCI, note 4, and compare the form biššo (bécho Salt, Appendix I, S. VIII) in the idiom of Harrar or Harrar.

Es ist gewiss auffallend, dass, während der Ausdruck für „Dieb" in beiden Sprachen gänzlich übereinstimmend lautet, die Namen für „Mann", B. deb, debe, gäba, Dör boodu (būdo); „Frau", D. né, D. koomara (kúma [ra, rä wahrscheinlich Ablativ, s. oben S. CCLXXIV, g und vergl. kāmo im Kanúri]); „Kind", B. gon, Dör neaté und andere einfache Ausdrücke so verschieden sein sollten; aber weitere Untersuchungen auf dem Gebiete der Dör und der benachbarten Sprachen werden unzweifelhaft dahin führen, weiteres Licht auf diese so interessante Beziehung zur Bágrimma-Sprache zu werfen und derartige Abweichungen zu erklären. Erwähnen will ich nur noch, dass die Form kuga im Dör für „Baum" der Form kúru (vielleicht kúyu) in der Für-Sprache sich sehr nahe anschliesst.

Zwölftes Kapitel.

Die Mába-Sprache: bora Mabá-ńg.

Ich gehe nun zur Behandlung des östlichsten meiner Vokabularien über, zu dem Wörter-Verzeichniss der Mába-Sprache. Schon in der, meinem Reisewerke (Reisen und Entd. Th. III, S. 501) einverleibten, ethnographischen Beschreibung von Wádai habe ich auseinander gesetzt, dass die bóra Mabá-ńg (über die Genitiv-Endung ang werde ich an betreffender Stelle sprechen) eben nur die Sprache der Kern-, ich möchte sagen Kron-Länder, jenes Reiches ist, in dem die grösste Mannichfaltigkeit der Sprachen herrscht, dass sie aber eben in dieser, ihrer Stellung als das officielle Idiom jenes ganzen Länder-Complexes betrachtet wird. Aber von einem Volksstamm scheint der Name Mába zur Zeit nicht mehr gebraucht zu werden.

In Betreff des Charakters dieses Wörterverzeichnisses selbst habe ich schon oben S. XIV angegeben, dass es nur äusserlich aus dem Munde einer einzigen Person niedergeschrieben wurde, ohne dass ich die Sprache auch nur im Allergeringsten beherrschte. Dies wäre einerseits ein entschiedener Nachtheil in Rücksicht der grammatischen Genauigkeit sowol, als auch der Vollständigkeit des betreffenden Vokabular's. Da aber auf der anderen Seite sowol jenes Individuum, der fakih Ibrahim, ein ungewöhnlich gescheiter und aufgeweckter Mensch war, als auch ich, meinestheils, damals volle Musse hatte, Alles bedächtig niederzuschreiben und zu kontroliren, so verdient auch dieser Theil meiner Sammlung volles Vertrauen, da es ungleich vollständiger und genauer ist, als das schon S. XIV, Note 2 erwähnte Seetzen's, gar nicht zu gedenken des viel kürzeren von Burckhardt, Travels in Nubia ed. II, App. II, p. 446. Übrigens sind beide keineswegs ganz unzuverlässig und ist in Betreff Seetzen's nur die völlig unsystematische, die Kontrole für den Sammler selbst so erschwerende Ordnung, so wie die fehlerhafte Orthographie zu tadeln; bedauern muss ich daher, dass ich zur Zeit keine Abschrift der beiden Wörtersammlungen bei mir hatte, um bei den einzelnen Fällen zu ermitteln, ob die betreffenden Abweichungen zwischen ihnen und mir auf Missverständniss von ihrer Seite, oder auf wirklicher Dialekt-Verschiedenheit beruhen. Die bezügliche Vortrefflichkeit meines Materials wird man besonders aus den mit reichster Fülle grammatischer Formen ausgestatteten Phrasen erkennen, die am Ende des Vokabular's gegeben werden sollen.

Indem ich nun zu der Analyse dieser Sprache nach meinem, in Obigem charakterisirten, Material übergehe, behandle ich

1. *Das persönliche und possessive Fürwort.*

	Singular.	Plural.
1ste	Person am	mańg.
2te	„ mi, me	kańg.
3te	„ ti, te	wańg.

Die 1ste Person Sing. scheint ihren Genitiv, der zugleich die possessive Form darstellt, in folgender mannichfaltiger Weise zu bilden.

It is, no doubt, remarkable, that, while the term for „thief" in both idioms is totally identical, the terms for „man", B. deb, debo, gāba, Dōr boodo (būdo); „wife", B. nē, Dōr koomara (kūma [ra, rā most probably being the form of the ablative case, p. CCLXXV, g. while kūma reminds one of the corresponding Kanúri-term kumo]); „child", B. gon, Dōr neaté, and so on should be totally different, but further inquiries into the Dōr and neighbouring languages, whose study will serve to throw a great light upon the Bāgrimma-idiom, will, no doubt, likewise illustrate these cases of discrepancy. The form kuga for „tree" in Dōr resembles very nearly the form kúru (perhaps kúγu) in the Fūr-language.

Chapter the twelfth.

The Māba-language: bōra Mabá-ňg.

I now proceed to treat of the Easternmost of the languages represented in my Collection, I mean the Māba-language. Already in the ethnographical description of Wádāy, inserted in the Narrative of my Travels and Discoveries (vol. III, p. 510), I have stated, that the bōra Mabá-ňg (ňg, aňg being a genitive form of which I shall have to speak in the proper place) is not the idiom of the whole country, where there is a great variety of languages, but merely that spoken by the ruling tribes in the chief provinces, or if I dare say so, the crown-lands, while on this very account it is to be looked upon as the official language of the whole kingdom. However, from all this it appears, that it seems doubtful, whether, at the present time, we ought to speak of a tribe or nation called Māba.

Now, with regard to the character of this vocabulary, I have already observed before p. XV, that I took it down from the mouth of one single individual, without myself dominating the language in the slightest degree. This, no doubt, is a decided disadvantage with regard to the grammatical accuracy as well, as the completeness of the vocabulary in question. But as, on the other hand, the individual mentioned, the fakih I'brahim, was an uncommonly clever and intelligent person, and as I myself commanded ample leisure at the time to write down and control every thing with great care and diligence, also this column of my collection claims full confidence, it being infinitely richer, and more exact, than the vocabulary of Seetzen's mentioned in the foot note 2 p. XV, not taken into account the much shorter one given by Burckhardt, Tr. in Nubia, app. II, p. 446. Nevertheless, neither of them is to be neglected, and I much regret, that at the time I had no copy of them with me, in order fully to examine, whether the discrepancies in some cases between them and me proceed from mistake on their part or be based on dialectical divergencies. With regard to Seetzen, in most cases, however, it is not but his deficient orthography which makes the words appear different from mine, while he himself has increased the difficulty of his task by throwing the words amongst each other in the greatest confusion, and not arranging them systematically. The relative excellence of my material will become best apparent from my phrases which, few and short as they are, exhibit a rich profusion of grammatical forms.

Proceeding now to an analytical review of the language from my own materials, such as they are, I first treat of

1. *The personal, and possessive pronouns.*

	singular.	plural.
1st person	am	maňg,
2nd „	mi, me	kaňg,
3rd „	ti, te	waňg.

The 1st person sing. seems to form its genitive case, which at the same time represents the possessive form, in various ways, thus:

am-

am de-i, „ich an mir", d. h. „ich selbst";
am a-né, „ich von mir", d. h. „ich habe";
em-bé-ti, „es ist von mir", d. h. „gehört mir";
tórrembok ám-be-go, „Kameel von mir", d. h. „mein Kameel";
em-be-h-ago, „Sache von mir", d. h. „mein Eigenthum";
torrémbo-si em-bé-ee, „Kameele von mir", d. h. „meine Kameele".

Unter diesen Beispielen ist der Formenreichthum auf den ersten Blick grösser, als bei näherer Untersuchung sich herausstellt, da sich die Form am-be, om-be, eigentlich an-be, eng an a-nó anlehnt, mit Einschiebung eines noch fernerhin zu besprechenden, zurückbeziehenden be. Auch die Form de-i wird wol im Verlauf dieser Untersuchung eine weitere Erklärung finden.

1ste Person Plur. Genitiv und possessive Form:
mang me-né, „wir von uns", d. h. „wir haben";
mang me-né-ti, „wir, es ist von uns", d. h. „es gehört uns".

me-nó oder me-ní kommt auch vor als selbständige Form des possessiven Fürwortes in Verbindung mit Substantiven, wie z. B. torrémbo-si me-ní ago-nó, „diese unsere Kameele", wo allerdings die nachfolgende Demonstrativform einen entscheidenden Einfluss geübt hat; sonst wird der Pronominalform selbst gewöhnlich, wie im Singular ein go, so in der Mehrheit ein ne, angehängt, also

tórrembok mé-ne-go, „unser Kameel";
torrémbo-si me-né-ne, „unsere Kameele".

1ste Person Sing. Dativ und Accusativ scheinen, wie das in vielen dieser Sprachen der Fall ist, meist nicht unterschieden zu werden; aber in einigen Fällen erleidet die Form eine leichte Veränderung,

lingák andé disa, „informire mich über, zeige mir den Weg";
and(-)asfinga, „lehre mich";
andén dokol, „zeige mir";
tabák andan tal, „der Leib läuft mir".

Dagegen scheint mir nur am-bé-ne, obgleich wir es mit „gib mir" übersetzen müssen, kein eigentlicher Dativ zu sein, sondern im Grunde zu bedeuten „gib (a-nár-ne, „ich gebe") (was) mein, das Meinige ist".

1ste Person Plur., Dativ und Accusativ, ist mir nicht ganz sicher. Der Accusativ ist aber wol mong. Der Dativ schien mir zuerst andó-go zu sein, nach der Phrase andé-go lingak hillegin disa, „zeige uns den Weg der Stadt". Dieses andó-go wäre aber, da andó die Singularform ist und go die Beziehung des Dativ's ausdrückt, als Pluralform sehr unsicher.

2te Person Sing., Genitiv und possessive Form:
mi mi-né, „du von dir", d. h. „du hast";
ne-né-ti (statt me-né-ti), „es ist von dir", d. h. „gehört dir".

Nun habe ich statt dieses ne-né-ti eine vollere, pleonastische Form ne-né-de-ti in meiner Übersetzung des Vater-Unser, nämlich güe ga dum daimen ne-né-de-ti, „alle Macht auf ewig ist dein", wo wir nun also schon eine leichte Erklärung des Gebrauchs der oben für die 1ste Person Sing. angeführten Form de-i haben.

tórrembok né-ne-go, „Kameel von dir", „dein Kameel";
torrémbo-si ne-né-ne, „Kameele von dir", „deine Kameele".

Ungewiss bin ich, ob das a-né-mi in der Phrase lilio-no ogo-nyére a-né-mi (S. 67 und 103), „diese Sache leihe ich von dir", als Genitiv zu fassen ist; doch scheint es so.

2te Person Plur., Genitiv und possessive Form:
kang ke-né, „ihr, von euch", d. h. „ihr habt";

am de-f, „I, as for me", i. q. „I myself";
am a-né, „I of me", i. q. „I have";
em-bé-ti, „it is of me", i. q. „it belongs to me";
térrembok ám-be-ge, „camel of me", i. q. „my camel";
em-be-k-ñgo, „thing of me", i. q. „my property";
torrómbo-si em-bé-se, „camels of me", i. q. „my camels".

This variety of forms, however, at a first superficial glance is greater, than it proves to be at a closer inspection, the forms am-bo, em-bo, properly an-bo, being intimately allied with a-né, the be having been inserted as indicative of the relative power of the pronoun, of which farther on we shall meet with some further instances. As for the form de-i also, in the course of our investigation we are to find some further points for explaining it.

1st person plur. genitive case, and possessive form:

mañg me-né, „we of us", i. q. „we have";
mañg me-né-ti, „we, it is of us", i. q. „it belongs to us".

The simple form me-né or me-ní of the possessive pronoun is also used in connection with substantives, as, for instance, torrómbo-si me-ní ego-né, „these our camels", the succeeding form of the demonstrative pronoun, no doubt, exercising in this case a decided influence upon it, while, in general, in the plural number go is added to the pronominal form itself, the same as no in the plural, thus:

térrembok mé-ne-ge, „our camel";
torrómbo-si me-né-ne, „our camels".

1st person sing. dative and accusative case, in general, do not seem to be distinguished from each other, as is the case with many of these languages; but in other instances the form of the dative case seems to undergo a slight change,

liñgák andé disa, „show me the track, inform me about the track";
and(-)esíñga, „teach me";
andán dokot, „show me";
tabdh andan tai, „the bowels run me", i. q. „my bowels run".

As for nar am-bé-se, on the other hand, although we have to translate it by „give me", it does not seem to be a regular dative case, but properly seems to mean „give (a-nár-ne, „I give") what is mine".

1st pers. plur. dative and accusative case are rather uncertain. For, while in the phrase andé-ge liñgak hillegin disa, „show us the track of the town", andé-ge seems to represent the dative case of the plural number; yet, as andé is the form of the singular, and ge appears merely to express the relation of the dative case, it seems a more than doubtful form of the plural number. The form of the accusative however seems to be mañg.

2nd person sing. genitive case, and possessive form:

mi mi-né, „thou of thee", i. q. „thou hast";
ne-né-ti (instead of me-né-ti), „it is of thee", i. q. „it belongs to thee".

Now, besides this form ne-né-ti, in my translation of our Lord's Prayer I have also a fuller form ne-né-de-ti, in the phrase güa ga dum daimen ne-né-de-ti, „all the power for ever is thine", this instance serving already in a certain respect for explaining the use of the form de-i, as mentioned above.

térrembok né-ne-ge, „camel of thee", „thy camel";
torrómbo-si ne-né-ne, „camels of thee", thy camels".

As for a-né-mi in the phrase lillo-ne ege-nyere a-né-mi (p. 67, and 103), „this thing I lend of thee", I am not certain, whether it is to be understood as a genitive case.

2nd person plur. genitive case, and possessive form:

kañg ke-né, „you, of you", i. q. „you have";

ka-né-ti, „es ist von euch", d. h. „es gehört euch";
tórrembok ká-ne-go, „Kameel von euch", d. h. „euer Kameel";
torrémbo-si ka-né-se, „Kameele von euch", d. h. „eure Kameele".

2te Person Sing. Dativ und Accusativ:
am me-gé búng-ayerík, „ich folge dir, verfolge dich" (N. 75);
am me-gé nayi-nyé-ni, „ich bin dir ungehorsam".

2te Person Plur. Dativ und Accusativ wahrscheinlich kong oder kom.

3te Person Sing. Genitiv und possessive Form:
ti te-né, „du von dir, du hast";
te-né-ti, „es ist von dir, ist dein, gehört dir";
tórrembok té-ne-go, „Kameel von dir, dein Kameel";
torrémbo-si te-né-se, „Kameele von dir, deine Kameele".

3te Person Plur. Genitiv und possessive Form:
wańg we-né, „sie von ihnen", d. h. „sie haben";
we-né-ti, „es ist von ihnen, ist ihr, gehört ihnen".

Auch für die volle, possessive Form der 3ten Person Plur. in Verbindung mit dem Nennwort habe ich ebenso häufig diese einfache Form we-né oder we-ní (zuweilen wie wüoni ausgesprochen) gehört, wie die mit angefügtem go, wie z. B.

sūk we-ní, „ihr Markt"; dréke-tū we-ní (wüöni), „ihre Kleidung"; šudda we-ní (wüoni), „ihre Einschnitte";
taúg-tū we-ní, „ihre Wohnungen";
tórrembok wé-ne-go, „ihr Kameel";
torrémbo-si we-né-se, „ihre Kameele";
bórik wé-ne-go, „ihr Pferd";
bóri we-né-se, „ihre Pferde".

Dagegen scheint mir onya we-ná-ba, „ihre Speise", einigermassen zweifelhaft, obgleich we-nó-ba, nach dem bei der 1ten Person Sing. über die Beziehung von b, be (ba) Angedeuteten, möglicher Weise richtig ist.

Unter den Phrasen am Ende dieses Kapitels werde ich noch ein Beispiel einer Form nu anführen, die sich an die Genitiv-Form des Nennwortes anschliesst.

3te Person Sing. Dativ und Accusativ ist mir unsicher.

3te Person Plur. Dativ und Accusativ wahrscheinlich wańg.

So gewinnen wir also folgendes Schema des persönlichen Fürworts:

	Singular.			Plural.		
	1ste Pers.	2te Pers.	3te Pers.	1ste Pers.	2te Pers.	3te Pers.
Nom.	am	mi, me .	ti	mańg . .	kańg . .	wańg,
Gen.	u-né . . . . um-be, em-be	mi-né no-né	te-né .	me-né, me-ní	ke-né . .	we-né, we-ní,
Dativ und Accusativ	andan . . audé .	me-gé .	te-gé? .	mońg? . .	kong, kom?	wońg?

2. Partikeln und Zahlwörter.

a) Mit Bezug auf die Partikeln, die, wie bei den meisten Sprachen, von substantivischen Begriffen abgeleitet sind, will ich hier nur bemerken, dass der grössere Theil derjenigen unter ihnen, welche eine Örtlichkeit anzeigen, mit dem lokalen gin zusammengesetzt sind, das wol seinerseits wieder mit dem bei dem Fürwort berührten, die dative Beziehung ausdrückenden, go verwandt ist, von dem ich weiterhin zu sprechen habe, wie z. B. we-gin, „hier"; illó-gin, „dort"; tinda-gin, „wo", u. s. w.

b) Auch in Bezug auf die Zahlwörter habe ich nur wenige allgemeine Bemerkungen, die

ka-né-ti, „it is of you", i. q. „it belongs to you";
tórrombok ká-ne-ge, „camel of you", i. q. „your camel";
torrómbo-ai ka-né-ne, „camels of you", i. q. „your camels".

2nd person sing. dative and accusative case:
am me-gé búng-nyerík, „I follow thee, pursue thee" (p. 74);
am me-gé nayi-nyé-ni, „I disobey thee".

2nd person plur. dative and accusative case most probably kong or kom.

3rd person sing. genitive case, and possessive form:
ti te-né, „thou of thee, thou hast";
te-né-ti, „it is of thee, is thine, belongs to thee";
tórrombok té-ne-ge, „camel of thee, thy camel";
torrómbo-ai te-né-ne, „camels of thee, thy camels".

3rd person plur. genitive case, and possessive form:
wang we-né, „they of them", i. q. „they have";
we-né-ti, „it is of them, is theirs, belongs to them".

The simple form we-né or we-ní (frequently pronounced wüeni), as the full possessive form of the 3rd person plur. in connection with the noun, I have heard quite as frequently as the other form with ge added to it, as for instance:

sūk we-ní, „their market"; dréke-tū we-ní (wüeni), „their dress";
ĭndda we-ní (wüeni), „their tattooings";
tang-tū we-ní, „their houses";
tórrombok wé-ne-ge, „their camel";
torrómbo-ai we-né-ne, „their camels";
bórik wé-ne-ge, „their horse";
bóri we-né-ne, „their horses".

As for the form enya we-ná-ba, „their food", I am doubtful, although, considered what I have said in connection with the 1st pers. sing. with regard to b, be (ba), it may be quite right.

Among the phrases at the end of this chapter I shall also have to mention an instance of a form na, connected, as it seems, with the genitive case of the noun.

3rd person sing. dative and accusative case uncertain.

3rd person plur. dative and accusative case probably wong.

Thus we obtain the following scheme:

	singular.			plural.		
	1st pers.	2nd pers.	3rd pers.	1st pers.	2nd pers.	3rd pers.
Nom.	am	mi, me .	ti . . .	mang . .	kang . .	wang,
Gen.	a-né . . . . / am-be, em-be	mi-né / ne-né	. te-né .	me-né, me-ní	ke-né . .	we-né, / we-ní,
Dativ. Accusative .	andan / andé .	me-gé .	te-gé? .	mong? . .	kong, kom?	wong?

2. *Particles and Numerals.*

a) With regard to the particles, which, as is the case with most other languages, are originally derived from independent substantive notions, I here do only remark, that the greater number of them, as far as they indicate a locality, are composed with the local termination gia, which, in its turn again, seems to be closely connected with the termination ge, above mentioned as forming the dative and accusative case of the pronoun, as, for instance, wa-gia, „here"; illó-gia, „there"; índa-gia, „where".

b) Neither with regard to the Numerals have I to offer many observations in this general

hier in dieser allgemeinen Analyse ihren Platz finden könnten, zu machen. Die Hauptsache ist, dass die Mába-Sprache in entschiedener Weise das Decimal-System befolgt; denn darüber kann nicht der geringste Zweifel sein, dass kanbir, „zwanzig", nur eine abgekürzte, populäre Form von átu̇'kán bir ist „zwei Zehner", von atúk, „zehn". Dann scheint zweitens das, wol sicherlich dem Arabischen entlehnte, settši für „sechs" deutlich zu zeigen, dass die Mába-Sprache ursprünglich nur bis „fünf" zählte, was schon an sich wahrscheinlich ist. Jedoch ist zu bemerken, dass im Mába die Zahlwörter über „sechs" nicht, wie wir das bei den meisten anderen derartigen Sprachen sehen, in enger organischer Beziehung zu dem Ausdruck für „fünf" oder den vorhergehenden Zahlwörtern zu stehen scheinen. Was dagegen einzelne verwandtschaftliche Beziehungen einiger Zahlwörter dieser Sprache mit den entsprechenden anderer Sprachen betrifft, so verweise ich auf den Schlussparagraphen dieses Kapitels.

3. *Das Zeitwort.*

Bevor ich bei der, gerade in dieser Beziehung, durch blossen Zufall, etwas grösseren Unvollständigkeit meines Materials, einige Bemerkungen über einzelne Erscheinungen des Zeitworts mache, halte ich für gut, einige möglichst vollständige Paradigmen desselben zu geben. Zuerst gebe ich am akal, „ich gehe", 2te Pers. Sing. des Imperativ's kokó, 2te Pers. Plur. kóko-yé.

Bemerkung. Ich würde der Formen des Imperativs halber am akkal schreiben, mit Reduplication des Konsonanten, wie ich auch an einer Stelle meines Vokabular's gethan habe, wenn nicht dadurch die gänzliche Umwandelung der Wurzelsilbe mit Verlust dieses Doppel-Konsonanten um so wunderbarer würde.

Gegenwärtige Zeit.

	Affirmative Form. Singular.	Plural.	Negative Form. Singular.	Plural.
1ste Pers.	am akal .	maṅg m-amal .	am aká-ta . .	maṅg m-atá-n [2]),
2te „	mi k-aká .	kaṅg k-ákayá .	mi k-aká-ta .	kaṅg k-atá-n,
3te „	ti t-atá .	waṅg w-áwawá .	ti t-atá-n? [1]) .	waṅg w-atá-n.

Unbestimmte Vergangenheit.

	Affirmative Form. Singular.	Plural.	Negative Form. Singular.	Plural.
1ste Pers.	am a-ká .	maṅg m-anė . .	am aká-endė .	maṅg m-amá-endė,
2te „	mi k-akó .	kaṅg k-akó . .	mi k-aká-endė	kaṅg k-aká-endė,
3te „	ti t-ató .	waṅg w-anė . .	ti t-atá-endė	waṅg w-awá-endė.

Zusatz: Unabhängig von diesem, im Zusammenhang niedergeschriebenen, Paradigma habe ich noch als vereinzelte Formen desselben Zeitwortes mi mi-aine für „wir gehen", aber in dieser Form wol gewiss falsch, vielleicht maṅg mi-aine, und dann als eine Art von Subjunktiv zu fassen; maṅg mí-are (mí-ya-ró) für „wir sind gegangen", und ma-nó, „lasst uns gehn". Die letztere Form ist entschieden richtig. Auch nyaite, „das Gehn, der Marsch", gehört nach dem, was ich weiter unten sagen werde, als Art Participial-Infinitiv unzweifelhaft zu demselben Zeitwort.

Ich gebe nun einige unvollständige Paradigmen, zuerst a) ein Paradigma der unbestimmten Vergangenheit von am a-nyi, „ich esse", 2te Person Sing. Imp. nyo, „iss".

	Positive Form. Singular.	Plural.	Negative Form. Singular.	Plural.
1ste Pers.	am á-nya-ró	maṅg mí-nya-ró	am a-nyá-endė .	maṅg mi-nyá-endė,
2te „	mi nya-ró .	kaṅg kí-nya-ró .	mi nyá-endė . .	kaṅg ki-nyá-endė,
3te „	ti tí-nya-ró	waṅg wí-nya-ró	ti ti-nyá-endė	. waṅg wi-nyá-endė.

¹) ti t-atá-n ist wahrscheinlich falsch durch Einfluss des Plurals, anstatt ti t-atá-ta.

²) maṅg m-atá-n und die nachfolgenden Formen des Plurals zusammengezogen aus maṅg m-áka-ta-n u. s. w.

analysis of the principal forms of the language. What I have to remark, is that the Mâba-language appears to follow the decimal system; for, there cannot be the slightest doubt, but that the term kanbir, meaning „twenty", is but an abbreviated form of átu)kán bir, „two tenths", from atúk, „ten", while the native terms for „thirty", and so on, have been supplanted by the corresponding Arabic terms. Further, the term sottal meaning „six", which, beyond a doubt, has likewise been borrowed from the Arabic, seems clearly to show, that the Mâba-language originally counted only as far as „five", a case very probable in itself. Moreover, I have to add, that the Numerals beyond „six" do not appear to stand in any organical way of connection with the term for „five", and the preceding ones, as is the case with most other languages of this class. Rather remarkable is the way of expressing the numerals above ten, „ten of one", „ten of two", atúk to-ñg, atúk bar-áñg, and so on; „ten above seven" atúk tal miudri, and so on, the smaller number being always regarded as the principal one.

3. *The verb.*

With regard to the relative incompleteness of my material, which in this case, I am sorry to say, just with regard to the verb is, by mere chance, a little more considerable, I think best, before offering some observations on single phenomena of the verb, to give a few paradigms of undoubtful forms. First, therefore, I place here a paradigm of the verb am akal, „I go", 2nd person sing. imp. kokó, 2nd person plur. kóko-yé.

Remark. With reference to the form of the imperative I should prefer writing am akkal, by doubling the consonant, as I have done so once in my vocabulary, if by doing so the total change of the verbal root, and the loss of the double consonant in other forms of this verb, would not be the more remarkable.

Present tense.

	affirmative form.		negative form.	
	singular.	plural.	singular.	plural.
1st pers.	am akal . .	mañg m-amal .	am aká-ta . .	mañg m-atá-n[2]),
2nd „	mi k-akā .	kañg k-ákayā .	mi k-aká-ta .	kañg k-atá-n.
3rd „	ti t-atā . .	wañg w-áwawā .	ti t-atá-n[1]) .	wañg w-atá-n.

Aorist.

	affirmative form.		negative form.	
	singular.	plural.	singular.	plural.
1st pers.	am a-kā . .	mañg m-anē . .	am aká-endē .	mañg m-amá-endē,
2nd „	mi k-akō .	kañg k-akō . .	mi k-aká-endē	kañg k-aká-ende,
3rd „	ti t-atō . .	wañg w-anē . .	ti t-atá-endē	wañg w-awá-endē.

Remark: Independently of these forms, written down conjointly from the mouth of my authority, my Collectaneous notes offer yet the following isolated forms of the same verb, as mi mi-aino, „we go", probably to be changed into mañg mi-aino (and then to be understood as a kind of subjunctive), mañg mí-arē, mí-ya-rē, „we are gone", and finally ma-nē, „let us go", this latter form, at least, no doubt, being correct. nyai-te also, „the going, the march", does belong to the same verb as a kind of infinitive, if we take into account, what I shall say further on with regard to this form in general.

I now, in the second place, give a few incomplete paradigms, and first a) a paradigm of the aorist of am a-nyī, „I eat", 2nd pers. sing. imp. nya, „eat".

	positive form.		negative form.	
	singular.	plural.	singular.	plural.
1st pers.	am á-nya-rē	mañg mí-nya-rē	am a-nyá-endē .	mañg mi-nyá-endē,
2nd „	mi nya-rē .	kañg kí-nya-rē	mi nyá-endē . .	kañg ki-nyá-endē,
3rd „	ti tí-nya-rē	wañg wí-nya-rē	ti tí-nyá-endē .	wañg wi-nyá-endē.

[1]) ti t-atá-n, instead of ti t-atá-ta, is probably wrong, being caused by the following plural forms.
[2]) mañg m-atá-n, and the following forms of the plural number, instead of mañg m-aká-ta-n, and so on.

b) Die affirmativen Formen der Gegenwart und des Aorist's von am arák-ne, „ich kaufe":

	Gegenwart. Singular.	Gegenwart. Plural.	Aorist. Singular.	Aorist. Plural.
1ste Prs.	am arák-ne	mańg m-arák-ne	am arko-ré-re	mańg m-arko-ré-re,
2te „	mi d-akko	kańg k-arák-ko	mi d-akko-ré-re	kańg k-arko-ré-re,
3te „	ti t-arák-te	wańg w-arák-ne	ti t-arko-ré-re	wańg w-arko-ré-re.

c) Negative Form des Aorist's am arká-endē, und mit doppelter Negation am ark-tá-endé.

d) Ich gebe nun die affirmative Form des Aorist's von dem eng verwandten am arki, „ich verkaufe".

Aorist, affirmative Form.

	Singular.	Plural.
1ste Person	am árko-rē	mańg m-árko-rā,
2te „	mi d-árko-rē	kańg k-árko-rā,
3te „	ti t-árko-rē	wańg w-árko-rā.

Jedoch muss ich bemerken, dass auch in der Pluralform das ē am Ende oft vorwiegt; auch muss ich hinzufügen, dass überhaupt die Formen von „kaufen" und „verkaufen" im Maba in vielen Fällen völlig gleichlautend sind. Ausserdem habe ich in den Phrasen mehrere Mal eine Form táka für „kaufen" ohne r, wie das ja auch in der zweiten Person verloren geht. Es kann aber wol ein Versehen bei einigen Formen dieses Zeitworts Statt gefunden haben.

Diesen umfassenderen, leider aber doch unvollständigen Paradigmen von Zeitwörtern füge ich noch vereinzeltere Beispiele hinzu.

e) am okoi, „ich sehe", 2te Person Imp. y-okoi, Aorist 1ste Person Sing. am okō-re, „ich habe gesehen", 2te Person mi m-okō-ro, negative Form am okō-yá-endé, „ich habe nicht gesehen".

f) Als Beispiele der Bildung des Imperativ's in seiner Beziehung zur verlängerten Präsensform gebe ich:

dańga, „nimm", von am a-dáńg-ne, „ich nehme";
yańga, „trink", von am a-yáńg-ne, „ich trinke", Aorist a-yáńg-e-rē;
kāra, „komm", Plur. kóro, von am a-kár-ne, „ich komme", Aorist am á-kare;
ukā, „wasche" von am a-ukā-ne (so zu verbessern S. 107), „ich wasche";
nar, „gib", von am a-nár-ne, „ich gebe", negative Form am a-nár-tá-endé;
dai, „stelle hin", von am au-dai, „ich stelle hin";
disā, „zeige", S. 71, etwas unsicher, aber wahrscheinlich von am a-dís-ne, „ich zeige";
tana, „steig auf", von am á-tan-i, „ich besteige", 3te Person Sing. Präs. t-átane (so S. 127; aber t-átari S. 131, wol aus Verwechselung mit der folgenden, ganz richtigen Form des Aorist's tara (ursprünglich tan-re);
fōa, „schlafe", mit der, diesen Sprachen eigenthümlichen, Verwechselung des f und h, von am a-bi, „ich schlafe" (am a-bōa, „ich bringe die Nacht zu, habe Nachtquartier").

Ausserdem habe ich in meinen Phrasen mehrere Beispiele von Formen der ersten Person Plur., wie mi-mesís-ne, „lasst uns einschlagen"; mu-šíš-ne, „lasst uns straff anziehn"; mu-sŏr-ne, „lasst uns absteigen"; mu-dénka, „lasst uns graben"; mu-ógōri, „lasst uns begrüssen"; ni-dé-teli, „lasst uns folgen"; dággaga m-ir-ne, „lasst uns aufschlagen (das Zelt)".

f, a) Als Beispiel einer negativen Form des Imperativ's führe ich an ańga gindana, „bleibe nicht, verweile nicht (lange)", von am ańgi, „ich verweile".

b) The affirmative forms of the present tense and of the aorist of am arák-no, „I buy":

	Present tense.		Aorist.	
	singular.	plural.	singular.	plural.
1st pers.	am arák-ne	mang m-arák-ne	am arke-ré-ro	mang m-arke-ré-ro,
2nd „	mi d-akke	kang k-arák-ke	mi d-akke-ró-ro	kang k-arke-ró-re,
3rd „	ti t-arák-te	wang w-arák-ne	ti t-arke-ró-ro	wang w-arke-ré-re.

c) Negative form of the aorist am arká-endō, and, with a double form of negation, am ark-tá-endē.

d) I now proceed to give the affirmative form of the aorist of the verb am arki, „I sell", the root of which is closely related to the preceding one.

Aorist, affirmative form.

	singular.	plural.
1st person	am árke-rē	mang m-árke-rā,
2nd „	mi d-árke-rē	kang k-árke-rā,
3rd „	ti t-árke-rē	wang w-árke-rā.

I must, however, remark, that also in the plural number the final ē often preponderates over the ā, and that, on the whole, the forms of the two verbs „I buy" and „I sell" in the Mába-language, in many instances are scarcely to be distinguished. Moreover, I have to remark, that among my phrases I have repeatedly the form táka for „to buy" without an r, as the r seems likewise to be lost in the forms of the 2nd person, although I think, some of the forms here mentioned may not be quite correct.

To these a little more copious, although themselves incomplete, paradigms of verbs I now add a few instances more of isolated verbal forms.

e) am okoī, „I see, look", 2nd person imp. y-okoī, „look", aorist 1st person sing. am okō-ro, „I have seen", 2nd person mi m-okō-ro, negative form am okō-yá-endē, „I have not seen".

f) I further give a few more instances of the formation of the imperative in its relation to the form of the present tense

dangа, „take", from am a-dáng-ne, „I take";
yanga, „drink", from am a-yáng-ne, „I drink", aorist a-yáng-e-rē;
kāra, „come", plur. kēre, from am a-kár-ne, „I come", Aorist am á-kara;
ukā, „wash", from am a-ukā-ne (sic p. 107), „I wash";
nar, „give", from am a-nár-ne, „I give", negative form am a-nár-té-endē;
dal, „put down", from am an-dal, „I put, place";
diesā, „show" p. 71, a little uncertain, but probably from am a-dís-ne, „I show";
tana, „mount", from am á-tan-i, „I mount", 3rd person sing. present tense t-átane vobly. p. 127, the form t-átari, p. 131, probably having arisen from confounding this form with the following tara (originally tan-ro) of the aorist;
fēa, „sleep", by means of a change of f and b, common to most of those languages, from am a-bī, „I sleep" (am a-bēa, „I pass the night, take quarters").

Besides these forms, I have among my phrases several instances of the 1st person plur. of the imperative, such as mi-mesís-ne, „let us fasten"; mu-šíš-ne, „let us tighten"; mu-eģr-ne, „let us dismount", from a-eģr-ne; mu-dánka, „let us dig"; mu-ngōri, „let us salute"; má-tetī, „let us follow"; dággaga m-ir-ne, „let us pitch (the tent)".

f, a) As an instance of a negative form of the imperative I mention ánga giadane, „do not stay (long)", from am angi, „I stay, remain".

4. *Einige allgemeine Bemerkungen über obige und andere, weniger sichere, Verbalformen.*

a) So unvollständig und keineswegs erschöpfend diese Beispiele sind, so gestatten sie doch einen ersten Einblick in die Abwandelung der Konjugation. Das Auffallendste bei derselben ist die bedeutende Umgestaltung der Wurzel in vielen Fällen durch Einwirkung der pronominalen Form. Auch das ist auffallend und unterscheidet diese Sprache von den meisten hier behandelten, dass zur Bildung der Form der Gegenwart kein Hülfszeitwort gebraucht wird; denn das in manchen Fällen der Form der ersten Person der Gegenwart am Ende hinzugefügte ne können wir kaum als solches ansehen, da es selbst in dieser Person keineswegs unumgänglich nöthig scheint und in den übrigen fast durchgängig verloren geht. Diese Form mit ne hielt ich eine Zeit lang für eine intensive, verstärkende, bin aber auch davon zurückgekommen, da sie im Allgemeinen ohne solche Beziehung Anwendung zu finden scheint; begründet übrigens schien jene Ansicht zuerst durch Vergleichung von am okol, „ich sehe" und am okol-ne, „ich suche, passe auf", und mit vorgesetztem d am d-okol-ne, „ich weise auf, zeige". Aber bei weiterer Untersuchung zeigte sich solche Unterscheidung nicht durchführbar.

a, α) Neben der Anfügung des ne unterscheidet sich die Form der Gegenwart noch besonders durch grösseres Festhalten des Hauptvokals der Wurzel und in manchen Fällen durch die Hinzufügung eines i-Lautes, den wir schon in anderen Fällen in derselben Stellung fanden; so z. B. ausser dem angeführten am a-nyī, „ich esse" (Wurzel nya), am á-nel-i, „ich höre".

b) Die negative Form des Präsens wird, wie es scheint — denn ob das durchgängig der Fall ist, kann ich nicht sagen — durch ein, an Stelle des ne, der affirmativen Form angehängtes, ta vertreten, dem in der Mehrheit ein n angefügt zu werden scheint [1]). Wir haben übrigens bei a-kal gesehen, dass das negative ta die ganze Wurzelsilbe des Zeitwortes, in der vulgären Aussprache wenigstens, verdrängt. Selbst bei Bildung der Nennwörter weiter unten werden wir dieses negative ta als integrirenden Bestandtheil wiederfinden. Dies ist sehr auffallend, da im Allgemeinen ta gerade „das Sein, Vorhandensein" zu bedeuten scheint, wie wir seiner Zeit sehen werden, und mir ist es keineswegs klar, wie die beiden zu unterscheiden sind; denn ursprünglich lang scheint das a im negativen ta nicht zu sein.

c) Die gewöhnliche Form der Vergangenheit scheint ein der Verbal-Wurzel angehängtes re oder ré zu sein, das im Plural gemeiniglich in ra, rā übergeht, obgleich das a auch schon in der ersten Person des Singular erscheint, wie in a-nel-á-ra (sie S. 49), „ich habe gehört", wo wir, neben dem angehängten ra, auch eine Veränderung der Präsensform in dem Übergange des i (á-nel-i) in a erhalten.

c, α) Eine ganz andere Bildungsweise der Vergangenheit durch Verkürzung oder blosse Vokalveränderung der Wurzel haben wir bei am akal gehabt, und ebenso haben wir t-io, „er ist gestorben" von am ūī oder cyī, „ich sterbe". Bei den Zeitwörtern dagegen, deren Wurzel auf r ausgeht, wird der letzteren in der Vergangenheit ein blosses u angehängt, also am a-kárne, „ich komme"; am á-kar-u, „ich kam". Ich habe auch Beispiele der Vergangenheit mit einem Konsonanten als Abschluss, wie dréko-tu fiddak, „die Kleider sind alt geworden"; dréke-tu tŭdmdak, „die Kleider sind zerrissen". Aber in Bezug auf diese und einige andere ähnliche Formen sind wir berechtigt, zu zweifeln, ob wir sie wirklich als Verbalformen anzusehen haben, da sie vielmehr nach dem, was ich an seiner Stelle über die Endung mit k, ak sagen werde, den Charakter von Adjektiven zu haben scheinen.

d) Die negative Form der Vergangenheit scheint durchgängig mit angefügtem adē, endē gebildet zu werden, so jedoch, dass zuweilen ein n zwischen dieser Endung und der Wurzel eingeschoben wird, wie z. B. okō-n-endē, „ich habe gesehen, (gut) gezielt".

---

[1]) Ob vielleicht das S. 49 mit der Bedeutung „ich stelle hin" angeführte Zeitwort am an-dóg-ta nichts ist als die negative Form von an-dóg-ne, „ich hebe empor", so dass es also eigentlich bedeutet „ich hebe nicht empor", „lasse stehn"? Oder sollte das ta hier eine ganz andere Bedeutung haben?

4. *Some general Remarks on the above mentioned verbal forms, and on some other less certain ones.*

a) Incomplete as are the foregoing paradigms, and although they are far from exhausting the matter, yet they open a first insight into the mode of conjugation of this language. The most remarkable feature, certainly, with regard to it is the considerable change, the verbal root does undergo in some cases, by means of the pronominal form. Another remarkable feature, and such as distinguishes this language from most of the others treated in this Collection, consists in the circumstance of no auxiliary verb being made use of in forming the present tense; for the syllable ne, which in many cases we find added to the form of the 1st person sing. of the present tense, we can scarcely look upon as such, as it is far from forming an essential part even of the 1st person, and is constantly lost in nearly all the others. However, for a long time I took this form in ne to be an intensive form of the verb, but was obliged to give up this opinion when ascertaining, that it is applied to most verbs without distinction, although the first impression seemed to be confirmed by comparing the verb am okoi, „I see, look" with am okoi-ne, „I search, pay attention to", the verb am d-okoi-ne, „I show" receiving a further development, and a more intensive meaning.

a, α) Besides the occasional adding of the termination ne, the form of the present tense is distinguished in a certain degree by preserving more distinctly the principal vowel of the root, and in many cases moreover by adding an i, which we have met with already in several similar instances; thus, besides am a-nyi, „I eat" we find the form am á-nol-i, „I hear".

b) As for the negative form of the present tense, in general it seems to be distinguished by ta *) being added to the root, instead of the ne of the affirmative form, an n being further added to the ta in the plural number. However, we have seen with regard to the verb a-kai, that in certain cases the negative termination ta obliterates and expels the whole root of the verb. The negative notion of this particle ta, which we find even in composite substantive terms, is the more remarkable, as in most other cases it seems, on the contrary, to express the notion of „to be, exist"; and I am not sure, how we are to reconcile these two opposite notions.

c) The past tense, in general, seems to be formed by adding the syllable re or rê to the verbal root, the e in the plural number being almost constantly changed into a, while in some cases it appears also in the singular, as, for instance, in a-nel-á-ra (sic p. 49), „I have heard", where, besides the adding of the ra, we see a change in the form of the present tense also in the circumstance of the a taking the place of the i, á-nel-i.

c, α) A totally different mode of forming the past tense by means of shortening the root, or by merely changing the vowel, we have met with in am akai, and thus likewise we have i-lo, „he died", from am eyi, „I am dying". On the other hand, we see, that with regard to verbs terminating in r, the past tense is formed by adding simply an a to the root instead of the ne of the present tense, as, for instance, am á-kar-a, „I came", from am a-kár-ne, „I come". I have also instances of the past tense terminating in a consonant, namely dréke-tŭ fiddak, „the clothes have become old"; dréke-tŭ tŭdmdak, „the clothes are torn". But with regard to these, and a few similar forms we may rather doubt, whether we have to look upon them as really verbal forms, while, from what I shall have to say further on with regard to the nature of the final k, they appear to exhibit rather the character of adjectives.

d) As for the negative form of the past tense, it seems constantly to be formed by adding the termination ndê, endê to the positive form, an n being inserted between it and the verbal root in such cases, where the latter terminates in a vowel, as, for instance, okô-n-endê, „I have (well) looked, aimed at".

*) I even think it possible, that the verb am an-dóng-te adduced p. 69 with the meaning „I put, place", may be nothing but the negative form of am an-dóng-ne, „I lift", the original meaning of the former being „I do not lift, let stand"; or, else, we ought to suppose the te in this instance to have quite another signification.

e) Nun habe ich aber mehrere Beispiele einer Vereinigung der beiden negativen Formen auf la und endĕ: ausser dem schon oben angeführten am ark-lá-endĕ, „ich habe nicht gesehen" auch am a-nar-lá-endĕ, „ich habe nicht gegeben" von am a-nár-ne, „ich gebe", und am angi-lá-endĕ, „ich habe nicht vergessen", „ich erinnere mich", von am angi.

f, α) Neben den, oben aufgeführten, sicheren Verbalformen habe ich nun auch noch einige andere weniger sichere, die ich hier für sich betrachten will. Dahin gehören zuerst einige fast sichere Beispiele eines Conditionell's, wie in der Phrase wulówulĕ tor-éĭka, „wenn, nachdem die Dunkelheit aufgehört hat", unzweifelhaft vom oben erwähnten Zeitwort t-átari (t-átane), „es hört auf", t-āra, „es hat aufgehört"; dann in der völlig identisch gebildeten zweiten Phrase bar-kir tor-éĭka, „wenn die Kühlung eingetreten ist". Vielleicht haben wir so auch zu verstehen und zu erklären yos tor-éŭga mit der Bedeutung „die Morgen-Zeit". So habe ich auch in den Phrasen wai hílle-go mánra-ka, „wenn, oder, nachdem wir in die Stadt gekommen sind". Überhaupt hat das ka die Bedeutung des Ungewissen und entspricht dem Kanúri yaie, wodurch es in weiterer Entwickelung die Bedeutung von „und — und" erhält. Unzweifelhaft gehört dahin auch die Redensart bong tir-ka χorio, „es möge heiss sein, oder, sei es auch heiss, das macht nichts".

Endlich finden wir diese selbe Form mit ka als eine Art von Imperativ gebraucht in der Phrase lĕ bori-ne far-ko-rō-ka, lölö ma-nē, „möchten wir, lass uns die Pferde schnell antreiben", oder „wäre es nicht gut, wenn wir die Pferde antrieben, lass uns schnell marschiren". Hieran scheint sich noch eine andere eigenthümliche, dem Subjunktiv sich nähernde, Konstruktion anzureihen, wovon ich ein Beispiel habe in der Form ka-t-andžú-ni, „dass" oder „ob er uns wol gastlich behandeln möge", in einer seiner Zeit aufzuführenden Phrase.

f, β) Eine bestimmtere Art von Subjunktiv finden wir wol in der Phrase bahar tin dă millía-te, „giebt es einen Fluss zu passiren", eigentlich „dass wir passiren", von am até-ni, „ich passire". So habe ich auch in den Phrasen als ganz verschiedene Form einer Art von Subjunktiv (mit der, zwischen Wurzel und Verbalform eingeschobenen, Genitiv-Endung ng) zu endži yū-toré, „das Wasser fliesst", endži ya-ūg-tă-ne, „damit das Wasser fliesse".

f, γ) Ich habe dann auch noch einige Beispiele einer ganz eigenthümlichen Form, die ich nicht näher unterzubringen weiss, die aber den Zweck anzuzeigen scheint, nämlich mit sun, wie kíro-sun, doggága-sun, fag-sun, „zum Miethen, zum Aufschlagen, zum Befestigen".

f, δ) Schon bei a-kal habe ich nyal-te als höchst wahrscheinliche Form eines substantivischen Infinitivs angeführt; davon habe ich nun noch ein anderes interessanteres Beispiel mit davon abhängigem Accusativ des Nennwortes, nämlich gŭdrie árda-te a-kal, „die Baumwolle zu pflücken, gehe ich", S. 119, von dem oben erwähnten am ardáng, „ich pflücke". So haben wir auch wol sicherlich die mir zur Zeit unverständlich gebliebene Phrase zu verstehen am mo-gó bungéri-te a-dal S. 49, wörtlich „ich dir zu gehorchen (búngnyorík S. 75) suche" (a-dal, „ich suche" S. 71), und demnach wol auch die S. 75 erwähnte und missverstandene Phrase am ganí-nya búrgo-te a-dal, obgleich ich sie noch nicht in ihren einzelnen Bestandtheilen erläutern kann. Ebenso habe ich die Phrase ans ágo-nó ta arák-te a-dal, „um die Hälfte suche ich es zu kaufen". So können wir aber auch die schon unter f, α) aufgeführte Phrase millínte verstehen, wörtlich „zum wir (we) passiren", wo der verbale mit dem substantivischen Begriff merkwürdig verschmolzen scheint. Als entsprechende passive Form zu diesem aktiven Infinitiv auf te werden wir bei Besprechung des Nennwortes (S. CCVIII, d) eine auf ti ausgehende Form finden.

f, ε) Eine Art von Gerundium erkennen wir in der Phrase nangan wang-nun t-ăka, „um, wegen dieses (im Genitiv), zu kaufen". Eine ganz eigenthümliche derartige negative Bildung des Gerundium's haben wir in der Phrase bodíd tóudrian feläo-n ŭdá-nda mín-ri-ni,

e) But now, I have also several instances, where both negative forms, as well that in ta, as that in endē, are used conjointly, viz, besides am ark-tá-endē, „I have not seen", mentioned above, am a-nar-tá-endē, „I have not given", from am a-nár-no, „I give", and am aŭgi-tá-endē, „I have not forgotten", „I remember", from am aŭgi.

f, α) These forms we may look upon as fully reliable and as well established; but, besides them, I have a few others less certain, which I want to consider now. To these latter belong a few probable forms of a conditional mood, as in the phrase walówalo tor-éñka, „when" or „after darkness has ceased", the verbal form, no doubt, having to be referred to the verb t-átari (t-átane) mentioned above, and meaning „it ceases", past tense t-āra, „it has ceased"; then, in another phrase formed in quite an analogous manner, bar-kir ter-éñka, „when the cool of the evening has set in". Perhaps, we have also to understand and to explain in a somewhat similar manner the phrase yos tor-éñga with the final meaning „morning", that is „before the sun obtains its full power". Thus, I have also among my phrases wal hílle-go mánra-ka, „after we have got to the town". On the whole, the ka conveys the notion of what is uncertain, what is supposed to be, and consequently is identical with the Kanúri ynió, receiving in a further development of that notion the meaning „and — and". Thus, beyond a doubt, we have also to understand the phrase boñg tir-ka χerte, „it may be hot", i. q. „although it be hot, it does not matter".

Finally, this same form with ka appears used as a sort of imperative in the phrase lō berí-no far-ke-rā-ka, lōlō ma-nē, „might we drive on, let us drive on our horses, let us march fast". Then I have a very remarkable phrase, where ka-t-undžiŋ-ni as a sort of subjunctive seems to mean „that, or whether he may give us a treat".

f, β) A more distinct kind of a subjunctive mood may possibly be contained in the phrase bahar tin dā mittís-te, „is there a river to cross", properly „that we cross", from am até-ni, „I cross". But this form shall be shortly examined from another point of view, while endži ya-ñg-tā-ne, if compared with the simple positive form endži yū-terē, seems to present another sort of subjunctive mood „that the water may run", although ñg. inserted between the root and the verbal termination, reminds of the form of the genitive case.

f, γ) Besides these forms I have a few instances of a very remarkable verbal form by means of sun, which I am uncertain where to refer to, as, for instance, kire-sun, deggéga-sun, fag-sun with the meaning „for hiring, for pitching, for strengthening".

f, δ) Already, when considering the verb a-kat, I have mentioned the form nyai-te as being most probably the form of a kind of substantival infinitive. Of such a form I have still another more interesting instance, joined to the accusative case of a noun, which it apparently rules; this is the phrase adduced p. 119 gñório ávda-te a-kat, meaning verbally „the cotton to pluck I go"; and thus, I think, we have likewise to explain the phrase mentioned p. 49 am me-gó buñgéri-te a-dat, and which at the time has remained unintelligible to me, explaining it now „I thee to obey (búñgnyerík p. 75) do endeavour" (a-dat p. 71). Probably, we have thus also to understand the phrase am ganí-nya bárge-te a-dat adduced likewise p. 75, and there explained wrongly, although I am not yet able to analyze the whole of it. In the same manner do I explain the phrase nus ágo-nó ta arák-te a-dat, „I want to buy it for half the sum". But, from this same point of view I have no doubt, we may also explain the form mittíste adduced under f, α), as being a combination of a verbal with a substantive notion, meaning verbally „for our crossing". Further on (p. CCCIX, d), when treating of the noun, we are to meet with a form in ti which seems to be a sort of passive voice in comparison with this termination te.

f, ε) But now, I think, we may recognise a sort of gerund in the phrase naŭgan waŭg-nun táka, „on account of buying this, for buying this" („this", waŭg being put in the genitive case); and a very peculiar negative form of a gerund of this kind we find in

„lasst uns ein Mittel machen, dass er (der Sattel) ein Geschwür nicht verursache", in der positiven Form felño t-údi, „er verursacht ein Geschwür".

f, ζ) Sonst wird bei Verbindung zweier Zeitwörter das zweite abhängige, keineswegs wie bei uns im Infinitiv, sondern gleichfalls in die bestimmte Zeit gesetzt, wie z. B. am gaó-nya á-tene, „ich will, ich besteige", anstatt „ich will besteigen".

f, η) Sichere Formen eines eigentlichen Particip's des Aktiv's kann ich nicht nachweisen; doch werden wir mehrfach einen Übergang dazu andeuten können, der dann zu Adjektivformen führt. Hier will ich nur auf die Phrase hinweisen kañg ago) litto t-ándí-rren, „diese Person) eine Sache spend-end", d. h. „freigebig".

g) Noch weniger entwickelt sind, wie in allen diesen Sprachen, die Formen des Passiv's. Als einen Versuch der Darstellung dieser Zeit führe ich hier an am-b-uñē-re, „ich bin geboren", von a-úño (sie S. 35), „ich zeuge, gebäre". Ich nenne es einen Versuch, weil es mir eine nicht recht entwickelte Form zu sein, und mehr zurückbeziehenden, medialen Charakter zu haben scheint, wie wir das b, be schon (S. CCXC) in den Formen des besitzenden Fürwortes der ersten Person gefunden haben und bei Bildung der Zeitwörter noch weiterhin finden werden. — Eine besondere passive Form scheint a-yō, „ich werde" von á-yi-ne, „ich mache".

g, α) Allerdings liegt hier eine Art passiver Bedeutung in dem verlängerten Vokal ē, da die Endung re vielmehr die Vergangenheit anzeigt. So haben wir denn auch teúg-ēre als Art Participium Passivi mit der Bedeutung „von dem Speer getroffen", und ebenso das, in Form wie Bedeutung, sich eng anschliessende odem-ēre, „mit dem Schwert getroffen".

g, β) Als weiteres Beispiel eines Particip's Passivi habe ich nun auch eine Form auf te oder vielmehr ēte. Denn wieder durch diesen langen Vokal unterscheidet sich diese Form äusserlich von der oben (S. CCC, f, δ) erwähnten Bildung des substantiven und transitiven Infinitiv's. So habe ich kése udē-te (wol als ud(e)-ē-te zu fassen), „geblendet", wörtlich „die Augen ausgestochen", von a-udá-ne, „ich steche aus".

g, γ) Dann aber habe ich auch die einfache Verbalwurzel mit der Bedeutung eines Particip's Passivi, nämlich uñé, „gebunden", von a-úñe-ne (sie S. 81), „ich binde", mit der entsprechenden negativen Form uñé-nde, „nicht gebunden".

h) Als eine Art von medialer Form möchte ich die Endung auf ön betrachten, wie z. B. am áfön, „ich habe mich verirrt" (térrembok tafain, „das Kameel hat sich verlaufen, ist verloren"), am állön, „ich bin ermüdet, bin matt"; und bei letzterem Zeitwort habe ich ein interessantes Beispiel einer, zur klareren Bezeichnung der zurückwirkenden Bedeutung, dem Zeitwort angehängten Pronominalform, nämlich mañg n-állod-mi, „wir haben uns ermüdet", d. h. „wir sind ermüdet".

i) Ich bespreche nun die impersonellen Verbalformen, oder solche Formen, die nur in der dritten Person gebraucht sind, auf die ich noch einmal ausführlich beim Eigenschaftswort zurückkommen muss.

i, α) Zuerst erwähne ich einige Formen, die durch Anfügung einer einfachen Verbalform an ein Nennwort entstanden sind, wie die S. 137 angeführten bur-sir, kókl-sir, koléksir, hanhán-syir, die alle bedeuten „es macht (= tšin in Kanúri in kógó-tšiu u. s. w.) den und den Ton". Diese Verbalform hängt wol mit dem weiter unten zu besprechenden Zeitwort srō zusammen und in weiterer Entwickelung mit dem unten, bei der Bildung zusammengesetzter Nennwörter, zu erwähnenden nenrik, mit der hiermit übereinstimmenden Bedeutung „machend".

i, β) Viel wichtiger aber als diese ist eine andere Bildung, wo dem Grundbegriff ein tá-ne, te-nā oder te-rē, te-rī angefügt wird. Diese Formen, besonders die ersteren, haben mir eine Zeit lang viele Bedenken gemacht, da ich nicht wusste, wie ich sie zu betrachten

the phrase bedíd tóndrian felüo-n ššá-sda mín-ri-ni, „let us contrive a remedy, in order (to prevent) that it (the saddle) may not cause an ulceration", from the positive verbal form felüo t-ődi, „it causes ulceration".

f, ζ) Else, when two verbs are joined, the infinitive does not seem to be made use of in the Mába-language, the second dependent verb being likewise placed in the definite tense, as, for instance, am gnó-nya á-tane, „I will mount", properly „I will, I mount".

f, η) As for a participle of the active voice, I am not able to point out some well established forms, but we shall find repeated opportunity of treating of a transitional form leading to the adjectives. Here I want only to adduce the phrase kaúg ago) litto t-úndš-eren, meaning „this person) spend-ing something", i. q. „liberal, generous".

g) As for the forms of the passive voice, they are even less distinctly developed, than these. First, I mention a-yō, „I become" (kolák-a-yō, „I become great, get old"), compared with á-yi-no, „I make", and as a further attempt at representing such a form I here mention am-b-uñō-re, „I am born", from am a-úño (sic p. 35), „I procreate, bear". I call it an attempt, as it does not seem to me to be a well developed form, representing the passive voice, but rather appears to convey a relative, medial notion, as we have had already opportunity (p. CCXCI) of meeting with the b, be in forms of the first person of the possessive pronoun.

g, α) In the form mentioned, the only sound really expressive of the passive notion seems to be the long vowel ō, the termination re rather indicating the past tense; thus, we have teñg-ēre as a sort of participle of the passive voice with the meaning „hurt by the spear", and the totally analogous odom-ēre, „hurt by the sword".

g, β) As a further instance of a participle of the passive voice, I have also a form terminating in te or rather ōte; for the long vowel seems to distinguish it from the form mentioned p. CCCI, f, δ) as representing a sort of substantival infinitive of a transitional character. Thus, I have káse udē-te, or rather ud(a)-ō-te, „blinded" (verbally „put out (as for) the eyes"), from a-udá-no, „I put out".

g, γ) But, besides these forms, I have also instances of the simple verbal root, perhaps with a slight change of the vowel, being used as a kind of participle of the passive voice, as, for instance, ušá, „bound, tied", from a-éše-no (sic p. 81), „I tie", with the corresponding negative form ušá-nda, „not tied".

h) As a kind of medial form I am inclined to look upon the termination ёa, as, for instance, am éfёa, „I am gone astray" (tórrombok tefaia, „the camel is gone astray, has been lost"); am állёa, „I am tired, ,worn out"; nay, with regard to the latter verb, I have an instance of a pronominal form being added to the verb, in order to express more distinctly the reciprocal power, namely mañg n-álleá-mi, „we have tired ourselves".

i) I now proceed to treat of the impersonal verbal forms, or those forms which on the whole, are not but used in the 3rd person, and to which I shall have to return once more, when speaking of the forms of the adjective.

i, α) First, I mention a few forms, which have been moulded by adding a simple verb to a noun, such as the terms adduced p. 137 bur-nir, kóki-nir, keldk-nir, hanhán-njir, all of them meaning „it (the animal) makes, produces such and such a sound". This verbal form nir, identical with the Kanúri tšin in kógō-tšin, and so on, seems to be connected with the verb aré to be mentioned further on; the participial, or adjective form nenrik with the analogous meaning „making, producing", which we shall meet with in a following paragraph, as forming a very important ingredient in the composition of nouns, being thence derived in a further development.

i, β) Much more important, however, than those ways of forming an impersonal verb, is another way of composition by adding the forms tá-no, te-nā or to-re, to-ri to the root expressive of the principal notion. These forms, especially those mentioned in the first place, have

hatte; jedoch bin ich nach hinreichender Erwägung aller Punkte zu der Überzeugung gelangt, dass sie als ursprünglich definite Zeiten des Zeitworts zu betrachten sind und erst allmählich, oder vielmehr bloss in äusserlicher Beiordnung, die Bedeutung von Eigenschaftswörtern erhalten haben. Ihr Grundbestandtheil ist te, das auch selbstständig für „ist" vorkommt.

Die Form te-ré, von der wir te-ri vielleicht bloss als Nebenform zu betrachten haben, obgleich, nach den beim Eigenschaftswort angeführten Bemerkungen, te-ré mehr den rein verbalen, te-ri mehr den adjektivischen Charakter zu haben scheint, erklärt sich nach dem oben von der Endung re Gesagten von selbst als Aorist, während das te, abgesehen von der unter c) besprochenen infinitiven Bedeutung, auch in anderen Verbal-Endungen wiederkehrt, wie z. B. anddóṅg-te, aróṅg-te. Diesen Gesichtspunkt ziehe ich demjenigen vor, von dem aus wir teré (t-are) vielleicht als dritte Person vom Hülfszeitwort aré ansehen könnten, das dem Alt-Egyptischen erí sich allerdings anzunähern scheint, das ich S. LXXIV erwähnt habe; auch fällt zu Gunsten dieser Annahme die oben unter f, η) angeführte Form t-ándž-eren gewaltig in's Gewicht, indem wir hier dieselbe Form in ihren aufgelösten Bestandtheilen zu haben scheinen.

So erklären sich also auf ganz natürliche Weise die unter den unpersönlichen Zeitwörtern erscheinenden Formen búm-teri, „riecht"; tugúl-teri, „riecht gut"; lúl-teri, „riecht schlecht". Am allerdeutlichsten aber ist das Beispiel von indži) kolák-teré, „das Wasser) ist gross geworden, tritt über", da wir kolák nicht allein als gewöhnliches Adjektiv haben, sondern auch in Verbindung mit der unter g) angeführten passiven Verbalform ayó in kolák-ayó, „ich werde alt". Einen völlig verbalen Charakter scheint auch zu haben das dāa endžíb-teré, „am Fuss verwundet er ist", obgleich es seiner Bedeutung „gelähmt" wegen unter den Adjektiven aufzuführen ist; so betrachte ich auch das später als selbstständiges Eigenschaftswort aufzuführende yó-teri, „lebend, lebendig" als verbalen Ursprungs. In dieser Anschauung werde ich bestärkt durch von te-ré wieder abgeleitete, entschieden verbale Formen mit terdóṅge, das seine volle Erklärung in einem nachfolgenden Paragraphen erhalten wird, wie indži) kir-terdóṅge, indži) boṅg-terdṅge S. 135, „das Wasser) wird kühl, wird warm".

i, γ) Die ganz regelmässig gebildete negative Form dieses verbalen te-ré oder te-ri geht auf tá-r-endé aus, wie fahem-tá-r-endé, „er ist nicht verständig", d. h. „thöricht", auf der einen, obgleich ich als positive Form dazu bloss das rein adjektivische fahém-te habe, und auf der anderen Seite komdl-tá-r-endé „er ist nicht stark", d. h. „schwach", obwol ich dann in positiver Form auch wieder nur das rein adjektivische komdl-ok, „stark" habe.

i, δ) Grammatisch etwas schwieriger zu erklären, als diese Endung te-ré, ist die auf tá-ne, oder was dasselbe zu sein scheint, te-né mit den negativen Formen tá-endé und te-ndai (irrthümlich sind te-né und te-ndai S. 123 als gleichbedeutend zusammengestellt), wie in ufmmoro tá-ne, „es ist gut, ist reif"; ufmmoro tá-endé, „ist nicht gut, ist unreif". Das einfache ta mit der Bedeutung „ist" scheint sich durch die am Ende dieses Kapitels aufzuführende Phrase mindži ta ba lel ta, „nahe ist oder fern ist", und mehrere ähnliche zu erklären.

i, ε) Wenn ich also diese Formen als eigentlich verbal ansehe und sie deshalb auch in diesem Paragraphen in Betracht gezogen habe, so halte ich dagegen Formen wie fiddak und tédumdak S. 127 mehr für adjektivisch, und dasselbe gilt von tórmerik, „ist ledig"; tamsáṅg, „es ist vorbei" S. 123, dagegen, wovon ich in den Phrasen eine andere, bestimmt verbale, Form tám-tere habe, so wie tiríṅg, „es fliesst" S. 131, mag wirklich verbal sein.

k) Ich will nun diesem Abschnitt über das Zeitwort in der Mába-Sprache noch einige Bemerkungen über Bildung neuer Zeitwörter hinzufügen, α) über solche, die dem Genius der Mába-Sprache selbst entwachsen, β) über solche, die dem Arabischen entlehnt sind.

α) Zuerst habe ich hier darauf hinzuweisen, dass, obgleich auf den ersten Blick der Vorsatz von a und an vor der ersten Person der Verbalwurzel gleichgültig und unterschieds-

caused me much embarrassement for a while, as I did not know exactly, what to make of them; but, after having weighed sufficiently all the points, finally I have convinced myself, that they are to be considered as being originally definite verbal tenses, their original root being ta, which even, when left by itself, means „it is", while they have not received the import of adjectives but by degrees, and even then merely through an outward juxtaposition.

Thus, the form te-ré, of which te-ri seems to be considered simply as a by-form, after what I have said in a former paragraph with regard to the verbal termination re, appears clearly to be looked upon as an aorist, the te returning also in other verbal forms, as, for instance, andóng-te, aróng-te. This point of view is, I think, more correct than to look upon the form teré (t-are) as the third person sing. of the auxiliary verb aré, although the latter may possibly be identical with the ancient Egyptian eri (see p. LXXV), and although this explanation appears to be recommended by the form i-úadž-eren mentioned under f, η).

Thus, therefore, the forms of impersonal verbs, such as búm-teri, „it blows"; tagúl-teri, „it smells well"; lúl-teri, „smells badly, has a bad smell", are explained in the most simple and natural manner. But the clearest, and most instructive instance of this formation is indži) kolák-teri. „the water) has become large, high", in consequence „inundates its banks", as we have kolák not only as a common adjective, but also in connection with the passive auxiliary verb ayō, in the form kolák-ayō. „I got great, old". A perfect verbal character is also apparent in the form dža endžíb-terī. „as for) the leg, lamed he is", although, as representing the general notion „lamed", it was to be ranged among the adjectives. From the same point of view I look also upon yō-teri as of verbal origin, although I shall have likewise to adduce it as an independent adjective, being confirmed in this view, in general, by comparing the evidently verbal forms terminating in teróngo, such as indži) kir-teróngo, indži) boúg-teróngo p. 135, „the water) gets cool", „the water) gets warm"; for these forms, no doubt, are again derived from the former.

i, γ) The regular negative form of this verbal te-rē or te-ri terminates in tó-r-endē, as, for instance, on the one hand fahom-tó-r-endē, „he is not prudent", i. q. „foolish", side by side with the affirmative form fahóm-te, and komól-tó-r-endē, on the other, „he is not strong", i. q. „weak", although as the corresponding affirmative form of the latter I have only the truely adjective form komól-ok, „strong".

i, δ) Rather more difficult to be explained from a grammatical point of view, than this termination te-rē, is the other one in tá-ne or, what seems to be the same, te-nā with the corresponding negative form tá-endē and te-ndai (the forms te-nā and te-ndai p. 123 being by mere mistake adduced as identical) as in nímmore tá-ne, „it is good, is ripe", with the negative form nímmore tá-endē, „it is not good, is unripe". In this case the real verbal root, expressive of the being, appears to be ta, the ne being nothing but a termination, this independent character of ta being best illustrated by the phrase mindži ta ba lel ta. „is it near, or is it far", and similar ones which I shall have to adduce further on.

i, ε) But, while I look upon forms, such as the above mentioned, as of a purely verbal character, and therefore have analyzed them in this paragraph, I consider other forms, such as fiddak and tšúmdak p. 127, rather as adjectives, and the same seems to be said of térmerik, „is leaky", while tamadúng, „it is passed" p. 123, of which among my phrases I have another truely verbal form tám-terē, and tiríng, „it runs" p. 131 may be in reality verbal forms.

k) To this chapter, treating of the verb in the Mába-language, I now subjoin a few remarks with regard to the moulding of the verbs themselves, α) such as are developed from out of the genius of the language itself, β) such as have been merely borrowed from the Arabic.

α) First, I have to point out, that, although at first sight the prefixing of a or an before the first person sing. of the verbal root, would seem to be entirely indifferent, and without

los zu sein scheint, das Beispiel von am a-dal, „ich suche, begehre", in Beziehung zu am a-a-dal, „ich schicke", doch einen solchen Unterschied aufzuzeigen scheint. Die Bedeutung des b, bo habe ich schon oben S. CCC, g) bei der Frage der passiven Form berührt und führe hier noch als Beispiel an am be-drine, „ich thue wohl" S. 77, im Vergleich zu am au-drine, „ich thue" S. 63, das Zeitwort b-aréṅgne (S. 73, 75, 77) zum einfachen aréṅgne, am teṅ b-irne, „ich verwunde mit dem Speer" (S. 99) in Beziehung zu am teṅg-árne, „ich stosse mit dem Speer" ebenda. Auch den scheinbaren Einfluss von de in am d-okoine habe ich schon oben S. CCXCVIII angedeutet; hier weise ich noch hin auf am d-erwā S. 107 in Beziehung zu am erwō-ne, „ich rasire".

k, β) Ich stelle nun die Art der Bildung der dem Arabischen entlehnten und der Muhn-Sprache nur anbequemten Zeitwörter zusammen. Diese Bildung geschieht vermittelst der Endungen aré, ar-ne, er-ne, eré-ne, erehē-ne, aréṅg-ne und a-nal. So habe ich am kil-aré, „ich messe", von كال u. a. كيل; am fám-(fáhem-)aré, „ich verstehe", von فهم; am héddiš-aré, „ich niese", von عطس; am ammer-aré, „ich lade (das Gewehr)", von عمر; am (χeme) dégeg-aré, von دقّ, „ich schlage (das Zelt) auf" (1ste Pers. Plur. Imp. χeme me-néno dégaga m-irne, was schon auf einen Übergang zur folgenden Form hinweist; am ōm-aree, „ich schwimme", von عام; am gér-eree, „ich lese", von قرا, daher gir-nir, „der Leser"; am kitib-eree, „ich schreibe", von كتب; am saim-eree, „ich faste", von صوم; am salla-(e)rēne, „ich bete", von صلى; am halfa-erēne, „ich schwöre", von حلف; am sudžid-erehēne, „ich werfe mich nieder", von سجد; am waras-erehēne, „ich erbe, bin der Erbe", von ورث; am dabá-aréṅg-ne, „ich schlachte", von ذبح; am tabák-aréṅg-ne, „ich falte zusammen", von طبق; am gaṭā-aréṅg-ne, „ich passire (einen Fluss)", von قطع; am fūl-aréṅg-ne, „ich blase an (das Feuer)", von فار u. a. فور, mit Übergang des r in l; am farhān-anal, „ich bin froh, zufrieden", von فرح; am hasdn-anal, „ich bin traurig", von حزن.

Wenn wir diese Bildungen mit den ähnlichen der Kanúri-Sprache vergleichen, so entsprechen die ersteren sechs Formen den Kanúri-Hülfszeitwörtern ni-skin, di-skin (S. LII), die letzte Form a-nal aber ganz entschieden der Medialform ṅgin (S. LIV), an welches sich jedoch das a-yō (S. CCCII, g) in kolák-a-yō, „ich werde gross, altere", noch näher anschliesst.

5. *Das Nennwort.*

Ich gehe nun zur Betrachtung des Nennworts über, indem ich mich an den vorhergehenden Paragraphen eng anschliesse und zuerst erwäge, in wie weit wir die Bildung des Nennworts aus verbalen Wurzeln erklären können. Beispiele einer solchen Bildung sehen wir nun

a) durch einfache Veränderung des wandelbaren Endvokal's, in uṅa, „Geburt", passivisch „das Geborene, das Kind", von am a-ṅōe, „ich erzeuge, gebäre" (am-b-uṅō-re, „ich bin geboren"); ferner in nyu, „Nahrung", nyū, „Fleisch", von am a-nyi, „ich esse";

b) mit hinzutretender leichter Abwandelung des Konsonanten, gini, „Marsch", von am a-kai, „ich gehe";

c) mit Vorsetzung eines Konsonanten, zuerst t (das Fürwort ti, „er"?), t-aṅg, taṅg, „Wohnstätte, Haus", von aṅgi, „sitze"; aṅga, „wohne, bleibe". Unzweifelhaft gehören hierher auch die ursprünglichen Ausdrücke für „Mutter" (miṅ) und „Vater" (maṅ), beide wieder von ṅōe, „gebären, zeugen". Diese beiden letzten Ausdrücke sind um so interessantere

any consequence, yet the instance of am a-dal, „I search", compared with am a-s-dal, „I send", apparently points to such a distinction. — With regard to b, be, I have already pointed out its import (p. CCCI, g), while treating of the passive form, and with regard to the question considered in this place, I mention the verb am be-drine, „I do well" p. 77, compared with the simple am an-drino, „I do" p. 63, as an instance of a form composed by means of this be; then the verb b-aróñgne (p. 73, 75, 77), compared with the simple verb aróñgne; am toñg b-irne, „I wound with the spear" (p. 99), compared with am toñg-árne, „I thrust the spear". Having pointed out already p. CCXCIX the apparent verbal influence of d, de in the verb am d-okolne, in this place I, moreover, mention am d-erwā p. 107, compared with am erwé-ne, „I shave".

h, β) I now proceed to give some instances of verbs borrowed from the Arabic, and accommodated to the laws of the Maba-language by means of the terminations arē, ar-ne, er-ne, orō-ne, orēñō-ne, aróñg-ne and a-nal. Thus, I have the verb am kil-aré, „I measure", from كال n. a. كيل; am fám-(fáhem-)arē, „I understand", from فهم; am héddiš-aré, „I succeed", from قدس; am ammer-arē, „I load (the gun)", from عمر; am (χéme) déğeg-arē, „I pitch (the tent)", from دقّ, 1st person plur. imp. χōme me-né-ne dágaga m-irne, forming already a transition to the following form; am ōm-eraé, „I swim", from عام; am gér-eraé, „I read", from قرأ, whence gir-nir, „the reader"; am kittib-eraé, „I write", from كتب; am saim-eraé, „I fast", from صام; am salla-(e)rēne, „I pray", from صلّى; am halfa-erēne, „I swear", from حلف; am sudžid-erehēne, „I throw myself down in prayer", from سجد; am waras-ereāñne, „I inherit, am the heir (of)", from ورث; am dabá-aróñg-ne, „I slaughter", from ذبح; am tabák-aróñg-ne, „I fold together", from طبق; am gaṭā-aróñg-ne, „I cross (a river)", from قطع; am fūl-aróñg-ne, „I blow (the fire)", from فار, n. a. فور, with a change of r into l; am farhān-anaī, „I am glad, content", from فرح; am hasān-anaī, „I am sad, sorry", from حزن.

On comparing these forms with the corresponding ones in the Kanúri-language we find, that the six former classes of them are identical with the Kanúri-terms composed by means of ní-skin, dí-skin (p. LIII), while the latter class terminating in a-nal decidedly corresponds with the medial form ñgin of the Kanúri-language (p. LV), to which the passive or medial form a-yō, however, mentioned p. CCCIII, g) with the meaning „I become", is still more closely related.

5. *The noun.*

I now proceed to consider the noun, taking for my starting point the very topic, where in the preceding paragraph I left the verb, in order to make those passive forms, which illustrate the derivation of the noun from the verbal root, the first object of my inquiry. Instances of such a formation occur

a) by means of a simple change of the final vowel, as, for instance, uña, in an active meaning, „birth", in a passive notion „what is born", „child", from am a-ñāe, „I beget, bear", (am-b-nñō-ro, „I am born"); nya, „food"; nyō, „meal", from am a-nyé, „I eat";

b) by means of a slight change of the consonant, besides adding a vowel, as, for instance, girai, „march", from am a-kaé, „I go, I march";

c) by means of prefixing a consonant to the root, as, for instance, t (ti, „it"?) t-añg, tañg, „dwelling, house", from añgi, „sit", náge, „remain, dwell". Most probably we have to look upon the terms for „father", muñ and „mother", miñ, as instances of a similar formation from the verb añe, although I am not yet able to show the import of the m; but

Beispiele dieser Bildung, als Burckhardt zwei ganz andere Formen anführt, nämlich ton oder tun (auch einmal bei mir) und tin, die also wieder dieselbe Verbalwurzel, nur mit anderem Vorsatz, eben jenem t, ti, aufweisen und sich auf das Ergato an tung anschliessen. Zu diesen Formen gehört auch das t-áka S. CCC vom Zeitwort ar-ák-ne S. CCXCVI. Dazu vergleiche auch noch yär-iṅg, „wach sein"; tär-iṅg, „Schlaf", obgleich wir hier wahrscheinlich nicht eine einfache substantive Umbildung, sondern die oben S. CCXCVIII, b) bei dem Zeitwort besprochene negative Bedeutung des ta zu erkennen haben, da Schlaf dem nicht Wachsein entspricht.

c, α) Als Beispiel grösserer Umgestaltung der Wurzelsilbe haben wir wahrscheinlich anzusehn das von demselben Zeitwort nögi (a-ṅgi) abgeleitete nyógo, „Ruhe".

d) Eine andere Bildung des Substantiv's, die sich jedoch in gewisser Beziehung der unter c) erwähnten anschliesst, besteht darin, dass eine bestimmte verbale Form zu einem substantiven Begriff geworden ist, wie z. B. t-lo, „er ist gestorben" S. 37, die 3te Person Sing. von am e-l, „ich sterbe", zu einem Nennwort, mit der Bedeutung „der Todte", „der Leichnam", geworden ist. Ähnlich ist yé-ti, „der Ackerboden", gebildet als eine Art passiven Infinitiv's (s. oben S. CCC, f, β), verglichen ti, „es ist"), von a-u-yĭ-no, „ich bebaue das Land".

e) Dadurch, dass man ein k der Verbalwurzel anhängt, wird die Bestimmung, der Zweck, das Mittel angezeigt, wie z. B. daṅga-k, „Handgriff, Handhabe", von daṅga, „nehmen, ergreifen"; yaṅga-k, „Trinkgefäss", von yaṅga, „trinken". Als ein anderes belehrendes Beispiel dieses Grundsatzes haben wir nyéro-k, im passiven Sinne „Speise", obgleich ich nicht ganz sicher bin, ob wir dies Wort als ein aus zwei verbalen Begriffen, nya und ero, zusammengesetzten Ausdruck, oder als ein einfach von nyéro, „das Essen", mit passiver Bedeutung, abgeleitetes Wort anzusehen haben.

f) Durch Anfügung der Silbe da an die verbale Wurzel scheint tĕul-da, „Husten", von tĕúl-aré, „ich huste", abgeleitet, wie auch andere Substantive, von denen ich keine entsprechenden verbalen Wurzeln besitze, in ähnlicher Weise gebildet scheinen, wie z. B. kul-da, „Rauch"; tak-da, „Händeklatschen"; wárek-da, „Sprache" (ein Synonym von bóra).

g) Eben dieses da soll mir auch den Übergang von der einfachen Ableitung der Nennwörter von verbalen Begriffen zu der Weiterbildung von substantivischen Begriffen geben, indem es auch hierzu benutzt wird. So z. B. haben wir džélka-da, „Tag, Tageshelle", als Weiterentwickelung des einfachen substantivischen Begriffes dželka, „Sonnenschein".

h) Eine andere Art solcher Weiterentwickelung finden wir vermittelst eines angehängten lik (mit zweifelhafter Bedeutung), wie z. B. ysi, „Urin", verglichen mit ysi-lik, „Speichel".

i) Indem ich nun die Bildung einfacher Nennwörter weiter betrachte, berücksichtige ich hier die dem Arabischen entlehnten Substantive, von denen die Mába-Sprache eine bedeutende Anzahl besitzt. Diese Wörter sind dem Geiste der Sprache angepasst dadurch, dass man gemeiniglich ein k ihnen anfügte, nicht allein in dem Falle, wenn sie auf einen Vokal ausgingen, wie z. B. hille: hille-k; kädi: kädi-k; räi: räyo-k, in welchen Fällen man vielleicht glauben könnte, dass sie das Arabische Schluss-h in k umgewandelt hätten, sondern auch bei solchen Wörtern, die auf einen Konsonanten endigten, indem man hier vor dem angehängten k, den Vokal o oder i einschob, z. B. nedžär: nedžär-ok; džesär: džesär-ik; merkeb: mérkeb-ek; delál: delál-ek. Jedoch ist dies nicht durchgängig der Fall, zumal wenn schon sonst eine leichte Veränderung mit dem Fremdworte vorgegangen ist, wie z. B. γarīb in harīb, „der Fremde"; árab in aram, „der Araber", wobei jedoch die Pluralform arám-ka wieder ein k aufweist.

k) Nun gehe ich weiter zu der Verbindung zweier Wörter, indem ich hier dem schon oben aufgeführten nyérok das in anderer Weise komponirte dža-ṅga-k an die Seite stelle mit der wörtlichen Bedeutung „Fuss-gäng-er", dann „Fusssoldat", von dža, „Fuss" und ka, ga, „gehn" (a-kai, „ich gehe", gi-ai, „Marsch"), mit dem angefügten, oben besprochenen k.

l) Einen direkten Übergang zu der bloss äusserlichen Verbindung zweier Substantive bildet

it is of considerable interest to compare with these forms, those adduced by Burckhardt, viz. ton or tun (appearing also once in my own phrases) and tin, where we have the same root with the addition of a t, ti instead of the m. Here we may compare the formation of the nouns yăr-ĭńg, „the being awake", and tăr-ĭńg, „the being asleep, the sleep", although I suppose, that we may have rather to recognise in the latter term the negative ta, of which I have spoken p. CCXCIX, b) in connection with the verb, the notion of „sleeping" being identical with that of „not being awake".

c, α) As an instance of a more considerable change of the verbal root we have, I think, to look upon nyŏge meaning „repose", from the same verb ăńgi (a-ńgi) mentioned above.

d) Substantives are further moulded by taking a certain verbal form for representing the general notion, as t-lo, for instance, „he died, is dead", the 3rd person sing. from am o-i, „I die, am dying", is used for representing the substantive „the dead, the corpse". In a different manner yĕ-ti, a sort of infinitive of the passive voice (see above p. CCCI, f, β) from o-uyé-ne, „I cultivate (the ground)" has become the substantive term for „field". To a certain degree this way of formation, and that mentioned under c) seem to be identical.

e) Substantives are formed by suffixing a k to the verbal root, in order to indicate the purpose, for which, or the means through which, something is done, as, for instance, dańga-k, „something) for seizing, laying hold of", „the handle", from dańga, „take, seize"; yańga-k, „drinking vessel", from yańga, „drink". As another instructive instance of a further development of this principle, we have nyéro-k, „food", although I am not quite sure, whether we have to look upon it as a compound term from nya and ero, meaning „prepared food" or as a passive notion „what to eat, to be eaten", compared nyéro, „the eating".

f) Substantives are, further, derived from verbal notions by adding the syllable da to the verbal root, as, for instance, tăul-da, „the cough", from tăul-ere, „I cough"; and, no doubt, many other terms, the corresponding verbal roots of which I have not become acquainted with, have been formed in the same manner, as, for instance kul-da, „smoke"; tak-da, „clapping of hands"; wérek-da (a synonyme of bŏra), „language, idiom".

g) This very suffix form da may serve me as a means of transition for considering the further development of substantives from other more simple substantives. Thus, we have dăélka-da, „time of sun-shine, daylight, day", from dźolka, „sun-shine".

h) As another means of further developing substantives we have to look upon the termination lik, as, for instance ytsi-lik, „spittle", compared with ytsi, „urine".

i) While now returning to consider other forms of simple substantives, I here take into account the terms borrowed from the Arabic, of which the Măba-language does possess a considerable number. These words, in general, have been accommodated to the spirit of the language by adding to them a final k, not only in these case, when they terminated in a vowel, as, for instance, hille: hille-k; kădi: kădi-k; răi: răye-k, in which instances we might suppose the native idiom to have changed the Arabic final h into a k, but also with those terms, which terminated in a consonant, by inserting in these instances the vowel e or i before the k, as, for instance, nedăăr: nedăăr-ek; dźosăr: dźesăr-ik; merkob: mérkeb-ek; delăl: delăl-ek. But, on the other hand, the fact, that such borrowed foreign terms do not necessarily undergo such a terminal change, is proved by some instances, where nothing is added to the original termination, especially when the word has undergone a slight change; thus, I have harib, „the stranger", from yarib; aram, „the Arab", from ărab.

k) I now proceed, further to consider the joining of two words, placing side by side with the above mentioned nyérek, the term dźa-ńga-k meaning „foot-passenger, foot-soldier", composed from dźa, „foot" and ka, ga, „go" (a-kai, „I go"; gi-ai, „the march"), to which the above mentioned k has been added.

l) A direct and highly illustrative mode of transition to the joining of two substantives

die Klasse zusammengesetzter Nennwörter, welche die Beschäftigung und Werkthätigkeit des Menschen beschreiben, wie bar-tū u-euri-k, „Schuhe Machender", d. h. „Schuster", von dem Zeitwort eurē, anrē, einer anderen abgeleiteten Form von arē, selbstständig gebraucht in der Phrase am tafi aurē (sie S. 121), „ich mache, flechte Matten" [tafi]); bottat u-euri-k, „Lederbüchsen-Macher". Ganz ähnlich ist die Komposition eines Nennwortes als Objekt mit einem derartigen verbalen Nennwort als Subjekt, wenn das letztere mit dem S. CCCII, i) besprochenen nir zusammenhängt, wie z. B. debórko-si k-ir-nir, „Felle der welcher bearbeitet", d. h. „Sattler" (über das der verbalen Form vorgesetzte k werde ich noch anderswo Einiges beibringen); hōt hautā-nir, „Fische Fangender", d. h. „Fischer". Ebenso begegnen wir bei dieser Art der Zusammensetzung der oben (S. CCIV, i, β) als definitive Verbalzeit auffällig befundenen Endung ṅg wieder, die hier nun eine ziemlich entschieden participiale Bedeutung zeigt, jedoch mit Benutzung eines vorgesetzten ti der 3ten Person Sing., nämlich in der Komposition nil (nimmere) t-andá-ṅg, „Indigo (gut) Bearbeitender", d. h. „der Färber", von am a-dal, an-dal, „ich mache". — Abweichend scheinen die Arten der Zusammensetzung der beiden folgenden Ausdrücke zu sein, einmal an Mâšy-Formen erinnernd, borok a-átal, „Pferd zum Rennen", von átala, „laufen" (in der S. 89 angeführten Verbalform wátala gehört w nicht zur Wurzel), das andere Mal mit vorangestelltem Objekt und zur folgenden Kategorie hinüberleitend, nyér telék, „Ess-messer" von dem oben erwähnten nya, „essen", nyó-ro, „das Essen".

m) Ich gehe nun zur einfachen Verbindung zweier Nennwörter über. Das letzterwähnte Kompositum hat uns ein Beispiel gezeigt, dass das Objekt — hier allerdings noch mehr verbal ausgedrückt — dem Subjekt vorangesetzt wird, und das ist nun durchgängig der Fall, wo beide Begriffe ohne weitere äussere Vermittelung an einander gereiht werden. Das schon wir besonders entschieden durchgeführt bei den mit molok („Meister, Herr von") zusammengesetzten Ausdrücken, die den Besitz von, oder die Beschäftigung mit, einer Sache anzeigen, wie z. B. táṅg-melék, „Haus-herr"; koṅgór-melók, „Bart-herr", d. h. „bärtige Person"; borl-molók, „Pferde-herr", d. h. „Reiter"; gó-melék, „Raub-herr", d. h. „Strassenräuber", und so weiter. Ja, bei diesem, so häufig wiederkehrenden, Begriff wird das Objekt sogar in solchen Fällen vorangesetzt, wenn es die im zweiten Falle zu besprechende Art Genitiv-Endung erfüllt, wie z. B. lingá-ṅg melók, „Weges-Herr", d. h. „Führer"; gangá-ṅg molék, „Trommel-Herr", d. h. „Trommler".

n) Bei anderen Verbindungen jedoch wird bei Veränderung der Endung des Objektes das Subjekt vorangestellt, wie z. B. gleich bei dem Namen der hier behandelten Sprache selbst bóra Mábá-ṅg, „Sprache von Maba"; tabg kóbol-aṅg, „Wohnung des Vogels", d. h. „Nest"; elu ber-t-aṅg, „Schweif des Pferdes" (ber-ek); ógedk torrómbe-s-áṅg, „Höcker von Kameelen" (tórrombok Plur. torrómbo-si); mókunór ingdárko-t-íṅg, „Schild von Rhinoceros(-Haut)".

n, α) Neben aṅg haben wir auch noch andere Arten der Abwandelung der Endung des Objektes, zuerst in, als einfachere, jedoch seltenere Form, z. B. liṅgak hillog-in, „der Pfad des Dorfes" (hillok). Viel häufiger jedoch geschieht die Abwandelung vermittelst eines angehängten nak, wie in gdrik nil-nak, „Urne zum Indigo" (nil); górik óndže-nak, „Urne für (zu) Wasser"; bórik sūk-nak, „Platz des Marktes", „Marktplatz"; šókal kāna-nak, „Rücken des Mundes", d. h. „Gaumen"; dolmik wasík-nak, „Zunge des Feuers", d. h. „Flamme", und andere. Aber bei dieser Art der Zusammensetzung geht keineswegs durchgängig das Subjekt dem Objekt vorher, sondern ich habe auch ein Beispiel des Gegentheils in odžílko-nak nyóre, „Nacht-Essen".

Die Bedeutung dieses, wahrscheinlich in sich selbstständig den Ursprung anzeigenden, nak erkennen wir erst recht deutlich aus Fällen, wo es einem längeren Begriffe beigeordnet ist, wie in der Phrase beléd em-bé nak ti, wörtlich „Stadt meine aus ist er", d. h. „mein Landsmann", und noch deutlicher in der längeren Phrase, wo es einer ein Objekt regierenden

is formed by those terms, which characterize the occupation and handicraft of man, as, for instance, bar-tū n-enri-k, verbally „shoes making", i. q. „shoe-maker", from the verb enrē, anrē, another derivative form from arē, and used quite independently by itself in the phrase am tafi aarē (sic p. 121), „I make, weave mats" [tafi]); bottāt n-enri-k, „leather-boxes making", i. q. „the maker of leather-boxes". Very similar is the way of composition in joining a noun (as object) to such a verbal notion (as a subject), in such cases where the nir mentioned p. CCCIII, i) forms an integrant part of the latter, as, for instance, debórko-si k-ir-nir, verbally „leathers he who works", i. q. „saddler" (to the mode of prefixing the k to the verbal form I shall return in another place); hōt hantā-nir, „fish catching", i. q. „fisherman". Further, in this sort of composition we again meet with the termination ńg, which, when found above (p. CCCIV, i, β) as a definite verbal tense, caused us some embarrassment, and which, in this situation, seems rather to bear the character of a participial mood, to which is prefixed the tl of the 3rd person sing., as, for instance the composite term nīl (nímmoro) t-andá-ńg, „he (who) works (a-dal, an-dal, andri-no, „I work") (well) in indigo", i. q. „the dyer". — Different is the mode of composition of the two following terms, on the one hand borok n-atal, „a horse that runs", „a race-horse", from átala, „run" (the w in the verbal form wátala mentioned p. 89, does not belong to the root) and, on the other, the object being placed before the subject, nyór-tolók, „eating-knife", from the above mentioned nya, „eat", nyé-ro, „the eating".

m) In the same manner, as the latter term exhibits an instance of the object being placed before the subject, we see also with regard to the general way of joining two nouns, that, although in general the subject precedes the object, the reverse is the case, where-ever two nouns are simply joined without the means of a particle or an outward change of the form of the object; thus, in the terms composed with mélek, „master (of)", and indicating the possession of, or the occupation with, something, the object constantly precedes this term, as, for instance, táńg-melók, „house-master", i. q. „landlord"; końgór-melók, „beard-master", i. q. „bearded person"; berí-melók, „horse-master", i. q. „horseman"; gā-melók, „robbing master", i. q. „highway-robber", and so on. Nay, this is even the case, when the termination of the object does undergo a slight change, and is placed in the genitive case, as, for instance, lingá-ńg melék, „road- (lingak) master", i. q. „guide"; gangá-ńg melék, „drum (gańga) master".

n) The commoner way, however, in the latter case seems to be, that the subject precedes the object, as, for instance, the name of the language itself which we are treating here bōra Mābá-ńg, „language of Maba", tańg kóbel-ańg, „the house of the bird", i. q. „the nest"; mókunór ingúrko-t-íńg, „shield of rhinoceros (-hide)", and by inserting a consonant between the object and the genitive termination ōlu ber-i-ańg, „tail of horse" (ber-ok); dgeók torrómbo-s-áńg, „bump of camels" (tórrembok, plur. torrómbo-si).

n, α) Besides this more common way of joining two nouns by changing the termination of the form of the object, I now mention some other modes, first by means of adding in to the object, as, for instance, lińgak hílleg-in, „the path of the town" (hillok). I give, further, some instances of such a composition by means of nak, sometimes the subject, at others the object preceding, as, for instance, görik nīl-nak, „urn of (for) indigo" (nīl); görik óndāe-nak, „urn of (for) water"; bórik sūk-nak, „place of market", „market-place"; šōkal kāna-nak, „backside of mouth", i. q. „palate"; delmik wasík-nak, „tongue of fire", i. q. „flame", and others; on the other side, edāílko-nak nyóro, „night's supper".

The real import of this suffix form nak is even more clearly illustrated by such instances, where it is added to a composite notion, as, for instance, in the phrase boléd em-bé nak tí, „town of me (mine) of (from) he is", i. q. „my countryman", and even more clearly in

verbalen Form beigegeben ist, sungok nyū karro-nda-ha nak, wörtlich „Holz Fleisch braten es zu von", d. h. „ein Bratspiess".

a, β) Es ist sehr möglich, dass das eben besprochene nak selbst schon in die oben (S. CCVIII, c) angegebene Kategorie der mit Anfügung eines k gebildeten Wörter fällt, wenn wir es auch nicht gerade als Nennwort bezeichnen können. Denn ganz in derselben Weise, wie nak, finde ich na gebraucht, und zwar bald mit Voranstellung des Subjekts, bald mit derjenigen des Objekts, z. B. dúkkunuk dōm-na, „Strick von Dōm(-Blättern)"; tang sēf-na, „Haus, Scheide des Schwertes"; andererseits dagegen sultān-na tang, „des Sultan's Haus"; súbbo-na giai, „Morgen's-Marsch"; matúk-na kalák, „des Freigelassenen Sohn". Ganz in derselben Weise haben wir zu verstehen nus-na nus, „von der Hälfte die Hälfte", d. h. „ein Viertel" (nus von dem Arabischen نصف).

a, γ) Eine andere Weise, zwei Nennwörter mit einander zu verbinden, besteht in der Benutzung des Wortes kelē. Das war offenbar ursprünglich ein selbstständiges Nennwort und bezeichnete „Art, Gattung", wie wir noch aus folgender Phrase erkennen böra we-nēno nyo kelē to genī, „welcher Art ist ihre Sprache"? Dieses kelē ist nicht zu verwechseln mit dem Nennwort kēlo, „Spiel, Gesang". Auch in dieser Verbindung mit kelē nun wird bald das Subjekt, bald das Objekt vorangestellt. So z. B. habe ich tang nišābok kelē, „Haus von Art des Pfeiles", d. h. „Köcher"; kórayat kelē kolák, „das Haupt (kolák) von Art der Königlichen Sklaven"; dann, mit vorangestelltem Objekt, die zugleich in anderer Beziehung noch einmal zu berücksichtigende Phrase kai áng kelē litto-no, „dieser Leute Angelegenheit".

a, δ) Nun habe ich noch eine andere Weise von dergleichen Verbindung zweier Nennwörter, nämlich vermittelst ná-no, das wahrscheinlich nichts Anderes ist, als das unter a, β) besprochene na, dem ein zurückbeziehendes no angehängt ist, wie wir ein solches dem Subjekte angehängtes und neben dem, die Beziehung schon vollständig ausdrückenden, kelē überflüssiges no in der eben unter a, γ) angeführten Phrase kai áng kelē litto-no haben. Weil erst vermittelst dieser Anhängungsform no das ná-no seine volle Erklärung findet, habe ich seiner Besprechung diesen Platz angewiesen, anstatt es unmittelbar hinter na folgen zu lassen, mit dem es eng zusammenhängt. So habe ich nun giai lēo ná-no, „Marsch zur Nacht" oder „zur Nachtzeit"; kai beldd áng ná-no, „die Leute von" oder „aus dieser Stadt"; und in Verbindung mit dem, oben unter b) besprochenen, auch zur Bezeichnung der Beziehung selbstständig gebrauchten in, litto sūk-le ná-no, „das Geschäft von wegen des Marktes". Vermittelst dieses ná-no haben wir aber auch wol unzweifelhaft die Form der 3ten Person Plur. des possessiven Fürwortes wo-nē-no zu erklären, als entstanden aus wang ná-no, „sie, von ihnen", d. h. „ihr".

6. *Deklination und Mehrheit des Nennwortes.*

a) Die so eben entwickelten verschiedenen Arten der Verbindung zweier Nennwörter stellen zu gleicher Zeit in der Weise, wie das Objekt abgewandelt wird, die Bildung des Genitiv's dar, und führe ich hier noch zur ferneren Beleuchtung desselben folgende Phrase an, wo diese Beziehung in ganz regelrechter Weise, sowol beim Nennwort, als beim Fürwort, ihren Ausdruck findet, nämlich kalák wago-n-fúg tun-dúg tafale, „der Sohn dieses (wago) Vater's (tun) ist gestorben".

b) Dagegen sind die anderen Kasus, so weit mein Material die Beurtheilung gestattet, sehr ungenügend ausgedrückt. Jedoch habe ich Beispiele von Versuchen, das Accusativ-Verhältniss auszudrücken durch die, dem Nennwort oder auch dem Fürwort angehängten Endungen en, ye, ta(?), ge. So habe ich (N. 93 des Vkbl.) bórek-en á-tani, „ich besteige das Pferd", aber gleich daneben bórek fár-aré, „ich treibe das Pferd an", ohne jedwede

a longer phrase, where it is added to a verbal form, ruling an object, suńgok nyū karro-nda-ha nak, verbally „a wood meat roasting it for", i. q. „a spit".

n, β) When I have just spoken of the termination nak as an independent particle of speech, I have here to add, that it seems possible, that it may closely be allied to na, which is used in a very similar manner, nak belonging possibly to the class of words, formed by means of k, and spoken under o). This na is always joined to the object, but in such a manner, that the latter sometimes precedes, at others is placed behind the subject, as, for instance, dúkkunuk dōm-na, „rope from dōm(-leaves)"; tańg séf-na, „house, sheath of sword"; on the other hand, sultān-na tańg, „the sultan's house"; sábbe-na gìai, „morning's march"; matúk-na kalák, „the Royal slaves' chief"; and quite from the same point of view we have to explain the term nus-na nus, „half of half", i. q. „a quarter", nus being the Arabic نصف.

n, γ) Another mode of joining two nouns consists in the employing of the term kolē. This term, no doubt, originally was an independent noun, signifying „species, kind", as we clearly see from the following phrase bōra wo-nō-no nyo kelē to gonī, „of what kind is their language"! This kolō, however, is not to be confounded with the other noun kōlo, meaning „play, song". Now, also in these phrases, which are composed by means of kelē, sometimes the subject, at others the object precedes. Thus, on the one hand, I have tańg nišābek kelē, „cover, kind (matter) of arrow", i. q. „quiver"; kórayat kelē kolák, „chief, headman (kolák) of the kind of Royal slaves"; and further the phrase kai ańg kelē lítto-no, „the affair on account of these people", which I shall have to consider presently from another point of view.

n, δ) Now, I have yet another mode of joining two nouns, viz by means of ná-no, which probably is nothing else but the very na, we have spoken of under n, β), to which a relative no has been added, the same no we have seen employed in the phrase just adduced under n, γ) kai ańg kolō lítto-na, in a rather redundant manner, side by side with kelē, the latter alone being already fully sufficient for expressing that relation. And the circumstance of the ná-no not finding its explanation but by way of this very termination no, is the reason why I have chosen this place for treating of the former, instead of making it to follow closely behind the na, to which it intimately belongs. Thus, I have the phrase gìai lře ná-no, „march of" or „at night, at nighttime"; kai boléd ańg ná-no, „the people of" or „from this town"; and, further, the phrase litto sūk-ln ná-no, „the business on account of the market", the latter showing it used in conjunction with the relative in, spoken of before under b). By means of this ná-no also, I have not the slightest doubt, that we have to explain wo-nō-no, the form of the 3rd person plur. of the possessive pronoun, as being originally wańg ná-no, „they, of them", i. q. „their".

6. *Declination and plural number of the noun.*

a) Three various modes of joining two nouns, in the manner of the flexion, which the object has to undergo, represent at the same time a sort of formation of the genitive-case; and this case, therefore, being already sufficiently illustrated, I here, for further exemplification, adduce only the phrase kalák wago-n-íńg tun-áńg tafaia, „the son of this (wage) father (tun) died", where the form of the flexion has been expressed twice, as well by the change of the noun, as by that of the pronoun.

b) As for the other cases, as far as my material admits of a final judgement, they are very imperfectly expressed. However, I have instances of attempts made by the language to express the relation of the accusative by means of the terminations en, yo, ta(?), go added to the noun, or even to the pronoun. Thus, I have (vebly. p. 93) bérek-en á-tani, „I mount the horse", but, also by, the other phrase bérek fár-aré, „I drive on the horse", without

Kasus-Änderung. In Verbindung mit demselben Zeitwort á-tani habe ich jene Endung en noch zwei Mal, einmal mórkob-en á-tani, „ich besteige das Schiff" (S. 117), dann in der S. 139 aufgeführten, aber hiernach zu verbessernden Phrase bórok móddžug-en i-átane, „das Pferd (der Hengst) besteigt das weibliche (móddžug, mit hinzugedachtem Pferd", d. h. „die Stute"); aber diese Accusativ-Endung en kommt in meinen Phrasen doch auch in Verbindung mit anderen Zeitwörtern vor, wie z. B. sorutl-en ukä, droke-(e)n ukä, „wasche die Hose, wasche das Hemd"; scheint also in ziemlich allgemeinem Gebrauch zu sein.

b, α) Dieselbe willkürliche Anwendung findet bei der Endung ye Statt, wie ich auf einer und derselben Seite (137) die beiden Phrasen habe óso-ye am asko, „ich lege das Samenkorn", mit jener Accusativ-Form und cso kil-aro, „ich messe", d. h. „ich kaufe, Korn", ohne jedwede Änderung der Form des Nennwortes. Bei der häufiger vorkommenden Accusativ-Form vermittelst go fällt, wenn das Nennwort auf k ausgeht, das letztere fort, wie in der Phrase sirre-go (von sirrek) bóro k-in-nerí dâdru, „nimm den Sattel vom Pferde". Dieses selbe go finden wir nun in der auffallenden Phrase hillok mamat-go, „die Stadt, wohin wir gehen", der Verbalform hinzugefügt, anstatt durch die davon direkt abgeleitete lokale Partikel, die wir unten finden werden, besonders ausgedrückt zu sein. Ein Beispiel aber, wo go dagegen eine entschieden ablative Bedeutung hat, kolä-go, „an Grösse", s. unter 7, l, α.

Eine dem demonstrativen Fürwort (ago) angehängte, allerdings uneigentliche, Accusativ-Form ta scheine ich mir in folgender Phrase gefunden zu haben lingah kolák ago-tá mé-tell, „lasst uns diesen grossen Weg verfolgen".

c) Auch von einem gelegentlichen Ablativ vermittelst eines dem Nennwort angehängten nerí, entweder allein, oder in Verbindung mit den Genitiv-Formen in, na, habe ich Beispiele, wie táng-nerí, „von dem Hause"; bórek-in-nerí, „vom Pferde (herab)"; lul-ún-nerí (das u in un wol durch die euphonische Einwirkung des vorhergehenden u, anstatt in), „von Westen her". Durch diese Endung wird aber auch die Zeit, wo etwas geschicht, ausgedrückt, wie glai ïše-ná-nerí, „Marsch zur Nacht-zeit". Auch die Partikel úgdanerí, „woher", S. 27, ist wol sicherlich in dieser Weise zu erklären anstatt gó-nerí, indem dieses go wahrscheinlich dem Zeichen des Accusativ's entspricht, und in Übereinstimmung damit scheint auch gin eine Art von Lokativ anzuzeigen, wie in der Phrase berí-ńg o-gin, „an welchem Orte"?, denn ich glaube kaum, dass ogín oder wogín, „welcher, welches" bedeuten kann. — Als eine verschiedene Form des Ablativ's haben wir wol entschieden anzusehn die Endung nen in der Phrase târiúg-nen móren(?) ávrińga, „vom Schlaf erhebe ich mich".

d) Im Anschluss an diese Formen bemerke ich über die Stellung der Präpositionen im Máha, dass sie zu Postpositionen werden, und als ursprüngliche Substantiv-Begriffe stets eine Abwandelung der Form des Nennwortes verursachen, wie z. B. χéme-nen kulü, „innerhalb des Zeltes", da es eigentlich bedeutet „Leib des Zeltes". So haben wir schon in der oben (S. CCC, ζ, γ) angeführten Phrase nańgan wáńg-nen táka, „um diese zu kaufen", wo es nicht sowol auf das Fürwort „diese", wang, sich zu beziehen scheint, denn es am nächsten steht, als auf den ganzen Begriff der Handlung, dieses nun als wirkliche Genitiv-Form gehabt. Allerdings kommt nun aber diese Anhängungssilbe nun auch alleinstehend als selbständige Präposition vor in der Phrase χeme-nen dal, „lege in's Zelt", mit ganz lokaler Bedeutung.

e) Die Bildung des Plurals geschicht auf ziemlich mannichfaltige Weise, obgleich die Abweichung der Formen eine bedeutende Einschränkung erleiden würde, wenn wir stets auf die ursprüngliche Form des Singulars zurückgehen könnten, da, wie wir schon oben (S. CCVIII, i) gezeigt haben, das Schluss-k in den Endungen ok, ik, uk nicht ursprünglich zu sein scheint. Als Beispiele der Abwerfung dieses k im Plural, während zugleich in den meisten Fällen der

the form of the object undergoing the slightest indication of flexion. However, in connection with the very verb á-tani, I have, besides the instance mentioned, the termination en in two cases, once mórkob-en á-tani, „I mount the boat", „go on board" (p. 117), the other time in the phrase adduced p. 139, but which has to undergo a slight correction in the following manner bórek móddžug-en t-átane, meaning „the horse mounts (covers) the female (móddžug, horse"); and this representation of the accusative case by means of en, in a few instances among my phrases appears also in connection with other verbs, as, for instance, serušl-en uks, droko-(s)e uks, „wash the trowsers, wash the shirt".

b, α) The same arbitrary use applies also to the termination ye, as on one and the same page (vcbly. p. 137) I have the phrases úsu-ye am anke, „I put in the seed", and ese kil-aré, „I measure", or „buy corn", the form of the noun in the latter phrase exhibiting no change whatever. As for the more common form of the accusative case by means of ge, the terminating k of the noun, if such exists, is thrown off, as in the phrase sírro-ge (accusative of sirrok) bóre-gín-nerí dǯóru, „take the saddle from off the horse". And now, in the remarkable phrase billek mamal-ge, „the town where we go", we find this very same ge added to the verbal form, instead of being expressed by the local particle thence derived, of which we shall speak a little further on. An instance, where this termination ge has a decidedly ablative meaning, viz, kolä-ge, „in size, as for size", we shall see further on under 7, 1, α.

A termination ta added to a pronoun (ago, „this"), in order to represent an accusative relation, I have found, I fancy, in the phrase líṅgak kolák age-tá má-toti, „let us follow this large track".

c) I have also a few instances of a certain representation of the ablative case by means of the termination nerí being added to the noun, either alone, or in conjunction with the forms in, na, expressive of the genitive relation, as, for instance, túṅg-erí, „from the house"; bórek-in-nerí, „from off the horse"; lul-én-nerí (the u, instead of i, in un most probably being caused by the euphonical influence of the preceding u), „from the West". But the time also, when something takes place, is expressed by means of this form, as, for instance giai ĭšo-ná-nerí, „march at night". The particle ṅgúnneri also (p. 27), I have no doubt, we have to explain in this manner, it having been originally gó-nerí, the ge most probably being identical with the sign of the accusative case, whence also a sort of locative particle gin seems to be derived, as in the phrase herí-ṅg o-gín, „at what place"?. For I scarcely think, that ogín, or even wogín, by itself may mean „which, what". As another different form of the ablative case, we have, I think, to look upon the termination nen in the phrase täriṅg-nen móren(?) ávriṅga, „I arise from sleep".

d) Following up the preceding observations, I remark with regard to the position of the prepositions in the Mába-idiom, that they become postpositions, and, as being originally substantives themselves, always produce a change in the form of the noun, to which they are joined, as, for instance, χóme-nun kulu, „inside the tent", it meaning originally „body of the tent". Thus, in the phrase already adduced p. CCXCI, f, γ) naṅgan waṅg-nun táka, „in order to buy this", we have met with this form nun as expressing a really genitive relation, although it does not seem to be joined to the pronoun wang exclusively, but rather to the whole notion involved in the phrase. But now, this termination nun occurs also as an independent preposition by itself in the phrase χómo-nun daí, „put into the tent".

e) As for the formation of the plural number, it takes place in a variety of modes, although the latter would certainly be greatly simplified, if we were able always to recur to the original form of the singular, the terminative k in ok, ik, uk, as stated above (p. CCLIX, i), in most cases not being original. As instances of nouns throwing off the k in the plural number,

Vokal eine leichte Veränderung erleidet, führe ich hier an: bérek, „Pferd", Plur. bérig; kánik, „Auge", Plur. káso; mášik, „Mann", Plur. mäso; guränek (von Gurán, s. oben S. LXVIII), „der Tobe", Plur. guräni; kodók, „Berg", Plur. kodö; sañgok, „Baum", Plur. sañgo; kobúk, „Blume, Blüthe", Plur. köbi. Eine grössere Veränderung des Vokallautes erleidet dok, Plur. dáye, „Kuh", obgleich die ursprüngliche Form des Singular's wol daik ist (bei Seetzen daig), wo dann der Plural ganz regelmässig gebildet wäre.

f) Als Beispiele von Wörtern, welche die Endungssilbe ik im Plural abwerfen und dafür tū der Stammsilbe anhängen, führe ich an bór-ik, „Sklave", Plur. bor-tū; mádž-ik, „Sklavin", Plur. madž-tū; kúl-ik, „Grobschmied", Plur. kul-tū; ár-uk, „Eunuch", Plur. ar-tū. — In dieselbe Kategorie fallen nun aber auch, nach dem schon wiederholt wegen der Anhängung der Silbe ik u. s. w. Gesagten, diejenigen Wörter, wo die Plural-Endung tū an die reine Form des Singulars angehängt wird, wie z. B. ossur, „Same", Plur. ossúr-tū; tañg, „Haus, Behältniss", Plur. tañg-tū; dróke, „Hemd, Tobe", Plur. droke-tū. Und nun ist es höchst lehrreich in Bezug auf die der ersten Klasse von Substantiven angehängte Endung auf ok, ik, als ein Thätiges, Lebendes bezeichnend, dass jene andere Klasse, die diesen Zusatz nicht zeigt, ausschliesslich sachliche Nennwörter zu umfassen scheint, bei denen also die Hinzufügung jener Endung nicht nöthig schien.

g) Als Beispiele abweichender Formation gebe ich: koñg, „Person", Plur. kai, „Leute"; múñgulak (eigentlich mun kolák), „Grossvater", Plur. múñgul-dže; koyé, „Ohr", Plur. kondži; ñgoñgo, „Tag", Plur. ñgondžo; hillek, „Dorf", Plur. billéinun (das nun jedoch vielleicht nicht dazu gehörend, sondern ein Genitiv-Verhältniss ausdrückend); kebél, „Vogel", Plur. kebél-nyo; árum, „Araber", Plur. arám-ka; torrembok, „Kameel", Plur. torrémbo-si; dúkunuk, „Strick", Plur. dúkun-si. Daran schliesst sich auch an mándakal, „Ziege", Plur. míndže-sí [*]), da die ursprüngliche Form von mándakal wahrscheinlich mandak lautete. — An dieses sí mit der bestimmten Vertretung der grösseren Anzahl haben wir, glaube ich, die Form der Zeitpartikel abín-dže-sí-(nun anzuschliessen mit der Bedeutung „vor zwei Jahren", im Vergleich und in enger Beziehung zu abin-džón mit der Bedeutung „im vergangenen Jahr", d. h. eigentlich „vor einem Jahr" (die Endung nun scheint genitivisch zu fassen zu sein). Hier will ich anführen, dass Burckhardt von dem oben erwähnten Ausdruck mar, „Stier" eine Pluralform marsha i. e. mar-ša hat, die ich nur auf seine Autorität gebe. — Was dagegen eine zuweilen vorkommende Plural-Endung ša betrifft, wie in bélod, „Dorf", Plur. bélod-ša; férig, „Araberweiler", Plur. forg-ša, so gehört sie nicht eigentlich hierher, da sie dem Arabischen entlehnt ist.

h) Das Geschlecht wird auch in der Mába-Sprache nur sehr unzureichend unterschieden, wie denn die Pronominal- und Verbalformen gar keinen Einfluss desselben zeigen. In Betreff von Menschen sowol als Thieren wird im Allgemeinen das männliche Geschlecht als vorwiegend angenommen und daher nur in solchen Fällen durch Hinzufügung von mar besonders unterschieden, wo die Beziehung zweifelhaft sein kann, wie z. B. bis mar, „männliche Katze, Kater"; bis módžam, „weibliche Katze"; borek allein oder borek mar, „Hengst"; borek módžam, „Stute". Interessant ist es nun, dass dieses mar eigentlich den „Stier" bedeutet, der bei diesen Völkern, wie auch bei vielen anderen, besonders Asiatischen, Völkerschaften das Symbol der Männlichkeit darzustellen scheint, und noch interessanter ist es nun in sprachvergleichender Beziehung, auf welchen Punkt wir unten zurückkommen müssen, dass die Dinka, deren Sprache noch andere Punkte der Verwandtschaft mit dem Mába aufweist,

[*]) Die Pluralform míndže-sí erscheint bei Seetzen in der Form mendschij als Singular, ebenso wie er den Plural džó-sí von džó, džok in der Form djösnik für „Ziege" hat. Allerdings aber hat auch Burckhardt zur Bestätigung des oben in Bezug auf mándakal Gesagten, dass die Endung sí eigentlich nicht zum Worte zu gehören scheint, eine andere Form für „Schaf", nämlich mindage Plur. mandji i. q. mendél.

while at the same time in most cases the vowel does undergo a slight change, I here mention the following: bérek, „horse", plur. béri; kásik, „eye", plur. káse; măšik, „man", plur. măse; gurănek (from Gurán, see above p. LXIX), „the Tódă-man", plur. gurăni; koddk, „mountain", plur. kodō; sañgok, „tree", plur. suñgo; kobúk, „flower, blossom", plur. kōbi. A more considerable change of the vowel appears in dok, „cow", plur. dáyo, although the original form of the singular seems to have been daik (daig with Seetzen).

f) As instances of nouns, which in the plural number throw off the termination ik, and instead add the syllable tū to the root, I mention bór-ik, „slave", plur. bor-tū; mádž-ik, „female slave", plur. madž-tū; kúl-ik, „blacksmith", plur. kul-tū; ár-ak, „eunuch", plur. ar-tū. But to the same category, after what I have said repeatedly with regard to the adding of the syllable ak, ik etc. to the root, also those nouns do belong, in which the termination tū, characteristic of the plural number, is joined to the very form of the singular, as, for instance, ossur, „seed", plur. ossúr-tū; tañg, „house, cover", plur. tañg-tū; dráko, „shirt, tobe", plur. dróko-tū. And now, it is not without interest to remark, that the latter class of nouns, which is without this termination in k, appears to contain almost exclusively nouns of a neutral character, while the former seems rather to embrace such ones, where, if not always a personal character, at least life and activity are more distinctly expressed.

g) As instances of a different formation I here give the following: kañg, „person", plur. kai, „people"; mángulak (originally mun kolák), „grandfather", plur. mángul-dže; koyí, „ear", plur. koudži; ñgoñgo, „day", plur. ñgondžo; billek, „village", plur. billélnun (the nun, however, perhaps not belonging to the form itself, but rather expressive of a genitive relation); kebél, „bird", plur. kebél-nyo; áram, „Arab", plur. arám-ka; tórrembok, „camel", plur. torrómbo-si; dúkuunk, „rope", plur. dúkun-si. And to these we may join mándakal, „sheep", plur. míndže-si[1]), the original form of mándakal being probably mandak. — To this termination si, involving the distinct notion of a larger number, we have, I think, also to refer the form of the term abíu-dže-si-(nun) with the meaning „two years ago", if considered in relation to the term abia-džén with the meaning „last year", to be understood as a singular number, and meaning „one year ago"; as for the termination nun, it seems to be understood as a sort of genitive case. I here also mention, that of the term mar, „bull", in Burckhardt's list appears a plural form marsha i. q. mar-ša. — With regard to a plural form in šn, occurring in some terms, as, for instance, in the term béled, „village", plur. béled-šn; fúrig, „a hamlet of Arabs", plur. forg-šn, it does not properly belong to the Mába-language, as being merely borrowed from the Arabic.

h) As for the gender, it is not expressed in the Mába-language but very insufficiently, just as we have seen, that neither the pronoun, nor the verb exhibits any distinction of that kind. As well with regard to human beings as to animals, the male sex, in general, is to be presupposed, if nothing is added, the term mar being only added in such cases, where the relation may be doubtful, as, for instance, bis mar, „male cat"; bis méžam, „female cat"; berek or berek mar, „(entire) horse"; berek méžam, „mare". Now, it is very interesting to observe, that the term mar originally means „bull", an animal which, as well with the people of this region as with some Asiatic tribes, serves as a symbol of manliness; and it is a circumstance of still greater interest, when we observe, that the Dinka on the white Nile, a tribe the language of which, as we shall see further on, exhibits also other points of linguistical relationship with the Mába, call the large-sized sacred bull, which they

[1]) This plural form míndže-si in Seetzen's Collection appears under the form mendschij, as the form of the singular, just as he gives the plural form djêssih i. q. dže-si, from dža, džek, as meaning „goat" in the singular number. I have to remark, however, that Burckhardt, in confirmation of what I have said in the text with regard to mándakal, has another form for „sheep", viz mindage plur. mandji i. q. mandži.

die grossen buntscheckigen Stiere, die sie als heilige Thiere verehren, mudr nennen [1]). Jedoch hat die Māba-Sprache auch einige besondere Ausdrücke zur Unterscheidung männlicher und weiblicher Individuen derselben Gattung, wie z. B. mun, tun, „Vater" im Vergleich zu min, tin, „Mutter", obgleich der erstere Ausdruck später durch den vielen Sprachen gemeinsamen, aber dem Māba ursprünglich wol ganz fremden, Ausdruck ba mehr verdrängt wurde und nur gelegentlich, wie z. B. in dem zusammengesetzten Ausdruck mṓṅgulak i. e. mun kolák, „Grossvater" (wörtlich „grosser Vater") sich erhalten hat, welche Form auffallender Weise selbst in Seetzen's Liste erscheint, obgleich er vereinzelt nur die Form tun, nicht mun kennt; bṓrik, „männlicher) Sklave"; mádžik, als Repräsentant des Weiblichen (mōdžam) überhaupt, und als leibhaftiger Beweis des uralten Bestehens der Sklaverei bei diesen Völkern, „die Sklavin".

7. *Das Eigenschaftswort.*

Ich wende mich nun zur Betrachtung des Eigenschaftswortes.

a) Indem ich hier an Dasjenige anschliesse, was ich oben (S. CCCIV) über verbale Formen mit to-rō bemerkt habe, schicke ich folgende allgemeine Bemerkung voraus. Bei dem bloss äusserlichen Abfragen der Bestandtheile einer illiterirten Sprache, wie diese Binnen-Afrikanischen sind, wird es im Allgemeinen äusserst schwer sein, die reine Form des Eigenschaftswortes zu erhalten, noch viel schwieriger, als die übrigen Redetheile; sondern es ist unumgänglich nöthig, dieselben aus längeren Phrasen zu abstrahiren, wo der verbale Fluss der Rede schon anderweitig seine lebendige Vertretung findet. Fragt man dagegen einen einfachen Menschen unabhängig nach einem Eigenschaftswort in seiner Sprache, wie „gut, schön, fern" u. s. w., so wird und kann er in vielen Fällen das gar nicht so einfach geben, sondern er wird es in eine verbale Form kleiden und wird sagen „ist gut, ist schön, ist fern". Manche Beispiele dieser Erscheinung haben wir schon bei den anderen, in meiner Sammlung vertretenen Sprachen beobachtet, z. B. beim Fulfúlde S. CLXII, und werde ich im Vokabular bei den einzelnen Ausdrücken stets darauf zurückkommen müssen. Nun gibt es aber allerdings auch eben von den verbalen, besonders den participialen Formen, abgeleitete componirte Adjektivformen, die an beiden Charakteren Theil zu haben scheinen und die Entscheidung in dieser Beziehung oft zweifelhaft lassen.

b) In Übereinstimmung mit diesen beiden Bemerkungen nun finden wir in Seetzen's Vokabular der Mobba- oder Māba-Sprache fast alle Eigenschaftswörter auf torib ausgehen, ja Seetzen gibt sogar zwei dieser Formen dortory i. e. dór-te-ri und mallery i. e. mál-te-ri als Nennwörter für „Donner" und „Blitz"; diese Endung te-ri aber ist nichts als eben jene verbale Form, die ich oben (S. CCCIV) besprochen und an die ich den Anfang dieses Paragraphen anzuknüpfen für richtig gehalten habe; wenigstens ist es eine ganz eng sich daran schliessende Form, indem hier allerdings ein Übergang in die Dauer des Adjektivs Statt findet, etwa wie im Deutschen „lebend" und „lebendig". So entspricht denn Seetzen's leterib, „bitter" oder vielmehr „bitter seiend, bitterlich", meinem laie; sein kamtorib, „sauer", meinem kāma. Ein sehr belehrendes Beispiel dieser Formen haben wir an dem schon oben (S. CCCIV, i, a) angeführten yū-te-ri, „beweglich, lebendig seiend", im Vergleich mit endăi) yū-te-rā, „das Wasser) fliesst, bewegt sich". Auch ich werde gezwungen sein, manche Eigenschaftswörter mit dieser mehr verbalen Endung zu geben, erstlich, weil wir diese Formen auch wirklich als zum Theil adjektivisch betrachten können, zweitens, weil ohne bestimmten Anhalt es nicht gerathen wäre, in den einzelnen Fällen den Versuch zu machen, die eigentliche Form abzulösen, da der Endvokal der letzteren gewöhnlich verloren gegangen ist und der Vokal der Wurzelsilbe häufig eine Veränderung erleidet. So macht bengo, „warm", bṓṅg-te-rō; kéra, „kalt", kír-te-rō.

[1]) Dr. Hartmann in der Zeitschrift für Erdkunde, Th. XIV, S. 39.

are worshipping, by this very name, under the form **mudr**[*]). The Mába-language, however, possesses likewise a few particular terms for distinguishing male and female individuals of the same class, as, for instance, **mun**, **tun**, „father", compared with **min**, **tia**, „mother", although the former term, in the course of time, has been superseded by **ba**, the term common to a great many languages, and has only been preserved occasionally, as, for instance, in the composite term **múñgulak**, i. e. **mun kolák**, mentioned above as meaning „grand-father", a term the more interesting, as it is given even by Seetzen, although he remained unacquainted with the simple form **mun** for „father"; **bórik**, „male slave", **mádžik**, „female slave"; the latter term being particularly remarkable, as it is evidently nothing but a mere personal form of **môdžum**, the general term for „female", and clearly serves to show the very ancient existence of slavery in those Regions, while **bórik** reminds me of **bóro** in Songai meaning „man".

7. *The adjective.*

I now proceed to investigate and analyse the character of the adjective.

a) While first of all referring to what I have said above (p. CCCV), with regard to verbal forms terminating in **te-re**, I introduce my individual observations on this paragraph with a general Remark. If, on the whole, it is very difficult to obtain the pure forms of words of an illiterate language by simply interrogating an individual of such a tribe, this difficulty touches in a yet greater degree the adjective, which can only be elicited from longer phrases, where the verbal forms of the speech have already found their full representation. But, if you ask an individual of a simple state of mind independently for an adjective in his own language, such as „good, fine, far", and so on, he in many cases neither will, nor can express such a term by a corresponding independent form, but will say „is fine", „is good", „is far". Several instances illustrative of this statement have already occurred to us with regard to other languages represented in my Collection, as, for instance, with regard to the Fulfúlde p. CLXIII; and I shall have to return to it, when speaking of each single term in the relative portion of my Vocabulary. But now, on the other hand, there are also composite adjectives, derived from verbal, and especially participial forms, which seem to partake somewhat of both characters, of that of the verb as well, as of that of the adjective.

b) Now, it is in perfect harmony with these two remarks, that in Seetzen's Vocabulary of the Mobba- or Mába-language we find almost the whole of the adjectives terminating in **terih**, i. e. **te-ri**; nay, Seetzen even gives two of these forms, viz **durtery** i. q. **dúr-teri** and **maltory**, i. q. **mál-tori**, as substantives with the meaning „thunder", and „lightning". But this termination **te-ri** is identical with, or at least closely allied to, the verbal form **te-ré**, which I have treated p. CCCV, and from which I have consequently chosen to take my start in the inquiry of this paragraph. Thus, **leterih** in Seetzen's list with the meaning „bitter", or rather „being bitter, bitterly", corresponds to my form **luia**; his **kamterih** „sour", to my **káma**. A very instructive instance of these forms, to which I have already called the attention on a former occasion (p. CCCV, i, *a*), is exhibited by **yū-te-ri**, „being alive, moving", therefore „lively", in comparison with, and in relation to, the strictly verbal form **ondii) yū-te-rē**, „the water) is moving, flowing". And I myself shall be obliged, to give several adjectives with this verbal termination, first as we may look upon these forms as really partaking some what of the character of adjectives, secondly because it is not advisable, without some unmistakeable point as a guide, to make the attempt at separating the original and simple form of each adjective, the terminating vowel being in general lost, while the vowel of the root often has to undergo a change. Thus, while from **boñgo**, „warm", the composite form **bóñg-te-rē** has been derived, from **kóra**, „cold", we have **kír-te-rē**.

*) See Dr. Hartmann in the Journal of the Berlin Geogr. Soc., „Zeitschrift für Erdkunde", v. XIV, p. 39.

b) Ganz dieselbe Erscheinung finden wir nun bei der einfacheren Endung des Eigenschaftswortes auf te und ti. Die Endung te fanden wir schon (S. CCC, f, δ) bei dem Infinitiv, und mit einem vorhergehenden langen Vokal (ö) bei dem Particip Passivi (S. CCCII, g, β); hier will ich aber zuerst die letztere besprechen, weil wir die verbale Form ti schon bei der Bildung der Nennwörter S. CCCVI besprachen. So wie wir da nun aber y ö-ti fanden mit der passiven Bedeutung „bebaut, beackert", daher „Feld", in ähnlicher Weise begegnen wir hier dem Ausdruck sö-ti, „bewahrheitet", dann jedoch, in weiterer Entwickelung, mit der scheinbar mehr aktiven Bedeutung „wahr seiend, aufrichtig", von der Wurzel se, sa [1]), woraus das entsprechende negative Adjektiv to-sö, „falsch, unwahr" und mit Hülfe eines negativen na (vielleicht ne-a) und einem angehängten k das persönliche Nennwort na-sö-k gebildet ist „der nicht Wahrhaftige", „der Lügner". (Vergleiche zu dieser negativen Form na-(a)lák-te, „untüchtig, träge", von alák, „thätig, tüchtig".)

Ganz dasselbe ti, wie in sö-ti, habe ich in der Phrase ondži nyïli-ti, „Wasser wenig seiend", d. h. „leichter Regen", so wie in dem anderen umschreibenden Begriff wäng lollo-ti, „diese dunkel seiend", d. h. „Dunkelheit".

c) Was nun die adjektive Endung te betrifft, wovon wir unter b) ein Beispiel in na-(a)lák-te gefunden haben, und die sich ganz der dritten Person Sing. des persönlichen Fürwortes nähert, so finde ich sie in meinem Vokabular nur selten einer noch ruhenden, so zu sagen adverbialen, Wurzel angehängt, wie in ser-te, „gerade seiend", von ser, „gerade aus", und ähnlich scheint die Bildung von toká-toká-te, „eins, eins seiend", d. h. „verschieden, mannichfaltig", von tok, „ein"; aber im Plural scheint das te verloren zu gehn, da ich da toké-toké-ye habe. In den meisten Fällen jedoch finden wir die Endung te einem Worte angehängt, das schon an sich eine volle Adjektivform besitzt, wie die weiter unten zu besprechenden Formen nímere-k, „gut" (nímerék-te); nískori-k, „spasshaft, scherzhaft" (nískorík-te), so wie einer hübschen Anzahl dem Arabischen erborgter, schon an sich selbstständiger, Adjektivformen, wie fáhol, „tüchtig" in fáhol-te; fahim, „verständig" in fáhom-te; adžob, „wunderbar" in ádžeb-te; korim, „grossmüthig", in kórok-te verwandelt, das vor dem Zusatz des te schon das einheimische Schluss-k erhalten hatte. Bei der, dem positiven fáhom-te entsprechenden, Negativ-Form fahom-tó-r(e)-ondĕ, „unverständig", finden wir sogar die andere noch pleonastischere Form mit te-re angewandt, ganz entsprechend dem negativen yar-tó-r(e)-endĕ, „nicht süss", d. h. „sauer". — Am deutlichsten erkennen wir die eigenthümliche Beziehung des te da, wo sie der S. CCCII, i, α) besprochenen verbalen Form nir, „er, sie, es macht", angesetzt ist, wie in dem componirten Ausdruck tińg-tińg-nir-te, wörtlich „Eklat macht, seiend" oder „Eklat machend", d. i. „ausserordentlich".

d) Ich gehe nun zur Adjektivbildung vermittelst tá-ne über und zu den daraus nur leicht veränderten Formen te-nä, te-nö. Auch diese Formen, die besonders dazu dienen, einen Besitz anzuzeigen, habe ich schon oben (S. CCCII, l, β) als eigentlich verbal bezeichnet, indem sie nur im Gebrauch selbst eine adjektivische Bedeutung erhalten zu haben scheinen. Sehr belehrend in dieser Hinsicht ist der Vergleich der beiden Phrasen, auf der einen Seite kolï tá-ne in Bezug auf die Eigenschaft von Bäumen, Äckern u. s. w., wo kolï als Objekt erscheint, „Früchte giebt es, sind da", d. h. „fruchtbar", auf der anderen kolï nímere tá-ne, wo kolï als Subjekt

[1]) Zur näheren Kennzeichnung der Wurzel sä führe ich hier noch die Phrase sa em ed yedlĭ e-z-sä-endĕ, wörtlich „ich [ob es] wahr (sä) oder falsch [sei] weiss (ed) ich nicht", d. h. „ich bezweifle es".

b) The very same observation we may make with regard to the more simple termination of the adjective in te, ti, the former of which as yet we have not found but in the form of the infinitive (p. CCCI, f, δ), and, joined to a long vowel, ē, in that of the participle of the passive voice (p. CCCIII, g, β). Leaving this, therefore, to the following paragraph, I here shall first treat of the latter, viz the verbal form ti which has already been spoken of p. CCCVII in connection with the formation of the noun. But, just as we have found there the term yē-ti with the passive meaning „cultivated", therefore „cultivated ground, field", in a similar manner we meet here with the term só-ti, meaning originally „verified", but, in a further development, conveying the rather seemingly active meaning „being true, sincere", from the root so, sa [¹]), whence the corresponding negative adjective te-sō has been formed with the meaning „untrue", „false", and by means of a negative particle na (no-a?) in connection with a k attached to its end, the term na-sō-k, „he who is not true", „the liar", with which latter we may compare the term na-(a)lák-te, „un-active", i. q. „lazy", from alák, „active, energetic".

The very same termination ti, which we have found in sé-ti, I have also in the phrase endši nyīli-ti, „water being few, little", i. q. „light rain", as well as wáñg lolte-ti, „this being dark", i. q. „darkness".

c) Now, as for the adjective termination te, an instance of which we have just seen under b) in na-(a)lák-te, and which closely approaches the 3rd person sing. of the personal pronoun, I have found it in my Vocabulary rather rarely joined to a quiescent root, or to a sort of adverb, as, for instance, in ser-te, „being straight", from ser, „straight on"; and a similar formation appears in the adjective term teká-teká-te, „being one, one", i. q. „different, manifold", from tek, „one"; but in the plural number this termination te seems to be lost, I having as plural form only teké-teké-ye. But in most cases we find the termination te joined to a word, which by itself has already a full adjective form. Thus, from the adjective form nímere-k, to be spoken of further on, I have nímerák-te, „goodly"; from níekeri-k, „playful", níekerík-te, „jocose"; and in the same manner those adjective terms, which have been borrowed from the Arabic, are accommodated to the spirit of the Māba-language, as fāhel, „energetic, active" is changed into fáhel-te; fahím, „intelligent" into fáhem-te; adžeb, „wonderful" into ádžeb-te; korím, „generous" into kérek-te, the latter, besides the rather verbal form te, having already received the purely adjective termination k. And now, as an instance of a further change, I here adduce the negative form of fáhem-te, viz fahem-té-r(e)-endē, „wanting of intelligence, imprudent", where we meet with the other yet more pleonastic form by means of te-re, exactly corresponding to the negative form yaw-té-r(e)-endé, „not sweet", i. q. „sour". — The peculiar character and nature of the te appears most clearly from such composite terms, where it has been joined to the verbal form nir, „it makes, renders", spoken of p. CCCIII, l, α), as, for instance, in the composite term tiñg-tiñg-nír-te, verbally „what (it) causes being", i. q. „extraordinary".

d) I now proceed to treat of the formation of the adjective by means of tá-ne, and the forms te-nē, te-nē thence derived by a slight change. Also these very forms, which serve especially the purpose of indicating some kind of possession, I have characterised above, p. CCCIII, l, β) as being properly of a verbal character, they seeming to have obtained an adjective notion merely through popular use. In this respect we have a rather instructive instance in the form exhibited by the two phrases, on the one side koli tá-ne with regard to the property of trees, fields, and so on, where koli appears in the character of an object, „fruits there are",

---

[¹]) For a clearer knowledge of the root sō, I here adduce the phrase am sō ye dēē a-n-sá-endē, meaning verbally „whether (it be) true (sō), or false (dēē), I do not know" (sa).

auftritt mit der Bedeutung „die Frucht ist gut", d. h. „sie ist reif". So scheinen nun auch die anderen, dermassen gebildeten Formen aufzufassen zu sein, obgleich ihre endgültige Bedeutung dem „haben, besitzen" entspricht. So heisst morū te-nā, „Schmutz ist da" = „Schmutz habend, schmutzig"; kang) mušóng tá-ne, „Person), Frau ist da" = „eine Frau besitzend", „verheirathet"; kańg) māli nolt tá-ne, „Person), Besitz viel ist da", d. h. „wohlhabend, reich"; hillek) kai nolt tá-ne, „Stadt), Leute viel gibt es", d. h. „volkreich"; mušóng) tábuk-in alák te-nē, „Frau), Leib von thätig ist", d. h. „schwanger". Obgleich also diese Form te-né der pronominalen Form der 3ten Person in te-né-no sich äusserlich nahe anschliesst, ist sie doch grundverschieden von ihr. — Auch unter den Phrasen werden wir einem sehr interessanten Beispiel begegnen, wo selbst die Präposition tal, „auf, über" durch eine solche Verbindung mit te-nā vollständig von dem Nennwort, zu dem sie gehört, abgelöst und zu einem verbalen Begriff, „oben sein", geworden ist.

e) Die, diesen positiven Formen tá-ne, te-nā, te-né, entsprechende negative Form ist tambai (das taubeij in Seetzen's Vokabular), d. h. „ist nicht da, gibt nicht", und sie wird in ganz derselben Weise benutzt, den Mangel an einer Sache anzuzeigen, wie tá-ne den Besitz anzeigt, also kańg) mušóng tambai, „Person), Frau ist nicht da, fehlt (ihm)", d. h. „unverheirathet", und eben so haben wir die Phrase zu erklären wańg-in (sie „von diesem", Genitiv von wańg, während mańgin S. 123 des Vokabular's verdruckt ist) faidok tambai, „von diesem Nutzen ist nicht da, fehlt", d. h. „diese ist nutzlos", und das Gegenstück zu wańg-in faidok tá-ne, „von diesem ist Nutzen da, diese ist nützlich".

Bemerkung 1): Dass diese Form tambai jedoch ursprünglich einen rein verbalen Charakter hat, erkennen wir aus ihren weiter unten (S. CCXXX) zu besprechenden verwandtschaftlichen Berührungen; zu beachten ist vielleicht, dass die negative Form zu der positiv verbalen Form kolt nímere tá-ne, „die Frucht ist reif", „die reife Frucht", nicht heisst kolt nímere tambai, sondern kolt nímere tá-endō.

Bemerkung 2): Anstatt der Form tambai habe ich auch ein Beispiel einer Form nambai, mit n als Anfangskonsonanten, in Verbindung mit dem Plural des Nennwortes, nämlich kańg) bar-tū nambai, „Person), Schuhe fehlen (ihr", d. h. „baarfuss". Diese Form scheint richtig zu sein; dagegen bezweifle ich, ob dasselbe von manbai gesagt werden kann, das in meinem Material in der Phrase lalal manbai erscheint, „Ermüdung gibt es nicht"; jedenfalls könnte es wol nicht bedeuten „ich bin nicht ermüdet", sondern „wir sind nicht ermüdet". — Auch der Ausdruck bétor-ambia, „umsonst, vergeblich", wo wir nun diese Form abgelöst von ihrem pronominalen Vorschlag, t, m, n, haben, hängt augenscheinlich mit dieser negativen Form zusammen, und scheint die wirkliche Wurzel anzudeuten.

Bemerkung 3): In ähnlichem Sinne haben wir nun auch wol aufzufassen die beiden zusammengesetzten negativen Eigenschaftswörter endāi-andot, eigentlich „welchem) Wasser fehlt", d. h. „durstig", und völlig analog a-dāō-andot, „welchem) Speise fehlt", d. h. „hungrig".

f) Nachdem ich nun so, a posteriori ausgehend, die uneigentlichen und mannichfach componirten Adjektivformen beseitigt habe, unterwerfe ich die eigentlichen und ursprünglichen Formen einer kurzen Betrachtung. Als interessantes Beispiel der einfachen Bildung des Eigenschaftswortes aus leicht erkennbarer Wurzel gebe ich kolák, „gross", das wol unzweifelhaft von derselben Wurzel abgeleitet ist, wie nolt, „viel", indem ich die beiden Wörter in analytischer Weise schreibe k-olá-k, „der gross ist" und n(e)-olt, „was gross, viel ist". Und nun erlangen wir ein weiteres, höchst belehrendes Licht über adjektive Wortbildung dadurch, dass wir dem positiven kolák gegenüber das negative kaldk haben, d. i. eigentlich k-a-old-k, mit der Bedeutung „nicht gross, nicht alt", d. h. „klein, jung", wie wir von dem

i. q. „fertile", on the other side, the phrase koll afmoro tá-ne, where koll appears as subject, meaning „the fruit is good", i. q. „is ripe". But I have to observe, that in English the true character of the phrase is less perspicuous, than in German. From the same point of view we have also to explain, I think, the other phrases formed in a similar manner, although their final notion means „possessing, having". Thus mora te-nā means first „dirt is there", consequently „dirty"; kaṅg) muňóng tá-ne, „person) wife is there", consequently „having a wife", „married"; kaṅg) māli noll tá-ne, „person) property much is there", i. q. „having much property, wealthy"; hilleh) kai noll tá-ne, „town) people many there are", i. q. „populous"; muňóng) tábuk-in alák te-nā, „woman) womb her there is labour", i. q. „pregnant, with child". Although this form te-nō, therefore, in outward appearance closely resembles the pronominal form te-ne-no, yet its intrinsic character and derivation is totally different from the latter. — Also with regard to the preposition tal, „on, above", we are to meet among my phrases with a very interesting instance, where, by means of such a connection with te-nā, it has been separated entirely from the noun, to which it belonged, and has become an independent verbal notion.

e) The negative form, corresponding to these positive ones tá-ne, te-nā, te-nō is tambai (written tanbeij in Seetzen's vocabulary), and meaning „there is not, is wanting", it being used in exactly the same manner for indicating the want of something, as tá-ne is used to indicate a possession. Thus, we have kaṅg) muňóng tambai, „person) wife there is not", „is wanting", i. q. „having no wife", „not married"; and thus also we have to explain the phrase waṅg-in (sic, „of this", genitive case of waṅg, maṅgin vebiry. p. 123 being a misprint) faidek tambai, „of this there is no profit", i. q. „this is useless", and the reverse of waṅg-in faidek tá-ne, „of this there is profit", i. q. „this is useful".

Remark I): That this form tambai originally does possess a purely verbal character, we see from the related forms in other languages, which I shall mention further on (p. CCXXXI); we have to remark, however, that the negative form corresponding to koll afmoro tá-ne, „the fruit is ripe", is not koll afmoro tambai, but koll afmoro tá-nadē.

Remark II): Instead of tambai I have also an instance of the form sambai, commencing by an s, in connection with the plural number of the noun, viz kaṅg) bar-tū sambai, „a person) shoes are wanting (him", i. q. „barefooted". But, while this form seems to be all right, I rather doubt, whether the same can be said of mambai, which appears in the phrase lalal manbai, „fatigue there is not", at all events, I am sure, it cannot mean „I am not tired", but rather we are not tired, the m, me representing the 1st person plur. — Also the form bóter-ambes, „in vain" appears to be connected with this negative term, while pointing out its real root amb.

Remark III): In a similar sense we have, I think, to look upon the two analogously formed, composite negative adjectives cadži-sadei, meaning properly „to whom) water is wanting", i. q. „thirsty", and a-džō-sadei, „whom) food is wanting", i. q. „hungry".

f) After having thus, by proceeding a posteriori, removed the rather improper and composite adjective forms, I now shall subject to a short inquiry the proper and original forms of the adjective.

As an interesting instance of the simple formation of the adjective from an unmistakeable root I give kolák, „great", which, there can be no doubt, has been derived from the same root, as noll, „much", these two words from my analytical point of view having to be written k-olá-k, „he who is great", and n(e)-oll, „what is great, much". And now, a further and most instructive light is shed over this formation of adjectives, when we consider the negative form kalák (properly k-a-olá-k, „he who is not old, not great", consequently „young, small", in relation to, and opposed to kolák, „great, old". Thus, by means

Neutrum noll das in anderer Weise gebildete Negativ nyllik haben, d. h. eigentlich ne-yl-oll-k, „was nicht gross, nicht viel ist", d. h. „gering". Nicht zu verwechseln mit kalák ist kálak, „Gott", im Für kalge. — Eine weitere Ableitung von kalák, „klein" ist dá-kalák, „kurz, niedrig".

f, α) Ein anderes, belehrendes Beispiel von der Bildung der Eigenschaftswörter ist das schon oben erwähnte niskerik, d. h. ne-iskeri-k, „scherzhaft", in weiterer, verbal-adjektivischer, unter c) besprochener, Entwickelung niskerik-te, „scherzhaft, lustig", von am áskeri, „ich liebe, scherze", mit der negativen, höchst merkwürdig componirten, aber deutlich an das negative endó (S. CCXCVIII, d) und die oben unter f, Bemerkung 3. erwähnte negative Form nodot sich eng anschliessenden, Form n-isker-endá-k-te, „nicht scherzhaft seiend", d. h. „ernst".

Bemerkung: Die mir bekannt gewordenen negativen Eigenschaftswörter entsprechen in ihrer Fortbildung keineswegs immer den ihnen der Bedeutung nach entsprechenden positiven Formen, sondern sind oft in ganz anderer Weise gebildet und setzen andere, mir nicht bekannt gewordene oder vielleicht selbst gar nicht einmal übliche positive Formen voraus. So habe ich zu dem, in einfachster, nach dem besprochenen Beispiel von kolák, bildender Weise, geformten positiven Eigenschaftswort k-omól-ok, „stark", das von der verbal-adjektiven Form abgeleitete k-omól-té-r(e)-endó, „nicht stark seiend", d. h. „schwach".

g) Eine blosse äusserliche, unorganische Klasse von Eigenschaftswörtern, die wir nach dem allgemeinen Charakter halb-barbarischer Sprachen überhaupt, gerade bei mehreren Sprachen meiner Sammlung stark vertreten gefunden haben, wird gebildet durch Wiederholung der Anfangssilbe eines substantivischen Begriffes, wie z. B. fa-fáda, „dünn, spärlich" (vom Baumbestande, Walde u. s. w.), sa-sála, „unfruchtbar, wüst" (vom Lande).

h) Zum Schluss der Besprechung der Bildung von Eigenschaftswörtern erwähne ich hier noch einmal in Kürze die mit melek, „Herr von", „im Besitze von", zusammengesetzten, obgleich ich diese Komposita ihres selbstständigen, substantivischen Gebrauchs halber schon bei Besprechung des Nennwortes S. CCCX berücksichtigen musste. Als seiner eigenthümlichen Zusammensetzung wegen mehr hierher gehörend erwähne ich noch besonders an dieser Stelle das umschreibende Adjektiv „gebirgig", als Prädikat einer Gegend (barik), kodó-noll-melék, wörtlich „Berge viele besitzend".

i) Was nun Stellung und Endung des Adjektiv's betrifft in seiner Beziehung zu dem von ihm charakterisirten Nennwort, so geht letzteres überall voran, scheint aber die Ausgangsformel des ersteren nur wenig zu beeinflussen, wie neben den, durch innere, selbstständige Bildung, nicht äussere Accommodation, in ihren Endungen übereinstimmenden seck gedík, „Mond neuer", d. h. „Neumond"; seck kolák, „Mond grosser", d. h. „Vollmond", folgende Beispiele zeigen, sunge faféda, „Bäume spärliche", d. h. „lichter Wald"; kodäde sásala, „Land wüst", d. h. „wüste Gegend".

k) Die Mehrheit scheint bei dem Eigenschaftswort nach dem mir vorliegenden Material so gut wie gar nicht ausgedrückt zu werden; denn munkúldže, der Plural von mánkolak, gehört nur uneigentlich hierher, obgleich das Wort ursprünglich aus einem Nennwort man und einem Adjektiv kolák besteht, da das Kompositum zu einem einigen, substantivischen Begriffe ganz verwachsen ist, weshalb ich gewiss mit Recht die Pluralform munkúldže den oben (S. CCCXVI, g) erwähnten Pluralformen des Nennwortes beigezählt habe.

l) Was die Vergleichungsgrade des Eigenschaftswortes betrifft, so können wir nach dem allgemeinen Stande der Entwickelung dieser Sprachen uns nicht darüber wundern, dass sie auch im Mába nur in höchst unvollständiger Weise zum Ausdruck kommen. Zumal erhält der Komparativ seine Bezeichnung nur durch ein besonders hervorgehobenes, demonstratives Hinweisen auf den Gegenstand, der den anderen in irgend einer Beziehung über-

of another negative form, from the neutral positive form noll, „much", we have the negative form nyllik, properly ne-yl-oll-k, „what is not great, not much", i. q. „scanty". A further derivative adjective form from kaldk, „small, little" is dá-kaldk, „short, low".

f, a) Another instructive instance of the formation of the adjective is the above mentioned nískerik, i. q. ne-ískeri-k, „playful", and in a further development nískerikte, „jocose", from am iskeri, „I do laugh, play", with the corresponding negative form n-isker-andá-k-te, „not being jocose", i. q. „morose", a form composed in a very remarkable manner by means of the negative form anda placed between the verbal root and the termination of the adjective, for anda no doubt is closely related to the verbal negative form endē mentioned above p. CCXCIX, d), as well as to andol mentioned under f, Remark III.

Remark: The negative forms of the adjectives, as far as they have become known to me, are by no means always derived from those positive forms in my Collection, to which they correspond, but are very often derived in a totally different manner from other forms, which either have not become known to me, or which are now not used at all. Thus, as the corresponding negative form of the simple positive form k-omól-ok, „strong", formed after the example of kolák, I have nothing but k-omól-lé-r(e)-endē, „not being strong", i. q. „weak".

g) Another class of adjectives of a rather unorganical character, but of which, in conformity with the general character of halfbarbarous languages we find rather numerous instances in my Collection, comprises such adjective terms as are formed by repeating the first syllable of a substantival notion, as, for instance, fa-fáda, „thin, scanty" (used of trees, forest etc.), sa-sála, „sterile, desert", said of a country.

h) In conclusion of this inquiry into the formation of the adjective in the Mába-language I here once more shortly mention the class of adjectives composed by means of molek, „master of", „in possession of", although on account of their being used as substantives I have already been obliged to consider these composite terms when speaking of the different classes of the noun p. CCCXI. In this place I will mention in particular the composite adjective term kedō-noll-molék, meaning verbally „possessing many mountains", i. q. „mountainous", and used of a district (barik), as belonging hither more truly with regard to the remarkable manner of its composition.

i) Now, as for position and termination of the adjective in its relation to the noun, which it serves to characterise, the latter always precedes the former, without, however, exercising any considerable influence upon its termination. For, while in the terms aeek gedík, „new-moon"; aeek kolák, „full-moon", the termination of both noun and adjective agree with each other, not in consequence of outward accommodation, but from innermost organization of each term independently, the terms suñge fafáda, „scanty wood", i. q. „trees far between"; kedāde adeala, „desert country", show clearly, that there obtains no rule in this respect.

k) As for the plural number of the adjective, my material seems to demonstrate, that it is scarcely ever expressed; the form munkáldže, the plural number of múnkolak, not belonging properly to this place; for, although this term is originally composed of the substantive mun and the adjective kolák, the whole in course of time has become one single substantive term; and thus, I have no doubt, that it is with good reason, that I have mentioned the plural form munkáldže p. CCCXVII, g) among the plural forms of the noun.

l) I as yet have to say a few words with regard to the degrees of comparison of the adjective. But in this respect, from the general state of development of these African languages, we may suppose a priori to find in the Mába-idiom likewise a very inadequate mode of expression. The comparative especially is not expressed but simply by means of a demonstrative way of pointing to the object, which excels another one in a certain respect.

trifft. Eine alleinige Ausnahme hiervon scheint zu machen der so gewöhnliche Komparativ „besser" von „gut", wofür die Maba-Sprache das Arabische خير in der schon oben S. CCC, f, α) erwähnten, national abgewandelten, Form χer-te oder χar-te eingeführt hat. — Was den Superlativ betrifft, so scheint der in gewissen Fällen eine ganz eigenthümliche Vertretung zu finden mit Hülfe des, an und für sich ohne Beziehung auf einen Vergleich, ohne Zweifel eigentlich eine Frageform mit der Bedeutung „was ist es"? darstellenden Redetheiles té-gent. So sehen wir in der Phrase „welcher Berg ist der höchste im Lande Wádai"?, Frageform und Begriff des Superlativ's auf die interessanteste Weise verschmolzen,

dār Mába koddk kolá-go nyá ori nun té-gent*),
(Land Wádai Berg gross an (an Grösse) welcher ist davon ist anders?)

Der Begriff des „Anderen" aber in dieser Form, das mit dem Vorhandenen verglichen wird, tritt noch deutlicher zu Tage in folgender Phrase „was sonst (also ein Vergleich) gebrauchen wir", d. h. „neben diesem welches Andere", litto andrí-te nu nye té-gent, wörtlich „was gibt es Anderes von (neben) der bedürftigen Sache", (nu, nun Genitiv).

Wenn nun in diesen beiden Beispielen die Bedeutung der Frage in der Form té-gent gänzlich vorzuwiegen scheint, so erhält dagegen dieser Redetheil in der Form tegen-ére durch Anfügung der Verbal-Endung ere, „seiend", die wirklich positive Bedeutung des Superlativ's, wie ich denn unter meinen Adjektivformen die Redeform tegen-ére kolák dō ganz einfach mit der Bedeutung „der grösste", von kolák, „gross", habe und ebenso tegen-ére nyllik dé, „der kleinste", von nyllik, „klein". In Bezug auf die eigentliche Bedeutung des do in diesen Formen bin ich nicht ganz sicher; ich hielt es zuerst für identisch mit dem do in der S. CCXC aufgeführten Form am de-t, „ich an mir", d. h. „ich selbst", glaube aber, dass es richtiger als do mit der Bedeutung „nur, allein" zu fassen ist und so die superlative Bedeutung des ausschliesslich Hervorragenden entschieden verstärkt.

8. Hiermit beschliesse ich diese vorläufige Analyse der Maba-Sprache, indem ich nichts eifriger wünsche, als dass recht bald ein noch reicheres Material nach Erzählungen aus dem Munde der Eingeborenen niedergeschrieben, weiteren Aufschluss über diese Sprache geben möge. Doch wird schon sowol der noch übrige Theil meines Vokabular's überhaupt manche neue Bemerkung bieten, als zumal wird die Erklärung meiner allerdings nicht sehr zahlreichen, aber doch mannichfach gegliederten Phrasen am Schlusse desselben mir selbst die Gelegenheit bieten, einige die Syntax betreffende Fragen noch näher zu erläutern. Hier will ich nur folgende zwei, zuerst die Satzgliederung mit „oder", dann die negative Gliederung mit „weder" — „noch" beleuchtende Phrasen aufführen und so die auf S. 9 meines Vokabular's gebliebene Lücke ausfüllen:

„reichen unsere Provisionen etwa (ka oben S. CCC, f, α) aus oder reichen sie etwa nicht aus"?,

zād mo-ali ágo-nō ka-tánrok ta ba ka-tánrok tá-endē;

„ist die Stadt, wohin wir gehen zu schlafen, nah oder fern",

hillo ma-uot ga góto mánrakí mindži ta ba lel ta;

„wir sehen (nicht) weder den Weg, noch die Stadt",

lingág(o) undžā mo-ko-yá-endē hillog(o) udžā mo-kó-yá-endē.

Über die ursprüngliche Form des udžā, undžā bin ich etwas zweifelhaft.

9. *Eine vorläufige Liste monosyllaber Wurzeln der Mába-Sprache.*

Nach der vorhergegangenen Analyse nun gehe ich mit Benutzung der so gewonnenen Resultate hier eine kurze Liste monosyllaber Wurzeln unserer Sprache, indem ich alles Unsichere fortlasse.

*) Über das hier als Art Ablativ gebrauchte go in kolá-go s. oben S. CCCXIV, b, α).

An isolated exception of such an inadequate mode of expression seems to consist in the common comparative form „better", for which the Māba-language has adopted the Arabic term خير in the form χer-te or χar-te, already mentioned p. CCCI, f, α), and changed in conformity with the rule noticed p. CCCXXI, c). — As for the superlative, in certain cases it seems to be expressed in a very peculiar manner by means of the form té-gent which, if placed by itself, without any reference to an intended comparison, evidently represents a form of question meaning properly, as it seems, „what is it"?. Thus, in the following phrase we see such a form of questioning combined in a remarkable manner with the notion of a superlative degree of comparison. This is the phrase „which mountain is the highest one in the Wádāy country"?, which in Māba is expressed thus:

dār Māba koddk kolá-go nyá orī nun té-gent *),

(country Wáday mountain great as for which is there-of is another one).

But the notion „another one", which by means of this form is compared with that what is present, appears perhaps yet more clearly in the following phrase „what else (besides this) do we want", litto andrí-te nu aye té-gent,

(thing necessary of what is else).

While thus, in these two instances, the character and notion of a question is evidently preponderating in the form té-gent, on the other hand in the form tegen-ére, by the affixing of the verbal termination ere, „being", it acquires the truely positive notion of a superlative, as, for instance, among my adjectives appears the form tegen-ére kolák dé, as simply conveying the notion „the greatest", from kolák „great", and further tegen-ére nyīlik dé, „the smallest", from nyīlik, „small". But, as for the proper meaning of the particle de, dē in these forms, I am not quite certain; for, while I first supposed it to be identical with the de in am de-i, „I by me", i. q. „I myself", I afterwards understand it to be identical with the dé meaning „alone, only", and thus strengthening the superlative notion.

8. I thus conclude this short analysis of the Māba-language from my limited material by giving expression to my sincere wish, that richer materials contained in Narratives taken down from the mouth of the natives may soon disclose more features of the character of this language. But the remaining portion of my Vocabulary will not fail to give me opportunity for offering many a new remark, and especially, while explaining the Collection of phrases at its end, I shall have ample opportunity of entering into some questions regarding the syntax of this language. In this place I will only adduce the following two phrases, illustrating first the juxtaposition of sentences by means of „or", then the negative position of „neither — nor", and thus forming a supplement to p. 9, where these forms of speech have been left unrepresented,

„may (ka p. CCCI, f, α) our provisions reach, or may they not reach"?,

sād me-nī ágo-nō ka-tánrek ta ba ka-tánrek tá-endā;

„is the town where we go to pass the night, near, or is it far",

hille ma-mot ga góto mánrakí mindžī ta ba lel ta;

„we see neither the track, nor the town",

lingag(o) undžū mo-ko-yá-endā hilleg(o) undžū mo-kó-yá-endā;

although, with regard to the original form of undžū I am rather a little uncertain.

9. *A list of monosyllabic roots of the Māba-language.*

Having, by means of the foregoing analysis, obtained an insight into the most original groundwork of the language, I now proceed to give a short list of monosyllabic roots, such as appear in my material, leaving away all what is uncertain.

---

*) With regard to the go in kolá-go, which is used as a sort of ablative case („in size"), see above p. CCCXV, b, α).

a: a (ā?), negatives Zeichen; am, „ich"; aṅg, „bleiben, sitzen"; ar, „verschneiden, kastriren".
b: ba die Frageform, dann „oder" (auch negativ?); ba (späterer, vielleicht vom Für entlehnter, Ausdruck statt des älteren mun), „Vater"; bak, „beseitigen"; bar, „zwei"; bar, „(Jahreshälfte?), Jahreszeit"; buk, „reiben, pressen"; bi, „schlafen"; bis, „Katze"; boß, „Nase"; boṅg, „heiss" (daher wol auch in weiterer figürlicher Entwickelung „Sporn").
d: dā, „fragen"; dan, „roh"; de, „von, an"; dē, „allein, nur"; dor, „Donner"; drek, „Hemd"; dum, „alles, ganz".
f: fi, „Boden"; fo, „Guineawurm"; fu, „Geschwür".
g: gan, „Sand, Fläche, Ebene"; gar, „Schwägerschaft"; gir, „liegend"; gñōn, „Elephant"; go, „Raub".
i, y: ye, „bebauen (das Feld)"; yos, „Morgen".
k: k (ek, ik, uk) Kennzeichen persönlicher Thätigkeit; ka, „vielleicht, ob, etwa, und"; kal, „Dreschstätte"; kam, kaṅg, Plur. kai, „Person"; kaṅg, „ihr", 2te Person Plur.; kir, „kalt"; kul, „Leib, Inneres".
l: la, „nicht"; lan, „Guineahuhn"; lar, „Antilope"; lel, „weit"; lul, „unten, Westen".
m: ma, andere Frageform, besonders selbstständigen Fragepartikeln hinzugefügt; mal, „Blitz"; mam, „ja"; maṅg, „wir"; mar, „Stier, männlich"; me, mi, „du"; meg, „Wild-Schwein" (daher meg-ik, „wildes Thier im Allgemeinen"); mog, „Hase"; nun vier, in höchst interessanter Weise sich gliedernde und die organische Entwickelung einfachster Beziehungen der Sprache in klarer Lebendigkeit darstellende Familienbezeichnungen min, „Mutter"; mir, „Bruder"; mug, „Schwester"; mun, muā, „Vater".
n, ny, ñ: na, nak, ṅg, nu, nun, („Geburt, Ursprung"), Genitiv-Verhältniss; nar, „geben"; ne, „er, es"(?); nye, nyo, „was"; nyō, „Hund"; nya, „essen"; nyu, „Fleisch".
r: rau, „nehmen".
s: sa, „wissen"; sā, sē, „wahr"; ser, „gerade aus"; si Zeichen der Mehrheit, s. S. CCCVI, g); sil, „Eidechse"; siṅg, „Thüre".
š: šim, „Büffel".
t: ta, te, „ist, seiend"; ta (tā?, ta-š, „ist nicht"?) negative Verbal-Form; tal, „oben, über, Osten"; taṅg, „Haus, Überzug"; tar, „Verschnittener"; te, ti, „er, sie"; tek, „einer, eine, eines"; til, „Floh"; tin, „fliegen"; tor, „fünf"; tun, Nebenform von mun, „Vater", dann in seiner ursprünglichen Bedeutung des Zeugen's, Gebären's (s. S. CCCVI, c), „Larve, Wurm".
u: uu, uā, „gebären"; ur, „singen".
dž: dža, „Fuss, Spur"; džā, „falsch, unwahr"; džik, „Raise"; dže, džok, „Ziege".

10. *Einige Punkte verwandtschaftlicher Berührung des Māba mit anderen Sprachen.*

a) Was verwandtschaftliche Berührungspunkte des Māba mit anderen benachbarten Sprachen betrifft, so scheinen solche, so weit mir bis jetzt bekannt, keineswegs zahlreich zu sein, weisen aber am meisten nach S.-O. Einige derartige Berührungspunkte sind schon in Verbindung mit anderen der hier behandelten Sprachen in der Analyse der vorhergehenden Kapitel besprochen worden, besonders was eine Berührung des Māba mit der, wenigstens seit zwei Jahrhunderten ihr benachbarten, Tédā-Sprache betrifft. Diese Punkte sind die folgenden: „Wasser", im Māba endži, im Tédā oyi (Kanúri ṅki); „Wind, Sturm", M. áffolō, T. ábonō (Wándala áffuya); „Vogel", M. kebdi, T. kobri; „Krieg, Schlacht", M. torre, T. tallo; „Wasserschlauch", M. átteri, T. teri (Bágrimma étili) und endlich die Verbalform arō, T. erík.

b) Als Berührungspunkte des Māba mit dem Kanúri erwähne ich, ausser dem oben angeführten Ausdrücken für „Wasser", M. delm-ik (verglichen mit Bezug auf die Endung ik das oben S. CCCXIV, e) in der Note Gesagte), „Zunge", Kanúri télam (Tédā tir-he, vergl. S. XCII, N. 6); „Besserung", M. ṅgā-ga, K. ṅgā-tši; „Strohdeckel einer Schüssel", M. ábilla,

a: a (ā?) negative sign; am, „I"; aṅg, „sit, remain"; ar, „castrate".

b: ba the form of questioning, „or" (also negative?); bā (later and less original term, perhaps borrowed from the Fūr-idiom, instead of mun), „father"; bak, „vanquish, beat"; bar, „two"; bar, („one half of year"?), „season"; buk, „press"; bī, „sleep"; bis, „cut"; boñ, „nose"; boṅg, „warm" (in a further development of this notion meaning „spur").

d: dā, „ask"; dan, „crude"; do, „at, in, by"; dē, „alone, only"; dor, „thunder"; drek, „shirt"; dam, „all, whole".

f: fi, „soil, ground"; fo, „guineaworm"; fu, „ulcer".

g: gan, „sand, plain, level"; gar, „affinity (by means of intermarriage)"; gir, „lying, prostrate"; gōōu, „elephant"; go, „robbery".

i, y: ye, „cultivate (the field)"; yes, „morning".

k: k (ek, ik, uk) personal sign of individuality; ka, „possibly, perhaps, and"; kal, „threshing floor"; kam, kaṅg, plur. kai, „person, individual"; kaṅg, „you" (plural); kir, „cold"; kul, „body, interior, inside".

l: la, „not"; lan, „guineafowl"; lar, „antelope"; lol, „far"; lul, „below, under, West".

m: ma, form of questioning, especially when added to interrogative particles; māl, „lightning"; mam, „yes"; maṅg, „we"; mar, „bull, male"; me, mi, „thou"; meg, „hog" (thence meg-ik, „wild beast", in general); mog, „hare"; now, four terms, all of them designating the various members of the family, and bringing to view the most interesting instances of organical development of the language, viz min, „mother"; mir, „brother"; mug, „sister"; mun, muñ, „father".

n, ny, ñ: na, nak, ṅg, nu, una („birth, origin") genitive relation; nar, „give"; no, „he, it" (?); nya, nyo, „what"; nyō, „dog"; nya, „eat"; nyū, „meat".

r: ran, „take".

s: sa, „know"; sā, sē, „true"; ser, „straight on"; si sign of plurality (p. CCCVII, g); sil, „lizard"; siṅg, „door, gate".

š: šīm, „buffalo".

t: ta, te, „is, being"; ta (tā?, ta-ā, „is not"?) negative sign; tal, „on, above, East"; taṅg, „house, cover"; tar, „eunuch"; tek, „one"; til, „flee"; tin, „(to) fly"; tor, „five"; tun, other form of mun, „father", almost exclusively known to Seetzen; then, in its general notion of „procreating" (see p. CCCVII, c), meaning „caterpillar, worm".

u: un, uñ, „bear, procreate"; ur, „sing".

dž: dža, „foot, footstep"; džā, „false, untrue"; džik, „rat"; džo, džok, „goat".

10. *A few points of affinity of the Māba-idiom with other African languages.*

a) As for points of contact and affinity between the Māba and other neighbouring languages, they do not seem to be numerous, but evidently point South-Eastward, as the original home of this tribe. A few points have already been mentioned in connection with the languages analyzed in the preceding chapters, especially the Tédā-idiom, the cases of harmony between the Māba-language and the latter being the terms for „water", Māba ondži, Tédā eyi (Kanúri ñki); „wind, storm", M. óffolō, T. ábonō (Wándalā óffeyā); „bird", M. kobél, T. kobri; „war, battle", M. torro, T. tullo; „waterskin", M. áttori, T. teri (Bágrimma étili), and finally the auxiliary verbal form M. arē, T. erik.

b) As instances of affinity of the Māba- with the Kanúri-language I mention, besides the terms for „water", „tongue", Māba dolm-ik (see with regard to the termination ik what I have said p. CCCXV, c), Kanúri télam (Tédā tir-he compare p. XCIII, note 6); „convalescence", M. ṅgá-ga, K. ṅgá-tāi; „straw-covering of dish", M. ábilla, K. fillē; „price", M. temman, K. tomman. Of this short list the two latter terms have merely

K. fille; „Preis“, M. temman, K. temman. Von diesen sind die beiden letzteren Ausdrücke von der Mába-Sprache dem Kanúri wahrscheinlich nur äusserlich entborgt worden, während auch Jeder sich überzeugen kann, dass bei einer solchen Entlehnung des Ausdruckes ñgā-ga die Bágrimma-Sprache ganz entschieden die Vermittlerin gebildet hat, wenn er das über den Bágrimma-Ausdruck tad ñgā-ga S. CCLXX, f) Gesagte vergleicht.

c) Als Punkte von äusserer Berührung oder innerer Verwandtschaft zwischen der Mába- und Bágrimma-Sprache, ausser dem schon Berührten und bloss äusserlich Aufgenommenen, erwähne ich die folgenden, die von grösserem Interesse und grösserer Bedeutung zu sein scheinen, Mába mug, mug-gu, „Schwester“, Bágrimma mudž, muddži, „Bruder“; „Herr von“, „im Besitz von“, M. mel-ek, B. mala, indem dieser Ausdruck in Zusammensetzungen im Mába dem Objekte nach-, im Bágrimma vorgesetzt wird (auch mal-na, „unser Herr“, d. h. „Gott“ im Lógone gehört hierher); M. bar, „Jahreszeit“, B. bárua (in dem der Bágrimma-Sprache eng verwandten Baṅg-Bai eben in der Form bar), „Regenzeit“; „Sklave“, M. bór-ik, B. bōli (im Nyamyam bei Petherick buroo, i. e. buru); „Elephant“, M. gñōn, B. kou; „Schatten“, M. indžgiák, B. indžili; „ich) breche auf“, M. á-)yiṅgi, B. máh)-ingi; „ich) schlafe“, M. a-)bi, „Schlaf“, B. bi.

d) Was Berührung des Mába mit der Wándalā-Sprache betrifft, erwähne ich hier, ausser dem oben angeführten éffuyā, folgende Ausdrücke: „Frau“, Mába mašóṅg, Wándalā mokea; „Salz“, M. údža, W. idža. Hieran will ich zugleich eine Bemerkung in Beziehung auf das Haussa anreihen. Während der Ausdruck mašóṅg der Form muso, „Frau“ in der Mande- (Mandingo)-Sprache sich näher anschliesst, als an den Haussa-Ausdruck matše, gleicht der analogisch gebildete Ausdruck mašik für „Mann“ in der Mába-Sprache auf das Entschiedenste dem entsprechenden Haussa-Worte meži.

e) Es gibt auch einige ganz augenscheinliche Berührungspunkte zwischen der Mába-Sprache und der Sprache von Für; jedoch sind sie weit weniger zahlreich, als ich nach früheren geringeren Proben (besonders aus Seetzen's Sammlung) vermuthete, da die mir gütigst von Herrn Werner Munzinger zugesandte grössere und zuverlässigere Liste von Für-Wörtern nur wenig mehr Ausbeute lieferte. So haben wir „ein“, im Mába tek, Für dik (Seetzen und Munzinger) (im Dinka tok[1]), Galla toko); „Gott“, M. kalak, F. kalge (Seetzen); lul im M. „Westen, unten“, im F. „Nacht“ (Munzinger); „Zunge“, M. delm-ik, F. dale (M.) oder dali (S.) (also ein Mittelglied zwischen der Téda-Form tirhe und der Kanúri-Form télam); „Haus“, M. taṅg, F. daṅg (M.) oder doṅg (S.). Auch erwähne ich hier den Ausdruck für „Berg“ in der dem Für verwandten Koldági-Sprache, kudou, auf das Engste sich anreihend dem Mába-Ausdruck kodó-k.

f) Manche Berührungspunkte des Mába, wie der anderen in dieser grösseren Sammlung behandelten Sprachen, werden wir noch bei Behandlung der kleineren Vokabularien besprechen müssen; hier erwähne ich nur das oben S. CCCXXII, c) besprochene negative tambai, „es ist nicht“, das auf das Engste mit aufai in Musgu, uahai in Bedde zusammenhängt; so wie das positive te-re, te-ri, „es ist“, in Form wie Bedeutung identisch mit tori im Kwána.

g) In Betreff der Mašiy-Sprache, mit der die grammatischen Berührungen hier gleich Null sind, erwähne ich nur „Leib“, Mába tabú-k, Mašiy tábutut (tábo ka Mašiy „pudenda muliebria“) und „Messer“, Mába télek, Mašiy télak.

h) Als ein vereinzeltes Beispiel von Wortähnlichkeit will ich noch erwähnen „kalt“, Mába kir, kéra („Hügel“, kikin), Ukámbani kiria. Solche einzelne Ähnlichkeiten aber, deren man leicht mehre auffinden kann, haben, wie bekannt, in der Sprachvergleichung gar kein Gewicht.

i) Sehr verschieden nun von solchen ganz äusserlichen sprachlichen Berührungen oder

[1]) Kaufmann „der weisse Nil“, S. 97; cf. Brun Rollet bei Petermann, Ergänzungsheft 7, S. 39.

been borrowed by the Bágrimma from the Kandri, in consequence of the external intercourse between the two tribes, while, from what I have said p. CCLXXI, f) with regard to the Bágrimma-term tad ñšš-ga, it must become evident to every body, that the Māba-language has borrowed this term likewise from the Kandri-idiom by means of the Bágrimma-language.

c) As points of contact between the Māba- and the Bágrimma-languages, besides the one just mentioned, which is the consequence of mere external relations of life, I in this place adduce as more remarkable and important the following terms, Māba mug, mug-go, „sister", Bágrimma mudž, múdži, „brother"; M. mel-ek, B. mala, „master (of)", in composite terms the former being placed after, the latter before the object or quality, the possession of which is indicated by those terms (the Lógone-term mal-na also „our Lord", i. q. „God", does belong hither); M. bar, „season", B. bárua (in the dialect of Dañgbai, which is closely related to Bágrimma, in the very form bar), „rainy season"; M. bōr-ik, B. bōli (in the language of the socalled Nyamnyam with Petherick buroo i. q. buru), „slave"; M. gūōn, B. kon, „elephant"; M. ándžglúk, B. indžili, „shade, shadow"; M. á-)yingi, B. mák)-iñgi, „I) start"; M. a-)bi, „I) sleep", B. bi, „sleep".

d) As for obvious instances of contact or affinity of the Māba with the Wándalā-idiom, besides éffnyā mentioned above, I still mention Māba mušóñg, W. moksa, „woman"; M. ūdža, W. idža, „salt"; and here I will at once offer a remark with regard to the Haussa-language. For, while the term mušóñg approaches more closely to the form muso in the Mande (Mandiñgo)-idiom, than the corresponding Hausa-term matšo, the Māba-term mālik for „man" resembles very closely the corresponding Hausa-term mēži.

e) There are some evident points of affinity between the Māba-idiom and the language of Für, although they appear to be much more scarce, than I at first thought probable from the few specimens given by Seetzen, the longer and more reliable list of Für-terms with which Mr. Werner Munzinger has kindly supplied me, not bringing to view but one or two more instances of affinity of this language with the Māba-idiom. Thus, we have in Māba tok, Für dik, with both Seetzen and Munzinger, (Dinka tok *), Galla toko), „one"; M. kalak, F. kalgo (Seetzen), „god"; lal in M. „below, West", in F. (Munzinger) „night"; M. dolm-ik, „tongue", F. dale (M.) or dāli (S.), this form standing in the midst of the corresponding forms tirbo in Téda, tólam in Kandri; M. tañg, F. duñg (M.) or doñg (S.), „house". I here mention also M. kodó-k, Koldági (which is closely related to the Für-idiom) kudou, „mountain".

f) Several other points of contact of the Māba-language with some of the dialects treated in my Collection of shorter vocabularies, which will serve to shed quite a new light over all the languages treated in this Collection in general, shall be treated in another place; here I mention only the negative verbal form tambai, „it is not" spoken of p. CCCXXIII, c), and which appears to be closely connected with the corresponding terms nafai in Musgu, nabai in Bedde, as well as the positive form te-rē, te-ri identical with the corresponding teri in Kwána.

g) As for the Māšiy-language, I mention only Māba tabú-k, „belly", Māšiy tábutut (táboka, „pudenda muliebria"); M. télek, Māšiy tolak, „knife", points of really grammatical relation between these two languages being wanting.

h) As an isolated instance of outward resemblance, such as may easily be met with among languages of the most divergent character, but which have very little importance for deciding linguistical affinities, I will mention by the way M. kéra, „cold" (kíkia, „hail"), in Chámbāni kíria.

i) Of a character, very different from such quite external linguistical resemblances, or

*) Kaufmann „the white Nile", p. 97, compared with Brun Rollet in Petermann's „Ergänzungsheft" n. 7, p. 39.

Entdeckungen scheinen die verwandtschaftlichen Beziehungen des Mäbe zum Dinka oder Denka, das am Weissen Nil in dem ausgedehnten Gebiet vom 5ten bis 12ten Grad N. Br. gesprochen wird, zu sein und hier eben eröffnet sich nun auch in ethnographischer Beziehung durch die Aufhellung des oberen Nil-Beckens ein ganz neuer Blick, wie in geographischer Beziehung hier die schönsten Entdeckungen der Gegenwart gemacht werden. So haben wir im Mäba mäšik, „Mann“, im Dinka moitš, „Gemahl“; „Leute“, M. kai, D. koitš, von einem im Mäba unbekannten Singular ran; „Hund“, M. nyok, D. tšyok; „Elephant“, M. gñön (Tédá kūu), D. kon, und nun das schon oben S. CCXVI, b) angeführte und als Beleg jener Verwandtschaft überaus interessante Substantiv „Stier“, das in beiden Sprachen zugleich Sinnbild der Männlichkeit ist, daher auch „männlich“ bedeutet, M. mar, D. muor. Zu diesen aus nur kurzem Glossar ausgewählten Beispielen kommen folgende bedeutsame grammatische Analogien hinzu, erstlich die Präposition de, die wir im Mäba nur noch vereinzelt bei am de-i, „ich selbst“ (S. CCXC) als Bildungsglied der possessiven Form des Fürwortes gefunden haben, die aber im Dinka fast ausschliesslich diese Formen bildet (s. dia u. s. w. bei Kaufmann S. 98); dann die Partikel „(vielleicht) und“, M. ka, D. ko; das fragende Fürwort „was“, M. nya, nye, D. ña, ñu; das persönliche Fürwort „ihr“ (Plur.), M. wong, D. wek, und das einfachste Zeitwort „sein“, M. ta, D. to. Diese verwandtschaftlichen Beziehungen zwischen beiden Sprachen würden sich bei vorliegendem vollständigeren Material über die Dinka-Sprache unzweifelhaft noch sehr vermehren lassen, aber leider hat der Missionar Kaufmann, der Verfasser des trefflichen kleinen Büchelchens über den Weissen Nil, zur Zeit Domvikar in Brixen, sein Material über jene Sprache seinen Kollegen am Oberen Nil bei seiner Heimkehr nach Europa zurückgelassen und hat mir daher auf mein an ihn gestelltes Gesuch nur ein Verzeichniss von etwa 300 Wörtern aus dem Gedächtniss gütigst mittheilen können.

Somit beschliesse ich die Einleitung zu diesen grösseren Vokabularien, indem ich am Schlusse des gesammten Werkes noch zu einigen allgemeinen Punkten zurückkehren und besonders einerseits die Beziehungen dieser Sprachen in ihrem Grossen und Ganzen zum Mäñy noch einmal betrachten, andererseits durch die Eintheilung der aus der Betrachtung der kleineren Vokabularien gewonnenen Resultate ein ethnologisches Gesammtbild dieses Theils von Afrika zu geben versuchen werde.

Nachtrag zu Kapitel XI,

(§. 8, S. CCLXXXVI „Verwandtschaft des Bágrimma mit dem Dôr“).

Obgleich Herr Petherick S. 400 seines äusserst schwach componirten Buches (Egypt, the Soudan and Central-Africa) ausdrücklich angibt, dass die Dôr eine von allen ihren Nachbarn verschiedene Sprache reden, so können wir doch schon nach den uns jetzt vorliegenden, höchst geringen Sprachproben jener Völkergruppe an dieser Behauptung einen wohlgegründeten Zweifel hegen. So z. B. ist einerseits kir, „Stern“, im Dôr, ganz identisch mit tšior im Dinka, und andererseits führen die mancherlei Berührungspunkte zwischen Bágrimma und jener dem Dôr benachbarten Sprache bei der an der bezüglichen Stelle nachgewiesenen engen Verwandtschaft zwischen Dôr und Bágrimma zu demselben Resultat, dass nämlich das Dôr keineswegs ohne Berührungspunkte mit seinen Nachbar-Sprachen sein kann. So z. B. ist bañgn, „Häuptling, Fürst“ im Bágrimma, ganz identisch mit beñg im Noaiglau (Petherick S. 436) und im Dinka (Kaufmann „der weisse Nil“, S. 96); bē, das im B. „Dorf“ bedeutet, heisst in der

terms merely borrowed by one language from the other, are the instances of really innate affinity between the Mába and the Dinka or Deńka spoken on the White Nile between 5° and 12° N. L.; and thus the Discoveries made in the basin of that Royal African River promise to shed quite a new light over that whole Region also in ethnological respect, as they form one of the most brilliant jewels in the crown of Geographical Research pursued by the present age. Thus, we have in Mába mäšik, „man", in Dinka moitš, „husband"; M. kai, D. koitš, „people", from a singular ran, not known in M.; M. nyoh, D. tšyok, „dog"; M. gñon (Téda kún), D. kon, „elephant", and now the most interesting glossarial instance of affinity, already adduced above p. CCXVII, h), viz M. mar, D. muor, meaning in both languages first „bull", and then „masculine". To these instances, picked up from a very short glossary, we have now to add the following most important grammatical analogies, first the preposition de, of which in Mába I have not found but one isolated instance in connection with the personal pronoun, in the form am de-i (p. CCXCI) meaning „I myself", but which in Dinka appears regularly to form the possessive forms of the pronoun (see dia, and so on with Kaufmann „the White Nile" p. 98); further, the conjunction „(perhaps), and", M. ka, D. ko; the interrogative pronoun „which, what", M. nya, nye, D. ńa, ńu; the personal pronoun „you" (plur.), M. wońg, D. wek, and finally the most simple and radical verbal form „to be", M. ta, D. to. These instances of affinity between the Dinka- and Mába-languages would, no doubt, be greatly increased, if we had before our eyes a richer material with regard to the former language; but I regret to say, that Rev. Mr. A. Kaufmann, the author of that excellent little volume „the white Nile", and at present Vicar of the cathedral in Brixen, to whom I have applied for that purpose, when returning to Germany from his station in Santa Cruce or Heiligen Kreuz, has left his labours on that language to his Colleagues, so that he was only able furnish me with a list of about 300 terms supplied by memory.

Thus I conclude the Introductory Remarks to my Collection of larger vocabularies, reserving me to return to a few points of general import at the conclusion of the whole work, where, on one side, I shall consider once more the grammatical relation of this group of languages to the Máziy or Berber, on the other, by summing up the individual results obtained from these and the smaller vocabularies, I intend to give a short ethnological account of this part of Central-Africa.

An additional remark to chapter XI,

(§ 8, p. CCLXXXVII „Affinity of the Bágrimma with the Dör").

Although Mr. Petherick on p. 400 of his book on „Egypt, the Soudan and Central-Africa", which, I dare say, is by no means a very careful composition, expressly states, that the Dör speak an idiom entirely different from that of all their neighbours, or from any that he himself had heard spoken, yet even from the very scanty linguistical specimens of that group of nations which are now before our eyes, we may with good reason call into doubt such an assertion. Thus, on the one hand, the terms for „star", Dör kir and Dinka tšier, are perfectly identical, while, on the other, the several points of contact intervening between the Bágrimma, on one side and the Dinka and other languages of that quarter, on the other considered the close affinity between the former and the Dör, which I trust I have fully proved, serve also to point out a certain degree of relationship between the Dinka and the Dör. Thus, for instance, banga, „chief, Sultan" in Bágrimma, is totally identical with beńg in Dinka (Kaufmann p. 96) and in Nouerglan (Petherick p. 436); bö in B. meaning

Sprache der (sogenannten) Nyamyam, d. h. der Mukaraka, in der Form baia, „Hütte", im Dińka als pai, „Dorf, Land"; „Leopard" heisst im B. kaga (im Für nach Munsinger gara [gaya?]), im Dińka kuatš; „Name" heisst in beiden Sprachen ri („dein Name", Dińka ri-a-ka im Paternoster bei Kaufmann S. 90); für „Hand", wofür wir schon oben (S. CCLXXXVI) im Bágrimma wie Dör denselben Ausdruck dži fanden, haben wir auch im Dińka das entsprechende tši, Plur. tšia; „schwarz" heisst im B. kolé, im D. tšol; „viel", B. otšo, D. tšuc-tš, und die Form des verbalen Futurum's im Dińka vermittelst eines angehängten bi wird auf das Schönste erklärt durch die Bedeutung „gehn" („ich gehe das und das zu thun", d. h. „ich werde thun"), welche das ganz identische be, a-be im Bágrimma hat.

„village" is identical with paia in Dińka, „village, country", and with baia in the language of the socalled Nyamyam, meaning „hut, cottage"; ri means „name" in Bágrimma as well as in Dińka (ri-a-ka, „thy name" in Our Lords Prayer, Kaufmann p. 90); the Bágrimma-term kaga for „leopard" (in Für with Munsinger gara (gaya?) resembles the corresponding Dińka-term kuatš; for „hand", which on p. CCLXXXVII we have found expressed in both Bágrimma and Dör by the term dži, also in Dińka we find the same term in the form tši, plur. tšia; „black" is kolé in B., tšol in D.; „much", otšo in B., tšuc-tš in D., while the form of the future tense in the Dińka verb, which is expressed by means of a bi added at the end of the root, is explained in the clearest manner by means of the notion „to go", which the very identical be, a-bé conveys in Bágrimma, just as most other languages are forming that tense.

Pronomina, Partikeln und Zahlwörter.

Pronomina, Particles and Numerals.

Deutsch und Englisch.	Kanuri.	Tédâ.	Hausa.	Fulfulde.
ich — *I*	ú-ma[1]	táni	ni[6] / nía	mi-hiñg / meñg
du — *thou*	ni-ma	nebrē	kai, m. / ki, f.	añg
er — *he* / sie — *she*	ši-ma	merē	ši, m. / íta, f.	kañ-ko
wir — *we*	ándi-ma	tinta	mú	míndoñg / énene
ihr — *you*	néndi-ma[2]	nebrai	kú	ónon / ónu
sie — *they*	séndi-ma	ánata	su	kam-be
ich selbst — *I myself*	ú nesko-ni[3] / ú kéla-ni	táni merē [5]	ni / nia da kai-na	mi hore-am[7]
du selbst — *thou thyself*	ni nesko-num[4] / ni kéla-num	nebrē merē [5]	kai da ka-ika / da kaine m. / ki da ka-iki f.	añg hore-ma
er selbst — *he himself* / sie selbst — *she herself*	ši nesko-nisé / ši kéla-nisé	merē [5]	ši da ka-na / da kai-ne / íta da ka-nía / da kai-ne	kañ-ko hore-ma-[ko]
wir selbst — *we ourselves*	andi nesko-ndē	tinta merē [5]	mú da ka-mu	(míndoñg) / (énene) hore-âmiñg
ihr selbst — *you yourselves*	nendi nesko-ndō	nebrai merē [5]	kú da ka-iku	ónon hore-mōn
sie selbst — *they themselves*	sendi nesko-nisá	ánata merē [5]	sū da ka-nsu	kam-bē hore-mābē

[1] ú-ma. Allerdings ist ú das eigentlich bedeutsame Lautzeichen für die erste Person und ma grammatikalisch unwesentlich, aber sachlich ist ma wichtig und darf in unabhängiger Stellung nicht fehlen. So würde es keinem Kanúri einfallen, auf die Frage: „wer hat das gethan?" zu antworten „ú", sondern ú-ma ist das durchaus Erforderliche. — Koelle schreibt für ú: wu, dazu ist aber gar kein Grund vorhanden. — Meiner Ansicht nach ist dieses ma, das erst nachher den Begriff des Haltens erhielt und so zu Zusammensetzungen besonders dienlich wurde, das ursprüngliche Wort für Mensch, Person, im Plural am. So würde die ursprüngliche Bedeutung von fír-ma sein „der Mann mit dem Pferd".

[2] néndi-ma. Für nendi schreibt K. nándi und der Vokal ist allerdings nicht immer ganz klar und bestimmt; es mag auch dialektische Verschiedenheit obwalten, aber in der Aussprache der gebildetsten Personen, mit denen ich zu verkehren hatte, wog das „e" vor.

[3] ú nesko-ni, ú kéla-ni, wörtlich „ich mit meiner Seele" (nesko), ich mit meinem Kopfe (kéla); nur wird kéla im Plural nicht gebraucht. Koelle schreibt kálá; nesko scheint bei ihm zu fehlen. Hier haben wir zugleich das pronomen possessivum suffixum, im nächsten Paradigma das selbständige pronomen kaší, das wieder ganz substantivisch abgewandelt wird.

[4] ni nesko-num. Der Vokal-Laut in dieser Pronominal-Endung ist nie ganz bestimmt, aber er nähert sich eher einem u als einem e, wie Koelle ihn gefasst hat und demnach nęm schreibt.

[5] Die Bedeutung des merē für „selbst" scheint auffallend und unsicher.

[6] Ursprünglich war nía wohl die Femininform und ni diejenige des masc. Das ist aber nicht so beibehalten worden.

[7] am. Reichardt in seinem Fulah Primer hat für die erste ps. des pron. pos. ein einfaches a. Darüber s. Prolegomena.

[8] Das k in dieser Form ist mir mehr als zweifelhaft und ich bin überzeugt, dass na-ídu die richtige Form ist. Der Lehrer brachte hier statt hámwuni ein kawuni hervor, aber das war wol nur Sprechfehler. In der Grundform der ersten und zweiten Pers. Pl. des pron. poss. hat das Lógoné auffallende Übereinstimmung mit dem Hausa.

[9] Ich hatte hier eine Femininform ibá-baha, aber sie ist mir zu unsicher, da sie in den Paradigmen gar keine Vertretung gefunden hat.

[10] g-írá-ngu. Das des Wohllauts wegen eingeschobene g ist wol richtig.

[11] g-ídá-koré. Der Übergang des r in íra in das verwandte d oder vielmehr ḍ ist ganz möglich wegen des eben vorhergehenden und bald nachfolgenden r.

[12] Die Formen, die ich hier erhielt, ma anhanma für die erste, yi mánalé für die zweite, ná mánali für die dritte Pers. S., drē malá für die erste Pers. Pl., sind zu unsicher, um sie hier in den Text selbst zu setzen.

[13] Die mir hier gegebene Form ni tagadelli kann nicht richtig sein.

Sonrai.	Lógonē.	Wándalā.	Bágrimma.	Mába.
ai-ta . . . . . . / ai-ga, é-ga . . . . \	indo	há-ya . . .	ma	am
ni-da	/ kan . . . . . / (kin . . . . . .)	bā-ka [9] . . .	yi	mi
áng-ain . .	ni	há-ngané . .	nē	ti
yiri . . .	mē	há-ngarē . .	dēē	mang
wiri . . . . / war-ia	wuni . . . . / onē	bá-korē . . / wó-korē . .	nē	kang
\ ingi-ta . / war-sa . .	tē . . . . . / tē-ti	hé-terē . .	dēigi	wang
ai-ta sāti .	indo hámwusi na-ū	hā-i irá-nā .	. . .	am de-l
ni-da sāti .	kin hámwusi na-kū	hā-ka g-irá-nga [10]		mi — ? [12]
áng-ain sāti .	ni hámwusi na-ni	há-ngané g-irá-ra	[13]	wāgo de-ti
yiri sāti	mē hámwusi na-mu	há-ngarē irá- [ngrona?		?
wiri sāti	wúni hámwusi na-kū	bá-korē n-idá- korē [11]		kang do-ki
ingi-ta sāti . . .	tē hámwusi na-kún [8] (na-lún?)	hé-terē irá-terē		wang u-dó-m

[1] ū-ma. There can be no doubt, that the significant word for the 1st pers. of the personal pronoun is ū and that ma is insignificant in a grammatical respect, but nevertheless as a part of speech the latter is important and cannot be omitted in some cases. Thus no Kanúri man would answer the question: „who has done that?" by a simple ū, but ū-ma is the only possible answer. Koelle moreover writes wu instead of ū, but there is no reason for doing so. According to my opinion this affix ma had originally the meaning of „man", „person", pl. am and only in course of time it has received the signification of indicating the possession of any thing, when it has become a very important word in compositions. Thus fir-ma properly would mean „the man of the horse" (fir).

[2] néndi-ma. Instead of nendi Koelle writes nándi as likewise sándi instead of sendi and I must acknowledge, that the vowel is not always clear and distinct, but with those people with whom I had to converse, the „e" prevailed decidedly; for I admit, that there may be a dialectical difference in pronunciation.

[3] ū nesko-ni, ū kéla-ni means verbally „I with my soul" (nesko), I with my head (kéla), but kéla is not used in the plural form. In this paradigm we have a specimen of the declension of the pron. poss. suffixum, while the next exhibits the changes of the full pronoun kakē, which is treated like a substantive.

[4] ni nesko-num. Also in the syllable num the vowel is not always clear, but at least it is nearer to the u, than to the e. Koelle writes nǝm.

[5] The signification of „morē" „self" seems awkward and uncertain.

[6] Originally it is probable, that nis was the fem. and ni the mascul. form, but such is not now the case.

[7] am. Rev. Reichardt in his Fulah primer represents the 1st pers. of the pronoun pos. by a simple a. See the Prolegomena.

[8] na-kún. The k in this form seems very doubtful to me and I am persuaded, that na-tún is the right form. My authority gave in this instance háwuel instead of hámwusi. The similarity of the 1st and 2nd form of the plural in H. and L. is apparent.

[9] I had here a fem. form ibā-kaka, but it cannot be correct.

[10] g-irá-nga. The g at the beginning I suppose added on account of euphony.

[11] n-idá-korē. The change of the r in ira into d or ḍ is probably caused by the influence of the preceding and following r.

[12] The forms which were given me in this instance, as ma nakauma for the 1st, yi mánalé for the 2nd, ná mánalā for the 3rd pers. sing. and dré malā for the 1st pers. plur., except the first appear very uncertain.

[13] The form mi tagodelli, which was given me in this instance, can not be right.

Deutsch und Englisch.	Kanúri.	Tédā.	Háusa.	Fulfúlde.
dies) (ist) mein — *this) (is) mine*	áte) kakĕ [1]	ai) tañ-go	éna) nā-wū [6] .	(ō-dum) am .
dies) (ist) dein — *this) (is) thine*	áte) kakĕ-num	ai) num [2] . .	éna) nā-ka, m. / nā-kī, f.	tō-dum) mā .
dies) (ist) sein — *this) (is) his* dies) (ist) ihr — *this) (is) hers*	áte) kakí-nisé	ai) añg-wadō [3]	éna) nā-sa . / nā-ta .	tō-dum) mako
dies) (ist) unser — *this) (is) ours*	áte) kakí-ndĕ	ai) tindau . .	éna) nā-mū .	tō-dum) ámmiñg
dies) (ist) euer — *this) (is) yours*	áte) kakí-ndō	? [4]	éna) nā-kū .	tō-dum) mōn .
dies) (ist) ihr — *this) (is) theirs*	áte) kakí-nisá	ai) teudō . .	éna) nā-sū .	tō-dum) mabê
dieser, diese, dieses — *this, this one*	áte-ma . . . / áte	ai	wo-nan [7] . . / a-wó-nan . / -nan . . .	dum dōo . .
diese — *these, these ones*	áni-ma . . . / áni	. . . . . .	wó-nan . . / nan	
jener, e, es — *that (one)*	tō-gnēi . . . / tuite . . .	té-merē . . .	wó-da-nan .	
jene — *those*	tōni	. . . . . .		. . . . . .
Jemand — *somebody* .	kōa . . . / lágā . . .	mer-ātra . .	wo-ne [8] . . / wo-ñga, pl. wo-dá-ñga; aga	ō-neddo, pl. heddo
eine Jemand — *some woman*	kāmo kōa . .	. . . . . .	wo-rga . . .	ō-debbo . .
einige — *some*	lágā	tent-ātra [5] .	wo-sú . . .	. . . . . .
die Einen — die Andern — *some — others*	lágā — lágā —	gorū — gorū —	wo-su — wo-sú —	bē — hē — .
die Einen gingen, die Andern blieben — *some went, others remained*	lágā lē-tsē, lágā neh-tsē	. . . . . .	wo-su sún-tafi, wo-su suna zamna	bē hi-dēōdi, bē hi-dilli

[1] kakĕ ist ein eigenthümliches Wort, das, ursprünglich offenbar ein einfaches Substantiv mit der Bedeutung „Besitz", allmählich zu einem Pronomen geworden ist, aber nur mit Zusatz des pron. pers. suffixum, das jedoch in der 1sten Pers. verloren gegangen ist; Koelle schreibt kágĕ.

[2] num ist wahrscheinlich nicht die ächte Tedā-, sondern eine Verwechselung mit der Kanúri-Form.

[3] añg-wadō ist wahrscheinlich nicht das eigentliche einfache pronomen possess., sondern wadō ist ein pron. demonstrativum.

[4] Mein Lehrer gab mir hier die Form ai) entém, aber er hat sich wol sicher auch hier nur mit dem Arabischen aus augenblicklicher Verlegenheit geholfen.

[5] Diese Form scheint mir mit tinta, „wir", zusammenzuhängen und also nicht ganz hierher zu passen.

[6] Man sollte anstatt nā-wū oder nā-n-ā eigentlich erwarten nā-na; vielleicht aber war auch im H. der einfache Vokal das Ursprüngliche für die erste Person.

[7] Wir haben in dieser Reihenfolge der Hausa-Kolumne Variationen des einfachen Lautes wo für menschliches Wesen, Mensch wo-ne, ein Mensch, irgend Einer, mit der Mehrheit wo-sú (sú: sie), wo-nan, dieser Mensch, wó-da-nan, Jener. — Die abgekürzte Form nan wird angehängt und ist häufiger im Gebrauch beim Plural als beim Singular. So „mútane-nan", diese Leute; doch auch mutumi nan, dieser Mann, mit einem dem Substantiv angehängten i. — éna wird nur in ganz allgemeiner Bedeutung gebraucht, wie oben éna nā-wū, dann anstatt mo-néne „was" in éna súné-ńka, „was ist dein Name!"

[8] Von wo-ne verschieden ist wol wā-ne mit der Bedeutung „ein Gewisser".

[9] Im Sokoto gehen h, f und fā stets in einander über.

[10] In der dritten Person Sing. und Plur. waren meine Quellen unsicher; für den Singular gaben sie die angeschickten Formen béro wonne, wal wonde, „das gehört einem Manne, einer Frau".

[11] gé-na-ul; gé-na-tún. Hier ist das n der Beziehung des Subjekts zum Objekt des nahe folgenden u halber in g übergegangen.

[12] Auch im Māba ist mir die dritte Person Sing. und Plur. unsicher geblieben. illége niakil, was man mir für das Erste, und illéñge oder illége lilli, was man mir für das zweite angab, können nicht ganz richtig sein.

Sonyai.	Lógoné.	Wándalá.	Bágrimma.	Mába.
wō-ki) (wō-lāe) [7] ē (wonne)	binne) na-ū . .	una) {zá-ruā . {zá-ronā	éna) á-miā .	waṅg em-bēti
wō-ki) nē (wonne)	binne) na-kū .	ūna) {zá-ṅga . {zá-ṅgona	éna) á-yi . .	waṅg te-nēti
[10]	binne) [11] gé-na-nī	ūna) {zá-tarē . {zá-ra .	éna) á-nyina .	[12]
wō-ki) yīro (wonne)	binne) na-mū .	ūna) {a-zá-mia {a-zá-ṅgrona	éna) á-dži .	waṅg me-nēti
wō-ki) war (wonne)	binne) na-kū .	ūna) {a-zá-korē {a-zá-ṅgre	éna) á-ṅē . .	waṅg ko-nīti
[10]	binne) [11] gé-na-tún	ūna) {a-zá-kar {a-za-károna	éna) á-džigi .	[12]
wō	{hanne . . . . {binne	bō-na (bá-ūna)		wá-goti
. . . .	bitki	béter-na . .	īna	wá-goni
. . . .	bin-tekénne . .	koyé-ṅganē .		illé-goti
. . . .	. . . .	. . . . . .		illé-ni
har afō	bill' áte-ma . .	dīžī-na . . .	kēde	andžēetē
waī afō	. . . .	. . . . . .	. . . . . .	. . . . . .
afō-di	. . . .	. . . . . .	kēde-gē . .	tōyi
afō-di — afō-di —	. . . .	. . . . . .	. . . . . .	. . . . . .
afō-di koi, afō-di gōro	. . . .	. . . . . .	. . . . . .	

[1] hakē is a remarkable word, which has evidently once been a noun with the signification of „property", but in course of time has become a pronoun, the derivation being effected by the aid of the pron. poss. suffixum, but so, that the 1st ps. s. hakē is left unchanged instead of hakē-ni. Koelle writes hágē.

[2] nam probably is not the original form belonging to the Tedá language, but is taken from the Kanúri.

[3] ság-wadé probably is not the simple possessive pron., but wadé is a demonstrative pronoun.

[4] My authority in this case gave me the form al) catôm, but I fear, that also in this instance he has recruited his memory from the Arabic to help himself out of momentary perplexity.

[5] It seems to me, that the form tent-âten is derived from „tinin", and I fear, that it has not such a general meaning.

[6] Instead of ná-wá or ná-n-á a person would rather expect „ná-na"; but it is not unlikely, that also in II. the simple vowel was the original form for the 1st ps. of the pronoun.

[7] In this succession of forms for the demonstrative pronoun in Hausa we have variations of the simple word wu for „human being", man; wo-ne, a person, a man, somebody, with the plural form wo- añ (añ = they), wo-nan, this person, wó-da-nan, that person. — The contracted form nan is used as a suffix and is of more frequent use in the plural, than in the singular. Thus mútanè nan, „these people", but also mutumi nan, „this man", the vowel I being appended to the final consonant of the preceding substantive. — éno, „that" and „what", is only used in a very general sense, as in éna ná-wá, „that is mine", éna súnā-ñka, „what is thy name?"

[8] Different from wa-ne may be wá-na, which seems to have the meaning „a certain person".

[9] In Songai h, ī and ü are constantly interchanged.

[10] With regard to the forms of the 3rd pers. sing. and plur. my authorities were not clear; for the sing. they gave me the imperfect forms of hōrn wonne, wai wonne, „that belongs to a man, that belongs to a woman".

[11] gé-nani; gé-na-tún. In these two forms the n expressive of the relation between subject and object is changed into a g on account of the neighbourhood of the following n.

[12] Also in Mába the 3rd pers. sing. and plur. has remained uncertain. People gave me illége niáhil for the first and illéōge or illége lītā for the second; ieñētí might seem to some to belong rather to the 3rd than to the 2nd ps.

Deutsch und Englisch.	Kanuri.	Tédā.	Hausa.	Fulfúlde.
Jeder, e, es — every body, each	ndu-ma[1] . .		kō-wo-ně . / kō-wo-tsě . / kō-wa[7] . .	koleínde .
Niemand, Keiner — nobody, none	ndu-ma -m	genā -n .	ba kō-wa ba	wala . . .
Niemand ging — nobody went	ndū-ma lē-tse-m	genā térerí-n	ba kō-wa yá-tafi ba	wala dżáhadò
Alle, Alles — all . . .	sem-ma .	gybri[6] . . .	dúkka . .	fū . . . .
sie alle — all of them .	su sem-ma	merā gybri fúlū	dúkka-nsú	hē-fu . .
zusammen, gemeinsam — together	yēro[2] . .	fúlū	tare[8]	táha . . .
unter einander, gegenseitig — one the other, amongst each other, mutually	katē-nisan[3] . / dābu-nisan .	marā-kudē	da džúná-nsu[9]	hi-hálde mā-bē / ódžune mā-bē
allein — alone	tilō[4] . . . / fal	trō-no . . .	dēa	?
nur (er — only (he, he alone	ši) temā[5] . .		(ši) kadē . . / sē (ši) dō .	sē (kaňko . . / kaňko) tā . .
ausser, ausgenommen — but	(— genia . . / (— genā . .	genia . . .		. . . .
wer, welche — who . .	ndū . . . . / ndū-sō . .	ñna	wo-ne (pl. wo- / wo-nē-neulán-da	dum) mói .
wer bist du — who art thou	ni-ma ndū-sō		kai wo-nē-ne	aig á-mói
wessen (ist dies — whose is it / wem gehört (dies — to whom does it belong	āte) ndū-be .	ñna-ū . . .	wá-na (éna .	dum tō-dum mói
was — what	áfi	índi	é-na . . . / me-nē-ne[10]	dum dumé
selbst, mit Einschluss — even	i-sā . . . . / i-yalē . . .		kō[11] . . . . / har	hódum .

[1] ndú-ma, s. was ich S. 7 n. 1 über das ma gesagt habe. Koelle hat sich hier versehen, indem er von ndū-ma auch die Bedeutung „Jemand" (some one, somebody) aufführt. — Für sem-ma schreibt er sum-ma.

[2] yēro. Beispiel: „gehe (zusammen) mit" yēro lō-nē, H. tafi tarē, F. yahhu tāba; „er sammt seinem Sohne wurde ergriffen", H. ái an-kāma-ši tarē dá da-nsa, F. ó-nnágidōamo kaňko hē biiko „er und sein Sohn".

[3] katē-nisan, dābu-nisan, eigentlich „in ihrer Mitte". Koelle hat von katē oder kátē, wie er schreibt, diese übertragene Bedeutung, von dābu scheint sie ihm unbekannt geblieben zu sein.

[4] Beispiel: „ich allein", ú-ma tilō-ni, T. tāni trō-no, L. Inde tehō; „er ging allein", ši-tse tilō-nisē, H. ši yá-tafi ši dēa, F. ó-dilli kaňko-tā.

[5] Die Partikeln temā, genia und genā scheinen bei Koelle zu fehlen.

[6] Ich habe hier auch die Form „genā-terón", aber sie ist unsicher, da genā schon eine negative Bedeutung zu haben scheint.

[7] Zu kō-wa ist das entsprechende Relativ „kō-mē", z. B. su-nyi me-sá kō-mē sú-ke-sé, „sie thaten ihm Alles, was sie wollten". Dieses kō-wa im H. hat nichts mit dem K. Wort kóa zu thun.

[8] tarē. Daven der militärische Zusammenruf „tarē-tarē", F. tebbeēde, tebbeēde.

[9] da džúná-nsú. Beispiel: sū-ne fā-da da džúná-nsú, auf F. e-bē-kēhde ó-džune mā-bē, S. efédie ókay afédie „sie bekämpfen sich unter einander".

[10] me-nē-ne. So „was ist das?" wo-ága me-nē-ne, auf Fulf. dum yó-dumē; S. mahióki-wā, im Wándalá ñeer-ñne.

[11] Das kō hat eine sehr umfassende Bedeutung und muss oft mit unserem fragenden „vielleicht" übersetzt werden. Beispiel „selbst ich", kō nia, im K. ú-ma yalē; „selbst, mit Einschluss des Fürsten", kō serki, har serki, im K. mai yalē. Der Gegensatz von kō ist „nur, allein", im H. sē — dē, im F. sē —, — tā. Beispiel: „es gibt keinen Regen, nur Wind", auf H. bābu rúa, sē iska dē, auf F. ndiam wála, sē hendu. Übrigens ist dieses sē wol erst aus dem H. in das F. eingeführt.

[12] hýte, i-hýte-nei nähert sich sehr dem Te-mášíyt-Wort i-kótené von derselben Bedeutung.

Sutyal.	Lógone.	Wandalá.	Bágrimma.	Mába.
boro-kul (h. Arb.)	?	. . . . . .	. . . . . .	
boro fö nó . .	bill' aši — sa .	aduka . . .	kède kau — li	. . . . . .
böru fö nó koi .	bill' aši nagir-sa	aduka bor-kení	kède kau kak-abē-li	tek-ten taiá-nde
. . . .	kyte	ba-dem-étere	pet	dum
. . . .	i-kyte-nai [12] . .	bé-demá . .	džä pet-kedē	. . . . . .
akól (Arb.) . .	billam	ámidúl kardē .	(džē) pet . .	dum barik téke
afódio — afódio	tauétufe namasúnsanámmo	abdugwátere .	dedún džä-džēmala	wógondē
	teku	bé-palle	se-kēle . .	tékē — tékē
		. . . . . .	. . . . . .	. . . .
	— sa-dá . . .	— mestika .		ñeta
mé-kun	bin-ta dá . .	war-áma . .	naóga	ñákai
	. . . .			. . . . . .
	binne ná-bakē .	áaa-u rö . .	éna) a-nánga	anga aikte genu
ménlu	ávemi	áze-rö . .	endun . . .	ñete gen
hárasén . . .		— kem		

[1] adü-ma. See what I have said p. 7 n. 1 with regard to the mo. Koelle in his vocabulary has made a mistake in attributing to this word besides the notion of „any body", also that of „some one", „somebody". — some-ma he writes ámmma.

[2] yèra. Ex. „go together", „go with me", yēra lé-nē, H. tafi tarē, F. yakka lèha; „he together with his son was seized", ži an-káme-ži tarē dá da-sen, F. ò-naágidōōma hadho bē bihe („he and his son").

[3] katē-ntsaa, dába-nisaa, mean verbally „in the midst of them". Koelle has the notion here given to katō or, as he writes kàtō, but of dába it seems to have remained unknown to him.

[4] „tilōž. Ex. „I alone", ū-ma tilō-ni, T. tani trō-ne, L. lado tokā; „he went alone", K. lū-tae tilō-ntaé, H. ži yá-tafi ži dén, F. ñ-dilbi hadho-ñā.

[5] The particles tomá, genia and gonā are wanting in Koelle's vocabulary.

[6] I have here also the form genā-terón, but it seems doubtful, as it appears, that genā has of itself already a negative signification.

[7] The corresponding relative pronoun to hō-wa is hō-mē. Ex. an-nyí ma-nā hō-mē nū-ke-nó „they did him all what they choose". This H. pronoun hō-wo has nothing in common with the K. pronoun hōa.

[8] „tarē". From this word the military expression has been formed „tarā-tarā", F. tabbarde, tebbarde.

[9] da dānā-nsú. Ex. „they fight amongst each other", sū-na fá-da da dānā-nsú, F. e-bē-kēbde ō-dāune má-ba.

[10] me-nē-ne. Ex. „what is that?" wo-dga me-nē-ne, F. dum yá-dumō, W. áar-úna.

[11] kō has a very wide signification and must often be translated by means of „perhaps". Ex. „even I, perhaps I myself", kamia, K. ū-ma yaiē; „perhaps even the king", kō serki, har serki, K. mai yaiē. — The contrary to kō is „only, but", H. sē — dō, F. sē — tū. Ex. „there is no rain, nothing but wind", H. babu rūa, sē iska-dē, F. ndiam wōla, sē hendu.

[12] [illegible]yte, i-kyta-nai has some affinity with the Te-máššyt word i-kētené of the same meaning.

Deutsch und Englisch.	Kanúri.	Tédá.	Hausa.	Fulfúlde.
was immer — whatever	áfi-sò . . . áfi yaiĕ . . ńgā-sò . .	gid-na . .	ko me-ne-ne	. . . . . .
entweder — oder — either — or —	— yaiĕ — yaiĕ	[2]	kò — kò — .	. . . . . .
und — and	— sò — sò .	. . . . . .	— da — . .	— bĕ — . .
nichts, gar nichts — nothing, nothing at all	áfi-nia gem .	. . . . . .	ba komi ba .	wōla [6] . . .
wie viel — how much, how many	ndà-go . . .	indi gorā . . ind-ukkur .	nawa .	dum) nōl . .
wie viel verlangst du dafür — what do you ask for it, what is the price	ndà-go nián-emin	ind-úkkur dano	nawa kurdi-nsa	no tiede nutko
1	tilo . . . . fal	trun . . . . toro [3] . . .	dèa [4] . . . . gudà	go
2	ndi	tĕu . . . . . kú	biu	didi [7] . . .
3	yásko [1] . . .	ágozò . . . óguzü . . .	oku	táti . . . .
4	dègu	tozo	fodu	nāi . . . .
5	úgu	fò; foo . . .	biet . . . . biel . . . . bier . . .	dāoī . . . .
6	rásko	disē; dis . .	šidda [5] . . .	dĕo-vĕ-gō [8] .

[1] Koelle hat in diesen Zahlenformen leichte Varianten, indem er schreibt pal, yāsge, dēga, ūrnsge, tālur, wāsge.

[2] Im Tédá wird das „entweder — oder" fast nie besonders ausgedrückt, sondern gewöhnlich durch den Ton der Rede angedeutet.

[3] In diesen Zahlwörtern ist, wie schon in der Einleitung gesagt, die nahe Verwandtschaft des Tédá mit dem Kanúri ganz klar in die Augen springend. Auch ndi und tĕu oder kú oder kiu stehen sich näher, als es auf den ersten Blick scheint. Dass auch bei ndi im K. die Variante mit u da war, ist aus der Form ndu-ri klar.

[4] dèa. Schön in der ersten, jetzt veralteten, Ausgabe seines Hausa-Wörterbuches, auf die ich deshalb weiter Rücksicht nehme, schreibt dein; in seinen neuen Übersetzungen schreibt er daia. Es ist ein sehr breites ĕ oder ae.

[5] šidda ist nach meiner Ansicht abgeleitet von ša dèa, „und eins", die fünf Finger der einen Hand und eins. Sitta, wie Schön schreibt, ist jedenfalls ganz falsch, und es ist sehr unwahrscheinlich, dass der Ausdruck für „sechs" allein aus dem Arabischen abgeleitet sein sollte, während die anderen ersten 10 Zahlwörter im H. gar keinen Arabischen Einfluss zeigen. Allerdings sehen wir gerade einen ähnlichen Fall in der Máha-Sprache. Die erwähnte Grundbedeutung hat sich sehr natürlich allmählich verloren und das ša dèa hat sich dann auf „elf" fixirt.

[6] wōla heisst eigentlich „es gibt nicht" und gehört daher als Verbalform nur uneigentlich hierher. Das ist auch der Grund, weshalb es eine so weite Bedeutung hat.

[7] Über die Übereinstimmung dieser Zahlwörter mit den entsprechenden der grossen süd-afrikanischen Familien s. die Einleitung.

[8] Die Zusammensetzung dieser Zahlwörter ist einem Jeden klar. Nur ist zu bemerken, dass das v vor dem ĕ (eigentlich bĕ, „und") ein blosser euphonischer Anlaut des o ist. In der contrahirten Form, die Reichardt in seinem Primer gibt, werden diese Zahlwörter in den weit ausgedehnten Landschaften, die ich besuchte, nirgend gesprochen.

[9] Diese Formen sind nach deutlicher Aussprache niedergeschrieben und ich brauche deshalb hier wie sonst nicht auf die sehr ungenauen Formen von Caillié (voyage à Timbouctou, Engl. Übers. II. Anh. II. S. 371 ff.) und Denham (Appendix zu Originalausgabe. 4. S. 182) stets hinzuweisen. Bei Caillié sind viele Fehler aus undeutlichem Schreiben in seinem fast verlorenen Tagebuch entstanden, so besonders (gou für „fünf", statt igou (ùgu), und dieselbe Form ist dann noch einmal für „sechs" wiederholt. Bei 15 und 16 hat er so ziemlich die richtigen Formen.

[10] In den östlicheren Landschaften Songai's ist diese national-einheimische Rechnung von 5 an durch das Arabische verdrängt worden. S. meinen Bericht über A'gades im Journal of the R. Geogr. Soc. of London, vol. XXI. p. 184.

[11] venághir ist wol entschieden zusammengesetzt aus „zweimal drei", ven-nághir, ebenso wie ven-yáde (eben deshalb schreibe ich so und nicht vehiade) aus ven und yáde.

[12] bòi, heyè und éfadè im Wándalá haben auf den ersten Blick eine grosse Ähnlichkeit mit den entsprechenden Hausa-Zahlwörtern biu, oku, fodu, wozu noch kommt, dass im W. auch für „eins" ursprünglich neben palle noch ein anderes, dem Hausa-Wort gudà verwandtes, Zahlwort gol oder ein ähnliches dagewesen sein muss; s. weiter unten.

[13] ngáomàdo-gò gòto bedeutet wörtlich „selbst nicht ein Ding ist da".

Sońyai.	Lógoné.	Wándalá.	Bágrimma.	Mába.
	hín-ta-belim . .	man ázerē-keni ázer-ūna . .	. . . .	. . .
?	?	(—magán) keni— (magán) keni	ēne — ēne — —kau — kau	— tá-ba — ta
— dē — . . .	— sāda — sāda	— bōna — bōna	— bāle — bāle	— ka — ka
. . . . . .	wadímadā . . .	man ázer-kē .	ngás kēde-gō gōto [13]	bateu (betúnde)
mergē	ganē	mágūora . .	kando . . .	ṅgōning
nel hakku tχímaiχin	gōra ganē . . .	kákalóng má-gūora	boi kando . .	ṅgōning kanmá-drakē
afō; fō [5] . . .	tekū . . . . serédiā . . .	palle . . .	kēde	tek
alfóka	kedē	búā [12] . . .	sab	bar
ahíndža; ahínza .	gáχkir	keyē	mutā	kuńgāl
atāki; táki . .	gāde	úfadē . . .	sō	asāl
igu [10]	sēni	ūdebē . . .	mī	tor
idu	venáχkir [11] . .	úúkohē . . .	migā	settāl

[1] Mr. Koelle has slight variations in these cardinal numbers, writing pal, yáego, dége, áraegy, wáegy.
[2] In Téda the „either — or" in general is not distinctly expressed, but merely indicated by the accent of the voice.
[3] The cardinals, as I have stated already in the introduction, show very clearly the near relation between the Téda and Kanúri languages. Even adi and tūō or ūn are more nearly related, than would appear at first sight. Thus it would seem from the form ada-ri, that for adi the K. possessed also the form adu.
[4] dia. Rev. Schön in the first edition of his Hausa-vocabulary writes dein and even in his recently published translations of the evangelists which he made with the assistance of the Hausa-boy, whom I brought to England, he writes sometimes dein, at others dais. It is a broad ā or [illegible].
[5] Kidda in my opinion is derived from ha dēa, „and one" (the five fingers of one hand and one), the original meaning of this form having gradually been lost, when the use of the (gōma) ha dēa formed the term for eleven. Schön writes Kitta which form approaches very near the Arabic term for „six", but the d sound is most distinct in all the dialects which I heard spoken. Moreover it is very improbable, that the term for „six" alone should have been taken from the Arabic, while the other cardinals from 1—10 show no Arabic influence whatever; however it is certainly remarkable, that this is the very case with the Māba cardinals.
[6] wóia properly is a verbal form, „there is not", and this is the reason, why the same word means „nobody" and „nothing".
[7] With regard to the similarity or identity of these numerals with those of the South-African families s. the Introduction.
[8] The composition of these numerals is clear to every body and I have only to observe, that the v which precedes the f or properly bē, „and", is a mere euphonical prolongation of the preceding e. Rev. Krapf in his Primer gives only a contracted form.
[9] These forms have been written down from very distinct pronunciation and it is therefore not necessary always to take notice of the forms of a few of them, such as given by Capt. Denham (Travels and Discoveries, Appendix p. 182) and Caillié (Voyage à Timbouctou, Engl. ed. vol. II. App. II. p. 392 ff.). In Caillié's list many mistakes have arisen from indistinct writing in his diary which was in an almost obliterated state; thus especially igou for „five" instead of igou (igu) and the same form has still been once repeated for „six". For „15" and „16" he gives nearly the right forms.
[10] In the Eastern districts of Sonyai this national system of reckoning beginning with five has been eliminated by the Arabic. S. my report on A'gades in the J. of the Royal Geogr. Soc. London, vol. XXI. p. 184 ([illegible] impression of the report p. 56).
[11] venáχkir, I have no doubt, is composed of „twice three", ven-gáχkir, just as ven-yāde of ven and gāde, and that is the reason why I do not write veāilde.
[12] The three numerals búā, keyē and úfadē in the Wándalá language at the very first sight bear a great resemblance to the corresponding Hausa numerals biu, ukú and fodū. Even for the first cardinal number the W. language appears to have possessed another term besides palle and nearer related to the Hausa-term dadé, although its form is not now quite certain. S. further on.
[13] ngás kēde-gō gōto means verbally „even not one thing is there".

Deutsch und Englisch.	Kanuri.	Tedā.	Hausa.	Fulfulde.
7	tųllur . . .	turrésiò . . . tųddesū . . .	bákoi . . .	dšō-vē-didi .
8	usku [1]	usō . . . . . yųsū	tókus . . .	džō-vē-tatti .
9	legár . . .	isī . . . . . yesē	tárn	džō-vē-nai . . .
10	mēgū [2]	mur-dō [5] . . . mor-dúm . . .	gōma . . .	sappo [7] . . .
11	mēgū n tilò n mēgū lag-ri [3]	mor summa torō	gōma ša dēa [6]	sappo ē gō .
12	mēgū n-ndī n mēgu ndu-ri	mor summa kiū	gōma ša biu .	sappo ē didi .
13	mēgū n yasko n	mor summ' águzū	gōma ša okū .	sappo ē tatti .
14	mēgū n dēgu n [4]	mor summa tozō	gōma ša fodu	sappo ē nai .
15	mēgū n ūgu n	mor summa fō	gōma ša biel .	sappo ē džōī .
16	mēgū n rasko n	mor summa disē	gōma ša šidda	sappo ē džō-vē-gō
17	mēgū n tųllur-ri	mor summa tųdesū	gōma ša bákoi	sappo ē džō-vē-didi
18	mēgū n usku n	mor summa yųsū	gōma ša tókus	sappo ē džō-vē-tatti
19	mēgū n legár-ri	mor summa isī	gōma ša tárn	sappo ē džō-vē-nai

[1] usku ist entschieden entstanden aus ūgu yasko, „fünf und drei".

[2] mēgū ist ebenso entschieden gebildet aus mē und ūgu, indem mē auch in anderen Wörtern mit der Bedeutung einer Wiederholung, einer Verdoppelung vorkommt. Daraus ergibt sich dann, dass die Ähnlichkeit dieses Zahlwortes mit dem entsprechenden meyāū im Temāšight ganz zufällig ist.

[3] mēgū lag-ri: lagri ist ohne Zweifel gebildet von laga, „Jemand, Einer", das aber nie für das bestimmte Zahlwort „eins" erscheint; also eigentlich laga-ri, aber das a wird nicht gehört.

[4] mēgū n dēgu n: Koelle, der bei allen diesen Zahlwörtern das mēgū weglässt, was nur unter bestimmten Verhältnissen Statt finden kann, hat für 14 dēri (zusammengezogen aus dēgu-ri) und für 15 ūri und wūri (ūgu-ri).

[5] mur-dō, mor-dúm: das dō oder dúm gehört entschieden nicht zum Stammworte. Da nun mor oder mur in keiner, auch nicht der entferntesten, Beziehung zu fō (fünf) steht, wie das Kanuri mēgū zu ūgu, so könnte es aus einer anderen Sprache herübergenommen zu sein scheinen, aber in fast allen diesen Sprachen hat der Ausdruck für „zehn" keine Ableitungsverwandtschaft mit dem für „fünf".

[6] In gewöhnlicher Rede sagt man nur ša dēa, ša biu, ohne das gōma zu nennen. Bei den Zwanzigern, Dreissigern aber ist das ašrin, tälatin u. s. w. unumgänglich nöthig.

[7] Die Entstehung von sappo ebenso wie diejenige von nogāš oder nogás ist mir nicht klar geworden; genug, das Erste ist die Einheit der Finger, in der Pluralform tšappande, das Zweite die der Finger und Zehen zusammengenommen.

[8] wařiha afō a)šī, eigentlich „zwanzig einer fehlt" oder „weniger eins", ist bei Caillié durch blosse Verschiebung an die Stelle von 20 gerathen. Das tohše aber, das er daneben für 80 anführt, ist mir im Soŋyai völlig unbekannt; dagegen ist es interessant, zu bemerken, dass es in der Pluralform bei mir unter den in der Provinz Māsina üblichen Fulfulde-Ausdrücken für 40, 60, 80 erscheint, tohē-dži didi, nai u. s. w., zwei Zwanziger, vier Zwanziger, also „ein Zwanziger" offenbar tohē, und es ist allerdings nicht unmöglich, dass die Fulbe diesen Ausdruck von den Soŋyai angenommen haben. — Übrigens ist wariáka (eigentlich wa-r-iáka), und die folgenden Zehner natürlich zusammengesetzt aus wa, der Grundwurzel von ewoei und ahiáka, ahiasa u. s. w. Dass das r nur eine euphonische Einschiebung ist, ergiebt deutlich sein Ausfallen bei wā-do, wā-ga, wā-ha, wā-ga.

[9] kolaua džuugtegol. Ich bin etwas ungewiss über die Zusammensetzung dieses Ausdruckes. Da „und" hier durch dža ausgedrückt erscheint, so muss man annehmen, dass das „eins" in „elf" (zehn und „eins") durch nagtegol ausgedrückt ist. Das sieht aber nicht wie eine einfache Form für das erste Zahlwort aus.

[10] duk-kamē ist, wie ich glaube, entstanden aus duk-kēde, „ein Zehner". Die Ähnlichkeit mit dem Haussa-Wort dikumi ist wol nur zufällig.

Sonyai.	Lógoné.	Wándalá.	Bágrimma.	Mába.
idž . . .	kătul	wūyo . . .	tšidī; tšilī . .	mindrī
yāha	venyāde . . .	tise	marta . . .	iya
yagga	disχiēn	masilmánne .	dōso	adoī
áwuai	χkán	kelaua . . .	duk-kemē [10] .	atúk
áwuai kindi fō .	χkan ka lekū	kelaua dżung-tegel [9]	duk-kemē kar kēde	atúk tong
áwuai kindi a)hiáka	χkan ka kadē .	kelaua dżu bua	duk-kemē kar sab	atúk baráng
áwuai kindi a)hinza	χkan ka gaχkir .	kelaua dżu keyē	duk-kemē kar mutá	atúk kungáng
áwuai kindi táki	χkan ka gádo .	kelaua dž(u)úfadē	duk-kemē kar sō	atúk asáng
áwuai kindi igu	χkan ka sesi . .	kelaua dž(u)íldelē	duk-kemē kar mī	atúk turáng
áwuai kindi idu .	χkan ka venáχkir	kelaua dž(u) un-kohē	duk-kemē kar migā	aták settáng
áwuai kindi idž .	χkan ka kătul .	kelaua dżu wūye	duk-kemē kar tšidi	atúk tal mindri
áwuai kindi yāha	χkan ka venyāde	kelaua dżu tise	duk-kemē kar marta	atúk tal iya
áwuai kindi yagga / wariáka afá a)ñi [8]	χkan ka disχiēn	kelaua dżu masil-mánne	duk-kemē kar dōso	atúk tal adoī

[1] uahu is undoubt formed from águ and yasko, „five and three".

[2] mégu is formed quite as certainly from mé and águ; me also in the composition of other words conveys the meaning of a repetition and we must therefore draw the conclusion, that the resemblance of the cardinal mégu with the corresponding one in the Temáshight language is but accidental, although it is remarkable, that also in the Tédā language it is nearly the same.

[3] mégu lag-rī: lag-rī undoubt is formed from laga, „some body", and which in this case is equivalent to „one". The original form therefore is laga-rī, but the „a" has been eliminated.

[4] mégu n dégu n: Koelle leaves out the mégu in all these cardinals, but such a use is only justified under certain conditions. For 14 he has the form dēri and for 15 ūri and wūri, evidently vulgar forms for dégu-rī, águ-rī.

[5] mur-dō, mor-dūm: the dō or dūm evidently does not belong to the root, which seems to be mur or mor. A great difference between the Kanúri and the Tédā cardinals is, that mor-dūm bears no relation whatever to fō (five), while mégu is intimately connected with águ. It might therefore seem probable, that mor-dūm has been introduced from another language. But almost in all these languages we find the term for „ten" without any connection with that for „five".

[6] In common conversation the terms ka dēo, ka bio are sufficient, without adding the góma; but with the terms (pl. tšappánde) connected with 30, 40 it is necessary to add the sáeria, télatio.

[7] Neither the origin of sappo, nor that of nogāī or nogáo has become known to me; but so much is clear, that sappo (pl. tšappánde) indicates the number of the fingers, the latter that of the fingers and toes taken together.

[8] wariáka afá (a)ñi, properly „twenty less one", in Caillié's list has got into the place of twenty. The term tuber however, which he gives likewise for „20", I have not met with in those provinces of Sonyai, which I have visited, but it is very interesting, that it appears as the plural form in my lists among the Fulfúlde-terms usual in the province of Másina for 40, 60, 80, tobē-dži didi, nai etc., two twenties, four twenties etc., consequently tobē, the singular form of tobē-dži, means „twenty", and it is not at all unlikely, that the Fulbe have overcome this term from their neighbours and subjects the Sonyai. — As for the origin of wariáka and the following cardinals expressing „ten" there can be no doubt, but that they are a combination of wa, the root of áwuai and ahiáka, ahinza, the r being inserted from euphonical reasons.

[9] kelaua dżungtegel. I am not quite certain as to the composition of this term; dżu no doubt meaning „and" we must conclude, that the notion „one" (ten and „one") is expressed in this compound term by ungtegel, although we can scarcely believe this to be a simple term for the first cardinal numeral.

[10] duk-kemē I suppose to have been corrupted from duk-kēde, „one ten". The resemblance with the corresponding term dikumī in Musgu is only accidental.

Deutsch und Englisch.	Kanuri.	Tēdā.	Hausa.	Fulfúlde.
20	fi-ndi[1] . . .	diggedim . . duk-kiū[3] . .	hanya[4] . . íšerin . . . lasso (Sok.) .	nogás; nogaï (Maa.) lasso (Góber)
21	fi-ndin tata tilō n	duk-kiū summa torō	íšerin da dēa	nogás ē gō lasso ē gō
29	fi-ndin tata legár-ni n	duk-kiū summa isi	íšerin da tāra	lasso ē džō-vē-nai
30	fi-yasko . .	mor-t(a)-águzū	télatin . . .	tšappánde-tatti woróndža (Soñy.) lasso ē sappo
33	fi-yasko n tata yasko n	mor-t(a)-águzū summa águzū	télatin da okū	tšappánde-tatti ē tatti
39	fi-yasko n tata legár nin	mor-t(a)-águzū summa isi	télatin da tāra	tšappánde-tatti e džō-vē-nai
40	fi-dēgu . .	mor-ta-tozō .	hanya biu . arbéin[5] . .	tšappánde-nai lassō-dži didi tobē-dži didi, Ms.
45	fi-dēgu n tata ūguu	mor-ta-tozō summ(a) afō	arbéin da biel	tšappánde-nai ē džōi
49	fi-dēgu n tata legár-nin	mor-ta-tozō summa isi	arbéin da tāra	tšappánde-nai ē džō-vē-nai
50	fi-gu[2] . . .	mor-ta-fō .	hanya biu da gōma hamsin . .	tšappánde-džōi lassō-dži didi ē sappo tobē-dži didi ē sappo
51	fi-gu n tata tilō n	mor-ta-fō summa torō	hamsin da dēa	tšappánde-džōi ē gō ·
59	fi-gu n tata legár-nin	mor-ta-fō summa isi	hamsin da tāra	tšappánde-džōi ē džō-vē-nai
60	fi-rasko . .	mor-ta-disē .	hanya okū . settin . . .	tšappánde džō-vē-gō lassō-dži tatti tobē-dži tatti
67	fi-rasko n tata tyllur-nin	mor-ta-disē summa týddesū	settin da bókoi	tšappánde-džō-vē-gō ē džō-vē-didi

[1] fi-ndi oder, wie Koelle aus anderer Dialektaussprache hat, pindi bedeutet unterbleiden „zwei Zehner". Wie aber dies fi oder pi, das auch in den folgenden Zehnern erscheint, zu der Bedeutung von „Zehner" gekommen ist, weiss ich nicht.

[2] fi-gu. Koelle gibt dafür píngu, aber obgleich fi-gu aus fi-ngu zusammengezogen ist, hört man doch das erste n nicht.

[3] duk-kiū ist eine ganz ähnliche Bildung wie fi-ndi; das duk im Bagrimma scheint ganz dasselbe Wurzelwort zu sein und ist vielleicht daher genommen, da es nur dies eine Mal in Tēdā erscheint.

[4] hanya. Dieser Ausdruck ist der alterthümliche und nationale, der das Rechnungssystem der Haussa abschloss als Gesammtzahl der Finger und Zehen, wie das auch bei vielen anderen Völkern der Fall ist. Bei dem gemeinen Mann schliesst die hanya das Rechnungssystem noch jetzt ab und er fängt dann wieder bei „eins" an; allerdings muss er dann bei grossen Summen, wie sie aber erst in später Zeit durch grösseren Verkehr unter seine Anschauung fielen, sich grösserer Zahlen als zwanzig bedienen, also 30 hanya, 40 hanya und so weiter; dazu nahm man denn die arabischen Ausdrücke zu Hülfe, die nun allmählich den nationalen Ausdruck verdrängten. — Schön schreibt in seinen neuen Übersetzungen íšerin, dazu ist aber nicht der geringste Grund vorhanden. — Der Ursprung des in Góber üblichen lassó ist mir ungewiss.

[5] arbéin. Ich halte es für unnöthig, bei diesen aus dem Arabischen aufgenommenen Wörtern das ain beizubehalten.

[6] tkam ist zweifelsohne zusammengesetzt und zusammengezogen aus tekŭ gham, „zwei Zehner", ebenso wie die entsprechenden Wörter in W., B. und M.; in letzterem ist kashir höchst wahrscheinlich eine populäre Korruption von atuhashir oder har.

Sońyai.	Lógoné.	Wándalā.	Bágrimma.	Mába.
warínka	tkam[6]	kul-búā . .	duk-sáb . .	kanbir
warínka kindi fō	tkam ka tekū .	kul-búā džung tegoi	duk-sáb kar kēde	kanbir toṅg
warínza afō (a)ši	tkam ka disχiēn	kul-búā džn masilmánne	duk-sáb kar dōso	kanbir tal adoi
warínza . . .	tkam-ka-χkan .	kul-keyē . .	duk-mutā . .	télatīn
warínza kindi (a)hínza	tkam-ka-χkan ka gáχkir	kul-keyē džu keyē	duk-mutā kar mutā	télatīn koṅgáng
warínza kindi yagga / war-táki afo (a)ši	tkam-ka-χkan ka disχiēn	kul-keyē džn masilmánne	duk-mutā kar dōso	télatīn tal adoi
war-táki . . .	tkam-kadē . .	kul-úfadē . .	duk-sō . . .	arbéin[5]
war-táki kind(i) ïgu	tkam-kadē ka sōsi	kul-úfadē džn ñdebē	duk-sō kar mi	arbéin toróṅg
war-táki kindi yagga / wē-gu afō (a)ši .	tkam-kadē ka disχiēn	kul-úfadē džu masilmánne	duk-sō kar dōso	arbéin tal adoi
wē-gu	tkam-kadē-ka-χkan	kul-ñdebē	duk-mi	hamsīn
wē-gu kind(i) ïgu	tkam-kadē-ka-χkan ka tekū	kul-ñdebē džn (u)ngtegoi	duk-mi kar kēde	hamsīn toṅg
wē-gu kindi yagga	tkam-kadē-ka-χkan ka disχiēn	kul ñdebē džu masilmánne	duk-mi kar dōso	hamsīn tal adoi
wē-du	tkam-gáχkir . .	kul-únkohē . / kul-unkōi .	duk-migā . .	settīn
wē-du kind(i) ïdu	tkam-gáχkir ka kátul	kul-unkōi džu wūye	duk-migā kar tšidi	settīn tal mindrī

[1] fi-adi, or as Koelle writes piadi, a mere slight variation of dialect and pronunciation, evidently means „two hands", although I am not able to say, how the fi or pi get this signification, which appears also in the following cardinals.
[2] fi-gu. Koelle writes plūgu, but although fi-gu is evidently contracted from fi-ŋgu, yet the n is not heard.
[3] dūk-hiū is quite a similar formation as fi-adi, the duk apparently being identical with the same term in *Bágrimma* and probably introduced from thence, as in Tēdā it appears only in this single instance.
[4] hanya: this expression is the ancient and national term, which concluded the original mode of reckoning of the Hausawa, being the joined number of the fingers and toes, a natural idea, which appears in the language of many nations. With the common Ba-hause man the hanya even at present is the end of his wit, where having arrived, he begins again with „one". Certainly for large sums, such as they become necessary in consequence of enlarged trade and intercourse, he is obliged to have recourse to other cardinals than twenty, but this he does in such a manner, as to subordinate these higher numbers to the term „twenty", as 30 hanya, 40 hanya; but the Arabic terms once introduced soon succeeded in ejecting the national term hanya to a great extent. — Rev. Schön in his translations writes ishirin, but there is not the slightest reason for the i. — Lasso is used in Góber, but I do not know its origin, as it does not seem to belong to the Sonyai-language.
[5] I deem it unnecessary with regard to these terms introduced into these languages from the Arabic to retain the Arabic ain.
[6] tkám, no doubt, is composed and contracted of tekū and χkan, „two hands", just as the corresponding terms in W., B. and M.; in the latter idiom kanbir most probably is a popular corruption instead of alakan bir or bar.

Deutsch und Englisch.	Kanúri.	Tédā.	Hausa.	Fulfúlde.
69	fi-rasko-n tata legár-nin	mor-ta-disē summa isi	settin da tára	tšappánde džō-vé-gō é džō-vē-nai
70 . .	fi-tyllur . .	mor-ta-týddesū	hauya okū da góma . . / sebéin . . .	tšappánde džō-vé-didi . / lasōdži tatti é sappo . . / tobēdži tatti é sappo . .
72	fi-tyllur-nin tata ndi-n	mor-ta týddesū summa kiū	sebéin da biu	tšappánde džō-vé-didi ē didi
79	fi-tyllur-nin tata legár-nin .	mor-ta týddesū summa isi	sebéin da tára	tšappánde džō-vé-didi ē džō-vē-nai
80	fi-t-usku . .	mor-ta-yysū .	hauya fodu . / témanin . .	tšappánde džō-vē-tatti . / lasōdži nai . / tobēdži nai .
88	fi-t-usku-n tata usku-n	mor-ta-yysū summa yysū	témanin da tókus	tšappánde džō-vé-tatti ē džō-vē-tatti
89	fi-t-usku-n tata legár-nin	mor-ta-yysū summa isi	témanin da tára	tšappánde džō-vé-tatti ē džō-vē-nai
90	fi-legár . .	mor-ta-isi .	hauya fodū da góma . . / teséin . . .	tšappánde džō-vē-nai . . / lasōdži nai ē sappo . . / tobēdži nai ō sappo . .
99	fi-legár-nin tata legár-nin / fi-legár legári [1]	mor-ta-isi summa isi	teséin da tára / dari bābo dēa	tšappánde džō-vē-nai ē džō-vē-nai . . / hémeredullel gō
100 . .	mie [2]	mie	dari . . . / zango [3] . .	hémere . . / temérre [4] . .
101 .	mie n tata tilō n	mie summa trō	dari da dēa .	temérre ē gō .

[1] fi-legár-legári. Dies ist die gewöhnlich übliche Form. Genau grammatisch sollte es allerdings heissen fi-legár-nin tata legár-nin.

[2] mie. Wahrscheinlich ist es nur durch allmählichen Gebrauch fixirt, dass yēro oder yōra, wie Koelle schreibt, wie ich es jedoch nie habe aussprechen hören, nie für „einhundert" gebraucht wird, ebenso wenig wie mie bei der Mehrheit von „hundert"; nur sonderbarer Weise sagt man wieder debū mie, jedoch scheint es nur in diesem einzigen Fall statt zu finden; denn bei 300000 tritt das yēro wieder in sein Recht ein und man sagt nur debū yēro ndi, nicht debū mie ndi. Vollkommen analog ist es der Tédā-Sprache ergangen, wo das nationale hēterа bei „einhundert" von dem Arabischen mia oder mīye verdrängt worden ist.

[3] zango ist gleichwie nambar den Hausaua von den ihnen im Handel und Gewerbebetrieb weit vorangeschrittenen Sonyai zugekommen. Solche Sprachverhältnisse beweisen Alles, was ich in meinem Reisewerk über die materiellen Beziehungen dieser Völkerschaften gesagt habe.

[4] temérre ist wahrscheinlich der Wolof-Sprache entlehnt.

[5] dermbe an-edle mfelle. an-edle scheint ein verstärktes „und" zu sein, etwa „und füge hinzu". In anderen Fällen erscheint an allein. In mfalle ist das p in palle (eins) in das engverwandte f übergegangen und hat ein euphonisches m zum Vorschlag bekommen. Etwas Ähnliches, in älteren Sprachen nur ein natürlicher Vorschlag, der im Schreiben vielleicht wegzulassen wäre, hat lldebē bekommen in dermbe bēā an hai-wōye an-edle er lldebē und so selbst masilmānse in 999.

[6] arú im Bágrimma ist wohl unzweifelhaft mit yēro im K. verwandt.

Sońγai.	Lógoné.	Wándalā.	Bagrimma.	Mába.
wē-du kindi yagga	tkam-gáχkir ka dis-χiēn	kul uńkōī dža masilmánne	duk-migā kar dōso	settin tal adoi
war-idž . . .	tkam-gáχkir-ka-χkan	kul-wūye . .	duk-tšidi . .	sebéin / méndigi (?)
war-idž kindi idž	tkam-gáχkir-ka-χkan ka kadó	kul-wūye dža búa	duk-tšidi kar sab	sebéin baráng
war-idž kindi yagga	tkam-gaχkir-ka-χkan ka disχiēn	kul-wūye dža masilmánne	duk-tšidi kar dōso	sebéin tal adoi
wē-ha . . .	tkam-gāde . .	kul-tise . .	duk-marta	témanin / égil (?)
wē-ha kindi yāha	tkam-gāde ka venyāke	kul-tise dža tise	duk-marta kar marta	témanin taliyá
wē-ha kindi yagga	tkam-gāde ka disχiēn	kul-tise dža masilmánne	duk-marta kar dōso	témanin tal adoi
wē-ga	tkam-gāde-ka-χkan	kul-masilmánne	duk-dōso . .	tesēin
wē-ga kindi yagga / zańgo fō asikuna	tkam-gāde-ka-χkan ka disχiēn	kul masilmánne dža masilmánne	duk-dōso kar dōso	tesēin tal adoi
zańgo fō . . .	mia	dermke . . .	arū[6]	dukák
zańgo fō kindi fō	mia ka tekú . .	dermke an-edže mfalle[5]	arū kar kēde	dukák tong

[1] ff-legár-legári is the usual form, but according to grammatical rules it should be ff-legár-nan tate legár-nin.
[2] mie. No doubt originally the national term also for „one hundred" was yēro — yéru, as Koelle writes, I never once heard pronounced —, but gradually it was established by common use, that for expressing this term the Arabic word mie alone should be employed, while the latter is never used for the plurality of „hundred", with the only exception of the notion „[illegible]", where debū mie" is the only term now in common use, while in [illegible] the national term yēro again vindicates its right, so that people say only debū yēro adī and not debū mie adī. It is remarkable, that we find quite a similar occurrence in the Tēda-language, where for the notion „one hundred" the Arabic term mie or miye has expelled the national term hēteru.
[3] zańgo just as the term sambar the Hausawa have adopted from their Western neighbours the Songhai, who have led the way and given them an example in trade as well as intercourse. Linguistic relations such as these illustrate the historical account, which I have given in my Travels and Discoveries.
[4] tamérre or témere I suppose to have been borrowed from the Wolof-language.
[5] dermke an-edže mfalle: an-edže seems to be nothing but a stronger form for „and", similar to our „and add thereto". In other combinations the particle an appears alone. In the word „mfalle" the p in palle (one) has been changed into the closely related consonant f or rather p, to which a euphonical m has been added. A similar additional sound, which in these illiterate languages is but too frequent and which, if they had been reduced to writing, would perhaps have cast off, the term [illegible] has received in the phrase „dermke bū an kul-wūye an-edže [illegible]" and even masilmánne in the term for 999.
[6] arū in Bagrimma is evidently related to the yēro in Kanúri.

Deutsch und Englisch.	Kanúri.	Tédá.	Hausa.	Fulfúlde.
143	mīe n fī-dēgu n tata yasko n	mīe mor-ta-tozō summ(a) águzū	darī arbēīn da okū	temérre tšappánde nai ē tatti
199	mīe n fī-legár-nin tata legár-ni n	mīe mor-ta-isī summa isī	darī temīn da tāra / darī bīu dēa bābo	temérre tšappánde džō-vē-nai ē džō-vē-nai / kēme didī dullel gō
200	yēro ndī . .	kátara kiū . .	darī bīu . .	témede didī / kēme didī[4] .
275	yēro ndī-n fī-tųl-lur-nin tata ūgu n	kátara kiū mor-ta tųddesū summa fō	darī bīu sebēī n da bīel	kēme didī tšappánde džō-vē-didī ē džōī
300	yēro yasko .	kátar(a) águzū	darī okū . .	témede / kēme tatti
400	yēro dēgu . .	kátara tozō .	darī fodū . .	témede / kēme nai
500	yēro ūgu . .	kátara fō . .	darī bīel . .	témede / kēme džōī
600	yēro rasko .	kátara disē .	darī šidda . .	témede / kēme džō-vō-gō
700	yēro tųllur .	kátara tųddesū	darī bókoi . .	témede / kēme džō-vē-didī
800	yēro usku . .	kátara yųsū .	darī tókus . .	témede / kēme džō-vē-tatti
900	yēro legár . .	kátara isī . .	darī tāra . .	témede / kēme džō-vē-nai
999	yēro legár-nin fī-legár-nin tata legárnin	kátara isī mor-ta-isī summa isī	debū dēa bābo	kēme sappo / udžunēre / zambar dullel gō
1000	debū[1]	debū	debū . . . / zambar[3] . . .	kēme sappo / udžunēre . / zambar . .
1852	debū n yēro uskun fīgun lokundīn[2]	debū kátara yųsū mor-ta-fō summa kiū	debū darī tókus hamsīn da bīu	debū da kēme džō-vē-tatti tšappánde džōī ē didī
2000	debū ndī . .	debū kiū . .	zambar bīu .	zambar didī / udžūne didī

[1] debú: Koelle schreibt débu. Dieses Wort ist in alle diese Sprachen aus derselben Quelle eingeführt.

[2] debū — loku ndīn. Dieses loku, das Koelle gar nicht gekannt zu haben scheint, wird bei längeren Zahlenquoten anstatt des tata gebraucht.

[3] Dieses zambar haben die Hausa wahrscheinlich erst von den Sonγai gelernt.

[4] kēme ist den Regeln der Fulfúlde-Sprache gemäss ziemlich gewöhnlich gebildeter Plural von hēme-re und doch stimmt es vollkommen mit dem Hausa-Ausdruck überein, während diese Sprache doch den Singular hēmere nicht zu kennen scheint. Hierüber muss die Zukunft nähere Aufschlüsse geben. — témede oder vielmehr témeđe ist ebenso regelmässig gebildeter Plural von témere.

[5] Das a in dakák scheint in der Mehrheit in o überzugehen. Das n vor hār ist augenscheinlich ein bloss euphonisches, um den Missklang eines Zusammentreffens von k und h zu verhüten.

[6] In deká lyo und deká ndol hat man das k am Ende fallen lassen, es scheint also unwesentlich zu sein.

Sedyal.	Légual.	Wándalä.	Bágrimma.	Mába.
zañgo fō warióka kindi bínza	mia ka tkam-kadē ka gáχkir	dermke an kul-úfa-dē an-edže keyē	arū duk-sō kar mutá	dakák arbēīn kuńgál
zañgo fō wē-ga kindi yagga . . . } zañgo bíńka fō asá-kunū . . . }	mia ka tkam-gáde -ka-χkan ka díaχiēn	dermke an kul-masilmánne an-edže masilmánne	arū duk-dōso kar dōso . . .	dakák teséīn tal adol
zañgo bíńka . .	mia kadē . . .	dermke búā .	arū sab	dekák [5] nbar
zañgo bíńka warīdā kindi īgu	mia kadē tkam-gáχ-kir-ka-χkan ka sēai	dermke búā an kul-wūye an-edž(e) er īldebē	arū sab duk-tšidi kar mi	dekák nbar ar-béīn toróńg
zañgo bínza . .	mia gáχkir . .	dermk(e) keyē	arū mutā . .	dekák kuńgál
zañgo taki . .	mia gāle . . .	dermk(e) úfadē	arū sō . . .	dekák asāl
zañgo īgu . . .	mia sēai . . .	dermk(e) īldebē	arū mi . . .	dekák tor
zañgo īdu . . .	mia venáχkir . .	dermk(e) úńkobē	arū migā . .	dekák settál
zañgo īdž . . .	mia kátul . .	dermke wūye	arū tšidi . .	dekák míndri
zañgo yāha . .	mia venyáde . .	dermke tīse .	arū marta . .	deká īya [6]
zañgo yagga . .	mia díaχiēn . .	dermke masil-mánne	arū dōso . .	deká adol
zañgo yagga wē-ga kindi yagga } zambar fo asákunu }	mia díaχiēn ka tkam-gáde-ka-χkan ka díaχiēn	dermke masil-mánne an kul-masilmánne anedž(e)er ma-silmánne	arū dōso duk-dōso kar dōso .	deká adol teséīn tal adol
zambar	debū	debū	debū	elf (Arab.)
zambar da zañgo yā-ha wē-gu kindi īgu	debū mia venyáde ka tkam-kadē-ka-χkan ka kadē	debū an dermke tīse an kul-īlde-bē an-edže búā	debū arū marta duk-mi kar sab	elf deká īya bam-sin baróńg
zambar bíńka .	debū kadē . . .	debu búā . .	debū sab . .	ellef bar

[1] dobū. Koelle writes dúba. It is evident, that this term has been introduced into all these languages from the same source.
[2] debû — loku ndi a. The term loku, which seems to have escaped Rev. Koelle's notice, appears to take the place of tete in longer forms of numerals.
[3] It is placed almost beyond a doubt, that the Housaas have introduced the term zambar from the Sedyal.
[4] hôme according to the laws of the Fulfúlde-language is a regularly formed plural of hóme-re; it is therefore the more remarkable, that the form hôme is totally identical with the corresponding Bámbara word, while that language does not appear to have the singular form hémere. — témede is the plural of témere or temérre, the latter being a contractedform of temédere.
[5] dekák nbar: the first a in dakák seems to have been changed into an e in the plural form. The n preceding the bar is evidently of a merely euphonic nature, in order to prevent the collision of a k and b.
[6] In the terms deka íya and deká adol the final k has been eliminated and we may thence conclude, that it does not belong to the root.

Deutsch und Englisch.	Kanúri.	Tédā.	Hausa.	Fulfúlde.
6347	debu n ūgu n yēro yasko n fi-rasko-n loku tyllurnin	debū fō kátarn ágozu morta-disō summan tydde su	zambar hul dari oku settin da bákoi	zambar dži kē-udžune me titi tšappánde dže-ve-gō ē dži-ve dīdi
10000	debu mēgu .	debū morduin	zambar goma	udžune sappo / zambar sappo
100000	debu mie . .	debū mie . .	zambar dari .	zambar temērre
129765	debū mie n fi-ndī n tata le-gari n yēro tyllurin fi-rasko-n tata ūgu n		zambar dari da debu āšerin da tara da dari bákoi settin da biel	
388243	debū yēro yas-ko n fi-t-usku n yēro ndi fi-dēgu n tata yasko n		zambar dari okū da debu tēmun-nia da tákus da dari bu ar-bēin da okū	
1,000000	debū debū .		debū baháu .	
der erste — *the first* .	lange [1] . . . / fugo-bē . . / burgō-bē [2] .	burdō . . .	na-fāri . . .	arraune [5] . . / fudōde . .
der zweite — *the second*	ken-ndi-bē [3] .	sōhi [4] . . .	na-biu . . .	gadādžo . . / dimmo . .
der dritte — *the third* .	ken-yasko .	águzū . . .	na-oku . . .	tokkndo ga-dādžo / tataibo . .
der vierte — *the fourth*	ken-dēgu . .	tozō	na-fudū . .	navēbu . . / nōbu . . .
der fünfte — *the fifth* .	ken-ūgu . .	fō	na-biel . .	džōgo . . . / džōābo . .

[1] lange führt Koelle auch mit der Bedeutung „eins" auf, aber so habe ich es niemals gebraucht gefunden.

[2] fúgo-bē, burgo-bē sind allerdings eigentlich Genitivformen, aber nur diese werden in den meisten Fällen gebraucht, wenigstens wo es sich von Menschen handelt, wo man sich „(ein Mann) des ersten (Gliedes oder der ersten Stellung)" denken kann. Der erste Tag des Monats heisst auf K. burgo kintáko-bē, auf T. suri burdó, auf B. mot-ne napoahi, auf M. čēk-na-tonil.

[3] ken-ndi-bē. Diese Ordinalform ist ganz allgemein in Gebrauch, und ich muss hier Koelle widersprechen, der in seiner Grammatik (p. 46) angibt, dass die Ordinalform mit ken nur für die Zahlen von 3—10 vorhanden sei, während für die erste und zweite Zahl keine solche existire.

[4] sōhi scheint beide Bedeutungen zu haben, „zweiter" (eigentlich „folgender") und „letzter".

[5] arraune hat eine mir unbekannte Wurzel.

[6] vōlanaáka und die beiden folgenden Ordinalien sind zum mindesten sehr unsicher. So sollte man meinen, dass thánaáka jedenfalls eher „der erste" bedeute als „der zweite", von tehū, „eins". Unmöglich ist es jedoch nicht, dass vōlanaáka doch der „erste" bedeutet, indem vala vom Arabischen auel abgeleitet wäre. In vahonkatkālle scheint wieder irgend eine Beziehung zu „Erster" zu liegen; thālle von tehū und ale? — Überhaupt zeigt die verschiedene, so ganz und gar abweichende Art und Weise, wie im Lōgonē, wenigstens so weit es mir bekannt geworden, diese Ordinalformen ausgedrückt werden, mit pēle, sal und mi, deutlich genug die unausgebildete Beschaffenheit dieser Redeform.

[7] akatafko ist mehr als ungewiss; dennoch könnte es ein militärischer Ausdruck sein, da es in gewisser Beziehung zu aka-tēllero, „Hintermann", zu stehen scheint.

[8] In g-lldm-lēē ist das d in lldebē ausgelassen worden und das b in ein m verwandelt.

[9] alf-kan dōkshān ist auffallend, aber, obgleich ganz ungrammatisch gebildet, doch vielleicht richtig.

Bak;al.	Lógonē.	Wándalā.	Bágrimma.	Mába.
zambar igu du zango hinza wē-du kindi idu	debū sēsi ka mia gizkir ka tkam-gizkir ka kátul	(debu ŭdebē an dermk(e) keye an kul-úúkohē an edže wŭye)	debu mi arū mutá duk-migú kar tšidi	ellef tor dekák kungūl settin tal mindri
zambar áwuat .	debū ẓkan . . .	debū keinna .	debā duk-kemē	allef atúk
zambar zańgo .	debū mia . . .	debū dermku .	debu arú . .	elf-kan dákakán[9]
. . . .	(debū mia ka tkam ka dïsziēn ka mia kátul ka tkam-gizkir ka sēsi)	(debū dermke an debū kul-búa an debū masibnán-ne an dermke wŭye an kul-úúkohē an edž(e)er ŭdebē)	(arū duk-sáb kar diso debū arū tšiū duk-mi-gā kar mi)	
	(debū mia gizkir ka tkam-gale ka venyáde ka mia kalē tkam kalē ka gizkir)	(debū dermk' keyē an debu kul-tise an debū edž(e)er tise dermke búa an kul-úfabē an edž(e)er keyē)	(arū duk-marta kar marta de-bū arū sab duk-sō kar mutá)	
	debū dóeakál debiya	debū-debū .	debū-debū	
	vōlanaúnka[6] . .	akatáfke?[7] .	nā	{džul aúcinā}
. . . .	tkánaúnka . . .	gu-bú-irē . .	mol-ga-nia . .	-bulò
	vakanhatkálle .	il-key-irē . .	mutā-nákena	-káyinga
	pēle-gádnlan uaua-káunlan	g-ufūd-irē .	sō-naki . .	-sal
	mal-sēsi-nē . .	g-ilém-irē[8] .	mi-naki . .	-tur

[1] lago with Koelle has also the meaning of „one", but I have never found it used so.

[2] fūgo-bū, burgu-bū no doubt originally designate the genitive case, although not but these forms are generally used, at least wherever there is the question of man, the proper meaning being „a man of the first rank or station". Different is the case in other connections, as „the first (day) of the month", K. burgo kintáke-bū, T. auri burdè, B. mot-na napnaki, M. éčh-na-tonti.

[3] ken-adi-bē: this ordinal is in very general and undisputed use and I am therefore obliged to correct Mr. Koelle, who states in his grammar (p. 41, § 46), that the form of the ordinal with ken is only used for the numbers from 3—10, while for „first" and „second" there is no proper ordinal, as he says.

[4] sĕbi also seems to have both meanings, that of „second" or „follower" and „last", „hindmost".

[5] the root of árrauna is unknown to me.

[6] vélanaúnka and the two following ordinals are, to say the least, uncertain. Thus we might rather suppose tkánaúnka to mean „the first", than „the second", as being apparently connected with tekū, „one". However it is not altogether impossible, that vélanaúnka means „the first", as vōle may possibly be derived from the Arabic term auel. Again in vakanhatkálle there seems to be hidden some relation to tekū; tkálle from tekū and ale? — Altogether the different and inconsistent manner, in which these ordinals are expressed in the Lógonē language, by means of an additional pēle, mal and mi, shows very clearly the imperfect character of this form of speech.

[7] akatáfke is more than uncertain, although it may possibly be a military term, as there seems to be a certain connection between it and aka-télliero „the last man of the rank".

[8] In the word g-ilém-irē the d of ŭdebē has been eliminated and the b has been changed into an m.

[9] elf-kan dákakán, if right, is very curious indeed.

Deutsch und Englisch.	Kanúri.	Tédā.	Hausa.	Fulfúlde.
der sechste — *the sixth*	ken-rasko . .	dinē	na-šidda . .	dšo-vē-gò-dšo (mā-be
der siebente — *the seventh*	ken-tgllur . .	turrésio . . . tújúdesu . . .	na-bókoi . .	dšō-vē-didī-dšō (mā-be dšē-dídábo .
der achte — *the eighth*	ken-usku . .	oso . . . . yusu	na-tókus . .	dšō-vē-tati-dšō (mā-be dšē-tatábo .
der neunte — *the ninth*	ken-legár . .	isó . . . . yesē	na-tára . . .	dšō-vē-nai-dšo (mā-be dšē-nayēbo .
der zehnte — *the tenth*	ken-mēgū . .	murdō	na-gōma . .	sappō-dšō (mā-be sappābo . .
der elfte — *the eleventh*	ken-lagri[1] .	. . . . .[9] .	na ša-dēa .	sappō-dšō ē-go-dšō (mā-be sappō ē-gōdšō
der zwölfte — *the twelfth*	ken-ndu-rī .		na ša-biu . .	. . . . . .
der dreizehnte — *the thirteenth*	mēgū-n yasko-n	. . . . .	na ša-okū .	. . . . . .
der zwanzigste — *the twentieth*	fī-ndī-n . .	. . . . .	na-āšerin . .	ikébindōbe lasso/ lassō-dšō (mā-be)
der mittlere — *the middle*	dābu-bē . .	dābu . . . . frēti	tsakka . . .	tšakka . . .
der letzte — *the last, hindmost*	derge; derēge-bē kadugu-bē[2]	sēhi	na-baia . . .	tokkaido bē-fū[4] gadādšō . .
der letzte Tag des Monats[6] — *the last day of the month*	gébligo kintáko-bē	auri sēbe . .	na-baia n wotia	. . . . .
der Hintermann — *the next man in rank*	kadūgu-bē .	sēhi	na-baia . . .	gadādšo . .
ein Mal — *once* . . .	tilō-ro . . .	trō; genē trōn	sō dēa . . .	dā gō . . .
zwei Mal — *twice* . .	ndi-ro . . .	kiū	sō biu . . .	dā didī . . .
drei Mal — *thrice* . .	yaski-ro . .	águzō	sō okū . . .	dā tāti[5] . .
vier Mal — *four times* .	dēge-ro[3] . .	tozō	sō fodū . . .	dā nai . . .

[1] ken-lagrī, ken-ndu-rī. Auch diese Ordinalformen für „elfter", „zwölfter", die Koelle unbekannt geblieben sind, sind in ganz allgemeinem Gebrauch; erst von „dreizehnter" an müssen die Kardinalzahlen aushelfen.

[2] kadūgu-bē ebenso wie na-baia hat auch, wie das nur zu natürlich ist, die Bedeutung von „Hintermann".

[3] dēge-ro, yaske-ro. Das e in diesen Formen möchte Koelle's Schreibweise von dēge, yaske in den Kardinalformen zu bestätigen scheinen, aber der Vokal in dieser Form verändert sich.

[4] tokkaido bē-fū ist eigentlich „der Hintermann von ihnen Allen", wie tokkaido gadā-dšō „der Hintermann des Zweiten", d. h. „der Dritte". Aber auch gadā-dšō allein schon erhält die Bedeutung „der Letzte", so dass es die beiden Bedeutungen hat, erster und letzter Hintermann. Ein ganz ähnliches Verhältniss sehen wir im B. mat-ga-nia „er, der dem Ersten folgt", mat-ga-dō „er, der Allen folgt".

[5] dā tāti. In Sokoto und an anderen östlichen Hauptplätzen der Fulbe scheint die Sitte eingerissen zu sein, von „drei Mal" an die Ordinalzahl der Hausa-Sprache mit dem dā des Fulfúlde zu verbinden.

[6] Man sollte vermuthen, dass auch koyē und ildebē hier durch eine besondere Form vertreten wären.

[7] kay-kēne-nahī. Das d in kēda ist durch Einfluss des nachfolgenden n ebenfalls in n übergegangen.

[8] oun-nahī. Auch hier wieder ist das h in nah in n übergegangen.

[9] tonhaia ist von tong, „und ein" (zehn und ein), abgeleitet, so auch ähnlich die folgenden, ganz wie im Hausa na ša dēa u. s. w.

Sonyai.	Lógoné.	Wándalá.	Bágrimma.	Mába.
. . . .	mal-venáχkir-nē	g-ùùkoh-irē .	migā-nakī .	-aili
	mal-kainl-nē .	w-uy-irē . .	ĉili-nakī . .	-mimri
	bille) venyádo nanaká-natán	wu-im-irē	maria-nakī .	-ēya
. . . . . .	mi-dīsχiēn . .	gin-masilmánn-irē	doso-nakī . .	-aduī
	mi-χkan-alē . .	kelau-irē . .	duk-komē . .	-atúk
	mi-χkan-ka-tekū-alē	ge-džung-teg-irē	kar-kēne-nakī [7]	-toūkaia [9]
. . . . . .	mi-χkan-ka-kadē-alē	ge-džu-bú-irē	san-nakī [8] . .	-baraúgkaia
. . . .	mi-χkan-ka-gáχkir-alē	ge-džu-key-irē	duk-komē kar mutā	-kungaúgkaia
. . . .	mi-waríaka . .	ge-kul-bú-irē	. . . . .	. . . . . .
. . . .	bille) námasé sé-natán-alé	amdukwē . .	dadán-nakī .	kang { óornak / úorok
	bille) bá-natán-alē	rō-akatelli-ĉakke	mot-ga-dó .	. . . . . .
. . . .	zála-nē ĉēli . .	malā terē . .	motšal napma	ĉek gabágin
. . . .	bille) nasmo yaltánāū	akatéllero . .	. . . . . .	gontiógna
. . . .	tekā	ge-fall-irē .	mó-t-kēde .	tek-ot akā
. . . .	kadē	ge-búš . . .	mó-sáb . . .	bul akā
. . . .	gáχkir	keyē [6] . . .	mó-mutā . .	kayáng akā
. . . .	gādo	g-ufad-irē .	mó-sō . . .	asi akā

[1] hen-legri, hen-ndu-ri. Also these ordinals, viz „the eleventh, the twelfth", are in very general use, although they appear to have remained unknown to Koelle. It is only beginning with „the thirteenth", that the cardinal numbers must suffice.

[2] haddugu-bē as well as na-bois has also the meaning of „follower", both words implying „he who is behind" (me, thee, all).

[3] dēge-re, tache-re. The e in these forms might seem to confirm Koelle's mode of writing the cardinal numbers, viz dēge, tache, but the vowel in this form is changed.

[4] tehhaide hē-fū means properly „the hindmost of them all", as tehhaide gadā-dīā, „he who is behind the second", that is to say, „the third". But also gadā-dīā implies already the meaning of the „hindmost (of all)" in the double meaning of „hind" or „behind", he who is behind the first as well as the last. Thus also in B. mot-ga-nie „he who is behind the first", mot-ga-dó „he who is behind them all".

[5] dā tāti. In Sókoto and other principal places of the Fulbe in the Eastern part of their empire it seems to have become the custom, from „three times" onward to combine the ordinal number of the Hausa-language with the dā of the Fulfúlde.

[6] We might presume to find also keyé and lidebē represented by a particular form.

[7] kar-kēne-nakī. The d in kēde has been changed into an n through the influence of the following n.

[8] san-nakī. In this word also the b in sab has been changed into an n.

[9] toūkaia has been derived from tong, „and one" (tan „and one" = eleven) and the following terms similarly from „and two" etc., just as in Hausa sa ša dēa etc.

Deutsch und Englisch.	Kanúri.	Tédā.	Hausa.	Fulfúlde.
fünf Mal — *five times*	úgu-ro	fō	sō biyel	dā dīōī
sechs Mal — *six times*	raske-ro	dise	sō šidda	dā dīō-vē-gō
sieben Mal — *seven times*	tullur-ro	turúsiu	sō bókoi	dā dīō-vē-didi
acht Mal — *eight times*	uskū-ro	osō	sō tókus	dā dīō-vē-tati
neun Mal — *nine times*	legár-ro	isi	sō tára	dā dīō-vē-nai
zehn Mal — *ten times*	mēge-ro	murdo	sō gōma	dā sappo
zwanzig Mal — *twenty times*	fi-ndī-ro	dú-kiu	sō āšerin	dā nogás
wiederum, noch ein Mal — *again, once more*	gadē-ro[1] kurū[2]	. . . .	sō na-bin[6] kuma	nombo
wie oft — *how often*	ndagu-ro	. . . . . .	sō nawa	dā noi
wann, zu welcher Zeit — *when*	yim-bi[3] saa-bi	kenā, S. nérua, N.	yau-še	nē[8]
in alter Zeit — *of old*	kúro	genē kubbu, S. ušiko, N.	zamáni nésa	bēbóima
einst (von der Vergangenheit) — *once*	burgón	. . . . . .	. . . . . .	. . . . . .
früher — *formerly*	burgó-ma tšā-man tšā men-tšē	gā	tuni	ólma . . . . . .
zuerst — *first, at first, in the beginning*	burgó-bē	burdō	da-fari	arro
eines Tages, im Laufe der Zeit — *once (of the future)*	. . . . . .	sēhi	wota rāna	dāgō
noch nicht — *not yet*	kurū[4]	garro, S. aúcui, N.	tókonā[7]	tāū, taho
immer, stets — *always, constantly*	saa-bi-sō[5] yim-bi-sō wátši-sō	genē-genē	kō-yauši	ko-indē

[1] gadē-ro. Koelle schreibt gadéró.

[2] kurū. Dieses Wort, das Koelle nur in der hier erscheinenden Bedeutung aufführt, bekommt in ganz natürlicher Entwickelung, „wiederum, ein ander Mal, später", auch die Bedeutung von „noch nicht".

[3] yim-bi, eigentlich yim-afi, „an welchem Tage"; saa-bi (afi), „an welcher Stunde". — Beispiel: „wann brechen wir auf?" yim-bi tši-nien, H. yau-še mu-ke-taši, S. han-fo ére-hoi, F. nö dille-ti.

[4] kurū. S. Note 2.

[5] saa-bi-sō, „an welcher Stunde immer"; yim-bi-sō, „an welchem Tage immer"; wátši-sō, „an welchem Morgen immer". Koelle hat wol ganz Recht, wenn er annimmt, dass wátši ursprünglich nur die Verbalform von wáṅgin war und erst allmählich Substantivbedeutung erhielt.

[6] sō na-bin kann nur von der Vergangenheit gebraucht werden.

[7] tókonā. Hier will ich die zusammengesetzte Redensart mit der verwandten Bedeutung „warte ein bischen" einschalten: K. dōge degö, T. tadgadāgo, H. sé sadēgana kadán, F. mayétale sadda.

[8] Neben nö scheint auch dē in gelegentlichem Gebrauche zu sein.

[9] han-fö. Das fö ist hier auf den ersten Blick sehr auffallend, es muss jedenfalls von dem fö, „eins", im später folgenden han-fö verschieden sein, aber dass es richtig ist, dafür bürgen die ganz selbstständig in Ágades erforschten Formen arendo-fö und alag-fö, also auch hier das fö. — Das folgende han-fö heisst ganz einfach „eines Tages".

[10] wat-erā scheint vom Arabischen Worte wakt, „die Zeit", abgeleitet zu sein. Eben daher wat-er-koni „zu welcher Zeit immer", und eben aus dieser selben späten Quelle, dem Anscheine nach, die Ausdrücke für „heute" und „heuer".

Sońγai.	Lógoné.	Wándalá.	Bágrimma.	Mába.
. . . .	sáxi	fidebē	mó - mī . . .	tur akā
. . . .	venázkir . . .	úúkoh - irē . .	mó - migā . .	setīī akā
. . . .	kátul	w - ny - irū . .	mó - tšili . .	ya - mindri akā
. . . .	ven - yále . . .	wu - tīs - irū .	mó - marta . .	ya - tya akā
. . . .	dis - ziēn . . .	masilmánn - irū	mó - domo . .	ya - (n)loī akā
. . . .	zkan	kelan - irē . .	mó - duk - kemē	ya - atúk osō
. . . .	tkám	kul - bó - irū .	mó - duk - sáb .	. . . . . .
. . . .	hin - sāne . . .	taā	ótpata . . .	
yérimi safō . .	. . . .		. . . .	
han - fō [9]	sinuá	wal - erā [10] . .	dungo . . . / yálin . . .	gotto
gōrai tāīni . .	zome	aknléfke . .	zemán tšā .	akóng
	bekū		zemán auō .	
agaī	. . . .	. . . . . .		
. . . .	bia zome bekū .	biiaré - kení .	tōga	
sāli	bekú - natán . .	zunge .	?	. . . . . .
han - fō . . .	. . . .	. . . . . .	gadō	serúg
džinne . . . . / tšinne	gánabē	leble . . .	aiki	lelle
. . . .	sinúá-blin . . .	ba wat-er-kenī	din - din - din .	daimen (Arb.)

[1] gedō-re. Koelle writes gaddrá.

[2] kavā. This word, to which Koelle attributes only the meaning, which we give in this place, by following up its various relations, „again, once more, another time", receives also the notion of „and yet".

[3] yim-bi, properly yim-afi, „what day"; saa-bi (afi), „what hour". — Ex.: „when do we start?" yim-bi tāī-nien, H. yan-ču mú-ka-táši, S. han-fé óra-kei, F. nò ditle-tī.

[4] kavā. S. note 2.

[5] saa-bi-ad, „what hour so ever"; yim-bi-ad, „what day so ever"; wātši-ad, „what time so ever". Koelle is right, I think, in supposing, that wātši was originally nothing but the verbal form of wedgin, having only by degrees usurped the character of a substantive.

[6] ad na-bin can only be used of the past.

[7] tòkenā. I think this the right place to adduce a related phrase with a similar notion „wait a while": K. dōga dogō, T. tabgodāge, H. sé and šumma kadán, F. mayétata eadda.

[8] Besides nō also dō seems to be used occasionally.

[9] han-fō. The fō may seem doubtful at first sight and it must evidently be totally distinct from fō, „one"; but its correctness is guaranteed by the two terms, which I have made out quite independently in A'gades, viz mende-fō and alár-fō. (The reason, why I have not introduced in these vocabularies the dialect of Agades, I have stated elsewhere.) The following term han-fō means simply „one day".

[10] wat-erā seems to have been derived from the Arabic word wakt, „time" and the same is the case with the term wat-er-kenī „at what-ever time" and with the terms signifying „to day" and „this year".

Deutsch und Englisch.	Kanúri.	Têda.	Hausa.	Fulfúlde.
ewig, in Ewigkeit — *in eternity, for ever*	ábadén (Arb.)[1]	. . . . . .	ábadá . . .	. . . . .
täglich, jeden Tag — *every day*	zibbed[2] . . .	tégena, S. bini gubbri, N.	kullum (Arb.)	ńande fū . .
niemals, nimmer — *never*	yim-bi man bágo	trón (deddo) bō[9]	dádai[10] . . .	. . . . . .
gegenwärtig, augenblicklich — *presently, immediately*	kirma-roā . malē-malē .	únnodē . . . nímmero . .	yenzā . . . yenzu-yenzā .	džōni . . .
heute — *to day*	kū	benā, S. . . benī, N. . .	yau	hande . . .
morgen — *to morrow* .	bāli	bekke, S. . tagal, N. . .	gobē	džóhango . .
morgen in der Frühe — *early to morrow morning*	subba (Arb.) wáltši-a[3] . .	tagal tógofū (N.)	gobē da sassā	. . . . .
übermorgen — *the day after to morrow*	wáge-rū[4] . .	karkō, S. . hógodē, N. .	džibi[11] . . .	fābi džáhango
gestern — *yesterday* . .	biskā . . .	woski, S. . . ṅgoski, N. .	žia[12] . . .	keńa . . . .
vorgestern — *the day before yesterday*	biskā-te[5] . .	ágodō, S. . benī dégená ugózū, N. .	šékare n žia[13]	hétši keńa
im letzten Jahre — *last year*	mindē[6] . . .	goróńko . .	šékara n bára	raúani . . .
vor zwei Jahren — *two years ago*	mindē-te . .	goróńko kadé, S. sāga kiū, N.	šékara n bára-utšen	ražáani . . .
vor drei Jahren — *three years ago*	sāga yasko .	sāga óguzū, N.	šékara okū .	rautiténni . .
heuer — *this year* . .	ki-mindé[7] .	mēdo, S. . . mēli, N. . .	šékara bána .	hika . . . .
im nächsten Jahr — *next year*	bāli min-wā[8]	sāga-hán bakēń-ga, S. . . sāga elńkidē, N.	bedī . . . . šékara mē zakwa	mauri . . .

[1] ábadén und die entsprechenden Ausdrücke der anderen Sprachen erhalten in gewissen Fällen die Bedeutung „niemals".

[2] zibbed. Koelle schreibt teębęd und gibt ihm fälschlich die Bedeutung „den ganzen Tag"; „einen ganzen Tag lang".

[3] wáltši-a ist eigentlich der Konjunktiv von wáltši (von waágin). „wenn" oder „nachdem der Morgen gedämmert hat".

[4] wáge-rū hat K. nicht, obgleich er wágē hat mit der Bedeutung „später, nachher, in der anderen Welt". Dagegen sagt er wunderbarer Weise zu biegātemi: i. q. wágeré, „on the day before yesterday". Die Wurzel von rū oder rē ist mir unbekannt. Unter bāli gibt K. bāli kótšin für „übermorgen".

[5] Koelle hat dafür biegātemi, aber das mi wird nur in gewissen Fällen angefügt.

[6] Koelle schreibt męndé; mendē-te aber hat er nicht.

[7] ki-mindé ist jedenfalls auffallend, da doch offenbar das min in diesem Worte und in mindē u. s. w. ganz dasselbe ist. Sollte die in mindé angezeigte Vergangenheit durch ki, kū (heute) wieder aufgehoben sein? Koelle hat es nicht.

[8] K. hat minwa und bāli minwa.

[9] trón (deddo) bō. Das deddo, „Mal", ist nicht nothwendig.

[10] dádai. Hierzu als Beispiel: „ich habe nie gesehen", H. dádai ba nágani ba, im F. nur durch misi ausgedrückt „ich habe nicht gesehen", da das „niemals" keine besondere Vertretung im F. hat.

[11] džibi. Im Hausa, Fulfúlde und Sonyai gibt es auch noch ein „über-übermorgen", H. gatta, F. fābiti džáhango, S. subba-ni hondu, und in den beiden ersten Sprachen selbst ein „über-über-übermorgen", H. čitta, F. fabitini džáhango.

[12] „Gestern Nacht", auf H. žia da derē, auf F. hańki džemma, auf Sonyai ižidži.

[13] „Vorgestern Nacht", auf H. šékaren žia da derē, auf F. hétši ži hańki.

[14] ki-fō. Wir haben hier nun wiederum fō in anderer Bedeutung, das Vorhergehen bezeichnend; übrigens haben die Sonyai noch einen besondern Ausdruck für den drittvorletzten Tag nämlich bibi fō handi.

[15] manna fō handu. Hier scheint das Vorhergehen in doppelter Weise ausgedrückt zu sein.

[16] Für „übermorgen" gab mir mein Lógone-Lehrer den Ausdruck „devéden hálineá"; aber aller Wahrscheinlichkeit nach heisst das „vorgestern". Eine Verwechselung dieser beiden Begriffe ist sehr gewöhnlich.

Sonγai.	Lógoné.	Wándalá.	Bágrimma.	Mába.
ábadén	. . . . . .	. . . . . .	din-din-din .	ábadúm
ban-kúl . . .	mawaiha . . .	wawā dippe .		gondžōdum
. . . . . .	ninta mašēnan .	ba wat-er-ken bāka	. . . . . .	. . . . . .
morēle; amorésker	madē-mandē . .	wasaúntsē . .	tšāna . . .	wai
{ hong (Tmb.) . / hanu wó (Agad.) }	am-di	wát-enā . .	džénnibi . .	woáing
šubba	diāse	makurálla . .	bīšerī . . .	sundar
. . . . . .	diāse-n fazr . .	wúrukeē maku-rálla	. . . . . .	. . . . . .
šubba { ki / si . . . }	[14]	gúrgogeē . .	nefū	sundar na kūsan
bi	devēde	áwayā . . .	tābre . . .	kúndan
bi-fō [11]	devēde ken . .	imbidda . .	tābre kōde .	kúndantóm
džiri k(e) abissa	wand kan . . .	emši fo . .	wāli	ábindžén
manna	wand kenánsa .	emšī fókwa .	{ wāli etkédenn / lūa sab . . }	abíndže sīnun
manna fó bendu [15]	. . . . . .	. . . . . .	wāli etkédenuna	. . . . .
{ hurán . . . . / džīro (Tmb.) . / giri wó (Agad.) }	wan	wát-enā . . .	bonibi . . .	wákién
{ giri wō k(e) wágo-ka / yēši . . . . . }	wūai mbillam .	emšī fá-bia .	lūa wa kalndžo	kúyan

[1] ábadén and the corresponding terms of the other languages in some cases obtain the notion of „never".
[2] sibbed. Koelle writes ìaybed and attributes to it the wrong notion of „the whole day", „all day long".
[3] wátši-a properly is the subjunctive mood of wátši (from wahyin), „when" or „after it has become morning".
[4] wágo-rá does not appear in Koelle's vocabulary; but he has wágé with the notion of „hereafter, afterwards, in the next world" and nevertheless under the term biogáteml he says, that this term is identical with wágeré, „on the day before yesterday". The origin and root of the final rá is not known to me. Under the term báll Koelle gives báll kóšša (that is properly „when to morrow is past") for „the day after to morrow".
[5] biokā-te: Koelle writes biogáteml, but the mi is only added in certain cases.
[6] mindé: K. writes męndé, but he has not mendé-te.
[7] ki-mindē is certainly remarkable, as it seems, as if the notion of the past contained in the term mindē were paralized by the preceding ki, perhaps from kū, „to day" but the root in both words is evidently the same. It is wanting in Koelle's vocabulary.
[8] Koelle has minwa and báll minwa.
[9] trân (deddē) bé. The word „dedde", „time" (one time, once) is not essential.
[10] dádai. Ex. „I have never seen", H. dádai ba nágané ba, expressed in F. by a simple [illegible], „I have not seen"; the term „never" not being distinctly represented in F.
[11] dšibi. In the Hausa, Fulfúlde and Sonγai languages there is also a peculiar term for „the day succeeding the day after to morrow", H. gatta, F. fabiti džábango, S. subba-ci bendu, nay in H. and F. there is even a term for the next following day, H. [illegible], F. fabititi džábango.
[12] „last night" in H. „Ĕla da deré, F. hakki džemma, S. [illegible].
[13] „last night but one" in H. šekaren Ĕla da deré, F. hekki ĕi habbi.
[14] bi-fó: here again we have the fó with a different notion, indicating the preceding of something; the Sonγai have even a peculiar term for the notion „three days ago", viz bibi fó bendi.
[15] manna fó bendu seems to contain a double notion of the „preceding" or „before".
[16] For the term „the day after to morrow" my teacher in Lógoné gave me the term devéden kéninsé, but it seems probable, that this means „the day before yesterday". A confusion however of these two notions is very common.

Deutsch und Englisch.	Kanuri.	Tēda.	Hausa.	Fulfulde.
in zwei Jahren — *the next following year*	bāli mín-wā-tē	sāga kú elíkidē	. . . . . .	. . . . .
im verflossenen Monat — *last month*	kintāge ngāfo-bē	auri kandžémma / auri ai kankéunsi	wotta n ēia .	lēura sabeíndu / lēura watúndu / lēura yautúndu
in diesem Monat — *this month*	kintāge ále .	auri ai . . .	tšikí n wotta nan	der lēura ndū
nächsten Monat — *next month*	kintāge fúgu-bē	auri augoríoge / auri ai gúhlaal(i) elíkia	wotta n gobé / wotta maitsía	lēura warrendū / lēura dzáhango / lēura daratóndu [12]
früh — *early*	. .	. . . . . .	da sa-sāfi [6] . / da dzedzīb .	bimbim . . . / súba-ka . .
spät — *late*	. . . .	. . . . . .	ba da-uri ba [7]	adauai . . .
wo — *where*	ndá-ra [1] . . / ndá-ran . .	indi	ina	toi, tō . . .
wohin — *where* . . .	ndá-rarō . / ndarrō . .	nókurdō . . .	urí-nda . .	toi, tō . . .
von wo — *from where*	ndá-ra . . / ndá-ra-gā .	nókurdō . . .	daga-ína . .	daga-dó [13] .
hier — *here*	ná-ten [2] . .	tša	daga-nán . .	doga-do . .
dort — *there*	ná-tun . .	nak	doga-tšān [8] .	doga-tón . .
hier ist es, sieh da — *here it is*	ungo-ši [3] . .	. . . . . .	ga-ši [9]	. . . . .
diesseits — *on this side*	ná-te-gan .	konágerī . .	daga-nán dagá [10]	doi-bī . . .
jenseits — *on the other side*	na-tu-gan . / tu-ten [4] . .	dogodéddo .	kétare	džultiki . . .
vor, voran — *before*	fūgo-n . . / fūgo-rō [5] . .	kūru	kabā	yēso . . . .
hinter, hinterher — *behind* . . .	ngāfo-a . . / ngāfo-rō . .	seggabúzo . .	baia . . . / na-baia [11] . .	gāda . . . .

[1] ndá-ra. Beispiele: „wo sind sie, sind sie geblieben?" K. ndá-ra neb-tsé, H. súna ina, F. tō be ngónni; „die Stadt, wohin wir gehen", K. billa ndá-ra lēnien, H. gari nel-nda zāmo, F. yaire tō min-dāāta.

[2] na-ten, eigentlich na-tten, „an diesem Platz, dieser Stelle".

[3] Die anderen Zeiten des Verbums ngin oder wngin habe ich nicht in Gebrauch gefunden.

[4] Bei Koelle scheinen diese Wörter zu fehlen.

[5] Beispiele: „gehe voran", K. fūgo-rō lē-né, H. taff kabā, F. yaha yēso.

[6] da sa-sāfi. Ich will bei Gelegenheit dieses Wortes ein Beispiel für die Partikel „seit" geben, das ich in den meisten dieser Sprachen nicht habe ausfindig machen können. „Seit der Frühe bin ich beim Schreiben", H. tun da sa-sāfi rúbutū ni kai, F. illa sóbaka mowinde. Auch will ich hier die Partikel „bis" anbringen, T. — tokár, H. har, F. háddum, W. amdo, M. — tondénge. So „er sprang, bis er fiel", H. yá-tsuma har ya-fádi, F. dumdi háddum yenni.

[7] ba da-uri ba, eigentlich „nicht am Orte".

[8] daga-tšān in H. und daga-tón in F. bedeuten auch „von dort".

[9] ga-ši ist eigentlich der einfache Imperativ von na-ga-ni „ich sehe".

[10] daga-nán dagá. „Diesseits des Wassers", H. daga-nán dagá gulbi, F. doi-bi máyo, S. ina-dí séda hére.

[11] na-baia. So: dúba na-baia, „sieh' hinter Dich", F. (orēra) yēyo gāda.

[12] lēura daratónde ist wol ein Provincialism und scheint im reinen Fulfúlde nicht bekannt zu sein.

[13] daga-dó so wenig wie daga-tón gehört der reinen Fulfúlde-Sprache an, sondern beide verdanken ihren Gebrauch dem Einfluss der Hausa-Sprache.

[14] Aus diesem binde ist der in den beiden letzten Bänden meines Reisewerkes so oft vorkommende Name Ari-binda (eigentlich Hari-binde) gebildet, (die Provinz) „jenseits des Wassers".

Sonyai.	Lógoné.	Wándalá.	Bágrimma.	Mába.
. . . . .	wai gáχkir . .	emši fá-džia .	?	kuyan na kūyan
bandu k(e)abissa / bandu díkabún .	těda billim . .	amégo tir-na á-dženа	kem naf godélle	šek niktin agin
handu wō . . .	těda gemá . .	an-fudē tir-ne	kem naf énnekl	šek agín
handu kō ago-ka	těda teká . . .	tir-nadžrggetefke	kem naf gó-wá-kedē	šek nanárgin
bíabia . . . . / subba-bēni . .	. . . . . .	. . . . .	. . . . .	
don	. . . . . .	. . . . .	. . . . .	
manábara . . .	ná-bakē . . .	ámmoěn . .		uṅgun
	. . . . . .	ad-ummen . .	éda	. . . . . .
néda	. . . . . .	anyé-berā?		ṅgánneri
néda	ná-mbanē . . .	áblaχna . .	lúlo	wagēn
bendu	nū-atkī . . .	koyénganē . .	et-nu . . .	illēgin
. . . .	. . . . . .	núngnué . .	. . . . .	. . .
— néda (hēre .	na-baui . . .	aχuuāra . .	et-džó-lolo .	alka
— binda (hēre [14]	na-banatki . .	koye k-eléfkara	ét-tera . . .	ukka
. .	na-hańatkan wetki	ak-atáfke . .	et-naigo . .	auel (Arb.)
. . . .	na-ihádg . . .	amiga	mólgadō . .	gánum

[1] ndá-ra. ex. „where are they?" K. ndá-ra nеb-teš, H. súna ian, F. tó haugáni; „the town where we go", K. billa ndá-rá lēnien, H. garí ari-nda ɐamo, F. yaire tó min-dāáta.

[2] ná-ten, properly ná ñten „in this place".

[3] nága-ēī: the other tenses of the verb nágia or wangia I have not found in use.

[4] The terms ná-te-gan, na-tá-gan and tá-ten seem to be wanting in Koelle's vocabulary.

[5] fūgo-rō: ex. „go before", K. fūga-rō lē-mé, H. tafī kabā, F. yōbe yēe.

[6] da na-séfi. I make use of this opportunity for introducing the particle „since", which I have not been able to make out in most of these languages: „since an early hour in the morning I am writing", H. tun da na-séfi rábutā ni kai, F. ille súbaka warinda. — I shall likewise introduce here the particle „till", T. — tokár, H. har, F. hádum, W. amde, M. — tondóngo; ex. „he jumped till he fell", H. yá-tuma har ya-fādi, F. dumdi hádum yrani.

[7] ha da-ari ba, properly „and in the (right) place".

[8] daga-tšán in H. and daga-tón in F. have also the meaning „from thence".

[9] ga-ēī is properly the simple imperative tense of na-ga-ni „I see, I look".

[10] daga-nán dagé: ex. „on this side of the river", H. daga-nán dagá gulbí, F. doi-ni máyo, S. isa-di néda-bēre.

[11] na-bain: thus „look behind you", dúba na-bain, F. (oráro) ybya góda.

[12] írura daratónda probably is a provincialism and does not seem to be used in the pure Fulfúlde idiom.

[13] neither daga-dó nor daga-tón belong to the pure Fulfúlde language, but owe their existence to the influence of the Hausa idiom.

[14] From this binda the name Ari-binda (properly Hari-binda) has been formed, which occurs so often in the last two volumes of my Travels and Discoveries and which designates the province „beyond the water".

Deutsch und Englisch.	Kanuri.	Teda.	Hausa.	Fulfulde.
über, auf — *on, over*	farin	ūli, S. / obrō, N.	bisa [10]	dō / lē
nieder, zur Erde — *down, on the ground* / unter — *under*	tsidī-gan [1]	wan / wannu	kása / kērkašē [11]	hi ledi / gurldu
neben, zur Seite — *beside, on the side of*	bétlagu [2]	lauda, S. / keri, N.	kusa-da [12]	badde
zwischen, unter — *between, among*	kalē-katēn	kwii / fereti-adē	tsakán [13]	hákkundē
in, hinein — *in, into* / innerhalb, *inside*	náši-rō [3] / tsorón [4]	yédero / fereti	tšikin	der / les
hinaus — *out of* / ausserhalb — *outside*	dēka-rō [5] / dēka [6]	yēga / agā	uke	yāsi / gadde
zur Linken — *on the left*	muskō ovín [7]	kōbe ánkia	hanū n hagu	dāmgo nanbo / nanne
zur Rechten — *on the right*	musko dul-nim / muskō kúmbe-rám-be [8]	kōbe bri	hanū n dama	dāmgo ñāmo
gerade aus — *straight on*	tsēg-rō [9]	kurímeo, S. / tévizē, N.	dēdē [14]	tāurō
in Windungen, Krümmungen — *meandering, roundabout*		. . . . . .	kēunyē [15]	filtōa / tārir

[1] tsidī-gan, wörtlich „zur Erde", entspricht völlig dem Hausa-Wort „kása" und dem F. hi ledi. Es ist aber entschieden ein Irrthum, wenn Koelle die Form tsédīga zu einem besonderen Substantiv macht.

[2] bétlagu fehlt bei Koelle. Allerdings ist es kein gewöhnliches Wort und seine Wurzel ist mir unbekannt.

[3] náši-rō fehlt auch bei Koelle, es hängt wol mit nalā zusammen.

[4] tsorón. Beispiel: „im Zelte", K. tsorón lēma-bē, H. tšikin lēma, F. lar lemāfu, S. hēgam dī-māea; „in der Stadt", K. tsorón billa-bē, H. tšikin garī, F. der gellūre, S. koree-dī dī-mā eo.

[5] dēka-rō. Beispiel: „gehe zur Stadt hinaus", K. dēka-rō billa-bē lē-aē, H. tafi uké a garī, F. dille gadda galdūre, S. kof koire dibánde bōra.

[6] dēka. Beispiel: K. dēka tšinna-bē nemne, H. zamna uké a kōfa, F. djōda yāsi dāmbogol, S. gōro hādi-mē dibánde bōre „bleibe vor der Thür".

[7] ovín fehlt bei Koelle, er hat dafür wōbi.

[8] muskō kúmberám-be ist wörtlich die Hand, womit die Speise — kúmbū — genommen wird. kúmbū ist wörtlich „das Ding zum Essen", kú-m-bū. Koelle schreibt weniger richtig kómbū und kómbūrám.

[9] Auch tsēg-rō fehlt bei Koelle.

[10] bisa. Beispiel: „lege das Buch auf das Bettgestell", H. aššē letáfi bisa gadō, F. reese dēftere lē lēeo; „es gibt Baumwuchs auf diesem Berg", H. a-kel itátua bisa dútsi a-we-nan, F. ledde bikkōde dō wamdē dō.

[11] kērkašē. Beispiel: „lege den Mantel unter das Kopfkissen", H. aššē al-kebba kērkāšē-n matšīnkai, F. reese alkebbāre les tīngāde.

[12] kúsa-da. Beispiel: „zu seiner Seite, neben ihm", H. kúsa-da ši, F. badde mā-ko.

[13] tsakán. Beispiel: „(auf dem Wege) zwischen Wurno und Gandi gibt es Kaib", H. tsakán-in Wurno da Gandi a-kai kaiō, F. hákkundē Wurno da Gandi wōdi nāffure; „unter uns gibt es nichts als Friede", H. tsakāni-mū bābo kōmī sai ál āfia, F. hákkundē ammiñ ed djam.

[14] dēdē. Beispiel: „folge der Strasse geradeaus, welche weder zur Rechten, noch zur Linken ab", H. bi hanīa n dēdē, hadda karkáta hanū n dáma, kō hanū n hagū, F. tokku laawol tāurō, ti āwwala dāmgo ñāmo, tā dawala dāmgo nanne. Der ursprüngliche Gegensatz zu dēdē scheint im H. tšāra zu sein.

[15] kēunyē hat auch die Bedeutung „rund herum". So „rund um den Berg herum", H. kēunyē da duddu, S. woine londi.

[16] tšīrē. Im Allgemeinen kann ich mein in Agades gesammeltes Vokabular ziemlich unberücksichtigt. Hier aber ist es wol interessant, als Dialektverschiedenheit des Songhaiischen hidō oder wol eigentlich kiōē zu vergleichen.

Sońyai.	Lógoné.	Wándalá.	Bágrimma.	Maba.
bēnc	nam	átirē	naúgc . . .	tul
tširē [14]	nalmúntin	anmnalára . .	rā	lul
{ amaniggn . . . / maaō . . . . . }	lungnu	etefk-ina . .	gálsch . . .	— tindagin
tširē gamē . .	naaxasa uánlco	amdugwátere .	dulāu . . .	ñoro
dimáso	nalálungún . ..	aubudara . .	net	kulū
— dibánde hōre	nafae	úgašē . . .	{ agla . . . / gadō . . . }	feriúg
kamba wano . .	θádr yalún . .	álabá . . .	dāī gēli . .	būna
kamba gummo .	θále zeul . . .	ádafā . . .	dāī kesā . .	kolón
nigúmnida . . .	telél	batséggc . .	abtál . . .	sérkoko
wañga		. . . .		

[1] toldi-gen means verbally „on the ground" and thus corresponds perfectly with the Hausa-term késa and the Fulfúlde hi lēdi. But it is certainly a mistake of Mr. Koelle's to make tardīyo (as he also writes tegdi instead of toldi) a distinct noun.

[2] háttagu is wanting in Koelle's vocabulary. It is certainly a word of unusual formation in the Kanúri language.

[3] nañi-rō likewise is wanting in Koelle; it may possibly be related to the word nekā meaning „side".

[4] tserón: ex. „inside the tent", K. tsorén léma-bē, H. tšikin lēma, F. nas lemára, S. bégam di-máse; „in the town", K. tsoréa bille-bē, H. tšikin garī, F. der gollúre, S. koire-di di-máse.

[5] dēga-rō: ex. „go out of the town", K. dēga-rō bille-bē lénō, H. fefi ušē a gari, F. diile gadde galdūre, S. koi koire dibánde hōre.

[6] dēbe: ex. „remain outside the door", K. dēka tšinne-bē nemna, H. esmne ušē a kōfe, F. dšēdu yōni dēmbegel, S. gōre hā(gu)di-mā dibánde hōre.

[7] wankā ovlu: ovlu is wanting in Koelle's vocabulary; he has instead the term wōbi, which I have never heard.

[8] nankē hámberám-be verbally is the hand, wherewith food — kamhú — is taken. kambé is „the thing to eat" ka-m-bū. Koelle writes kómhō and kómbūrám.

[9] taēg-rō is likewise wanting in Koelle's vocabulary.

[10] biese: ex. „place the book upon the bed", H. ašē latšif biese gadō, F. resse dēftere lā lēeo; „there are trees on this mountain", H. a-koi itšine biese dūtsi n-wo-nan, F. ledda hingbde dā wamde dē.

[11] kárkašē: ex., „place the cloak under the cushion", H. ašē al-kabba kárkašē-n matāsani, F. resse silkebhére les tlegánda.

[12] kūsa-da: ex. „near him, at his side", H. kūsa-da ši, F. badda mā-ko.

[13] tsakán: ex. „between Warno and Gandi there is (much) mire", H. tsakān-in Wurno da Gandi a-koi kafō, F. hakkundē Wurno da Gandi wōdi nōffuro; „between us there is nothing but peace", H. tsakáni-mū bābo komē sē al āfia, F. hakkundē amming sō dšam.

[14] dēdē: ex. „follow the road straight along, do neither keep to the left nor to the right", H. bi hanya dēdē, kadda karkato hanú n dáma, ko hanú n hagú, F. tokka laawol tāuro, tā ávarla dšunāgo bāme, tā ávarla dšunāgo nanna. The contrary of dēdē in H. originally seems to have been taēra.

[15] kēwayē has besides the meaning „round about". Thus „round about the mountain", H. kēwayē da taddo, S. wonga londi.

[16] tšīrē. Although in this Sońyai vocabulary in general I do not take into regard my Note made in A'gades on account of the impure character of the dialect there spoken, yet in this case it is interesting to compare the term kidē or rather kidō of that dialect as an example of the frequent exchange of k and tš, d or ō and r.

Deutsch und Englisch.	Kanúri.	Tédā.	Haussa.	Fulfulde.
weshalb — *wherefore, why*	afi-ro [1] . . .	inya, S. . . / négai, N. . .	do-mé [3] . .	gam-du-mē [5]
deshalb *therefore, on that account*	áte naúga [2] .	adō yené, N. / ni bimardé, S.	doúg hákka-ná	gam-du . .
ja, so ist es — *yes, so it is*	áte-na ā [8] . .	fal . . . . / á-meré . .	tō . . . . . / hákka-ná . . .	dum wódi . .
nein, so ist es nicht — *no, it is not so*	áte geni	án . . . . / merē genín .	um ba hákka-ba	wóna-nún [6]
wie — *how*	áfī gaī . . .	négedī, S. . / négai, N. . .	kaká	noé . . . .
so — *thus*	áte gaī . .	. . . . . .	hákka-ná [4] . / hákka-dā .	non . . . . / hadu . . . .
vielleicht — *perhaps* .	. . . . . .	. . . . . .	wolta kila . .	wóna-nun dum wóni [7]

[1] afi-rō bedeutet wörtlich „[illegible]".

[2] So „deinetwegen", K. nima naúga, H. domin-ka, F. gam-mā; „seinetwegen", Ki-ma naúga, H. domin-sa, F. gam-mā-ko.

[3] do-mé, eigentlich doúg mé, „wegen wessen!"

[4] hákka-ná und hákka-dá im H. sind nicht ganz gleichbedeutend, da hákka-dá grössere Bestimmtheit zu haben scheint: „gerade so". Ich will hier auch die fragende Partikel aufführen: H. hakka-ná-ne, „ist es so?", F. non dung wonnu.

[5] gam-du-mé; man sollte eigentlich erwarten gam-mé.

[6] wóna-nún. Das ó in wóda ist des Wohllautes halber offenbar in o übergegangen; ebenso in der weiter unten folgenden Phrase.

[7] wóna-nun dum wóni soll offenbar eigentlich heissen: „es ist nicht oder es ist".

[8] [illegible] ist nicht leicht zu analysiren.

[9] [illegible] wird nur von den Gebildeten hinzugefügt; [illegible] ist hinreichend.

Šabyal.	Lógané.	Wándalá.	Bágrimma.	Mába.
mè-nénne . .	gigger-gerám .	hád-abò-ŕ .	din-dží-na	sebéh)[9] tenáng hĕta
. . . .	ógr hénne gagĕ .	hád-abò-no .		waág hĕta
mbĕ . . . . . / ógă . . . . . / nitšĭm	hasse yl . . .	man-abò-no .	éne	man
ánnetši tšimi[8] .	hasse lĕsa . .	man-kōno . .	én(e)-alĕ . .	lă
. . . .	ávrrnl	sétara . . .	dīya	ganoroita
. . . .	. . . .	. . . . . .	. . . . . .	
. . . .	. . . .	. . . . . .	. . . . . .	

[1] afi-rĕ means verbally „in what", „for what".

[2] ale nangu: thus „on thy account", K. eĭma nanga, H. domíā-ka, F. gam-mi; „on his account", K. ši-me nanga, H. domiasa, F. gam-mi-ko.

[3] do-mĕ, properly dang-mĕ.

[4] hákka-na and hákka-dā are not quite identical in Hausa, hákka-dā having to all appearance a more distinctly affirmative character and approaching the notion of our „just so". I make use of this place to introduce the interrogative particle: H. hákka-ne-ne, F. non dang wonne, „is it so?"

[5] gam-du-mĕ: a person might rather expect nothing but gam-mĕ. It seems to be properly „for (gam) this (du or dum) which (mĕ)", that is „wherefore this?"

[6] wōna-ndn: the d in wōdu has evidently been changed into a n from euphonical reasons.

[7] wāna-nna dum wānl seems to mean originally „either it is not, or it is".

[8] ánnetši tšimi is not easy to analyse.

[9] sebĕh tenáng hĕta. The Arabic word sebéh is only added by the higher class, but the tenáng hĕta is sufficient.

Zeitwörter.

Verbs.

Deutsch und Englisch.	Kanúri.	Tédā.	Hausa.	Fulfúlde.
ich gebäre — *I bear* ich zeuge — *I procreate, beget*	t-e-amb-iskin [1]	. . . .	ina haif-o . . na-i dā [9] . .	médo-deōi . médo-rimmi . médo-wōdi biñgel
die Frau gebiert — *the woman bears, gives birth to*	kámo t-e-amb-in	ádi-bi ye-fúsni	matše tána haif-o	debbo o-deñi / rimmi
ich bin geboren — *I am born*	ka-tamb-ú-ako	tánō fuss-erdō [7]	an-haif-ēni .	mē-rimm-āma
er ist geboren — *he is born*	ka-tamb-ō .	. . . . . .	an-haif-ē-ši	. . . . .
ich heirathe, mache Hochzeit — *I marry, consummate a marriage*	larúsa dí-akin [2] nigá dí-akin [3]	táne adē-m-rik táne ádi-bi ma-rik	ni ina amrē [10]	médo-bòa .
ich vollziehe den Beischlaf — *I cohabitate*	nigá-ngin . nigá kélag-n-iskin [4]	negánto-rik .	ina gāmu da matše	medórni debbo
ich beschlafe (eine Frau — *I sleep, lie with a woman*	bōg-iskin [5] bō-akin . .			
ich bin lebendig, ich lebe — *I am alive, live*	ŭ ngā [6]	táne níri . .	ina da rai [11] .	mō mōdi yuñki
er lebt — *he lives, is alive*	ši ngā . . .	merē níri [8] .	ši šina da rai	kañko ó-mōdi yuñki

[1] t-e-amb-iskin ist das aktive und transitive Verbum zu tambú-akin. Die transitive Bedeutung ist neben dem aktiven iskin „ich gebe" (eigentlich tamba-iskin „ich gebe Geburt") noch ausgedrückt durch die Einschaltung des e, das auch in der Mâsi-Sprache so prinzipiell durchgeführt ist. Koelle hat in seinem Vokabular das Wort in dieser Form nicht, aber in der Form von yambúskin mit derselben Bedeutung. Das aber halte ich für einen entschiedenen Irrthum, der daher stammt, dass die 1ste Person so gut wie nie gebraucht wird und seinem Lehrer die richtige Ableitung von tambin unbekannt war; tambú-akin hat er nur in der Bedeutung „ich komme heraus (wie aus einem engen Loch)" und doch fragt es sich sehr, ob nicht in tamb gleich die Grundbedeutung „Geburt" war, vielleicht „die Gebärmutter"; dann könnte allerdings das Wort nur von der Frau gebraucht werden. Das wird wahrscheinlich durch das Wort kan-tambú, „ein Eingeborener" mit Beziehung auf irgend einen Ort.

[2] larúsa dí-akin, 3te Person larúsa tsí-din, L. bâll' ale gant' eni, W. ámagá larúsa gené, B. [illegible] udanne (eine unabhängige Verbalform, die mit monda „reife Jungfrau", zusammenhängt). Von der Frau auf Tédā ádibi mári.

[3] nigá dí-akin. Obgleich das Wort nigá aus dem Arabischen herübergenommen ist, wo nikâ eigentlich den wirklichen Beischlaf bezeichnet, so ist doch bei der Redensart nigá dí-akin nur der allgemeine Begriff der Heirath festgehalten; nicht so beim folgenden Worte. Koelle schreibt nigā.

[4] nigá kélag-n-iskin hat Koelle nicht, eben so wenig, wie nigá-ngin, aber er hat kélágin, „ich verbinde, ich begegne", was wahrscheinlich nur eine andere Form desselben Verbums ist.

[5] bōg-iskin. Diese Form und diese Bedeutung hat Koelle nicht; bóngin hat, so viel ich weiss, nie die Bedeutung des Beschlafens. Ich will hier das begriffsverwandte Wort bibin-iskin oder bibiá-gin anführen, „ich thue Gewalt an" einem Mädchen (féro), auf W. [illegible], H. mai-odi mon-nē. Auch will ich hier einige andere verwandte Redensarten anführen, für die ich nur in den wenigsten Sprachen Ausdrücke erfahren habe. So „die Frau hat empfangen", T. ádibi [illegible], H. matše ta-kāma tšeki, F. debbo ó-nāngi réda; die Kanúri gebrauchen für die Niederkunft der Frau den euphemistischen Ausdruck fáto gâgin, „sie geht in's Haus ein", auf T. [illegible], in W. erste Pers. ye-dámbre. „Die Frau säugt das Kind", H. matše ta-bā yarīli nóno, F. nedda ó-hókko [illegible] omóssona; „das Kindlein saugt", H. yarīli šina šā mamma (ganz wie wir sagen „trinkt die Brust") — F. biñgel [illegible] omósseno yandi.

[6] ŏ ngā. Allerdings ist dies keine Verbalform, aber in den entsprechenden Sprachen ist es zum Theil so.

[7] táne fuss-erdō. „Wo bist du geboren?", gámtebi fusss, auf H. ina an-haifé-ka, auf F. to on-dim-ãdo.

[8] merá níri. So ábbē neme níri-mi, „ist dein Vater am Leben?"

[9] na-i dā. So: „er hat zehn Kinder gezeugt", H. ši ya-i dia gōma, F. kanko rimmi bibe sappe oder ó-wōdi bibe sappe.

[10] ni ina amrē. „Ich habe nicht geheirathet, bin unverheirathet", bā ni amrē bā, F. mē-bōa-ta.

[11] ina da rai, daher das Adjektiv „lebendig, am Leben", H. mai-rai, F. gudódo yuñki, Plur. wodóbe yuñki.

[12] Die doppelte Bedeutung von ni-haif, „ich gebäre" und „ich bin geboren", ist auffallend und, wenn richtig, nur durch eine Verschiedenheit der Betonung zu erklären.

[13] billē ngā. Dies sieht nicht sehr originell aus, da ngā entschieden das Kanúri-Wort ist. In der ersten Person habe ich es nicht erfahren können.

[14] ba láfia genē gehört eigentlich nicht hierher, da es eher heisst „er ist bei Wohlsein".

[15] adádde-ma zeigt ein Beispiel einer Reduplication des dā-Lauts. Das k in na-k-eddāe muss des Wohllauts halber eingefügt sein.

Sonyai.	Lógoné.	Wándalá.	Bágrimma.	Mába.
aí-hal [12]	. . . .	ye-ya . . .	. . . . . .	. . . . . .
ni-da-n izzo . .	. . . .	. . . . . .	. . . . . .	av-ñõ
. . . .	ganám davẽúli .	á-ya-ne muksa	nẽ na-k-oddžo	mežóng tu-ñár
ai-hal	yane-ẽ	yeyim bã-ya	maandžódžo-ma [15]	am bu-ñẽro
. . . .	yaue-ní . . .	yeye bá-ñganẽ	džódžum . .	. . . . .
ambẽk (y) . . .	gunto 'nlo nĩ .	{yé-magã larúsaa / y(e)-igaẽ larúsaa}	mak-un manda	
	. . . .	{yé-kela . . / yú-ñela gúñeiẽ}	mát-odĩ . .	am buddu (kolini
áfunã (?) . . .	. . . .	ye láña . . .	ma kotško .	am lekai andĩ
	bille úgã [13] . .	be láña genẽ [14]	nẽ kotško . .	iĩ lekaĩ tendı

[1] ṭ-a-amb-lakin is the active and transitive form of the verb tambá-akin, the transitive character being expressed besides by the verbal form lakin (properly tamba-lekin „I give birth") by means of the a, which also in the Máaly language bears such a conspicuous part. The word in this form is wanting in Koelle's vocabulary, but he gives it under the wrong form of yembáakin with the notion „I bring forth, beget", the error originating in the circumstance, that the 1st person of this verb is very rarely used, so that the true derivation of teambin remained unknown to his teacher. The passive form tamb-á-akin Kl. has only with the notion „I come out (as of a narrow hole)" and although this might seem to be a fit notion for barbarians, from which „to be born" might be derived, I yet doubt very much, whether the original notion of tamb was not „womb". In this case however the word can only be used of women and that seems really the case. Intimately connected with this notion is the term kam-tambũ, „a native" of such and such a place.

[2] larúsan di-akin, 3rd person larúsaa tei-din, L. bill' ale gunt' eni, W. ámagã larúsaa genẽ, B. nẽ nadánne (a verbal form, from which the noun manda „a ripe virgin" appears to be derived). Of the woman the Téda say ádibi mári.

[3] niga di-akin: although the term niga has been introduced from the Arabic, in which language nika means the actual cohabitation, yet the phrase niga di-akin in Kanúri expresses only the general notion of marriage; but the same cannot be said of the following term.

[4] The term niga ḳéleg-a-lakin is wanting in Koelle's vocabulary, but he has the word ḳéligin, „I join, I meet", and that is probably only another form of the same verb.

[5] bõg-lakin. This form of the verb with this notion is wanting in Koelle's vocabulary; the form bõngin, which he gives, has, as far as I know, never the notion of cohabitation. — I shall in this place adduce a term of a similar notion, viz bibia-lakin or bibiá-gin, „I debauch a girl" (fóra), in W. itdãgoagwã, B. mai-odi mon-nã. I shall likewise mention in this note some other terms, which I can only represent in a few languages. Thus „the woman has conceived", T. ádi-bi lẽmi, H. mataẽ ta-háma tãchi, F. debbo ó-nãági rẽdu. — The Kanúri use for the confinement of the woman the euphonic expression fãto gágia, „she retires into the house", T. aekbia, W. ia pera yo-dámbra. „The woman suckles the baby", H. mataẽ ta-bã yarĩli núna, F. neddo ó-hóhko sũkaira hetšel oméeeena; „the baby sucks", H. yarĩli šina ñõ mamma, F. biágel hetšel oméeeena yandi.

[6] ñ ágã: in Kanúri this is certainly no verbal form, but in other languages it is.

[7] ñánõ fuaa-ardõ: „where are you born?", gámichi fuaea, H. ina aa-haifã-ka, F. tõ oa-dim-áda.

[8] mardõ nĩri: thus „is your father alive?", dãehã neme niri-mĩ.

[9] aa-i dã: thus the phrase „he has begotten ten children", H. ñĩ ya-i dia gõma, F. hadho rimmi bibe sappo or ó-wádi biba sappo.

[10] ni laa amrẽ: I here give the phrase „I have not married, am not married", bã ni amrẽ há, F. mõ hóa-te.

[11] laa da raf: thence the adjective „alive", H. mai-raf, F. godõdo yuáki, pl. wadõbe yuáki.

[12] The double meaning of ai-haĩ, „I bear", „beget" and „I am born" or „begotten", is remarkable and, if correct, can only be explained by way of a distinct and very different intonation of these two words.

[13] bille ágã has not a very original look about it, especially as ágã belongs to the Kanúri idiom. In the first pers. I was not able to make it out.

[14] be láña genẽ does not properly belong to this place, as it means only „he is well".

[15] adžódžo-ma is an example of a reduplication of the sound „dž". The k in the form na-k-oddžo appears to have been inserted from euphonic reasons.

Deutsch und Englisch.	Kanúri.	Tédā.	Hausa.	Fulfulde.
ich altere, werde alt — *I get old, grow old*	keāri-niskin / keāri-ñgin .	búggoli [6] . .	na-I súfa [8] .	mē-naui . . / nai-ēdžo . .
er ist alt geworden, hat gealtert — *he has got old*	keāri-dāí . .	. . . . .	ši ya-I súfa .	kañko ó-naui
ich sterbe — *I am dying*	nu-skin . .	tánē te-nās-ik	ná-mutū . .	m(e) omaI . .
er ist gestorben, ist todt — *he died, is dead*	nu-I [1] . . .	merē nōs . .	yá-mutu [9] .	kañko(ma)ó-omu
er liegt in den letzten Zügen — *he is breathing his last*	nesko-nisé kariñgu taú-lugin / ši kariñgu tímmotšin	merē kerkúkinI	. . . . .	
ich esse — *I eat* . . .	bú-skin . .	tánē bó-rik .	Ina-tšI . . .	mēdo-nyūma .
iss — *eat*	bú-I	. . . . .	tšI	yaúg . . . .
er hat gegessen — *he has eaten, finished eating*	zé-bi [2] . . .	. . . . .	ya-tšI [10] . .	kañko ó-nyāmi
ich schmecke — *I taste*	támbu-skin [3] .	tánē tōbe-rik	ina tebba-wa / ina tamma-wa / ina dándana	mēdo-mēdaseídu
er schmeckt — *he tastes*	ši tamb-in .	. . . . .	ši sina tebba-wa u. s. w.	kañko ú-mēdo seídu
ich bin hungrig, empfinde Hunger — *I am hungry*	ū-ma kenā-wa [4]	tánē agaI tšedI	ina-žin yung-wa	mēdo-nanna wēlo
ich bin satt, es genügt mir — *I am satiated, satisfied*	ū-ga se-tI [5] / se-tI ū-ga .	agal-ter [7] . . / túsede . . .	ná-koši . .	mē-hāri . .

[1] na-I. Die Kanúri haben für dieses Wort mehrere euphemistische Ausdrücke, wie fētsibI („er hat sich verirrt"), lē-teō („er ist davongegangen") und kóla-tsē („er hat verlassen"). — Ich bemerke hier, dass in den meisten hier gegebenen Paradigmen auch die erste Person in der Vergangenheit ist.

[2] Ich führe hier noch das Substantiv „die Speise" an: K. ke-m-bá, H. tšī-ma, F. kō-nyāme-te oder nyāma-ndē, L. wai-ejummi, W. mé-sanē, B. ngás-ke-sé, M. ša. Auch gehört hierher das Kanúri-Wort bá-ai („Fisch"). Ich will hier noch bemerken, dass das Wort „essen" in den meisten dieser Sprachen auch von leblosen Dingen gebraucht wird, wie besonders vom Kriege, kerigu zé-bin, „der Krieg isst, zerstört"; kasuku zé-bin, H. kasuwa tána-tšI, „der Markt isst, wird gehalten", oder auch „ich esse den Markt, d. h. benutze ihn zu Einkäufen".

[3] támbu-skin ist ein Beispiel, wie zwei Wörter einander so ähnlich sehen können, wie dies Wort und das vorhergehende, ohne etwas mit einander gemein zu haben. Denn tambu ist wol entschieden auf das Engste verwandt mit dem entsprechenden Hausa-Wort tebba oder tamma und der Tédā-Ausdruck ist eine blosse Variation davon; auffallend ist jedenfalls die 3te Person ši tamb-in. Ich führe hier noch das verwandte Wort gei-skin, „ich kaue", an, im W. ye-kepépedē.

[4] ū-ma kenā-wa. Der Form nach gehört diese Phrase ebenso wenig wie ū-ma gūd-wa hierher. Koelle schreibt kṳnā. s. w.

[5] ū-ga se-tI, eigentlich „es genügt mir" (se-tI impersonal von ti-skin); 3te Person, „er ist satt" (es genügt ihm), K. se-tI šiga oder šiga se-tI.

[6] búggoli ist in dieser Form mehr als zweifelhaft.

[7] Über agal-ter bin ich nicht ganz sicher; die volle Form würde sein agal-ter-ik und dann würde das von mir auch niedergeschriebene agal-teri-e dem als negative Form erscheinen.

[8] na-I súfa. Ich führe hier die begriffsverwandte Redensart auf „ich bekomme graue Haare", H. na-I fárfara, F. mē-wōdi dasándi oder mē-wōdi dendéndi.

[9] yá-mutū: „ist er todt oder lebt er?", H. ši yá-mutū kō šina da rai, F. ó-mōdi kó gé ó-mal.

[10] Ich will hier die beiden verwandten Redensarten aufführen: „ich speise zu Mittag", H. ina kala-tšI (wahrscheinlich erst aus der Verbindung mit dem Arab. kelá entstanden), und „ich frühstücke", H. ina káriu n komállo, wörtlich „ich breche die Bitterkeit", F. medde kóyom.

[11] tō ozinee mewē kedám. ozinea in diesen beiden Redensarten, obgleich auffällig, muss wol richtig sein. bille heisst „Mensch, Person", demá und mawē (im B. máhi) sind verschiedene Ausdrücke für „alt"; aber was kedem bedeutet, weiss ich nicht.

[12] néfa-ni esáfne: néfa-ni „seine Lunge", „sein Lebensathem", das Nomen vom Arab. abgeleitet; esáfne ist mir unbekannt.

[13] dadimne entspricht vielleicht eher dem Kanúri-Ausdruck bal-nískene; denn für die 3te Person, „er ist satt", habe ich den ganz besonderen vielleicht mehr hierher gehörigen Ausdruck dógde gonéko.

[14] Dass ši-ša zwei getrennte Redetheile sind, ergibt sich aus der Form für die 3te Person, ša-n šI-n gané.

[15] mab-ga. Auch hiervon habe ich in der 3ten Person die selbstständige Form á-ai galé.

Sońγai.	Lógoné.	Wándalá.	Bágrimma.	Mába.
ai-dáru	indo agínse bille demā	gaa ṅgum džikō	man-gádagā / man-tal gádagā	am kolák nyō
a-džen	tē agínse mawū kadám [11]	gab) ṅgum džikē gań-kenī?	. . . . . .	. . . . . .
ai-bū	indo amli . . .	yo-misa . .	mak-oigu . .	am ei
a-bū	ni ni-ámti . .	a-misa bá-ṅganē	n(ō)-oigu . .	lio
. . . . . .	néfa-ni asáfne [12]	am tdggirzē .	ṅgilne lekō .	túrmouū?
éga-gnā . . .	indo u-zym . .	yo-zā (bā-ya	mak-e-sā .	am aōl
gnā	zymmi	zā	sā	ōn
úńg-aia a-gnā .	na-zym . . .	ta-zā (bá-ṅganē	ni nak-e-sā .	. . . . . .
. . . . . .	ū-dim	ye-tapāna bā-ya	man-dáṅga .	am aináṅgne
. . . . . .	sigē-dim? . . .	. . . . . .	nen-dáṅga .	
. . . . . .	av-yendrā		ōdžo andol .	
éga-mántu . . / éga-húṅgu . .	dadímna [13] . .	ēl-ēn [14] . . .	mab-ga [15] . .	a-silo

[1] nu-i. The Kanúri people have several euphemic expressions for this word, as fétsikī („he has strayed"); lá-isé („he is gone"), hálo-isā („he has left"). I remark, that in most of the languages here exhibited also the first pers. of this word is given in the past tense.

[2] I mention here in the note also the substantive „food, eatables", K. bu-m-bá, H. tīl-ma, F. kó-nyáma-le or nyámadō, L. wai-ugmmi, W. má-nazā, B. ugás-ka-nā, M. ōa. Also the Kanúri word bú-ai („fish") belongs to this place. I will also observe here, that the term „eat" is used in most of these languages also in the case of inanimate subjects, as especially that of war; thus kerigu sé-bin, „the war eats, devours"; kásuku sé-bin, H. kasuwa tána-tsī, „the market eats, takes place", and likewise „I eat or frequent the market".

[3] támbu-shin may serve as an example, how words may be very similar one to the other, like this word and the preceding one and nevertheless have nothing in common. The term tambu probably derived from or related to the corresponding Hausa word and the T. term is a mere dialectic difference of the same; remarkable is the 3rd pers. sing. Si tamb-in. I also adduce in this place the term ṅgri-shin, „I chew", W. ye-kapápadā.

[4] ū-ma kanā-ma: properly neither this phrase nor that of ū-ma gūd-wa, as not being a verbal, but an adjective formation, belong to this place, but I was obliged to introduce them here. Norris writes kyné and so on.

[5] ū-ga nō-tī, properly „it suffices me" (no-tī being the 3rd pers. of ti-shin); „he is satiated, satisfied", K. no-tī Siga or Siga no-tī.

[6] hággoli is certainly a very doubtful form.

[7] agal-tes: I am not quite certain with regard to this form, but I suppose it to be a popular abbreviation of agal-ter-ih, of which the term agal-teri-n, which I have also taken down would seem to be the negative form.

[8] nu-i súfu. I shall here adduce the related phrase „I get grey hairs", H. na-i fúrfura, F. mó-wódi dandádi or mó-wódi dendéndi.

[9] yé-mutū; here the phrase „is he dead or does he live?", H. Si yé-mutū kō šina da rai, F. é-mādi kó gō é-mal.

[10] I shall here adduce two related terms: „I dine", H. ina kalá-tsī (probably, a compound word of the indigenous H. term and the Arabic kalā), and „I breakfast", properly „I break the bitterness (the bitter taste of fasting)", H. ina kária n komilio, F. modda kōyam.

[11] tō agínse mawū kadám: agínse is remarkable, but probably is correct. bille means „man, person", demá and mawū (in B. mābī) are different terms signifying „old"; but I do not know what may be the meaning of kadám.

[12] néfa-ni asáfne: néfa-ni „his breath, his lungs", the noun being derived from the Arab.; asáfne is unknown to me.

[13] dadímna perhaps rather corresponds to the Kanúri term bai-nishena; for the 3rd pers. „he is satiated" I have found expressed by the independent phrase ságde genáho.

[14] ēl-ēn evidently does consist of two distinct roots, as appears from the form for the 3rd person, Fe-n ēl-n ganā.

[15] mab-ga. For this word also in the 3rd person I have the independent term t-ai galā.

Deutsch und Englisch.	Kanúri.	Tēda.	Hausa.	Fulfúlde.
Ich habe keinen Appetit — *I have no appetite*	kul-niskena [1]	. . . . . .	(ba nī sō ábe-n-tšī [9]	mēdo-dóñere?
Ich bin durstig, empfinde Durst — *I am thirsty*	ŭ-ma gŭd-wa [2]	tánē godō . .	ína-ží-n ki-šī-n rūa [10]	mēdo-nauna doňka
ich trinke — *I drink* .	yā-skin [3] . .	tánē yā-rik .	ína šā . . .	mēdo-yā-ra [12]
er trinkt — *he drinks* .	tsē-nin . . .	merē í-yā .	šína šā . . .	kaňko ó-yā-ra
trinke — *drink*	yā	yā	šā	yāra . . . . .
ich rauche (trinke Tabak — *I smoke (drink tobacco*	tāba yā-skin .	tánē tāba yā-rik	ína šā tāba .	mēdo-yāra tāba
ich bin betrunken — *I am drunk*	karábi-skena [4]	egé-hedē [7] . .	nia ná-bogū [11]	bam fū-mi [13]
er ist betrunken — *he is drunk*	karábt-ena .	büri e-iyā-de	šī yá-bogū .	bam fū-mō / kaňko fáddakē
ich schlafe — *I sleep* .	len-niskin [5] .	tíse-rik [8] . .	ína bertšī . .	mēdo-dāni .
	3te Pers. lei-tšin	nékkini . . .	šī šína bertši	kaňko ó-dāni
ich liege, lege mich nieder — *I lie, lie down*	bō-niskin [6] . / bō-ngin . .	girlítidik? . .	nī-ko kontše .	mē-fukko-to

[1] kul-niskena. Dieses Wort hat Koelle nicht, aber er hat das nahverwandte Wort kulágin mit der Bedeutung „ich bin stark, fett, korpulent".

[2] ŭ-ma gŭd-wa. Koelle schreibt ŭgáðñ, ŭgáðña.

[3] yā-skin. Die 3te Person dieses Verbums, die so ausserordentlich unregelmässig ist, scheint dafür zu sprechen, dass in der ursprünglichen Form das Kanúri- und Hausa-Verbum sich einander näher standen, als yā und šā. Der Wurzelkonsonant š erscheint auch in dem Substantiv ken-tsā, „das Getränk". So ist denn die Übereinstimmung zwischen Kanúri und Fulfúlde (yā-skin — mēdo-yā-ra) in diesem Falle wol nur scheinbar, indem ausserdem, wie der Imperativ zeigt, das ra in der späteren ausgebildeten Form schon zum Worte selbst gehört; aber das war wol nicht der Fall in der ursprünglichen Form. Koelle hat im Vokabular anstatt yā-skin yáskin; die 3te Person Plur. ist tsa-tsi.

[4] karabt-iskena. Dies Wort fehlt bei Koelle; die Ableitung ist auch mir unbekannt.

[5] len-niskin ist, wie ich glaube, die einzige gebräuchliche Form für das Präsens dieses Zeitworts; wenigstens habe ich eine Form lēn-gin dafür nie gehört, sondern nur als Präsensform des so ähnlich lautenden Wortes lēn-iskin oder lēngin, „ich gehe"; Koelle schreibt das Letztere, um zu unterscheiden, léngin. Dass t zur Wurzel gehört, scheint sich aus dem Worte leti-orom, „Schlafgemach", zu ergeben.

[6] bō-niskin, bō-ngin. Dass das n nicht zum Stamme gehört, scheint sich aus den Formen bō-tšin u. s. w. und bō-gata, „liegend", „schlafend" (W. áldenā) zu ergeben. Eine enge Verwandtschaft dieses Wortes mit búnē, „die Nacht", kann dabei doch bestehen; Koelle schreibt búnyé. Koelle's Wort bun, „das sich Niederlegen", ist mir aber auffallend und zweifelhaft. Auch ein ben, „schlafen", mit den abgeleiteten Wörtern, die ich ebenso wenig wie die Form búnyē je gehört habe, möchte ich bezweifeln.

[7] egé-hedē ist mir mehr als zweifelhaft. Offenbar ist das büri e-iyā-de eine ganz andere Redeform.

[8] tíse-rik: ganz sicher bin ich über diese Form nicht; „wir schlafen" heisst tise-t, auch tīš-t, cond. tīš-tat. Die folgende Form nékkini gehört natürlich einer ganz anderen Wurzel an und heisst wahrscheinlich nur „er liegt", nicht „er schläft".

[9] ba nī sō ábe-n-tšī, eigentlich „ich mag keine Nahrung", aber ein anderer prägnanterer Ausdruck ist mir unbekannt.

[10] ína-ži-n ki-šī-n rūa. Das Wort ki-šī, „Durst", hängt, wie schon gezeigt, mit der Wurzel šē zusammen.

[11] nia ná-bogū, wörtlich und eigentlich „ich bin geschlagen (am Kopfe getroffen) worden", ist mit bugga, „schlagen", verwandt.

[12] mēdo-yā-ra. S. Note 3 über die scheinbare Übereinstimmung in diesem Falle zwischen Fulfúlde und Kanúri.

[13] bam fū-mi, wörtlich „das berauschende Getränk (bam) hat mich getroffen"; fū-mō „hat ihn getroffen".

[14] a-jirbi. Ich habe mir in diesem Falle erlaubt, den Konsonanten, den ich sonst mit dš wiedergebe, mit einem blossen j zu schreiben, da er hier nur eine Erweichung des g-Lautes ist.

[15] wō-sē tāba; dazu die negative Form „ich rauche nicht", wōnē tāba-sā (die negative Partikel dem Substantiv, anstatt dem Verbum angehängt), im W. ye-šē-ke tāpa.

[16] bili(e) āla hankal-nsē šē, wahrscheinlich „dieser Mensch hat seinen Verstand vertrunken".

[17] bá-ya lagú. Das lagū ist allem Anscheine nach keine eigentliche Verbalform.

Šebyal.	Légumē.	Wándalā.	Bágrimma.	Mába.
. . . .	. . . .	a-öćàg-neaā?	mirga? . . .	. . . .
. . . .	av-yóća . . .	. . . . . .	andži andoī .	. . . . . .
éga-haṅg . . .	wū-sē	ye-šenne . .	mak-ai . . .	á-yaṅg-nē
. . . .	ní ya-tē . . .	a-šenne . .	nō-ai . . .	. . . .
haṅg	sē-o	šenne . . .	ai	yaṅga
	wu-sé taba [13] .	ye-šenne tápa	mak-ai taba .	kui á-yaṅg-nē
. . . .	. . . .	y(o)-ėumanē .	mam tárkarál fagā	am ámmaril
. . . .	bill(e) ále haukal-anē šē [16]	a-'mmamá-n-genē	nē tárkarál fagā	t(e) ámmaru
éga-girbi, džírbi	wu áwisā . . .	yō páharó . .	ma-tod bi-ga	á-bi
(imp. a-jirbi [14]) .	bill(e) ále áwisen	há-ńganē páharē	nē nē-tod bi-ga	(imp. fen)
éga-kanní . . .	. . . .	bá-ya Ingā [17] .	mam tod-ga .	. . . . . .

[1] k a l - a l a h e n a is wanting in Koelle's vocabulary, but he has the nearly related verb h a l á g i n, „I am stout, fat, corpulent".

[2] ṅ-ma gúd-wa. Koelle writes á g á d ā, á g é d ā n.

[3] y á - a h i n: the 3d person of this very irregular verb seems to favour the assumption, that its root was nearer related to the Hausa language, than appears from the modern form of the present tense. The consonantal root ša appears also in the form of the noun š e n - l a ā „beverage". It is therefore to be regarded, I think, as merely accidental, that the form of the Fulfúlde verb is seemingly so clearly allied to the Kanúri, besides that the syllable ya in y á - r a evidently belongs to the root, at least of the present form of the verb which is now before our eyes. I must still remark, that Koelle writes y é a h i n and not y á - a h i n. The 3rd pers. pl. is t e a - t a l.

[4] k a r a b i - l a k a n a is wanting in Koelle's vocabulary.

[5] l e n - a l a h i n, as far as I was able to learn, is the only usual form of the present tense of this verb; at least I have never heard the form g i n used of this verb, but only of the almost identical, but totally different verb l ē n - i a h i n or l ē n - g i n, „I go". Koelle distinguishes both forms merely by the adding of a dot over the n in the latter word. That t belongs to the root, seems to be confirmed by the form of the noun l e n t - e r a m, „bed room".

[6] b ó - a l a h i n, b ó - á g i n. That the a does not belong to the root, seems to be clearly demonstrated by the forms b ó - t á d a, „he sleeps", and b ó - g a t a, „lying", „sleeping" (W. á l d e w ā). A close relationship between this verb and the noun b á n ē „night" may nevertheless exist. K. writes, b á n y ē; but the term b u n, which appears in Koelle's vocabulary with the notion of „lying down", appears doubtful to me. I even feel inclined to reduce to the same root the term b u n, „sleep", in Koelle's vocabulary with the terms thence derived, which I have never heard, as little as the form b é n y ē for b á n ē.

[7] e g é - b a d ē is more than doubtful. At least thus much is certain that b ū r i k e - i y ā - d u is a totally different phrase.

[8] t i a r - r i k: I am not quite certain as to this form of the pres. tense; „we sleep" is t i a - i, sometimes also t i ā - i, cond. t i ā - i a l. — The following term n é k k i n i of course does belong to a totally different root and means probably only „he is lying down", not „he is sleeping".

[9] k a u l a ó á b e - n - t ā l, properly „I do not like any food".

[10] l a a - š i - a k i - š i - a r ū a: the word k i - š i „thirst", is evidently nearly related to the root š i „drink".

[11] n i a n á - h o g ā has probably the original meaning of „I am struck" (in the head) and is closely allied with „h a g g a", „to beat, strike".

[12] m ó d a - y ā - r a: see note 3 on account of the seeming harmony between the F. and K. languages in this instance.

[13] b a m f i l - m i means verbally „the intoxicating beverage (b a m) did strike me".

[14] a - j i r b i: in this instance I have taken the liberty to render the consonant, which in general I represent by means of a dž, by a simple j, as it is a merely softened form of g.

[15] w ū - s ē t á b a: thereof the negative form „I do not smoke", w ū - s ē t á b a - s á, the negative particle s a being attached to the noun, instead of to the verb; in W. y e - š e - k e t á p a.

[16] b i l l (e) á l e h a u k a l - a n ē š ē has probably the original meaning: „this man has drunk down his intelligence."

[17] b á - y a l a g ā: the term l a g ā according to all appearance is not a verbal form.

Deutsch und Englisch.	Kanuri.	Tédā.	Hausa.	Fulfulde.
ich bringe die Nacht zu — *I pass the night*	bō-nískin . .	tíse-rik . . .	ína kwāna [9] .	mēdo-weldi .
er liegt, legt sich nieder — *he is lying, lies down*	bō-tšin . . .	nékkini . . .	ši yina kontāo	om-ó-fukki .
wo schlafen wir, bringen wir die Nacht zu? — *where do we pass the night*	ndára bō-nien	nō-kordē tišī	dagá ína mūna kwāna	tō mim-baldi
ich schnarche — *I am snoring*	tánguri yūk-lskin [1]	kirkékini? . .	ína hánsari [10]	mēdo-harra .
ich gähne — *I am yawning*	snaśngo yūk-lskin [2]	. . . . .	ína hamma .	mēdo-gābi .
ich bin schläfrig, Schlaf überkommt mich — *I am sleepy*	kenám ū-{se-tal [3] gn {gō-tsin}	ūne-šilli ke-mú-k [6]	ína gíógedi .	mēdo-waánga
ich träume — *I dream*	nešín-nískin [4] .	tánō mešénne-rik	na-ī má-falki	. . . . .
ich bin wach — *I am awake*	ū-ma fā-gata [5]	{ása nepík . ūne-šilli ke-mú-ēn [7]}	. . . . .	. . . . .
ich erhebe mich vom Schlaf — *I arise from sleeping*	ū tšī-nískin ke-nám-nin	{yer-dik [8] . . . une-šilli árne-rik}	ína tāši dagá berišī	. . . . . .

[1] tánguri yūk-lskin hat Koelle nicht; vielleicht ist tánguri verwandt mit tnágin, „ich [illegible] aus“. yūk-lskin, das Koelle in dieser Form nicht hat, ist entschieden verwandt oder vielmehr identisch mit yengin, „ich bewege, drehe“, und yēágin, „ich antworte“. — 3te Person tánguri tse-kin.

[2] Auch snaśmge yūk-lskin, 3te Person snaśmgo tse-kin, hat Koelle nicht; snaśmgo hängt entschieden zusammen mit sámgin.

[3] kenám ū-ga se-tal: 3te Person, „ihn überfällt Schlaf, er ist schläfrig“, kenám šī-ga se-tal; Koelle schreibt kanám.

[4] nešín-nískin: wörtlich „ich mache Traum“. Koelle hat die Form náślngin. Sonderbar ist, dass das offenbar verwandte Wort im Tédā mit einem m und nicht mit einem n anfängt.

[5] ū-ma fā-gata. Koelle schreibt págata, so wie er auch pángin schreibt. Dieses Wort in der Bedeutung „aufwachen“ ist allmählich zu einem ganz abgesonderten von (fangin) pángin, „ich höre, vernehme“, geworden; denn der Kanúri scheint sich unter dem Wachen nichts Anderes gedacht zu haben, als seiner Sinne mächtig zu sein, besonders des Gehörs, wie denn das Aufwachen bei ihm sachlich und sprachlich identisch ist mit dem Hören des Hahnengeschrei's.

[6] ūne-šilli ke-mú-k: ūne-šilli muss wol richtig sein, da ich es mehre Male habe; ke-mú-k, 3te Pers. sing. von ma-rik „ich ergreife“. Die pronominale Beziehung scheint hier nicht besonders ausgedrückt zu sein; das ist sie aber in der Phrase mará ūne-šilli ke-mú-de „ihn erfasst Schläfrigkeit“.

[7] ke-mú-ēn, „erfasst nicht“, ist die negative Form vom vorhergehenden ke-mú-k. — ása-ne-pik ist keine rein nationale Redensart; ása ist Arabisch.

[8] yer-dik. Der Imp. yer soár, „wache auf und rühre dich“, scheint richtig zu sein.

[9] ína kwāna. Ich will hier in dieser Note die eigenthümlich prägnante Phrase aufführen na-kwan da rhu, „nachdem man unter Regen die Nacht zugebracht hatte“. Ähnlich sagt man im F. mē-waldi hi ndiam, Plur. im-baldi hi ndiam.

[10] ína hánsari. „Ich schlief, so dass ich schnarchte“. H. na-ī beríšī har na-ī hánsari, F. madánshē hámide harre.

[11] wá áwieén-eá ist die negative Form zu wá áwinan, „ich schlafe“.

[12] wūn-tinló; dazu Imp. [illegible]. „stehe auf“.

[13] ya-bedhrá, vielleicht richtiger ye bédderá.

[14] ya awa; 3te Person áwa bá-égané.

[15] ye pabárud yé-megén muká-nište, wörtlich „ich schlafend ich machte ein Traumgesicht“. Das muká-nište zeigt entschiedene Verwandtschaft mit dem Kanúri-Wort nešin, „der Traum“ und ist wol ein erkünsteltes Wort.

[16] teé-na-teé pábaré. Dazu habe ich als 3te Person die etwas unsichere Form teb-teé pabgue pábaré.

[17] bi-hem-gá; 3te Person nē bi-heg-elē, wörtlich „er, der Schlaf erfasst ihn“. bi ist „der Schlaf“.

[18] sangeidek wie met-ed šeamgá im B. scheinen mit dem Kanúri-Wort snaśmgo Verwandtschaft zu haben, aber man muss wol bedenken, dass alle diese Wörter keine ursprünglichen sind.

[19] ay-ering-tá-al, wiederum die negative Form.

Sonyai.	Lógoné.	Wándalá.	Bágrimma.	Mába.
óga girbi, dzirbi	wū-sénabó . .	. . . . .	mam-tód-ga	am ábrea / am ándani
. . . . . .	ya-sénabé . . .	bá-ñganē lagā	í-tod-ō . .	. . . . . .
. . . . . .	amdil mu-senáhayen banta	me-hāram ámmōe	éda tód-gena	. . . . . .
óga hanzūru . .	wū gúmguma .	ye bedbrā [13] .	mal-ad írga / mam-girna .	gukúrda
	. . . .	ye áwa [14] . .	mat-ad ásamgā	sañgaidek [18]
	álan kotliwá wū-sénabē	áwēn hāre . .	bí-kom-gā [17]	tāriñg andoī
	. . . .	ye paháruā yémagán maká-nišin [15]	mam-aklúi .	am-óleli
. . . . . .	wū áwisón-sā [11] .	yo-nitše . .	mal-onnal-lí mak-indžira	ay-āriñg-tā-ni [19]
á-tun dzírid-gā	wū-θnié [12] . .	taá-na-tsē pá-harē [16]	m(a)-in-grāge / m(a)-in-ro bí-ga	tāriñgnen mēren ávringa

[1] tóñguri yēk-lekin is wanting in Koelle's vocabulary. It is however not impossible, that tóñguri is related to the verb taígin, „I squeeze, press". Koelle, as usual, has not the form yēk-lekin, but he has the two distinct forms yangin, „I move, turn", and yéñgin „I answer", though these are evidently one and the same word, the one term expressing the material and the other the spiritual effect of the same action. 3rd pers. tóñguri tse-kin.

[2] sectámge yēk-lekin also is wanting in Koelle; 3rd pers. sectámge tse-kin. The word probably is connected with the verb sámgin.

[3] kenám ñ-ga se-tal: 3rd pers. „sleep overtakes him, he is sleepy", kenám šī-ga se-tal; Koelle writes keném.

[4] nežin-niskin „I make dream": Koelle has the form nāžingin. It is remarkable, that the corresponding Tēdā word, which evidently bears close relation to the former, does begin with an m instead of an n.

[5] ñ-ma fā-gata: Koelle writes pāg-áta, as he writes also páñgin: that is a mere variety of dialect, and I think, this verb implying the notion of „to awake" originally was not distinct from pāñgin (faúgin), „I hear", „learn", but on the contrary it seems, that the Kanúri identified the notion of „to awake" with that of „hearing the cock's first crowing".

[6] ñne-žitti ke-má-h: ñne-žitti probably is correct, as I have taken it down several times; ke-má-k is 3rd pers. sing. from ma-rik „I catch, lay hold of". The pronoun is not so distinctly expressed in this phrase as it is in the following word ñne-žitti ke-mó-de „him sleep catches".

[7] ke-má-ta, „does not catch", is the negative form of the preceding ke-má-h. — āsa ne-pik does not appear to be a purely indigenous phrase, āsa being evidently introduced from the Arabic.

[8] yer-dih: imp. yer sedr, „awake and move", seems to be right.

[9] ina kwina. Here in this note I give the remarkably concise phrase an-kwan da rūa, „after having passed the night under rain", in F. mā-wēldi bi ndiam, pl. im-báldi bi ndiam.

[10] ina hánsari: „I slept, so that I snored", B. na-i heržil har na-i binsari, F. medánakā hámido harre.

[11] wū áwisén-sā is the negative form of wū áwisén, „I sleep".

[12] wū-θalē: imp. θal, „rise".

[13] ya-hedbrā, perhaps more correctly ye hédderu.

[14] ye áwa. 3rd pers. áwa bá-ñganē.

[15] ye pahárnā yé-magan maká-nišin, verbally „sleeping I have a dream"; the word maká-nišin no doubt is intimately allied with the Kanúri word nežin, „dream".

[16] taá-na-tsē pāharē: of this phrase I have in the 3rd pers. the doubtful form tsē-tsē pasgar (bá-ñganē) páharē.

[17] bí-kom-gā; 3rd pers. nē bí-kog-nié verbally „he, sleep catches him". bí means „sleep".

[10] sañgaidek as well as the Bágrimma term mat-ad ásamgā seems to be closely allied with the Kanúri term sectámge; we must bear in mind however, that all these are not original words, but introduced at a later period.

[19] ay-āriñg-tā-ni: here again we have the negative form.

Deutsch und Englisch.	Kanuri.	Tédā.	Hausa.	Fulfulde.
ich stehe aufrecht — *I stand upright*	ū dāg-ata [1] .	tánē te-túzzedē	ni na-tsaia dēdē	{ mēdo-darro / mē-darr-ekē }
er steht aufrecht — *he stands upright*	ší dāga-ta .	merō túzzedē .	ši šína tsaia dēdē	kaňko ó-dárro
ich bleibe, sitze — *I remain, am sitting*	nem-niskin [2] .	{ tóbnaik [6] . . / tōzik . . . }	ina zamna . .	mēdo-džōda-kē
er bleibt, sitzt — *he remains, is sitting*	{ nem-tšin . / nep-tšin . . }	. . . . . .	ší šína zamna	kaňkoó-džōda-kē
sitzend — *sitting, seated*	ném-kata . .	. . . . . .	an-zamna . .	. . . . . .
ich stütze mich auf, lehne mich an — *I lean on, lean against*	rā-niskin . .	. . . . . .	na-žingena .	{ mēdo-wāha-kē / mē-wakka-hó }
ich falle — *I fall* . .	(dū-ruskin, impera.)	. . . . . .	ina-fād-wa .	mēdo yenni .
ich huste — *I cough* .	kásagē yasráskin [3]	mórte kemúk [7]	ina tūari . .	mēdo-džel .
ich niese — *I sneeze* .	wádlinā yēk-iskin [4]	síne-rik [8] . .	na-i { átiša . / átišēya . }	mē-islakē . .
ich putze meine Nase — *I clean my nose*	kin- { tin-nískin [5] / tsā-nītin-gin }	susúkkerúk ? .	ina gerta hantši	. . . .
ich schwitze — *I perspire*	. . . . . .	tánō dehī . .	na-i žēbi . .	{ mē-zúvveni [9] / mēdo-wūli . }
mir ist übel — *I am qualmish*	. . . . . .		nai komilo .	{ mēdo-nanna / mēdo-wōdi } kē-fa

[1] dāg-ata kommt von der Wurzel dāngin, das ich zwar nicht in Gebrauch gefunden habe, das aber in der dritten Person als impersonelle Form dā-tši, „es steht still, ist vorbei", allgemeine Bedeutung hat. Auch kommen verschiedene abgeleitete Formen von diesem Zeitwort her. Koelle führt unter dem Worte rāngin, S. 368, eine Phrase an, wo dā-tši in der Bedeutung „er stand aufrecht" erscheint, aber so habe ich es nie gebraucht gefunden.

[2] nem-niskin. Koelle, der es in der Genauigkeit gar zu weit treibt, sucht zwei Wörter zu unterscheiden, nám-gin, „ich sitze, warte", und nēm-gin, „ich bin ruhig, still". Das ist aber ein und derselbe Begriff in verschiedener Fassung und ein und dasselbe Wort. Das a und e ist blosse Dialektverschiedenheit. „Bleib' aufrecht stehen", nem-ne dāg-ata, auf H. tsaia dēdē.

[3] kásagē yasrá-skin fehlt bei Koelle ganz und es findet sich dort auch gar nichts Ähnliches. yasrá-skin könnte eine verstärkte Form von ra-skin sein, dessen Grundbedeutung wahrscheinlich identisch ist mit rāngin, „ich zerspringe, zertheile" (so bei Koelle). 3te Person Sing. „er hustet", kasagē tserōnin.

[4] wádlinā yēk-iskin; 3te Person wádlinā tse-kin. Koelle schreibt wádlīša yākēskin.

[5] kin-tsā-ni tin-nískin; 3te Person: „er reinigt seine Nase", kin-tsā-ntse tin-dšin. Koelle hat tin-niskin nicht. Dann schreibt er kentsā oder kentsā für „Nase". Die erste Form ist aber jedenfalls zu verwerfen, weil sie jeden Unterschied zwischen „Nase" und „Getränk" aufhebt. S. Prolegomena über das i als Zeichen der Activität. So ist ki-n-tsā das Ding oder Werkzeug zum Athmen, ke-n-tsā das Ding zum Trinken, passivisch, d. h. was getrunken wird.

[6] tóbnaik, dazu Imp. tobōs. — Die Endung ik ist eine abgekürzte Form von erik.

[7] mórte kemúk. Ich bin nicht ganz sicher hinsichtlich dieser Form; morte kemo-dē muss die 3te Person sein.

[8] sine-erik; 3te Person Prät. sin-erdē.

[9] mē-zúvveni ist nicht originell einheimisch, sondern vom Arabischen abgeleitet.

[10] ā-wádlinā; 3te Person as an-wádinā. — In Bezug auf das Vorhergehende nēfa-ū vergl. S. 36 N. 12 nēfa-ni.

[11] ā-sōāge yeeni ist zweifelhaft; der ohne Etymologie aufgefasste Laut der Phrase war nasánganī; zum aber heisst die Nase yeeni; aber dagegen gab man mir als 3te Person Sing. einfach yieeni.

[12] ye-fong wádlīā; 3te Person á-fóng-ne bá-ág(an?) wádlīā. Dagegen gehört yē in der vorhergehenden Phrase zum Stamme, wie die 3te Person zeigt a-yē-kadē.

[13] ye-fong múkkodlō; 3te Person á-fóng-ne bá-ágane múkkodlō.

[14] mam-eikēne; 3te Person a(e)-eikēne.

[15] nak-ombānī; wahrscheinlich gibt es für dieses Wort noch einen ganz anderen Ausdruck, da ich für die 3te Person die Form nē ar-ied ēnin habe.

Šedyal.	Légwol.	Wándalá.	Bágrimma.	Mába.
Á-tun kagni . .	wa-bígarā . .	bā-yu tšē . .	mam-darrā-ga	gonsaī andoī
. . . .	. . . .	bá-ńganē tšē .	nē darrā-ga .	. . . . . .
éga-gōru . . .	. . . .	ye-ndžā . .	mam-ak-índži	am-angi
	a-zógalen	báńganē nē-ndžā	a-ak-índži .	
	úngani	andža . . .	índži-nánge .	
	. . . .	. . . . . .	. . . . . .	
éga-kang (ganda	. . . .	. . . . . .	. . . . . .	. . . . . .
éga-tókkoto . .	néfa-a dikkwai .	yē-na wéksöē	mam-otkēse [14]	am tšúl-arē
	ā-wádiša [10] . .	yo-fong wádiša [12]	mak-osbāni . / mam-wadiesa	am beddiš arē
	a-súnga χaeni [11] .	ye-fong múk-kodiē [13]	mak-ombāni [15]	sing arúng?
		. . . . . .	. . . . . .	
. . . .		. . . . . .	. . . . . .	

[1] dég-ata is derived from the root dágia, which however I have not found in use, while the 3rd pers. dá-tšī is very common as an impersonal form „it stops, is spent". Rev. Mr. Koelle p. 208 of his vocabulary under the term rágia gives a phrase, where dā-tši appears with the notion of „he stood upright", but such a use is not known to me. There are several derivative forms of this verb.

[2] nom-aiakin: Mr. Koelle, who pushes accuracy rather too far, tries to distinguish between two words, viz ném-gin, „I sit down, wait", and ném-gin, „I am quiet, silent". But this is one and the same notion and one and the same word and the difference between the a and e is merely difference of dialect. I still adduce here the phrase „remain in an upright posture", nem-no dág-ata, H. tenia dódd.

[3] kásagē yaerá-skin is wanting in Koelle. yaerá-skin may possibly be a stronger form of ra-skin, whose original notion is probably identical with rágia, „I divide, rend in two". — 3rd pers. „he cough's", kásagē taeerdoia.

[4] wádiaš yōk-iskin; 3rd pers. wádiaš tee-kin. Koelle writes wódiša yākéskin.

[5] kin-taá-nī tin-aiskin; 3rd pers. „he cleans his nose", kin-taá-ntee tin-dāin. Koelle has not tin-aiskin. Besides instead of kintaš (properly ki-n-taā) he writes kentaš and kantaš indifferently, but I think it better to distinguish between the term meaning „nose" and that meaning „drink, beverage", and therefore write the one ki-n-taā, „the thing or instrument for breathing or respiring", and the other ka-n-taá, „a thing for drinking" or rather „to be drunk, a beverage".

[6] tóbnaik; imp. sobta. — ik at the end of a word is an abbreviated form of erik.

[7] mérte komák: I am not quite sure of this form; merte kome-dē, what I have, must be the 3rd pers.

[8] sim-erik; 3rd pers. of past tense sin-ordē.

[9] mā-nárvenī is not derived from an indigenous source, but has been borrowed from the Arabic.

[10] ā-wádiaš; 3rd pers. na an-wádiaš. — With regard to the preceding néfa-ā „my breath, my lungs" see p. 37 n. 13.

[11] ā-súnga yeeni is doubtful. The sound caught without regard to etymology was aséágueaī; but the noun is yeenī. But in the 3rd pers. I heard the simple form yieenī.

[12] yo-fong wádiše; 3rd pers. á-fóng-ne bá-ág(anē) wádiša. As for the yō in the preceding phrase it belongs to the root, as appears from the 3rd pers. sing. a-yō-hašē.

[13] yo-fong múkkodiē; 3rd pers. á-fóng-ne bá-ńganē múkkodiē.

[14] mam-otkēse; 3rd pers. a(a)-othése.

[15] mak-ombáni; probably there is still another term for this word and that a very different one, as for the 3rd pers. I have the form nē na-tad énia.

Deutsch und Englisch.	Kanuri.	Tedā.	Hausa.	Fulfulde.
ich breche mich, habe Erbrechen — *I am vomiting*	fi-niskin[1] / tsûno niskin[2]	yerâg-eri	na-i amai	medo-tuta .
ich speie Blut — *I spit blood*	bu fi-niskin[3]	. . . . . .	na-i tôfi-n-ženi	medo-tuta iyam
ich magere ab — *I become lean*	dérî-niskin[4] .	. . . . . .	na-i râme[9] .	mēdo-fōdi .
ich werde fett — *I become fat*	. . . . . .	. . . . . .	na-i kibba[10]	mē-me fai .
ich werde geblendet — *I am dazzled by the glare*	. . . . . .	. . . . . .	na-i mákabtše	mē-wumi . .
ich werde schwindelig — *I become giddy*	. . . . . .	. . . . . .	na-iyadime(Arb.)	mē-fáddaké .
ich zittere (vor Kälte) — *I shake, tremble (of cold)*	kôgo-lôlō-niskin / rō lôlō-ñgin	lôlo-tekeni .	ina makárkata	mēdo-dinna[11]
ich wärme die Hände am Feuer — *I warm my hands at the fire*	kannu gōt-iskin[5]	koko-neri . .	ina gasaa hanú-na	mēdo-írfo . .
?	kumbo-niskin[6]	kôba-neri[8] .	. . . . . .	. . . . . .
ich fühle mich krank, unwohl — *I am sick, feel unwell*	döndi-ñgin .	wāšerik . . .	inaži n tšio .	mēdo-nanna ōñaudo
ich bin bettlägerig, liege auf dem Krankenlager — *I am sick abed*	döndi-ñgi bō-niskin / döndi-niski bō-ñgi	táné derénigiu (kerin?)	ná-kontše dong tšio	
3te Person — *3rd pers.*	döndi-ñge bō-tšin	merē derénkindē	yá-kontše dong tšio	. . . . .
ich fühle mich besser, fühle Erleichterung — *I feel better*	mēre-skin[7] .		na-i da-dama / na-i rññgumé / na-sāmo sauki	mē-nenni / mē-bebbi dēam / mē-bebbi hóyendē

[1] fi-niskin. Koelle hat piogin, was dasselbe Wort in anderer Form ist, er gibt jedoch unter den vier Bedeutungen nicht die von „erbrechen" an. — 3te Person fi-tšin.

[2] tsûno-niskin; 3te Person tsûn-tšin. Koelle hat dasselbe Wort in der Form tsúñgagin (3te Person ši tsuñšin).

[3] Ich bin nicht ganz sicher, ob bû fi-niskin „ich speie Blut" heisst; jedenfalls hat es daneben die Bedeutung von „ich vergiesse Blut".

[4] dérî-niskin oder dérîñgin, wie Koelle hat, ist sehr schwer zu unterscheiden von dem ganz gleich geschriebenen, nur etwas anders accentuirten Worte, bei Koelle derîñgin, „ich drehe herum". Auch die von diesen beiden Verbalformen gebildeten Adjectiva dérî-gâta (Koelle dérî-gâta), „abgemagert", und dérî-gata, „rund", sind sich ganz ähnlich.

[5] kannu gōt-iskin fehlt bei Koelle; denn natürlich ist gōt-iskin ein durchaus verschiedenes Wort von gō-niskin.

[6] Über die Bedeutung von kumbo-niskin bin ich etwas unsicher. Auf den ersten Blick würde man dieses Verbum mit der Wurzel kumbû, „Speise", zusammenbringen; aber es hat hier offenbar eine dem vorhergehenden Verbum verwandte Bedeutung. Dass kôba-neri im Tedā diesem Worte genau entspreche, ist eine blosse Annahme von mir, aber eine sehr wahrscheinliche, da ich eigentlich kôba-neri, koko-neri als eine zusammenhängende Phrase aufgeschrieben hatte.

[7] mēre-skin oder mēre-shin scheint nicht eben sehr allgemein im Gebrauch zu sein. Daher das Substantiv merē, „die Genesung".

[8] S. Note 6.

[9] nai râme: dazu die Phrase „das Pferd magert ab", dôki ya-i râme, F. putšu fódi.

[10] nai kibba: dazu „das Pferd wird fett", dôki yai kibba, F. putšu gueisi.

[11] mēdo-dinna. Davon das Substantiv dinñgol dinñhengo, „das Zittern der Hand".

[12] ina(e) ale ele fū-ai ist mir in seinen einzelnen Theilen nicht ganz klar; das Feuer heisst fū.

[13] ñgā-ee, „krank", ist die negative Form von ñgā.

[14] yé-besā fuā; 3te Person ti-besā fuā.

[15] auře wārne lidawā. Diese und die nächste Phrase scheinen nicht ganz richtig zu sein; lidawā ist ganz richtig und heisst „liegend", also müsste auře wārne die Verbalform von „krank" sein; für „krank" habe ich aber den Ausdruck „auž névena" und dem nähert sich ánovō in der folgenden Phrase.

Sonγai.	Lógoné.	Wándalá.	Bágrimma.	Mába.
éga-yéri . . .	néfa-u ábra-ya	yé-bezā fuā [14]	mak-ōmo . .	kúlik andúng burma
éga-yōri kúri .	. . . . . .	. . . . .	. . . . .	. . . . .
. . . . . .	. . . . . .	. . . . .	. . . . .	. . . . .
. . . . . .	. . . . . .	. . . . .	. . . . .	. . . . .
. . . . . .	. . . . . .	. . . . .	. . . . .	. . . . .
. . . . . .	. . . . . .	. . . . .	. . . . .	
éga-bargu . .	flemadé (?) . . .	ye-gegille wokse	. . . . .	
. . . . . .	ind(o) ālo ōle fu-zi [12]	ye-kerā karā .	. . . . .	
. . . . . .	wóγfia	gágulē . . .	. . . . .	
éga-gezánge . .	. . . . . .	. . . . .	mangāli . .	
. . . . . .	indō-(ma) ŋgā-sa [13] wasé-nahē	auča wárua lída-wā [15]		am andár banō
	ni ŋgā-sa awénahō	yánhará barē ávnovō	. . . . . .	wádža ágonō an-dór-munō
élu-bāni . . .		. . . . .		

[1] fi-niskin: Koelle has píngin, which is merely another form of the same word, but among the four meanings, which he gives, we miss that of „vomiting". — 3rd pers. fi-tšin.

[2] taššo-niskin; 3rd pers. tašo-tšin. Koelle has the same word in the form tedecágin (3rd pers. ši tenššin).

[3] hū fi-niskin may possibly not have the meaning „I spit blood"; at least I am certain, that it means also „I spill blood".

[4] déri-niskin or, as Koelle writes, dérlégin is not very easily to be distinguished from the same word written with the same letters and only slightly distinguished by pronunciation, but the meaning of which is „I turn round". Also the two adjectives derived from these two verbal forms, viz déri-gáta (Koelle déri-gáta), „lean", and déri-gata (Koelle dérigata), „round", are extremely like each other.

[5] kanne gét-iskin is wanting in Koelle; the verb gét-iskin is of course totally different from gé-niskin.

[6] kumbo-niskin: I am not quite sure with regard to the meaning of this word. At first sight one should feel rather inclined to suppose a connexion between it and the root kumbū, „food", but in this case it has evidently quite a different meaning and almost identical with the foregoing. However it is a mere supposition of mine, that the Téda-word kōba-neri corresponds exactly to this one, as taking down these words from the mouth of the natives I connected this term with the preceding one and wrote kōba-neri, koko-neri as one phrase.

[7] mōra-skin or mére-skin does not seem to be a word of very general use, but to be restricted to more refined society as well as the noun morō, the „recovery".

[8] kōba-neri: see the sixth note.

[9] nal rāme: hither belongs the phrase „the horse becomes lean", dōki yal rāme, F. putšu fādi.

[10] nal kibba: thereto the phrase „the horse becomes fat", dōki yal kibba, F. putšu gaafoi.

[11] mōdo-diúna: thence derived is the substantive diūŋgel diábange, „the trembling of the hand".

[12] ind(o) ālo ōle fú-zi: this phrase is not clear to me in all its single parts; fú is „fire".

[13] ŋgā-sa, „ill", is the negative form of ŋgā.

[14] yé-bezā fuā; 3rd pers. tá-bezā fuā.

[15] auča wárua lídawā: this one and the following phrase do not seem to be quite right; lídawā is all right and means „lying", so that auča wárua ought to be the verbal form of „sick"; but for „sick" I have the term „aue névrua" from which ávnovō in the following phrase is not far remote.

Deutsch und Englisch.	Kanúri	Tédā.	Hausa.	Fulfúlde.
Ich genese — *I get well*	úgā-niskin [2] . / gəskē-úgin .	kau-erik . . / túnē lenī killahā	un-wúrki [10] .	mē-bōi . . .
Ich harne, lasse Wasser — *I make water*	hòbul-iskin / hòbul-úgin [3]	kohós am-erik / gumó suu-erik	fun fitsarē [11] .	mēdo-silla [16] .
Ich leere aus — *I clear my bowels*	kälem yēn-iskin [4]	. . . . . .	fua kāše . .	mē-džōdi do selgu
Ich gehe hinaus (um ein Bedürfnis zu verricht.) — *I go out*	dēka-rō lūg-iskin [5]	fēšu am-erik	fua genaie bāya n gida [12]	mē-hai gāda südo
Ich habe dringend. Bedürfnis — *I have a pressing business*	. . . . . .	. . . . . .	fua gaddu n daua [13]	mē-sükkita .
Ich habe Durchfall — *my bowels are loose* [1]	tooro-ńe-tšin / ni (nō-ka-šin [6])	bešī nerē ke-yaii	tšeki-na šina guddu n daua [14]	mēdo-dogga rēdu / rēdo-am hi-dogga [17] / rēdo-am hi-sāno
Ich lasse Wind — *I let a fart*	kā-sām / kargi fi-niskin [7]		fua tusa . .	mēdo-ridi . / mēdo-nenna ride
Ich sehe, schaue — *I look, see, regard*	ru-skin [8] . . / ru-úgin . .	dō-derik [9] . .	fun gani . . / ina dūba [15] . / ina dubi . .	mōdo-rāra .

[1] Diese beiden Ausdrücke im Deutschen und Englischen stellen ungleich die verschiedenen Wendungen in den entsprechenden Sprachen dar.

[2] úgā-niskin hat Koelle, wie es scheint, nicht. Ich verstand erst, wenn ich dieses Wort hörte, gewöhnlich ágillenískin; das scheint jedoch ein Irrthum zu sein.

[3] hòbul-úgin; 3te Person hòbul-tšin; aber Koelle bemerkt wol nicht ganz richtig, dass es nur in der 3ten Person gebraucht werde.

[4] kälem yēn-iskin fehlt bei Koelle, obgleich er zwei Formen für yēn-iskin hat, yēngin und yēngin, die er will S. 40 N. 1 angegeben, gänzlich von einander trennt, die erste mit der Bedeutung „ich bewege, drehe", die zweite mit „ich antworte".

[5] dēka-rō lūg-iskin; 3te Person dēka-rō lua-lūg-ena. Koelle hat diese Redensart nicht.

[6] tooro-ni nē-ka-šin ist die 3te Person von kasoskin; daher das Substantiv kasō, „das Laufen", und in Verbindung mit kälem „Diarrhöe"; kurgún kälem kasōhe, „Öffnung verschaffende Arznei".

[7] kā-sām fi-niskin, kargi fi-niskin. Koelle hat weder die eine Redensart, noch die andere. Allerdings hat er den Ausdruck kāsām, aber nur in der Bedeutung „Wind, Brise". kargi möchte etwas auffallend erscheinen wegen seiner Ähnlichkeit mit karge (Koelle kárge), „das Herz".

[8] ru-skin; 3te Person Sing. tsu-ri-n. úngin oder, wie Koelle schreibt, núngin habe ich nur in der Imperativform in Gebrauch gefunden: unge-ši, „siehe da". Es ist übrigens eigenthümlich, dass Koelle, der sonst nie die Form auf skin oder ískin gibt, sie allein bei ru-skin hat, offenbar zum Unterschied dieses Zeitworts von rúngin, „ich verwerfe, verachte".

[9] dō-derik: vielleicht schreibt man dies Wort richtiger mit einem d, wodurch es der Kanúri-Wurzel näher kommt.

[10] un-wúrki. Davon „genesen", an-wárke, F. dum bōī.

[11] ina fitsarē. Ich führe hier die verwandten Redensarten an, die ich nur im H. und F. kennen gelernt habe, die eine „ich kann kein Wasser lassen, der Urin will nicht fortgehen", ba nīya fitsarē, bōli yaki fitta, auf F. nasa-ta sēlbone, selēkke wártakō, die andere „ich habe Urinbeschwerden", ina-zi n mai-yasa n fitsarē, F. mēdo-nanna selbōa.

[12] ina genaie bāya n gida, eigentlich „ich biege seitwärts hinter das Haus".

[13] ina guddu n daua heisst wörtlich „ich eile in den Busch, in die Wildniss" und bildet daher den natürlichen Übergang zu der folgenden Phrase.

[14] tšeki-na šina guddu n daua. Verwandte Phrasen scheinen na-i lumfāši, na-i tšēda, na-i fukka, auf F. mēdo-fopte zu sein. — Ich will hier auch die begriffsverwandten Redensarten aufführen: tšeki ya-i sāš, „ich habe Leibschmerzen", und tšeki ya-i kumburi, „mein Leib ist geschwollen", auf F. rēdu uffi oder utti.

[15] ina dūba. Dazu die Phrase „ich beschaue mein Gesicht im Spiegel", ina dūba fuska-na tšiki n mādubi, F. mōdo-rāsa yēsa der dārorgel; „ich sehe nach Flüssen" H. ina dūbi n kolkōtta, F. mēdo-rāra tendi.

[16] mēdo-silla. Ich bin über diese Form nicht ganz sicher; für die Hausa-Redensart sāni fitsarē, „ich bin im Begriff, Wasser zu lassen", habe ich im F. mēdo-salha.

[17] mēdo-dogga rēdu, „ich habe Fluss im Leibe", rēdo-am hi-dogga, „mein Leib hat Fluss".

[18] ēga-gāna. Neben diesem Worte muss es noch ein anderes, ganz verschiedenes, geben, da ich für die Phrase „lasst uns sehen" yerga-tšenai habe.

[19] úngawaši. Davon 1ste Person Perf. ungasiā.

[20] y(r)-ánnc-ha. Das h wol mag zur Wurzel gehören und in den anderen Formen nur in der Aussprache verschluckt werden; so mag auch die 3te Person, die ich als ánnar aufschrieb, richtiger heissen ánneha-ne mit nachfolgendem bā-ágand.

[21] ella-dum táfie ist keine Verbalform.

Sońyai.	Lógoné.	Wándalá.	Bágrimma.	Mába.
ćga-han . . .	wáñe { dagahia . / lappiaya . }	maoba . . .	(alla-dum láña[21])	am tébeō
	wuakaui . . .	ye-dźí-korē .	mam-akidźi .	Isi á-aiknē
	wálbaiá . . .	ye-dźíbodō .	mattegágela .	. . . . .
	. . . . . .	. . . . . .	mam-dummo	fīriñg akkai
	. . . . . .	. . . . . .		. . . . .
	ungo-nau dikkun	ogźa bōda-ruā	mam-brá-nokō	tabúk-an dantal
	uχpan	ye-pišárde .		
úgn-gōna[18] . .	uńgówuai[19] . .	y(e)-únne-ha[20]	m-áka . . .	am okkoi

[1] The two different ways of expression in English and German correspond exactly with the different turn of the phrases in the corresponding languages.

[2] ágā-niskin is wanting in Koelle's vocabulary. In the beginning, when I heard this word, I thought, I understood ágilla-nishkin, but I afterwards convinced myself, that I was mistaken.

[3] bóbul-ágin; 3rd pers. bóbul-tšin, but I doubt, whether Koelle is right in stating, that the 3rd pers. alone is used.

[4] kálom yōu-iskin: this phrase is wanting in Koelle, although he has two verbal forms yéngin and yéágin, between which according to his custom, as stated p. 61 n. 1, he distinguishes strictly, attributing to the first the exclusive notion of „I move, I turn" and to the second that of „I answer".

[5] dėķo-rō lúg-iskin; 3rd pers. dėka-rō tee-lúg-ene; this phrase also is wanting in Koelle.

[6] kasro-ni cé-ka-sin: céka-šin is 3rd pers. of kaseskin, and thence the substantive kasō, „the running" and in connexion with kálom „diarrhoea": kargáa kálom kasōbe, „aperient medicine".

[7] ká-ním fi-niskin, kargi fi-niskin. Koelle has neither the one nor the other phrase. He has indeed the word kánám, but only with the notion „wind, breeze". The word kargi might seem to have something remarkable about it on account of its close resemblance to kargo (Koelle kárgę), „heart", but that may be merely accidental.

[8] ru-skin; 3rd pers. tee-rin. The verb núgin or wúágin, as Koelle writes, I have only found used in the imperative form núgu-ńi, „look there". I must remark however as a peculiarity of Koelle's, that while in general he never gives the form of the pres. tense in skin or iskin, in this case he has only the form ru-skin, I suspect, in order to distinguish this word from ruágin, „I reject, despise".

[9] dó-derik: perhaps we would do better to write this word with a ḍ, when it resembles more the Kanúri-root.

[10] na-warki; thence „recovered", na-warke, F. dam-báf.

[11] ina fitsarō: I here shall mention some phrases of a similar notion, which I have only learnt in the Hausa- and Fulfúlde-languages, the one „I cannot make water, the urine does not come forth", H. ba nīya fitsarō, bāfi yāhi fitta, F. nena-in sélbana, seidhko wéríabó; the other „I suffer from strangurie", ina-ńi n mai-yana n fitsarō, F. mődo-nanna selbōa.

[12] ina gannie báya n gida, properly „I go aside behind the house".

[13] ina gudda n dana means properly „I hasten into the bush, into the wilderness" and thus forms a natural transition to the following phrase.

[14] tšeki-na fina guddu n dana: I have some phrases in Hausa, which seem to have a meaning of a similar import, but with the proper notion of which I have not become acquainted: na-i tumfāki, na-i tšēda, na-i fakka, to all of which seems to correspond more or less the F. term mődo-fopia. — I shall also mention here some other phrases as „the bowels pain me", tšeki ya-i tšā, and „the belly is swollen", tšeki ya-i hámbori, F. rēdu uffi or utti.

[15] ina dūba. thereto the phrase „I look at my face in the mirror", ina dūba fuska-na tšíki n madobí, F. mődo-rīra yēso der dáreręri; „I look at (I search) them" H. ina dūbi n koikōtta, F. mődo-rāre tondō.

[16] mődo-silla: I am not quite sure of this form, as I have a rather different form, mődo-selba, to express the Hausa-term ašai fitsarō, „I am about to make water".

[17] mődo-dogga rēdu, means properly „I have diarrhoea (in my) bowels", rēdo-am hi-dogga, „my bowels have diarrhoea" or „are in a running state".

[18] égn-góna: besides this word the Sońyai-language must possess another very different term, as is apparent from the word yerga-tšduni, „let us see".

[19] uńgówuai: 1st pers. of past tense núgánit.

[20] y(e)-iune-ha: it is possible, that the h belongs to the root and that in the other forms it has been only lost through the carelessness of pronunciation, so that instead of ánnana, which I wrote down as 3rd pers., we ought to write more correctly aanaha-na with the following pronoun bá-águuá, „he".

[21] alla-dum láña does not appear to be a verbal form.

Deutsch und Englisch.	Kanúri.	Tédā.	Hausa.	Fulfúlde.
sieh — *look*	rū-i	lau[1]	dūbi	darde[16] . .
ich höre, vernehme — *I hear*	fān-iskin[1] . / fān-gin . .	tebās-erík[8] .	ina-žī . . .	mēdo-nenna .
hörst du? — *do you hear?*	fān-im-bā .	sebás . . .	ba kāna-žī ba	fada-nénna . / won ada-nénna
ich horche, behorche — *I hearken, overhear*	kirre-nískin[2] / kirre-ngin .	sinmīu néruā-de tebās-erík	. . . . .	. . . . . .
ich spreche, rede — *I speak, talk*	manna-nískin[3] / manna-ngin	. . . . . .	na-ī mágana[11] / na-ī batū .	mē wólui . .
ich sage — *I say, tell* .	gúl-iskin[4] . / gúl-ngin . .	nohād-erík[9] .	na-tšē[12] . . / ina fádda[13] .	mē-wī . . . / mēdo battu .
ich antworte (dir) — *I answer (thee)*	nīro) gúl-untsqa-ko lanno[5]	. . . . . .	na-ámsa[14] .	mēdo-džebbi .
ich schweige — *I am silent*	kodák ném-nis-kin[6]	dángerik[10] .	na-ī kurúm .	idē inēao[17] . / adédda . .
ich überrede (dich) — *I persuade (you)*	. . . . . .	. . . . . .	na gaskánta (ka	mēdo-góndini(ma
ich bitte, erbitte — *I beg, pray*	logō n-iskin / ngin . / gódō n-iskin / ngin .	lantán-erík .	ina rōko[15] .	mēdo-tórrotō

[1] fān-iskin, das pán-gin von Koelle.

[2] kirre-niskin. Dieses Wort steht mit solcher Bedeutung ganz vereinzelt in der Kanúri-Sprache, doch scheint es mir mit dem Hausa-Wort kirra, „rufen", eine entfernte Verwandtschaft zu haben, aber vielleicht würde man dann besser kere-niskin schreiben (Koelle kérengin). — 3te Person Sing. kirre-tšin (Koelle kécentšin).

[3] manna-niskin. Es ist auffallend, dass die beiden Wörter für „sprechen" und „sagen" in der Kanúri-Sprache fremden Ursprungs sind, das erstere der Hausa-, das zweite der Arabischen Sprache entlehnt. Denn es ist kein Zweifel, dass manna eine Zusammenziehung aus mágana ist, und eben deshalb ziehe ich die Schreibart mit doppeltem n der von Koelle befolgten mit einfachem n vor; manna-niskin ist also wörtliche Übertragung von na-ī mágana, „ich mache Rede, mache Worte"; 3te Person Sing. manna-tšin.

[4] gúl-iskin ist unzweifelhaft von dem Arabischen kūl abgeleitet und man könnte daher auch kúl-iskin schreiben; 3te Person Sing. gúl-tšin. — „Was sagst du?" afi gúl-nemin, H. mē ka-tšē, F. nam-bida.

[5] nīro gúl-untsqako lanno, nicht einfache Redensart, sondern nur in gewissen Fällen anzuwenden; wörtlich „ich will dir sagen, nachdem ich (deine Rede) verstanden habe".

[6] kodák nem-niskin. Koelle schreibt kadeg und kedeg.

[7] lau setzt offenbar eine Präsensform lau-erik voraus, die aber nicht in Gebrauch ist.

[8] tebás-erik, wol nur populär abgekürzte Form; davon kommt tēbnik, das ich auch notirt habe.

[9] nohád-erik. Neben diesem Wort habe ich die Phrase geschrieben tanō kē tefádembó, aber dies bedeutet wol „ich sage dir an", entsprechend der Hausa-Phrase ina fadda mahā.

[10] dángerik; Imp. dángir.

[11] na-ī mágana. Ich führe hier einige verwandte Redensarten auf: H. ina tabbatawa mágana und ina kāenaš mágana, „ich plaudere", F. mēdo-yēa bollde; H. ina ayanana mit ähnlicher Bedeutung, F. medérni bollde, „ich eröffne meine Rede", H. ina būde mágana nāwa, F. mēdo-firto bollde-am. „ich unterrede, bespreche mich", H. na-ī batū, F. mē-wólui; „lasst uns uns besprechen", H. mu-ī batū, F. mim-bólui.

[12] na-tšē gehört zu den einfachsten Grundwörtern der Hausa-Sprache: tšē, sein, tšū, essen, tšī, essen.

[13] ina fádda ist viel stärker als na-tšē und heisst „ich sage an, sage aus".

[14] na-ámsa erhält nachher die verwandte Bedeutung „ich nehme an, genehmige", so die Redensart na-ámsa batū, F. mēdo-džebbi bollde ma-ko, „ich stimme deiner Rede bei".

[15] ina rōko. Hierher die Phrase „du bittest viel, bist zudringlich mit Bitten", kāna rōko dōwa, F. anne dūdi tórrandi.

[16] darde ist allem Anscheine nach ebenfalls von einer anderen Wurzel als yára; von unterschieden ursprünglicher Wurzel ist wiederum das Präterit. mo-ī, „ich habe gesehen".

[17] idē inēao kann ich nicht erklären.

[20] wáttenā hū-an ganī; 3te Person áffenā hē-nāū.

[21] u-nkānī; 3te Person nē aukāni.

[22] Ich habe hier als erste Person inde hahā und als 3te aim-aluā.

[23] ye tšenēn išenā. Die folgende Form zeigt, dass das išenā keineswegs unumgänglich nöthig ist.

[24] ye-ndang-na bāyo; 3te Person a-ndang bá-āganó.

[25] mak-wō; Imp. dembi, offenbar von ganz anderer Wurzel.

[26] mam-dēga-ī mah-ar deh-kit „ich antworte nicht", „ich schweige".

[27] am-ánr-ī; 1ste Person Perf. am ane-ldra; Imp. nēla.

[28] am bayárne, etwas unsichere Form; 3te Person Plur. kai bairne.

[29] am mēgo biágfeita adai ist zweifelhaft.

Sonyai.	Lógone.	Wándalä.	Bágrimma.	Mába.
gòna	. . . .	enna (énneha)	āka	yokoī
éga-má . . .	wáθenādi . . .	yé-tšenén tšená[21]	mam-ōga . .	am-áne-li[25]
í-mō	gáθenālia-dā .	ká-tšenén-ka	w-ōga-lē . .	
. . . . . .	wáθenā bē-au ganī[18]	ye-ndúng-na bā-ya[22]	mak-wō[23] .	
. . . . . .	w-ukáni[19] . .	yé-ndaná bá-ya	mam-allāwo .	am buyárne[26]
éga-sílle . . .	[20]	yé-banē bā-ya	mam-dēga (ga	
éga-tā	w-aka-kū kaksín-nani	yú-ndaná kátše-nón-tšená	yī mam-dēga	. . . . . .
	wu-faïšok . . .	yé-nōde bakírke	mam-dēga-li mak-av dok-kik[24]	am illi arne
		. . . . . .	. . . . . .	. . . . . .
éga-ṅgwáre (hayō	w-ámaonī . . .	yé-ṅgalā . .	mam-nakī . / mam-dugō .	am mēgo bingé-rite adal[27]

1 fāu-iskin, the pán-gin of Koelle.

2 kirre-niskin: this word seems to stand quite alone in the Kanúri-language without any radical connection with other words, but I am convinced, that it is allied to the Hausa verb kirra, „to call", so that we have here the active and transitive form of the Kanúri-verb. From this point of view my mode of writing seems by far preferable to that of Koelle's, who writes kare-niskin. — 3rd pers. sing. kirre-tšin.

3 manna-niskin: it is remarkable, that the two words for „to speak" and „to say, tell" in the Kanúri-language are of foreign origin, the 1st being borrowed from the Hausa and the second from the Arabic language. For there can be no doubt, but that manna is a contraction of the Hausa-term mágana, and it is on this account, that I prefer writing manna with a double n to writing it with a single one like Koelle; manna-niskin therefore is a verbal translation of the term na-i mágana, „I make a speech". — 3rd pers. sing. manna-tšin.

4 gúl-iskin is, as I just observed, evidently derived from the Arabic ḳál, ḳâl and might therefore be written as well kúl-iskin; 3rd pers. sing. gál-tšin. — „What do they say?" afī gúl-nemin, H. mī ka-tšē, F. nun-bida.

5 niro gál-natenske fanne is not a simple phrase, but only to be employed under certain conditions, its proper meaning being „I shall tell you, after having understood (your words)".

6 kodák nem-niskin. Koelle writes ködeg and kydeg.

7 lan evidently makes us suppose another form of the pres. tense, viz lan-erik, but this does not seem to be used.

8 tabás-arik: I have also the form tánsik, but it may be nothing but a popular abbreviation of the same word.

9 nobád-arik; besides this word I have written down the term tanē hō tefádembō, but this means probably „I tell, announce you (in an authoritative manner)", and thus corresponds to the Hausa-phrase ina fádda maká.

10 dángerik; imp. díngir; therefore the full form of the pers. tense ought to be dánger-erik.

11 na-i mágana. I shall here mention some other phrases of a similar meaning: H. ina tabbatana mágana and ina hánaná mágana, „I chat", F. mēdo-yēn hollde; H. ina ayenana with a similar meaning, F. medéyni hollde. Then „I open my speech", H. ina búde mágana ná-wa, F. mēdo-firte hollde-am. To na-i batū I shall mention here the 1st pers. plur. imp. „let us have a talk", H. mu-ki batū, F. mim-bólut.

12 na-tšē belongs to the class of most primitive radical verbs in the Hausa-language: tšē, „to be", tšē, „to say", and tši, „to eat".

13 ina fádda is a much stronger term than na-tšē and means „I announce, declare".

14 na-ámsa receives further the meaning „I accept, approve"; thus „I approve thy speech", na-ámsa batū, F. mēdo-dšabbi hollde má-ko.

15 ina rōko: hence the phrase „you beg much, are troublesome", kāna rōko dīwa, F. anne dádi tórremdō.

16 darda according to all appearance is derived from another root than rāra and again another and no doubt more primitive root is seen in the past tense na-i, „I have seen".

17 idō lašo I am not able to explain.

18 wáθaná bé-au gani; 3rd pers. sing. áθená bē-nāā.

19 w-ukáni; 3rd pers. sing. nē nukáni.

20 I have here as 1st pers. sing. indo kakú and as 3rd pers. sing. nim-akaū, so that I am not sure of the right form.

21 yé-tšenén tšená: the following form shows, that the tšená is not at all essential.

22 ye-ndáng-na bá-ya, 3rd pers. sing. a-ndang bá-ganá.

23 mak-wō; imp. ámabī; evidently derived from another root.

24 mam-dēga-li mak-av dok-kik, „I do not speak, I am silent".

25 am-ane-li; 1st pers. of the past tense am ane-lára; imp. ačla.

26 am buyárne; also this form is not quite certain; as 3rd pers. plur. I have kai buirne.

27 am mēgo bingérite adal is doubtful.

Deutsch und Englisch.	Kanúri.	Tédā.	Bagrma.	Fulfúlde.
ich rufe / ich nenne } *I call* . .	{ bobó-niskin[1] / bobó-ngin . }	tánē kolln-erík[5]	ni ína kirra[9] .	mēdo-nóddi-mō[15]
wie nennst du (dies? — *how do you call this?*	álo agō) á-fi bo-bú-nemin	(ína ai indi) .	{ sū-na abi-nga[10] / wo-ne menēne / kāna kirra-ši }	kō nō-inde mā-dāum[16]
ich frage — *I ask* . .	kōre-skin . .	mōdi) ennōd-erík[6]	ína lam-bēa .	mēdo-yamma
ich frage um Rath, berathe — *I ask advice, consult*	nšaur-niskin[2]	nebra) šaur-én-erík[7]	ína šaura[11] .	mē-dōdi šaura
ich überlege, bedenke — *I consider*	gangan-fakin[3]	(dabanar bádi modiód-erík[8]	{ ína túnanē . / ni-tuna . . }	mēdo-mítšilo
ich bin aufmerksam, achte auf — *I attend, pay attention to*	hánkal-nin dí-akin[4]	{ lan-erík . . / rōwa-(e)rík . }	ína maida hánkali (da kaya[12]	mē-hōre hakkíllo (der kaya
pass' auf, gib Acht — *attend to, mind*	hankal dē . .	{ lan . . . . / gal hánkalō . }	ka-maida hánka-lín-ka (da kaya	hōru hakkíllo[17] mā-da (der kaya
ich ersinne, finde einen Ausweg — *I devise*	. . . . .	. . . . . .	na-ī debbára (h. A.)[13]	mē-derri . .
ich gestehe — *I confess*	. . . . .	. . . . . .	na-beñēma? .	mē wángini .
ich läugne — *I deny* .	. . . . .	. . . . . .	na-ī gérdama[14]	mē-iddi[18] . .
ich meine, muthmasse — *I presume, suspect*	. . . . .	árrodō? . .	ína tamnába	mēdo-támmohē (S.)

[1] bobó-niskin, K. bóbángin. Dass das zweite o kurz ist, ergiebt der Imperativ bóbo-nā ši-ga, „rufe ihn".
[2] nšaur-niskin. Alle diese Sprachen haben das Arabische Wort in mehr oder minder individualisirter Form aufgenommen. — Es fehlt bei Koelle.
[3] gangan-fakin fehlt bei Koelle. Ich bin über seine Ableitung ungewiss; vgl. jedoch die Wándalā-Phrase yé-ṅgánga miri, S. 63.
[4] hánkal-nin dí-akin. Dass das Pronomen poss. nicht unumgänglich nöthig ist, sieht man aus dem Imperativ, wo es weggelassen ist. Somit entspricht das Wort wol jedenfalls dem ṅgaltiskin bei Koelle, das er für identisch mit ṅgáltágin erklärt und ihm die Bedeutung „ich handle klug" beilegt. Vergl. haṅkal.
[5] tánē kolln-erík. Über diese Form und besonders über die reine Wurzel bin ich nicht ganz sicher, da ich als Imperativ hóbu, „rufe ihn", habe. Jedenfalls hat die folgende Phrase, ína ai indi, nichts damit zu thun und heisst „was ist das?"
[6] mōdi ennōd-erík: mōdi „Wort" scheint nicht nöthig zu sein; vielleicht aber ist das eigentliche Verbum nur ōd-erík.
[7] nebra) šaur-én-erík: nebra, „dich".
[8] dabanar bádi modiód-erík. Das eigentlich hierher gehörende Wort scheint das Verbum modiód-erík zu sein. Vielleicht aber sollte es heissen: dōke-nir („mit meinem Kopfe") bádi mōdi („diesem Wort") ōd-erík („frage ich").
[9] ni ína kirra. Zu kirra vergl. S. 48, N. 2.
[10] sū-na abi-nga, wörtlich „sie nennen das Ding", mit hinzugedachtem menēne, „was?".
[11] ína šaura. Ich will hier die begriffsverwandte Redensart anführen „ich habe dir etwas anzuvertrauen", H. ína da ganana, F. mēdo-wōdi gida.
[12] ína maida hánkali (da kaya. — da kaya, F. der kaya, „in" oder „auf das Gesicht".
[13] na-ī debbára. Begriffsverwandt ist „ich habe Auswege, bin erfinderisch in Auswegen". H. nāya da debbára, F. mō-yoftī débbere. Auch will ich hier die Phrase anführen „vermittelst eines guten Auswegs" oder wörtlich „gemacht eine gute List", H. nād debbára néggari, F. dum darbi débberdē bádum.
[14] na-ī gérdama. Die Bedeutung dieses Wortes ist nicht ganz sicher, da ich dasselbe Wort auch für „ich misstraue" aufgezeichnet habe.
[15] mēdo-nóddi-mō, „ich rufe ihn"; Imperativ noddōī-mō, aber das Wort hat nicht die Bedeutung „nennen".
[16] kō nō-inde mā-dāum, „was ist sein Name?"
[17] hōru hakkíllo mā-da. Ich habe für den einfachen Imperativ die Form kōre hakkil, aber dies scheint, nach dem h zu schliessen, jedenfalls die Pluralform zu sein.
[18] mē-iddi; 3te Person Sing. haṅko giddi.
[19] ēge-akoike. Dazu habe ich als Imperativ ēhia aka, aber der ist jedenfalls zusammengezogen.
[20] ēga-há(n)i; Imperat. „frage ihn", há-nee.
[21] á-kai seilei heisst wahrscheinlich „ich gehe in den Rath", aber vielleicht liegt ein Missverständniss zu Grunde.
[22] bóboléíkō ist mehr als unsicher; für „rufe ihn" habe ich billē-ni.
[23] yé-dabá oder yé-dahá bá-ya, „ich rufe". Die Wurzel ist wol da oder daba; als Imperativ habe ich da nana.
[24] mei-herá; Imperativ „rufe ihn", heré-hā.
[25] ágás-nen atne zei déiiemhī. Diese Redensart scheint wörtlich zu bedeuten „ich lege alle Sachen auf (oder unter) meine Zunge"; delmih oder déiiemih, „die Zunge".
[26] am (hon) geria; Imperat. „frage ihn", nin geria.

Sońyai.	Lógoné.	Wándalá.	Bágrimma.	Mába.
égu-akoike[19]	búbolé(kú[22] . .	yé-dahá[23] . .	mot-baré[24] .	{am-dĕe kūre / am awaigne
. . . . . .	{hénne rónidā . / niffelē rónidā . }	mokka ka-dá-ngwe (?)	. . . . . .	beled ágonō) gā-som owū
éga-hā(ni[20] . .	wásamā(ni . .	yé-ndana . .	mam-lumno .	am (bon) gerin[26]
(ú-koi sellet[21]) .	wóha(-nī) šauarī	mōko sanalī (?)	mam-áta saura	bin) gēria
éga-hungo (hayō	wāde naúgul kā-nāū	yé-sasátsatsē	ṅgás-nen etne net délemki[25]	. . . . . .
	. . . .	yé-banín bihkalo	{ma-tad áṅkal-mō / mák-indā aṅkal-ammu}	am okoī-nē
mēdam lakkal .	run aṅkal na-nī	. . . . . .	{tad / dā} áṅkali	nimmore) okoi
	. . . .	. . . .	. . . . . .	. . . . . .
. . . . . .	. . . .	. . . .	. . . . . .	
. . . . . .	. . . .	. . . .	. . . . . .	
. . . . . .	. . . .	. . . .	. . . . . .	

[1] bobó-niskin, Kl. bóbágin. That the second o is short, we learn from the form of the imp. bóbo-nó šī-ga, „call him".
[2] nšaur-niskin. All these languages have adopted the Arabic word, accommodating it in a different way to their own principles.
[3] gaágan-iskin is wanting in Koelle's vocabulary and I myself am uncertain as to its origin, but compare the Wándalá-form yé-ńgéńga miri, p. 53.
[4] háškal-nin dī-skin. The form of the imp. mood shows, that the pers. pronoun is not essential, and it thus appears, that this word is identical with the angaltiskin of Koelle, although he identifies the latter with angálógin, attributing to both the meaning „I act wisely".
[5] táné kolln-erik. I am not quite certain with regard to the root and the primitive form of this word, especially as I have kóha in the imp. mood for „call him". Of course the following phrase, ina ai indi, has no connexion whatever with this root and means „what is that?"
[6] mōdi) enuód-erik: mōdi (word, language) does not constitute an essential part of the phrase and the proper verb may be ód-erik.
[7] nebra) šanr-én-erik: nebra, „then".
[8] dahanar hádi modiód-erik: evidently not a simple phrase, the verb modiód-erik being the word more properly belonging to this place. hanar may have some connexion with the verb hanán-erik; but I suspect it to be a totally different phrase, thus: dáho-nir („with my hand") hádi mōdi („this word") ód-erik („I ask").
[9] ai ina širra. With regard to the verb širra see p. 49. n. 2.
[10] sū-ne ahi-ágo, verbally „they call this article", monéne, „what?" being added in thought.
[11] ina šanra. I shall adduce in this place another phrase with a similar meaning: „I have something to confide to you", H. ina da gunnua, F. mōdo-wādi gide.
[12] ina maida háshali (da kaya. — da kaya, F. der kaya (at least in the corrupted dialect of Sókoto) means „in" or „on the luggage".
[13] na-i dabbāra. Closely allied to this phrase is another one: „I have expedients, subterfuges", H. máya da dabbára, F. mō-yofti dábbare. I likewise adduce here the phrase „by means of a good expedient", H. ané debbára séggari, F. dum derbi débbardō bédum.
[14] na-i gérdama. The meaning of this phrase is not quite certain, as I have noted it down also with the meaning of „to mistrust".
[15] mēdo-noddi-mō, „I call him"; imp. noddōi-mō, but the word has not the meaning of „giving a name".
[16] hō nō-inda má-dāmu, „what is his (or „its") name?"
[17] hōra hehkillo má-da. For the simple imperative mood I have the form hōre hekkil, but as the change of h into h in hōre seems to indicate, this is the plural and not the singular.
[18] mā-iddi; 3rd pers. sing. haho giddi.
[19] égu-akoika. To this present tense I have the imperative mood ákin aku, but that is certainly not a simple verbal form.
[20] éga-hā(ni; imp. „ask him", há-nan.
[21] ú-koi sellet probably conveys the original meaning of „I go into council", but there may be some misunderstanding.
[22] bóbolé (kú is rather doubtful; for „call him" I have bilié-ni.
[23] yé-dahá or yé-dahá bá-ya, „I call". The root is daba or da; I have the imperat. da anne or dabo anne.
[24] mat-baré: imp. „call him", baré-nō.
[25] ṅgás-nen etne net délemki. This phrase seems verbally to mean „I lay all things on (or under) the tongue"; delmik or délemik means „the tongue".
[26] am (ban) gerin; imp. „ask him", nin gerin.

Deutsch und Englisch.	Kanuri.	Tedá.	Hausa.	Fulfúlde.
Ich glaube daran, bin damit einverstanden — *I believe, confirm*	žirē-níškin [1] žirē-ṅgin .	(mödi nēma (búdi) war [7]	ná-yirdá (da ši [14]	mēdo-yāfa [17] .
ich glaube nicht — *I do not believe*	žirū-níškin bāgo	(mödi nēma war yenín [8]	ba na-yírda ba	
ich zweifle — *I doubt* .	šek-níškin [2] . šek-ní mbēdži	táne bádi šekkēn-erik	. . . . . .	. . . . . .
ich erinnere mich, habe im Kopf — *I remember*	kōla-n té-skena [3]	yā-den [9] . . bádi yā-te tenī	ína tuná . . ína túnawé .	mēdo-mítšito .
ich habe vergessen — *I have forgotten*	sibh-ískena [4] gōseu-ískena	yimbétto [10] . . tigge féne-dē [11]	ná-mantšē [15] .	mē iggiti . .
vergiss mich nicht — *do not forget me*	uten góseuī-mi [5]	yēsun ke-féne-ten [12]	kadda ká-mantšé-ni	. . . . . .
ich verstehe — *I understand*	fā-níškin [6] . fā-ṅgin . .	hanán-erik [13]	ína-ži [16] . . ína utte . .	mēdo-nanna .

[1] žirē-níškin heisst wörtlich „ich halte für wahr"; es fehlt bei Koelle, der überhaupt žirē sehr verschieden schreibt.

[2] šek-níškin fehlt auch bei Koelle, wenigstens in dieser Form; es ist halb Arabisch. šek-ní mbēdži, „mein Zweifel ist da".

[3] kōla-n té-skena. Koelle hat diese Redensart nicht, obgleich er beide einzelne Ausdrücke hat, die er kōlā und tá-skin schreibt, wie ich selbst auch meist schreibe.

[4] sibh-ískena. Koelle schreibt síbgeskin, scheint aber gōseu-ískena nicht zu haben.

[5] ūten schreibt Koelle wōte und allerdings habe ich dieses Wort in gewissen Verbindungen auch so aussprechen hören.

[6] fā-níškin, fā-ṅgin müsste eigentlich mit einem aspirirten p geschrieben werden. Das p ist jedenfalls der Grundlaut, wie man deutlich am pá-ṅgéske sieht, das auch ich in den von mir bereisten Landschaften Bornu's nur mit p aussprechen hörte, dagegen aber würde es Niemandem einfallen, pā-nemin oder pā-nim-bá zu sagen. Vgl. S. 40 N. 5.

[7] mödi nēma war gehört eigentlich nicht hierher, da es keine Verbalform ist, sondern wörtlich heisst „dein Wort ist wahr"; bádi ist „dies". Ebenso die folgende Redensart.

[8] mödi nēma war yenín, „dein Wort ist nicht wahr".

[9] yā-den ist vielleicht eine abgekürzte populäre Form und wahrscheinlich ganz gleichbedeutend mit der folgenden vollständigeren Phrase bádi yā-te tenī, „dieses ist im Kopfe". Wenigstens ist dies wahrscheinlicher, als dass yāden eine abgekürzte Verbalform wäre. Für „Kopf" habe ich freilich in den Nominallisten dāba.

[10] yimbétto ist mir als erste Person zweifelhaft, kann aber doch richtig sein, da es ja die vergangene Zeit ist; die negative Form dazu ist, glaube ich, yimbétte-na.

[11] tigge féne-dē. Der Beisatz tigge ist offenbar Nebensache, aber ich kenne die eigentliche Bedeutung des Wortes nicht.

[12] yēsun ke-féne-ten ist grammatisch vollkommen genau zu analysiren: yēsun, „dass nicht", ke-féne, „du vergissest", ten, „mich".

[13] hanán-erik. Einige Formen dieses Zeitwortes siehe weiter unten.

[14] ná-yirdá ist aus dem Arabischen abgeleitet.

[15] ná-mantšē. Ich will hier die begriffsverwandte Redensart anführen „ich habe übergangen", ná-kétare, ná-nikē.

[16] ína-ži, „Verstehst du Hausa?", kána-ži máganan Hausa, im F. ad-andana hadāre, oder bolide, Hausāre, „ich verstehe nicht", H. ba ína-ži ba, F. mēdo-nānna-ta.

[17] mēdo-yāfa ist offenbar der Sonyai-Sprache entnommen.

[18] éga-má. „Verstehst du die Sonyai-Sprache?", aiga-má Sonyai hi-ni; „ich verstehe nicht", éga-má.

[19] nágénke žerān ist entschieden keine Verbalform; aigunke ist vielleicht naagul na-hú. Das letzte Wort scheint jedenfalls žerē zu sein; žerū, „wahr". — Das folgende haaganhalle bin ich gar nicht zu analysiren im Stande.

[20] sāga gilte kelā-na. Diese Phrase kann ich nicht analysiren; sollte sāga der Imperativ von wu-sha sein? Man sollte aber erwarten, dass die Negation voranginge.

[21] ganébke as žiro. ganébke oder ganéfke ist entschieden die negative Form von gefke, das also an sich eine negative Bedeutung haben muss, die durch die andere Negation wieder aufgehoben wird, also verwandt mit „zweifeln".

[22] yé-héganó bū-ya šiggāra. šiggāra ist wol Substantiv, „der Zweifel".

[23] wenā-ka. Das ka ist die Negation und es scheint „mich" nicht ausgedrückt zu sein.

[24] mam-dīčīlle-āga scheint nichts Anderes zu bedeuten, als „ich weiss es".

[25] ión ga-ndi ist jedenfalls eine positive Phrase, ganz unabhängig von der vorigen.

Sonyai.	Lógoné.	Wándalá.	Bágrimma.	Mába.
éga-yáfa . . .	nágúnko šerēa [19]	ganébke se žire[21]	ma-tad žirē-ga	. . . . . .
. . . .	kangankálle? . .	gefke žire . .	. . . . . .	. . . .
	wáku álo šekke na-ū lalí	yé-béganá bá-yu šiggāra[22]	ma-tad šegga	am avaá-eadē
. . . .	nangul kā-nāū .	yé-ngánga miri	mam-džélle-nga[24]	am aungi tandi
ég(a) Ini bayō .	wu-ske kelā-ya	wenā-via . .	mam-dúnga .	am aunge-sō
. . . . . .	sāga gilte kelā-sa[20]	wenā-ka[23] .	. . . . . .	lōn ga-ndi[25]
éga-mā[18] . . .	wusenária . . .	yé-tšinén tšiná	mam pemlúa .	am fúmarē

[1] širé-nishin means verbally „I take for true"; it is wanting in Koelle's vocabulary, who besides writes šéré in a very different manner.

[2] šok-nishin at least in this form is likewise wanting in Koelle; it is half Arabic. — šok-ni mbódši, „my doubt exists".

[3] kéla-n té-shena means verbally „I have caught it with the head". The phrase is wanting in Koelle, although he has each of the two terms singly, writing kéjá instead of kéla and tá-skin, as I myself spell the verb in general; but the a in this verb is changeable, the form of the imperative tense being té-i.

[4] sibb-ishena: Koelle writes séhgeshin, but seems not to have géseb-ishena.

[5] átan, „that not, not", is written wóte by Koelle and I myself have heard the word pronounced in this way in certain conn-

[6] fá-nishin, fá-ágin we ought properly to write with an aspirate p. Evidently p is the radical sound, as we are clearly from the verb pá-á gésho, which I myself heard pronounced with a p in all those districts of Bornu, over which I travelled, but nobody there would have taken it into his head to pronounce pá-nemin or pá-nim-bá.

[7] mádi néma war properly does not belong hither, as it is not a verbal form, but means „thy word is true"; bádi means „this". — The same is to be said of the following phrase.

[8] mádi néma war yamin, „thy word is not true".

[9] yá-dam may be an abbreviated popular form and nothing else, but the following full phrase bádi yá-le temi, „this be in the head". At least this is more probable, than that yádam be an abridged verbal form. In what relation yi may stand to dābo, I cannot say, and it may not mean „head" at all; for among the nomism the term „head" in T. is represented by dábo.

[10] yimbéite is doubtful to me as 1st pers., but it may possibly be right, as it is the past and not the present tense: the negative form is, I think, yimbéite-ae.

[11] tigge féne-dē: the adding of tigge is evidently unessential, but I do not know its proper meaning.

[12] yénnu ka-féne-ten is grammatically easily to be analysed and perfectly correct: yénnu, „that act", ko-féne, „thou forgettest", ten, „me".

[13] haunn-ayin. Some forms of this verb see lower down.

[14] ná-yirdē is derived from the Arabic.

[15] na-mantšā: I here adduce two terms of a similar meaning, via ná-hétare and ná-nišē, which have also the meaning of „I have left out".

[16] lma-ši: thereto the phrase „do you understand the Hausa-language?", hans-ši mágana a Hausa, F. nd-naénna hadūre, or hollde, Hausára: „I do not understand", H. ba lma-ši ba, F. médo-nánna-ta.

[17] mēdo-jáfa: the word yáfa has been evidently borrowed from the Sonyai-language.

[18] éga-mā: „do you understand the Sonyai-language?", niga-mā Sonyai ki-ni; „I do not understand", éna-mā.

[19] nágúnko šerēa has not much the appearance of a verbal form. The last word seems to be šerēa or šere a, šeré meaning „true".

[20] sága gilte kelā-sa. I am not able to analyse this phrase grammatically; might sága be the imperative mood of wu-ska? In this case I should expect the negative particle to precede.

[21] ganébke se žire: ganébke or ganéfke is evidently the negative form of gefke, which itself must be of a negative meaning, such as „doubting", so that this negation becomes annulled by a second one in the positive phrase „I believe".

[22] yé-béganá bá-yu šiggára: šiggāra seems to be a noun.

[23] wená-ka: ka being the negative particle, the pronoun „me" does not seem to be expressed.

[24] mam-džélle-nga according to all appearance means only „I know it".

[25] lōn ga-ndi, although its root is not known to me, is evidently a positive phrase totally distinct from the preceding one.

Deutsch und Englisch.	Kanúri.	Tédă.	Hausa.	Fulfúlde.
ich lerne[1] — *I learn* . .	pá-ngésko[2] . / fā-ngin . .	hénnerik[8] . .	ína kòya	médo-ékketo .
ich lehre dich — *I teach thee*	ni-rō yeke-li-skin[3]	táné hē tiáffa	ína kōya máta	médo-ékketā-mo
du lehrst mich — *you teach me*	ū-rō yeke-li-min	yīrin fáda(?) .	kai kā-na kōyá meni	an-ékketi-mi
ich weiss, kenne — *I know, am acquainted with*	nō-niskin[4] . / nō-ngin . .	banán-erik .	ná-sani[9] . .	médo-andi .
ich weiss, kenne nicht — *I do not know*	nō-ngin bagó	táné banán-erin	ba ni-sáni ba	médo and-a .
weisst du nicht? — *do you not know?*	nō-nemin bá	banán-in-meni	kai ba ka-sáni ba	ana and-a .
ich bin gewohnt — *I am accustomed*	. . . . . .	. . . . . .	ní na-sába[10]	médo-wōa .
ich fürchte — *I fear* .	rī-niskin[5] . / rī-ngin . .	auz-erik . .	ína tsorō . .	médo-hulla .
was fürchtest du? — *what do you fear?*	áfi-rō rī-nemin[6] / áfi rī-min .	négnie auz-emi	mē kaná tsorō	hó-fúlla-ta[11]
ich bin vergnügt, zufrieden — *I am glad, content*	ardi-niskin[7] .	táné bérnē . / lari . .	na-ī murna .	médo-welwélta
mein Herz ist guter Dinge[1] — *my heart is light, at ease*	kárge-ni ketšī	konó-n-erik .	zūtšia(-na) ya-ī dádi	bérrende anwēli
	3te Pers. kárge-nisé ketšī	konó-kindé .	zūtšia-nisé ya-ī dádi	bérrende mā-ko an-wēli

[1] Diese Phrase, obgleich in den meisten Sprachen nicht verbal ausgedrückt, musste ich doch hier aufnehmen.

[2] pá-ngésko ist die vierte Verbalform von pá-ngin oder fā-ngin, fehlt aber bei Koelle.

[3] yeke-li-skin, wörtlich „ich mache (dich) lernen". Koelle hat yikélitskin und yekélitskin.

[4] nō-niskin. Daher das Substantiv nō-te, „Kenntniss".

[5] rī-niskin. Davon rī-gata, „gefürchtet", rī-te, „die Furcht".

[6] áfi, áfi-rō. Hier ist die verschiedene Konstruktion des Verbums genugsam angezeigt; so auch abá-ni rī-niskin und abá-ni-rō rī-niskin.

[7] ardi-niskin, wo natürlich das Stammwort ardi aus dem Arabischen abgeleitet ist, fehlt bei Koelle.

[8] hénnerik vielleicht hén-erik. Ich habe ausserdem noch tefékki, aber das kommt Arabischen Formen zu nahe, als dass ich es für richtig halten könnte.

[9] ná-sani. Dies ist eins der Verben im Hausa, die entschieden aus der Temáshyt-Sprache aufgenommen sind; in der letzteren heisst „ich weiss" sau-agh.

[10] ni na-sába, „ihr seid gewohnt", ké ka-sába, F. euom ombéfti; „sie sind gewohnt", „man ist gewohnt", H. sū sa-sába, F. hē habáfti und in Sokoto mit anders gewendeter Phrase gandaude halā. Dahin gehört auch das Hausa-Sprichwort aikin dúnia dáka sé sába, „jedes Werk der Welt nur durch Gewohnheit". Auch hat man im Hausa noch eine andere begriffsverwandte Phrase, nämlich na-ī Jimma da Jī, „ich habe mich lange damit abgegeben", im F. mé-yaule dāke hē mā-dāe oder mé-gáddi hē mádde. Die Phrase im Hausa sé an-ĵimma kadán hat einen etwas anderen Sinn, eigentlich „nur nachdem man ein bischen dabei geblieben", d. h. „warte nur ein bischen".

[11] hó-fúlla-ta. Davon Pluralform hó-hulléttn.

[12] aiga-hába. In diesem Dialekt, der in der Stadt Sai und dort am Niger gesprochen wird, vertritt aiga die Stelle des ēga in der ersten Person des Verbums.

[13] Ich habe auch hier wieder w-ósená-rin, aber obgleich dieses Wort eine weite Bedeutung für alles geistige Erfassen zu haben scheint, kann es doch nicht „lernen" selbst ausdrücken. Der Grund des Missverständnisses liegt wahrscheinlich in der nahen Verwandtschaft der Kanúri-Ausdrücke fā-ngin und pá-ngésko; denn auch im W. habe ich wieder denselben Ausdruck wie für „verstehen".

[14] Ich habe für „du lehrst mich" im Lógoné die Form kenágohán, und die erinnert an das kínüā in der Phrase nangol hénüā, „ich erinnere mich", wofür ich jedoch há-nüā geschrieben habe, da ich es mit hā, „Kopf" in Beziehung gesetzt habe.

[15] wé-sená. Davon dritte Person Sing. nim-ásená.

[16] inta-hō erwangd-ārnā. inta-hē, „es freut sich", davon negative Form inta-n-hē; erwangde, „das Herz".

[17] mam-dāali-adesna ist eine zusammengesetzte Zeitform von mam-dāelle, „ich weiss", etwa „ich mache mich wissen", d. i. „ich lerne". Das ádesna hat eine auffallende Ähnlichkeit mit dem entsprechenden ádeiágá im Mába.

[18] dérmahum. Unter den Musgu habe ich dieses Wort nicht und für „Herz" ein anderes Wort.

Sońyai.	Lógoné.	Wándalā.	Bágrimma.	Mába.
. . . . .	[12]	yé-tšimen tšinā	mam-džell-aú-sena [17]	am aúsiñgā
. . . . . .	san wurbélnkū (?)	yé-mbā-gaa bā-ya	mam-an-daža	am asiñg-mē
am a-dénden hayō	[11]	ka-mbī-se bā-ka	i-dang ka-dīžo-ma	and' asiñg-a
óga-bē	wú-senā [13] . .	dien-dī-ya .	mam-dželle .	am aus-e
ésa-bē	wú-sen-nā . .	dień-ka bā-ya	mam-dželle-lī	am aus-andē
nina-bō . . .	gū-sen	dień-ka bā-ka	in-dželle-lī .	
óga-fūdži . . . / aiga-bābu [12] .	. . . .	. . . . . .	. . . . .	. . . . . .
óga-hámboru .	wádebál . . .	wē-va yana .	mam-bōlo .	am ásko
mēkin ká-hámboru	kádebál la ram .	á-vaka hád-abō yana	i-bōl endī .	. . . . . .
óga-ba hayō . .	wugóm	hēnin hāya .	mam-ofte . . / martag askénagō	am farhānnai (Arb.)
ébena gakán . .	nefā-ī delē . .	inta-kē erwañgd-árnā [14]	dérmakum lēlē [18]	
. . . .	nefā-nī delē . .	inta-kē erwañgd-āra	. . . . .	

[1] This phrase, although not expressed by a verbal form in most of these languages, I was yet obliged to introduce here.
[2] pā-ágéske is the 4th verbal form of pá-ágin or fā-ágin, but is wanting in Koelle, at least in his vocabulary.
[3] yaka-lī-skin, verbally „I make thee learn". Koelle however writes yikēliskin and yekēliskin.
[4] nó-niskin: from the root nó-tu, „knowledge".
[5] rī-niskin: thence rī-gatu, „feared", and rī-tu, „the fear".
[6] áfī, áfī-rō: we have here a specimen of the different mode of construing this verb. Thus both is right, as well abá-nī rī-niskin as abá-nī-rō rī-niskin.
[7] ardi-niskin is wanting in Koelle. The root of this word is the Arabic redā, from which has likewise been derived the Hausa-word na-yirdā.
[8] hénnerik, perhaps hén-erik: besides this verb I have still the form tefékki, but that approaches too closely to some Arabic forms and has too little of the 1st pers. of a Tédā verb, so that I think, it is wrong.
[9] ná-sani. This is one of the verbs in the Hausa-language, which without the least doubt have been derived from the Temāšiyt, where we have ssn-agh.
[10] ai na-saba: „you are accustomed", sū ka-saba, F. onon ambófīl; „they are accustomed", H. sū sa-saba, F. bē bebéfīl and in Sońyai by a different mode of expression gandaude hayō. To this place belongs also the Hausa-proverb aiki n dénia dáka sē saba, verbally „every work or handicraft of the world only by custom". — In Hausa there is also another phrase of a similar meaning, na-i Iimma da šī, „I have dealt with it", in F. mē-fauta dāka bē mē-dāo or mō-nēddi bē mēdio. But the Hausa-phrase sē na-Iimma kadán has the somewhat different meaning „wait a little", but properly it is „only after having dealt a little with it".
[11] kó-fúlla-án: thence the plural form kó-bulléita.
[12] aiga-bābu: in this dialect, which is spoken in the town of Say and in the neighbouring district along the Niger aiga takes the place of óga in the 1st pers. of the verb.
[13] Here also I have the same term w-ásenā-ria, but although this word seems to have a wide range, comprising various ways of mental conception, I yet doubt very much, whether it can possibly have the meaning of „to learn". The reason lies in the close proximity of the two Kanúri-terms fā-ágin and pā-ágéske, as it was by means of the Kanúri-language that I became acquainted with the corresponding terms in the other languages. Thus it is explained, how it happens, that also in the Wándalā-language I have the same term for understanding and learning.
[14] For the phrase „you teach me" in the Lógoné-language I have the phrase kenágebén and that reminds one of the term kénkā in the phrase nangui kénkā, where however I have exchanged the kénkā for ká-nkā.
[15] wú-senī, thence 3rd pers. nim-asenā.
[16] inta-kē erwañgd-ārnā: inta-kē, „it is glad", negative form inta-n-kē; erwañgde, „the heart".
[17] mam-džell-aúsena is likewise formed of mam-dželle, „I know", with the addition of aúsena, the meaning being „I make myself to know". The aúsena bears a remarkable resemblance to the aúsiñgā in the Mába-language.
[18] dérmakum: among my list of terms this word is wanting and for „heart" I have another term.

Deutsch und Englisch.	Kanúri.	Tédā.	Hausa.	Fulfúlde.
ich bin traurig — *I am sorry*, mein Herz ist betrübt — *my heart is afflicted, sad*	kárge-nī kuttu / kárge-nī bíbiti [1]	anár tánge kōsu genē [6]	zūtšia-na yá-baté	mēdo-ennna .
ich trage etwas mit Geduld — *I bear with patience*	. . . . . .	. . . . . .	na-ī hánkora da abū dauya [10]	. . . . . .
ich bin einer Sache überdrüssig — *I am tired of, disgusted with some thing*	. . . . . .		ina-ši n tšlo wo-ne abū [11] / ná-rēne . .	mēdo-nannanau-dum dūmadóm mē yábbekē .
ich zürne, bin böse — *I am angry*	girgā-nískin / girgā-ógin [2] .	tánē anár-nerí	na-ī fuši . .	mē-tókki . .
er zürnt — *he is angry*	girgā-tšin . .	anár-kindē .	šina yi-n fūši	kanko ó-túkki
?	. . . . . .	. . . . . .	ina daure . .	mēdo-moňdo
ich lache — *I laugh* .	kásulū (gō-nískin / gō-ógin [3])	káz-erík [7] . .	ina dária [12] .	mēdo-džella .
ich weine — *I weep* .	yīr-eskin . .	yód-erík . .	ina kūka . .	mēdo-wōya .
was weinst du? — *what do you weep?*	áfī yīr-emin .	nēgaie domī [8]	mē ásamē-ka kā-na kūka [13]	kó bem-ma ad-auēā
ich schreie — *I cry* . .	yíl-ískin [4] . / yíl-ógin . .	kórroro dún-erík	. . . . . .	. . . . . .
ich bin beschäftigt — *I am occupied*	kidā-nī mbēžin	ēne kanno tári bēn-erík [9]	ina da (ai-ki [14] / šággeli)	mēdo-oidi kūgel
ich lese — *I read* . .	kará-nískin . / karā-ógin .	karán-merík, S. / karán-erík, N.	ina kára-tū .	mēdo-džangu
ich schreibe — *I write* .	rubū-nískin [5] .	rū-erík, S. / arbū-nerík, N.	ina rūbu-tū [15]	mēdo-winda .

[1] kárge-nī bíbiti von bíbi-nískin, bíbi-ágin, „ich verderbe", und fast wörtlich in derselben Auffassung wie die Hausa-Phrase zūtšia-na yá-baté. — Anstatt kuttu schreibt Koelle kótū.

[2] girgā-ágin. Koelle schreibt gergá-ágin.

[3] kásulū gō-ágin. Koelle unterscheidet zwischen zwei Ausdrücken, nämlich kásutū gō-ágin, „ich beginne zu lachen", und kásutū dī-skin, „ich lache".

[4] yíl-ískin. Koelle hat für das Wort yīlágin zwei Bedeutungen, einmal die von „laut schreien" oder „jauchzen", dann die von „brüllen" wie ein Löwe.

[5] rubū-nískin schreibt Koelle rufángin: es ist dies, wie schon oft erwähnt, nur unbedeutende Dialektverschiedenheit. Das Participium rubū-gata oder rufū-gata habe ich nicht in Gebrauch gefunden.

[6] anár tánga kōsu genē, „mein Herz ist nicht süss". Die Tédā haben auch noch eine andere Phrase, die aber in der ersten Person nicht gebräuchlich zu sein scheint; dagegen haben sie die Phrase nēgai anár rómmī, „warum ist das Herz traurig?", „warum bist du traurig?" Die Ableitung von rómmī ist mir nicht bekannt.

[7] káz-erík. Die Wurzel káz ist augenscheinlich identisch mit derjenigen von kás-u-tū.

[8] nēgaie domī ist wol unzweifelhaft eine populäre Abkürzung von nēgaie yód-emī.

[9] ēne kanno tári bēn-erík. Diese Phrase ist mir in ihren einzelnen Theilen nicht deutlich.

[10] na-ī hánkora da abū dauya. da abū dauya, „mit einer schweren, unangenehmen Sache".

[11] ina-ši n tšlo wo-ne abū, wörtlich „ich fühle unwohl (wegen) dieser Sache".

[12] ina dária. Ich will hier auch die Redensart „ich lächle" anführen, H. ina mūimušī, F. mēdo-mōso.

[13] mē ásamē-ka, „was ist dein Verhalten?", „was ist dir?", kā-na kūka, „du weinst" oder „dass du weinst".

[14] ina da ai-ki, „ich habe Arbeit"; ai-ki von ai, „machen", šággeli vom Arabischen šogl.

[15] ina rūbu-tū. „Dieser Brief ist gut geschrieben", a-wó-nan utíke an-rūbu-tū néggari [illegible], F. [illegible] wind-āma windol [illegible].

[16] Agahē. Nach dieser Form sollte man schliessen, dass die Wurzel hē wäre, das wird aber mehr als zweifelhaft durch die folgende Phrase, aus der sich gahé als Wurzel zu ergeben scheint, also eigentlich ēga-gahé.

[17] [illegible] hat nicht das Aussehen einer reinen Verbalform.

[18] kórbais kann kaum die erste Person Präs. sein.

[19] nō andī. Die äusserliche Übereinstimmung dieses andī, „wer", mit dem nachfolgenden verbalen ándī muss Niemanden verwirren.

[20] kōte yell: die Verbalform ist nicht bestimmt ausgedrückt.

Sónyai.	Lógoné.	Wándalá.	Bágrimma.	Mába.
. . . .	nefā-n delē-sa .	tnta-n-kē er-wangd-áruā	dérmakum oño	am bazánanai (Arab.)
	. . . . . .	. . . . . .	. . . . .	. . . . . .
. . . .	. . . . . .	. . . . . .	. . . . .	
ága-bírringā . . / ben-éga kasángendā	w-ó-mtsakā . .	vranga vranga bā-ya	mam-kollo . / mam-tadžbérga	
ága-bírringā . .	nī m-á-mtsakā .	vranga vranga bá-nganō	. . . . .	
. . . .	. . . . . .	. . . . . .	. . . . .	. . . . . .
éga-hāre . . .	θāli inθē [17]	yé-zekka bā-ya	mam-ákkogō	am óskeri
éga-bē [16] . . .	w-usē	yé-kuā . . .	mam-a-nō .	am óyoli
kin gahē . . .	g-usē gagám .	ká-kuē . . .	nō andī [19] . .	ēēte yoli [20]
. . . .	w-ūθa θenāne demā	yohúl bá-ya .	mam-ándi-ki	. . . . . .
. . . .	badže nāū lalī .	. . . . .	ngás-em ētu .	am lītto kēne
éga-kán (kián) . / éga-tšán . .	wé-aofū . . .	yé-ndalēa . .	mám-doyō .	am ger-úrne
éga-hántum . / éga-ntum . .	bārbata [18] . . .	yé-polēa . .	mám-džangā .	am kittib-érne

[1] kárga-al bibili, derived from bibi-alakin, bibi-ágin, „I spoil", and thus almost verbally identical with the Hausa-term aûtšía-na yá-hatšé. — Koelle writes kátû instead of katin.

[2] giegā-ágin: Koelle writes gergá-ágin.

[3] késantá gé-ágin: Koelle distinguishes between two different terms, viz késantû gé-ágin, „I begin to laugh", and késantû di-ekin, „I laugh".

[4] yil-lekin: Koelle does not mention the meaning of „crying", but attributes to this word, which he writes yilágin two somewhat different meanings, first that of shouting or hallooing, then that of roaring as a lion.

[5] ruhū-afakin: Koelle writes rufángin, only the common slight variation of dialect. — The participle rufá-gata or ruhū-gata I have not heard used.

[6] anár tán-go kōan gené, verbally „my heart is not sweet". The Tédā have also another expression for this phrase, which however does not seem to be used in the 1st pers.; but the common phrase for „why are you sad?" is nōgai anár rámmi, verbally „why is the heart sad?" rámmi however is not else known to me.

[7] kán-erik: the root kán is no doubt intimately allied with that of kán-n-tû.

[8] nōgain domi, I have no doubt, is a popular abbreviation of the phrase nōgais yód-emi.

[9] ōna kuano tári kén-erik: the different parts of this phrase are not clear to me.

[10] na-i báskora da abû dauya: da abû dauya, „with a difficult, disagreeable thing".

[11] ina-ši n tšie wo-na abā, verbally „I feel sickly (on account of) this thing".

[12] ina dárin: I shall here adduce the phrase „I smile, simper", H. ina mélmuli, F. mōdo-mōso.

[13] mē ásamē-ka, „what is the matter with thee?", kā-na kūka, „thou weepest" or „that thou weepest".

[14] ina da ai-ki, „I have work", ai-ki being the indigenous Hausa-noun derived from ai, „make"; šaggali is a later word introduced from the Arabic šugl.

[15] ina ráhu-tā: „this letter is well written", a-wé-naa atika an-ráhu-tā néggari ši-kē, F. daréni windi-āma windoi hádum-gan.

[16] éga-bē: from this form we might conclude the root to be bē, but that becomes doubtful in consequence of the next phrase, which seems to indicate gabē as the root; it therefore might be better to write éga-gabē.

[17] θāli inθē has not the character of a pure verbal form.

[18] bárbata can scarcely be the 1st person of the present tense; but it may be w-árbata.

[19] nō andī: the similarity of this andi with the following ándi must perplex nobody; the former is the pronoun „what", the latter is a verbal form.

[20] ēēte yoli: the verbal form is not distinctly expressed.

Deutsch und Englisch.	Kanúri.	Tédā.	Hausa.	Fulfúlde.
ich schreibe ab, kopiere — *I copy*	fal-nískin[1] . / fug-niskin[2] .	. . . . .		. . . . .
ich zähle — *I count* . .	tamísse-nískin / tamisse-ŋgin[3]	táně kit-erik / táně badin kit-erik	ni ina ked-aia[12]	médo-limma .
ich bete, verrichte mein Gebet — *I pray, offer up my prayers*	sál-I-nískin / sál-I-ŋgin[4] . / sálā dí-skin .	salĭ-n-erik . / sel-n-erik .	ina-yi-n salla	médo-dūūl-a[15]
ich verbeuge mich im Gebet — *I bow, stoop (in prayer*	ungum-ískin[5] .	réka-n-erik[10]	ina dūk-ana	mē-sujjúda-kē / mē-tūra-kē[16]
ich werfe mich zur Erde nieder (im Gebet — *I throw myself down (in prayer*	súdžu-ŋgin[6] .		na-I rolla[13]	mē-neúgi nangérdi
ich knie nieder — *I kneel down (in prayer*	gorúm-gorúm-nískin[7]			. . . . .
ich verehre, bete an — *I adore, worship*	ábād-nískin[8]		. . . . . .	. . . . .
sie verehren, erzeigen göttliche Ehre — *they adore, worship*	séndima ábād-tsē-nin	wóteri . . .	sun-mai da taáfi[14]	bokōri torūrel bena Alla mā-be[17]
ich befehle meine Seele zu Gott — *I recommend my soul to God*	lāmer semma Alla-rō tsellem-niskin[9]	ron né-ruš Alla sadáng-irdē[11]		. . . . .

[1] fal-niskin. Dies ist dasselbe Wort, das Koelle pálŏgin schreibt, obgleich er diese besondere Bedeutung nicht hat, aber der Grundbegriff des Abschreibens entspricht dem Begriff „durch Tausch etwas Anderes erhalten".

[2] fug-niskin fehlt bei Koelle; es ist aber eng verwandt mit fog-niskin, bei Koelle fóŋgin, „ich verbinde" (zwei Sachen).

[3] tamisse-ŋgin. Da das Substantiv nach Koelle's eigener Schreibweise tamisse, „die Zahl", heisst, so halte ich die Schreibart mit doppeltem s für richtiger als die mit Einem s. Participium: tamisse-gáte, H. an-kad-ała, F. dun limi. „Sind diese Muscheln gezählt oder nicht?", H. kurdi a-wà-nan an-kad-ała kó ba an-kad-ała ba, F. tšede dō limá-ma kó lima.

[4] sál-I-ŋgin. Koelle hat neben dieser einfachen Phrase auch die ungewöhnlichere sálā sálingin (sic).

[5] ungum-iskin fehlt bei Koelle; vielleicht richtiger ungum-niskin.

[6] súdžu-ŋgin. Auch dies Wort fehlt bei Koelle; es ist natürlich aus dem Arabischen سجود von سجد abgeleitet und durch Abwerfen des finalen d der Sprache accommodirt.

[7] gorúm-gorúm-niskin fehlt gleichfalls bei Koelle, ebenso wie das Substantiv gorúm-gorúm.

[8] ábād-niskin fehlt auch bei Koelle; es ist natürlich auch aus dem Arabischen eingeführt und kein ursprünglich einheimisches Wort. Das d wird in gewöhnlicher Aussprache auch hier weggelassen und das Wort wie die in den entsprechenden Sprachen meist vom heidnischen Kultus gebraucht.

[9] lāmer semma Alla-rō tsellem-niskin, wörtlich „ich übergebe den ganzen Befehl (lāmer الأمر) an Gott". Hierher will ich auch die Redensart setzen, die unserem Begriffe des Hoffens und Wünschens nahe kommt: „Alla hegimtsin (i. e. hokkum tsin), „wenn Gott es (so) befiehlt", im Tédā hakkum kyénwō, L. málagin, W. mašēn wilélle.

[10] réka-n-erik, natürlich aus dem Arabischen abgeleitet und mit einheimischer Verbalendung versehen.

[11] ron né-ruš Alla sadáng-irdē. Die Verbalform steht im Präteritum, sonst ist Alles richtig.

[12] ni ina ked-aia. Die Wurzel von ked-aia und kit-erik ist offenbar identisch.

[13] na-I rolla. Wir haben hier ein unabhängig gebildetes Wort für einen fremden Begriff.

[14] sun-mai da taáfi heisst wörtlich „sie machen sich (einen Gegenstand) zu einem Götzen", (taáfi, bei Schön dafi).

[15] médo-dūūl-a. Daher dūūl-do, Plur. dūūl-be, „der Muslim". Dieser Name hat in Bezug auf die sogenannten Mandingos Anlass zu vielen Missverständnissen gegeben.

[16] mē-tūra-kē ist ein interessantes Wort, das wahrscheinlich mit dem den Mairi bezeichnenden Namen tūri zusammenhängt. S. Reisen, Bd. I, S. 516. (Engl. Ausg. I, S. 471.)

[17] bokōri torūrel bena Alla mā-be; die ersten drei Wörter kann ich nicht analysiren; Alla mā-be, „zu ihrem Gott".

[18] indo ayesnaséché; 3te Person Sing. ni nan-ayesnaséché.

[19] tōtim alla-mū ist auffallend und wol falsch.

[20] te-magists hētere ist von einer andern Wurzel abgeleitet, als die vorhergehende Phrase.

[21] nam-damasi. Die Bagirmier haben auch einen Ausdruck für „ich falte die Hände", noh-na dilimnáfra, im M. am barringáfne ōred.

Sonyai.	Lógoné.	Wándalá.	Bágrimma.	Mába.
. . . .	ind(o) alúχeahé .	ye-yakúlmabā-ya	. . . . .	. . . .
óga-kabbu . .	wúdia	yé-kelē kolāra	mam-bodžó .	am aiēne
óga-džinger . .	wú-salā . . .	yō-magā salla / yéd-sebō (ye-daebō?	ma(m)-salla .	am salla-rēne
. . . .	madémgazī (?) .	yé-gana . .	mam-dugnánga	am báker-rinēne
. . . .			mak-ingųmna / mak-indanaī	am sųdžide-ri-nēne
. . . .	indo aχsenzézehā [18]	yó-kelábdže .	mam-dumnai [21]	am akki orúngne
. . . .	indo dum alla-kon	yé-ngis . .	. . . . .	gáso) abád eretčti
. . . .	tētim alla-mā [19]	te-magánia bé-tare [20]	. . . . .	waṅg abád erāni
. . . .	lemár-ne kųtie-ne rōna gimmelwā	béddeme lāmer áruā yé-mága-nan mag Alla	lammar ámana tasālem Allakō	

[1] fal-niekin: Koelle writes this word pálágin, although he has not the meaning here mentioned, but the notion of copying corresponds to that of „exchanging" or rather „obtaining another thing by change".
[2] fug-niekin is wanting in Koelle; but it is, no doubt, closely allied to, or rather identical with fog-niekin (Koelle fóngin) „I join" (two things).
[3] tamlece-ńgin: As according to Koelle's spelling the form of the substantive is tamlasa, I am of opinion, that it is more correct to write this word with two than with ones. The form of the participle tamlee-gāte, H. na-ked-aia, F. dum limi. I add the phrase „are these cowries counted or not (counted)?", H. kardi a-wó-nan na-ked-aia kō ba na-ked-aia ba, F. tšēde dā limá-ma kó lima.
[4] sal-l-ńgin: Koelle has besides this simple phrase the compound and more unusual form sálā sálingin.
[5] núgun-lekin is wanting in Koelle's vocabulary; perhaps it is more correct to write núgun-niekin.
[6] sádžu-ńgin is also wanting in Koelle. Of course this word has been derived from the Arabic سجود from سجد, the final d having been elided and the form of the word having been accommodated to the rules of the Kanúri-language.
[7] gorám-gorám-niekin is also wanting in Koelle, as well as the noun gorám-gorám.
[8] abád-niekin is likewise wanting in Koelle. Of course it is no indigenous word and has been introduced from the Arabic, but nevertheless it is generally applied to the worship of the heathens as well as the corresponding terms in the other languages. Also in this case the final d is elided in common pronunciation.
[9] lámer somma Alla-rō tsellem-niekin means verbally „I surrender the whole order to God", but lámer (الأمر) has obtained a very comprehensive meaning. Here I shall also adduce a phrase, which approaches very near our notion of „to wish" and „to hope": Alla hagimtein (i. e. hokkum tein), verbally „if God ordains", in T. hakkum kyénwō, L. malagin, W. mažen wižélla.
[10] róku-n-erik of course is derived from the Arabic and provided with an indigenous final form.
[11] ron né-rań Alla endáng-írdō: the verbal form seems to belong to the past tense; ron né-rań is „my life".
[12] ni ina ked-aia: the root of this Hausa-word and of the corresponding term in the Téda-language kit-erik is evidently identical.
[13] na-i rolia: we have here an indigenous term for a foreign notion.
[14] sun-mal da tsáfi means verbally „they placed (or took) as an idol"; tsáfi is written by Schön dsáfi.
[15] módo-džūl-a: thence džūl-do, plur. džúl-be, „the moslim". This name especially, in connection with the Mandingoes, has given rise to numerous misunderstandings.
[16] mé-tūra-kó is an interesting word, which probably may have some connexion with the name tōri, given to an individual of the Maleki sect; s. Travels, Vol. I, p. 471.
[17] hokōri torūrel hono Alla ná-be: the first three words I am not able to analyse; Alla nā-be, „their good".
[18] indo aχsenzézehā, 3rd pers. sing. ni nan-aχsenzéreha.
[19] tātim alla-mā seems remarkable and more than doubtful.
[20] te-magánia bétere is evidently derived from a different root than the preceding phrase.
[21] The people of Bagirmi and Wádāi have also an expression for the term „I fold my hands in prayer", mok-ne dšim-náfra, in M. am kerringūēne šored.

Deutsch und Englisch.	Kanúri.	Tédā.	Hausa.	Fulfulde.
ich faste — *I fast, keep a fast*	ū sum-niskin[1]	e-zúm-erik .	ni ina ázemi .	mēdo-sūm-otō
ich schwöre — *I swear, affirm by an oath*	lukrán bú-skin[2]	{ūne / lúkerān} bō-rik	na-I rinswa[11]	mēdo-búnnakē
ich spiele — *I play* . .	biskō-{niskin[3] / ńgin .}	{uwám-erik . / abina-(e)rik[8]}	ina wargī . .	mēdo-fidža .
	3te P. S. biskō-dzin	. . . . . .	šī ší-na wargi	kañko ó-fidža
ich singe — *I sing* . .	kaigagō-{niskin[4] / ńgin}	{debōna / dona} yud-erik[9]	ina wāka . .	mēdo-yimma .
	3te Pers. kaiga gō-tšin	. . . . . .	šī ší-na wāka	kañko ó-yimma
ich tanze — *I dance* .	far-niskin[5] .	{yemō-apék . / abina-(e)rik .}	ina rawa . .	mēdo-womme
	3te Pers. far-tšin	. . . . . .	šī ší-na rawa	kañko ó-womme
ich springe — *I spring, jump*	. . . . . .	. . . . . .	ina-tumā . .	mēdo-diwa .
ich schlage die Trommel — *I beat the drum*	sā-{niskin . . / ńgin[6] . .}	banga bāb-erik[10]	ina bugga ganga	
	3te Pers. sā-tšin	. . . . . .	. . . . . .	
ich blase (ein Instrument — *I blow (an instrument*	fū-{niskin[7] . / ńgin . .}	. . . . . .	ina fūra . .	

[1] ū sum-niskin. Koelle schreibt dsúmgin und tsúmgin, wie er sich denn in dem ersten Laut fast durchgängig versehen hat. sum ist das Arabische [illegible], wörtlich „ich mache Fasten“.

[2] lukrán bú-skin (lukrán wird gewöhnlich lógerán ausgesprochen), wörtlich „ich esse den Kurán“, weil der Moslim beim Schwören die Hand erst auf den Kurán und dann an die Stirn und Brust legt.

[3] biskō-niskin. Koelle schreibt bángē und erklärt es „eine Tanzpartie der jungen Leute, ein Ball“, und allerdings ist es wahr, dass der Haupt- und erste Begriff des Spieles bei diesen Völkern im Tanzen liegt; das sehen wir auch aus dem entsprechenden Ausdruck in anderen dieser Sprachen. Aber für das eigentliche Tanzen habe ich in den Provinzen, die ich bereist habe, diesen Ausdruck nicht in Gebrauch gefunden.

[4] kaiga gō-niskin. Koelle schreibt kaiga und kelga und verbindet dieses Substantiv nicht mit gō-ńgin, sondern mit yōńgin. Das heisst aber wörtlich „ich beantworte den Gesang“ und kann eigentlich nur von Wechselgesängen gesagt werden, ist also wol nicht das einfache und ursprüngliche Wort für „singen“.

[5] far-niskin hängt unzweifelhaft auf das Engste mit fare, „in die Höhe“, „über“, zusammen und heisst wörtlich „ich mache in die Höhe“, also in weiterer Entwicklung „ich fliege auf“ (vom Vogel), „ich springe, tanze, passire über“ u. s. w.

[6] sā-ńgin hat Koelle nicht in dieser Bedeutung, aber der Grundbegriff des Ausdehnens, Ausziehens, Spannens ist festgehalten, da das ja die unmittelbare Folge des Schlagens der Trommel und Ursache des Schalles ist.

[7] fū-niskin, wörtlich „ich mache Luft, Wind“, hat die allgemeine Bedeutung „blasen“, die sich ebenso gut auf das Anblasen des Feuers als auf das Blasen eines Instruments beziehen kann.

[8] abina-(e)rik, siehe an der Doppelbedeutung dieses Wortes Note 3.

[9] debōna yud-erik. yud-erik wird mit Dialektverschiedenheit auch yus-rik geschrieben. Es muss dafür aber noch ein anderes Wort in Gebrauch sein, da ich für die 3te Person debōna yofádi habe.

[10] banga bāb-erik: für „die Trommel“ habe ich im Tēdā dangara.

[11] na-I rinswa. Ein begriffsverwandtes Wort ist na-I hapāra, F. mēdo-būnnakē hunnōre faure, „ich schwöre einen Meineid“.

[12] ēga-gannu. Die Ähnlichkeit dieses Wortes mit dem Arabischen [illegible], „singen“, kann wol nur zufällig sein. gannu [illegible] und [illegible] scheinen Ein und dasselbe Wort zu sein und bestätigen, was ich Note 3 gesagt habe.

[13] nelá-dabō, nalá-kali haigē. Über diese verlängerte Form des Präsens mit la, die auch weiterhin in der Phrase ludo ála dē-āli erscheint, s., was ich in den Pronomen gesagt habe.

[14] lud(o) ála dō-āli ganga. Dō-āli oder zusammengezogen dāli muss eine sehr allgemeine Bedeutung haben, da wir es auch in der Phrase dāli fe dē, „ich lache“, gehabt haben, vielleicht eigentlich, wie wir sagen, „ich schlage ein Gelächter auf“. Dass aber das Wort dāli aus zwei selbstständigen Theilen besteht, dō und āli, sieht man aus der Form für die 3te Person t-āli dē ganga.

[15] ludo dāli ist wieder jenes ganz allgemeine Wort und es giebt für den Ausdruck „ich blase ein Instrument“ einen ganz anderen, offenbar viel prägnanteren Ausdruck, wie man aus der 3ten Person Sing. wámbere) daawēa sieht.

[16] á-kasa tsbángalkai. Das Substantiv ist offenbar vom vorhergehenden verschieden und bezeichnet vielleicht eine andere Art Gesang.

[17] yé-dān; 3te Person a-dān-na.

[18] Ein begriffsverwandtes Wort zu mam-dángo ist plesénya, aber ich kenne seine nähere Beziehung nicht.

Seŋyul.	Lógonē.	Wándalā.	Bágrimma.	Kūka.
éga-mĕhan . .	am diwáse ašām	yé-tsu fándera	mal-ad asiámo	am saim-erŏ
éga-džŏ . . .	wumo lákorān .	yé-zel el kurān	mak-ayérge .	am halfa-eróne
éga-ganno [12] . .	wū-θabā . . .	yó-gágusā . .	mam-daṅgo [18]	am ayélo-ne
. . . .	3rd pa. s. nalá-θabá [13]	a-gágusā . .	. . . . . .	3rd pa. pl. kai welo
éga-dun . . .	wū-kolā balgē .	yé-keroā búlayē	mot-akā . . / mok-uṅkā . .	am úrarī
. . . .	3rd pers. nalá-kolā balgē	á-kean tabáṅgalhai [16]	. . . . . .	. . . . . .
éga-gan . . .	wū-kenā . . .	ye-šikle (bá-ya	mam-ápia . / mam-ándabē	am aiṅgi
. . . .	3rd pers. ná-kenā	a-šikla (bá-ṅgauē	. . . . . .	. . . . . .
éga-gāre . . .	. . . . . .	. . . . . .	. . . . . .	. . . . . .
	ind(o) ālu θŏ-āli (gaṅga [14]	yó-dža [17] . .	mam-akkos (gaṅga	am ádumĕ
	. . . . . .	. . . . . .	. . . . . .	. . . . . .
	indo θāli [15] . .	yé-fríttala .	mak-ub gosso	ferre) am-ávao

[1] ŏ aum-nizkin: Koelle writes dubúmgin and teámgin, as he is generally mistaken with regard to the first consonant.

[2] lakrān hé-ekin (the word lakrān being vulgarly pronounced lógorān) means verbally „I eat the Kurān", an account of the Moslim, while taking an oath placing his hand on the holy book and then resting it on his front and chest.

[3] bleké-nizkin: Koelle writes bēogā and attributes to it the meaning „a dancing party of young people, a ball". Certainly there is no doubt, that the chief notion of play with these people is dancing; that is proved also by the corresponding term in other of these languages. Nevertheless in those provinces of Bórnu, through which I have travelled, I have not found bleké-nizkin used to express the distinct notion of dancing.

[4] kaiga gō-nizkin: Koelle writes kaiga as well as koiga, while he scarcely ever uses the diphtong ai; but this noun he does not join with the verb gō-ńgin, but with yéōgin. But kaiga yē-ńgin means verbally „I answer the song" and can properly only be used of alternative songs and I therefore doubt, whether it is the original term for singing.

[5] fer-nizkin without any doubt is intimately connected with the particle fare, „above, on high", and means verbally „I make (myself) high", consequently „I fly, I jump, I pass over, cross, dance".

[6] sá-ńgin is wanting in Koelle with this meaning, but the original notion of extending, stretching out, has been preserved and only amplified in this word.

[7] fū-nizkin has the general notion of „to blow" applying as well to the fire as to the instrument; properly „I make wind".

[8] ubisa-(a)rik: on the double meaning of this word see note 3.

[9] dabōna yuḍ-erik: yuḍ-erik with a dialectical variation is also pronounced yuu-rik. But there must still be used another word, as for the 3rd pers. I have the phrase debōna yefōdi.

[10] haṅga hāh-erik „I beat" is undoubtedly right; but, what haṅga means, I do not exactly know. The term „drum" is represented in my lists by the term dáṅgara.

[11] ua-l rinewa: I here insert the H. and F. term for „I swear a false oath", „I perjure myself", H. na-i kapáre, F. mōdo-kāunakō haunōre faure.

[12] éga-ganno: the similarity of this word with the Arabic term غنى for „to sing" must be merely accidental, as for that notion we have éga-dun in S., but ganno and gan seem to be identical and confirm, what I have stated in note 3.

[13] nalá-θabā, nalá-kulā balgē: with respect to the lengthened verbal form with la, which appears also further on in the phrase indo ālu θo-āli, see what I have said in the Prolegomena.

[14] ind(o) ālu θŏ-āli (gaṅga: θŏ-āli or θāli in the contracted form must convey a very general meaning, as we have had it also in the phrase θāli indō, „I laugh". That the word θāli does consist of two separate portions, θŏ and āli, we see from the form of the 3rd pers. ā-āli θā gaṅga.

[15] indo θāli: here again we have the term θāli, but evidently the L. idiom has besides an entirely different term for „I blow an instrument", as for the 3rd pers. sing. I have the phrase wāmbere) daewān.

[16] á-kean tabáṅgalhai: the noun is evidently quite distinct from the preceding one.

[17] yó-džā: thence 3rd pers. á-džā-na.

[18] mam-daṅgo: a term of a meaning closely related to this one is plaeṅya, but its precise nature and notion are unknown to me.

Deutsch und Englisch.	Kanúri.	Tédā.	Hausa.	Fulfúlde.
ich will, liebe — *I will, like*	rāg-ískin . / rā-skin . .	tánē de-rík[4] . / tánē dāro . .	ína sō . . .	mēdo-ídi . .
	3te P. tse-rāg-ena	me(rē) ke-da-de	ší ší-na sō .	kaṅko ó-ídi .
ich liebe dich — *I like you*	ní-ga-nze rāg-iskena	tánē nébre-hé dāro	ína sō-ńka .	mēdo-ídi-mā
ich will kaufen — *I will buy*	rāg-iskin ísi-skena	. . . . .	ína-sō én-sáā[10]	mēdo-ídi mē-sāda
ich will nicht — *I will not, dislike*	wā-nískin[1] .	tánē mas-erík[5]	bā ni-sō . .	mída[12] . . .
ich widerstrebe, fühle Abneigung — *I am disinclined*	wā-ígin . .	tánē ínai wan-erík[6]	nā-ki-a . .	mē-sálla-kē .
er will nicht — *he does not like*	wā-tsena . .	merā ardí-keni-n[7]	bā ší sō . .	kaṅko ó-ída .
er hat Abneigung — *he is disinclined, abhors*			yā-ki . . .	kaṅko ó-sálla-kē
ich kann — *I can, am able*	rāg-sásko[2] .	a-róng-erík[8]	ní íyā . . .	mēdo-aua . .
ich kann nicht, bin unfähig — *I cannot, am unable*	rāg-sásko bāgo	tánē róng-erí-n	ba ni íyā ba .	mēdo-ana-ta
ich übertreffe — *I excel*	. . . . .	. . . . . .	nā-fi[11] . . .	mē-būri . .
ich thue, mache — *I do, make*	dí-skin[3] . .	tánē ibén-erík[9]	ína yí . . .	mēdo-oddi .
	3te Pers. tsi-din	. . . . . .	ší ší-na yí .	. . . . .

[1] wā-nískin: wir können jetzt noch nicht entscheiden, ob die Verbalform dieses Wortes von ískin, dí-skin oder ní-skin ist; wā ist aber wol einerlei mit ba.

[2] rāg-sásko. Die einfache Form rásgin, die Koelle hat, habe ich nie gehört; dass sie aber wenigstens früher in Gebrauch gewesen ist, sieht man schon aus der engverwandten Tédā-Form a-róng-erík.

[3] Von diesem Wurzel-Zeitwort gebe ich weiter unten ein Paradigma.

[4] tánē de-rík. Die Wurzel scheint da zu sein; also vielleicht richtiger zu schreiben d(a)-erík. — merā ke-da-de unsicher; niedergeschrieben hatte ich me kiddadā.

[5] tánē mas-erík. Ich bin nicht ganz sicher über diese Form, da ich nur die Form des Präterit. mas-erdē habe.

[6] tánē ínai wan-erík. Da das k in dieser Form in alltäglicher Rede abgeworfen und auch das i häufig verschluckt wird, so hörte ich bei diesem sehr gewöhnlichen Worte nur die Form waner, doch zweifle ich nicht, dass wan-erík die richtige Form ist; ínai ist wol ín-ai, „dieses".

[7] merā ardí-keni-n. Dieses Verbum hängt offenbar mit dem Gesammte zusammen mit dem oben S. 56 aufgeführten Kanúri-Verbum ardí-nískin, das ganz wie das entsprechende Hausa-Wort nā-yirdā, das wir S. 52 aufführten, leicht die Bedeutung gewinnen kann „ich bin zufrieden" und mit der Negation „ich bin dagegen".

[8] a-róng-erík. Ich habe den euphonischen Vorschlag, der schon bei der Verbindung mit dem Pronom. pers. tánē verloren geht, hier nicht aufheben wollen.

[9] tánē ibén-erík. Daneben habe ich auch das Wort mandir (mand-erík?), setze es aber als ungewiss in die Note.

[10] ína-sō én-sáā. Ich will hier einige verwandte Ausdrücke hersetzen, die ich nur in der Hausa- und Fulfúlde-Sprache erfahren habe; so „ich wähle", H. na-sába, F. mō-subido; „ich ziehe vor", H. ni ná-fiesó (wo-ze abū), F. mō ma-bûri iggo, und dann die Phrase „wir ziehen Schöpsenfleisch vor, es ist besser als Rindfleisch", H. mū-óku fiesó nāma n rago, yā-fi nāma n sāno, F. handēl mín-bûri iggo tēó dḗodir, dum bûri tēó nai. In der letzten Phrase haben wir das Wort bûri in transitiver und in intransitiver Bedeutung.

[11] nā-fi. Dazu: „er übertrifft an Grösse", H. ší yā-fi girma, F. kaṅko ó-bûri mauudo; „sie übertreffen an Zahl, sind zahlreicher", H. sū sū-n-fi dówa, F. kombe bē-bûri dūde, S. ai biesa irkabā. — Begriffsverwandt sind auch die Worte ína basí(ka) im H., mē-sallóru(mā) im F. „ich bin stärker als du".

[12] míde, eigentlich mē íde.

[13] óga-biesa (bayó: bayó, „die Sache, etwas", drückt den Lokativ aus, wenn das Ausstechen Statt findet.

[14] inde-m-ógemi. Das m gehört nicht zum Worte, sondern ist der Akkusativ des demonstrativen Pronomen.

[15] wā-boka. Ich schreibe hier mit Bestimmtheit k, weil das einfache k doch wol nicht in g übergehen kann.

[16] wō-yá-wuá, „er liebt mich".

[17] ší ba-nyí; die Person Plur. kai wong-ya-nyí.

Sonyai.	Lógoné.	Wándalá.	Bágrimma.	Mába.
éga-bā	indo-m-ógomi [14]	wē-n-wéa .	mam géu . .	am áwe-ni
. . . . . .	ni-m-ágemi . .	wē-yá-weā [16]	. . . . . .	tí to-nyi [17]
. . . . . .	ógom-nī . . .	wē-na-wéa .	. . . . . .	. . . . . .
éga-hā tadé . .	. . . . . .	. . . . . .		
ésa-bá . . . . } éga-windi . . . }	wá-beka [15] . .	wē-n-ka . .	{ mam-gêi-lī . { mam-bátga .	} am (bon)gioyendī
. . . . . .	. . . . . .	. . . . . .	. . . . . .	
é-windi . . .	nī má-bega . .	wé-eu-ka . .	. . . . . .	. . . . . .
. . . . . .	indo ma wúdemnī	yé-bekén-beñā	mal-igība .	am ēgin
. . . . . .	. . . . . .	. . . . . .	. . . . . .	. . . . . .
éga-hima (hayō [13]	. . . . . .		. . . . . .	. . . . . .
éga-borínde (hayō	woyán(i	yé-magā . .	mát-ada . .	am andrīne
. . . . . .	noyán	á-magá-ne bá-ñganē	. . . . . .	. . . . . .

[1] wá-nishin: we are not able to decide, whether the verbal form of this word has been derived from ishin, di-shin or ni-shin; wā is most probably identical with ba.

[2] rág-sásho: I have not heard the simple form rāágin, which is found in Koelle's vocabulary, but I have no doubt, that it is used, as is shown already by the closely allied Tédā-form n-róág-erih or róág-erih.

[3] dí-shin: of some forms of this and the corresponding verbs in the other languages I give a paradigm lower down.

[4] tánō da-rih: the root of this word seems to be da and perhaps we ought to write d(a)-erih. — meri ba-da-de is uncertain.

[5] tánō mas-erik: I am not quite certain of this form, as I have only the form of the pret. más-ardā.

[6] tánī inai wan-erih. The final h being commonly elided and even the i being often slurred over in vulgar pronunciation, I heard the word wan-erih, which has passed into the most vulgar use, only pronounced as wanar, but I have not the slightest doubt, that wan-erih is right. — What inai is, I do not know.

[7] merā ardi-basi-n: this verbal form evidently is most closely allied with the Kanúri-word ardi-nishin cited above p. 64. For ardi-nishin, „I am content", as well as the corresponding Hausa-word na-yirdá p. 58 can easily obtain the meaning of „I agree with it" and in the negative form „I do not agree, I am opposed to it".

[8] n-róág-erih: I did not like to leave out the euphonic alliteration of n in the beginning of this word, although it does not belong to the root and is lost in the connection with tánō.

[9] tánō ibéu-erih: besides this word I have another one mandir (mand-erik!), which I prefer putting in the note.

[10] ina-cā ém-sīā: I think this a fit place for mentioning a few related terms, which I have only learnt in the Hausa- and Fulfúlde-languages: thus „I choose", H. na-zāba, F. mé-subide; „I prefer" (some-thing) H. ni na-fiasó (wa-ne abû), F. mō ma-bùri iggo, and thereto the phrase „we prefer mutton, (as) it is better than beef", H. mû-ñka fiesā nāma n regō, yā-fi nāma n šānū, F. handši min-bùri iggo tšé dāādir, dum bùri tšē nai. In this latter phrase we have the word bûri in a transitive as well as in an intransitive or neutral sense.

[11] nā-fiā: thereto the phrase „he excels in greatness, size, is greater", H. ŠI yā-fi girma, F. kaōko é-bùri mawnde; „they excel in number, are more numerous", H. sū sū-n-fi dūwa, F. hambe bē-bùri dūde, S. ai bisse irkaña. A similar meaning have also the words ina boai (ka) in H. and mé-sallōra (má) in F., „I am stronger (than you)".

[12] mīda, properly mé ida.

[13] éga-bīssa (hayō: the term hayō, „the thing, some-thing", represents the object, in which the excelling takes place.

[14] indo-m-ógomī: the m does not belong to the word, but is the accus. of the demonstrative pronoun.

[15] wá-beka: I have write on purpose k, as I scarcely think, the simple k can be changed into a g.

[16] wē-yá-weā, „he likes me".

[17] tí to-nyi: 3rd pers. plur. kai weóg-ye-nyi.

Deutsch und Englisch.	Kanúri.	Tēdā.	Hausa.	Fulfulde.
was wollen wir thun? — *what shall we do?*	á-fi di-yen .	fui indi kisseri[3]	mē-nēne mū-nyi	kō { min-gadī / min-hádli }
ich habe, besitze — *I have, possess*	ū-ma nā-ndin[1]	tánē tá-rik[4] .	nī ína da (wo-ne abū[6]	meng mē-dōdi (dum
du hast, besitzest — *you have, possess s.*	nī-ma nā-nemin	nebrē ta-m .	{ kai ká-na da (wo-ne abū / ki kí-na da (wo-ne abū }	ang áda-wōdi (dum
er hat — *he has* / sie hat — *she has*	šī-ma ná-nisin	mere ye-tá .	{ šī ší-na da (wo-ne abū / ita tá-na da (wo-ne abū }	kaṅko ó-mōdi (dum / kaṅko debbo ó-mōdi (dum
wir haben, besitzen — *we have, possess*	ándi-ma nā-ndin	tinia ta-tá .	mū mū-na da (wo-ne abū	enne[9] mēdong gōdi (dum
ihr habt — *you have, pl.*	nándi-ma ná-ndun	nebrai kye-tá-wen?	kū kū-na da (wo-ne abū	ónom ōdun gōdi (dum
sie haben — *they have* .	séndi-ma ná-nisan	ánala yo-tá-wen	sū sū-na da (wo-ne abū	kam-bē ōdun gōdi (dum
ich halte, halte fest — *I hold, hold fast*	tá-skin[2] . . . 3te Prs. S. tsa-tin	kába tá-rik[5]	{ ína kāma . / ína riki[7] . . }	{ mēdo-wōdi . / mēdo-džōgi . }
halte, halt' fest — *hold, hold fast*	tči	tó-rō . . .	{ kāma . . . / rike . . . }	. . . . . .
ich nehme — *I take* .	{ gō-ńskin . / gò-ngin . . }	tánē { ma-rik . / ma-rik . }	ína kāma . .	mó-nanga (hunde
nimm — *take*	gō-ne . . .	. . . .	kāma	. . . . . .
ich empfange, nehme in Empfang — *I receive*	. . . . . .	. . . . . .	{ ína karba . / ína amsa[8] . }	mēdo-džobba

[1] ū-ma nā-ndin. Koelle hat diese höchst gewöhnliche Phrase nicht, obgleich er das Substantiv nā in den verschiedensten Beziehungen erklärt. Ob daher unsere Phrase abgeleitet ist, ist allerdings nicht gewiss, scheint aber doch der Fall zu sein, obgleich ich selbst lange gezweifelt habe und es eine Zeit lang mit dem Arabischen [illegible] in Verbindung bringen wollte. Die Phrase hätte also substantivische Form, „ich, Besitz von mir", u. s. w. Die Form der 1sten Person Sing. ndin ist auffallend.

[2] tá-skin. Das s nähert sich sehr dem c, wie man aus dem Imperativ sieht. Koelle hat dieses Wort zweimal, einmal in dieser Form, dann als tángin (mein kúla-n tá-ngin), „ich erinnere mich"; denn die Form Ki tákšíin ist wol unrichtig.

[3] kisseri ist offenbar von einer ganz anderen Wurzel, deren Gebrauch mir aber sonst nicht bekannt geworden; ob 3te Prs. S.?

[4] tánē tá-rik scheint mir eigentlich nicht die Bedeutung „haben" zu besitzen, und es gibt wol noch einen besseren Ausdruck dafür; im gewöhnlichen Leben aber sagt man sogar ta-ré wie ta-m.

[5] kába tá-rik; 3te Person kába yo-tá-de. Auch tá-rik allein wird in der Bedeutung „festhalten" gebraucht.

[6] nī ína da (wo-ne abū, wörtlich „ich bin mit" oder „von (dieser Sache)".

[7] ína riki ist eigentlich keineswegs gleichbedeutend mit ína kāma, sondern es ist der Gegensatz zu sehi, „loslassen".

[8] ína amsa. Beispiel: „er hat das Geld in Empfang genommen", H. 31 ya-ámsa kurdi, F. ó-džebbi džōde. In weiterer Folge hat amsa die Bedeutung „antworten" erhalten.

[9] enne mēdong gōdi. Wir haben hier beide Formen für „wir", énne(ne und mē-dong; vgl. S. 2.

[10] kére agénde kayō ist eine sehr ungrammatisch und unkünstlerisch konstruirte Phrase, und die gebildeteren Bórnui, zumal in den noch unabhängigen Provinzen müssen andere Ausdrücke dafür haben.

[11] ŕga-kerénde kayō ist noch barbarischer als das Vorhergehende.

[12] nī ná-ta-kā ist eine höchst zweifelhafte Form; wahrscheinlich nī nág-nāi.

[13] wāk-ena. Für die 3te Person habe ich die Form nī nág-nāi, offenbar = nág-nai.

[14] y(e)-ikawá-wán; 3te Person ikawa ká-áganē.

[15] ágés én matédíŋ. ágés bedeutet „die Sache", und in én (wol = én-din) muss das Pronomen interrog. enthalten sein.

[16] á-mé ēta, „bei mir ist".

[17] y-á-ī ēta. Das Pronomen yī, „Du", ist durch Einschaltung des Vokals á, der „mit" bedeutet, in zwei Wörter getheilt = á-yī, S. 5.

[18] Ich habe hier die Form ncaé-ágé, aber sie gehört wenigstens der Wurzel nach keinesfalls hierher.

[19] ga-moréágte genl. genī heisst „was?"; ga-moréágte ist mir unbekannt.

Sonγai.	Lógoné.	Wándalá.	Bagrimma.	Mába.
mē girlena bantaē?	moyán wúö-na .	núndže luē? .	ngáséu matádiā [15]	ga-marúgle-genī [19]
egónde (hayò	nág-a-ú . . .	azé-ruā	á-mā ētu [16] .	am a-nē
	kan nág-a-kú .	azé-úga . .	y-á-ı ētu [17] .	mī mi-nē
bōro egónde (hayō [10]	ní ná-te-kā [12] .	azé-ŭgarē . .	nesé-ŏge [18] .	tī te-nē
éga-barándo (hayō [11]	mē nág-a-mu .	azé-ŭgerē . .	á-džō ētu . .	maúg me-nē
. . . .	wuni nág-a-kū .	azé-kur wókorē	á-sē ētu . .	kaúg ke-nē .
bor (flaume egónde hayò	dúngyu) nág-a-tén	azé-terē . .	á-džigi ētu .	wang we-nē
éga-yári . . .	wák-ena [13] . .	y(e)-ikswá-wēā [14]	mani-úngā .	am adáwe
. . . . . .	. . . . . .	ganáŭga . .	. . . . .	. . . . . .
éga-hayò-(e) di	indo wa-sé-(ni .	y(e)-ikaán duksa	mak-nuu . .	maláŭgne
éda	sé (ni	ikaán duksa .	nuu	daŭga
éga-tūnta . . .	. . . . . .	. . . . . .	. . . . .	. . . . . .

[1] á-me nā-ndin: This very common phrase is wanting in Koelle, although he gives the substantive nà with a good many different notions. I myself am not quite sure of our nā-ndin being thence derived, but it is more than probable, nā having a very general signification, comprising possession, dwelling, place etc. If this is right, the phrase á-me nā-ndin would properly mean „I, property of me", „it belongs to me", „I have". I once thought that the phrase might be connected with the Arabic ﻋﻨﺪ, but that is scarcely possible. However in our case the d in the 1st pers. sing. nā-ndin is, no doubt, very remarkable and perhaps not correct.

[2] tá-ekin: the a approaches closely to an e, as is seen from the form of the imperative. Koelle has this word twice, once in this form, and besides in the form tágin (= my kéla-n té-ekona); the form for the 3rd pers. sing. ši takšūn which he gives is, as far as I know, not correct.

[3] kiecetel evidently belongs to a root totally different from that of the preceding word. It may be the 3rd pers. sing.

[4] tánē té-rik does not seem to me to imply the proper meaning of „to have" and the Tédā may have another more distinct form for expressing this notion; in common life they use the form ta-ré for the 1st, and ta-m for the 2nd pers.

[5] kāba té-rik; 3rd pers. sing. kāba ye-té-de. Even té-rik alone is used with the notion of „I hold fast".

[6] ni lan da (we-ne ahū, verbally „I am with" or „of this thing".

[7] ina riki properly is not identical with ina kāma, but is the decided reverse of ochi, „to let loose".

[8] ina emna. As an example illustrating this meaning of „I receive" I here insert the phrase „he has received the money", H. ši ya-émoa hurdi, F. ó-dšebbi taōde.

[9] onne mēdoñg yēdi: onne is not the common form of the pronoun, although p. 3 we have ánne(ne besides mē-doñg.

[10] bóro egónde hayò is construed in a most ungrammatical and imperfect manner. Indeed some other phrases in the S. language were so rude, that I did not even venture to write them down, nevertheless they are used. But the higher class of Sonγai-people in the provinces, which are still independent, must possess other forms.

[11] éga-barándo hayò is a phrase still more barbarous than the preceding one.

[12] ni ná-te-kā is a remarkable form and probably not right; we expect ni nag-nu.

[13] wák-ena: for the form of the 3rd pers. I have ni nág-alé, evidently identical with nag-ani.

[14] y(e)-ikswá-wēā: 3rd pers. ikswa ká-ŭganē.

[15] ŭgáo én matádié: ŭgao means „thing, object", and én (= ēn-dia) therefore must represent the interrogative pronoun.

[16] á-mā ētu, „there is with me".

[17] y-á-ī ētu: the pronoun yī, „thou", has apparently been separated in two by intruding between them the vowel a signifying „with"; therefore y-á-ī is = a-yī, p. 5.

[18] I have written down the form nesé-ŏge, but although it may have the meaning of „he has", it does not properly belong hither.

[19] ga-marúgle genī: genī means „what?"; ga-marúgle I am not able to analyse.

Deutsch und Englisch.	Kanuri.	Tēdā.	Hausa.	Fulfulde.
Ich gebe (dir — *I give (thee*	ni-rū) yí-akin [1]	yé-rik [6] / nin-rik	nī bā (ka)	mĕdo-hokku (má
Ich gebe (dir) nicht — *I do not give (thee*	ní-rū) yí-skin bágo	yé-ri-n	ba ni bá (ka) ba	mĕdo-hokka-tá-(ma
gib (mir — *give (me*	ñĕ / tšĕ ú-rō	ye-n [7]	bā (ni	hokk(a) (am
Ich gebe mehr, lege zu — *I add, give more*	yirgá-skin [2]	sirkás-erík [8] / kodín nin-rik	ína kāra	mĕdo-bĕde / mĕdo-beuda
Ich ziehe ab, gebe weniger — *I give less, withdraw*	fulū-ñgin [3]	fulū-n-erík [9]	ína ragĕ	mĕdo-busta
Ich gebe zurück, bezahle — *I return, pay back*	rambú-skin	samór-n-erík	nī bā (ka) abí-n-ka [11] / nī māyes (ma-kā [12])	mĕdo-hokku-mā dum-mā [14]
Ich leihe, verleihe (dir — *I lend (you*	ní-rō) tégeri dí-skin [4]	tánĕ yeńkai-n-erík	ína ramtšĕ (ma-kā	mĕdo-hókku-(mā) ramtšĕ
leihe (mir — *lend (me*	tégeri sege nĕ(?)	yeńkai ti-n	ramtšĕ me-ni	ramtšĕ dumĕ
Ich entlehne (von dir — *I lend from (you*	nā-nemin [5]) tégeri niskin	tánĕ éreni ren-erík [10]	zāni ramtšĕ(garĕ-ka [13]	mĕdo-ramtšo(ho-mā [15]

[1] yi-skin. Koelle schreibt gleichfalls yiskin, und führt als Beispiel an wu nirō nem tšiskin, „ich gebe dir ein Haus", wo tšiskin die durch nirō motivirte objective Inflection sein soll, die ich aber in dieser so gewöhnlichen Phrase nicht ein einziges Mal gehört habe.

[2] yirgá-skin. Ich hatte irgá-skin geschrieben, aber die Vergleichung mit dem eng verwandten Tēdā-Wort hat mich bewogen, das y besonders auszudrücken. Dasselbe Wort scheint auch beinahe anzuzeigen, dass das s mit zum Stamme gehört und dass wir daher auch im Kanúri richtiger yirgás-skin schreiben würden; doch könnte die Wurzel [illegible] sein.

[3] fulū-ñgin hat Koelle nicht. — Für rambú-skin hat er drei Formen, rambúskin, rembúskin und rumbúskin.

[4] ní-rō) tégeri dí-skin. Diese Phrase hat Koelle gleichfalls nicht. Es scheint mir, dass tégeri kein einheimisches Wort ist, sondern dass es mit dem Berberischen Vorschlag te vom Arabischen kerā abgeleitet ist. Die volle Form mit nirō nach der objectiven Inflection ist tégeri tatdi-skin, ntsédeskin bei Koelle, Gr. §. 108. Im Übrigen entsprechen sich di-skin als Activum und ni-skin als Passivum vollkommen. Nur sollte man im Imperativ für „leihe mir" anstatt tegeri segé né, tégeri ú-rō dē erwarten; aber wir haben hier wirklich ein Beispiel der objectiven Inflection. Koelle Gr. §. 94.

[5] ná-nemin ist wörtlich „an deiner Stelle" = Koelle's nánémmé; tégeri ní-skin, „ich mache" oder „ich nehme ein Anlehen".

[6] yé-rik. Anstatt yé-rik ist der Gebrauch von kúrt-erík auch für „geben" sehr allgemein, wie eine Verwechselung dieser beiden Ausdrücke auch in anderen Sprachen ganz gewöhnlich ist.

[7] ye-n. Für diesen Imperativ wird neben kurtn auch die Form ti-n gebraucht, deren Ableitung mir aber nicht bekannt ist.

[8] sirkás-erík, s. Note 2. Das s im Anfange steht dem y auch so nahe, dass der Imperativ deutlich yirkás lautet.

[9] fulū-n-erík. Neben diesem Ausdruck habe ich einen andern, in Kānem gebräuchlichen, nämlich nōn kirdinne, über dessen nähere Beziehung ich jedoch unsicher bin.

[10] tánĕ éreni ren-erík. Ich bin fest überzeugt, dass éreni eigentlich égereni heissen sollte, also mit dem entsprechenden tégeri eng verwandt ist.

[11] ni bā (ka) abí-n-ka, wörtlich „ich gebe dir deine Sache"; Imperativ: „gieb mir das Meinige", bā-ni abí-na.

[12] nī māyes (ma-kā. Beispiel: „geh' nur, gieb es mir morgen oder übermorgen zurück", H. taff, ka-māyes gobĕ kō djībi, F. hoffi hōra kō dāngo kō fābi dāngo.

[13] zāni ramtšĕ garé-ka, eigentlich „ich komme, von dir zu leihen".

[14] mĕdo-hókku-mā dum-mā; „gieb mir das Meinige", hokk(a) am dum-ang.

[15] mĕdo-ramtšo (ho-mā. Von dieser Redensart gebe ich am Ende ein Paradigma.

[16] ĕga dĕchbu sieht mir aus, als wenn es aus der Fulfúlde-Sprache übertragen wäre.

[17] é-garéwa. Die Wurzel ist garáwa und es sollte eigentlich ĕga-garáwa heissen.

[18] wa-bá (ni, ni, „ihm", also die Wurzel ba identisch mit dem Hausa und eins der nicht häufigen, aber sicheren Beispiele einer Übereinstimmung zwischen diesen beiden Sprachen. Siehe die Einleitung. — mu[illegible] ba-kō weiterhin heisst „deine Schuld".

[19] wá-nta-ā nág-akū, „ich entlehne deine Sache", scheint richtig, aber in der zweitvorhergehenden Phrase ist nág-akū kaum richtig.

[20] Für „ich gebe nicht" habe ich im W. ye-wilka, aber dies gehört wenigstens der Wurzel nach nicht hierher.

[21] mak-ád-a; Präter. m-ád-iga. — mándago (mam-ándago) vgl. weiter unten, eigentlich „ich kaufe eine Schuld".

[22] am ba taháí-ne. Das ba gehört nicht zum Worte selbst; Imperativ: táhaia.

[23] [illegible]) ar-mángadi, mit der folgenden Phrase verglichen, lässt mich über die Wurzel in Zweifel.

Sonyai.	Lógonē.	Wándalā.	Bágrimma.	Mába.
ég-em-íno (hayō	wu-bá (ni[18] . .	yo-sō (hāya .	mak-ád-a[21] .	am a-nár-ne
és-em-íno (hayō	wu-bá (nī)-sā .	[20]	mak-ád-ó-lī	am a-nár-tā-ndo
éno (hayō . . .	ha-n	í-sā	ád-im-džo .	nar (ambēne
éga-tónta (nisse	wu-bá kōfa narē	ye-kuírikse .	mak-órna . .	am ba takúl-ne[22]
éga-džebbu (hayō[16]	w-áχdilbā . . .	yé-gunáguna .	ngáa ne) mak-imbāsa	am anyáng-ne
ég-ení (háyo-te(o)	{wúse-rū wúleku uwákulgō / indo ma wu-bī mu(?)lím na-ku}	y-ápelā . .	mam-ák ad-1	
é-garáwa (ni)[17] .	wú-nta-ū roiši nág-akū	yé-ke(u) al tekse gemá	ma-tilka-džō	litto ne-nángedi[23]
gárawāt . . .	í-nta-ūgo . . .	ksé tekse gemā-ra	tilka-m-džō .	. . . . .
. . . . . .	wú-nta-ū nág-akū[19]	yé-kse ázena	{mándugo rēgi mok-un kada ruiki}	litto) ne-égu-nyēro unnami

[1] yi-akin: Koelle likewise writes yiakin, and adduces as an example the phrase wa nirō nem tiliakin, „I give you a house", in which case tiliakin or rather atiliakin (see his gr. § 107, p. 130) is to be taken as an example of euphonic inflection caused by nirō, but I have not instanced a single time such a change in this very common phrase. See the Introduction.

[2] yirgá-skin: I had written irgá-skin, but a comparison with the corresponding Tédā-word has induced me to express the y sound by an express sign; compare note 8. The same Tédā-word seems to show, that the root itself has a final e, and it might therefore perhaps be better to write yirgáe-skin.

[3] fulē-ágin is wanting in Koelle. Root not known to me. rambú-skin he writes in three different ways rambúskin, rembúskin and rumbúskin.

[4] ni-rō) tégeri di-skin: this phrase is wanting in Koelle. However I am almost sure, that tégeri is not an indigenous term, but that it has been derived from the Arabic word kerā giving it the Berber prefix te. The full euphonical form of the phrase in connection with ni-rō is tégeri tai-diskin (ntedeskin with Koelle; see his gr. § 112); while on the whole di-skin as the active, „lending", „giving a loan", and ni-skin as the passive notion, „taking a loan", correspond perfectly. As for the form tégeri segē nē we have here a remarkable example of that objective inflexion which Rev. Koelle calls one of the most remarkable peculiarities of the Kanúri-language. See his grammar § 98.

[5] nē-nemin (the nánemme of Kl.) verbally means „(in) thy place"; tégeri ni-skin, „I make" (in a passive sense) or „take a loan".

[6] yé-rik: instead of this word the use of kár-terik in this sense is very general, and we find a confusion of these two terms common with many people.

[7] yo-n: besides this imperative and kurtu also the form ti-n is used, the derivation of which however is not known to me.

[8] sirkáe-srik: see note 2. The e in the beginning of this word is so clearly a mere corruption of the y, that the form of the imp. mood is still yirkáe.

[9] fulū-n-srik. besides this term I have noted down another one, which is used especially by the Tédā population of Kánem, viz nōn kirdinue, but I am not able to analyze it and am uncertain as to its form.

[10] tané évent ren-srik: I am fully persuaded, that évent should be égrent or égerent and is intimately allied by a common root with the Kanúri term tégeri.

[11] ni bá (ka) sbi-á-ka verbally „I give thee thy thing"; imp. „give me my thing", bá-ni sbi-ae.

[12] ai méyen (me-kī; as an example I cite the following phrase: „go, (but) return it me to morrow or the day after to morrow", H. taffi, ka-máyee gobé kō djibi, F. betši hára kō diángo hō čibi diángo.

[13] sáni remtšē garē-ka, properly „I come to lend from you".

[14] médo-hékhu-mā dum-mā, „I give thee thy property"; „give me my property", hokk(a) am dum-áng.

[15] médo-ramtšo (he-mī; of this phrase I shall give a grammatical paradigma further on.

[16] éga džebbu has the appearance, as if it were taken from the Fulfúlde-language.

[17] é-garáwa; the root is garáwa and the full form of the 1st person of the present tense is éga-garáwa.

[18] wu-bá (ni: ni, „him", so that we have the root ba fully identical with the Hausa-word and one of the few examples of a near relation between these two languages. See the introduction. — mu(?)lím na-kū further on means „thy debt".

[19] wú-nta-ū nag-akū, „I lend thy thing", seems to be right, but in the preceding phrase nág-akū can scarcely be right.

[20] For the phrase „I do not give" in the Wándalā-language I have the form ya-wiika, but this does not belong to this place, at least as far as regards the root.

[21] mak-ád-a, past tense m-ád-iga. — mándugo (mem-andugo) régi, further on, properly means „I buy a debt".

[22] am ba takúl-ne; the ba does not belong to the verb; imp. tákala.

[23] litto) ne-nángedi compared with the following phrase leaves some doubt about the root.

Deutsch und Englisch.	Kanuri.	Tedâ.	Hausa.	Fulfulde.
ich bringe — *I bring* .	kot-ískin [1] . 3te P. S. tši-kot-in	kurt-erik . .	ina kāu . .	mēdo-wadda .
bringe — *bring* . . .	kot-é . . .	kurta . . .	kāu	waddu . . .
ich verweigere, stosse zurück — *I refuse, reject*	dēm-nískin [2] . 3te P. S. dem-tšin deb-tšin	[6]	ina kōra	mēdo-riwi . . . . . .
ich entlasse, scheide mich von einer Frau — *I divorce a (my) wife*	kāmo dem-nískin	ádi-bi söb-erik	ina kōra māta [8]	mēdo-dotárfa raabe
ich hebe (in die Höhe — *I raise*	fari-rō) am-nískin [3]	gon-erik [7] . .	ina dauki (bisa	mēdo-hōya . / mēdo-boiše .
hebe (in die Höhe — *raise*	fari-rō) am-nē	gōno	dauki (bisa .	hoi / boiše } dō .
ich nehme ab, lade ab — *I take down, unload*	šāg-ískin [4] . .	. . . . . .	ina sebkás [9] .	mēdo-džippini
nimm (das Gepäck) ab — *take down (the load*	šāg-ē (kerre) .	gōne (faṅgo . / yēte (fakko .	sebkás (kaya .	džippe (kayádžibe / dāga doug gelōba
ich stelle, lege hin — *I put, place*	genā { nískin / ūgin [5] . }	tánē nák-erik	ní ina ažā . .	mēdo-yawa . / mēdo-rrsan . / mēdo-rōto .
stelle hin — *put down* .	genā-nē . .	nak	ažō	rōla . . . . / rrs . . . . .

[1] kot-iskin hat Koelle in der Form kóskin, kótçskin; es hängt wol jedenfalls mit kaw im H. zusammen.
[2] dem-nískin hat eine viel weitere Bedeutung, als die meisten der gegenüberstehenden Wörter der anderen Sprachen, aber es wird doch wol nur vom moralischen „Lassen" oder „Loslassen" gebraucht und kommt am gewöhnlichsten in der Phrase vor dem-nē li-gá, „lass' ihn, lass' ihn machen was er will". In weiterer Entwickelung dieses moralischen Loslassens bekommt der Ausdruck die Bedeutung der Ehescheidung, die Koelle, der das Wort démgin schreibt, gar nicht erwähnt, aber doch in der Phrase barge kámmó débgeskin, die er dann anführt, berührt, indem sie, kámo, kámo-rō anstatt kám-mō gesetzt, heisst „ich (verstosse die Frau nicht im Zorn", sondern) „entlasse sie mit einem Segen". Koelle's démgin ist dasselbe Wort.
[3] Koelle hat die Form ám-gin als die gewöhnliche, aber ich zweifle, ob sie in dieser Bedeutung je in Gebrauch ist, da sie die einzig gebräuchliche Form für das fast gleiche Verbum ist, das „ich bin kalt, werde kalt" bedeutet, obgleich ich dieses letztere Wort ham-gin mit h schreibe, wie ich auch ham-sa (Koelle amása) schreibe. Die 3te Person unterscheidet diese beiden Verba auch in Koelle's Schreibweise sehr deutlich, indem sie bei unserm Verbum aptšin lautet, beim andern aber amtšin.
[4] šāg-iskin. Koelle schreibt ság-eskin und hat auch einen anderen Ausdruck waséágin.
[5] genā-ūgin. Koelle schreibt genéngin und genáágin.
[6] Die Tedâ scheinen kein allgemeines Wort für diese Bedeutung zu haben; in gewissen Beziehungen gebrauchen sie dafür kúrt-eri-n, „ich bringe nicht, gebe nicht" (3te Person Sing. merō ye-kúrt-eni-n), ganz ebenso, wie im Máha am-e-nár-tā-nde gebraucht wird.
[7] gōn-erik hat nur missbräuchlich die Bedeutung des Emporhebens erhalten, so wie es auch in seiner allgemeinen Bedeutung des Aufnehmens vom Herabnehmen gebraucht werden kann. Die Tedâ besitzen dafür wol noch ein ungleich prägnanteres Wort.
[8] ina kōra māta, māta im H., wie raabe im F., ist Pluralform, aber ich habe das Verbum mit dem Singular matše oder debbo (Sing. von raabe) nie gebraucht gefunden. — Verwandte Ausdrücke sind im H. sarro(?) bada de māta, im F. mēdo-walzi raabe.
[9] ina sebkás ist die transitive Form von ina sébka, „ich steige ab". Das s finden wir im Anfang des Wortes mit solcher Bedeutung auch in anderen Sprachen, am Ende des Wortes kann es aber wol diese Bedeutung nicht haben, sondern ist wol ursprüngliche Abkürzung von si, „es".
[10] ēga-fōnen ist eine kleine Dialektverschiedenheit von dem vorhergehenden.
[11] gimenē weist natürlich eine ganz andere Wurzel voraus als ēga-donde, aber es wird in den anderen Modis wol nicht gebraucht.
[12] walnādija. Das Wort „Frau", genem, scheint nicht besonders ausgedrückt werden zu müssen.
[13] Ich hatte hier debe niedergeschrieben; vielleicht ist es (?) imbi, imbi, „das Gepäck", wie oben imbi nie, „dieses Gepäck", „diese Sachen".
[14] Ich habe schon oben bemerkt, dass die Máha kein allgemeines Wort für „verweigern" haben. In gewissen Fällen sagen sie am-a-nár-tā-nde, „ich gebe nicht".
[15] ma-nía dáng ist völliger Gegensatz zu ma-nia kadawa, „ich lade auf"; nur scheint mir beides 1ste Person Plur. und nicht Sing.

Sekyani.	Légumi.	Wándala.	Bágrimma.	Mába.
égu-hámse-ne (hayō	wa-dō	yé-senā . .	mam-desínya .	. . . . . .
	3rd prs. s. ni ya-dō	á-senā . .	. . . . .	. . . . . .
éga-fúnsu [10] . .				
hamse . . . . / funsu	dō	senā . . .	desínya . . .	. . . . . .
éga-gáro (hayō .	wú-malá . . .	yé-džahā . .	mák-ogō . .	[11]
. . . . . .	3rd pers. sing. ni yá-malá	3rd prs. s. á-džahā	. . . . .	. . . . . .
éga-yénde wai .	wa-isādžia [13] . .	yé-balá-balá mukső	mok-ung ne-ua	am alaig-ne
éga-zau (he . .	wa-si wa . . .	ye-kē kántekán (dúmdžiglā	mam-úkurā .	tal uudúng-ue
zau(ṅga bōne . .	si(gi) wa-hā . .	kánteká . .	. . . . .	. . . . . .
éga-simínde (hayō	imbialetzom wa-tēn	ye-ksanáksa .	ma-dís (kálkouā	ma-nín dāori [15]
			dis yú (kálkonā	
éga-donde . .	indo wa-lēn . .	yé-fofā . . .	mam-ak-fuda	andúng-ta
gissenē [11] . . .	[12]	fofō (χenā . .	índa	. . . . . .

[1] kot-lokin: Koelle has this term with the form kúskin, kútṣekin; it can scarcely be doubted, that it is connected with the Hausa-word kau.

[2] dem-niakin: this term has a far wider notion, than most of the corresponding words of the other languages, but it is mostly used in a moral sense of letting or forsaking a person, as one of the most common phrases of daily life is dem-nā ži-gā, „let him alone, let him do what he chooses" and it is only a further step in this direction that the term obtains the notion of divorcing a wife, although Koelle who writes démgin, does not mention the latter; but at the same time he adduces a phrase horge hámmé děhgrokin, which with a slight change, hámo, hámo-yé being written instead of hámmé means „I (do not divorce my wife in a fit of rage, but) dismiss her (in peace) with a blessing".

[3] am-niakin: Koelle has the form ám-gin, but I doubt, whether this form is ever used in the sense, of which we are here treating, while it is the only form used of the almost identical verb with the meaning „I am" or „grow cold", although I prefer writing the latter ham-gin, as I write also ham-on, „cold", the amáoe of Koelle. However the 3rd pers. distinguishes these two verbs, even in the way, in which Koelle writes them, our word forming áp-tšin and the other one ámtšin (ham-tšin).

[4] ság-fokin: Koelle writes ság-ṣekin.

[5] genī-ágin: Koelle writes gandágin and gnaágin.

[6] The Tédā do not seem to have a word for this rather comprehensive notion and in certain cases use the term kárí-erí-n, „I do not give" or „bring" (3rd pers. sing. merō ye-kárí-rai-n) just as in Maba om a-nár-ti-nde is used.

[7] gán-erik, „I grasp, take", only abusively is used with the notion of „I raise", as it is even used for „I take down". But I suspect, the Tédā possess other more expressive terms.

[8] fan kára máta: máta in H. as raube in F. are plural forms of matše and debbo, but I have never heard this verb used with the singular. A phrase of a related notion is in H. aurro(?) bnda da máta, F. médo-wairi raube.

[9] ine sahkén is the transitive form of ine sébba, „I descend". The s in the formation of verbal clauses has very frequently such a transitive influence, at least when added in the beginning, but here I suspect it to have arisen originally from II., „it".

[10] éga-fúnsu is a mere dialectical difference of the preceding form.

[11] gissenē of course has nothing to do with éga-donde, but it is not used in the other moods.

[12] wateādžia: it seems, as if the word „woman", genem, need not be distinctly expressed.

[13] I had written down the form debe, but I suppose, it ought to be tō imbi, imbi meaning „luggage", „things".

[14] I have already observed before, that the Mába do not seem to have a general word for „I refuse"; in certain cases they say om-a-nár-ti-nde, „I do not give".

[15] ma-nin dāori is the distinct reverse of ma-nin kudáwe, „I load upon"; but I suspect both forms to be the 1st pers. plur. and not sing.

Deutsch und Englisch.	Kanúri.	Tédā.	Hausa.	Fulfúlde.
ich suche — *I search, look for*	mā-nískin [1] . / mā-ágin . .	táné fúlonū .	ina nēma . / ina bidda .	mēdo-dabbo . / mēdo-rarta [12]
was suchst du? — *what are you looking for?*	áfī mān-emin	indi kúrmidē .	mē ká-na nēma [8] / mē ká-ke bidda	kō on-dárta-ta
ich finde, erreiche, erlange — *I find, get, reach*	fand-iskin [2] .	táné fáng-erík [6] / ū-báng-erík	ina sāmo [9] . .	mēdo-hebbi [13]
hast du gefunden? — *have you found?*	fánd-emī . .	ū-báng-emī .	ka-sámo-sī .	hebbī-mō . / áyetī-dum .
ich bringe Nachrichten, benachrichtige — *I inform*	labár { nōt-iskin / kú-skin	nobád-erík . / nefád-erík .	ina kāu labári	mēdo-wadda hábbaru
ich schicke, ich sende — *I send, despatch, forward*	nōt-iskin [3] .	dōgo derík? . / kón-erík . .	ina aiko . .	mēdo-nīla .
ich zeige (dir — *I show (thee*	felē- { nískin . . / ágin [4] .	n-ūkedús-erík / korús-erík [7] .	ina { núna [10] / góda } (ma-) ká	mēdo-bolli (má
ich zeige nicht — *I do not show*	felē-ágin bágo .	n-ūkedús-erī-n	ba nūna (ma-kā) ba	mēdu-bólla-tá (má
zeige (mir) den Pfad — *show (me) the path*	dibbel (ú-rō) felē-nē	ī-úkedús tériā	ka-gōda (me-nī) hanya	bolla am { dattal / lawel
ich führe — *I conduct, lead*	yāt-iskin [5] . .	táné nkúrk-erík	ina kāu . . / na-ī ma-ka rék-kia [11]	mēdo-dōptu-ma

[1] mā-nískin. Auch derí-nískin (dérīágin bei Koelle), im Tédā derí-nerík, eigentlich „ich mache einen Umkreis, ich gehe herum", hat die Bedeutung „suchen". So áfī deri-tšin, „was sucht er?"

[2] fand-iskin. Koelle schreibt pánd-eskin. Ganz auf denselben Begriff des Erreichens, Findens beruht die Redensart áfī ni-gà (ī-gà u. s. w.) tsé-fand-ĕ, „was hat dich (ihn) befallen?"

[3] nōt-iskin. Koelle schreibt nōt-eskin mit dem unbestimmten e, aber ich halte das i hier für sehr wesentlich, da es eine Handlung, nicht einen passiven Zustand anzeigt. nō-te, „die Kenntniss", von nō-nískin, nō-ágin; nōt-iskin, „ich gebe Kenntniss, melde"; nōtō, „das Kenntniss-Geben, die Botschaft".

[4] felē-ágin, Koelle pelēágin.

[5] yāt-iskin. Koelle schreibt yá-skin und yát-eskin, und, indem er es mit dem ganz verschiedenen ya-skin verwechselt, giebt er ihm Bedeutungen, die es nicht hat, wie „nehmen, wegnehmen".

[6] táné fáng-erík. Auch hier sind die gewöhnlichen Formen fánger, ū-bánger; 1ste Person des Präterit. in negativer Form ū-báng-erī-n.

[7] korús-erík ist vielleicht nur eine dialektische Verschiedenheit des ūkedús-erík, besonders wenn wir das letztere mit dem weichen d schreiben.

[8] mē ká-na nēma. Ich will hier auch noch die Redensart hersetzen „suche sorgfältig", K. mánē ngilla, H. nēma néggarī, F. dábbitē-mā oder rartu bōdum, S. tamba húre (hayō.

[9] sāmo in Verbindung mit karfi ist auch ein Kriegsausdruck: sū sun-sāmo karfī, „sie haben Kraft gefunden", „sie haben sich verstärkt", F. be-hébī sembē.

[10] ina núna ist der in Kátsena, ina góda der in Góber übliche Hausa-Ausdruck.

[11] na-ī ma-kà rékkia ist allerdings nicht das gewöhnliche Wort vom gemeinen Führer, sondern von einem grösseren Geleit zur Ehre oder zur Sicherheit; Imperat. ka-ī me-nī rékkia, F. dopta.

[12] mēdo-rarta. In Sókoto wenigstens ist noch ein drittes Wort in Gebrauch, nämlich mō-dēna, aber mit der üblen Nebenbedeutung vom „Nachlaufen hinter den Frauen". Ähnlich wird auch das Hausa-Wort na-ī nēma gebraucht, und daher das Adjektiv ma-ī-nēma.

[13] mēdo-hebbi. Daher das Substantiv hebbel, „der Fund", Gegensatz zu „Verdienst", wie das Sprichwort sagt: hebbel búrī bamka, „finden ist besser als verdienen", auf H. sámo yáfī ī-rewa.

[14] ādu sieht nicht wie die richtige Form der 1sten Person Präs. aus.

[15] maltšaba fondo hat nicht das Aussehen einer Zeitform.

[16] ai mála-kū. Ich habe hier auch die Form wúhakū, aber ich bin ihretwegen noch ungewiss.

[17] awa heisst „he da!" und gehört nicht zur eigentlichen Phrase.

[18] marīa mérmele āngulō. maria ist wahrscheinlich eine verkürzte Form von mánskin; „mir" heisst marā. was ist nun mérmele? āngulō heisst „der Weg".

[19] dies ist wol ein anderes Wort für dekel, „zeige"; andē = andén, „mir".

Sónyai.	Lógoné.	Wándalā.	Bágrimma.	Mába.
éga-hūre (hayō .	wú-wanē . . .	yé-katā	mam-hoyō .	am adaī
mē hinne gauri .	gō wanī . . .	ká-katáwe .	. . . . . .	
ēdu [14]	wá-se-nīa . .	yé-šenūā . .	mam-gaó-na	am ókkonō
yelándu (?) . . .	gá-se-ol . . .	ká-šenūā . .		. . . . . .
. . . .	wá-doku labāria	ye-zinse lábare	. . . . . .	anárga kásaingā (am(be) dinne
éga-nidónto . .	wálle (nī . . .	yé-belā . . .	mak-usalnya .	am andai
éga-kǫbbere (nisse hayō	aī mála-kū [16] .	yé-máraka .	mak-indádāum	am dokoine
ése-kǫbbere (nisse hayō	aī. mála-kū-sa .	yé-māraka-ñ-ka	. . . . .	. . . . . .
kǫbbere (sē) fondo (maltāaba fondo [15]	awa [17]), mála-n zíbbelo	marín mérmele úngulē [18]	indādžum debna	lingák (andé) dinā [19]
		. . . . . .	. . . . . .	

[1] má-nishin: also deri-nishin, in the T.-language deri-nerih, with the original meaning „I go about" has the secondary notion of „I look for". Thus áfi deri-tīin, „what is he looking for?"

[2] fand-ishin: Koelle writes pánd-gekin. Here the phrase áfi ni-gá (ñi-gā) tsé-fand-ō, „what is the matter with you?", is based on this meaning, it being properly „what has reached thee (him).

[3] nát-ishin: Koelle writes nát-gekin with an indistinct e, but I think, the i is essential, as it indicates an action and not a passive condition. nóte, „knowledge", from ná-nishin, ná-ágin: nót-ishin, „I give knowledge, send"; nótē, „the giving of knowledge", „the message".

[4] falē-ágin. Koelle pǫlēágin.

[5] yāt-ishin: Koelle writes yá-ekin as well as yát-gekin, but confounding this term with ya-ekin attributes to those forms the meaning of „take away, take", which they do not properly possess.

[6] tánē fáng-erih: also in this case I found the vulgar forms fángee, ū-bángee; 1st pers. of the past tense in the negative form ū-báng-eri-a.

[7] korēa-erih probably is nothing but a slight dialectic variation of ókadāa-erih, especially if we write the latter with a soft d.

[8] mē kā-na nāma: I shall also give in this place the phrase „search carefully", K. nāne ágilla, H. nēma néggari, F. dábbitoi-mē or reete bódum, S. tamba hūre (bayō.

[9] sámo in connection with karfi, „iron, strength", has become a technical expression of warfare: H. sū san-sámo karfi, F. be-kōbi sembē.

[10] ina nūna is the term of the Hausa-language, as spoken in Kátsena, inā yóda that of the dialect of Góber.

[11] na-ī ma-kā rēkkia is not the vulgar term used of a common guide, but rather of a larger escort or an honorable company; imp. ka-ī ma-ni rékkia, F. depta.

[12] mádo-raria. In Sókoto at least a third word is also much used, via mē-dāraa, but it implies a bad action, via the „running after women".

[13] mōdo-habbi: thence the form of the noun habbel, „the finding, discovery", also „getting by chance", in opposition to „merit, desert", as in the proverb „finding (getting by chance) is better than deserving", F. hebbel bāri banka, H. sāmo yáfi iyáwa.

[14] ēdu does not look like the right form of the 1st pers. of the present tense.

[15] maltāaba fondo has not the appearance of a verbal tense.

[16] aī mála-kā: for this word I have also the form wókakā, but I am not certain about it.

[17] awa means „ho, there!" and does not belong to the original phrase.

[18] marin mérmele ángulē: marin probably is an abridged form of mérahin, if it is not perhaps said for marí, „me". ángulē is the „track, path"; then we have mérmele, which is not quite clear to me.

[19] lingák andé dinā: andé = andán, „we"; dinā perhaps is another term for dokol, „show".

Deutsch und Englisch.	Kanúri.	Tédā.	Hausa.	Fulfúlde.
ich versammele — *I assemble*	sám-{nískin . / gin [1] . . }	kiám-erik . .	ínā tára [11] . .	mēdo-mopta [16]
ich gehe mit, gehe bei, vereinige — *I join, bring together*	fog-nískin [2] .	. . . . .	. . . . .	. . . . .
ich begegne ihm — *I meet him* / wir begegnen, vereinen uns — *we meet (face to face*	andi-ma kélan fóg-nien [3]	hénneri nokórdu kiáb-tentī	ína iskē-šī [12] .	mēdo-tau-mo [17]
der Markt hat sich gefüllt, ist voll — *the market is full*	kásukū dam-tšī [4]	kásukū dī teyim fidē?	háswa ta-tšíka	lūmu {bēbi . / bēvi . }
wir trennen uns, gehen auseinander — *we separate*	gedē-niyen [5] .	girterī . . .	. . . . .	. . . . .
die Leute haben sich zerstreut, sind auseinander gegangen — *the people have scattered, dispersed, separated*	ām tartai [6] .	ánnata árkedē	mótane sun-wasu	yimbe tšenkétekē
ich begrüsse (ihn — *I greet (him*	ši-gá{láfia-nískin [7] / wúse-nískin }	táuē kalē hanán-erík	nī ína agai-swa [13] .	mōdo {homna / himna }
wir verbinden die Hände (ich schüttele (deine) Hand) — *we shake hands*	múskō fóg-nien [8]	kubba turtúnti	ína-kāma hanú (ú-ka [14]	menéndi dāungo má-da
ich küsse seine Hand — *I kiss his hand*	múskō-ntse taun-taú-ngin [9]	tutumai diáb-erík [10]	[15]	[15]

[1] sám-gin, 3te Person ši sáp-tšin. Koelle führt neben diesem sám-gin noch zwei andere auf, sámgin, „ich rathe" (3te Person ši samtšin), und sámgin, „ich theile aus".

[2] fog-nískin. Koelle schreibt fóngin und man muss sich hier eigentlich denken, dass das zur Wurzel gehörige g ausgefallen ist.

[3] andi-ma kéla-n fóg-nien, wörtlich „wir vereinen (uns) mit dem Haupte". kéla-n ist Ablativ; Koelle schreibt kala (kéla), fasst es also als Akkusativ, und das ist allerdings der Fall in der Phrase múskō fóg-nien, scheint hier aber nicht an der Stelle zu sein.

[4] kasukū dam-tšī. Das Wort damtšī kommt von dam-gin, dem Koelle zuerst die Bedeutung „Strömen, laufen" beilegt, „nur von Flüssen gebraucht", dann aber in zweiter Instanz auch vom Versammeln der Menschen.

[5] gedē-niyen kommt von gedē-ngin oder, wie Koelle schreibt, gadéngin. Koelle hat aber die hier angeführte Bedeutung gar nicht, obgleich sie dem Begriff des „verschieden Machens" nahe kommt, wenn man sich nämlich das Pronomen hinzudenkt: „wir machen uns verschieden", d. h. wir geben uns eine verschiedene Richtung, gehen auseinander.

[6] ām tartai. tartai ist entschieden die 3te Person Plur. Prät. von tar-ngin, obgleich Koelle von diesem Wort, dem er eine ganz richtige Bedeutung beilegt, in der Vergangenheit nur die Form mit e angiebt, tartse, tartse].

[7] láfia-nískin. Koelle hat die Form láfiángin, die aber nach meiner Ansicht weniger richtig ist, weil láfia ein einfaches Substantiv und nískin keine blosse Verbalendung, sondern das Verbum „ich mache" selbst ist.

[8] múskō fóg-nien, „wir vereinen die Hand"; s. N. 3.

[9] tauntaú-ngin. Koelle schreibt ntsáutsungin, das er aber nur vom Saugen des Kindes erklärt.

[10] tummai diab-erík. Ich habe allerdings nur die Form diab-irdē gehört. „Ich küsse" heisst táuē nódnkā.

[11] ínā tára. Daher tarē, „Versammeln", tāri, „viele".

[12] ína iskē-šī. Diese Hausa-Redensart entspricht dem Kanúri mehr dem Sinne als der Form nach; wörtlich „ich begegne ihm", Präteritum: na iskē-šī; „gehe ihm entgegen", taff iskē-šī.

[13] nī ína agai-swa. Dahin gehört die verwandte Redensart agai-šē-ka, „ich danke dir" (F. mōdo-héfau-ma). Imperat. agai šē (F. hefau-mō, hiane-mō). Das Hausa-Wort erhält zuweilen auch die Bedeutung „danken". Hierher will ich auch die Phrase na-i léddabi, „ich verbeuge mich", F. mēdo-weddi daddeh, setzen.

[14] ína-kāma hanú (ú-ka, „ich ergreife deine Hand"; ebenso ist es im F. aufgefasst.

[15] Ich habe diesen etwas ungewöhnlichen Ausdruck im H. und F. nicht, dafür aber habe ich einen anderen, nämlich „ich umfasse den Fuss", H. na-i kāmen kaffa, F. mēdo-naāgi koido.

[16] mēdo-mopta. Neben diesem Wort ist noch ein anderer Ausdruck vorhanden, wie der Púlo sagt mēdo-hanratima yimbe, „ich versammele Volk", H. ína tára mótane, und yimbe hauye-tšē, „die Leute haben sich versammelt", H. mótane sun-tára.

[17] mēdo-tau-mō, gleichfalls „ich begegne ihm"; in der vergangenen Zeit mē-taī-mō.

[18] Die Sonrhay scheinen diese Art des Ausdruckes nicht zu haben, wol aber sagen sie „gieb mir die Hand", ćane kambe-di

[19] wába mát-abē scheint, wenn wába mát-edē einfach heisst „ich vereine, gehe mit", nicht ganz bezeichnend zu sein.

[20] awe, mehhia ttada-mō. Über das awe s. S. 70, N. 17. Es scheint also die 1ste Pers. Plur. des Imperativs.

[21] yé-gan dāem arwa. arwa ist „die Hand", yé-gan, „ich mache", dāem, „zusammen".

[22] diē-nid-nēē. Der Wohllaute wegen scheint hier ein e die Stelle des ī eingenommen zu haben.

[23] fárriánnē ist ein aus dem Arabischen eingeführtes und der Mebn-Sprache accommodirtes Wort.

[24] ám tanbar nyéta kalak ist vielleicht nicht ganz richtig. Für Hand habe ich kerrifagnk.

Sonγai.	Lógone.	Wándalá.	Bágrimma.	Mába.
éga-merdži .	wāha (míslemé) mát-adē	ye-gán wegē .	mét-kolū (debge	
. . . .	wāha mát-adē .	yá-wetšē . .	má-kobō . .	
ég(a)-crui . . .	wōha mát-abē[19]	ga-wetšē-na bá-ngarē fetīre	džā-kobō dála-dšē	
hēbu kádu . .	káskū dekéša	debā debā kosk-we	kaskō n(e) and-olā-ga	kai taisingā / tai lrringu
. . . .	má-farē kelā . .	ga-nāte ganā	dšū-sid-nāē[22]	. . . . .
hōr raū	ingum kįje tíllie yé-farū kelā-ya	té-kiš . . .	deb-go šid-ga	nan fárringnē[23]
éga-fūyo firo . . [14]	wúngol-(uī . . awe[20]), mubbin šadá-mū	yé-gan wétšia	mat-ad láfia .	am angoine
		yé-gan džem erwa[21]	dšī bō dže-dšī	am kaṅkar nyēla kalák[24]
	šadá-ni wa-sí-n alga kalgē niki	ye-bētše erwa	ma-súm dšī-na	am dšuṅg ba-róngne

1 sám-gin; 3rd pers. ši sáp-tšin. Koelle mentions two other similar verbs besides this sám-gin sámgin, „I rub" (3rd pers. ši sámtšin), and sámgin, „I distribute".
2 fog-nichin: Koelle writes fóngin, which I have never heard; at least in this form we have to suppose the g left out.
3 andi-ma kéla-n fóg-nien means verbally „we join, meet with the head". kéla-n is the ablative case, but Koelle writes kalā (kéla), and supposes therefore the accusative case. The latter is certainly expressed in the phrase múskō fóg-nien, but does not seem applicable to our case.
4 káskō dam-tši: the word damtši is derived from dam-gin, the same word, to which Koelle attributes in the first instance exclusively the meaning of „to flow, run", „used only of fluids"; but in the second explains it also as meaning „to assemble".
5 gedō-niyen is derived from gedé-ngin or, as Koelle writes gadéógin. Koelle however does not mention the notion, which we have here, although even this meaning may be derived from „to make different", if we refer this to the direction, thus „we make us (our direction) different, take a different direction".
6 ám tarial: tarial is decidedly the 3rd pers. plur. of the past tense of tar-ngin, „I scatter, disperse", although Koelle attributes to this word a different form of the past tense, viz tarteq, tártaei.
7 láfia-nichin: Koelle also in this case has the form with ágin (láfiángin), which however I think here wrong, láfia being a pure noun and nichin not being in this case a simple verbal termination, but the verb itself, „I make".
8 múskō fóg-nien, „we join hand", see n. 3.
9 tenniseh-ngin: Koelle writes ntsahntenngin, explaining it only of the sucking of children.
10 tummal diáh-erik: I have only heard the form diáh-erdé. For the simple term „I kiss" I have in the T.-language sánó nódakó; but kissing with Negroes is not a very common affair.
11 ina tára: thence tarō, „together", tári, „many".
12 ina iaké-ši: this Hausa-term corresponds to the Kanúri one more properly in sense, than in form; verbally it means „I meet him"; past tense: na iakō-ši; imp. „go and meet him", tafi iakē-ši.
13 ni ina agai-ewa: thereto belongs the related term agai šé-ha, „I thank thee" (F. médo-béfan-mā); imp. agai šá (F. béfan-mé, kisne-mé). This Hausa-word sometimes has the notion of „to thank". I have also added the phrase, H. na-i iréddehi, F. médo-weddi deddeh, „I bow to, make a bow".
14 ina-hima bani (á-ke, „I take, grasp thy hand"; just the same sort of expression we have in F.
15 In M. and F. I have no term for „I kiss hand", but instead of that I have another term, viz „I embrace, grasp the feet", H. na-i hime n kaffa, F. médo nangi koide.
16 médo-mupte: besides this word there must still be another term, as the Fulbe say mido haaretime yimbe, „I gather, assemble people", H. ina tára mótane, and yimbe haare-tšā, „the people have assembled", H. mótane sun-tára.
17 médo-tan-má: past tense „I went to meet him", mé-tai-mé.
18 The Sonγai do not seem to have this sort of expression, but they say „give me (your) hand", ónee kombe-di.
19 wōha mát-abē does not seem to be fully expressive, supposed wāha (perhaps wa-ha) mát-adē means only „I join".
20 awe, mubbin šadá-mū: awe see p. 71, n. 17, mubbin (mu-bi-n) seems to be the 1st pers. pl. of the imp. mood from wu-bá.
21 yé-gan džem erwa: erwa is „hand", yé-gan, „I make", džem, „together" i. e. „I join".
22 dšá-sid-nāē: from euphonical reasons the s seems to have taken the place of the š.
23 fárringnē is a term introduced from the Arabic into the Mába-language and accommodated to the rules of the latter.
24 ám kaṅkar nyēla kalák is perhaps not quite right; for „hand" among my list of nouns in M. I have kárringak.

Deutsch und Englisch.	Kanuri.	Tédā.	Hausa.	Fulfulde.
Ich umarme ihn — *I embrace him* / wir umarmen uns — *we embrace each other*	ngándži fóg-nien[1]	tinta lú-t-cri?[6]	na-ī rúnguma	mō-húfli-(mō
Ich werfe Staub auf mein Haupt — *I sprinkle dust upon my head*	kalī gōn {fakin / gin .}		na-ī affi[10] .	mē-búkkak[F] .
Ich ziehe mein Hemd von der Schulter — *I draw my shirt from the shoulder*	húlgū[2] múskō-n-ben lugú-akin		. . . . . .	
Ich nehme Abschied — *I take leave*	. . . . . .		na-ī ma-kā babán kwāna[11]	médo-wúnilō (mā
Ich danke, bedanke mich — *I thank, render thanks*	godē-ngin . .	. . . . . .	ína-gōde[12] .	mēdo-yella .
Ich folge — *I follow* .	gá-skin[3] . .	{táné ea-gā[7], táné ifū-hénnā tedēdi}	ína-bī[13] . .	mēdo-tokke .
Ich gehorche, folge — *I obey, follow*	gnabi-fakin[4] .	{malō . . . / buddi keučir[8]}	ína-bī[14] . . / ína-bīn . . .	mēdo-tokke . / mēdo-bīo . .
Ich bin ungehorsam, aufsässig — *I am disobedient*	ní-gā ac-gá-akin bāgo[5]	táné dunna kás-crik[9]	oī ba ína-bī merādi (úka	mēdo-túkki-ta (merādi mā-da

[1] ngándži fóg-nien, „wir vereinigen die Brust". Anstatt ngándži schreibt Koelle ngántši, hat aber unsere Phrase nicht.
[2] húlgū. Koelle schreibt kálugū und hálgū. Die ganze Phrase bezeichnet einen Akt der Unterwürfigkeit, der jedoch nicht in allen Ländern der Schwarzen üblich ist, weshalb diese dann natürlich auch keinen Ausdruck dafür haben.
[3] gá-skin; Imperat. gai. Verber schreibt Koelle gádóngin.
[4] gnabi-fakin fehlt bei Koelle; 3te Pers. Sing. gnabi-in.
[5] ní-gā ac-gá-skin bāgo. ac-gá-skin, eine durch objective Infixion entstandene Umwandelung für ye-gá-skin. „Er gehorcht ihm nicht", ac-gā bāgo ší-gā.
[6] tinta lú-t-cri ist sehr zweifelhaft; niedergeschrieben nach dem Gehör habe ich tutto láttedā, wol lú-t-ardē, 1ste Person Plur. Prät.
[7] táné ea-gā. ea-gā scheint mit dem Kanúri-Wort eng verwandt zu sein. táné ifū-hénnā tedēdi, „ich gehe hinter ihm".
[8] buddi keučir heisst vielleicht „Alles soll geschehen (wie du sagst)"; deshalb habe ich es nicht in keučirik verwandelt; malō ist wol nicht verbal.
[9] táné dunna kás-crik, „ich breche den Befehl", ein etwas unbehülflicher und wol nicht eigenthümlicher Ausdruck (von كسر !).
[10] na-ī affi ist ein höchst eigenthümlicher, prägnanter Ausdruck.
[11] na-ī ma-kā babán kwāna, wörtlich „ich mache dir ein (grosses) langes Nachtlager, lange gute Nacht".
[12] ína-gōde. Dieser Ausdruck hängt unzweifelhaft mit dem Kanúri-Wort zusammen, aber ich glaube, dass das Hausa-Wort das ursprüngliche, das andere das abgeleitete ist. „Ich danke sehr, sage tausend Dank", H. ina-gōd-ia korā, F. mēdo-yella bēdum.
[13] ína-bī, „ich folge", hat auch die Bedeutung „ich schlage ein" von einer Strasse, so H. ína-bī hanja n Kanō, „ich schlage die Strasse von Kanō ein". Dies ist theilweise der Gegensatz zu nī na-rādla, „ich weiche ab", F. mē-seli, Plur. min-tāēdo; min-īdōde hat auch die Bedeutung „wir trennen uns", Gegensatz von mēdeng-gendi, wir gehen zusammen".
[14] ína-bī, wieder in dem Sinne „ich gehorche". So „ich gehorche deinem Willen", H. ína-bī merādī-ā-ka, F. mēdo-tokke merādi mā-da; „sie gehorchen dem Herrn von Kanō", H. sú súka-bī serki n Kanō, F. kambe tókkite lámido Kanō. Das H. ína-bīn und das F. mēdo-bīo sind intransitiv. Hierher will ich auch noch einen anderen Ausdruck setzen: H. na-mai-ar kamān obā-na, „ich stelle, verehre ihn wie einen Vater", F. mō-mannsel-mō bāne bāba-am. — Hier will ich auch die Phrase hersetzen „ich diene, leiste Dienste", H. nī ína bautá, F. mēde-wira.
[15] ēga-hángani ist eigentlich nichts Anderes als ēga-hai.
[16] hōya-ha na-kū na mát-adē. hōya-ha habe ich nicht unter meinen Substantiven, es muss aber „Brust" oder etwas Ähnliches bedeuten, vielleicht verwandt mit hai, „nahe"; na-hū heisst „dein", mát-adē, „zusammen", und das vorhergehende na ist wahrscheinlich falsch, vielleicht wa-há.
[17] wa-sabēnia, Imperat. sabēni, hat, wie man aus der negativen Form deutlich sieht, auch die geistige Bedeutung des Gehorchens.
[18] wa-angángibā; 3te Person nú-ian angángibā.
[19] yē-gan dēem ahawe. Unter den Substantiven habe ich für „Brust" im W. ahawe; dēem, „zusammen" (s. S. 70, N. 21).
[20] ā-dēedši báng-nifā ist wol unzweifelhaft die 3te Person. Sing.; la báng-nifā steht bā-ágané, „er".
[21] yē-deh-ka ist die einfache negative Form von yē-deha.
[22] dāā-kobē kadši-an. kádši, „die Brust"; dāā-kobē ist 1ste Person Plur. von má-kobē.
[23] man sá-(yī-ga, „ich folge (dir)"; Imperat. „folge (ihm)", só frāa. Das ga scheint eine Art Accusativform zu sein, die aber nur selten gebraucht wird, wie man aus der negativen Form man od-yī-ll ersieht.
[24] am geni-nya hūrgete adaf, „ich folge ihm, der voran geht".

Sońyai.	Lógoné.	Wándalá.	Bágrimma.	Mába.
egánde-(nī . .	boya-ha na-kū na mát-adē[16]	yé-gan džem akewe[19]	džá-kobŏ kádži-na[22]	am kerĭb (barúngne
	wa-sī níbra?	yé-kae gūra .	mam-okku nanga	géaínga kŏdži-n á-wonī
. . . . . .	wŭ-safoé nangu lebū	. . . . .	mat-igdži bŏlu	am karkáyo
éga-kenni kélgomŏ	. . . .	. . . . .	. . . . . .	. . . . .
éga {foni . . . / fonga . . .}	. . . .	. . . . .	. . . . . .	. . . . .
éga-bánga-nī[15]	wa-zebénia[17] . .	yé-deba (bá-ya	mam sá-(yí-ga[23]	am gonī-nya búrgeto adaī[24]
éga-baī . . .	wa-angángibā[18] .	á-džedži báng-nifá[20]	mat-ad genībdžŏī	{am burke / am (megó) bŭng-nyerik
ésa-baī . . .	wa-zebéni-sā .	yé-deb-ka[21] .	mam sá-(yí)-lī	am (megú n) áyinyĕni

[1] ágándĕi fég-aian, „we join breast". Koelle has not this phrase and writes ágáatĭl.

[2] kálgū: Koelle writes kálngū and kálgū. The whole phrase describes an act of respect, which is not in use among all the various nations of Negroland, the others of course having no term for it.

[3] gá-ckin; imperat. gai. Instead of godō-ngin; Koelle writes gādéngin.

[4] gánkt-ickin is wanting in Koelle's vocabulary; 3rd pers. sing. gánkt-in.

[5] ní-gā ye-gá-ckin bāge: ye-gá-ckin variation caused by what Koelle terms objective inflection for yo-gá-ckin; „He does not obey him". ye-gā bāgo ĭi-gā.

[6] tinta lé-t-erĕ is very doubtful; my Manuscr. gives the form tatte láttedĕ, probably lé-t-erdĕ 1st pers. plur. praet.

[7] tánā en-gā: en-gā seems to be closely allied to the Kanúri. tánó ífū-bénná tedĕdi, „I go at his back, go behind him".

[8] heddi kaeĭir may possibly mean „all shall be done, be attended to" and it is on this account, that I do not write kaeĭrik. malé probably is not a verbal form.

[9] tánā dĭnaa háe-erik, „I break the command", probably not the only term used for disobeying and not original.

[10] na-ĭ effĭ is a very peculiar expressive national term.

[11] na-ĭ ma-há hahán kwána, verbally „I make thee a long or great night's rest or good night".

[12] ínā-gáde: the Hausa-term is no doubt closely related to the Kanúri one, but the former is, I think, the original, the latter the derived one. „I thank (you) much, say a thousand thanks", H. ina-gód-ia kerĕ, F. mŏdo-yetta bŏdem.

[13] ína-bi, „I follow", has also the meaning „I take (a road)", as „I take the road (leading) to Kanó", H. ina-bi hańa n Kanó. This is in some respect the reverse of the phrase nī na-gádŏe, „I turn out (of a road)", F. mŏ-acli, plur. min-tĭāde. This latter term has also the meaning „we separate", forming the reverse of médoeg-goadi, „we travel in company".

[14] ina-bĭ in the sense „I obey". Thus „I obey, follow thy inclination", H. ina-bĭ merádi-áka, F. mĕdo-tokke merádi mā-da; „they obey the governor of Kanó", H. sú súka-bi serki n Kanó, F. hambe tékkite lámido Kanó. The Hausa form ina-bia and the F. médo-bie are not transitive. I adduce another term: H. na-mai-ne kamán ubá-na, F. mŏ-monaenī-mé bāne bābā-am, „I place (respect) him as my father"; likewise another term „I render service, serve", H. nī ina baránta, F. mĕdo-wiea.

[15] éga-bánga-nī properly is nothing but éga-bai with the pronoun.

[16] bóya-ba na-kū na mát-adē: bóya or bóya-ba I have not in my list of nouns, but it must mean „breast" or have a similar signification (boi, „near, close to"); na-kū means „thine", mát-adē, „together"; na is wrong, perhaps na-kā.

[17] wa-zebénia (imperat. zebénī) has also the meaning „I obey", as is clearly seen from the negative form.

[18] wa-angángibā; 3rd pers. ná-ina angángibā.

[19] yé-gan džem akewe: yé-gan džem (s. p. 73, note 21): akewe, „the breast".

[20] á-džedži báng-nifá is doubtless the 3rd pers. sing., há-ágená, „he", being concealed in the form báng-nifá.

[21] yé-deb-ka is the simple negative form of yé-deba.

[22] džá-kobŏ kádži-na: kádži, „breast"; džá-kobŏ is 1st pers. plur. from má-kobā.

[23] mam sá-(yi-ga, „I follow (thee": imperat. „follow (him", sá (sha. The affix ga seems to strengthen the form of the inventive, but is not necessary, as is seen from the negative form mam sá-yi-li.

[24] am gení-ñya búrgeto adai, „I follow him, who goes before".

Deutsch und Englisch.	Kanúri.	Tédā.	Hausa.	Fulfulde.
ich bemitleide, bedaure — *I feel compassion with* —	¹		na-ī tausai (da ĭī nī na-ī taëlo	mēdo-yįrmenī mēdo-nanna yįr-mendĕ (má-ko) mēdo-hebbi yá-foë má-ko
ich erbarme mich Jemandes — *I take pity of, show mercy to* —			na-ī taúlefi⁷ garë (ĭī) ina-kámna (ĭī)⁸	mēdo-wŏdi gigē-te(-má
ich helfe (dir), leiste Hülfe — *I help, assist, aid*	nī-gā) bána tai-dī skin²	nébra-hē) girná-n-erīk⁵	na-ī taimăko na-táya⁹ . . na-ī guddu-mana	mēdo-welli .
hilf mir, zu Hülfe! — *aid, assist me! help*	ú-ro bána se-gē	tánē-hē girna-téo kórrorŏ dýnneri⁶	ka-ī taimăko . guddu-mana .	well-am .
ich thue (ihm) wohl, erzeige (ihm) Wohlthat — *I do (him) well, do (him) a benefit*	ĭī-gā) ṅgilla dí-skin	terin kót-erīk? morā-ha gāli ibén-erīk	na-ī néggari larĕ da (ĭī	mĕdo-wăddi kŭdi hauta do-mo
ich segne (dich — *I bless (thee*	nī-gā) barkā-ṅgin³	. . . . . .	na-ī (ma-kā) ad-dána¹⁰	mēdo-dokō (má
ich empfange dich gut, bereite dir einen guten Empfang — *I give thee a good reception*	nī-gā) sábāg-iskin?	. . . . . .	na-ī ma-kā tér-ria¹¹	mē-tábakī-mā
ich erhebe (ihn), erhöhe den Rang — *I elevate, raise the rank*	ĭī-gā) zaṅg-lakin⁴		na-ī (ma-sā) gir-ma¹²	mēdo-em (mō) maṅgo

¹ Ich bin über die Phrase im K. nicht ganz sicher; ich selbst habe die Redensart gebraucht: kan-dālimeli, „Mitleid", (s. das Verzeichniss der Substantive, wo auch die entsprechenden Ausdrücke im H., W. und B. angegeben sind), á-gā (mich), se-tal (erfasst), Ĭī-gā naṅga (seinetwegen). Mitleiden ist ein den Negervölkern nicht zum klaren Bewusstsein gekommenes Gefühl.

² nī-gā bána tai-dī-skin (tai-dī-skin, objective Infinition statt dī-skin) fehlt bei Koelle, jedoch hat er es nebenbei aufgeführt unter márteṅgéskin, nämlich in der Phrase mártegenē bandeygnē, „sei doch so gut und hilf mir". Siehe Beispiele zu dieser Phrase unter den Verbal-Paradigmen in der Einleitung. Statt bána hört man oft bána.

³ barkā-ṅgin. Koelle schreibt bargangin. Es ist natürlich ein Fremdwort.

⁴ zaṅg-lakin scheint bei Koelle ganz zu fehlen.

⁵ girná-n-erīk. Aus der Form des Imperat., tánē-hē girna-téo, ersieht man, dass das zweite n nicht zur Wurzel gehört. Daneben scheint übrigens noch ein anderer Ausdruck, turhá-n-erīk, zu existiren.

⁶ kórrorŏ dýnneri: kórrorŏ könnte von kárt-erīk, „ich bringe", abgeleitet zu sein scheinen, aber das t im letzteren Wort gehört mit zur Wurzel, wie der Imperat. kurtu zeigt. Ich bin über die ganze Phrase etwas unsicher.

⁷ taúlefi ist aus dem Arabischen abgeleitet.

⁸ ina-kámna Ĭī ist ein eigenthümlicher Ausdruck; kámna heisst sonst „schneiden".

⁹ na-táya und noch entschiedener na-ī guddu-mana (vgl. guddu n dana S. 46, N. 13) haben den Begriff der kriegerischen Hülfe.

¹⁰ na-ī (ma-kā) addána: addána stammt aus dem Arabischen [illegible]. Ja Koelle hat selbst im Kanúri ein hiervon abgeleitetes Verbum, adŭṅgin, das ich aber nicht in Gebrauch fand.

¹¹ na-ī ma-kā térria. So „der Fürst hat dir einen guten Empfang bereitet", H. serki ya-ī ma-kā térria korē, F. lámido tábakī-mā bodum.

¹² na-ī (ma-sā) girma und die Ausdrücke im F. und S. haben etwas allgemeinere Bedeutung, als die entsprechenden in den anderen Sprachen.

¹³ éga-gā nárnese. nárnese scheint mit dem Fulfulde-Ausdruck yįrmendĕ in der vorigen Phrase verwandt zu sein.

¹⁴ éga-fába-(al hat mehr die Bedeutung der kriegerischen Hülfe, daher Imperat. Plur. „helft, helft", wá-fába, wó-fába.

¹⁵ Ich habe hier die Form ébue nfor, aber ich bin zu ungewiss, um sie in den Text zu setzen, vielleicht ist es égn-bur, bur mit o-bári „ist gut, schön" verwandt; vielleicht ist es auch nicht die erste Person Sing. Präs.

¹⁶ ége-sém bérkol. sum ist offenbar das Verbum und bérkol aus barka verdorben. Oft genug habe ich das Wort sum bérkol von den um Segen bettelnden Bóuyai hören müssen.

¹⁷ woyá-n-hŭ dawa heisst wol sicherlich „ich thue, gebe dir (hŭ, ŭku) Arznei" (dawa statt des einheimischen moyán) und ist also identisch mit der Phrase S. 83. Über woyá, woyán habe ich etwas Weiteres in der Einleitung gesagt. Das Missverständniss beruht offenbar darauf, dass der W.-Bursche das K.-Wort bána nicht recht verstand.

¹⁸ Ich habe hier wieder eine entschieden falsche Phrase inde ta kúṅgu lā, vielleicht inde tal-hā-n-ya-lā als letzte Person Sing. Präs.

¹⁹ woyá-n-hŭ dibbi. Ich habe eine andere Form inde me oan (oā-ŏ!) gunkŏ dibbi. Über die auffällige Übereinstimmung des dibbi mit der Bedeutung „gut" im Logone mit dibbi, „schlecht", im Kanúri siehe die Einleitung. yé-magā la-hŏ melĕ ist wiederum eine sehr volle Form, für die man im gewöhnlichen Ausdruck auch yom-la-hā (hā-ya) sagen kann. Dagegen lautet der Imperativ „helft, helft" nur melĕ, melĕ.

éga-gā súrneso [13]				
éga-hamne . . } éga-fāba-(n)ī [14] . . }	woyá-ū-(kū dawa [17]	yé-magā la-kū melē [20]	mam-ákc-ma-(ī	am dabā (ba-róngne
wū-fāba . . .	[18]	melē-melō .	mā-mā . . .	karún dalā ánda-róng
[15]	woyá-ū-(kū dibbi [19]	yé-magā mogg(e) irō	mat-aḋ ngilla-gā	am kerro bedríne
éga-súm búrkoi [16]	. . . . . .	. . . . .	. . . . .	. . . . .
. . . . . .	. . . . . .	. . . . .	. . . . .	. . . . .
éga-hánsene (ní-ne) hai béri	hōma dōma wóya-(n)?	yé-χodā . .	mak-ínya . .	

[1] I am not certain of this term in K. I myself have used the following phrase: han-dīlimmeïi, „compassion" (see the list of nouns where the corresponding terms in L., W. and B. are also given, though mostly Arabic) ā-gá, „see", or-tal, „vision", ēl-gā naáge, „on his account"; but compassion is not a feeling of which the Negroes have become perfectly conscious.

[2] ni-gá bána tsi-di-ekin (tsi-dí-ekin caused by objective inflection, instead of di-ekin) is wanting in Koelle, although he has mentioned the term under the verb mártegéehin in the phrase mártegené bánáegené. Nevertheless it is a very common expression, of which I have given some examples in the introduction among the paradigms of conjugation.

[3] barké-ágin: Koelle writes bargángin. It is of course a foreign term.

[4] sadg-ishin seems to be wanting in Koelle's vocabulary.

[5] girua-n-erik: from the form of the imp., tánē-bá girnatén, we see, that the second n does not belong to the root. Besides this term a second one, turké-n-erik, seems to be used.

[6] kérreré dáneri: kérreré might seem to be derived from kúrt-erik, but the t in the latter word belongs to the root, as is seen from the imp. kurtn. Indeed I am not sure of the exact meaning of the phrase.

[7] taálefi has been derived from the Arabic.

[8] ina-kámma ñī is a peculiar expression; kámma in general meaning „to cut".

[9] na-tkya and still more decidedly na-ī guddu-mana (cf. guddu n dana p. 46, n. 13) convey the meaning of a military assistance.

[10] na-ī (ma-hē) addána: addána is a foreign word introduced from the Arabic [illegible]. Koelle has even a verb addángin.

[11] na-ī ma-hā térria: thus „the prince has given you a good reception", H. serki ya-ī ma-kā térria karē, F. lamido tábaki-mō bódum.

[12] na-ī (ma-sá) girma has a more general meaning than the corresponding terms in the other languages, except those in F. and S.

[13] éga-gā súrneso: súrneso seems to be somehow related to the F.-term yermendé in the preceding phrase.

[14] éga-fāba-(n)ī almost exclusively has the meaning of a military assistance; thence plur. imp. „help, help", wó-fābo, wó-fāba.

[15] I have written ébar nlee, but I am not sure, whether it be right; it may be éga-bur (bur related to abúri „it is well").

[16] éga-sūm búrkoi: sum is evidently the verb „make" and búrkoi is corrupted from barka. The common people in Ñgáyai being most anxious of obtaining my blessing, I had frequent opportunity of hearing the words sum búrkoi, sum búrkoi.

[17] woyá-ū-kū dawa, I am almost sure, means „I make" or „give thee medicine" and therefore is identical with the phrase adduced p. 83, the misunderstanding probably having originated in the term bána. kū or ákū is „thee", woya, „I make" and the foreign term has been employed, although the L. idiom has a native one for „medicine" via moyóa.

[18] indo ta kánga lū, what I had taken down, is evidently false; perhaps it ought to be indo tal-kū-ā-ya-lū as 1st pers. sing. of the present tense.

[19] woyá-ū-kū dibbi: I have another form, indo ma saa (sā-ū?) guákū dibbi. With reference to the accidental agreement of the different terms, dibbi meaning „good" in Lógone and dibbi meaning „bad" in Kanúri, see Prolegomena.

[20] yé-magā la-kū melé again is a fuller form, instead of which the people generally say yem-la-kā (ká-ya); but the form of the imperative is nothing but melé, melē.

Deutsch und Englisch.	Kanúri.	Téda.	Mába.	Fulfúlde.
Ich setze in ein Amt ein — *I invest (with an office*	ši-gā (gálā {níakin / ngin)	ámu ai) tegē-hé-muā hín-erik [7]		. . . . . .
Ich entkleide meines Amtes, setze ab — *I deprive of his office, depose*	ši-gā ka-gálā n tolug-úskin [1]	tírk-erik . . .	. . . . . .	. . . . . .
Ich verläumde — *I calumniate*	gader-níakin [2]	táně něne nirki [3]	{ína-rída [7] . / zání (ma-sā) zambar [8]	mědo-nyūra . / mědo-zámbo-mō
Ich verspotte, verhöhne (dich — *I abuse (thee*	. . . . . .	. . . . . .	{na-ī ma-kā halbi [9] / na-ī ma-kā būlāfa / na-īma-kā dāentūi [10]	mō-fidī-ma {na / mědo-nimakohā / mī-dācntī-mā
Ich mache (ihm) Schande — *I cause shame to*	ū (šl-rō) núngū dí-ukin	. . . . . .	na-ī(ma-sā) kóm-mia [11]	mědo-sénia-mō
Ich verrathe — *I betray*	hayen-níakin [2]	táně χien-erik	. . . . . .	. . . . . .
Ich störe (dich — *I disturb (thee*	. . . . . .	. . . . . .	ína-gámaššō-(ka [12]	mědo-hótta-(mā
Ich hindere — *I prevent*	. . . . . .	. . . . . .	ína-hanna . .	mědo-heddi ..
Ich bin (dir) lästig — *I am troublesome*	?	. . . . . .	ína-álalō-(ka [13]	mědo-wánna-(mā
Ich verzeihe dir — *I pardon thee*	ní-rō grabángena [4]	[4]	nī gáfertá ma-hā [14]	mědo-yáffaku-mā lèiñ mā-ila

[1] ši-gā ka-gálā n tu-lug-úskin. Koelle schreibt kágalla mit zwei l, was offenbar falsch ist, da er selbst gálāgia mit Einem l schreibt. Statt tu-lug-úskin schreibt er túleskin und túlāgeskin. Ich will hier auch den technischen Ausdruck für das „Wiedereinsetzen in's Amt" hersetzen: K. ši-gā ka-gálā-a-tee-rō (oder bei höheren Statthalterschaften ker-mai-ntee-rō) yed-weigiskin gedé-rō (gedū-rō, „ein zweites Mal", „noch ein Mal", s. oben S. 23), T. áma ai („diesen Mann"), tegé hénuē sám-erik.

[2] gader-níakin hat Koelle nicht, es hängt, wie das Nomen-Wort, unzweifelhaft mit dem Arabischen [illegible] zusammen.

[3] hayen-níakin fehlt auch bei Koelle; natürlich ist es kein einheimisches Wort, sondern aus dem Arabischen eingeführt.

[4] grabángena hat Koelle auch nicht. Allerdings ist es aus dem Arabischen eingeführt ([illegible]) und wenig nationalisirt. Wir sehen hier von einer Afrikanischen Nation, ganz wie es die Franzosen so oft thun, das Arabische γ durch g r dargestellt.

[5] táně něne nirki sieht als erste Person Sing. Präs. etwas verdächtig aus.

[6] Ich hörte hier nur die Form nyenīwáde und das ist wol der Imperativ, „verzeihe (mir".

[7] ína-ríde. Hier haben wir eine ganz andere Form des Arabischen Wortes, das auch dem gader-níakin zu Grunde liegt.

[8] zambar. Es ist auffallend, dass dies Wort sich in allen drei Sprachen findet, in H., F. und S.

[9] na-ī ma-kā halbi. Das einfache ína-halbé-ka habe ich im Präsens nicht gehört, wol aber in der Vergangenheit; so „er hat mich verspottet", H. yá-halbé-ni, F. ó-fidī-ya.

[10] na-ī ma-kā dāentūi hat ursprünglich, glaube ich, die Bedeutung „ich mache dir Grimassen".

[11] na-ī ma-sā kómmia. „Er hat mir viel Schande gemacht", ya-ī ma-ni habá-n kómmia.

[12] ína-gámaššō-ka. „Du störst mich", H. kai gámaššē-ni, F. an-fatta-niya. Dem Sinne nach entspricht diesem im Sonyai die Phrase hayē sabba, d. h. „ich habe etwas zu thun".

[13] ína-álalō-ka. Die Phrase kai álalē-ni entspricht unserem „du bist mir lästig", F. an-wannī-ya. Auf das Lästigwerden bezieht sich im H. der Ausdruck béhe rúa-nan, „nicht ist sein Wasser", d. h. er ist nicht zugänglich.

[14] ni gáfertá ma-hā. „Verzeihe mir", H. gáfertá ma-ni, F. yaffe, S. maná-fe aihákha. „Ich bitte ihn, er möge mir verzeihen", H. ina-rōho-nsa ši gáfertá ma-ni, F. mō-torre hómo ó-yaff-ō-a. „Rache ist nicht gut, verzeihen ist besser, damit uns verzeihe unser Herr Gott", H. rāma béhe hyau, gáferta yēfi, dóng ši gáferta ma-nā Ubangídši n Alla, F. beire wōde, yaffā-mo dum bûri, gam Dšomirēē yaffē-mē. Ich will hier die Phrase hersetzen „ich habe Geduld mit ihm", H. na-ī hákuri da ši, F. mō-unnī-mo. Zu gáfertá will ich das wurzelverwandte gáffara anführen, „mache Platz", F. farronnu; dafür sagt man auch hā-ni uri, z. B. „mache Platz, dass ich (frische) Luft schöpfe", H. hā-ni uri ina-šā iska, F. hoh-am yeire yōre henda.

[15] Siehe Note 13.

[16] ína-mána nīse aihakha, „ich erinnere ihm das Recht". Vergl. hierzu die Phrase égo-mána hanee hai fūta, „ich verzeihe ihm eine schlechte Sache".

[17] hill' ále, „dieser Mensch", wó-ha-ni, „ich gebe ihm", moyel, hier offenbar = orm-maiyal, sonst „die Königinerde", während teilbia die Einsetzung eines Beamten bedeutet; maiyal, „der Hofbeamte". dérrelea (i. e. dérdēē), „das Amt".

[18] Ich habe hier als 3te Person Sing. hill(e) ále gálge-ni.

[19] yé-ssnoē ám-nhoē. Ich bin eigentlich nur unsicher über die Richtigkeit dieser Phrase, weil ich sie verstellt und es der Bedeutung „ich entkleide seines Amtes" geschrieben hatte; die Bedeutung konnte es aber nicht haben, da yé-ssnoē oder yé-ssnoē yé-ssnoē S. 69 ist; dagegen heisst die andere Phrase y(e)-ófel(a) ám-nhoē, offenbar „ich gebe das Amt zurück", indem y(e)-áfela identisch ist mit y(e)-ápelī S. 67 „ich gehe zurück". Das Wort ám-nhoē von mohee, mohee, „die Frau" kaum zu unterscheiden, verwirrte mich eine Zeit lang, doch kann es das Amt des t-nhoē, „Häuptling" bezeichnen, obgleich ich dafür ein anderes Wort tákeirū habe und dies erscheint in einer anderen Phrase, die ich niedergeschrieben, ohne für ihre genaue Beziehung einstehen zu können, ye-htee-nehtee adem? táheir(e)-āre.

Sonyai.	Lógonē.	Wándalā.	Bágrimma.	Mába.
	{billi(e) ále wó-ha ni} mayal (retsa[17] {maiyal wó-banī dér-}	yé-senaŝ ámuk-sō(?)[19]	mat-adiu garā	χalīfa am adóng-ne
. . . .	wüdāin dérretai na-kū		moh-udī-se garā-gē	am óndingō
éga-kīne (bórēō {éga-samba (hayō}	woyá-n-kū n gadér	{yé-magā-nan goderīre ye-tālas sérarā}	mam-tad gádarī	am ognū sirēne
. . . .	. . . .	. . . . . .		
. . . .	. . . .	. . . . . .	. . . .	
. . . .	[18]	yó-nahā . .	mam-ṭad háye-ńga	mangmasā?
[15]	. . . .	. . . . . .	. . . .	
émongónde (hayō	. . . .	. . . . . .	. . . .	
égurá-nga hayō hanse	. . . .	. . . . . .	. . . .	
éga-māna nisse alhakku[16]	woyá-n-kū gráffera	yé-magā hábera	mam-átadī gá-braga	

[1] ši-gā ha-gálā n ta-ing-áshin: Koelle writes hágalla with a double l, although he himself writes gálágin with a single l. Instead of ta-ing-ishin he has the two forms táishin and táingashin. — I here give the phrase for „I restore him again to his office": K. ši-gā ha-gálā-n-tea-rā (or, if the speaker refers to the Royal dignity, ker-mai-n-tea-rā) yed-weigishin gedā-rá (gedā-rā, „a second time", c. p. 77), T. ámn ai („this man"), tagā hénnā sém-erih.

[2] gadar-nishin is wanting in Koelle; it is probably connected with the Arabic غفر, as is also the case with the Hausa-word.

[3] hayen-nishin also is wanting in Koelle. It is not an indigenous word, but introduced from the Arabic.

[4] grabángana has Koelle neither. This word, being likewise of Arabic origin, from غفر, has not become a common term. We see here the Arabic γ represented with an African native by gr, just as Europeans use to represent this sound.

[5] tánā nána nirhi has rather a suspicious appearance as the 1st pers. of the present tense.

[6] Of this word in the Tédā-language I heard only the form nyenāwáde and that may be the imperative, „pardon (me)".

[7] ina-rédu; here we have another form of the Arabic term, which forms also the root of the Kanúri-term gader-nishin.

[8] sumbar is a foreign word, which on this account is almost identical in H., F. and S.

[9] na-i ma-hó baibé, verbally „I make thee a shot (with the bow)". Besides this form there is a more simple one, at least in the past tense: ná-baibé-ka: „he has abused me", H. yá-baibē-ni, F. á-fidi-yo.

[10] na-i ma-hé dientši has originally, I think, the meaning „I make thee a wry face".

[11] na-i ma-sā hámmia: „he has caused me great shame", ya-i ma-ni babá-n hámmia.

[12] ina-gémašō-ka: „thou disturbest me", H. kai gémašō-ni, F. an-faita-niyo. Identical in sense, but not in grammatical construction, with this is the S.-phrase hayā ashba, „I am busy".

[13] ine-áiaib-ka: the phrase kai áiaiā-ni corresponds in sense to the vulgar phrase „thy presence nauseates", F. an-wan ni-ya. Hither belongs also the H.-term bābo rūa-sea, properly „there is not his water", i. e., „he has no leisure", „is not accessible".

[14] ni gáfería ma-kā: „pardon me", H. gáfería ma-ni, F. yaffa, S. mandā-ie alhákku. „I entreat (implore) him, that he may pardon me", H. ina-róka sea ši gáfería ma-ni, F. mā-torra hémo é-yaff-ā-a. „Revenge is not good, to pardon is better, in order that our Lord may pardon us", H. ráma bābo kyau, gáfería yáfi, domi ši gáfería ma-ad Ubangidšin Alla, F. hoire wódu, yaffā-mo dum búri, yam Dšomiraō yaffō-mē. I likewise adduce here the phrase „I have patience with him", H. na-i báāhori da ši, F. mā-nani-mā; „have patience with him", H. ka-yi báāhori da ši, F. mayā-mē. In reference to the term gáfería I also adduce here gáffara, which is derived from the same Arabic word, although it means „make place (F. farronam) = bā-ni uri, thus „make place, that I may inhale a little air", H. bā-ni uri ina-šā iska, F. hoh-am yaira yére hendu.

[15] see note 12.

[16] Compare the phrase éga-mina hanse kai fāta, „I pardon him some mischief".

[17] billi ála, „this person", wó-ha-ni, „I give him", mayal in this instance evidently = mém-miayal, which properly means „the royal dignity", while teliķia is the general term for „office", or mayal may be the office of the malyal, „courtier of second rank"; dérretsa is from the Arabic درجة „ordo dignitatis".

[18] I have here as the form for the 3rd pers. sing. billi(e) ála gálga-ni.

[19] yé-senaŝ ám-nkaō: I had written this phrase in the wrong place, as if it meant „I deprive of his office"; but yé-senaŝ or yé-sanaŝ is evidently identical with the yé-senaŝ of p. 69; as for another phrase which I have written down y(e)-áfel(e) ám-nkaō, it means evidently „I restore (him) to (his) office", y(e)-áfela being identical with y(e)-ápela p. 67 „I give back, return". As for ám-nkaō, it bears some resemblance to mokna, „women", but it may be quite right, indicating the dignity of the ä-nkaō or chief, although I have the peculiar term táheiré and have an example of its being employed in the phrase ye-hias-nahtsa adem(?) táheir(e)-āre.

Deutsch und Englisch.	Kanúri.	Tēdā.	Haussa.	Fulfúlde.
ich tadele (ihn — *I blame, reprehend (him*	šī-gā gádeskin[1]	. . . . . .	nī-balā-šī	mēdo-bunnī-mò
ich bestrafe (ihn — *I punish (him*	yō-tárig-ískin[2]	. . . . . .	nī bā-šī tsorò[11]	mēdo-búlni-mò
ich räche (eine Mordthat — *I take revenge for (a murder*	kusū bū-be rum-bú-skin[3]	grarē yēd-erík	ina-rāma kašē[12]	mēdo-hōre wá-riṅgo
ich schlage — *I beat, slay*	{ lrag-nískin . / sug-nískin . }	kórkede hāb-erík	ina-bugga . .	mēdo-fiye
ich gebe eine Ohrfeige — *I give a box on the ears*	ram-nískin[4] .	áflatī-erík . .	. . . . . .	. . . . . .
ich tödte — *I slay, kill*	yē-dží-skin[5] .	táné néd-erík	nī-kašī[13] . .	{ mēdo-wára[17] / mēdo-marro }
	3te Prs. S. tšē-tšin	. . . . . .	šina kašē . .	kaṅko ó-wára
ich binde — *I tie* . .	gūr-ískin[6] .	táné { tukín-erík / tím-erík }	ina-damrē . .	mēdo-habba .
	Prt. P. ter-gēr-ina	tukín-tedō .	án-damrē[14] .	. . . . . .
ich enthaupte (ihn — *I behead (him, cut off his head*	kélā-nze kam-nískin[7]	dāho kōb-erík	ina-dēbe ka-nsa[15]	mēdo-itše hōre mā-ko
ich blende, mache die Augen aus — *I put out one's eyes*	{ kúmbu-rō gē-dísko[8] / šim-ze tu-lug-úskin }	semmo tér-erík		
ich hänge (Jemanden — *I hang (some body*	{ sen-ískin[9] . / rōg-ískin . }	lónt-erík[10] .	ina-ratša-šī (bisa itšē[16]	mé-dillī-mō (do lekke

[1] gádeskin. Koelle construirt gádeskin in dieser Bedeutung mit širō und gibt ihm auch noch andere Bedeutungen.

[2] yō-tárig-ískin fehlt bei Koelle, ist aber nur eine verstärkte Form von terángin, das er erklärt „ich drohe".

[3] kusū bū-be rumbú-skin ist etwas doppelsinnig, da es eigentlich heisst „ich trage dir Schuld des Blutes ab", also auch vielleicht von dem gesagt werden kann, der den Mord begangen hat. Etwas ganz Ähnliches finden wir aber auch in anderen Sprachen, so gleich hier im H. und F., wo dasselbe Wort mit geringer Abwandlung — ja im F. mit gar keiner — „ich gebe Rache" und „ich nehme Rache" heisst. Übrigens hörte ich in diesem Falle nur rambú-skin, nicht rambú-skin.

[4] ram-nískin fehlt bei Koelle, wenn es nicht einerlei ist mit seinem rángin, „ich erhebe die Hand, um zu drohen".

[5] yōdžī-skin. Koelle schreibt yēteskin. Diesem Worte legt Koelle auch die Bedeutung „betrügen" bei.

[6] gūr-iskin. Koelle hat gēreskin und yirgēreskin.

[7] kélā-nze kam-nískin (Koelle kámgin), eigentlich „ich schneide seinen Kopf ab".

[8] kúmbu-rō gē-dísko hat Koelle nicht; dabei schreibt er für „blind" kámpū. gē-dísko, eine aoristische Form für „ich mache" habe ich sonst nicht. šim-ze tu-lug-úskin heisst wörtlich „ich mache sein Auge herauskommen".

[9] sen-ískin fehlt bei Koelle, aber rōgeskin hat er, auch führt er als 3te Konj. rōtegeskin, „ich hänge mich selbst", an. „Sie haben ihn gehängt", šī-gá rōtsa-gal.

[10] lónt-erík: 3te Person Plur. Prät. tekintedō.

[11] nī bá-šī tsorō, wörtlich „ich gebe ihm Furcht". Ich führe hier noch eine ähnliche Redensart an, die aber nur von Herrschern oder anderen Personen hohen Ranges gebraucht wird: H. nī-nafórē-šī, „ich bestrafe ihn", F. mēdo-ēlta-mō; H. na-ī ma-kā hókkum-tšī, „ich spreche ein Urtheil über dich", F. mēdo-nī-ma hókkum-tšī.

[12] ina-rāma kašē. „Er rächt den Mord seines Vaters", H. šī-na rāma kašē n ubá-ne, F. ō-m-ohāre wāringo bába ma-ko. Ich will hier noch eine andere verwandte Phrase hersetzen, die ich auch nur in diesen beiden Sprachen habe: „ich muss ihm Rede stehen, bin ihm Rechenschaft schuldig (wegen der und der Sache)", H. nī-yi rāma ma-sā da wo-ne abū, F. mēdo-hōre ai-mo hālu wēnde mā-ko.

[13] nī-kašī. „Tödte ihn", H. kašē šī. F. warai-mō; „nachdem ihm viele Leute getödtet waren", H. an-kašē ma-sā mútane dōwa, F. imberre ādune dúlbe.

[14] ān-damrē. Ich führe hier die nur im H. mir bekannt gewordene Phrase na-kubtšē an, „ich bin dem Gefängniss entsprungen".

[15] ina-dēbe ka-nsa. Ich will hier die kräftigere Redensart anführen nā-fašē ma-sā kai, obgleich nā-fašē oder nī-martša, F. mēdo-fussi, die allgemeine Bedeutung des „Zerschmetterns" hat. Der Bedeutung des Enthauptens steht, glaube ich, ein anderes Wort sehr nahe, obgleich mir dessen nähere Beziehung unbekannt ist, nämlich na-ma korē-šī, F. mēdo-eddī-mō. Diese Redensart scheint mir unserem „ich schicke ihn zum Teufel" am nächsten zu entsprechen.

[16] ina-ratša-šī (bisa itšē, „ich hänge ihn auf — an einem Baum".

[17] mēdo-wāra. Von diesem Verbum ist wāringo abgeleitet.

[18] yo'idesāngaa (ha-ya. Für die 3te Person Plur. Prät. habe ich die Phrase līngelar diggela, die jedoch schwerlich richtig sein kann.

[19] magon kélā dem-na, vielleicht mak-ogē, „ich verweigere", kodā, „die Schuld, Ablösung durch Geld", dem-na, „des Blutes". Es wäre hier das Arabische dem gebraucht und nicht das einheimische múso für „Blut", weil es eine religiöse und richterliche Bedeutung hat.

[20] sam, „ich", háar, „die Augen", Plur. von kaslh, sontsa, „deine" Plur., gō Form des Aoristus, a-ndó-nn, „ich nehme weg". Davon Particip. Passiv. háso udō-te.

Sońyai.	Lógoné.	Wándalá.	Bágrimma.	Mába.
. . . .	. . . .	. . . .	. . . .	. . . .
	wá-tebál-nī . . .	yenánte ye-džawa	mam bolldžnga	. . . . . .
	bī mádīlim-nā wofū?	y(e)-ápela gomo-dāe	magog kélā dem-na [19]	am badžaine
. . . .	wa-tā-kū	yé-džena bá-ya	{ mam-tukí-nya / mam-rutī . }	am budduṅg
ye-dzenánbe verver	. . . .	. . . .	. . . .	. . . .
. . . .	waylan-nī . . .	yé-dža . . .	ma-dōi . .	am barēne
. . . .	3rd pers. sing. a-ylán	á-dža bá-ugané	. . . . . .	. . . . . .
ága-haugn-ndu korfo	wóben-hā . . .	yé-ṅgdo bā-ya	mam-dāoki-nya	{ am ánšene / am gēda-arne }
. . . .	part. p. yábení-nahā	a-úgdo . . .	džoki-nya .	. . . . . .
. . . .	wúpin kan-bénuā	ye-tšē yīr(e)-āra	. . . . . .	. . . . . .
	wū-debāla (kē .	yó-serai itā-āra	mam-átadē gúlu	am káse nonēno-gō á-ndá-ne[20]
	indo asgwa . . .	yo ʾldegáṅgna (bā-ya[18]	ma(m)-līldebrā	korroṅg arrúṅga

[1] gádeskin: Koelle writes gádeskin and construes it with Kirā, attributing to it also other significations.
[2] yé-tárig-íshin appears to be nothing but a stronger form of Koelle's tárīṅgin, but which I have never heard.
[3] kueṅ bá-be rambá-skin is rather a little ambiguous, as it seems properly „I return, pay the debt of the blood", so that it may possibly apply also to the person, who has committed the murder and has to bear the consequence. But something very similar we find also in other languages, as just here in H. and F., where the same term with none or only a slight variation has both meanings, „I give revenge" and „I take revenge".
[4] rem-níshin may be identical with Koelle's rángin, „I check or restrain by waving the hand.
[5] yé-dāī-skin: Koelle writes yōterskin, a term, to which he attributes likewise the meaning of „to cheat".
[6] gēr-íshin: Koelle has the two forms gérçskin and yirgérçskin.
[7] kēlī-nne kam-níshin, verbally „I cut off his head".
[8] kúmbu-rā gē-dinko is wanting in Koelle; kúmbu alone he writes kámpū. I have no more examples of the form gē-dinko, as far as I know. Sim-ne tu-ing-áskin means verbally „I make his eyes come out".
[9] son-íshin is wanting in Koelle, but rágçskin he has, and of the latter verb he adduces as 3rd conjugation rótegçskin, „I hang myself". „They have hanged him", ši-gā rótem-gel.
[10] lónt-erīn: 3rd pers. plur. of past tense lokintedé.
[11] ni bū-ši toorō, verbally „I give him fear", I must here adduce another phrase of a similar meaning, H. ni na-fúre-ši, „I punish him", used only of governors or other persons of high rank, F. mēdo-ēlte-mō; H. na-I mahá hókkum-šīf, „I pronounce sentence upon thee", F. mēdo-ni-mā hokkum-tīl.
[12] ina-rámo kaśē: as an example take: „he revenges the murder of his father", H. ši-na rāma kašé n ohá-ne, F. é-m-ohōre warrigo báha mā-ko. In this place I also mention another related phrase, for which I cannot give the corresponding terms, but in the H.- and F.-languages: H. ni-yi rāma ma-ei da wo-ne shā, F. mēdo-bōre ni-mā hēlawēndr mā-ko.
[13] ni-kaši: „kill him", H. kašē ši, F. waraf-mó; „many people having been killed him", H. ān-kašā ma-ei mótane dēwa, F. imberre ádune dúlbe.
[14] an-damrē. With regard to the captive I will here adduce a phrase, for which I have learnt the corresponding term only in Hausa, viz nā-kubššē, „I have made my escape".
[15] ina-dóbe ka-naa: I here also mention a stronger phrase nā-faššē ma-eá kai, although H. ná-fašē or ni-marēho, F. médo-fussi, has the general meaning of „to crush, dash to pieces". Another phrase must be adduced here, the exact meaning of which I have not made out, but which appears to me to correspond closely to our „I send to the devil", H. na-ma borō-ši, F. mēdo-eddi-mō.
[16] ina-rataa-ši (bisa itāe, „I hang — him on a tree".
[17] mēdo-wāra of course is the root, from which wárīgo has been derived.
[18] yé ʾldegáṅgna (bā-ya for the 3rd pers. plur. of the past tense I have the phrase tlágeler diggela.
[19] magog kēlā dem-na probably is not right, perhaps it ought to be mak-agō, „I reject", kedé, „the credit, debt", dem-na, „of the blood", the Arabic term dem being used in this instance instead of the native word mākū on account of a religious and juridical action being here implied.
[20] am, „I", káse, plur. of káelk, „the eyes", nonēno (plur.-form of núnego), „thine", gō sign of the accus. case, á-udá-ne, „I take away", thence participle passiv. káse udō-te.

Deutsch und Englisch.	Kanuri.	Tédā.	Hausa.	Fulfulde.
ich mache einen Verstoss — *I commit a mistake*	ágēse-diskin[1]	(buddi) berkín-erik	na-ī kówaĭšĕ[11]	mēdo-tĕti . .
ich sündige — *I sin, commit a sin*	bīgu-diskin[2] .		na-ī lēifi[12] .	mē-wōdi lēifi
ich stehle, begehe einen Diebstahl — *I commit a theft*	berbo-diskin[3]		na-ī sáta . .	médo-wūdĕi[16]
ich gehe mit einem Menschen vor Gericht — *I take the law of our*	ū-ma šī-wa šérĕa lén-fen	. . . . . .	ína kāa šeria ta-rē[13] da wo-ne mutúm	mēdo-yába kita bē ó neldo,
ich bereue — *I repent* .		. . . . . .	na-túba (Arb.)	mē-tubi . .
ich presse die Glieder — *I press the joints, rub*	gambú-skin[4] .	gám-erík . .	ína tausa[14] .	mēdo-nódžoki
ich fächele, wedele — *I fan*	sabút-iskin[5] .	báb-erík . .	. . . . . .	. . . . . .
ich gebe dir Arznei (du wirst besser), ich kurire dich — *I give thee medicine, cure thee*	ní-rō kurgún dí-skin (ngá-ne-min[6]	súro kurt-ún-erík[9]	ína léka mágani[15] .	mēdo-takka sa-fare
ich lasse zur Ader — *I take, draw blood*	(bū to-lug-úskin) (bēdžim kāse-gúiskin[7])	furkyī lér-erik	ína déhe ženi	(mēlo-bīre .) (mē-iltai īyam)
ich bekehre (dich) zum Islam — *I convert (thee) make (thee) a Moslim*	ní-gā) mislem-iskin[8]	tánē (ne)brà guf-fúr-n-erik[10]		. . . . . .

[1] ágēse-diskin ist wol sicherlich identisch mit gesen-iskena, S. 52. Koelle gibt dem Zeitwort ágē-sāgin nur die Bedeutung von „vergessen", aber ágēse, „Fehler", das Koelle nur als „Hautkrankheit" erklärt, hängt damit zusammen.

[2] bīgu-diskin, Koelle bīge diskin.

[3] berbo-diskin. Koelle hat dies Zeitwort nicht, aber er hat barbāngin, „ich werde zum Räuber".

[4] gambú-skin hat Koelle mit der Bedeutung „ich bräune", indem er den Sinn wol nicht recht gefasst hat.

[5] sabút-iskin fehlt wieder bei Koelle. Es ist jedoch kein ursprünglich einheimisches Wort, sondern dem Stamme nach aus dem Arabischen eingeführt.

[6] Das hinzugesetzte ngá-nemin, „du wirst gesund", drückt das Kuriren der Krankheit aus. In anderen Sprachen wird dies angedeutet durch den Zusatz „gut" zu „Arznei". Koelle hat für „ich genese", dámāngin.

[7] bēdžim kāse-gúiskin. Das Verbum hat Koelle in der Form kāsegin (3te Person kī kāšin); bēdžim hat er nicht, und ich selbst kenne es auch nur in dieser Verbindung.

[8] mislem-iskin hat Koelle nicht; übrigens schreibt er mōslem.

[9] súro kurt-ún-erik: súro, „Arznei", kúrt-erik, „ich bringe", S. 64, kurt-ún-erik wol nur verstärkte Form.

[10] tánē (ne)brà guffúr-n-erik. guffúr-n-erik hängt wol unzweifelhaft mit dem Arabischen kāfir, „Ungläubiger", zusammen und es wäre dann die Grundbedeutung „ich entkafere dich". Das ne in nebra wird im gewöhnlichen Leben wegen des vorangehenden ne in tánē verschluckt; eigentlich ist es nebrá-ne.

[11] na-ī kówaĭšĕ. Ich bin nicht ganz sicher über die Bedeutung dieses Wortes. Als passive Form habe ich anyī me-nī kówaĭšĕ, F. mētotá-mā.

[12] na-ī lēifi. Negative Form: „das ist nicht mein Fehler", H. ba ni lēifi ba, F. mā-wōdo-ī lēifi.

[13] Ich will hier die begriffsverwandten Phrasen aufführen „ich besiegte vor Gericht", H. ná-kašĕ (ŠI) da šeria, F. mōdo-yī (mā) ke kita: „ich habe meinen Process verloren, ich bin ruinirt" (wörtlich: „der Gerichtsort hat mich getödtet, mein Vermögen ist zerstört"), H. yá-kašĕ-ni ari-n šeria, yá-rossa dúkiá-ta, F. odōyī-am yaire kita, mé-eolti dāondi. Hierher gehört auch gewissermassen die Phrase H. ína rossa gaskia, F. mé-eolti gonga mé-ko, „ich verdrehe, verderbe das" oder „sein Recht".

[14] ína tausa. Ich will hier das begriffsverwandte Wort ína rēda hersetzen, F. mēdo-baren, „ich streichele".

[15] ína léka mágani wird eigentlich nur von äusserlich applicirten Heilmitteln gesagt. Ich will hier noch eine andere Phrase aufführen „ich träufele Arznei in die Augen", H. ína tsīe mágani tšikin idonū, F. mēdo-tobbe.

[16] mēdo-wūdĕi; davon das Substantiv gūdĭo, Plur. wuībe, „der Dieb".

Sónγai.	Lógonē.	Wándalā.	Bágrimma.	Mába.
. . . .	wuγsē kalā . .	yé-návia . .	mam-ándangā	am angna-rène
éga-hín ħai futu	wa-gimbekē . .	yé-magā {bikrr / maγaipa}	mam-índ biggéa	
. . . .	. . . .	. . . . . .	. . . . . .	
éga-sáya? . .	. . . .			
	. . . .			
éga-múse . . .	wum[illegible]? . .	yé-swa . . .	mam-gak . .	{am búka-rē / am konye-erè}
. . . .	wuħisse zau . .	yé-weta . .	mam-ak obrúmma	am yáwerē
	woγá-ñku daúa ká ke-ñaiñga	yé-magā kurgún kamba	ma mat-ad-ī kurgūn tád-en gāga	
éga-kau kuri .	wu-firmi	yé-sa wudže .	mat-ad mūsenāgla	am šeddier baróñgne
	índo tī woyá-ñku mislim	yé-gāgwo-ga míslema	mat-ad-ī mislim	am mislim éyinè

[1] ágēse-diskin most probably is identical with gesen-iskene p. 52, although Koelle attributes to the verb ágéśęgin nothing but the notion „I forget", but the substantive ágése which he mentions with the notion „cutaneous disease", probably is the root of that verb, signifying every sort of „fault".

[2] bíga-diskin: Koelle bíge diskin.

[3] berbe-diskin: Koelle has not this verb, but he has barbúngin, „I become a thief", as he also writes barbu.

[4] gambú-skin: Koelle has this term with the meaning „I scratch", but does not seem to have caught the right meaning. Koelle himself has other by far more expressive terms for such a notion.

[5] sabát-iskin: also this word is wanting in Koelle. It is however not an indigenous word, but of foreign importation, having been derived from the Arabic.

[6] ní-rē kurgún dí-skin ingā-nemin: the addition of ngā-nemin, „thou getst well", expresses the „curing" of the disease. In others of the corresponding languages this notion has been expressed by adding to the word „medicine" the adjective „good", „efficient".

[7] héddim kase-gúiskin: Koelle has the verb under the form of kasęngin (3rd pers. sī kaššin), but the noun héddim he has not and it is certainly not a common word and I have never met it in any other connection, but this one.

[8] mislem-iskin is wanting in Koelle who, instead of mislem writes mósęlem.

[9] sóro kart-ín-erik. sóro, „medecine", kart-ín-erik probably another form of kárt-erik, „I bring", p. 68.

[10] táné (ne)brā guffúr-n-erik: there can scarcely be the least doubt, that the verb guffúr-n-erik has been derived from the Arabic term káfir, „the infidel", so that the original meaning seems to be „I make thee cease to be a pagan". The ne in nebrā in vulgar dialogue is absorbed by the preceding ne in táné; the full secus. form is nebrā-ne.

[11] na-í kówatšē: I am not quite certain of the original meaning of this term. In the passive tense I have the form nayī me-nī kówatšē, F. métetá-mb.

[12] na-í lōtfí: negative form: „that is not my fault", H. ba nī lōtfí ba, F. mē-wāda-ī lōtfí.

[13] I shall here adduce some phrases of a similar meaning, as „I win a suit of law" (properly „I kill him by law"), H. nakašē (šī) da šerí́a, F. mēda-yī (mō) he kita; „I have lost a suit of law, I am ruined" (properly „the place of law has killed me, my property is absorbed"), H. yá-kaše-nī ori-n šeria, yá-rasse dúkiá-ta, F. odóyi-om yaire kita, mē-seiti dānadi. To this place belongs likewise in some respect the phrase H. ina resse gáskia, F. mē-seiti gongo mā-ho, „I spoil the (or „his") right".

[14] ina tausa. I here adduce a term of a similar meaning, via ina rēda, F. mēdo-bursa, „I stroke, caress, handle".

[15] ina lēka māgani properly is only used of medicine applied externally. I adduce here also another phrase of a similar meaning: „I drop medicine into the eyes", H. ina tarfa māgani [?] […] idanū, F. mēdo-tobba.

[16] mēdo-wūdī: thence gúdio, plur. waibe, „the thief".

Deutsch und Englisch.	Kanuri.	Tëda.	Haussa.	Fulfulde.
ich beschneide — *I circumcise*	kadža-tiskin [1]	. . . . . .	nia kátšia . .	mēdo-dul-na .
ich entmanne, verschneide — *I unman, castrate, geld*	{údim-i-rò kam-n-iskin [2] / yé-sa-ṅgin [3]}	togór kaser-erík [10]		
ich begrabe — *I bury* .	rum-niskin [4] .	setrá-nt-erík	ina bisne-(ši [12]	mēdo-mabbi-(mo
ich beerbe — *I inherit* .	wúrnta-niskin [5]	rizi bénnā gön-erík [11]	. . . . . .	. . . . . .
ich folge nach, sitze auf dem Throne meines Vaters — *I succeed to, sit on the throne of my father*	kirte[6] diggel {olā-ni-bē nam-nis-kin}	. . . . . .	ina-bi-(ma)tšikin sarauta	
ich warte — *I wait* . .	gurē-niskin [7] .	tinē kenéu-erík	ina žira [13] . .	medo-hetti .
ich habe Geduld — *I have patience*	kúnnudi gön-iskin [8]		na-i háukora	. . . . . .
ich gehe — *I go*	lē- niskin [9] . .	to-dêdi . . .	{ni-zāni . . / ina tafi-a .}	mēdo-dilli
ich reise — *I travel* . .	lē- ṅgin . .			
gehe, reise — *go, travel*	lé-né . . .	{owū . . . . / yesu . . . .}	zāni . . . . / tafi	{dillu . . . . / yābo . . . .}
ich gehe nicht — *I do not go*	lē-ṅgin bago .	te-dêdi-n . .	ni ba {ni-zāni / ina ta-fi-a} ba	mēdo-dilla-ta
ich gehe umher, mache einen Spaziergang — *I go about, take a walk*	derī-niskin .	derī-derī-n-erík	na-i kilisa .	{mēdo-waigoi / mé-wantšeto}

[1] kadža-tiskin. Koelle hat dieses Wort in der Form katšáṅgin und katšiáṅgin. Für die 3te Person Plur. habe ich kádža-sē. — Übrigens habe auch ich für „Vorhaut" die Form katšā.

[2] ûdim-i-rò kam-n-iskin, eigentlich „ich schneide zu einem Eunuchen". Koelle hat hierfür die Form udim-ö yàkéskin.

[3] yé-sa-ṅgin wird, glaube ich, selten anders als von Thieren gebraucht; Particip. Passiv. ye-sáhhate.

[4] rum-niskin: Koelle rēmgin; daneben šitęrēágin.

[5] wúrnta-niskin ist wieder ein vom Arabischen ورث eingeführter und der Bórnu-Sprache angeeigneter Ausdruck, der wol nicht so leicht in die Provinzialsprache übergegangen ist und daher bei Koelle fehlt.

[6] kirte ist wol unzweifelhaft das Arabische kursi; diggel heisst das einheimische Rohrbett, zugleich Diwan.

[7] gorē-niskin. Koelle hat dieses Wort in der Form gureṅgin, und davon ist das andere Wort, gēṅgin, welches er auch mit derselben Bedeutung hat, wol nur eine volksthümliche Abkürzung.

[8] kúnudi gön-iskin. Koelle hat neben dieser Phrase auch das Zeitwort kunudiṅgin für die verwandte Bedeutung „ich ertrage mit Geduld".

[9] lé-niskin ist wol die einzig richtige Schreibweise dieses Wortes zum Unterschiede von len-niskin S. 38, N. 5. „ich schlafe".

[10] togór kaser-erík. togór heisst der Eunuch; kaser-erík das Arabische كسر mit einheimischer Endung.

[11] rizi bénnā gön-erík, wörtlich „ich nehme, erhalte sein Vermögen".

[12] ina bisne-(ši wird auch vom gewöhnlichen Verstecken gesagt, besonders unter der Erde.

[13] ina žira. Beispiel. „sie sind fortgegangen, ohne auf mich zu warten", H. sún-tafi, ba sú-žira-ni ba, F. bē-dilli dó kettāke-am. Ich will hier die begriffsverwandte Phrase anführen „ich lauere auf" (b. Koelle mbēli-niskin), H. ina tsarō, F. mēdo-rēma; „worauf lauerst du?", H. mē ka-kè tsarō, F. kò ondēmata; „sie lauern ihm auf der Strasse auf", H. sú-na tsaró nsa šíhi-n hanya, F. bdum hēdema oder betāšāho-mo dé laawol.

[14] Als 3te Person Plur. habe ich im Lógonē für „sie beschneiden" die Form yafiane kaša.

[15] y(e)-edé-ka, offenbar nicht von y(e)-él dulá, sondern von y(e)-edé. Ich habe von diesem Zeitwort ein ganzes Paradigma niedergeschrieben, aber leider sind viele Formen unsicher.

[16] am ar-ēmne; Imperativ lemma.

Bedyal.	Lógonē.	Wándalā.	Bágrimma.	Mába.
. . . .	"	yé-dimtšé-dekwē	mam-ákoll .	am tar arúṅgne
	wú-piakū meláxim	ye-gán wédilima	m(am)-ákol ádim	am átam maṅgne
éga-fige . . .	wú-χa belémna .	yé-χedā . .	mam-tad džúfūgā	am amíanc
. . . .	wa-zúm wurótayā	yé-zavre tāra	m(am)-úkum wor-ret-maá	am wārax-ercñē-ne
	wa-zúm rāne bē-nūā	yé-džan bāde-ruā	mak-indži god babá-ma	am koldum ūl-mo-núṅg nagó-naya
éga-hattu . . .	wú-dakúlni . .	yé-pakā . .	mak-odi-nya	am ar-énne [18]
. . . .	. . . .	yé-magā-n-magā kam-dire	mak-un kanādi	
éga-koi . . .	wú-gir.	y(e)-él dalā / yé-dela . .	mak-abē . .	am akāī
koi	gulu	él dalā	abē	koko
éna-koi . . .	wu-gir-na . .	y(e)-edo-ka [15]	mak-abé-li .	am áka-ta
	indo wú-guri .	ye-dámmala .	mak-gogrī .	am akaī

[1] kedša-tiskin appears in Koelle's vocabulary under the form katšángin and katšiángin; as 3rd pers. plur. I have kédša-nō. However for the term „prepare" I myself have the form katšā.

[2] ádim-í-rā kam-a-iskin means properly „I cut as (or „to") a eunuch". Koelle has the form ádimmā yókéskin.

[3] yé-ea-ngin, I think, is scarcely ever used except of animals; particip. passiv. ye-nákkain.

[4] ram-niskin: Koelle rémgin and besides šátęrángin, identical with the T.-term.

[5] wúrata-niskin again has been taken from the Arabic ورث and has been adapted to the grammatical rules of the Kanúri-language, without becoming a common term used in the country and in the provinces, whence it happens, that it has remained unknown to Koelle.

[6] kirie is most likely the Arabic kursi; diggol is the term for the native bed or diwan of reeds.

[7] gorō-niskin: Koelle has this word under the form gurōngin and I suppose, that another word, góngin, to which he attributes the same meaning, is nothing but a vulgarly contracted form of the same word.

[8] kánadi gön-iskin: besides this phrase Koelle has the verb kanadingin with the meaning „I bear patiently".

[9] lē-niskin is, I think, the only, right way of spelling this term, in order to distinguish it plainly from the verb lenniskin, „I sleep", p. 38, note 5.

[10] togór kasear-erik: togór is „the eunuch"; kasear-erik is the Arabic قصر, an indigenous termination being added.

[11] rini kénaá gán-erik means verbally „I take, receive his property".

[12] ina hinge-(ži is also used of a common hiding, especially underground.

[13] ina Sira: as example I cite the phrase „they are gone, without waiting for me", H. sún-taff, ba sú-Sira-ni ba, F. hé-dilli dó ketšike-am. — In this place I must also adduce a phrase of a similar meaning: „I lurch, am on the watch for somebody" (K. Koelle mbélániskin), H. ina teará, F. módu-réna: „what are you on the watch for!", H. mō ka-kē teará, F. ké andénata: „they are lurking for him on the road", H. sū-na teará maa šikki-n hanya, F. adanr héddas or ketšókko-mó dó laurl.

[14] As 3rd pers. plur. for „they circumcise" in Lógonē I have taken down the form yafiané kaši.

[15] y(e)-edó-ka evidently is not derived from y(e)-éldalá, but from y(e)-edó. Of the verb y(e)-él dala I have a complete paradigm, but unfortunately many forms are uncertain.

[16] am ar-énna; imperat. trans.

Deutsch und Englisch.	Kanuri.	Tedâ.	Hausa.	Fulfulde.
ich breche auf — I rise, start	tšī-nískin[1] .	táně yár-n-erík	ína tāši[13] . .	mēdo-úmmoto[16]
ich komme, komme herbei — I come	ísi-skin[2] . .	táně { girg-erík / tír-erík[8] }	ína { tafē . . / zakka[14] . / zūwa . . }	{ mēdo-wára . / mēdo-iba . . }
komm — come	arē[3]	yíro	yāka	wárol . . .
ich gehe ein, komme herein — I go in, enter	gāg-ískin[4] .	{ védero girg-ērík / táně tózzoti[9] }	ína šigga . .	mēdo-nāta .
ich gehe hinaus, bin im Hinausgehen — I go out, am going out	lug-áskin[5] .	{ agā rórik[10] . / táně lurde . }	zāni fitto . .	médo-wurto .
ich kehre zurück, heim — I return, get home	welt-ískin[6] . 3te Prs. S. weltšin	táně záftot-erík[11]	{ ína-kōmo . / ína-dauiö . }	mēdo-wárti . kaúko ó-wárti
ich nähere mich — I approach	káring-nískin[7]	{ edíňke / nerkai } tíg-erík[12]	na-i kūsa[15] .	mī báda-kē .

[1] tšī-nískin. Koelle schreibt tšīágin. Das l in der Wurzel ist nicht ganz klar und ich hörte oft tšē-niskin, wie denn die 3te Person Sing. wol durchgängig tšē-tšin lautet.

[2] ísi-skin. Koelle schreibt íseskin und iskin. — 3te Person Sing. íšin.

[3] arē, ein nur im Imperativ gebräuchliches unvollständiges Zeitwort, das mit dem T. yár-n-erík verwandt ist.

[4] gāg-iskin; 3te Person Sing. gāg-in. Koelle schreibt gāgqskin.

[5] lug-áskin; 3te Person Sing. lué-lug-in. Koelle schreibt lúskin und lúgqskin.

[6] welt-iskin. Diese Form, die in den Landschaften Bórnu's, die ich besuchte, die alltägliche ist, hat Koelle nicht, dagegen hat er die Form wol-ágin. Es hängt wol jedenfalls mit ولى zusammen; als 3te Person Sing. hat er davon woltšin. Zu diesem Worte wird ausdrucksvollerer Bezeichnung halber oft das Wort ágife-ró, „rückwärts", hinzugesetzt.

[7] káring-niskin. Koelle schreibt auffallender Weise kárgágin, was doch keine Verbalform von kárangy oder kárqangu sein kann und dabei auch dem ganz ebenso geschriebenen und doch so verschieden abgeleiteten Wort für „ich lese" gleich ist.

[8] tánē girg-erík, tír-erík. Dies sind nach meiner Vermuthung die grammatisch richtigen Formen; aber ich habe nur tánē girge, tánē tírri gehört.

[9] táně tózzoti; Imperativ „gehe, komm herein", ozzout; tózzoti wahrscheinlich populäre Form für tózzot-erík.

[10] agā rórik. Für die Form des Imperativs habe ich yaráh. — lurde, vielleicht ursprünglich lugde, wol für lúgd-erík.

[11] Ich will den verwandten Ausdruck táně yefúbeu igáe-erík anführen.

[12] edíňke, nerkai tíg-erík: edíňke heisst „nahe".

[13] ina tāši. Ich will hier auch eine einschlagende Redensart anführen, die ich nur im H. und F. vertreten kann, nämlich „ich treffe Vorkehrungen zur Reise", H. na-šárie tafia, F. mēdo-bebbi (oder mēdo-yérinde) dāñhangel; „es gilt jetzt die Reisezurüstung" (wörtlich „zur Reisezurüstung"), H. sō šēra u tafie, F. dagē ánnie dāñhangel.

[14] ina zakka, ina zūwa. Zuweilen können diese beiden Wörter auch eine dem „Hingehen" sehr ähnliche Bedeutung erhalten, wie in der Redensart „wohin gehst du?", H. ina zakka, ina ka-zō, F. tō a-dāta, Plur. tō on-dāta, S. máne kal, während „woher kommst du?" H. ina ká-fitto, F. tō yóhedd, S. máni bau heisst. Für „ich komme an" haben einige dieser Sprachen noch besondere Wörter, wie das H. nī ní-isá, F. mēdo-áttakē; in den anderen Sprachen vertritt das eine Wort auch diese Bedeutung. tafē wird besonders in der populären Phrase ga-ni nan tafē, „siehe, da komme ich, da bin ich", gebraucht.

[15] na-i kūsa. Ich will hier die begriffsverwandte Redensart anführen „ich rücke näher", H. ina gúrgusa, F. mē-fóttahē, mēdo-hikki torro; „rücke ein bischen näher", H. gúrgusa kadán, F. fóttero sedda oder bádwa. Gegensatz zu na-i kūsa ist H. na-i nēsa, F. mē-wóddakē.

[16] mēdo-úmmoto gebrauchen die Fulbe nicht eben häufig vom Aufbruch zur Reise, da sie besondere Ausdrücke für das Aufbrechen je nach der Tageszeit haben. So sagen sie für „ich breche früh Morgens auf" (H. ina tāši da sassáfi) mēdeui oder mēdo-fina, für den Ausdruck „ich breche am Abend auf" (H. ina tāši da márайčē) mēdo-hírindē, für „ich breche zur Nachtzeit auf" (H. ina tāši da derē, ina dauka-n derē) mēdo-bēdāi.

[17] ága-hūra. Ich bin der Meinung, dass sowol dieses Wort, wie das folgende mit hū (hagā) zusammenhängt.

[18] wo'ale hängt möglicher Weise mit wó-sa zusammen, wäre also richtiger mit a zu schreiben.

[19] índo lāgukā. Im Lógone muss hierfür noch ein ganz anderes Wurzelwort vorhanden sein, da ich für die 3te Person Sing. ní násaló habe.

[20] wá-sa ēn. Nicht von diesem Zeitwort, sondern vom vorhergehenden ist awa ēn, „komm herein", abgeleitet.

[21] wálame aló. aló heisst „nahe"; das a scheint aber in anderen Formen in ą übergegangen.

[22] ye-sā bí-ya; „er kommt", a-sā bá-nganá.

[23] á-berten. Für „er kehrt um, geht zurück", habe ich á-berten degatélile (gigs-téllia').

[24] mák-fúri. Dazu die Phrase „ich brach auf und ging", mak-i mak-sbē.

[25] masa-ah indáā. Eine vollere Form für „komm herein" ist andáe dāóngaia.

[26] Für „ich gehe hinaus" habe ich im Mába wieder á-yihgi aufgeschrieben, „ich stehe auf, breche auf", was natürlich durch den Zusammenhang oft diese Bedeutung erhalten kann.

Sońyai.	Lógoné.	Wándalá.	Bágrimma.	Mába.
éga-tun	índo woñaia [18] .	yé-tsetšē . .	mák-iúgi [24]	á-yiúgi
éga-kā	índo (nia) wu-lógu-ku [19]	ye-só bá-ya [22]	mam-dēga . / mák-anā . .	am úndirkō / am áka-(e)rnē
kā	awa	sáwa	abdžō . .	kāra, plur. kēre
éga-hūra [17] . .	wú-aa én [20] . .	y(e)-ïdo . .	mam-ák indžā [25]	am aynī
éga-húntarē . .	wú-aa fúne . .	ye-ségešē bá-ya	ma-leká galá	[26]
. . . .	wa-kag-áya . .	yé-betsa . .	madúng-gulō / madúng-bē-ta	am wai akaī
. . . .	3rd ps. s. ná-la kog-a	á-betsa [23] . .	. . . . . .	. . . . . .
éga-mán . . .	wálone aiō [21] . .	herdža y(e)-endi-gredžē	mal-ad boi-ga	am mindži akaī

[1] tšī-nichin: Koelle writes tšī-ágin; the ī in the root tšī is not quite clear and I heard often pronounce tšē-nichin and thus the 3rd pers. sing. seems to be constantly tšē-tšin.
[2] lel-chin: Koelle writes leqchin and lchin. — 3rd pers. sing. llin.
[3] arō, a defective verb, used only in the imperative mood, but evidently from the same root, as the T.-word yar-n-erik.
[4] gág-ichin; 3rd pers. sing. gág-in. — Koelle writes gágéchin.
[5] lug-áchin; 3rd pers. sing. tsé-lug-in. — Koelle writes láchin and lúgechin.
[6] welt-ichin: this form, which in those provinces of Bórnu, which I have visited, is the only one used, is wanting in Koelle; on the contrary he has a form, which I have never heard, viz wel-ágin: in any case it is derived from [illegible]. In order to impart a more expressive character to this word the adverb ágáfo-rō, „backwards", is often added.
[7] háríág-nichin: Koelle has the shorter form hāréngin, which seems by no means a regular verbal form derived from hárange or hárangen, besides that it is so easily to be confounded with the almost identical word conveying the totally different meaning „I read".
[8] tanē girg-erik, tir-erik: these according to my opinion are the true grammatical forms of the two verbs, but I heard only tanē girge, tanē tirri.
[9] tanē tásaoti is probably a popular form for tásant-erik; imperat. „go in", „come in", susent.
[10] agā rōrik: for the form of the imperat. mood I have yerōk. — lurde, perhaps originally lugde, which might be the popular form of lúgd-erik.
[11] I must here adduce a phrase of a similar meaning: tanē yetūben igés-erik.
[12] adiáke, nerhel alg-erik; adiake means „near".
[13] ina tāši: I must here also adduce a phrase of a meaning pertaining to this subject, but which I can only give in H. and F.: „I make preparations for the journey", H. na-šárie tafia, F. mōdo-hebbi (or mōdo-yérindo) dáabangel; „(there remains) nothing but preparations for the journey", H. sē šēra n tafia, F. dagā innie dáabangel.
[14] ina nakka, ina sáwa: in some cases these two words can receive a signification very nearly approaching to notion of „to go", as is the case with the phrase „where do you go?", H. ina nakka, ina ka-nā, F. tá a-dāta, plur. tá on-dāta, S. mána hoi, while the phrase „whence do you come" is in H. ina ká-fitō, F. tō yūhedā, B. ndal bun. — The verb tafē is particularly used in the popular phrase ga-ni nan tafē, „see, there I come, there I am".
[15] na-i hūsa: I must here adduce a phrase of a similar notion: „I draw near", H. ina gárgasa, F. mē-fóttahē, mōdo-hibbi terre: „draw a little nearer", H. gárgasa kadān, F. fōttore sedda or hédwa. The reverse of na-i hūsa is in H. na-i nēsa, in F. mē-waddahō.
[16] mōdo-ámmato is not a word so frequently used by the Pulbe, as one might suppose, as they have particular terms signifying the starting at different times of the day. Thus they express „I start early in the morning" (H. ina tāši da sassāfi) by the term mōde'ul or mōde-fini, „I start in the evening" (H. ina tāši da márailē) by mōdo-hirrindō, „I start by night" (H. ina tāši da darē or ina dauka-n darē) by mōdo-hēdāi.
[17] éga-bāra: I am of opinion, that this word as well, as the following is connected with bā (hogū).
[18] woñala is possibly connected with wá-sa, so that it might better be written with a instead of an ().
[19] indo lógahē: besides this word there must still be in use another one derived from a totally different root, as for the 3rd pers. sing. I have the form ni ásealē.
[20] wá-sa én: for the term „come in" awa én is used, which is not derived from this verb, but from the preceding one.
[21] wálone alō: alō means „near", but the latter a in other tenses of this verb seems to be changed into a g.
[22] ya-sō bá-ya: „he comes", sué bá-ĝanē.
[23] á-betsa: the meaning „backwards" distinctly expressed makes á-betsa degatéllia (yiga-téllia!).
[24] mák-iúgi: compare the phrase „I started and went", mak-i mák-ahō.
[25] mam-ák indžā: for „come in" I have the fuller form andže dáángala.
[26] For „I go out" I have in Mába again á-yiági, which properly means „I arise, start", but in certain cases may convey the other meaning.

Deutsch und Englisch.	Kanuri.	Tédā.	Hausa.	Fulfúlde.
ich laufe — *I run* . .	ingrim-níškin [1]	táne yák-erík / ya-rík [6].	ína guddu [10] .	mēdo-dugga .
	3te Prs. S. ingrím-tšin	. . . . .		
ich fliehe — *I escape, flee*	kás-iskin [2] .	[7]		
	3te Pers. S. se-kás-in	. . . . . .	. . . . . .	. . . . . .
ich habe mich verirrt — *I have gone astray*	fat-iskena [3] .	morrin tíri-dē [8]	ná-hatši . .	mé-meddži [12] .
ich habe den Weg verloren — *I have lost my way*	3te Prs. S. fét-sikī	morkin	ná-hatús da hanya	mē-med-dži dattal / lauel
ich fühle Ermüdung — *I get tired*	tsimbar-iskin [4]	táne gallauye?	ina ži n gažia	mēdo-nanna tšómmeri
ich bin ermüdet — *I am tired, fatigued*	tsimbar-iskena	lóbtekin [9] . .	ná-gaži . .	mē-sómmi .
	3te Pers. S. tsím-barī	lóbkindē . .	. . . . . .	. . . . . .
ich mache Halt, halte an — *I stop, make a halt*	dā-nískin . / dā-ngin . .		ina tsaia . .	mēdo-dárrekē
halt an, Halt — *stop* .	dā-né . . .	. . . . . .	tsaia	darra . . .
	Plur. dā-né de-gō	. . . . . .	. . . . . .	. . . . . .
ich verweile, bleibe — *I abide, tarry, remain*	nem-nískin [5] .	táne te-búz-erík	ina da ganánna	mē-mélodó .
ich habe meinen Aufenthalt, wohne — *I dwell*		némai tóm-erík	[11]	

[1] ingrim-níškin, bei Koelle ngérgmgin, 3te Person Sing. ngérgmtšin.

[2] kás-iskin. Koelle schreibt kásaskin und in der 3ten Person ksegásin; in Betreff des Überganges des k in g hat er der Aussprache wegen Recht, nur bezweifle ich, dass beim Schreiben der Konsonant zu verändern ist.

[3] fat-iskena. Koelle schreibt pádzeskin und 3te Person Sing. pátsegi.

[4] tsimbar-iskin hat Koelle in der wol älteren Form mbáreskin und führt sogar die Phrase za wu nirō mbáreskī. Ich habe nur noch die Form yimbar-iskin gehört.

[5] nem-níškin hat Koelle in der Form namgin. nem-níškin hat beide Bedeutungen, weil nem eine sehr umfassende Bezeichnung hat, „Ort, Stelle, Haus", also nem-níškin wörtlich „ich mache einen Ort, mache eine Wohnung"; Participium néb-kata.

[6] táne ya-rík. Diese Form nimmt das Zeitwort in der gewöhnlichen Umgangssprache an; dass aber die eigentlich grammatische Form yák-erík ist, zeigt der Imperativ yak.

[7] Für kás-iskin hörte ich in der Tédā-Sprache nur die Form táne yarde und in der 3ten Person Plur. ho yárhodē; beide Formen sind von ya-rík abgeleitet.

[8] morrin tíri-dē; tíri heisst „der Weg".

[9] lóbtekin ist eine etwas auffallende Form; aber ich habe auch 1ste Person Plur. lóbtaygō, 3te Person Plur. lóbygō.

[10] ina guddu. Imperativ „laufe, eile", H. guddu, F. dugga. Verwandt ist damit dem Sinne nach die Phrase na-i gúrmusia, die, so viel ich verstanden habe, unserem gewöhnlichen „ich reise aus" entspricht; F. mēdo-báeseda.

[11] Die Hausa-Sprache hat, so viel mir bekannt, keinen eigentlichen Ausdruck für „ich wohne", und sie können es nur umschreiben mit „mein Haus ist (da und da)", gída-na nkai. — ina da ganánna hat die Nebenbedeutung von Langsamkeit und wird, glaube ich, besonders von Nachzüglern gebraucht; es gehört also, genau genommen, nicht hierher.

[12] mē-meddži. Es ist auffallend, dass wir hier und in der folgenden Phrase dieselbe Form des Zeitwortes haben, da es doch so verschiedene Bedeutungen hat, im ersteren Falle „ich habe mich verloren", im zweiten „ich habe den Weg verloren".

[13] Über den geistigen Zusammenhang der Sprachbildung bei den Verbalformen ēga-kō, ēga-hai, ēga-hai s. Prolegomena.

[14] naugin. Ich habe hier als 3te Person Sing. skhu, das wäre aber eine ziemlich unregelmässige Form.

[15] á-kudá-kodē. Ich habe auch noch die Form kódauwó-kodē.

[16] wátein kogó ist wol unzweifelhaft der Imperativ; kogó kohó, „geh", also ist vielleicht am wátein nkai die 1ste Person Sing., aber für die 3te Person Plur. habe ich dum („alle") wátele.

Sónyai.	Lógoné.	Wándalá.	Bágrimma.	Mába.
		yó-digaā . .	má-nyurū . .	am áviai
éga-zorū . . .	wó-gobī . . . . , 3. pers. sing. á-gobī			
		yé-džéga-dē	mák-anyā . .	wátala kogō[16]
	. . . .	. . . .	. . . .	. . . . . .
éga-áddere . .	waugía[11]	yé-kedá-n kedā 3. pa. s. kedá kedā	mam-īga . . ēga	am áffēa táffēa
si farā	wa-mberīa . .	yé-kudú-kodē	mam-ókkorō mam-orga .	am állēa
	3. pers. sing. nī na-mberīa	á-kudú-kodē[15]	. . . . .	
éga-kai[13] . . .	. . . .	. . . .	. . . .	. . . .
kai	. . . .	. . . .	. . . .	. . . .
. . . .	. . . .	. . . .	. . . .	. . . .
. . . .	wúse wātin . . wúsena (na rō-na átema	yé-džindžā .	mak-indžī	am akálle am bāle taṅg-andā-ne

[1] ingrim-nískin: Koelle ńgéremgin, 3rd pers. sing. ńgéremdšin.

[2] kás-iskin: Koelle writes káseskin and in the 3rd pers. sing. tsegásin. With regard to the latter form involving a change of the k into g he is right, as far as pronunciation is concerned, but I doubt, whether in writing the same rule has to be adopted.

[3] fat-iskena: Koelle writes pádgeskin and pátsegi.

[4] tsimbar-iskin has Koelle in the very different form mbéreskin for which he adduces the phrase wa síró mbáreski; it may be the original form, as is seen from L. Another form yimbar-iskin I have sometimes heard.

[5] nem-nískin has Koelle in the form nómgin. — The term has both notions „I remain" and „I dwell" on account of the wide signification of the word nem, „place, order, house", in consequence whereof nem-nískin means „I make a place, dwelling" etc. — Partizip. néh-kein.

[6] táné ya-rik is the form, which the verb adopts in general conversation; but that yák-erik is the right grammatical form, we see from the imperative yak.

[7] For the Kanúri-verb kás-iskin in T. I only heard táné yardē and in the 3rd pers. he yárkedé. Both forms are evidently derived from ya-rik.

[8] morrin tirí-dē: tiri means „path", „road".

[9] íóhtekin is a remarkable form; for the 1st pers. plur. I have íóhteyó and 3rd pers. plur. iobgó.

[10] ina guddu: imperat. „run, make haste", H. gaddu, F. dagga. A similar meaning approaching closely to that of „I desert" is conveyed by the phrase na-i górmanlā, F. médo-bóserdo.

[11] The Hausa-language has no distinct term for „I dwell" and the Hausa-people circumscribe it by means of the words „my house is (at that place)", gida-na shiī. — ina da zaúna involves a meaning of slowness, and I think, is especially used of stragglers.

[12] mé-meddēi: it seems remarkable, that in this and the following term we have the same verbal form, although in the first case it has an intransitive and in the second a transitive notion.

[13] With regard to the mental connection between the verbs éga-hē, éga-kai and éga-koi s. the Prolegomena.

[14] waugía: I have here as 3rd pers. sing. ahhe, but, if right, that would be a rather irregular form.

[15] á-kudú-kodē: kodá-n gorá kodē, „we are tired"; kodé-n wó-kodē, „you are tired".

[16] wátala kogō is, I think, the imperative (kogō: kokó, „go"), and I suspect the 1st pers. sing. therefore to be am wátala akíl, although for the 3rd pers. plur. I have dum („all of them") wátala.

Deutsch und Englisch.	Kanúri.	Tédā.	Hausa.	Fulfulde.
du bist lange geblieben, hast dich lange aufgehalten — *you have remained long, have tarried*	ngubbu-rō } nēm- kurūgu-rō } ne-mī[1]	negēen enō múzedé	kai ká-dedē .	ang a-nēbi .
ich bleibe zurück — *I remain behind*	gábō-niskin[2]	tánē séhet búzerik	ina tāke rawa[9]	mēdo-šōbbito
ich ruhe, ruhe aus — *I rest, pause*	tus-niskin[3] .	bóbiya-rik[7] .	ina fótawa[10] .	{ mēdo-siūta . { mēdo-fofta .
	3. Prs. S. tus-tšin .	. . . . . .	. . . . . .	. . . . . .
ich bringe die Mittagshitze zu, ruhe am Mittag aus — *I pass, rest the heat of the day*	dēbdō-niskin[4]	{ duggúdigī . { tiddógedī[8] .	ina ēni . . .	. . . . . .
	1. Pers. Pl. Imp. dēbdō-nīyen	tuddugultar .	mūna ēni . .	. . . . . .
ich gehe zu — *I go on*	ham-niskin[5] .	gubūdi tedēdi	zāni kaura .	{ mēdo-barta { mēdo-éggoto
	3. Prs. S. hab-tšin	. . . . . .	. . . . . .	. . . . . .
ich gehe vorüber, passire — *I pass (on the road)*	kō-niskin[6] .	gubūdi kón-erik	{ ina utše[11] . { zāni utše . .	mēdo-yauta .
	3. Prs. S. kō-tšin	. . . . . .	. . . . . .	. . . . . .
ich gehe zu Fusse — *I go on foot*	šī-ni lē-ngin	sāye né-ruā tedēdi	ina tafia da kafa	. . . . .
	3. Pers. S. šī-u-taš lē-tšin	sāye hé-nuā tedēdi	. . . . . .	. . . . .

[1] ngubbu-rō nēmne-mī. Ich will hiernach die Bedeutung bestimmen „halte dich nicht lange auf", K. wotte s kurūgu-rō nēmne-min, H. kadda ka-dedē, F. tā ansiba. Dasselbe Wort hat im H. und F. auch die Bedeutung „langwierig sein"; so „die Krankheit ist recht langwierig", d. h. hat jetzt lange gedauert, H. tšīwōta yá-dadē, F. nyau nōbi oder bōne nōbi, S. warki a-dīē.

[2] gábō-niskin bei Koelle ngáfúngin. 3te Person Sing. gábō-tšin.

[3] tus-niskin. Das erste s wird durch den Einfluss des vorhergehenden u mehr wie ein ṣ gesprochen. Koelle hat die Form tusúngin, die sich scheinbar dem Worte túsu, „die Pause", näher anschliesst, als meine Form, und dass es damit zusammenhängt, ist wol nicht zu läugnen. Koelle hat für die 3te Person die Form túšin. Das t in dieser Form bewährt sich aber durch die substantivischen Ableitungen tŭste, „die Ruhe", tústē-ma, „der Ausruhende", tústeram, „die Ruhestätte".

[4] dēbdō-niskin. Koelle hat dieses Wort in der Form debdóngin, erklärt es aber falsch mit „ich verlebe einen Tag", wie er denn débdō „den wirklichen Tag von Sonnenaufgang bis Untergang" erklärt, während es nur „die heisseste Tageszeit" bedeutet oder vielmehr „die Ruhe während der heissesten Tageszeit". Er erklärt dasselbe Wort sogar in der Form von dĕbdō für gleichbedeutend mit kătširi, „Abend".

[5] ham-niskin. Koelle hat diese Form nicht, aber dem Wort entspricht, was er an ámgin, „ich hebe auf" sagt: „2te Konjugat.: ich breche auf, stehe auf, gehe ab, reise ab, setze zu einer Reise aus".

[6] kō-niskin hat Koelle wieder in der Form kóngin. Das Wort hat auch die Bedeutung „übertreffen".

[7] bóbiya-rik. Imperat. „setze dich und ruhe aus", sobdŭ) bóbiya. Als vulgäre Form der 1sten Person habe ich wō-yarge.

[8] Ich habe diese Formen nicht ändern wollen, weil ich über die eigentlich richtige grammatische Form in Ungewissheit bin.

[9] ina táke rawa. Über die ursprüngliche Bedeutung bin ich nicht gewiss. Heisst es vielleicht „ich gehe zu Fuss"?

[10] ina fótawa. „Lasst uns ausruhen", H. mū mūna-fútawa, F. bē min-tšīfōta-kā.

[11] ina utše. „ich' voran", H. utše kabā, F. yaháteri yāse. Begriffsverwandt hat die Bedeutung „ich komme ihm zuvor", H. ina rigan-šī, F. mēdo-eriu-mā.

[12] mó tamba kabā ist mehr als zweifelhaft; mā, „was", tamba, „schnell", kā, „kommen". Der Sinn soll wol sein „warum kommst du nicht schnell!".

[13] wagélemī. Neben diesem Wort muss es wol noch ein etwas verschiedenes geben, da ich in der 3ten Person Sing. die Form walaléyekā habe.

[14] wā-l-bakā; 1ste Person Plur. Imperat. muOā-bakā.

[15] yé-delē sará-ruā. Neben dieser Form muss es wol noch eine andere geben, da ich für die dritte Person ēnnu bé-ágand sorá-ra habe.

[16] mak-ab e-indša-mā. indša heisst im B. „der Fuss"; a(e) ist die Präposition „mit".

[17] dša-nyi am bákan akši: dša-nyi wol versprochen statt dša-sō, „mein Fuss"; was bákan bedeutet, weiss ich nicht.

Šoŋni.	Lógunā.	Wándalā.	Ságrimma.	Hāba.
mē tamba kakā [12]	kō na-úsene íiya	ódžedža kóiγia	indži otšga .	mē angā ginrī
éga-hoī . . .	wagólomī [13] . .	yedse átega téllia	madúng adō .	. . . . . .
éga-hunzam . .	wú-dū wālan (tābu	ye-še-gāš-kwā	mak-um rōmo	{ am angā ándanī { am ávli
. . . .	. . . .	á-še-gāš-kwā	. . . . . .	. . . . . .
. . . .	índo wabē . . .	y(e)-awā . .	ma-wāī . .	am ávaenī
. . . .	mú-wabē . . .	. . . . . .	. . . . . .	. . . . . .
éga-ganna . .	wugír	y(e)-aγha . .	. . . . . .	. . . . . .
. . . .	3. prs. s. nī ná-segír	aγha	. . . . . .	. . . . . .
éga-bisma . . .	wū-ī-hakā [14] .	yé-dedē . .	mák-ab-nā .	am atēni
. . . .	. . . .	. . . . . .	. . . . . .	. . . . . .
. . . .	wugír am(e)-āū .	yé-delāserā-ruā [15]	mak-ab a-indža-mā [16]	dža-nyi am bēkan akāī [17]
. . . .	3. prs. s. negír am(e) anē	. . . . . .	. . . . . .	. . . . . .

[1] agqbba-rō némne-mi: I shall here also adduce the phrase „do not be (remain) long", K. wolla a hurāgu-rō ném-aomin, H. hedde há-dedē, F. tī a-nalba. The same word ná-dedē in H. and mó-nóhi in F. has also the meaning „to be tedious, lengthy"; thus „the disease is of very long standing", H. tšiáta yá-dedē, F. yea nóhi or bōna nóbi, G. wurki a-dīā.

[2] gábā-niskin with Koelle ágāfšágin; 3rd pers. sing. gábā-tšin.

[3] tun-niskin: the first i in consequence of the preceding u in the first syllable is generally pronounced something like ų. Koelle has the form tunáágin, which certainly approaches nearer to the word táun, „the pause, rest", from which there is no doubt the verb has been derived, than the form given by myself, but nevertheless I heard only the latter. Koelle gives as the form of the 3rd pers. sing. tálšin, but of the correctness of the t there cannot be the slightest doubt, if we take into regard the nouns hence derived, viz tánle, „repose", tánle-ma, „he who reposes", tánla-rom, „the place of repose".

[4] dóbdō-niskin has Koelle in the form of dębdōágin, but attributes to it the wrong meaning „I spend a day", as he attributes also a totally false meaning to the noun dębdō, „the actual day from sunrise to sunset", while in reality it means only the hottest time of the day or rather the repose during that hottest time. The very same word in the slightly varied form of dúbdō he supposes to be identical with hełāiri and to mean „evening".

[5] hum-niskin: Koelle has not this form, but the meaning, which he attributes to the 3rd conjugation of the verb łmgin, „I break up, rise, start, depart, set out on a journey", belongs to it.

[6] hō-niskin has Koelle again in the form hóágin. The word has also the meaning „to surpass" and thus takes the place of the comparative and superlative forms.

[7] bóbiya-rik: imperat. „sit down and rest", sobáé) bóbiya. Besides bóbiya-rik I have as a vulgar form of the 1st pers. wó-yarge.

[8] duggádigi, tiddágadi: I did not like to change these forms, as I did not know, which of them was the most correct in grammatical respect.

[9] ina tāke rewe: I am not quite sure of the original meaning of this phrase and I suspect, it means „I go on foot".

[10] ina fálawa: „let us repose, take a little rest", H. ež-ména-fálewa, F. bē min-išiáta-bē.

[11] ina niša: „go before", H. ntše habā, F. yadtori yēon. I shall here adduce a phrase of a similar meaning, viz „I am beforehand with him, anticipate him", H. ina rigan-ži, F. mōde-árta-mē.

[12] mē tamba kakā I suspect to mean „why do you not come swift"; mē, „why", „tamba, „swift"; kakā is wrong.

[13] wagólomī: besides this word there must be still another different term, as for the 3rd pers. sing. I have the form molalóyabā.

[14] wū-ī-hakā; 1st pers. plur. imperat. mufá-hakā.

[15] yé-dalā sarā-ruī: besides this term there must be another one, as for the 3rd pers. I have asan bá-āgenā serā-ra.

[16] mak-ab a-indža-mā: indža means „feet" in B., a(e) is the preposition „with".

[17] dža-nyi am békan akāī: dža-nyi certainly a mistake instead of dža-mā, „my feet"; what békan means, I do not know.

Deutsch und Englisch.	Kanúri.	Tédā.	Hausa.	Fulfulde.
Ich steige hinauf, aufwärts — *I ascend* Ich steige zu Pferde — *I mount on horseback* Ich reite — *I go on horseback*	bé- / lá- skin [1] . 3· P. S. m-bē-nin	kón-erík . . aski kón-erík [6] twīgi [7] . . .	zāni hawa [11] ína hawa . [12]	mēdo-waddo . mē-waddo-tō
Ich steige hinab — *I descend* Ich steige vom Pferde ab — *I dismount*	zem-nískin [2] . 3· Ps. S. zeb-tšin	tšám-erík . fān-erík . .	ína sásabō . ína sebka . .	mēdo-írta-kē mēdo-bīdo . mōdo-džippa-kē
steig' ab — *dismount* .	zem-nō . . .	fan-ō . . .	sebka . . .	džippa . . .
Ich treibe das Pferd an — *I spur, drive on the horse*	fir yog-nískin [3]	aski tuffúrku [8]	ína kōre dōki	. . . . . .
Ich passire einen Fluss — *I cross a river*	komádugu) fal-nískin [4]	īya-n) kōb-erík	ína kétare (gulbī [13]	mē-dēōdi (māyo) mōdo-yarta (māyo)
Ich besteige ein Boot, schiffe mich ein — *I get into a boat, go on board*	mákará-rō bé-skin	mákara túz-erík [9]	ína šigga žirgī	mēdo-nāta lāna
Ich steige aus, schiffe mich aus — *I get out of a boat*	mákara n lúg-nskin	. . . . . .	ína fito daga žirgī	mēdo-wurto lāna
Ich schwimme — *I am swimming*	bā-nískin [5] . ka-m-bō dískin	eyī wón-erík [10] īya bāb-erík	nī ína īyo [14] .	mēdo-īno . .

[1] bé-skin hat die allgemeine Bedeutung „ich steige empor" und man muss sich hier eigentlich fir-rā, „auf das Pferd", hinzudenken, es wird aber besonders und auch ohne Zusatz in dieser Bedeutung gebraucht.

[2] zem-nískin. Koelle schreibt taégmgin, und obgleich ich das ts im Anfange nie gehört habe, spricht doch die Form tšám im Tédā für die Richtigkeit als dialektische Verschiedenheit. Es kommt aber der Umstand hinzu, dass das Wort in dieser Form mit dem der Bedeutung nach ganz und gar verschiedenen taégmgin, „ich ersticke", gleich lautet.

[3] yog-nískin; 3te Person Sing. yóg-tšin. Koelle hat zwar yóāgin mit der Bedeutung „ich treibe, jage in die Flucht", ich bin aber überzeugt, dass das Verbum tsóāgin, dass er unmittelbar ganz unabhängig hat, eben dasselbe Wort ist, nur mit dem dialektischen Übergang des y in ts, wovon wir schon mehrere Beispiele gesehen haben, und alle Bedeutungen, die er dann anführt, kommen auf das „Steuern", „Antreiben" hinaus; ganz ausser Zweifel stellt aber die Frage die letzte oder fünfte Bedeutung „mit daggānan (Sporn), „ich treibe an", also eben unser Wort.

[4] fal-nískin (3te Person Sing. fál-tšin) entspricht offenbar Koelle's pálágin, obgleich er unsere Bedeutung nicht anführt. Aber die Grundbedeutung ist auch beim Übersetzen eines Flusses der „Wechsel", nämlich der Austausch des einen Ufers für das andere.

[5] bā-nískin ist wol dasselbe Wort wie „ich schlage", hier gedacht „ich schlage das Wasser", wie auch das pudelhafte Schwimmen der Schwarzen nichts Anderes ist; es ist identisch mit Koelle's mbángin. Statt ka-m-bó sollte man ke-m-bó erwarten, ke oder ken die „Handlung", „Eigenschaft", hier des Schwimmen's.

[6] aski kón-erík. „Sie steigen zu Pferde", aski-a kiotšē; „macht, steigt auf", kórrerī, kon-ta. Dann habe ich aber von einer noch ganz anderen Wurzel den sehr einfachen Imperativ sūa.

[7] twīgi muss eine populär abgekürzte Form sein.

[8] aski tuffúrku ist eine ungrammatische Form.

[9] mákara túz-erík. Ich hörte nur túz-etī oder túz-edē. Natürlich ist der ganze Ausdruck den im Binnenlande hausenden Tédā fremd; eben daher habe ich auch kein Wort für den nächsten Ausdruck.

[10] Für „schwimmen" habe ich im Tédā noch die Redensart gehört am wuai baddi-mā genē íntabbbi, „dieser Mann versucht zu schwimmen".

[11] hawa. „Steige auf", H. hau, F. wadda, Plur. badde.

[12] Für den eigentlichen Begriff des „Reitens" haben die Hausaua so wenig wie die übrigen hier aufgeführten Völker einen bezeichnenden Ausdruck. Aber die Hausaua haben mehrere Ausdrücke für besondere Arten des Reitens: so „ich galoppire", das die Kanúri ebenfalls durch ingrim-nískin wiedergeben würden (auch fir ingrim-tšin, „das Pferd galoppirt"), H. ína sukwa, F. mēdo-samma; „ich reite kurzen Galopp", H. na-i giddiripti oder na-i kukwáfa, F. mē-dōda azāgol; „ich halte das Pferd zurück", H. ína rike dōki (K. fir rān-iskin?), F. mē-nērga-hē putšu; „ich lasse das Pferd Kapriolen machen", H. ína tebbia dōki, F. mēdo-mōmo putšu.

[13] ína kétare (gulbī. „Ich passire einen Fluss zu Boot", H. ína kétare gulbī tšiki-n džirgī, F. mē-dēōdi māyo der lāna.

[14] nī ína īyo. Ich will hier eine begriffsverwandte Redensart aufführen, die ich nur im H. und F. vertreten kann: „ich überschlage mich im Wasser", H. na-nūte tšiki-n rūa, F. mē-nūtta-hō oder mē-nūtī der ndiam.

[15] wó-fēā (ayám: 3te Person Sing. n(I) aiē fēā. Das Schwimmen ist wol der Grundbegriff.

[16] atani, Imperat. tán-a.

Bedyal.	Lógone.	Wándalá.	Bágrimma.	Mába.
éga-kar (béri . .	wuʼá-ika buskwán 3ᵉ pra. s. nī naʼá-ika buskwán	yedō-to belis-a adō bá-ngaue 3ᵉ pers. s. belissa	mak-al (sinda Imperat. alla	bérek-en)á-tani[16]
éga-sumbu . .	wuʼá wāten . .	yé-tsekwā . .	(mak-um sindo-rā) (mám-disē .) (mam-disená-nge)	am a-surne
sumbu	ʼá wāten . . .	. . . . . .	disena . . .	surne
. . . . . .	wúgala buskwán	yé-bakā belissa	mam-attur sinda	am bérek fūr-arē
éga-dang (ísa .	wú-fēā (layám[15]	yé-de-sē bā-ya	mak-áltera .	am gatia-árungē
éga-būra bī . .	wuʼá ungu layám	yé-dō bā-ya to mákara	mak-índēe tokō	mérkeb-en á-tanī
éga-búntare bī .	wuʼá fēno layám	ye-ségešén má-kara	matékken gal tokō	mérkeb-en a-súr-ne
éga-džia har-ga	wú-fēā layám .	yú-gin . . .	mam-ákala .	ómarnē (b. Arb.)

¹ bá-akin properly has the general meaning of „I ascend, mount", and in our sense fir-rō, „the horse", has to be understood, but is rarely added.

² sem-niskin: Koelle writes taémgin, and although I have never heard the first letter pronounced as a ts in Kanúri, yet the form tšam in Tédā confirms this mode of writing as a really dialectic difference. But, besides that this way of spelling is now only used in certain provinces, we must take care, not to confound this word with another one of a very different meaning, viz taémgin, „I sigh".

³ yog-niskin; 3rd pers. sing. yóg-tšin: Koelle has yóngin in the sense of „I drive, turn to flight", but I am convinced, that even the verb londígin, which he gives as a totally independent verb, is nothing but this same word with the only dialectical difference of a y instead of a l in the beginning, of which we have already seen several examples. All the meanings, which he attributes to the word londígin, proceed from the notion of „to pull, stir up", and the last notion, which he gives, is exactly the one, which corresponds to our fir yog-niskin; for he says: „with dugganan, „I spur". dšagána meaning „the spur", it is just contrary.

⁴ fal-niskin (3rd pers. sing. fal-tšin) is evidently identical with the pálágin of Rev. Koelle, although he does not attribute to it the meaning, which we have here. But even with regard to the crossing of a river the chief idea is the „changing" of one shore against the other.

⁵ bé-niskin probably is the identical word as „I beat", „the water" being here taken into prime consideration, as the doglike swimming of the native blacks is in reality nothing else, but „beating the water". It is identical with the mbángin of Koelle. ka-m-bē he has not. Instead of this form we might rather expect kam-bā, from ka or kan and bā, mbā, „the act of swimming", but I have not heard it.

⁶ nahí kón-erih: „they mount on horseback", sokí-a kiotšē; „make haste, mount", kórrezi, kon-te. But I have also the very simple imperat. són, derived from quite another root.

⁷ twigi appears to be a popularly abridged form.

⁸ nahí tuffárka seems to be an ungrammatical form.

⁹ mákara tša-erih: I think, this is the right form for the present tense, although I heard only tša-eti or tša-adē. Of course the whole idea is rather strange to people living in the interior like the Tédā and that is the reason, why in this language I have no expression for the following term.

¹⁰ eyl wón-erih: besides the two terms here given I have still in T. the phrase am woal buddi-mē genē intabōhi, „this man knows swimming".

¹¹ hawa: „mount", H. hau, F. wadda, plur. badde.

¹² For the meaning of „to go on horseback" neither the Hausawa nor the other people, whose languages are here represented, have an expressive term. But the Hausa-people have several terms for special ways of riding: thus „I gallop", which the Kanúri would render by the word ingrim-niskin, is in H. ina sukwa, F. médo-samma; „I canter", H. na-i gidiaripti or na-i hohwāfa, F. mē-dōda sadgol; „I stop the horse", H. ina rike dōki (K. fir rōn-iskin!), F. mé-nérga-kē patšu; „I make the horse prance", H. ina tabbi n dōki, F. mēdo-mēmo patšu.

¹³ ina kétare (gulbī: „I cross a river in a boat", H. ina kétare gulbi tšiki-n dširgi, F. mē-dšōdi māyo der lāna.

¹⁴ ni ina iyo; I shall here adduce another phrase of a similar meaning, which I can only represent in H. and F.: „I jump about, I tumble over in the water", H. na-nāta tšiki-n rūa, F. mé-nótta-kē or mē-nātl der ndiam.

¹⁵ wú-fēā (layám; 3rd pers. sing. n(i) aié fēā.

¹⁶ átani: imperat. tán-a.

Deutsch und Englisch.	Kanúri.	Tédā.	Hausa.	Fulfúlde.
ich wandere umher — *I wander about*	guzá-nískin [1] .	. . . . . .	. . . . . .	. . . . . .
ich verändere meinen Wohnort — *I change my dwelling place, migrate*	bör-ískin [2] .	táně zukko .	ína mosaia urí-n gida-na	. . . . . .
ich gehe in den Krieg, führe Krieg — *I go to war*	kerige-rō lē-nískin [3]	yebúr tedēdi / más-erik [11] .	zāni yāki [18] .	mēdo-bonno [19]
ich kämpfe, fechte — *I fight, do battle*	libāla-nískin [4]	músol-erik .	ína ſadda [16] .	mēdo-habba [20]
ich greife (stürme) an — *I attack, charge*	ū-ma borgo fir yog-nískin [5]	táně burdu totiu bó-rik	. . . . . .	. . . . . .
ich werfe zurück — *I throw back, drive back*	kālang-nískin [6]	[12]	ína korē-sū [17] / ína tanīē-sū	S. Pajbē-terſībe / Plur. ſeebē-dauko
ich schlage, verfolge sie — *I beat, pursue them*	dū-nískin [7] . / séndi-gā aglam-nískin [8]	hobút-erik . / táně bēder [13] . / táně bur . .	. . . . . .	. . . . . .
der Krieg ist siegreich, hat Erfolg — *the war is victorious, victory is gained*	kerigu násar-tī [9]	yebúr násar-tín-tedē	yāki násar-tāī / sun-sāmo [18] .	bē-kebbi [21] .
ich führe in Sklaverei, mache zu Sklaven — *I enslave*	kindāi-rō dí-skin [10]	bódera ta-rik [14]	. . . . . .	

[1] guzá-n ískin hat Koelle nicht.
[2] bör-ískin hat Koelle auch nicht.
[3] kerige-rō lē-nískin. Koelle hat für diesen Begriff noch den besonderen, mir unbekannten Ausdruck teámen sāngyekin.
[4] libāla-ní-skin oder libāla dí-skin, wol ohne allen Unterschied. Die Phrase fehlt bei Koelle; das Substantiv erwähnt er lebāla.
[5] ū-ma borgo fir yog-nískin, wörtlich „ich treibe zuerst das Pferd an", also eigentlich nur von Kavallerie zu gebrauchen, die im Bórnu-Heer stets die Entscheidung gibt.
[6] kālang-nískin. Koelle hat kálangin, erste Bedeutung „ich richte, ziele", zweite Bedeutung „ich wende, drehe rückwärts". Die Grundbedeutung ist wahrscheinlich „ich mache Front, leiste kräftigen Widerstand".
[7] dū-nískin. Koelle hat dúngin.
[8] aglam-nískin ist Koelle's ágelámgin, „ich beunruhige, ermüde".
[9] kerigu násar-tī. Die erste Person nasar-tískin wird wenig gebraucht.
[10] kindāi-rō dí-skin. Koelle hat diese Phrase nicht; kindāi schreibt er kéndíl.
[11] más-erik ist ein auffallendes Wort; ich habe an anderer Stelle auch wáne-erik.
[12] Dem kālang-nískin entsprechend habe ich im Tédā in der 3ten Person Plur. írdi sánfirdē; írdi heisst „die Feinde".
[13] táně bēder, táně bur, gewöhnlich abgekürzte Zeitformen, bur = bú-rik, bú-rik. „Wir haben die Feinde besiegt", tinta erdí-n bú-t-urdē. Daneben habe ich noch die zweifelhafte Phrase für „sie besiegten ihn", um morá gókurdi.
[14] bódera, Plur. von bóderi, „der Sklave"; ta-rik, „ich nehme", das Kanúri tá-skin.
[15] zāni yāki. Ich will hier einige stammverwandte Phrasen hersetzen: „sie führen Krieg", H. sūna yāki, F. [illegible]-bonna, S. wonga dāza; „der Fürst von Kátsena ist in Krieg verwickelt", H. serki n Kátsena na-yāhē-[illegible], F. lamido Kátsena bonnā-ma; „ich fange Krieg an", H. [illegible] damre yāki, F. mēdo-habba bonno, S. ēga wonge mirgi (wonge, „Krieg" muss es wol heissen, aber müdge habe ich niedergeschrieben, mirgi, „versammeln"); „der Krieg ist eröffnet, hat angefangen", H. yāki ya-bāde, F. bonno ámtokē.
[16] ína fadda. Ich will hier auch die verwandte Redensart hersetzen „ich werde handgemein mit ihm", H. na-[illegible], F. mé-[illegible] mé-ka, S. ēga-tōri.
[17] ína korē-sū. Alle diese Wörter werden selten oder nie in der ersten Person Sing. gebraucht, ich setze sie daher meist in der 3ten Person Plur. her. Vergl. auch die ausdrucksvolle Phrase „nachdem sie verfolgt waren, warfen sie (die Feinde) wieder zurück", H. [illegible] sūna kōra. Ich will hier auch die Phrase hersetzen „ich leiste Widerstand, halte (den Kampf) aus", H. ína tsaye fadda, F. mē-dērro-tum habba; dann noch folgende Phrase: „sie haben sich zusammengerottet und sich durchgeschlagen", H. [illegible] oder [illegible], F. [illegible] (in der Präsens-Form) oder bē-[illegible] bra-gōrti, S. wonge [illegible].
[18] sun-sāmo, ebenso wie der entsprechende Ausdruck im F., eigentlich „sie haben gefunden"; S. „der Krieg hat gefunden".
[19] mēdo-bonno; davon das Substantiv bonno.
[20] mēdo-habba. Es ist zu bemerken, dass diese Phrase, wenn allein gebraucht, die Bedeutung „ich kämpfe" hat, 3te Pers. Plur. bē-habbai, aber in Verbindung mit bonno „ich fange Krieg an" bedeutet.
[21] bē-kebbi ist die 3te Person Plur. von mēdo-kebbi, „ich finde".
[22] Für „sie kämpfen" habe ich im S. [illegible].
[23] bugga ist der Plural von baki, „Sklave".
[24] um bárik kagia nerí ávnagi: bárik ist „Platz", kagia oder agia, „Aufenthalt" und neri = ávnā, „mein".
[25] um nyaráno. Daneben muss es wol noch einen anderen Ausdruck geben, da ich in der 3ten Person Plur. sabbangira habe.

Sonyai.	Lógoné.	Wándalá.	Bágrimma.	Mába.
. . . .	(wógobī?) . . .	yé-kildā . .	mam-ásodū .	. . . . .
. . . .	wulgun ádemā? .	yé-keli akelē .		am bárik kagin nerí ávrungī [24]
ćga-koī woági .	woyá runā . . .	ye-dō(u) ńgwā	mak-a wāya .	wēre-n akāī
[22]	1st prs. pl. mekávkelē mim-sakwā	ye-dō awa .	mam-adō . .	am ayarōne [25]
. . . .	índo bó-bekū wágala buskwán na-ü	yé-bákana bā-ya bellasa zuńgo	mam-áltur síndanā ávlemā	1st prs. pl. mang-auel má-nē
3d prs. íri-gáre . plur. ígāre wán-guti	wágala ádo wákuna	ye-tacnán tibaā	adū-na mam-kalóńga	. . . . .
. . . .	wágala tanna .	yé-bakā . .	mam-atāilla .	am bak-árnē
woógo a-dō . .	yagénka nasaérea	. . . . . .	wai netā ka-nássar	kai) nōba ko-írne
. . . .	wú-kulā yolímazā	yé-gá-n wawē	mam-lō bagga [23]	bortu ran-árnē

[1] gasá-n-íshin is wanting in Koelle.
[2] hār-íshin is wanting likewise in Koelle.
[3] korigo-rá lbá-íshin: Koelle expresses this notion also by the term teáman mángeskin, but the latter has remained totally unknown to me.
[4] líbála-níshin or líbála dishin are totally identical terms, but wanting in Koelle, who writes the noun lebála.
[5] ā-ma borgo fír yog-níshin means verbally „I drive on or spur my horse first" and properly is only used of cavalry, which however in general decides the fate of any battle in Africa.
[6] kálaág-níshin: Koelle has kálaágin with the primitive notion „I direct, point", and the secondary „I turn, turn back". But I suspect, that in reality the primitive notion is „I make front, make (successful) resistance".
[7] dú-níshin: Koelle has dúágin.
[8] agism-níshin or agelam-níshin has Koelle of course in the form of ágelámgin with the notion „I tremble, harass".
[9] korigu nácar-tī: the first person naanr-íshin is but rarely used.
[10] kindāl-ró dí-shin: this phrase is wanting in Koelle's vocabulary; the noun kindāl he writes kendál.
[11] mác-erik seems to me a remarkable word; I have also the term wáne-erik.
[12] As a Teda-term corresponding to the Kanúri kálaág-níshin I have in the 3rd pers. plur. írdí („the enemy") sénfirdē.
[13] tanó béder, tanó bur are vulgar forms. tanó bur or bor = bá-rik, bó-rik, „I eat, devour, vanquish". Besides for the phrase „they vanquish him" I have the term am merē gúburdī.
[14] bódera ta-rik: bódera, plur. form of béderi, „the slave"; ta-rik, „I take", the Kanúri tá-shin.
[15] abai yáki: I shall here adduce some phrases of a similar meaning: „they are waging war", H. súna yákí, F. ibe-honne, S. woága dáse; „the governor of Katsena is engaged in war", H. serkí n Kátsena anyáká-ší, F. lámido Kátsena honná-me; „I begin, enter upon a war", H. ina damre yáki, F. módo-habba honne, S. éga woáge mirgi (I have written móńge, but I am sure, that it ought to be woáge; mirgi, „gather, collect"); „the war has begun" (verbally „has opened"), H. yákí ya-búde, F. honne ómtahé.
[16] ina fadda: I have also adduce the related phrase „I fight hand to hand with him", H. na-tárit-ší, F. mé-haare má-ko, S. éga-téri.
[17] ina herá-vea: all terms of a similar notion are mostly used in the 3rd pers. plur., in which I therefore write them down. I here adduce also the expressive phrase „after having been pursued they (turned round and) threw (them) back", H. ana-bí-naā súna hóra. I here adduce also the phrase „I stand the brunt", H. ina tsaya fadda, F. mé-dérru-tam habba; then also the following phrase: „they have formed a compact mass and have fought their way", H. sún-giwa sún-fitá or sún-gamū sún-fitá, F. giwé-yeré é-wárta-hē (pres. tense) or bē-mépta-hē hen-gárti, S. moáge fortíóterē.
[18] saa-sámo, just as the corresponding terms in F. and S. means verbally „they have found".
[19] módo-hoane: hoane is the root of the noun honne.
[20] módo-habbe: it seems remarkable, that this term, if alone, has the notion „I fight", 3rd pers. plur. bē-hebbai, while in connection with honne it means „I commence (war".
[21] bē-hebbi is the 3rd pers. plur. of módo-hebbi, „I find".
[22] For the term „they fight" in S. I have the word irgáce.
[23] bagga, plural mode of bahi, „the slave".
[24] am bárik kagin nerí ávrungī; barik is kagin or agin, „dwelling, residence" and nerí = nérué, „my", „mine".
[25] am ayaróne: besides this term there must still be another one, as I have subbengire in the 3rd pers. plur.

Deutsch und Englisch.	Kanúri.	Tédā.	Hausa.	Fulfúlde.
Ich plündere eine Stadt — *I plunder, ravage a town*	ä billa bú-skin [1] 3. P. Pl. billa zé-bu-in	nómai(trö)-he bú-rik [11]	ína-täī garī [13] búna-tèī garúewa	mēdo-yāme gel-lūre bē-yāme gellōdže
der Krieg plündert, frisst — *the war devours, destroys*	kerīgu zé-bin	yebúr tú-bo-dē / erdi a-bú-t-erdé [12]	yāki šina-täī .	konno ó-yāme
ich theile die Beute — *I divide the spoil*	dager-niskin [2]	. . . . . .	. . . . . .	. . . . .
ich verbrenne — *I burn, destroy by fire*	kannuwar-niskin [3]	némai) wúēni yén-erík	. . . . . .	. . . . . .
ich zerstöre, vernichte — *I upset, destroy, ruin*	far-niskin [4] .	némai tiggir-erík	ína-falĕ [14] . / nī-marēka .	mēdo-fusni .
Alles hat die Flucht ergriffen — *all the people have taken to flight*	kām sèmma só-kás-i [5]	amma kubrī ke-yá-röén	mótane dukka sún-godū	. . . . .
der Krieg, die Schlacht ist verloren — *the war is spoilt, the battle is lost*	korigu bíbi-tī [6]	yebúr tuggúr-kodē	yāki yá-watšē / yāki yá-faab	konno o-fúsui / konno saúkétaké
die Expedition ist umgekehrt (unverrichteter Sache) — *the expedition has returned (having had no success*	kerīgu welt-i [7]	yebúr forúm-tindē	yāki ya-kōmo	
ich ziehe das Schwert — *I draw the sword*	kasákkar fī-niskin [8]	akāsu ter-erík	ína-fitt(ö) kanák-kali / ina-sāra	mēdo-warti káfebi . / lebbi .
ich stecke das Schwert ein — *I put in the sword*	kasákkar yēk-iskin [9]	akāsu dun-erík	ína-maida kan-ákkali / ina-fiana kanák-kali tšiki-n gi-dá-ma [15]	mēdo-haure káfebi / lebbi . / mēdo-wotto ká-febi der súdo má-ko
ich schlage, verwunde mit dem Schwert — *I strike, wound with the sword*	taal-iskin [10] .	táné nöb-erík / táné akāsu-de köb-erík	ina-sāre (ī .	mēdo-fēdēi [16] .

[1] ä billa bú-skin, eigentlich „ich esse, verschlinge die Stadt".
[2] dager-niskin fehlt bei Koelle.
[3] war-niskin. Koelle hat uóragin. — kannu für kannu-a.
[4] far-niskin, „ich mache (unterst) zu oberst". Koelle schreibt fáragin und páragin, „ich trenne, löse auf, zerstöre".
[5] so-kás-i, 3te Person Plur. von dem oben aufgeführten kás-iskin.
[6] korigu bíbi-tī, bíbi-tī, 3te Person Prät. Pass. von bibi-niskin, Koelle bibí-ngin, „ich verderbe". Anstatt kerīgu schreibt Koelle krigu und kerigu.
[7] kerīgu welt-i, welt-i ist „zurückgekehrt", von welt-iskin.
[8] kasákkar fī-niskin. Koelle schreibt kásagar píngin; 3te Person Sing. [illegible] pittšin. Siehe die Einleitung.
[9] kasákkar yēk-iskin. yēk-iskin ist aller Wahrscheinlichkeit nach Koelle's yekéskin („ich stecke, stecke ein" oder „an"), obgleich er die besondere Phrase mit kasákkar nicht hat.
[10] taal-iskin hat Koelle wieder in der Form tsálngin.
[11] nómai (trö)-he bú-rik; trö oder terö ist offenbar das Zahlwort „eins", „eine"; he ist die Accusativ-Endung, die, wenn man trö auslässt, zu némai rechnen kann; bú-rik oder bó-rik heisst „ich esse, zerstöre".
[12] erdi a-bú-t-erdé, „die Feinde zerstören", andere Wendung der vorhergehenden Redensart.
[13] ína-täī garī. So auch die Phrase „nachdem ihm viele Pferde erbeutet, abgenommen (gegessen)", H. ána-tšī [illegible] dáwaki déwa, F. enyáme nō-mé putšī dúdī, und die ausdrucksvolle Redensart im H. an-tšenyé dúkiá-asú, án-kaššé-sú da ka-nsú, „nachdem ihr Vermögen geplündert und sie selbst getödtet waren".
[14] ína-falĕ. Ich will hier die Phrase anführen „die Stadt ist zerstört und verheert", H. garī tá-falĕ, böbe kōwī tšikí-n (Niemand ist darin), F. gorīri fusni, B. heire-di sú. Das falĕ wird auch vom geistigen Zerschmettern gebraucht, so sún-falĕ, sún-godū, „sie sind auf das Haupt geschlagen und haben die Flucht ergriffen".
[15] tšiki-n gidá-nsa, F. der súdo mé-ko, „in sein Haus", d. h. in die Scheide.
[16] mēdo-fēdēi. „Schlage, verwunde ihn mit dem Schwert", fēda-n-má.
[17] wongu bó heire, wörtlich „der Krieg verschlingt die Stadt".
[18] wúne fá īgo uágoin wonée. fá ist „Feuer".
[19] wa-wil rö-a-ya: rá, „die Stadt".
[20] wún-ándu, „(in) sein Haus". wüne (méverám) ist die „Schwertscheide".
[21] yé-hünsá n herá. herá, „das Feuer".
[22] mál-wal-na man-ékalá. mál-wal-na, „das Besitzthum des Krieges" (mál ist das Arabische mál).
[23] bénu) n wóngu féde-gu. bénu, „die Stadt", fádu, „das Feuer".

Šaiyal.	Légeañ.	Wándalá.	Bágrimma.	Mába.
. . . .	wa-z(á) úngo-yá	yé-zagaē . .	mak-casina .	am anyáne
. . . .	. . . .	. . . . . .	. . . . . .	. . . . . .
woñgo hō koire [17] / woñgo diága .	ma-zújm wyaná-ya / wyaná dezengúnna	ságeru saúga? / la-zā uñgwa .	wai nasī tšagá / wai sáulže . .	waugkalimgo inyi
. . . .	y(e)-ifse dagér .	yé-fa / yē-χa dágare	mál-wai-na mam-ákalá [22]	
. . . .	wa-zí fú 'lge wágala wunēa [18]	yé-bšená n kará [21]	bēne) n wónga fóde-ga [23]	
	wa-wil rō-a-ya [19]	yé-pyēka (ikse	bōne ma-setinya	am arám-ne
	ngum kytte daχ-wúmba	béddeme (wan?) džégadē džégadē	. . . . . .	. . .
woñgo-di hássarē	wyaná béldžia . / wyaná n-étkogá .	. . . . . .	wal n(e)-adúm godō	. . . . .
	wá-debā máverám-ma	yé-pon kašékkare	musi káskar(a) ága	am ardággi
éga-etle tábogu	wa-zi máverám wen-ánēa [20]	yé-fák kašékkare ám-brē?	mus káskara bē-nyi-ga	am andai
éga-hēri . . .	woyá-fiya-ni en má-verám	yé-tšišá . .	mak-adžá . .	am balá maigne

[1] ā bitle ká-shia: verbally „I eat, devour the town".
[2] duger-aiskin: the verb as well as the noun, from which it has been derived, is wanting in Koelle's vocabulary.
[3] war-aiskin: Koelle has the form wárágin.
[4] far-aiskin: Koelle has both forms, fárágin and parágin, with the notion „I separate, dissolve, destroy".
[5] sa-kás-i, 3rd pers. plur. of the verb kás-iskin, which we have had before.
[6] kerigu bibi-ti: bibi-ti is 3rd pers. pret. passiv. of the verb bibi-aiskin (Koelle bibiágin), „I ruin, spoil". Instead of the fuller form kerigu Koelle writes krigy and kerigy.
[7] kerigu walt-i: walt-i, „has returned", from welt-iskin.
[8] kasákker fi-aiskin: Koelle writes kásager pingin; 3rd pers. sing. fi pittšin. See the Introductory remarks.
[9] kasákker yōk-iskin: yōk-iskin is identical with the yakéskin of Koelle, to which he gives the notion of „I put", „I put in" or „on", although he has not the particular phrase in connection with kasákkar.
[10] tsal-iskin has Koelle in the form tsálágin.
[11] némal (trá)-ho bú-rik: trá or torá evidently is the cardinal number „one"; ho is the form of the accusative which, if we eliminate trá, we may join to némal; bú-rik or bó-rik is „I eat, destroy".
[12] erdi a-há-i-erdē, „the enemy destroys", another turn of the preceding phrase.
[13] ina-tši guri; I compare the phrase „after many horses had been taken from him" („been eaten" by the enemy), H. ána-tši ma-ed dáwaki déwa, F. an-yáma ná-ma patki dūdi, and the very expressive phrase „after their property had been plundered (taken possession of) and they themselves had been slain", H. an-tšēnyé dúkia-sa, an-kašē-sá da ka-sa.
[14] ina-fašē: I will here adduce the phrase „the town has been destroyed and become desolate", H. gari ta-fašē, bábe kōmi tšikí-n („no body is there in"), F. garixi fusal, S. koire-di aū. The term fašē is also used of annihilating in a more spiritual sense, as in the phrase sún-fašē, sún-godē, „they have been totally defeated and have taken to flight".
[15] tšiki n gidá-sa. F. der súde mi-ho, „in its house", i. e. into the sheath or scabbard.
[16] sáde-fidšē; „strike, wound him with the sword", fídšē-u-má.
[17] woñgo hō koire, verbally „the war devours the town".
[18] wa-zá fú 'lge wágala wunēa: fú is „fire".
[19] wa-wil rá-a-ya: rá means „the town".
[20] wēn-ánēa: wēne (máverám) is the sheath of the sword.
[21] yé-bšená n kará: kará, „fire".
[22] mál-wai-na mam-ákalá: mál-wal-na properly means „property of war", i. e. booty; mál has been introduced from the Arabic.
[23] bēne) n wónga fóde-ga: bēne, „town", fóda, „fire".

Deutsch und Englisch.	Kanúri.	Tédā.	Hausa.	Fulfúlde.
ich werfe den Speer — *I throw the spear*	kasúkka gem-niskin [1]	fill kusún-erík	ina žéfa māši	médo-húba-kē lebbo
ich stosse mit dem Speer — *I thrust the spear*	kasúkka za- { níski / úgin [2] }	gugū ze bāb-erík [8]	ina sóka . .	médo-inn . .
ich verwunde (mit dem Speer — *I wound (with the spear*)	{ za-nískin . . / za-úgin . . }	yéb-erík . .	(ina sare-ši ?)	. . . . . .
ich parire mit dem Schild — *I ward a blow with the shield*	ńgawa n fai-nískin [3]	kifi ti-kin-erík	ina kária [9] . .	médo-kāre-kē wōali [12]
ich schlage den Schild — *I beat the shield*	ńgawa bag-nískin [4]	kifi bāb-erík	ina bugga gerkwa	médo-fido wówadē
ich kniee nieder (zum Schiessen — *I kneel down*	gorúm-gorúm níkin	. . . . . .	ina dúrkusa .	mēd(o)-ítāa-kē
ich schiesse den Pfeil ab, ich treffe mit dem Pfeil — *I let fly the arrow, I strike with the arrow*	kenīgi n za-nískin		ina halbi [10] .	médo-fiddai .
ich bestreiche den Pfeil mit Gift — *I poison the arrow*	kenīgi lem-nís-kin [5]	. . . . . .	. . . . . .	
ich lade das Gewehr — *I load the musket*	béndega yem-búlu-skin [6] .	{ ngúl džénrige / béndugo kyém-erík }	ina dúra béndega [11]	médo-bowa béndega
ich ziele — *I take my aim*	béndega tū-g-ú-skin [7]	{ yerón-erík . / béndugo tún-erík }		
ich feuerte, ich habe ihn getroffen — *I fired, I hit him*	bag-níski. ši-gā fan-díski	{ tánē yéb-erdē, S. / bāb-erdē, N. }	ina ba-ši kuskuréwa	mē-hebbī-mó [13]

[1] gem-niskin. Koelle schreibt gémgin; 3te Pers. Sing. ši gēptšin. Anstatt kasúkka schreibt er kátsága.

[2] za-úgin hat Koelle in der Form tsáúgin, dann aber nicht diese erste Bedeutung, sondern nur die von „durchbohren, erstechen".

[3] fai-níski scheint bei Koelle zu fehlen.

[4] bag-niskin. Koelle schreibt bágin.

[5] lem-niskin entspricht wol Koelle's lémgin, obgleich er es nur auf das Waschen des Gesichts bezieht.

[6] yam-bálu-skin hat Koelle, aber nicht in der Bedeutung „ich lade eine Flinte". Ausserdem habe ich auch noch ein besonderes Wort für „ich stampfe den Ladestock nieder", béndega tsenug-níski, wol Koelle's dzúngin entsprechend.

[7] tū-g-uskin, transitive Form von tū-níski = Koelle's túngin.

[8] gugū ze bāb-erík: gugū ze ist unsicher, vielleicht skúza; bāb-erík ist richtig.

[9] ina kária ist ein besonderer technischer Ausdruck, der nichts mit kária, „Lüge", zu thun hat.

[10] ina halbi. Dann „(er) vom Pfeil getroffen", H. an-halbē-ši, F. fiddi-mó. Die Hausa-Sprache besitzt aber noch den oben angeführten, sehr schönen, prägnanten Ausdruck für „treffen", eigentlich freilich nur das Negativ des „Fehltreffens" (kuskuréwa), ina ba-ši kuskuréwa. — Vergl. S. 7[illegible], N. 9.

[11] ina dúra béndega. Dann die Phrase „ist die Flinte geladen oder ist nichts darin?", H. béndega an-dúra ši-kē kō bābo kōmi, F. béndega halái kó gódum wóla.

[12] médo-kāre-kē wōali. Ich weiss nicht, ob wōali oder wówali eine Nebenform von wūnde oder wówadē ist, oder nur eine populäre Korruption.

[13] mē-hebbī-mó, wörtlich „ich habe es (ihn) gefunden". „Ich feure" ist médo-fiye béndega.

[14] águ-nabgu ist mir verdächtig.

[15] ága-téndigu mélfa-ga. mélfa ist aus dem Arabischen medfá gebildet, das von den Maurischen Stämmen um Timbuktu in der Bedeutung „Gewehr, Flinte" gebraucht wird.

[16] á-g-a-bartá-ága ist die Negation: „ich habe ihn nicht verfehlt", ganz analog wie im H. „ich feure", ága-kār melfa.

[17] wa-sā (n)lri-i ágálo galákē-a heisst wol unzweifelhaft wörtlich „ich schlage den Speer gegen den Schild".

[18] wá-lemē nāku taúgē. taúgē heisst „Pfeil", nāku wahrscheinlich „Leib, das Innere".

[19] wáta morén gaa daré-n. Vielleicht wa-tla, „ich lege", mor(?) nākun, „in", daré-n, „das Gewehr". Daneben habe ich für „ich stampfe mit dem Ladestocke" den zweifelhaften Ausdruck dará wūagodu ralla (wuagu doré ale?).

[20] bará másaare, wörtlich „das Ägyptische Rohr".

[21] moa gán-igā. Das Wort moa steht in keiner Beziehung zum folgenden tégena, vielleicht zu móh-eal, „ich verwunde".

[22] am teng-birns steht offenbar im nächsten Verhältniss zu am tuúg-áras, aber ich kann das birne nicht analysiren.

[23] am ammér-arē ist von dem Arabischen ámmer mit einheimischer Endung gebildet.

Sonyai.	Lógoné.	Wándalá.	Bágrimma.	Mába.
éga-kilto-nī . .	wa-hī (e)lrā-i .	yé-pyō ūpa .	mam-agōni-gā	am adiāno
éga-gur-nī . .	wá-selī (e)lrā .	y(e)-awan ūpa	mam-gab nyeńga	am teńg-árne
. . . .	wu-ñā-ni . . .	tsákanwā tsekā	mók-osī . .	am teńg-birne[22]
éga-nánga[14] . .	wa-kúmna háńg galákō	yé-bedán n guloko	mók-erís ńgawa na-kí	am war eríńgnyéne
éga-kár korál .	wa-sā (e)lrā ńgōlo galákē-a[17]	yé-džo gulóko .	mal-ún ńgáwa-na	. . . . .
éga-tšéngere . .	indo agsenzézchā	ye-kelálalže .	mam-dumnai	am akki oróúgne
éga-kár hangum	. . . . . .	. . . . .	. . . . .	
. . . . . .	wú-lemē uńku tańgē[18]	yé-gegwō áte gurnē	kesē mák-indā kurgún-na	
éga-túndiga mélfaga[15]	wūta morún gun darē-a[19]	yé-tšimawa karā mássare[20]	mam-dódžigel búndug-ná	am anmér-arē[23]
. . . . . .	{wá-ndanē ayā / wa-ze dará-le}	yé-palán an karā mássare	mam-dadž búndug-ná	nímmereyokō-yin andžem-únne
é-s-a-bartá-nga[16]	wá-θanē wa-θénia	ya-wo tšenánša	mos gía-igā[21]	am okó-nye

[1] gam-nishin: Koelle writes géngin; 3rd pers. sing. ši gēptšin; instead of hoeéhha he writes hátsága.

[2] sa-ágin appears in Koelle's vocabulary under the form of tsáágin, but only with the meaning of „to pierce, stab".

[3] fain-ishin seems to be wanting in Koelle.

[4] bag-nishin: Koelle writes báágin.

[5] tem-nishin is identical with Koelle's támgin, although he refers that notion only, to the washing of the face.

[6] yem-búlu-shin is found in Koelle, but not with the express notion of loading a musket. Besides this term I have still a peculiar one for the phrase „I ram down the charge", béndege tsuong-nishin corresponding with the dangágin of Koelle.

[7] tō-z-nshin is the transitive form of tū-nishin = Koelle's tūágin.

[8] gugū ae bāb-erih: gugū ae is uncertain; perhaps it ought to be nkásu, bāb-erih is right.

[9] lan bárin is a peculiar technical term, which in a slightly changed form appears also in the Fulfulde-language and has nothing to do with the identical term bárin, „lie".

[10] lan balbi: thereto the phrase „struck by an arrow", H. án-balbō-ší; F. fiddā-mō.

[11] lan dūra béndega: „is the gun loaded or is it empty?", H. béndega an-dúra ši-kē kā babu komi, F. béndege belól ko godum wóla.

[12] méda-hárn-hé wōali: I do not know, whether wōali or wówali be another form for wówadō or whether it is only a popular corruption.

[13] mō-hebāl-mó means verbally „I have found it".

[14] éga-nanga is perhaps not right.

[15] éga-túndiga mélfa-ga: the term mélfa is a corruption of the Arabic word medfā, which by the Moorish tribes round Timbuktu is used with the meaning of „musket".

[16] é-s-a-bartá-nga is the negative form of the verb éga-barta, „I have missed", just in a similar manner, as is the case in H.

[17] wa-sā (e)lrā-i ńgōlo galákē-a means verbally „I beat the spear against the shield".

[18] wú-lemē uńku tańgē: tańgē means „arrow", uńku probably „body, inside".

[19] wūta morún gun darē-a: the phrase is not certain; it may be wa-tía, „I put", mor(?) unkun, „inside", darē-a, „the musket". I have also a peculiar, but doubtful term for „I ram down with the ramrod", darā wásyoda ralla.

[20] karā mássare means verbally „the Egyptian reed".

[21] mos gía-igā: the term „mos" has no relation to the following „iágeau", but may be related to mók-osī, „I wound".

[22] am teńg-birne evidently has a close relation to the phrase am teńg-árne, although I am not able to analyze the word birne.

[23] am anmér-arē has been derived from the Arabic by adding an indigenous termination.

Deutsch und Englisch.	Kanúri.	Tédā.	Hausa.	Fulfúlde.
ich fürchte, ich habe ihn verfehlt — *I erred, I missed him*	bug-nískí, šī-gā fand-iski-nī	táne käye, S. / wu-bánde bāb-e-nī, N.	ina ku-kuréwa	me-woli . .
ich treibe Handel — *I trade, make commerce*	libáya dī-skin [1]	táne kasō-kasō [5] / yōb-eri(k) nī / kyuás-eri(k) [6]	nī na-i tšinaki [7]	médo-waddi tšoggo
ich treibe keinen Handel — *I do not trade*	libáya dī-skin bágo	. . . . .	nī ba na-i tšinaki ba	médo-waddi-a tšoggo
ich kaufe — *I buy* . .	ī-fi-skin [2] . .	yōb-erīk . .	nin nasēa [8] .	mēdo-sodi .
	3. Pers. S. tši-bín	. . . . .	. . . . . .	. . . . . .
ich kaufe nicht — *I do not buy*	ī-fi-n bágo .	yōb-erí-n . .	ba nī-sāi . .	mēdo-sóda-ta
ich verkaufe — *I sell* .	ū lád-īskin [3] .	tánē köäs-erīk / tšöäs-erīk	nīn na-sāis .	mēdo-sotti .
	3. Pers. S. šī tsi-lád-in	. . . . .	. . . . . .	. . . . . .
ich verkaufe nicht — *I do not sell*	ū lád-in bágo	tánē köäs-erí-n / tšöäs-erí-n	ba nī sáwwa ba [9]	mēdo-sótta-ta
ich wechsele, vertausche, mache Tauschhandel — *I exchange, barter*	fal-īskin [4] . .	táne forós-erīk	zāni músayn . / zāni fúrfuré .	mēdo-wot-ïuïre [10]

[1] libáya dī-skin. Koelle schreibt lebáya. Der Ausdruck ist unzweifelhaft nicht einheimisch und hat keine einheimische Wurzel, sondern ist erst in späterer Zeit durch den Verkehr mit den Arabern eingeführt; eigentlich el biā (البيع). Der gewöhnlichen Aussprache nach würde man es wol ebenso richtig líbeia schreiben.

[2] ī-fi-skin. Koelle schreibt yifeskin und yibuskin, und diese letzte Form steht offenbar der Tédā-Form ungleich näher als die meinige, und die 3te Person zeigt zur Genüge, dass das b zur Wurzel gehört; doch hörte ich selbst nur ī-fi-skin gebrauchen.

[3] Koelle schreibt ladēskin, aber das aktive, transitive ī ist in diesem Verbum offenbar von Bedeutung; es ist wahrscheinlich eine blosse Contraction von libáya dī-skin. In den von diesem Verbum abgeleiteten Substantiven wiegt das ō des Präteritums (tšī-lád-ō) durchaus vor, so lódō, „der Verkauf", ládō-ma, „der Verkäufer".

[4] fal-ískin. Koelle schreibt palēgin. Übrigens gebrauchen die Kanúri und die meisten dieser Völker für das Wechseln eines Geldstückes den Ausdruck lád-ískin, da dies ein wirklicher Verkauf ist und man nicht einmal kleinere Münze, sondern nur andere geartete Gegenstände, wie Muscheln, Baumwollstreifen, dafür einzutauschen kann. Die L. umschreiben es und sagen z. B. „ich gebe einen Dollar hin, ich nehme Muscheln", wū-gir riāl, wū-ga lēmbeaī oder weldaliā. Im W. aber und im B. hat man einen eigenen Ausdruck, dort yé-welon riál, im B. riál magistana. Die Tédā gebrauchen auch hierfür forós-erīk.

[5] kasō-kasō ist eine unvollständige Verbalform, von der Wurzel der Substantiva kas-wa und kás-uhā gebildet.

[6] yōb-erī(k) nī kyoás-erī(k). Das Abwerfen des k in der gewöhnlichen Sprache habe ich schon mehrmals bemerkt, das nī aber für „und", wie es hier gebraucht scheint, ist mir sonst nicht vorgekommen. Jedenfalls heisst unsere Phrase wörtlich „ich kaufe und verkaufe".

[7] nī na-i tšinaki. tšinaki ist ein eigenthümliches Wort.

[8] nin nasēa. Höchst eigenthümlich ist, dass das Verbalsubstantiv „das Kaufen" saī-ewa lautet, wie in der Redensart „hier ist Gelegenheit zum Kaufen", dága-nán arī n saī-ewa.

[9] ba nī sáwwa ba. Vergl. die Phrase „es gibt hier weder Kauf noch Verkauf", d. h. „es fehlt dem Orte an Verkehr", H. dáganán bābo saī-ewa bābo sáwwa; „das Ding des Verkaufs" (d. h. was man für Geld thut) „hat keine Kraft", d. h. keinen Bestand, H. abū sáwwa bābo karfi, F. hó sott-eló-dum yola-fóda; „verkauft", H. s-sōa-sod, F. sött-ō-dum. Ich will hierher auch einige Ausdrücke setzen, die ich nur im H. und F. vertreten kann, so „ich überlasse dir" (nach übereingekommenem Kaufpreis) „dieses Hemd", H. ina sállemō-ka s-wō-nan riga, F. mēdo-nī-mā sállema toggóre; „ich lasse dir etwas ab, gebe dir Erleichterung", H. na-i ma-kā rángomō: „lass mir etwas ab und überlasse mir dieses Hemd für Geld (Muscheln)", H. ka-i ma-nī rángomō, sállemó-nī s-wō-nan riga da sambar kúdde, F. bástana yúpiánam toggáre sambar dáō-vō-ga.

[10] mēdo-wot-ïuïre. Neben diesem einheimischen Ausdruck ist auch das Wort fúrfuré im Gebrauch, das wie das Hausa-Wort seinen Ursprung im B. zu haben scheint.

[11] yer-ma-barbar ist die 1ste Person Plur.

[12] Das semā, „ganz und gar nicht", gehört eigentlich nicht zur Phrase.

[13] semā, siehe die vorhergehende Anm.

[14] ye-gā goné: gono, „Handel".

[15] Ich habe hier die Phrase simbille tanyia bága, „Hirse gegen Butter vertauschen", aber ich bin nicht sicher über die Form der ersten Person, die jedoch wahrscheinlich mam-bille lautet.

Soáyat.	Lógone.	Wándalá.	Bágrimma.	Mába.
éga-harta (éga .	wá-thauã wa-tféni-ka	yawe tšenáška	túgena gas-inyéli	am okó-n-endē
éga-dam hebbu	ind(o) alrá kasku	ye-gá gané [14]	mam-a-tád gi-an-na	am tádžar-na akai
é-s-a-dam hebbu	ind(o) alrá-n kasku (semá [12]	yé-ge-ká gané	. . . . .	am tádžar-na aka-tánde
éga-de	wo-tu (mánkoné-ši	ye-šé-kwā .	mam-úndugo	am ark-erīri
. . . . . .	3 ps. s. ni-na né-tu-a	a-šé-kwā . .	. . . . .	. . . . .
é-s-a-dē . . .	wo-tu-a (semá [13]	ye-šé-n kwa	mam-úndugó-li	am ark-tá-endē
éga-nēre . . .	ind(o) á-urī . .	yé-welā . .	magirta . . / mándugó koro	am arki / am árakné
. . . . . .	3 pers. sing. ni ná-uri	á-welā . . .	. . . . .	. . . . .
é-s-a-nēre . .	. . . .	. . . . . .		. . . . .
yer-ma-barbar [11]	wu-nta-hal . .	y(e)-émbedá .	[15]	am odeléne

[1] libáya di-skin: Koelle writes lebáya, but the a is not at all pronounced long, and it would perhaps be more correct to write libeia. However there cannot be the slightest doubt, that the word is not indigenous, and that it has been introduced from the Arabic in consequence of the intercourse with the North — the original form being [illegible] (el beá).

[2] l-fi-skin: Koelle writes yifuskin and yibuskin and it is remarkable, how near the latter form approaches the Tédá-term, which is evidently related to it, and the b of the 3rd pers. shows, that it is original and belongs to the root, but nevertheless I heard only the form l-fi-skin.

[3] Koelle writes ladéskin, but the l expressing the active and transitive notion is evidently not without importance in this verb. In the nouns, which have been derived from it, the ó of the past tense (tšl-lád-ó) prevails; thus ládó, „the sale", ládó-ma, „the seller".

[4] fal-lebás: Koelle writes pálágén. I must here observe, that the Kanúri and most of these people regard the changing of a dollar rather as a selling — the Kanúri therefore says à riál lád-lebis — it being really rather a sale, than an exchange and the seller obtaining instead a totally different material, such as shells and cottonstripes. The people of L. circumscribe it and say „I give a dollar and take shells (instead)", wú-gir riál, wú-ga lémdená (or melóke ttá). In W. however and in B. there is a peculiar phrase for an exchange of this kind, W. yé-welan riál, B. riál ma-girtana. The Tédá also in this instance use the term forós-erik.

[5] kasó-kará is scarcely to be called a verbal form, as it is a vulgar derivation from the root kas, which appears in the K.- and T.-term kás-yakó and in the H.-word kas-wa.

[6] yób-eri(k) ni kyoás-eri(k) in vulgar pronunciation sounds yobri-ni kyoáseri. The throwing out of the k at the end of the verbal form of the 1st pers. I have already remarked upon. ni seems to be used here for „and", but of such a use I have not found another instance. At any rate the phrase means „I buy and sell".

[7] ni na-l tšlnchi: tšinchi is a remarkable word.

[8] nia nanda: I here adduce the remarkable form bal-awa for the verbal noun „the selling, sale", as in the phrase „here is an opportunity for selling", dága-nán eri-a bal-awa.

[9] ba ni séawa ha: compare the phrase „there is neither selling nor buying", that is to say „the place has no commerce", H. dágaská bábo bal-awa bábo séawa; „the thing (object) of sale has no strength" i. e. „what a person does for money has no value", H. ábú séawa bábo karfi, F. kó sotl-oló-dum yrla-fódu; „sold", H. a-adó-ará, F. ikotl-é-dum. I shall also adduce in this note some terms, which I can only give in the H.- and F.-languages, as „I cede to you" (by sale) „this tobe", H. ina séllemé-ka a-wá-nan riga, F. médo-ni-má séllema toggére; „I abate (a little)", H. na-l ma-ká rángemá; „abate (me) a little and sell me this tobe for (cowries (shells)", H. ka-i ma-ni rángemá, séllemá-ni a-wá-nan riga da sambar šiddu, F. bástana yéptanam toggére sambar dšá-ré-gó.

[10] módo-wel-inlve: besides this indigenous term the word fárfaró also is in common use. This word has evidently been introduced, both into the F.- and the H.-language, from the Soáyal.

[11] yor-ma-barbar is the 1st pers. plur.

[12] The word semá, „by no means", properly does not belong to the phrase.

[13] semá in a strict sense does not belong to the phrase.

[14] ye-gá gané: gané means „commerce".

[15] I have here written down the phrase nimbille tenyle hágu, „to exchange millet against butter", but I am not quite certain with regard to the 1st pers.; probably it is mam-bille.

Deutsch und Englisch.	Kanuri.	Tēda.	Hausa.	Fulfulde.
ich leihe dir — *I lend you*	ni-rō tégeri-n tai-dī-skin [1]	tánē yaúkai-n-erik	ina ramtšo ma-ka	mēdo-bokku-mā ramtše [14]
leihe mir — *lend me* .	tégeri sé-genō [2]	yaukai teo .	ramtšo me-nī	ramtše damē .
ich entlehne von dir — *I lend from you*	nā-nemin tégeri-niskin [3]	tánē égreni reu-rík	zāni ramtšo garē-ka	mēdo-ramtšo ho-mā
ich miethe — *I hire* .	ágeri-niskin .	tánē egrén-erík	na-ī súfuri [10] .	. . . . .
ich bezahle — *I pay* .	alū-nískin [4] .	tánē belím-erík [7]	nī-bā da kurdī [11]	mēdo-hokko tšē-de
ich bin (ihm) schuldig — *I owe him*	kusu-rō gá-skin [5]	tánē šer táre-dē [8]	ina bī-ma bā-šī	mēdo-téffu-mō ya-mánde [15]
er ist (mir) schuldig, hat Schulden — *he owes me*	šī-ma adīn-wa [6]	merē yaúkai bud-di ye-tā [9]	šī šī-biā-nī [12]	óyobá-mī . .
ich fange an — *I begin*	badī-niskin .	. . . . . .	ina fāra [13] . .	mēdo-fūda .

[1] ni-rō tégeri-n tai-dī-skin. tégeri ist ein Substantiv, gebildet von einer Wurzel, die auch dem Verbum ágeri-niskin zu Grunde liegt und mit dem Arabischen kerā eng verwandt ist, wenn nicht direkt davon abgeleitet. Die verstärkte Form tai-dī-skin ist verbale Inflexion.

[2] tégeri sé-genō. Das sé-genō ist ebenfalls verbale Inflexion, durch vorhergegangenes, hier aber fortgelassenes ü-rō motivirt.

[3] nā-nemin tégeri-niskin, wörtlich „deiner Stelle Schuld nehme ich".

[4] alū-niskin fehlt bei Koelle, ebenso das Substantiv alūa.

[5] kusu-rō gá-skin, wörtlich „ich folge der Schuld". Der sehr interessante Ausdruck fehlt bei Koelle.

[6] šī-ma adīn-wa gehört eigentlich nicht hierher; denn adīn-wa, davon abgesehen, dass es ein Fremdwort ist, abgeleitet vom Arabischen dīn, ist eine Adjektivform; aber die entsprechenden Ausdrücke sind zum Theil Verbalformen.

[7] belím-erík ist natürlich eng verwandt mit dem in N. 4 besprochenen Kanuri-Wort. Daneben habe ich im T. noch šerra nán-erík, das mit dem folgenden Ausdruck zusammenhängt.

[8] tánē šer táre-dē. Ich bin über die Schreibart nicht sicher. Zuerst hatte ich geschrieben tánē šēe tála-dō, aber, wie ich es oben geschrieben, ist es wol richtiger. So habe ich für „ihr schuldet uns" die Phrase šer tára-tal.

[9] merē yaúkai (oder yeúkai) buddi ye-tā heisst wörtlich „er Schuld ganz hält" (ye-tā von tá-rik, „ich halte", S. 61), d. h. „er ist sehr verschuldet".

[10] na-ī súfuri. Ich will hier ein paar verwandte Redensarten aufführen: „ich trete in deinen Lohn, biete dir meine Dienste an", H. zāni ma-kā súfuri, F. mēdo-hokki-mā genāri mādo geāgal; „vermiethe mir dein Kameel", H. ka me-nī súfuri rākumī-n-ka, F. hokk-am genāri gelōba mā-da.

[11] nī-bā da kurdī ist eigentlich wie die entsprechende Fulfulde-Phrase ein unbeholfener Ausdruck. Ich will hier eine Redensart heraussetzen, deren genaue Beziehung ich nicht kenne, H. na-ī ma-nā gamme, F. mōdo-hanti-bē.

[12] šī šī-biā-nī. Dann „ich bin dir schuldig", H. nī ina biā-ka, wörtlich „ich, es ist Schuld gegen dich", F. mēdo-yébbu-mā; sonderbar ist die Redensart: H. ana-biā-ka da Kanō, F. to mindāō-ka hanō adahiye, „dir verschuldet von Kanō"; „er ist sehr verschuldet, hat viele Schulden", H. ana-bī-ana bā-šī dēwa, F. ó-téffu ya-mánde ko dūdi; adjektivisch „verschuldet", H. ma-l-yawa-n danke-n bāšī, F. hotše a ya-mánde, S. gōro bōha gadālnde. Ich will hier auch einige andere Phrasen anführen: „ich gebe dir Handgeld", H. nī bā-ka arē, F. mēdo-hokku-mā wūdāo, S. ēga-tambe ferahán; „ich leiste Bürgschaft", H. nī na-ī lāmo, F. mō-lu-múntu-kō, S. al-damē boro fó. Die Ausdrücke für „ich nehme ein Versprechen auf mich" habe ich schon früher angegeben.

[13] ina fāra. „ich beginne die Lektüre des Koran", H. ina fāra karatū n el kurān, F. mōde-fūda dīnāgde el kurān.

[14] ramtše ist natürlich nur Fremdwort und es muss daneben noch ein einheimisches Wort existiren.

[15] mēdo-téffu-mō ya-mánde. ya-mánde ist Substantiv.

[16] gōro goi dālnde ist mir undeutlich.

[17] wā-nta-ū reiši nág-ahū kann wol nur eine vollere Form der zweitfolgenden Phrase sein; nág-ahū, „deine Sache".

[18] gaba wokālle ist mir nicht deutlich. Vollkommen richtig ist und gehört hierher indo ma wa-bi mu[illegible]lim na-kā, S. 67.

[19] wange hēla mi[illegible]lmaū. Es müsste vielleicht heissen bill' āle, „diese Person" und mu[illegible]lim na-ū oder na-nī.

[20] bill' āle) hille adīn, wörtlich „dieser Mann (ist) ein verschuldeter Mann".

[21] yé-ku(ā) ni-tekeē gemā. tekeē ist augenscheinlich das Substantiv vom Verbum yé-kob.

[22] ne adīn tšīla hadda, „er ist sehr stark verschuldet".

[23] am eginabre yalean bodāngne ist offenbar „ich mache den Geliehene quitt".

[24] munde am gin-lendī ist mir nicht deutlich.

[25] riaik neil-teal. riaik ist das Arabische rizik, das ursprünglich eine allgemeinere Bedeutung hat.

Sońyai.	Lógoné.	Wándalá.	Bágrimma.	Mába.
égu-gára na-ni	wú-nia-ū roiši nág-aku[17]	yé-ka(ē) ni-tekaē gemá[21]	nam-tílka-dže	litto-n) endúnge-di
gára na-ni . .	i-niá-ńge . . .	kaē le-kaē gema-ra	tílka-ra-dže .	. . . . . .
	wú-nia-ū nág-akū	yé-kaē áte-nā	máadugo régi / mok-na kadá-rwiki	litto égonō) ne-éginuére anná-mi
	wu-ni agrī . .	yé-magā nan-ákria	mat-ákri . .	am héren barónghe
. . . . . .	ruba wokúlle[18] .	yé-magā móggena ndwá-ra	mara-eggo yásem	am eginnére gal-aan hodóngne[23]
góro goi džinde[16]	wunge héla miθθimau[19]	yé-debanak gemá	másai kadá-nya	mundo am gin-tendi[24]
	bill' óle) bille adin[20]	á-na din-aknē	nō adin táila haddo[22]	risik noli-teni[25]
. . . .	. . . .	. . . . . .	. . . . . .	. . . . . .

[1] ai-rā tégari-n tai-dí-shin: tégeri is a noun formed from a root, from which has been derived likewise the verb ágeri-nishin and which is related to, if not identical with, the Arabic kerá. The form tai-di-shin is an instance of objective verbal inflection.

[2] tégari aé-genē: aé-genē again objective inflection, caused by a preceding á-rē, which however is suppressed.

[3] nān-emin tégari-nishin means verbally „thy place loan I make".

[4] alā-nishin is wanting in K., as well as the substantive alā.

[5] kūan-rē gé-shin means verbally „I follow the debt". This very expressive term is wanting in Koelle.

[6] Ki-ma adin-wa properly does not belong to this place; for adin-wa, besides, that it is an imported word of foreign origin, derived from the Arabic word din, is an adjective; but some of the corresponding terms in the other languages are verbal forms.

[7] baiān-erīk of course is closely related to the K.-word just adduced. Besides I have in T. the term šerra nāu-erīk, which, I suspect, has some relation to the following term.

[8] tánē šer táre-dē: I am not quite certain of the spelling of this phrase; in the beginning I had written tánē šēr táia-dē, but, I think, it is more correct, as I have given it; thus I have šer táre-tai for the phrase „you owe me".

[9] merē yahkai (or yeákai) haddi ye-tē means verbally „he debt whole holds" (ye-tē from tá-rik, „I hold" p. 84) i. e. „he is very much in debt".

[10] na-í aáfuri: I shall here adduce some phrases of a similar meaning, as „I enter into your salary, offer you my service", H. sáni ma-kā séfuri, F. médo-hokki-mā genári mádo gaégal; „give me thy easeri for hire", H. ban me-ni aáfuri ráhemi-á-ka, F. hokk-am genári gaiba ma-da.

[11] ni-hā da kardi, as well as the corresponding F.-phrase, is rather an awkward expression. I will here adduce a phrase, H. na-í maaá gamma, F. médo-hauti hē, the exact meaning of which I do not know.

[12] Ki ši-biá-ni: thereto „I owe thee", H. ni ina biā-ka, verbally „I, I have debt to thee", F. médo-yóhhe-ma; there is a peculiar phrase „having debt to thee from Kanō, having contracted a debt with you (by your agent or correspondent) in Kanō", H. ána-biā-ka da Kanō, F. to mindāē-ha Kanó adabiya; „he is greatly in debt, has many debts", H. ana-bi-aaa bā-ši dówa, F. ó-téffe ya-mánda ko dūdi; adject. „(greatly) indebted", H. ma-i yawa-n danke-n bā-ši, F. kotšo n ya-mánda, S. góro bóho gadáinde. I will here also adduce some other phrases, as „I give thee earnest-money advance-money", H. ni bá-ka arō, F. médo-hókka-mā wúdle, S. águ-tamhe órraha; „I stand security", H. ni na-í lāmo, F. mé-lamáute-hē, S. ai-damē horo fō; as for the related phrase „I make a promise" I have given it in some other place.

[13] ina fára: „I begin reading (studying) the Kurán", H. ina fára kárantá n al kurān, F. médo-fúde dākyde al kurān.

[14] ramtšē of course is a word of H. import and there must certainly exist beside it an indigenous F.-term.

[15] médo-téffe-mā ya-mánda: ya-mánda is substantive.

[16] góro goi džinda is not quite clear to me.

[17] wú-nia-ū roiši nág-akū seems to be a more complete form of the second phrase, but one; nág-akū, „thy thing".

[18] ruba wokúlle is not clear to me; but the phrase cited p. 87 inde ma wu-bi muθθim na-kā belongs to this place.

[19] wunga héla miθθímaú: it should probably be bill' óla, „this person" and muθθim na-ú or na-ni, „my (his) debt".

[20] bill' óla) bille adin means verbally „this person (is) an indebted person (a person in debt)".

[21] yé-ka(ē) ni-tekaé gemá: tekaé is apparently the substantive formed of the verb yé-kaé.

[22] nō adin táila haddo, „he is very greatly in debt".

[23] am eginnére galaan hodóngne evidently has the original meaning of „I acquit (restore, pay back) what I have lent".

[24] mundo am gin-tendi I am not able to analyse.

[25] risik noli-teni: risik is the Arabic rizk, which however has a far more comprehensive signification.

Deutsch und Englisch.	Kanúri.	Tēdā.	Hausa.	Fulfulde.
ich beendige — *I finish, absolve*	tumó-niskin [1]	. . . . . .	na-wánió [11]	mē-lenyi [15]
ich binde — *I tie, bind*	gōr-iskin [2] .	táné tún-erík	{ ina damrē . / { ina dérme-wá }	mēdo-habba .
ich öffne, löse — *I loosen, open*	ferem-niskin [3]	táné { kár-erík, S. / fúr-erík, N. }	ina bude . .	mēdo-omti .
ich mache zu, schliesse — *I shut, close*	dāgg-niskin [4] .	{ (ivē-kai) tum-erík, S. / yetši) yén-erík, N. }	ina rūfe [12] . .	mēdo-maddi .
ich verschliesse — *I lock up*	gumbal-iskin [5]	ivē kai hé-nuā [8]) kokō dibāli-erík	ina serka-féwa	mēdo-billa .
ich ziehe mich an — *I dress*	{ mas-skin [6] . / { kulgū yēk-iskin }	kuhū más-erík [9] / más-erík . . }	ina-žē túfa [13] .	mēdo-ruma kú-džulē
ich lege die Kleider ab — *I pull off the shirt, undress*	kulgū li-niskin [7]	{ algi / kisár [10] ner-wā } tér-erík	ina dēbe rīga [14]	mēdo-horta tog-gōre

[1] Diese beiden gewöhnlichen Ausdrücke habe ich in den meisten Sprachen niederzuschreiben vergessen.

[2] gōr-iskin. Koelle schreibt gērgskin. Ich habe dieses Wort schon oben einmal (S. 80, N. 6) in der Bedeutung „in Fesseln legen". Dort findet man auch die Participialformen für „gebunden", „gefesselt".

[3] ferem-niskin. Koelle schreibt pērymgin; auch hat er ein besonderes Wort für „lösen", nämlich pēpōgin, das ich nicht gehört habe.

[4] dāgg-niskin scheint bei Koelle zu fehlen, jedoch sieht man aus der 3ten Pers. Sing. tsāktšin, dass es sein tsāgin ist; nur macht er das Verbum, dass er die ganz geistige Bedeutung a fāro tsāgin oder vielmehr dāgg-niskin dem „Schliessen der Thüre" voransetzen lässt, da doch jene abgeleitet ist: „ich verschliesse das Mädchen", nämlich für Andere, indem ich sie für mich gewinne, mir antraue, wie wir sagen würden.

[5] gumbal-iskin ist halb Arabisch, von kufl, „Schloss", mit einheimischer Accommodation. Es fehlt bei Koelle.

[6] mas-skin. Dass das s zur Wurzel gehört, sieht man aus der Tēdā-Form. Allerdings, wenn man die Verbalendung mit der Wurzel zusammenzieht, kann man auch einfach maskin schreiben, wie Koelle thut. Das Verbum wird fast ausschliesslich in der ersten Person gebraucht. Für kulgū yēk-iskin schreibt Koelle kālagū (auch kālgū) yākēskin.

[7] li-niskin hat Koelle in der Form ilngin; 3te Pers. Sing. šī ilntšin, allerdings von der passiven Form; activisch eigentlich šī-li-n.

[8] ivē kai hé-nuā, „das Haus seine Öffnung" . . dem zusammengezogenen ivē-kai = yetši in den südlichen Dialekten.

[9] kuhū und algi, „das Hemd", „die Tobe".

[10] kisár ist corrumpirt aus dem Arabischen kiswa, كسوة.

[11] na-wánió. Ein eigenes Wort haben die Hausa für das Beendigen der Lektüre des Koran, was durch einen besonderen Festtag gefeiert wird, nämlich den kwána a séddaga, auf F. wolánde yullma; also „ich habe den Koran beendigt", H. na-dāidda el korán, F. mé-renyi el kurān. Ich will hier auch den Ausdruck unterbringen „ich habe (es) verbraucht", H. na-kāre-šī, F. mé-rēldā. Das Impersonelle „es ist verbraucht" siehe weiter unten.

[12] ina rūfe. „Ist die Thüre zugemacht?", kófa an-rūfe ši-kē.

[13] ina-žē túfa. Vergl. den allgemeinen Ausdruck H. ina-sā káya-nā, F. mēdo-borna kayādže: „ich habe meine Waffen angelegt", H. na-šigga káya n yáki (wörtlich „ich bin hineingegangen in meine Kriegsgeräthe"), F. mē-metti kāyadši konno. Dann „ich lege Staat oder Staatskleider an", H. ina-yin adō, F. medda hawāddi, S. hadēmde dorha konte (hier ist die Verbalform ungenau). Hier noch einige verwandte Redensarten. „Ich gürte den Leib", ina damrē tšēki, F. mēdo-tánda-kō; „ich binde das Hemd auf dem Nacken auf", H. ina mēde riga da ūya, F. mēdo-tánda-kō bē hāō; dann H. ina sanya riga, F. mēdo-olte dánde toggōre, S. ai herá kasába.

[14] ina dēbe riga. „Ich kleide mich aus", H. ina tōbe, F. mēdo-horta.

[15] mē-renyi ist das Präteritum.

[16] ūga-fér. Imperat. „öffne die Thür", far hō-di-mi; Passivum aūga fer-ga.

[17] ai-damē kasába ist keine einheimische Phrase und es giebt daneben wol noch eine bessere. kasába ist ebenfalls von kiswa = elšába, dem in Timbuktu gebrauchten Ausdruck für „Tobe".

[18] wa-lúgae lubāsei. wa-lūyas, „ich ziehe aus, lege ab", mag mit dem Kanúri-Wort lūg-āskin zusammenhängen. lubāsei ist wol das Arabische lebes. Für „Hemd" habe ich im L. lebō. Ob hiermit lesiā in der nächsten Phrase zusammenhängt, weiss ich nicht.

[19] yē-išékwā. Der Gegensatz der Bedeutung zu der vorhergehenden Phrase ist auffallend.

[20] māh-as (bōie nähert sich fast ganz dem K. mas-iskin.

Sónγai.	Lógonē.	Wándalā.	Bágrimma.	Mába.
éga-tímmi . .	. . . .	. . . . . .	. . . . . .	. . . . . .
éga-hangá-nda (horfo	wú-henhā . . .	yé-úgdo há-ya		
éga-fér [16] . . .	wó-láhiā . . .	y(e)-ávrurō .	ma-tie-nye .	am arlotúngne
éga-dābu . . .	wágiā	yé-χedā	má-dib (tārn	am kilsi
éga-kuffel . . .	wa-hō kukō (a-γā-ū		mádib-jūa . / málal-iún .	am kerker aróng-ne
si-damē kasāba [17]	wa-lúχae lubúmi [18]	yó-taekō . .	mák-us (bōlo [20]	am ayaine
	wa-dehā lúviā .	ye-taékwā zanē [19]	mók-od korō	am andóngne

[1] These two terms, although of so general an import, have not been written down by me in most of these languages.
[2] gér-fehia: Koelle writes gíreskin. I have given this word already once (p. 80) with the notion of „to put in fetters". In that place I have also given the forms for the participle „bound", „fettered".
[3] farom-nishin; Koelle writes pérgmgin; he has also a peculiar term for „loosen", viz pépbégin, which I have not heard.
[4] dieg-nishin: a person would look in vain in Koelle for this term under this form, but he has it under the form tsáṅgin, 3rd pers. sing. tsektšin; but, besides confounding dš and ts, Koelle commits the mistake of giving first the peculiar signification ā féro tséṅgin (dieg-nishin), „I engage a girl", properly „I shut up a girl", namely for others, by attaching her to myself, the term being only derived from the idea of shutting a door.
[5] gumbal-ishin is half Arabic, being derived from the Arabic word kufl „lock" and accommodated to the laws of the Kanúri-language; it is wanting in Koelle.
[6] muo-shin: From the corresponding Tédā-term we see, that s belongs to the root, but, if as Koelle does, we do not separate the root, we may write mushin. The verb is almost exclusively used in the 1st pers. sing. — Instead of kulgū yōk-ishin Koelle writes kálugù (also kálgù) yákfskin.
[7] li-nishin has Koelle in the form língin; to this form belongs the 3rd pers. sing. li lintšin, while the active form tši-li-n is obsolete.
[8] ivō kal bé-nah means verbally „the house its opening" and is identical with the composite term ivō-ḫal = yetši in the Southern dialects.
[9] kubū and nigí, „the shirt" or „the tobe".
[10] kisaér is a corrupted form from the Arabic word kiswa.
[11] na-wánió: in H. there is a peculiar term for the absolving the lecture of the Kurān, H. na-dākidda el kurān, F. mō-roqyi el kurān. The day, on which this first lecture of the holy book is finished, is celebrated as a holiday, being called kwāna n sáddaga, F. wolánda yellma. — I will here also adduce the expression „I have consumed it", H. na-kāre-ši, F. mō-réidō. As for the intransitive form „it is consumed, it is gone", see lower down.
[12] ina rāfe: „is the door shut?", kōfa an-rūfe ši-kō.
[13] ina-šē tūfa: compare the other term of a more general import „I put on my things", H. ina-sā kāya-nā, F. mōdo-borna kayēdžo; „I have put on my arms", H. ná-šigga kāya n yáki (verbally „I have entered my things of war"), F. mō-natti kāya-dāi konno; „I put on full dress", H. ina-yi n adō, F. modde hawādāi, S. ho dóndo derba bente. In the latter phrase the expression of the verbal form is incomplete. Here also a few phrases of a similar notion „I gird myself (the body)", H. ina damrē tšehi, F. mōdo-tánde-kē; „I tie the shirt behind the neck", H. ina mōdo riga da ûya, F. mōdo-tánda-kō hō bāō; then H. ina sanya riga, F. mōdo-otta dāude toggāra, S. ai-berā kasāba.
[14] ina dōhe riga: compare the phrase „I undress", H. ina tūbe, F. mōdo-borta.
[15] mō-bonyi is not the present, but the past tense.
[16] éga-fér: imperat. „open the door", fer hō-di-mō, passive nōga fer-ga.
[17] ai-damē kasāba is not a purely indigenous phrase and I have no doubt, that there exists another more original one beside it. kasāba is likewise from kiswa = ri[illegible]ha, the term for shirt which is used in Timbúktu and the neighbourhood.
[18] wa-lúχae lubúsei: wa-lúχae, „I take off" may be connected with the Kanúri-word lúg-ishin. lubúsei probably is the Arabic lebes, „clothing, dress"; it cannot well mean „shirt", as I have it represented by the word lebū. Whether the term lúvia in the next phrase be connected with the latter, I cannot say.
[19] ye-taékwā: the verb being nearly identical, the difference of the meaning in reference to the preceding phrase is remarkable.
[20] mák-us (bōlo very closely approaches the Kanúri-word muo-(shin.

Deutsch und Englisch.	Kanúri.	Tédā.	Hausa.	Fulfúlde.
ich falte das Hemd zusammen — *I fold the shirt*	taam-nískin [1] .	tánē kilīn-erík	ína nedde rīga [10]	mōdo-tegga toggōre
ich entfalte, öffne — *I unfold, open*	fefē-nískin [2] .	tánē firín-erík	ína būde (rīga	mēdo-onta (toggōre
ich rasire (mich — *I shave*	kum-nískin [3] .	kyūso tér-erík [6]	ína aski [11] . .	mēdo-fémbo-to
ich rasire den Kopf — *I shave my head*	kélā-nī kum-nískin	dáho né-ruā kyūso tér-erík	ína aski kai-na	mēdo-fembo hōre-am
ich schneide das Haar — *I cut the hair*	kúnduri kam-nískin [4]	kyūso kúb-erík	ína yanka gāši	. . . . .
ich ordne, bessere — *I arrange, mend, repair*	yēná-skin . .	yén-erík . .	ína {gēra . . / gyarta [12] . .}	mēdo-wúdyinē
ich reinige, fege — *I clean, sweep*	farán-nískin [5]	{sárd-erík, S. / farán-erík, N.}	ína šāre [13] . .	mēdo-wūa .
ich reibe — *I rub* . .	gámbu-skin [6] .	gám-erík . .	ína gōga . .	mēdo-dogga .
ich wasche — *I wash* .	tul{úskin [7] . / úgin . .}	{túld-erík, S. [9] / kēs-erík, N. .}	ína woñko . .	mēdo-lōti [14] .

[1] taam-níakin hat Koelle mit dieser Bedeutung nicht, aber er hat támgin (3te Pers. Sing. šī saptšin), „i. q. tsámgin", mit der Bedeutung „ich dränge zusammen" oder „häufe zusammen", wo sich denn unser „zusammenfalten" unterordnete. Für „falten", „aufrollen" hat er kéllúgin.

[2] fefē-níakin bei Koelle pēpēúgin.

[3] kum-níakin hat Koelle nicht. Die Ähnlichkeit mit kam-níakin ist ganz äusserlich.

[4] kam-níakin allein werden wir später wieder haben. Koelle schreibt kamgin und gibt neben der gewöhnlichen Form der dritten Person, kamtšin, auch eine seltenere, kaptšin, die ich aber nie gehört habe. — Geistig abstrahirt von „schneiden" ist der Begriff des „Bestimmens, Festsetzens".

[5] farán-níakin kommt offenbar von faráñ, „offen", „rein", also eigentlich „ich mache offen, rein". Deshalb wiederhole ich das n. Allerdings ist das Schluss-ñ von faráñ ein ganz nasales und man hört sogar oft faráq, aber dieser Nasenlaut wird durch das darauf folgende n wieder aufgehoben. Koelle pēráñgin, obgleich er fáraá schreibt.

[6] gámbu-skin hat Koelle mit der Bedeutung „ich kratze", dagegen hat er für „ich reibe", sámgin, was jedoch nur vom „Einreiben" (mit Butter, Fett) gebraucht zu werden scheint.

[7] tul-úskin hat Koelle unbegreiflicher Weise, wie es scheint, in dieser allergewöhnlichsten Bedeutung nicht. Zwar hat er túlnskin, aber nur als zusammengezogene Form von túlúgeskin. Dass er das Wort gar vergessen hat, sieht man daraus, dass er túlagin bei kasálúgin, einem ganz ungewöhnlichen Wort für „waschen", eigentlich nur zum Gebete (kasalla), neben lámgin erwähnt.

[8] kyūso tér-erík, „ich nehme das Haar ab"; kyūso (kūso) oder tšūso, „das Haar"; dáho né-ruā kūso, „das Haar auf meinem Kopfe".

[9] túld-erík, kēs-erík. Hier haben wir einmal ein Beispiel, dass der dem Kanúri am nächsten verwandte Ausdruck der Tédā-Sprache in den südöstlichen Landschaften gesprochen wird, während der ganz fremde Ausdruck kēs-erík im Thale Kauār und nördlicher zu Hause ist, also in Landschaften, die dem politischen Einfluss der Kanúri am meisten ausgesetzt waren. „Ich wasche mein Gesicht", bérí né-ruā kēs-erík; zugleich scheint die Form tuld-erík im Tédā anzuzeigen, dass das d oder t ursprünglich zur Wurzel gehörte, obgleich es in der 3ten Person auch im Tédā nicht erscheint.

[10] ína nedde rīga. „Ich rolle das Hemd auf", H. ína ribe rīga, F. mēdo-nōn toggōre; „ich kehre das Hemd um", H. ína birkotšši, F. mōdo-wallita toggōre.

[11] ína aski. Dazu die Redensart „ich beschneide meinen Bart", H. ína šāta gēme, P. mēdo-tšánte wāre-mā.

[12] ína gerta. „Setze dies in guten Stand", H. gerta a-wá-nan néggari, F. wōdin dum bōdum; „du hast das nicht gut gemacht oder ausgebessert", H. kai ba ka-gérta-šī néggari ba, F. a-wōdin-ai dum bōdum.

[13] ína šāre. „Kehre die Wohnung sorgfältig aus", H. šāre daki néggari, F. hu-wā-ki sūdo.

[14] mēdo-lōti. Dieses Wort hat eine auffällige Ähnlichkeit mit dem Lateinischen Particip. lotus von lavere.

[15] ōkwa síbidi ist eigenthümlich und auffallend. Das ōkwa ist wahrscheinlich unrichtig; vielleicht sollte es ēga heissen.

[16] w(a) ūta kelmétadē. Das letzte Wort kann ich nicht erklären.

[17] w(a) ūdo mtsúlkā. imtsúlis heisst „das Haar"; imtsúlkā statt imtsúle nā.

[18] inūē-rohé ist keine Verbalform; vielleicht sollte es wuūē-rohé heissen.

[19] wa Thā könnte Manchem ein Missverständniss scheinen, da tebā „das Hemd" heisst; auch habe ich in der ersten Person daneben das mir nicht ganz klare Wort rūšī, aber die folgenden Zeitformen lassen keinen Zweifel.

[20] yé-aská yíre. yíre heisst „das Kopfhaar".

[21] yé-tloguo. „Haar" ist hier nicht besonders ausgedrückt.

[22] binšadā, vielleicht yé-'nšadā.

[23] am derwá ist auffällig.

[24] am ēnde(nin)-nyé. Das nin kann nicht zum Verbum selbst gehören, weil der Imperat. a-ēndenyé heisst.

Sónyai.	Lógoné.	Wándalá.	Bágrimma.	Mába.
. . . .	w(a)-ū(a kalmáta-dē[16]	yé-džahā . .	mam-ákabā .	am tabák-aróng-ne
. . . .	w(a)-uwíle angolla	yé-pelā . .	mak-idnánga	am firtik-aróng-ne
éga-dāirfe . .	ind(o) álu-gī .	yé-sehā . .	mádissa . .	am crwēne
éga-dāirfe bongo	ind(o) álu-gī kā nāū	yé-sehā yīre[20]	mádissa dalám-nā	am derwā[23]
	w(a)-ūðe mtaslāū[17]	yé-ðogue[21] .	mokal bī-nā .	am atámuc
éga-bīnsa-gā .	luðē-rohō[18] . .	yé-méganā magā	maládla . .	am sorser-aróng-ne
čkwa sibidi[15] .	wa-tambánčā .	hínšadā[22] . .	máscrēū . .	am énde(nín)-nyē[24]
éga-dēēriga . .	wu' mðaðāū . .	yé-swā . . .	mam-gak . .	am búkarē / am konye-erē
éga-bīmai . .	wu' lbū[19] . . .	yé-barā (barē	mándžugō . .	am avkāne

[1] tasm-nichin with this signification and with this form is wanting in Koelle, but he has samgin (3rd pers. sing. Ii soptēin), which he states expressly to be identical with tsámgin, while the notion, which he attributes to it, namely „I crowd or heap together", has some connection with our „I fold together".
[2] faff-nichin: Koelle pépágin.
[3] kam-nichin has Koelle not. No doubt this word looks very like kam-nichin, but such a resemblance is merely seemingly.
[4] kam-nichin will occur further on in my lists as an independent verb. Koelle writes it kámgin and has besides kámtšin, the common form of the 3rd pers. a rarer form, kápšin, but this I have never heard used. — Derived from this material notion in a spiritual sense is that of „deciding, settling".
[5] faran-nichin is evidently derived from the adjective faráñ, „open, clean", and the original notion is apparently „I make open, clean". That is the reason, why I write the n twice. Now in the word faran the ā is evidently a nasal one, and it very often sounds like faráŋ, but through the following simple n the nasal sound has been changed. Koelle has this verb under the very different form peránġin, although he writes faran.
[6] gámbu-shin has Koelle with the notion „I scratch", while for „I rub" he gives sámgin, although I think, the latter is used only of the rubbing of fat or butter into the skin.
[7] taj-ūshin: Koelle most unaccountably has not this common word, at least not with this notion, for he has téjnshin only as the contracted form of téjāgeshin; but from the circumstance that, when explaining the term hasálġin, not the common term for washing at all, but only for the washing before a prayer (kasálla), he mentions téjāgin, we see that he has forgotten to mention the latter in the right place.
[8] kyáso tér-erik, „I take off the hair"; kyāso (kāso) or tšāso, „the hair": dībe né-rnā kāso, „the hair of my head".
[9] táld-erik, hés-erik: here we have an instance of the case, that the term, which is nearest related to the Kanúri, is spoken in the south-easterly provinces of the dominion of the Tédā, while the term hos-erik, which has no connection whatever with that language, is used in the valley Kawár and more to the North, that is to say, in those provinces, which have been most exposed to the political and moral influence of the Kanúri. „I wash my face", bírī né-rnā hés-erik. I will also mention, that the form of the Tédā-verb táld-erik seems to indicate, that the d or t originally did belong to the root and has been lost in the Kanúri-language, although even in T. it is lost in the 3rd pers.
[10] ina nedde riga: „I roll up the shirt", H. ina ribe riga, F. médo-sówa toggóra. „I turn the shirt", H. ina birketšši, F. médo-wallita toggóre.
[11] ina aski: I here insert the phrase „I trim my beard", H. ina Ždia síme, F. médo-tšaute wáre-mā.
[12] ina gerte: „repair this nicely", H. gerta n-wé-nan néggari, F. wódia dum bódum; „thou hast not arranged or repaired it well", H. hai ba ka-górta-ši néggari ba. F. a-wódin-ai dum bódum.
[13] ina šāre: „sweep or clean the house carefully", H. šāre díki néggari, F. hu-wā-ki súdo.
[14] médo-lóti: this Fulfúlde-word bears an accidental resemblance to the participle lotus of the Latin verb lavare, „to wash".
[15] čkwa sibidi is remarkable and can scarcely be right. Perhaps instead of čkwa it ought to be éga.
[16] w(a) ūta kalmátadē; the last word I am not able to explain.
[17] w(a)-ū(ð)e mtaslāū: imtašle means „the hair"; imtašlāū instead of imtašle nāū.
[18] luðē-rohō is not a correct verbal form and perhaps it ought to be wuððē-rohō.
[19] wu lbū might seem a misunderstanding to some one, as lobē means „shirt", and in the first person I have added the word rāūšī, the exact meaning of which I do not know, but the following verbal forms leave no doubt as to the correctness of the verbal form wu lbū.
[20] yé-sehā yīre: yīre means „the hair of the head".
[21] yé-ðogue: „hair" is not expressed in this phrase.
[22] hinšadā is possibly not correct and may be corrupted from yé-'nšadā.
[23] am derwā is remarkable.
[24] am énde(nín)-nyē: that the syllable nín does not form an intrinsic part of the verb, appears from a-éndenyē, the form of the imperative tense.

14*

Deutsch und Englisch.	Kanúri.	Tédā.	Hausa.	Fulfulde.
er wäscht — *he is washing* / sie wäscht — *she is washing*	tál-tšin	merē tól-kent	ši ši-na woñkej / ita tā-na woñkej	kanko ó-loti .
gewaschen — *washed* .	túl-gata . .	. . . . . .	an-wóñke [10] .	lotā-mo . .
ich trockene, mache trocken — *I dry*	tar-nískin [1] .	táné { intšórdu [8] / inkoērke }	ina kékašē [11] .	mĕdo-yōri .
ich koche — *I cook* . .	dē-nískin [2] .	táné { bórt-erik / dē-n-erik [9] }	ina deffa . .	mĕdo-deffai [13]
ich röste — *I roast* . . / ich schmore — *I fry, broil*	kayō-nískin [3] .	wŭeni yē-n-erik	ina sōya . . / ina gasea . .	mĕdo-sōya [14] . / mĕdo-džúdu .
ich schlage Feuer — *I strike fire*	kannu bag-nískin [4]	wŭendē wŭeni tér-erik [10]	. . . . . .	. . . . . .
ich zünde Feuer an — *I light the fire*	kannu yēk-ískin [5]	wŭeni akāu [11] .	ina hasaa uta	mĕdo-hobba yīte
ich blase das Feuer an — *I blow up the fire*	kannu fū-nískin [6]	wŭeni fū-n-erik	ina fūra uta .	mĕdo-hobba yīte
ich lösche das Feuer aus — *I put out the fire*	kannu yēdž-ískin [7]	wŭeni yē-n-erik [12]	ina kašē / ina tuši } uta	nil-ĕ yīte . .

[1] tar-nískin, „ich mache auseinander", „ich breite aus", daher „ich trockene". Koelle macht zwei Verba tárgin daraus; 3te Pers. Sing. tar-isín, Partizip. Passiv. tár-gata.

[2] dē-nískin, wörtlich „ich mache leer, entlee". Koelle dēgin; 3te Person Plur. séndi-ma dē-sé.

[3] kayō-nískin hat Koelle in der Form káyōgin.

[4] kannu bag-nískin ist eigentlich auffallend und ganz analog der prägnanten Deutschen und Englischen Phrase: „ich erzeuge Feuer durch Schlagen des Stahles".

[5] kannu yēk-ískin. Koelle erwähnt kannu yikēskin. Die Grundbedeutung ist wol dieselbe wie bei „ich lege das Kleid an", wo ich oben kalgú yēk-ískin habe; denn man sagt fáto-rō kannu yēk-ískin, „an das Haus lege ich Feuer".

[6] kannu fū-nískin oder fū-ágin; 3te Person Sing. kannu fū-tšin.

[7] kannu yēdž-ískin; 3te Person Sing. kannu tšē-tšin.

[8] táné intšórdu oder inkoērke sind nur verschiedene dialektische Formen desselben Wurzelwortes.

[9] dē-n-erik. In diesem, wie im folgenden Verbum und fū-n-erik, ist n des Wohllautes wegen zwischen die beiden Vokale eingeschoben.

[10] wŭendē wŭeni tér-erik. wŭendē heisst „der Feuerstahl".

[11] wŭeni akāu ist eine unvollkommene Verbalform.

[12] wŭeni yē-n-erik, im Imperativ wŭeni yi. Hier ist wŭeni Objekt, in der obigen Phrase ist es Mittel.

[13] an-wóñke, Plur. an-wóñke-su, F. dé-lotā-ma.

[14] ina kékašē. Ich will hier die begriffsverwandte Redensart hersetzen: „ich hänge an die Luft, lüfte", H. ina kényē, F. mĕdo-rille, B. égu-yéndige; „hänge diesen meinen Teppich an die Luft, damit er auslüftet" (wörtlich „damit er ein wenig Wind trinkt)", H. kényē ewá-nan kilīšī nā-wā, dōmi ši-šā iska kadan, F. rilu-bē kétti-bē gambe, dūerel hendu sadda; „ist das Hemd trocken geworden, oder noch nicht?", H. riga yé-kāše, kó tókonā. F. toggōre yōr-i, kó tahónde yōr-ai (yōr-ai, „ist nicht getrocknet)".

[15] mĕdo-deffai könnte scheinen der Hausa-Sprache entlehnt zu sein, aber es ist doch ursprünglich; selbst im Tomba ist es ähnlich.

[16] mĕdo-sōya ist wol nicht der einheimische Fulfulde-Ausdruck.

[17] égu-hōr nāne-di. Das eigentliche Verbum ist wol dasselbe, wie in der vorhergehenden Phrase, in der das gu eigentlich nicht zur Wurzel gehört, und nāne-di, „mit dem Feuer", wird bei dieser zweiten Phrase hinzugefügt, weil hier die Einwirkung des Feuers ganz direkt ist. Die Wurzel hor oder hur haben wir weiter unten, nur ist sie da zu kohúr verstärkt.

[18] ikolām ist eine auffallende Form für die 1ste Person; 3te Person Plur. te-tikolām.

[19] indéle Ol sonāda. tē muss hier für nē oder inē, „die Flamme, der Funken", stehen; indéle ist wol sicherlich contrahirt aus indo wile, also wörtlich „ich mache Funken mit dem Feuerstahl".

[20] wanu fū igrē heisst wol ursprünglich „ich mache Feuer an dem Zunder".

[21] wá-fadā fuyē; 3te Person Sing. al-na fedá fuyā.

[22] wa-öyelā fuyē; 3te Person Sing. al-na öyelā fuyē. Das ö ist hier offenbar ein integrirender Theil der Wurzel.

[23] yé-dlan kárā; 3te Person Sing. á-dlane bé-ngaré kārē.

[24] mal-ok pod-na. Wir haben hier eine ausgebildete Accusativ-Form; dagegen haben wir in der weiter unten folgenden Phrase mal-ūwe pódo die einfache, dem Nominativ entsprechende Grundform des Wortes.

Sonyai.	Logoné.	Wándalá.	Bágrimma.	Mába.
. . . .	nŏ na-n-ulbū	á-barā . . .	ám-džŏgŏ . .	. . . . . .
hímai-ndi . . .	yélbia	annó-barā .	. . . . . .	. . . . . .
éga-kók . . .	wú-kabē . . .	yé-pelā . .	mán-adžā . .	am ondodžēre
éga-kór-ga . .	íkolám [18] . . .	yé-giyā . .	mán-džu-dŏ .	am(nyērek)andri
éga-kór nūne-di [17]	wú-sáwalŏ . .	yé-selā . . .	man-dža-bínya	am áwasnē am ándžikē
. . . .	indála θŏ senáde [19]	yó-džo kárā .	mal-uk pod-nu [24]	senád ginnon du-nyérga enye-múnne
éga-fúnsu nūne .	waza fŭ 'lgēā [20]	yé-fón tofŏ kárā	mak-na pod-na	am adal
	wú-fedā fuyā [21]	yé-mebán kárā	mal-ūwo {póda / fóda}	am fui arúgne
éga-wūi nūne-di	wa-ōyelā fuyā [22]	yé-džan kárā [23]	ma-tol pódu .	am avgi

[1] tar-nískin or terágin, as Kanúri has it, means properly „I take asunder, I spread out" and thence „I dry", wherefore there is not the slightest reason, why Kanúri should make it two distinct verbs; 3rd pers. sing. tar-isin, partic. pass. tár-gata.

[2] dŏ-nískin: Kanúri of course has the form dŏágin; 3rd person plur. séndi-ma dŏ-sŏ.

[3] kayē-nískin has Kanúri under the form kāyēágin.

[4] kanna bag-nískin is quite as pregnant a phrase, as the English „I strike fire", „I make fire by striking the flint with the steel".

[5] kanna yŏk-iskin: Kanúri writes kanna yŏkéskin, just as he writes above p. 106 kalgŭ yākéskin, for the original notion is the same in both phrases, viz „to apply, application"; thus fáto-rŏ kanna yŏk-iskin, „I apply fire to the house", „set the house on fire".

[6] kanna fŭ-nískin or fŭ-ágin; 3rd person sing. kanna fŭ-tšin.

[7] kanna yādi-iskin; 3rd person sing. kanna tšŏ-tšin.

[8] téoā intšŏrdo or intsŏrdo are only different dialectical forms of the same root.

[9] dŏ-n-orik: in this, as well as in the following verb, and in fŭ-n-orik the letter n has been inserted between the two vowels on account of euphony.

[10] wŏendŏ wŏeni tér-orik: wŏendŏ is „the fire-steel".

[11] wŏeni) ukŏā is an imperfect verbal form.

[12] wŏeni yŏ-n-orik: as most of these Tédā-forms are greatly abridged and corrupted in common life, I am not quite sure of the form of the present tense; wŏeni yi is, I think, the imperative. wŏeni in this phrase is the object.

[13] an-wóhle: plur. an-wóhle-sŏ, F. dé-Iŭtŭ-ma.

[14] Ina kóhalē: I will here insert a phrase of a similar meaning: „I air, expose to the air", H. ina šiayē, F. mŏdo-yile, S. éga-yéndigu: „expose this my carpet to the air, that the wind may penetrate it" (verbally „that it may drink a little wind)", H. šiayē a-wó-nan bi[illegible] nā-wa, dung [illegible] isha kadan, F. yiin-bŏ br[illegible]-bŏ gambe, dāerri henda sedda; „has the shirt dried or not yet?", H. riga yá-būšo kō tōkona, F. toggōre yōr-i, kŏ tabónde yōr-ai (yōr-ai, „has not dried)".

[15] mŏdo-daffal might seem to be borrowed from the Hausa-language, but nevertheless it is an indigenous Fulfúlde-word.

[16] mŏdo-siye most probably is not the national Fulfúlde-term, although it is the only one used at present by the Fúl-be of Sókoto.

[17] éga-kór nūne-di: the verbal root seems to be the same, as in the preceding phrase. For, while ga there appears not to belong to the root, in the instance before us nūne-di is added, in order to express the direct action of the fire. The same root kor or kur we have lower down in the lengthened and emphatic form kuhár.

[18] íkolám is remarkable as the form for the 1st pers. sing.; 3rd pers. plur. te-tíkolám.

[19] indála θŏ senáde: indála, I have no doubt, is the contracted form of indo wila; θŏ seems to be the nθŏ or lnθŏ in my list of nouns, meaning „spark, flame", so that the original meaning is „I make sparks by means of the steel".

[20] waza fŭ 'lgēā seems to mean originally „I make fire to the tinder".

[21] wú-fedā fuyā: 3rd pers. sing. ni-na fedā fuyā.

[22] wa-ōyelā fuyā: 3rd pers. sing. ni-na ōyelā fuyā; the ō is evidently an integral part of the root.

[23] yé-džan kárā: 3rd pers. sing. á-džane bé-áganá kárā.

[24] mal-uk pod-na: in this instance we have a full form of the accusative, while a little lower down in the phrase mal-ūwo póda we have the simple form pódu unchanged.

Deutsch und Englisch.	Kanúri.	Tēda.	Hausa.	Fulfúlde.
ich verbrenne — *I burn*	war-nískin[1] .	wūeni yē-n-crík[8]	ína kōne[15]	mēdo-dāne . / mēdo-wāli .
ich zerbreche — *I break*	nam-nískin[2] .	kir-crík[9] . .	ína kárië . .	mēdo-yawa .
zerbrochen — *broken* .	núm-gata . .	te-kir-kedē .	an-kárië . .	dum yawá-ma
ich schneide — *I cut* .	kam-nískin[3] .	kōb-crík[10] .	ína yanka[16] .	mēdo-hirsa .
geschnitten — *cut* . .	kám-gata . .	tó-góppedē[11]	yánka-kē . .	kirsā-do . .
ich giesse ein — *I pour in*	fī-g-ískin[4] .	tánē { bīer[12] . / suri . . }	ína zūba[17] .	mēdo-wondža
ich giesse aus — *I pour out, I spill*	fī-nískin[5] . .	{ bérik[13] . . / tánē bīer butta }	ína yūis . .	mēdo-wañlita
ich stülpe um — *I overthrow*	filī-nískin[6] .	forúm-crík .	ína žirgitta .	mēdo-wañlitáki
ich schöpfe Wasser — *I draw water*	ńkī gulú-skin[7]	gōn-crík[14] .	ína { žā rūa . / dēbe rūa }	mēdo-afōdi ndiam / mēdo-nokka ndiam

[1] war-niskin. Koelle unterscheidet dieses Wort durch ein langes ā von einem anderen Worte, wāragin, „ich greife an, ergreife hastig", aber ich habe unser Wort nur mit kurzem a aussprechen hören und ich bin der Ansicht, dass beide Wörter identisch sind; denn bei der Bedeutung „ich verbrenne" muss man sich eigentlich k a n n a hinzudenken. Auch im L. gibt es kein besonderes Wort für „verbrennen", so wie überhaupt wol in wenigen ausgebildeten Sprachen.

[2] nam-niskin: 3te Person Sing. nam-tšin, während nam-niskin, „ich setze", das Koelle ebenfalls námgin schreibt, in der 3ten Pers. Sing. nab-tšin hat (nach Koelle náptšin und zuweilen námtšin). — Für nám-gata schreibt Koelle nomgáte.

[3] kám-niskin, siehe S. 108, Anm. 4.

[4] fi-g-iskin: 3te Person Sing. fīegin, 3te Person Sing. Perf. fītene. fī-g-iskin ist die verstärkte, transitive Form von fī-niskin.

[5] fī-niskin; 3te Person Sing. fī-tšin; zuweilen wird in diesem Sinne dēka-rā hinzugefügt. Koelle hat pīngin.

[6] filī-niskin ist wol unzweifelhaft verwandt mit firim-erik im Tēdā S. 108, da „umstülpen" und „entfalten" auf denselben Begriff zurückkommt. Entschieden hängt es zusammen mit fille oder filō (Koelle pēlei), „der Deckel, die umgestülpte Schüssel" und vielleicht sogar mit felē-niskin, S. 70, „ich steige", d. h. „ich mache offen".

[7] ńkī gulú-skin. Koelle schreibt gūtsgin. Das Wort hat zugleich in sehr natürlicher Weiterentwickelung die Bedeutung „ich bewässere (den Garten)".

[8] wūeni yē-n-erik scheint hier in seiner eigentlichen Bedeutung zu stehen, während es für „rösten" nur uneigentlich gebraucht wird. Ich habe hier auch eine vulgäre Form wūeni yāë. — wūeni ist Ablativ.

[9] kir-erik; die gewöhnliche Form ist tánē kir.

[10] kōb-erik. Wir haben hier den b-Laut in der Wurzel, der sich auch noch bei dem entsprechenden Kanúri-Zeitwort in der allerdings seltneren Form der 3ten Person Sing. kāb-tšin oder kāp-tšin zeigt.

[11] tó-góppedē ist eine unregelmässige Verbalform, in der sich die drei Umwandlungen aus dem Wohllaut erklären.

[12] tánē bīer. Dies ist die gewöhnliche, aber ungrammatische Form, die ich brauche, weil ich über die richtige nicht ganz sicher bin, bīer-erik oder bēr-erik, wahrscheinlich das letztere, wie die folgende Form zeigt.

[13] bērik, wahrscheinlich abgekürzt statt bēr-erik. Für „ausgiessen" scheint auch noch ein dem Kanúri näher stehendes Wort in Gebrauch zu sein, da ich für „er giesst aus" die Phrase morō fehēnde habe.

[14] gōn-erik. „Wasser", eyi, sollte wol besonders ausgedrückt ist.

[15] ina kōne. Dazu die Phrase „du hast dein Hemd verbrannt", H. kai ka-kōne riga-nka, F. anñ loggóre má-da, K. ni kukde-ni karabō-di.

[16] ina yanka. Ich will hier die Phrase einschieben: „ich schneide die Feder", ina gyeta alkálemi (eigentlich „ich mache die Feder zurecht").

[17] ina zūba. „Giesse darüber", H. zūba ka-nan, F. wondže da mādla.

[18] ēga-bīga tūri-di ist vielleicht nicht richtig; tūri = tāguri ist „Holz", „Baum".

[19] ēgu-kō bangó-di kóna bāri, „ich schöpfe Wasser (bāri) aus (kóna) dem Brunnen oder Teich" (bangō).

[20] w(a)-āgele. Ich bin nicht ganz sicher, ob das a zur Wurzel des Verbums gehört. Übrigens haben die Leute von Lōgone kein besonderes Wort für „verbrennen" und w(a)-āgele, das nur den allgemeinen Begriff des Zerstörens hat, erhält nur dadurch jene Bedeutung, dass wane fā 'Igrā vorgesetzt wird, „ich zünde Feuer an und zerstöre (auf diese Weise)".

[21] w-agōē fe-nēa. Die Form der 3ten Person Sing. die ich niedergeschrieben habe, nen-agōē-nē, scheint zu zeigen, dass die Sylbe fe keinen integrirenden Theil dieser Phrase bildet.

[22] w(a)-anfē wagōēa, wol sicherlich zwei gesonderte Zeitwörter, „ich stosse an, ich giesse aus".

[23] yē-bēšenē bā-ya. Das erste e wird gar nicht gehört; so 3te Person Sing. ā-bšenē bā-āgenā.

[24] yē-pwa; 3te Person Sing. ā-pwa bā-āgenā, 3te Person Sing. Perf. pépwa.

Sónγai.	Lógonē.	Wándalā.	Bágrimma.	Mába.
éga-kukúr (ganda) nūne-dī	w(a)-ágela[20] . .	ye-bēšenā bā-ya[23]	ma-nyúnga .	wasík tinyēre
éga-bāga tūri-dī[18]	w(a)-āga . . .	ye-kélda . .	ma-tókking korō	am termēre
. . . .	dāgēā	anne-kēlda .	. . . . .	. . . . . .
éga-dumbu . . / éga-dungu . .	w(a)-áfēā . . .	yé-tši-aá . .	mam-nkol .	am atámne
dungu	dápiā	an-itāā . . .	. . . . .	. . . . .
éga-béri . . .	w-ayōe annánguná	yé-pwa[24] . .	mak-om ùgalle	am endži áwanē
éga-manga . .	w-ayōē fe-nēa[21]	yé-púnfa bā-ya ágnāē	mak-om korō / ma-dás korō	am yū-arrónge
. . . . . .	w(a)-anōē waχōēa[22]	yó-póne ruppwe	má-nagā . .	. . . . .
éga-kō bańgō-dī kōna hāri[19]	w(a)-úlowā am .	yé-billēwe .	motkod manē	am andánge

[1] war-niskin: Koelle distinguishes this verb by means of a long ā from another verb, wárāgin („I grasp, seize hastily"), but I have heard our word only pronounced with a short vowel and am of opinion, that both words are identical; for properly „I burn", that is „I seize, destroy by fire", is not war-niskin, but kannu war-niskin. Also in L. there is no particular term for „to burn", and the same is the case in most of the languages of uncivilized people.

[2] nam-niskin: 3rd pers. sing. nam-tšin; but nem-niskin, „I sit down", which Koelle writes likewise námgin or némgin, has in the 3rd pers. sing. nep-tšin (according to Koelle néptšin and sometimes némtšin). — nám-gata is written by Koelle namgáta.

[3] hám-niskin: see p. 107, note 4.

[4] fi-g-iskin: 3rd pers. sing. fisgin, 3rd pers. sing. perf. fitena. fi-g-iskin is the stronger, transitive form from fi-niskin.

[5] fi-niskin: 3rd pers. sing. fi-tšin; sometimes the particle déha-rō is added, in order to express the meaning more distinctly. Koelle writes plágin.

[6] fili-niskin undoubtedly is related to the T.-term firin-erik p. 106, the notion of turning over and that of unfolding, proceeding from the same idea. To the same root does also belong the term fille or filē (Koelle pélet) „the cover", i. e. „the dish turned over" and perhaps even fréē-niskin, „I show" i. e. „I make open".

[7] ńhi gutá-skin; Koelle writes gútçekin. The word conveys also the notion of „irrigating (a garden)".

[8] wūeni yē-n-erik seems to appear here with its original signification, while it is only improperly used for „to roast". I have also in this instance the vulgar form wūeni yōē.

[9] kir-erik: the vulgar form is tánē kir.

[10] kōb-erik: here we have the b sound appearing in the root, while in the corresponding Kanúri-word it has disappeared, remaining only in the rare form of the 3rd pers. sing. káb-tšin or káp-tšin.

[11] tó-gáppedē is an irregular verbal form.

[12] tánē bier: this is the vulgar and ungrammatical form, which I give here, as I am not quite certain with regard to the right form, whether it be bier-erik or hér-erik; probably it is the latter, as is shown by the following phrase.

[13] hérik, probably an abbreviated form for hér-erik. However for the term „I pour out" the Kanúri-language seems to possess also another phrase, which approaches more closely the corresponding Kanúri-word; thus for the phrase „he pours out" I have written down meré fekénde.

[14] gōn-erik: I suspect, that the word ayi, „water", ought to have been added.

[15] ina kāne: compare the phrase „thou hast burnt thy shirt", H. kai ka-kōne riga-nka, F. auli toggōre mā-da, S. ni kobér-ni kásnhā-di.

[16] ina yanka: I have heard the phrase „I cut the pan", ina gerta alkáleml (properly „I arrange, mend the pan").

[17] ina rūba: „pour over it", H. zōba ka-nen, F. wondāe da wádāe.

[18] éga-bōga tūri-di probably is not quite correct; tūri = tágari means „tree", „wood".

[19] éga-kō bangō-di kōna hāri, „I draw water (hāri) from out (kōna) the well or pond" (bangō).

[20] w(a)-ágela: I am not quite sure, whether the a belongs to the verbal root. However I have to observe, that the L.-language does not possess a particular term for „to burn", and the term w(a)-ágela properly conveys only the general notion of to destroy and obtains the particular one of to burn merely in consequence of the phrase wane fū 'igūā being prefixed, so that the meaning is „I light fire and destroy (by means of the fire)".

[21] w-ayōē fe-nēa: the form of the 3rd pers. sing., which I have taken down, viz nen-ayōē-nē, seems to show, that the syllable fe does not form an integrant part of the phrase.

[22] w(a)-anōē waχōēa most probably are two distinct verbal forms, „I push against, I overthrow".

[23] yé-bēšenā bā-ya: the first e is not heard at all, so that the 3rd pers. sing. is á-bšenā ba-ágnaē.

[24] yé-pwa; 3rd pers. sing. á-pwa bá-ágnaē, 3rd pers. sing. of the past tense pápwa.

Deutsch und Englisch.	Kanári.	Tôdâ.	Sanna.	Pulfolde.
Ich tränke (das Pferd) — *I water (the horse*	fir) yē-t-iskin[1]	aski) eyī ênrigē[7]	nī-hā (dōki) sā[9]	{ mēdo-yérrinu / médo-hokku } putān ndiam
tränke das Pferd, führe das Pferd zur Tränke — *water the horse*	fir yāte yē-tē		bā dōki sā .	bokku putān ndīam
Ich melke — *I milk* . .	kiām gan-iskin[2]	{ yō-rīk . . / tánē yorge . }	ina tām sánia[10]	mēdo-bīrra negge
Ich rühre die Milch um — *I stir the milk*	kiām sang-iskin[3]	yému lēt-erík	ina dāma nōno	. . . . .
Ich buttere — *I butter* .	kiām land-iskin[4]	yému tér-erík[8]	ina tungwanōno[11]	mēdo-fīya neb-bum
Ich rühre um (die Speise — *I stir (the food*	dī-niskin[5] .	barē) berán-erík	{ ina dorvā[12] . / ina tūka n tūo }	mēdu-lellntúkki / mēdo-lawal nyīri
Ich mische, menge durcheinander — *I mix up*	tuksa-niskin[6]	manint-erík .	ina dāmu . .	mēdo-suita .

[1] yē-t-iskin fehlt bei Koelle; es zeigt sehr schön die Verbalbildung, yē oder yā, „trinken", t das transitive, übertragende Zeichen und iskin, „ich gehe". Für yē-t-iskin hört man oft yā-t-iskin; dass aber das e richtig ist, sieht man aus der folgenden Phrase, wo das Wort mit dem so ähnlich klingenden yāt-iskin, „ich führe", in nahe Verbindung kommt. — Von Personen wird yē-t-iskin wol eben nicht gebraucht, sondern man sagt da mehr ēhī iskin, „ich gebe Wasser".

[2] kiām gan-iskin. Koelle hat ágángin allein und kiám ágángin in dieser Bedeutung.

[3] kiām sang-iskin. Koelle hat sángin (3te Person Sing. Fī sáhiBin) nur in der Bedeutung „ich presse durch, filtrire, seihe durch".

[4] land-iskin. Koelle hat lándegin und zwar selbstständig, ohne kiām.

[5] dī-niskin. Koelle hat dīgin mit der Bedeutung „ich reibe, knete".

[6] tuksa-niskin, bei Koelle tógesāgin oder tóyesāgin.

[7] aski) eyī ênrigē. Die Verbalform ist hier sehr unvollständig ausgedrückt; vielleicht ên-erík.

[8] yemmu tér-erík. Neben tér-erík habe ich die unvollkommene Verbalform tér-ahal.

[9] nī-hā (dōki) sā. Bei dieser Phrase wird rūa, „Wasser", selten ausgedrückt, aber bei Personen wird es gewöhnlich hinzugefügt; so „ich gebe dir zu trinken", nī-hā-ha rūa sā; „gib mir zu trinken", H. bā-nī rūa sā, F. hokk-am ndiam nyēre, S. nēye oyin bāri. Ich will an dieser Stelle einige begriffsverwandte Phrasen anführen: „ich benetze dich des Wassers", H. ina hanna ma-hā rūa, F. mēdo-bádde-má ndiam; „ich schwämme das Pferd (durch den Fluss)", H. ina na-ī dōki ratō, F. mēdo-billini putān; „schwimme mir mein Pferd (durch den Fluss)", H. ka-ī ma-nī dōki-na ratō, F. a-billa-ne putān āgun; „ich füttere das Pferd, gebe ihm Korn", H. nī-bā dōki hatsi, „ich nehme dem Pferde den Hafersack ab", H. ina dōbe īēka n dōki, F. mēdo-hitte hāen putān; „ich sattele das Pferd", H. nī ina sad sirdi bisa dōki, F. mēdo-yōl hirke putān; „ich sattele das Pferd ab", H. ina koutse sirdi diga bāya n dōki, F. mēdo-firta hirke hō hāē n putān (wörtlich „ich löse den Sattel von dem Rücken des Pferdes").

[10] ina tāsa sánia. Im H. wie im F. und S. ist „Kuh" besonders ausgedrückt.

[11] ina tungwa nōno. Ich will hier zwei begriffsverwandte Redensarten anführen: „ich rahme ab", H. ina dēba yāda n nōno, F. mēdo-huhta hébtungol; „ich schöpfe die Butter ab", H. ina dauka mai, F. mēdo-hetta pollo S. ēgu-hō bāra kūru-dī.

[12] ina dorvā. Ich will hier die begriffsverwandte Phrase anführen: „ich schüttele das Trinkgefäss", H. ina motsī da korīa, F. mēdo-sunyi támbadé.

[13] ēgu-nyin dī bāri-dī. Das erste dī ist offenbar überflüssig.

[14] wa bushwan am, „ich dem Pferde Wasser"; das Verbum scheint zu fehlen, man sollte wobāni bushwan am erwarten; auch das dī in der folgenden Phrase ist mir auffällig.

[15] defān afē hēllesa. Der erste Theil der Phrase ist unsicher.

[16] mah-ee el-na: el-na ist der Accusativ von el, „Milch"; die Wurzel von mah-ee ist etwas unsicher, da ich in vulgärer Rede mahāline aussprechen hörte.

[17] am elgō, vielleicht am melgē.

Kaáyal.	Légoná.	Wándalá.	Bágrimma.	Mába.
éga-nyin dī bári-dī[13]	wa bųskwan am[14]	yé-ida bélima	ma: man sinda	
nyin bári-dī . .	dī bųskwán-en am	defán ufē bélisa[15]	. . . . . .	
éga-sorō hau-dī	w(a)-unim ēne .	yé-pašō ūba .	mak-os sī-na[16]	am cigō[17]
. . . .	wa-laf ēne . .	ye-šē ūba .	mak-osl sī-na	am kurūl-arū
éga-zenna wā-dí.	w(a)-úẓla ēne .	ya-ūba . . .	matúk sī-na .	
. . . .	wa-úrbusa (inabaī)	ye-avšúvša .	mak-gógodé-nya	am furgo-arónge
éga-kúlla-ga .	wudáma-ttido .		mok-usī (na-gá	am kųddúd-a-rōngo

[1] yá-t-lekin is wanting in Koelle's vocabulary. Nevertheless it is a very interesting word, which may serve as a fair example of the formation of a verb, as its root is yā or yá, „to drink", to which is appended lekin, „I give", both being joined by means of a t as the sign of transitive notion. Instead of yā-ṭ-lekin I sometimes heard the form yá-t-lekin, but that the e is the right sound, we see most clearly from the following phrase, where the word is combined with the closely resembling term yāt-lekin, „I conduct". However yé-t-lekin does not seem to be used of human beings, but only with reference to horses and cattle, while with regard to the former the common term is shi lekin, „I give water".

[2] kiām gas-lekin: Koelle has the verb ngángin with this notion with and without adding kiām.

[3] kiām casg-lekin: Koelle has the verb cángin (3rd pers. sing. ſī cáktšin) only with the meaning „I strain, filter, percolate".

[4] lend-lekin: Koelle has lándęskin as an independent verb without adding kiām.

[5] dī-alekin: Koelle has diágin with the signification „I rub, knead".

[6] imkes-alekin is to be looked for in Koelle under the form tégesángin or tégeškágin.

[7] ashi) syī énrigē: the verbal form has been expressed very imperfectly: perhaps it ought to be én-erik.

[8] yamma tér-erik: besides tér-erik I have another verbal form tér-ahal.

[9] ni-hē (dóki) šá: in this phrase the word rún, „water", is rarely expressed, as horses or cattle drink nothing but water, but if the term is used of human beings, it is generally added, thus „I give thee to drink", H. ni-há-ka rún šá; „give me to drink", H. hā-ni rún šá, F. hokk-am adiam nyēre, S. néye ay in bári. — I must insert in this place some phrases of a similar meaning: „I deprive you of water", H. ina hana ma-há rún, F. mėde-héddu-ma adiam; „I swim the horse across the river", H. ina na-i dóki ratē, F. mėde-billini putšu; „swim my horse across", H. ka-i ma-ni dóki-na ratē, F. a-billo-ne putša bgan. — „I give corn to the horse", H. ni-ba dóki hatsi; „I take the nose-bag from the horse", H. ina dóbe šákan dóki, F. mėde-bille báan putša. — „I saddle the horse", H. ni ina sai sirdi bisse dóki, F. mėde-yōt kirke putšu; „I take the saddle from the horse", H. ina kontše sirdi dága bāyan dóki, F. mėde-lirte kirke kē kāō a putšu (verbally) „I loosen the saddle from the back of the horse").

[10] ina tšas sánia: in this phrase as well as in the corresponding one in F. and S. the word „cow" is distinctly expressed.

[11] ina tangwa nóno: I will here insert two phrases of a similar meaning: „I take off the cream", „I skim", H. ina dábe yādo a nóno, F. mėde-hubte kébtinágal; „I skim the butter", H. ina danka mai, F. mėde-kotše polle, S. ēga-kō bíre hāra-dī.

[12] ina doría: I here insert a phrase of a similar meaning: „I shake the drinking vessel", H. ina motšā da kória, F. mėde-senyt témbudē.

[13] éga-nyin dī bári-dī: the first dī is evidently superfluous.

[14] wa bųskwan am: „I (to) the horse water"; the verb is apparently wanting and we should expect wa-bé (wokšo in the German note opposite is a mistake) bųskwan am. The dī also in the following phrase seems doubtful; perhaps it ought to be dā, „bring".

[15] defán ufē bélisa: the first part of this phrase also is uncertain.

[16] mak-os sī-na, sī-na is the accusative case of sī, „milk", but as to mak-os, the root of this verbal form is somewhat uncertain, as in vulgar pronunciation I heard generally makóšina.

[17] am cigē: perhaps it ought to be am meigō.

Deutsch und Englisch.	Kanúri.	Tédā.	Hausa.	Fulfulde.
ich weide — *I tend (cattle*	nóg-iskin [1]	ngaí) felé-n-erík [7]	ina kíwo . .	mēdo-durra .
ich schlachte — *I slaughter (cattle, sheep*	debā- { níśkin . / ngin [2] . }	debā-n-erík .	ina kašè [10]	. . . . .
ich schinde, ziehe das Fell ab — *I skin, flay*	kai-níśkin [3] .	ádže tér-(er)ík [8]	nī na-fēde [11] .	mēdo-hulla .
ich reinige den Acker — *I clean the ground*	kúlō farán-níśkin [4]	kinnera sarám-erík [9]	ina girbi gōna [12]	mēdo-rugga gessa
ich säe, pflanze — *I sow, plant*	nā-t-iskin [5] .	{mchínne rōd-erík} / {kosínne lōp-erík}	ina šibka [13] .	mēdo-awa .
ich gäte — *I am weeding*	bāre { níśkin . / díśkin [6] . }	{ wōnar rōd-erík, S. / óberi(?) berónt-erík, N. }	ina nōma . . / ina džinni káka }	mēdo-remma

[1] nóg-iskin; 3te Person Sing. tse-nóg-in. Koelle schreibt nógeskin und gibt ihm die allgemeine Bedeutung „ich achte auf etwas, halte auf etwas", aber ich glaube, dass diese allgemeine Bedeutung, wofür er als Beispiel anführt von dem Warten des Kindes von Seiten der Mutter, abgeleitet ist von der besonderen des Wartens des Viehes, und fast möchte ich die Wurzel nóg in Verbindung bringen mit dem Fulfulde-Wort nagge, „Rind"; denn die Viehzucht in Central-Afrika scheint von dem Stamm der Fulbe ausgegangen zu sein und das Wort nagge selbst ist in viele andere Sprachen der Umgegend übergegangen. Allerdings haben die Kanúri für „Rind" ein anderes Wort, nämlich fē, das entschieden mit dem na in den benachbarten Sprachen zusammenhängt, aber gerade das „Weiden" selbst ist auch jetzt noch bei grösseren Heerden der Kanúri ganz in den Händen der Fulbe. S. Reisen, Bd. II, S. 251.

[2] debā-ngin ist aus dem Arabischen eingeführt und der Kanúri-Sprache accommodirt.

[3] kai-níśkin vielleicht Koelle's kángin. Ich bin nicht sicher, ob das n zur Wurzel gehört.

[4] kúlō farán-níśkin. Koelle hat pérángin nicht in dieser Bedeutung; gewiss hängt es mit farán, „offen, frei, eben", zusammen: „ich mache frei, räume weg, was im Wege liegt", s. S. 100, N. 5. 3te Person Plur. kúlō farā-tsai.

[5] nā-t-iskin, verstärkte Form von nā und yi-skin, „ich mache Platz nehmen", d. h. „lege in die Erde", „säe". Koelle schreibt nályeskin.

[6] bāre-níśkin und bāre-díśkin wird ohne Unterschied gesagt und diese beiden neben einander gebrauchten Formen zeigen wol, dass meine Form auf níśkin, die ich der Koelle'schen auf ngin vorziehe, ihre gute Begründung hat. Das Gäten des bāre erfolgt, wenn die Saat noch klein ist; wenn sie grösser ist, halb ausgewachsen, folgt ein zweites Gäten, die tšūa, daher tšūa-níśkin, bei Koelle tšuángin und tšoángin.

[7] ngaí felé-n-erík; 3te Person Sing. frié-kini. ngaí bedeutet nicht „Vieh", wofür ich unter den Nominibus ai habe, sondern „Ziegen", im S. ingé oder ngó.

[8] ádže tér-(er)ík. Das zweite er wird gewöhnlich verschluckt, so dass man nichts weiter hört als terík; es soll entschieden bedeuten „ich fasse, ziehe ab die Haut". Unter den Nominibus habe ich für „Haut" aber, sowol von Menschen wie von Früchten, nur die Form ádi und ich bin unsicher, was das Richtige ist.

[9] kinnera sarám-erík. Neben diesem Verbum hat die Tédā-Sprache offenbar ein anderes, dem Kanúri-Wort ganz nahe stehendes, da ich die 3te Person Plur. mеrá kinnera ferá-kinti habe.

[10] ina kašè. Ich habe hier den Ausdruck einzufügen „ich drehe den Hals (des Hammels) um", H. ina kōma nya a ragō, F. mēdo-ubbga hōre dānudirl.

[11] nī na-fēde. Dazu die Redensart: H. ina dōbe asika, F. mēdo-worta semmálle, „ich ziehe das (ganze) Fell als Schlauch ab". Dies geschieht auf äusserst künstliche und geschickte Weise, besonders in Kátsena.

[12] ina girbi gōna. Verwandt sind die Ausdrücke: H. ina láke gōna, ina gēra a gōna, F. mēdo-tánnanō.

[13] ina šibka. „Ich pflanze den Baum", H. ina šibkawa n itšē, F. mēdo-awa ledde (Plur. von leggel).

[14] ága-kár. Daher „der Hirt" kér-koi.

[15] ága-na dámmo. Über die Form und Bestandtheile der Phrase bin ich nicht ganz sicher; niedergeschrieben hatte ich nach dem Gehöre áganadámmo.

[16] ága-fērl. Daher „der Garten, der Acker" fērl.

[17] ind(o) ále mangá mork. Hier ist offenbar mehr als die einfache Verbalform: „er weidet", nángana.

[18] iéfiā marō sieht auch nicht wie eine Verbalform aus.

[19] dálnhai ist auch keine Verbalform; vielleicht ind(o) ále hat.

[20] wa-lá syrā. Für die 3te Person Plur. habe ich mōší tále-ta ugrū.

[21] wa-bō gálā. gálā ist auffallend: vielleicht ist es gyóla.

[22] aégura kann nicht richtig sein, vielleicht nā wégura.

[23] yé-piā (Oā. Oā, „das Rind".

[24] ve-lé-da fē. Dass lē-dā aus zwei verschiedenen Theilen zusammengesetzt ist, sieht man aus der Form der 3ten Pers. Plur. ta lē-na-dā bétere fē.

[25] m(a)-angámma, Imperat. angóm.

Šekyal.	Lógoné.	Wándalá.	Bágrimma.	Mába.
éga-kúr [14] . . .	ind(u) ālo mungá morē [17]	yō-piē (fá [23] .	m(a)-angúmmo [25]	am akol
. . . . . .	lúfiā-marē [18] . .	yé-tāi-tāā .	ma-m-ákolō / ma-tólfita .	am dab-arónguo
éga-forga . . .	dálohul [19] . . .	yé-χarā . .	ma-svoña . .	am atā
égn-na dúmmo [15]	wu-tā syrē [20]	ye-šé-dā fē [24]	má-sarā . .	am sungo ásimnuē / kóruk-arē / ī orróngno / avyēne
éga-fīgi . . .	wu-bō (gálā [21] .	ye-dāchiā . .	mak-obaia . / m(a)-ét-kogō	am melle arne
éga-fēri [16] . . .	núgura [22] . . .	y(e)-áhardā .	m(a)-et-atšídda / m(a)-ét-nabō	am nimmere ni-tēne

[1] nēg-ishin: 3rd pers. sing. tse-nēg-in. Koelle writes nēgeshin and attributes to it the general notion of „I mind, attend to, keep", but it is my opinion, that this general meaning, which he fully establishes by means of an example referring to the tending of a child by his mother, is rather a secondary one, being derived from the primary one of the tending of cattle, and I am inclined to suppose, that the root nēg is intimately connected with and related to the Fulfúlde-term negge, „cow"; for the breeding of cattle, as I have had frequent opportunity of observing in my Travels and Discoveries, seems to have spread over most parts of Central-Africa through the influence of the Fulbe, so that the term negge has penetrated into many languages of the interior (s. vol. II, p. 230). Certainly the Kanúri-language has another term fē, which, I have no doubt, is but another form of the term fā in Lógoné and some of the neighbouring languages, but even in Bornu the breeding or tending of the cattle even at the present time is almost entirely in the hands of the Fulbe or, as they here called, Fellāta.

[2] dabā-ágin has been introduced from the Arabic and accommodated to the rules of the Kanúri-language.

[3] kai-nishin perhaps Koelle's kéngin, „I draw aside". As for the n I am not certain, whether it belongs to the root or not.

[4] kálā ferān-nishin: Koelle does not attribute this notion to his identical verb pērāngin. I have already, stated p. 101, note 5, that it is connected with the adjective ferēn, „open, plain", and that the original meaning is „I make plain" (by taking away any thing, that may cause obstruction). 3rd pers. plur. kálā ferā-tsai.

[5] nō-t-ishin is the stronger, causative form from nō, „place" and yi-shin, „I give", „I make take a place" i. e. „I put in the ground". Koelle writes nátsshin.

[6] bára-nishin and bára-dishin are terms used without distinction and serve well to show, that the form nishin used by me in preference to the ágin of Koelle is based on sound reasons. The weeding of the bára takes place, when the corn is as yet small, but when it is nearly full grown, a second weeding takes place, the tšūn, whence the verb tšūn-nishin or tšnāgin and tšeāgin, as Koelle writes.

[7] ngal folō-n-erin: 3rd pers. sing. folō-kin. ngal does not mean „cattle", which term in my list of nouns is represented by ay, but „goats", in the singular form ingē or égē.

[8] adāe tér-(er)in: the second er seems generally to be slurred over, so that terin is alone heard; the phrase evidently means „I take the skin off", but among my list of nouns I have only the form ādi for „skin" and therefore am not certain, what of the two may be the right form, ādi or adāe.

[9] kinnere earém-erin: besides this verb the Tédā-language evidently possesses another one, as I have the phrase morā kinnere ferá-kinti for the 3rd pers. plur.

[10] ina kašē: I here have to insert the term „I wring the sheep's neck off", H. ina kōma fiya n ragō, F. médo-nanga bāre dāendiri.

[11] ni na-fēde: hereto add the phrase: H. ina dōba oelka, F. mēdo-worte sammálle, „I draw off the (whole) skin (in order to use it as) a waterbag". This is done in a very clever way, especially in Katsena.

[12] ina girbi gōna: of a similar meaning are the terms: H. ina tāke gōna, ina gēra n gōna, F. médo-tšunnuné.

[13] ina šibba: „I plant a tree", H. ina šibbawa n itše, F. mēdo-awa leddo (plur. of lygal).

[14] égn-kúr: thence „the shepherd" kúr-kol.

[15] égn-na dúmmo: as to the form of the verb I am not quite certain, as I had taken down ágnanadúmmo.

[16] égn-fēri: thence „the garden, field" fērī.

[17] ind(o) ālo mungá morē: here we have evidently more than the simple verbal form; for „he tends" I have nothing but nángana.

[18] lúfiā marē does also not look like a simple verbal form.

[19] dálohul likewise is not a verbal form; perhaps it ought to be ind(o) ālo hul.

[20] wu-tā syrē: for the 3rd pers. plur. I have the phrase mēšī tāle-tā syrē.

[21] wu-bō (gálā: gálā seems uncertain, perhaps it ought to be vyálā, „corn".

[22] núgura cannot be right; perhaps nú núgura.

[23] yé-piō (fā: fā, „the cattle, cow".

[24] ye-šē-da fē: that šē-dā does consist of two different particles, we see from the form of the 3rd pers. plur. ta šé-na-dá hēlere fē.

[25] m(a)-angúmmo: imperat. angám.

Deutsch und Englisch.	Kanúri.	Tédā.	Hausa.	Fulfúlde.
ich schneide (Korn — *I cut (the corn)*	argúm kam-niskin / argúm kúrem-niskin	kóp-erík . . / húm-erík . .	ína dēbe hatsi[12]	mēdo-teddāe gauri
ich haue (Korn — *I chop off (the corn)*[1]	argúm taal-níakin	. . . . . .		
ich stampfe das Korn — *I pound the corn*	argúm kókō-niskin[2] / argúm wúse-nískin[3] / argúm bá-skin[4] / argúm gubúr-úgin[5]	bedē tōp-erík / bedē dolónt-erík / bedē tōp-erík[11]	ína dakka hatsi	mēdo-ūna . .
ich worfele Korn, scheide die Spreu aus — *I winnow, fan the corn*	sābú-skin[6] .	(kabai) bedō ibén-erík	ína bákatšē .	mēdo-yessa .
ich mahle — *I grind* .	nē-niskin[7] .	tūgu kín-erík	ína níka . .	mēdo-namma
ich kaufe (messe) Korn — *I buy (measure) corn*	argúm gal-ískin[8]	. . . . . .	. . . . . .	. . . . .
ich messe — *I measure*	gal-ískin . .	ingél-d-erík / bāb-erík(?) .	ína auna[13] .	mēdo-etta . .
ich theile — *I divide, rend in two*	girt-iskin[9] . / rō-nískin[10] .	girt-erík . . / gúrd-erík . .	ína rába . .	mēdo-edda[14]

[1] „Ich haue Korn" (ganz derselbe Ausdruck wie vom Holzfällen) klingt für unsere Ohren sonderbar, aber keineswegs für denjenigen, der das dicke Rohr des Sorghum und Pennisetum gesehen hat. Koelle tsalágin, vorher kérgmgin.

[2] kókō-niskin, bei Koelle kógoágin, „ich schlage". Dieser Ausdruck ist mit dem gleich folgenden keineswegs identisch, sondern bezeichnet das erste rohe Stampfen der Kornähren oder vielmehr der Ähren des Sorghum und Pennisetum, um die Körner von der Kolbe abzulösen; es entspricht also dem Begriffe nach vollkommen unserem „dreschen". Aber allerdings unterscheiden nicht alle hier vertretenen Sprachen diese beiden Ausdrücke.

[3] argúm wúse-niskin (3te Pers. Sing. wúsein, 3te Pers. Plur. wúseai), bei Koelle wúsegágin (3te Pers. Sing. wússin), bezeichnet das Stampfen der schon ausgelösten Körner, um die Hülse davon zu lösen.

[4] bá-skin bedeutet das gänzliche Zerstampfen zu Teig für die Mahlzeit. Hiervon gibt es keine Nebenform und auch Koelle hat báskin.

[5] gubúr-úgin bedeutet das nur theilweise Zerstampfen, um aus dem so gestampften Korn ein Getränk zu bereiten. Koelle hat das Wort nicht, hat dagegen aber ein anderes Zeitwort túrgágin, dem er allerdings eine etwas abweichende Bedeutung gibt, als das Reinigen von der zweiten, feinen Spreu, und von dem ich nur die substantivische zusammengesetzte Form tsete-kumbé hörte, als unserem Worte gleichbedeutend.

[6] sābú-skin fehlt bei Koelle.

[7] nē-niskin, bei Koelle nyégin. 3te Person Sing. nē-tšin.

[8] gal-ískin (bei Koelle kgálágin) scheint mir kein einheimisches Wort zu sein, sondern abgeleitet von dem Arabischen kál mit der Kanúri-Endung. Ich musste den Ausdruck argúm gal-iskin als besonderen technischen Terminus hierhersetzen, weil die Anschauung der verschiedenen hier vertretenen Völker verschieden ist.

[9] girt-iskin. Koelle hat gértgskin.

[10] rō-niskin, rōngin bei Koelle; Particip. Pass. rō-gata, zusammengezogen rō-ta, das gewöhnliche Wort für „halb".

[11] bedō tōp-erík. Anstatt tōp-erík gibt es die zusammengezogene gewöhnliche Form tō-rík.

[12] ína dēbe hatsi. Vergl. die Phrase „bei Sókoto ist alles Korn geschnitten", hatsi n Sókoto dakka an-dēbe šihē; an-dēbe = kerémgata im K. Ich will hier noch ein paar begriffsverwandte Redensarten anführen, zuerst zwei, deren genaue Beziehung mir unklar geworden: H. ína figō hatsi, F. mēdo-erta gaari; H. ína bōbe-aun, F. mēdo-bārt bembe; „ich mache Kornhaufen", H. ína gēra n būšin, F. mēdo-wódymi súdo gaari.

[13] ína auna, nur von trockenen Sachen gebraucht.

[14] mēdo-edda. Dieses Wort zeigt jedenfalls eine grosse Ähnlichkeit mit dem eben vorhergehenden, wenn es nicht gar dasselbe ist; dies erklärt sich jedoch ganz natürlich, da „messen" und „theilen" von demselben Begriff ausgehen. Dieselbe Erscheinung sehen wir auch in den Ausdrücken der Bágrimma-Sprache: mam-ákala, „ich theile", mam-akílla, „ich messe".

[15] ēga-dambu, „ich schneide" (S. 111), hénī, „Negerhirse", ist wol sicherlich richtig, aber in meinem Manuscript steht ēga-haine dambu.

[16] wal nyū̆ū vyōlī. Das wal ist offenbar eine Verbalform für sich.

[17] mam-bodī tago. Ich bin nicht ganz sicher über die Verbalform und wollte zuerst m(a)-ambodī schreiben, [illegible] man gewöhnlich nur dann die 1ste Pers. des persönlichen Fürworts verkürzt, wenn ein Vokal folgt, aber es hängt wahrscheinlich mit mām-bodiō, „ich säbe", S. 50 zusammen.

Sońyai.	Lógoné.	Wándalá.	Bágrimma.	Mába.
éga-dumbu bēni [15]	wu-tū vyóla . wa-dīsum . .	y(e)-áwardá biā yé-tšitšā . .	m(a)-ōkolteńg-na, má-katšā . .	am orrougne csē-ye) súkun-tang nudái-n)
éga-dúr bēni-dī	wu-dá vyólá .	yé-džegā biā ye-fā biā .	ma-tud teńgo	(csē-ye) am aske
	wu-dir . . . wá-tuxsū . .	yé-džegā biā yé-tasá biā .	múk-udū . . ma-seb teńgo	
	wu-díktekē . .	yé-sapā . .	mak-gavdé-nya	am ambúlle
éga-fufūgu . .	wu-χā	y(e)-okχo . .	m(a)-okkwō .	am óngost
. . . .	wul uχōū vyólā [16] wul kaskū-tu vyólā	yo-džā biā .	mam-bodž teńgo [17]	
éga-nēai . . .	wul kaskū-tū .	ye-džā . . .	mam-al-akilla	csē kīl-aré am dér-ané
éga-zémma-gā .	wu-fríkalā . .	yé-χa . . . yé-tegán falle	mam-ákala .	am bā-arē

[1] „I chop off (the corn" sounds rather peculiar to our ears, but not so to the ears of those, who are aware of the thickness and strength of the reed of the sorghum and pennisetum.

[2] hóbá-niskin; Koelle hógdágin, „I flog, beat". This term is by no means identical with the one immediately following, but indicates the first rough pounding of the ears of corn or rather of sorghum and pennisetum, in order to separate the grains; it therefore corresponds in some respect very well with the notion of the European „to thrash". But not all the languages of Negroland make such a nice distinction between these different notions.

[3] argém wúse-niskin (3rd pers. sing. wús-sin, 3rd pers. plur. wús-sei), in Koelle wósengin (3rd pers. sing. wóžšin), indicates the pounding of the grains, after they have been separated from the ear, in order to separate the husk from each single grain.

[4] bá-skin means the thorough pounding of the corn, in order to prepare from it the common daily meal; of this verb there is no form in ágin and Koelle also has the form báskin.

[5] gubár-ágin indicates the partial and softer pounding of the grains for the preparing of a beverage, such as the bulóbuló. Koelle has not this term, although it is very common, but he has instead another term tásengin, „I clean from the second, fine chaff by beating" of which I heard only a popular composite form tasin-hambā.

[6] sûbe-skin is wanting in Koelle.

[7] nē-niskin (Koelle nyéngin); 3rd pers. sing. nē-tšin.

[8] gal-iskin (in Koelle's vocabulary ágálágin) seems to me not to be an indigenous word, but to be derived from the Arabic kāl, to which has been added the Kanúri verbal termination. I saw myself obliged to insert here the phrase argém gal-iskin as a peculiar technical term on account of the different mode, in which the different languages express it.

[9] girt-iskin: Koelle writes gértṣekin.

[10] rō-niskin, réngin with Koelle, participle pass. rē-gein and in the contracted form rō-in, which has become the common term for „half".

[11] badē lōp-erik: for tōp-erik there is a contracted vulgar form tó-rik.

[12] Ina dêbe hatsi: compare the phrase „in the environs of Sókoto all the corn has been cut", hatsi n Sókoto dukka an-dóba šikā; an-dêbe = keyémgata in K. I shall here insert a few terms of a similar notion, although I am not quite certain with regard to the exact meaning of the two first: H. ina figē hatsi, F. mēdo-orta gauri; H. ina hêbe-awa, F. mēdo-bāya hamhe; „I heap up the corn in stacks", H. ina géia n hāšin, F. mēdo-wódymi oûdo gauri.

[13] ina ouna is only used of dry things.

[14] médo-oddu evinces a striking similarity to the verb just preceding, if in fact it is not the very identical word, but this we can easily explain, as the terms „to measure" and „to separate" proceed from the very same idea. The same is the case with the terms mam-ákala and mam-al-akilla in the Bágrimma-language.

[15] éga-dumbu, „I cut" (p. 111), bēni, „Negromillet", no doubt is right, but my Mscr. has éga-baine dumbu.

[16] wul uχōū vyólā: the syllable wul is evidently a verbal form.

[17] mam-bodž teńgo: also in this case I am not quite certain of the verbal form, and I wanted first to write m(a)-ambodž, as the form mam is generally only used for the 1st pers. of the pronoun pers., when it is followed by a vowel; but the term is most probably derived from mám-bodžē, „I count", p. 59.

Deutsch und Englisch.	Kanúri.	Tédā.	Hausa.	Fulfúlde.
ich pflücke ab (eine Frucht) — *I pluck (a fruit*	lúta késka-bé) dör-ískin [1]	(inne) máng-erík [9]	ina dēbe da n ītše [12]	. . . . . .
ich pflücke, sammele die Baumwolle — *I pluck, gather the cotton*	kal- (dör-ískin) kútta (lau-nískin [2])	kolkúttun máng-erík	ina dēbe ábulega	. . . . . .
ich pflücke die Baumwolle von dem Samenkorn — *I pick the cotton*	kalkútta so-nískin [3]	kolkúttun fúz-erík	ina gurdže ábdega	mēdo-namma pöttolo [15] / mēdo-buraa
ich ziehe den Faden — *I spin yarn*	grasán fī-nískin [4]	gráhanu ferīn-erík [10]	ina sobbi . .	mēdo-fittotō .
ich drehe den Faden — *I twine thread*	sāgá-nískin [5] .	(gráhanu) sagán-erík, N.	ina zarē [13] . .	mēdo-motta .
ich webe — *I weave* .	tand-ískin [6] .	tóm-erík, S.	ina sāka . .	mēdo-saña .
ich nähe — *I sew* . .	dutu-skin [7] .	táně sö-rík [11]	ina dīmki [14] .	mēdo-nyōa .
ich klopfe das Hemd (gebe ihm Glanz durch Klopfen) — *I calender the shirt*	kulgu) bag-nískin	köbu tob-erík	ina bugga (rīga	mēdo-fīyai toggōre
ich färbe das Hemd — *I dye the shirt*	kulgu) dé-langin [8]	kobu lán-erík alin-do	ina rinna (rīga	mēdo-b-alinna [16]

[1] dör-iskin. Koelle schreibt dörgekin und scheint die Bedeutung „abpflücken" dem Worte nicht beizulegen.

[2] lau-niskin. Koelle schreibt lángin oder laúgin und bemerkt ausdrücklich, dass lau entweder zweisilbig oder als Diphthong ausgesprochen werden kann. kalkútta schreibt er kalgátan.

[3] so-niskin scheint Koelle nicht zu haben, wenn es nicht seinem ságin entspricht, das er freilich nur in der Bedeutung „ich quetsche, hane, schlage" gibt; aber man muss bedenken, dass dieses Pflücken der Baumwolle vermittelst eines kleinen Eisens geschieht.

[4] grasán fī-niskin. Wir haben hier wieder ein sehr interessantes Beispiel der nahen Verwandtschaft der Tédā- und Kanúri-Sprache. Koelle nämlich hat anstatt meiner Redensart gerásan pérlngin, und obgleich ich dieses Verbum im gewöhnlichen Leben nicht gehört habe, wird seine Richtigkeit eben durch das entsprechende, nahe verwandte Tédā-Wort völlig erwiesen. Koelle hat selbst den Ausdruck péri dískin.

[5] sāgá-niskin fehlt bei Koelle; er hat dafür berémgin.

[6] tand-ískin; Koelle schreibt tándeskin, 3te Person Sing. tegtándin; dem Begriffe nach wenigstens ist dieses Wort verwandt mit tendere, und oft hört man es auch im K. mit einem e ausgesprechen.

[7] dútu-skin. In diesem Worte habe ich ein deutliches u gehört; es scheint also zur Wurzel zu gehören. Koelle hat dútćskin.

[8] kulgu) dé-langin. Ich hatte ursprünglich dé-langin niedergeschrieben, glaubte dann aber, es müsste délngin heissen, und ich bin nicht ganz sicher, ob ein Vokallaut nach dem Konsonanten da ist. Jedenfalls aber gibt es von diesem Verbum keine Endung auf skin oder iskin. Koelle hat die Form délngin. Aber einen höchst merkwürdigen Aufschluss über die eigentliche Wurzel scheinen wir hier wiederum durch die Tédā-Sprache zu erhalten, wo wir sehen, dass lan die eigentliche Wurzel ist, das de mag nun im Kanúri dazugekommen sein, wie es will.

[9] máng-erík. Ich bin nicht ganz sicher über die Form und fast scheint es, als wenn ein e zur Wurzel gehörte, wenigstens hörte ich nur die vulgäre Form mángeri.

[10] ferī-n-erík, s. N. 4.

[11] táně sö-rík. Die Wurzel sö ist wol mit dem so im Kanúri so-niskin einerlei. — alin-do weiter unten „mit Indigo".

[12] ina dēbe da n ītše. Das so allgemeine Wort ina dēbe muss auch vorhalten beim Abschälen, so H. ina dēbe bawo n da n itše, „ich ziehe die Schaale der Frucht ab", F. mēdo-woria bāddi, S. ēga-hōe-ogá.

[13] ina zarē. Im H. und F. habe ich noch einen besonderen Ausdruck für „ich hänge die Faden zum Weben auf", H. ina wöddari, F. mēdo-yēna oder mēdo-yeona garādže.

[14] ina dīmki. Ich will hier den begriffsverwandten Ausdruck hersetzen „ich schneide zu", H. ina fāsali (aus dem Arabischen [von demselben Wort ist in Folge der Kreuzzüge das Französische façonner hergeleitet]), F. mēdo-wādyiaaleppi, S. ēga-fasal hāaabá-dí.

[15] mēdo-namma pöttolo ist auffallend in Vergleich mit mēdo-namma auf S. 116 mit der Bedeutung „ich mahle", aber ich glaube, es ist richtig.

[16] mēdo-b-alinna. Hier haben wir vielleicht eine Verbalbildung durch Vorsetzung eines b vor dem Substantiv; alin, „Indigo".

[17] ēga-hó hābu nédi. Was nédi bedeutet, weiss ich nicht.

[18] ēga-dám da kasāha aini kōna scheint wieder eine sehr unbehilfliche Redensart zu sein, wie so viele im Songai: wörtlich heisst sie „ich ziehe das Hemd aus dem Indigo".

[19] Ich bin nicht ganz sicher über die Verbalform, da ich hámbe niedergeschrieben habe.

[20] ya-teákha tāže. Hieraus ergab sich, dass das in der vorhergehenden Phrase dem tenbhe angehängte h nicht dahin gehört.

[21] y(e)-indera tāže. Ich bin nicht sicher, ob diese Phrase nicht an den unrechten Platz gekommen ist.

[22] mam anyére. anyére scheint hier Zeitwort zu sein.

Sońγai.	Lógoné.	Wándalá.	Bágrimma.	Mába.
. . . .	wu-húmbo gale (hú-dugwā[19]	ye-taúkka(k) fdža-n afū	. . . . .	. . . . . .
	wu-lūám fáltakí	ye-taúkka tūže[20]	mám-okód nyēre	guório ávdate-akūī
óga-kō hābu zōdi[17]	wu-sien fáttaki-hē	yé-šetā tūže .	mám-akid gigí-nyo nyēre	am kúdžkodžin-nēre avdáng
óga-bī hābu-dī	wu-dim fáttaki-hē	yé-po tūže .	{ mam-anyēre[22] / mak-anyēre }	am alge
óga-kaigo . . .	wu-síkahū fáttaki-hē	y(e)-éndera tūže[21] }	mak-odžō . .	am aske (?)
óga-hínas-gā . .	wu-hī fáttaki-hē	yó-ayā . . . }		
óga-tā-ga . . .	wushā	y(e)-ídaebē .	mam-ákurū .	am séhare
óga-kár kasāba	w(a)-ábugū lebū	yé-džegén zonne	. . . . .	. . . . . .
óga-dám da kasāba sīni kūna[18]	w(a)-áze lebū .	yé-berā zonne	mak-us álimi .	am nīl-nun adāī

[1] dār-iekin: Koelle writes dōrgekin and does not seem to have become aware of the notion of „to pinch".
[2] lan-niskin: Koelle writes lénágin or laúágin and makes the express remark, that lan may be pronounced as two syllables or as a diphthong. Instead of kalhútta he writes kalgálan.
[3] so-niskin seems to be wanting in Koelle or it may be his súágin, although he attributes to the latter only the notion „I whip, flog, beat", but we must bear in mind, that this picking of the cotton is done by means of a small sharp iron point.
[4] grasán fī-niskin: we have here again a very interesting and, taken into account the source from whence it is derived, a most striking example of the close relation of the Tédā- and Kanūri-languages. For Koelle instead of my phrase has the term gerlean pérlágin, and although I myself have not heard the latter used, yet its correctness is sufficiently proved by the corresponding Tédā-term.
[5] sāgá-niskin is wanting in Koelle; he has instead hęręmgin.
[6] tand-iskin: Koelle writes tándgekin, 3rd pers. sing. teçtándin; in regard of the meaning this term seems to have some connection with the Latin word tendere.
[7] dūtn-ekin: in this word I have heard decidedly the sound of an n and I conclude therefore, that it belongs to the root. Koelle has the form dūtçekin.
[8] kalga) dé-lengin: this is the form, which I have written down, and I think, that it is right, although I thought a moment, it might be delágin. That the syllable lan is right, we find a most remarkable proof in the corresponding word of the Tédā-language, although I do not know, whence may have been derived the de, which has been added before the lan. There is no form in skin or iskin of this verb. Koelle writes dálágin.
[9] māng-erik: I am not quite certain as to the form of this verb and it would almost seem, as if the root contained an o; at least I heard the form mángori.
[10] feri-n-erik: see note 4.
[11] táné sō-rik: the root sō may be identical with the so in the Kanūri-word so-niskin.
[12] ina dōbe da a ilže; the verb dōbe conveys such a general notion, that it forms part of many different phrases. Thus also „I peel off, pare", H. ina dōba bawa n da a ilbe, F. mēdo-woria bādli, S. óga-kás-agā.
[13] ina savē: in H. and F. I have still another term of a related meaning, H. ina wóddari, F. mēdo-yēne or mēdo-yoana garīdāe.
[14] ina dimki: I will here adduce another term of a related notion: „I cut out", H. ino fássali (derived from the Arabic, from which even the French façonner has been derived), F. mēdo-wádyine leppi, S. óga-fassal hásabá-dī.
[15] mēdo-namma pōttolo seems suspicious, if we compare it with the independent term mēdo-namera (p. 116), conveying the totally different meaning „I grind", but, I think, it is right.
[16] mēdo-h-alinan: in this case, according to all appearance, we have a verbal formation by prefixing h before the substantive (alin, „indigo") and giving it a verbal termination.
[17] óga-kō hābu zōdi: I am not certain with regard to the meaning of the zōdi.
[18] óga-dám da kasāba sīni kūna seems to be another example of an awkward and unfinished phrase, of which the Sońγai-language offers so many examples; the verbal meaning is „I draw the shirt from the indigo".
[19] wu-húmbo: I am not quite certain of the correctness of the verbal form, as I have taken down nothing but húmbo.
[20] ye-taúkka tūže: from this instance it appeared, that the k, which in the preceding phrase before a vowel had been appended to the term taúkka, does not belong to the root.
[21] y(e)-éndera tūže: I am not quite certain, that this phrase has not got into the wrong place.
[22] mam anyēre: anyēre seems to be a verbal form in this case.

Deutsch und Englisch.	Kanúri.	Tédā.	Hausa.	Fulfúlde.
ich fälle einen Baum — *I fell a tree* ich spalte Holz — *I cleave wood*	keuka taal-niskin[1]	nkō / ide } kōb-erik (kōrik)	ina sāra itše ina fāskara itše	mēdo-feddže lekki
ich schleife (ein Messer — *I grind (a knife*	kara-niskin gel-niskin[2] .	kelās-erik . .	ina wāši ūka .	mēdo-welli lebbi
ich grabe einen Brunnen — *I dig a well*	. . . . . .	. . . . . .	ina hakka rižia[9]	mēdo-wossa bundu
ich schlage das Zelt auf — *I pitch the tent*	lēma kog-niskin[3]	lā hóng-erik .	ina kaffa lēma	mēdo-tasi lēmū-ro
ich schlage das Zelt ab — *I take down the tent*	lēma mag-niskin[4]	lā terik[7] . .	ina dēbe lēma	mēdo-itte lēmū-ro
ich baue (ein Haus — *I build a house*	fāto) ger-niskin[5]	ive tóm-erik .	ina ginni[10] . ina šūfe . .	mēdo-māha .
er hat eine Stadt gebaut — *he has built a town*	billa gér-tso .	merē némaī ivégendē[8]	ya-ginni / ya-górta } gari	. . . . . .
ich drehe das Tau — *I make the rope*	džē yē-t-iskin	. . . . .	ina tumka egia	mēdo-walla boggul
ich flechte die Matte — *I make the mat*	būži tand-iskin[6]	kawal tóm-erik	ina sāka tabérma	mēdo-saña dāgo

[1] keuka taal-niskin, s. S. 116, N. 2.

[2] kara-niskin, gel-niskin fehlen beide bei Koelle; das erste Wort hat eine auffallende Ähnlichkeit mit dem Ausdruck für „ich lese", aber auch hier erhalten wir einigen Aufschluss durch die so eng verwandte Tédā-Sprache, aus der wir erkennen, dass in dem Worte für „ich schleife" ursprünglich ein e in dem Stammwort sich befand, es also von jenem Worte sehr verschieden war; gel-niskin ist wol nur eine sehr zusammengezogene Form.

[3] lēma kog-niskin entspricht dem kógin Koelle's (ēl kóktšin), obgleich er den besonderen Bezug an lēma nicht erwähnt. Die Wurzel scheint, nach dem entsprechenden Tédā-Wort zu erklären, hong zu sein.

[4] lēma mag-niskin. Das mag-niskin entspricht wol dem mágeskin und máskin Koelle's „nehme, nehme weg, ergreife", obgleich er auch hier die besondere Beziehung auf lēma nicht angibt.

[5] ger-niskin. Koelle schreibt gérgin und scheint es mit garū oder, wie er schreibt, gáru, „die Stadtmauer", etymologisch in Verbindung zu setzen.

[6] būži tand-iskin, s. S. 116, N. 6. Koelle schreibt búži tándeskin. Das Zeitwort wird auch in Verbindung mit ngē, „der Topf", gebraucht, und dies erscheint auf den ersten Blick höchst sonderbar, aber man muss bedenken, dass auch die Arbeit des Töpfers in einer rundenden, drehenden Bewegung besteht.

[7] lā terik. Die abgekürzte Form terik für tér-erik, ganz wie kōrik für kōb-erik, haben wir schon oben (S. 114) gehabt.

[8] merē némaī ivégendē. Das ivégendē ist auffallend, da ich für „ich baue eine Stadt" den Ausdruck némaī tóm-erik habe.

[9] ina hakka rižia. Dazu die verwandte Redensart „ich fasse den Brunnen ein", H. ina tōna rižia oder ina yāsa rižia, F. mēdo-irta bundu.

[10] ina ginni. Ich will hier einige begriffsverwandte Ausdrücke herzusetzen: „ich nehme (grabe) Thon zum Bau", H. ina hāba n kása, F. mēdo-tšīe lēdi; „ich mache Bausteine", H. ina yi-n tūbali, F. mēdo-tamba lēdi oder mēdo-wodda tūbalīdže; „ich beschmiere, bestreiche (die Wand, das Haus)", H. ina yābe, F. mēdo-makka lēdi; und für „ich glätte (die Wand)" wieder das so oft wiederholte ina dēbe, offenbar mit der Grundbedeutung „ich nehme (die Unebenheiten) weg", F. mēdo-harsa.

[11] (ēga-tšén hōgu di) ist hier uneigentlich, da hōgu oder hō in der späteren gewöhnlichen Bedeutung wenigstens nur „Haus" bedeutet, nicht „Zeit", aber ich habe im Sońγai gar kein besonderes Wort für „Zeit" erfahren.

[12] ēga-na kāmdi. Auch hier hege ich einige Ungewissheit über die Wurzel.

[13] ēga-tšén (hō. hō ist contrahirt aus hōgu, „Haus".

[14] ēga-hinna tándšera bēla. Der Zusatz bēla gibt hier eine nähere Bezeichnung.

[15] w(a)-ódasī hodógnā. Ich habe hódnaā hodógnā niedergeschrieben.

[16] wa-ōŋ ra-hō. re, yo, „das Haus"; rā, pō, „die Stadt".

[17] am gāme dogég-arē. Das dogég ist wol ohne Zweifel vom Arabischen dakka mit derselben Bedeutung abgeleitet.

Sedyal.	Lógoné.	Wándalá.	Bágrimma.	Mába.
éga-duṅgu bâdu	w(a)-óduaǒ hodú-gui [15]	yé-tše-n afī	mam-ótkalžá ka-gā	am sańgo asimme
éga-fār būri-dī	wudélde . . .	yé-gan óterē	mat-us kía-nā	am áńfilógē
éga-hinsa boṅgo	. . . .	. . . . . .	. . . . . .	. . . . . .
(éga-tšén bōgu-dī [11])	w(a)-otkū lēma-hā	yé-daebē lēma	mat-uk lēma-nā	am gēme degég-arē [17]
éga-na-kám-di [12] / éga-na-kanán-di bō-gu-dí	w(a)-otkū uṅgūna lēma-hā	yé-petā lēma	mák-odō lēma-nā	am gēmo firtik-arē
éga-tšén (bō [13] .	wa-ǯǧ ra-hū [16] .	ye-dǯā (hā .	. . . . . .	. . . . . .
. . . .	na-ǯǧ rō-bē . .	a-dǯē-ne bá-óga-nē ekaē	. . . . . .	. . . . . .
éga-hinsa korfo	. . . .	. . . . . .	. . . . . .	. . . . . .
éga-sōga tándže-re-dī / éga-hinsa tándže-re bāla [14]	wú-ragā . . .	y(e)-éndera būtše	m(a)-ókodž rāga	am tāfi anrí

[1] kaeka taal-niskin: see above p. 117, n. 2.

[2] kara-niskin, gel-niskin are both wanting in Koelle. The first term bears a remarkable resemblance to the identical one for „I read", but also in this case we obtain much light through the closely related Tédā-language, and we may thence conclude, that the Kanúri-term for „I grind" contained originally an e before the second a, the whole word being kerāe- or kelāe-niskin, of which gel-niskin may be nothing but a contracted form.

[3] lēme hog-niskin: the word hog-niskin corresponds to the hóagin of Koelle, although he does not mention the term in connection with lēma. The root seems to be hoág, if we may draw a conclusion from the corresponding Tédā-term.

[4] lēma mag-niskin: the verb mag-niskin seems to be identical with móggskin or móskin of Koelle „I take from, take out", although also in this case he does not mention a distinct reference of this verb to lēma.

[5] gar-niskin: Koelle writes gárágin, which has some probability of correctness on account of its close connection with garū or, as Koelle writes the word, gáru, „the wall of the town".

[6] būdi tand-iskin: see above p. 119, note 6. Koelle writes būdži tándgokin. The verb is also used in connection with ágō, „the cooking pot", which seems rather remarkable at first sight, but the original notion of tand or tond (for even tond-iskin is used) appears to be „round" or „turning round" the business of the potter, also consisting in the rounding of the pot. Even the Hausa-word tanda, „the (round) box", seems to be derived from the same root.

[7] iā terik: terik is the contracted form of tér-erik, just as hōrik is the abridged form of hōb-erik, and we have had an example of it already before this (p. 114).

[8] merā némal iségendā: iségendē is remarkable, as for „I build a town" I have also the term tóm-erik (némal tom-erik).

[9] ina hakka rījia: I adduce here another phrase: „I wall in the well", H. ina tōne rījia or ina yāna rījia, F. mōdo-irta banda.

[10] ina ginsi: I shall here insert a few phrases of a similar meaning: „I take (dig) clay for building", H. ina kāba u kāsa, F. mōdo-tōto lōdi; „I make bricks", H. ina yi-n tūbali, F. mōdo-tamba lōdi or mōdo-wadda tūbaliddē; „I besmear (a wall with clay or something else)", H. ina yābe, F. mōdo-mabba lōdi; the term „I smooth, polish" again is expressed by the general term ina doke, evidently implying the fundamental notion „I take away" (via the uneven, rough parts), F. mōdo-barsa.

[11] (éga-tšén bōgu-dī): this phrase does not correspond exactly to the other terms, bōgu or bō being rather the term for „house", but the Sedyal do not seem to have any peculiar term for „tent".

[12] éga-na kámdi: in this case likewise I am not quite certain of the root.

[13] éga-tšén (bō: bō is contracted from bōgu, „house".

[14] éga-hinsa tándžere bála: the bála, which has been added, gives to the phrase a more distinct expression.

[15] w(a)-óduaǒ hodúgui: of the w(a)-óduaǒ I am not quite sure, as I had written down hóduaǒ.

[16] wa-ǯǧ ra-hū: ra, ya, „the house"; rō, yō, „the town".

[17] am gēme degég-arē: the root degég is beyond a doubt derived from the Arabic dakka, which has the same meaning.

16

Unpersönliche Zeitwörter.

Deutsch und Englisch.	Kanúri.	Tédā.	Hausa.	Fulfúlde.
es verdient, ist werth — *it deserves*	tšándena [2] . .	(áyander . . / (á-merēdakker [11]	yá-kammäta [16]	mē-dum) hāni
es bedarf, ist nothwendig — *it is necessary*	mbō-tšī [3] . .	. . . . . .	ší-na sō . .	. . . . . .
es übertrifft, ist grösser — *it does exceed*	kō-tšī [4] . . .	ai kankin [12] .	yā-fi [17] . . .	mē-dum) būri
es ist besser — *it is better*	áte) ngélkō [5] .			
es ist vortheilhaft, nützt — *it is useful, advantageous*	ambá-sonó [6] .	ambal dženigē [13]	(á-koi ánfanē-naa) / á-koi rība . / ší-na da ánfanē / (ší-na da rība)	mē-dum) wódi néfné / ágo-mai el fé-de [19]
es ist genug, reicht hin — *it is enough, does suffice*	(tšiī . . . / (tai-te-na [7] .	bū . . . . . / ĭi	yá-isa . . .	dum fotti . .
es ist abgemacht, dabei hat es sein Bewenden — *that is it, it is done*	áte-ma ši [8] .	á-merē . . .	(ší-ke nan . / (ší kagā . .	káñkana [20] . .
es ist zu Ende, ist verbraucht — *it is finished, it is at an end*	dā-tšī [9] . .	fudák [14] . . .	ya-kāre . .	dum réi . .
es gibt, ist da¹ — *there is, it exists*	mbē-tši [10] . .	(tšī . . . . / (ĭi [15] . . .	á-koi [18] . .	mē-dum wódi

[1] „Es gibt, ist da". Über „es gehört" s. oben unter den Fürwörtern S. 4 „das ist mein", und S. 64 „ich besitze".
[2] tšándena. Das Wort fehlt bei Koelle, sowol im Vokabular als in §. 113 der Grammatik.
[3] mbō-tšī konnte ich auch bei Koelle nicht finden.
[4] kō-tšī, wörtlich „es ist vorbei-, vorangegangen", von kō-niskin S. 90, N. 6. Daher nicht eigentlich unpersönlich.
[5] ngélkō ist wahrscheinlich aus ngal, ngilla kō (tšin entstanden. Anders Koelle, Grammatik §. 197, 1, Note, indem er ngalgō schreibt.
[6] ambá-sonó scheint ein zusammengesetztes Wort zu sein, dessen erster Theil, ambá, dem Arabischen yenfá zu entsprechen scheint, der zweite aber, sonó, die Form des Futurums ist (bei Koelle tsonó), die auch weiter unten in makán sóne-ra wiederkehrt. Koelle hat das Wort nicht; dagegen mit unserem šempá, „Aufmerksamkeit, Sorge" hat es wol nichts zu thun.
[7] tšiī bei Koelle (tsai). Für tai-te-na hat er taçtī (Grammatik §. 113, 4). Die Wurzel von beiden Wörtern scheint aber dieselbe zu sein, ebenso wie die des ĭi in der Tédā-Sprache.
[8] áte-ma ši ist eigentlich mehr eine Pronominalform, „das da (ist) so", aber in einigen dieser Sprachen wird der Begriff durch ein Zeitwort ausgedrückt.
[9] dā-tšī ist eigentlich kein unpersönliches Zeitwort, da dā-niskin oder dā-ngin in der Bedeutung „ich mache Halt", „ich stehe still" gebraucht wird. Siehe S. 84.
[10] mbē-tšī. Koelle nimmt in seiner Grammatik (§. 267) wol mit Recht eine Wurzel be an. Über diesen bē s. Prolegom.
[11] á-merē dakker. Das dakker ist auffallend.
[12] ai kankin kann ich leider nicht durch Beispiele erläutern.
[13] ambal dženigē. Das ambal ist deutlich, aber nicht so das dženigē.
[14] fudák. Neben diesem Ausdruck, der besonders bei den südlichen Stämmen in Gebrauch ist, habe ich noch zwei andere, nämlich mórkin und tna, die mehr in den nördlichen Landschaften üblich sind.
[15] tšī, ĭi. Es ist auffallend, dass wir hier denselben Ausdruck für „es gibt" haben, wie oben für „es reicht hin".
[16] yá-kammäta. Dazu die negative Phrase „es verdient nicht, ist nicht werth", H. yá-kammäta ba, F. mē-dum hāni-a.
[17] yā-fi. Zu diesem yā-fi wird die Eigenschaft, worauf die Vergleichung beruht, hinzugesetzt, als yā-fi girma, „es übertrifft an Grösse", „ist grösser"; yā-fi yawa, „ist tüchtiger, vortrefflicher".
[18] á-koi. Die Wurzel dieses einfachen Zeitwortes ist mir zweifelhaft.
[19] mē-dum wódi néfné, ágo-mai el féde. Beide Redensarten sind nicht ganz einheimisch, wenigstens die Substantive in beiden sind Arabischen Ursprungs, das eine von nefá, das andere von faida abgeleitet.
[20] káñkana stammt offenbar von kañko, „er", „das".
[21] Für „ist werth" habe ich im Sonyai den Ausdruck aitšim, aber er kann kaum richtig sein.
[22] ábal. Dazu die Redensart „es ist besser, wir gehen jetzt", ábal érma-koi merēdar.
[23] wó gänafal hat auch kein ganz einheimisches Ansehen und ist vielleicht eine Verdrehung des Arabischen نفع.
[24] gadáne, auch mit Vorsetzung von atimmi: atimmi gadána.
[25] débi kadam ist mir zweifelhaft; das débi scheint fast nichts Anderes zu sein, als das adibi.
[26] teal (maiá. Das teal ist wahrscheinlich aus der Kanúri-Sprache herübergenommen.

Impersonal verbs.

Sónyai.	Lógonē.	Wándalā.	Bágrimma.	Mába.
[21]	débi kadám [25] .	lenlēa . . .	safkila badda manē	mangin faidik tambai
. . . .	dággedī . . .	tsáwagtsē . .	mánkonfē . .	litto ago) oágo-nyéri
ábal [22]	(hanne) diffen (han-)tikenē / (hanne) ndíbi . .	degdē . . .	éna dillega .	
wò gánafaí [23] . .	ñdáyinī lalí . .	ámagēn mága-nán pirē?	gassónka hámba-kī	nó fanda-róngte
ágō tónton . .	taní (malá [26] . .	tšášya . . .	éma áalga . .	méte
gadāne [24] . . .	hanne-ī . . . / ninnedē . . .	gñanna bōno .	énenē	wágo-ti
abén	dagáya . . . / šéna	dolde . . .	darga . . . / góttoga . . / dimgaga . .	dum tamsúng
agá-kunō . . .	nāli . . . . / nāli-dā . . .	ankwa . . .	ētu	téndai / tenā

[1] „There is, exists". As for the term „it belongs to" see the pronouns p. 4 „(this is) mine" and the verb „I possess" p. 64.
[2] tšándena is wanting as well in Koelle's vocabulary, as in his grammar §. 112.
[3] mbō-tšī I have looked for in vain in Koelle.
[4] kó-tšī means verbally „it has passed", therefore „exceeds", from kó-nlokin p. 80, note 6 and therefore is not properly an impersonal verb.
[5] ágéllō probably is contracted from ágal, ágilla kó tšin, although Koelle, who writes ágalgō, explains it in a different manner (gr. §. 197, 1, note).
[6] ambá-sonō seems to be a compound word, the first part of which, ambá, would seem to correspond to the Arabic yenfá, while the second one, sonō is the form of the future tense (Koelle i-sonō), which returns also further on in the term makin sóso-ra. Koelle has not the word, although his ámpi which, he explains „attention, care", may have something to do with it.
[7] tsēī appears in Koelle, while for tsi-ts-na he writes tsētī. However the root of both terms is probably the same as well as the ti in the Tédā-language is to be derived from the same root.
[8] áte-ma tī properly is a pronominal form, „that (is) it", but in some of the other languages we have a verbal form.
[9] dá-tšī properly is not to be regarded as an impersonal verb, the verb dá-nlokin or dá-ngin being used also with the signification of „I stand still", „I make a halt". See above p. 58.
[10] mbō-tšī: Koelle with great probability assumes a root be (bē) (in his grammar of the Kanúri-language, §. 207).
[11] á-merē dakker: dakker is remarkable and suspicious.
[12] ai kohkin: this term I am not able to illustrate.
[13] ambal dēénigō: the ambal is clear, but not so dēénigō.
[14] fudōk: besides this term, which is especially in use with the Tédā-tribes settled in the South, I have still two another ones, mórkin and tue, which are more common in the North.
[15] tšī, tī: it is remarkable, that we have here the same term for „there is", as we had a little before for „it is enough".
[16] yá-hammáte: thereto the negative phrase „it does not deserve, is not worth", H. yá-hammáta ba, F. mō-dum hán-a.
[17] yā-fi is not an impersonal word in a strict sense, as nā-fi, kā-fi, mun-fi, kun-fi, sun-fi may also be used. Of course the property, in regard to which the comparison is made, is added in the form of the substantive, such as yā-fi girma, „it exceeds in greatness, is greater"; yā-fi yawa, „it excels in strength, is more excellent".
[18] á-hoī: I am doubtful as to the root of this common word.
[19] mō-dum wódi néfaō, ágo-mal ol fédo: neither the one, nor the other of these phrases is indigenous, at least the noun in both being imported from the Arabic, the one being derived from nefá, the other from faida.
[20] kóbkana is formed evidently from kokko, „it", „that".
[21] For the phrase „it is worth" I have in Sónyai the term altilim, but it can scarcely be correct.
[22] ábal: compare the phrase „it is better we go now", ábal érma-koi moréden.
[23] wó gánafaí has not the character of an indigenous word and may possibly be a corrupted form of the Arabic ينفع with the same meaning.
[24] gadáne: also with the addition of atimmi: atimmi gadáne.
[25] débi kadám looks rather suspicious, and débi might seem nothing else but ndibi.
[26] taní (malá: the term taní probably has been borrowed from the Kanúri-language.

Deutsch und Englisch.	Kanúri.	Tédā.	Hausa.	Fulfúlde.
es gibt nicht, es fehlt — *there is none, is wanting*	bā-gō [1] . . .	bē . . . . / yēko . . .	babō	dum wōla . . / faráki [16]
vielleicht ist es, vielleicht auch nicht — *perhaps it is, perhaps not*	makān sóno-ra, makān san-nī [2]	tegiasegē [8] . .	ko á-kol ŝī [11]	mō-ánda ko-ī dum hòri [17]
es hat nichts zu bedeuten — *it is of no consequence, is indifferent*	lárū lrā-gō [3] / afī-ma genī	tikkesi yēko .	bābō kō-mō .	[18]
es ist zerbrochen — *is broken*	nam-tī [4] . .	tegirta [9] . .	yá-karē [12] . .	dum yōri . .
es ist verdorben — *is spoiled*	bibi-tī [5] . . / á-tsena [6] . . / zíb-tsena . .	bibi-tfude . . / dwi-kfude . .	yá-batšē [13] .	(dum) wōni .
es hat einen schlechten Geruch — *it has a bad smell*	kaino dibbi [7] .	gurī bénnāsanto [10]	ya-ī doī [14] .	dum luba-ī [19] / ó-mo-batši .
es hat einen guten Geruch — *it has a nice smell*	kaino ketšī .	gerī bónuā kussu	šī-na da kamši [15]	ó-mo-luba . / dum wōdi úruñ-gul

[1] bá-gō scheint mir zusammengesetzt aus bā agō, „nicht eine Sache"; allerdings kann man nicht leugnen, dass es auch mit dem so ähnlich klingenden entsprechenden Hausa-Wort in Beziehung steht, worüber in den Prolegomena das Nähere. Man hört mitunter bā-kō ausgesprochen.

[2] makān sóno-ra, makān san-nī ist eine höchst interessante Phrase, auf eigenthümliche Weise aus Arabischen und Kanúri-Elementen zusammengesetzt, die zu mich einige Zeit gekostet hat, zu analysiren. makān nämlich ist unzweifelhaft das Arabische إمكان, possibilitas, sono ist die Form des Futurum vom Zeitwort „sein", ra ist die Partikel der Ungewissheit, san-nī statt sóno-nī die negative Form des Zeitwortes. Koelle hat sie nicht.

[3] lárū hat Koelle in sehr weiter Bedeutung, es bedeutet nach ihm jede Art Schaden, selbst mit Einschluss von „Mord", aber in diesem Sinne ist es offenbar ein euphemistischer Ausdruck. — genī, Koelle genī, eigentlich gen-nī, Neg. von geno.

[4] nam-tī von nam-niskin, „ich breche".

[5] bibi-tī. Koelle hat ausser dem transitiven bibingin (bibi-niskin) nur das Neutrum bibite, oder wie er accentuirt, bibíte, „Verderben", wie z. B. bibite kargeho, „Unzufriedenheit, Gram, Kummer".

[6] á-tsena, zíb-tsena werden beide, so wie die ihnen gegenüberstehenden Ausdrücke in den anderen Sprachen, vom Verderben des Fleisches gebraucht. Koelle scheint weder den einen, noch den anderen Ausdruck zu haben. Ich will hier noch auch den verwandten Begriff einschieben: „es ist verschimmelt, mit Schimmel bedeckt", K. mitsena, W. hadeébbené.

[7] kaino dibbi. Diese wie die folgende Phrase im Kanúri gehören ihrer Form nach eigentlich nicht hierher, da sie adjektivisch ausgedrückt sind: „(es ist) an Geruch schlecht", „an Geruch angenehm". — kaino, Koelle keino.

[8] tegiasegē heisst eigentlich „es ist möglich", wogegen die Negativform tegiaseno lautet.

[9] tegirta ist keine gewöhnliche Form.

[10] gerī bénnā santo, wörtlich „Geruch von ihm schlecht".

[11] kó á-kol ŝī. Über das kó, „vielleicht", „möglich" s. S. 8.

[12] yá-karē ist eigentlich die passive Form von Ina-kárió, „ich zerbreche", s. S. 110, es ist daher wol zu unterscheiden von ya-kāre, „es ist verbraucht", „es ist zu Ende".

[13] yá-batšē hat im H. verschiedene Bedeutungen, die nicht alle dem Kanúri-Ausdruck entsprechen; so heisst rakumi yá-batšē „das Kameel hat sich verirrt", K. kargimá fétsiki; dieser Bedeutung entspricht eigentlich im F. der Ausdruck múdši. Dagegen entspricht die Bedeutung dem bibi-tī völlig in der Phrase tuo yá-batšē, „die Speise ist verdorben", F. ńīri madše (also hier auch in diesem Sinne), S. tšau hanni.

[14] ya-ī doī. „Das Fleisch riecht schlecht", H. náma ya-ī doī, F. tšo hi-lúba oder hassel geiwódu, S. ham do fumbu. Auch will ich hier noch eine begriffsverwandte Redensart hersetzen: „der Ghussub-Trank ist sauer geworden", H. fúra ya-ī yámi, F. tšōtem lommi.

[15] šī-na da kamši, wörtlich „ist von Wohlgeruch".

[16] dum faráki. faráki kommt mir nicht wie ein einheimisches Wort vor, und fast möchte ich glauben, dass es mit dem Arabischen faraga, „es ist zu Ende", zusammenhängt.

[17] mō-ánda ko-ī dum hōri, wörtlich „ich weiss nicht, (ob) dies ist oder nicht".

[18] Ich will hier einige Ausdrücke einreihen, die ich nur im H. und F. habe: „es passt mir, ist mir gelegen", H. ya-gamšē-nī, F. (mōdum) hándi-mā; „es passt mir nicht, ist mir ungelegen", H. ba yá-gamšē-nī ba, F. dum handaya; „es gleicht, ist einerlei", H. šī-na dédé, F. mī-dum fotti, S. wonda kol tye fo, „es ist verschieden", H. šī-na hambámta, F. mō-dum durrī. fotti und durrī sind wirkliche Verbalformen, im H. hingegen ist die Ausdrucksweise adjektivisch. Im S. wonda wool himma.

[19] dum lúba-ī ist die negative Form der folgenden Phrase.

[20] dáffa beldšia. Ich bin nicht sicher, ob das dáffa einen integrirenden Theil der Redensart bildet.

[21] devī heisst offenbar „es riecht", wie die beiden folgenden Phrasen deutlich zeigen.

[22] kenti, „die Sonne", „das Gewand" aus „Baumwollenzeug".

[23] bidbede sára, eigentlich „riecht (nach) Wohlgeruch".

[24] ćom ōto wie nie lōle sind mir nicht ganz deutlich; lōle bedeutet „süss", aber nie sieht nicht wie eine Verbalform aus

Sónyai.	Lógonē.	Wándalā.	Bágrimma.	Mába.
naá-kunū . . .	ĩèn	bāka	góto	{kai / tambai}
ahánko agá-kunu / aaá-kunu	lúgo ále aránna andi / gang-alá arán-sa	ádzegún segúmtu / ádzegim-to	gas é-nan etíkkeli / av lan tíkkeli	. . . . .
. . . .	{hanavaéna . . / wáŝiaā . . . .}	bāka lakó-úka	{larú / lavno} góto .	. . . . .
akairi	tónā	ázenā)galóbgelē[22]	tadīga . . .	kútu
{adano . . . . / kanui . . . .}	{dáǹa bóldžia[20] . / devī[21] . . . .}	badzóbbazē . / waṅgō . . .	natúddzō . . / indžúmga . .	nenyīli / kalolati
ahōogo fumbu .	devī kadámna .	mandžo sāra .	ósn ēle[24] . .	lúl-teri
ahōogo {bente . / kān . .}	devī doló . . .	bídbede sāra[23]	nia lēle . . .	tugát-teri

[1] kā-gō appears to me to be composed of kā agō, „not a thing", while on the other side I have shown in the Prolegomena, that it is closely related to the corresponding Hausa-term bābō. But I must not forget to mention, that the word is frequently pronounced bā-kā.

[2] makán séne-ra, makán san-ni is an interesting phrase, formed in a very remarkable manner of Arabic and Kanúri-elements which it has cost me some time to analyse. makān no doubt is the Arabic إمكان, „possibilitas", sane again in the form of the future tense of the verb „to be", ra is the particle „either", san-ni contracted from sene-ni the negative form of the verb. Koelle has not the phrase.

[3] lárú appears in Koelle with a very wide signification, every sort of „damage", including even murder; but in cases, where the latter is understood, the use of the word is certainly a euphonic one.

[4] nem-ít from nem-nískin, „I break".

[5] bibi-ti: Koelle besides the transitive form of the verb bibíngin (i. q. bibi-niskin) has only the noun bibite or, as he writes bibitę, „spoiling", as bibite kárgebe, „dissatisfaction, grief, vexation".

[6] á-tsena, alá-tsena are both used particularly of the spoiling of meat, as well as the corresponding terms in the other languages. Koelle seems to have neither the one nor the other of these terms. I shall here also insert another term of a related meaning, viz „it has got mouldy, has been covered with mould", K. mtásena, W. badzóbbazā.

[7] kaine díbbi: this as well as the following Kanúri-term properly does not belong to this chapter, the expression being in the form of an adjective: „(it is) bad (díbbi) of smell (kaine)", „(it is) pleasant of smell)".

[8] tegleszgō means verbally „it is feasible" and has as negative form teglesanā. They say also ki-ni yéko labár teria.

[9] tegirta is not a common form.

[10] geri kénuá aante means verbally „smell of it bad".

[11] kó á-kol li: with regard to the kó, „perhaps", may be", see p. 8.

[12] ya-kerō properly is the passive form of ina-kárīō, „I break", which see above p. 110. It is consequently not to be confounded with ya-kāre, „it is consumed, is come to an end".

[13] ya-batšē in H. has various meanings derived from the notion of receding from its nature, from the right path, which do not all correspond to the Kanúri-term; thus rákomi ya-batše means „the camel has been lost" „has strayed", corresponding to the Kanúri-term kargimō fétaiki. To this notion of the Hausa-term corresponds the Fulfúlde-term mādši. On the other side the Hausa-term corresponds entirely to the K. bibi-ti in the phrase tûo ya-batše, „the food is spoiled", F. ñiri medši, S. táen kanui.

[14] ya-i doi: compare the phrase „the meat has a bad smell", H. nāma ya-i doi, F. tēo bi-lāba or kasaol seiwōda, S. ham de fumbu. I shall also adduce here another term of a similar meaning: „the ghussub-water has become sour", H. fūra ya-i yámi, F. tšōtam lemmi.

[15] Ii-na da kamší means verbally „is of a good smell".

[16] dum faráhi: faráhi does not bear the character of an indigenous word and I am inclined to suppose, that it is derived from the Arabic فرح.

[17] mō-ánda ko-i dum bibri means verbally „I do not know, (whether) this be or not".

[18] I shall here insert a few phrases, for which I have corresponding terms only in H. and F.: „it suits me", H. yá-gamšé-ni, F. mē-dum) bándi-mē; „it does not suit me, is inconvenient to me", H. ba yá-gamšé-ni ba, F. dum) bondáyo; „it is one and the same, resembles each other", H. ki-na dé-dē, F. mō-dum fotti, S. wonda kul iga fó; „it is different, does not resemble", H. ki-na kamkámta, F. mō-dum durri. — fotti and durri are really verbal forms, while in H. the term is formed by means of the adjective. In Sónyai wonda woei hinna.

[19] dum lúba-i is the negative form of the verb lúba.

[20] dáǹa boldžia: I am not quite sure, whether the word dáǹa forms an integral part of the term or not.

[21] devi means evidently „it smells", as is distinctly shown by the two following phrases.

[22] ázená, „the straw" or „covering of cottoncloth".

[23] bídbede sāra means properly „smells fragrancy".

[24] ósn ēle as well as nia lēle is not quite clear to me; lēle means „sweet", but nia has not exactly the appearance of a verbal form.

Deutsch und Englisch.	Kanúri.	Tēda.	Hausa.	Fulfulde.
es hat sich gespalten, hat eine Öffnung bekommen — is rent	ré-tí[1] . . .	far-tínde . .	túlu) ya-fúde[18]	áde) ulku . .
der Schlauch leckt — the waterskin leaks	ágirke) / sakti } ákí fi-tšin[2]	lúli kerúde[13] .	selka tá-na zubba rúa	. . . . .
es ist zerrissen — it is torn	ham-tí[3] . .	farta	ya-sáma {regga / summa}	o-hebbi bite .
das Hemd ist zerrissen — the shirt is torn	kulgu kerī-tena[4]	kubū fafār-tinde	rīga ta-sámo regga[19]	. . . . .
die Kleidung ist alt geworden — the dress grew old	kázum dín-sina[5]	térkeni gíbi-kinde	tōfa tá-na súfa	. . . . .
es hat sich verändert, wird zu — it has changed (its nature), becomes	fal-tí[6] . . .	for-islinde[14] .	ši-na kōmo[20]	dum warti .
es schmilzt — it melts .	fá-tsena[7] . .	yīi-kinde . .	ya-nérki . .	dum tal . .
das Eisen ist angerostet — the iron has grown rusty	sū teídi-yé súb-ena[8]	ásubu busāfu kúf-cédē[15]	kasa ya-tšī karfi	lēdinyāmidžamdi
es (meine Haut) juckt — my skin itches	(tigge-ni) lilim-tšin[9]	lilūeni . . .	. . . . . .	. . . . .
es (die Wunde) schmerzt — it (the wound) pains	zau-tšin[10] . .	iśántak[16] . .	ší-na tšīo . .	dum onyando
es (die Wunde) trocknet, heilt — it (the wound) dries up, heals	ham-tšī[11] . .	. . . . . .	ya-wárki . .	ó-böl . . .
die Sonne ist aufgegangen — the sun has risen	kau tse-lúg-ena[12]	{esō grū, S.[17] / yezē korúk, N.}	rāna yá-fittō[21]	nañge fūdi .

[1] ré-tí von ré-nishin, ré-ngin.
[2] ágirke, sakti ákí fi-tšin, wörtlich „der Schlauch lässt das Wasser los".
[3] ham-tí von ham-nishin oder ham-gin, „ich zerreisse, scheide", kann nur von harten Gegenständen gebraucht werden, während das folgende Wort, kerī-tena, von weichen gebraucht wird.
[4] kulgu kerī-tena. Der Kanúri-Ausdruck ist allerdings kein unpersönliches Zeitwort, da kerī-nishin oder kerī-ngin ein gewöhnliches transitives Zeitwort ist, aber im H. u. B. ist der Ausdruck ganz unpersönlich.
[5] kázum dín-sina. dín-sina (dín-tsena) hat Koelle nicht, sondern nur das Adjektiv dín; kázum bei ihm kátsumá.
[6] fal-tí ist auch eigentlich kein unpersönliches Zeitwort, da fal-nishin gewöhnliche transitive Bedeutung hat. Koelle schreibt palngin, paltí, und das Letztere hat er sogar von der Frau in ihrem (veränderten) Zustande der Schwangerschaft.
[7] fá-tsena, vulgär faddena scheint bei Koelle zu fehlen; Grundbegriff wol „es rührt sich".
[8] sū teídi-yé súb-ena, wörtlich „die Erde (teídi) hat das Eisen gegessen". Weil hier das Objekt vorangestellt ist und so leicht ein Missverständniss entstehen konnte, ist dem Subjekt das ye angehängt, das ich sonst im gewöhnlichen Leben zu beobachten so gut wie gar keine Gelegenheit hatte, während es bei Koelle eine Hauptrolle spielt.
[9] (tigge-ni) lilim-tšin. Koelle hat lilim-tšin nicht und schreibt anstatt tigge: tigi oder tige.
[10] zau-tšin, wörtlich „macht schwer". Das tšin wird auch oft weggelassen. Anstatt zau schreibt Koelle tsau, so auch tsau tigebē, „das Fieber". Vergl. kálu zau tšin, „Leibschmerzen", tšim zau tšin, „Augenübel" u. s. w.
[11] ham-tšī, wörtlich „ist kalt geworden" von ham-gin, d. h. „ist getrocknet, geheilt", vollkommener Gegensatz zu zau-tšin, „ist warm, brennt, schmerzt". Man hört oft am-tšī und auch Koelle hat ámgin oder hamgin (3te Pers. Sing. [illegible]), mit der ersten Bedeutung „ich werde kalt" u. s. w. und der zweiten „ich genese", „ich werde wohl".
[12] kau tse-lúg-ena. tse-lúg-ena von lúg-nskin, „ich komme heraus". Derselbe Ausdruck wird auch in allen diesen Sprachen vom Monde gebraucht.
[13] lúli kerúde. Unter den Nominibus habe ich für „Wasserschlauch" im Tēda lini. S. die Note zu dem Worte.
[14] for-islinde. Ich sehe als Wurzel for an = fal im Kanúri.
[15] asubu busāfu kúf-cédē. Für „Eisen" habe ich zwei Formen: asú und ásubu.
[16] iśántak ist eine auffallende Form.
[17] esō grū. Das Zeitwort grū ist wol nur eine populäre Korruption.
[18] túlu, F. áde, „die Wasserurne". Ich will hier eine begriffsverwandte Phrase hersetzen: „ist entzwei (in zwei Theile zerspalten)", H. ya-rába biu, F. dum sendi dē didi; „der Weg hat sich getheilt", H. hanya ta-ráha, F. laual tšēdi; „der Weg hat sich verloren", H. hanya rátša, F. laual sēli, S. fondo áfal.
[19] rīga ta-sámo regga, wörtlich „das Hemd hat einen Riss gefunden".
[20] ši-na kōmo. Im Hausa sowohl wie im Fulfulde wird für „werden" derselbe Ausdruck gebraucht, wie für „zurückkehren", ganz wie im Arabischen [illegible].
[21] rāna yá-fittō. „Die Sonne ist noch nicht hervorgekommen, ist noch im Aufgehen", H. rāna tšikonā ba yá-fittō ba, F. nañge urtwáki, S. wēne [illegible]; „der Morgenstern ist aufgegangen", H. gamodži yá-fittō, F. [illegible] arlikke, S. alfedšr [illegible] difátta.
[22] áteri lérmerih hat etwas Zweifelhaftes.

Sonyai.	Lógoné.	Wándalá.	Bágrimma.	Mába.
. . . .	dálaa	tapie . . .	páge	áteri térmerik [23]
. . . .	. . . .	. . . . . .	. . . . .	létiere
. . . .	dápia	itšewltši . .	nol-korōga .	tétumō
. . . .	. . . .	. . . . . .	bal famili . .	drékeiā {ñddak / tšúmdak
. . . .	lobā dáakia . .	. . . . . .	búle hoúga .	mandžil tšo
. . . .	farékalā . . .	bedém-wedē .	doleŋga . . .	. . . . . .
. . . .	avlésia	parnāpa . .	ganmáñga . .	airtáriñgē
. . . .	. . . .	. . . . . .	. . . . . .	. . . . . .
. . . .	zawa zimin . .	áso írua wárua	. . . . .	. . . . . .
étše gadōri . .	dukku	awa nūā . .	ónyoma . . .	ándanē
awō	iχθéχθiā . . .	. . . . . .	kóbuñgō . .	. . . . . .
wōne difâlta . .	aāyo dásvoyā . .	aexa wétšia .	kai tegga . .	cidk tatúnne

[1] rē-ti from rō-nishin, rē-ágin.
[2] égirke, sakti áhi ſi-tšin means verbally „the waterskin lets loose the water".
[3] ham-ti from ham-nishin or ham-gin, „I cut".
[4] kuign keri-tene: the Kanúri-verb is certainly not an intransitive one, the form keri-nishin or keri-ágin being in common use, but the corresponding Hausa-term belongs entirely to this place.
[5] kāgm din-nina: the verb din-nina (perhaps more correctly to be written din-teena) is wanting in Koelle, who has only the adjective din. The word hāgm appears in his vocabulary in the form hátaumé.
[6] fal-ti is not exactly an intransitive verb, as fal-nishin or, as Koelle writes, pálágin is a common transitive verb. Koelle uses even páiti of a woman in her (changed) state of being with child.
[7] fā-teena, in vulgar pronunciation fádānna, is wanting in Koelle.
[8] sū toidi-yé sáb-ana means verbally „the earth (or soil) has eaten the iron". On account of the object being placed here before and a misconception being easy, the termination ye has been added to the subject, while in general I had very little opportunity of observing the use of the ye.
[9] (tigge-ni) lilim-tšin: Koelle has not this verb and instead of tigge writes tigi or tige.
[10] aan-tšin means verbally „makes heavy, disagreeable", but tšin is often left out. Instead of aan Koelle writes teon, thus teon tigebē, „the fever". Compare the terms kálem aan tšin, „the bowels pain", šim aan tšin, „the eye is sore".
[11] bam-tši, „has become cold", from bam-gin l. q. „has dried up, has healed" the exact reverse of aan-tšin, „is warm, burns". One hears frequently am-tši and Koelle has both forms ámgin or hámgin (3rd pers. sing. ši ámtšia).
[12] kau tee-lág-ana; tee-lág-ana from lág-nakin, „I come forth". The same term is also used with regard to the moon in all these languages.
[13] ldit koriāde: among my list of nouns I have the Téda-term šiai for „waterskin". See what I shall say there.
[14] for-latinde. I derive this word from a root for, corresponding to the fal in Kanúri.
[15] áenbu bacáfa báf-sáb: áenbu is one of the two forms for „iron" in Tédā, which I have noted down; the other is saā.
[16] iaāntak is rather a remarkable form.
[17] saá grā: the verb grā seems to be a popular corruption.
[18] tšila, F. ādo, „the arm", „jar". I shall here adduce a phrase of a related meaning: „has split in two", H. ya-rāba biu, F. dum sandi dē-didi; „the path has divided", H. hanā ta-rāba, F. lauol tšédi; „the path has disappeared", H. hanā ráitšē, F. lanol eéli, S. fondo áfal.
[19] riga ta-sáme rugga means verbally „the shirt has found a rent".
[20] ši-na kōmo: in Hausa as well as in Fulfúlde we have for „to become", „to become by change", the same term, which means „to return", just as in Arabic رجع.
[21] rāna yá-fittā: compare the phrase „the sun has not yet risen, is rising", H. rāna tákonā ba yá-fittā ba, F. nadge urtwáki, S. wōne dinafátta; „the morningstar has risen", H. gomaški yá-fittā, F. dšabira urifáko, S. alfedár sanáj difátta.
[23] áteri térmerik looks somewhat suspicious.

Deutsch und Englisch.	Kanúri.	Tédā.	Hausa.	Fulfúlde.
die Sonne ist untergegangen — *the sun has set*	kau tšó-kurī [1]	yezē tobúr [10] .	rāna ya-fādi .	nañge mutī .
die Sonne ist noch nicht untergegangen — *the sun has not yet set*	kau tšo-kúr-nī [2]	yezē kórukē .	rāna tókonā ba ya-fādi ba	nañge mutta .
der Mond ist verdunkelt, es ist Mondfinsternis — *the moon has been eclipsed*	kumbal teer-gör-in [3]	. . . . .	rāna ya-kāma wóta [16]	nañge nebgi lēuru
der Mond kommt (wieder) hervor — *the moon shines forth (after the eclipse*	kumbal wī-tī [4]	. . . . .	rāna yá-sekī wóta [17]	nañge yanāi lēuru
der Monat geht zu Ende — *the month draws to its close*	kintāko tamōle [5]	anri {ennōs-edē / túz-edē [11]}	wóta tá-na mútua	. . . . .
der Wind weht — *the wind blows*	kárwa só-gasin [6]	{auen irē [12] / ābonō kebābi}	iska ya-búgga [18]	hendu hi-biffa
es donnert — *it thunders*	dū̧nya gir-tšin [7]	eskónuō ké-yodī [13]	[19]	. . . . .
es blitzt — *the lightning flashes*	dū̧nya {tsenltin [8] / molúk-tšin}	yumár-konī [14]	. . . . .	. . . . .
Gewitterregen kommt — *a storm gathers*	délāgo līšin [9] .	níngeli [15] fe-kénde	hádderi ší-na zúa	yoōnde wāra .

[1] kau tšó-kurī, wörtlich „die Sonne ist gefallen". Dieselbe Anschauung liegt auch dem Hausa-Ausdruck zu Grunde. Koelle hat das Wort, wie es scheint, nicht.
[2] tšo-kór-nī, „ist nicht gefallen".
[3] kumbal teer-gör-in, wörtlich „der Mond ist gebunden", von gér-iskin, „ich binde". Eben dieser Grundanschauung liegt auch den Ausdrücken im Lógonē und Bágrimma zu Grunde. In den anderen Sprachen konnte ich den entsprechenden Ausdruck, da er den Leuten nicht eben geläufig ist, nicht erforschen. Substantivisch sagt man „Ergreifung" ken-tā (kúmbal-bé, „des Mondes").
[4] kumbal wī-tī. Der Ausdruck fehlt bei Koelle.
[5] kintáko tamōte. Hinsichtlich der Verbalform bin ich nicht sicher. Koelle hat ein Verbum tamóngin, „ich beendige, schliesse ab", in der dritten Konjugationsform „ich nehme ein Ende, sterbe", aber da würde man in der 3ten Person Sing. tamōtse erwarten. Koelle hat tamóte als Substantiv, „Ende", „Beendigung".
[6] kárwa só-gasin. só-gasin ist die 3te Person Sing. von kás-iskin, „ich fliese", „ich fliege", s. S. 88. Koelle schreibt toegáfin. Anstatt kárwa schreibt Koelle kárūa.
[7] dū̧nya gir-tšin. Koelle hat diese Phrase weder in seiner Grammatik, § 57, wohin sie gehört, noch in seinem Vokabular unter dem Worte gerágin (gir-niskin), wohin sie der Ableitung nach gehört, obgleich er den Ausdruck komadúgu gértšin (komádugu gir-tšin), „die See tobt" hat, noch unter dem Worte dúnya, das er diniā, dúnyā oder dinia schreibt.
[8] dū̧nya tsenltin und molúk-tšin fehlen auch bei Koelle. Hinsichtlich ihrer Wurzel und Ableitungsart bin ich nicht ganz sicher, aber das erstere scheint in gewissem Zusammenhang mit wélkin zu stehen.
[9] délāgo līšin. Bei délāgo (Koelle schreibt délāgo und déläge) ist der Endvokal so unsicher, dass ich beinahe selbst délāge schreiben möchte. līšin kommt von leiskin.
[10] yeзē (ezē) tobúr. Über die genaue Bedeutung des tobúr bin ich nicht ganz sicher.
[11] anri túz-edē. Vergl. tuz S. 177, N. 14; beide Zeitwörter stehen hier im Präteritum.
[12] auen irē. Ich hatte aue nirē niedergeschrieben, aber unter den Substantiven habe ich auen für „Wind".
[13] eskónuō ké-yodī: eskónuō, „der Himmel"; für „Donner" habe ich eskoinu (girgé-konī), wo das letztere Wort offenbar die Verbalform ist = K. gir-tšin.
[14] yumár-konī; yumár heisst „der Blitz".
[15] níngeli. Über die ursprüngliche Bedeutung dieses Wortes s. bei den Substantiven.
[16] rāna ya-kāma wóta, wörtlich „die Sonne hat den Mond ergriffen"; ebenso im Fulfúlde.
[17] rāna yá-sekī wóta, wörtlich „die Sonne hat den Mond losgelassen".
[18] iska ya-búgga, eigentlich „der Wind schlägt".
[19] Sonderbarer Weise habe ich diesen und den folgenden Ausdruck im Hausa nicht niedergeschrieben, ich glaube aber, „es donnert" heisst ya-i barádu. Ich will hier noch die begriffsverwandte Redensart hersetzen „die Wolken haben sich zusammengezogen", K. gideŋŋéddé nou-gámu, F. dúle he-haura [illegible].
[20] séma-dé. séma ist ein Wort von allgemeiner Bedeutung, das „Wind" und „Regen" zusammenbegreift, dann auch „die Regenzeit", obgleich hierfür auch noch ein besonderer, mit dem Hausa-Wort damana zusammenhängender Ausdruck, nämlich dēman, vorhanden ist; aber für „Wind" scheint dem Worte séma gewöhnlich dé angehängt zu werden.
[21] éffeyā ist vielleicht nicht ganz richtig oder drückt nicht die volle Phrase aus. Unter den Substantiven habe ich éffayé für „Wind".
[22] rānan delē und morgám watélle sind mir zweifelhaft. morgám delé habe ich unter den Substantiven für „Donner".
[23] wolda. Unter den Substantiven habe ich moldeh für „Blitz".

Sońyai.	Lógoné.	Wándalá.	Bágrimma.	Mába.
wēne kam . . .	säye déba-bē .	amba wétšia .	gótema kadī-ga	ëñík seríug-nēre táya
wēne á-si-hám	säye dindlana dūibō	bišbiä wétšia .	hadže útšoga .	eñík téa
. . . .	yēlin tédi-a . .	. . . . . .	nap-ne dži-džoki-ùga	
	yäibē tédi-a . .		nap-ne dži-ti-ùga	
. . . .	tēli á-gaya . .	. . . . . .	nap-ne darga	ēēk loti-nyetū
. . . .	séma-dē a-bā [20]	éffeyā [21] . .	lēl babā . .	aulék ágo búm-leri
. . . .	indelgäle a-kú .	. . . . . .	ränan delō [22] .	. . . . . .
	bárakē (Arab.) . .	. . . . . .	morgúm watálle	wolda [23]
engtäerinna a-kā	. . . .	. . . . . .	. . . . .	

[1] kan tšé-kari means verbally „the sun has fallen". Koelle has not the verb. The same meaning is expressed in the Hausa-term.
[2] tše-hér-a l, „did not fall".
[3] kumbel tser-gēr-in means verbally „the moon is tied". The same notion is expressed by the corresponding terms of the Lógoné- and the Bágrimma-languages. In the other idioms I was not able to make out this term, which of course is not a very common one. For „eclipse of the moon" the term ken-tšē, „the seizing" (kúmbal-bē, „of the moon") is used.
[4] kumbel wi-ti is wanting in Koelle's vocabulary.
[5] kistáke temáte: I am not quite certain of the verbal form. Koelle has a verb temágin, „I finish, dissolve", in the 3rd form „I come to an end, die", but if our word were derived from this root, we should rather expect temátse. Koelle has temóte as a noun with the notion „end", „termination".
[6] kárwa sé-gesin: sé-gesin is the 3rd pers. sing. from kés-ískin, „I run, fly": see above p. 85. Koelle writes tesgeskin and instead of kárwa- kárše.
[7] dúnye gir-tšin: Koelle has not this phrase, neither in his grammar of the Kanúri-language, where it ought to have found its place among the phrases cited in §. 52, nor in his vocabulary under the verb gerágin (gir-nishin), to which it belongs, although he mentions the term komedágu gertšin (komádugu gir-tšin), „the sea makes a noise", nor finally under the word dúnye or, as he writes it, dinià, dúnyé and dinie.
[8] dúnye tenšíkin and melék-tšin are also wanting in Koelle. As for their root and mode of derivation I am not quite certain, but there seems to be some connexion with wélkin.
[9] délége lšin: as to the final vowel of the word délige I was uncertain, whether it be rather an e or an e, but the latter may be more correct. Koelle writes délige and délige. lšin is from íšekin.
[10] yaeō (seō) tehár: with regard to the exact notion of tehár I am not quite certain.
[11] suri téa-edē: compare tua p. 193, note 14; both verbs are here in the past tense.
[12] enen irē: I suppose iyé to be the only verbal form of the phrase, as among the nouns I have enen for „wind".
[13] asténuē hé-yedi: astéunē, „the heaven"; among the nouns I have given „thunder" by aekelne (gir-gé-keni, where the latter word is evidently the verbal form, identical with the K. gir-tšin.
[14] yumár-keni: yumár means „lightning".
[15] ulúgeli: with regard to the original meaning of this term I shall say something in another place.
[16] rána ya-káma wóta means verbally „the sun has seized the moon" and in Fulfúlde it is the same.
[17] ráne yá-sehi wóte means verbally „the sun has let loose the moon".
[18] isha ya-hágge means verbally „the wind beats" or rather „has beaten".
[19] By accident I have not noted down this and the following phrase in Hausa; for „it lightens", I think, they have a peculiar term, but to express the term „it thunders", I suspect, they have only the substantive berádu, derived from the Arabic, to which is added ya-L. I think this a fit place for inserting a phrase of a related notion, viz „the clouds have gathered", H. gidegiddši ene-gámu, F. dúle hé-hauts.
[20] séma-dē: séma is a term of a general notion, comprising „wind" as well as „rain", nay even „rainy season", although for the latter notion I have the peculiar term démen, closely related to the Hausa-term dámane; but in the case of séme meaning „wind" the syllable dē is generally added.
[21] éffeyā, I think, is not quite correct or does not express the whole phrase. Amongst the nouns I have éffeyā for „wind".
[22] ränan delō and the following phrase, morgúm watálle, look rather suspicious to me. morgúm delō appears in my list of nouns for „thunder".
[23] wolda: among my list of nouns I have moldeh for „lightning"; the root therefore seems to be old.

Deutsch und Englisch.	Kanúri.	Tédā.	Hausa.	Fulfúlde.
der Regen giesst, es regnet — *the rain pours, it rains*	délāgo fī-tšin[1]	níngeli fē-kénde[8]	ta-ī rūa[10]	dum tobbi[15] .
das Sturmwetter, der Regen hört auf — *the storm, the rain ceases*	délāgo tsi-dūrin[2]	níngeli ēli . .	rūa sun-kāre[11]	ndīam réi . .
die Regenzeit hört auf — *the rainy season is drawing to its close*	níngeri tsi-dūrin[3]	níngeli nerkak-fode	dámanaya-kāre[12]	duńgu réi . .
der Fluss ist im Steigen — *the river, the lake is rising*	komá-dugu (tsī-tšin[4] / išin[5] . / tsirgainin[6])	eyī fū-kínde[9]	gulbī ī-nasūwa[13]	māyo hi-wāra[16]
der Fluss ist voll, hat seinen höchsten Stand erreicht — *the river is full, has reached its highest level*	komádugu tsi-mbúl-ena[7]	. . . . . .	gulbī ī-na tšī-ka[14]	māyo hēvi . .

[1] délāgo fī-tšin. fī-tšin ist hier augenscheinlich intransitiv, obgleich Koelle unter plágin (entsprechend meinem fī-nískin) dem Worte nur transitive Bedeutungen beilegt.

[2] délāgo tsi-dūrin. Über diesen und den folgenden Ausdruck bin ich nicht ganz sicher; dūru-skin heisst „ich falle", also sollte man délāgo tsi-dūrin, „der Regen fällt", erwarten, und so fasst es Koelle unter dem Worte délāgo auf (er schreibt tsédurin), und dass es diese Bedeutung hat, darüber lässt der Ausdruck bún-durō délāgi-bē, „ein Regenschauer", gar keinen Zweifel; aber was fällt, hört auch auf; dahin gehört auch die schon von Koelle angeführte Phrase kágara tsédurī, die er übersetzt „es fand ein Orkan statt", und die von mir gleich im Folgenden angeführte Redensart níngeri tsi-dūrin hat gar keinen Sinn, wenn man tsi-dūrin in der einfachen Bedeutung „fallen" nimmt; wenn níngeri allerdings, wie die Tédā-Sprache zeigt, ursprünglich auch die allgemeine Bedeutung „Regen" hatte, so hat es dieselbe doch allmählich verloren.

[3] níngeri tsi-dūrin, s. die vorhergehende Note.

[4] komádugu tsi-tšin, von tsī-nískin oder, wie Koelle schreibt, tšīngin. Koelle hat diese Bedeutung nicht, er hat aber die nahe verwandte vom Aufkeimen der Saat.

[5] išin, s. oben S. 86, N. 2.

[6] tsirgainin, eigentlich tsi-irgá-inin ist eine etwas ungewöhnliche Form von yirgá-skin (S. 86, N. 3), wie tsa-hé-inin von hé-skin, „ich besteige".

[7] komádugu tsi-mbúl-ena. tsi-mbúl-ena, auch vom „Leibe" gebraucht, wie tšīrō-ni tsi-mbúl-ena, „mein Leib ist voll", kommt von der Wurzel mbúl, die sich bei Koelle nur in der Zusammensetzung tsarómbulē (d. i. tšīrō-mbulō) findet.

[8] níngeli fē-kénde. Wir haben hier, wie in S. 129, N. 15, ein Beispiel des fē im T., während das K. fī so vieldeutig ist.

[9] eyī fū-kínde. Das fū-kínde scheint mit dem fē-kénde der vorhergehenden Phrase verwandt zu sein. Dabei liegt ein offenbarer Gegensatz der Wurzeln fū und nē klar zu Tage. Die Tédā, die grössere Wasserbecken kaum kennen, haben theils gar keine, theils nur unbehülfliche Ausdrücke für solche Phrasen. eyī heisst „Wasser" überhaupt.

[10] Ich habe hier im Hausa keinen dem Kanúri entsprechenden Ausdruck; denn der gewöhnliche Ausdruck für „es regnet", H. ta-ī rūa, F. dum tobbi, entspricht nicht ganz. Hierzu vergl. die passivisch ausgedrückte Redensart: „nachdem es zum Regen gekommen ist", H. anā rūa oder an-yi rūa, F. médum-tobbe ndīam.

[11] rūa sun-kāre, wörtlich „die Wasser hörten auf", entspricht auch dem Kanúri-Ausdruck nicht völlig, da hier von der Gesammtnatur des Sturmwetters abgesehen ist. Hier schiebe ich die Phrase ein „der Regen ist in's Haus eingedrungen", H. rūa yá-šigga tšīki-n gida, F. ndīam nātoi dar úro, S. hāri āgo-būr hōgu.

[12] dámana ya-kāre. Dieses der Gegensatz dámana ya-fāra slāma, „die Regenzeit hat ihre Vorzeichen angefangen", allerdings ein erst spät aus dem Arabischen eingeführter verfeinerter Ausdruck, F. duńgu fuddi slāma, S. kaidiye s-kā. Hier will ich auch die Redensart einfügen „die Kälte (die kalte Jahreszeit) will eintreten (anfangen)", H. dári kasó n šigga, F. débundé hódi nāttinkē.

[13] gulbī ī-na sūwa. In meiner Handschrift steht suwa, aber es ist unzweifelhaft ī-na sūwa, ganz gleichbedeutend mit išin, „er kommt".

[14] gulbī ī-na tšīka. Ich will hier eine verwandte Phrase hersetzen: „die Muscheln sind vollzählig", kurdī sun-tšīka, eigentlich „sind vollzählig geworden". „Sind die Muscheln vollzählig oder nicht?", H. kurdī sun-tšīka ko bá sun-tšīka bá, F. tšēdī dō hēv-i ko dō hēv-apē.

[15] Siehe Note 10.

[16] māyo hi-wāra entspricht genau dem Kanúri-Ausdruck komádugu išin.

[17] nēma-dē na-tobā, s. S. 118, N. 20.

[18] yōō yēvia. Über das Gleichgültige des Vor- oder Nachsetzens des Zeitworts im Wándalā siehe die Einleitung. Für „Regenzeit" habe ich unter den Substantiven den besonderen Ausdruck wiya.

[19] manē ēī-hedō, wā-hedē. Diese und die folgenden Formen sind in dem das Bágrimma betreffenden Kapitel der Einleitung besprochen.

[20] bā ēī-hedē heisst, wie eine Vergleichung mit manē ēī-hedē zeigt, offenbar eigentlich „der Fluss fliesst auf, ergiesst sich". Auch das Deutsche Wort „ergiessen" hat diese beiden Beziehungen.

[21] ne-bōla ist wahrscheinlich von derselben Wurzel wie mbúl im Kanúri.

[22] óffolo maágin túra. maágin ist ohne Bedeutung als unbestimmtes Pronomen.

Sonyai.	Lógonē.	Wándalā.	Bágrimma.	Māba.
ágo-bána . . .	séma-dé léhiā .	puápuē yōē .	manē ét-kedē[19]	indēl {tiriñg / anmañgin / tiriñg}
bāna a-bíssa . .	séma-dé ná-lehā[17]	a-χē-yōē . .	man(ē) wá-kedē	óffolo mañgin tára[22]
kaidīye {a-bin . / a-bíssa .}	séma ná-lehā .	yōē χévin[18] .	bārwa dēga .	kolēri t-álari
isa-di-n ága-temāli	layam al-añáya .	séma / ánawō} guwō .	bā {ét-kingī . / ét-kedē[20]}	. . . . . .
isa-dī {top . / tonton .}	layam dúkseā .	nátima guwō .	bā ne-bēle[21] .	. . . . . .

[1] délāgo fī-tšīn: fī-tšīn is here evidently an intransitive verb, „rushes, pours down", else we ought to understand délāgo as meaning the stormclouds and supply ēhī, „the stormclouds pour out (the water)". Koelle at least attributes to the verb fī-nishin or, as he writes, pīšgin, only transitive meanings.

[2] délāgo tsi-dūrin: I am not quite sure of the exact meaning of this phrase. dūra-shin means „I fall"; we should therefore expect délāgo tsi-dūrin or, as Koelle writes, tsúdurin, to mean „rain falls", and the term kóndurō délāgi-bē, „rainfall" or „shower of rain", scarcely leaves any doubt as to the correctness of such a meaning, but then we must take into regard, that délāgo has a rather wide meaning and that, what falls, ceases. Thus Koelle himself translates the phrase kógura tsúduri, „there has been a tornado". This certainly might seem not so clear, but the following phrase nīāgeri tsi-dūrin has no proper meaning, if we explain tsi-dūrin by „it falls"; for „the rainy season falls" is nonsense. No doubt the Tédā-language shows the term nīāgeri to have had originally the general meaning of „rain", but that notion has been lost in Kanúri, where, as Koelle himself has it, it means at present nothing, but „rainy season".

[3] nīāgeri tsi-dūrin: see the preceding note.

[4] komádugu tsi-tšīn, derived from tsi-nishin or, as Koelle writes, tšīšgin. Koelle has not this peculiar meaning, but he gives the nearly related one of the coming forth of the seed.

[5] tšīn, see above p. 87, note 7.

[6] tsirgaiain, ts-irgá-iain from yirgá-shin (p. 67, note 2) like tsu-ké-iain from ké-shin, „I mount".

[7] komádugu tsi-mbúi-ena: tsi-mbúi-ena, used also of the belly or the bowels, as tšīrō-ni tsi-mbúi-ena, „my belly is full", evidently is derived from a root mbūi, which appears in the composite word tšīrō-mbuiō or, as Koelle writes, tsuvómbuió, the name of a festival.

[8] nīāgeri fē-kénde: we have here and p. 129, note 15 an instance of the Tédā fē, while the corresponding fī in Kanúri is so much more frequent.

[9] eyī fū-kinde: fū-kinde seems to be closely related to, if not identical with, the fē-kénde of the phrase in the preceding note. Besides we may advert to a distinct opposition of the roots fū and mé. eyī means simply „water", the Tédā having no proper term for lake or river, or having lost it in consequence of their migration into the desert region.

[10] In Hausa I have no term, which fully corresponds with the Kanúri-expression; for the common term for „it rains" viz. H. ta-i rūa, F. dum tobbi, „it makes water", does not correspond exactly. Compare also the phrase expressed in a passive form: „after it had come to rain", H. ané rūa or an-yi rūa, F. mōdum-tobba ndīam.

[11] rūa sun-kāre means verbally „the waters cease or have ceased" and does not correspond exactly with the Kanúri-term, as in the latter the notion of the whole character of the storm has been emphatically expressed. Here I insert the phrase „the rain has penetrated into the house", H. rūa ya-šigga tšīki-n gida, F. ndiam nātoī der ūro, S. hārī ágo-hār hōgu.

[12] dámana ya-kāre: the contrary phrase is dámana ya-fāra alēma, „the rainy season has begun her signs", of course an Arabicised and not indigenous phrase, the term alāma at least being of Arabic origin. F. dadge fuddī alāma, S. kaidīye a-hē. In this place I will also insert the phrase „the cold (cold season) will come in", H. dārī hanē n šigga, F. dēhandē hēdi nāttakē.

[13] guibī šī-na sūwa: my Msc. in this place exhibits sawa, but that, no doubt, is a mistake and it must be sūwa = the Kanúri-term tšīn, „it comes, arrives".

[14] guibī šī-na tšīka: I will here adduce a different meaning of this verb, viz. „the (number of) cowries or shells are (is) complete", H. kurdī sun-tšīka. „Are the cowries complete or not?", H. kurdī sun-tšīka ko bá sun-tšīka bá, F. šēdī dē hēv-i ko dā hēv-ayē.

[15] See note 10.

[16] máyo hi-wāra corresponds exactly with the Kanúri-term komádugu tšīn.

[17] séma-dē ná-lehā: see p. 119, note 20.

[18] yōē χévin: with regard to the indifference of the Wándalā-language to the position assigned to the verb see the introduction. For „rainy season" in Wandalā I have among my list of nouns the particular term wīya.

[19] manē ét-kedē, wá-kedē: with regard to these verbal forms see that chapter of the introductory Remarks which treats of the Bágrimma-language.

[20] bā ét-kedē, as is seen from a comparison with the term manē ét-kedē, has originally only the meaning of „the river flows", pours forth".

[21] ne-bēle is probably from the same root as tsi-mbúi-ena in Kanúri.

[22] óffolo mañgin tára: mañgin is the indefinite pronoun.

Deutsch und Englisch.	Kanúri.	Tédā.	Hausa.	Fulfúlde.
der Fluss tritt über. — *the river rises over its borders*	komá-dugu {zé-bi[1] . / laú-lug-ī}	eyī agā ke-rū-de	gulbī šī-kōwa[11]	māyo modde manum[17]
der Fluss ist zurückgetreten, hat zu sinken angefangen — *the river has begun to recede*	komádugu wel-tī[2]	eyī mō-kinde	gulbī ya-fāra eckī[12]	māyo fūdi džūbo
der Fluss hat abgenommen, ist abgeflossen — *the river has lowered*	komádugu fúlū-tī[3]	. . . . . .	gulbī yá-ulāé[13]	{māyo bēbi . / māyo ya-ūle}
der Fluss ist ausgetrocknet — *the river is at its lowest, has dried up*	komádugu gulū[4]	. . . . . .	gulbī ya-būše[14]	māyo yōri . .
das Kraut kommt hervor, schiesst auf — *the herb comes forth*	kāžim tse-lúg-ena[5]	óberī barāzi ke-rū-de[8]	bakki ši-na fitto	fūdo fuddi .
der Baum treibt Blüthen — — *the tree is in blossom*	késka kámbe-ri {gō-tse-na[6] / tsi-de-na}	{grōgo . . / akā ēderi kinnā-de[9]}	itše ya-tūfe[15]	leggel wfliti .
die Frucht reift — *the fruit ripens*	táta késka-bē būf-in[7]	{tinni ebāf-edē, N.[10] / unnubahange, S.}	da n itše ši-n(a) ánona[16]	biñgel leggel ō-béndi

[1] komádugu zé-bi, laú-lug-ī. Der erste Ausdruck heisst wörtlich „der Fluss hat gegessen" (nämlich „seine Ufer"), von bé-skin, S. 34, N. 3, der zweite „der Fluss ist ausgetreten" („aus seinen Ufern"), von lug-ískin, S. 34, N. 5.

[2] komádugu wel-tī, wörtlich „der Fluss ist zurückgekehrt", von wal-ískin, S. 36.

[3] komádugu fúlū-tī. fúlū-tī kommt von fulū-ógin, „ich ziehe ab", „ich nehme ab"; s. oben S. 66, N. 3.

[4] gulū fehlt bei Koelle; es ist jedenfalls eine ungewöhnliche Form.

[5] kāžim tse-lúg-ena, wieder von lug-ískin; man sagt auch kāžim li-tšin.

[6] késka kámberi gó-tsena oder tsi-dena. Diese beiden Phrasen hat Koelle nicht, aber er hat kámberi, das er kámpeli schreibt. gó-tsena kommt von gō-nískin (s. S. 64), „ich fasse", tsi-de-na von di-skin, „ich mache".

[7] táta késka-bē búf-in: búf-in oder káb-in. Koelle hat eine transitive Form bufískin, „ich koche", obgleich er selbst das Wort für ein intransitivum erklärt; allerdings wird es auch vom Fleisch gebraucht, welches gar geworden ist, wie wir gleich sehen werden.

[8] óberī barāzi ke-rū-de. óberi, vielleicht káburē, „Regenzeit"; unter den Substantiven habe ich für „Kraut" [illegible].

[9] ēderi kinnāde. Über die Bedeutung von ēderi bin ich unsicher. grōgo vielleicht vulgär ke-rū-de.

[10] tinni erscheint in meiner Liste der Substantiva mit der Bedeutung „Dattel"; unnu dagegen habe ich nicht, aber es wird auch wol eine besondere Frucht bezeichnen.

[11] gulbī ši-kōwa bezeichnet eigentlich nicht das Übertreten, sondern das Bewahren des höchsten Niveau's, ähnlich der Fulfúlde-Ausdruck.

[12] gulbī ya-fāra eckī, wörtlich „der Fluss hat angefangen loszulassen".

[13] gulbī ya-ulāé, wörtlich „der Strom ist vorbeigeflossen". Ich will hier die Phrase einschieben „diese Flüsse vereinigen sich, der eine nimmt den anderen auf", H. gúlabé a-wó-nsu su-óka gámu, F. mádde ondém heuri, S. les-di-n ihabé.

[14] gulbī ya-būše. Vom Austrocknen eines Brunnens gebraucht man denselben Ausdruck, so in der Phrase „dieser Brunnen hat nur Wasser zur Regenzeit, in der trockenen Jahreszeit trocknet er aus", H. ridžia a-wó-nsa bābo rūa, sē lotto-n dámana, lotto-n dári ta-na būšo-wā, F. bundu wōle ndiam sē der duñgu, yérra-ndū [hier ist der einfachen Verbalform ein euphonistischer Auslaut angehängt] der dēbbundū; aber man hat auch noch einen anderen Ausdruck, so z. B. „der Brunnen trocknet nicht (niemals) aus", H. ridžia bā kékašē-wa, F. bundu dū hérent-a, S. bongo-di á-ni-hé ábadén.

[15] itše ya-tūfe ist von der Kleidung des Menschen hergenommen und wird wol allgemeiner vom Laube als von den Blüthen verstanden.

[16] ši-n(a) ánona; Präteritum y(a) ánana.

[17] māyo modde manum heisst wörtlich „der Fluss bewahrt sein Grösstes".

[18] bīri-di surba (a)biena kann nicht heissen „der Fluss tritt über", sondern bedeutet wahrscheinlich „der Fluss hört auf (a-biena) zu steigen".

[19] iayam alé ohágaye. Das ohágaye hat, wie der gleich folgende Ausdruck iayam ohágaye zeigt, eine ganz allgemeine Bedeutung, und das „Übertreten" muss allein durch alé ausgedrückt sein.

[20] dek iniabie. Unter den Adjektiven habe ich für „trocken" die Form dekwa.

[21] dádrali; Präteritum derécli.

[22] [illegible]-ga. „ist reif", [illegible]-edi.

[23] bohū tine, simmere tāne siehe das die Mába-Sprache betreffende Kapitel der Einleitung.

Sońyai.	Lógoné.	Wándalá.	Bágrimma.	Mába.
hári-dī zurka (a)bisa[18]	layam la-zúm . . / alā akágaya[19]	paspa guwō .	bā et-kissa .	indžl kolák-terō
faa ágo-sém . .	layam wā . . .	billabūllo guwō	bā esfirro . .	. . . . .
faa-dī kōsi . .	layam akágaya .	billabūllo guwō	bā esfirro . .	
	layam dak intabīa[20]	zabégise guwō	bā ne-dúnge .	. . . . .
sūbo a-fārta . .	ϑowinna róeowā (dúsvoyā?)	yāya kútsepē .	mū tegga . .	lōwa túnguri
	hódugū dawerēlia		kag-ne tádž piña-gā	sungo nō kobū tāne[23]
túguri-iddže nīnin	galī hodúgwā dádraši[21]		kan-kag-ne idž-ga[22]	kolī nimmere tāne

[1] komádugu eé-bi means verbally „the river has devoured (its borders)", from hé-skin (which see above p. 36), komádugu taé-ing-i means „the river has come forth (from its borders)", from ing-éskin (see p. 84, note 3).
[2] komádugu wal-tī means verbally „the river has turned back", from wal-ískin, which see above p. 86.
[3] komádugu fálā-tī: fálā-tī from falā-niskin, falā-ágin, „I take off, diminish"; see above p. 87, note 3.
[4] guiō is wanting in Koelle; it is, no doubt, not a very common form.
[5] kālim tsa-lág-ona, again from ing-éskin; people say also kálim lī-tīia.
[6] kínka kámberi gō-tsena or tal-da-na: Koelle has not these two phrases, but he has the noun, which he writes kāmpeli. gō-tsena is from gō-niskin, gō-ágin (see p. 54), tal-da-na from di-skin, „I do, make".
[7] táta késka-bō bāf-in: bāf-in or báb-in. Koelle gives the verb under the form bāfāskin, „I cook", although he himself declares it to be of an intransitive character; nodoubt it is also used of meat, which is (well) done, but I much doubt, whether the original notion has any thing to do with cooking.
[8] óberi barási ka-rú-de: among my nouns I have lili for „herbage"; óberi may be béberé, „rainy season".
[9] éderi kinnáde: I am uncertain about the meaning of éderi; grōge may be a corruption of ka-rū-de.
[10] tinal appears in my list of nouns with the meaning of „date" tēnī is Mālīy, and I have no doubt, that anne likewise designates some kind of fruit.
[11] gulbī ki-kōwa properly does not denote the inundating of the river, but the preserving of its highest level; the same is the case with the Fulfúlde-term.
[12] gulbī ya-fāra saki means verbally „the river has begun to let loose".
[13] gulbī yá-utšē means verbally „the river has passed by". I will here insert a phrase of a related meaning: „these rivers join", H. gúlabē a-wé-nan sa-áka gámu, F. mádže ondám kenri, S. Isa-di-n ihuhā.
[14] gulbī ya-būše: the same term is used also of a well, which has dried up, as in the phrase „this well has only water during the rainy season, in the dry season it dries up", H. ridžia a-wé-nan bábo rūa sí latte-n dámana, latte-n dāri tá-na būše-wā, F. bandu wóla adíam sí dar dungu, yorre-ndū [here an alliterate termination has been added to the verbal form] dar déhbandū; but besides there is another expression, as in the phrase „the well does not (never) dry up", H. ridžia ba kékašō-wa, F. bandu dū kéreui-š, S. beágo-di á-si-kō bhadén.
[15] itša ya-tūfa: the term ya-tūfa has been adopted from the dressing of men and probably is more generally applied to the foliage, than to the blossom.
[16] Ĭi-n(a) ānona; past tense y(a) ānona.
[17] māyo modde mannam means verbally „the river preserves its greatness, size".
[18] hári-dī zurka (a)bisea can not mean „the river rises above its borders", but means probably „the river ceases to rise".
[19] layam alā akágaya: the term akágaya, as is shown by the directly following phrase layam akágaya has a very general signification, whence we must conclude, that the notion of „the rising above the borders" is alone expressed by the particle alā.
[20] dak intabīa: among my list of adjectives I have the form dakwa for „dry".
[21] dádraši: past tense darásid.
[22] idž-ga: past tense, idž-adī.
[23] kobū tāne, nimmere tāne: see the chapter of the Introductory Remarks, which treats of the Māba-language.

Deutsch und Englisch.	Kanúri.	Tédā.	Hausa.	Fulfulde.
die Frucht ist (noch) nicht reif, ist noch unreif — *the fruit is not (yet) ripe*	táta kúnka-bē bāſ-e-nī	timni {bāſ-e-nī[8] / aweni bāſ-in}	da n itše tókonā ba y(a) ánoná ba	bingel leggol bend-ā
die Frucht ist süss — *the fruit is sweet*	táta kúska-bē lēle-tšin[1]	búdi kēsu[9] .	da n itše ya-ī dādi	. . . . .
das Wasser kühlt sich ab — *the water cools*	ūkī hám-tšena[2]	eyī {wab-tše, S.[10] / wob-kinde, N.}	rūa ya-ī sañi[14]	ndīam fōvi .
das Wasser wird warm — *the water gets warm*	ūkī zimzim-sena[3]	eyī {wálterī, S.[11] / wūeni ki, N.}	rūa ya-ī zāfi	. . . . .
das Wasser kocht — *the water boils*	ūkī to-lár-ena[4]	eyī {tšerauge, S.[12] / ekillak, N.}	rūa yá-tafása	ndīam wūli[17]
das Wasser kocht über — *the water boils over*	ūkī ngēn tau-lár-ō fī-ndžin[5]	. . . . .	rūa yá-tafása har ší-nazuba[15]	ndīam wūli bā-dum ruffi
das Feuer brennt — *the fire burns*	kannu sambin[6]	wuēni artšē[13]	ūta ya-fūra[16]	hīte hubb-āma[18]
das Feuer ist ausgegangen — *the fire is out*	kannu nu-ī[7].	wúēni nós-edē	ūta yá-mutu.	hīte nyifī . .

[1] lēle-tšin fehlt bei Koelle, ist aber doch ganz gewöhnlich im Gebrauch. Auffallend ist nur, dass das einfache Adjektiv lēle, woran es offenbar angelehnt ist, in Bornu gar nicht mehr bekannt ist, während es doch in Bagirmi in derselben Form und im Logone in der nur leicht veränderten Form dēle sich erhalten hat.

[2] hám-tšena ist wol die einzige, grammatisch richtige Schreibweise, obgleich ich gewöhnlich ham-dšina hörte. Ohne deutlichen h-Laut im Anfange habe ich das Wort nie gehört, aber Koelle hat beide Formen, āmgin und hāmgin. Siehe S. 126, N. 11.

[3] zimzim-sena hat Koelle nicht. Das Wort zimzim scheint mir ein Onomatopoietikon und von dem Singen des Wassers hergenommen zu sein.

[4] to-lár-ena. Die Wurzel von diesem Worte ist offenbar lár, und vielleicht identisch mit lag, „herauskommen", wie auch im Logone dasselbe Wort beide Bedeutungen hat. Koelle hat es nicht. Die Form tau-lár-ena scheint nicht gebräuchlich zu sein.

[5] ūkī ngēn tau-lár-ō fī-ndžin, wörtlich „das Wasser läuft oder giesst im Kochen aus dem Kochtopf heraus". Für tau-lár-ō hörte ich gewöhnlich toállero, aber das ist offenbar eine Korruption. fī-ndžin ist eine etwas ungewöhnliche Form für fī-tšin.

[6] kannu sambin. Die Wurzel ist mir ungewiss.

[7] kannu nu-ī, wörtlich „das Feuer ist gestorben", von nú-skin.

[8] timni bāſ-e-ni. bāſ-e-ni ist keine eigentliche Tédā-Form. aweni, „noch nicht" = garre.

[9] búdi kēsu. kēsu heisst „süss", búdi, „sehr"; „Frucht" ist nicht ausgedrückt.

[10] wab-tše, wob-kinde. S. über diese beiden verschiedenen Formen die Prolegomena.

[11] wūeni ki, eigentlich „macht Feuer".

[12] tšerauge. Die Form erinnert an babauge S. 138.

[13] artšē. Wir haben hier einmal eine ganz auffällige Identität mit dem Lateinischen; ardere und besonders das Perf. arsit liegt nahe genug.

[14] rūa ya-ī sañi. Dass die Bedeutung „lass das Wasser im Schlauch abkühlen", H. bar rūa ya-ī sañi tšiki-n salka, F. atšu ndīam dum fōvi der samálle, S. nan hāri-di mayō hambar.

[15] rūa yá-tafása har ší-na zuba, wörtlich „das Wasser hat gekocht, bis es überläuft"; ebenso im Fulfulde.

[16] ūta ya-fūra. Wir haben sowol in diesem Ausdruck wie in dem anderen H. ūta yá-bassa, F. hīte he-bábbi die passive Bedeutung der S. 108 aufgeführten transitiven.

[17] ndīam wūli. Dazu die Negation „das Wasser kocht nicht", H. rūa ba yá-tafásna ba, F. ndīam wūl-di.

[18] hīte hubb-āma steht in engem Verhältnis zu dem in N. 16 aufgeführten he-bábbi und zu dem mōdo-hobba S. 108 als Particip. Pass.

[19] ninin giné, „reift nicht", ist eine ganz ungewöhnliche Form. giné erinnert an das Kanúri genī.

[20] gall tin dádabō. Ich bin hier nicht ganz sicher; vielleicht ist es dindan, „unreif", gánabō, „noch", obgleich das letztere gewöhnlich dem negativen „noch nicht" entspricht.

[21] ámi fú šatáblabī heisst wahrscheinlich in der ersten Bedeutung „das Wasser hat das Feuer in sich aufgenommen".

[22] fú d-aſféya. d-aſféya bietet ein interessantes Beispiel von Verbalbildung; aſféya, „kochen", d-aſféya, „aufkochen".

Bodyal.	Lógoné.	Wándalá.	Bágrimma.	Mába.
nīnín-giná [19] . .	galī tin dádabē [20]	. . . . .	kan-kag-ne ídic-lī	kolī nimmere tā-ūndē
	galī dēlo kadám		kan-kag-ne lēle	. . . . .
hāri-dī yē . .	āmi tēθe . . .	yōē kaša . .	man(e) ōlu .	indži kir-terónge
. . . . . .	āmi fū kalábtabē [21]	yoē ómbra .	man suúgo bāsa-bāsa	indži bong-terón-ge
hāri a-wāsn . .	āmi aθáya . . .	yōē béttukhā .	man tegga .	indži walákte-riógi
hāri a-wāsn bar a-mún	āmi skwōla iθáfne	. . . . .	. . . . .	indži bul-úk-toré
nūne á-fonús .	fū d-aθáya [22] .	tšaūtšuā karā	pō sága . .	waaík nimmere tuni
nūne a-bún . .	fū dámtšá . . .	. . . . .	pō nōēgn . .	waaík tiyo

[1] lōte-tšin is wanting in Kanúri, although its use is very general. However it is remarkable, that the simple adjective lōle, from which it has been derived, is not known in Bórnu, while even in Bagirmi it has remained unchanged and in Lógoné it has been preserved in the slightly changed form dēle.

[2] hám-tšena seems to me to be the only right form from a grammatical point of view, although I heard generally pronounce hám-dšina. At least I always distinguished clearly a h-sound at the beginning of the word, while Kanúri has both forms, ámgin and hámgin. See p. 126, note 11.

[3] almolm-sena is wanting in Kanúri. The term almolm seems to me to be an onomatopy and to be derived from the singing of the water.

[4] te-lár-ena: the root of this verb is evidently lár which may be identical with lag, „to come out", as we see also in Lógoné the same verb to have both meanings. It is wanting in Kanúri. The form ten-lár-ena, which we should expect the more so, when we compare ten-lár-ō of the following phrase, I have never heard.

[5] pkī ágio ten-lár-ō fī-ndšin means verbally „the water pours out from the cooking pot by boiling". Instead of ten-lár-ō however I heard the vulgar form tellore, but I have no doubt, that that is a corruption. fī-ndšin is a rather unusual form for fī-tšin.

[6] kannu nambin: I am not certain of the root of the verbal form.

[7] kannu nu-i means verbally „the fire died", from nú-skin.

[8] tlmai bāf-e-nī: bāf-e-nī is not properly a Tédā-form. ewonī, „not yet" = garre.

[9] bádi kōen: kōen means „sweet", bádi, „very", „fruit" is not expressed.

[10] wab-tša, wab-kinde: the latter is the indigenous form, the former is introduced through the influence of the Kanúri. See the Prolegomena.

[11] wēcni ki properly means „makes fire".

[12] tšerange: the form reminds one of babange p. 132.

[13] ardāō: we have here an example of an accidental identity of the Tédā with the Latin; for ardere and especially ardet are very near at hand.

[14] rūa ya-i sahī: I here subjoin the phrase „let the water cool in the skin", H. bar rūa ya-i sahī tšiki-n salka, F. ñda ndiam dam fēvi der semétie, S. nan hāri-di mayā bumbar.

[15] rūa yá-tafáasa bar ši-na zūba means verbally „the water has boiled, till it pours over", and the same is the meaning of the Fulfúlde-phrase.

[16] ñta ya-fūra: we have as well in this phrase, as in another one H. ñta yá-basan, F. bīte be-bóbbi the passive mood of the forms of the active mood mentioned p. 108.

[17] ndiam wālī: compare the negative form „the water does not boil", H. rūa ba yá-tafáasa ba, F. ndiam wāl-ī.

[18] bīte babb-āma: babb-āma is the participle of be-bóbbi mentioned in note 16, while móde-bobba p. 108 is the active mood.

[19] nīnín-giná, „is not yet ripe" is a very uncommon form in Bodyal, giná reminding one of the Kanúri genī.

[20] galī tin dádabē I am not quite certain of the form being correct: perhaps it ought to be diadan, „unripe", gáaabē, „as yet", although the latter more generally conveys the negative meaning „not yet"; the negation may be expressed twice.

[21] āmi fū kalábtabē in the first signification means probably „the water has absorbed the fire".

[22] fū d-aθáya: the form d-aθáya exhibits an interesting instance of verbal formation; aθáya, „it (the water) boils", d-aθáya, „it (the fire) burns".

Deutsch und Englisch.	Kanúri	Tedā.	Hausa.	Fulfúlde.
der Vogel zwitschert, singt — *the bird is singing*	úngudu tšīr-in[1]	kébri ke-yúḍ-i	tsuntsu šī-na kuka[12]	sundu bivēa
der Hahn kräht — *the cock is crowing*	gábugum kókore se-kín[2]	kókolwadán-kenī	zákara šī-na ka-ka-rāko	dīaka-{ekōwa / ēdi nód-dina} rāri
die Henne gackert — *the hen cackles*	kokī kaká-šin[3]	kóko-ya {tšáḍege / kaká-kenī}	kāza šī-na kér-karu	gértogel édowō-de botšōde[15]
die Henne hat ein Ei gelegt — *the hen has laid an egg*	kokī gibbel kólo-tšī[4]	kókoya sul afúa	kāza tána-yín koī	gértogel herīma botšōde
der Hund bellt — *the dog barks*	kéri tšāmbutin[5]	kédī wōenī	kerre šī-na habši	rauandu hi-wōfa
der Hund beisst — *the dog bites*	kéri {tšī-nándin[6] / tse-tš}	kédī {intšōš / ke-yābi}	kerre šī-na tšizo	rauandu hi-gétta
der Hund wedelt mit dem Schwanz — *the dog wags with the tail*	kéri ngábbere sé-gindin[7]	kédī ām ai hille hákkeni[10]	kerre šī-na rāū da ntšia	rauandu hi-ffyo bokkórde
das Pferd wiehert — *the horse neighs*	fir gugū-tšin[8]	aski {yinni-kenī[11] / yin-yinni}	dōki haninia[13]	putšu hi-hídžia
das Pferd spitzt die Ohren — *the horse pricks the ears*	fir summo fal-tšin[9]	aski summo kinši	dōki šī-na dauki kunne nsa[14]	putšu o-sónyi noffi

[1] tšīr-in, 3te Pers. Sing. von yīr-iskin, das wir vom „Weinen" des Menschen oben S. 56 hatten. Koelle erwähnt die hier gegebene Bedeutung des Wortes nicht.

[2] gábugum kókore se-kín. Anstatt gábugum hat Koelle die sehr verschiedene Form gábōgem oder gábōgum und schreibt die Phrase unter dem Worte kokóreō folgendermassen: gábōgem kokóreō tsekī, das Zeitwort im Präteritum.

[3] kokī kaká-šin fehlt bei Koelle ganz; statt kokī schreibt er kágui.

[4] kokī gibbel kólo-tšī. Statt gibbel schreibt Koelle ágeŋgul, hat aber diese Phrase nicht, dafür hat er kágui ágepel kaltšin, „die Henne brütet Eier", von einem mir unbekannten kalágin.

[5] kéri tšāmbutin. Die Wurzel ist mir unbekannt.

[6] kéri tšī-nandin von dem ungebräuchlichen persönlichen Zeitwort nándeskin, woher nandō, „der Biss". Koelle schreibt tsenándin. — tse-tš, „hat ergriffen" kommt von tsé-skin S. 64.

[7] ngábbere sé-gindin. sé-gindin von gind-iskin, das aber selten gebraucht wird. Koelle hat zwar dieses Zeitwort in der Form gendiskin, aber meine Phrase hat er nicht.

[8] gugū-tšin scheint ebenfalls bei Koelle zu fehlen. Vielleicht hängt es mit kógō, „Stimme, Laut" zusammen.

[9] fir summo fal-tšin. Koelle hat diese Bedeutung von fal-niskin oder palágin, wie er schreibt, nicht; denn weder stimmt sie zu seinem „ich tausche", noch zu der Bedeutung „ich theile, schneide entzwei, spalte", obgleich sie sich der letzteren anschliesst.

[10] kédī ām ai hille hákkeni heisst wol eigentlich „der Hund begrüsst diese Leute"; „Schwanz" hōde.

[11] aski yinni-kenī oder yin-yinni. Das Zeitwort steht dem Arabischen sehr nahe, braucht deshalb aber eben so wenig wie das entsprechende Hausa-Wort von ihm abgeleitet zu sein, da diese Ausdrücke [illegible] dem natürlichen Laute nachgeahmt sind.

[12] tsuntsu šī-na kuka. Es ist eigenthümlich, dass sowol das lebhafte Hausa- wie das melancholischere Kanúri-Volk das Singen der Vögel als ein Weinen oder Jammern auffassen; denn auch kuka heisst in Bezug auf den Menschen „weinen", obgleich Schön es auch vom „rufen" gebraucht. — Ich will hier ein paar andere Redensarten vom Vogel einschieben: „der Vogel fliegt, fliegt auf", H. tsuntsu na-šaági [šī-na šaági?], F. sundu bi-wolēda, S. tšēre é-tuse; „der Vogel senkt sich herab", H. tsuntsu šī-na sabka, F. sundu dīippoka.

[13] dōki haninia, s. Note 11.

[14] dōki šī-na dauki kunne-nsa. Ich will hier zwei begriffsverwandte Phrasen im H. und F. einschieben, die ich n den anderen Sprachen nicht vertreten kann: „das Pferd fürchtet sich", H. dōki šī-na tsorō, F. putšu hi-happa, und H. dōki šī-na seántsamo, F. putšu helémno.

[15] gértogel édowōde botšōde scheint die ursprüngliche Bedeutung „die Henne schreit nach Eiern" zu haben.

[16] kolá tšō sawā scheint mir bei einer Vergleichung mit tšila tšō sawā einigermassen verdächtig.

[17] hérsh hemim ist sehr prägnant und kurz.

Sotyal.	Logone.	Wandala.	Bagrimma.	Maba.
. . . . . .	šíšiá θē suwē	ódχwā giyó .	el nō . . .	koäfk burnir
. . . .	kuskū na-bē ladán	. . . . . .	ṅgab kindže lá el-nū	
. . . .	ku-kū tokálkal .	ókulā kaka .	kindša na-nálkoi	kārik kékimír
gorúṅgu a-dán gún-gori	ku-kū dabél θalā	beláblimača (o)ku-lā	kindā(n) élal kab-ga	kārik nado
hanši dō-sū . .	kalá (o)ṅger . .	kr(ē) ámbuχā	bīse-no ol-káṅge	ṅuk wógnir
hanši {ága-nā-madā / dō-nam .}	kalá θenni θenda	áwa krē . .	bīse-ne dāónyi	ṅuk níserók
hanši ága-kár ága-dāra	kalá θē suwō [16] .	. . . . . .	bīse-ne tugdž ēl(a) aṅga	ṅuk kelók kelók-nir
búri {ága-kāti . / dō džaṅga .}	buakwán ālamlím	ádžemā bélimā	sinda hirinya .	bérek hanhányir
béri aká-indíṅgo haṅga	buakwán ántata šemáye	. . . . . .	sinda ná étker imbī-nya	bérek bemím [17]

[1] tāir-in, 3rd pers. sing. from yir-iakin, the same verb, which we have had p. 56 for the „weeping" of man. Koelle does not even mention that meaning of this verb, which we give in this place.

[2] gábugam kókore ao-kin: instead of gábugam Koelle has the very different form góbógem or góbógum and writes the whole phrase in the past tense (sub voce kokóreō): góbógem kokóreō taáhi.

[3] koki koká-kin is wanting in Koelle. Instead of koki he has kágai.

[4] koki gibbal kóle-tāi: instead of gibbal or ágibbal Koelle writes ágopal, but he has not this phrase, while he gives another one, which I have not, via kágai ágopai kaltšin, „the hen is brooding eggs" from a verb kalágin.

[5] kéri tšámbatin: root unknown to me.

[6] kéri tšē-nándin from the verb nándąkin, whence also nandā is derived, „the kite". Koelle writes taqnándin. — tao-tō, „has seized" is from tā-akin p. 64.

[7] ágábbere aé-gindin: aé-gindin from gind-iakin, which however is very rarely used. Koelle has the verb in the form gendýakin, but he has not the phrase.

[8] gagā-tšin seems likewise to be wanting in Koelle; it may have some connection with kógó, „voice, sound".

[9] fir aqmmo fai-tšin: Koelle has not this notion of fai-niakin or pelágin, as he writes it; for neither does it agree with the notion of „I change", nor with the other one of „I divide, cut in two, split", although it approaches in some degree the latter one.

[10] kédi ám ai bilio bákkeni: I have no doubt, means „the dog salutes, bids welcome these people".

[11] aoki yianí-kani or yia-yinai: the verb approaches very nearly the corresponding Arabic term, but that is no proof of its being thence derived, so little as the Hausa-verb, as all these terms are formed in imitation of the natural sound.

[12] tsuntsu ši-na kūka: it seems remarkable, that as well the lively Hausa-people, as the more melancholically disposed Kanúri regard the singing of the bird rather as a weeping or lamenting; for even kūka, if used of human beings, means „to weep", „to cry". — I shall insert in this place a few other phrases with reference to the bird, such as „the bird flies, soars", H. tsuntsu na-šanági (perhaps ši-na šanági), F. sonda ši-walóda, S. tšēra á-tunu; „the bird descends", H. tsuntsu ši-na sabka, F. sonda dāippakō.

[13] dāki hauainia, see note 11.

[14] dóki ši-na dauki kāsas-aaa: in this place I will insert two phrases of a similar meaning in H. and F., as I have not learned the corresponding terms in the other languages: „the horse is frightened", H. dóki ši-na tsorá, F. puttšu hi-káppa, and H. dóki ši-na tudntsuma, F. puttšu helámno.

[15] gértogel ádawáde bokšōde seems to have the original meaning „the hen cries for eggs".

[16] kalá θē suwō seems rather a little suspicious, if we compare it with the term šíšiá θē suwō.

[17] bérek bemím is so short as pregnant a term.

Deutsch und Englisch.	Kanúri.	Tédā.	Hausa.	Fulfúlde.
das Pferd macht Capriolen — *the horse is capering*	fir biskē-dšin [1]	aski áfi kinâi [7]	dōki ší-na tumtuma dōki ya-lála-tšē [8]	putšu be-lúmmo putšu umlaláta-kē
das Pferd (der Hengst) belegt — *the horse covers*	fir felē-ze [2] .	aski súbozī .	dōki ší-na bāl [9]	putšu é-bóllina
das Pferd wälzt sich — *the horse is rolling*	fir fīwi-din [3] .	aski ulétinī .	dōki na-bérkida / ya-ī bérgima	putšu bi-tállo
die Kuh kalbt — *the cow is calving*	fē tsambin [4] .	furā tšerérre .	sánia tá-na haifo	negge rimi .
die Kuh — *the cow* / das Kamel — *the camel* } käut wieder — *is ruminating*	fē . . / kargimmo } dšū-gō-tšin [5]	furā / gōne } tšuggo kāki	sánia / rákomi } na-tuke [10]	negge / gelōba } yákkito
das Kamel schnäuzt sich — *the camel throws up its muzzle*	kargímmo kin-zā bak-tšin [6]	gōne fúrtšenfk	rákomi ší-na bugga kai [11]	gelōba be-dímba bōre

[1] biskē-dšin, „spielt" ist eins der vielen Wörter, die, auch vom Menschen gebraucht, bei den Thieren in unseren technisch so ausgebildeten Sprachen anderen Ausdrücken entsprechen. Koelle schreibt, wie schon oben S. 60, N. 5 erwähnt ist, das Substantiv bēgō, und das davon abgeleitete Zeitwort begōngin.

[2] fir felē-ze ist ein sonderbarer Ausdruck: er ist doch wol von felē-ziekin oder, wie Koelle schreibt, pélōgin abgeleitet, welches ich sonst nur in der Bedeutung „entfalten", „zeigen" gefunden habe; was hat aber das Bespringen des Pferdes damit zu thun? Vielleicht „er zeigt, entfaltet seine Kraft, zeigt sich".

[3] fīwi-din fehlt wieder bei Koelle. din kommt offenbar von di-ekin und vertritt tsī-din.

[4] tsambin (t-s-amb-in) ist das gewöhnliche, auch für das Gebären des Menschen gebräuchliche Zeitwort, S. 34, N. 1.

[5] dšū-gotšin. Dieser Ausdruck fehlt bei Koelle, ist aber wol nur eine andere stärkere Ausdrucksweise, gō-tšin von gō-niskin, „nehmen, fassen", für dšū-niskin oder, wie Koelle schreibt, dšūngin, „ich stopfe, drücke etwas vorwärts". S. die Einleitung.

[6] kargimmo kin-zā bak-tšin, wörtlich „das Kameel schlägt die Nase", kin-zā hier wegen des folgenden tš statt kin-tsā (kin-tšī). Koelle hat den Ausdruck nicht; übrigens schreibt er einzeln kaligimó, kéntsá und baktšin.

[7] aski áfi kinâi steht offenbar in engem Bezug zur vorhergehenden Phrase und heisst vielleicht „das Pferd bewegt die Beine".

[8] dōki ya-lálatšē entspricht, glaube ich, nicht ganz genau der Bedeutung des biskē-dšin, sondern hat mehr die Bedeutung „scheu-, störrig sein", aber einen völlig entsprechenden Ausdruck habe ich nicht. Ich führe hier aber einige andere begriffsverwandte Ausdrücke an, die ich nur im Hausa und Fulfúlde habe: „das Pferd hat sich auf die Hinterbeine gestellt", H. dōki ya-tāši biana, F. putšu fáido; „das Pferd springt", H. dōki ší-na tumā, F. putšu be-diwāli; „das Pferd hat Tücke", H. dōki ší-na gúrmantā, F. putšu hi-lelddāa; „das Pferd geht rückwärts", H. dōki na-géwayá, F. putšu hí-táro; „das Pferd scharrt den Boden", H. dōki ší-na ginna kasa, F. putšu be-irte lēdi; „das Pferd schlägt hinten aus", H. dōki ší-na bugga da kaffa, F. putšu be-fi be kolāgel, und fast in ganz gleicher Bedeutung H. dōki ší-na da šúri, F. putšu gaégu latte.

[9] dōki ší-na bāl, wörtlich „das Pferd steigt auf".

[10] sánia na-tuke. Ich will hier einige andere Phrasen einfügen, die ich nur im Hausa und Fulfúlde habe: „die Kuh brüllt", H. sánia tá-na kūka (ein etwas allgemeiner und unbestimmter Ausdruck), F. negge hénnki, S. hau dgákurū; „die Kuh ist scheu geworden, ist fortgelaufen", H. sánia ta-firgitta tá-godā, F. negge faidāl; „die Fliegen haben sie verwirrt gemacht", H. kudā sun-báukatá-ši, F. būbe báugakí negge; „die Kühe stehen verwundert still", H. šāno na-bōda, F. nai be-bōra; „die Kühe grämen", d. h. „kommen neugierig heran", H. šāno su-nyi márhaba, F. nai dšabbāko; „die Kühe sind zur Tränke gegangen", H. šāno sún-tafi ari n madšekaré, F. nai dōmoi (ein sehr prägnanter Ausdruck); „die Kühe sind in's Gras gegangen", H. šāno sun-táši, sún-tafi ari n hekki, F. nai berti di šōdoi; „der Stier wühlt den Boden auf", H. bádšini ší-na ginna u kasa, F. kalhálde he-irte lēdi.

[11] rákomi ší-na bugga kai. Ich will hier noch zwei Ausdrücke vom Kameel anführen: „das Kameel kniet", H. rákomi ya-mike káfafū, F. gelōba forti koide; „das Kameel legt sich, kniet nieder" (um die Last aufzunehmen), H. rákomi kása na-šefa, F. gelōba be-witše lēfe.

[12] bushwán á-owohāl bushwán ālgaaám, „das (männliche) Pferd besteigt das weibliche Pferd (die Stute)". In dieser Phrase haben wir „die Stute" besonders ausgedrückt, sonst aber in keiner anderen dieser Sprachen, ausser im Māba, wo es aber keineswegs so deutlich ist.

[13] intšā daó. Danach können wir nun verbessern S. 35 gabám daó wále, „die Frau gebiert einen Sohn" anstatt des falschen darbāli.

[14] ádšire légomā. Über die Ableitung von légomā habe ich in der Einleitung gesprochen.

[15] bérek módši ginin-táne. Unter den Substantiven habe ich für „Stute" bérek módšum, also ist módši wol der Accusativ, wenn bérek nicht wiederholt ist, obgleich módšum ein Adjektiv und der Gegensatz dazu, nämlich mar. „männlich", bei bérek gar nicht besonders ausgedrückt ist.

Sonyai.	Lógoné.	Wándalá.	Bágrimma.	Mába.
. . . .	bąskwán á-θabā	bélimā guaā .	sinda et-nánga	bérek ágtelē
. . . .	bąskwán á-swokál) bąskwán alganám[12]	takā bélimā .	sinda da-kinya	bérek módši ginta-táno[15]
béri dö billim billim	bąskwán abútkala	. . . . . .	sinda netbábla	bérek tatóngulō
hau bai . . .	inθā duē[13] . .	yaiā θā . . .	mang ét-kodžō	dek wai tunti
. . . .	inθā . } áwegen kúrguma } áwegen	ádida θā . . ádžire légomē[14]	mang } etgúldža lúguma } etgúldža	dok tángaro tórrombok yer-rek tenēri
	kúrgum(a) á-deašk gaenī	légom(o) adžék tarō	lúguma etúk omí-nya	tórrombok fúr-terī

[1] bishō-dšin, „is playing" is one of the many terms, which are applied as well to human beings as to animals, but with regard to the latter correspond to very different words in our languages. Koelle, as already mentioned on a former occasion, writes the substantive bęsgō, and the verb, which has been thence derived, bęsgōngin.
[2] fir felō-an is a remarkable expression. It is, no doubt, an intransitive form of felō-nishin or pélóngin, as Koelle writes the verb, but that has only the meaning of „I develope, unfold, show", and it is not easily to be seen, what the covering of a stallion has to do with that meaning, if we do not supply something like the following „it shows (itself as a horse)", so that it approaches the import of the English word „to horse".
[3] fiwi-din is also wanting in Koelle's vocabulary; din is evidently the 3rd pers. sing. of di-shin and takes the place of tsi-din.
[4] tsambin (t-s-amb-in), 3rd pers. sing. of tsmbó-shin, is the term generally used also of women, p. 85, note 1.
[5] dšā-gōtšin is wanting in Koelle, but probably is only a stronger term for dšā-nishin or dšāngin, as Koelle writes it, giving it the meaning of „I push, press, move a thing forward". ni-shin, „I make", gō-nishin, „I seize, take".
[6] kargimme kin-sā bah-tšin means verbally „the camel beats the nose". Koelle has not this expression, while he writes the single words kaligimé, kéntsā and bahtšin.
[7] nehi šīl kindši has evidently a close relation to the preceding Tédā-phrase and, according to all probability, means originally „the horse moves the legs".
[8] dōki ya-iálatšē, I think, does not correspond exactly with the notion of the Kanúri-term bishō-dšin, but has rather the meaning of „being skittish"; but, I think, the Hausa-people do not employ the term ši-na orgi of the horse in the same sense, as the Kanúri do their bishō-dšin. I here adduce a few more terms of a related meaning, for which I have learnt the corresponding terms only in Hausa and Fulfúlde, such as „the horse is prancing", H. dōki ya-tšši biese, F. putšu fáido; „the horse is springing", H. dōki ši-na tumá, F. putšu ho-diwātši; „the horse plays tricks", H. dōki ši-na gármantá, F. putšu hi-taládde; „the horse is going backwards", H. dōki na-gēwaye, F. putšu hi-táro; „the horse paws (the ground)", H. dōki ši-na giana kása, F. putšu ho-irte lōdi; „the horse is kicking", H. dōki ši-na hugga da kaffa, F. putšu ho-fi ho koingel, and almost conveying the same meaning H. dōki ši-na da šári, F. putšu guágu letta.
[9] dōki ši-na hāi means verbally „the horse mounts".
[10] sánia na-ihke: I will here insert a few other phrases, for which I have the corresponding terms only in Hausa and Fulfúlde: „the cow is lowing", H. sánia tá-na kūka (a rather vulgar and inexpressive term), F. nagge hāenki, H. has égá-kurú; „the cow has taken fright (and) is running away", H. sánia ta-firgitta tá-gudú, F. nagga faidši; „the flies have started her (the cow)", H. budá sun-hánkalá-ši, F. bōhe hánghō nagge; „the cows are standing gazing", H. šāno na-háda, F. nai ha-hōre; „the cows are saluting", that is to say „approach from curiosity", H. šāno su-nyi márhaba, F. nai dášhháke; „the cows are gone to water", H. šāno sún-tafi uri n waší-karō, F. nai dúmol (a short and very pregnant term); „the cows are gone grazing" (especially used of distant pasture-grounds), H. šāno sún-táši, sún-tafi uri n hákki, F. nai borti di tšōdoi; „the bull paws the ground", H. bádšani ši-na giana n kása, F. balhálde ha-irte lōdi.
[11] ráhomi ši-na hugga hal: I will adduce in this place two other expressions with regard to the camel, first „the camel is limping", H. ráhomi ya-mike háfafū, F. golōba footi koldei „the camel kneels down" (in order to take up the load), H. ráhomi kása na-šáfa, F. golōba ha-witše láfe.
[12] bąskwán á-swokál bąskwán alganám, „the (male) horse covers the female horse"; in this phrase the word „mare" is distinctly expressed, while of the corresponding languages the Mába alone has something of the sort.
[13] inθā duē: from this phrase we are able to correct another phrase, writing with certainty p. 35 ganám duē wála, „the woman bears a child" instead of davéšli.
[14] ádžire légomē: of the source, whence the term légomē has been derived, I have spoken in the Introductory Remarks.
[15] bérek módši ginta-táno: in my list of nouns I have bérek módšum for „mare"; módši therefore may be taken to be the accusative case, bérek being not repeated a second time, although módšum is merely an adjective and opposed to mar, „male", which is not expressed.

Deutsch und Englisch.	Kanúri.	Tēdā.	Hausa.	Fulfúlde.
der Hammel blökt — *the ram, the sheep is bleating*	ŋgelārō tšīrin[1]	sádege tšǵdege	ragō šī-na kūra	karrōri } be-wōyn
der Ziegenbock mäckert — *the goat is bleating*	dal búlolē-džim[2]	. . . . . .	búnsuru } šī-na kūka	belōri } be-wōyn
die Hyäne schreit — *the hyena howls*	bultu tšīrin[3] .	múlohul tšūdi	kūra } šī-na kūka	džāro } be-wōyn
der Löwe brüllt — *the lion roars*	kúrguri nuk-tšin[4]	dúguri tšǵdege	zāki šī-na rūori[8]	džágge-re {be-útta / be-únuan}
der Skorpion sticht — *the scorpion stings*	kelándži tse-nán-din[5]	étū kyābi . .	kunāma šī-na halbi[9]	yáhare (be-)fiddi
die Mücke sticht — *the gnat stings*	kántana tši-nán-din[6]	entēki kyābi .	sábbero šī-na tšīzo	boṅgu bi-gāttu
die Schlange kriecht — *the snake creeps along*	kādī tsorō-ntse lē-tšin	auso derōno tē-din[7]	[10]	

[1] ŋgelārō schreibt Koelle ŋgelárá. — tšīrin natürlich wieder von yīr-tšin (S. 136, N. 1), das, während es eine sehr beschränkte Bedeutung in Bezug auf den Menschen besitzt, sobald es in den Thierkreis gezogen wird, die weiteste Beziehung erhält und die mannichfaltigsten Töne vertreten muss.

[2] dal bólolē-džin. Koelle hat weder das Substantiv dal, noch das Zeitwort.

[3] bultu tšīrin. Über tšīrin s. N. 1. Von den Hyänen, der einen Species wenigstens, ist der Ausdruck „weinen" eben nicht unpassend.

[4] kúrguri nuk-tšin. Das Zeitwort in dieser Form fehlt bei Koelle, aber er hat nundúngin ganz in derselben Bedeutung vom Löwen und Büffel: statt kúrguri in dieser Bedeutung schreibt er kúrgull oder kurúgulō, wol besonders, um es von dem Adjektiv kúrguri, „weiblich" zu unterscheiden.

[5] kelándži tse-nándin, wörtlich „der Skorpion beisst", tse-nándin hier des Wohllautes halber statt tši-nándin, s. oben S. 136, N. 6. Koelle hat die Phrase nicht.

[6] kántana. Koelle accentuirt kantána.

[7] auso derōno tēdin. Über das derōno bin ich nicht ganz sicher; tēdin, „geht".

[8] rūori sieht dem Englischen roar merkwürdig nahe, aber es ist eine in der Sache und Anschauung begründete Ähnlichkeit.

[9] kunāma šī-na halbi. „Hat mich gestochen", H. yá-halbē-ni, F. fiddi-yá. halbi vom Pfeil gebraucht. S. 88, N. 10.

[10] Den Ausdruck „die Schlange kriecht dahin" habe ich auf Hausa nie gehört, dagegen aber habe ich den Ausdruck „die Schlange beisst (den Menschen)", H. mátšidži šī-na tsára (mutúm), F. bógul leadi („der Erdstrich") múmtsaki.

[11] nasmio ist auffallend und mir sonst unbekannt; unter den Nennwörtern habe ich für „Hammel" sōgl, aber das mag auf einer Verwechselung beruhen, da es dem Ausdruck für „Löwe" sehr ähnlich sieht.

[12] sil págin bābu kann ich auch nicht erklären; für „Ziegenbock" habe ich mampōli.

[13] imfagē affūntal. Wahrscheinlich ist die letzte Silbe ein Wort für sich und bedeutet „Stachel" oder sonst etwas und dasselbe gilt von der nächsten Phrase.

[14] ātyiō indule. ātyiō wird häufig wie ātšo gesprochen.

[15] ātyiō ērwora. Eine solche Umstellung des Zeitworts, wie ich sie hier ausdrücklich in den beiden Phrasen gegeben, könnte man fast bei jeder Phrase vornehmen.

[16] sābe didalā hod(ē)-āra. Die beiden letzten Wörter habe ich aus Conjectur geschrieben, aber sie ist wol völlig sicher. didalā, „(er) geht", hod(ē)-āra, „mit seinem Leibe". adálba ledára, was in meiner Handschrift steht, ist durch vulgäre Aussprache verdorben.

[17] ayaégo. Unter den Substantiven habe ich für „Hyäne" nur ayīgo.

[18] katš. Der End-Vokal ist wegen des folgenden o in sī-nō weggefallen; wenn es ein a ist, so haben wir hier offenbar nur eine andere Form für kagn, aber unter den Substantiven habe ich dieses Wort für „Leopard", während für „Löwe" tōhlo erscheint.

[19] hokēš ist Arabisch.

[20] drehēk tšil. Unter den Substantiven habe ich für „Hyäne" die Form drehēk.

[21] gērringak tlaīrō. Für „Skorpion" habe ich unter den Substantiven die Form tērringah.

[22] ēgalah. Unter den Substantiven habe ich dafür die Form āgalah, und zwar aus demselben Munde; so schwankend ist die Aussprache in diesen ungeschriebenen Sprachen, und solche Verschiedenheiten kehren bei allen Wörtern wieder.

Sońyai.		Lógoné.	Wándalā.	Bágrimma.		Mába.
ága-tónton	fēgi .	uxemla tsuwō[11] .	kiane étχōē .	bāl(a) .		kebéš[19] álebléb-terē
ága-tónton	hantšin	ail gágin bābu[12]	wúsalē ūksūa nauc	bāl(a) .	et-nō	mūdāl hólulū-terē
kōro . .	ága-hēng	dādu tsuwō . .	átχiō índale[14]	nyuńgo[17]		drebék tōli[20]
gengin mūši	ága-hēng	zéweni tsuwō . . / zéweni adíyakū .	érwere tχiō . / átχiō érwere[15]	katš[18]		amrek tériyē
donton bīre . .		ímθagē aθántal[13]	wīw óritaš . .	. . . . . .		tórringek tísirē[21]
. . . .		bíllaθē dodávtal .	wīw úgdžindža	ēlu θamma .		égelek tinyēri[22]
. . . .		mār(c) alu uńgunnénni	zāhe éldalā bod(ē)-āra[16]	kelā ne-kanya		. . . . .

[1] ágelárō is written by Koelle ágalárō. — tīlria: here we have again this term (yīr-lakin), which, while applied to human beings it has such a restricted meaning, obtains such a wider range of notion, at least, when compared with the great perfection of our technical terms, as soon as it is applied to the animal kingdom, in consequence of all the different sounds having been regarded by the natives from one and the same point of view.

[2] dal hélelō-dīla: Koelle has neither the term dal, nor the verb.

[3] holla tīlria: with regard to the verb tīlria see note 1.

[4] hárgarī anā-tšin: the verb is wanting in Koelle in this form, while he has another one aaaárāgin, which has remained unknown to me, with the very same meaning; instead of hárgarī with this meaning he writes hárgalī or harágalī, perhaps only in order to distinguish it from the adjective hárgarī, „female".

[5] kalándšī tee-nándia means properly „the scorpion bites", tee-nándia here from reasons of euphony instead of tšī-nándia; see above p. 136, note 8. Koelle has not the phrase.

[6] kántaua: Koelle places the accent on the second syllable, thus: kantáua.

[7] auso deršaa lōdia: with regard to the term deršao I am not quite certain; lōdia, „walks".

[8] rūarī bears a remarkable resemblance to the English to roar, but that resemblance is not based upon any identity of origin, but upon an identity of mental conception.

[9] hundma šī-na halhi: „it has stung me", M. yé-halhō-nī, P. fiddī-yé. — halbi of the arrow p. 98, note 10.

[10] I have not learnt the Hausa-term for „the snake creeps along", but instead I have taken down another expression, viz „the snake bites (the man)", H. mátšidšī šī-na ledra (mutúm), F. bōgal leadī (verbally „the earth-rope") mómlaká.

[11] uxomla is not known to me, as among my nouns I have „ram" represented by the term alfgī, but the latter may be wrong, as it bears some close resemblance to the term meaning „lion".

[12] ail gágin bābu: I am not able to explain this phrase; for „goat" in my list of nouns I have mampōtī.

[13] ímθagē aθántal: I suspect, that the last syllable does not belong to the verb, but is a word by itself, meaning „sting" or something else and the same seems to be the case with the following phrase.

[14] átχiō índale: átχiō is frequently pronounced like átšo.

[15] átχiō érwere: such a transposing of the verb, as is here expressly represented by the two phrases, might almost take place with every single phrase in the Wándalā-language.

[16] zāhe éldalā bod(ē)-āre: the two last words I have written from conjecture, but I am fully convinced that I am right: éldalā, „in going, walking", bodō-āra, „with" or „on his belly". What my Mscr. exhibits, adālha lodāre is undoubtedly corrupted in consequence of vulgar pronunciation.

[17] nyuńgo: among my list of substantives I have only the form nyīgo for „hyena".

[18] katš: the final vowel has been absorbed by the following e in et-nō; if it was an a, then we have here another form for kaga, but in my list of nouns that term represents „leopard", while for „lion" I have another term tóbio.

[19] kebéš is Arabic.

[20] drebék tōlī: among my nouns I have the form drabák.

[21] tórringek tísirō: also in this instance I have a slightly different form for the noun, when written alone, viz térringek.

[22] égelek: here again I have a slightly different form, viz ágalák, and all this from the same mouth. So great is the wavering of sounds in these illiterate languages; and such differences occur almost with every word.

Sammlung und Bearbeitung
Central-Afrikanischer Vokabularien

von

Heinrich Barth.

Dritte Abtheilung.

Nennwörter.

Collection

of

vocabularies of Central-African languages

compiled and analyzed

by

Henry Barth, C. B. D. C. L.

3^d part.

Nouns.

Gotha: Justus Perthes.

1866.

Nennwörter.

Nouns.

Deutsch und Englisch.	Kanúri.	Téda.	Hausa.	Fulfúlde.
Gott, unser Herr, unser Vater — *God, our Lord, our Father*	Alla (Arb.) . kémā-ndē [1] .	Alla kénuō . . .	Alla	Alla . . . Dīomirāo tše-nīdo [12]
Welt — *world*	dunya [2] (Arb.)	dúnya . . .	dunya [9] . . .	dūnyāro . .
letzter Tag, Weltgericht, andere Welt — *last day, day of judgement, next world*	láhira [3] (Arb.)	lária	al áhira . .	al áhira . .
Paradies — *paradise* .	dženna [4] (Arb.)	aldženna . .	aldženna . . alitšana [10] . .	aldženna . .
Hölle — *hell*	kannu džānem [5] (h. Arb.)	wūēni lária [7] .	aldžehénnema	al džehénnema
Teufel — *devil*	džin [6]	mōši [8] . . . eldžēnū . .	seitāna [11] . .	alseitānu . .

[1] kémā-ndē, wörtlich „Herr, Gebieter von uns", „unser Herr". Selbst kémā ist aber entschieden nicht das ursprüngliche Kanúri-Wort für „Gott", und auch hier war es wol unzweifelhaft ein Wort, das zugleich den Himmel mit bezeichnete, vielleicht Kāma. Denn der Islam hat, wie S. XXIV und XXVIII der Einleitung ausgeführt, die ursprünglichen Ausdrücke für diese heidnischen Begriffe verdrängt. Vergleiche dazu, was Bile in seiner Vorrede zu den Elementen der Otjo-Sprache S. VII und VIII Treffliches über diesen Gegenstand sagt, den ich noch weiter bei den kleinen Vokabularien besprechen muss, die eben, weil sie vom Islam noch nicht berührt sind, durch die Vergleichung mit den hier repräsentirten verwandten, aber mohammedanisirten Sprachen den schönsten Aufschluss geben. Einige Hauptbegriffe musste ich hier hersetzen, dagegen lasse ich andere, als rein dem Islam angehörig, wie die Beinamen Gottes, z. B. „Schöpfer", K. aläkte-ma (von aläkte, wieder von aläk [خلق]-aläkin) u. s. w. hier fort, da sie alle dem Arabischen entnommen sind.

[2] dunya. Koelle schreibt, als klares Beispiel schwankender Orthographie in diesen Sprachen, dinie, dinie und dūnyā.

[3] láhira unzweifelhaft aus dem Arabischen الآخرة; Koelle schreibt lāira und láhira, giebt aber die eigentliche Bedeutung gar nicht, da er „Grab und andere Welt" nur in zweiter Instanz bezeichnet; Koelle hat aber ausserdem noch für „die andere Welt, Ewigkeit" den mir in dieser Form wenigstens unbekannten Ausdruck ligāma.

[4] dženna auch dzanna geschrieben. Über diese Orthographie s. Einleitung S. XXXVIII und XLII. Koelle schreibt tšannā.

[5] kannu džānem ist eine nicht ganz grammatische Komposition und soll eigentlich heissen kannu džānem-be, „das Feuer der Hölle". Koelle verleiht schon dem Ausdrucke kannu allein in zweiter Instanz die Bedeutung „Höllenfeuer, Hölle", das kann aber nur durch den Zusammenhang der Rede geschehen.

[6] džin ist das Arabische جن. Koelle hat für dieses Wort zwei ächt nationale Ausdrücke, keliram, „Waldteufel" und ágameram, „Wasserteufel"; ausserdem giebt Koelle noch als selbstständigen Ausdruck kériram mit langer Erklärung, das ist aber unkritisch, da kériram nur dialektische Nebenform von, und völlig identisch mit keliram ist. Dies sind nur zwei concrete Darstellungen des böswilligen verderblichen Naturgeistes, dessen Vorstellung allen Naturvölkern neben der Ansicht von einer guten, daher nicht gefürchteten und kaum verehrten, Gottheit, die sie mit dem Firmament, mit der Sonne und den Gestirnen identificiren, so überwiegend eigen und das zu versöhnen ihr Hauptbestreben ist. Ganz dasselbe haben wir nicht allein bei anderen Afrikanischen, sondern auch bei den meisten Amerikanischen und Asiatischen Völkerschaften, so den Tschuktschen im äussersten Asien, ja selbst noch heut zu Tage eigentlich bei unserem gemeinen Volke selbst. Auf diesem Glauben beruht das ganze Princip der Zauberei, der Menschenopfer und der Gottesgerichte.

[7] wūēni lária eigentlich „Feuer des letzten Gerichtes".

[8] mōši scheint ein originelles Wort zu sein, eldžēnū dagegen ist wol nur eine corrumpirte Form des Arabischen Plurals.

[9] dunya. Ich will hier noch den Ausdruck für „Schöpfung" im H. und F. hersetzen, H. tahalitta, F. tagafōdi.

[10] alitšana. Diesen der Arabisch-moslimischen Sprache und Vorstellung mit der höchst irdischen Anschauungsweise des Paradieses vollkommen eingebürgerten Ausdruck hat Schön in allen seinen Übersetzungen biblischer Stücke zur Darstellung des christlichen Himmels gebraucht, aber solche Anwendung hat etwas entschieden Missliches, wovon Schön auch seinen eigenen Bemerkungen, Niger-Expedition S. 180, sich überzeugen muss.

[11] Schön giebt in seinem Wörterbuch 1843 für Teufel „the evil one" ein Wort alaki, das mir aber eben so wenig bekannt geworden ist, wie das Adjektiv und Substantiv alahaki, „teuflisch, Teufel".

[12] dīomirāo, das wol mit emir zusammenhängt, für sich heisst allerdings nur „Herr" und erhält die Bedeutung von „höchster Herr" eigentlich nur durch den Beisatz tšenīdo, doch wird auch schon das Erste allein in der Bedeutung von „Gott" gebraucht. Reichardt schreibt gēmirādo und hat daneben noch einen besonderen Ausdruck für „Gott", nämlich rewetēdo, den ich aber in den von mir bereisten Gegenden nie gehört habe.

[13] yer-kei, „unser Herr", yer, „unser", kei, „Herr", also wörtlich dem Kanúri- und Lógoné-Ausdruck entsprechend. der Wándalá-Ausdruck dadá-mia dagegen hat die für unsere christlichen Gefühle höchst interessante, dem Moslim ganz fremde Bedeutung „unser Vater" (mia, „unser" S. CCXXXII). Davon ist dáme wol nur eine populäre Verkürzung.

[14] larde bé-deme, „die gesammte Erde" entspricht nur in einem Sinn dem Worte dúnya, da das letztere auch den Begriff des Irdischen in geistiger Bedeutung einschliesst.

[15] kálnā in dieser Bezeichnung scheint dem Geiste der Mába-Sprache sonst ganz fremd zu sein, denn kalák, „klein" heisst im Gegensatz von kolák, „gross" (S. CCCXXII, f); es ist wol dem Für kalge entlehnt oder gehört einer anderen beiden Sprachen gemeinsamen Wurzel.

[16] kásang wol ähnlich unserem Ausdruck „die Zukunft"; daher sundar na kásang, „übermorgen", von sundar, „morgen".

[17] wasiyi ist entschieden nichts Anderes, als der Plural von wasih (Burckhardt waseyh), „das Feuer"; im Kanúri (Burckhardt) heisst wassik, „Stern", wieder ein höchst interessantes Bruchstück von Feuerdienst bei diesen Völkern.

Sonγai.	Lógoné.	Wándalá.	Bágrimma.	Mába.
yer-koi [12] . . .	mál-uš	{dadá-mia . / dáme . . .}	alla	kälak [15]
andūnya . . .	dụnya	larde bé-deme [14]	dụnya . . .	dụnya
. . . .	láherā	faya ? . . .	láhera . . .	kūsang [16]
andženna . . .	dženna	dženna . . .	dženna . . .	dženne
. . . .	fú (a)l džehánnama	kāra džānem .	pōdu džehénnema	{džehánnem / wasīyi [17]}
[{korle / kóte} Idol] .	aldžinne . . .	džinni . . .	{kau . . . / džinnige . .}	džin / šetán

[1] kémā-ndē verbally „Lord of us", „our Lord". kémā itself, however, does not seem to have been the original Kanúri-term for the Supreme Being, this being probably a word, signifying at the same time „heaven", perhaps Káma. With regard to the religious notions of African pagans, in general, are some very excellent Remarks of Rev. Riis in the Preface to his Grammatical outline of the Oji-language, Basel 1854. While these larger Vocabularies of mine represent languages, more or less influenced by Islamism, which, as I have exposed p. XXV and XXIX of my Introductory Remarks, has brought a great change over them, my smaller vocabularies, which represent idioms, part of them closely related to the former, but not at all influenced in such a manner, will, as far as they reach, tend to shed much new light over many of these points. A few of these Arabicised religious terms I was obliged to give here; others I pass by, such as the surnames of God, f. i. „Creator" alkhte-ma (from alákte which again has been derived from alák [خلقْ]-alakin.

[2] dụnya: Koelle writes dinīš, dinie and dúnyá.

[3] láhira, beyond any doubt, is identical with the Arabic الآخر. Koelle writes leira and láhira, but does not notice the original meaning of „the last day, day of judgement", the meaning of „next world, grave" being only second hand.

[4] dženna is also spelt deenna, this change being spoken of in my Introductory Remarks p. XXXVIII and XLII. Koelle writes tekand.

[5] kannu džānem properly is not composed correctly according to grammatical rules, as it ought to be kannu džānem-be, „the fire of hell". Koelle attributes to the simple term kannu the meaning of „hell, hellfire", and, no doubt, in certain cases, when illustrated by the context, it may be so employed.

[6] džin no doubt is derived from the Arabic جن. Koelle has not this word, but gives instead two other terms of a similar meaning and of truely native origin, viz koliram, „wood [-or earth-] demon" and ṅgamaram, „waterdemon", while a third term, which he gives, viz kárīram, explaining it in a long article as something quite independent and original, is nothing but a slight dialectical change of koliram. These are only two notions of that malignant natural principle, the idea and fear of which overawes the mind of the pagan much more, than that of the benevolent spirit, as manifested in heaven, sun, stars and so on, and which former, therefore, they contrive to befriend by all means. The same we find to be the case with all rude tribes, nay, with our common people this is the origin and source of all superstitious belief. See with regard to the Chukches the remarks of Mr. Ditmar in the „extraits des publications de la Soc. Imp. Géogr. de Russie p. 13 „Les Tschoukktchis et les Koriakes sont idolâtres; ils croient à l'existence d'une divinité bienfaisante qu'ils nomment „Apapeis" et à celle de mauvais esprits qui tourmentent les hommes et dont il faut s'efforcer de satisfaire l'avidité par de nombreux sacrifices".

[7] wāšal lárla means properly „fire of the last judgement".

[8] mōbi seems to be a purely native term, while aldžonē is, no doubt, derived from the Arabic.

[9] dụnya: I have heard the terms for „creation", in Hausa tahalitta, in F. tagefádi.

[10] alidžene: this term the Rev. Schön has adopted in all his translations of biblical stories, in order to express the Christian idea of „heaven", but such a use is certainly precarious and liable to serious misunderstandings, the term alidžene being too closely and exclusively connected with the idea of the Mohammedan paradise (el dženna), on which point Mr. Schön himself seems to be perfectly clear, when he remarks in his account of the Niger-Expedition p. 120 „the influence which Mahomedanism has gained over the people in the interior has supplied it (the Hausa-language) with many religious terms and words which we sought for in vain among the vocabularies of Pagan nations".

[11] Schön gives in his vocabulary (1843) a term alaki, meaning according to him „the evil one", but such a term has remained totally unknown to myself as well as the adjective and substantive alaheki, „evil".

[12] džomirāo (a term probably connected with emir) alone conveys the general idea of „master", and properly obtains the meaning of „our Lord" only by adding to it the term tšenido, „most High", but, where there cannot be any doubt as to what is meant, it is also used by itself. Rev. Reichardt writes gōmirādo, and, besides this one, has another peculiar term for „god", namely eswetyido, which I did never hear in any of these regions, through which I travelled.

[13] yer-koi, means „our master", yer, „we, our", koi, „master"; and, therefore, exactly corresponds to the Kanúri as well to the Lógoné-term, while dadá-mia in Bágrimma appears to convey the interesting meaning of „our father" (mia, „our", Intr. Remarks p. CCXXXIII), dáme, according to all appearances, being a popular form of the same term.

[14] larde bé-deme, „the whole earth" does not express but one side of the import of the term dúnya, the latter in a wider sense comprising both earth and heaven.

[15] kälak is identical with the Fūr kalge, while it seems to have no root in the Māba-idiom, kaláh in the latter meaning „small", „little", and being the reverse of koláh, „great"; see Introductory Remarks p. CCCXXIII, f).

[16] kūsang corresponds almost exactly with our term „the future", whence ganduer en kūsang, „the day after to morrow".

[17] wasīyi apparently is nothing else, but the plural of wasīh, „the fire". In Kordofal (Burckhardt) wusīh means „star".

Deutsch und Englisch.	Kanúri.	Tédā.	Hausa.	Fulfúlde.
Himmel, Firmament — sky, heaven	samma [1] (Arb.) / semmi . . .	čakenō [9], Plur. ce-kénuā	semmi . . .	kámū-dži . / somma-ädži [13]
Sonne — sun	kan [2] . . . . / kengal, kangal	yedē; yenē . .	rāna	nañge . . .
Mond — moon	kumbal [3] . .	avri, auri [10] .	wotta . . .	lēuru . . .
Neumond — new-moon .	kintāgo birrin [4]	auri burdu .	farfila . . . / sabō n wotta	kolyōa . . . / lēuru kéeu .
Vollmond — full-moon .	kumbal bul [5] .	auri lābu . .	fāri n wotta .	lélewel . . .
Stern — star	tšeltūgo [6] . .	teskī [11] . . .	temrāro . . .	hódere Pl. kōde
Morgenstern — morning-star	kuwáshil [7], Knr. / tingúrmi, Knm.	teskī al fedīr	gomzāki . .	džabire . . .
Nord — north	yālā [8]	mā	árewa . . .	so-birre [12] . .

[1] samma. Koelle hat unter pátō einen wol entschieden noch heidnischen (vergl. S. 146, N. 1) Ausdruck für „Himmel", nämlich pátō rámbhe. Der Grund davon, dass diese Völker einen fremden Ausdruck für einen ihnen so nahe liegenden Gegenstand annahmen, liegt eben darin, dass ihr altes einheimisches Wort für Himmel, gleich dem Chinesischen thian und den Wörtern bei den verwandten noch heidnischen Stämmen Central-Afrika's, die wir in der nachfolgenden Sammlung kleiner Vokabularien vertreten, auch die heidnischen Begriffe der Gottheit selbst enthielt.

[2] kan, kengal. Diese beiden Ausdrücke sind allerdings, wie Einleitung S. LX, N. 3 bemerkt, ursprünglich nicht gleichbedeutend gewesen, indem der erste Ausdruck von der hoch am Himmel stehenden, einem glühenden „Steine" gleichenden, der zweite nur von der aufgehenden oder untergehenden Sonne als „schönes Naturschauspiel" gebraucht wurde, und auch der heutige Gebrauch macht noch solche Unterscheidung. Koelle hat übrigens noch einen besonderen Ausdruck teri für „Sonnenschein", der mir unbekannt geblieben ist; er nähert sich sehr dem V. yel S. 150, N. 10 und L. eel S. 164, N. 11.

[3] kumbal kommt wol unzweifelhaft von der Wurzel mbal, „voll sein" (kamádugu tsi-mbál-sna S. 130). Daraus erklärt sich von selbst, dass dieser Ausdruck nicht vom Neumond gebraucht werden kann. Koelle schreibt kémbal.

[4] kintāgo, Koelle kentāgo — Die Wurzel ist tāk oder tág.

[5] kumbal oder kémbal bul hat Koelle nur in der Bedeutung von „Mondschein" und allerdings ist durch das bul der Begriff des Leuchtenden besonders hervorgehoben, da kumbal allein schon eigentlich „Vollmond" heisst, wie N. 3 gezeigt.

[6] tšelūgo fehlt bei Koelle; es zeigt entschiedene Verwandtschaft mit ailhe, aïlge, aillege der verschiedenen Kótokó-Dialekte und im Lógonē.

[7] kuwáshil. Koelle schreibt kwāshil und košegil; tingúrmi hat er nicht: das steht dem B. tungūmi sehr ähnlich.

[8] yālā, vermittelt durch yēle, scheint eine blosse Dialekt-Verschiedenheit des Kótokó-Ausdruckes wēle zu sein, wie wir denn deutlich sehen, dass die Kanúri alle diese Ausdrücke für die Himmelsgegenden aus uns bis jetzt noch unbekannten Gründen mit ihren weiter vorangeschrittenen östlichen Nachbarn, den Kótokó, gemeinsam haben.

[9] čakenō steht unzweifelhaft mit kenuā, „Gottheit", in engster Beziehung, wahrscheinlich als „Wohnsitz der Gottheit".

[10] auri zeigt einige Verwandtschaft mit dem Te-māšiy-t und dadurch mit dem Koptischen. S. die Einleitung S. XCVI, N. 15.

[11] teskī, wol ursprünglich „das Leuchtende, Glitzernde", im Gegensatz zu yoskī, „Dunkelheit"; teskī al fedīr ist ein nur halb nationaler Ausdruck, neben dem es sicherlich noch einen der Tédā-Sprache durchaus eigenthümlichen geben wird.

[12] kámū-dži wie somma-ädži scheint nach semitischen Begriffen mehr in der Pluralität aufgefasst. Reichardt hat sommā und kāmu.

[13] so-birre und so-banda haben einen entschiedenen Parallelismus der Beziehung, obgleich ich ihre ursprüngliche Beziehung nicht mit voller Sicherheit darlegen kann; wahrscheinlich ist so-birre (mit dem das vorhergehende džabire vielleicht zusammenhängt) die „Gegend der Wüste", wie so-banda die „Gegend der Landschaft Banda"; sie würden also die Sitze der Fúlbe in jener Gegend am Senegal seit alter Zeit fixiren. Solche lokale Ausdrücke sind oft von der allerhöchsten Bedeutung zum Auffinden der Ursitze der Völkerschaften und zur Geschichte ihrer Wanderung. — Der von den in Adamaua angesiedelten Fúlbe gebrauchte Ausdruck wēla ist dem benachbarten Kótokó-Dialekten entnommen, wie andere dort übliche Ausdrücke, obgleich Dr. Baikie in seinen Berichten an die Engl. Regierung (Reports 5, n. 5, p. 11) gerade den in Adamaua gesprochenen Dialekt, und nicht ganz mit Unrecht, für sehr eigenthümlich hält, vgl. Einl. S. CXI.

[14] banda erinnert an das gleichbedeutende Hindi yand, Singhal handa, wie wir solche Anklänge des Sonyai mehr finden.

[15] hálaka erinnert ganz entschieden an das gleichbedeutende kálega im Nūba und Berbēra, wie ólage, „Süd" an Nūba órogo.

[16] dádedem ámdšigiā hängt offenbar genau mit dadá-mia, dem Namen für „Gott", zusammen. Der Ausdruck dšigiā kehrt in dem Kompositum für Ost wieder und in der Form yagiā für „Nord" wol mit der generellen Bedeutung „Gegend".

[17] tré yóhua wol sicherlich „der kleine Mond"; aber für klein habe ich sonst die Form tšiko, tšikua.

[18] kadim-yagiā und die folgenden Bezeichnungen der Himmelsgegenden im W. sind offenbar beziehungsreich, aber mir noch nicht ganz verständlich, vielleicht yagiā = daigiā, „Wohnung, Aufenthalt", wie auch in até-daigiā. watšin átirō heisst „die Sonne" (wetšia) „oben", átirō S. 79, d. h. „zur rechten Hand".

[19] neppa džeppe. Wir haben hier eine durch Euphonie begründete Nebenform von néfa. S. CCLXXVIII, 5, a). Zu eef al kigge ibid. 5, e).

[20] plāe-plāe wol zu erklären „die Himmelsflammen"; plāa, „Flamme".

[21] ákih (Burckhardt saykh) und ékh (Burckhardt ayk) stehen wahrscheinlich in enger Beziehung der Bildung zu einander, wie etwa „grosses" und „kleines Licht". Für „Sterne" (stars) gibt Burckhardt die Form meniet; für „Nord" Seetzen das von meinem melašéy ganz verschiedene, wol falsche tarru.

Sonyai.	Lógoné.	Wándalá.	Bágrimma.	Mába.
bīni . . . . / bēne	áanma	dádedem émdži-glā [16]	aaémma . .	somma
wōnu . . . . / wōno	sáyo	wátšia . . . / wótšia . . .	kádža . . .	éōik [21]
handu; hendu [14] .	tōdi	trē	náfu	ōik
handu { tāo / kai . .	tōdi aigá-mdi .	džotángwoaīrin(?)	naf al kiggo .	ōōk gedík
handu { dē / kōre . .	tōdi aigá-fabám .	(trē) daaye .	neppo dāappo [19]	ōōk kolák
sanūi Plur. sanōyu	silkín	trē yōkna [17] .	piōe-piōe [20] .	minwō
subha-sanāi . .	silkín īro fezr .	. . . . . .	taógūml . .	. . . . . .
siggi-bōre . . .	húlaka [15] . . .	kadīm-yaglā [18]	mēla	minūāg

[1] samma: Rev. Koelle s. v. pátā gives another term for „heaven" of apparently pagan origin (compare p. 145, note 1), viz pátē rámábo, „the domicile of Rima". For, in general, the reason, why these people on their being converted to Mohammedanism adopted also another term for „heaven", was, that their original term was too intimately connected with the pagan notion of the Supreme Being itself.

[2] kan, kaágal: these two terms, as stated p. LXI, note 2, originally seem to convey a different meaning, kan being employed to signify the sun, as the full Luminar orb (compared with a stone), and kaágal to indicate the planet in its vicissitudes of rising and setting; and even at the present time such a distinction is generally observed. Koelle has also a peculiar term for „sunshine", viz tool which I have never heard; it bears a slight resemblance to the identical F.-term yol.

[3] kambal most probably has been derived from the root mbal, „be full" (kamádugu tel-mbál-ena p. 130) whence it becomes clear, how it happens, that this term cannot be used of the new-moon. Koelle writes kę̄mbal.

[4] kintāge, Koelle kéntāge. — The root is tāk or tāg.

[5] kambal, or kémbal bul appears in Koelle's vocabulary only with the notion of „moonlight", and, no doubt, both meanings coincide in many respects, especially as kambal by itself means rather „fullmoon".

[6] sīlāgo is wanting in Koelle's vocabulary; it is evidently akin to the terms silka, silge, sillage in the various Kótokó-dialects and in Lógoné.

[7] kuwákkil: Koelle writes kwáckil and kaágil; tingármi, which is wanting in his collection, looks very much like the B.

[8] yálā seems to be a mere dialectical variation of the form wēla in several dialects of Kótokó (yéla in Ndifu), the terms for the other points of the compass also being identical in these idioms, from reasons as yet unexplained.

[9] áchaud, no doubt, bears a close affinity to the term kamno, „god", and probably means „God's abode".

[10] auri seems to be related to the Temáshight-term ayór, as well as to the Coptic. See Introductory Remarks p. XCVII, note 16.

[11] tooki al fedār is a term of mixed native and foreign origin, besides which there is probably a more expressive one in the pure dialects of the Tédā-language; as for tooki, it appears clearly to express the reverse of yaski, „darkness".

[12] kamā-dāl and somma-ádāl represent the plurality of heavens, according to Moslem notion. Reichardt has asamān and kámu.

[13] so-hirre and so-bundu exhibit a most decided parallelism of terminology, although I cannot explain their original meaning with perfect certainty, but I myself do not entertain any doubt, that so-bundu meant originally the side towards Bundu, the country to the S. of the Upper Senegal, while so-hirre meant the side of the Desert (bur). Thus we should have here another proof of the original seats of the Fúlbe, at least in historical times, having been in the region of the Senegal. Such local terms are of the very highest importance, indeed, for investigating the original seats of nations and for following their wanderings through different regions. — As for the term wēla, used by the Fúlbe of Adamawa it has been borrowed from the idiom of the neighbouring Kótokó, and is not recognized by their countrymen as a term belonging to their language, as is the case also with many other expressions of that dialect, though it may, as Dr. Baikie thinks (Reports 5, n. 6, p. 11), and does really contain many original elements; see Introductory Remarks p. CXII.

[14] handu in Songai reminds one of the corresponding cand in Hindi, handa in Singhalese.

[15] húlaka reminds one decidedly of the corresponding term káloga in Nuba and Berābra, just as ilage, „South" does of the corresponding Nuba term áraga.

[16] dádedem émdžiglā: this term is, according to all appearance, intimately connected with the term dadá-mia, „god", and seems to mean „habitation of god"; the term dāiglā, which returns in the composition for East and, in the form yaglā, for North, seeming to convey the general notion of „region".

[17] trē yōkna most probably means „little moon", although for the adjective „little" I have the form tšiko, fm. tšikna.

[18] kadīm-yaglā and the following terms, indicating planetary regions in the Wándalá-language, are evidently full of meaning and instruction. The term for south wátšia átirē means „sun above", i. q. „to the Right".

[19] neppo dāappo: we have here another form of náfu, occasioned by laws of euphony, which in these illiterate languages it would be very wrong to obliterate; see Introductory Remarks p. CCLXXVIII, 5, a), and, as for naf al kiggo ibid. 5, c).

[20] piōe-piōe seems to be understood as „the Flowers (of heaven)", piōa meaning „flower".

[21] éāik (Burckhardt ayk), and ōok (Burckhardt ojk) are apparently closely related terms, indicating some comparison between one another, such as „big" and „little planet". For „stars" Burckhardt gives the form mniat; for „North" Seetzen gives tarra, a term widely different from mine.

Deutsch und Englisch.	Kanúri.	Tédā.	Hausa.	Fulfúlde.
Süd — south	ánum[1] . . .	onúm[6] . . .	gusum . . / kódu . . .	so-bandu . / hōre būdo . / hōre fūdo .
Ost — east	gedī[2] . . .	yē . . . . / fōto	gabbes . . .	fū-nange[11] . / lītogel . .
West — west	futē[3] . . .	yalā[7] . . . . / dī	yamma . . .	hir-nange . / gorgal . . .
Nord-West (zwischen Nord und West) u. s. w. — north-west	yálā-futē . .	. . . . .	taskán n árewa da yamma	lēkkere so-birre dē gorgal
Erde, Land — earth, country	tāidī[4] . . . / lardo (Arb.)	dunya kerō[8] .	kása	lezdi . . . / lēdi . . . .
Wasser — water . . .	ńkī[5]	eyī; īya; yīe; yō	rūa[10] . . .	ndīam . . .
Feuer — fire	kannu . . .	wūēni[9] . . .	ūla	yīte; hīte Pl. kīte

[1] ánum steht bei Koelle in der Form von ányem.

[2] gedī oder, wie Koelle weniger richtig accentuirt, gédi, hat wol in seiner Bedeutung von „Ursprung, Anfang" auch die weitere Bezeichnung von „Osten" bekommen, so wie die von „Bedeutung, Meinung" in Bezug auf Rede.

[3] futē schreibt Koelle pátē und pátē.

[4] tāidī. Koelle schreibt teádī und anstatt lardo: lárdq. Das te anstatt tā ist allerdings das gewöhnliche in der Präposition teidī-ga, „auf der Erde, unten".

[5] ńkī, T. eyī, H. ruaī stehen in äusserlich engster Beziehung zu den entsprechenden Ausdrücken in vielen der Mandinga-Sprachen dei, dsē, davi, adsē, yi u. s. w.; aber doch ist solche Ähnlichkeit wol nur Schein, s. S. LX, N. 5.

[6] onum. Neben diesem, gewiss erst durch enge Berührung mit dem neueren Kanúri eingeführten, Ausdruck gibt es wol noch einen anderen einheimischen, der den monosyllaben Ausdrücken der anderen Himmelsgegenden entspricht: má, yē, dī.

[7] yalā, offenbar identisch mit yálā im Kanúri, hat auffallender Weise im Tédā die Bedeutung „Westen" erhalten, wie fōto diejenige von „Osten". — dī heisst im Tēdiná „Ost". Beispiele solcher Verwechselungen kommen auch sonst vor, wie mit den Ausdrücken gibli und šerki bei den Maurischen Stämmen der Westlichen Wüste und glaube ich nicht, dass ich geirrt habe.

[8] dunya kerō ist ein nothbehelfender Ausdruck: daneben gibt es wol einen besseren.

[9] wūēni nähert sich sehr dem entsprechenden Ausdrucke einiger der Akū-Dialekte und der Nūoh-Sprache.

[10] Weder von rūa noch rāna habe ich Dialekt-Verschiedenheiten der Hausa-Sprache beachtet, so dass man lūa, lāna sagte (Koelle Polygl.), das möchte aber Einfluss der Yorúba-Sprache auf die südwestlichsten Dialekte am unteren Niger sein.

[11] fū-nange, hir-nange bedeuten eigentlich „Sonnenaufgang", „Sonnenuntergang".

[12] lee-bēre bedeutet eigentlich „die Flussseite", von lee, „der Fluss"; siggi-bēre heisst daher wahrscheinlich „die Seite der Wüste". Wir hätten also hier einen ganz deutlichen Beweis vor uns, dass die ursprünglichsten Sitze der Sonyai wenigstens schon in sehr alter Zeit nördlich vom Flusse lagen. Freilich sind diese Ausdrücke nicht gültig für A'gades und Umgebung, aber die dort üblichen, dem Temāšīyt entnommenen Ausdrücke, die ich in meinem Kangi-lemi-Wörterbuch aufgeführt, musste ich hier übergehen. S. Einleitung S. XVIII.

[13] gonda, gande, kanda bezeichnet im gewöhnlichen Leben „Boden, Landgebiet", daher so viele Sonyai-Namen von Ortschaften mit der Endung ganda oder kanda, wie z. B. Sōma-kanda. dē scheint die ganze Erde zu bezeichnen (dē, „voll, genug"), aber im Zusammenhang der Rede habe ich es nie gehört.

[14] nōne. Dieser Ausdruck scheint nur in Tímbuktu und den umliegenden Provinzen üblich zu sein und rührt fast unzweifelhaft von dem im Süd benachbarten Tombo her, die, wie in meinem Reisewerk ausgeführt, Th. IV, S. 569, grossen Einfluss auf die Geschicke der Stadt ausgeübt haben. Auch Denham hat nōne, Travels II, App. XX, Timbuctoo vocabulary p. 188, nur hat er dasselbe mit jorree, i. e. dāri, „Tag" den Platz zu tauschen. Ich hörte auch noch gelegentlich ein Wort tō für „Feuer", aber diesen wollten Andere für durchaus nicht der Sprache eigenthümlich anerkennen; es nähert sich dem entsprechenden tā, tē in den Mandinga-Dialekten, so wie andererseits dem entsprechenden Dahōme-Ausdruck und ebenso der Barba-Sprache und ist wahrscheinlich von den in Gurma wohnenden Sonyai aufgenommen worden.

[15] sa ist mit dem entsprechenden Ausdruck in der zweiten Gruppe der Sprachen des Niger-Delta's in Koelle's Polyglotta und in der Fika und den benachbarten Sprachen eng verwandt, worauf ich bei den kleinen Vokabularien zurückkomme.

[16] fā, „Feuer" steht, abgesehen von dem mit Lógonē eng verwandten Kōtokō-Sprachen, und ausser mit dem B. pódu, in entschiedenem Zusammenhang mit dem Ausdrucke für „Sonne" im Bedōnga (fā-yo) und im Ndīfu (fu-ne).

[17] Auf rā und hangri werde ich an der betreffenden Stelle der kleinen Vokabularien zurückkommen. Das erstere besonders ist sehr bedeutend, weil es in dem eng verwandten, vom Islam noch nicht entstellten, Dialekt von Kebga auch „Gott" und „Himmel" bedeutet; hangri hängt höchst wahrscheinlich mit ha, „Fluss" zusammen, also „Flussseite".

[18] mané. man, manē, á-man ist einer von jenen Ausdrücken, die einer Menge Afrikanischer Sprachen gemeinsam sind.

[19] talám ist offenbar abgeleitet von tal (in Tumale delläg), „über", lálen von lal, „unter", daher das letztere im verwandten Für „Nacht" bedeutet; eben daher stammt auch die Benennung der beiden Stadtquartiere von Wara tér-talé und tér-lalé und eben daher „Ober"- und „Unterlippe", tal-na und lal-na. — Zu „Erde" bemerke ich, dass Burckhardt für „ground", dordjob gibt.

Sońγai.	Lógoné.	Wándalá.	Bágrimma.	Mába.
ise-hāre [12] . .	álage	wátši(a) átirō .	rá [17]	mōta
wēne hunal . .	kusé wenī . . .	alé-džiglā . .	džonsu . . .	talūm [19]
wēne kańgal . .	madō	atir-zalā . . / futā . . .	bańgri . . .	lálan
džińgur siggi-hēre dē ise-hēre	. . . . . .	. . . . . .	. . . . . .	. . . . . .
dō; dōbo . . . / genda; kanda; gande [13]	loāde	χāχa	ardu	gésióga / ard
ari; hari; héri .	am [15]	yōē	man; manē [18]	endže; indži
korū . . . . / nōne, Tb. [14] . .	fū [16]	kárā	pódu, fódu .	wasík

[1] ānum: Koelle writes ânym.

[2] gedi, or gédi, as Koelle writes, seems to have conveyed originally the meaning of „bottom, origin", from whence the other meanings have been derived, „east" („origin of the sun"), as well as „meaning, import" („bottom of the speech").

[3] futé: Koelle writes pótō and pótē.

[4] tšídi: Koelle writes taédi, and instead of lardo: lárdo. The ta in the former of these two terms is certainly prevailing in the preposition taidi-ga, „on the earth, down, below", but not in the simple term tšídi.

[5] áhi, T. syi, M. sadši seem to evidence close connection with the corresponding terms in many dialects of the Mandingo-language, such as doi, dob, deei, udeé, yi, although áhi in its close affinity to ágé, „alive" (Introductory Remarks p. LXI, note 5) rests completely in the Kanúri-idiom.

[6] ondon seems to be intimately connected with the Kanúri-term ānum, and I do not doubt, that the Tédā-language possesses another more characteristic and monosyllabic term, corresponding in form and originality to the other terms má, yá, di for the various points of the compass.

[7] yalá, which is evidently identical with the Kanúri yálā, through some unaccountable change of relation seems to have obtained with the Tédā the signification of „west", while the term fōte obtained that of „east". Something similar is not a rare occurrence, as the Arabic term gibli meaning originally „south" has obtained the notion of „west" with the Arabs or Moors of the Western Desert, while šerki (east) with the latter means „south".

[8] dunya heré is a very awkward expression, besides which there is, no doubt, a better and more expressive one.

[9] wōrai bears a remarkable resemblance to some terms of the Akú-dialects and in the Ndob-language.

[10] róa, róna. Koelle in his Polyglotta gives lóa and lána, but, although r and l are frequently interchanged in the various dialects of the Hausa-language, yet I have never observed such a change in these two words.

[11] fā-wange, hir-nange mean „rising of the sun", „setting of the sun".

[12] ise-hēre properly means „the side of the river" (isa, „river"); it is more than probable, therefore, that siggi-hēre means „side of the desert", and we should thus have a proof more, that the seats of the Sońγai lay to the north of the river from very ancient times, the latter being towards the south. — The terms here exhibited are not used in Á'gades and the neighbouring country, where they have given way to other terms taken from the Máśiγ-language, which I have adduced in my vocabulary of the Emγédesi-language, but which I cannot admit in this place. See Introductory Remarks, chapter I, p. XIX.

[13] ganda, gande in daily life signifies „ground", „territory", which is the reason, why so many Sońγai-names of places and districts close with a final ganda or hande as, for instance, Sāme-kanda. The term dō seems to signify the earth as a whole (dō, „full, entire"), but I have never heard it used in connection with other words.

[14] nōne: this term seems only to be used in the Sońγai-provinces in the neighbourhood of Tímbuktu, and most probably was there introduced by the people of Tombo, to whose idiom it seems to have originally belonged; it appears also in Denham's Timbuctoo vocabulary (Travels II, App. XX, p. 182), where it has to change place, however, with the other term jarree, i. e. džári, „day". I heard also occasionally another term for „fire", namely tā, but this term most of the Sońγai, with whom I had occasion to converse, would not acknowledge as belonging to their language. tā resembles in some degree the corresponding Dahómi term, as well as that of the Bariba-idiom, whence it has, no doubt, been borrowed by the Sońγai settled in Gurma.

[15] am is nearly related to the corresponding term in the second group of languages, belonging to the Niger-Delta (in Koelle's Polyglotta), as well as in the Fīka and neighbouring languages.

[16] fū, „fire", besides being nearly related to the corresponding term in the Lógoné- and Kótokō-dialects and to the Bágrimma-term pódu, appears closely connected with the term fū-yo for „sun" in Bedańga and fa-ne in Ndifa.

[17] rá, hańgri: with regard to these terms I shall say something more in the proper place of my smaller vocabularies, rá especially being of very great interest, as in the dialect of Kénga, which has not been influenced by Mohammedanism, it means both „god", as well as „sky, heaven"; as for hańgri, it may indicate the side of the „river" (ba).

[18] manē: man, mané, á-men is one of those terms, which are common to a considerable number of African languages.

[19] talūm has been evidently derived from tal, „on, above", as well as lálan from lal, „below", thence again being derived the names tár-talō and lár-lalā designating the East- and West-quarters of the town of Wára, as well the terms designating „upper"-, and „under-lip", tal-ne and lal-ne.

Deutsch und Englisch.	Kanúri.	Têda.	Hausa.	Fulfúlde.
Flamme — *flame* . . .	tẽlam kámnu-be [1]	tirmésu wũlẽzi	haltši n ũta .	demgal yĩte .
Rauch — *smoke* . . .	kantšo [2] . .	kangia . . .	háyaki . . .	{ tšéroki . . / tšúreli . . }
Asche — *embers*	būgu . . .	tifi	tõka	kāla . . . .
Feuerkohlen — *cinders* .	kentíbel [3] . .	galfi	garwãši n ũta	farĩrdži . . .
Licht, Helligkeit — *light, brightness, shine*	nūr [4] (Arb.) .	. . . . .	haske . . .	{ džẽengol Plur. džẽli / yildo [10] . . }
Dunkelheit — *darkness, obscurity*	kilmíske [5] . .	yeski . . .	duffu . . .	ñĩbre [11] . . .
Schatten — *shade, shadow*	{ káfia [6] . . . / kaimi . . . / gerë . . . }	arkoĩ . . .	énũa	dōdi Plur. dōle
Tag, Tageslicht — *day, daylight*	kábu [7] . . .	{ bã Plur. bĩa / yum (Arb.) . }	rāna [9] . . .	nyálloma . .
Nacht — *night*	búnẽ [8] . . .	dógesõ Plur. dó-gesã	derẽ	dĩemma Plur. džemmãdže
Monat — *month* . . .	kintágo; kintáge	auri	wotta Plur. wát-lane	lẽuru Plur. lebbi

[1] tẽlam kánnu-be, wie fast alle entsprechenden Ausdrücke der anderen Sprachen, wörtlich „die Zunge des Feuers".
[2] kantšo. Koelle schreibt kentši.
[3] kentíbel hängt wol entschieden, als von gleicher Wurzel abgeleitet, mit tíbel, „kleines Kind" zusammen, in so fern als Kohlen die Keime des Feuers enthalten; es fehlt bei Koelle.
[4] nūr ist, obgleich rein Arabisch, doch ein ganz gewöhnliches Wort in Bornu geworden. — Ich will hier bemerken, dass ich für den Begriff „Luft" in keiner dieser Sprachen einen nationalen, prägnanten Ausdruck gefunden habe, sondern meist hilft man sich mit dem Arabischen hawa, aber ein Kanúri umschrieb mir den Begriff mit den Worten nemmi n sai-di-ga-n katẽ, „der Raum (katẽ) unter dem Himmel".
[5] kilmíske fehlt bei Koelle.
[6] káfia (Koelle kafia) ist der Schatten eines Baumes oder sonst eines Gegenstandes, so fern es zum Schutze gegen die Sonne dient; kaimi (fehlt bei Koelle) ist der Schatten lebender Wesen; gerë (fehlt auch bei Koelle) ist der Schatten, den eine Mauer wirft; man sagt also gerẽ subba, gerẽ kátšeri, „Morgenschatten, Abendschatten".
[7] kábu. Koelle accentuirt kābū; kū ist wol eine blosse populäre Abkürzung dieses Wortes, hat dann aber die Bedeutung erhalten „dieser Tag, heute".
[8] búnẽ. Koelle schreibt bũnyẽ oder bẽnyẽ, aber solche Aussprache habe ich nie gehört. S. Note 1. — Zu kintágo s. S. 146, N. 4.
[9] rāna. Dieser Ausdruck bezeichnet nur den von der Sonne beschienenen Tagesabschnitt und er wird nicht gebraucht bei längeren Zeitabschnitten, sondern da gebraucht man lieber den Ausdruck kwāna, „Schlaf", „Nachtquartier", zumal bei Entfernungen auf der Reise, also „wie viele Tage, Tagemärsche", kwāna nawa. Eben so ist es im Fulfúlde, wo man in dieser Beziehung den Ausdruck walláнde gebraucht. Plur. balde (balde nei); im Sonyai gebraucht man girbi (girbi merge). In gewisser Beziehung kann man den Türkischen Ausdruck konak vergleichen.
[10] yildo wird, wie es scheint, nur von der Helligkeit und dem Scheine des Feuers gebraucht. Die Wurzel ist yel, „leuchten", die auch wol nyálloma bildet.
[11] ñĩbre, Reichardt ñure.
[12] áyessi; so sagt man „euer Schatten", áyessi na-hũ u. s. w.
[13] nāyeli, nágeli hängt entschieden zusammen mit náye, „die Sonne".
[14] hãka tiẽ, „da ist kein Mondschein" bezieht sich eigentlich nur auf die Dunkelheit der Nacht. — tšilkõ. So sagt man tšilkõ n afi, „der Schatten des Baumes"; tšilkõ rã, „der Schatten eines lebenden Wesens"; tšilkõ n gadiã, tšilkõ dãã wéškie u. s. w.
[15] wégia: die nahe Verwandtschaft von wégia und wétšie bei so entgegengesetzter Bedeutung ist sehr lehrreich. Das Princip des Lebens und der Bewegung ist augenscheinlich durch tše ausgedrückt, wie S. CCXL, 4, b) ausgeführt.
[16] edšilli. Die grosse Übereinstimmung dieses Ausdruckes mit dem entsprechenden im Māba ist bemerkenswerth, s. Einleitung S. CCLXXXIV, c). — kéda bei naf heisst „ein", wie im W. pella.
[17] Für „Flamme" gibt Seetzen das (vielleicht dialektisch) ganz verschiedene fitirngõk, „für „Rauch", kondik, für „Kohlen", kikimik. — Zu meinem wung lolfati vergl. S. CCCXX, b); zu délba-dẽ S. CCCVIII, g).

Sonyai.	Lógoné.	Wándalá.	Bágrimma.	Mába.
{ kord n / nōne } dēne .	inōe-fū	wa kárā . .	dźōlo fódu .	delmik waaik-nak [17]
{ dulla . . . . . / sisi Tb. . . . . }	dūn-al-fū	gīre [?] . . .	{ sā . . . . / sáa-fódu . . }	kulda
bōso	gufū	dābtšia . . .	burgu . . .	avnu
{ deṅgi . . . . / zdiendźi . . . }	ťinne-fū . . .	ďáfalā kárā .	nála	. . . . . .
gai	nūr	. . . . . .	annūr . . .	
{ kobāye . . . / gum . . . . }	tū	[bāka trē [14]] .	gotīli . . .	waṅg lolloti
bī	ǵyeaaī [12] . . .	tšilkō . . .	ndźili [16] . . .	ándźulúk
{ dźāri Plur. dźário / zāri Plur. zário }	{ sáyeli . . . . / sáṅgeli [13] . . . }	har	{ kádźa . . . / wai . . . }	délka-dā / ingúṅgo
kīgi; kīdźi; tāīdźi	imwāde	{ wégia [15] . . / wágia . . . }	dźō	ťāc
hendu	tōdi	tīr (palle . . .	naf (kéde . .	. . . . . .

[1] tēlam kánnu-be, just as all the other corresponding terms means verbally „tongue of fire".
[2] kaatše: Koelle writes kontšī.
[3] hratibel most probably is etymologically connected with the term tibel, „baby", just as „embers" in English is connected with „embryo"; it is wanting in Koelle.
[4] nūr, although a pure Arabic word, is in common use in Bornu. — I shall here remark, that I have not met with a truly national term for „air, atmosphere" in any of these languages; in general, more civilized people use the Arabic term haua, but a Kanúri-man once rendered to me the meaning by the phrase sammi n teidi-ge-n hatō, „the space (hatō) below the sky".
[5] kilimiske is wanting in Koelle.
[6] káfia (Koelle káfia) signifies the shadow of a tree or any other object and the protection thus afforded against the sun; kalmi (a term wanting in Koelle) is the shadow of animate beings; gerō (likewise wanting in Koelle) is likewise the shadow of any object, but merely as indicating time; thus the K. say: gerō subbe, gerō kātferi, „the shadow (of a wall) in the morning", „the shadow in the evening".
[7] kābū: Koelle writes kábū; as for the term kū, it is probably nothing, but a popular abbreviation of kābū, and only by and by has obtained the meaning of „to day".
[8] bánē: Koelle writes bányō and bényō, but such a pronunciation I have never heard; — as for kintāgo see p. 147, note 4.
[9] rána: this term signifies the day, as far as it is illuminated by sunshine and it never comprises day and night together; accordingly, where longer periods of time are to be expressed, the term kwána is used, especially with regard to the length of a journey, as f. i. kwána nawa, „how many nights rest", i. q. „how many days' journey"; the Turkish term konák can only be partly compared. The same is the case with the term wollánde, plur. balde in the Fulfúlde-language (balde nol, „how many days (journey)"), as well as girbi in S. (girbi merge).
[10] ylide seems to be used especially and almost exclusively of the luminous appearance of the fire; the root being yel, „to shine", from which ayēlōma also seems to have been derived.
[11] ēlhre, Reichardt writes hurę.
[12] ǵyeaaī: thus the Lógoné-people say ǵyeaaī na-kū, „your shadow", and so on.
[13] sáyeli, sáṅgeli apparently has been derived from sáye, „sun".
[14] bāke trē meaning verbally „there is no moon-shine", properly designates only the darkness of night. — tšilkō: thus they say tšilkō n ofā, „the shadow of the tree"; tšilkō rō, „shadow of a living being"; tšilkō n gadźa, tšilkō dlō wátšia and so on.
[15] wégia: the close resemblance of wégia and wátšia, wātšia being only distinguished by one single sound, while their meaning is so decidedly different, is certainly remarkable and very instructive, tšu no doubt expressing the moving and living principle, as stated in the Introductory Remarks p. CCXLI, 4, b).
[16] ndźili: the great similarity of this term with the corresponding one in Mába is remarkable, especially as the languages in general have so little in common; see Introduct. Remarks p. CCLXXXV, c). — kéde with naf means „one", as palle in W.
[17] For „flame" Fresnel gives the totally different term fitirngéh, which whether it be wrong, or due to a dialectical variety, I cannot tell; for „smoke" he has haudik, for „cinders", kitimih. — As for the term waṅg lolloti compare Introductory Remarks p. CCCXXI, b); as for délka-dā ibid. CCCLX, g).

Deutsch und Englisch.	Kanúri.	Tedá.	Hausa.	Fulfulde.
Jahr — year	sága [1]	sága	šékara [12] . .	hitánde . . / dungu, Pl. dúbi
Morgendämmerung — morning twilight	fedžr [2] (Arb.) / fedžr date n; / kurū ágilla wātší-ni [3]	al fedžr . . / awenne fiyúkkenen	gāri yausi .	bedgul . . .
Morgenfrühe — morning	wālo . . . / dunya wātši .	balkē[?] . .	assubba . .	bimbi . . . / súbaka . .
Sonnenaufgang (nur verbal) sun-rise (verbal phrase)	kańgal kau / tsú-lug-in [4] / tambin	yezé / korúk . / kéyorúk	lattu n rāna šina litto	nańge fūdi .
Morgen (vor der grossen Hitze) — morning (before the great heat sets in)	bálte [5]	baltē	hantai . . .	[hantai [13]] . .
Mittagshitze — midday-heat	dibdu [6] . . .	kun? [11] . . .	êni	nyélloké . .
Mittag, Sonnenhöhe — midday, noon	kau dābu [7] .	dyski (lābo .	rāna tsakka .	tšakka nyelōma / bottadlo . .
Dhohor (um 2 U. N. M.) — Dhohor (about 2 ocl. p. m.)	dohor, dōar [8] (Arb.)	eddóhor . .	zohor . . .	zúhura . . . / sallifánna (Ms.)
'Asr (gegen 4 U. N. M.) — 'Asr (about 4 ocl. p. m.)	áser [9]	aláser . . . / adér . . .	aser	alāsera . . .
Nachmittag (die Zeit nach dem 'Asr) — afternoon (the time after the 'Asr)	kátšeri [10] . .	dénno-kú . .	máretšé . .	kikide . . .

[1] sága. Koelle hat noch einen Ausdruck kérbū oder kerfā für „Jahr", wenigstens mit Bezug auf das Lebensalter der Menschen und auch noch einen dritten ágall oder ágeil; das ist aber nur sehr uneigentlich und beruht nur darauf, dass diese Völker, anstatt nach Jahren, nach „Regenzeiten" rechnen.

[2] fedžr. Koelle schreibt fatsar. date n ist von dángin, „ich stehe auf, bleibe aufrecht stehn".

[3] kurū ágilla wātší-ni, wörtlich „es ist noch nicht gehörig Tag geworden", woran sich eng die folgende Phrase schliesst dunya wātši, „die Welt hat (nun) getagt".

[4] tsú-lug-in von lug-ískin, s. oben S. 88; tamb-in von tamb-ískin, „ich krieche hervor", „werde geboren", s. S. 31. — In allen correspondirenden Sprachen habe ich diesen Ausdruck nur in verbaler Form darstellen können.

[5] bálte. Das letzte e habe ich im Kanúri nie lang gehört, wie Koelle es schreibt, baltē, aber stets so im Tedá.

[6] dibdu. Diesen überaus gewöhnlichen Ausdruck gibt Koelle in der Form dúbdō irrig für „Abend" = kátširi, wie er auch wol irrthümlich dem davon abgeleiteten Ausdruck díbdi-fú die allgemeine Bedeutung von „heisser Jahreszeit" beilegt.

[7] kau dābu, wörtlich „die Sonne im Mittel". Diesen Namen gibt Escayrac de Lauture (1856) dem von ihm (von Kanúri-Leuten) erforschten „equatorialen See" in der falschen Form Koel-Dabo. S. Petermann und Hassenstein, Karte von Inner-Afrika, Blatt 7.

[8] dōar ist die gewöhnliche Form im gemeinen Leben, während die Gebildeten das h zu bewahren suchen, schrieben sie ihre Sprache, sie würden es sicher ausdrücken. Koelle schreibt dúar, hat aber dasselbe Arabische Wort noch einmal in der kaum kenntlichen Form altšifer.

[9] áser. Koelle schreibt alnháser.

[10] kátšeri. Koelle schreibt kátširi.

[11] kun in der Phrase kun wa pylaššā, S. LXXVI, „wenn die Hitze vorbei ist".

[12] šékara. Ich will hier den Ausdruck kwāna n šékara anführen, entsprechend unserer „Sylvesternacht" und dem Begriffe nach wenigstens auch unserem „Neujahrstag", auf F. wolánde hitánde.

[13] hantai ist das Hausa-Wort, aber die in Sókoto und den umliegenden Landschaften angesessenen Fulbe scheinen ihren heimischen originalen Ausdruck für „Morgen" ganz vergessen zu haben.

[14] tédi yhan-ka-hedé, „12 Monate"; die Lógone-Sprache hat keinen eigenthümlichen Ausdruck für „Jahr"; doch, wo es sich auf Alter bezieht, scheint ein solcher Ausdruck da zu sein, wenigstens habe ich unter meinen Phrasen bayan-kō gené (gané, „wie viel", S. 9), „deine Jahre wie viel" dem H. šékerú-n-ka nawa.

[15] móea ist in seiner Entstehung mir nicht ganz deutlich.

[16] wétšin átiró heisst eigentlich „die Sonne oben". — itše wétšin, „Nachmittag", eigentlich „Auge des Tages".

[17] kai tegga. kai ist offenbar eine populäre Abkürzung für kadóa, wenn es nicht die ursprünglichere Form ist, da dša die zweite Hälfte des letzteren Wortes allein „Tag" heisst und eine enge Beziehung zu dšš, „die Nacht" zu haben scheint.

[20] abin ist auffallend und beruht vielleicht auf Missverständniss, da es sonst heisst „es hört auf". Seetzen's kaddris für „Jahr" ist also vielleicht richtig. — Zu walō-walé toróáka, eigentlich „nachdem Dunkelheit aufgehört hat" siehe Einleitung S. CCC, f, a); ebenso von tor-ángu. — Neben delba wird wahrscheinlich noch har bango für „heisse Tageszeit" gebraucht, von Seetzen als „heisse Jahreszeit" missverstanden, während bar-kir, „die kühle Tageszeit", in meinen Phrasen vorkommt und sich wieder an kirranda, „Winter" bei Seetzen anschliesst. — kondo kóro erinnert lebhaftig an den Namen der bekannten Missionsstation am oberen Nil und das ist gar nicht so ohne Grund, da, wie Einleitung S. CCCXXXII gezeigt, das Bari mit dem Mába mehrere Berührungspunkte hat. kóro heisst „oben".

Fulful.	Lógonē.	Wándalā.	Bágrimma.	Māba.
dĭri	tĕdi χkan-ka-kadē[14]	Iwo	lōa	[abín[15]]
bía-bía	fedĭr . . . . / rō al fedĭr . .	sircuíodža . . / wūra fayaē wozóze	fedĭr . . . / na fedĭr rakī; / fedĭr tšatšātša	weréddo
subba	rō dataia . . .	róroksē . . .	godlífga . . .	walō-walo to-rónka[16]
wēne-di falta .	sāyo dáswoyā .	acssa wétšia .	kai tegga[17] .	añik tmgūri
dóbade	máhalē (mawóahā alē?)	gúserō . . .	balte . . .	yes terúnga
wēnu akórron .	sáyeli wlán . .	gofga wótšia .	kadž sungo .	delka[18]
džāri māsu . .	mawéahā . . .	wétšia átirō[16]	gal kádža . .	delka kibbi
lúla	dohor	dohor . . .	dohor . . .	dohor
útšeri	aser . . . . / máse[15] . . .	aser . . . . / ltše wétšia .	asar . . . . / dantágri . .	asar / kondo kóro[18]

[1] sága. Koelle besides this one has yet another term, viz hérbā or hérfā with regard to human age, and even ágoll or ágoll, but the latter at least, which means but „rainy season", very improperly belongs to this place, the Africans, as well as many other nations under the Tropics, very naturally reckoning by „rainy seasons".

[2] fedĭr. Koelle fatear: and no doubt the Arabic ج is easily changed into ts. — dāte a is from dāāgia, „I stand upright".

[3] horō ágilio wétši-ni means verbally „day has not yet well dawned". Thus also the following term dunya wétši, means „the world has dawned".

[4] teb-jug-in, 3rd person sing. prs. from jug-ńakio, see p. 86; tamb-in, 3rd person sing. prs. from tamb-ńakin, „I am born", see p. 33. I have not found in any of these idioms an expressive substantival term for „sunrise".

[5] bálte: Koelle writes baltē, but the final e is not long in Kanúri, while in Tĕdā certainly it is long.

[6] dibdo: this most common term of daily life Koelle wrongly gives in the form dábdē as meaning „evening" = hátširi; then he has another term dibdi-fū, evidently thence derived, to which he wrongly attributes the general meaning of „hot season".

[7] kou dábu means verbally „the sun in the middle, in the zenith", and this is the very name, which the Nilotic traveller Brun-Rollet de Lauture in the wrong form Koel-Dabo gives to an Equatorial lake of which in the year 1855 he obtained information, evidently from Kanúri-pilgrims, and which Mr. Petermann has laid down in his large Map of Central-Africa, about n. 7.

[8] dóar is the usual form in daily life. Koelle writes dúar, but has besides, the totally different form alšifer.

[9] āser, Koelle alabáser; that is certainly wrong, although we might express the Arabic ع by a double a, thus aaser.

[10] kátšeri; Koelle hátširi.

[11] kuu I have only in the phrase kuu wo pyindō, „when the heat of the day is past".

[12] Šēhara: I here adduce the term kwána n šēhara, which corresponds to the English term „new-year's night", and in some respects even to that of „new-year's day", F. wolánde hitánde.

[13] hantai is the Hausa-term, but I never learned the original Fulfúlde expression, which the Fúlbe settled in Sókoto and the neighbouring provinces seem to have entirely forgotten.

[14] tĕdi χkan-ka-kadē, „twelve months"; it is however possible, that there is another term for „year" in the Lógonē-language, which was unknown to my authority, and such a term I have obtained myself in the phrase ániya-kā ganē, „thy (kā) years how many" (ganē, „how many") = H. šékarú-n-ka nawa.

[15] máse is of unknown origin to me.

[16] wétšia átirō properly means „the sun above". — ltše wétšia, „afternoon", originally „eye of day".

[17] kai tegga: kai is apparently a popularly abbreviated form for kádža or it may rather be the original form, meaning „day", dža alone having a certain relation to dža, „night".

[18] abín probably is caused by a misunderstanding, and means nothing but „it is finished, is at an end"; the term kaddeia therefore given by Seetzen with the notion of „year" may be right. — As for the phrase walō-walō torónka meaning properly „after darkness has ceased", as well as with regard to the form yes ter-ánga see Introductory Remarks p. CCCI, f, a). — Besides the term delka probably another one is used with the same meaning, viz bar buhgo, which Seetzen has given as meaning „hot season", while my term har-hir meaning „cooler part of the day, afternoon" reminds us of the term hirraoaka given by Seetzen as meaning „winter". — The term kondo kóro reminds one of the name of the wellknown Missionary station on the Upper Nile, and such resemblance is not a mere phantom, the Bari-idiom, as shown Introductory Remarks p. CCCXXXIII, having certain points of affinity with the Māba; kóro means „above".

Deutsch und Englisch.	Kanúri.	Tédā.	Hausa.	Fulfulde.
Sonnenuntergang — *sunset* (meist verbal s. S. 128 ff.)	nisukúrō kén-gal-be ken-tsúrō .	yezē tobúr . .	rāna fādua .	naúge múti .
Maghreb, als Zeit des Gebets — *Maghreb, as time of the evening prayer*	mógreba (Arb.) mogárifū [2] .	mābor . . . almuyreb . .	almúyreba [8] .	kikīde . . . fúttura . .
el 'Ašā — *el 'Ašā* . . .	lēšā (Arb.) . .	lasā	al ašā . . .	ēšai . . . .
Mitternacht — *midnight* .	dyrtu bunē [3] .	dógoso labo .	tsakka derē .	tšakka dženma
Stunde — *hour*	sáa (Arb.) .	sáa (Arb.) . .	sáa (Arb.) . .	saáa . . . .
Woche — *week*	mágo [4] . . .	dógesā tyddesa [7]	kwāna bókoi .	. . . . .
Sonntag — *Sunday* . .	lāde [5] . . (Arabisch)	lábadu . . .	láhade . . .	láhade . . .
Montag — *Monday* . .	léteriñ . lételin . .	eltnin . . .	áltenin . . .	áltenin . . .
Dienstag — *Tuesday* . .	telāgo . .	tlōta	attalāta . . .	attalāta . . .
Mittwoch — *Wednesday* .	láraba . .	láraba . . .	aláraba . . .	aláraba . . .
Donnerstag — *Thursday*	lamīsu . .	lamīsu . . .	alamīsu . . .	alamīsu . . .
Freitag — *Friday* . . .	zymma . .	eldzymma . .	aldžymma . .	aldžymma . .
Sonnabend — *Saturday* .	sibde . .	essébdu . . .	assebdu . .	assebdu . . .
Januar — *January* [1] {1845, 1878}	moharrem (mā-ram [6]	Arb.	ovō [9]	ahāram . . .

[1] Monatsnamen des Mohammedanischen Jahres, als Mondmonate mit unserem Kalender nur jedes 33ste Jahr correspondirend.

[2] mogárifū. Koelle schreibt mágarifū.

[3] dyrtu bunē. Anstatt dyrtu schreibt Koelle dértę und gibt anstatt meines Ausdruckes für „Mitternacht" den allgemeinen dinīá dértę. Ja, in seiner Grammatik §. 115 hat er dértę allein für „Mitternacht".

[4] mágo bedeutet sowol 7 als 8 Tage. S. Koelle's Grammatik §. 108.

[5] lāde u. s. w. Alle diese Namen sind natürlich dem Arabischen entnommen und daher ist ihre Schreibweise sehr unsicher, da die Eingeborenen je nach dem Grade ihrer Bildung sich dem Vorbilde näher oder entfernter halten. Deshalb führe ich hier die abweichenden Formen bei Koelle nicht an.

[6] moharrem u. s. w. Dies sind die ziemlich rein Arabischen Formen der Monatsnamen, welche die gelehrten Städter gebrauchen; die bei dem Land- und gemeinen Volke üblichen sind mehr oder weniger verdorben; ich habe in Klammern die von Koelle unter kantágę gegebenen Formen mit Fortlassung der mir überflüssig erscheinenden Zeichen beigesetzt. Dabei will ich nur vorübergehend bemerken, dass es natürlich grundfalsch ist, wie Koelle diese Mohammedanischen Monate denen des christlichen Kalenders entsprechen lässt, da der ganze Kreislauf des Mondjahres in 33 Sonnenjahren ein Jahr verliert, so dass also die Monate im Mohammedanischen Kalender sich fortwährend verschieben.

[7] dógesā tyddesa, eigentlich „7 Nächte", wie denn viele dieser Völker nach Nächten rechnen. Der entsprechende Ausdruck im Wándalā, Bagrimma und Móba heisst „7 Tage", der zweite Móba-Ausdruck ngendān ēye, „8 Tage".

[8] almúyreba. Ich will hier die Ausdrücke für „Abendröthe" angeben, so weit ich sie erfuhr. H. dāā, F. bodēri, S. nāri-yē. Die Hausa haben auch noch einen eigenthümlichen Ausdruck für Abenddämmerung, nämlich gadlimarē, sowie sie viele andere individuelle Ausdrücke haben, die ich in den anderen Sprachen nicht vertreten habe.

[9] ovō. Dieser, so wie manche der nachfolgenden Namen sind offenbar beziehungsreich, aber es ist jetzt schwer, ihre ursprüngliche Bedeutung aufzufinden. Besonders fand ich Niemand, dem die Bedeutung von ovō bekannt gewesen wäre und selbst der Name war den meisten Hausaen entfremdet. kanē, eigentlich „jüngerer Bruder", bedeutet hier „der darauf folgende"; dasselbe bedeutet bawa, „Sklave", und wenn das bei dem Namen bawa n watta n lēa nicht der Fall zu sein scheint, indem der watta n lēa selbst erst nachfolgt, so ist das offenbar nur scheinbar, indem es nicht zweifelhaft ist, dass ursprünglich der hārāma salla als watta n lēa, „der Monat des Lammschlachtens" gedacht wurde".

[10] dādeh kann ich nicht mit Bestimmtheit erklären; auch hier ist der nachfolgende Name als der „kleine", d. h. „der jüngere Bruder" gefasst.

[11] sol scheint eine volksthümliche Abkürzung aus sāyeli, sāgeli zu sein.

[12] léde moharrem. Die eigentlichen Monatsnamen im Lógonē und den beiden folgenden Sprachen habe ich nicht erfahren und gebe hier nur die bei den Gebildeteren üblichen, ziemlich rein Arabischen Formen.

[13] ēdžolkē ist ein eigenthümlich selbstständiger Ausdruck für „Mitternacht" und hängt vielleicht mit hoenāga zusammen, das Burckhardt für „Nacht" gibt.

[14] dēba-sēn steht in engem Zusammenhange mit dabbo, ganz wie fátter-ān zu fatter, „der auf die dabbo, auf den fatter folgende Monat" und dient also zum klaren Beweise, dass im National-Kalender der Móba der Moharrem nicht den Anfang bildet. Das s scheint nur aus euphonischen Gründen eingeschoben zu sein.

Sońyai.	Lógoné.	Wándalá.	Bágrimma.	Mába.
safúkko	sáye dáyiha . .	biá-biá wétšin	katš otšō-ga .	añik tai
fútiero . . . . ⎫ almāri . . . . ⎭	múgreba . . .	mógreba . .	mógreba . .	almágreba
fúttero būno . .	. . . . . .	. . . . . .	. . . . . .	. . . . . .
kīgi (tšīdži) māsu	wāde adán . .	⎧gefga⎫ ⎨kúda⎬ wágia ⎩bōda⎭	gal n džō . .	ódžolkō [13]
. . . . . .	. . . . . .	. . . . . .	. . . . . .	. . . . . .
. . . . . .	semálge	har wūye . .	dža marla . .	ngóndžo ⎧mindri ⎩ēya
láhade	sal lāde [11] . . .	lāde	láhadi . . .	ahád
áltenīn	sēle telēn . . .	létenīn . . .	letnīn . . .	étleuīn
attalēta	sel teláko . . .	telágo . . .	dža taláki . .	öttelēt
aláraba	sel láraba . . .	láraba . . .	láraba . . .	áraba
alamīsu . . .	sel lamīsu . . .	lamīsa . . .	lamīsi . . .	ɣamīs
aldžumma . . .	sel demā . . .	ṣumma . . .	ūdžimma . .	džumma
assebdu . . .	se' sibde . . .	sibda . . .	síbbedī . . .	sab
dādeb [10] . . .	tēde moharrem [12]	moharrem . .	moharrem . .	débe-tēn [14]

[1] The names of these Mohammedan months, as belonging to the Lunar system, do not correspond with the names of our months, but every 33rd year.
[2] mugérifā: Koelle writes mégerifā.
[3] durin bunē; instead of durin Koelle writes dérię and gives for „midnight" the general and inexpressive term dinia dérię; nay, in his grammar § 115 he attributes the notion of „midnight" to the term dérię alone.
[4] mágo means as well a period of seven, as of eight days. See Koelle's grammar § 208.
[5] lóde etc. All these names of the days of the week, of course, have been borrowed from the Arabic, and that is the reason, why the mode of writing them in these illiterate languages is very uncertain, each of the natives according to the degree of his state of civilization approaching nearer to the origin, or receding further from it. It is on this account, that I do not mention here the forms given by Koelle.
[6] moharrem etc. I here give the almost pure Arabic forms of the names of the months, such as they are used by the more learned people; while those used by the country-people are more or less corrupted; although, no doubt, many native terms might still be learned in this respect; I have added in brackets the terms given by Koelle under the name kanáge. But I have to remark, that it is a great mistake of Koelle's to make correspond these names of the Mohammedan calendar to those of the Christian one, each period of 33 Lunar years, such as those of the Mohammedan calendar are, losing one whole year, so that the correspondence of the relative months is continually changed.
[7] dégeaó tyddeen, „seven nights"; the corresponding terms in Wándalá and Bágrimma meaning „7 days", while in Mába, besides this one, we have ngendže ēya meaning „8 days".
[8] almáyreba. I will here adduce the native terms for „evening-sky", as far as I was able to make them out, H. dīš (red), F. hodéri, S. sári-yō. The Hausa-people have besides a peculiar term for twilight, viz gedšímaró.
[9] ovā: this one, as well as several of the following terms may possibly be very expressive and highly interesting for national customs, but it is difficult at present to make out their original meaning. Thus I did not find a single Ba-kanáe man, who was able to tell me the meaning of drarī; nay, the name itself has almost become obliterated. — kané means properly „younger brother", and means here „he who follows upon" the preceding one; just the same is the meaning of buna (properly „slave"), and the exception to this rule, which seems to be contained in the term buna n welle n lēe is only seemingly; for there cannot be the slightest doubt, that originally the kárama sallā was regarded as the welle n lēa, „the month of the slaughtering".
[10] dādeb I am not able to analyze; also in this language the succeeding month is called „the younger brother", kaine.
[11] sel seems to be a popularly abbreviated form from esyeli, ségeli.
[12] tēde moharrem: in Lógoné as well, as in the two following languages I did not learn the popular names of the months and therefore here give merely these nearly pure Arabic forms, which are used by the people of the higher classes.
[13] ódžolkó is a remarkably independent term for „midnight" and may have some connection with keoshga the term given by Burckhardt as meaning „night".
[14] débe-tēn is intimately connected with debēr, the name of the succeeding month, clearly showing, that the native calendar of the Mába does not begin with this month.

Deutsch und Englisch.	Kanúri.	Tédā.	Hausa.	Fulfúlde.
Februar — February . .	saffer (šāfer) .	Arabisch	kané n ovō .	min - hāram,[4] .
März — March	rebī el auel (lafeloúal)		gani	gani . . . .
April — April	rebī el āgir (lafelāyer)		kané n gani . / úrorí n farī .	min - gani . .
Mai — May	džumāda auel (wōtšimadaloúal)		auta . . . . / úrorí n tsakka	boddāre . .
Juni — June	džumāda agir (wotšimadaláyer)		úrorí n kárewā	džatiru . . .
Juli — July	radžeb (rádzab)		azōni n sōfi .	sumatāndu néhebe
August — August . . .	šabān (sabán)		baua n azōni n sōfi / ša n rūa n sōfi	gādže . . . / džaudiaungel .
September — September .	rámadān (ármalán)		wotla rámmala	sūmayō[5] . .
Oktober — October . .	šauāl (soúal) .		kárama salla[3]	džūldendu . .
November — November .	zulkēde (kide)		baua n wotla n lēa	siūta rāndu[6] .
Dezember — December .	hadž (átši) .		wotla n lēa . / babá n salla	leyādži . . .
Zeit, Jahreszeit — time, season (adverbiale Zeitbegriffe s. S. 22 ff)	lokte[1] (Arb.) .	káare . . .	lókatši . . / lattu . . .	wákkati . .
trockene, heisse Jahreszeit — dry, hot season	bē[2] . . . . / dunya-bē, nembē	borō . . . . / bē noekinde .	rāni	tšēdu[7] . . .

[1] lokte. Koelle schreibt lókte und lókta. Ich will hier den Ausdruck girgám anführen, der unserem Begriffe von „Datum" zu entsprechen scheint; so „was ist sein, ihr Datum (in Bezug auf eine Begebenheit)", a-fi girgám-tee oder sāga a-fi girgám-tee, „welches Jahr sein Datum", also auch kāba a-fi girgám-tee, „an welchem Tage hat es sich zugetragen"?. Ähnlich sagt man im Lógonē sanhē dikēmi dē und im Wándalá saor yéh-avé oder sare girgáme tsakka (in der letzteren Phrase ist der Einfluss des Kanúri unverkennbar, obgleich für girgam im Wándalá ein eigner Ausdruck rámmalé vorhanden zu sein scheint); im Bágrimma entspricht lōen konde, „wie viele Jahre" nicht ganz.

[2] bē ist jedenfalls eines der ursprünglichsten Kanúri-Wörter, die einen der Hauptbegriffe ihrer Anschauung auf die kürzeste und prägnanteste Weise ausdrücken. Vielleicht stehen binem und bigelā dazu in natürlicher Beziehung. Dabei scheint der Ausdruck bē nāgeli im Tédā anzudeuten, dass bē ursprünglich den ganz allgemeinen Begriff von „Jahreszeit" hatte. Vergl. die Bemerkung über die Begriffs-Entwickelung von bē S. LVIII, N. 2, die jedoch dahin zu modificiren ist, dass bē nicht eigentlich „die Regenzeit" selbst, sondern der Übergang dazu ist.

[3] kárama salla, wörtlich „das kleine Gebet"; als „Geburtsmonat", džāl-dāndu (von médé-džūla, s. S. 55) wird der Schauāl auch im Fulfúlde aufgefasst.

[4] min-hāram ist eine höchst eigenthümliche Zusammensetzung, indem hier das s in der aus moharrem verkürzten Form zhārem abgeworfen und diesem Worte min (von minye, „jüngerer Bruder") vorgesetzt ist. In diesem, wie in den beiden folgenden, Monatsnamen ist ein grösseres oder geringeres Anlehnen an das Hausa klar ersichtlich. Andere Dialekte werden eigenthümlichere Formen haben.

[5] sūmayō, „Fastenmonat", welcher Begriff weiter unten noch seine besondere Vertretung findet.

[6] siūta rāndu kann ich nicht erklären.

[7] tšēdu. Reichardt hat dafür die offenbar nur in dialektischer Aussprache verschiedene Form dšētu und dann wieder eine andere Form setu, die er sonderbarer Weise als besonderes Wort für „Sommer" giebt. Primer in the Fulah-language p. 5.

[8] ben-mé oder mé-ben, „Fastenmonat", von éga-mében, „ich faste". Offenbar hat fer-mé eine ähnliche Beziehung, wo auf das kleine Fest mit seinem öffentlichen „Gebet", obgleich ich für „beten" kein Zeitwort wie fer habe.

[9] kipel banda, wahrscheinlich „der letzte, der Schluss-Monat".

[10] leyte. Allerdings habe ich niedergeschrieben leyterinne, aber rinne oder wol erinne ist unbestimmtes Fürwort.

[11] kaye, „die Zeit der Sonne, der Hitze".

Sonyai.	Lógoné.	Wándalá.	Bágrimma.	Mába.	
dādeb kaine . .	tēde šaffer . .	saffar . . .	saffer . . .	ubéd	
almuddu . . .	tēde lebbi el auel	rebī el auel .	lebī el auel .	tom el auel	ímila el arbá
almuddu kaine .	tēde lebbi el áχir .	rebī el áχir .	lebī el áχir .	tom bārik	
akaine binkánte .	tēde džumāda auel	džumāda auel	džumāda el auel	tom kuńgōšk	
akaine himsánte .	tēde džumāda áχir	džumāda áχir	džumāda el áχir	tom asālik	
errédžeb . . .	tēde rádžabu . .	rádžeb . . .	radžeb . . .	radžeb	
tšekórno . . .	tēde šabān . .	šabān . . .	šabān . . .	geeār	
ban-mē [8] . . / mē-ban . . .	tēde rámadān .	rámadān . .	rámadān . .	rámadān	
fer-mē	tēde sauel . . .	šanāl . . .	sūwel . . .	fāttor	
bonénzem . . .	tēde sulkedē . .	sulkēde . . .	sūlkīda . . .	fāttorēn	
kipsi [9] / tšipsi } handu .	tēde sulhádži .	hadž	sūlhadž . . .	debēe	
wāti	loχte [10]	χepše	lokte . . .	wakket	
kóron, kúron wāti / korān	kodēze	gelga) kāye [11]	kirui	áruńgók	

[1] lokte: Koelle writes lókte and lókta. I will here adduce the term girgám, which seems to correspond to our notion of „date"; thus the Kanúri express the phrase „what is its date", „when did it happen" by a-fi girgám-tse or, by adding the term ngaa, „year", ngaa a-fi girgám-tse; thus a person can also say kābu a-fi girgám-tse „on what day did it happen"?. The same meaning is expressed in Lógoné by the phrase [illegible] dikémi di and in Wándalá [illegible] or [illegible] girgámma [illegible] (the latter phrase bearing evident traces of the influence of the Kanúri, which is remarkable, as the Wándalá seems to have the peculiar term [illegible] corresponding to the Kanúri girgám); in Bágrimma the phrase is rendered by [illegible] kaude meaning „how many years (ago)".

[2] bē, as shown Introductory Remarks p. LIX. note 2, is evidently one of the most primitive terms of the Kanúri-language, which expresses one of the principal notions of the natives, „the full measure of existence", in the shortest and most concise manner. Probably also the term binem (bē-nem) and bigelā (bē-gelā) may be connected with this term bē, while the term bē ningeli in the nearly related Tédā-language seems to indicate, that the original meaning of bē was the general notion of „season", just as we have it there with the notion of „day".

[3] hárama salla means verbally „the little prayer"; also the Púlbe regard the month of shawāl as „a month of prayer", dūāl-dándu (from móddō-dūāla, „I pray", see above p. 88).

[4] min-hárana is a term of peculiar composition, the a in the word ahárana, which represented the syllable ma in the original Arabic form, having been thrown off as a mere superfluous addition and min (the root of the term minye, „younger brother") having been prefixed to it. The two following names bear a close resemblance to the corresponding [illegible]-terms, while other purer dialects of the Fulfúlde-idiom probably may exhibit more original forms.

[5] sūmayē, „month of fasting".

[6] sidīn rēodu is a term, which I am not able to explain.

[7] sēēdu: Rev. Reichardt for this term gives the form dīēu, which evidently is a merely dialectical variation, while a little farther on he gives the same word once more in the form of ceto for „summer". Primer in the Fulah-language p. 5.

[8] ban-mē or mē-ban, „month of fasting", from ége-mēban. Evidently the term fer-mē likewise has a similarly significative meaning, and probably means „month of prayer", although I have no such verb as for for „to pray" in Sonyai.

[9] kipsi handu probably means „last month".

[10] loχte: I wrote down loχtarinna, but rinna or rather arinna must be the indeterminate pronoun.

[11] kāye, „the time, period of the sun, the heat".

Deutsch und Englisch.	Kanúri.	Tédā.	Hausa.	Fulfulde.
Hitze — *heat*	kamméguā [1] .	úneki	(zāñ) zuffu . .	galli . . . .
Kälte — *cold*	kágo	kéri; adj. kéridē	dāri	dźangol . . .
kalte Jahreszeit — *cold season*	bīnem . . .	{ donso, S. . } { domóskin, N. }	dāri	{ dźangol . . } { débbundē . . }
Regenzeit — *rainy season*	nìngeri [2] . .	{ ngēle . . . } { hē nìngeli . }	dámana [10] . .	dungu . . .
Erntezeit, Ende der Regenzeit — *harvest-time, end of rainy season*	bígelā, bíggela [3]	{ héberē . . . } { kéberē . . }	kaká [11] . . .	nyāmendē . .
Wind — *wind*	kárna [4] . . .	{ auen . . . } { ábonō . . . }	iska	{ bendu . . . } { kenne . . . }
Wirbelwind — *whirl-wind*	múlteruā . .	ábonō derékini [8]	gúgua . . .	dulúru . . .
Gewitter — *thunder-storm*	délágo [5] . .	{ auen bum, S. } { ábonō níngeli manē [9] }	hádderi [12] . .	{ yōnde . . . } { yonde . . . }
Donner — *thunder* . . .	sergagālo [6] . .	{ éskenō . . . } { eskoine girgékini }	harādu [13] . .	falmángu, Plur. falmāli
Blitz — *lightning* . . .	dunya tsuēltin [7]	{ kindéele, S. . } { yumár, N. . }	wélkia [14] . .	mátyerē . .

[1] kamméguā ist auffällig, es fehlt bei Koelle.
[2] níngeri wol kein ursprüngliches Wort, das wol nur erst später für den verloren gegangenen monosyllabischen Ausdruck für „Regen", „Regenzeit" gangbar wurde. Koelle schreibt nìngeli und nàngali.
[3] bígelā, bíggela. In Betreff der Übereinstimmung dieses Ausdrucks mit dem entsprechenden des Bágrimma siehe S. CCLXXXII, 6, a).
[4] kárna. Koelle schreibt kárnā und gibt unter diesem Wort den Ausdruck kárna tsumaria für „Wirbelwind", entsprechend meinem múlteruā.
[5] délágo ist das mit Regen verbundene Gewitter, wie es in den Tropen üblich ist. Koelle schreibt délágo und déláge.
[6] sergagālo ist ein sehr zweifelhafter Ausdruck. Koelle hat für „Donner", rálma, das habe ich nie gehört.
[7] dunya tsuēltin. Dieser verbale Ausdruck gehört eigentlich nicht hierher, aber einen nationalen substantivischen Ausdruck scheint es nicht zu geben, obgleich das Arabische ráde zuweilen in dieser Bedeutung gebraucht wird.
[8] ábonō derékini ist keine substantivische, sondern eine verbale Redensart, „der Wind dreht sich herum, wirbelt".
[9] ábonō níngeli manē ist ein unbehülflicher Ausdruck „Wind mit Wasser", für den es wahrscheinlich einen besseren gibt, obgleich man bedenken muss, dass wir im Gebiete der Tédā kein Tropenland, sondern ein durchgängig wüstes Hochland vor uns haben, wo Wind mit Regen und Regen überhaupt eine Ausnahme ist.
[10] dámana ist entschieden verwandt mit den Ausdrücken der Kótokó-Dialekte dáman u. s. w. (S. CCVI) und ist wol später aufgenommen worden. Die Hausa- und Fulfulde-Sprachen besitzen übrigens noch besondere Ausdrücke für besondere Abschnitte der Regenzeit und wahrscheinlich besitzen die meisten der anderen Sprachen deren auch, sie sind mir aber nicht bekannt geworden. „Anfang der Regenzeit", besonders mit Bezug auf die Zeitigkeit der Hirsesaat, H. bácara, F. séte oder koreal, B. mária; „heftigster Theil der Regenzeit", H. malka, F. loddo oder déákam; „das die Regenzeit abschliessende Gewitter", H. hádderi n kaká, F. birorādu. Etwas zweifelhaft ist mir die Bedeutung von H. agadāri, F. agadārie, aber allem Anscheine nach bedeutet es die ungesunde Zeit am Ende der Regenzeit.
[11] kaká. So „Erntezeit der Negerhirse", H. kaká n góro, F. nyāmendē gauri; „Erntezeit des Sorghum", H. kaká n dawa, F. nyāmendē bairi.
[12] hádderi. Schön schreibt hādari. „Ein Gewittersturm hat sich erhoben", H. hádderi ya-tāso, F. yonde ámmahé.
[13] harādu. Schön hat arádu, wie denn der beginnende Anlaut des h im Hausa sehr wechselnd ist. So schreibt Schön hicha anstatt icha und hohhādo anstatt ūhada.
[14] wélkia. Schön walkia.
[15] ?i-ma kommt wol von wu-?ō, „ich schneide (Korn)", Einleitung S. CCX, a) und ist grundverschieden von sema, sima, „Kälte", das aber wol mit sìmadē zusammenhängt. wélfuni könnte, da der Wirbelwind mehr ein heisser Wind zu sein pflegt, mit maifū, „warm" zusammenhängen.
[16] tagadāō ist wahrscheinlich falsch, gehört wenigstens nicht hierher. dāōe erinnert an yōe, „Wasser", und taga, das auch vom Aufgehn der Sonne gebraucht wird, heisst wahrscheinlich auch „es hebt sich, steigt" (springt auf, kommt empor) vom Wasser. Der Ausdruck gehört also wol nach S. 134, wo mir der entsprechende Ausdruck fehlt.
[17] wiya ist höchst wahrscheinlich auf das universale wa, wa und yōa, „Wasser" zurückzuführen. Wāg-Ongā hängt vielleicht mit yó-dāogē, „ich dreschte" (S. 117) zusammen.
[18] semta, das neben dem eigenthümlich nationalen Bágrimma-Ausdruck kárna (vielleicht ba, „Wasser, Fluss" und rna = ... lāa, „Zeit, Jahreszeit") gebraucht zu werden scheint, ist wol den Kótokó-Sprachen entnommen. — delé in dem zusammengesetzten Ausdruck morgám delé ist sicherlich nichts anders als lela, „Wind", indem die vorhergehende Liquida die nachfolgende umgewandelt hat, also eigentlich „die Sturmwolke".
[19] marrā „Blitz" ist wol mehr als zweifelhaft, indem es dem mau-rā, „Regen" gar zu ähnlich sieht.

Téda.	Lógoné.	Wándalá.	Bágrimma.	Mába.
korno	mutkin	tagadžöē(?) [16]	kurbu	boṅgo adj.
fofō	aimāde(?)	. . . . . .	kúlú	kéra (adj.?)
fofō wāti	aima(?)	ikθe; ékyie .	kúlō	nānik
kaidīye . . . / kaidīye wāti .	déman	wīya [17]	semán (? [18]) . / bárua	kelēri
liyé	θī-ma [18]	θág-θagē . .	biggela . . .	káre
hēu . . . . . / híyau	sémadē	éfuyā	léle	avlik
hēu hére(?) . .	mátfuni	wé-lelē . . .	léle n okko . / otāo .	avlik nōlik / dokúðel
bāna	sémadē	samā	morgúm delé .	óffolō
bāna dundum . / bāna tondi . .	rāde	rāde	morgúm delé(?)	ðar-ða
mellu	bárak (Arb.) . .	. . . . . .	marrā [19] . . .	moldak

[1] kammégnā (ka-mégnā?) is of an origin unknown to me, and not a common formation; it is wanting in Koelle.
[2] aiāgeri; Koelle writes nγágeri as well as ngágeli. The root is evidently ger, as is plainly seen from the term kégerā (ka-ger-a) p. 160 „heavy rain"; ningeri (ne-égeri) therefore is „the space, the time of rain".
[3] bigelā, biggela; with regard to the identity of this term with the corresponding one in the Bágrimma-idiom see Introductory Remarks p. CCLXXXIII, 8, a).
[4] hárma; Koelle, who writes hérūa, gives the composite term haráa mamarla for „whirlwind" instead of my mát-farnā.
[5] délēgo means the storm or tornado, coming on with a drenching rain, such as are peculiar to the Tropical regions. Koelle writes délāge as well as délēge.
[6] aergagālo is a rather doubtful term. Koelle has rélma for „thunder", which I myself have never heard.
[7] ānaya tezēltin; this verbal form of expression properly does not belong to this place, but except the Arabic rāde, which is sometimes used, I have not heard a substantival term for expressing this notion.
[8] āhonō derékini, of course, is not a substantival, but a verbal form of speech, meaning properly „the wind turns round".
[9] āhonō aiāgeri manō is an awkward form of expression, meaning „wind together with water", and it is not at all improbable, that there is another more expressive one, although we must take into consideration, that the country of the Tēdā is not a Tropical region, but an almost total desert or rocky waste of considerable elevation, where rain is extremely rare.
[10] dámana is evidently related to the term déman of the Kótokō-dialects. The Hausa- and Fulfúlde-languages possess also peculiar terms for various periods of the rainy season, and probably most of the other languages have similar terms, but they have not become known to me. Thus, „the beginning of the rainy season", especially with regard to the proper period of sowing, is expressed in Hausa by means of the term bázara, F. cèto or korzel, A mário; „the most violent part of the rainy season", H. maiko, F. loddo or dūdkam; „the storm, which concludes the rainy season", H. hadderi n kakā, F. hirorédde. As for the proper meaning of agadēri, F. agadéria, it seems to signify the most unhealthy period at the end of the rainy season, although it may also signify the disease (dysentery?) itself.
[11] kakā: thus „the season for harvesting the negro-millet", H. kakā n géro, F. eyámendē gauri; „the season for harvesting the sorghum", H. kakā n dawa, F. eyámendē bairi.
[12] hadderi: Schön writes hadari; „a storm has gathered", H. hadderi ya-tāso, F. yonde ámmakā.
[13] haráda; Schön spells aráda, and, no doubt, the h in the beginning of the Hausa-words is very changing and uncertain. Thus Schön writes bisku instead of isku and habbada instead of ábada.
[15] wálkia; Schön writes walkia.
[16] θī-ma seems to be derived from wu-θē, „I cut (the corn)", Introductory Remarks p. CCXI, a), and seems to be totally distinct from aema, aima, „cold", which, no doubt, is connected with sémadē, „wind", „thunderstorm". As for mátfuni, it may be derived from matfā, „warm", the whirlwind being rather a warm blast of wind.
[16] tagadžöē may be wrong, at least may not belong strictly to this place, džöe reminding us of yāo, „water", while taga, which is also used of the forthcoming, or the rising of the sun, means probably „the water) starts up, boils"; the term, therefore, rather seems to belong to p. 136, where its place has been left vacant.
[17] wīya most probably has been derived from the generic wo, wa (Introductory Remarks p. CCXLI, b) and yīo, „water". — θág-θagē may possibly be connected with yē-θlagé, „I thrash" (p. 117).
[18] semán, which is used occasionally besides bárua, seems to have been borrowed from the Kótokō-languages, while bárua itself seems to be composed of ba, „water, river" and rua = lāa, „season". — delē in the composite term morgúm delē is a slight euphonical change from lele, „wind", and therefore properly means „storm-cloud".
[19] marrā with the notion of lightning is rather doubtful, resembling as it is does so very closely the term mau-rā, „rain".

Deutsch und Englisch.	Kanuri.	Tēda.	Hausa.	Fulfulde.
Regen — *rain*	níngeri . . .	eyī alla . . / níngeli . .	rūa n Alla . / rūa	tōberínde . . / ndīam tōbi .
heftiger Regen — *heavy rain*	kúgera [1] . .	níageli . . .	baki kirri n .	ballēdīum kurrum
leichter Regen — *light rain* / Tropfenfall — *dropping*	zémzemī [2] . .	níngeli kouü konū	taśasafa . . / yinyiffe . .	mismam . . .
Hagel — *hail*	māfi [3] . . .	grēni níngeli?	kánkara . .	tīammam [13] .
Thau — *dew*	kuláñgo [4] . .	beśāfu nubtū [9]	rāba [10] . . .	saaure . . .
Nebel — *fog*, *mist* . . .	bánteně [5] . .	kōboi . . .	hazū [11] . . .	tăuddi . . .
Halo (Hof am den Mond) — *halo*	. . . . .	. . . . . .	zénsenē . . .	timō-timōñgel / sebe . . .
Wolke — *cloud*	fagāū [6] . . .	kedi, S. . . / koū, N. . .	gidagidže . . / gadūimarē (?) .	ruide Plur. dūle
Regenbogen — *rain-bow*	kemárma [7] .	eyī dágara .	ma-ša-n rua [12] / baká n alla .	ñolōñgel . . / dāeredu ndīam
Echo — *echo*	. . . . .	. . . . . .	kūwa . . .	sautu (Arb.) . / sautu bamle [14]
Tropfen — *drop* . . .	lakte [8] . . .	. . . . . .	alnukta Arb. .	alnukta . . .

[1] kúgera (ku-ger-a) von derselben Wurzel wie níngeri (n-nger-i). Koelle schreibt kúgere und erklärt es mehr in der Bedeutung, in welcher ich delēge gebrauchen hörte.

[2] zémzemī fehlt bei Koelle. Es ist wol onomatopoëtisch.

[3] māfi, „Hagel" ist, obgleich in den von mir bereisten Gegenden viel seltener, als es in den von Burton und Speke bereisten, viel höher gelegenen Landschaften des südlichen äquatorialen Afrika's der Fall zu sein scheint, doch nichts Unerhörtes in Central-Afrika, und alle diese Völker haben eigene Ausdrücke für diese Erscheinung. Im Kanuri heisst „es hagelt", māfi tei-dúria („Hagel fällt").

[4] kuláñgo, „Thau" fehlt bei Koelle. Die Wurzel ist lan, lañg.

[5] bánteně. Koelle schreibt bánteṇyé.

[6] fagāū. Koelle schreibt fágoṇ und gibt auch als besondere Gattung von Wolken lálām (cirrus).

[7] kemárma scheint ungewöhnlich zu sein. Koelle hat dafür mármo mit der Phrase délēge mármo kurtši, wörtlich „das Sturmwetter hat einen Regenbogen gemischt", d. h. „da ist ein Regenbogen". Es scheint mir aber nicht unmöglich, dass in eben dieser Phrase das ke als Anfangssilbe von kemarme durch den Einfluss des vorhergegangenen ge in délēge nur verloren gegangen ist. Aber auffallend ist es, dass marma zwei so ganz verschiedene Dinge bezeichnen soll, wie das nach Koelle der Fall sein würde, einen Offizier und einen Regenbogen, während durch ke ein Vergleich angedeutet wird.

[8] lakte ist nach meiner Ansicht eine blosse populäre Verderbung des Arabischen nukta. Koelle hat eine eigenthümliche Form téłoktę, die er nicht richtig als reines Substantiv fasst mit der Bedeutung „Tropfen", wie schon die Konstruktion der angeführten Phrase zeigt, während es als mehr verbale Form anzusehen ist vom unpersönlichen Zeitwort tiloh-tāin, „es tröpfelt".

[9] beśāfu heisst „Erde, Land"; der Ausdruck „Thau" ist also umschrieben, vielleicht „Befeuchtung der Erde"; zu nubtū vgl. beśāfu bū-mede, „feuchter Boden" S. 168. — grēni níngeli heisst wahrscheinlich nur „grauer, heftiger Regen".

[10] rāba mit der Bedeutung „Thau" scheint abgeleitet von der Bedeutung „theilen" des identischen Zeitwortes rāba oder rāba.

[11] hazū. Die Hausaua und Fulbe haben auch einen eigenthümlichen Ausdruck für den in den südlichen Landschaften nach dem Benue zu häufigen „Höhenrauch", nämlich H. hayehi-hayehi, F. tšurtšúrle.

[12] ma-ša-n rua, „Wasser- oder Regentrinker"; baká n alla, „der Bogen (Flitzbogen) Gottes".

[13] tīammam. Ich hörte von den in Adamaua ansässigen Fulbe auch den Ausdruck Delnere für eine Art gefrorener Feuchtigkeit, und es mag möglicher Weise „Schnee" bedeuten, der auf den höchsten Bergen jener Landschaften gelegentlich vorkommt, aber auf der anderen Seite sieht er dem Ausdruck saaure so ähnlich, dass er vielleicht eher „Reif" bedeutet.

[14] sautu bamle, wörtlich „der Schall der Berge"; bamle ist der Plural von waṃde.

[15] her endáñg. her, „Wasser", endeñg ein Partizip; Koelle (Polyglotta) hat hárēnde, Barth'sche als Arama sée arende.

[16] bāne gō hāne, wörtlich „der Regen, der oben (in der Luft) ist". In analoger Weise scheint der folgende Ausdruck gebildet zu sein, indem ein n zwischen dem Nomen und dem relativen go eingeschaltet ist, obgleich ich nicht sicher bin.

[17] man-rē hat aller Wahrscheinlichkeit nach ursprünglich die interessante Bedeutung „Wasser vom Süden" (rē).

[18] māfi: die Originalität gebührt hier wahrscheinlich dem Bägrimma, wenn anders hier kein anderer Ausdruck üblich ist.

[19] man-al-kódo, wörtlich „Wasser zu eins", ein einzelnes Wassertheilchen.

Kanúri.	Lógoné.	Wándalá.	Bágrimma.	Mába.
bána . . . . . . / eṅgläerinna . .	sáma	wlya	man-rā [17] . .	endži / mäirek (Arb.)
bāna bēre . . .	sáma denyi . .	ašēve	man okko . .	endži nolīti
misimíssi / ago-tólle (verb.)	sáma dūdebē .	andžáme . .	man woke . . .	endži ñlliti
garī	ïha	állanzē . . .	mafi [18]	kíkin (?)
har andáṅg [15] . .	mū	angolžīre (?) .	tāla	der kíki
. . . .	balkūwun . . .	kočē	bútutū . . .	tíye
. . . .	. . . .	. . . . . .	. . . . . .	. . . .
bāne gō bēne [16] .	bulki	kumba	morgúm . .	ábiō [D. ábuya]
bāna n-go ntāl .	maróm delgā (?) .	uktur-vré . .	morgúm kékorā	badžás
	. . . .		. . . . . .	. . . . . .
	lugte		man-al-hēde [19]	ledda [S. tlak-täñk]

[1] kégora (ka-ger-a, see p. 160, note 8): Koelle writes kégara, and attributes to it the meaning, for which I usually found the term delágo to be used, viz „a heavy storm, a tempest, tornado, covering the whole sky with clouds and often accompanied by hail-stones".

[2] adeweṅi is wanting in Koelle's vocabulary; it seems to be an onomatopoetical form.

[3] máfi, „hail". Hail, although much less common in the regions traversed by myself, than seems to be the case in those more elevated regions to the south of the Equator visited by Captains Burton and Speke, nevertheless is not at all unusual even in the lower Equatorial regions of Africa, as appears already from the fact of all these people having a peculiar term of their own for this phenomenon, although in a few instances I may have been misunderstood. As for the phrase „it hails", it is expressed in Kanúri by máfi tsi-dūrin, („hail falls").

[4] kelāṅge, „dew" is wanting in Koelle. The root evidently is lan, laṅg.

[5] kántenō: Koelle writes kántenyé.

[6] fogáū: Koelle writes fágge and, besides, gives the term lálēm for the peculiar kind of clouds called „cirrus".

[7] kemárma. Koelle has instead the form márma with the phrase délágy márma kurtšî, „there is a rainbow", and I am inclined to think, that, as he has probably derived the simple term from this very phrase, the beginning syllable ke (ke-marma) may have been lost through the influence of the preceding ge in délágo. Koelle himself gives the simple term marma as conveying a totally different meaning, viz „an officer next in rank to the mainta, and always a slave"; but while it is very improbable, that the same term should have two so totally different meanings, it seems more probable, that from marma the term kamarma has been derived, in order to express some similarity between the rainbow and that officer.

[8] lakta, I think, is a popularly corrupted form of the Arabic term nukta. Koelle has a peculiar form, viz kélakta, which he wrongly looks upon as a simple substantive meaning „drop", while it is rather a verbal form from kélak-tšin, „it is dropping".

[9] kasáfu nabīū: kasáfu meaning „earth, ground", it is evident, that we have here not a simple term, but rather a circumscribing form, which is further illustrated by comparing the term kosáfu ka-nabó, „humid ground" p. 158.

[10] rába: the notion of „dew" seems to have been derived from its character of a [illegible] partition of water, the verb raba or rába meaning „to divide", p. 116.

[11] hacū: The Hausa and Fúlbe have also a peculiar term for signifying the thick yellowish fog covering the tops of the mountains, H. hāyaki-hāyaki (properly „smoke-smoke"), F. tšuriāría.

[12] ma-ša-n rūa properly „the drinker of water or rain"; baká n alla, „god's bow".

[13] tšammam: From the Fúlbe settled in Adamaua I heard, besides, the term dalaare, as signifying some sort of frozen or crystallized humidity, and it is not impossible, that this expression means „snow", which occasionally falls on the highest mountain-tops in that region; but, on the other side, dalaare bears such a close resemblance to the term saaara, „dew", that it very possibly means „hoarfrost".

[14] sanin bemle means verbally „the sound of the mountains", bemle being the plural number of wamda. — sanin is not indigenous, but taken from the Arabic.

[15] har andáṅg: har, „water", andáṅg a participial form. Koelle in his Polyglotta gives the contracted form hárāndu, Raffenel aév arande as the corresponding Arame-term.

[16] bāne gō bēne means verbally „the rain, that is above (in the air)"; and in quite an analogous manner the following term appears to be formed, an n having been inserted before the relative go.

[17] man-rā, according to all appearance, means „water from the South", a form of expression very interesting from a physiological point of view.

[18] máfi; the originality with regard to this term no doubt belongs to the Bágrimma-language.

[19] man-al-hēde verbally „water (one) to one", i. q. „a single drop".

Deutsch und Englisch.	Kanúri.	Tédā.	Hausa.	Fulfúlde.
kurzer Brunnen — *short well*	⎰ ńúwa . . . ⎱ dedē [1] . . .	yigō koraī . .	mármaru [7] . .	sebōre Plur. čēbōdže
Loch, wo Wasser geschöpft wird — *hole, from whence water is scooped out*	kékenū . . .	bíreni . . .	. . . . . .	. . . . . .
tiefer Brunnen — *deep well*	barrem [2] . . ⎱ bélkaši . . ⎱ kašim . . .	yigē [6] . . .	ridžia [8] . . .	bunda Plur. bulli
Quelle — *source* . . .	šim úkí-be [3] .	galle	idanú n rúa .	⎰ bítere n ndīam ⎱ bōgul ndīam
Quell-Bach — *living brook*	komádugu [4] .	fōdi; foti . .	⎰ kogi	wúrruǹgō . .
Fluss — *river*			⎱ gulbi . . .	māyo Pl. mādže
todter Flussarm, Hinterwasser — *dead river-arm, back water, mallah*	ngaldžam [5] .	. . . . . .	fádama [9] . .	⎰ illāgul . . . ⎱ fadamāre .

[1] dedē. Der dedē ist noch kürzer, als der núwo. Koelle hat das letztere nicht und schreibt den ersteren bald nḗu bald ńḗā, das er erklärt „ein Brunnen von 2—7 Faden Tiefe". Anstatt kékenū schreibt Koelle kékēnu. Es ist die flache Grube im Flussbett, wo das Wasser mit der flachen Hand geschöpft wird.

[2] barrem fehlt bei Koelle; für bélkaši schreibt er belgáši. Der feine Unterschied, den er ausserdem zwischen dieser Art Brunnen und dem ńḗu macht, abgesehen von der Tiefe, indem der Quellsprudel des letzteren sich stets im Sande, der des ersteren unter einem Felsen finde, möchte sich nicht immer bewähren. Übrigens ist von diesem Worte bélkaši die Brunnenstation Bélkaši fárī, d. h. „der obere Brunnen" genannt, wo dem Corporal Macguire 1856 getödtet wurde.

[3] šim úkí-be fehlt bei Koelle. Ich bin nicht sicher, ob kašim nicht vielleicht von diesem šim, „Auge" abgeleitet ist. Neben dem einfachen kášim hat Koelle auch das zusammengesetzte kášim belgášibē und hat noch einen anderen Ausdruck kádam mit dem Kompositum kádam nḗibé für „Quelle" oder „Quellsprudel" im Brunnen, aber den habe ich nicht gehört.

[4] komádugu. Koelle schreibt kómodūgu. Die Ableitung des Wortes ist ungewiss. Die Endung mádugu erinnert an dasselbe Wort im Hausa mit der Bedeutung „Karawanenführer". Das Wort hat eine sehr weite Bedeutung und begreift so auch vollkommen das wádi im Arabischen, das nur gelegentlich in einen Wasserlauf verwandelt wird. — Die verbal dargestellten Ausdrücke vom Anschwellen, Sinken des Stromes u. s. w. s. bei den unpersönlichen Zeitwörtern S. 130 f.

[5] ngaldžam fehlt bei Koelle. Über diese Wasserbildungen habe ich wiederholentlich in meinen Reisen gesprochen, besonders bei Gelegenheit der Musgu-Expedition Th. III, S. 199 u. 202; sie entsprechen in gewissem Sinne den indischen nullah. Sie sind fast immer mit reichem Baumwuchs besetzt.

[6] yigē ist ohne Zweifel zusammengesetzt aus eyí, „Wasser" und gē. — Hodgson gibt in seiner kurzen Liste von Tédā-Wörtern (Notes on Sahara p. 108) für „Brunnen" (well), ekai; für „Fluss" (river), ea.

[7] mármaru fehlt bei Schön.

[8] ridžia, bei Schön rijia. — idanú n rúa, wörtlich „Augen des Wassers".

[9] fádama. Diese schöne Hausa-Bezeichnung war Schön unbekannt geblieben, aber selbst kogi scheint er früher nicht gekannt zu haben. Verschieden von der fádama ist der kórremi, im Fulfúlde dellal, „ein sandiger, höher gelegener Thalboden" mit gelegentlichem Wasserlauf, und von letzterem wieder in näherer Beziehung verschieden die kováwma, ein Name, der besonders denjenigen Theil eines solchen kórremi bezeichnet, wo Wasser in geringer Tiefe gefunden wird, F. gōbul, Plur. gobādži. Beide Begriffe werden im S. durch bari-har, „Wasserbett" ausgedrückt.

[10] hari kaina, „kleines Wasser" ist ein sehr unvollkommener und wenig bezeichnender Ausdruck. Es erklärt sich jedoch von selbst, dass die an einem grossen Flusse wohnenden Sonyai keinen eigentlichen Namen für Brunnen haben. So könnten auch wir die offenen ungeheuren Wassergruben bei Tímbuktu nur sehr uneigentlich mit dem Namen „Brunnen" bezeichnen; der Name bango, den ihnen die Eingeborenen geben, entspricht mehr dem Begriff eines Wassertümpfels. Daher nennen auch die dort angesessenen Araber dieselben nicht bír, sondern dhaie. Im folgenden Ausdruck bango-mé finden wir dieses Wort wieder, in Verbindung mit mó, „Auge".

[11] Isa, Iša. Diess sind daher die besonderen Namen des Niger geworden, als des besonderen Flusses der Sonyai; s. Reisen IV, S. 243. — Für Isa, marigot, also so ziemlich meinem dšende entsprechend, gibt Raffenel das Wort hó, womit mein góru weiterhin vielleicht zusammenhängt, das ich allerdings auch noch in anderer Bedeutung für „rauhe Passage" habe. S. 161, N. 10.

[12] kaié-foll. kaié hängt wol sicher mit kallá oder galiá, „kurz" zusammen; dann wäre die folgende Form gé-fali vielleicht nur eine populäre Abkürzung, obgleich gé, „Bett" (gé-iayámí S. 166) hier Berücksichtigung finden könnte.

[13] gá ní oamá ist mir in seiner Entstehung nicht ganz deutlich; ró ist nai = roádo, „Erde"; es heisst sonst gewöhnlich „Stadt".

[14] iáyam-ášinhá: ášinhá scheint mit dem S. 41 aufgeführten Zeitwort ášnahé, „ruhen, liegen" zusammenzuhängen. iáyam selbst scheint eine Zusammensetzung mit am, „Wasser" zu sein.

[15] adwa. Ich glaube kaum, dass dieser Ausdruck aus der Kanúri- so völlig in die Wándalā-Sprache übergegangen ist, aber man kann sich wol erklären, dass diese kleine Gebirgsvölkchen für derartige Brunnen, wie sie trockenen Gegenden eigen sind, keinen eigenthümlich nationalen Ausdruck haben. yétāna yōr, „das aufsteigende Wasser"(?), von yeteé, „ich stehe auf".

[16] kámmané ist vielleicht zusammengesetzt aus kar-mané, „die Hand oder der Finger des Flusses".

[17] bōtuh ist eine nationale Umwandelung des Arabischen bat-ḥá. bahar scheint in allgemeiner Bedeutung für „Flussthal" gebraucht zu werden, wie folgende Phrase zeigt, bahar ágono barik té-na-go dakalal, „dieser Fluss, Stromthal", „sein Strom(?)" (barik) ist „seicht", dakalal. barik selbst hatte ich eine Zeit lang mit bahar zusammengestellt.

Sońγai.	Lógonē.	Wándalā.	Bágrimma.	Mába.
hāri kaina[10] . .	kalé-felī[12] . . / gé-felī . . .	sûwa[15] . . .	irbi	gúlayē [S. kulläb]
. . . .	tāhe am . . .	gōa	man anségna .	
. . . .	felī	. . . . .	malā	
hari bango -mō . .	rò al aamā[13] . .	yétŭua yōē . .	man kindži .	kasī (kodók-na [S. tjaltjáll])
ísa, ília[11] . . .	láyame; lárame .	γāye . . .	bā	bētak[17]
sai		guō		babar (Arb.)
džende	láyam-ásinhā[14] .	mrá guō . .	kámmanē[16] . / gúgulī . . .	bētak

[1] dedō: the dedō is a still shorter well, than the sûwa. Koelle does not mention the former and writes the latter sûn or sóń, which he interprets rightly as a well of from 2—7 fathoms. hóhenū, which by Koelle is written hóhŭne, is a small hole in the sandy bed of a fiumara, where people are able to reach the water with their hand.

[2] borrom is wanting in Koelle; instead of bélkaši he writes belgáši, and makes a rather nice distinction between this kind of well and the other one, which is called sôs or sûwe, even besides the greater depth of the former, this one differing, as he says „also by its spring (hášim) being underneath a rock, whereas the spring of the sôs (hádam) is in the sand". He has also the composite term hášim belgášibé, as well as another one hádam sóbé.

[3] Fim shi-be is wanting in Koelle. I am not sure, whether hašim be derived from the term Sim, „eye". From the term bélkaši the well bélkaši fávi, „the upper Well" on the highroad from Kano to Fumm, where Corporal Maguire was killed in 1856, has received its name.

[4] kowádagu: Koelle writes kómodágu; I am not sure, whether the latter part mádugu, which in Hausa means „leader of a caravan", and which might seem to indicate, that the original meaning is „water-channel", has really that origin. The term has a wide signification and comprises also the Arabic wādi, which only occasionally is changed into a watercourse.

[5] ngaldšam is wanting in Koelle's vocabulary. In my Travels and Discoveries, especially vol. III, p. 203, I have described repeatedly these shallow watercourses, which bear the same character as the Indian nullahs. Almost constantly their border is lined by rich vegetation.

[6] yigē, beyond a doubt, is composed of the term eyi, „water" and gō. — Hodgson in his short list of Tédá-words (Notes on Sahara p. 106) gives akai for „well", as for „river".

[7] mármara is wanting in Schön's vocabulary.

[8] ridžio: Schön writes rîjia.

[9] fádama: this most expressive and beautiful Hausa-term has remained unknown to Rev. Schön, and even the most common term kogi is not mentioned by him. — Distinct from the fádama is the kárrcmi, called dallul in F., a term which denotes a more elevated valley with a sandy bottom, which in consequence of heavy rains occasionally is changed into a watercourse, and again distinct from the kárrcmi is a closer sense is the karémma, a term designating that part of a kárrcmi, where water is found at little depth, in F. gébal, plur. gebádši. Both notions are expressed in S. by the term hari-har.

[10] hari kaina, „little water", is a very defective and not at all expressive term, but we can easily understand, how the Sońγai-nation, whose territory stretches along a large and navigable river, has no peculiar name for „well". It would be even improper, to give this name to those large open cavities in the neighbourhood of Tímbuktu, from whence the natives of that place take their supply of water; the name bango, which is given to them by the natives, expresses more correctly the notion of „pond" or „pool", while neither the Arabs settled in those regions call them bīr, but dhaia. — The same term bango in connection with mō, „eye" appears also in the following term.

[11] Isa, īša: it is this generic term for „river", which has become the proper Sońγai-name of the Niger, Tr. and Disc. vol. IV, p. 590. As for the term „marigot, lac" corresponding with dšende in my list, Mr. Raffenel renders it by hō, which may be connected with my góru, although the latter term appears in my list p. 160, note 10 also with the meaning „rough passage".

[12] kalé-felī: kalé, I have no doubt, is intimately connected with the term kellé or galié meaning „short"; in this case the following form might be a popular abbreviation of the same, although I have a term gē meaning „bad".

[13] rò al aamā: the composition of this term is not quite plain to me; rò in this case may be an abbreviated form of roōde, „earth".

[14] láyam-ásinhā: As for láyam, it seems to be compound with am, „water"; ásinhā appears to be closely connected with the verb ásinhē mentioned p. 43 with the meaning „to lie, repose".

[15] sûwa: I do not think, that this term has passed so completely from the Kanúri into the Wandalá-language, as to be in general use, but we have here a similar case, as that just mentioned with regard to the Sońγai-language, and it is very natural, that the small tribe of the Wandalá living in a mountainous region, well irrigated with living water, has no national term for such sort of wells, which are peculiar only to dry regions.

[16] kámmanē possibly is composed of the terms ka and manē, meaning „the hand" or „the finger of the river".

[17] bētak is a Mába-form of the Arabic term bat-hā, just as for a while I thought berih (bahrik) to have been derived from bahar and thought it interesting to see both terms, the Arabic form bahar and the derived Mába-form berih used side by side with a different meaning in the following phrase bahar agone berih té-ar-go dabalai, „the watercourse (berih) of this rivervalley (bahar) is shallow". But berih probably means nothing else, but „place, room".

Deutsch und Englisch.	Kanúri.	Tédā.	Hausa.	Fulfúlde.
irgend welche Ansammlung von Wasser — *collection of water of whatever dimension*	birrim[1] . . .	belle	bāki n rūa .	. . . . . .
Pfuhl, Tümpel — *pool, puddle*	kúlūgu . . .		tebki n rūa .	vendu (ndīam) Pl. bēli (ndīam)
Thal mit Tümpeln stehenden Wasser's — *valley with pools of standing water*	komádugu . .	hénderi[7] . .	rāfi Plur. rafafúkka	lúggere Pl. lugge
weit offenes Flusswasser — *wide open river-water*	ńki bul[2] . .	eyī tšópuki .	bakī n rūa .	ndīam ballēdam
Strom, Kanal — *stream, canal*	ńgāda[3] . . .	[8]	tágua[9] . . .	yorāki . . .
Wellen — *waves*	kazaua . . .	. . . . . .	tóšāī n gulbi .	bampēdže . .
Furt — *ford*	fāl-teram komádugu-be[4]	. . . . . .	kaffa n gulbi[10]	koñgel māyo .
flaches Ufer — *flat shore*	tšī komádugu-be[5]	. . . . . .	gāba n gulbī .	{ñoñgo / foñgo} māyo
steiles Ufer — *steep shore*	ńgarmómogō[6]	kerī foīī-en .	gāba mai-surūñ	{ñoñgo / foñgo} džotúngo

[1] birrim ist, wenn auch wol nicht im Ursprunge, so doch im Gebrauche völlig verschieden von barrem und hat den allgemeinen Begriff von jedweder Wasseransammlung, für den wenige der anderen Afrikanischen Sprachen einen entsprechenden Ausdruck besitzen. Es fehlt bei Koelle.

[2] ńki bul. Die Ausdrucksweise der Kanúri ist hier derjenigen der Hausa und Fulbe entgegengesetzt; die Ersteren nämlich bezeichnen ein offenes Wasser, wie dasjenige nach der Mitte des Tsād-Beckens hin als „weiss", während sie das von Inseln und Flachstellen unterbrochene seichte Wasser ńki tsilim oder „Schwarzwasser" nennen; die Letzteren dagegen, wie auch die Sonyai und Andere, bezeichnen das offene Wasser als „schwarz". Denn dass dieses bakī n rūa wirklich diese Bedeutung hat und nicht die von „Wassermund", von bákī, „Mund", wie der in erster Zeile dieser Seite aufgeführte Ausdruck, zeigt deutlich die wörtliche Übersetzung in der Fulfúlde-Sprache ndīam ballēdam. Der Missionar Schön in seinem Bericht der ersten Niger-Expedition (Niger-Expedition 1842) giebt den Namen „Schwarzwasser" dem Tšadda, d. h. dem unteren Lauf des Bénuē, und diesem Gebirgswasser gebührt auch dieser Name ganz vorzüglich im Gegensatz zu dem weissen thonreichen Wasser des Niger. S. meinen Aufsatz über Dr. Baikie's Thätigkeit am Unteren Niger in der Zeitschrift für Erdkunde XIV, 1863, S. 106.

[3] ńgāda fehlt bei Koelle, ebenso wie kazaua.

[4] fāl-teram komádugu-be, „Übergangsort des Flusses", von fal-ńiskin S. 93, mit der ursprünglichen Bedeutung „ich mache ein anderes", dann „ich wechsele, tausche".

[5] tšī komádugu-be, eigentlich „der Mund, die Lippenöffnung des Flusses", muss man nicht verwechseln mit šī komádugu-be, „Arm (eigentlich „Bein") eines Flusses, Nebenfluss".

[6] ńgarmómogō fehlt bei Koelle, seine Ableitung und Zusammensetzung ist mir unbekannt.

[7] hénderi: daher heisst das bei den Arabern als Wadi Kauār bekannte „Hauptthal der Tédā": hénderi Tédā.

[8] Es ist nicht verständlich, warum den Tédā diese bezeichnenden Ausdrücke von Wasser fehlen, da es ihrem ganzen Lande fast an jedem fliessenden Wasser gebricht.

[9] tágua. Hierzu will ich einen begriffsverwandten Ausdruck hersetzen, nämlich „tiefe Stelle" im Fluss oder See, H. gurbi, F. wéndewō, Plur. gendéppe.

[10] kaffa n gulbī, eigentlich „Bein des Flusses", kann nur sehr uneigentlich „Furt" bedeuten, aber doch ist es so. Bezeichnender im Hausa ist der Ausdruck für den Punkt, wo man einen Fluss zu Boot passirt, „Fähre", nämlich mai ketare, F. džáldugal oder regórde.

[11] bul pisuen kann ich nicht analysiren.

[12] polá-leyām. Hier habe ich selbst etwas systematisirt; denn, was ich nach dem Gehör niederschrieb, war polau erāmmal.

[13] sse-légaiš tibbus. Das Wort sse-légaiš klingt wol genau mit dem vorhergehenden ádäga zusammen. S. 93 habe ich freilich yé-de-nō, „ich überschreite einen Fluss".

[14] máhala. Die Übereinstimmung des Lógonē- und Bágrimma-Ausdruckes in diesem Falle kommt wol nur darauf zurück, dass die eine Sprache von der anderen mit nur geringer Umbildung das Wort aufgenommen hat.

[15] hálterá kann kaum von reinem Bágrimma-Ursprung sein; es ist vielmehr vielleicht nur eine verunstaltete Form des Kanúri-Wortes fálteram.

[16] marga bā. Wir haben hier eine vollständige, aber doch ganz zufällige Übereinstimmung eines Afrikanischen Wortes mit einem Lateinischen, marge mit merge.

[17] barih gatā arāaya, „die Stelle (barih, das wol wie schon S. 152, N. 17 angegeben, nichts mit bahar, „Fluss" zu thun hat) des Furten's", von um gajā-arāaga, „ich passire (einen Fluss)", Einleitung S. CCCVI, h, β).

Kanúri.	Lógoné.	Wándalá.	Bágrimma.	Mába.
bango	surí	dirwe . . .	. . . . . .	. . . . . .
	láyame . . .	dirwe . . .	hedā . . . / abīli . . .	lāsu
gōru	. . . . . .	. . . . . .	. . . . . .	bētak
hari bībi . . .		yō eče (daáye?)	man džappe .	. . . . . .
. . . . . .	ámawa	guš	man kelá . .	endži tantálle?
. . . . . .	(a)má-(wa)-belévia	ádžaga dēve .	mábala [14] . .	. . . . . .
fuа-di džiōdi . .	bal plauen [11] . .	ase-žégalé tibbua [13]	káltera [15] . .	barík) galá (arúnye [17]
. . . . . .	gólarā [gē-layám?]	wa guō . . .	marge bá [16] .	džurí (Arb.)
. . . . . .	pelá-layám (?) [12]	zella ńgwai (?)		

[1] birrim is a term totally distinct from kasrem, if not by origin, at least by usage, and signifies any sheet or collection of water, a meaning of so wide an application, that only few of the other African languages have any thing corresponding to it. It is wanting in Kanúri.

[2] áhi bal: in this instance the terminology of the Kanúri is just the reverse of that of the Hausa and Fúlbe; the former giving to an open sheet of water like that towards the midst of the Tsād the name of „white", while they call áhi tsilim or „black water" the shallow water broken by islands and sandbanks near the shore; the Hausas and Fúlbe, on the contrary, give the name of „black" to the open water. For there can be no doubt, that the Hausa-term bahi n rúa has this meaning and does not mean „mouth or gulf of water" (from báki, „mouth"), as some travellers have misunderstood this term, while such is really the case with the first Hausa-term mentioned in this page; for the Fulfúlde-term ndiam ballēdam is a mere translation of the Hausa-name bahi n rúa. Rev. Schön, Niger-Expedition 1842, p. 111 applies the term „black water", to the Tśadda (the lower part of the Bénué) and, no doubt, that river is particularly designated by that name. See „Zeitschrift für Erdkunde" XIV, 1863, p. 106.

[3] ágáda is wanting in Kanúri, as well as the term kasowa.

[4] fál-terem komádugu-be, „place of crossing the river", from fal-niskin, „I change, I cross (the river)" which see p. 91.

[5] tál komádugu-be must not be confounded with fí komádugu-be, „aley of the river, a creek" or „tributary river".

[6] ágermómogá is wanting in Kanúri; whence it has been derived as well as its mode of composition is not known to myself.

[7] hénderi: thus the largest and most renowned valley in the territory of the Tédā, which with the Arabs is known by the name of Wadi Kawár, is called hénderi Tédā.

[8] It is but natural, that those terms relative to various expanses of water should be insufficiently expressed in the Tédā-language, as there is scarcely a single running water in the whole extent of their territory. No doubt, the neighbours of those few localities, where there is something of the kind, must have distinct terms; but these it is difficult to obtain.

[9] tágna: I here will adduce another related term, viz „a spot of great depth in a river or sea", H. gurbi, F. wúnduwō, plur. gundáppe.

[10] kaffa n gulbi means properly „leg of a river", and only improperly means „ford", the place of fording, a shallow place being compared to the leg of a man. More significative in H. is the term for the spot, where a river is crossed in a boat, viz. uri n kétare, F. dāáldugal or ragérde.

[11] bal plauen I am not able to analyse.

[12] pelá-layám: in this case I have rather changed a little from theory; for from hearing I wrote down pelán erámmal.

[13] ase-žégalé tibbua: the word ase-žégalé seems to be intimately connected with the preceding term ádžaga, but not being certain I do not like to change. For „I cross (a river)" I have yé-da-aö p. 93.

[14] mábala. Probably we have here an instance of an intrinsic harmony between the Lógoné- and the Bágrimma-idiom, but it is evident, that the one language has simply adopted the term of the other, changing it but very slightly. For Bágrimma is so extensively spoken in the small territory of Lógoné, that some terms belonging to the former idiom could have been easily be introduced into the daily use of the latter.

[15] káltera seems do me not to belong to the Bágrimma-language, but to be a corrupted form of the Kanúri-term fál-terem.

[16] marge bá: in this instance we have a perfect, but nevertheless totally accidental harmony between an African and a Latin, nay the very English term marge and marge, „margin".

[17] baríк gajá arúnye, „the spot, place" (barík, a term which, as already stated p. 152, note 17 probably has not been derived from bahar, „river", though in some cases it might seem to be so) of fording" (see gajá-aréágue, „I cross a river", Introductory Remarks p. CCXVII, b, β).

Deutsch und Englisch.	Kanúri.	Tédā.	Hausa.	Fulfúlde.
Confluenz (Zusammenfluss) — *confluence*	ná komádugu fogtain	. . . . . .	ma-gángamu [8]	{ follírde mādže / těpe [12] . . . }
Salzsee, Meer — *salt-sea, sea*	nkī mánda-be [1]	cyī grönde? .	rūa n giśerī .	ndīam lamdam
Insel — *island*	tšukko [2] . .		gungu [9] . . .	{ bulur . . / dūnde [13] . . }
Land, Gebiet — *country, district*	{ lardo [3] . . . / tšidī . . . }	{ besāfu . . . / dunya kerō . }	kasa	lědi; leadi . .
steinige Ebene mit spärlichem Baumwuchs — *stony plain with a scanty growth of trees, with trees far between*	{ kabē [4] . . . / kabē bul tel }	{ dylle . . . / bi forān . . }	fili [10] . . .	džairi . . .
sandiges (bewaldetes) Hügelland — *sandy hilly-country*	. . . . . .	āri [6]	diegana . .	{ džarengol Plur. džarendi / yolde Pl. yōle / bulbúlde [14] . / hainārē . . }
Wildniss, Wald — *wilderness, forest*	karāga [5] . .	{ hónderi [7] . . / ónneri . . . }	{ dāži [11] . . . / daua . . . }	ledde [15] . . .

[1] Es ist leicht erklärlich, dass diese Binnenvölker bei ihrem fast gänzlichen Mangel eines unmittelbaren Verkehrs mit der Küste nur sehr ungenügende Ausdrücke für „Salzsee", „Meer" haben; sie helfen sich mit dem allgemeinen Namen „Salzwasser".

[2] tšukko fehlt bei Koelle; es ist allerdings kein ganz gewöhnlicher Ausdruck.

[3] lardo. Koelle schreibt lárdę. Es ist natürlich aus dem Arabischen el árd. Anstatt tšidī schreibt Koelle tsédi.

[4] kabē bei Koelle kápē; meine Schreibweise durch die enge Beziehung zum entsprechenden bi im Tédā gerechtfertigt. — kabē bul tel bezeichnet diejenige steinige Ebene, die „ganz weiss", ganz nackt ist.

[5] karāga. Koelle accentuirt kárāgā.

[6] āri entspricht dem Arabischen Ausdruck érg, érg, áreg (eigentlich „Adern"), dem Máḍīy (Targi) ádehī Plur. édeyen.

[7] hónderi bezeichnet nur uneigentlich den „Wald", da es eigentlich nur „Waldthal" bedeutet S. 164, N. 7, aber die Bewohner der Wüste können sich keinen anderen Wald vorstellen, als eben in den Thälern.

[8] ma-gáugamu, „Vereinigungspunkt", von ina gámu, „ich vereinige", mit Reduplication der ersten Silbe, vgl. maráraba.

[9] gungu. Diesen Ausdruck haben die Hausaua unfehlbar von den Sonyai aufgenommen, da sie selbst bei den kleinen Flüssen ihres eigenen Gebietes nur uneigentlich von Inseln reden können. Aber jene Gegenden haben dagegen ihre eigenthümlichen Inseln und diese ist das, was die Hausaua tšéberi nennen, die Fulbe dādda, die Sonyai gungu keina, eigentlich „kleine Insel", nämlich eine zeitweilige Insel, wie sie von Flussarmen gebildet werden, die einen Theil des Jahres austrocknen, wie die berühmte Tšébori, wo die frühere Hauptstadt des Góber-Gebietes lag.

[10] fili ist vielleicht kein ursprüngliches Hausa-Wort. Die Hausaua und Fulbe haben noch besondere Ausdrücke für „Ebene" im Allgemeinen, H. sáreri, F. bōhel, sowie auch für „Hochebene", H. fáko, F. keronel, und dann auch für „Hochebene von rothem Sandstein", worauf sie gewöhnlich bestehen, H. dāe n fáko, F. kaedidāl.

[11] dāži bezeichnet mehr die „bewaldete Wildniss", denn die „nackte Wüste".

[12] těpe ist ein nicht in allen Provinzen der drei Fulbe-Reiche bekannter Ausdruck, aber in Adamaua ist er so völlig eingebürgert, dass er der alleinige Name des Zusammenflusses des Bé-nué mit dem Faro ist. S. meine Reisen Th. II, S. 555; Auszug I, S. 437. Von einem Orte Namens Tépe habe ich nie gesprochen.

[13] dūnde steht in enger Beziehung zu der Pluralform rūde, der Inselgruppe im oberen Laufe des Máyo balléo, die den Kern des Reiches von Másina bildet.

[14] bulbúlde scheint mir ein nur unter den Fulbe Adamaua's üblicher Provincialismus zu sein.

[15] ledde, eigentlich der Plural von leggel, „der Baum".

[16] guré ist dasselbe Wort mit gourein, das Raffenel in seinem Arama-Verzeichnisse mit „montagne ordinaire" widergibt, vgl. sein toundi gourein, „montagne rocheuse".

[17] am līū mit ursprünglicher Bedeutung „Wasser der Finsterniss", von lū, „Finsterniss".

[18] horāhe Légemé, bolō Wándalā, petrnal Bágrimma sind wol entschieden unter einander verwandt, weniger farra (fára) Sonyai, das mit der einheimischen Wurzel for, „öffnen" unzweideutig zusammenhängt (Einleitung S. CXC, N. 1).

[19] ilen tšitel: ilen hat auch Barth mit dem Begriffe „Sandwüste", wogegen er hibeih für „Steinwüste" hat. — tšitel ist mir sonst nicht vorgekommen und deshalb in seiner ursprünglichen Beziehung undeutlich, erinnert aber an das tautālle in endāl tautālle S. 165. — hodāde sāeale, „Baumwuchs (vgl. unten hadādi, „Wildniss") spärlich", scheint ein integrirender Bestandtheil derselben Phrase, keine neue Form zu sein.

Sonyai.	Lógoné.	Wándalá.	Bágrimma.	Mába.
. . . .	. . . .	. . . . . .	[siba fatāa] .	. . . . . .
ma { horno . . / bonno . . }	am itū [17] . . .	yo daṅgo . .	babar il mála	babar īl mála
guṅgu	sēyi	derra . . .	gōro	džezīra (Arb.)
genda; gande .	{ lóáde . . . . . / rōda . . . . . }	gāga	ardu (Arb.) .	{ géuiṅga / ard (Arb.) }
farru, fára . .	barāhe [18] . . .	balē	páruaī (fū . .	ilan téltal kedásle sásala [19]
hundu . . . . / gurē [20] . . . . }	. . . .	. . . . . .	. . . . . .	. . . . . .
{ geṅgi . . . . / saii . . . . . . }	gēui	kōmba . . .	korō	hadādi

[1] It is easily to be understood, how these nations settled in the interior and destitute of any direct intercourse with the coast, have not but very insufficient terms for „sea"; indeed, almost all of them express the notion by the term „saltwater".
[2] tšakko is wanting in Koelle.
[3] tarde: Koelle writes tardę.
[4] babó by Koelle is spelt kápé. — Another, composite term kabó bultal, „desert quite white" designates the perfectly stony and barren plain.
[5] harága. Koelle writes kéragá. As to the probable mode of composition of this term given on a former occasion I am now rather uncertain.
[6] ári corresponds to the Arabic term árg, árg, áreg (originally „veins"), the Tamašiyt ádehi plur. ídeyan.
[7] hóndari only improperly signifies the forest, such as they are characteristic of Tropical Regions, but properly means a valley clad with vegetation, the inhabitants of the desert being only able to fancy larger clusters of trees growing in valleys.
[8] ma-gágamo, „place of junction", from ina gámu, „I join"; ma (mai) signifying „possessing, master of", and the first ga being a repetition of the principal root, just as ra in ma-rá-raba, „the crossway", from rába, „to divide".
[9] guṅgu: the Hausa-people have borrowed this term from the Sonyai-language, there being no islands properly so called in their own territory. On the other hand, these regions contain a peculiar kind of islands of their own. This is, what the Hausa-people call tšóbari, the Fúlbe diádu, the Sonyai guṅgu kaina, viz. a piece of ground encompassed by two branches of a river valley, which part of the year are flooded and the other dry, as is the case with the well-known Tšíbari, which contained the former capital of the territory of Gōber. Travels and Disc. IV, p. 535 f.
[10] fíli; the Hausa and Fúlbe have also peculiar terms with the general meaning of „plain", H. sárari, F. bábal, as well as another one expressive of „plateau", or „elevated plain", H. fáko, F. karasal, and again for „plaines of red sandstone", such as is the general feature of these regions, H. dān u fáko, F. kardidši.
[11] dāši properly signifies the forest, dana rather the naked desert.
[12] tūpa is a term not generally known in the other provinces of the three Fúlbe-empires, while in Adamawa it has become so generally and exclusively used, that Tōpa is at present the only name of the place of junction of the Bē-nuē with the Fāro. See my Travels and Discoveries II, p. 465. — I never said, that Tōpa was the name of a place or village, as Dr. Baikie (Exploring Voyage p. 186) seems to have misunderstood me.
[13] dūnde is evidently intimately connected with the name rūde, given to the principal island in the Upper course of the māyo kalióo, and forming the nucleus of the empire of Másina.
[14] kalbálde seems to be a term used only among the Fúlbe of Adamawa.
[15] ladde properly is the plural of luggal, „tree".
[16] garé is identical with ganrein, the term given by Raffenel for „montagne ordinaire", with which we may compare his tondi genrein, „montagne rocheuse".
[17] am itū, „the black water", or „the water of darkness", tū meaning „darkness".
[18] barāhe in Lógoné, balē in Wándalá, páruaī in Bágrimma seem to be closely related amongst each other, while farru or fára in Sonyai is evidently to be referred to the indigenous root far (Introductory Remarks p. CXCI, note 1).
[19] ilan téltal: the term ilan appears also in Seetzen's list with the notion „sandy waste", besides which he gives kibalh as meaning „stony desert". As for téltal, it is not quite plain to me, not having occurred to me in other relations, but it reminds of tontélle in the phrase ondši tantélle p. 165. — hadáde sásala means „scrubby growth of trees", hadáde being closely related to, if not identical with, the term hadádi, „wilderness", a little further on, and evidently forms an integrant portion of the whole phrase.

Deutsch und Englisch.	Kanúri.	Tédā.	Hausa.	Fulfúlde.
Hoher Wald — *high forest*	dérìdē[1] . . .	bénderi ídaákonō	dāēdāi . . .	ledde terre .
dichte Waldung — *dense forest*	karága tsilim[2]	bénderi tēfi baī	kumtsi . .	gūbe . . . .
dichter Wald von jungen Bäumen — *dense forest of young trees*			sahō n kumtsi	fitto-fittōru .
undurchdringliches Dickicht *impenetrable thicket*	fāme[3] . . . / pāme . . .		kumtsi . . .	. . . . . .
Hügel — *hill*	kau[4] ganā .	. . . . . .	tsauni . . .	komel; kótšel
Berg — *mountain* . . .	kau kurā .	ēī . . . . / ēmi . . . . / yēmi[9]	tuddu[10] . .	yolde Plur. yōle / tondi[13] . .
Fels, Stein — *rock, stone*	kau	. . . . . .	dūtsi / dūtsi Pl. dūatsū[11]	wamde Pl. bamle / haire Pl. kādāe / hosēre Pl. kosē-dāe / tiffāre
Loch, Grube — *hole, cavity*	bulāka[5] . .	fōti	rāmi Pl. rámuna	gaska Plur. gasde
Grube (Bergwerk) von Eisen, Salz — *cavity (mine) of iron, salt* .	sirge[6] (sū-be, mánda-be	fōti grēni (?) .	rámin karfi, gišeri	. . . . . .
fruchtbarer Boden — *fertile soil*	tsidi dyunoa[7] / tsidi kúrguri	besāfo dyunedē	kása mai-kiaa[12] / kása mai-albáraka / kása mai-yáa n hatsi	lēdi di-yúūki .
feuchter Boden — *moist ground* .	tsidi keri[8] .	besāfo bú-nebō	kása mai-rūa	

[1] dérìdē fehlt bei Koelle, obgleich er ein Adjektiv dérī hat „trocken, mager", mit dem es möglicher Weise zusammenhängt; auch hängt mit meiner Form vielleicht die Bedeutung von dē, „leer" noch zusammen, so dass die eigentliche Bedeutung wäre „trocken und leer". Sonst könnte auch dē eine blosse Endung sein, wie sie dem verwandten Tédā gewöhnlich ist (Einleitung S. LXXXII, vgl. S. XC, N. 2), obgleich ich sie im Kanúri sonst nicht gefunden habe.

[2] karága tsilim, wörtlich „schwarzer Wald".

[3] fāme fehlt bei Koelle.

[4] kau. Koelle schreibt diesen kau mit der Bedeutung von „Stein" kou, irriger Weise es von kau, „Sonne" unterscheidend, wie Einleitung S. LX, N. 2 näher ausgeführt. kau kurá, „grosser Stein, Berg", kau ganā, „kleiner Stein, Hügel".

[5] bulāka. Koelle schreibt bulúga. Es kommt offenbar von bu-ngin, „ich grabe".

[6] sirge fehlt bei Koelle.

[7] tsidi dyunoa, „kräftiger Boden". Koelle schreibt dunōwa. kúrguri heisst eigentlich „weiblich", in weiterer Entwickelung „fruchtbar". Koelle führt bei diesem Adjektiv unsere Bedeutung, die sich aus jener ergiebt, nicht an.

[8] tsidi keri. keri, „grün, frisch, feucht". Ich will hier noch einen besonderen Ausdruck anführen für „geebneter Boden, Ebene, Terrasse", tsidi kāre, im W. serana, d. h. wahrscheinlich sera wōn, „der Fuss des Gebirges", denn die Bewohner von Wandalā haben in ihrem kleinen gebirgigen Ländchen eigentlich keine Ebene von grösserer Ausdehnung.

[9] ēmi, yēmi. Ausser diesen verschiedenen Formen habe ich noch anderswo den ganz verschiedenen Ausdruck tu, der mit dem entsprechenden Koptischen tau eng verwandt zu sein scheint. — fōti grēni heisst wahrscheinlich „grosse Grube".

[10] tuddu bezeichnet ursprünglich alles Runde und bedeutet „Berg" in Folge seiner Bezeichnung der Wölbung.

[11] dūtsi. Ich will hier einige verwandte Nebenbegriffe anführen, die ich nur im Hausa, Fulfúlde und Sonyai erfahren habe; „Berggipfel" (K. kéla kau-be), H. kai n dūtsi, F. hōre wamde, S. tondi bōna; „Bergpass, Défilé", H. hōgo n dūtsi, F. lāvi oder kommódde, S. gūsu (eine arme Ausdrucksweise, wie die ganze Sonyai-Sprache so arm ist, da gūsu nur die allgemeine Bedeutung von „Loch" hat); „Steingerümpel", H. mardāi oder dūtsi sa tsōkua tsōkua, F. meraiel; „rauhe Passage", H. hautsasché, F. hogáddi oder fogáddi, S. gōru; „steiler Abhang", H. gēbe mai-surāfi, F. gēhal mangal oder gērol, S. yāre tēre.

[12] Für „unfruchtbarer Boden" haben die Hausaua den ganz besonderen Ausdruck mutsattse n kasa, entsprechend dem lēdi tsfanda im Fulfúlde.

[13] tondi ist aus der Sonyai-Sprache in's Fulfúlde herübergenommen worden. Übrigens muss ich bemerken, dass ich nicht daran denke, hier eine genaue Unterscheidung von Fels und Berg zu machen; auch haire und wamde bedeuten oft Berg.

[14] tugáddie heisst eigentlich „die Bäume".

[15] ka kōdu, kōdu, kōde, „ein Baum einzeln, einzeln, einzeln".

[16] godgam dāuphiāg mihā-ga, „ein Loch zum graben Eisen" (miha).

[17] kodōb, daher der Name des Stammes der Kodoi eigentlich „Bergbewohner" (Reisen Th. III, S. 501).

[18] maha, „Eisengruben" (Reisen III, S. 543, 544), burik fēddatsch, „Stelle, Fundgrube des Silbers"; keine solche vorhanden.

Sọṅyai.	Lógonē.	Wándalā.	Bágrimma.	Māba.
ingúdēio[14] . . .	gēmi bētu . . .	bāla	ka kēde, kōde, kēde[15]	suógo fafádda
	gēmi(i-)tū . . .	derba duṅge .	dēūru . . .	suógo kárkurō
. . . .	bóďugi	hinda kāmba .		
tondi kaina . . tondi bēre . . . tondi	inkúnhi	wūa	tōde . . . tōto . . .	kodók Pl. kodō[17]
gunu	báṅgole . . . zirge (lá χaafū) .	. . . . . . lígerē . . .	búkuan . . . godyam dēapkiṅg (miiā-na)[16]	. . . . . . mōku[18] barík fúddalek
. . . .	rōda tū . . .	(χāγa)-zínsedā ōir dígdegē .	aōe yīli . .	gésingā lélīō
	lōad-ándan . .	ágawaī . . .	kurbu . . .	barak [barík?] nówota

1 dérìdē is wanting in Koelle, although he has the adjective dérì with the meaning „dry, lean, emaciated, wasted", with which I think dérìdē may be connected; perhaps also the latter half of the word is related to the term dē, „empty", and thus the original meaning of dérì-dē would be „dry (and) empty". But dē may also be a mere termination very common to the Tédā (Intr. Rem. p. LXXXIII), although I have not met with it in Kanúri. Compare Intr. Rem. p. XCI, note 8.

2 korāge tellim means verbally „black forest".

3 fāme is wanting in Koelle.

4 kau: Koelle writes kạu, to which he only attributes the meaning „stone", but, as stated on a former occasion (Intr. Remarks p. LXI, note 3), the very same word kau both means „stone" as well as „sun". kau kurá properly means „big stone, mountain", kau ganā, „small stone, hill".

5 bulāko: Koelle writes bụlága. The root, at any rate, seems to be la-ágin, „I dig".

6 sírge is wanting in Koelle.

7 tšídi dąnnoa, „properly „the strong, powerful soil". Koelle writes daaówa. — kárgaeī properly means „female", and Koelle does not even mention the notion, which is here given and which has been derived from the former.

8 tšídi korī: korī, „green, fresh, moist". I here will also mention a peculiar term for „uncultivated ground", tšídi kárē, W. serena, or rather, as I think será wūa, „foot of the mountains" („Piedmont"), the Wandalā-people not possessing any plain of some extent in their mountainous country.

9 ēmi, yēmi: Besides these various forms of the same term among my phrases I have yet another totally different term, viz tu, which may be related to the corresponding Coptic tau.

10 taddu has the meaning of „mountain" in consequence of its indicating any thing convex.

11 dūtšī: I shall here adduce some related notions, for which I have learned the corresponding terms only in Hausa, Fulfúlde and Sọṅyai; „top of mountain" (K. kéle kau-ba), H. kai n dūtsi, F. hōre wamde, S. tondi bāṅo; „mountainpass, defile", H. hāgo n dūtsi, F. lāāī or hommáddo, S. gūan (a rather poor and not very expressive term, as the Sọṅyai-language, in general, is not very rich, gūan having the general notion of „hole, hollow"); „very rough ground", H. merdāi or dūtsi cō teákue teákua, F. merelel; „rough passage", H. kasáeccbó, F. bogéddi or fogéddi, S. gūru; „steep descent", H. gōbe mai-surūfi, F. gōhul maāgul or gōrel, S. fāre tšire.

12 For „sterile soil" the Hausa-language has the peculiar term matsáttsa n kása, corresponding to lédi léfanda in Fulfúlde.

13 tondi has been introduced into the Sọṅyai-language from the Fulfúlde. I must remark, however, that I do not intend to distinguish accurately between the terms meaning „rock" and „mountain"; for hairo and wamde both often mean „mountain".

14 ingúdēio properly means nothing but „trees".

15 ka kōde, kēde, kēde, „a tree single, single, single", i. q. „trees far between".

16 godyam dēapkiṅg miiā-na, „a hole for digging iron" (miiā).

17 kodók: this is the origin of the name of the tribe of the Kodoi, properly „mountaineers", Trav. and Disc. vol. III, p. 540.

18 mōku, „iron mines" (Trav. and Disc. III, p. 578); barík fúddalek, „site, place of silver", i. q. „silver-mines".

Deutsch und Englisch.	Kanúri.	Tédā.	Hausa.	Fulfulde.
Koth, Schlamm — *mud, slime*	káli	. . . . . .	kafō	nāfferi . . .
schwarzer, vegetabilischer Humus — *black vegetable soil*	firki[1] . . .	yeako . . .	. . . . . .	. . . . . .
schwarzer, vegetabilischer Boden von der Sonne zerklüftet — *black vegetable soil cleft by the sun*	ange[2]			
Thon zum Bauen — *clay for building*	kāti	lū; lō . . .	yumbu . . .	lōfe[13] . . .
rother Thon — *red clay* .	kāti kemē . .	breáfu mádo[7]	dāa n yumbu	. . . . . .
Sand — *sand*	kéaa	. . . . . .	rerē	dilarēnde . .
Staub — *dust*	. . . . . .	. . . . . .	kurā	sallāre . . .
Acker, Gartenfeld — *field, garden-field*	kūlō	kinair[8] . . .	gōna Pl. gōnaki[20]	gesa Plur. gese
Bewässerungsdamm — *small dike for purposes of irrigation*	dumba[3] . .	. . . . . .	. . . . . .	. . . . . .
Rohr, Halm — *reed, blade*	kangálle[4] . .	. . . . . .	kárā[11] . . .	kombel Pl. kombe
Gras, Kraut — *grass, herb*	hādžim[5] . .	illi[9]	tšiaua . . .	fúdo[14] / gĕnel } hetšo
trockenes Gras — *dry grass*	hādžim ngamdu	. . . . . .	hakki . . .	fúdo / gĕnel } yorko .
Pennisetum distichum — *pennisetum distichum*	ngibbu[6] . .	. . . . . .	karéngia[12] . .	kebbe . . .

[1] firki. Koelle hat diesen Ausdruck nach der irrthümlichen Angabe seines schon 25 Jahre seiner Heimath entrissenen 'Ali Eisāmi in der Form Fergi für den Eigennamen des Distriktes von Dikoa gegeben, wo jener Boden allerdings gerade vorwaltet. Vergl. meine Reisen Th. II, S. 363, 437.

[2] ange fehlt bei Koelle. Eigentlich übrigens ist der ange vom firki nicht seiner inneren Natur, sondern nur der Jahreszeit nach verschieden.

[3] dumba fehlt bei Koelle.

[4] kangálle. Koelle schreibt kángalei und erklärt es etwas zu speciell. Auffallend ist die äussere Ähnlichkeit der Form mit kregél, „Sonne" (beim Aufgang).

[5] hādžim. Koelle schreibt hádžim.

[6] ngibbu fehlt bei Koelle. Die Kanúri-Sprache hat auch einen besonderen Namen für das dem Reisenden in einigen Gegenden Central-Afrika's gleichfalls so lästige dris (arthratherum pungens).

[7] breáfu mádo. mádo heisst „roth".

[8] kinair. In Betreff der ungewöhnlichen Endung der Substantive auf r im Tédā s. Einleitung S. LXXVIII, 9.

[9] illi. In der Tédā-Sprache habe ich noch folgende besondere Benennungen für Grasarten erfahren: mull (Arb. neṣī, „arthratherum plumosum"); adau (Arb. ṣgreî); serī (Arb. hād, „Anabasis alopecuroides"); móyoyo (Arb. sebâd); genti (Arb. hû rékkeba, „Panicum colonum") und endlich sibō (Arb. agûl, „Hedysarum Alhagi").

[10] gōna bedeutet auch Pflanzung; so „Palmenpflanzung", H. gōna n dabino, F. geese dabinaadje, S. garbe farī.

[11] kárkara, der Plural von kárā, bedeutet „Stoppelfeld", und davon haben die in Hausa angesiedelten Fulbe das Wort karkarāre gebildet.

[12] karéngia. Der bei einigen Stämmen am Rande der Wüste viel gegessene Same dieser Pflanze heisst bei den Hausaua irri n karéngia, bei den Sonyai dāne lōdde. — Ich will hier auch die Namen einiger anderer Futterkräuter angeben: erstlich „die schwarzstachelige derīsa", H. cuida, F. coldaddi oder tāpe, S. ingórfu; „eine Art Crucifera", H. domenkadda, F. wabábbo, S. tenélle; „eine Liliacea", H. kinera, F. kinaréhe; dann „die Sennapflanze", H. filásko, F. bulbulahi.

[13] lōfe. Ich will hier noch die Ausdrücke für „Kalk oder Gyps" im F. und S. angeben, F. nomérde, S. tibi.

[14] Für fúdo ist die Dialektverschiedenheit húdo.

[15] Zu der Pluralform faró s. Einleitung S. CLXXXIV, d, a).

[20] sireádo, wahrscheinlich nur besondere Form des allgemeinen Ausdrucks für „Erde".

[21] yè-li von e-n-yéne, „ich baue das Land"; s. Einleitung S. CCCVIII, d). — gonar heisst eigentlich „Saat" und wird wol nur uneigentlich für „Acker" gebraucht, besonders insofern er besäet ist. — Anstatt láwa hat B. die wenig verschiedene Form lowa.

Sonyai.	Lógoné.	Wándalá.	Bágrimma.	Mába.
tíbi	. . . .	γáγa	aho	urá
. . . .	balge	fíkō . . . / delwa fíkō .	bángela . . / pandóga . .	kákmerō
lábo	elroáde [16]	γáγa	aho	urá
. . . .	róda sé	γáγa n γánge	añe atšē . .	urá kókōáb
táai . . . . . / dō kōri . . .	aífa	šiggo	. . . . . .	. . . . . .
kúso	. . . .	. . . . . .		. . . . . .
farí Plur. farē [15]	aγrē	fē	baya	yē-ti / ossur [17]
. . . .	tγúm	úwaka fē . .	ágena	hobbua
hēni) kári	gem	wogwe	dīēdža	díffelē
sūbo (gēni T . / táō . . .)	tárbi	masā	(mū . . . . / džē . . . .)	lúwa
sūbo (kōgo . . / kōu . .)				
dáne				

[1] firki: Koelle has given this term under the form Pérgi as the proper name of the district of Dikwa, where that sort of ground really prevails to a very great extent. See Travels and Disc. vol. II, p. 345. But this is not Koelle's fault, but that of his authority 'Ali Eisámi, who during his long absence from home must have forgotten a good many things.
[2] ságe is wanting in Koelle. — The ságe, however, rather differs from the firki only according to colour.
[3] damba is wanting in Koelle.
[4] kaságilla: Koelle writes kásgalei and attributes to it a rather particular and restricted meaning.
[5] kádlim: Koelle writes kátšim.
[6] ngibbe is wanting in Koelle. The Kanúri have also a peculiar term for another sort of very annoying plant in this Region, the drin or arthratherum pungens.
[7] kosáfu mádo: mádo means „red".
[8] kinnir: With regard to the rare instances of nouns terminating in r in the Tédā-language see Intr. Rem. p. LXXIX, 9.
[9] kilil: I have still the following particular Tédā terms for special varieties of herbage, which are of considerable importance with regard to a nation, scattered over a vast extent of desert country and principally of nomadic habits: mall identic with the Arb. nsil („arthratherum plumosum"); adus, Arb. ágrel; sarí, Arb. hád („Anabasis Alopecurum"); wáyoyu, Arb. nebid; goeti, Arb. hú rákeba („Panicum colonum"), and finally elbó, Arb. agúl („Hedysarum Alhagi").
[10] gáno means also „plantation"; thus, „plantation of date-trees", H. gána n dabino, F. gonna dabinódže, S. garbe farí.
[11] kárá: kárkara the plural-form of káré, „road" means „stubble-field", and this term the Fúlbe settled in Hausa have slightly changed into kárkaráre.
[12] karéngia: as for the seed of this plant, one of the greatest plagues of the traveller in these regions, which is used as a chief article of food by several tribes settled on the border of the desert, it is called irri n karéngia in Hausa, dáne léddi in Sonyai. — I will here adduce the names of some other plants used for fodder, first „the sharp pointed drin", called in H. ssida, F. selbáddi or tópa, S. segérin; „a variety of Crucifera", H. damesbadda, F. wabábbe, S. tandílo; „a Liliacea", H. kinara, F. kinarábe; „the Sennaplant", H. filasko, F. balabalébi.
[13] láfa: I learned also the term for „chalk" and „gypsum" in F. (nanmérde) and in S. (šíbi).
[14] fúdo, is often pronounced húdo.
[15] With regard to the plural form faré, see Introductory Remarks p. CLXXXV, d, e).
[16] elroáde seems only to be a peculiar form of the general term for „earth, soil".
[17] yé-ti from a-n-yéne, „I till the ground"; see Intr. Rem. p. CCCIX, d). — ossur seems properly to mean „seed", while it may be used to designate a field, as far as it has been sown. Instead of lúwa B. has lowa.

Deutsch und Englisch.	Kanúri.	Têda.	Hausa.	Fulfúlde.
Asclepias gigantea — *Asclepias gigantea*	krúnka . . . kais (?) . . .	. . . . . .	tumfáfia . . .	bambámbi . .
Korn (im Allgemeinen) — *corn (in general)*	argúm . . .	bedō ? . . .	hatsi [5] . . . / sáaba . . .	gauri . . . / togauri . . .
Negerhirse — *negro-millet (pennisetum typhoideum)*	móro [1] . . . / argúm móro	ánnere [3] . .	gēro	gerōri [6] . . .
Sorghum (Sorgho) — *sorghum*	ngáberi [2] . .	funtun . . . / ingáfuli [4] . . .	daua	bairi [7] . . .

[1] móro. Koelle accentuirt mōró und beschränkt den Ausdruck unrichtiger Weise auf die Bezeichnung der „rothen" Negerhirse im Gegensatz zu argúm, oder wie er schreibt, árgem mátla (weiterhin S. 268 schreibt er matōa oder motia), während er in Wirklichkeit die beiden Sorten der rothen und gelben begreift. Allerdings mag man einen solchen Unterschied in der Provinz Gēnir machen, ganz wie bei uns auch so verschiedene Benennungen ganz lokal sind, aber in der Hauptstadt Kúkaua oder sonst im eigentlichen Bornu geschieht das nicht. Der häufige Vorsatz des argúm scheint anzuzeigen, dass móro ursprünglich adverbial gedacht war. argúm, als das einheimische ächt Afrikanische Korn bezeichnend, bildet den allgemeinen Gegensatz zu dem erst im Laufe der Zeiten aus der Fremde eingeführten ngáberi. — Hier muss ich noch anführen, dass Koelle einen Ausdruck járō mit sehr weiter Bedeutung hat, als jedes künstlich Angepflanzte und nicht wild Wachsende bezeichnend, sei es Baumfrucht, Korn oder Gemüse. Es ist mir aber unbekannt geblieben und kann ich nichts darüber sagen.

[2] ngáberi. Koelle schreibt ngáfeli, sagt aber, dass die Einwohner von Dikōa es mit b aussprächen; aber nicht allein diese, sondern alle Einwohner des eigentlichen Bornu sprechen es mit b. Es scheint mir nämlich wahrscheinlich, dass dieses Korn, jetzt das Hauptkorn von Bornu, daher seinen Namen hat, dass es der eigentliche, dichterisch der „lebendige" (ngá), „Lebensunterhalt" oder die alltägliche „Kost", bēri, der Kanúri ist. Die diese Landschaften bereisenden Araber haben daraus ihren Namen gafāli gemacht. Koelle bezeichnet es auch fälschlich als Hirse. Übrigens will ich hier noch die besonderen Namen verschiedener Arten von ngáberi angeben, die Koelle aufzählt und die mir selbst nicht bekannt geworden sind, auch selbst unsicher scheinen, abgesehen von seinem cábēde, das meinem chbaode entspricht, maságba meinem masákua und kéliram, das ich als kériram habe, und das er richtig als besondere Art von masákua bezeichnet; die beiden letzteren Arten entsprechend dem Lógone- und Wándalá-Ausdruck sá ferá und dem Bágrimma wā bark. Die von Koelle s. v. ngáfeli noch ausserdem erwähnten Arten sind die folgenden: bárga („morsch"?); ligórum; sémbul („rein weiss", sem, „ganz, alles", bul, „weiss"); káfugaram (in Dikōa wōlō-gana) (offenbar nur durch seinen kurzen, gedrungenen Wuchs ausgezeichnet (káfuga oder kabuga, „kurz", gana, „klein")); kelakaliae (in Dikōa kéli kētēl) (augenscheinlich nur eine „süsse" Abart des kériram); ngáfeli tearmé. Dann hat er noch besonders ein mátāl oder ngáfeli mátāl, woraus auch der rothe Farbestoff gemacht wird. — Ich habe sonst nur die Unterscheidungen nach der Farbe in einigen der hier verglichenen Sprachen erfahren: so „weisser Sorghum", K. ngáberi bul, H. fari n daua, F. bairi danuēri, S. bāme korō; „rother Sorghum", K. ngáberi kemé, H. dja n daua, F. bairi badfel, W. guacā, S. bōme tōeré oder aōha (der letzte der alltägliche Name in Tímbuktu); „schwarzer Sorghum", H. baki n daua, F. audumēri, S. dīfbi.

[3] ánnere scheint mit dem entsprechenden Ausdruck in der Máśiy-Sprache verwandt zu sein (Einleitung S. XCVI, 16.) als eines der wenigen Beispiele einer solchen Übereinstimmung; ja, in Bilma ist die reine Máśiy-Form āneli im Gebrauch. Das will aber sprachlich wenig sagen, da die Bewohner von Bilma ihren ganzen Vorrath von Negerhirse eben von dem Máśiy-Stamme, den sogenannten Tuareg, als formelle Abgabe bei der Ausbeutung der dortigen Salzlager erhalten.

[4] ingáfuli. Ich schreibe absichtlich nicht ngáfuli, weil ich in der Têda-Sprache den nasalen Vorschlag nicht gefunden habe.

[5] Es ist ein Unterschied zwischen hatsi und sáaba; das letztere ist der ausgelesene hatsi mit der Hausa-Erklärung: hatsi bābe baiba taibā. — Ich will hier noch einige auf das Korn bezügliche Ausdrücke anführen, die ich nur in wenigen Sprachen vertreten kann. „ein grosser Haufen Korn", K. bugge (bei Koelle teérnīō, ein mir unbekannt gebliebener Ausdruck), H. tummo, F. mámmuri; „ein Bündel ungedroschenen Kornes", H. damme, F. bulāre; „ein kleiner Bündel", H. gumma karami, F. gommel. — Hier will ich den Namen für die „Hülse des Kornes" angeben, H. eurfō, F. tōoltāndo, S. sáanba.

[6] gerōri ist natürlich nicht das ursprüngliche Fulfúlde-Wort, aber es ist der einzige bei den in den früheren Hausa-Landschaften angesiedelten Fúlbe jetzt übliche Ausdruck.

[7] bairi ist ein höchst bemerkenswerther Name, der uns ganz besonders einer jener wenigen Reste des muthmasslichen Zusammenhanges dieses merkwürdigen Stammes der Fúlbe mit Asien, und Indien im Besondern, scheinen möchte; aber doch auch mit Bezug auf ihn müssen wir vorsichtig sein. Ich komme auf diese Frage bei der ethnographischen Übersicht zurück.

[8] bēul hat zuweilen diese weitere Bedeutung als „Korn" im Allgemeinen.

[9] mákala ist auffallend durch seine äussere Ähnlichkeit mit dem Arabischen mákala, aber wol nur dem Scheine nach.

[10] medī-ēhuō und med-ējuē stehen offenbar in naher Beziehung zu einander, aber ich kann ihre nähere Beziehung zur Zeit noch nicht ergründen, obgleich ich glaube, durch Vergleich mit mao ehoē, dass es bedeutet „trockene und feuchte Saat". Anstatt medī-ēhuō scheint man im gewöhnlichen Leben nur medī zu sagen, ja ich habe in einer Redensart den Gegensatz von medī und bō; Kire bēters guo imtū, „was ist ihre Art von Saat" oder „welche Art von Saat haben sie", medī ga bō, „Hirse oder Sorghum").

[11] kolaua für „Negerhirse" habe ich in den Phrasen. Burckhardt gibt für „Korn", ali (ēll Arb.), für Dhurra koēme.

Sonγai.	Lógoné.	Wándalá.	Bágrimma.	Mába.
turdža	. . . . . .	. . . . . .	. . . . .	. . .
bēni [8]	vyōla	bīa . . . . / χia	nyŏ	casur (?)
hēni	wīyo	medž - ébuš .	lšcógo . . . / tcúg . . .	cuŏ / kelana ? [11]
hāme . . . . / hummo . . .	mákala [9] . . .	med - ékuš [10] .	wŏ	kóšimū

[1] móro: Koelle writes móró and wrongly restricts the signification of the term to the „red millet" in opposition to argém or, as he writes, árgəm mátla (p. 356 he writes the latter term mátša or mátla). No doubt, the circumstance, that argém — the term expressing the indigenous African corn and forming the general opposition to ngáberi, at a remote period the corn introduced, from abroad, as it seems — is frequently added, appears to indicate, that móro originally was an adverbial form, but in Kúkawa and in Bornu Proper in general, the móro at present comprises both species or rather indicates only the common yellow millet, there being no red millet at all cultivated in that country. However it is very possible, that in the province of Gházir, the dialect of which is especially represented in Koelle's vocabulary, such a distinction is made. In Bornu, however, the matla is expressly looked upon as a kind of ngáberi, Travels and Disc. II, p. 318. — I here mention, that Koelle, besides, has another term, viz lárá, to which he attributes a very comprehensive notion, as meaning „fruit, corn, vegetables, any thing planted and not growing wild", but which has remained unknown to myself.

[2] ngáberi: Koelle writes ngáfəli, but adds, that the inhabitants of Dikwa, that is to say, of Bornu Proper, pronounce it with a b. And I have scarcely any doubt, that the sorghum, forming at present the staple food of Bornu Proper (see my Travels and Discoveries vol. II, p. 313), while the móro is principally used for the horses, has received its name from that very reason, because it constitutes the „living", ngá, that is to say the principal, „food" (béri) of the Kanúri. Moreover, Koelle very wrongly explains the term as meaning „millet". From this Kanúri-term the Fezzáni's who frequent these markets, have formed the term yafáli. — In this note I will also adduce the various terms of particular varieties of ngáberi, as mentioned by Koelle, but which have remained unknown to myself, although they are easily explained. First, as for his sábáde, it is identical with my sébbade and his masakúa with my mashkuá, his kélíram with my kériram, a particular variety of mashkuá, called sí fará in Lógoné and Wándalá, wi bará in Bágrimma; but besides these varieties he has the following, which I have not: bárgu (? „first"); Bigéram; sámbul [„all white"?, sam bul]; káfeguram (in Dikōa wálóguná) [no doubt distinguished on account of its „short" (káfuga or kábuga) or „small" (ganá) growth], kalakaláno (in Dikōa kéli kétši) [evidently nothing but a „sweet" (ketši) variety of the kélíram or kériram]; and finally ngáfəli tsárma. Besides these terms all mentioned by Koelle s. v. ngáfəli he has another term mátši or ngáfəli mátši, whence a red dye is prepared. — Probably the latter term is identical with my ngáberi kemé, H. dāwa dawa, F. bairi badéri, W. guasá, S hāme téeré or sába (sába being the common term of daily life in Timbuktu); besides this variety I have the „white sorghum", K. ngáberi bul, H. farí n dawa, F. bairi danéri, S. háme korō, and „black sorghum", H. baki n dawa, F. ondumúri, S. dímbí.

[3] auncre, as stated Introductory Remarks p. XCVII, 16., seems to be related to the corresponding term in the Máših-language, and may thus be one of the few instances of such a harmony intervening between these two languages: nay, in Bilma and probably in the whole of the wádi Kauár, in general, the pure Máših-form éneli is exclusively in use. But that is no proof for linguistical connection, the inhabitants of Bilma receiving from the Máših-tribe, the so called Tawárek, their whole supply of negro-millet in exchange for their salt.

[4] ngáfuli: Intentionally I do not write ngáfuli, as I have not observed this nasal sound to be peculiar to the Tédá-language.

[5] batal and sásaba have not exactly the same meaning: sásaba signifying the batal, as far as it is cleared (batal báho kaika taiki). — I shall here adduce a few other terms having some relation to corn, for which I have learned the corresponding terms only in some of the languages of my list „a large stack of corn not yet thrashed", K. hagga (Koelle gives instead a term legrale not known to me), H. tumma, F. mámmarí; „a bundle of corn in the stalks", H. damme, F. bulére; „a small gavel", H. gomma hárami, F. gommel. — I here also give the name for „husk", H. surfō, F. tšottánde, S. nóoba.

[6] gerést, of course, is not the original Fulfúlde-term, but is the only one, which at present is used by the Fúlbe settled in the provinces of the former Hausa empire.

[7] bairi is a very remarkable name, being one of those scanty vestiges of a connection between the mysterious tribe of the Fúlbe on the one, and the Indian tribes on the other side, and it is a point of great interest, when we consider, that the sorghum altogether was not indigenous to Africa, but, according to all probability, introduced from India.

[8] bēni in certain cases really seems to have this general meaning of „corn".

[9] mákala at first sight is remarkable, but I do not know, whether it has any connection with the Arabic term mákela.

[10] medž-ébuš and med-ékuš appear to have some intimate relation one to the other, but I am not able to explain with certainty the point of comparison, although by comparing these terms with mée-akud, which certainly is of Wándalá, and not of Bornu origin, it seems, that they mean, the one „seed growing on dry", and the other „seed growing on wet ground". In common life people seem to call the former only by the name of medž, and in one phrase I have this term opposed to bō: ñire bétera goe imtā, „what is their kind of seed", or „what kind of seed have they", medž go bō, „millet or sorghum".

[11] Among my phrases I have kelana for „negro-millet". — Burckhardt gives the term sī (the Arabic 'īš?) as meaning „corn"; instead of kóšimū he has košme.

Deutsch und Englisch.	Kanúri.	Tédă.	Hausa.	Fulfúlde.
Egyptischer Mais — *Egyptian corn; Zea mais*	masar [1] . .	másarmi . .	daua n Másara [10]	bútali [16] . .
Holcus cernuus — *[illegible]*	masákuă [2] . .	. . . . . .	maiwa . . .	maiwári . . .
Sorghum saccharatum — *sorghum saccharatum*	séblade [3] . .	. . . . . .	takánta . . .	takantádés .
Reis — *rice*	fúrgami [4] . .	šinkafa . . .	šinkáfa [11] . .	maróri . . .
Sesamum — *sesamum* .	márraši [5] . .	. . . . . .	nómo . . .	márasin [13] . .
Baumwolle — *cotton* . .	kalkútia [6] . .	kulkútton . .	{ ábulega . . / báda Bok. . }	púttolo [16] . .
Same der Baumwolle — *seed of cotton*	témmali [7] . .	kulkútton miga hena [9]	yangúria [12] .	. . . . . :
Indigo — *indigo* . . .	arin [8] . . .	alin	baba	{ tšaliári . . / babábo . . }

[1] masar heisst eigentlich nichts Anderes als „Egypten" oder „Kairo", hier „Korn aus Egypten", weil es von dort aus nach Central-Afrika eingeführt wurde, obgleich es Amerikanischen Ursprungs ist, wie wol trotz Schleiden's Einsprache jetzt feststeht. Es wird übrigens in den von mir besuchten Gegenden nur in kleiner Menge gebaut, gewöhnlich nur in

Sońyai.	Lógoné.	Wándalá.	Bágrimma.	Mába.
massar hāme . .	báherā	{iya / hia} mássare [18]	mássara . .	. . . . . .
. . . . . .	massákuā . . .	mas-ákuā . .	{bar ndžáppe [20] / bar alñe . .}	. . . . . .
tšenéuke . . .	kanaē	wómtekē . .	lúśsurū . . .	. . . . . .
mō [16]	inkā	kúdžer(e) ákire [19]	ingérde . . .	rūs (Arb.)
namie	makámme . . .	serwa . . .	karru . . .	wonánge
há-bu	mpátakī . . .	sūže	ūēre	gnório
. . . . . .	inkoāī mpátakī .	témmari . .	inga ūēre . .	. . . . . .
šīni, sīni [17] . .	{mógonē . . . . / mōn . . . .}	{unē / anyē}	alīni	nīl

[1] massar properly means nothing else, but „Egypt" or „Cairo", but in this instance signifies „Egyptian corn", it having been introduced into Central-Africa by way of Egypt, although of American origin. In those regions, however, which I myself have visited, it is only cultivated in very small quantities, generally only in the courtyards round the cottages.
[2] masakuā. With regard to the mode of cultivating this kind of corn see my Travels and Discoveries vol. II, p. 353.
[3] sóbbadu: with regard to the „sorghum saccharatum", or „holcus saccharatus", which at present has begun to become a general article for feeding the cattle even in many parts of Europe, see my Travels vol. III, p. 59.
[4] fórgami: this national term for rice, which seems to prove, that rice is indigenous in certain parts of Bornu, is wanting in Koelle, who gives instead a slightly changed form of the Hausa-term, namely šingáfa or šinkáfa, and, no doubt, this term is used in many districts of Bornu, and has been so from ancient times, as is sufficiently shown by the Tédā-language using the same term. Rice growing wild almost exclusively on that sort of soil called forki or firki mentioned above, and from which Koelle by mistake, as stated, has formed the name of a district Férgi, it is not at all improbable, that this is the original meaning of fórgami or fórkami, namely „corn growing in firki soil".
[5] márrakī seems to be wanting in Koelle's vocabulary, although it constitutes such an important ingredient in the staple food of these Regions, less so however in Bornu, than further to the South and East.
[6] kalkâtie is a remarkable name, although the similarity, which it bears to the name of the Indian capital is only seemingly; and it would be very wrong and highly absurd, to draw thence the conclusion, that cotton was introduced into Negroland from India. But on the other hand it is not improbable, when we consider the Tédā-form, that the name has been derived from the Arabic kutton, the Negroes having certainly learned from the Arabs the use of the cotton, while the native terms, which we find in the other languages, fully prove its original growth there. The term appears in Koelle only in connection with kénder and úgur kénderbé, „the cottoncapsule", with regard to which he makes the remark, after opening it is called kalgáteu, „cottonshrub".
[7] témmali, which is wanting in Koelle, is probably borrowed from the Wándalá-idiom, and not the reverse (see Intr. Remarks p. CCLIII), but the native name is very important, as the cottonseed forms a most common and almost necessary ingredient in the food for cattle in Negroland.
[8] aylu is identical with the šilu of Koelle, although the latter was not aware of the identity of this plant with the indigo-plant.
[9] kalkáttou mige hené, „cotton its child", with regard to which form see Introductory Remarks p. LXXXI.
[10] dauu u Mássara: we here see a proof, that the Hausa-people do not distinguish the Zea from the sorghum, but consider the former as a mere variety of the latter.
[11] šinkáffa: I here give the particular terms of two varieties of rice; „a peculiar kind of black rice", H. dūimmoro, F. marōri ballēri; „the best variety of white rice", H. fari n irri n šinkáffa, F. marōri daneeri, S. gammi. Besides, there are peculiar terms for the „rice in the husk", H. šinkáffa sánšorā, F. marōri n dorúnde, and for „cleaned rice", H. šinkáffa sárfafé, F. marōri sattándi. — As for the terms for „wheat" and „barley", I have left them out on purpose, as in all these languages they are expressed by means of the Arabic term el šaïr, ul gámo with some slight variations, lokómo in Bágrimma, gomone in Mába.
[12] yangárid seems to be composed of ya („child") and gária, in which case gária would seem to represent the term cotton in some other respect.
[13] bátoli seems to me a little doubtful, as it is the regular plural-form of batándu with the general notion of „cornstalk", corresponding to the Sońyai-term sengárne; but from some reason unknown to ourselves the term may have really received that particular meaning.
[14] mórasin: this term by the Eastern Fulbe has evidently been borrowed from the Kanúri, and I have therefore no doubt, that it is totally unknown to their Western countrymen; I do not even know, whether cresses be cultivated there to any extent.
[15] péttolo: in the Eastern provinces of the Fulbe empire an h seems to take the place of the p in the beginning of this word.
[16] mō as a monosyllable has a very primitive character and does not seem to be derived from foreign origin (see Introductory Remarks p. CXCV, note 1): it is, therefore, of considerable weight with regard to the question, whether rice be indigenous in the countries of the Niger and in Central Africa in general, and I begin to doubt the truth of what I supposed in my Travels V, p. 194, viz. that the rice was introduced into the region of the Niger from Egypt at a relatively late period.
[17] šini: this term properly seems to mean only the indigo-colour called šūni in Koelle, not the plant itself.
[18] iya or hia mássare, no doubt, means „corn from Egypt", iya or hia being = giya.
[19] kúdžer(e) ákire is a name given to the rice from a comparison with the common Pea, which is simply called kúdžere.
[20] bar ndžáppe: I am not quite sure of the bar.

Deutsch und Englisch.	Kanúri.	Teda.	Hausa.	Fulfúlde.
Gemüse — greens . . .	kalu [1] . .	zīlu	gabe Plur. gáñaye	hákodžī . .
Bohne — bean; Vicia Faba	ŭgālo [2] . . .	gallu . .	wáki Pl. wakōki	ŏēblere Pl. ŏebbe
Erdmandel — groundnut; Arachys hypogaea.	koltše . . .	. . . . .	yáro da dária [6]	bírio Pl. birīdži [9]
andere, bittere Art Erdmandel — other, bitter kind of groundnut	ngúngala [3] . .		yerkúrga [7] . .	
Melone — melon; cucumis melo		. . . . .	gunna . . .	dennaldžo . . / tšekīlže . .
Coloquinthe — coloquinthe	. . . . .	tabérka (?) . .	dža n gunna [8]	denne kadde [10]
Cucurbita melopepo als Gemüse im gekochten Zustande — cucurbita melopepo, used in a cooked state	gubásko . .	. . . . .	. . . . .	basko-džo [11] .
Cucurbita pepo — cucurbita pepo	ságode . . .	kebéwa [5] . .	kubéwa . . .	kobōul . . .
Flaschenkürbiss — cucurbita lagenaria	gubēto [4] . . .	kolu	kória	túmbudē . .
Cucurbita maxima? — calabash	kúmō . . . / kummu . .		dumma . . .	fandu Plur. pali

[1] kálu. Koelle kálü, von dem er aber als ganz besonderes Wort kálne mit der Bedeutung „Gras" [illegible], obgleich es ganz dasselbe Wort ist. Vergl. [illegible], S. 180 kálu kéeka-be, „das Gras des Hauses", d. h. „Blätter".

[2] ngála. Koelle, der ngálo schreibt, führt (in dem von ihm vertretenen Dialekt) mehrere besondere Arten von Bohnen an, ngálo tšīgar, „kleine rothe Bohnen"; ngálo mánkó Fulátá, „eine andere Sorte rother (nach den Fúlbe benannter) Bohnen"; ngálo koyam kálē (in Dikoa kullmi genannt), „eine Art bunter (besonders in der Provinz Kojam gebauter) Bohnen"; ngálo káfi, „eine andere Art bunter Bohnen".

[3] ngúngula fehlt bei Koelle mit dieser Bedeutung; er hat es nur für „bent" (sperkind). Anstatt koltše schreibt er kultši. — Ich will hier auch die Benennungen des sehr häufigen cyperus esculentus, Arb. habb el ’aziz, anführen. K. [illegible] oder [illegible] (Koelle núfu als „Art kleiner Erdmandeln"), H. gedžia und vielleicht F. birio Plur. biridži.

[4] gubēto. Koelle schreibt kapeto und erklärt es für den Baum, der die als kúmō, d. h. „Schalen" benutzten Kürbisse trägt. Das ist aber eine Verwechselung, obgleich kumma oder kúmō, wie wir hernach noch näher sehen werden, nicht allein die Pflanze, sondern auch die daraus bereitete Schale oder Kumme bedeutet.

[5] kebéwa gehört nur uneigentlich hierher, da diese Pflanze im Tédā-Gebiete, wenigstens in den von mir besuchten Theilen, gleich den meisten der hier aufgeführten Pflanzen fehlt; kabéwa nennen auch die [illegible] diese Pflanze.

[6] yāro da daria, wörtlich „ein Bube zum Lachen". Vergl. Reisen Bd. II, S. 17.

[7] yerkúrga. Aus dieser bitteren Art Erdmandeln wird ein eigenes Nationalgericht bereitet, Namens paṡō oder fuñē, dessen Zubereitung ich hier auf Hausa mittheile. yerkúrga [illegible] ga ráma yō [illegible]; yo [illegible] da [illegible] kudan, [illegible] addbba [illegible] dūtsi, [illegible] spaṡé-ta, Sina paṡō, „nachdem die Erdmandeln zu einem Brei gestampft sind(?), bringt man sie und schüttet sie in die Sonne, damit sie trocknen; sind sie dann getrocknet, so wird etwas Wasser darauf gegossen und mit etwas Sand(?) gekocht; wenn es fertig ist, giesst es auf einen heissen Stein und röstet es, so ist es das paṡō genannte Gericht".

[8] dža n gunna, eigentlich „rothe Melone"; eben dieser engen Anschliessung des Namens halber habe ich die Coloquinthe an dieser Stelle unterbringen zu müssen geglaubt; vergl. Reisen Bd. I, S. 480.

[9] bírio. Ich bin nicht gewiss, ob bírio eine oder beide Arten der Erdmandeln bezeichnet, oder ob dieser Ausdruck vielleicht gar eigentlich nur die gedžia bezeichnet (Note 3). Reichardt in seinem Primer S. 9 gibt tigáre für „Erdmandel".

[10] denne kadde heisst wahrscheinlich „weisse, helle Melone", denne = dannéu und kadde vielleicht dem S. [illegible].

[11] baskō-džo ist unzweifelhaft der nur äusserlich der Fulfúlde-Sprache anbequemte und im Anfang abgekürzte Kanúri-Ausdruck gobásko und ist daher ebenso unzweifelhaft in den westlichen Landschaften der Fúlbe völlig unbekannt.

[12] kóen, S. 181 für „Blatt", heisst eigentlich „frisch, jung" und erscheint daher noch einmal als Eigenschaftswort.

[13] mátiya. So hat auch Kaffenel in Arama, d. h. dem von den Hausa angenommenen Songhai-Dialekt, mátiba für „pistache de terre", und eben aus diesem mátiya ist unzweifelhaft das nach Reichardt in den westlichen Fúl-Dialekten gebrauchte tigáre abgeleitet (Note 9), mit Abwerfung der Anfangssilbe ma, ganz wie baskódže von gobásko abgeleitet ist.

[14] kan-kenna u. s. w. Ich überlasse es einem späteren Reisenden, diese vier Species zu identificiren; eine derselben entspricht möglicher Weise dem K. gobasko. kanna scheint mit H. gunna eng verwandt, wie auch die Ausdrücke dža n gunna und kanne [illegible] in den beiden Sprachen sich völlig entsprechen.

[15] [illegible] heisst eigentlich „die Erdmandel der Heiden", weil sie nur in den südlicheren, von den Heiden bewohnten Landschaften vorkommt.

[16] Ich habe hier niedergeschrieben bálēl déberē, aber es scheint mir, abgesehen von einer an sich unwesentlichen Ähnlichkeit mit dem entsprechenden Wándalá-Ausdruck libberé, dem wéle lebrē S. 170 für „Bamia" so ähnlich, dass ich es an unserer Stelle für mehr als zweifelhaft halte.

[17] angab kúdah. Der erste Theil erinnert an Burckhardt's [illegible], „gourds", der letztere ist mir unsicher.

Sóṅyai.	Lógoné.	Wándalā.	Bágrimma.	Mába.
kōsu [12]	wōnan	dālo	goṅgo . . .	dedrīya
dáṅguri	magōro	gīro	mondžo . . .	mmo (?)
mátiya [13] . . .	{ indáral kerdi [15] .	yin(a) ímbana	būli búbera .	. . . . . .
	{ indáral Logón .	yína kosōkosō	būli ugórgoli .	
{ kan-kanna [14] . / kóra-kanne . . / musse-músse . . / mulli . . . . }	. . . . . .		górlaka (?) . .	[andádji D.]
kanno tīro . .	. . . . . .	. . . . . .	. . . . . .	. . . . . .
. . . .	bólōl débere [16] .	íbbere . . .	kurtši ? . . .	molūwon
lebiíndo(?) . . .	wumbógo . . .	bōgo	bō	dántegit
gāsu . . . . . . / kulba . . . . . }	gil	uwā	pallo? . . .	kāli
maríkašē . . .	kalha	efga	górlakā . . .	aṅgab kūduk [17]

[1] kāla, Koelle kálā, from which he wrongly diverses kalua meaning „grass" as a totally distinct term, although it is the very same word. Compare kālu késka-ba p. 180.

[2] ágilo: Koelle writes ágálá and mentions several varieties of beans, as ágálā tšigar, „small red beans"; ágálā múskā Fulátā, „another kind of red beans" [called after the Fúlbe or Fulata]; ágálā kóyām kálā (called kulimi in Dikoa), „a kind of speckled beans" [principally cultivated in the province of Koyām]; ágálā háfi, „another kind of speckled beans".

[3] ágáágula is not mentioned by Koelle, but with the meaning of „speckled". Instead of koltšo he writes koltšī. — I shall here also adduce the native terms for the very common and (even by myself) much liked cyperus esculentus, Arb. habb el ázīz, as far as I was able to make them out, K. nifu or nibu (Koelle náfō, „a kind of small groundnuts"), H. gaž̄ia and perhaps F. birio plur. biridži.

[4] gobōto: Koelle writes kāpetā and explains it wrongly as meaning the plant which bears the gourds used as kámō i. e. „calabashes" although kamma or kámō not only signifies the plant, but also the bowl or dish thence prepared.

[5] kebéwa properly does not belong to this place, the plant being rather foreign to the territory of the Tēda and used of the latter calling it by the Kanúri-term. However, also the neighbouring Imóšay call it kabéwa.

[6] yāro da dária means verbally „a boy for laughing", see Travels vol. II, p. 15.

[7] yerkúrga: from this bitter kind of groundnut a peculiar national dish is prepared, called palō or fašō, the mode of preparing which I here give in Hausa with the English translation. yerkúrga intonkta akune azábba ga rána ye kékaše; ya kékaše azábba rúa kadán azúye-ta da verē kadán, t(a)-ánina azábba táikí-n dútsi, sána da-sáfi ápašō-ta, šina palō, „you first blanch the groundnuts, and you then place them in the sun for drying, and when they are dried, you pour a little water upon them and boil them mixing therewith some sand (?); when it is done, you pour the whole upon a hot stone and roast it, and thus you have what is called palō".

[8] dāo n gunna properly means „red melon", and it is on this account, that I have assigned to the colocynth this place. See Trav. and Disc. vol. I, p. 393. I here remark, that the natives, especially the Tēda, prepare a tolerable dish from the seeds of the colocynth.

[9] birio: I am not quite certain, whether the name birio is given to one or to both kinds of groundnut, nor even, whether it may not possibly mean exclusively the cyperus or gažia (compare note 3). At least Rev. Reichardt in his Primer p. 8 gives the name tigare for „groundnut", a term which, beyond the least doubt, has been derived from the corresponding Sonyai-term mátiya, by throwing off the first syllable ma.

[10] dunno kadde means probably „white melon", dunno = dunnéo and kadde = the Sonyai kaane.

[11] boskó-dža has beyond a doubt been derived from the Kanúri-term gobásko, exactly in the same manner, as tigáre has been derived from the Sonyai-term mátiya, and is therefore probably unknown to the Fúlbe of the Western provinces.

[12] kōsu properly means „fresh, young" and on this account has to be mentioned in another portion of this vocabulary.

[13] mátiya: this term appears as well in Koelle's Polyglotta in the form of matiya as in Raffenel's Aruma-list as mátiho meaning „pistache de terre".

[14] kan-kanna etc.: one of these terms may be identical with the variety called gobásko. kanna, no doubt, is clearly related to gunna in Hausa, as also the expressions dāo n gunna and kanno tīro correspond with each other exactly.

[15] indáral kordi properly means „the groundnut of the pagans", on account of their being generally grown only in the countries to the South, exclusively inhabited by pagans.

[16] bólōl débere, which I have written down, bears such a close resemblance to wéle lebre, „hibiscus esculentus" p. 179, that I am rather doubtful as to its correctness, although the corresponding W.-term seems to show, that it is here in its right place.

[17] aṅgab kūduk: while the first term clearly resembles the anka of Burckhardt with the meaning „gourds", the latter seems rather a little uncertain.

Deutsch und Englisch.	Kanúri.	Tédā.	Hausa.	Fulfúlde.
Gurke — *cucumber; Cucumis sativus*	maĭă[1]	. . . . .	korús-korús[7]	deppi . . . .
Patate — *sweet potatoes; Convolvulus Batatas*	[2]	. . . . . .	dánkali . . / kúdaku H. S.	kúdakūdže .
Kräb, Gramineen mit [illegible] Samen — *Poa Abyssinica (?)*	kalā[3]	[6]	. . . . . .	. . . . . .
andere Varietät von Poa — *other variety of the same*	. . . . . .	. . . . . .	. . . . . .	. . . . . .
Bamia; Corchorus olitorius — *Corchorus olitorius*	gumsēno[4] . .	kébbelu . . .	miya[8] . . .	līyo . . . .
Blätter der Adansonia als Gemüse — *leaves of the Adansonia used as greens*	kālu kūka . .		miya n kūka .	līyo bokko .
Garten-Bamia — *garden-Bamia, hibiscus esculentus, L.*	gobálgo fāto-be	. . . . . .	. . . . . .	
wilde Bamia — *wild Bamia*	gebálgo déri-be / gádegir . .	. . . . . .	. . . . . .	. . . . . .
Jatropha Manihot — *Jatropha Manihot*	karēsa, karāsa	karāsu . . .	rōgo[9] . . . / ruăla . . .	rogōhi Plur. rogōdže
Baum, Holz — *tree, wood*	késka[5] . . .	akā	itatše . . . / itše Plur. itātua	leggel Plur. ledde
gewaltiger Baumstamm (zum Brennen) — *big old stump to be used as firewood*	gógō? . . .	. . . . . .	gúngumē . .	leggel mangal

[1] maĭă. Ich bin nicht ganz sicher, ob maĭă dem gegenüberstehenden Hausa-Ausdruck entspricht; jedenfalls entspricht es dem Lógonē- und Wándala-Ausdruck. — Die Gurke findet sich eigentlich nur an der Gränze der Wüste und des Tropenlandes.

[2] Die süsse Kartoffel findet sich nicht im eigentlichen Bornu und in den östlich angränzenden Landschaften, aber freilich in den westlichen an Hausa gränzenden Provinzen, jedoch auch dort habe ich keinen nationalen Namen dafür erfahren, da dort eben die Hausa-Sprache vorwiegt. — Die Ausdrücke für die mit Weizen zugleich von den Arabern in diese Länder eingeführte Zwiebel will ich nicht aufführen, weil sie mehr oder weniger rein Arabisch sind (albossal, albassar, albásasare); nur im Fulfúlde ist er etwas eigenthümlich in albásle eingewandelt.

[3] kalā fehlt bei Koelle. Mir wurden zwei Varietäten bekannt, kalā ungórgo und kalā magala. Dann gibt es noch eine verwandte Poa mit essbarem Samen, kerēs genannt, und noch eine andere mit dem halb Arabischen Namen abu-sábe, deren Same durchgeweicht und mit Negerhirse gemischt gegessen wird.

[4] gumsēno fehlt bei Koelle, ebenso wie gebálgo und gádegir. Bei den beiden Arten der gebálgo ist das „Haus", fāto, der „offenen Wildniss", déri (S. 168 déri dē, so zu schreiben und zu trennen) entgegengesetzt. Die Bamia ist übrigens in Bornu vielleicht erst von Bagirmi aus eingeführt.

[5] késka. Ich hörte stets zwei scharfe k in diesem Worte, nur zuweilen näherte sich das zweite k einem g-Laut. Koelle dagegen, der aber, wie oft erwähnt, nur eine einzige Autorität, einen Provinzialen 'Ali Aísē-mi Gasirmu, hatte, schreibt gégē und gibt kēgā als Ausnahme.

[6] Im Lande der Tédā gibt es, wie es scheint, in den von mir besuchten Gegenden keine Poa, daher auch keinen Namen dafür; im Hausa, Fulfúlde und Sonγai dagegen habe ich nur durch Zufall den entsprechenden Namen nicht erfahren.

[7] korús-korús ist kein eigentlicher Hausa-Name, sondern scheint nur in Asben gebraucht zu werden, Reisen 1, S. 470.

[8] miya. Der Corchorus hat diese Bezeichnung miya wol nur deshalb, weil die daraus bereitete „Brühe" die in Hausa und fast im ganzen Negerlande volksthümlichste ist und gehört er deshalb in der Bedeutung von „grüner Brühe" in mancher Beziehung mehr einer späteren Abtheilung dieses Wörterbuches, das die Speisen behandelt, an.

[9] rōgo. Ich will hier auch die Specialbenennungen für verschiedene Varietäten von Maniok oder Brodfrucht im Hausa und Fulfúlde einschalten: H. riaga, F. riagōdže oder bogámdēl; H. tomāgu, F. mattawelie; H. gwáse, F. gwasádže oder taudaudža oder auch kibe (der letzte Ausdruck nur in Masina am Oberen Niger üblich oder vielmehr von Masina an westlich; denn es ist kein Zweifel, dass kibe identisch ist mit dem kapo. „yams" in Reichardt's A-B-C-Buch S. 4, wenn man bedenkt, dass Reichardt seine Sprachstudien eben in dem Dialekte der westlichsten Fúlbe machte); H. dōya, F. dōyádže.

[10] Rafīenel gibt für „Patate" im Azena, d. h. dem von den Hausa angenommenen Sonγai, dourbé oulé (durbē ulē).

[11] sansan. Diese, sowie die Wándala-Form sind blosse leichte Variationen des Bágrimma-Ausdruckes, da diese Poa wesentlich von Bagirmi nicht einheimisch zu sein scheint. Von ihrem ausgedehnten Gebrauch in Bagirmi habe ich in meinem Reisebericht gesprochen Th. III, S. 362 und 399.

[12] daságe. Von dieser Poa lernte ich im Mába die Namen dreier bestimmter Varietäten kennen: tilikāt, korōk und taufáfanāng.

[13] Da ich den Mába-Namen für die in diesem Lande in so allgemeinem Gebrauche stehende Bamia nicht erfuhr, erwähne ich, dass Burckhardt für „rohe Bamia", gorenu (gorūn) gibt und für „ein Gericht aus Bamien", oeo, das an mein nese, „Bohne", erinnert.

Sónyai.	Lógoné.	Wándalá.	Bágrimma.	Mába.
demsi (?) . . .	ralle yiri	taúasa . . .	. . . . . .	[saboro B.?]
[10]	. . . . . .	. . . . .	. . . . . .	. . . . . .
. . . . . .	kalligibi	kúdžere . . .	tšenna . . .	denáñg [12]
. . . . . .	zauzau [11] . . .	zózó	džódžó . . .	felš
molunkīya (Arb.)	sobandīya . . / lōgum	umbé . . .	godérmo . .	moluxīa (Arb.)
kō foi . . . / hoi . . .	. . . . . .	. . . . .	. . . . .	. . . . .
. . . . . .	wēle-lebrē . .	. . . . .	gobállo . . .	[13]
. . . . . .	wēle-gemī . .	yobér bodá .	géddegir . .	. . . . .
labdundu . . .	bēri	šiá	. . . . .	. . . . .
túgudži Pl. tugúdžio / túguri Plur. tūri	hodúguā . . .	afā	kagā	sungók Pl. sungō
tūri bēri (Plur.) .	. . . . . .	. . . . .	. . . . .	. . . . .

[1] maššá: I am not quite sure, whether maššá corresponds exactly with the Hausa-term, but thus much I know, that it conveys the identical meaning as the Lógoné- and Wándalá-word. — As for the cucumber, it is not proper to the fertile Regions of Negroland, but rather to the border districts of the desert.

[2] Sweet potatoes not being grown in Bornu Proper and in the adjoining provinces, but only in the Western districts bordering on Hausa, where the term belonging to the latter language does prevail, I have not learned the proper Kanúri-term. — As for the terms for „onion", I have omitted them on purpose, the onion having been introduced into these regions together with wheat and in consequence thereof being called by its Arabic name „el basal", but slightly changed „albasal, albassar, albássare"; only in Fulfúlde a more peculiar form has thence been derived, albásle.

[3] kalá is wanting in Koelle. I learned the names of two varieties, kalá ngégge and kalá magala. — Besides, there is another kind of Pea, containing likewise an edible seed, called kertšu, and another one called by the half Arabic name abú-sáke, the seed of which is often mixed with Negrocorn.

[4] gamasóne is wanting in Koelle, as well as the terms gabálgo and gédegir. As for the two kinds of the former, fáto, „the house" has been opposed to déri, „the open country, wilderness" p. 160 (where déri dē have to be separated from each other). It seems however, as if the use of the hemp has been introduced into Bornu from Bagirmi.

[5] káshu: I always heard distinctly two h's in this word, only rarely the second h approaching the g sound. Koelle, on the contrary, following the sole authority of his 'Ali Ahmad not a native of Bornu Proper, but of the province of Gúmir, writes gógeh, giving kógeh as an exceptional form.

[6] The Tédá seem to have no proper term for the Pea, although it may grow in some of the Southernmost districts of their territory. — In the Hausa-, Fulfúlde- and Sónyai-languages it is merely by accident, that I did not learn the proper terms.

[7] kerda-kerda is a term not properly belonging to the Hausa-language, but seems to be used exclusively in the country of Asben (Travels I, p. 405).

[8] miya: this name seems to be given to the carcharus olitorius only on account of it constituting the most common „sauce" of the natives, and has to be mentioned once more among the articles of native food.

[9] róge: I shall here insert the names proper to the Hausa- and Fulfúlde-languages for some varieties of yams the Dioscorea, H. riago, F. riagódše or hogámdši; H. tomágu, F. mottawolla; H. gwóza, F. gwozúdše or tondondše or kábu, this latter term being used in Masina, and as it seems, also in the F. provinces W. of Masina; for there can be but little doubt, that kábu is identical with the term hope, „yams" in the Primer of Rev. Reichardt p. 4, this Missionary having made his linguistical studies from the dialect of the Western-most Fúlbe. As a further variety I mention H. dóya, F. dóyádše.

[10] I here mention for the use of future travellers, that Raffenel in his list of Arama, a dialect of Sónyai, gives the term dourbé oulé (durbé ulé) for „potato".

[11] zauzau: this as well, as the corresponding Wándalá-term, is a mere slight variation of the Bágrimma-name, this Pea apparently not being so common in the provinces West of Bagirmi, as in the latter country, with regard to which I have spoken repeatedly of the extensive use, which is made there of this article of food, Travels and Discr. III, p. 405 und 447.

[12] denáñg: of this Pea I learnt the names of three varieties in Mába, namely liliháñ, korók and tanfafanáñg.

[13] As it is by mere accident that I did not write down the name given to this plant in Wadái which there forms a most important article of food, I here mention, that Burckhardt gives the term gerenn (gerku) for „bamia" itself, and one which reminds a little of my term ussu meaning „bamia", for „a dish of bamia".

Deutsch und Englisch.	Kanúri.	Tédā.	Hausa.	Fulfúlde.
Rinde — *bark*	kerre (?)	. . . . . .	baua; bambar	kobbe ledde
Wurzel — *root*	furtu[1]	dāīru	séwua n itše	dádul leggel, Pl. dadidži ledde
Gabelast — *forked bough*	fárage késka-be[2]	. . . . . .	. . . . . .	. . . . . .
Ast — *branch, bough*; Zweig — *twig*	déllemi[3]	akā) kobā benā[12]	sebga Pl. semādži; rēfe n itše	lōsol Plur. lōtši; lítšal Plur. lítše
Blatt — *leaf*	kálu késka-be[4]	hóhori; hófori	kunno n itše[14]	baroūtiol Plur. baroūtiin; nōpi leggel
Palmblatt — *palm-leaf*	úgille[5]	. . . . . .	kába Pl. kébobī	balli
Baumkrone — *crown of tree*	kógiö késka-be[6]	akā) dābo benā	koāya?; kai n itše	gēdžu[15]; hōre leggel
Dorn — *thorn*	kárage késka-be[7]	šimberi	káya n itše	gīyel Plur. gīye
Blume, Blüthe — *bloom, blossom, flower*	kámberi[8]	bō; kobo	furē Plur. fúrnyē	pindi, findi; lokke
Samen — *seed*	kásanī (?); ngúr	. . . . . .	irri	aúrode ledde Pl. aude ledde
(Baum)-Frucht — *fruit*	túta késka-be[9] Pl. tatanan késka-be	akē médondig[13]; orma; timni	dan itše Pl. yāye n itátua	biúngel leggel, Pl. biko ledde
Schote — *pod, cod*	. . . . . .	. . . . . .	tūšia	túggerē
Nuss-Schale — *nut-shell*	kāma[10]	āši	kússeri	sotōre Pl. sotōdže
Hülse, Schale — *husk, peel*	kerre[11]		kautši	

[1] furtu, Koelle púrto, daneben aber noch pérte mit der Bedeutung „Baumstumpf"; er hat mit dieser Bedeutung auch noch [illegible] und ausserdem yā gēgābō für „Baumstamm".

[2] fárage késka-be. fárage ist offenbar abgeleitet von farágin, „ich theile, vertheile"; es erscheint bei Koelle nur s. v. gēgā [illegible] kaska als párage gēgābē, „die Stelle des Baumes, wo die niedrigsten Zweige vom Stamme ausgehen".

[3] déllemi hat eine mir unbekannte Ableitung und ist auffallend wegen seiner Übereinstimmung mit dem entsprechenden Mába-Ausdruck (Note 19).

[4] kálu késka-be s. oben S. 176, N. 1.

[5] úgille erscheint bei Koelle unter der Form ugelei, „Palmen, aus der Stricke gemacht werden".

[6] kógiö késka-be. kógiö allein (die bei Koelle daneben angeführte Form kóge ist mir nicht vorgekommen) hat die allgemeine Bezeichnung eines Kopfschmuckes und bezeichnet keineswegs allein, wie Koelle angibt, den Federbusch gewisser Vögel; Koelle ist aber unser Ausdruck unbekannt geblieben.

[7] kárage késka-be. Dieser Ausdruck fehlt bei Koelle. kárage ist offenbar ganz ebenso von karágin, „ich verwirre" abgeleitet, wie fárage von farágin, N. 2. Ich möchte hiernach meinen, dass auch karága, „Wald", hiermit zusammenhänge, wegen des „verwirrenden" Charakters der hiesigen Dickichte, wenn es wirklich karagā gesprochen würde, wie Koelle schreibt; aber ich habe es stets nur karāga mit einem entschiedenen langen zweiten á sprechen hören.

[8] kámberi. Koelle schreibt kámpeli und gibt ihm neben unserer Bedeutung auch die Bezeichnung von „Ringen". Ich glaube aber, die beiden Wörter sind grundverschieden.

[9] túta késka-be, wörtlich „Kind des Baumes".

[10] kāma fehlt bei Koelle in dieser Bedeutung.

[11] kerre fehlt auch bei Koelle.

[12] akā) kobā benā (bénuā), wörtlich „Baum, seine Hände" (ganz wie S. tūguri kamba und im W. craw n afa). akā) dābo benā, „Baum sein Kopf", vergl. Einleitung S. LXXX.

[13] akē oder akā médondig. Zusammensetzung unbekannt und so vollständig kaum richtig.

[14] kunno n itše, wörtlich „das Ohr des Baumes", ganz wie nōpi leggel in F. — Koelle in seiner Polyglotta gibt [illegible] für „Blätter", als Dialekt in Sókoto gebräuchlich.

[15] gēdžu und hōre leggel sind nicht ganz identisch; der letztere heisst eigentlich „Kopf des Baumes".

[16] [illegible]. Danach also haben wir zu verbessern die Phrase [illegible] (sic), „ich pflücke die Wolle vom Baume", S. 119, N. 11.

[17] sokóigo hággu ist mir im Einzelnen unsicher. Statt háugnā sollte man hodúgnā erwarten.

[18] lohā n al llohān. lohā, „Kleid, Bedeckung", al, „Kind, Frucht" und llohān sind sicherlich identisch mit dem obigen dū n) elohān.

[19] dilmi sikáwuā. Die Übereinstimmung des Mába-Wortes dilmi mit déllemi im Kanúri ist bei der sonstigen geringen Übereinstimmung der beiden Sprachen höchst auffallend.

Sonyai.	Lógoné.	Wándalá.	Bágrimma.	Mába.
bergi	. . . .	álabā n afā .	. . . . . .	. . . . . .
turi {lindže, lińgo} . .	imbelō bodúguā .	táluā n afā .	yīri	urrug (Arb.)
. . . .	mságarā . . .	χemā n afā .	dadá n kirī .	serdi (? Arb.)
túguri kamba .	impelilám (?) . .	erwā n afā .	kīya	dilmi alkáwuā [19]
fita, kösu	pafal bodúguā .	dalē	kamō	koüi
końgo	. . . .	. . . . . .	. . . . . .	. . . . . .
túguri bońg . .	onkúlgu báńguā [17]	átirā n afā .	dála kirī . .	. . . . . .
kardži; kargi .	dū	. . . . . .	konō	aāk
[lákaka ?] . . .	dūu álohán . .	úbenē n afā .	piña	kobúk Pl. kobī
zē [16]	. . . .	. . . . . .	. . . . . .	. . . . . .
túguri iddže Plur. turi iddže	galī bodúguā . .	edza n afā .	kán-kogō . .	kolli
kūri	. . . .	. . . . . .	. . . . . .	. . . . . .
bergi	lēye . . . . . / lobú n ul ilohán [18]	álabā džinē .	godiyamū . .	makám-kamā

[1] farin, páriq with Koelle, who, besides gives pérte, which is nothing but another form of the very same term, with the different meaning „stump of a tree", while the former notion he attributes also to the term tear or rather tear gęgąbé.
[2] fárage kécha-ba: fárage evidently is derived from farágin, „I divide, separate"; in Koelle it appears only s. v. gęgą (i. q. kecha) as párage gęgąbé, „the place where the lateral boughs or branches grow out of the trunk of a tree".
[3] déllemi has a root unknown to me and is rather remarkable on account of its close relation to the corresponding Mába-term (see note 19).
[4] kálu kécha-be see p. 177, note 1.
[5] égilla appears in Koelle's vocabulary under the form ügalei, „plant of which ropes are made".
[6] kóglō kécha-be, verbally „top, tuft of a tree"; the term kóglō alone has the general meaning of ornament of the head, and is by no means restricted to the bunch or tuft of feathers on the head of certain birds, as Koelle says, who, besides, appears to have ignored the meaning explained in this place. The other form of this word kógē, which Koelle gives, has remained unknown to me.
[7] kárage kécha-be is wanting in Koelle. kárage, beyond a doubt, is derived from karágin, „I tear" in the very same manner, as fáraga has been derived from farágin. If the term karaga, „forest" had the second vowel short, I should certainly be inclined to derive it from the same root on account of the „tearing" character of a forest in these regions, but I have only heard it pronounced karága with the second a decidedly long, although Koelle writes káraga.
[8] kámbari: Koelle writes kámpeli and besides the notion here adduced attributes to it also that of „wrestling"; but I think, the two terms are decidedly different.
[9] tála kécha-be, means verbally „child of the tree".
[10] káma with this notion is wanting in Koelle.
[11] karra is likewise not mentioned by Koelle.
[12] akā) kohá bend (kénuō) means verbally „the tree, its heads" exactly as the corresponding terms in Wándalá and Sonyai, while the following term akā) dābe bená means „the tree, its head". See Introductory Remarks p. LXXXI.
[13] akō or akā mádandig: the second part of this phrase I am unable to explain and it may be wrong.
[14] kunna n itān, verbally „the ear of the tree". Koelle in his Polyglotta gives a term canasámi as used with this meaning.
[15] gódīn and bāre leggel are not quite identical, although I am not able to point out the exact point of difference.
[16] zē: from this form of the noun we have to correct the phrase adduced p. 119, note 17 ága-hā hába zē-dé (sic), „I pluck the cotton from the seed".
[17] onkúlgu báńguā seems to me not quite certain. At least instead of báńguā we should expect bodúguā.
[18] lobú n ul ilohán: lobú, „covering, dress", ul, „child, fruit", while ilohán, no doubt, is closely connected with dū n) álohán which we have had before.
[19] dilmi alkáwuā: The perfect harmony between the Mába-term dilmi and the Kanúri-word déllemi is rather remarkable, as the two languages, in general, have very little similarity one with the other.

Deutsch und Englisch.	Kanúri.	Tēdā.	Hausa.	Fulfúlde.
Fleisch der Frucht — *flesh of the fruit*	{sūsu [1] . . . / nāgo . . . }	īni	. . . . . .	. . . . . .
Kern — *kernel*	ṅgúr	kau	dutši . . .	
Talha — *Acacia Arabica*	kindil [2] . . .	tehī; tefī . .		. . . . . .
Saaf, Gerred — *Acacia Nilotica*	kingar . . .	{gui . . . . / gabbur . . }	tsáda . .	tšabúlli . . .
andere Mimosen — *other species of Mimosa; Acacia albida?*	gayō	. . . . . .	{bagga-rúa [7] . / aganò . . . }	gauāri Pl. gauāri
Sidr; Zizyphus spina Christi — *Zizyphus spina Christi*	kurna . . .	kurru . . .	kurna . . .	{kúrnahi Pl. kurnādže
Zizyphus lotus — *Zizyphus lotus*	kúsulū . . .	. . . . . .	magáriā [8] . .	džābi . . . }
Hadžlīdž, Hadžlīdž — *Balanites Aegyptiaca*	bīto [3] . . .	alō	áddua [9] . . .	tanni Pl. tanne
Frucht der Balanites Aegyptiaca — *fruit of the Balanites Aegyptiaca*	nāge bītohe .	alau [álōb Arb.]	da n addua .	
Afrikanischer Pflaumen-Baum — *African plum-tree*	birgim [4] . . .	. . . . . .	gandži . . .	dúndehi . .
Ficus — *kind of fig-tree*	{termo . . . / džēdža . . }	. . . . . .	{kaiwa [10] . . / alléluba . . }	nelbi Pl. nelbe
Dšimmie — *Sterculia cinerea Rich.*	{ṅgáborē [5] . . / kāgō . . . }	. . . . . .	bōre, baure? .	ibbi . . . .
andere Varietät von Ficus — *other variety of fig-tree*	kaña	. . . . . .	dúmmia . .	búmmehi Plur. bummēdži

[1] sūsu hat Koelle nicht, nāge gibt er für „Kern", und das mag zuweilen richtig sein; vergl. weiter unten nāge bīto-be.
[2] kindil. Diese Mimose scheint ihren Kanúri-Namen daher bekommen zu haben, weil sie im Lande der Kindin oder Tuarek ganz besonders eigenthümlich und verbreitet ist. Der Name fehlt bei Koelle so gut wie die beiden folgenden.
[3] bīto. Über die grosse Bedeutung dieses Baumes mit seiner, die Dattel vertretenden, allerdings einen bitteren Früchten und seinen den Salzmangel gewissermassen ersetzenden Blättern im Leben des Volkes s. Reisen Th. II. S. 284 und 398, wo er der Milchkuh gleichgestellt wird; III, S. 513, 600 und sonst, sowie über die den, vielleicht erst im Gefolge des Islam eingeführten kurna und seinen in den verschiedenen Sprachen fast unveränderten Namen ebenda III, S. 260. Zu bemerken aber ist als besonders wichtig und wirft ein ganz neues Licht über diese Fragen, dass im Fūr kurna, „Baum" überhaupt heisst, während bīto dem hatte, bel-(g), fette im Fandā und Kranāi entspricht.
[4] birgim, Reisen II, S. 248, 649. In Bezug auf die Selbstigkeit des gandži und dúndehi, deren Einerleiheit unter sich feststeht, mit dem birgim und den im Lógone, Wándalā und Bágrimma ihnen gegenüberstehenden Baumarten bin ich nicht ganz sicher. — Alle diese Baumnamen bis auf tōsō fehlen bei Koelle.
[5] Der ṅgáborē selbst, der als einer der herrlichsten Bäume dieser Zone (vergl. v. Barnim's Reise durch Nord-Ost-Afrika S. 517) mit seinem grossartigen Kronendach sich ausschliesslich am Rande von Sümpfen ausbreitet, ist mir, wie ich glaube, im eigentlichen Hausa-Lande nicht vorgekommen. Dafür ist dort, so wie in den Landschaften südlich von Bornu die andere grossartige Ficus-Art häufig (Reisen I, S. 410; II, S. 34), H. baure, F. ibbi, die mit dem auf Mosgu hāgā genannten Baum identisch ist. Diese baure ist aber eine Afrikanische Species und kann nicht, wie Schön that, das sycē (ficus carica) Evang. Joh. I, v. 49 so übersetzt werden. Der dúdōn ist besonders reich an elastisch-gummiartigen Absonderungen.
[6] Ich habe theils durch Zufall, theils in Folge der Naturverhältnisse nie einen achten Hausa-Namen für die Mimosa Arabica erfahren können; sie geht allerdings selten über 13° N. Br. südlich hinaus.
[7] bagga-rúa. Diese Mimose hat daher ihren Namen, weil sie fast ausschliesslich an Winterströmen wächst, wo sie „vom Wasser geschlagen" und in Folge der grösseren Anschwellung derselben oft merkwürdig zugerichtet wird.
[8] magáriā. Eine besondere Varietät dieses stattlichen Baumes, dessen kirschgrosse Früchte zu einem tūo n magáriā genannten, von mir mehrfach genossenen Brod verbacken werden, ist die magáriā n kūra, F. gulīe n džābi, S. kōra dīgo.
[9] áddua. Ich will an dieser Stelle noch drei andere Baumarten aufführen, deren Europäische Bezeichnungen mir unbekannt sind: H. taura, F. kōlhehi Plur. konkōdže, S. fonte; H. takkarúa mit sehr leichtem schwartigen Holz, woraus besonders die Lagergestelle bereitet werden, F. takkarúddže, S. dī.
[10] kaiwa. Ich will hier noch den Namen eines anderen Baumes (auch eine Ficus?) einschieben, H. dōki, F. gaéki, S. bōgi.
[11] garbe korna, eigentlich „die bittere Dattel", ein Name, der besonders interessant ist im Vergleich zu der Weise, wie die Fúlbe umgekehrt der Dattelpalme ihren Namen tanne darádže von dem Vergleich mit der Balanites gegeben haben.
[12] ádda haūō kann kaum richtig sein.
[13] kaláh tenéh: kaláh, „Kind". tenéh ist mir nicht bekannt.
[14] kōhorō koli. Ich bin nicht völlig sicher, ob dies die Frucht der Balanites oder die des Zizyphus ist, da ich kōhorō eigentlich als den der kurna entsprechenden Namen aufgeschrieben hatte.

Soṅyai.	Lógonē.	Wándalā.	Bágrimma.	Mába.
. . . .	serni	ódza bušū(?) [12]	sirni	kalák lenék [13]
. . . .	gerém	udsa n afá(?)	gerém . . .	. . . . . .
. . . .	bolúgna kindīl .	. . . . . .	kelaia . . .	yēri
tanza	roál	ógwula . . .	kiägar . . .	
bāni / bisso	. . . .	mádželē . . .	gayō	
däre	yīfi (a)l kirna .	kurna	kirna . . .	
	yīfi	ulwa	sebbid . . .	. . . . . .
garbe borno [11] .	zim	džūwa . . .	džanga . . .	kókorō
garbe borno iddze	gerém	némnakē . .	kliganа . . .	kókorō koli [14]
. . . .	ábanā	kurdā	kurme . . .	
düō	laдlan	žēžn	termo . . .	. . . . . .
	gerra . . . . (búske(? Tr. v. III, p. 215))		bili	džimmēsek (Arb.)
bōō	. . . .	. . . . . .	. . . . . .	. . . .

1 aūan is wanting in Koelle, while náge is explained by „kernel", a meaning which, in certain cases, where the kernel forms the principal part of the fruit, may be right; compare below náge bīto-be.

2 kindil: this species of Mimosa seems to have obtained this name as the dominating tree all over the country of the Mázly, who by the Kanúri are called kindin. This term, as well as the two following ones, are wanting in Koelle.

3 bīto: with regard to the great importance of this tree, with its rather bitter fruit, which in a certain respect takes the place of the date, while its leaves have to replace the salt, see my Travels vol. II, p. 314; III, p. 384; and with regard to the importance of the kurna vol. III, p. 300. As to the remarkable circumstance of the latter name occurring in all these languages almost without any change, we have to consider, that in Für kurne means „tree" in general, while bito appears to be closely allied to the corresponding term batta or fatte in Pandā; batta, bat, faiti in Kanúri.

4 birgim: with regard to the identity of the gandāl and dōndebi with the birgim in Kanúri, and the names mentioned in Lógonē, Wándalā and Bágrimma, I am not quite certain, but about the identity of the latter among each other there is no doubt. — All these names of trees, with the single exception of the tóso, as he writes it, are wanting in Koelle.

5 The ngáborō itself, one of the most splendid trees of Negroland, which spreads its magnificent foliage almost exclusively on the border of swamps and lakes, has not occurred to me in Hausa Proper, where the other variety of ficus called baure is rather frequent. Whether the latter be called kágō in Kanúri Proper, I am not sure, but at least it is so in Mašgo (Trav. and Disc. vol. III, p. 230). But it is not justified at all, to translate the συκῆ (ficus Carica) in Ev. Joh. I, v. 48 by baure, as Schön has done. As for the dūddūs, it is very rich in secretions of Indian rubber and caoutchouc.

6 I have never heard a proper Hausa-name for the Acacia Arabica, which in the more fertile districts does not seem to go further South, than about 13° N. L.

7 hagga-rūa: the Acacia Nilotica has obtained this name on account of its growing almost exclusively on the border of torrents or fiumara's, where it is „beaten by the water", and is often greatly damaged in consequence.

8 magárii: a peculiar variety of this useful tree, the fruits of which are made into a kind of bread called in Hausa tūo n magárië, and often eaten by myself (Tr. and Disc. vol. I, p. 522), is called magárië n kūra, F. yalla n dīabi, S. kōre dāre.

9 áddua (ádwa?): in this place I am going to mention three other species of trees, the scientific names of which are not known to me: H. tsara, F. kóohehi plur. konkédde, S. fenta; H. takhurōa, a tree of a very light sort of wood, from which the common bedsteads of the country are generally prepared, F. takhuruádde, S. di.

10 kaiwa: I here adduce the name of another tree, called dāki in Hausa, gaáki in Fulfúlde, and hōli in Soṅyai.

11 garbe borno properly means „bitter (sort of) date", a name which is particularly interesting in comparison with the manner, in which the Fúlbe from the opposite point of view call the datepalm tanne daródde, „the noble balanites".

12 ódza bošō, I suspect, is not quite right.

13 kalák lenék: kalák means „child, fruit", but with regard to the meaning of lenék I am rather uncertain.

14 kókorō koli: I am not perfectly sure, whether this term does signify the fruit of the balanites, or that of the zizyphus; but, having noted down kókorō as the corresponding Mába-name of the kurna, the former appears to be the case.

Deutsch und Englisch.	Kanúri.	Tédā.	Hausa.	Fulfúlde.
Bassia Parkii — *Shea-butter-tree; Bassia Parkii*	tóso[1] . . .	. . . . . .	kadéña[8] . .	kárehi Pl. karē-dži
Parkia — *Parkia biglobosa*	[2]	. . . . . .	dorōa[9] . . .	narrēhi . . .
Tamarinde — *Tamarindus Indica*	tomsúka[3] . .	temsúka[7] . .	tsámia . . .	džatámmi . .
Bombax — *Silk-cotton-tree; Eriodendron Guineense*	. . . . . .		rīmi[10] . . .	bénte-hi[13] . .
Brodfruchtbaum — *monkey-bread-tree; Adansonia digitata*	kuka	. . . . . .	kūka[11] . . .	bokki Pl. bodódže
Dûmpalme — *Cucifera Thebaica*	kirzim[4] . . .	sōbu N. . . / ob N. . . .	gōreba . . .	gellēhi Pl. gellē-dže
Delébpalme — *Borassus flabelliformis Aethiopicus, v. Martius*	kamolútu . .	. . . . . .	gigiña . . .	dugbi Pl. dugbe
Dattelpalme — *date-tree; Phoenix dactylifera*	káska n debíno[5]	ake timbi . / timmi . . .	itatše n debíno	tanne darādže[14] / leggel debínodže
Carica Papaya — *Common Papaw-tree; Carica Papaya*	bambūs Massar-be[6]	. . . . . .	gonda n gida[12] / gonda Masr .	dukūdže . .

[1] tóso. Dieser überaus wichtige und schöne Baum ist nicht im eigentlichen Bornu einheimisch. — Ich will hier noch einen anderen Baumnamen anführen, K. kemaua, W. süs, Arb. bemid.
[2] Die schöne und werthvolle Parkia kommt nicht in Bornu vor und bedienen sich die Kanúri daher des Hausa-Namens.
[3] tomsúka. Koelle schreibt tamsúgū. Der Baum ist auch in Bornu von solcher Bedeutung, dass die Kanúri ihn die „Kuh des Armen" nennen, fē talakka-be. Über die heilsame blutreinigende und kühlende Wirkung der Früchte habe ich in meinen Reisen wiederholt gesprochen, besonders Th. III, S. 334, 400 und sonst. S. das Register Th. V, S. 736.
[4] kirzim. Koelle hat diesen Namen und den folgenden nicht, führt aber eine andere Art von Fächerpalme auf, die er gōgū nennt und die unzweifelhaft meinem kamolútu entspricht, der auf Ngaruam gōgu heisst, woran sich H. gigiña anlehnt. Über die Dûmpalme s. besonders Reisen Th. II, S. 220.
[5] káska n debíno. Da die Dattelpalme nur künstlich in einigen Gegenden des Negerlandes eingeführt ist, so ist es interessant, zu sehen, wie auch hier das Kanúri diffē-(gi), an das sich das Tédā timbi angeschlossen, ein neues Licht über diese Namengebung verbreitet (Th. II, S. 264). Interessant ist es immerhin zu bemerken, dass auch noch die Auér-Sprache im fernen Westen unter 16° den eigenthümlichen Namen itu für die „Dattelpalme" hat. Koelle schreibt dibino und difunō.
[6] bambūs Massar-be bedeutet „Egyptischer oder Orientalischer Melonenbaum", indem er unzweifelhaft aus Indien über Egypten eingeführt ist. Denn, wie die Logonē-, Wandalā- und Bagrimma-Formen deutlich zeigen, ist bambūs aus bangūs, bagūs und wahrscheinlich aus dem Arabischen fagūs entstanden und bezeichnet wol eigentlich die recht wohlschmeckende Frucht, die einer Melone so ähnlich sieht, dass auch Europäer den Baum gewöhnlich als Melonenbaum bezeichnen.
[7] Die Tédā gebrauchen wol nur den Kanúri-Ausdruck, da in ihrem Lande die Tamarinde zu fehlen scheint. Dagegen ist die Dûmpalme so recht der echte Vertreter der Tédā-Oasen-Vegetation.
[8] kadéña. Das werthvolle Produkt dieses Baumes, die mai kadeña kommt in einer späteren Abtheilung vor.
[9] dorōa. Die Fruchtkolben dieses wichtigen Baumes heissen kálluá und die daraus durch Rösten, Zerstampfen und bis zur Fäulniss in Wasser Gährenlassen bereiteten chokoladenartigen aber übelriechenden Kuchen, aus denen die von mir oft erwähnte wohlschmeckende Brühe bereitet wird, heissen daddāwa, F. máheri, S. mári; wenn mit den Früchten der baggarūa gemischt H. daddāwa bosso, F. máheri bosso. — Ich will hier noch die Namen dreier anderer Baumarten einschieben H. maddāe, F. kaiřehi; H. madotši, F. kabi (Afrikanisches Rothholz?) und H. rōāia, F. daušé Plur. daušódži.
[10] rīmi. Die Hausa und Fulbe unterscheiden bei diesem wichtigen Baum (Reisen Th. II, S. 103) das Geschlecht, indem die Letzteren für den männlichen Eriodendron, H. rīmi né-medī, sogar den ganz gesonderten Namen bantorlāhi haben.
[11] kūka. Die Übereinstimmung des Namens in diesen verschiedenen, doch sonst so stark gesonderten Sprachen für diesen jetzt durch das ganze breite Central-Afrikanische Binnenland verbreiteten und für das Volksleben so unendlich wichtigen, wie das Land selbst so eigenthümlich charakterisirenden Baum, nach dem sogar die Hauptstadt von Bornu, allerdings erst in allerneuester Zeit, benannt ist, ist im höchsten Grade merkwürdig, und man könnte fast zu dem Schlusse kommen, dass seine Einführung erst von den Sonyai herrühre, s. Einleitung S. XXXII. Ich komme hierauf bei den kleinen Vokabularien zurück.
[12] gonda n gida, „die gonda des Hauses", gonda Masr, „die Egyptische gonda", indem die Eingeborenen den Namen dieses ursprünglich fremden Baumes sonderbarer Weise in ein verwandtschaftliches Verhältniss zu einer bei ihnen heimischen Annone setzten, deren schöne Waldfrucht ich oft in meinen Reisen erwähnt habe; s. Th. II, S. 88 und 606. Dieser Busch wurde von mir „wilden Gonda", gonda n dāji. — Ich will hier noch die Namen einiger Pflanzen anführen, die ich nur in Hausa und Fulfúlde erfahren habe, zuerst den „Bananenbaum", H. itatše n ayaba, F. ayabádže; dann die nur dem Rande der Wüste und den tropischen Fruchtländern angehörige „Capparis sodata", Sodada decidua, Forskal, H. ablega, F. asawāki (Arb.), S. tēasi; H. kalgo, F. bárkehi; „Schlingpflanze" Cissus quadrangularis, H. gráffeni, F. ganaforiro; H. sábara, F. gellōhi. Auch K. ganó oder karíge, Th. II, S. 206, 271, kann ich nicht identificiren.
[13] bénte-hi, daher auch Mungo Park's Vorgang oft Bentang-Baum genannt; s. Reisen Th. II, S. 103.
[14] tanne darādže. Die Dattelpalme ist hier offenbar der Frucht wegen in Vergleich zur Balanites gesetzt s. S. 183, N. 11.
[15] balánga aya, „Mutter der balanga", d. h. „der aus den Früchten bereiteten Butter" (Reisen IV, S. 404 u. f.), wie die Sonyai die Bäume gewöhnlich als „Mutter" (nya) ihrer Frucht bezeichnen. Anstatt hōne nya hat Raffenel bohonno.
[16] Die Deléb-Palme kommt im ganzen Gebiete der Sonyai, mit Ausnahme der Landschaften am Débu-See (R. V, S. 481), wol kaum vor.

Sedyai.	Lógoné.	Wándalá.	Bágrimma.	Mába.
bulánga nya [15] .	. . . .	. . . . .	. . . . .	. . . . . .
dóa hamno . .	. . . .	. . . . .	. . . . .	
bōso nya	mai (?)	ūre (?) . . .	más	
damba (?)	. . . .	. . . . .	. . . . .	. . . . . .
kō nya	hólugi (a)l kuka	kókuā . . .	kúka	wurēk
kongom / kondži . . .	garūru	. . . . .	kolóngo . . .	dōm (Arb.)
[16]	murgúm . . .	ávragā . . .	kauo	delāb (Arb.)
gerba nya . . .	difino	. . . . .	. . . . .	. . . . . .
. . . .	baúgūs	baúgūs . . .	baúgūs . . .	baúgūs

[1] tōso: this beautiful and most useful tree not being indigenous in Bornu, it is rather remarkable, that a peculiar name has been given to it. — I here mention another name of tree (Arb. hamēd), K. kemane, W. nāa.
[2] The Parkia not growing in the Bornu territory, the Kanúri, whenever they speak of this tree, make use of the Hausa-name.
[3] ármeúka: Koelle tamaágā. The beneficial effect of the fruit of this tree has been praised by me repeatedly, and the tree is even called by the natives of Bornu: fē talákba-be, „the cow of the poor".
[4] kirsim: this name, as well as the following one, is wanting in Koelle; but he mentions instead another kind of fan-palm, which he calls gángā, and which is evidently identical with the kamelútu, the latter being called gaaga in Ngamam.
[5] késka ndebino: Koelle writes dibanó and difanó. The datepalm having been introduced from abroad into all the countries of Negroland, where it at present grows, it is highly interesting to see, that the Kanúri-term diffē-(gi), if we compare the Tédā timbi, throws a full light upon the origin of our term, as well as upon the road, which the introduction of the tree took. But in some languages we find original terms of expression, as f. i. in Sedyai and in Anēr (ita).
[6] bambús Massar-be means „melon-tree of Egypt", for the forms usual in the L.-, W.- and B.-languages seem clearly to indicate, that the original form of this name is baúgūs, this name being most probably derived from the Arb. fagūs. For even Europeans, in general, call the Carica Papaya „melon-tree"; so much does the fruit resemble the melon.
[7] The Tédā make use of the Kanúri-term for signifying the tree, which is wanting in their own territory.
[8] kadéna: as for the celebrated and most valuable butter mai kadanā itself, which is prepared from the nuts of this tree, it will be mentioned in another chapter.
[9] doróa: the fruitstalk of this highly important tree bears the name hóllan, and the brown chocolate-like cakes thence prepared by roasting, bruising and fermenting in water, which notwithstanding their bad odour prepare a very tasteful broth, bear the name doddōa, only one consonant in the name of the tree being changed. — I here still insert the names of three other species of trees, one of them called in H. mádža, in F. kalrlekī; another one called in H. mádotšī, in F. kōhī (rosewood?), and the third one called rólla in Hausa, danēā in Fulfúlde, plur. danēdži.
[10] rimi: the Hausaua distinguish between the male, rimi námedži, and the female specimens of this tree, the Fúlbe calling the former by the peculiar name kontariāhi.
[11] kúka: it is very remarkable, that the name of this tree, which is of such vast importance to the whole life of the African, while it exhibits one of the most characteristic physical features of the country, should be almost identical in most of these idioms, which in other respects are so totally different, and we might almost feel induced to adopt the conjecture proffered in the introductory Remarks p. XXXIII, that it is the Sedyai, who have introduced the Adansonia into these Regions. I hope, I may find opportunity of returning to this question, when treating of my shorter vocabularies.
[12] gonda n gida means „gonda of the house", „domestic gonda", gonda Masr, „Egyptian gonda"; the native Hausaua having put this tree, which was totally new to them, into a certain relation with the custard-apple indigenous in their country, calling the latter in consequence the „wild gonda", gonda n dáži, while it had been originally their only gonda. — I here mention also the Hausa- and Fulfúlde-names of some other species of trees, first „the plantain-tree" (Musa Paradisiaca), H. ituéē n ayaba, F. ayabádže; then „Capparis sodata" or Sodada decidua, Forskal, H. abiega, F. ssaušhi (Arb.), S. téaak; H. kalgo, F. kérkehi; „Cissus quadrangularis"? a creeper, called gráfoni in Hausa, ganaforire in Fulfúlde; and finally another plant called cábara in Hausa, galldhi in Fulfúlde. As for the large tree called karága or gaoó in Kanúri, Tr. vol. II, p. 186, I think, it is the locust-tree.
[13] bántekī, this is the original and indigenous form of what Mungo Park calls the „bentang-tree"; see Tr. and Disc. II, p. 89.
[14] tanne deradže: the date-palm, as stated p. 183, note 11, on account of its fruit, which bears some exterior resemblance to that of the balanites Aegyptiaca, has been brought into close relation to that tree.
[15] bulánga nya, „mother of the bulánga", that is of the butter prepared from the fruit of this tree, as mentioned Tr. and Disc. vol. IV, p. 400, as the Sedyai in general use to designate the tree as the „mother" (nya) of its fruit or produce, the latter being considered the prime object of the nation. — Instead of bōso nya further on Hoffman has bakasso.
[16] The deléb-palm does not seem to grow anywhere in the whole extent of the territory of the Sedyai, with the sole exception of the district close to the lake of Débu, Tr. and Disc. vol. V, p. 478.

Deutsch und Englisch.	Kanúri.	Tédā.	Hausa.	Fulfúlde.
Hausthiere — *domestic animals*	kā̆su [1] . . .	ai(?); úgai? . / zádeni [8] . .	bímaāč [10] . . / dúbbubī . .	debbauel Pl. debbálži
Kameel — *camel; camelus dromedarius*	kargimo [2] . .	gōnc, gōmi .	rákomi Pl. rákoma	gelōba [10] Pl. gelōdi
Kameelstute — *she-camel*	ĭlge [3] . . .	dūi Plur. dīí .	tágua . . .	gelōba devva Pl. gelōdi debbi
junges Kameel — *young of camel*	úōgwa kargímobe [4]	errēmi . . .	da n tágua [11]	gélobe . . .
Rind, der Sudanesische Dschelorbe — *cattle; bos Zebu Aethiopicus*	fē [5]	fur, for . . .	sa [12] Pl. šāno	kalhálde Pl. kalhúlli
Bull — *bull*	fē kōú-ngā [6] .	fur domár N. / dur S. [9] . .	badīšni . . .	neggo Pl. nai / gári . . . / garwāri . .
gewöhnlicher Lastthier — *common ox of burden*	kanēmo [7] . .	. . . . . .	takórkeri Pl. takérkerai	dandi Pl. dáli

[1] kā̆su, dessen genaue Übereinstimmung mit Bágrimma kā̆sĭa bemerkenswerth ist, fehlt bei Koelle; dafür hat er ein anderes mir unbekannt gebliebenes Wort tśāgen für „Thier, besonders dessen Fleisch vom Menschen gegessen wird".

[2] kargimo. Koelle schreibt kalgimá, ganz wie er statt meines kargi, „Dorn" kálgal schreibt; denn dass das erst vor wenigen Jahrhunderten in Nigritien eingeführte Kameel, vergl. den Bornu-Historiographen Imam Ahmed, Account of expeditions conducted by the Sultan of Bornu, Journal of the Asiatic Soc. vol. XIX, p. 251, etwa von seiner grossen Liebhaberei für die jungen, selbst schärfsten Dornen der Mimosen seinen Namen erhalten habe, kann nicht zweifelhaft sein, eine Vorliebe, die den Eingeborenen bei ihrer Bekanntschaft mit ihm auffallend genug erscheinen musste.

[3] ĭlge hat Koelle nicht. Er hat dafür mátsei oder kalgimá mátsei, das „weibliches Kameel" bedeuten soll. Dies ist aber ein Irrthum. mátsei nämlich heisst nichts Anderes als „(er) sucht", von ma-nichin oder mágin, und der Irrthum beruht auf einem Missverständniss, indem Koelle's Autorität offenbar von einem männlichen Kameel gesprochen hatte, das eine Kameelstute „sucht", und als Koelle ihn fragte, was er mit mátsei meine, erklärte er, dass es brünstig

Sónghai.	Lógoné.	Wándalá.	Bágrimma.	Mába.
almán [11] . . .	morō(? p. 115) .	sillewa . . .	kātšu . . .	. . . . . .
yō Pl. yowō . .	okurgémma . .	eldegōme [15] .	lúkuma . . .	tórrembo(k [17] Pl. tarrémboal
yō wai	kurgúmma genám	muks' algōme	lúkuma nē	tórrembo mōdžam
yō kidžo . . .	kurgúmma n tāo	cls(c) algōme	on gona lúkumá-nda	tórrembo kalák
hau Pl. hauō .	#a, n#a . . .	#ā	mango [16] . .	dek Pl. dáye
yāro	. . . . . .	. . . . . .	. . . . . .	mar [18]
yēgi . . . . / yēgi kāro . .	dur-ui	kauc	mang digi-n-ále	dek

1 hāan, the close relation of which to the corresponding Bágrimma-term is remarkable, seems to be wanting in Koelle, who has another term unknown to me, viz tšágon, „animal, living creature, especially those whose meat is eaten by man".
2 kergimo: Koelle writes kelligimō, just as he writes kéligi (instead of kergi, „thorn"); for, that the camel on being introduced into Negroland, some centuries ago, received its name from the circumstance of its being peculiarly fond of the young thorns of the Mimosa, there can scarcely be the least doubt. With regard to this introduction of the camel, see Imam Ahmed, Account of Expeditions conducted by the Sultan of Bornu, Journal of the Asiatic Soc. vol. XIX, p. 121.
3 Kige seems to be wanting in Koelle; but instead he has mateel or kelligimō mateel, which he explains „a female camel", but which means nothing else but „it, he seeks, looks after", the error having originated in a misunderstanding between Rev. Koelle and his authority, the latter having spoken of a he-camel, who being in the rut, searched (mateel) for a she-camel, when Koelle thought, the she-camel was the mere explanation of the term mateel.
4 ságwa kergimo-be is wanting in Koelle. — The root, as well as the mode of derivation, of ságwa is unknown to me.
5 fē is one of the most important memorable terms of the Kanúri-idiom, proving the original importance of cattle for that nation. Koelle writes pē with a slight and very common dialectical difference. — He, moreover, mentions three kinds of pē, first the pē modere, distinguished by its small horns, but which in reality seems to mean the cattle kept merely for the sake of its milk (H. madera), then the kári, and finally another kind of cattle, which he calls abóri. But this latter kind is not in itself a peculiar kind, the term meaning in reality nothing else, but the foreign cattle kept by the Ó'bere, excellent cattle-breeders from the tribe of the Fúlbe. See Travels and Disc. vol. II, p. 279.
6 fē hōā-ágā, „cattle male, alive", that is to say „a strong bull". Koelle has instead hanlamē mbélan or h. búširi.
7 hanēmo: Koelle writes kanlamō, and attributes to the term the general meaning of „bullock" or (s. v. ogóardi which he explains as meaning the ox „which was castrated when quite young") as an ox „which was castrated when older", the particular meaning of „beast of burden" not being expressed according to him, but by adding the term lapiyram, „taking up" (viz „burdens"); but as for me, I have never found the term hanēmo used, except with the meaning of „beast of burden". Be this as it may, the bullock in former times served as the beast of burden, or rather as cattle for draught, even on the highroad of the Great Desert, as Mr. Duveyrier (Exploration du Sahara T. I, p. 273) has had full opportunity of corroborating my own statement, Tr. and Disc. vol. I, p. 200.
8 nadeni seems to mean especially the small cattle, such as sheep and goats.
9 dor might seem to be a contracted form from domar, but may be rather an original form.
10 bleaná plur. of bleen, débbobi plur. of debba. — I here insert, besides, the term gerke for „herd", to which the Fulfúlde-term hoggo corresponds in a certain sense, although the latter seems also to mean „hurdle".
11 da n tágna means properly „child of the she-camel".
12 su, sénio, Káno resembles very closely the Galla sā, saal. See, what I have said on account of this name with regard to the introduction of the cattle into the various countries of Central-Africa, Travels vol. II, p. 200.
13 golōbe: the Fúlbe have, besides, the term amáliri for the full male camel, H. rakomi na-mijí, S. yō har.
14 almán seems to be a foreign term, probably derived from the Arb. al māl, meaning originally „property", and in consequence that which with nomadic tribes more particularly constitutes the property, viz. horned or small cattle; and thus Hodgson may be quite right in attributing to our term, under the form elman, the special meaning of „goats", goats constituting the chief property with many tribes on the Niger, as f. i. the Kél-ulli. — Instead of yō Raffenel has hué.
15 eldegōme: the proper term for „camel" in Wandalā, as appears from the following forms, being algōme, this might seem to be identical with the Mósiy-term niyom, which in the Southern dialects of that language has made place to the more recent term ámeníe; but it is by far more probable, that the root is simply gōme, being identical with the corresponding kam in Kondái, and some other languages of the Nile, whence possibly also the H.-term ra-komi has been derived.
16 mango is closely allied to mandšo in Fūr. — As for mang digi-n-ále, compare it with diga-n mang-ne, „load of ox". — With regard to nda, the form of the genitive case in lúkuma-nda, see Intr. Remarks p. CCLXXII, d).
17 tórrembok appears to have no relation. Burckhardt in the S.-number has torbok, but in the plural tormboey.
18 dek, Burckhardt dafg, plur. dae-y, is closely related to Kondai tigi, tyg, Berber tiga, Dungola tig. — With regard to the ethnological importance of the term mar, as a symbol of manliness and manhood, see Introductory Remarks p. CCCVII, b).

Deutsch und Englisch.	Kanúri.	Tédā.	Hausa.	Fulfúlde.
Lastthier der Kūri — *ox of burden, called Kūri*	kūri [1] . . .	. . . . . .	takérkeri n kūri	. . . . . .
verschnittener Stier — *castrated bull*	kanēmo . . .	. . . . . .	fūrtumi . . .	búdšeri . . / tafándi . .
Kuh — *cow*	fē kámo [2] . .	for S. . . . / furá N. . . .	sánia Pl. šāno	negge Pl. nai
milchgebende Kuh — *milk-cow*	fē mádara-be	. . . . . .	sánia da aka-tšea [9]	negge biretéinge
Kalb, männl. — *he-calf*	dālo	derībi . . .	kúrsanā . .	bígel Pl. bídši
Kalb, weibl. — *she-calf* .	kirna [3] . . .		márekī . .	šéllahál . .
Pferd — *horse*	fir [4]	aski Pl. áskin / áskida [8]	dōki Pl. dawáki / dawákai	putšu Pl. put-šēdši [12]
Wallach — *gelding* . .	fir tirrin [5] . .	aski togór . .	fiddaēyo . .	putšu budšángo
Staatspferd, Ross — *state-horse*	fir ketši [6] . .	aski aukir . .	dōki ingérma [10]	tšaadu . . / tšaadu gordi
Schnellläufer — *race-horse*	fir doi . . .	aski ohúmde .	dōki mai-gúdu	. . . . . .
Trotter — *trotter* . . .	kerīsa [7] . . .	. . . . . .	. . . . . .	. . . . . .
Schnellschreiter — *horse of a swift pace*	kamándara .	. . . . . .		
schlechtes Pferd, Klepper — *nag*	kádara (Arb.)	kádara . . / aski zaulo .	kádara [11] . .	

[1] kúri ist der stets hellfarbige, durch seine Grösse, Stärke, erhabenen Nacken, ganz ohne Fetthuckel, und besonders in ihrer unteren Dicke gewaltige lyraförmige Hörner ausgezeichnete Stier von den Inseln der Kúri im Sumpflande Kargu's, s. Reisen Th. II, S. 381; von dieser ganz besonderen Art, gleich der in Egypten auf den Monumenten vertretenen, in Folge wiederholter Kreuzungen aber jetzt ausgestorbenen, altegyptischen Race ist noch kein Exemplar nach Europa gekommen.

[2] fē kámo. Nach Koelle scheint der Ausdruck kenage, „die Gelbe, die Braune" selbstständig für „Kuh" gebraucht zu werden, obwol er s. v. kenáge ausdrücklich angibt, dass dieses Eigenschaftswort ausschliesslich von Pferd oder Kameel gebraucht werde. — Zu fē mádara-be s. S. 186, N. 6.

[3] kirna fehlt bei Koelle; dālé hat er.

[4] fir, das sich von dem Tédā for, fur für „Rind" abschliesst, zeigt wol eben das ursprünglich Fremdländische und die späte Einführung des Pferdes in diesen Gegenden, wo es dann erst nach dem Rinde benannt wurde. Koelle schreibt per.

[5] fir tirrin fehlt bei Koelle, tirrin ist wol vulgäre Form. Ich musste übrigens diese zum Theil adjektiven Ausdrücke hierhersetzen, weil sie in vielen Sprachen substantivirt sind. Aber viele andere Bezeichnungen des Pferdes gebe ich erst unter den Eigenschaftswörtern bei den Farben.

[6] fir ketši bedeutet eigentlich „angenehmes Pferd".

[7] kerīsa wie kamándara scheinen bei Koelle zu fehlen.

[8] aski. Hodgson hat ashee. (aski) wol nur Schreibfehler. Bei der sonst so gänzlich abweichenden Form dieses Wortes von dem entsprechenden Kanúri ist es über alle Massen interessant, das fast ganz identische Koptische zu vergleichen, htho nach Brugsch und Kircher. Die Tédā also lernten das Pferd nicht vom N. her, sondern vom Osten, vom Nil her, kennen, woher offenbar viele Stämme und Bildungsmittel in jene Gegenden eingewandert sind.

[9] sánia da aka-tšea, wörtlich „die Kuh zum Gemolkenwerden", von tšea, „melken" S. 119. Der Gegensatz davon ist dālya mit der Umschreibung sánia bābe haifua, „die Kuh, die nicht gebiert" = F. negge fedinga.

[10] dōki ingérma. Das ingérma ist wol ohne Zweifel aus der Kanúri-Sprache herüber genommen worden von ngirma, „gross", da alle Hausa-Provinzen mit einem schöneren Schlag Pferden von Bornu aus versorgt wurden.

[11] kádara. Ich will hier noch einen besonderen Ausdruck anführen für den kleinen Poni aus Yóruba oder Yáriba: H. kūru Yáriba, F. opagiáli.

[12] putšu. Reichardt schreibt pútšu.

[13] nila āpēn rámmia, buskaa āpēn rámmia, wörtlich „Rind ausgeschnitten die Hoden", „Pferd ausgeschnitten die Hoden", s. Einleitung S. CCVIII, g).

[14] bárea bóyama. Nach diesem Kompositum scheint es, als wenn für „Lastthier" im Allgemeinen neben kane auch der Name bárea üblich sei; denn bóyama bezieht sich offenbar auf die Provinz Koyám oder Koiám (s. Reisen Th. II, S. 300; Th. IV, S. 16), deren Bewohner sich dieser Stiere neben dem Kameel auf ihren Reisen besonders bedienen.

[15] bérch, Burckhardt barah. Die völlige Übereinstimmung des Namens des Pferdes in Bagirmi und Mába, die sonst so gut wie gar nichts gemein haben (S. CXCIV), wird sich wol erst aus bis jetzt noch unbekannten, eigenthümlichen historischen Verhältnissen erklären. — bérch u átal s. S. CCCX, f); bérch dárik-dárik-nir verbal S. CCCX, l, a); bérch nimmere kalte, „das Pferd gut im Lauf".

Sońγai.	Lógone.	Wándalá.	Bágrimma.	Mába.
. . . . . .	dókame kūri . .	bárea kóyama [14]	mang kūri . .	dek kúrik Pl. dáye kauári
dāsu	n°a ápēa rúmmia [13]	. . . . .		. . . . .
hau wal . . .	n°a genfu . . .	muksa ńā . .	mańg-nē . .	dek mödžum
hau wāri . . .	. . . . . .	. . . . .	. . . . .	. . . . . .
hau iddžo { sŷŋ	dūlo	dūlo	on mańga . .	dā-n kalúk
{ bende	rúmm	muksa (e)l dūlo	kirna . . .	trūmba
{ béri Pl. bériō . / bári Pl. báriō . }	byskuán . . .	bélissā . . .	sinda . . .	bérek Pl. béri [15]
gū	byskuán ápēa rúmmia	. . . . .	sinda-n-ádemi	bérek hemik
. . . . . .	býskuán á°laba .	agússa . . .	sinda tétkadā	bérek gélabik
. . . . . .	býskuán dúggo-mī	adžégedē . .	sinda áyen-wége	bérek n átal
. . . . . .	býskuán agéedžogo	tásala bélissā .	sinda neb-kiba	bérek džerík-džerík-nir
. . . . . .	býskuán akáte-mī	áhlurám kándarē	sinda dzuágda	bérek ulmmere ŝaite
. . . . . .	kúdaro	kádara . . .	kádara . . .	bérek kedár

[1] kūri is the peculiar kind of bull of large size, great strength, immense lyre-shaped horns, a most powerful neck without a hump, and resembling altogether the bull, as represented on the old Egyptian paintings, such as it is indigenous in the islands of the Kūri, in the swampy district of Karga on the S. E. shore of the Tsad. See Travels vol. II, p. 300.
[2] fā hāmo: according to Koelle the adjective kunāge, meaning „yellow, brown", seems to be used (in some provinces), in order to designate the cow, although in his vcbl. c r. kunégy he states expressly, that this adjective is „used only of a horse or camel". — As for fā mōdere-be, see p. 187, note 5.
[3] kirne is wanting in Koelle; instead of dūlo he writes dūlō.
[4] fir, which is closely allied to the Tédā-term fer, fur meaning „cattle", and which has been applied at a later period to the horse, seems to show the late period of introduction of the latter into these regions. Koelle writes per.
[5] fir tirrin is also wanting in Koelle. I was obliged to insert these terms in this place, as, notwithstanding the adjectival form of most of them, in some languages they are expressed by a substantive. But many other varieties of horses, distinguished on account of their colour, I shall have to mention among the adjectives.
[6] fir kelāī properly means „nice, pleasant horse".
[7] kerien, as well as kamándere, seems to be wanting in Koelle.
[8] aski, totally isolated as it is with regard to relationship with the Kanúri, is highly interesting on account of its close affinity with the corresponding Koptic-term hešhi, according to Brugsch and Kirchner, the Tédā having evidently made acquaintance with the horse from the side of the Nile. — Hodgson has sebes (sebi), probably only from a lapse of the pen.
[9] sánia da aka-tāsa means verbally „the cow to be milked", aka-tāsa from tāsu, „to milk" p. 142; the contrary thereof being dūūye, a concise and pregnant term, which can also be rendered by the phrase sánie bābo heifae, „the cow which does not bear (young)" = F. nagge fodinga.
[10] dōki ingérma: the term ingérma has apparently been borrowed from the Kanúri-language, where ágirma means „large", almost all the Hausa-provinces being supplied with a finer race of horses from the side of Bornu.
[11] kádara: in this place I shall mention also a peculiar term designating the small pony of Yóruba or Yáriba: H. kūru Yáriba, F. apagidāi.
[12] patāu: Reichardt in his Primer spells pódšo.
[13] n°a ápēa rúmmia, byskuán ápēa rúmmia, means verbally „ox, horse cut out (as for) the testicles"; see Introductory Remarks p. CCIX, g).
[14] bárea kóyama: from this phrase it would appear, as if, besides the term haua meaning „beast of burden", there were still another one in use, namely bárea; for, as to the term kóyama, it evidently relates to the province Koiám or Koyám (see Trav. vol. II, p. 300; IV, p. 24), the inhabitants of which make particular use of this kind of beast of burden.
[15] bérek (Burckhardt barek): the perfect identity of this term in the Sońγai- and Mába-idioms, which in general have nothing whatever in common (Intr. Remarks p. CXCV), is very remarkable, and most probably will be explained by way of historical relations at the time not yet known to us. — As for the verbal form bérek džerík-džerík-nir, see Introductory Remarks p. CCCXI, I, e) and as for bérek n átal (ibid. p. CCCXI, I); bérek ulmmere ŝaite means „the horse good for running".

Deutsch und Englisch.	Kanúri.	Tédā.	Hausa.	Fulfúlde.
Stute — *mare*	fir kāmo [1] . . / kāmo fir . .	aaki-édī . .	gódia . . .	putīu dēu . / teffe Man. .
Füllen männl. / weibl. — *colt* . .	kúnta . . .	. . . . . .	dúkuši na meēī / na matše	mollu . . . / mollil . . .
Esel — *ass; Asinus Africanus*	kōro [2]	ágar S. [6] . . / ar-mai N. .	žakī Pl. žákona [8]	babba Pl. bamdi
Eselin — *female ass* . .	kāmo kōro .	ágar édī S. . / ar-mai édī N.	žaka	babba dēu .
Maulthier / Maulesel — *mule* . . .	alfáddara [3] .	alfáddara N. / lóhurā S. . .	alfáddara . .	alfaddarire . / lambāna [11] .
Fettschwanz)-Schaaf — *sheep; Ovis Aries platyura*	dimī	irō S. . . . / irōmo N. . . / hádwi . . .	túmkia Pl. tumáki [9]	bālu Pl. bāli .
Hammel — *wether; ram*	ágelāro [4] . .	[7]	ragō Pl. rágona	džaudiri Pl. džaudi
Ziege — *goat; Capra Hircus*	káni	arō	akūya Pl. aúakai [10]	beōwa Pl. beēōdži
Ziegenbock — *he-goat* .	dāl [5]	ingē	búnsuru Pl. búnsurai	dámdiri Pl. damdi / elōri Pl. elōdžī
Zicke, Zicklein — *kid* .	tāta kánibē .	. . . . . .	da n akūya .	bingel beēwa .

[1] fir kāmo. Das sonst für „weiblich" übliche Adjektiv kárgari, das nach Koelle auch von Pferden gebraucht wird, habe ich nicht ein einziges Mal so anwenden hören.

[2] kōro. Koelle schreibt kóró. — In Bornu hat dieser, für Nord-Afrika sonst wichtigste, Einhufer (s. N. 6) in Folge der ausgedehnten Pferdezucht denselben alle Bedeutung verloren. Aber die Eselin gilt in Bornu neben der Sklavin als das Sinnbild zärtlichster, mütterlicher Liebe, agō dúnya-nyin kóro-n kir-nyin-ne tata tesrégena gā hēgo, „in der (ganzen) Welt gibt es Nichts, das sein Kind so liebt, wie die Eselin oder die Sklavin". — Die Übereinstimmung des Namens in Kanúri und Bágrimma ist sehr bedeutend und findet vielleicht durch weitere verwandtschaftliche Beziehungen Erklärung, indem wir selbst im Kaffa (nach Charles Beke) kórō haben, und die besten Esel kommen unzweifelhaft von Osten.

[3] alfáddara. Koelle schreibt alfátera und alpátera und gibt auch eine vollere Form, kórō alfátera, die ich aber nie gehört habe. Woher ist der Name?, wol nur Korruption von al bayla, el báyela. Auffallend aber ist lóhara im Tédā. Das Maulthier ist jedenfalls nicht einheimisch im Negerlande und sehr selten (Reisen Th. II, S. 170): der Maulesel etwas häufiger.

[4] ágelāro. Koelle schreibt ágalárē und ágalārō.

[5] dāl fehlt bei Koelle; die Beziehung zu dāle, „Kalb" ist auffallend.

[6] ágar. Ich habe hier die bei den südlichen Tédā übliche Form vorangestellt, weil sie mir die ursprüngliche zu sein scheint, woraus die erste Silbe in ar-mai durch Zusammenziehung entstanden ist; der letzte Theil der letzteren, mai, gehört wol ursprünglich gar nicht dazu, besonders, wenn wir das entsprechende hieroglyphische ā a vergleichen (Brugsch, Zeitschrift für Egyptische Sprach- und Alterthumskunde, 1864, S. 27). Esel fanden sich nämlich schon unter den ältesten Dynastieen der Egypter als Hausthiere, nach Dr. Hartmann (a. a. O.) eben der durch seinen schwarzen Rückenstreif und die schwarze Schwanzquaste gekennzeichnete Nord-Afrikanische domesticirte Wildesel: vergl. Brehm „Ergebnisse" S. 142.

[7] Ich habe hier wóšai niedergeschrieben; da aber dies Wort sonst „Feuer" bedeutet, zweifle ich an seiner Richtigkeit: für ingē hat Hodgson endie und zwar mit der Bedeutung „Schaf".

[8] žakī. Schön schreibt zaki oder žakī. Die Haussaua und Fulbe haben eine ganz besondere Bezeichnung für den besonders „grossen und starken Eselhengst", H. hingi, F. bingiri. Dann haben die Fulbe auch noch zwei Ausdrücke für den „verschnittenen Esel", nämlich tapándi und hadkándi, der im Sonyai farka márkaba oder ki-dúmba heisst, von dumbu, „schneiden".

[9] túmkia. Schön schreibt dunkia und tunkia, im Plural dumaki und tumaki.

[10] akūya. Schön schreibt akwia Plur. awaki.

[11] lambāna ist wol sicher von dem Sonyai entlehnt und nicht umgekehrt, um so mehr, als Reichardt, als dem westlichen Dialekt angehörig, ein ganz anderes Wort angibt, nämlich kampadēu, das unzweifelhaft mit putīu (bei ihm pudēu), „Pferd" zusammenhängt.

[12] byehnén el genóm. Über die Einschiebung des el s. S. CCXIV, h). Anstatt genám hörte ich bald genám, bald gen im aussprechen.

[13] édik (d. e. ad-ik) schliesst sich ziemlich eng dem Mátiy-Namen für den „Esel" an, ehed (Decryrier eyhad).

[14] mindže-el, s. Einleitung S. CCXXVI, N. 3.

Sonyai.	Lógonē.	Wándalā.	Bágrimma.	Māba.
béri téfe . . . . téfe	bųaknán el genám[12]	āma bólimā .	sinda { nō . . / bárkemē }	bérek mōdžum
béri iddže . . .	nl bųakuán . .	édma n bólimā	knala . . .	bérek kalák
farka Pl. fárkayō	būri	éangā . . .	kórō	ādik[13]
farka wai . . .	būri (e)l genám .	ūma (e)sungā	kórō nō . .	ādik mōdžum
lumbāna . . .	lárafún	alpádare . .	bátara . . .	baylah (Arb.)
fīgi wai Pl. figiō	wūfu	ki-anē . . .	bāla	dēō, dēok Pl. dēō-si
{ figi bar . . . / gāru . . . . }	sifgī	šéggara . . .	kalta-kalta .	kebbeš (Arb.)
hantši nē . . .	temē	anē	biña	mándakal Plur. míndže-sī[14]
hantši bar . .	mam-pēti . . .	úsalē . . .	bāla	mūdžul
džindi	. . . .	. . . . . .	. . . . .	. . . . . .

1 fir hāmo: hérguri, in other respects the common Kanúri-adjective for „female", which Koelle applies also to horses, I have never heard used in this connection.

2 hāge: Koelle writes hórō. The identity of the term in Kanúri and Bágrimma is remarkable, and may find an explanation in the identity of the corresponding Kāfa-term (Beke) hāro. But, while the donkey, in general, is an animal of the utmost importance for the whole of Northern Africa (note 7), in Bornu, on the contrary, it has entirely lost its value in consequence of the extensive breed of excellent horses having been introduced there. At present, the ass is only remarkable in that country on account of the tenderness, with which the female cherishes her young, in which respect the Bornu-people compare the ass with the female slave, saying ngó dųnya-nyin kóro-n kir-nyin-ne tata teerágena gó bāge, „in the whole world there is nothing which cherishes its young like the ass and the female slave".

3 alfáddara: Koelle writes alfátera and alpátere, and gives as the more complete term kórō alfátera, which, however, I have never heard. There cannot be any doubt, however, that the mule is not indigenous in Negroland, as it is very rare even at the present day (Travels and Disc. vol. II., p. 200); and probably the name is nothing, but a corrupted form of al beghale. The Tédā-name lóhuru, however, is remarkable.

4 ágeláre: Koelle writes ágalárē and agalárē.

5 dāl is wanting in Koelle.

6 ágar: in this instance, contrary to my general arrangement, I have placed in the first rank the form used by the Southern tribes of the Tédā, as it seems to be the original one, whence the first syllable in the term ar-mai has been formed by contraction; the second part of the term, mai, probably conveying some other, totally distinct notion. In this respect it is not without interest, to compare the corresponding term of the ancient Egyptian, vis ān, especially if we remember, that the ass was an domestic animal in Egypt, even under the very first dynasties, and the very same animal, as distinguished by the black stripes across the back, and by the black end of the tail, as at the present day we find to be the case with the wild ass of Northern Africa.

7 I have taken down wuēņi as the Tédā-name; but, as this term means also „fire", I rather doubt, whether it be here in its right place. — Instead of ingō, Hodgson has the form eddān with the different meaning „sheep".

8 kahī: Schön writes ookī or kahī. The Hausawa and Fúlbe, besides, have a peculiar name for distinguishing the strong and powerful male ox, namely H. blágī, F. blágirī; and the Fúlbe have, besides, two terms for distinguishing „the castrated ox", vis tupeudī, and budžandī, S. farka márbehe or hl-dámbe (from dambu, „to cut").

9 támkie: Schön writes dunkie and tunkie, both forms with e n, while in the plural-form he himself preserves the m, writing dumeki and tumekī.

10 akhye: Schön writes ekwia plur. awakī.

11 lambāna: this term, I am sure, has been borrowed by the Fúlbe from the Sonyai, and not vice versa, the more so, as Reichardt has a totally different term, vis bempudān, which, no doubt, has been derived from, or is a composite term in connection with, puttio, „horse".

12 bųaknán el genám: With regard to the el inserted, see Introductory Remarks p. CCXV, b). Instead of genám I heard sometimes genám, at others genīm.

13 ādik i. e. ad-ik, seems to be closely related to ehed in Māšy (Dureyrier eyhad).

14 míndže-sī: with regard to this irregular plural-form, see Introductory Remarks p. CCCXVII, note 1.

Deutsch und Englisch.	Kanúri.	Tédā.	Hausa.	Fulfúlde.
Hund — *dog*	kéri [1] . . .	kedī	karē [7] . . .	ramándu Pl. dandi; kútaru Pl. kutūdže [9]
Hündin — *bitch*	kāmo kéri . .	kedī edī . .	kárea . . .	raundu rāoru
Kater — *male cat* . . .	ngām [2] . . .	ingām . . .	mūse . . .	mūsūru Pl. musūdže
Katze — *female cat* . .	ngām tsilim .	intšī . . .	keúngwa . . .	fāturu . . .
Ratte — *rat*	gúrguma [3] . .	kūr	gáfia [8] . . .	. . . . . .
wilde Thiere — *beasts of prey*	bondi [4] . . . ; dā karāga-bē	úrurā . . .	nāma n dana	barōde . . . ; túktake; tetke
Löwe — *lion*	kúrguri [5] . . ; mína	dúguri; dúguli	záki Pl. zákona, zakuōki; Löwin — *lioness* zakainia	džággere Plur. džagge; maunde [10] . ; šebbe . . .
Leopard und Gepard — *leopard and hunting-cat; Felis leopardus; Cynailurus guttata*	džazórma [6] . ; ngām karāga-bē		damísa . .	tšírgu . . ; mállehul [11] . ; džámmalu . ; dondôru Plur. dúndohul ; musūru . .

[1] kéri, Koelle kéri. S. in Betreff der übereinstimmenden Formen dieses Namens in den verschiedenen Sprachen, als Beweis für die Einführung des Hundes aus derselben Gegend, Einleitung S. XC, N. 4, wozu noch Koama ágidde, und Dāgga [illegible] hinzuzufügen. Der Hund dieser Gegenden übrigens ist fast ausschliesslich ein grosses schlankes Windspiel, meist falb-gelbfarbig, nach Süden immer seltener, vielleicht in Folge des Leoparden. Am Niger ein schmutziges, feiges Thier.

[2] ngām bei Koelle in der Zusammensetzung ngampátū, eine Form, die mich anfangs verwirrte, indem ich pátu mit fáto, „Haus" für identisch hielt und diesen Ausdruck für die einzig richtige Bezeichnung der „Hauskatze" oder gezähmten Kater auffasste, bis ich erkannte, dass pátu eben der Wandalá- und Bagrimma-Ausdruck für Katze ist, der auch im Fulfúlde fátu-ru erscheint, so dass hier zwei ganz verschiedene Namen der Katze kombinirt sind. — ngām tsilim für „Katze" erlaubt vermuthen, dass das weibliche Thier im Gegensatz des Männchen meist schwarze Farbe hat, vergl. Brehm „Ergebnisse" S. 113.

[3] gúrguma fehlt bei Koelle, wenn es nicht vielleicht in ngurgu-ma, „[illegible]" zu suchen ist, da wirklich aus den Rattenfellen ganz vorzugsweise „kleine Säcke", ngurgu, gemacht werden.

[4] bondi. Koelle accentuirt bóndi und unterscheidet zwischen den bóndi dálibe, „den Thieren des Feldes" und den bóndi karagábe, „den Thieren des Waldes", s. v. [illegible] scheint er bóndi als Singular zu geben; es wird aber nur in der Mehrheit gebraucht — dā karāga-be, „das Fleisch des Waldes", ganz wie H. nāma n dana und B. [illegible].

[5] kúrguri. Koelle schreibt kúrgull und karágull, vielleicht nur, um dieses Wort einigermassen von dem kúrguri, „weiblich" zu unterscheiden; aber l und r sind bloss dialektische Verschiedenheiten desselben Lautes, und das entsprechende Tédā-Wort scheint zu zeigen, dass die ursprüngliche Form des Kanúri-Namens für Löwe eine ganz andere war, indem das k im Anfang nicht ursprünglich ist; denn es fiel mir Einleitung S. LXXXII, wo ich die beiden Formen dúguri und kúrguri als nahe verwandt hinstellte, nicht ein, zu meinen, dass d und k in einander übergehen könnten. Auch Tédā úrurā hängt mit diesem Namen des Löwen auf's Engste zusammen. Der Löwe wird so übrigens nur in den östlichen Provinzen genannt, während in den westlichen sein gewöhnlicher Name mína ist.

[6] džazórma. Koelle schreibt dešírma und šírma. — Ich bemerke hier, dass ich den Leoparden und den Geparden in den Afrikanischen Idiomen nicht habe unterscheiden können; der letztere ist jedenfalls viel seltener. ngām karāgabe, „Katze des Walddickichts", entspricht dem Fulfúlde-Namen musūru.

[7] karē. Schön schreibt kerreh und giebt als Pluralform karnuka, dagegen Grammatik (1862) §. 29, karnuka.

[8] gáfia. Ich führe hier die Hausa-Namen von drei besonderen Arten von Mäusen an: „Baummaus", [illegible]; „Feldmaus", [illegible]: „Feldspringmaus", [illegible], Plur. [illegible].

[9] kútaru hängt vielleicht mit dem Kanúri kútoru zusammen, obgleich dieses letztere eigentlich nur von Hündchen, Ferkelchen gebraucht wird; wahrscheinlicher ist es eine verstärkte Form von kútu, das sich dem kédi u.s.w. eng anschliesst.

[10] maunde, maundu, Plur. maudi, eigentlich „der Grosse".

[11] mállehul scheint hier auffallend, da das offenbar verwandte mélehul im Tédā die Hyäne zu bezeichnen scheint. — Koelle in seiner Polyglotta hat drei ganz andere F.-Namen für den „Leoparden", [illegible] (das auch Reichardt hat), [illegible] und [illegible], ein deutlicher Beweis, eine wie hervorragende Rolle der Leopard in der Afrikanischen Fauna spielt, d. h. wenigstens in den gebirgigen Landschaften; denn in Bornu ist er seltener. Vgl. Brehm „Ergebnisse" u. s. w. S. 100 ff.

[12] [illegible], „die Thiere des Waldes", [illegible], „das Thier, er", d. h. „das Thier vorzugsweise", „der König der Thiere".

[13] [illegible], wie [illegible], [illegible] und andere sind wol von besonderen Eigenschaften hergenommene Namens-Formen.

[14] [illegible]. Koelle in seiner Polyglotta hat hier, wie so oft in Bagrimma, den H.-Ausdruck in der leicht veränderten Form [illegible].

[15] bie mádlum. Für „Katze" giebt Seetzen das ganz verschiedene wonjeng; für „Hund" hat er (njōh) und Burckhardt (nyonh) fast eben dasselbe, wie ich.

Sonyai.	Lógoné.	Wándalá.	Bágrimma.	Mába.
hansi har . . . . [1]	kalê	krē	bísi	ńö, ńök
hansi wai . . .	kalê (e)l genim .	muksa krē .	bísi nē . . .	ńö mödžum
müsu	mamlígiā . . .	ŏwa	džaura	bis mar
	daθī	pātu	batū . . . / méla batū .	bis mödžum [15]
. . . . . .	ú"yaemī (u"yaéyemi?)	dígelô . . .	wāge . . .	dšik
džéri Pl. džériō .	suvé-gemī [12] .	édia érvē . .	džá-korô . .	mĕgik (Pe. merg p. 109)
gengi { haie . . / gun . . / n müši . }	séve-nī	érvalē [13] . . / árverē . . .	tóbiō [14] . . .	amrek / [B. amarak]
mār	si"ti	wúbelār . . .	hāga	yirri

[1] hári: see Introductory Remarks p. XCI, note 4, with regard to the closely allied forms of this term in the several languages, to which we may further add ngidde in ki-Kamba, kite in ki-Dóngge, as a clear proof of the dog having been introduced into these Regions from one and the same quarter. The dog, however, in these quarters, in general, is a fine strong grey-hound, mostly of a yellowish-grey colour, becoming rarer towards the South, probably on account of the prevalence of the leopard; but in the quarter of the Niger the dog is a dirty, cowardly animal.

[2] ágām, ágem with Koelle appears in the composite form ágampátū, a term which first tended thoroughly to confound me, as I understood pátu as páto, fóto, „house", and thought the form identical with ágem fóto-bē, „the domestic cat", till at length I found, that two different terms had been combined here, pátu being the very same term which we find in Wándala, and in a slightly varied form in Bágrimma (batū), as well as in Fulfúlde, fátu-ru. ágám teilim „black cat", for „female cat", is a proof of the female, in general, distinguishing itself from the male by its black colour.

[3] górgoma is wanting in Koelle, if we have not perhaps to look for it in the form ágergé-ma, „bag-maker", the small bag called ágerge being in truth generally made out of the skin of the rat.

[4] bundi: Koelle writes búndī, and distinguishes between the búndi délibē, „the beasts of the field", and the búndī kárngābō, „the beasts of the forest". s. v. cámōli he gives búndi as a singular form, but that is an error.

[5] hárgari: Koelle writes kárgalī and karágalī, perhaps from no other reason, but in order to distinguish this term from hárgari with the notion „female"; but we must remark, that r and l are mere dialectical differences of the same sound. However, the corresponding Tédā-term seems to show, that the name given to the lion, was not originally hárgarī, the h not belonging to the root, which is also to be recognized in Tédā ururē, „wild beasts", but that it assumed this form only in course of time. Moreover, the king of the forest is called by this name only in the Eastern provinces, while in the Western part of Bornu its common name is nina.

[6] dšusérma: Koelle writes dašsirma and sásirma. — I here remark, that I have not been able to distinguish in the African idioms between the common leopard and the hunting leopard, the latter being apparently much more rare.

[7] karê: Schön writes karreh, and gives as the plural-form karrenai, but in his recent grammar (1862) § 77 kárasha.

[8] gáfio: I here add the Hausa-names of three peculiar varieties of muridae; one living in the trees called miyáusa, a kind of jerboa called kúsu plur. kusoci, and another one, breeding in rocky ground, and called rámo.

[9] hátaru may seem to be connected with the identical K.-term hátaru, although the latter, generally, is only used of young dogs and pigs; but it is by far more probable, that it is nothing, but huta with the termination ra, ru, see Intr. R. p. CXLIX, CLI.

[10] manadu, manado plur. manadi properly means „large, big".

[11] mólichal seems remarkable, as the nearly related term mólobal in Tédā, according to all appearance, signifies a totally different animal, the hyena. — The important part, which the leopard bears among the Central-African Negro, at least in the more hilly and mountainous regions, is fully born out by the fact of Koelle in his Polyglotta not mentioning any of my numerous Fulfúlde-terms, but three other ones, viz batóri (a term mentioned also by Richardson), ténga and enidu.

[12] suvé-gemī, „the beasts of the forest", séve-nī, „the beast", i. e. „the king of the forest".

[13] érvalē, as well as ind-alē, „hyena", ée-alē, and other terms, are forms of adjectives, derived from certain qualities.

[14] tóbiō: here we have an instance of how little reliance is to be placed for special purposes in the terms given in Koelle's Polyglotta, especially with regard to the Bágrimma; for here he gives the Hausa-term nāki in the slightly varied form nakí.

[15] bis mödžum: Seetzen gives a totally distinct term for „cat", viz wonjeng, while for „dog" he has only a slightly varied form from that given by myself (ńjōk), as well as Burckhardt (nyokb).

Deutsch und Englisch.	Kanúri.	Tédā.	Hausa.	Fulfúlde.
wilde Katze — mountain-cat	kiyāl[1] . . . súmoli . .	. . . . . .	sára	. . . . . .
(Gefleckte) Hyäne — (spotted) hyena; Hyaena crocuta	búlta[2] . . .	mólobúl . .	kurā . . . ábi n dawa[7]	ranándu ledde[11] Pl. ðauádi ledde ðiiro Pl. ðiuri-dži fauru . . . buru . . . búi S. . . . lesadógge . . wásondū[12] .
Schakal — jackal; Canis mesomelas	delā (Arb.) .	turke . . .	dilā[8] . . .	. . . . . .
Elephant — elephant . .	komāgun . . komāun[3] . .	komōgun . . kūn	gīwa[9] . . .	ǹīwa Pl. ǹībi
Rhinoceros — rhinoceros; Rhinoceros Africanus, Rhinoceros simus?	kárgadán[4] . bárkadžán .	[6]	marili[10] . . .	lillifóri . . .
Nilpferd — River-horse; Hippopotamus Africanus	ńgurūtu[5] . .	. . . . . .	dórina . . .	ṅgabbo Pl. ṅgabbi

[1] kiyāl fehlt bei Koelle, erscheint bei ihm als ŋgampitə adurwal. — Den höchst merkwürdigen súmoli beschreibt Koelle als ein fabelhaftes Thier, von dem man annähme, dass es eine grosse Menge Ohren habe und alle Geheimnisse wisse, s. Reisen III, S. 153. Mir scheint es nicht unmöglich, dass dieses der von Schimper und Brehm l. c. S. 107, leider ohne Bezeichnung der Ohren, angegebene Abessinische weba, ein wirklicher Tiger, ist, „das grausamste aller wilden Thiere".

[2] búlta. Koelle hat daneben noch bálte. Die Eingeborenen scheinen die verschiedenen Arten der Hyäne nicht zu unterscheiden — im Allgemeinen ist es wol die Hyaena crocuta; im Tēda-Gebiet dagegen mag die Hyaena striata vorwiegen — obgleich das Thier somit eine grosse Rolle in ihren Anschauungen spielt. So sagen sie von dem, der sich bei Tagesanbruch in Ruhe wälzt: bálte-rö ŋgule wátši sibbelan, „die Hyäne hat auf ihrem Weg den Morgen überrascht".

[3] komāun. Koelle schreibt kamáun, kamáun und kamágun. Zu der ursprünglichen Form vgl. Einleitung S. XCII, N. 1.

[4] kárgadán. Es ist auf den ersten Blick höchst wunderbar, wie dieser Indisch-persische Name nach Bornu kommt; man muss jedoch bedenken, dass das Rhinoceros im eigentlichen Bornu keineswegs einheimisch ist (s. Reisen Th. III, S. 313), so dass die Gelehrteren unter den Bewohnern den von den Reisenden aus dem Orient ihnen angeführten Namen wahrscheinlich adoptirt haben. Der Indisch-persische Name nämlich war schon so früh im Orient und Occident allgemein geworden, dass er schon von Arrian erwähnt wird in der Form καρτάζωνος. Auch hatte im äussersten Westen der Mohammedanischen Welt heute keinen anderen Namen. bárkadžán scheint ebenfalls nur eine populäre Verdrehung des ersten Namens. Beide Namen fehlen allerdings bei Koelle, der dafür einen mir unbekannt gebliebenen einheimischen Namen kamarima gibt (von kamár, „Mond"?), den Baikie (s. N. 10) in der falschen Form kamarami als den Namen seines eingebildeten Einhorns aufgefasst hat; der andere vermeintliche Name dieses vermeintlichen Thieres bundié-ru ist wahrscheinlich nichts als bundi ngō, „irgend ein wildes Thier". Burton gebraucht den Ausdruck kargadan auch für die Equatorial-Länder an der Ostküste Afrika's; da ist er jedoch nicht einheimisch.

[5] ŋgurūtu. Koelle accentuirt ŋgúrutū.

[6] Für solche Thiere, wie Rhinoceros, Nilpferd und Krokodil haben die Bewohner der Wüste im Allgemeinen keine Namen.

[7] ábi n dawa. Dieser allgemeine Name „das Ding (Ungeheuer) der Wildniss", so wie die vielen der Hyäne in der Fulfúlde-Sprache beigelegten Namen zeigen wol deutlich, wie gefürchtet das Thier in jenen Gegenden ist.

[8] dilā. Ich führe hier noch die Namen eines verwandten Raubthieres an, vielleicht Canis pictus, H. söwandu oder karémbiki, F. söwando (Plur. sōði) oder basáru ledde; dann habe ich auch noch die Hausa-Ausdrücke für zwei Wolfsarten kélkatel (Canis lupaster Ehrenberg?) und döbbegi (Canis Anthus?). Ich will hier auch noch die Namen für „Fuchs" (Vulpes famelica) anführen, H. buáderi, F. fatōro; dann ein Thier auf Hausa genannt matl[illegible], F. dlaldu, und ein anderes H. buderri. Eins von diesen beiden ist wol die Megalotis.

[9] gīwa. „Der weibliche Elephant", H. gīwa na matše, F. ǹīwa dewo; „der ausgewachsene, grosse Elephant", H. tōro (wol aus dem Kaddïga, der Sprache des Reiches Ghámla, wo Elephanten gezähmt wurden, tōro Plur. tōro), F. tóróri; auch, glaube ich, wird der „junge Elephant" im Hausa mit dem besonderen Namen kurunkū bezeichnet.

[10] marilī. Dr. Baikie hat den marili oder marlei (Athenaeum 1860, Nr. 1816, Zeitschrift für Erdkunde Th. XIII, S. 228), den yillifé oder dáharbálewal der Fulbe, für das Einhorn gehalten. Die gänzliche Verkehrtheit dieser Deutung hat ein Zoologe Rev. W. Haughton in den Annals of Natural History 1868 dargethan; ich kann sie von sprachlicher Seite vertreten.

[11] ranándu leddr. Dieser, so wie der zweite der Sonyai-Namen bezeichnet die Hyäne als „Hund der Wildniss".

[12] wásandū ist wol ein nur in Adamaua üblicher Provincialismus.

[13] ke-bérí hängt wol sicher nicht mit béri, „Pferd", sondern mit bóro, „gross" zusammen und bezeichnet den Elephanten als das Riesen der Fauna. Dieses bestätigt die entsprechende Logone-Bezeichnung bam ro béro, „das grosse Fleisch (Wild)".

[14] gavó verhält sich zum Hausa gīwa, fast wie Logone ŋevi zum Fulfúlde ǹīwa. — ind-alé, „der Räuber".

[15] drabák. Burckhardt murfan (Arb.) und dabah. — Burckhardt hat auch einen M.-Namen für „Tiger" (?) nämlich tomory.

[16] gōón. Burckhardt hat das ganz verschiedene kuhoty und dagegen für ógár-kutl, „Rhinoceros", das fast Arb. amhorn.

[17] gariuttye ist das Magrebinische gerinti (s. N. 5). Burckhardt hat den einheimischen Namen celeen; ist zu controliren.

Sonyai.	Lógoné.	Wándalá.	Bágrimma.	Mába.
. . . .	mamtigiá . . .	yira	malá-korö .	. . . .
kōro . . . . . . / harmi n geúgi . / haile (?) . . .	dādu	ind-alē . . .	ūlgo . . . / nyungo . .	drabák [15]
. . . .	berkazeńgzeńg .	bádela . . .	berkiúgdžéńg-dżeńg	sagár'
tarkónde . . . / ke-béri [13] . . .	novī	guvē [14] . . .	kōdži . . .	guōn [16]
. . . .	íngirmē	asemmīmo . .	birni	ńgúr-kulī
bańya	niyō	bībi taúgurā (?)	āba	gerintiyo [17]

[1] kiyál may be identical with Koelle's ógampítú adarwai. — With regard to the very remarkable animal, called sámoli (Koelle sámóli and búndi sámóli), see Travels vol. III, p. 164. This most ferocious animal may be identical with the wobo, a real tiger, represented by Abessinian travellers as „the most ferocious of animals", although unluckily they say nothing of the form of the ear, which, with its pointed shape, and black edges, is so very characteristic of this animal. Koelle also describes it as „a fabulous animal supposed to have a great number of ears all over its head, and to know all secrets".
[2] báltu: Koelle, besides this form, has also bálty. As for the different varieties of the African hyena, I have not found any distinguishing names, although the hyena, in general, plays a most conspicuous part in the life of the Natives, as, for instance, we see from the K. dictum bálta-ró dunia wátši albbelaa, „morning has surprised the hyena on her road".
[3] komáon: Koelle writes kemdan, komdoo and komágan. As for the original form, see Intr. Remarks p. XCIII. note 1.
[4] kárgadan: At first sight it is quite wonderful, how and why there should exist a perfect harmony between the Kanúri-term of the rhinoceros, and the name used in Persia and India; but, when we reflect, that the rhinoceros is not indigenous in Bornu Proper (see Trav. vol. III, p. 313), while the name kárkadán had become common in all countries of the Orient and Occident at so early a period, as to be even mentioned by Aelian in the form καρτάζωνος (neither did Edrisi know any other name), we can understand, how the more enlightened Natives of Bornu adopted the name brought to them by the travelling merchants from the North and East; as for the name kárkadán, it is evidently a mere popular corruption of the Persian name. Both names are wanting in Koelle, who, instead, gives a native term kamarimo, a name which Baikie in the corrupted form kamarami has misunderstood as meaning the Unicorn (see note 10), his bundiá-ru, which he gives as a synonym of the same, being nothing but bundi ngō, „some wild beast". Burton uses the name kárgadán in speaking of the rhinoceros in the Equatorial Region on the East coast of Africa: but there it is not indigenous.
[5] ngaráte: Koelle writes ngáratū. — From this term the modern Arabs of Barbary seem to have formed their gerinti.
[6] The inhabitants of the desert, of course, have no indigenous name, neither for the rhinoceros, nor the hippopotamus, or crocodile.
[7] áhi n daua; this name of so general an import, „the thing (beast) of the wilderness", as well as the great number of names given to the hyena in the Fulfúlde-language, show clearly, how much feared this animal is in these regions.
[8] dilā; I here adduce the names of another beast of prey of a related species (Canis pictus?) H. sáwandu or karémbikí, F. (at least in Sókoto) sówandu (plur. sóíí), or bosáru ladde. I here also mention a few other names of animals, first „fox" (Vulpes famelica), H. baúdoyi, F. fulóro; then an animal called maššantši in Hausa, and dšolda in Fulfúlde, and another one called badévri in Hausa. I have finally, besides, the Hausa-terms for two species of wolf, as it seems, viz kólkotši (Canis lupaster, Ehrenberg?), and débbegi (Canis Anthus?).
[9] giwa: „the female elephant", H. giwa na matše, F. níwa devva; „the full-grown big elephant", H. tōro, a very remarkable term and, no doubt, borrowed from the Kadšiga, the official language of the once glorious empire of Ghánata, the inhabitants of which seem to have known the art of taming the (African) elephant, called tūre plur. tōru, F. tórāri; even „the young elephant", if I am not mistaken, has the peculiar Hausa-name kunkuá.
[10] mariri: Dr. Baikie in a communication dated from the Niger, published in the Athenaeum 1862, n° 1816 has described this very same animal H. mariri or mariri, P. yillifá (my lillifári), or dákarbáleewal as the Unicorn. But, while my linguistical information clearly shows him to have taken the rhinoceros for that fabulous animal, Rev. W. Houghton, in the Annals of Natural History 1862, has justly reproved him for such nonsense from a zoological point of view.
[11] raváadu ladde, as well as the second of the two terms given in Sonyai, denotes the hyena as „dog of the wilderness".
[12] wánsundē, probably, is a mere provincial term, used by the Fúlbe settled in the far remote country of Adamáwa.
[13] ke-béri, no doubt, derived from béro, „large, big", in Emghédesi ham ro béro, „the largest beast".
[14] guvē seems to bear the same relation to Hausa giwa, as Lógoné navī bears to Fulfúlde níwa.
[15] drabák: Burckhardt gives merfaa [Arb.] and dabak. — He also gives a Mába-name for „tiger" (?), tomery.
[16] guōn: Burckhardt has kookoty i. e. kū-koti, and instead of ńgúr-kulī, „rhinoceros", the Arabic amhorn.
[17] gerintiyo is from the Maghrebine gerinti. Burckhardt, however, gives a totally different indigenous term oaleen.

Deutsch und Englisch.	Kanúri.	Tédā.	Hausa.	Fulfúlde.
Krokodil — crocodile; Crocodilus Niloticus	kĕram[1] . . .	. . . . . .	káda	nóda[9] F. H. nórua F. F. . gillaĭêro . .
Büffel — buffalo . . .	ŋgăran[2]	. . . . . .	bauna . . .	mbanna Pl. banni edda Pl. eddi
Giraffe — giraffe; Camelopardalis	kindžer[3] . .	kindžer . . .	rákomi n dana[6]	gelōba ledde dĭdi ledde[10] tiréwa . . .
eine grosse Varietät von Antilope — a large species of antilope; Antilope bubalis	kargúm[4] . .		gada . . . gádu . . .	haogăre H. . hammafúrde F.[11] duggewīre Plur. duggewīdĕe
Tétel — A. Soemmeringii?	forto	grasĕ . . .	delli[7] . . .	. . . . . .
Ovis tragelaphus — Ovis (Onager?) tragelaphus	kirtšíge . . .	. . . . . .	rāgo n dūši .	. . . . . .
Leucoryx Antilope — Antilope Leucoryx	komásunū . .		welusidži . .	. . . . . .
Oryx — Oryx	. . . . . .	. . . . . .	márrē . . .	imbáda Pl. imbarādĕ
Art von Wasser-Antilope — waterbuck	kelóra . . .	turbuī . . .	gouki[8] . . .	kōba Pl. kōbi
Gazelle — gazelle; Gazella Dorcas	ingerl[5] . . .	udén; udēno .	beréwa . . .	léllua F. H.) Pl. lĕlel F. F.) lelli

[1] kârem. Koelle accentuirt kárem. — Ich will hier noch eine Art Gnúnu oder wenigstens ein verwandtes Thier erwähnen, das ich leider nicht selbst gesehen habe (s. Reisen Th. V, S. 161, vgl. S. 188); in Bornu scheint es gútiken genannt zu werden und von den westlichen Fúlbe zagariwal, in S. onúgwai. — Mit Bezug auf agéliti im Yóruba s. N. 12.

[2] ŋgăran. Koelle schreibt ŋgéran.

[3] kindžer. Koelle kéntegr.

[4] kargúm. Koelle kérgum. — forte fehlt bei ihm, ebenso wie kirtšíge und komásunū. Bei dem sehr eigenthümlichen Kopfe dieser Antilope ist nichts natürlicher, als dass Koelle's Ali Eisámi den Angaben Clapperton's gegenüber mit Hartnäckigkeit darauf bestand, dass es nicht eine Antilope, sondern eine Kuh sei. So sagt Denham selbst von diesem Thier (Denham und Clapperton I, S. 176, hier korookoo geschrieben), dass es ein Mittelding zwischen einem Ochs und einer Antilope sei.

[5] ingerl. Ich schreibe so absichtlich und nicht mit Koelle ŋgérī oder ŋgárī. — Über die kelára s. meine Reisen Th. II, S. 333. — Hier erwähne ich noch die tigdim genannte, ganz kleine Antilope (Antilope pygmaea? Thbg., A. spinigera?) Reisen Th. III, S. 277.

[6] rákomi n dana. Auch die Kanúri gebrauchen zuweilen den entsprechenden Ausdruck kérgimō karáge-bē, „Kameel der Wildniss". Bezeichnend ist der Name deshalb, weil er zeigt, dass einige dieser Völker noch eher mit dem Kameel, als mit der Giraffe bekannt wurden, also sicherlich nicht ursprünglich Bewohner des tropischen Afrika sind.

[7] delli. Mit dem delli ist wol identisch der dorri, von dem ich in anderen Gegenden hörte, obgleich man ihn mir als ein büffelartiges Thier beschrieb.

[8] gouki. Über die Selbständigkeit dieser Antilope mit der kelóra bin ich nicht ganz sicher.

[9] nóda, nórua. Reichardt hat den ganz verschiedenen Ausdruck modóri, der bei den westlichen Fúlbe in Gebrauch sein mag.

[10] dĭdi ledde. Die nähere Bezeichnung von dĭdi ist mir unbekannt; denn mit dáŋdiri, Plur. dĭandi, „der Hammel" hat es doch wol nichts zu thun; jedenfalls ist es wol eine Pluralform.

[11] hammafúrde ist wieder ein Ausdruck, der durchaus auf Fómbina oder Adamaua beschränkt scheint und den übrigen Fúlbe wahrscheinlich unbekannt ist.

[12] ékarai; vergl. den Yóruba-Namen für die Afrikanische Gnúnu agéliti.

[13] táhoš würde, die merkwürdigen Beziehungen gerade der Sonyai berücksichtigt, wol an den entsprechenden tahaš des Alten Testamentes erinnern.

[14] adye-pértueeé hat offenbar eine nähere Beziehung, die mir aber nicht deutlich ist; in pérúnsé steckt wol forte.

[15] forte. Da der Tétel, der eigentliche Bewohner der marsch- und brunnreichen Niederungen in Bagirmi, wie ich aus eigener Erfahrung weiss, häufig ist, in Bornu dagegen selten, so ist wol sicher, dass die Kanúri-Sprache den fremden Ausdruck sich angeeignet hat. Ob eben dasselbe mit dem Ausdrucke kergúm der Fall ist, bin ich nicht im Stande, zu entscheiden.

[16] hondla. Burckhardt hat das Egyptisch-Arabische temsah; für yílir hat er ófer.

[17] ler, „Gazelle" möchte die Wurzel von Kanúri kelóra sein.

Sedyai.	Lógoné.	Wándalá.	Bágrimma.	Mába.
ákarai[12]	mítigē	kirwē . . .	māra . . .	kondžu[16]
hīra	dógomē [dúggo-mi?] (gemī)	taá-kilē . . .	dōgo	šīm
boróng	mzá-dakē . . .	kéntaerē . .	korio	yīfir
. . . . . .	gária	ki-yekē . .	kargúm . . .	
. . . . . .	adye-pártouaē[14]	avyanē . . .	forto[15] . . .	. . . . . .
. . . . . .	hária	. . . . . .	hária . . .	derángal
siné (?)	. . . .	íranē . . .	. . . . . .	. . . . . .
gēri hengēr . .	. . . .	. . . . . .	. . . . . .	. . . . . .
. . . . . .	mazā	bugia . . .	kāla	. . . . . .
táboē[13]	úfulū (gemī) . .	zāra kamba .	džóbēb . . .	lar[17]

[1] hīram: Koelle writes hárum. — I think this a fit place for mentioning that kind of genius, of which I have spoken as living in some African rivers, without, however, catching a glimpse of any (see Trav. vol. V, p. 146; compare p. 186). In Bornu it seems to be called gúttlea, while the Western Fúlbe call it eagariwal, and the Sedyai anágwal. With regard to the agéliti in Yóruba see note 12.

[2] ngáran: Koelle writes ngéran.

[3] kindīlsr: Koelle kéntaçr.

[4] kargám: Koelle writes kárgam, and in opposition to Capt. Clapperton states, that it is a cow and not a species of Antilope, an error, which is very natural, as he had to rely entirely upon the statements of a single individual, and the head of this antilope being really so very much like that of a cow, that Major Denham himself, who writes koreakoo (Denham and Clapperton, Travels I, p. 176), says, that that animal is something between an ox and an antilope. As for the terms forto, as well as kirikigo and komaesnō, they are wanting in Koelle.

[5] ingari: I write so on purpose, and not ágiri or ággri with Koelle. — With regard to the kalára, see Travels vol. II, p. 333. — I here mention, besides, the diminutive little antilope called ligdim (Travels vol. III, p. 877), which may be identical with the Antilope pygmaea of Thunberg, or with the Antilope spinigera.

[6] rákomi n dass: the Kanúri also sometimes use the corresponding term kárgimé haréga-bé, „camel of the wilderness", and this name is of importance in some respects, as it seems to show, that some of these tribes, at least, made earlier acquaintance with the camel, than with the giraff. Consequently, there cannot be the slightest doubt, but that they migrated into the Tropical Regions of Africa at a comparatively very recent date, posterior to the Arab immigration, vol. VII.

[7] delli: I have occasionally heard also of an animal called derri, which the people described to me as somewhat resembling the buffalo, and I am almost sure, the same is a mere dialectical variety of delli.

[8] gaṅhi: I am not quite certain with regard to the identity of this antelope with the kalára.

[9] nádo, nárna: Reichardt has the totally different term moddīri, which seems to be in use with the Western Fúlbe.

[10] dīādi ledde: the original meaning of the term dīādi, if used by itself, is not known to me; for it can scarcely be identical with the term dīaádiri plur. dīandi, „the rain".

[11] bowwanférde, again, is a term, the use of which seems to be limited to the Fúlbe settled in Fúmbina or Adamawa, while it is unknown to those sections of this widely spread tribe, settled farther to the West.

[12] ákarai: this term may have something in common with the Yóruba agéliti, which Rev. Crowther understood as meaning a „genius".

[13] táboē, if we consider the various relations of the Sedyai, may remind us of the corresponding term tsebi in the old Testament.

[14] adye-pártouaē evidently includes the relation to some other object (pártouaē = forto?) which I have not made out.

[15] forto: the Antilope Soemmeringii or Léfel being frequent in Bagirmi, as I know from my own experience, while it is rather rare in Bornu, it seems most probable, that the Kanúri-language borrowed the term from her neighbour, and not the contrary; but I am not sure, whether the same be the case with the name kargám.

[16] kondžu: Burckhardt has, instead, the Egyptian-Arabic term tamsah, while instead of yīfir he has éfar.

[17] lar may seem to be the root of the Kanúri-form kalára.

Deutsch und Englisch.	Kanúri.	Tédā.	Haussa.	Fulfúlde.
Eber — *boar; sus Senna-rensis*	gadō [1] . . .	gōdu	gadō [9] . . . . gúrsuná Pl. gur-sunnā	gursunúre Plur. gursúndži
Erdschwein — *Orycteropus Aethiopicus ?*	ṅāšī [2] . . .	. . . . . .	. . . . . .	. . . . . .
Ameisenbär — *ant-eater* .	džorō . . .	. . . . . .	[10]	. . . . . .
Schleichkatze, gestreifte Manguste — *herpestes fasciatus*	kélege [3] . . .	. . . . . .	kurēge	džīre Pl. dži-rēdži; safándu . .
Hase — *hare; lepus Aethiopicus, Ehrenberg*	lárgonā [4] . .	tšomár . . ; tšōar . . .	zōmo . . .	bōdžel Pl. wó-džere
Affe, Meerkatze — *monkey; Cercopithecus, Erxleben*	dāgel [5] . . .	maugo [8] S. . ; dāgel . . .	bēri Pl. borōri	wandu Pl. bādi
Schlange — *serpent* . .	kādi	auso . . . ; gōle . . .	matšidžī . .	bōdi Pl. bolle; modóndi . . ; bōkul lōdi [12]
Schildkröte — *turtle* . .	kūdu [6] . . .	nir	kúṅkurū [11] . .	buṅāre . . .
Eidechse — *lizard* . . .	dárimī . . .	dorū	kadángerē . .	falándi Pl. falánde
Skorpion — *scorpion* . .	kaléndži [7] . .	éti	konāma . . .	yáhare Pl. džāhe [13]

[1] gadō. Koelle schreibt gádu. — gadó allein heisst immer „Eber", obgleich eigentlich nur der kī, „der männliche", gemeint ist, im Gegensatz des gadō kárgari, „der Sau". — Ich will hier auch die betreffenden Namen für „Stachelschwein" hersetzen, soweit mir bekannt. K. kimō, H. begōa.

[2] ṅāšī fehlt bei Koelle, ebenso džorō; dagegen hat er gárgum für ein derartiges Thier, das er aber dann doch für identisch hält mit dem von Clapperton I, S. 390 erwähnten koorigum, der S. 196 erwähnten Antilope kargúm.

[3] kélege hat Koelle, erklärt es aber fälschlich als „eine kleine Art wilden Hundes". — Ich will hier auch den Namen des Ichneumon (Herpestes Pharaonis) hersetzen, der im Kanúri sowohl wie im Bágrimma tširóma heisst, im Haussa tsári. Von diesem in die Erde sich eingrabenden tširóma kommt unzweifelhaft der Ausdruck im Kanúri für ntširóma n tsógin, d. h. „ich befestige das Pferd nach Weise eines Ichneumon's", woraus Koelle irrthümlich ein Substantiv ntšíróma gebildet hat, „ein tiefes Loch im Sande".

[4] lárgonā. Koelle schreibt targúna und erklärt es neben „Hase" auch für „Kaninchen", aber die gibt es hier nicht.

[5] dāgel, ursprünglich nur der „rothe Affe", Cercopithecus ruber, woher es denn die Bedeutung von „roth" überhaupt erhalten hat. Wie der dunkelfarbige, „schwarze Affe", auf H. bēri baki oder bika, F. wandu ballēru, H. bolsiu, auf Kanúri genannt wird, weiss ich nicht; jedoch glaube ich kaum, dass man sagen kann dāgel tsilim. Der eigentliche dāgel, der rothe Affe, heisst dža u bēri auf Haussa, wandu bodēru auf Fulfúlde. — Ich habe ausserdem noch bēri maléōdi in Haussa, yibbíru Plur. yibbídži in Fulfúlde, vielleicht dāgel bulāgā bei Koelle.

[6] kūdu fehlt bei Koelle; so auch dárimī; anstatt kādi schreibt er kādi.

[7] kaléndži. Der Name des Skorpions im Kanúri scheint von seiner kennzeichnendsten und verderblichen Eigenschaft, des „Stechens" mit dem Schwanz abgeleitet zu sein. S. das Zeitwort kálundgin bei Koelle.

[8] maugo im südlichen Dialekt der Tédā verdient wol Beachtung bei der grossen Verbreitung dieses Namens.

[9] gadō. Die Haussa-Sprache hat einen eigenthümlichen Ausdruck für „Sau", nämlich gadónia. Übrigens bin ich unsicher über den Unterschied des gadō und des gúrsunā; eins von ihnen entspricht jedenfalls dem Phacochoerus Aeliani. Auch habe ich noch einen darauf bezüglichen Ausdruck mugúndo n, dessen genaue Beziehung mir entfallen ist.

[10] Anstatt des entsprechenden Ausdrucks für džorō will ich hier zwei Haussa-Namen für „Dachs" angeben: tsáku und degge.

[11] kúṅkurū. Ich führe hier den Namen eines verwandten Thieres an, das ich aber nicht näher identificiren kann, nämlich H. kúmtsurtši, F. tōnlándi.

[12] bōkul lōdi heisst wörtlich „das Erdtau", ebenso wie der entsprechende Songai-Ausdruck.

[13] yahare Plur. džāhe. Rev. Reichardt hat hiervon zwei verschiedene Wörter gemacht; denn zuerst führt er in der Liste zweisilbiger Wörter S. 6, h) an yáre mit der Bedeutung „Spinne" und in der Übersetzung der drei Fúlah-Bücher gibt er džahe, das er Arabisch جاه schreibt, durch „Skorpion" (s. Arab. Text S. 4, v. 49 und die Übersetzung S. 21), aber sowohl džahe wie das daneben stehende bolli, بلي sind Pluralformen, wie wir gesehen haben.

[14] meg. Wenn der Ausdruck megih oben S. 193 wirklich die allgemeine Bedeutung „wildes Thier" hat, so können wir wol mit Recht annehmen, dass er sie eben von dem Vorwiegen des Wildschweins in den Wildnissen Wadái's erhalten hat.

[15] tédžom. Burckhardt hat das sehr ähnliche tajoun l. c. tadžūn, dagegen hat Seetzen das ganz verschiedene delbak und kúdžimit, wol als besondere Arten von Schlangen.

Sonyai.	Lógoné.	Wándalá.	Bágrimma.	Mába.
binka	sime	ebdĕi	gari	meg [14]
. . . .	máǹceǹi	kúšebē . . .	ōmo	. . . . . .
. . . .	mavidli	moila	. . . . . .	dĭlnserík
. . . .	. . . . . .	. . . . . .	. . . . . .	
. . . .	{ tóruš . . . . / swēka . . . . }	awīra	. . . . . .	mog
fóno	wagila	bašú-alē . .	bēti	górik Plur. gortu
ganda karfu . .	māre	zābe	kelā	tēdĭlom [15]
. . . .	kinálahám	fīrfe	{ yikko . . . / man . . . }	ābu gāda (Arb.)
. . . .	dágarā	mopálalā . .	{ kékeli . . . / kikil-māla . }	{ sil / garúmbel / torgól / endindíggere }
donton	{ lméāge (p. 141) . / mesákian . . . }	erítaā	yīnl	tar-angág

1 gadó: Koelle writes gádu. — gadō, if used by itself, always means „boar", male, bī, not being particularly expressed, in opposition to the gadō kérgeri, „sow". — I here adduce the names for „porcupine", K. kimā, H. begón.
2 cédi is wanting in Koelle, as well as the term dīeró; he has gérgum for an animal of some such kind, although he is inclined to identify it with the koorigum (the antilope korgúm p. 106) mentioned by Capt. Clapperton I, p. 370.
3 hélege: Koelle has this name, but explains it wrongly as „a small kind of wild dog, which are a little larger than a cat and live in holes which they dig in the ground". — I here also adduce the name of the „ichneumon", which in Kanúri, as well as in Bágrimma, is called tšīrōme, in Hausa tsíri. From the manner in which the tšīróme buries itself under ground, I have no doubt, that the Kanúri-phrase fir ntšīróme n tségin has been borrowed, that is to say „I fasten a horse (by a rope underground in the manner) of the ichneumon", whence Koelle by mistake has formed a substantive ntšīrōme, „a hole dug in the ground from two to three feet deep for the purpose of tying horses".
4 târgenā: Koelle tergūna, to which, and besides the meaning of „hare", he attributes that of rabbit also, though there are none.
5 dīgel originally appears to mean nothing, but the red or brown monkey; and it is on this account, that the term dīgel is generally used as an adjective, especially in connection with horses, in order to indicate the red colour. As for the „black monkey", H. bíri bakī, or biki, F. wandu baliēro, S. hulele, I do not know, how it is called in Kanúri; at least, I do not think, that the term dīgel tsilīm is ever used. The dīgel proper, or the red monkey, is called dāo n bīri in Hausa, wandu bodēru in Fulfúlde. — I have, moreover, the name of a peculiar variety, called bīri mairódi in Hausa, yibbire (plur. yibbīdši) in Fulfúlde; and it is possible, that this name is identical with the peculiar species, called dīgel balángū by Koelle who, however, does not further explain the name, but as „a kind of baboon".
6 búdu is wanting in Koelle, as well as dévimī.
7 kaléndāi seems to be derived from kalóógin, „I direct, point", with Koelle.
8 mégo: this term, occurring in the Southern dialect of the Tédā deserves peculiar attention.
9 gadó fm. gadénia, „sow". I am not quite certain, however, with regard to the difference existing between the gadō and the gáraunī, one of which must be identical with the Phacochoerus Aeliani. I have also, besides, a term ma-géndo n, the exact reference of which is not now known to me.
10 I have not learnt the term, which in Hausa corresponds to the Kanúri-term dīeró; but I here give two terms, tsóka and dogge, which seem to denote an animal like the badger.
11 hábharō: I here adduce the name of a related animal, called H. kómtoarīdī, F. tšulándi.
12 hákal lēdi, as well as the corresponding Sonyai-term, means verbally „the rope of the earth".
13 yábere plur. dīēbe: Rev. Reichardt has made two different terms of this one word; for in the first place, in the list of dissyllabous words p. 6, b) he gives yére (i. e. yábere) with the notion „spider", and in translating the three Fulah pieces he translates dīebe (i. e. (dīēbe) [illegible] by „the scorpion", see the Arabic text in his Primer p. 4, v. 42, and the English translation p. 34. But dībebe or dīebe, as well as belli, [illegible] with which it is joined, are plural-forms.
14 meg: the frequency of the hog in the Mába-territory is fully born out by one and the same term serving to indicate the „wild beast" in general (p. 106), meg-ik being nothing, but the full and complete form of meg.
15 tēdíbom: Burckhardt tojoon, i. q. tedšūn, while Seetzen gives, instead, two totally distinct terms delbeh, and hédšimit.

Deutsch und Englisch.	Kanúri.	Tédā.	Hausa.	Fulfúlde.
Frosch, Kröte — *frog, toad*	kōgo [1] . . .	. . . . . .	kowáddu . .	fabru Plur. fābi
Fisch — *fish*	bū-ni [2] . . .	fósu [8] . . .	kīfi Plur. kīfayē [10]	lingo Plur. līdi
Vogel — *bird*	úngudū [3] . .	yáborē N. . / kóbri S. . .	tsuntsu Pl. tsún-tsayē [11]	sondu Plur. čolli
Huhn, Henne — *fowl, hen*	kokī [4] . . .	kúkora, kúkoya	kāza Plur. kāši [12]	gértogel Pl. gertóde
Hahn — *cock*	gábugum [5] . .	kóki ankir .	zákara . . .	zakkarāri Plur. zakkarādže
Küchlein — *chick, chicken*	fiyógma . . .	kókoi miá-honā [9]	da n kāza . .	bingel gértogel?
Gans — *goose*	géde-gabū [6] . / gámana beri-nana	. . . . . .	gabá	gabādže . .
zahme Taube — *pigeon* .	katábora [7] . .	kátabar . .	tantábora [13] .	tantabarāru Plur. tantabarādži
Turteltaube — *turtle-dove*	. . . . . .	. . . . . .	kúrtšia kárami	hondu Plur. fōli

[1] kōgo. Der Frosch führt diesen Namen ganz natürlicher Weise von seinem Quaken, kōga, „Stimme, Geräusch". Koelle handelt daher nicht konsequent, wenn er letzteres Wort kōgé, den Namen des Frosches dagegen kōhō schreibt. Übrigens versteht er unter letzterem nur die gewöhnliche bittere Kröte mit dunklem Rücken und weisser Stirn, und unterscheidet davon eine besondere Varietät, die er berîtege nennt, auch têtege, als die grüne Art wohlriechender Kröte mit gelber Stirn.

[2] būni, „Fisch" leite ich mit voller Überzeugung von bú-nkin, „ich esse" ab (s. Einleitung S. LVIII, N. 3), und finde darin, dass der Fisch vorzugsweise als „die Speise" bezeichnet ist, einen Beweis, dass die Kanúri seit sehr alter Zeit an einem fischreichen Gewässer angesessen gewesen sein müssen; allerdings keineswegs am Tsād, sondern wol am Nil. Diese sprachlichen Berührungen, mit Kandol u. s. w., sind noch nachträglich auszuführen; hier ist die Verwandtschaft des entsprechenden fūn oder būn im Für von grosser Bedeutung. Vergl. auch den buzni, „Barbus Bynni", Cuvier, eben im Nil.

[3] úngudū. Koelle schreibt úgúdú.

[4] kokī. Koelle schreibt kógui; die von ihm angeführte Verbindung mit kárguni, „weiblich", am „Henne" zu bezeichnen, habe ich nie gehört, und bezweifle sehr ihre Richtigkeit.

[5] gábugum, bei Koelle in der Form gáhógom und gáhógum. Aber gábugum hängt wahrscheinlich mit kabugu, „kurz, klein" zusammen, und ist dem so prätentiösen Hahn als Spottname gegeben; anstatt fiyógma hat Koelle hógú.

[6] géde-gabū und der andere Ausdruck kommen bei Koelle nicht vor. Das gede vor dem eigentlichen, dem Hausa entlehnten Namen bezeichnet vielleicht das „Fremde, Ausländische" (gedé, „verschieden") dieses Wasservogels.

[7] katábora. Koelle hat kálapar und kátafar, die er aber eigentlich nur als adjektivische Unterscheidungen von ágigi (S. 202) angibt. Diese Zuchttaube ist wahrscheinlich von den Schuāh aus Egypten eingeführt.

[8] fósu. Dieser vom Kanúri ganz und gar unabhängige und grundverschiedene Ausdruck für „Fisch" im Tédā ist weniger auffallend, wenn man bedenkt, dass im eigentlichen Gebiete der Tédā der Fisch, wenigstens der lebende, so gut wie unbekannt ist, und dass fósu ursprünglich gar nicht den lebenden, sondern nur den getrockneten Fisch bezeichnet; vergl. Reisen Th. V, S. 407. — Für „Vogel" im Tédā hat Lyon woggha (s. Einleitung S. LXVIII, N. 7); zu yáborē, „Vogel" vergl. unten (S. 208) täckurīye, „Nest".

[9] kókoi miá-honā, „die Henne, ihre Kleinen"; s. Einleitung S. LXXX. Zu miá vergl. miga, „Name", me, „Enkel".

[10] kīfi. Ich führe hier den im Hausa, Fulfúlde und Sońγai gleichlautenden Namen des wunderbaren ayú an, den Richard Owen nach der Beschreibung Dr. Eduard Vogel's, dessen Aufmerksamkeit ich bei seiner Reise nach dem Bénuē ganz besonders auf dieses Thier gelenkt, Manatus Vogelii genannt hat. — Ich habe auch noch gaiwa für „Schlammfisch".

[11] tsuntsu. Schön gibt die Form tsuntsu Plur. tsuntsayē und tsuntsaye.

[12] Für „Henne" gibt Schön, ausser kāza, tšiako, und dem entsprechend für „Küchlein", da n tšiako neben tšakoa.

[13] tantábora. Schön gab früher tantaba als Singular, tantabaru als Plural. Allerdings endigen die Hausa-Wörter selten oder nie auf einen Konsonanten, dieses aber ist kein Hausa-, sondern ein Fremdwort. Grammatik, zweite Ausgabe, S. 19, hat er noch herde, Plur. herdaye für „Taube".

[14] hári hum, eigentlich „Wasser-fleisch", ein sehr unbeholfener Ausdruck, der, wenn wirklich die unabhängigen Sońγai keinen prägnanteren besitzen, wol darauf hinzuweisen scheint, dass dieses Volk ursprünglich nicht an einem Flusse angesessen war.

[15] kilfō. Hier haben wir wieder eine ähnliche Übereinstimmung zwischen Wándalā und Hausa; s. Einleitung S. CCLIII.

[16] tákala. Es ist in allen diesen Wörtern eine deutliche Analogie, und offenbar sind sie alle nach einem Gesichtspunkt gebildet, wákala, téakala, lákala, tákala. Ebenso scheinen mir dūckra (wol dūc hera) und dūrud (vielleicht dūc rud), in innerer Beziehung zu einander zu stehen.

[17] handūe. Für alle diese Ausdrücke, wo Koelle in seiner Polyglotta entsprechende Namen hat, gibt er Hausa-Wörter anstatt Bágrimma-Wörter.

[18] hoš ómbu heisst wol „der grüne Vogel". Burckhardt nämlich hat anstatt meines kabéi: hoš, haši, und so hat auch Seetzen kušik.

Sońrai.	Lógoné.	Wándalá.	Bágrimma.	Mába.
korobáta . . .	bártiťī	mugdaa . . .	karro . . .	áńkalák
hāri ham [14] . .	kī, kīi	kilfē [15] . . .	kandža [17] . .	hōt (Arb.)
koru; tšeru . .	sisia	gīye, gáye . .	ōla	kebél Pl. kebél-ńe
gorúńgu . . .	kusku Pl. kúsokai(?)	wúkula . . .	kindža . . .	kārik
gorúńgu har . .	kusku kúlkuldī .	taákala . . .	kindža kāla .	koš úmba [18]
. . . . . .	kusku-n tabū .	ede(e) wúkula	ńun kindža .	. . . . .
gab	maaī . . . . / moyā	wotšē . . .	dabā	wūsinaīk
túldaber . . . / túrun	gūgu-n massar .	tákala [16] másere	der másaara .	hammam (Arb.)

[1] kágo: the frog bears this name most appropriately from his constant noise, kāgo meaning „voice, cry". From this point of view Koelle does not act consistently in writing the latter word kágó, while he writes the name of the frog káká. By the latter, however, he understands only the common toad, with a dark back and a whitish front, and of a very bitter taste, while he distinguishes from it a peculiar variety, which he calls hertétege, also tétege, „the larger kind of toad (kákó), with a dark back and yellow front, said to be very fat, and much relished even by the Moslems".

[2] há-ni, „fish", I derive with perfect confidence from the verb há-chin (see Introductory Remarks p. LIV, note 3), and find in the circumstance of the fish having been designated as „(the) cut-able (thing)" in particular in the Kanúri-language, a distinct proof, that the Kanúri-people were settled from very ancient time on the border of a large sheet of water; on purpose I do not say, the Tsád, but rather mean the Nile. However, the close relation of the corresponding Fúr-term, fún or þún is of great importance, besides which we may also compare the name bunnī of the particular kind of fish of the Nile, called by Cuvier accordingly „Barbus Bieni".

[3] dágudū: Koelle writes ágádó.

[4] koki: Koelle writes kági, and, in order more distinctly to express the female sex, adds hérgari, „female": but such a use of that adjective in this connection I have never found.

[5] gábugam in Koelle appears in the form gábágom and gábógum, but my form, I think, is perfectly right, being derived from kábugu, „short, small", and being a nickname given to the cock on account of its noisy and pretentious character. Instead of fiyágma Koelle has kágū, which may be a mistake, although I have nothing to explain fiyágma.

[6] géde-gubá, and the other term are likewise wanting in Koelle. gubú is the proper term, while géde has some secondary meaning, probably indicating the foreign character; gedé means „different".

[7] katákora: Koelle writes kátapor and kátafor, but considers them as mere adjective distinctions of the various varieties of ágiri (p. 207). This domestic pigeon has, beyond a doubt, been introduced into Negroland by the Sońrai.

[8] fóan: this peculiar Tédā-term for „fish", totally independent and different as it is from the Kanúri, is rather remarkable, especially as there is no living fish in the territory of the Tédā. But I am quite sure, that fóan originally does not mean the living, but the dried fish, which is a great delicacy with the Tédā, Travels vol. V, p. 406.

[9] kákai mia-kani, „the hen, her young ones"; see Introductory Remarks p. LXXXI, and with reference to the term mia, compare migo, „seed", as well as mr, „grandchild".

[10] kīfi: I here mention the name of the remarkable Cetaceous animal, called by the identical name ayú in all the languages, in which I heard of its existence, namely the Hausa, Fulfúlde and Sońrai, and to which Richard Owen in honour of Dr. Edward Vogel, whose attention I had particularly called to this great object of wonder to the natives, has recently given the name of Manatus Vogelii.

[11] tsanlon: Schön has the form cansns plur. cansnī and cansnaī.

[12] For „hen" Schön besides kása gives tšiako, and for „chicken", accordingly dan tšiako, beside tšahne.

[13] tantábara: Schön in the first edition of his grammar gave the form tantabr as the singular, and tantabarn as the plural-form; and, no doubt, the general rule of the Hausa-language requires the vocables not to terminate in a consonant, but here we have a foreign term. In the second edition he gives for pigeon also a term hordo plur. hordaye.

[14] hári ham properly means „water-meat", a very barbarous term, which would seem to prove, that the tribe of the Sońrai was not originally settled on the border of a river; it is not improbable, however, that the independent section of that tribe, which has preserved its original character in a purer state, uses another more expressive term.

[15] kilfē: in this instance, again, we have a tolerable harmony between the Wándalá- and Hausa-languages. Introductory Remarks p. CCLIII.

[16] tákala: in all these terms, such as wúkula, taákala, tákala, tákala, there is a remarkable similarity, and it does not seem doubtful, that all of them have been formed from the same point of view. In the same manner dáabra (probably dáa bara) and dáirab (perhaps dáa rab) seem to be connected with one another by an intimate sort of relation.

[17] kandža: instead of this, and almost all these Bágrimma-names of animals, Koelle in his Polyglotta gives the corresponding Hausa-terms. So little confidence is to be placed for particular purposes in this collection, made in that Babel of African tongues, Sierra Leone.

[18] koš úmba probably means „large bird", Burckhardt giving koš, koši, and Seetzen having kašik, instead of my kebél.

Deutsch und Englisch.	Kanúri.	Tēda.	Hausa.	Fulfúlde.
junge Turteltaube — *young turtle-dove*	. . . . .	. . . . .	da n kúrtšia .	bingel hondu .
wilde (kleine) Taube mit zwei schwarzen Ringen um den Hals — *small dove with two black rings about the neck*	ngígi[1] . . .	áyer	kúrtšia habá / hamsebiya .	hondu tókotšel
Rebhuhn — *partridge* . .	kulye[2] . . .	. . . . .	fákara . . .	gerlal Pl. gerle
Perlhuhn — *guinea-fowl; Numida meleagris*	kāži . . . .[a]	kāži	zabō . . . . / kāza n Yáriba[6]	džaungel Plur. džaule
Strauss — *ostrich* . . .	kergŏko[3] . .	soēn S. . . / kedō N. . .	ďimmena[7] . .	dau Plur. debbi
junger Strauss — *young ostrich*	. . . . .	. . . . .	da n ďimmena	bingel dau .
Aasgeier — *vulture; Vultur Cinereus, gyps Rueppellii?*	kōgo[4] . . .	zinkī	úngulū . . .	žiga / žigauel žigadže
andere Varietät — *other variety; Neophron percnopterus*	. . . . .	. . . . .	mīkia . . .	dutal Pl. dutte / maikiadže .
Steppenrabe — *Corvus scapulatus?; Philostomus Senegalensis, Gmelin*	ngágu . . .	. . . . .	hankáka[8] . .	daungel Pl. daule
Rinderhüter — *Buphaga bubalus, B. leucorinchus*	farátše? . .	. . . . .	belbēla . . .	nyálel Pl. nyalde
Papagei — *parrot* . . .	džidžim-agō[5]	. . . . .	akū	džidžimakōro / sandu laide (ledde?)
Storch — *stork*	gāňo	. . . . .	ďámua[9] . . .	tamuádže . .

[1] ngígi. Koelle betrachtet dies Wort als die allgemeinste Bezeichnung der Taube, und unterscheidet die „wilde Taube" dann nur durch den Beisatz malam (ngigi malam im Gegensatz des ketafar). Ausserdem unterscheidet er noch ngigi gàlà als besondere grosse Varietät der wilden Taube und ngigi bullam als weisse Varietät.

[2] kulye fehlt bei Koelle; anstatt kāži schreibt er kàtši.

[3] kergŏko. Koelle kyrgōgo. Zur richtigen Erfassung der Wurzel und ursprünglichen Form ist der Tēdā-Name kedö überaus wichtig.

[4] kōgo ist wol nur der äusseren Form, nicht der Grundbedeutung nach mit kōgo, „Frosch" S. 200 identisch. Koelle kōgo; ebenso statt ngágu: ngágo.

[5] džidžim-agō scheint bei Koelle zu fehlen; agō ist augenscheinlich das Hausa-Wort akū; worauf džidžim sich bezieht, das eben so in Fulfúlde džidžimakōro erscheint, weiss ich nicht. Man muss aber bedenken, dass der Papagei in ganz Bornu nicht einheimisch ist, und dass auch die Haussaua ihn nur von den südlichen Grenzländern her kennen lernten.

[6] kāza n Yáriba, „das Huhn von Yóruba" (in der Hausa-Form Yáriba) erklärt Schön irrthümlich für „Ente".

[7] ďimmena. Dies ist Schön's tchimmia.

[8] hankáka. Ich will hier in der Note die Namen einiger anderer Vögel in Hausa und Fulfúlde einschalten: „Fledermaus", H. džemāge, F. džemagéru, S. teiraoui und taflrflr; „kleiner schwarz und weisser Vogel mit langem Schnabel und langem Schwanz", H. tšulleköa, F. kiyátorel; „Corropis rufifrons, Le Vaillant", H. saalwa, F. wilwildu.

[9] ďámua. Ich führe hier die Namen mehrerer Wasservögel auf Hausa und Fulfúlde an: „Pelikan" (K. kāgem?), H. maišiha („der Beutelherr"), F. džindžimlen Plur. džindžimldži; „Ardea Goliath, Rüppell", H. gomráha, F. komaréwel Plur. komarédži, S. hemáre; dann den schönen, scharlachrothen Vogel, H. serbe, F. tšēdal Plur. tšēle, und endlich den „Taucher", Podiceps minor, Latham(?) H. dušie, F. tšeigel.

[10] einžin, „das Täubchen", ist bei der ausserordentlichen Liebhaberei der Sonyai für junge Tauben (s. Reisen Th. V. S. 3) von grosser Bedeutung, besonders in Timbuktu.

[11] tšerë bi eigentlich „der schwarze, schwarzgraue Vogel". — tultel lautet im Dialekt von A'gades taral-tarel.

[12] tšerë hēre, tšerë bōra. Die Sonyai unterscheiden diese beiden Geierarten nur durch den Beisatz von „grau" und „weiss". Auffallend ist es allerdings, wenn die Sonyai wirklich den Geier als „den grauen Vogel" anerkennen, da doch, ganz abgesehen vom Strausse, der im mittleren Niger so zahlreich vertretene Pelikan ihn an Grösse übertrifft.

[13] sohhirià bezeichnet jedenfalls einen Vogel, der, wenn mit den durch die gegenüberstehenden Namen der anderen Sprachen bezeichneten nicht ganz identisch, so doch ihnen sehr verwandt ist.

[14] tōhul' adë, „die rothe (adë) Taube".

[15] gēdogata scheint ein eigenthümlich nationaler Name zu sein.

[16] šili. Barth oder der Herausgeber seiner Papiere hat hier eine Umstellung und Verwirrung verschiedener Ausdrücke veranlasst, wodurch adeh für „Strauss" in seiner Liste erscheint. Es muss aber l. c. S. 447 folgendermassen heissen „birds", kasby; „ostrich", elyl; „locust", adeh.

Sonyai.	Lógone.	Wándalá.	Bágrimma.	Mába.
nisiim[10]	. . . . . .	. . . . . .	. . . . . .	. . . . . .
. . . .	gūgu	tákala	der-re . . . / der bóteram	ermil
. . . .	mágralē . . .	tókul' sēö[14] .	kóya	. . . . . .
tšerö bī[11]	zanan	džabra	tandža	lan
taitai	akclē	= dšīroë	bū	alū[16]
taitai hidža . . .	. . . . . .	. . . . . .	. . . . . .	. . . . . .
tšerö bēre[12] . .	mario	silla	mario	arak
tšerö kōre . . .	. . . . . .	. . . . . .	. . . . . .	. . . . . .
. . . .	ŋgāk	zelke	gā	águrúk
. . . .			. . . . . .	
. . . .	agō	gédegata[15] .	akoī	
tekkiriā[13]	. . . . . .	. . . . . .	. . . . . .	. . . . . .

[1] ógigi: Koelle considers this term as designating any kind of pigeon, in general, and merely distinguishes the wild pigeon by adding málem (ógigi málem), which, however, I have never heard, in opposition to boletar. Besides, he distinguishes the ógigi gotā as a peculiar large variety of the wild pigeon, and ógigi buliam as a variety of white colour.
[2] kulye is wanting in Koelle; instead of kāji he writes kātši.
[3] kergike: Koelle kęrgágę. The corresponding Tédā-form kēdü evidently is by far more original.
[4] kógo: Koelle kógę, just as instead of ngigu he writes ŋgágę.
[5] dšidšim-agō seems to be wanting in Koelle; agō is evidently a slightly changed form of the Hausa akō; but I do not know, what dšidšim may mean. The parrot, however, is not at all indigenous in Bornu, and even the Hausa-people have made its acquaintance only through the inhabitants of the regions bordering on them towards the South.
[6] kāsa n Yariba, „the fowl of Yóruba", which country by the Hausawa is called Yáriba, by Schön is wrongly explained as meaning „duck".
[7] Simmone is Schön's tahimnia.
[8] benkóho: in this note I am going to mention the Hausa- and Fulfúlde-names of some other kinds of birds, which I have not had occasion to learn in the other languages: „bat", Vespertilio, H. džemāgr, F. džemágēre, S. toirēnai and tefirfir; another „small bird of black and white plumage, with long bill and long tail", called tšallebóe in H., and kiyātorel in F.; and another one (Corvopis rufifrons, Le Vaillant?) called in H. ensōme and wilwilde in F.
[9] kamus: I here mention the names of some other waterbirds in Hausa and Fulfúlde; „pelican" (K. bōgam?), H. maišiho („master of the bag"), F. džiladšimire plur. džiladšimidži; „Ardea Goliath, Rüppell", H. gamrāke, F. homaréwal plur. homarēdži, S. homāre; then a beautiful bird with azure plumage, H. oorbe, F. tšādel plur. tšóle; and finally the diver (Podiceps minor, Latham?), H. dabío, F. tšelgel.
[10] nisiim is an article of great importance with the Sonyai, especially with the inhabitants of Tímbuktu, the great predilection of whom for young pigeons has been repeatedly mentioned by me in my Travels, especially vol. V, p. 3.
[11] tšerö bī means „black, grayish bird". — taitai is the Kingiríemi-dialect of the Sonyai-language sounds terel-terel.
[12] tšerö bēre, tšerö kōre: the Sonyai distinguish these two totally different species of birds of prey simply by adding the adjectives „big" and „white", although it is remarkable, that they call the vulture simply „large bird", notwithstanding it is excelled in size by several other birds, common of that region, not only the ostrich, but also the pelican.
[13] tekkiriā means a kind of bird, which, if it is not identical with those indicated by the corresponding names in the other languages, is at least nearly related to them.
[14] tókul' sēö means „red dove".
[15] gédegata seems to be a peculiar national name, or may be a composite form.
[16] ālū: Burckhardt, or the editor of his papers, has here misplaced several terms of his list l. c. p. 447, in consequence of which edek appears there as meaning „ostrich". But the terms have to be arranged in the following manner: „birds", kooby; „ostrich", alyl; „locust", edek.

Deutsch und Englisch.	Kanuri.	Tédā.	Hausa.	Fulfúlde.
Fliege — *fly*	kigī	{ aosín S. . . / sidëno N. . . }	kuše Plur. kudā	būbu Plur. būbi
Biene — *bee*	kāli kemágen-bē[1]	{ ēbibī (?) S. . . / sidēnoédžimfi N. }	kudā n súmmua[4]	ñākel Plur. ñāke
Mücke — *gnat*	kántanā . .	intēki	sábberō . . .	{ boūgu Pl. bōdi / tšūñ . . . }
Heuschrecke — *locust* .	kāli[2]	gamāru . . .	farā[5]	babátta Pl. ba-hátti
kleine Ameise — *ant* . .	šīšegun[3] . .	. . . . . .[10]	turúrua . . .	horreudólde[7] Pl. korreudónde
kleine rothe Ameise — *small-sized red ant*	kíla-kíla . .	waršē . . .	kōatšī . . .	metellu Plur. me-telli
grosse schwarze Ameise mit grossen Vorrathskammern — *large black ant, building ample store-rooms*	kingíbbu . .	{ mēlo- S. . . / edžíugeri . . }	tšírnāka . . . }	ñuñu Plur. ñūdi[8]
andere Art grosser Ameise — *another kind of large ant*	kamāri . . .	. . . . . .	túma da gaie[6] }	

[1] kāli (Koelle kālī) kemágen-bē heisst wörtlich „das Insekt des Honigs", und hat kāli ursprünglich eine ganz allgemeine Bedeutung, aber das Wort hat sich fast nur in Beziehung auf die Biene erhalten, als das Insekt, das etwas Eigenthümliches erzeugt, den Honig. Dagegen sind die anderen Zusammensetzungen von kāli mit den Gegenständen, worin das Insekt lebt, wie kāli argám-bē, „das Insekt des Hirses", kāli ŋgálo-bē, „das Insekt der Bohne", nicht so allgemein gebräuchlich, sondern wird dafür das bezügliche Eigenwort gebraucht. Nur wiederum, wo irgend eine Art Insekt mit einem anderen Gegenstand unter gewissem Gesichtspunkte verglichen wird, wie mit dem Kameel, seiner langen Beine halber, oder mit dem Málle m, dem bescheidenen Gelehrten jener Gegenden, da hat sich wieder diese Ausdrucksweise ihres pikanten Charakters halber im volksthümlichen Sprachgebrauch erhalten. So gibt es für Schmetterling wirklich keinen anderen Namen als kāli mállem, auf H. letáfi mállem mit einem doppelten Vergleich, mit dem Gelehrten sowohl, wie mit seinem Buche, indem die lebhaften Hausua die Flügel des Schmetterlings mit einem Buche, den gesammten Habitus des Thieres mit einem armen Gelehrten verglichen haben. kántanā accentuirt Koelle kántena.

[2] kāli. Koelle gibt folgende 7 verschiedene Arten von Heuschrecken an, die mir nicht bekannt wurden, und die ich daher der Kontrolle zukünftiger Forscher empfehle: kāli kaman oder kamaewe; k. kāli kēcderma, „grüngestreifte Heuschrecken", die besonders auf Baumwollstauden (kánder) leben; k. difū, „dunkelfarbige Heuschrecken"; k. lagará oder lagere, „eine grosse Art bunter Heuschrecken"; k. ságundā oder sugúndórám, „eine ähnliche Art, ausgezeichnet durch Schönheit der Farben"; k. kāli ságume, „eine Art grüner Heuschrecken", und endlich die k. kazáálma, „eine Art weisser Heuschrecken", die auf dem kazáli-Baume leben sollen. Einige dieser Namen kommen mir sehr zweifelhaft vor; die Heuschrecken verdienen aber freilich sowohl ihrer verheerenden Eigenschaften, als auch besonders ihrer Bedeutsamkeit als Nahrungsartikel halber, grosse Aufmerksamkeit und haben solche bei den Eingeborenen natürlicher Weise in vollem Maasse angeregt. — „Grille, Heimchen" gibt Koelle mit ŋgikī.

[3] šīšegun nicht ganz sicher, fehlt bei Koelle; kingíbbu schreibt er kəŋgə́fū und kəŋgə́fū; kamāri fehlt bei ihm.

[4] kudā n súmmua ist die Pluralform, aber den Singular kuše n súmmua habe ich nie gehört.

[5] farā. Ich habe keinen anderen Ausdruck gehört, Schön gibt hobé fm. babánia, und das wird durch den entsprechenden Fulfulde-Ausdruck, der davon möglicher Weise abgeleitet, anscheinend bestätigt. — kōatšī ist das kiuchi in Koelle's Polyglotta.

[6] túma da gaie, wörtlich „springe und schreie", ein sehr phantasiereicher Name für ein Insekt mit so schmerzhaftem Biss. — tšírnāka der Name hängt wol sicherlich zusammen mit dem Laute tšer, tšir, der so ziemlich allen Ameisen gemein ist. Die von den Kanúri eben daher tšermo genannte Gattung gehört zu den Erdameisen. Schön schreibt fälschlich tšínaka und leitet es von tšī, „essen" ab. Koelle in seiner Polyglotta gibt den Namen in zwei leicht verschiedenen Formen für zwei ganz verschiedene Thiere, als dgirnégo im Dialekt von Kátsena für „Schmetterling", und als cernāko im Dialekt von Kano für „Wespe".

[7] horreudólde. Reichardt hórudoll.

[8] ñuñu Plur. ñūdi. Die Fulbe Adamaua's haben noch einen anderen Ausdruck, dšotti hāli; der gilt aber als Provinzialismus und nicht als der Fulfulde-Sprache eigentlich angehörig.

[9] tšoi gáreg-en ima. ima heisst „Honig"; gáreg-en ist Participialform, s. Einleitung S. CCXL, c).

[10] kiŋ tšdāī. Wir haben hier ein Beispiel der Abwandlung des n in Verbindungen, kin, kiŋ.

[11] kin-ntšō. ntšō heisst wirklich „roth", aber für „schwarz" allein habe ich unter den Eigenschaftswörtern iii, nicht ino, aber dennoch kann kin-ino richtig sein für die schwarze Ameise, indem die Bezeichnung von einer anderen Eigenschaft hergenommen ist.

Sonyai.	Lógoné.	Wándalá.	Bágrimma.	Mába.
hámmeni Plur. ham-ménid	zü	ndžanga . .	kin	añín
yū hámmeni . . / yō nya . . .	matian yīman (éman)	tšoi géreg-en ama[9]	kiñg tédži[10] .	kemín
taráma	háladše	úgdžindžä . .	ēlu	ágelák
tangam-bāra . .	imbillum . . .	ívol	. . . . . .	alák
. . . . . .	limmadš . . .	arvánuā . .	béhemā . . .	gúrgurik
in-tánda . . .	meõé 'lhanzä . .	gódepō . . .	kíe-atšē[11] . .	gúrguri' kúkiák
in-kóndo . . .	márodā . . .	wurtša . . .	kíe-ino . . .	gúrgurik lylliók
	méše-vā . . .	tšédžaklē . .	túturu . . .	oidúk

[1] hûli (Koelle hêli) homágen-hé means verbally „the insect of the honey", hûli having quite a general meaning. Nevertheless, the term is not in frequent use, except in this case, where the produce of the insect's activity, the honey, characterizes it sufficiently, and better, than any other description could do, while, as for the other cases, where the name hûli has been joined to the names of those things wherein the insect lives, such as hûli orgûm-hé, „the insect of the millet", hûli ngálo-hé, „the insect of the bran", this general term is rather rarely used, a proper name being preferred. But, as for such cases, where some kind of insect is compared with another object from a certain point of view, as f. i. with the camel, on account of its long legs, or with the mállem, the unpretending and humble teacher of those regions, in such cases these phrases have been preserved on account of their popular character; thus, there is scarcely any other term now used by the inhabitants of Bornu Proper and Kánem with regard to the butterfly, except hûli mállem, H. letáfi mállem, the latter from a double point of comparison, the Hausa-people comparing the wings of the butterfly with a book, letáfi, on account of the manner, in which they fold up; we might, therefore, best render this popular term by the phrase „the professor with his book". Instead of hóntenā Koelle writes kuntána.

[2] kéfi: Koelle mentions the following seven varieties of locusts, with which I did not become acquainted, and therefore recommend their names to the control of future travellers: kéfi, or as he spells kéfi kámen or kámenwe; k. kéli (i. e. keri) kéndenma, „green cotton locusts"; k. difū, „dark coloured locusts" (this name being more than suspicious to me; diffa means „the darkness"); k. legérā or legeré, „a large kind of speckled locusts"; k. ségundé or ségundérem, „a large kind of beautifully speckled locusts"; k. kéli ségema, „green locusts living in the grass called ségu" (the two latter varieties seeming to me to be identical), and finally the k. kasálima, „white locusts", which feed on the leaves of the kasági-tree. The locusts, indeed, are worth all the attention of explorers, not only on account of their destructive habits, but also from the circumstance, that they form a considerable portion of the life-stock of the inhabitants. — I have mention, that Koelle gives ngiki for „cricket", which is wanting in my list.

[3] Jiñegan, as well homári, is wanting in Koelle; instead of kiágibbo he writes kéágófū and kaágífū.

[4] hadá a ségmma is the plural-form, but the singular kaši a sémmua I have not once heard.

[5] fará: I have never heard another Hausa-term, although what Schön gives, hebé fm. hahénia seems to receive some confirmation from the corresponding Fulfúlde-term, which may thence be derived. — kéeiši is the kinshi of Koelle.

[6] tûme do gela means verbally „jump and cry", a very appropriate and witty name for an insect, the bite of which is very painful indeed. — tširnoka: the name appears to be derived from the second tšar, tšil, common to almost all kinds of ants; the Kanúri-term tšer-me also, designating a peculiar kind of termites, belongs thither. Schön writes tšinaha, and derives the name from tši, „eat", while Koelle in his Polyglotta gives the same term in two slightly different forms for two totally different kinds of insects, first as dzirnége, in the dialect of Katsena, for „butterfly", and secondly as aeraiko, in the dialect of Kano, as meaning „wasp"; the kind, however, called tšer-me by the Kanúri, as stated before, belongs to the termites.

[7] barreadéide: Reichardt héyndull.

[8] boho plur. bódi: the Fúlbe settled in Fúmbina have still another name for this kind of ants, viz déetti bélé, but this seems to be a mere provincialism, and not to belong to the pure Fulfúlde-language.

[9] tšoi géreg-en áma: áma means „honey"; géreg-en is the participial form of the active voice, see Introductory Remarks p. CCXLI, e).

[10] kiñg tédži: we have here an instance of the change of the simple n, when brought into connection with other words.

[11] kie-atšē: atšē means „red", but as for kie-ino designating a kind of black ant, I have to remark, that for „black" in my list of adjectives I have ili, and not ino; nevertheless kie-ino may be right.

Deutsch und Englisch.	Kanúri.	Tédā.	Hausa.	Fulfúlde.
wandernde Ameisen — travelling ants	. . . . . .	. . . . . .	korkása [8] . .	korkādīe . . / malla-mallēri
Erdameise — termite; termes fatalis, termes destructor	kánām . . .	tšonō . . .	garā	mōyo Plur. mōyi
Varietät besonders grosser Ameisen — variety of very large termites	kánām gálgelma [1]	. . . . . .	. . . . . .	. . . . . .
Termitenhügel — ant-hill	gotkum [2] . .	. . . . . .	sūri [9] . . .	wālde Plur. bādi
Wurm — worm	kēntšī [3] . . .	kolē S. . . / karmi N. . .	sūtsa . . .	gillíngu, gilingu Plur. gilye
Mistkäfer — dung-beetle .	talkórkoriā .	ábebō S. . . / totō N. . .	buzūsu [10] . .	hosure Pl. kovōi
Floh — flea	tirgāfo [4] . .	[7]	kolkótta . .	teńgu Plur. tendi
Laus — louse	kangúsu [5] . .	masko . . .	komā . . .	damme . . / pilpil . . . / komādīe . .
Wanze — bug	bérmede [6] . .	. . . . . .	kedī . . . / kazinaemi [11] .	kazūdāl . . / burúmmudī .
Kameellaus — camel-louse	kāri	medāso . . / malāsu . .	. . . . . .	. . . . . .
Pferdeungeziefer — vermin infesting the horse	. . . . . .	kirke . . .	kaska . . .	kōtu Plur. kōti

[1] kánām gálgelma. Diese verwandeln sich am Ende der Regenzeit und werden zu „beflügelten Ameisen", auf K. kánām dendeā. Koelle erwähnt ausserdem noch als besonders unterschiedene Varietäten kánām burei, „die kleinen weissen Termiten" und kánām leiebbē, „rothe Termiten", die besonders die Leichen verzehren. Der letzte Name kann wol kaum richtig sein, da leire d. i. láhira eigentlich der Tag des Gerichtes, nie aber das Grab oder die Leiche heisst; s. oben S. 144.

[2] gotkum fehlt bei Koelle und ist mir auffallend.

[3] kēntšī, vielleicht von kēngia, „neben fort, entfernt", scheint ebenfalls dort zu fehlen, ebenso talkórkoriā.

[4] tirgāfo. Koelle tirgafū. Man nahm früher an, dass Flöhe gar nicht über den nördlichen Theil von Fesān südlich hinausgingen, aber ich habe diesen Irrthum berichtigt. Im Lande der Tédā allerdings scheinen sie fast ganz zu fehlen, woher es kommt, dass ich in der Sprache dafür auch keinen besonderen Namen erfahren habe, und sie sind auch höchst wahrscheinlich nach Bornu nur von den Arabern eingeschleppt worden.

[5] kangúsu. Koelle kęngúsų.

[6] bérmede. Koelle bęrmędę.

[7] S. Note 4 über das Fehlen der Flöhe im Wüstengebiet der Tédā.

[8] korkása ist allem Anscheine nach eine blosse volksthümliche Abkürzung des gewöhnlicheren Ausdruckes kaúre-kása, obgleich ich in einigen Gegenden die letztere als besondere Gattung unterscheiden hörte, wo dann der Fulfúlde-Name [illegible] mir als ihnen entsprechend angegeben wurde.

[9] sūri hat Schön offenbar missverstanden, indem er es für Holztermiten, also gleichbedeutend mit garā erklärt. Freilich gibt er in seiner neuen Grammatik (1862) einen ganz anderen, aber höchst zweifelhaften Namen für Erdameisen, nämlich sárie n Illuri, wo Illuri wol gleich meinem sūri ist.

[10] buzūsu. Ich führe hier noch einen allgemeineren Ausdruck burgāngume an, der dem Begriffe „Käfer" zu entsprechen scheint. Auf Fulfúlde wurde mir diesen durch gilga mouga wiedergegeben, aber ich möchte die genaue Gleichstellung der beiden Ausdrücke bezweifeln; vielleicht heisst das letztere nur „grosse Würmer".

[11] kazinaemi scheint mir einen merkwürdigen Anklang an das Kanúri-Wort kahidhedi zu haben, „Wohlgeruch", womit auch eben die Wanzen hier zu Lande besonders bezeichnet werden, indem merkwürdiger Weise der Geruch der Wanze als überaus wohlriechend angesehen wird.

[12] dālī ekomī etc. Diese sind besondere Varietäten, ebenso wie die drei entsprechenden Namen in der Móba-Sprache.

[13] mala n [illegible] wahrscheinlich „Leucht des Viehes", weil die Lebens-Thätigkeit des Mistkäfers ganz an den Viehdünger gebunden scheint; für „Vieh" habe ich sonst allerdings die Form lha.

Sońyai.	Lógoné.	Wándalá.	Bágrimma.	Mába.
. . . . . .	. . . . . .	. . . . . .	. . . . . .	. . . . . .
dusso	dāli	tér-ewē . . .	ŏö	annugŏók.
. . . . . .	dāli ekemī [12] . dāli géve-nī . .		. . . . .	síosanāt annugŏók kokiák annugŏók kŏsok
kŏmo	. . . . . .	. . . . . .	dilba . . .	óngudík
nōni	duló-adū . . .	gébekē . . .	kiddže . . .	ton
. . . . . .	mata n ebī [13] . .	subaegúrima .	kúmmangē .	. . . . .
genni	kúfkufū	tšotā-úkulā .	bŭbim . . .	til
nōni(?)	ingírsa	tšētāa . . .	ingírša . . .	ménelék
. . . . . .	tuggúlatsē . . .	šedaie . . .	bóborō . . .	dárderík
. . . . . .	búrgomē n kúrgumma	džāgo . . .	meŏge . . .	gíngerík
kandža	. . . . . .	. . . . . .	. . . . . .	

1 kánām gálgelma: These kind of termites at the end of the rainy season change their habit, and become winged, in which state they are called in Kanúri kánām kedádeū. Koelle, besides this name, mentions as peculiar varieties of termites, the kánām karai of small size and white colour, and another one, which he calls kánām leirábe, „a kind of red termites, fond of consuming dead bodies in the grave (leira)". But lairo i. q. lábira, as stated p. 144, rather meaning „the day of judgement, the next world", and never meaning „dead body", that term can scarcely be right.

2 galkam is wanting in Koelle, and I myself am not quite sure of its being correct.

3 kōatšī, perhaps from kádgin, „I remove, take away", seems likewise to be wanting in Koelle, as well as teikárkeriā.

4 tirgófa: Koelle térgafū. In former times people supposed, that there were no fleas H. of the Northern districts of Fezzán, but I have had the opportunity of correcting this error. No doubt, they may be there imported by the Arabs, while in the desert country of the Tédā they seem, indeed, to be wanting and this is the reason, why the Tédā-language does not seem to have a peculiar name for them.

5 kaŋgáou: Koelle kaŋgąoa.

6 kérmeda: Koelle bįrmáde.

7 See note 4 with regard to the circumstance, that fleas are wanting in the country of the Tédā.

8 korkāso, according to all appearance, is a mere popular abbreviation of the common term kuára-kaáse, although in some districts I heard the latter to be distinguished from the former as a variety of its own, even the Fulfúlde-term lomdam hēli being given me as corresponding to the latter especially and exclusively.

9 sūrì evidently has been misunderstood by Rev. Schön, who explains it as being identical with gorá, the common term for wood-termites. But in the second edition of his grammar, recently published (1862), he gives quite a different term for termites, viz sária n Eiári, where Eiárì seems to correspond to my sūrì.

10 bashea: I here give another term of a more general import, viz kargángumo, and perhaps indicating all kinds of beetle, although the Fulfúlde-term gilga mańgo, which I learned as corresponding to the former, would seem to have the meaning of something like „big worms".

11 kasinceml seems to me to have a great similarity, or at least analogy in form and composition, to the Kanúri-term kebidbedi, meaning properly „perfume, fragrance", and which notion the Kanúri-people particularly entertain of the smell of the bugs, much in opposition to our own feeling.

10 dāli ekemi: these, no doubt, are peculiar varieties of the insect, as well as the corresponding term in the Mába-language; as for the form géve-nī, compare edve-nī p. 193, note 12.

11 mata n ebī, most probably, means „insect of the cattle", although for „cattle" I have lba, the life and activity of the beetle being perfectly dependent on the dung of cattle. The same is the case with B. kummange (meŏge, „ox").

Deutsch und Englisch.	Kanúri.	Tédã.	Hausa.	Fulfúlde.
Schweif, Schwanz — *tail*	kádui [1] . . / ngáberè [1] . .	bōde	wūtsia . . .	bohórrde . . / witāo [12] . .
Horn — *horn*	kángadī [2] . .	yaya	kafō Pl. kafōni	luel Plur. lae / walādu Pl. galādi
Fuss, Huf, Klaue — *foot, hoof, claw*	kólo-ram [3] . .	tárkonā . . .	kófatō . . .	kolaēre Pl. koltēe / kóngoli? . .
Fusspur — *foot-step, trace*	šī	šō-fame . . .	kōfa n taki [11]	kósséngel . . / balte . . .
Höcker (Kameel-) — *hump (of camel)*	súgure [4] . . .	gūsu	. . . . .	. . . . .
Mähne — *mane*	demsāri [5] . . .	dīya	gezā	sáhaúgo . . / salekōbe Plur. salekōdži
Stirnhaar bei Pferden — *front-hair of horses*	. . . . .	. . . . .	namza . . .	yáhire . . .
Euter — *udder*	tiggam [6] . . .	tuggum . . .	nōno(n sánia	yendu Pl. yendi
Brustwarze, Zitze — *teat, dug*	tillo [7]		. . . . .	. . . . .
Augenkrankheit des Pferdes — *sore eyes of horse*	tpnúngudū [8] .	semmoke-džāni [10]	dōki) (dawú-nna sūna da t-lo	
Katarrh (des Pferdes) — *catarrh (of horse)*	keláterō [9] . .		. . . . .	
Räude (von Kameel, Pferd) — *scab (of camel, horse)*	kumkun . . .		. . . . .	

[1] kádui bedeutet den Schweif, wie vom Pferd, Esel, Giraffe; ngáberē den Schwanz, wie beim Kameel, Rind. Das letztere Wort, wol von ngáfe, „der Rücken" abgeleitet, fehlt bei Koelle. Die Fulbe aber, obgleich sie zwei verschiedene Ausdrücke besitzen, gebrauchen demnach bohórde sowohl vom Pferd, wie vom Rind.

[2] Statt kángadī accentuirt Koelle kangádi.

[3] kólo-ram. Koelle schreibt kóléram und erklärt es als den Fuss und die Fussspur von Pferden, Eseln und Maulthieren. Obgleich das entsprechende S. kóle zu berücksichtigen, scheint es doch, dass kólo-ram abgeleitet ist von kolo-niskin (eigentlich koló-taram), also bedeutet „das im Boden Gelassene, Zurückgelassene" und wäre dann die Fussspur das Erst- und der Fuss selbst erst das Zweitverstandene. Gegenwärtig aber im alltäglichen Gebrauch ist šī das Gewöhnliche für „Fussspur". pergani („Nagel"), das Koelle ebenfalls in dieser Bedeutung anführt, habe ich so nie gehört.

[4] súgure. Koelle schreibt tsúgurē.

[5] demsāri. Koelle dámsāli.

[6] tiggam. Koelle schreibt dies Wort tégam und gibt ihm die allerweiteste Bedeutung von Frauenbrust und Thiereuter, nur ausgenommen das „Euter von Stuten und Kameelen", wofür er den Ausdruck bobu hat, das ich selbst jedoch nie gehört habe.

[7] tillo scheint bei Koelle zu fehlen.

[illegible]	Lógoné.	Wándalá.	Bágrimma.	Mába.
dára (? S. 137) . .	. . . .	áktuvé . . .	gála	ólu
	. . . .	devmá . . .	kadžemmómo (?)	kemfk
	kábu(n θa . . .	θirbá . . .	kólo	delúl
	ayá so wáteu	será	dáb-laka . .	dšá
	zarká	abbadžógené .	gála (lúkumá-na)	ógoók (torrém-buaáng)
. . . .	kótal (al bóakóán)	patsa . . .	maiga . . .	téñyé sogúl
. . . .	. . . .	. . . . . .	. . . . . .	. . . . . .
faffa Pl. ifáffayo	yiwayé	wubé . . .	mbá-mang . .	ngúk
. . . .	kálgiwal [13] . . .	her-θa . . .	. . . . . .	ángoáI
	wurí	awá n itáo bélinsa	dú	hióa (yúlere)
	mágar al bóakóán	kelátero . .	sinda báni etkó-ña [14]	furda
	χaan	indúgulá . .	kúra	džerúb (Arb.)

[1] kádni means a bushy tail, such as that of the horse, ass, giraffe; ágáberé the tail of the camel, and that of the cattle. The latter term, which most probably is derived from ágáfo, „the back", is wanting in Koelle. The Fulfúlde-term bokérde, however, means both sorts of tail, while witšo is used only in the Eastern provinces and, no doubt, is a mere corruption of the corresponding Hausa-term.

[2] káágadí: keágádi with Koelle.

[3] kólo-rom: Koelle writes kálbrám, and explains it not only as the foot, but also as the track of horses, asses and mules. kólo-ram indeed, although as to outward form rather resembling the corresponding Mába-term kólo, is derived, I think, from kole-nichie, „I leave behind", the proper form being kolé-terem and originally meaning „that which has been left behind"; the meaning of „track, footprint", therefore, would be the primary, „foot" the secondary notion, although at present, in the daily use of common life, it has become the common term for „footprint". As for pergéni (firgéni, „nail of finger, toe"), which Koelle also gives with this notion, I have never heard it in this way.

[4] ságare: Koelle teágará.

[5] demsávé: Koelle dámesli.

[6] tiggem: Koelle writes tégem, and attributes to it a very wide meaning, as indicating the breast both of man and beast, with the only exception of the „udder of mares and asses", for which he gives the peculiar term kokó, which, however, I have never heard.

[7] tillo seems to be wanting in Koelle.

[8] tuntágadá is evidently composed of the two words tean or tgan, „sore, ulcer", and ágadá; it is wanting in Koelle.

[9] kelátero is wanting in Koelle; supposed, that it is of true Kanúri origin, which may even doubtful, if we consider the identical term in Wandalá, it may be derived from kéla, „head", as it seems distinctly to express „the running of fluid matters towards the head (kéla)", thence the accusative form ró. — kochou is likewise wanting in Koelle.

[10] semmo ke-dléni, according to all appearance, is a verbal form of speech, meaning „the eye is running".

[11] kófo o tábi means verbally „the door, the opening of the footprint".

[12] witšo, as stated in note 1, appears to be used exclusively by the Fúlbe settled in the former Hausa-provinces, bokérde with the other Fúlbe expressing, as well the bushy tail of the horse, as the bare tail of the cattle, although Rev. Reichardt has another peculiar term as belonging to the Western Fúlbe, viz ladšol.

[13] kálgiwal, almost beyond a doubt, is contracted from kéo, „head", el the particle of conjunction, and yiwayé, „breast, udder".

[14] sinde báni etkóho is a verbal form of speech.

Deutsch und Englisch.	Kanúri.	Tēdā.	Hausa.	Fulfúlde.
Flügel — *wing*	fefēto [1] . . / pepēto . . .	hēri S. . . . / kobaī N. . . .	fikafikentsuntsu [9]	lillōal Pl. lillidž
Feder — *feather*	ligtiga . . .	. . . . . .	. . . . . .	. . . . . .
Schnabel — *bill*	tšì ngúdu-bē [2]	. . . . . .	baki n tsuntsu	. . . . . .
Vogelnest — *bird's-nest*	fāto n ngúdu-bē	tšohoríye [6] . .	gida n tsuntsu	sūdu sondu .
Ei — *egg*	gibbel; ngubbel	ńgubbel . . .	kwai	otšōnde . . .
Flosse — *fin*	pepēto bûni-bē	. . . . . .	fikafiko n kīfi	lillīdši lidi [13] .
Gräten, Knochen des Fisches — *fish-bone, bone of the fish*	kardži bûni-bē [3]	. . . . . .	kāya n kīfi [10]	dongal lingo Plur. dongle lidi
Leichnam, Skelett — *dead body, skeleton*	rība [4] . . .	ágafúr . . .	mūšo [11] . . .	tšādum Plur. sādi
Mensch, menschliches Wesen — *man, human being*	kām [5] . . .	ai [7] . . . . / am	mutúm [12] . .	nédo . . . .
Menschen, Leute — *people*	ām	amma [8] . . .	mútane . . .	yimbe . . .

[1] fefēto. Koelle hat pepēto in der Bedeutung von Feder, die wirklich nur ligtiga zukommt, woraus er dann erst die Bedeutung von Flügel weiter entwickelt. Dass pepēto aber nur als „bewegendes Ruderwerk" gefasst ist und nichts mit dem nur auf Vögel anwendbaren Begriffe von Federn zu thun hat, zeigt völlig deutlich seine Anwendung auf die Flossen der Fische. ligtiga hat Koelle in anderer Form, nämlich tèhtigi.

[2] tšì ngúdu-bē, „Mund des Vogels"; fāto n ngúdu-bē, „Haus des Vogels".

[3] kardži bûni-bē. kardži scheint nichts Anderes zu sein als kargi, das kâlligi bei Koelle, so dass wir hier dieselbe Ausdrucksweise haben, wie im Hausa, „die Dornen des Fisches".

[4] rība. Dies riba ist mit dialektischer Abweichung identisch mit Koelle's rífā, beide mit dem Arabischen [illegible] zusammenhangend; denn sein ribā, „Vortheil, Gewinn" ist ein ganz verschiedenes Wort, zu dem wir erst viel später kommen.

[5] kām. Ich theile nicht die Ansicht Koelle's, der meint, dass dieses kām einen nahen Zusammenhang mit dem Namen Cham's „des grossen Vorfahren der Neger" habe und ich bin überzeugt, dass sehr wenige Sprachforscher seine Ansicht theilen werden. Dahingegen bin ich der entschiedenen Ansicht, dass die jetzige Form des Plurals ām das Ursprüngliche ist, verwandt mit dem entsprechenden semitischen Wort, und dass kām (ke-ām) erst die spätere Bezeichnung des einzelnen Individuums ist. Dies wird ganz deutlich durch das entsprechende Tēdā-Wort am, Plur. amma, das dem semitischen ganz nahe rückt. Die von Koelle neben ām angeführte Pluralform kām habe ich nie gehört. Vergl. Einleitung S. XLVII und S. LVIII, N. 1. Bei den kleinen Vokabularien, wo in mehreren Sprachen am für „Mann", ama für „Frau" erscheint, komme ich auf diesen interessanten Punkt zurück. Im Kanem und Yēdi heisst kām, „Frau".

[6] tšohoríye scheint den Namen für „Vogel", yāhorā zu enthalten; s. S. 200, N. 3 am Ende.

[7] ai ist zweifelhaft; es mag alles Lebende bezeichnen. Vergl. S. 156, N. 8.

[8] amma. Merkwürdig ist dazu die Nebenform anna für „Leute, Bewohner von", anna Borno, anna Māba; s. weiter unten, also ähnlich wie Ama-Xōsa u. s. w. bei den sogenannten Kaffernstämmen Süd-Afrika's.

[9] fikafiko. Einen Singular fiffikeh oder fifiko, wie Schön angibt, habe ich nie gehört.

[10] kāya n kīfi, eigentlich „die Fischdornen"; vergl. N. 3.

[11] mūšo. Ein begriffsverwandtes Wort ist gidše, F. sabbinirde.

[12] mutúm hat, wie Schön ganz richtig bemerkt, entschieden die ursprüngliche Bedeutung „Sterblicher". Sehr interessant aber ist es, hiermit das gleichbedeutende und nahe verwandte muntu, umtu der Süd-Afrikanischen Sprachen zu vergleichen.

[13] lillīdši lidi. lidi ist ebenfalls Pluralform, im Singular lingo: „Fisch".

[14] bingu tekō, „eine Feder", während bingā allein die Pluralität der Federn, „den Fittig" bezeichnet.

[15] hillam, wol zusammengezogen aus hille, „Wesen, Geschöpf", ganz in allgemeinster Beziehung auch von Thieren gebraucht, und am, „Mensch" (s. oben N. 5). — ya, „Leute" erscheint in meinen Phrasen; (ein mir zweifelhaftes mea heisst vielleicht „Männer", Plur. von mēnt, „Mann").

[16] rífdi. Die nahe Übereinstimmung des Wándalá mit dem Kanúri in diesem Falle ist eben aus der Arabischen Ableitung zu erklären; s. N. 4.

[17] yimde. Die scheinbar nahe Übereinstimmung dieses Wortes mit dem entsprechenden Fulfúlde-Ausdruck ist bloss zufällig. yimde ist wahrscheinlich Plur. von emda, das jedoch im Singular selten gebraucht wird. Die Endung ne in dāsi-ne gehört nicht zum Worte; Dasselbe gilt ...

[18] kebēi-kolai ist mir in dieser Bedeutung auffallend und scheint mir eher „Vogelbrut" als „Feder" zu heissen.

[19] tang kébel-āng. Seetzen gibt für „Nest", isā, das ist aber wahrscheinlich nichts Anderes, als isa, „Gras", woraus der Vogel sein Nest bereitet. — wámaré hängt unzweifelhaft auf das Genaueste mit am ām-araē, „ich schwimme" zusammen. Einleitung S. CLXVI, h, β).

[20] mālo bedeutet eigentlich Männer, ist aber neben dem gewöhnlicheren kai auch der Ausdruck für „Menschen".

Sónγai.	Lógonē.	Wándalā.	Bágrimma.	Mába.
. . . .	bisγā	dánbakē . .	gīya	kébel-dšō
kiro hambe . .	bisγa tokū [14] . .	ima-ókulā . .	bīyi	kubēl-kolai [18]
. . . .	. . . .	wa-gīye . .	keleñēra . .	kanā
. . . .	wenā šišiā . . .	hā-gīye . .	tšīra	tang kébel-áng [19]
gungūri	. . . .	ϑīya (?) . . .	. . . . . .	. . . . . .
. . . .	mwákka-kī . .	keta kilfai . .	džandža . .	wōmarē
. . . .	yiwe-kī	keke kilfai .	tšungo kindža	kandīyi
. . . .	fádi af	rifāl [16] . . .	gēa . . . . / latis	
bōro	billam [15] . . .	dāil(-na . .	deb	kam, kang / mašik
bórēō	γa	yimde [17] . .	deb-ge . . .	kai / māšo [20]

1 fefōte: Koelle attributes to popēte or fefōte the meaning of „quill, feather" (from which that of wing he supposes to be developed), which by right seems to belong only to the word tigtiga. For, that popēte originally means the instrument, in general, by which animals are moving, without any regard to the feathery nature of wings, is shown sufficiently by the fact of it being applied as well to the fins of fish. The following term tigtiga Koelle has in the form téktigi.

2 tšī nágádu-hā, „mouth of bird"; fóta n nágádu-hó, „dwelling of bird".

3 hardāī būni-bā: hardāi seems to be nothing, but kargi, „thorn", kāligi with Koelle, the proper meaning being „thorns of fish", exactly the same sort of expression, which we have in Hausa.

4 riba with this notion is identical with, and only a dialectical variation of, the lífō of Koelle, both of these forms being probably derived from the Arabic [illegible]; for his ribā with the notion of „gain" is a totally different word. See further [illegible].

5 hām: I am not of the same opinion, as Rev. Koelle, who supposes, that this word hām is intimately connected with the proper name of Khām, „the great ancestor of the Negroes", and I am persuaded, that very few persons, who have pursued linguistical studies, are of his opinion. On the contrary, as stated in the Introductory Remarks p. XLVIII compared with p. LIX, note 1, I am almost sure, that the present form of the plural, via ām, is the original term, intimately connected with the corresponding Semitic word, while hām (ha-ām) the term for the single individual is of later origin. This opinion finds a strong corroboration in the corresponding term am plur. amme of the Tedā-language, as well as in the form am, „man", fm. āma, „woman" in some of the idioms in my Collection of shorter vocabularies, where I shall return to this question. In Kanem and Tīšī hām means „woman". — The plural-form hām which Koelle mentions in Kanūri besides ām, I have never heard.

6 tšoberiye: this term seems to contain the general name for „bird", yáberō; see p. 200, note 8 towards the end.

7 ai is rather doubtful, but may convey the general notion of all living beings. See p. 187, note 8.

8 amma: Here we have to remark the secondary form anna for „people, inhabitants of", as f. i. anna Borno, anna Māba.

9 fikefike: the form fifikeh or fifike given by Schön in the singular number I have never heard.

10 kāya n hifi properly „the thorns of the fish"; see note 3.

11 múše: a term of a similar meaning, but which I cannot define very distinctly, is gidže, P. ŏabbinirdu.

12 mutám, as Rev. Schön justly remarks, originally means „mortal"; and it is of very great interest to compare the identical muto and umtu in several dialects of the great South-African family.

13 ļiiiidāī ļidi: lidi likewise is a plural form of the singular liégo, „fish".

14 bisγa tokū means „one feather", while bisγá means „the feathers", and in consequence „the wing".

15 billam probably is formed by contraction from bille, „creature" of any kind, including even animals, and am, „man, human" (see above note 5); it therefore means exactly „human being". — γa with the meaning „people" occurs among my phrases, and seems to be placed beyond even the slightest doubt, while with regard to another form mea, I doubt, whether it be not rather the plural of méni, „man".

16 rifál: the close resemblance of the Kanūri- and Wándalā-languages in this instance is to be explained by means of the Arabic; see note 4.

17 yimde: the close resemblance of this word with the corresponding one in Fulfūlde, I am sure, is merely accidental, yimde most probably being the plural number of emde, which, however, appears rather obsolete. As for dāil-na, the na does not belong to the root; Denham has the form gila.

18 kebél-kolai is remarkable, and may rather mean „young of bird", than something like „feather".

19 tang kébel-áng: Seetzen gives tan with the meaning „bird's-nest", but probably that is nothing else but tán, meaning „grass, herbage", whereas the nest is prepared. — The following term wōmarē, beyond a doubt, has been derived from ōm-orrō, „I am swimming"; see Introductory Remarks p. CCLVII, h, β).

20 māšo is the proper term for „men", but is also used for „people" instead of the usual kai, the plural of kāng, „person".

Deutsch und Englisch.	Kanúri.	Tēda.	Hausa.	Fulfúlde.
Mann, Gatte — *man, husband*	kóa Pl. kóawa [1]	omri [6] . . .	meĭl Pl. máza [7]	gorko Pl. wor-be
Frau, Gattin — *woman, spouse*	kāmo Pl. kámüa [2]	{ ádi Pl. ádiyā { ádibi Pl. ádibā	matše Pl. máta [8]	débo Pl. raube
Vater — *father*	ába Pl. ábawa	{ ába . . . . { aebē Pl. aemai	bāba	bāba [11] . . .
alter Mann — *old man* .	kiári [3] . . .	bógedī; búgetī	. . . . .	. . . . .
Mutter — *mother* . . .	yā	{ aiya . . . { de; dā . .	wā	{ dāda . . . { inna [12] . . .
alte Frau — *old woman* .	kumúrŏu . .	{ atše . . . { aĭi	. . . . .	. . . . .
Grossvater — *grand-father*	kagá [4] . . .	dizzu . . .	kakā ná-meĭl	mama gorko .
meine Grosseltern, Vorfahren — *my ancestors*	kagáwa-(uī .	dizzu-dizzūle .	kaká-(nī) máza [9]	mamirābe worbe
Grossmutter — *grand-mother*	kagá (kāmo .	kagā	kakā ná-matše	mama dēbo .
die Sippen, Sippschaft, Familie — *kindred, family, domestics*	ayāli (Arb.) [5] .	. . . . . .	{ mútane n gida { eyāli . . . { deúgi [10] . .	{ yalúdĭam . . { mardi . . . { leñul . . . .

[1] kóa. Es bieten sich hier mehrere Verwandtschaften, so das gleichbedeutende kwe im Dalla, während koá im Fūr „Menschen" heisst. Es zeigt übrigens die Robheit der Familienverhältnisse unter diesen Völkern, dass sie kein Wort für Gatte und Gattin haben, als die allgemeinen Geschlechtsnamen, obgleich auch wir gewöhnlich nur die allgemeinen Ausdrücke Mann und Frau auf die ehelichen Verhältnisse anwenden. So sagt eine Frau im Kanúri nur kóa-nī, „mein Mann". Ein verheiratheter Mann heisst kóa kāmū-a; eine verheirathete Frau kāmo kóa-na. Nur die Fúlbe, die überhaupt höchst eigenthümliche und interessante Familienverhältnisse haben, besitzen auch ein besonderes Wort für „Gatte", tīngágūre und für „Gattin", ewīldo, offenbar mit aūto, eūde, „Haus" zusammenhängend, obgleich auch hier für Ehefrau nur der allgemeine Ausdruck débo gebraucht wird. So eine „freie Ehefrau", H. matše diya, F. dimo débo Plur. rimbe raube; eine „unfreie Ehefrau", H. baiya matše, F. kordo débo Plur. horbe raube, im Sokyal mit dem besonderen Ausdruck hoāgo bezeichnet. — Die Kanúri haben aber ein besonderes Wort für „Mitweib", kōmi.

[2] kāmo, Koelle kāmū, ist die einfache Femininform zu kóa; Koelle führt davon Gr. §. 38 noch eine besondere Pluralform āmūa und āmwa an, die sich also der S. 206, N. 5, als in verwandten Sprachen vorkommend, erwähnten Formen ama, „Frau" anschliessen. — Ich führe hier das gleichbedeutende kamore im Dār (nach Petherick) an.

[3] kiári. Koelle schreibt keári; für kumúrŏu gibt er drei verschiedene Formen an, kəmérəó, kəmérəo und kəmúrəó.

[4] kagá. Koelle accentuirt kāgā.

[5] ayāli ist dasselbe, was Koelle's abgekürzte Form yal, über dessen umfassende Bedeutung als „Familie, Sippe, Hausgenossen, Gesinde" und endlich „Stamm, Nation" er eine längere richtige Erläuterung giebt.

[6] omri ist das embri Hodgson's, der ausserdem noch ein sehr zweifelhaftes embiador für „Ehegatte" (husband) hat. — Anstatt aebē, „Vater" habe ich auch dāchē.

[7] meĭl. Schön schrieb mitshe (mĭtše) und mīni, indem er auch in diesem Wort den rechten Laut nicht erfasst hat. Das ursprünglich bloss adjektivische na-meĭl wird gleichfalls häufig substantivisch gebraucht.

[8] matše. Ich führe hier das identische matša im Gonga an, Wandala mĭdeta. Ich will hier auch noch den Ausdruck für „junges Eheweib" hinzufügen, H. matše kārama, F. dēl tākotšel und „vor Kurzem vermähltes Weib", H. sābua amrē, F. amariādāo heseo (wenigstens in Sókoto, offenbar aber nur abgeleitet vom Hausa-Wort amariā, eigentlich „Braut"), H. (zum wenigsten in Tombuktu, wo der junge Ehemann den Beinamen Sultān führt) Sultān wal.

[9] kaká-(nī), ebenso bei dem andern kakā für „Grossmutter", „meine Grossmütter", H. kakā-nī máta, F. mamirābe raube. Dass das kakā im Plural nicht abgewandelt wird, ist allerdings auffallend, ich habe aber die von Schön in seiner neuen Grammatik angegebene Pluralform kākənī nie gehört und halte sie für unrichtig.

[10] deúgi. Dieser Ausdruck bezeichnet dann auch die Stammverwandtschaft, den gesammten Stamm, so H. deúgi n mútane, F. lenyílo yimbe; die Sokyal aber haben für diese Verhältnisse den Arabischen Ausdruck el kabīle aufgenommen.

[11] bāba. Ich will hier den mit der eigenthümlichen Verwandtschaftsform erāo, Einleitung S. CXXXVIII, l) vgl. S. CXL (a Plur. erābe) und S. CXLVI (e Plur. erābe), gebildeten Ausdruck anführen, den die Fulfúlde-Sprache für „die Verwandten von väterlicher Seite, die Oheime" hat, bāberābe; im Hausa ist diese Verwandtschafts-Verhältniss anders gefasst und man sagt īayē mana; wenigstens entspricht dieses dem Fulfúlde-Ausdruck in gewisser Beziehung.

[12] inna. „Tante", F. inna-rābe, H. īayē máta. Zu īayē (von H. al!) vergl. Einleitung S. CXCVI, N. 2.

[13] wal. Raffenel giebt im Azawa (ähnlich wande mit der Bedeutung „Gattin, épouse". S. Einleitung S. CLXXXVI, a).

[14] kaga. Diese Übereinstimmung zwischen Sokyal und Kanúri in diesem Falle ist höchst auffallend und findet wol ihre Erklärung nur durch die Vermittelung des Hausa.

[15] ēmdāngē ist sehr interessant, da es im Wandalā ein ursprünglich vorhandenes am für „Mensch", im Amharisch am an in den anderen Sprachen, zu beweisen scheint; denn es kann kaum zweifelhaft sein, dass dāngē nichts ist als dāchē, „gross, alt". — Statt āma, „Mutter" hat Denham mama, ganz wie er statt meines ēdda, „Vater", dada hat.

[16] mbà, „Vater" (daher mbāgeiāk i. e. mbà kolāh), mìà, „Mutter" (daher mìāgelāk i. e. mìà kolāh), mag, „Bruder", mir, „Schwester". Über diese Formen, so wie die entsprechenden bei Burckhardt s. Einleitung S. CCVI, 8, c) vgl. mit S. CCXXVIII. In der S. CCXII, e) aufgeführten Phrase habe ich selbst tna für „Vater".

Sonyai.	Lógoné.	Wándalá.	Bágrimma.	Mába.
har	méni	wurā	ngába . . .	maźik Pl. mášo
wai Pl. waidīo [12]	genóm	mokua . . .	nē Pl. nē-ge .	mušóng Pl. mušō
bāba	bā	edda	bāba	{ muā [16] / ba
. . . .	gúχ-u-bā . . .	úmdžugē [15] . .	gāda	kam kolák
nya	mas	ōma	kuō	miā
. . . .	guχ billom . .	úmdžugē mokaa	mābi	mušóng kolák
kaga [14]	dīya	ég-gi	kakī	múngulák
kága-yō	. . . . . .	. . . . . .	. . . . . .	múnguldšā
kaga wai . . .	dīya (genóm . .	ég-gi	kakī	miūgelák
kille	. . . . . .	. . . . . .	. . . . . .	

[1] hōe exhibits several points of contact with other languages, as f. i. the identical hwa in Dalla, and hoá in Fūr, meaning „people". It shows the barbarous character of family ties among these people, that they have scarcely any other term for husband and spouse, but the general terms indicating man and woman, although it is true, that even civilized nations in common life are only to apply the general terms of man and wife to the relations of husband and spouse. Thus a Kanúri-woman says kōa-ni, „my man"; „a married woman" is called kāmo kōa-ne; „a married man", kōa kāmá-e. Only the Fúlbe, with whom family relations altogether bear a very remarkable and interesting character, possess a peculiar term for „husband", viz. iémégūre, and for „spouse", entúdo, probably derived from sūdo or súdu, „the house"; but even with this tribe débo is used, in general, when „spouse" is meant. Thus „a spouse of free origin", in H. matše díyo, in F. is called dimo débo, plur. rimbe reube; „a spouse of slave origin", H. baiya matše, F. horde débo, plur. horbe reube, in S. kaga. — The Kanúri have a peculiar term kōmi for „fellow-wife".

[2] kāmo, is the simple feminine form of kām. Koelle has kāmū, and in his grammar § 28 as another plural-form he mentions āmko and āmwo, which seems to be derived from a form ame, „woman" mentioned above p. 203, note 5.

[3] hīārī: Koelle kēri, and instead of kamárin he mentions three different forms kamérsō, kamérsō and komérsō.

[4] kaga: Koelle writes kāgā.

[5] ngāli is identical with Koelle's yai, to which word he makes some very just remark with regard to the wide range of its meaning, so as to signify „house, family (including servants and slaves), relationship, and even tribe or nation".

[6] amrī is the ambri of Hodgson, who has besides a peculiar, but very doubtful, term ambinder with the notion „husband". — Besides the form aobō, „father", I have also dābā.

[7] moli: Schön did not catch the right sound of this word, while writing mitaba (mitšo) and miel. ná-molī also, which originally was nothing but the form for the adjective, often is used as a substantive.

[8] matše: I have adduce the identical mutše in Gadge, mišoto in Wanika, and I have also add the term for „young spouse", H. matše kárama, F. dēi tēhotāni, as well as for „a recently married woman", H. sabuo amrō, F. amarīādōo haaen (at least thus used in Sókoto, although it has evidently been derived from the Hausa-term amaria, meaning „bride"), S. Sultān wai, at least in Timbúktu, where the young husband bears the peculiar title Soltān.

[9] kaká-(ni): It is remarkable, that kaká is not changed in the plural-number; thus „my grandmothers", H. kaká-ni maia, F. mamirābe reube. At least, I have never heard plur. kákoki mentioned by Schön in the II edition of his grammar.

[10] dengī: this term means also „tribe", especially when mútane, „people" is added, H. dengi n mútane, F. lēnyīlo yimbe; but the Sonyai in this sense employ the Arabic el kabīla.

[11] bābe: I have mention the peculiar term, by which the Fúlbe call their „relatives from father's side, in some way their uncles", hīborābe, the termination arāo particularly indicative of such a family relation having been spoken of in the Introductory Remarks p. CXXXIX, D, p. CXLI (a plur. arābe) and p. CXLVII (a plur. arābe); the Hausa-term leyā maca, corresponding in a certain degree to F. hēborābe, has been formed from another point of view.

[12] ínne: „relatives from mother's side, aunts", F. inne-rābe, H. leyō-māla. leyā (plur. of nī?) see Introductory Remarks p. CXCVII, note 2.

[13] wai: Raffenel in his list of Azenna-words has a term waude with the notion „spouse" (épouse); but that is an error. See Introductory Remarks p. CLXXXVII, a).

[14] kaga: the similarity between the Sonyai- and Kanúri-language in this instance is very remarkable, and probably may have been brought about through the interference of the Ilassa.

[15] úmdžugē is an interesting term, as it evidently indicates the existence in W. of a term um meaning „man", identical with the um mentioned above (p. 211, note 5); for there can be but little doubt, that the second half džugē is nothing else, but dāchá, „great, old". — Instead of ōma, „mother", Denham has moma, just as he has edde instead of my deda, „father".

[16] With regard to the forms muā, „father" (whence múngulák i. q. muā kolák, „grandfather"), miā, „mother" (whence miūgelák i. q. miā kolák, „grandmother"), mag, „brother", and mir, „sister", see Introductory Remarks p. CCCVII, b, a) compared with p. CCCXXIX. In the phrase adduced p. CCCXIII, c) I myself have the form tua for „father".

Deutsch und Englisch.	Kanúri.	Tédā.	Háusa.	Fulfúlde.
Embryo — *embryo*	. . . . . .	. . . . . .	dăindĭeri . .	bingel pámarol
Knäblein — *baby, little boy*	ubal	. . . . . .	dĭarili[7] . . / yarili . . .	bingel ketšel Pl. bībe ketšc
Sohn, Kind — *son, child*	táta[1] Pl. tátawa	kalle Pl. añga S.[5] / átsyo Pl. áta N.	da[8] Pl. yaiya	bí-do[12] Pl. bī-be / bingel . . .
Tochter — *daughter*	fēro[2]	dōs S. . . / dōbu N. . .	dīya	bī-do débo . / bingel dēl .
Enkel — *grand-child*	dígo[3] . . .	me . . . . / dégu . . .	ĭīka[9] . . .	tan-irāo Pl. tan-irābe
Älterer Bruder — *elder brother*	yayā[4] . . .	dē-n inge[6] .	wā	maun-irāo Plur. maun-irābe
mein älterer Bruder — *my elder brother*	yayā-ni . .	. . . . . .	wā-na[10] . .	maun-am . .
Jüngerer Bruder — *younger brother*	kerāmi . . .	dē-n inge . .	kanē	miñerāo Pl. miñe-rābe
Ältere Schwester — *elder sister*	yayā fēro . .	dé-n derdō .	yā	maunirāo débo Pl. maunirābe raube
Jüngere Schwester — *younger sister*	kerāmi fēro .		kánnua . .	miñerāo débo Plur. miñerābe raube
Zwilling — *twin*	. . . . . .	. . . . . .	tauai[11] Pl. tauaiyo	tšūto Pl. aiūtube

[1] táta. Die Zusammensetzungen mit táta, welche Eigenschaften der Menschen bezeichnen, gebe ich unter anderen betreffenden Abschnitten.
[2] fēro. Koelle pēre.
[3] dīgo. dīgo fēro, „Enkelin".
[4] yayā. Ursprünglich war dieses Wort wol nicht verschieden von yāya, „Urgrosseltern" und der Ton ist auch oft derselbe. ya ist ein Naturname von der allgemeinsten Bedeutung, an dem man erst später an [illegible] Beziehung etwas geknüpft hat.
[5] kalle Plur. añga ist nicht so auffallend, wie es zuerst scheint. Unzweifelhaft ist añga das Ursprüngliche.
[6] dē-n inge und dē-n derdō sind wol unzweifelhaft von dē, „Mutter" abgeleitete Begriffe und dē-n inge heisst wahrscheinlich nichts anderes als „Kinder der Mutter", als Pluralform. Lehrreich ist der Vergleich dieser Bezeichnungen mit den von Hodgson gegebenen dembree (i. e. dē-embri [omri vgl. S. 213, N. 6]), „Mutter-Sohn", „Bruder", dedebea (i. e. dē-debe), „Mutter-Tochter", „Schwester". Vgl. Einleitung S. C.
[7] dĭarili oder yarili. Ein Ausdruck von verwandter Bedeutung ist yayai, F. yentāde Plur. yentābe.
[8] da. „Sohn einer Freien", H. da n diya, F. bi-dimo; „Sohn einer Sklavin", H. da n bauya, F. bi-horde, S. [illegible]. Ich will hier auch noch einige bildliche Ausdrücke anführen: „ein Mann von Familie oder aus einem alten Hause", H. da n asali (wörtlich „ein Kind von Ursprung"), F. bi asali oder H. da n [illegible] („ein Kind von vielen Sippen, Ahnen vergl. oben S. 212, N. 30), F. bi [illegible]. Dazu ist der Gegensatz der „Emporkömmling", [illegible], „der Mensch, welcher seine Sache (selbst) angefangen hat", F. [illegible].
[9] ĭīka. Schon alīka für „Enkel" und [illegible] für „Enkelin".
[10] wā-na. Ich führe hier auch einen verwandten Ausdruck an H. [illegible], F. [illegible].
[11] tauai. Die Übereinstimmung dieses Ausdruckes mit dem Namen, mit dem die Haussa ihre Nationalfeinde bezeichnen, ist vielleicht nur zufällig, doch muss man allerdings bedenken, dass bei diesen Völkern Zwillinge meist als ein Unheil angesehen und oft sogar getödtet werden. S. Waitz, Anthropologie.
[12] bi-do. Das eigentliche Wurzelwort für „Sohn" ist bi, verwandt mit der entsprechenden Wurzel in den Indogermanischen Sprachen. bi-do ist ursprünglich „ein Kind", bi-ngel, „irgend ein Kind".
[13] [illegible]. [illegible], „der Mutterleib", [illegible] mir nicht klar.
[14] [illegible]. [illegible] ist wol nur eine populäre Veränderung des gewöhnlichen [illegible], „Kind", durch den Einfluss des [illegible].
[15] [illegible] kann ich nicht sicher erklären, doch ist es vielleicht nichts Anderes als [illegible].
[16] [illegible], „Kind, Sohn der Mutter", d. h. „Kindes-Kind" ohne Autorität, ganz wie [illegible], „Tochter der Mutter".
[17] [illegible], „meine Ältere, Frau sie", d. h. „meine ältere Schwester"; ebenso unten [illegible]. S. Einleitung S. CCXLIV, g).
[18] [illegible] ist das Wort, das das männliche Geschlecht des Kindes in ausdrücklicher Weise bezeichnet, in gewöhnlicher Rede aber ist es [illegible]; auch für [illegible] habe ich häufige Varianten [illegible] gehört.
[19] [illegible]. Seetzen hat [illegible] für „Tochter", während er für „Sohn" [illegible] gibt.

Sónyai.	Lógoné.	Wándalá.	Bágrimma.	Mába.
áberi n guñgu [13]	. . . .	. . . . . .	. . . . . .	. . . . . .
aidža kaine [14] .	. . . .	. . . . . .	. . . . . .	uña
idža Pl. ídžëö . / iza	wúl-e-mení . .	édze	mon-gāha [18] . / gon	kalák
idža wai . . .	wul ganám . .	yāle	mon-nĕ . . / gon-nĕ . .	ká-kalák [19]
nidžĕdže [15] . . .	ke; ken (?) (nāŏ .	eg-ye . . .	nāni	kóliún kolák?
ai bĕre	dis dekín (?) . .	manné . . .	mudĕ ṅgōlo .	mir kolák
ai-me bĕre . .	. . . .	manné-ruā .	. . . . . .	mir (ambe)-go kolák
ai kaine . . .	wúl-e-más [16] . .	kudde . . .	mudĕ mbāsa .	mir
ai bĕre wai . .	mágazī(nāŏ . .	manne (ruā) múk-sa-kĕ [17]	mudĕi-nĕ ṅgōlo	muk
ai kaine wai . .	úχt-e-más . . .	kudde (ruā) múk-sa-kŏ	mudĕi-nĕ mbā-a	
kári Pl. kárió .	. . . .	. . . . . .	. . . . . .	. . . . . .

[1] tóte: terms originating from a combination with the term tóte, and describing certain qualities of man will be mentioned in another chapter.
[2] fêre: Koelle pēre.
[3] digé: digé fêre means „granddaughter".
[4] yeyá originally, no doubt, was identical with the name given to grandfather and grandmother, although the latter term at present is more commonly pronounced yéye, ye being a root of most general import.
[5] kalle plur. ṅága is remarkable; also in this case, however, the plural-form seems to be the original one, from which the other has been derived by prefixing k.
[6] dō-n ṅáge and dō-n derdé most probably have been derived from dē, „mother", dō-n-ṅáge meaning nothing else, but „children (ṅage) of mother"; and we have in this instance a very instructive comparison with the corresponding terms given by Hodgson, viz dembree, i. q. dē-embri (embri = emri, p. 213, note 6), „brother", and dedeboe, i. q. dē-debo, „daughter of mother", i. q. „sister".
[7] dāri̇̄li or yarīli: a term of nearly related import is yeyel, F. yeniādo plur. yeniāba.
[8] da: I am going to adduce in this place some terms combined with da, „the first born", dan forī; „son of a free woman", H. dan diya, F. bi-dimo; „son of a female slave", H. dan houya, F. bi-kordo, S. hong-iddé; „a man of family", H. dan asali (verbally „a child of origin"), or dan dañgi dewo („a child of many ancestors, see above p. 213, note 11), F. bi asali, bī lenyol. These terms form the reverse to what the Hausa call mutúm wonē ya-fāra abi-nea, „the man who has begun his affair (by himself)", „the upstart", F. fudūdu dum héro mé.
[9] ilka: Schön has ailka, „grandchild", and ailkata for „granddaughter".
[10] wā-na: I here adduce another term of a similar notion, H. cāgirma mūzi, F. mauvulūme.
[11] tanal: the identity of this term with the name, by which the Hausa-people designate their national enemies, is perhaps not merely accidental, twins with most of these people being rather looked upon as an abomination, than otherwise, and in many cases being even killed on the spot.
[12] bi-de: the proper root of this word, as seen from the composite terms, is bi, bī, nearly identical with the corresponding term in the Indo-Germanic languages; I have, however, a phrase where yō-ma seems to mean „thy son". — As for moan-eráe compare the corresponding hand-eráe in Timbo and Salum.
[13] áberi n guñgu: guñgu, „the womb"; as for áberi, it is probably closely related to the roots fer, far, farī, and so on, Introductory Remarks p. CXCI, note 1.
[14] aidža kaine: aidža seems to be nothing, but a popular corruption of idža, „child", being influenced by the ai in kaine.
[15] nidžēdže most probably is nothing, but n-idža-idže, „the child's child". — ai seems to mean „kindred of any kind".
[16] wúl-e-más, „child, son of mother" = aktoem in W. (Koelle Pol.) i. e. akiee (= edze) mā, just as úχt-e-más, „daughter of mother".
[17] manne-(ruā) múksa-kĕ, „my elder parent, woman she", i. q. „my elder sister", just as kudde ruā muksa-kĕ, „my younger parent, woman she", i. q. „my younger sister", and p. 217 muksa dā ruā. See Introductory Remarks p. CCXLV, g). — Koelle in his Polyglotta gives aktoem for „brother" (see note 16), yāwé for „sister".
[18] mon-gāha is the term, which is used, when the male sex of the child is to be distinctly indicated, but in other ways the simple gon is employed, and even instead of mon-nĕ I often heard gon-nĕ.
[19] ká-kalák: Nachtigal has kalák kóklak for „daughter", while for „son" he gives kalák kembak.

Deutsch und Englisch.	Kanúri.	Tēda.	Hausa.	Fulfúlde.
väterl. Oheim, älter als der Vater — *uncle from father's side, older than the father*	ába kúra . .	ába-dō[4] . .	wa n obā . .	ba-díko[6] . .
erster Oheim nach dem Vater — *first uncle, younger than the father*	ába ganá[1] . .		kané n obā .	sambo . .
zweiter Oheim nach dem Vater — *second uncle, younger than the father*				ba-yérro . .
dritter Oheim nach dem Vater — *third uncle, younger than the father*				ba-páño . .
vierter Oheim nach dem Vater — *fourth uncle, younger than the father*				ba-fáte . .
fünfter Oheim nach dem Vater — *fifth uncle, younger than the father*				ba-kóda . .
mütterl. Oheim, älter als die Mutter — *uncle from mother's side, older than the mother*	rába / ráfa kúra[2]		ya n wā . .	ya-díkko . .
erster mütterlicher Oheim nach der Mutter — *first uncle from mother's side, younger than the mother*	rába / ráfa ganá .		kané n wā .	ya-kúmbo .
zweiter mütterlicher Oheim nach der Mutter — *second uncle from mother's side, younger than the mother*				ya-féndo . .
dritter mütterlicher Oheim nach der Mutter — *third uncle from mother's side, younger than the mother*				ya-táko . .
vierter mütterlicher Oheim nach der Mutter — *fourth uncle from mother's side, younger than the mother*				ya-moini . .
Tante — *aunt*	yonā(n)[3] . .	dā-dō . . .	kanú n obā matāe[5]	goggo Pl. gogge-rābe

[1] ába ganá. ába, „Vater" (S. 312), allerdings auch als gewöhnliche vertrauliche Anredeform gebraucht, kann nur in der speciellen Beziehung als „grösserer und kleinerer Vater" die Bedeutung von „Onkel" erhalten.
[2] rába ist offenbar die ursprüngliche Form, von ába und re als Zeichen der Wiederholung, „zweiter Vater". Koelle ráfa.
[3] yonā. Koelle hat dafür bábā (s. N. 8); bábā kúra, „Vaters ältere Schwester"; bábā ganá, „Vaters jüngere Schwester".
[4] ába-dō, dā-dō u. s. w. Zu diesen Formen vergl. Einleitung S. LXXX, 10.
[5] kanú n obā matāe ist nur „die Tante väterlicher Seite", und zwar eigentlich nur die „jüngere Schwester des Vaters". Dabei ist die männliche Form kané auffallend anstatt kánnua.
[6] ba-díko u. s. w. Alle diese Namen haben gewiss eine höchst interessante ursprüngliche Beziehung, die vielleicht den allerreichsten Aufschluss über die ethnographische Verwandtschaft dieses merkwürdigen Stammes geben könnte. sambo, der ursprüngliche Eigenname des Onkels, ist nun ganz allgemeinster Eigenname bei den Fúlbe geworden. ba-díko, wahrscheinlich „der grosse Vater" (ba = babá [bāgel baba S. 312], wie ya in diesem Namen für Mutter statt inna, dáda = H. nya), wie ba-panya entschieden „der jugendliche Vater" heisst, und wie ba-fáte wol Beziehungen hat zu dem verwandten Timbo-Ausdruck páti, „Grossmutter" (Koelle Polyglotta) und ba-kóda zu kóṣo (obwodo) „älterer Bruder". — Zu den im Text angeführten Verwandtschafts-Namen muss ich hier noch den eigenthümlichen Namen des „Hausfreundes" oder „Freund des Vaters" anführen (H. áboki-n-wá) dend-iráo, wo also dieser wol ausschliesslich zu verwandtschaftlichen Beziehungen benutzte Kadung („der Freund meines Vaters", dend-am, s. oben S. 312, N. 12) ihn gewissermassen zu einem eigentlichen Mitgliede der Familie stempelt, wie er auch einen grossen Einfluss in dem gesammten häuslichen Leben der Fúlbe übt. Bei solcher individuellen Ausbildung der Familienverhältnisse wäre es wunderbar, wenn die Fúlbe keinen eigentlichen Namen für „Schwiegersohn" hätten (S. 316, N. 10).
[7] Für „Onkel" in dem dem Songai verwandten Arama gibt Raffenel aeeie mit der sonderbaren Erklärung „qui n'a pas fait enfant", also wol a-al idae; für „Tante", aená (awá).
[8] babá-(ama. babá ist wol eine kindliche Bezeichnung der Tante statt muddā-nē bába, „Schwester des Vaters". Vgl. N. 3, wo Koelle auffallender Weise dasselbe Wort im Kanúri gibt.
[9] mungad. Anstatt dessen hat Burckhardt mamunk, Seetzen mónungēh; anstatt meines malmik, „mütterlicher Oheim" hat Burckhardt mamnak und anstatt meines mínége, „Tante" hat Seetzen das offenbar componirte mannugajúh.

Sokyud.	Lógonê.	Wándalá.	Bágrimma.	Mába.
	[bakunarli??] . .	dĕ(-ruā . . .	nanó (-ama (?)	mungad [9]
	kenĕku (?) . . .	dĕ-ŏe (ruā .	mudé-kuó . .	malmik
	máñgann . . .	muksa dé(-ruā	babā-(ama [8] .	miñrge

[1] âba gonŏ. âba, „father" (p. 512), which has gradually become not only an honorary title, but also a common confidential form of addressing any respectable elderly person, obtains the meaning „uncle" by adding „elder", „younger".
[2] râba, „the second father" is probably the original form, derived from âba, and ra the sign of reiteration. Koelle râfâ.
[3] yenâ: Koelle bâbâ, „father's sister", bâbâ bâre, „the father's elder sister", bâbâ yenâ, „the father's younger sister".
[4] âba-dĕ, dé-dŏ. As for the derivation of these terms see Introductory Remarks p. LXXXI, 10.
[5] hané n ohâ matĭe means originally „the younger sister of the father"; hané instead of fm. hânnae is remarkable.
[6] ba-diho: It would be highly instructive, to know the original meaning of all these characteristic names of parentage with the Fúlbe, as they may tend to throw a clearer light upon the ethnological connection of this very curious tribe, than any other specimen of linguistical relationship; but I am sorry, I can as yet not explain all of them. Thus, as for ba-diho, I think, diho means „big", or something like it; while, as for ba it evidently means „father" in these composite terms, just as ya means „mother". Thus ba-diho would form a kind of opposition to ba-patyo, which, no doubt, means „the youthful father". As for sambo, this original title of uncle has become a proper name of the most general application with the Fúlbe. Further, as for ba-fâle, it may be related to the term pêll in the related idiom of Timbo (Koelle's Polyglotta), meaning „grandmother", just as ba-hâde appears to be related to the Timbo-term hâjo meaning „elder brother". In this note I still add the peculiar term dend-irâo, by which the „father's friend" (H. âbohi-n-wâ) is called in Fulfúlde, who exercises a very great influence in the relations of domestic life of that remarkable nation, and is even looked upon as a member of the family itself, this kind of relationship being expressed by that very termination erâo, irbo (see p. 212, note 12) („my father's friend" dend-am). — Such being the very characteristic development of degrees of family life with the Fúlbe, it would be very odd indeed, if they had not a more expressive term for „son-in-law", than appears in my list p. 516.
[7] For „uncle" in the related dialect of Aramo Raffenel gives ascie, but which according to the very curious explanation „qui n'a pas fait enfant", would seem to be nothing else but a-ei Idae; for „aunt" he gives aoné (awé).
[8] babā-(ama: babā seems to be an infantile term given to the „aunt" instead of madĭl-né bâba, „father's sister". We therefore have here the very term, Koelle gives in Kanúri: see note 3.
[9] mungad: B. gives monmâh, S. mónoogâh; and instead of my malmik B. masaak; instead of miñrge S. menangatâh.

Deutsch und Englisch	Kanúri	Tédā	Hausa	Fulfúlde
Vetter — *cousin* . . .	tála ába ganá	baader [2] . .	da n kané n obā (na [6] da n wā . .	bingel bāba . baúdiko (s. N. 6)
Nichte — *niece*	fēro ába ganá	. . . . . .	. . . . . .	. . . . . .
Schwiegervater — *father-in-law*	kiaaī [1] kōa .	. . . . . .	sorúkko Pl. sorúkki	es-erāo Pl. eserábe [9]
Schwiegermutter — *mother-in-law*	kiaaī [1] kāmo .			
Schwiegersohn — *son-in-law*	kiaaī kōa . .	aurō	meži n dīa [7].	gorko bī (am [10]
Schwiegertochter — *daughter-in-law*	kiaaī kāmo .		matšc n dā (na	dēbo bingel (am
Bräutigam — *bridegroom*	lariíaaa [3] . .	áfandē . . .	ango [8] . . .	angōdīo . . dīom-bādīo .
Braut — *bride*	lariíaaa [3] . .	ádi áfandē .	amáriā . . .	débo bangādo sūdo mā-ko [11]
Wittwe (während der 4 ersten Monate nach dem Tode ihres Mannes) — *widow (during the first four months after the death of her husband)*	kāmo kámbā [5]	. . . . . .	. . . . . .	. . . . . .
Wittwe, wieder fähig zum Heirathen — *widow, fit for contracting another marriage*	kāmo zauar .	. . . . . .	góburo(?) . .	
Waise, Verwaiste — *orphan*	ingenī [4] . . .	lūhi	marain . . .	yatīme Pl. atimēdži (Arb. ginīdīo . .

Sonyai.	Lógoné.	Wándalá.	Bágrimma.	Mába.
dżóri fö idše[12] .	bauán	edze dĕ(-ruā .	[bāb(a) adžégene müdžu[14]]	mir-ak
. . . .	ágt-umán . . .	mukaa edze dĕ(-ruā	gonnē amúdžu-ma	mir-ǎan halák
hanyöre . . .	sǎam	ǎöle[13] . . .	mōmo . . .	man-gar[16]
			mōmi . . .	miúek[17]
			gab n gonne	tan-gar
. . . .			nē n gon? .	. . . . .
. . . .	bille larúasa . .	larúasa . . .	. . . . . .	káilengék; ke-dán-gar-ak
. . . .	geném el larúasa	larúaseri . .	nē ňěka . .	muǎóng kédangák; kákalak arūs
a-si bīgi . . .	geném al ulda (Arb.)	tágaba . . .	nomēda . . .	mašík tenék teyók[18]
. . . .	mó-sinnén . . .	záware (Arb.)	kedábokō . .	. . . . .
yetīm (Arb.) . .	milgēn [me-el gēn]	tabē	gon-Alla[15] .	sāyik

1 kisaf: Koelle writes kéaaf, and does not attribute to it the general notion of all degrees of affinity, but merely the exclusive notion of „son" or „daughter in law". In order to decide this question, we ought to know the root of kisaf.

2 larúasa: Koelle instead of this term, introduced from the Arabic has a very peculiar term tarlaiže, which looks suspicious on account of the almost identical term tárgaiže, to which he attributes the totally divergent meaning of „fog, dew".

3 kámbā, I have no doubt, means originally „there is no (ba = ba ugó, bágó, Introductory Remarks p. LXIII. note 1) man, husband" (kám), that is to say „she has no husband". But, as the original notion of kám comprises also the woman, kámbā can also be said of the husband, who has lost his wife. But for the latter the state of being kámbā is without moral or juridical consequences, while the kámo kámbā is prevented from marrying during the first four months after her husband's death, nay she is even not called kámbā after that time, but then becomes a kámo) azzar, a term, which is borrowed from the Arabic, and is wanting in Koelle.

4 lagoni: Koelle writes ágoni, but shows himself by adding the accent over the á, that that is rather a syllable by itself.

5 hauder, if right, is a vulgar corruption; it ought to be ába-dō halle bé-nai, „the uncle his son", or something like it.

6 da n baad n wá (na, „son of the younger brother of (my) father", da n wá, V. baddiko (ba-d-diku?), „son of the ba-diko" p. 218), „son of the elder uncle".

7 mašī n dīa, „the husband of (my) daughter", matže n dá (na, „the wife of (my) son".

8 ságo: the derivation of this term is unknown to me, amárīā is from amrē, „to marry".

9 en-aráo: „my father in law", se-am. — The Fúlbe, however, have a more general term comprising all degrees of affinity (K. sigáí?), sing. kávo (kav-erāo not used) plur. kaiveráho, to which the Sonyai-term hasaal seems to correspond. In Hausa I sometimes heard the term ráfani (ráfa-ni? compare Kanúri ráfa p. 217, note 2) used in this respect, but I am not quite sure of it.

10 gorko bí (am, „husband of (my) daughter", débo bingel (am, „wife of (my) son". But see my remark p. 216, n. 6 at the end.

11 débo bangáda aádo (ma-ko, means either „the woman to be brought into his the bridegroom's house" or „the woman shut up in her own house".

12 dżóri fö idše seems rather to convey the notion „a child of one (fö) year (yéri) of age".

13 ǎöle: this term denoting the various degrees of affinity, most probably is nearly related to šela, „coitus, marriage".

14 bāb(a) adžégene müdžu can only mean „the fathers their (a-dže-gene Intr. Remarks p. CCLVII) brothers", therefore „uncle", not „cousin". — gon-nē a-médžu-ma seems to mean „daughter of my brother".

15 gon-Alla means verbally „child of God", the orphan being placed under the particular protection of God.

16 man-gar means properly „father by affinity" (gar), tan-gar, „son by affinity". While by mischance not learning the corresponding M.-term for „daughter in law", I learnt that for „sister in law", hamayak, probably vulgar form of hama-gar-ak

17 miúek seems to be one and the same word with miáege, „aunt" p. 217.

18 mašík tenék teyók: mašík, „man, husband"; tenék teyók, therefore must convey the notion of not „being allowed to have or obtain (a husband".

Deutsch und Englisch.	Kanúri.	Tédā.	Hausa.	Fulfúlde.
ein Knabe vier Spannen hoch — *a boy four spans high*	rubbai [1] (Arb.)	. . . . . .	da n mōgodántši karamī [7]	dōkel tókotšel
ein Knabe von fünf Spannen — *a boy five spans high*	ẏomāi (Arb.)		mōgodántši Plur. mōgodántai	dōko Pl. dōbe
ein Knabe von sechs Spannen — *a boy six spans high*	sedāsi (Arb.) .	. . . . . .	da n ẏāro . .	sūkaēl darēl .
ein Knabe von sieben Spannen — *a boy seven spans high*	subbai (Arb.) .	. . . . . .	ẏāro [8] . . .	sūka / sūkaēl, Pl. sukābe
Mädchen — *girl* . . .	fēro [2] . . .	dōē / dōbu . . .	yārīña [9] . . .	sūka dēbo . .
reifes Mädchen — *maid* .	fēro débūgu [3]	. . . . . .	buderūa [10] . .	paño débo Pl. fambe raube / dēīo Pl. dēūbe
junger Mann — *young man*	sēro [4] . . .		sermaī Plur. sermāri [11]	paño (faño) gorko Pl. fambe worbe
junger bartloser Mann — *young beardless man*	(sēro)		meran-kāto [12]	dōko faño . .
junger bärtiger Mann — *young bearded man*	gurzem . . .		kāto Pl. katta	katōru Pl. katōdēe [14]
Freund — *friend* . . .	sōba [5] . . .	sardo [6] . . .	ābokí Pl. ābokoi [13]	bīgo Pl. bīgo-terābe [15]

[1] rubbai u. s. w. Diese, allerdings dem Arabischen entlehnten, aber doch, zumal für die Sklavenverhältnisse, sehr gewöhnlich gewordenen vier Ausdrücke fehlen bei Koelle. Dagegen hat Koelle in seiner Grammatik p. 20 den Ausdruck tsairo für „Knabe", den ich nie gehört habe, vielleicht verwandt mit dem Hausa-Wort yāro.

[2] fēro, bei Koelle pēro; s. oben S. 214 „Tochter".

[3] débūgu fehlt bei Koelle; es kommt offenbar von débū, dēbū, „die Taille", „das Mädchen mit der vollen Taille".

[4] sēro und gurzem fehlen beide bei Koelle.

[5] sōba, Koelle sābā; es bekommt auch häufig die Bedeutung „Gefährte", wofür die Kanúri aber oft den Ausdruck hēma gebrauchen, der jedoch etwas unbestimmte Beziehung hat und eigentlich „gleich, ähnlich" zu bedeuten scheint. — Für „*Wohlthäter*" hat Koelle ausserdem yerma (yer-ma).

[6] sardō. sardō-nir, „mein Freund"; für „Freundin" habe ich den besonderen Tédā-Ausdruck terhaeē.

[7] da n mōgodántši karamī. Das da, „Kind von" drückt die, wenn man von dem Höheren ausgeht, in dem Hauptprädikat ausgedrückte nachfolgende Stufe aus (vergl. S. 184, N. 9 über hané und bawe), obgleich sie in meiner Anordnung vorhergeht. mōgodántši scheint aber ursprünglich „kleiner Hohe" zu bedeuten, weil die Knaben in diesem Alter am durchtriebensten sind.

[8] yāro, obgleich es die allgemeine Bedeutung „männliches Kind" hat, bezeichnet doch vornämlich den ausgewachsenen Knaben, ehe er in das Jünglingsalter eintritt. In dieser Bedeutung scheint der Plural nur yāra zu lauten, nie yāya.

[9] yārīña. Schön, der yarinia schreibt, hat den auffallenden Plural yemmata.

[10] buderūa. Schön bēderuā Plur. bederai. Auffallend, und vielleicht nicht ohne inneren Grund, ist das Zusammentreffen dieses Hausa-Ausdruckes mit bodarud im Tédā, Plur. von bodir, „(Lieblings)-Sklavin".

[11] sermaī (Schön sarmāyi) scheint, der höchst unregelmässigen Form des Plurals zu Folge, ein fremdländisches Wort zu sein.

[12] meran-kāto, so wie kāto selbst, scheint nicht reinen Hausa-Ursprung zu haben; beide Wörter stammen wahrscheinlich aus der Sonyai-Sprache, daher die Negation ca in mer-ca-kāto. Die Hausa-Umschreibung des ersten Wortes lautet bābo gēma, ya-i girma, „er hat (noch) keinen Bart, (aber) er hat die (gehörige) Grösse erreicht"; die Hausa-Erklärung von kāto: mai-gēma, „Herr eines Bartes".

[13] ābokí (s. N. 16), daher „der Reisegefährte", āboki n tafia, für den die Fúlbe den besonderen Ausdruck dīade-dōb haben.

[14] katōru ist in den westlichen Fúlbe-Landschaften wahrscheinlich nicht gebräuchlich.

[15] bīgo-terābe ist offenbar von einer Singularform bīgo-terāo, die in den Bereich der Verwandtschaftsverhältnisse fällt.

[16] ubākoi. Die Ähnlichkeit des Hausa- und Sonyai-Wortes ist um so wahrscheinlicher Weise daraus zu erklären, dass das erstere aus dem letzteren entstanden ist, als das Sonyai abā-koi, aus dem Geiste der Sprache erklärt, einen ganz vortrefflichen Sinn hat, nämlich „Herr des Vaters"; keineswegs ist das Umgekehrte der Fall. Vergl. Einleitung S. CXCVI.

[17] manda von ando, „heirathen"; vgl. S. 35 mak-an manda.

[18] kaūgár-melék, „Herr des Bartes".

[19] sofīkeh ist das später eingeführte Arabische Wort. Daneben aber scheint das einheimische kolāh gebraucht zu sein, wenigstens bei Asraden „Du Freund". Hierfür gebraucht man aber auch kaúg ēga, „dieser Mann", „Du da".

Sonyai.	Lógonē.	Wándalā.	Bágrimma.	Mába.
. . . .	wul e rubbai . .	édze rubbai .	gon-dẽĩ-sò .	?
. . . .	wul e bomāsi . .	édze bomāsi .	gon-dẽĩ-mí .	romāsik (Arb.)
. . . .	wul e sedāsi . .	édze sedāsi .	gon-dẽĩ-migā	sedāsik (Arb.)
. . . .	wul e subbai . .	édze subbai .	gon-dẽĩ-tšilĭ .	?
wai kalna . . .		yāle . . . / édzirík . . .	mon-nĕ . .	ká-kalak
hondía	áli gosē . . .	édzirík zaknā	manda [17] . .	ká-kalak düd / šeršerāye
kōso	wul e zevē . .	zérria . . .	ingán-gab-gē(?)	
. . . .	mábi [me-a-bi] .	māfi davle .	bélkazā . . .	kungúr-melék [18]
etšōre . . . . / abákoi [16] . . .	wul goféfnāū . .	ðiggetc . . / tsákkatē . .	kafá (am . .	refíkek [19] (Arb.)

[1] rabbei etc.: these terms, which here, indeed, been borrowed from the Arabic, but are nevertheless in very general use, are wanting in Koelle, who on the other hand in his grammar § 80 has a peculiar term tsairo for „boy" which may be related to H. yáro, but which I have never heard.

[2] fēro: Koelle pēro; see p. 214 s. v. „daughter".

[3] débūge is wanting in Koelle; it is evidently derived from débū, dàbū, „the waist"; it therefore means „girl of a full waist".

[4] aīro and gurasem are both wanting in Koelle.

[5] sōbe (Koelle zóbā) frequently has also the meaning of „companion". The latter notion, however, is often expressed by the term háme, although this latter term has a rather indistinct meaning „any thing which is like, and belongs to somebody", and a wide sense accordingly. — I here mention, that Koelle has a term yerme (yer-me), „benefactor".

[6] sardē: sardē-nir, „my friend"; for „female friend" I here the peculiar Tédā-term terkoabi.

[7] den mōgodéntši karami: the den, „child of" expresses the degree following upon the state expressed by the chief predicament, such as here mōgodéntši, although in my arrangement it precedes the latter. — mōgodéntši seems to mean originally „naughty boy", because children of this age, in general, are rather cunning and vicious.

[8] yáro, although it has the general notion of „boy", nevertheless preeminently designates the fullgrown boy, and when employed with this notion has the plural-form yára, not yāya.

[9] yērīān: Schön writes yerinia and has the remarkable plural-form yemeata.

[10] bedorān: Schön bédurwā plur. budarai. The coincidence of this term with the Tédā bedoran, being the plural of hedir, „female slave" is perhaps not accidental.

[11] sermai (Schön sarmāyi) according to the very irregular form of its plural-number, seems to be a term of foreign origin.

[12] merce-hāte, as well as the term hāte itself, does not seem to be of pure Hausa origin; the latter term at least would seem to be borrowed from the Sonyai-language, and thence probably also the negative particle ce in mer-ce-hāte has to be explained; translated into pure Hausa the former means bābo gēmo, ya-i girma, „he has not (yet) a beard, (but) he has reached (the right) size", while hāte means mai-gēme, „master of a beard".

[13] āboki (see note 16): „friend of the journey", „travelling companion", āboki n taffe, expressed in Fulfúlde by dīnde-dāō.

[14] batōre probably is not usual in the country of the Western Fúlbe.

[15] higo-terābe: This form of the plural; the corresponding singular of which higo-t-erāo is not used, places „the friend" in the category of relatives, see above p. 216, note 6. As for the t, it seems to be added merely from reasons of euphony.

[16] abākoi: the similarity of this Sonyai-term with the corresponding Hausa-word āboki most probably has to be explained from the circumstance, that the latter has been borrowed from the former, abá-koi in Sonyai meaning „master of the father".

[17] manda from nada, „to marry"; see p. 55 mah-ne manda.

[18] kungúr-meléh, „master of the beard".

[19] refíkek is the Arabic term, besides which kaláh seems to be used, especially when addressing a person, in which case use is made also of the form kaág ágo, meaning properly „this man".

Deutsch und Englisch.	Kanúri.	Tédā.	Hausa.	Fulfúlde.
Gast, Fremder — guest, stranger	kusótō[1] . . .	arzē S. / arnē N.	bakō[9] Pl. bákona	koddo Pl. hobbe
Nachbar — neighbour . .	kemóši (nī[2] .	. . . . .	[10]	. . . . .
Landsmann — country-man	táta búlla-bē[3]	ámu nemā-nír[7]	da n gari . .	. . . . .
Hausherr — landlord . .	kúra fāto[4] .	bó-n-torō[8] .	ōba n gidši[11]	džomírdo[12] .
Hausfrau — landlady . .	kumā kindži-bē[5]	ádi-bō . . .	war-gida . .	dāda sāre / džom-sūdo / inna ūro
Herr (in Anrede) — Sir	ába	máyirdē / mori (nír .	. . . . .	. . . . .
Feind — enemy	kel-ādu[6] (h. Arb.)	irdī	tauai[13] . . .	konnōdžo[14] / bónnubē / túrtubē / pírtubē (Plur.)

[1] kusótō ist ein bezeichnender und umfassender Ausdruck. Koelle hat von derselben Wurzel sogar ein Wort ausótō, „fremdes Land, die Fremde", und ein Zeitwort ausótōgin.

[2] kemóši bei Koelle kemōšī.

[3] táta billa-bē, „Sohn der Stadt"; ausserdem habe ich noch mit derselben Bedeutung billa gana, wörtlich „die kleine Stadt", mit dieser Bedeutung für „Landsmann, Landsleute" zu auffallend und unsicher, um es in den Text zu setzen. Koelle hat diese zusammengesetzten Ausdrücke nicht; anstatt billa schreibt er bēlā.

[4] kúra fāto, eigentlich kúra fāto-bē, „der Grosse des Hauses". Koelle hat dafür kémā pātōma.

[5] kumā kindži-bē, „die Grosse, Gebieterin der Sklaven"; kumā ist nichts Anderes, als kémā in kémā-ndē S. 144. Allerdings drückt dieser Ausdruck die Bedeutung von „Hausfrau", welcher der Hausa- und Fulfúlde-Ausdruck wirklich entspricht, nur unvollkommen aus, aber die Kanúri scheinen dafür nichts Anderes zu haben, während dem K. kumā kindži-bē wörtlich entspricht H. baba n bauya, F. horga mauga. — Zu āba mit der Bedeutung „Herr" s. oben S. 214, N. 1.

[6] kel-ādu (Koelle kelládo) ist unbedingt entstanden aus dem Arabischen el ādū mit dem Vorsatz des Kanúri ke, „Einer von". So ist denn das kel nicht durch Einfluss des Mūsy-Wortes kēl, „Leute" hineingekommen, wie ich früher glaubte (R. Th. II, S. 297 N.). Das rein Arabische Wort ohne Artikel ist in L., B. und M. eingebürgert worden. Übrigens haben diese Sprachen jedenfalls noch eine populäre Weise, einen in Privatverhältnissen feindlichen Menschen zu bezeichnen.

[7] ámu nemā-nír, „Leute meiner Stadt".

[8] bó-n-torō hängt wol mit yēbo, „Haus" zusammen, indem beide Bestandtheile ye und bo sogar selbständig mit dieser Bedeutung vorzukommen scheinen, so dass es „Kater (torō) des Hauses" heisst. Ähnlich, aber in umgekehrter Stellung, ist das Folgende.

[9] bakō. „Der Gast aus fernem Lande", H. bakō mai-nēsa, F. koddo góddudo Plur. bobbe wóddu-bē. Schön übrigens gebraucht bakō ganz allgemein in dem Sinne „fremd", wie er Exodus „ich bin ein Fremder in fremdem Lande gewesen", übersetzt na kasa bako gatšikin kasa bakua; solche Bedeutung hat es aber nie.

[10] Schön in Exodus III, v. 22 hat ein Wort makofta für „Nachbarn", das ich aber nie gehört habe und das mir verdächtig erscheint; in der II. Ausgabe der Grammatik gibt er Singular mákoptā.

[11] ōba n gidši. Ich will hier den begriffsverwandten Ausdruck anführen baba n gida, „Ältester des Hauses", gegenüberstehend dem karami n gida, „Jüngster des Hauses". Schön schreibt für ōba n gidši fälschlich ubangiżi, wobei die Beziehung auf das Haus, gida Plur. gidadže, gänzlich verloren gegangen ist, wie er es auch ganz allgemein durch „Herr" erklärt. In Verbindung mit Alla ist es dann ein gewöhnliches Beiwort von Gott geworden, als der Hausherr der ganzen Welt, Oba-n gidši n Alla.

[12] tauai hat nicht die allgemeine Bedeutung von „Feind" in öffentlichen und Privatbeziehungen, sondern wird nur gebraucht von öffentlichen Feinden und zwar besonders von den unabhängigen Hausa-Stämmen, welche die Sicherheit des Verkehrs in den von den Fulbe unterjochten Staaten gefährden. Vgl. oben S. 214, N. 11. Schön führt in seinem Wörterbuch mit der allgemeinen Bedeutung von „Feind, Gegner" auf makiotši, makiyi Plur. makiya; das kann aber höchstens vom Privatfeind gebraucht werden, von dem, der einen Andern nicht mag. S. naki oben S. 62.

[13] džomírdo. Ich bin nicht ganz sicher, ob irdo, die zweite Hälfte des Wortes, noch eine besondere Beziehung andeutet, oder ob diese Form mit džomirōo für „Gott", S. 144, zusammenfällt. — Für „Ältester des Hauses" hat die Fulfúlde-Sprache die beiden, zu verschiedenen ethnographischen Beziehungen (vgl. weiter unten zu ūro und sāre) stehenden Ausdrücke ūro maūgo und sāre maunde und das Gegentheil gūrel tōkotšel.

[14] konnōdžo von konne, „der Krieg". Die drei anderen Ausdrücke haben lokale Beziehung und nur ganz lokalen Gebrauch.

[15] bōre-hol hat wieder eine specielle lokale Beziehung.

[16] mayāni gibt wol die an einen Gast gerichtete Frage „was (ist) seine Stadt", ma rō (na-)ni, d. h. „woher ist er gebürtig".

[17] billa lorāāda kommt unserem Ausdruck „Landsmann" wörtlich ganz nahe.

[18] mābob layámasē. māhoš fm. von mābi S. 221, layámasē wahrscheinlich Verdrehung von yálemasē, „die Sklavinnen". — al wayē hängt wol sicher mit dem Namen šiwa, etwa der einheimischen Arabischen Bevölkerung zusammen.

[19] dadá-ui aed. arō, „die weiblichen Sklaven". dada hatten wir oben S. 213, N. 16 = edda, „Vater"; diese Bedeutung kann es hier jedoch wol kaum haben.

[20] mausel, vielleicht zusammenhängend mit manean, „schlecht".

[21] kariba, verdorben aus dem Arabischen yarib.

[22] baléd ambé-neh ti, „er ist (ti) von, aus" (nah Genitiv- und Ursprungsverhältniss, S. CCCX, n. e), „Ort von mir", „meiner Stadt", baléd ambé; d. h. „er ist mein Landsmann".

[23] ódu. Dafür hat Gaetan ein vielfach zusammengesetztes mungenjiedij, in dessen letztem Theile unser ódu zu stecken scheint.

Sonyai.	Lógoné.	Wándalá.	Bágrimma.	Mába.
yo	marõni ?[18] . . .	waivĕ . . .	ingā	kang hartba[21] (h. Arb.)
[alaime ?] . . .	bille gimmg(ãã .	riáng irfälle .	bókoma . . .	. . . . . .
. . . . . .	bille loröäde[17] .	édu(e) ákse .	gon nanga . .	beléd embú-nak ti[22] (h. Arb.)
hõgu-koi . . .	mal-yaã . . .	mãlo-yekẽ [dãjkẽ]	māla-bĕ . .	tang-meléh
hõgu-koi wai(?)	máboã layómazẽ[18]	dadā-ni evē[19]	mála-baina .	. . . . . .
. . . . . .	elwayẽ	adda	bāba-ain . .	ba
bẽre-koi[15] . .	ãdu	manzol[20] . .	ãdu	ãdu[23]

[1] kuaólé is a very important and common term with the Kanúri. Koelle has even made thereof a central term, the real existence of which, however, I doubt, viz nuaólá, „foreign country", and even the verb nuaólóngin.

[2] hamóẽi with Koelle is hamãẽi.

[3] fáta billa-bé, „son of the town"; another term billa gana meaning verbally „the small town", which I have likewise written down for „countryman" seems rather uncertain. Koelle has not these terms; instead of billa he writes bĕlā.

[4] kára fáto properly kára fáto-bé, „the great (man), the chief of the house". Koelle gives instead kámá pátómu.

[5] kumá kiadái-bé, „the great (woman) of the slaves", kumá being identical with kúmá in kúmá-ndé, „our Lord" p. 144. But this term does not properly express the idea of „landlady", to which the terms given in the Hausa- and Fulfúlde-language correspond exactly, while the meaning properly expressed in the Kanúri-language is exactly rendered by the Hausa-term baba n bauye, F. horga mańga.

[6] kel-ádu (Koelle keliádo) has certainly been formed from the Arabic el ádû by adding the Kanúri-pronoun „one of", ka, ba. For, although the first syllable kel greatly resembles the Mãsy-word kĕl, „people", yet I do not now think, as I once did, that it has been borrowed from that language. The pure Arabic form of the term has been adopted by the Lógoné-, Bágrimma- and Mába-languages, without adding the article. But I have no doubt, that the Kanúri-language does possess a more original and national term for denoting a hostile person, at least with regard to private affairs.

[7] áma nemá-air, „people of my town".

[8] hó-n-toró seems to be connected with yóbo, „house", the two portions of which, ye as well as bo, seem to be used independently with the same meaning, so that it means „the first (toró) of the house", and then likewise ádi-bá is = ádi-yobo.

[9] bahá; thence „the guest from a far-distant country", H. bahó mai-nésa, F. koddo gáádado plur. hobbe wóddo-bé. But Schön is wrong in attributing to bahó the general notion of „foreign", as f. i. he translates the passage in Exodus „I have been a foreigner in a foreign land", by na kawa baho gatśikin kasa baiwa.

[10] Rev. Schön in his translation of Exodus III, v. 22 has a word makofia for „neighbours", and in the new edition of his grammar in the singular makoptśi, which I have never heard, and which is very suspicious to me, indeed.

[11] óba n gidá: I here mention the term báha n gida, „eldest of the house", the contrary of karami n gida, „the little, youngest of the house". Schön writes wrongly obangiset instead of óba n gidái, and thus entirely sacrifices the intimate relation, which the term bears to gida, „house", as he explains it also by means of the general word „master". From a sensible point of view this epithet is joined to the word Alla, „God" and then becomes Oba-n gidá n Alla.

[12] tanai has not the general meaning of „enemy", in private as well as public relations, but is merely used of public enemies, and especially of those independent Hausa-tribes, that infest the peaceable intercourse of the other Hausa states, which have been subjugated by the Pálba. Compare also, what I have said p. 210, note 11. Schön has, besides, another term makiotśi, makiyi, plur. makiya, with the meaning „enemy, adversary", but which can only be used in exceptional cases, as a person that does not like, or rather hates another one, and not as an independent term.

[13] dãamirdo: this word, the chief portion of which is dĩom, in the form dĩomirdo which exhibits the important termination irdo often spoken of, has been applied to God, just as the corresponding Hausa-term (p. 144). — „Eldest of the house" is rendered in Fulfúlde by the two terms ôro mańgo and ôere manude and the contrary by gûrel tókotšel.

[14] konnédão from konno, „the war". The three other terms have quite a local relation unknown to me, as yet.

[15] bére-koi [béri-koi?, „horseman"] again has quite a local relation, as is very natural with these terms. — Instead of yo (not to be confounded with yó, „camel" p. 187) Koelle Polyglotta has yon, Rafenel in Arama hiá.

[16] marõni can scarcely be the term denoting the foreigner himself, but seems to express the query „what is his town (or country)", ma, „what" rô, „town", (na-)ni, „of him".

[17] bille lorãõde is exactly the English „countryman".

[18] máboã layómazẽ: máboá fem. of mábi p. 221, layómazẽ probably a corrupted form of yólomazẽ, „the female slaves". — elwayẽ seems to be derived from elwa, ĕlwa, the name given to the indigenous Arab population.

[19] dadá-ni evé: evé, „the female slaves"; dada in this place can scarcely be identical with dada given p. 213, note 16 = eddo, „father".

[20] manzol, evidently is derived from manzan, „bad".

[21] hartba is corrupted from the Arabic yarib.

[22] beléd embó-nak ti, „he is (ti) of" (nak relation of genitive case, p. CCCXI, w, α), beléd embó, „town of me", „my town", i. e. „he is my countryman".

[23] ãdu: Seetzen has a curious compound word manganjiadij (in his own writing), which seems to contain our word.

Deutsch und Englisch.	Kanúri.	Tédā.	Hausa.	Fulfúlde.
freier Mann — free-man	kām-bē[1] . .	morī	dā Pl. dīa . .	odímo Pl. rimbe
Sklave (ohne Unterschied des Geschlechts) — slave (in general)	kindži Pl. kindži-wa[2]	agrē	baua Pl. bai .	birde . . .
Sklave (männlich) — slave (male)	kária Pl. kári-wa[3]			mátšodo Plur. mátšubē[13]
Sklavin — female slave .	kir Pl. kir-wa	bodír Pl. bodéruā[7]	bauya[10] . .	. . . . . .
der Freigelassene — liberated slave	kām-bē-tšin[4]	kamaī[8] . . / nē morī entér	bárrerē[11] . .	rimdinádo . .
Sohn eines Freigelassenen — son of a liberated slave	tšútšana[5] . .	kámayē S. . / kīkenī N. .	bā-tšútšān[12] .	dimādio . . / bī-romde[14] .
Diener — servant . . .	wúledī[6] (Arb.)	berē[9] . . .	baraie . . .	barayēro . .

[1] kām-bē, eigentlich „freier Mann"; Koelle kámbē. Er hat ausserdem noch den Ausdruck mágāmi für „Freigeborner"; der ist mir aber unbekannt geblieben.

[2] kindžī. Koelle schreibt kēntšī, vielleicht der Wurzel näher kommend. — „Die königlichen Sklaven", K. kindžiwa mai-bē, T. agrē derdai, H. bai n serki, F. mátšubē lámido, B. bahlāg en bānga, M. mit dem besonderen Namen kōrayāt bezeichnet.

[3] kária, Koelle kálīa; er müsste dann konsequent auch kīl schreiben und nicht kir.

[4] kām-bē-tšin ist ursprünglich weder Substantiv noch Adjektiv, sondern Verbalform: „er ist frei geworden", von kām-bē-ngin, „ich werde frei", wird aber als substantivischer Zusatz gebraucht. Der Verbalform kām-bē-ngin giebt Koelle übrigens fälschlich auch die Bedeutung „ich mache frei", das heisst kām-bē-nīskin oder kām-bē-dīskin.

[5] tšútšana fehlt bei Koelle. Auch die Maghrebiner gebrauchen Kuban in diesem Sinne.

[6] wúledī fehlt bei Koelle; es wird auch kaum in allgemeinem populären Gebrauch sein. Für „Diener", „Gesinde" gebrauchen die Kanúri oft in engerem Sinne ayāl fēto-bē, was ich oben für die ganze Familie angeführt habe; s. S. 219, N. 5.

[7] bodéruā. Über die Ähnlichkeit dieses und des Hausa-Wortes bodurúe für „Mädchen", s. oben S. 270, N. 10.

[8] kamaī ist auffallend und vielleicht erst spätere Ableitung aus dem Kanúri, da die Form kam für „Mensch" im Tédā nicht gebräuchlich ist. nē morī entér ist eine umständliche Ausdrucksweise, „er ist frei geworden".

[9] berē und die verwandten Ausdrücke, mit Einschluss von bēli, „Sklave" im Bagrimma, scheinen dem Alt-Egyptischen entlehnt; im Amhára barja, „Sklave".

[10] bauya. Ich will hier in der Note die besonderen Namen gewisser Unterabtheilungen der Sklavinnen im Hausa und Fulfúlde-Haushalt anführen: „die Sklavin, die als Verwalterin oder Wirthschafterin das ganze Vertrauen ihres Herrn besitzt", H. bauya amíni, F. mátšudo kelādo; „die alte (treue) Sklavin", H. sūfue a bauya, F. korde nēdāi; „die Sklavin zum Kornstampfen", H. bauya n dakka, F. tšadido; „die Sklavin, die das Haus rein hält", H. maitšāre n gida, F. korde dēno-āre; „die Sklavin zum Wassertragen", H. kuyángi (offenbar ein fremdländisches, wahrscheinlich dem Songhai entlehntes, Wort, das auf Hausa umschrieben wird mai-baete mai-daukī n rūa), F. kopangēdāo.

[11] bárrerē, Participium passivi von ina ber, „ich lasse frei"; ich führe hier noch an „die freigelassene Sklavenfrau", wie solche Freilassung durch Geburt eines Kindes nach dem Koran gewissermassen eintritt, H. bauya maile bárrerē, F. korde dēbo rimdinádo.

[12] bā-tšútšān. Ich führe hier einen anderen begriffsverwandten Ausdruck an, nämlich bā-gadāo, Plur. bē-asaī, „Sohn eines Sklaven mit einer Freien".

[13] mátšudo. Reichardt hat mádūdo.

[14] bī-romde heisst eigentlich „Kind des Sklavenwallers" (romde).

[15] tam wird, glaube ich, nur in der allgemeinsten Bedeutung für Sklave gebraucht, während bei Unterscheidung des Geschlechts bauya, im Kugédeni baina, gebraucht wird, wofür Denham bunnua hat. — birtšīa bei tam birtšīa ist wahrscheinlich dasselbe mit berkia, „freier Mann". — Für „Sohn eines Freigelassenen" habe ich im Kugédeni avei-kai; für „Diener", bogā-n kēgei.

[16] bille dana kedám. bille, „Mensch", kedám aus dem Arabischen entstellt.

[17] edsa tīle, „Kind eines Mannes".

[18] ēve, ēwe. Daran wol die S. 95 angeführte Pluralform wawō. — kōttana scheint mir zweifelhaft, vgl. oben S. 216 kodde, „jüngerer Bruder". Ich will hier aber nachholen, dass Koelle (Polyglotta) für „Bruder" einen ganz verschiedenen Ausdruck gibt, nämlich aktsam, offenbar in seinem Dialekt „Sohn der Mutter", aktac-mō, ganz völlig dem wāl-o-māa im Logoné entsprechend. In Bezug auf unser Wort hier ist es mir auffallend, dass Koelle in seiner Polyglotta zwei ganz verschiedene und sehr charakteristische Ausdrücke hat, nämlich bāka (das an das Alt-Egyptische bāk erinnert) für „Sklave" und āfi für „Sklavin". Vielleicht ist das erstere das allgemeine Wort für „Sklave" als Beutē; das letztere = ēve.

[19] billa nāhila gefga tse ēlle, eine lange, unbeholfene Redensart, die wahrscheinlich heisst „ein Individuum, das angefangen hat (gafga) ein (freier) Mann zu sein". bille, „Mensch" aber gehört nicht der Wándalá-Sprache, sondern dem Logmó an.

[20] bēli s. N. 9. Für das ganze Sklavengesinde, besonders im fürstlichen Haushalt, haben die Bagrimma den Ausdruck kojil, die Miba koil.

[21] māla-tšiddāgu. Das tšidda scheint nur eine leichte Veränderung des kidda, „Arbeiter", zu sein.

[22] maddīk. Barchkardt, der dasselbe hat, gibt als Plural mayto (maito). — Übrigens kann dasselbe Wort wol kaum „Sklavin" und „Diener" heissen. Seetzen hat für „Knecht, Bedienter", kambah.

Sońyai.	Lógoné.	Wándalá.	Bágrimma.	Mába.
bor kin(?) . . .	(kam-bō sir) . .	edze žile[17]	(kam-bē) . .	. . . . . .
tam[15]	yolémazā Plur. yall-mazē	ōve, ōwe[18] . .	bēli[20] . . .	bōrik Pl. bortu
banya har(?) . .				
banya wai(?) . .		kóttena[? [18]] .	bōlo	madžik[22] / džuńgur
tam birtšin . .	haiták (Arb.) . .	billa nábila gef-ga tse žile[19]	háitaká (Arb.)	bōrik mátúkte (h. A.)
. . . .	súsunā	tsúntsana . .	tšútšana . .	mátúk-na kalák (h. A.)
. . . .	bille dana kadám[16]	žil wúledi . .	mála-tšiddánge[21]	madžik Pl. madžiu

[1] kám-bē (Koelle kámbē), „free (bē) man". Koelle has, besides, another term, viz mágōmi, „one who is free-born", but that I have never heard and recommend the term strongly to the control of future travellers.

[2] kindāi: Koelle writes kéntšī, which may approach somewhat nearer to the root. — „The Royal slaves", K. kindāi-we mei-bē, T. ngrō derdai, H. bai n serki, F. mátšubē lámido, B. bakińg na bańga, in M. with the peculiar title kóyayát.

[3] kavia: Koelle kália, but then he ought to have written also kil, and not kir for „female slave".

[4] kám-bē-tšin, originally, is neither substantive, nor adjective, but is a verbal form from kám-bē-ágin, meaning „he is free" or rather „he has become free", which, however, may be added to a substantive with the power of an adjective: „this man, he or who has become free"; kám-bē-ágin, however, cannot convey at the same time the active or rather transitive meaning „I make free, liberate", as Koelle states, but that is rather kám-bē-niskin or kám-bē-diskin.

[5] tšátšana is wanting in Koelle. Also the Maghrebine Arabs use the word šušān with this meaning.

[6] wúledi is wanting in Koelle and may really not be a word in common use. The whole idea of what we call „servant" is, of course, rather strange to these people, and for the plural „servants" comprising all the domestics of one household, the Kanúri employ the half Arabic term ayál fāto-bē; compare p. 313, note 5.

[7] badérma: As for the close resemblance of this word with the Hausa-term budurua meaning „girl", see what I have said p. 270, note 10.

[8] hamni is a remarkable term, and may simply be borrowed from the Kanúri. ná mori entér means „he has become a free man".

[9] berē and the related terms in the other languages here represented, including bēli, „slave" in Bágrimma, bára in Ambára, seem to have been borrowed from the ancient Egyptian.

[10] banya: I here am going to mention the peculiar names in Hausa and Fulfúlde of certain subdivisions of the female slaves in an African household. First „the trusty female slave, who keeps the house", H. banya emini, F. mátšudo ko-lúdo: „the old female slave", H. sófua n baiya, F. kordo nyēdii; „the female slave, who pounds the corn", H. banya n dakka, F. išodido; „the female slave, who sweeps the house", H. mai-taire n gida, F. kordo dēno-ūra; „the female slave, who serves as watercarrier", H. kuyángi (no doubt a word of foreign origin, probably borrowed from the Sonyai which, translated into pure Hausa means mai-banta mai-dauki n rūa), F. koyangéde.

[11] bárrorē properly is the participle of the passive voice from ina her, „I liberate", but sometimes it is used as a substantive. I here mention still the name given to „the freed slave wife", the female slave becoming free by right, after having given birth to a child, H. banya mutšo bárroré, F. korde dibo rimdiņādo.

[12] bá-tšátšán: I here mention another term of a related import, viz bā-gadše, plur. bá-sanā, „son of a slave and of a free woman".

[13] mátšudo: Reichardt writes madšudo.

[14] bi-rumdo means properly „child of a slave hamlet" (rumde).

[15] tam, I think, is only used to indicate slaves in the most general sense as property, while, when looking upon them as human beings, and distinguishing the sex banya (baina in Emghédesi) is used, which is identical with the bannu of Denham. — As for birtšin in the composite term tam birtšin, it is probably identical with borkin meaning „free man".

[16] bille dana kadám: bille, „man", kadám perhaps a corruption of the Arabic.

[17] edze žile, „son of a man".

[18] ōve, ōwe: there are, no doubt, the plural-form wawā, adduced p. 95. — As for kóttena, „female slave", it seems doubtful to me, especially if we compare kadde, „younger brother" p. 215. As for the meaning „brother", which is not expressed in that term, I must here mention, that Koelle (Polyglotta) has for „brother" the very expressive term ahtema (ahtes-má in his dialect i. e. „son of mother"). Now, Koelle has also two totally different terms for „slave" and „female slave", viz báke and áfi, the former of which reminds us of the ancient Egyptian bōk, while the latter may be identical with my ōve.

[19] billa nábila gefga tse žile means probably „an individual, who has begun (gefga) to be a (free) man" (žil).

[20] bēli; as for this term see note 9. — For the whole community of slaves, especially in a Princely household, the Bágrimma have the term kolli, the Mába kolī.

[21] mála-tšiddánge: the tšidda seems to be nothing, but a slight variation of the word kidda, „work-man".

[22] madžik: Burckhardt, who has the same, gives in the plural mayte (maite), while Seetzen for „servant" has the totally different term kambah.

Deutsch und Englisch.	Kanúri.	Tédā.	Hausa.	Fulfúlde.
Stallknecht, Pferdejunge — *groom, horse-boy*	muli-ma [1] . .	. . . . . .	maggi [10] . . .	dòko putšu .
Arbeiter, Tagelöhner — *work-man, journey-men*	kída-kída-ma [2]	. . . . . .	ma-aiki . .	baráđio Plur. - bárué dakáre . .
Lastträger — *porter, carrier*	ágerl-ma [3] .	. . . . . .	mai-dauki-n kāya	. . . . .
Pförtner — *porter* . . .	tšégā-ma [4] . .	iwē-ka-dē [8] .	mai-kōfa . .	. . . . .
Herr, Gebieter, Häuptling — *master, chief, chieftain*	mai [5] . . .	dirdē . . . / derdaī . . .	serkí [11] Pl. sára-kai, sarákona	lámido Plur. lalámbe [13]
Oberherr, Fürst, Sultan — *sovereign, liege-lord, sultan*	mai kúrā . .	dirdē buī . .	babá n serkí .	lámido maundo
Königin, Sultanin — *queen, sultana*	mai kāmo . .	dérdayē dē hé-nuā [9]	serkí matše . / sarauniā . .	. . . . .
Königin-Mutter — *queen mother*	mágerā [6] . .	. . . . . .	. . . . .	. . . . .
Thronerbe, Kronprinz — *heir apparent, crown-prince*	tšila mai kúrā / tšírō-ma [7] .	. . . . . .	tšírō-ma [12] .	

[1] muli-ma von mulí, „Pferdestall".

[2] kída-kída-ma. kída-ma (von kí-da, „die Arbeit", von di-skin, „ich thue, mache") wäre eigentlich vollkommen genug; die Wiederholung des kída ist aber im gewöhnlichen Leben ganz allgemein, um das Ausschliessliche zu bezeichnen. Ich will hier noch anführen, dass ich irgendwo kídama in der Bedeutung von „Lieblingssklavin" gefunden habe, das scheint jedoch nur missbräuchlich.

[3] ágerl-ma von ágerl, „Lohn", das wol mit dem Arabischen kerá zusammenhängt. Beide Wörter fehlen bei Koelle.

[4] tšégā-ma (Koelle tšígāma) kommt allerdings von tšéga oder tšíga, „das Stadtthor" her, letzteres Wort aber habe ich im alltäglichen Gebrauch nie gehört und schliesse daraus, dass es nur eine verschiedene Form von tšínna ist.

[5] mai, Koelle mai. Von mai ist der Titel mai-na abgeleitet, der ursprünglich „Prinz" bedeutet und ausser den Söhnen des Königs selbst ehemals nur noch denen des Kaigamma gegeben wurde (s. Reisen, Th. II, S. 318 Note), jetzt aber weniger Bedeutung hat.

[6] mágerā Koelle mágira. Das Wort gehört wol sicherlich der Lógonē-Sprache an, wo es eben „Mutter des Königs" heisst.

[7] tšírō-ma fehlt bei Koelle. Der Ursprung dieses auch in andere Sprachen übergegangenen Wortes ist mir unsicher.

[8] iwē-ka-dē von iwé, „Haus", ka = kai, „Thür", und dē, eigentlich „Mutter", dann die Postposition der Beziehung. S. Einleitung S. LXXX, 10.

[9] dérdayē dē hé-nuā, wörtlich „der König seiner Mutter". S. Einleitung S. LXXX.

[10] maggi. Daneben gibt es noch den begriffsverwandten Ausdruck sayāyo, dessen genaue Beziehung mir jedoch unbekannt ist.

[11] serkí entspricht dem sarikí oder salikí bei Schön.

[12] tšírō-ma. Über die frühere Reihenfolge der Hofämter in den Hausa-Reichen, die noch jetzt auch in den meisten Gegenden des mittleren Negerlandes beibehalten ist, s. meine Auseinandersetzung in der aus dem Jahrgang 1851 des Journal of the R. Geogr. Soc. of London ausgezogenen Berichterstattung über die Central-Afrikanische Expedition: Progress of the Mission to Central Africa p. 64. Eine als Autorität anerkannte „Königin-Mutter" gibt es in den Hausa-Staaten nicht.

[13] lámido. Der Plural la-lambe ist nur durch euphonistische Wiederholung der ersten Sylbe la entstanden.

[14] kol. Raffenel gibt in Arema für „prince", Almohadem, das klassischen Arabischen Einfluss deutlich zeigt.

[15] mírā, eigentlich mé-ya-rā. Dass übrigens das r sich mehr einem y nähert, sieht man aus wál-à-yal, „Königssohn".

[16] wál-à-yal. Über die Reihenfolge der Hofämter im beschränkten Lógonēer Staatsleben s. Reisen, Th. III, S 217. In ihr entspricht eigentlich der malàyuma dem yaladi-ma; der wál-à-yal folgt in seiner Amtsstellung erst hinter dem maraleyā, der als „Herr des Flusses" in diesem kleinen, von zwei schiffbaren Flüssen eingeschlossenen, befruchteten und dem Verkehr eröffneten, Herrschaft besonders grosse Bedeutung hat. Ein solcher Hafenmeister, „Herr des Flusses oder Herr der Boote" erscheint auch in manchen Hausa-Staaten, besonders aber in Nūfe (unter dem Titel [illegible]) auch als ein Beamter ersten Ranges; H. heisst er serkí n rūa oder serkí n žirgi, F. lamído ndiem oder lamído lanádde, auf S. hio koi, der in Timbuktu bei dem damals so lebendigen Flussverkehr einst grosse Autorität besass.

[17] kídda-kídda. Dieser Ausdruck, so wie der davon abgeleitete im Bagrimma sind nur dem Kanúri entlehnt. — Zu tšéndakri, d. i. tše-nd(e)-akri vgl. Einleitung S CCXLII, c. b). — Anstatt tahaē hat Koelle Polyglotta die abweichende Form olēhoe, wo ol wol den eigenthümlichen O-Laut darstellen.

[18] mal-ted-kídda-kídda-ma. Dazu vgl. Einleitung S. CCLXXIV, f).

[19] baāga. Zu den verwandtschaftlichen Beziehungen dieses Wortes s. Einleitung, Nachtrag, S. CCCXXXII am Ende.

[20] kárih siág-ne melék, „der Mann, Herr (melék) der Thür (siág)". Daher der Titel des ersten Vezirs am Hofe von Wadāï, worüber ich, wie über die übrigen Hofämter, in meiner Abhandlung über jenes Land, Reisen, Th. III, S. 215, gesprochen habe. Dieser Siágmelék eben ist es, der auch in den Berichten über Vogel's Tod eine bedeutende Rolle spielt.

Sónyai.	Lógonē.	Wándalā.	Bágrimma.	Mába.
. . . .	. . . .	. . . . . .	. . . . . .	. . . . . .
. . . .	káre kárebá . .	kidda-kidda [17]	mal-tad-kidda-kidda-ma [18]	. . . . . .
. . . .	bill(e) ákeri . .	θéndakrí . .	mála-diggi .	. . . . . .
. . . .	me-siátima . .	tāegāma . .	tāegāma . .	borik sing-ne me-lék [20]
koi . . . . . . / Amīro . . .	mlarā [15]	tuksē . . .	. . . . . .	. . . . . .
koi bēro . . . / ko-koi [14] . . .	mlarā demá . .	tuks-u-malē .	banga [19] . .	sultān (Arb.)
. . . .	mlarā (e)l ganúm	. . . . .	banga-nē . .	. . . . . .
. . . .	mágirā	mágerā . . .	kuā banga .	moma
koi izze	wúl-ā-yal [16] . .	edze-tuksē .	tāirōma . . .	kolōtu

[1] mall-ma from mall, „stable".
[2] kida-kida-ma: kida-ma (from ki-da, „work", from di-skin, „I do work") would be sufficient to express the idea of „work-man", but it is quite common in this case to repeat the substantive, thus saying kida-kida-ma, in order to express the exclusiveness of the occupation. I will here mention, that I have somewhere found the term kidama used as meaning „favorite female slave"; but such seems rather an abuse.
[3] ágerī-ma from ágeri, „wagon", which seems to be derived from the Arabic kerī. Both words are wanting in Koelle.
[4] tšégá-ma (Koelle tšigāma), no doubt, is derived from tšéga or tšīga, „the gate of the town", but I have never heard such a term to be used, and I therefore conclude, that it is only a different form of tšiima.
[5] mai: Koelle writes mei. From mai the title mai-ma has been derived, which originally meant „prince Royal", and besides to the sons of the king, in former times was given also to those of the kaiyá-má, but at present has become a title of minor importance.
[6] mágerā: Koelle mágira. — The word evidently has been borrowed from the Lógonē, where it simply means „king's mother".
[7] tširō-ma is wanting in Koelle. — With the origin and original meaning of this term, which has also passed into other languages, I am not acquainted.
[8] iwō-ka-dō from iwō, „house", ka = kai, „dear", and dō (originally „mother"), the term expressing origin and relation, and spoken of Introductory Remarks p. LXXXI, 10.
[9] dérdayē dē ká-nal means verbally „the king his mother". See Introductory Remarks p. LXXXI.
[10] saggi: the Hausa-language has another term sayēye, of a similar meaning, but the exact import of which is not known to me.
[11] serki: Schön gives the form sariki or saliki.
[12] tšīrō-ma: with regard the former order and rank of the offices in the Royal household of the Hausa-states, which even at the present time has been preserved in most of the provinces in the central parts of Negroland, see my remarks in the „Progress of the Mission to Central Africa" (forming part of the Journal of the R. Geogr. Soc. 1851) p. 64.
[13] lamide: the plural-form la-lambe seems to owe its origin to a merely euphonical repetition of the first syllable la.
[14] koi: Raffenel in Arama gives the term Almohadem for „prince" which clearly exhibits its Arabic origin.
[15] mlarā: the root is rā, yō (thence wūl-ā-yal, „son of king", kim-rā-yō, „persons belonging to king", i. q. „courtier" p. 331).
[16] wúl-ā-yal: With regard to the list of offices of the Royal household in the small principality of Lógonē, see Travels, vol. III, p. 306. Here the title of the malayuán originally corresponds to that of the yaladī-ma, while the wúl-ā-yal follows according to his rank behind the marāleyá, „the Sire of the river", the latter exercising a great deal of authority in this small community, hemmed in towards the East and West by large navigable rivers. — However, such a master of the river, or master of the harbour or the boats, H. serki n rūa or serki n jirgi, F. lāmīdo ndiam or lāmīdo laoōēe, exercises also paramount authority in several of the Hausa-states, especially in Nūpe, where they bear the titles soāa and lēēi; even in Tímbuktu the hi koi in former times was a person of first rank and authority.
[17] kidda-kidda: this term, as well as the corresponding one in Bágrimma, seems to have been borrowed from the Kanúri. — As for θéndakrī i. e. θe-nd(a)-akri, „he who takes hire", see Introductory Remarks p. CCXLIII, e, b). — Instead tuksē Koelle (Polyglotta) has the curious form siéken, where si probably are intended to convey the sound of θ.
[18] mal-tad-kidda-kidda-ma: as for this mode of composition, see Introductory Remarks p. CCLXXV, f).
[19] banga: as for the affinity of this term, originally meaning „chief of village" (ba), with the corresponding terms of other languages of East Africa, see Introductory Remarks, Appendix p. CCCXXXIII.
[20] bōrik sing-ne meléh, „the son, master (meléh) of the gate (sing)". This is the origin of the title of the Vizier at the court of Wadāi, as I have more fully explained in my Travels, vol. III, p. 545. Also in the reports with regard to the death of Mr. Vogel this Síngmeléh plays a conspicuous part.

Deutsch und Englisch.	Kanúri.	Téda.	Hausa.	Fulfúlde.
Reihenfolge der Hofämter an den verschiedenen Höfen eines jeden dieser Völker — List of courtiers according to the rank which each of them holds at the court of each of these nations.	kalyá-ma[1] .	buyá dérdayé[5]	yáladī-ma[6] .	yáladī-ma . / bátšido lámido maundo
	yerī-ma . .		burda n Kano[7]	. . . . . .
	yáladī-ma . .		serkí n daúakai[8]	lámido putši / bōre putši .
	fugū-ma . .		alkāli[9] (Arb.)	alkāli . . .
	káyarī-ma . .		serki n bai[10]	. . . . . .
	aintel-ma . .		gadō[11] . .	. . . . . .
	kásal-ma[2] .		serkí n šāṅo[12]	džōro nai . .
	kayustē-ma .		. . . . . .	. . . . . .
	árdžinō-ma[3] .		. . . . . .	. . . . . .
	mestrē-ma .		. . . . . .	. . . . . .
	yirō-ma . .		. . . . . .	. . . . . .
Anführer — *Commander* .	kažélla[4] . .	. . . .	serkí n yáki[13]	lámido konno

[1] Ich habe hier die Reihenfolge der Würdenträger an den verschiedenen Höfen einander gegenübergestellt, obgleich sich ihre Titel in den meisten Fällen keineswegs genau entsprechen. Die Kanúri-Ordnung ist die Reihenfolge der 12 grossen Ämter (mit Einschluss des tširóma) im alten Reiche der Séfua, die in der neuen Dynastie der Kánemiyin allerdings ganz umgeworfen ist. S. über sie Reisen, Th. II, Anhang S. 328 ff.; dort habe ich auch die ursprüngliche Bedeutung jedes Titels einzeln erläutert und theilweise schon die von Koelle in seinem Wörterbuche unter dem Worte [illegible] gegebenen Abweichungen berücksichtigt.

[2] kásal-ma. Koelle hat kásalma.

[3] árdžinō-ma. Koelle árdžinōma.

[4] kažélla. Koelle hat kátsella und gibt ihm eine nicht ganz richtige Bedeutung. Als Titel bedeutet es nämlich nur den Kriegshauptmann, der allerdings zuweilen auch die Regierung eines Bezirkes erhält, wie wiederholte Beispiele davon in meinem Reiseberichte gegeben sind. — Über die untergeordneten Ämter des ká-ma und gó-ma s. Reisen, Th. II, S. 330.

[5] buyá dérdayé, „die Grossen des Königs".

[6] yáladī-ma. Diese, dem Kanúri-Reiche entlehnte Würde ist in den Hausa-Staaten stets die erste nach dem Herrscher selbst, was durch die Fulfúlde-Phrase bátšido lámido maundo, „der Nächste nach dem Grossherrn", bestimmter ausgedrückt ist, und entspricht so ziemlich derjenigen eines ersten Ministers, weshalb sie auch in den Niger-Berichten so unaufhörlich wiederkehrt.

[7] burda n Kano. Dieses Amt hat allerdings direkt nur Anwendung auf die Provinz Kano, erscheint aber auch an anderen Höfen.

[8] serki n daúakai, wörtlich „Herr der Pferde", „Anführer der Reiterei".

[9] alkāli, aus dem Arabischen al kádi, „der Richter", hat grosse Bedeutung in dem Hofpersonal der Hausa-Staaten, und ich habe ihn hier in seiner Rangordnung eingeschoben, obgleich ich ihn unten noch einmal bringe.

[10] serki n bai, wörtlich „Herr der Sklaven".

[11] gadō, „der Schatzmeister". — Irgend Jemand möchte glauben, dass diesem Titel der Gadādo in Sókoto entspricht, den Clapperton so häufig als Würdenträger daselbst aufführt, aber das war der Eigenname des damaligen ersten Ministers daselbst, kein Titel.

[12] serki n šāṅo, ganz wie der entsprechende Fulfúlde-Titel, wörtlich „Herr der [illegible]", d. h. „Quartiermeister".

[13] serki n yáki, gleichwie F. lámido konno, wörtlich „Herr des Krieges oder Kriegszuges", entspricht nicht eigentlich dem kažélla, sondern in manchen Beziehungen eher dem kalyá-ma, obgleich es kein stehendes Hofamt ist, sondern mehr zeitweiliges Amt während der Dauer jedes einzelnen Kriegs- oder Raubzuges.

[14] bérie kol entspricht wörtlich dem serki n daúakai; gabi kol-ni entspricht dem serki n karfi, „eine Art Polizeimeister" im Hausa. — Für „Minister" im Allgemeinen (ministre) gibt Raffenel im verwandten Azenaga [illegible], dessen zweiter Theil an den im Bagirmi gebräuchlichen Titel ka-kol) gerē-gerē für den ersten Minister erinnert. — Über die Hofämter im alten Sonyai-Reiche, besonders über den Titel ferreng oder forma, s. Reisen, Th. IV, S. 4[illegible].

[15] ibálaynán, d. i. iba-balaynan, scheint in entsprechender Beziehung zu bálaynán zu stehen, das den hauptsächlichen Bestandtheil des letzten der folgenden Titel bildet; iba scheint der Haupttitel zu sein, vgl. Reisen l. c. S. 278, Note. Merkwürdig ist dabei im höchsten Grade, dass ibálaynán äusserlich fast ganz genau dem Titel der entsprechenden Würde in der Yóruba-Sprache gleicht, wo er nach Crowther bálogun heisst.

[16] Über den fatša und die übrigen Würdenträger in Bagirmi s. Reisen, Th. III, S. 403.

[17] [illegible], s. oben S. 226, N. 16; die übrigen Titel der Würdenträger in Wadái habe ich nicht hierher gesetzt, weil dort keine stehende Rangordnung herrscht, sondern Alles mehr vom persönlichen Einflusse und von Zeitumständen abhängt. S. die nähere Beschreibung der einzelnen Ämter in Reisen, Th. III, S. 516 ff. — [illegible] ágíd, dieser altarabischen Würde des Kriegshauptmannes, die auch von den Abābde und [illegible]-Beduinen bewahrt wurde, vgl. die vortrefflichen Bemerkungen Burckhardt's, Beduinen und Wahábi, Weimar 1831, S. 239—242.

Sońγai.	Lógone.	Wándalā.	Bágrimma.	Mába.
bério koi [14] . .	ibálayuán [15] . .	θagámma . .	fatša [16] . . .	mairam / siñg-melék [17]
gabi koi-ni . .	maláyuán . . .	θe-dé-gonē .	ńgar-māne . .	. . . . . .
. . . . . .	mairáī	edzōfa . . .	gelétma . .	. . . . . .
. . . . . .	madám	θéwomō . .	gar-moyenmańga	. . . . . .
. . . . . .	mará-leyā . .	θimdalā . .	milma . . .	. . . . . .
. . . . . .	maraī-marbā . .	θéwela . . .	gar-ńgōde .	. . . . . .
. . . . . .	madám-atiā . .	θiggerēa . .	gar-ńgińgo .	. . . . . .
. . . . . .	madám-uχθám .	θudžā (θe-udžā)	. . . . . .	. . . . . .
. . . . . .	fnθawā	iaégge . . .	. . . . . .	. . . . . .
. . . . . .	mage wenī aχθám	. . . . . .	. . . . . .	. . . . . .
. . . . . .	másayē aχθám .	. . . . . .	. . . . . .	. . . . . .
woñgo bońgo . .	mage wenī halaguán	bérgoma . .	barma . . .	kámkolák / ágīd Pl. ágade

[1] I have here arranged the titles of the chief dignitaries at the courts of the various African states in parallel order, although but in a few cases they correspond to each other exactly. The list given in Kanúri is the order and rank of the chief offices under the old dynasty of the Séf-wa, which offices have been totally overthrown under the new dynasty of the Kánemiyīn, where no such rank does exist at all. See my Travels, vol II, p. 640, where I have explained at the same time the original meaning of each title. A person who takes some more serious interest in the matter, may also compare the list of these charges as given by Koelle in his vocabulary under the word ślam, where there are, however, some mistakes.

[2] kéal-ma: Koelle writes kéealmá.

[3] árdšiné-ma: Koelle ártšinéma.

[4] kalēila: Koelle writes kåtealla and gives it a rather wrong meaning; for, if a kaléila is made the governor of a district — he is never a magistrate —, it is merely from certain political reasons, principally on account of the dangerous state of the province, of which I have given several instances in my Travels, but such a governorship is not indicated by the title itself. As for the inferior offices of the bú-ma and gá-ma, not mentioned here, see Tr., vol. II, p. 660.

[5] bayā dérdayó, „the great (men) of the king".

[6] yéladī-ma: the charge of this officer in the Hausa-states is always the first after the ruler himself, a relation which has been expressed more distinctly by the Fulfúlde-title kátšīdo lámido maudo, „the first following upon the Sovereign", and is almost identical with the authority of a Prime Minister in a despotical state.

[7] borda n Kano: this office properly has only reference to the province of Kano, but is also represented in the other provinces.

[8] serki n dáúchaī means verbally „master of the harem".

[9] alkāli from the Arabic el kádi, „the supreme judge". I have inserted the name of this officer here on account of his rank and authority in the Royal household of several Hausa-states; but I must render it also in another place.

[10] serki n baī means verbally „master of the slaves".

[11] gadó is nearly identical with our „treasurer". — To this gadó somebody might think, the Gedádo in Sókoto mentioned by Clapperton as a sort of title, to correspond; but Gedádo was the proper name of the Prime minister at the time of the visit of that distinguished traveller, not his title or rank.

[12] serki n šāno, just as the corresponding Fulfúlde-term, verbally „master of the cattle" or rather „care of herds", that is to say „the quarter-master general".

[13] serki n yākí, properly „master of the war or warlike expedition", does not exactly correspond to the office of the kaléila, but in some respects rather to that of the kalyá-ma, although it does not range among the statute offices of the court, but is rather a mere temporary charge.

[14] bério koi is verbally identical with the serki n dáúchaī. — Compare Travels, vol. IV, p. 417, with regard to the scanty acquaintance we have with the offices of the Royal household in the old empire of Sońγai, especially also with regard to the farma or feréńg. — I here mention still the office of the gabi koi-ni, which is identical with that of the serki n hardī in Hausa as a sort of „minister of Police". I further mention, that Raffenel in Arvma gives tiékéré for „minister", in general (ministre), the second part of which term seems to correspond to the title ka-kol geré-geré mentioned by me in Bagírmi as that given to the first minister.

[15] ibálayuán: this title, contracted from iba-balayuán, iba being the proper title, as mentioned Tr. vol. III, p. 306, seems to have some close relation to that of bálayuán, which forms the chief ingredient of one of the following titles. But, besides, it is curious to see, that ibálayuán is almost identical with bálogun, the corresponding title in the Yóruba-language.

[16] With regard to the fatša and the other dignitaries in Bagírmi, see Travels, vol. III, p. 462.

[17] siñg-melék, see p. 227, note 16; as for the other titles of dignitaries in Wádāi, which I have not inserted in this place, as they relate more to personal qualities, and do not bear the character of a systematical order of rank and authority, see vol. III, p. 443. — As for the truly Arab dignity of the ágīd or „war-chief", preserved also by the tribes of the Abábde and Bíshārīn, see the excellent remarks of Burckhardt in his „Bedawins and Wahabys".

Deutsch und Englisch.	Kanúri.	Tédā.	Haussa.	Fulfúlde.
Kriegshauptmann — Captain	grē-ma [1] . .	. . . . . .	. . . . . .	. . . . . .
Minister des Innern — minister of the household	digga-ma . .	. . . . . .	mágadži [10] . .	maudo . . .
Hofmann, Hofrath — courtier, member of the council	kókana Pl. koka-náwa [2]	. . . . . .	múlomi n serki	. . . . . .
Rathsversammlung — council	nókana, nógana [3]		. . . . . .	. . . . . .
Amtmann einer Stadt — bailiff of a town	bílla-ma [4] . / tšī-ma [5] . .	. . . . . .	serki n gari / mai-gari [11] .	lámido [15] . .
Kādhi — judge, Kádhi .	rekāli [6] (Arb.)	gaídua [9] . .	alkāli . . .	alkāli [16] . . .
der Imam — the Imam .	rimám [7] (Arb.)	limán . . .	. . . . . .	al imāmu . .
königlicher Bote — royal messenger	kiṅgalam [8] . .	. . . . . .	manzō n serki Pl. manzonin serki	nilādo / lilādo / Pl. nilābe lámido — lámido [15]
königlicher Diener, Adjutant — royal servant, aide de camp	kām mai-bē .		žāka fāda [12] .	džoltinbe lámido

[1] grē-ma. Koelle gérēma. — digga-ma ist ein neuer Titel, der am Hofe Schaich 'Omar's grosse Bedeutung hat.
[2] kókana. Koelle, der kógana schreibt, erklärt es fälschlich für „Soldat".
[3] nókana, nógana steht offenbar in engster Beziehung zum vorhergehenden Worte, als der Ort, wo die Rathssitzung Statt findet oder auch als die Rathsversammlung selbst. Koelle erklärt es eben so unrichtig wie das vorhergehende Wort als „Handwerk des Soldaten".
[4] bílla-ma. Koelle schreibt bəlāma.
[5] tšī-ma (tšīma) erklärt Koelle für den Einnehmer der Abgaben.
[6] rekāli schreibt Koelle lagāli, das er aber dann doch nicht bestimmt auseinanderhält von dem ursprünglich gänzlich verschiedenen lagāri. Übrigens ist der Kādhi im Negerlande eng mit der Moschee verbunden.
[7] rimám. Koelle schreibt limān, das er aber nicht sicher verstanden zu haben scheint, da er es nur auf Mekka bezieht. es ist eigentlich „der Vorbeter" in jeder Muhammedanischen Gemeinde.
[8] kiṅgalam. Koelle hat dafür als Wort kóngama mit der Bedeutung „follower", das eng damit zusammenzuhängen scheint.
[9] gaídua scheint mir verdächtig, da es mit dem kāid oder politischen Verwalter mehr Verwandtschaft zu haben scheint als mit dem kādi oder Richter.
[10] mágadži (erklärt in H. durch die Worte šina gádiewa gida n serki, nicht wie auch Schön, der (Gr. ed. II, p. 9) mágaiši schreibt, von ga. gaši, „erben"), entspricht im Kanúri Hofstaat der Sache nach fast genau dem digga-ma. Der Anklang des mágadži an die Abessinische Würde des magazat, des vom König den einzelnen Emiren beigegebenen Gehülfen, ist nur scheinbar.
[11] serki n gari, mai-gari. Das letztere Wort hat eine allgemeinere Bedeutung und bedeutet gewöhnlich „Städter". — Ich will hier noch einige auf Stadt und Land bezügliche Amtstitel aufführen, die ich nur in Hausa und Fulfúlde erfahren habe. So „Amtmann eines offenen Dorfes", H. serki n ráḡga, F. dšo-[illegible] (dieser Titel ist oft ein Bestandtheil in der Bildung von Ortsnamen geworden); „Amtmann der Fulbe", H. serki n Fúlani, F. ardo Fulbe; „Amtmann der Sullebawa" (s. Reisen, Th. IV, S. 145), H. serki n Sullebawa, F. ardo Sisilbe; „Vogt oder Konsul der zeitweilig als Handelsreisende sich aufhaltenden Araber", H. serki n turawa, F. lámido túrēe (über den Ausdruck ba-túre, Plur. turawa, s. weiter unten); „Steuereinnehmer" (K. tšī-ma, s. oben N. 5), H. serki n [illegible], F. lámido [illegible] (zweifelhaft, [illegible] heissen die Boote und über den lámido [illegible], „Hafenmeister", s. oben S. 226, N. 16); „Zolleinnehmer", H. serki n tafárki, F. lámido [illegible] oder [illegible]; „Marktvogt", H. serki n kāsuwa oder alkāli n kāsuwa, F. lámido lūma, S. [illegible].
[12] žāka fāda, „der nach dem Palast kommt". Statt manzō schreibt Schön manzoh. Ich will hier noch eine eigene Klasse königlicher Leibwächter aufführen, genannt auf H. sárome (Schön sarumi, Plur. sarumai) n serki, Plur. saromawa n serki, F. Plur. [illegible] lámido, und den tálakka n serki, F. [illegible] lámido, eine Art königlicher

Sońyai.	Lógoné.	Wándalá.	Bágrimma.	Mába.
. . . .	máyalé mulō . .	. . . . . .	. . . . . .	agíd
. . . .	. . . .	mágadži [17] . .	zerma . . . / kadamángr .	džerma
. . . .	himrayē (p. 227, note 15)	kókona tekwē .	. . . . . .	adžuādi Plur. adžauid
. . . .	táluha	akúñirē (akúñi [re?])	gar-m-bange .	fāšer / fāšer-melō [19]
kōra koi . . . / Amiro . . .	níaadā	bílla-ma [18] .	gar . . . . / gol-n-nánge .	hillek melek (h. A.)
Alkāli [16] . . .	lekāli	erkāli . . .	alkāli . . .	kādik
al Imāmu . . .	limán	limán . . .	limán . . .	imám
. . . .	billa mianrē . .	edze šefka	kangéam-m-bań-ga	mesin

[1] gré-ma: Koelle gérēma. — As for the digga-ma (perhaps more correctly dige-ma), it is a recent title, the present diggama, although a man of the most narrow views, exercising paramount authority with Sheikh 'Omar.
[2] kóhana: this term is wrongly explained by Koelle, who writes kógana, as meaning „soldier".
[3] núkana, nógana: this term bears evident traces of a close relation to the preceding one, meaning originally „the place (no, na), where the council is held, or the sitting of the council itself". Koelle explains it wrongly as the profession or occupation of a soldier.
[4] billa-ma: Koelle writes bélēma.
[5] tšī-ma (čīma) is explained by Koelle as meaning „collector of taxes".
[6] yakóli: Koelle writes legāli, which he explains „chief justice of a whole country", and wrongly distinguishes from the very identical legári, „a Muhammadan dignitary in rank between a common schoolmaster and a gāsi".
[7] rimám: Koelle writes limán, but does not seem to have understood the whole import of that term, referring it exclusively to Mecca, while its proper meaning is „he who leads in prayers", be the congregation ever so small.
[8] kiagaiam seems to be identical with Koelle's kágáme with the meaning „follower".
[9] galdma with this notion is suspicious to me, as it seems to be more closely related to the term kāid meaning the governor, than with the term kādi, or the judge.
[10] mágadši: the office of the mágadši (šima gádiewa gide n sarki, while Rev. Schön, who writes magaši (grammar ed. II, p. 9) derives it from ga, gani, „to look") corresponds almost exactly with that of the digga-ma in Kanúri. But, as for the similarity of our term with the Abyssinian magaset, the inspector associated by the king to every provincial governor, it appears to be merely accidental.
[11] sarki n gari, mai-gari: the latter of these terms has rather a double meaning, and is commonly understood as „the inhabitant of the town". — I am here still going to adduce several names of offices, respectively titles, which I have only learnt in Hausa or Fulfúlde. Thus: „the bailiff of an open village", H. sarki n rúgga, F. dāo-ūro (a title, which in many instances has become an integrant part of local names); „the baily of the Fúl-o portion of the inhabitants of a place", H. sarki n Féllani, F. ardo Fúlbo; „the baily of the Syllabawa" (see Trav. vol. IV, p. 144), H. sarki n Syllabawa, F. ardo Sielibe; „the baily of the Arab residents", H. sarki n turawa, F. lámido tūrēa (as for the term ba-túre, plur. turawa, see farther on); „collector of taxes" (K. tšī-ma? see note 5), H. sarki n fitto, F. lámido lanádšo (the latter rather doubtful, lanádša meaning „the boats", and the lámido lanádša having been already explained p. 227, note 16 as „master of the harbour"); „collector of the toll or passage-money", H. sarki n fatárki, F. lámido lanel or dattal; „bailiff of the market", H. sarki n kásua or alkāli n kásua, F. lámido lūmo, S. dōbba-hoi.
[12] šuba fada means properly „he who comes to the palace". — Instead of manso Rev. Schön writes manseh. I here also am going to mention a peculiar class of „Royal body-guard", called in H. sáromo n sarki, plur. saromawa n sarki, F. saŋubé lámido, and finally the baiákka n sarki, F. táihoŕa lámido, a sort of „Royal serfs".
[13] lámido: the Fulfúlde-language is wanting in a more significative term for „governor or bailiff of a town".
[14] alkāli; the Fúlbe possess a peculiar term, via alkāli alkalāti (al kādi al kadāti), for the chief-kādhi, called alkāli babá in Hausa, which may be identical with the very important title Alfa (a corruption of the Arabic yalifa) occurring in the kingdom of Masina, the present Alfa having played a most conspicuous part in the recent history of that Region.
[15] allādo, plur. allōbe, is also used by itself, without adding lámido.
[16] Alkāli: Raffenel for „judge" (juge) in Arama gives the very interesting title sara-tiga-hoi, which most clearly explains the title Saratik, of so general a use in the several states of Senegambia, sara being nothing, but the Arabic Serd, Serīe.
[17] mágadši: The identity of this name in Hausa and Wándalá is remarkable, especially as these terms were obtained in a totally independent manner. However, I have to remark, that the mágadši in W., according to his rank, precedes the bérgoma.
[18] billa-ma: the country people of this small principality do, I expect, possess a more peculiar term, besides this Kanúri one.
[19] fāšer-melō, „the masters (members) of the council". With regard to the kambánjib given by Seetzen as meaning „Royal servant", compare his kambak, „servant", above p. 225, note 72.

Deutsch und Englisch.	Kanúri.	Tédā.	Hausa.	Fulfúlde.
Eunuch — *eunuch* . . .	ádim [1] . . .	togór . . .	bāba n serkí [8] Pl. bābane serki	tšortādo . . / bodžo Pl. bulbe
Aufseher der Sklaven — *overseer of the slaves*	kária marma kúllo-bē [2]	agrē bui hentū [7]	serkí n gandó [9]	hōrēdžo džiābe [12] / maundo džiābe / lámido gándua
Henker, Scharfrichter — *executioner, hangman*	. . . . . .		dūka? . . . / dógali . . .	džom loptaido / dogarīdžo . . / mátšudo lámido
Gelehrter ersten Ranges — *learned man of first rank*	góni [3] (Arb.) .	mállem wār .	mállemi mai-kárratū déwa [10]	módibo džángado
Gelehrter, der den Koran auswendig weiss — *learned man, who knows the Koran by heart*	legāri [4] (Arb.)			módibo maúdudo
Gelehrter im Allgemeinen — *learned man in general*	alfáki (Arb.) / mállem [5] (Arb.	mállem . . .	mállemi . .	módibo . . . .
angehender Gelehrter, der auswärts geht; fahrender Student — *scholar, who does go abroad: wandering student*	fókara [6] (Arb.)		almádžiri [11] .	ahídžo Pl. ahīye

[1] ádim. Koelle ádim. Allerdings vielleicht vom Arabischen خـدم, obgleich dieses Wort „Diener" überhaupt bezeichnet.

[2] kária marma kúllo-bē, wörtlich „der Sklave, der Aufseher des Feldes". Auch Koelle hat márma für den Titel eines Beamten, zunächst im Rang nach dem meinta (maínta), und fügt hinzu, dass es stets ein Sklave sein muss.

[3] góni ist an dem Moslemisirten Negerhof von Bornu mit sehr prononcirter After-Arabischer Bildung zu einer vollkommenen Titulatur geworden, die vom Faki verliehen wird. Koelle góni.

[4] legāri von القاري, „lector, praelector Corani".

[5] mállem (Koelle málam and málǎm) hat eine engere und eine weitere Bedeutung; in jener Beziehung bezeichnet es den wirklichen Gelehrten, zu dem auch der góni, legāri und fáki gehören, daher oft mállem góni u. s. w. gesagt wird; in weiterer Bedeutung aber wird so ein Jeder genannt, der ein Paar Gebete schreiben kann und die kleinen Schulknaben unterrichtet. Dann ist auch mallem in vielen dieser Sprachen auf den Schmied „den Doktor des Eisens" (Casalis, the Basutos p. 131) übergegangen; s. N. 13. Für „Schulmeister" hat Koelle noch das mir zweifelhafte Wort gádager. — alfáki, durch Einfluss des schlechten Meghrebinischen auch häufig figi genannt, ist für die allgemeinen Beziehungen des Lebens mehr der Rechtsgelehrte, als der Gottesgelehrte; aber beide Begriffe fallen hier fast genau zusammen.

[6] fókara (Koelle fugurá), eigentlich Plural von فقير, Plur. فقراء, aber hier als Singular gefasst, bedeutet in Bornu nie, wie Koelle angibt, den gewöhnlichen Schulknaben, sondern den in die Fremde gehenden, bettelnden jungen Studenten, bei dem allerdings die Armuth ein begleitendes Attribut ist, aber keineswegs, wie das bei dem Arabischen Worte, wo es „der Gottbedürftige" im reinsten ausschliesslichsten Sinne bedeutet, der Fall ist, das charakteristische Kennzeichen. Der Begriff dieses Ausdrucks fällt also in vielen Beziehungen mit dem eines Mallem ... zusammen und so nennen die Tédā sie.

[7] agrē bui hentū, „die Sklaven, ihr Ordner"; s. Einleitung S. LXXX, 9.

[8] bāba n serki. Dieses bāba hat nichts mit babá, „gross", gemein, es bedeutet wol ursprünglich „der Alte"; der Beisatz serki gibt ihm allerdings einen näheren Bezug und macht es dem K. ádim mai-bē näher entsprechend, als dem ádim im Allgemeinen; aber das kommt so ziemlich auf dasselbe hinaus, da nur Fürsten Eunuchen haben.

[9] serki n gandó. gandó scheint mir kein ursprüngliches H.-Wort zu sein, sondern aus der Sonyai-Sprache herübergenommen.

[10] mállemi mai-káratū déwa, wörtlich „der Gelehrte von viel Belesenheit".

[11] almádžiri. Dem Arabischen entnommen (s. N. 14), mit leichter Veränderung der Bedeutung.

[12] hōrēdžo džiābe. hōrēdžo ist wol sicherlich von hōre, „Kopf, Haupt", gebildet, das allein erben in dieser übertragenen Bedeutung gebraucht wird.

[13] kohol kaina, eigentlich „der kleine Herr", ist wol ein allgemeiner verbreiteter Ausdruck für „königlicher Eunuch", obgleich ich ihn nur in A'gades gehört habe. Die übrigen dort üblichen Ausdrücke aber lassen gar keine allgemeine Anwendung im Sonyai zu, sondern haben eine ganz lokale Beziehung, ausgenommen vielleicht kohol gorégoré für serki n turaka.

[14] asm. Dieses Wort entspricht sehr eigentlich dem Begriffe eines mállem, da die Benennung des Letzteren, ganz wie im Temáshyt, auf den „Grobschmied" übergegangen ist; s. N. 5. So wird man denn auch weiter unten S. 238 dasselbe Wort asm für „Schmied" finden.

[15] bēla n gotbain. bēll, „Sklave". Das letzte Wort dagegen ist mir unsicher.

[16] māla n dóyō, „Herr des Lesens", von mam-dáyō, „ich lese".

[17] giraír allein ist vielleicht nicht richtig, obgleich es heissen könnte „er, der Lektüre (gir) macht"; s. über dieses eigentlich rein verbale nir Einleitung S. CCX, 1). Dieses gir-nir wäre also verschieden von k-ir-nir, das nur eine allgemeine Thätigkeit ausdrückt (ebenda).

[18] mohādžer, مهاجر, „qui discessit a suis, de regione in regionem migravit", von هجر.

Sonyai.	Lógonē.	Wándalā.	Bágrimma.	Mába.
kókoi kaina [13] .	bílla me-l-ázim* .	wúsala takeē .	ádeme . . .	árak Pl. artu
. . . ¹ . . .	ulomazē ayē . .	mála n ēve .	béla n gothaia [15]	kórayāt kelē ko-lák
. . . . . .	. . . . . .	. . . . . .	. . . . . .	
. . . . . .	goní	goní	el góno . . .	góni
. . . . . .	legári	legári . . .	mála n dóyō [16]	girnir [17]
zem [14]	mállem	mállem . . .	mállem . . .	. . . . . .
aga-náro (verb.?)	wúle fókara . .	pókara . . .	gon-fukaraie .	mohádžar [18] (Arb.)

[1] ádim. Koelle writes ádim. Perhaps it is derived from Arb. خدّام, although this term means „servant" in general.

[2] kária marma kálle-bé means verbally „the slave inspector of the Saida". Koelle also has máyma, and explains it as the title of an officer next in rank to the meinta (i. e. „a Royal commissionary or treasurer and always a slave").

[3] Instead of góni Koelle writes góni. The authority and position of this religious dignitary is characteristic of the Mohammedan white-wash, with which the whole machinery of the Bornu kingdom, or rather the former dynasty of the Sefua, has been plastered over in so very conspicuous a manner. The dignity is conferred by the fakih.

[4] legári from the Arabic القارى, „lector, praelector Corani".

[5] mállem (Koelle málam and málám) has a narrower and a wider meaning, in one respect denoting the really learned man, such as the góni, who on that account often is called mállem góni, in the other comprising all such people, who are able to write down, and to say, or dictate a few prayers, and who as such teach the school-boys, the term in many Mohammedan countries being moreover applied to the blacksmith, „the doctor of iron" (Caulie, the Sahara p. 131 compare note 13 further on). — As for alfakī or, as the term is often spelt through the influence of the so-called Moghrebine dialect, fíqi, he is rather the Doctor of law; but in many parts of Negroland, both notions coincide.

[6] fókara properly is the plural-form of فقير, plur. فقراء, but has been adopted by the natives of Negroland as the singular, and, though originally conveying the notion of voluntary poverty, which proceeds from an application to divine matters, has been almost exclusively applied to the class of young scholars, who go abroad, and while endeavouring to increase their small stock of learning, generally gain their living by begging. The Tédà call this class mállem. But, as far as my experience goes, the name never indicates the simple schoolboy, as Koelle explains the name, which he writes fugurá.

[7] agrē bul hentá, „the slaves their chief", see Introductory Remarks p. LXXXI, 8.

[8] bába a serkī: the term bába has nothing to do with bobá, „great", and designates the „papa" or „aged surveyor of the harim", while the term serkī being added identifies him more closely with the ádim mal-bē in Kanúri, than with the simple ádim; but none but kings (abstraction being made from the temple of Mecca) are allowed to have eunuchs.

[9] serki n gandé: gandé seems to me to owe its origin to a foreign language, probably the Sonyai.

[10] málljami mal-kératā dówa means verbally „a learned man of much reading".

[11] alkádiri is borrowed from the Arabic (see note 14) with a slight change of the original meaning.

[12] bérédlo dáiske: bérédlo is evidently derived from bére, „head, chief".

[13] kókoi kaina means properly „the little master", a very appropriate term for the influential Royal eunuch, and which on this account may be in general use in most of the Sonyai-states, although I heard it only in A'gades. But, as for the title kókoi gerégeré used likewise in A'gades, identical with the Hausa-term serki n turawa, it may be an exclusively local expression, which, therefore, I dare not to introduce into the general vocabulary of the Sonyai-language.

[14] zam: this word does not correspond exactly to the notion of a mállem, on account of the latter term having been employed by the Sonyai in imitation of the neighbouring Arabs to denote the „blacksmith" (see p. 137), the doctor of iron, who in most of the African communities is quite an exceptional and highly important character: see note 5.

[15] béla n gothaia: bél means „slave", but, as for the latter part of the phrase, I am not quite certain.

[16] mála n dóyō, „master of reading", from mam-dóyō, „I read".

[17] girnir may be only the latter part of the term, if the first syllable gir be not a corruption from kara, „reading", so that girnir would by itself mean „he who makes (as for the termination nir, see Introductory Remarks p. CCXXI, 1) reading", and would be totally distinct from kirnir (k-ir-nir, ibid.), which expresses nothing but the general state of action.

[18] mohádžar, مهاجر, „qui dimisit a suis, de regione in regionem migravit", from هجر.

Deutsch und Englisch.	Kanúri.	Tēda.	Hausa.	Fulfúlde.
Schulknabe — *school-boy*	tála dári kárā-bē[1]	kará-kenī[5] . .	da n káratū .	. . . . . .
Hirt — *shepherd, neat-herd*	sími[2] . . . / súnyē-ma . .	dībedir . . . / dēdir[6] . . .	ma-kiaii Pl. má-su-kīvo[7]	(gaináko Pl. wai-nábe / doró Pl. doróbe[9])
Jäger — *hunter, huntsman*	bárá-ma[3] . / san-ma . .	kédedá . . . / ezekīnai . .	mai-faranta Pl. másu-faranta	lóhogel, lógel Pl. lohákki
Schütze — *marksman* . .	tēte-ma . .	. . . . . .	mai-halbi Plur. másu-halbi	pipido Plur. fifi-be[10]
Schiffer, Bootführer — *boatsman*	kām mákara-bē Pl. āmmákara-bē	. . . . . .	mútumi n īirgī Pl. mútane n īirgī	(himbe lāna . / yimbe kómbo-dže (Pl.)[11])
Fischer — *fisher-man* .	kendíbin[4] . .	. . . . . .	(ma-kāmi-n kīfi[8] / mai-faranta-n ruā)	(tšūo . . . / nango līdi[12] / sórkoï[13] (Man.))

[1] táta déri kárá-bē ist ein zusammengesetzter Ausdruck, über den ich nicht völlig sicher bin, mit der spöttischen Bezeichnung entweder „das bessere Kind" oder „das Kind der Lektüre im Freien". Ich bin nämlich nicht sicher, ob déri Substantiv oder Adjektiv ist. Vgl. S. 166, N. 4, wo déri dē als zwei ganz getrennte Wörter auseinander zu halten sind. Allerdings kommt kárē sonst selten so substantivisch vor; dass es aber doch ursprünglich von den Kanúri so aufgefasst wurde, sieht man aus dem Zeitwort kará-niskin S. 66, das eigentlich nichts Anderes heisst, als „ich mache Lektüre". Ich glaube übrigens, dass auch ma-kárá-n-tīl von ma-kárá-n-ti, „die Schule", für „Schulknabe" gebraucht wird.

[2] sími ist etwas vornehmer, als súnyē-ma und bedeutet auch „Heerdenbesitzer", während letzteres nur den wirklichen Hirten bezeichnet, von súnyē. Den eigentlichen Schafhirten bezeichnet man auch noch besonders mit dimi-ma.

[3] bárá-ma von bárē, „Jagd". Koelle hat zwar nicht die Form bárá-ma direkt für Jäger, sondern er giebt dafür die vollere Form bárātę-ma, die erst wieder von dem Subst. bárātę (wieder von bará-niskin abgeleitet) gebildet ist, aber er giebt doch selbst kēri bárāma für „Jagdhund", d. h. eigentlich „der Hund Jäger". — san-ma fehlt bei Koelle; er hat sonst noch kandīra für „Jäger", das mir nicht vorgekommen, aber vielleicht von dirngin, „ich erlege" (Fleisch) abzuleiten ist; es könnte auch in engstem Gegensatz zu kendíbin stehen.

[4] kendíbin fehlt bei Koelle; seine Ableitung ist mir ungewiss; die Wurzel aber ist unzweifelhaft dib oder dif.

[5] kará-keni, „er macht Lektüre"; vgl. Einleitung S. LXXVIII, 5.

[6] dēdir gleichwie dībedir scheinen auf ein dir für „Thier" hinzuweisen.

[7] ma-kiaii. Schön führt eine Pluralform makiaya an, die ich nicht gehört habe.

[8] ma-kāmi-n kīfi, eigentlich „der Ergreifer (von ina-kāma) von Fisch".

[9] dorō. Ich will hier noch zwei besondere Ausdrücke anführen, die bei den Fúlbe üblich sind zur Bezeichnung der Rinderaufsicht der Wildniss: déen und heroredio, Plur. herorédil. Den letzteren Ausdruck, der eng mit har-i-édši, „das Austreiben des Viehes in die Wildniss" und wol auch mit mbaroga Plur. berédi, „Löwe" in Solum (Koelle) zusammenhängt, gebrauchen die Hausa-Leute gleichfalls, während ihn die Sonyai durch gandēi bóro, „Mann der Wildniss" umschreiben. In Masina wird der Ausdruck harorédil nicht gebraucht, sondern man sagt statt dessen berimanki.

[10] pipido. Die in Adamaua angesiedelten Fúlbe haben noch den besonderen Ausdruck dirzmīdio, der jedoch der Fulfúlde-Sprache im Allgemeinen fremd zu sein scheint, wenn er nicht vielleicht mit dem Namen der Provinz Dirma, Dirama zusammenhängt.

[11] yimbe kómbodže. Auch das Wort kómbodže (Plural) scheint der reinen Fulfúlde-Sprache fremd zu sein.

[12] nango līdi. Die in Adamaua ansässigen Fúlbe haben noch die Ausdrücke gantódo und kaltóro, die aber von

Sonyai.	Lógoné.	Wándalá.	Bágrimma.	Mába.
. . . .	ámbae fū-honán [14]	dándale ankámbe [16]	ingánge dneb god n dóyō [20]	múkulúf [22] (herānik Pl. heráni
kur-koi . . .	bille gémen-ŧa [15]	apénōē [17] . .	súnui . . .	rāyeh (Arb.)
. . . .	bille gel-al-kille	mátsame [18] .	tébo kóddada [21]	ningivyirék [23]
. . . .	. . . .	. . . . . .	. . . . . .	. . . . . .
. . . .	. . . .	. . . . . .	. . . . . .	. . . . . .
tam-koi . . . } sorko . . . . }	máguwál . . .	manzau [19] . .	māla-handže .	hōt hánlanir [24]

[7] tāta déri hárā-bō is a rather unusual term, with regard to which I am not quite certain, it meaning either „the associated (déri) child of lecture or reading", or „the child of lecture in the open air": see the term déri dé (the two words are to be kept separated) p. 16[?]. Certainly the term hárā is not generally used as a substantive, but even the verb hárā-niskin (p. 66) shows, that such was really the case at a former period, that verb meaning originally „I make lecture". However, another term ma-hárā-n-tēl is also used, I think, for the „scholar", just as ma-hárā-n-ti denotes the „school".

[8] oūni seems to be a class of shepherd superior to the eānyē-ma, and occasionally means possessor of a herd, while the latter more distinctly and exclusively designates him, who exercises the eānyē, „the tending of the herd". However, the real shepherd is more particularly indicated by the term dimi-me.

[9] bárā-ma from bárā, „chase, hunting". Koelle has not the form bárā-ma for „sportsman", but, while he translates the latter term by means of the fuller form horátq-ma, which again has been formed from bárā-niskin, „I make chase", he translates „sporting dog" by the very term hēri barāma. The term eaa-ma is wanting in his vocabulary, but, instead, he has another one handira, which may be a very original term, opposed to hendihin.

[4] hendihin is wanting in Koelle.

[5] haré-heni, „he (who) makes lecture"; see Introductory Remarks p. LXXXIX, 8.

[6] dédir seems to be a popularly contracted form of dibedir; see Introductory Remarks p. 71.

[7] ma-kieli: Rev. Schön has a plural-form makiaye, which I have not heard.

[8] ma-hāmi-n hifi, properly „the catcher (from ins-hóme, „I catch") of fish".

[9] dovō: I here adduce two peculiar terms, dōse and hevoróddo, plur. bereróddi (compare ber-t-ōdē, „the driving out of the cattle into the wilderness"), used by the Fúlbe, in order to denote „the cattle-breeders of the wilderness". The latter of these two names, which may be connected with the term mberóge plur. berōdi meaning „lion" in the Salum-dialect (Koelle, Polyglotta), although it is not used by the Fúlbe of Másina, who instead use the term herimondi, is in use also with the Hausa-people, while the Sonyai translate it literally, saying yendēi hére, „sons of the wilderness".

[10] pipido: the Fúlbe settled in the province of Fómbina or Adamawa have, besides, another peculiar term, dirawáddo, which however seems to be foreign to the pure Fulfúlde-language, but might be derived from the name of the province of Dirma on the Niger, the inhabitants of which were most excellent archers and distinguished marksmen. Compare note 12.

[11] yimbe hámboddo: the term hámboddo (plur.) also seems to have been borrowed from another idiom.

[12] nango lidi: that portion of the Fúlbe settled in Fómbina uses, besides, the terms gaudóo and kuttóvo, which, however, are not understood by the other sections of that widely scattered nation; but, nevertheless, taken into consideration what I have said in another place (Introductory Remarks p. CXII), a remark which has entirely been confirmed by the observations of Dr. Baikie (Reports 5, note 8, p. 11), may be considered as belonging to the Fulfúlde-idiom, and may even turn out to be of very great ethnological interest.

[13] sórkoī: this name does not properly belong to this place, as it is not a generic term, but originally the name of a tribe, which in course of time has accommodated itself to one peculiar kind of living. See Travels, vol. IV, p. 604.

[14] ámbae fū-honán means verbally „he who is learning by the fire-side" (fū, „fire"), these poor children having to make their exercises very early in the morning long before dawn.

[15] bille gémen-ŧa properly only designates the „cattle-herd", „he who tends (Introductory Remarks p. CCXVII, c) the cattle" (ŧa).

[16] dándale ankámbe: I am as yet not able to explain, except, that dandal means the public square or Palmall.

[17] apénōē undoubtedly is to be derived from the verb ya-pié, „I bend" p. 115.

[18] mátsame has still to be controled.

[19] manzau with this notion seems suspicious, it meaning „bad" in other respects, while for „fish" I have hilfē.

[20] ingánge dneb god n dóyō means „he who goes to the place (god) of reading" (dóyō).

[21] tébo kóddada has evidently been derived from the corresponding Tédā-term kódadá, adding the name of that tribe itself, to which the huntsmen frequenting the Northern provinces of Bagirmi do almost exclusively belong.

[22] múkulúf properly means the boy, who is sent (as a pensionary) to a teacher dwelling abroad, while heránik designates the poorer school-boy, who has to learn his lesson early in the morning at the fireside.

[23] ningivyirék I am not able to explain as yet.

[24] hōt hánlanir: hōt, „fish"; hánlanir (less correctly hantánir), „he who catches", Introduct. Remarks p. CCCXL, D.

Deutsch und Englisch.	Kanúri.	Téda.	Hausa.	Fulfúlde.
Städter — [illegible]	kâm billa-bé [1] Pl. âm billa-bé	. . . . . .	mai-gari Pl. má-su-gari	džom gari Plur. džombe gari
Ackerbauer — husbandman	barē-ma [2] . .	baré [8] S. . . . / bonokímmui N.	mónomi Pl. mónoma [11]	demmōvo Plur. remmōbe
Schmied — black-smith .	kâgil-ma [3] . .	âsé [9] . . . / dûti	mákeri . . .	kiládio Pl. kilâbe / babillo Pl. babîlbe
Schlächter — butcher . .	mínori [4] . . .	[10]	má-fauti . .	pano . . . / bangâro Plur. wangárbe
Sattler, Lederarbeiter — saddler, leather-dresser	ndžeri-ma [5] .		má-šemi [12] . . .	[illegible]-gûri / bodino-gûri [13]
Sattler, Verfertiger von Pferdegeschirr — harness-maker	múndel-ma [6] .		. . . . . .	. . . . . .
Sattelgestellmacher — carpenter who makes the frame-work of the saddles	sírde-ma [7] . .			

[1] kâm billa-bé. Den von Koelle angeführten Ausdruck barni-ma, „Bewohner einer Hauptstadt", habe ich nie gehört, er mag aber vor 20 Jahren ganz gebräuchlich gewesen sein. Koelle gebraucht auch belá-ma (billa-ma, „Amtmann, Schultheiss", s. S. 230, N. 4) für „Städter" mit dem unerhörten Plural belá-ba, Grammatik §. 40, 4.

[2] barē-ma fehlt bei Koelle, der aber barē hat.

[3] kâgil-ma, „Herr des Ambosses" (kâgil oder, wie Koelle schreibt, kêgel).

[4] mínori scheint nach Koelle's nánari dáma (von dá, „das Fleisch", also „Fleischer") ursprünglich eine allgemeinere Beziehung zu haben, wahrscheinlich (vgl. námé-ma S. 235, N. 1) „der das Fell abzieht". Übrigens schreibt Koelle bald nánari, bald nánóri, ein Beispiel unter vielen, wie wenig sicher seine doch so in's Minutiöseste durchgeführte Accentuirung ist.

[5] ndžeri-ma, bei Koelle ndžirima; auch hat er mit derselben Bedeutung kátigima, was ganz richtig von kátigi gebildet ist, d. h. ka-tigi, „was den Leib bedeckt", „rohes Fell", im Gegensatz zu ndžeri, „bearbeitetes Fell".

[6] múndel-ma fehlt bei Koelle; das Stammwort scheint dem Logone entlehnt zu sein.

[7] sírde-ma. Statt sírde-ma hat Koelle sirdę-ma. Die Aufnahme des aus dem Arabischen [illegible] abgeleiteten sirde in allen diesen Sprachen erklärt sich von selbst. Vgl. übrigens zu dem Begriff „Tischler" auch S. 242.

[8] baré für „Landbauer", verglichen mit K. barē, „Landbau" ist auffallend; bonokimmui bleibt zu bestimmen oder zu analysiren; es ist wol verbale Form.

[9] âsé. „Die Schmiedsfrau" (H. makério), die in vielen Gegenden gleichfalls grossen Ansehen geniesst, heisst âsé-lû.

[10] Bei den Stämmen der Wüste gibt es eigentlich keinen Schlächter, sondern Jeder schlachtet für sich.

[11] mónomi scheint ein Wort zu sein, das wegen seiner noch zu erforschenden Abstammung wol Beachtung verdient. Für „Pflanzer", wofür die Kanúri-Sprache kein besonderes Wort besitzt, hat die Hausa-Sprache auch den Ausdruck mai-gôna, eigentlich „Gartenbesitzer", Plur. másu-gôna, F. dâm-gesse, Plur. dâmbe-gesse, S. fêri-kol.

[12] má-šemi. Dies ist der kurze terbmische Ausdruck für das umständlichere ma-sihi-n fáta, „Arbeiter in Leder oder Fellen".

[13] bodino-gûri. Die Fúlbe Adamaua's haben auch den eigenthümlichen Ausdruck hóppoho-lárral.

[14] [illegible]. Vgl. die Bemerkung S. 237, N. 13. — Rafouri gibt im verwandten Aramo dKam.

[15] mogôi ist entschieden verwandt mit H. mákeri (s. Einleitung S. CCXXVI) und kann wol dessen Entstehung erklären.

[16] ẽhirdâ. ye-ẽbardâ, „ich gâte" S. 115.

[17] Θ(e)-ẽgda von egda, „Amboss".

[18] Θé-tšitš von yé-tšitšé oder yé-tšité, „ich schlachte". Übrigens scheint das Θ vor dem tš des Wohllautes halber mehr in einen d-Laut überzugehen.

[19] Θó-megé gégo ruá; für „Grasbirr" allein habe ich gégue (wol im Plural), ruá also gehört nicht zum Worte, sondern heisst „mein", Einleitung S. CCXXX, 2, a).

[20] umde sirdi. umde, „Mann, Person".

[21] barē-ma. Die Übereinstimmung dieses Ausdruckes mit dem entsprechenden Kanúri-Wort ist auffallend (Einleitung S. CCLXXXII, g, α); die Bágrimma-Sprache besitzt aber dafür wol auch einen einheimischen Namen.

[22] hótĩ-mógó. hót oder hótĩ ist „der Arbeiter", mógó „der Amboss".

[23] móla-téd holéd gebé, „der Meister, der in Sandalleder (ndára) holóda, „Sandalleder") arbeitet".

[24] hol-dum ist vielleicht nicht vollständig; dasselbe hol haben wir doch wol in móla-hol-su, wo es „Schuh" bedeutet, hol also „arbeiten" bezeichnen würde. Vielleicht fehlt nur móla im Anfang, also móla-hol-dum.

[25] altoh autum ist mir in seinen Bestandtheilen ganz unverständlich. — Seetzen gibt für „Bauer" halibaih.

[26] dahórhoal kirair s. Einleitung S. CCCX, 1).

Sonyai.	Lógoné.	Wándalá.	Bágrimma.	Mába.
. . . .	. . . .	. . . . . .	. . . . . .	. . . . . .
(féri-koi see note 10)	bille guraneu . .	ábirdā [16] . .	harē-ma [21] . .	aitok nnium [25]
žem [14] . . . . . / garāsa	megél [15] . . .	θ(e)-égda [17] .	kútā-mógō [22] .	kālik Pl. kultu
. . . .	bille súnnri . .	θé-tšitā [18] . .	kót-kuru . .	dēczārík (Arb.)
. . . .	bille hardō . .	θé-magā-n-án-tšīrī	māla-tód kulód genā [23]	debórkosi kir-nir [26]
. . . .	bille mindil . .	θé-magā gógo ruā [19]	kol-dum [24] . .	. . . . . .
. . . .	bille téboie . .	emda sirdi [20] .	kotia sirde .	sedāārek (Arb.)

[1] hām bille-bō: the term horni-me, „native of a capital", adduced by Koelle, I have never heard. Koelle attributes also the notion of „townsman" to the word holā-me (i. e. bille-me, „mayor" p. 230, note 4) with the unheard of plural-form holā-he, §. 40, 4.

[2] barā-me is wanting in Koelle, though he has barā.

[3] hāgil-me, „master of the anvil" (hágél or, as Koelle writes, hágel).

[4] sánnri according to Koelle's sánnri dáma (dá-me from dā, „meat") seems mean originally „he, who takes off the skin". I must remark, however, that Koelle at times spells sánnri, at others sángri, an instance of, how little confidence is to be placed into the exaggerated degree of accuracy exhibited by him in his mode of spelling.

[5] ndáeri-me: niširime with Koelle, who besides, has, the term hátigime, which is regularly formed from hátigi, i. e. ha-tigi, „what covers the body", „raw skin", in opposition to ndáeri, „worked leather".

[6] mándel-me is wanting in Koelle and may not be a pure native term, mundel apparently being borrowed from the Lógoné.

[7] sirde-me: Instead of sirde-me Koelle writes sįrdę-me. It is easily understood, how sirdi derived from the Arabic سرج has been introduced into all these languages. Compare also „carpenter" p. 242.

[8] barā with the notion, of what in Kanúri is horē-me, seems deficient, while bonohimmai has still to be analysed.

[9] šaé: the wife of the blacksmith, who very often exercises the art herself (called in H. maheria), and who in many regions, just as is the case in the Tawárek-country, enjoys herself great respect, bears the name šaé-lā.

[10] Among the tribes of the desert there is generally no butcher, but every one does that business by himself.

[11] móhomi is a remarkable word, which I am not able to analyse from out of the elements of the Hausa-language, and which deserves attention in an ethnological respect. To express the term „planter", the Kanúri-language does not possess a peculiar term, while the Hausa has the term mai-gōna, „master of a garden" (plur. masu-gōna), F. dīem-gesse, plur. dīembe-gesse, S. féri-koi.

[12] má-šemi is the technical name of the ma-aīki-n fāta, „the workman in leather or skins".

[13] hadime-gūri: the Fúlbe settled in Yōmbina have also the peculiar term hóppoho-iārrol.

[14] žem: compare the remark p. 238, note 13.

[15] megél must probably is nearly related to H. mákeri, and may serve to explain its origin; see Introductory Remarks p. CCXXVII.

[16] ábirdā has been plainly derived from ye-ábardá, „I wend" p. 115.

[17] θ(e)-égda from θe, „he who works in" and egda, „the anvil".

[18] θé-tšítā from yé-tšitšā or yé-tšitá, „I butcher", the following harsh sound tš serving rather to give the sound of d to the preceding θ.

[19] θé-magā gógo ruá: the term „harness" in my vocabulary being expressed by the term gógua (probably in the plural-form), ruā evidently is the possessive pronoun „mine". Introductory Remarks p. CCXXXI, 3, a).

[20] emda sirdi properly means „person (emda) of the saddle".

[21] harē-ma: the identity of this term with the corresponding one in the Kanúri-language is remarkable (see Introductory Remarks p. CCLXXXIII, g, e)); but the Bágrimma-language may possess another peculiar term.

[22] kótā-mógō: kōt or kótā means „the workman", mógō „smith".

[23] māla-tód kulód genā, „the master, who works in prepared leather" (ndára) kaléda).

[24] kol-dum is remarkable and perhaps not quite complete, for there seems to be little doubt, that this kol is identical with the kol in mále-kol-se (se, „shoes"), „the master of working shoes"; but perhaps only māle is wanting.

[25] aitok nnium in its ingredient parts is not clear to me. — Seetzen for „peasant" gives the term halinaih.

[26] debórkosi kirnir: see Introductory Remarks p. CCCXI, I).

Deutsch und Englisch.	Kanúri.	Tédā.	Hausa.	Fulfúlde.
Schuhmacher — shoemaker	súnō-ma[1] . .	ŏsa	me-takálme[7] .	bādo-fadde . / gano-fadde .
Lederbüchsenmacher — maker of boxes made of bull-hide	tendū-ma[2] .	. . . . .	. . . . .	. . . . . .
Mattenflechter — mat-braider	kasár tendu-ma[3]		. . . . .	. . . . . .
Weber — weaver . . .	tendū-ma . .	. . . . .	mai-sáki[8] . .	tšantšándo Plur. sansambe
Näher, Schneider — seamster, tailor	kun-dútá-ma[4] / ribrā-ma[5] (b.A.)	yunō-hide . .	mai-dimki n fāta[9] . / wendu / fúla . / rīga .	ŏo-wōo[11] gūri . . / salládže / kummēdži / togōdže
Färber — dyer	árin-ma[6] . .	. . . . .	mai-rinni[10] .	tšinōwo . . / máripnīdžo[12]

[1] sánō-ma (Koelle sanōma) von sánō, „Schuh" hängt etymologisch mit sánori, „Schlichter", eigentlich „Schinder" zusammen.

[2] tendú-ma. Koelle tándūma. Dass tendū oder tendū nicht, wie Koelle erklärt, ein viereckiger Lederwerk, sondern eine Lederbüchse zum Aufbewahren von Butter ist, darüber an bezüglicher Stelle mehr. Hier will ich nur bemerken, dass es ein so eigenthümliches Kanúri-Produkt ist, dass die anderen Sprachen kein besonderes Wort dafür haben.

[3] kasár tendū-ma ist sehr auffällig wegen seiner grammatischen Konstruktion, indem das Objekt kasár mit dem Subjekt in verkürzter Weise verbunden gedacht ist und deshalb im Accusativ erscheint. Übrigens ist dieses tendū in seiner näheren Entwickelung ganz verschieden vom vorigen, indem nur der Begriff des Abrundens beiden gemeinsam ist, und kommt von tend-iskin (Koelle tándeskin), „ich webe". Über kasár später.

[4] kun-dútá-ma, eine doppelte Zusammensetzung; dūt-eskin, „ich nähe", ist die erste Wurzel, dann ist daraus offenbar ko-a-dūte und mit euphonischem Übergang des ersten e in a kun-dūte oder kun-dúte geworden, „das Nähhandwerk", und daraus erst kun-dūtá-ma, „der Meister des Nähhandwerks"; es fehlt bei Koelle.

[5] ribrā-ma, bei Koelle lifgráme, von ribrá (Koelle liferá), „die Nadel". Das r im Anfange wird zuweilen weggelassen, wie denn das eben das Ursprüngliche ist, da r unzweifelhaft nur aus dem l des Arabischen Artikels entstanden ist; denn natürlich ist ribrá nichts als das Arabische [illegible].

[6] árin-ma fehlt bei Koelle; von árin, „Indigo", bei Koelle ília.

[7] me-takálme. me, ma sind Verkürzungen von mai. Ich will hier noch den besonderen Ausdruck für „Schlauchmacher" anführen: H. mai-salkoae, F. dūom somellédžī. Die besondere Geschicklichkeit der Bewohner von Kátsena im Präpariren solcher Wasserschläuche durch kunstvolles Abziehen des genannten Felles ohne Aufschneiden, ist berühmt.

[8] mai-sáki. Ich will hier zwei begriffsverwandte Ausdrücke anführen: „Fadenzieher", H. mai-sará, F. mottōwo „Rohrschläger", H. mai-wóddará, F. wadderīdžī oder geeobōwo.

[9] mai-dimki n fáta, „der Schneider in Leder"; m. wendú, „der Hosenschneider"; m. fúla, „der Mützenmacher" m. rīga, „der Näher von Hemden". Die entsprechenden Fulfúlde-Wörter haben dieselbe Bedeutung.

[10] mai-rinni. Hier will ich den verwandten má-bugū anführen, F. piōwo togōdže, Plur. [illegible] togōdže, wörtlich „der Schläger oder Klopfer der Hemden", der Arbeiter, der diesen Baumwollzeugen durch regelmässiges Klopfen ihren eigenthümlichen Glanz verleiht. Dieses Klopfen der Hemden verleiht den Afrikanischen Baumwoll-Industrieplätzen einen eigenthümlich regen und lauten Charakter und ist überaus charakteristisch.

[11] ŏowōo von [illegible], „ich nähe".

[12] máripnīdžo ist ein nur in den jetzt den Fulbe unterworfenen Hausa-Staaten üblicher und aus der Hausa-Sprache abgeleiteter Ausdruck, in den westlichen Provinzen ist er unbekannt.

[13] Raffenel gibt im verwandten Arama für „Weber" (tisserand) dar' [illegible] [illegible]. Übrigens kann man sich alle diese Ausdrücke vermittelst bei und den betreffenden Zeitworten und Objekten selbst zusammensetzen.

[14] [illegible] kann kaum richtig sein. Die Matte heisst ragā, also vielleicht ragā-ne-monām.

[15] [illegible], „Person des Nähens (nabá) das Kleid (lebá)". — mōn, „Indigo".

[16] [illegible]-mogā himmokā. Ich bin nicht ganz sicher über diesen Ausdruck, da ich aus Versehen bloss himmokā niedergeschrieben hatte und das [illegible]-magi aus blosser Analogie anderer ähnlicher Phrasen hinzufügte.

[17] tindare kássere. Für „ich webe" habe ich allerdings S. 119 das ganz verschiedene yé-eye, dagegen aber habe ich ebenda für „ich drehe (den Faden)", y(e)-ėndera ([illegible]) und von diesem ėndera ist unser tindare abzuleiten.

[18] [illegible]-magā-l-ripre, „der Werkmann mit der Nadel"; s. Einleitung S. CCXLII, c, b).

[19] [illegible]-uayé, „der Mann des Indigo"; uayá, uaé, „Indigo".

[20] [illegible] tendaág heisst „er bereitet die Indigofarbe ([illegible]) gut". Siehe S. CCCX, b) der Einleitung. Eben so verbal ist die folgende Redensart und bezeichnet den, „der seine Sache, d. h. seine Waaren (zum Verkauf) zubereitet".

Sonyai.	Lógoné.	Wándalá.	Bágrimma.	Mába.
. . . .	bille rálabē . .	θé-magā kímmakē[16]	māla-kol-sa .	bartu-nenrik
. . . .	bille tandu . .	dētše tanda .	kótā-tanda .	māšik bottat-nenrik
. . . .	bille rannemonám[14]	tindare kámere[17]	māla-kúdže-rága	daffārik
(himsa-koi?)[13] .	. . . .	. . . . . .		
ta-koi	bille nabá lebé[15]	θé-magā-l-ripre[18]	māl(a) ákurú ngásaa	χayātik (Arb.)
. . . .	bille mōn . . .	džīl-unyē[19] .	kótā-álini . .	nīl nimmere tandang[20]

[1] sáne-ma (Koelle sánéma) from sáné, „shoe", etymologically connected with sánefi, „butcher", properly „flayer".

[2] tendū-ma: Koelle tándū-ma. However, whether you spell tendū or tandū, the word does not mean „a square leatherbag", as Koelle explains, but a peculiar cylindrical vessel of various shape made of untanned hide for containing butter, and so peculiar to Bornu, that the neighbouring tribes have adopted the same term.

[3] kasár tendū-ma is remarkable on account of the mode, in which the noun kasár (with regard to which term I shall say more lower down) has been placed in the accusative case before the noun tendú-ma, „the weaver", from téndiskin (Koelle tándeskin), as if it were a verbal form; for grammatically we ought to expect tendú-ma kasár-be. This term tendú, however, we must remark, in the further development of its notion is entirely distinct from the preceding similar term, nothing but the notion of the rounding of, or twisting, being common to both of them.

[4] kan-dúlá-ma the root is the verb dút-askin, „I sew"; from which has been derived a substantive kan-dúte (originally ka-n-dúte) or kan-dúla, „the needle-work", and from this latter the term kan-dúlá-ma, „the master of the needlework", i. e. „the tailor" has been formed; it is wanting in Koelle.

[5] ribrá-ma (Koelle lifrámа) from ribrí (Koelle liferí), „needle". I also heard sometimes ibrá-ma, which is nearer to the root, although the r in the beginning may represent the l of the Arabic article, ribrí having evidently been borrowed from the Arabic إبرة.

[6] árin-ma is wanting in Koelle, from árin, „indigo" (Koelle ális).

[7] ma-tabáluse. ma and ma are shorter, and perhaps more original forms of mal. I am going still to adduce in this note the peculiar name given to the „worker in waterskins": H. mai-salkuna, F. dǎum sumalliédǐi, the ability of the inhabitants of Kátsena in preparing waterskins from the hides of goats, without cutting them up, being most remarkable.

[8] mai-sáki: I here am going to adduce two terms of a similar meaning, viz: „thread-maker", H. mai-sarē, F. motlówo; and „ropemaker", H. mai-wéddaré, P. wadderīdǐi or gasanāwa.

[9] mai-dinki n féta, properly „the sewer of the skin"; m. wando, „the tailor, who makes trowsers"; m. fúla, „the sewer of caps"; m. riga, „the sewer of shirts", the corresponding Fulfúlde-terms conveying the same notions.

[10] mai-rinsí: I here mention the related term má-hogú, F. piōwe togédia, plur. fi-bébe togéddo, properly „the beater of shirts", or the man, who by subjecting the shirts to a regular kind of beating gives them the peculiar and beautiful lustre, which distinguishes the splendid dark blue cottons of Kanó, while the manipulation of the beating itself constitutes one of the most striking, and I may add, most noisy features of the industrious centres of Negroland.

[11] ňowān from mé-dē-ňōn, „I do sew".

[12] márinuldšo is a term derived from the Hausa-language, and is used only by the Fúlbe settled in the Hausa-states, while it is unknown to the inhabitants of the Western provinces.

[13] While I have not been able to get a fit term for „weaver", except the mode of composition by means of koi and the verb hinsa, Raffenel in the related Arama represents this term (tisserand) by dar' bekete koi.

[14] rannemonám scarcely can be right, or at least exhibits a high degree of vulgar corruption, „mai" being ragé.

[15] bille nabá lebé means properly „person of sewing (nabá) the dress" (lebé). — bille mōn, „person of indigo".

[16] θé-magá kimmakē: I am not quite sure of the meaning of this term, having written down the word kimmakē alone, and adding afterwards the θe-magá from mere analogy.

[17] tindare kásere: For „I weave", certainly, I have the totally distinct verb yé-ngá (p. 119), but instead for „I twist (the thread"), I have the very verb y(e)-éndere (tíde, from which our term tindare has been derived.

[18] θé-magā-l-ripre, „the workman with the needle"; see Introductory Remarks p. CCXLIII, c, b).

[19] džīl-unyé, „the man of the indigo"; unyē, uné, „indigo".

[20] nīl nimmere tandang has rather a verbal meaning: „he who spreads the colour well" (nīl = nileh); see Introductory Remarks p. CCCXI, I). The following phrase andžī lifto ,tenéne tondéng seré, likewise has a verbal meaning: „he who spreads out his merchandize for sale".

Deutsch und Englisch.	Kanúri.	Tédā.	Hausa.	Fulfúlde.
Trödler — *fripperer*	feikē-ma[1]	. . . . . .	mai-talla	géo Pl. geyēbe
Trödler in einer besonderen Waare — *fripperer, trading in a particular article*	selā-ma[2] (h. A.)			gadēdo yaínuki
wohlhabender angesiedelter Kaufmann — *settled merchant, being well of*	libáyá-ma[3] (h. A.)	béruē S. / birbē N.	tádžeri (Arb.) / mai-dúkia[8]	tūra-džō[10] / dīom-dēaudi / diskurantēdžo[11]
reisender Händler, der seine Waare auf dem Kopf trägt — *travelling dealer, who carries his merchandise upon his head*	dangarúmba[4]	. . . . . .	da n garúnfa	. . . . . .
reisender Händler mit Packthieren, in Natron, Gurunüssen u. s. w. — *travelling dealer in natron, guronuts etc. with pack-oxen and asses*	togúrtši[5]	éraki téde[7]	mai-falkī Pl. fatáki[9]	tiggarādže Pl. tiggárbe[12] / fātakēdžo
reisender Sklavenhändler — *travelling slave-dealer*	kómboli			
reisender Kaufherr — *travelling merchant*	sáfer-ma[6] (h. A.)	béruē S. / birbē N.	mai-fatautši	. . . . . .

[1] feikē-ma. Koelle pathéme, von feikē, „Waare" (bei Koelle pathé).

[2] selā-ma fehlt bei Koelle und ist allem Anschein nach kein reines Kanúri-, sondern ein aus dem Arabischen abgeleitetes Wort.

[3] libáyá-ma (bei Koelle lebáyima) von libáya, einem ebenfalls aus dem Arabischen abgeleiteten Wort ([illegible]).

[4] dangarúmba ist unzweifelhaft der verdorbene Hausa-Ausdruck da n garúnfa, indem diese mit geringstem Verdienst zufriedenen wandernden Kleinhändler fast ausschliesslich dem Hausa-Stamme angehören.

[5] togúrtši und kómboli, beides fremdartig aussehende Bezeichnungen, scheinen bei Koelle zu fehlen. Der letztere Ausdruck kómboli ist durch den Vergleich mit dem ursprünglichen Bagrimma-Wort imboli, dem nur das charakteristische K. ke (s. Einleitung S. XLVI) vorgesetzt und dann der Vokal unter Einfluss des zweiten o verwandelt ist, von grossem Interesse.

[6] sáfer-ma bei Koelle in der Form sáherma, wie er auch sáher u. s. w. schreibt. Dass es aber allerdings dialektische Verschiedenheit ist, sieht man aus der Logoné-Form desselben Wortes. Ausser diesem Ausdruck unzweifelhaft Arabischen Ursprungs hat Koelle ein ganz heimisches Wort gárwa für „Kaufmann", das ich nicht gehört habe, das aber vielleicht sich an das weiter unten aufzuführende Tédā-Wort gará für „Stadt" anschliessen mag, wonach gárwa eigentlich „der Städter" wäre, der nach dem Charakter jener Landschaften auch eben der eigentliche Kaufmann ist. Auffallend ist dann nur, wenn nicht auch die Tédā diese Bedeutung bewahrt hätten und neben dem auffallenden, mir noch unerklärlichen birbē das gárwa gebrauchten.

[7] éraki téde ist mir unverständlich, enthält aber wahrscheinlich sehr interessante ethnologische Andeutungen.

[8] mai-dúkia, wörtlich „Herr des Reichthums".

[9] mai-falkī zeigt in seinem so ganz unregelmässigen Plural fatáki noch deutlich seine Ableitung vom ursprünglichen Logoné-Worte fatkē, das noch im Logoné und Kanúri erhalten ist. Schön hat als Einzelform von fatakeh, wie er den Plural schreibt, falkeh.

[10] tūra-džō ist ein ähnlich wie marinaidžo (s. S. 238, N. 12) gebildeter Ausdruck vom Hausa-Wort ba-túre (welches, s. S. 250, N. 11), eigentlich „der Araber", hier aber als Arabischer Grosshändler gefasst.

[11] diskurantēdžo ist ein auffallender, mir in seiner Ableitung noch nicht klarer Ausdruck.

[12] tiggarādže scheint mit dem Kanúri-Wort togúrtši in irgend welcher, wenigstens äusseren, Verbindung zu stehen.

[13] dē-hoi, „Herr des Verkaufens", von dē, „verkaufen".

[14] mi-pathē. mi-patkē in seiner reinen, dem Logoné angehörenden Bildung zeigt deutlich und unwiderleglich, eine wie grosse Priorität dieser Sprache, der alten Kultur und frühen Siedelung der Kotokō-Völkergruppe halber, vor dem Hausa und Kanúri in vielen Beziehungen gebührt. S. Einleitung S. CCXXIV.

[15] Ge-šē-kalā von ye-šē (šekō, šekwā S. 101, vgl. Einleitung S. CCXLII, c, b), „ich kaufe", und kalá, „Waaren", „Dinge". Dieses Wort, das in gewöhnlicher Rede vielfach abgekürzt und verdorben wird, habe ich in den drei Formen tešēkalā, tešeškalā und aleškalā niedergeschrieben. Es tritt nämlich hier vorwiegend der Fall ein, dass das folgende š auf das vorhergehende e etwas modificirend einwirkt, während schon sonst im Logoné e und š schwer zu unterscheiden sind.

[16] Ge-gé-gaē ganz ähnliche Ableitung von ye-gé gaē, „ich treibe Handel".

[17] hakeeiáke dabga-miri ist im ersten Theil entschieden korrumpirt und hat sonst unbekannte Beziehungen.

[18] mála-gáhav-tšinshi ist ein durch den Handel der kleinen Hausa-Krämer nach Bagirmi (s. Reisen, Th. III, S. 342) entstandener Mischlingsausdruck: tšinchi ist das Hausa-Wort für „Handel".

Šukyal.	Lógoné.	Wándalá.	Bágrimma.	Mába.
dē-koi[13] . . . dīri-koi . . .	bille aúená . .	ōe-ŝē-kalā[15] .	mála-fatki .	endži litto tenēno tondóng serē
mosébbeb (Arb.)	mi-patkō[14] . .	ōe-gā-ganē[16] .	delāl . . . mála-tšincki	tadžāre kāgo tángdetē tín-dael
		(kakuetāka dab-ga-mīri[17])	mála-kalko . mála-dig džóngi	. . . . . .
	bille sāber . .	tsitsákalā (s. n. 15)	ímboli (s. n. 8)	tádžering-malék
		siaákalā (s. n. 15)	mála-gākav-tšíneki[18]	

[1] fatkō-ma: Koelle pathima, from fatkā (Koelle patkē), „merchandise".

[2] selā-ma is wanting in Koelle, and, according to all appearance, is not a pure Kanúri-term, but has been derived from the Arabic.

[3] libāya-ma (Koelle lebāyāma) from libāya, which, beyond a doubt, has been likewise borrowed from the Arabic [illegible].

[4] dangarámbe appears to be a mere corruption of the Hausa-term da n garánfa, those petty travelling traders almost without any exception belonging to the Hausa-tribe.

[5] togártši and hémboli seem to be wanting in Koelle. Both are rather strange looking terms, the term hémboli being evidently derived from the B. imboli, by adding the characteristic Kanúri personal prefix ke, and therefore of considerable interest with regard to the history of that idiom.

[6] sāfer-ma: Koelle sāberma, just as he writes sāber, and that such a form is indeed used in some parts of Bornu, we see from the corresponding term in Lógoné, which has evidently been borrowed from the Kanúri. Besides this term of undoubted Arabic origin, Koelle has another one of pure native make, viz gérwa, which has not become known to me, and which accordingly, has as yet to be controled. But I suspect, that it may be a term belonging to the old stock of Garamantic ethnology, in which garama indicates the „capital", while gerē still in the Tédā-language at the present day means „town", whence garwa may be derived, as originally indicating the towns-man, who in those Regions is at the same time the „merchant".

[7] áyuhi tédo I do not understand, as yet, but expect, it may disclose in the course of farther inquiry some ethnological hints of great importance.

[8] mai-dúkia means verbally „master of wealth".

[9] mai-falki in its irregular plural-form falāki clearly exhibits evident signs of its origin from the Lógoné-term fatkā. Rev. Schön has for the singular case the form falakeh, and in the plural falakeb.

[10] túra-dāō is a term of similar formation as márinaidžo (see p. 239, note 12), derived from the very curious Hausa-word ba-túre (which see p. 251, note 13), meaning properly „the Arab", but in this case being understood as „Arab merchant".

[11] diakarantédže is a curious name of an origin as yet unknown to me.

[12] tiggarádže may in some way or other be connected with the Kanúri-term togártši.

[13] dē-koi, „master of selling", from dē, „sell".

[14] mi-patkō in its whole character and way of composition, entirely belonging to the Lógoné-idiom, most clearly serves to prove the priority of that language with regard to a certain state of civilisation, connected with the early settlement of the tribes belonging to the Kótokō-nation. See Travels and Discoveries vol. III, p. 270, 302, and passim, compared with Introductory Remarks p. CCXXV.

[15] ōe-ŝā-kalā from ye-ŝā (šehē, šēhwā above p. 101 compared with Introductory Remarks p. CCXLIII, c, b), „I buy", kalā, „merchandise", „things". — This term is perfectly identical with the several forms tsāhalā, tsitsákalā and siaákalā which I have given on purpose, in order to exhibit an instance of the uncertain state of orthography of these illiterate languages.

[16] ōe-gā-ganē from ye-gā ganē, „I make commerce".

[17] kakuetāka dabga-mīri is evidently a corrupted form, at least is totally unintelligible to me as yet.

[18] mála-gākav-tšíneki is a curious term, which by way of the mixture of its various parts represents the lively intercourse of various nations of those Regions. For here we have the direct influence of the commerce of the Hausa traders (tšinchi being the Hausa-word for „trade") with Bagirmi, with regard to which compare Travels, vol. III, p. 394.

Deutsch und Englisch.	Kanúri.	Tédā.	Hausa.	Fulfúlde.
Führer — *guide*	dibel-ma [1] .	teski-dē [7] . .	má-dogu [10] .	maundo tiggár-bo [12] / maundo fāiakēn
Mäkler — *broker* . . .	dilál-ma (h. A.)	delai	da n kásua [11] / dilali . . .	hī lūmo . . / dilālidžo . .
Schuldner — *debtor* . .	küse-ma [2] . .	büde gäli lirkin-tidē [8]	. . . . . .	. . . . . .
Baumeister — *builder (of huts), architect*	ūgim-ma [3] . / madán-ma . / katī-ma . .	ivē yetómpi [9] .	mai-ginni . .	mále [13]. . . / ma-hōwo lādi / lōpe
Töpfer — *potter* . . .	ṅgē-ma [4] . .	. . . . . .	mai-diba yumbu	no-hōwo lōpe [14]
Tischler, Verfertiger von Thüren — *carpenter who makes doors*	tábarā-ma [5] .	mégenē . . .	masáschi? . .	. . . . . .
Arzt, Quacksalber — *physician, quack*	kurgún-ma [6] .		mai-mágani .	džom-safāre [15]
Barbier — *barber* . . .	wanzémma [6] .	wanzām . .	mai-áski . .	pembōwo Pl. fembōhe

[1] dibel-ma von dibel (Koelle dibal), eigentlich „Herr des Weges", fehlt bei Koelle; er hat dafür in seiner Grammatik, §. 40, N. 8, S. 24 den mir unbekannt gebliebenen, aber wol richtige pelēgema von pelēngin (felé-elokin), „ich säge".

[2] küse-ma von küsa oder küse, „die Schuld", fehlt bei Koelle.

[3] ūgim-ma von ūgim, ochen nem. dem einfachsten Ausdruck für „Wohnung", „Hütte" (Strohhütte); madán-ma, „der Errichter des ūgim madán", einer besseren Art von Hütte; katī-ma, ganz allgemein „der Meister in Thon", aber hier mit der Bedeutung „Errichter von Lehmwohnungen". Alle drei Ausdrücke fehlen bei Koelle, der dafür aber einen ganz andern, mir unbekannt gebliebenen Ausdruck aufführt, nämlich tēmtema vom Zeitwort tēmgin (T. tóm-erik), „ich baue".

[4] ṅgē-ma von ṅgē, „Topf".

[5] tábará-ma (Koelle táberā-ma) von tábará, dem historisch in Folge des Holzhandels adoptirten Arabischen Wort für das Lateinische und Italiänische *tabula*, *tavola*, „die Planke", woraus die Thüren verfertigt werden.

[6] kurgún-ma (Koelle kúrgunma), „der Meister der Arznei" (kurgún). — wanzémma, Koelle wanzámma.

[7] teski-dē, wörtlich „der Mann von den Sternen", s. Einleitung S. LXXXII.

[8] büde gäli lirkintidē ist ein unbeholfener Ausdruck mit passiver Participialform; vgl. Einleitung S. LXXX.

[9] ivē yetómpi verbal unbeholfener Ausdruck von ivē, „Haus", und tóm-erik, „ich baue".

[10] má-dogu, sowie das entsprechende Fulfúlde-Wort, bezeichnet eigentlich nicht den Führer im Allgemeinen, sondern den Führer oder Hauptmann einer Karawane, den Karawanenführer.

[11] da n kásua, wörtlich „Sohn des Marktes".

[12] maunde tiggárbe, „der Grosse der Handelsreisenden".

[13] mále. Die genaue Beziehung ist mir undeutlich; sie ist vielleicht national.

[14] no-hōwo lōpe ist offenbar mit dem vorhergehenden Ausdruck der Wurzel nach ganz einerlei.

[15] džom safāre. Der Ausdruck safāre ist unzweifelhaft von den Fulbe der Sonyai-Sprache entlehnt und nicht umgekehrt. Die Folge davon ist, dass der Ausdruck den westlicheren Fulbe, die mit den Sonyai nicht in Berührung gekommen sind, nicht bekannt sein wird.

[16] saúnse welala ist mir in seiner Entstehung noch unklar; vgl. S. 71.

[17] Ich habe an dieser Stelle den Ausdruck mohárreme dibbealli niedergeschrieben, der aber wol kaum hierher passen kann, da mohárreme „Sänger" heisst.

[18] billi lubwe: lubwe kann ich nicht erklären.

[19] Bédégolē von fle, „Meister, Herr" und dégolē, „der Weg".

[20] gimma scheint mir zweifelhaft.

[21] fle-nder-āwā heisst „Meister (fle) vom Flechten (undera S. 119, vgl. S. 239, N. 17) der Hütten", wie denn bei den meisten der einheimischen Hütten und bei einem grossen Bestandtheile selbst der Thonhütten aber vom Flechten (des groben Rohrmattenwerkes, aus denen sie bestehen), als vom eigentlichen Bauen die Rede sein kann.

[22] makas n toonlēre, „die Frau", weil die Töpferei fast ausschliesslich von Frauen betrieben wird; toonlēre gleich dem bald darauf folgenden dordre, scheint eher eine passive als aktive Form zu sein.

[23] fle-gá-n-efā, „der Arbeiter in Holz"; Einleitung S. CCXLII, c, b).

[24] lingáng-melēh, „Herr des Weges".

Ṡoṅyai.	Logone.	Wandalā.	Bagrimma.	Māba.
	asáneo welaia[16] .	Ɓángolē[19] . .	māla-debbu .	lingáng-melék[24]
. . . .	bille dilél . . .	Ɓe-dilélli . .	ádim dalāla .	dalálek
. . . .	bille mesíllim (h. A.)	gimma[20] . .	māla-keda .	
. . . .	"	Ɓe-nder-áwuā[21]	{ māla-tod-kūdži / māla-kotā-egérra }	kokónne
. . . .	bille iskwa[18] . .	muksa n tesiēre[22]	māla-kū džúgarn	darómtu
. . . .	tigāma	Ɓe-gā-n-afā[23]	kotā-totāo .	goddūm
safári-koi . . .	. . . . . .	. . . . . .	. . . . . .	. . . . . .
wandžām . . .	wanzām . . .	darēre . . .	māla-diaā . .	

1 dibel-ma from dibel (Koelle dibal). „the road", therefore meaning properly „master of the road", is wanting in Koelle, who has instead another characteristic term pelégema from pelāngin (felè-niskin), „I show, exhibit".

2 kūea-ma from kūea or kēea, „the debt", is wanting in Koelle.

3 ágim-ma from ágim, besides nem, the simplest term for „dwelling", especially the common conical hut of the country; madān-ma, „the architect of the ágim madan", a better sort of hut; kuli-ma a more general term, „the master of (building in) clay". None of these three terms is mentioned by Koelle, while he has, instead, another term témtema from the verb témgin, „I build", with which I myself have not become acquainted, but which we find in T. tém-orih.

4 ágō-ma from ágō, „pot".

5 tābaré-ma (Koelle tāberé-ma) from tābarē, the Arabic term derived in consequence of commercial relations from the Latin and Italian word *tabula*, *tavola*, „plank" (from which doors are made).

6 kurgán-ma (Koelle kárganma), „the master of medicine" (kurgán). — wasérmma: Koelle wentsámma.

7 tocki-dā verbally „the person of the stars", see Introductory Remarks p. LXXXIII.

8 hāde gōli tirkintidō is a very awkward expression in a passive form, with which compare Introductory Remarks p. LXXXI.

9 ivē yutémpi from ivē, „the house", and tém-orih, „I build".

10 ná-dogu, just as the corresponding Fulfúlde-term, properly does not indicate the guide in general, but only the leader, or headman of a caravan.

11 du n kāsua means verbally „son of the market".

12 maunāo tiggérbe, „the great (man) of the travelling merchants".

13 mālr: the exact meaning of this term is as yet unknown to me.

14 go-kōwa lōpe appears to be identical with the preceding term.

15 dēem safāre: the term safāre has undoubtedly been borrowed by the Fúlbe from the Sonyai-language, and not the contrary; the consequence is, that this term is not known to the Western-most Fúlbe, who have had no intercourse with the Sonyai.

16 asénee welaia I cannot explain as yet compare the terms adduced p. 71.

17 I have here the term mobárrema dibbealli, but it can scarcely be right, mobárrema meaning „singing man".

18 bille iskwa: iskwa also remains as yet to be explained.

19 Ɓángolē from Ɓe and ángolē, „the road".

20 gimma seems doubtful.

21 Ɓe-nder-áwuā properly means „the master (l'e) of braiding (endere p. 139 compared with p. 229, note 17) the huts", most of the native African huts being rather more like a wicker-basket, than a house, and consequently the braiding being by far a more essential portion in erecting them, than any thing, which may be called building.

22 muksa n tesiēre: muksa, „the women", on account of the art of pottery being almost exclusively exercised by females. As for tesiēre, it seems rather to exhibit the form of a participle of the passive voice, especially if we compare darére farther on.

23 Ɓe-gā-n-afā, „the workman in wood"; see Introductory Remarks p. CCXLIII, r, b).

24 lingáng-melék, „master of the road".

Deutsch und Englisch.	Kanúri.	Téda.	Hausa.	Fulfúlde.
Reiter — *man on horseback*	kām fīr-wa[1] Pl. ām fīr-wa	aski-dŏ . .	mai-dōki . . / má-an-dōki	džom-putšu . / badyāko . .
Infanterist — *foot-soldier*	sātl[2]	ángbidi[10] . .	da-kāro[12] . .	koidādžo Plur. / hoedābe / da-karēdžo .
schwerer Reitersmann — *heavy cavallery*	lībbedi[3] . .		liffedi . . .	tĕuddúngu Plur. tĕunddudi
Bogenschütze — *archer* .	kenīgi-ma[4] .	. . . . . .	mai-kébia . .	pipído Pl. fiffbe
Fahnenträger — *ensign-bearer*	além-ma[5] . .	. . . . . .	. . . . . .	. . . . .
Gefangener — *prisoner* .	kám tergērina	tukýntidĕ . .	mutúm ān-damrē[13]	. . . . . .
Trommelschläger — *drummer*	gangá-ma[6] .	kénia ganga ki-bāppi[11]	oba n gīžī n gānga[14]	dšanmo baggu / gimmōro Plur. / yimmōbe
verschiedene Arten Musikanten — *various kinds of musicians*	zózo-ma[7] . / mangúm-ma[8] / fumfúm-ma[9]	. . . .	mai-džódžua[15] /	fino džodžīra / fifido kādža .

[1] kām fīr-wa. Koelle hat pírma, d. i. fīr-ma, das ich, obgleich es vollkommen regelmässig gebildet und wol nur veraltet ist, nie so gebraucht gefunden habe, während er fīr-wa (bei ihm pírwa), jedenfalls irrthümlich erklärt „voll von Pferden", also nur auf Örtlichkeiten zu beziehen, während es eine viel allgemeinere Bedeutung hat. Er hat auch hémhīma.

[2] sātl, vielleicht von sángin, „ich strecke aus" (hier verstanden „die Beine").

[3] lībbedi. Koelle lófędę oder lóhędę, das er jedoch nur von dem Zeug erklärt, womit jene Kürass-Soldaten bekleidet ist; allerdings ist das die erste Bedeutung, wol sicher vom Arabischen لبس, wie der Stahlpanzer im Grunde noch jetzt heisst, während in Bornu allerdings auch der dick wattirte Streitanzug darunter verstanden wird; dann aber ist das Wort auch auf den so gepanzerten Mann selbst übertragen. Eine Darstellung solcher Reiter s. Reisen, Th. III, S. 184 in der Scene des Ngaljam bei Demmo.

[4] kenīgi-ma. Koelle kaṅígema, obgleich er auch die Form kęnigę für „Bogen" hat.

[5] além-ma hat Koelle nicht, obgleich er ālam hat. — kám tergérina: tergérina Participium passivi „gebunden" von gérinkin.

[6] gangá-ma. Koelle hat hierfür den volleren Ausdruck dúgū gaṅgima. Danach würde dúgū die allgemeine Bedeutung „Musikant" zu haben scheinen, obgleich er es selbst an der betreffenden Stelle schon an und für sich als „Trommler" erklärt. Es ist aber wol nichts Anderes als mein duggu, „Sänger, Bänkelsänger", der dann unterschieden wird je nach dem jedesmaligen Instrument, womit er seinen Gesang begleitet.

[7] zózo-ma, „der Musikant, der das zózo spielt" (s. weiter unten), fehlt bei Koelle.

[8] mangúm-ma, „der Hornbläser"; Koelle mágūmma.

[9] fumfúm-ma, „der Trompetenbläser", von fumfum oder fomfom (Koelle pómpom).

[10] ángbidi ist wol nicht ganz richtig; ein Zeitwort ladádi, „ich gehe" aber habe ich als Synonym góbedi, das etwas Ähnliches enthalten mag.

[11] kénia ganga ki-bāppi ist 3te Person Plur. der verbalen Umschreibung.

[12] da-kāro. Der Titel des Anführers der Infanterie ist: H. serki n karma, F. lámido karmáddi.

[13] mutúm ān-damrē ebenso wie der Kanóri-Ausdruck und die meisten der entsprechenden bedeutet „gebundener Mensch". — Ich führe hier noch einige auf den Krieg bezügliche Ausdrücke an, die ich nur im Hausa und Fulfúlde vertreten und selbst da nicht völlig erklären kann: H. ma-dāwel (Spion?), F. dāvotōdo; H. mai-gaāglue, F. honnāwo, Plur. honnōbe; H. mai-šēn yāki (der im Hinterhalt Liegende?), Plur. máoū-šēn yāki, F. hodōde honno, Plur. fodéhe honno, und einen Ausdruck, den ich nur in der Pluralform habe: H. máoū na-gāba da yāki (wahrscheinlich „die vor der Fronte Kämpfenden", „Tirailleure"), F. ardīhe honno.

[14] oba n gīžī n ganga, eigentlich „der Herumtaler der Trommel".

[15] Anstatt des dem mangúm-ma im Hausa entsprechenden Musikanten führe ich hier den mai-kiddi auf (K. kagū-ma?), F. pīōwo, Plur. fīhōbe, und den kīndo, F. pillāel.

[16] maeha, höchst wahrscheinlich ma-asha; mit den in meiner Liste vorkommenden Ausdrücken für „Bogen" und „Pfeil" hat es freilich nichts gemein. Dagegen will ich hier anführen, dass die Fúlbe im nahen Adamaua noch den diesem sich eng anschliessenden und wol von ihm abgeleiteten Namen maohíddo für „berittenen Bogenschützen" haben.

[17] aléwenk. Für „Fahne" habe ich in Logoné além; das n ist also ausgefallen oder abgeworfen.

[18] magaláhke, „Gefangener", eine Zusammensetzung, die wol mit galáhke, „Schild" zusammenhängt.

[19] Hugárme von gurma, „Pfeil", ebenso wie mála-heaē in Bágrimma von heaē.

[20] darrim-dūša ist mir in seiner Ableitung und näheren Schreibweise unsicher.

[21] haogáh ośáhtī ist offenbar „der Mann (haóg) mit dem Bogen", obgleich ich für „Pfeil" in Móba nur das vom Arabischen abgeleitete alšāhoh und für „Bogen" fidah habe. — ráyek meléh, „Herr der Fahne" (rāyoh).

Sońrai.	Lógoné.	Wándalá.	Bágrimma.	Mába.
....	....	......	......	......
	....	......	......	
....	....	......	......	......
....	masku [16] ...	θugúrme [19] ..	māla-keeō ..	kangák eráktí [21]
....	aléwenā [17] ...	além-ma ..	māla-ún-alémma	rāyek melék
nédo / wāne } habbāma	magalákke [18] ..	derrim-dūra [20]	bang džokkinge	kang múhobūs (b. A.)
ganga-koi ...	bille ganga ..	džil-ganga .	koi-ganga .	gangánk melék
....	{ bille takā-takā / bille mfōro .. }	pompómme .	{ māla-kádžena / kotā-gosso . }	......

[1] hām fir-wa: Koelle has, instead, the form pérme, i. e. fir-ma, which, although regularly formed, and probably only obsolete, I have never found used. On the contrary fir-wa (pérwa) is erroneously explained by Koelle as an adjective meaning „containing horses, full of horses", while it has a far more general meaning, viz „having any connection of whatever kind with horses". Besides Koelle has also a different term kémbéma from báshin, „I mow".

[2] nūti may possibly be derived from sángin, „I stretch out", in this case to be understood of „the legs".

[3] libbedí: Koelle léféde or lébede, which he explains as meaning nothing but the thick covering, by which that peculiar class of heavy cavalry is distinguished, and such, no doubt, is the original and primary meaning of the term, derived as it is from the Arabic [illegible], a term which is still used in Sennár at the present day for denoting the coat of mail; but in the vulgar idiom, at least, it signifies also the man clad in such an armour. See a representation of these men, Travels, vol. III, plate p. 208.

[4] kanigí-ma: Koelle kenigama, although besides kenige he gives also the form kyuige for „bow".

[5] além-ma is wanting in Koelle, although he has álam. — hām tergérina: targérina is particip. passivi from gérishin, „I tie, bind".

[6] gángá-ma: Koelle has the fuller form dágū gángáma, from which we might conclude the term dágū alone to have the general meaning of „musician", although Kl. himself (under the term dágū) attributes to it the particular meaning of „drummer". But his dágū, I think, is nothing else but my duggu, „singing men", of which several kinds are distinguished according to the instrument, by which they accompany their song.

[7] náno-ma means the musician, who plays the náno, an instrument described lower down; it is wanting in Koelle.

[8] mangám-ma: Koelle mégūmma, „the man who blows the horn, the cornetor".

[9] fumfúm-ma, „the trumpeter", from fumfum or fomfom (Koelle pómpoū).

[10] ághbidī may not be quite right; but in my Mscr. list of verbs, I have as an additional term to teddí, „I go", the word gáhodi, meaning evidently „on foot" and serving probably to explain and correct our own term in this place.

[11] kónin ganga bi-báppi is 3rd person plur. of the verbal form of expression.

[12] da-káre: I here adduce the title of the commander in chief of the infantry: H. serki n karma, F. lámido karmádíi.

[13] maíém ún-damró, as well as most of the corresponding terms means „a man bound, tied up". — Besides, I here adduce a few other terms, which have reference to war, but which I can only give in Hausa and Fulfúlde, and even in these two languages am not able fully to explain them: H. ma-dšówai (spy?), F. džéotádo; H. mai-gáógána (a similar class of men), F. honnóvo, plur. honnóbe; H. mai-šén yáki („he, who is lying in ambush"?), plur. masú-šén yáki, F. hodédo honne, plur. fodábe honne; and finally another term, which I have learnt only in the plural-form: H. mbašu na-gába da yáki (perhaps „they, who fight in front of the battle", or „the sharpshooters"), F. ardíbe honne.

[14] ohe n gíli n gánga, properly „the landlord of the drum".

[15] Instead of the Hausa-name of the peculiar class of musician, corresponding to the Kanúri mangám-ma, I here adduce the name of the fiddler. H. mai-biddí (K. kogū-ma?), F. piówo, plur. fibóbe, and another sort of musician, called bindo in Hausa, pillóni in Fulfúlde.

[16] masko, most probably, is a composite term of me and sake, although it has no connection with the terms for „bow" and „arrow", given in my list, while on the other side the Fúlbe of Adamaua most probably have derived the term mashōdžo, „the mounted archer" from this term, belonging to the idiom of their North-Eastern neighbours.

[17] aléwenā is perhaps not quite correct; for „ensign" in Lógoné I have the term além.

[18] magalákke, „spearman", a composite term, probably connected with galákke, „shield".

[19] θugúrme from gurme, „arrow", just as mála-keoō in Bágrimma has been from keoō meaning likewise „arrow".

[20] derrim-dūra: As for the elements, of which this term has been composed, I am not quite certain.

[21] kangák eráktí means evidently „the person (kang) with the arch", although for „arch" in Mába I have quite another term, viz fidak, and also for „arrow" have only the term nišábah, simply derived from the Arabic. — rāyak melék, „master of the ensign".

Deutsch und Englisch.	Kanúri.	Tédā.	Haúsa.	Fulfúlde.
Sänger — *singing man*	duggu[1] . . .	debûne gúkkeni[6]	mai-wāka . .	bambādo . . gimmōo Plur. yimmōbe
Zauberer — *sorcerer* . Taschenspieler — *juggler*	móngolō[2] . .	. . . . . .	mayí fm. máyia	. . . . . .
singender Bettler — *singing beggar*	gódō-ma[3] . .	bézerē . . .	. . . . . .	. . . . . .
Bettler — *beggar* . . . Gesindel, armes Volk — *poor, miserable people*	ngúdi[4] . . .	láuta-dē[7] . .	mai-rōko[8] . matšiata . .	rogōdē . . torotōdo . . tšoido Pl. soibe sewindādšo .
Schlemmer — *glutton* . .	. . . . . .	. . . . . .	mai-lōma[9] .	džom-lóngere mò-lóngere maundo
Jähzorniger Mensch — *irascible person*	. . . . . .	. . . . . .	mai-cbilisse[10]	džom-ginni[12] kangáldo Plur. hangābe
Hundesohn — *son of a dog*	táta kéri-bō[5]		da n kerré[11] .	bi rauándu[13] .

[1] duggu. Koelle dúgū; s. S. 244, N. 6.

[2] móngolō fehlt bei Koelle, wie es auch entschieden kein eigentliches Kanúri-Wort, sondern dem Lógonē entlehnt ist, wie ich Einleitung S. CCXXIV gezeigt habe. — Für „Hexe" (witch) hat Koelle kareme.

[3] gódō-ma. Das gódā, gódō-niskin ist nach meiner Ansicht kein einheimisches Kanúri-Wort, sondern vom Haúsa-Wort (na-)gódo abgeleitet „ich lobe, preise", weil diese Art Bettler eben unter Lobpreisungen [illegible] betteln. Dieses selbst gódo ist sogar in's Temádjyt übergegangen.

[4] ngúdi hat eine sehr allgemeine Bedeutung und bezeichnet Alles, was mit Elend und Armuth verbunden ist, daher auch wol, wie Koelle richtig vermuthet, die Bedeutung des Guinea-Wurmes (vgl. weiter unten), weil dieser gerade zur Regenzeit, wo in diesen Gegenden die einzige Arbeit Statt findet, diejenigen, die davon befallen sind, mehr oder weniger zum Elend verdammt.

[5] táta kéri-bō. Dieser Ausdruck, „Sohn des Hundes", ist zum allergewöhnlichsten Schimpfwort bei den Kanúri geworden.

[6] debûne gúkkeni heisst vielleicht „er stimmt den Gesang an"; jedenfalls ist gúkkeni (gúk-keni) verbal.

[7] láuta-dē, eigentlich „die Person von den Lumpen"; s. Einleitung S. LXXXII.

[8] mai-rōko begreift auch den keineswegs Armen, der aber durch sein Bitten zudringlich wird. So nähert sich dieser Begriff oft demjenigen des Schmeichlers, wofür die Haúsa-Sprache die beiden eigenthümlichen Ausdrücke hat: baba-n-bōde und tórōdo; der letztere (wol nicht von ursprünglicher Haúsa-Abkunft) ist im Fulfúlde in der Form torá-torāo aufgenommen. — matšiata, freilich keine Singularform, entspricht ziemlich genau dem ngúdi.

[9] mai-lōma. Ein verwandter Ausdruck ist ragō (vom „Hammel" hergenommen, obgleich die Pluralbildung verschieden scheint), auf F. [illegible].

[10] mai-cbilisse, wörtlich „Herr des Teufels" (vom Arab. eblis). — Ich will hier einige begriffsverwandte Ausdrücke anführen: „Streithammel", H. mai-[illegible], mai-ma-fádda-[illegible] (eine doppelte Zusammensetzung: „der Herr des vielen Streit-Machens"), auf F. [illegible] oder [illegible]. Dann ein anderer Haúsa-Ausdruck von ähnlicher Bedeutung kebā-kebā; dann H. keri-keri und (kemōme) mesómiata, F. kābelīdo, und endlich „der Spottvogel", „Lustigmacher", H. mai-wōsa (da wólasa), F. [illegible].

[11] da n kerré entspricht vollkommen dem gegenüberstehenden Kanúri-Ausdruck; viel gewöhnlicher aber und das lockere Leben bei den Haúsawa bezeichnend ist der Schimpfname „Hurensohn", der in verschiedener Weise ausgedrückt wird. der gewöhnlichste Ausdruck ist da n farka, F. bi n dōōin; dann H. da n sēni (eigentlich „Sohn der Ehebrecherin"), F. bi n dēdnu; H. da n nēma (eigentlich da n mai-néme, „Sohn der [Männer] Suchenden", F. bi mzrōdlo. H. da n banenze („Sohn der nichtigen, nicht rechtmässigen (Väter)", F. bi wāla.

[12] džom-ginni, wol wörtliche Übersetzung des Arabischen sīdi džennūn, „Herr der Geister".

[13] bi rauándu wird wol von den in den früheren Haúsa-Staaten ansässigen Fúlbe gebraucht in Nachahmung des Haúsa-Ausdruckes, aber sonst wol weniger, da der strengere Charakter der reinen Fúlbe solchen Schimpfwörtern einigermassen abhold ist, während sie bei den Haúsawa den dritten Bestandtheil der ganzen Sprache bilden.

[14] dšehénnem(e) iddžo, „Sohn der Hölle".

[15] mohárreme ist auffallend wegen der hier ihm beigelegten Bedeutung, die es wahrscheinlich besonderen, uns unbekannten Umständen zu verdanken hat, wahrscheinlich dem von der Religion „verbotenen" Charakter seiner oft unzüchtigen Umzüge.

[16] móngalō. Über die echt Lógonēische Zusammensetzung dieses Namens s. Note 2 und die daselbst angeführte Stelle der Einleitung. — Den Zusatz wenialyén in der folgenden Phrase, der das „Singen" ausdrücken muss, kann ich nicht erklären, da ich S. 61 für „singen" ein grundverschiedenes Wort habe.

[17] [illegible] verdient Beachtung.

[18] dāli taléggu. taléggu ist der Haúsa-Sprache entnommen.

Sonyai.	Lógonē.	Wándalā.	Bágrimma.	Mába.
	mohárreme[15] . .	duggu . . .	mála-búrba .	lĕbib amböni saffári
kerkò(?)	móngolò[16] . . .	wóngola . .	bêli	kaňg-mankĕrib
. . . .	áholnī waniaiyūn	ńngalā[17] . .		
	áholnī	džil talágga[18]	mála-gōdo .	meskīn (Arb.)
. . . .		. . . .		
. . . .	. . . .			
džehénnem(e) lo-dže[14]				
. . . .	. . . .	. . . .	. . . . . .	. . . . . .

[1] duggu: Koelle dúgū; see p. 245, note 6. — Koelle has also a term ngarima, „deceiver, jester, joker, one who tells stories to entertain people".

[2] móngolò is wanting in Koelle, as it, no doubt, is not an original Kanúri-term, but has been borrowed from the Lógonē, as shown Introductory Remarks p. CLXXV.

[3] gódé-ma: gódé, gódé-niskin, according to my opinion, is not an indigenous Kanúri-word, but has been derived from the Hausa-term (na-)gódē, „I praise", a term which has even been introduced into the Tamāšiyt, these sort of beggars accompanying their begging phrases with chanting the praises of the Almighty.

[4] ngādi has a very general meaning, denoting every thing connected with misery and poverty, whence the word has even obtained the notion of Guinea-worm, most probably, as Koelle rightly conjectures, on account of this grave sickness disenabling the people just during the rainy season, which is the very period of the year, when almost all the agricultural labours must be absolved in these regions, so that it becomes easily the cause of their misery.

[5] tata kéri-bè: this term, „son of a dog", has become an abusive term, in most common use with the Kanúri.

[6] debóne gákkinī perhaps means „he who begins a song"; at any rate gákkenī is (gák-kenī) a verbal form.

[7] lente-dĕ properly means „the person of the rags"; see Introductory Remarks p. LXXXIII.

[8] mai-róko: the term comprises also that class of people, who, although they are not poor, are absolutely given to begging. Thus, the meaning of this term approaches that of a flatterer, or sycophant, for which the Hausa-language possesses at least two distinct terms, viz baba-n-bāde and tórādo, the latter of which (probably of foreign origin), in the form tórō-tórōwe has passed into the Fulfúlde-idiom. — The term matālāta corresponds tolerably well with the Kanúri-term ngādi, and, although representing a plural-form, is not declinable.

[9] mai-lúma: a term of similar meaning is ragó (a person of such habits being, compared to a „ram"), F. láfudō.

[10] mai-sbilless means verbally „master of the devil" (from the Arabic iblīs). — I here do adduce a few other terms of a similar meaning, such as „quarrelsome person, wrangler", H. mai-tsédanni or mai-ma-fádda-lāi (a double mode of composition, meaning „the master of making much quarrel"), F. tšatindo or tšátudo. Then, another Hausa-term: habō-habó, the exact meaning of which I am not acquainted with, and another term, H. keri-keri (or kemóma) masémtata, F. kabatūdo, and finally „merry-Andrew", „derider (of other people)", H. mai-wása (da mótane), F. tédi-rēdo.

[11] da n karrē corresponds exactly to the Hausa-term, but much more common is another abusive term, „whore-son", expressed in many different ways, and by means of this common abuse characterizing the easier way of life of the Hausa-people: the most common term is da n farka, F. bi n djála; then H. da n eānī (properly „son of the adulterer"), F. bi n dšónu; H. da n nēma (properly da n mai-nēma, „son of the searching", meaning the woman, who runs after the men), F. bi n errāddo; further, H. da n kanuaka („son of the naughty or illegitimate [fathers]"), F. bi n wāla.

[12] dšom-giani seems to be a verbal translation of the Arabic term aldi džennūn, „master of the spirits".

[13] bi rananda is actually employed by the Fúlbe settled in the Hausa-states in imitation of the corresponding Hausa-term, but it will scarcely be used, I think, by their other compatriots of pure descent, the whole character of the Fúlbe-nation abhorring apparently from the use of such terms, while they form almost the third part of the speech of the common Hausa-people.

[14] džehénnem(e) loddža, properly means „son (offspring) of hell".

[15] moharrame: the meaning of this term, whose Arabic origin seems to be placed beyond a doubt, is curious, and probably owes its origin to some peculiar circumstances.

[16] móngolò: with regard to the true Lógonē origin of this term, see note 2, and the relative chapter of the Introductory Remarks there adduced. — As for the additional term waniaiyūn in the following phrase, I presume, it must express the singing, although in my list of verbs p. 61 I have expressed the latter by another quite distinct verb.

[17] ńngalā seems to merit peculiar attention.

[18] džil talágga: talágga has been borrowed from the Hausa-language.

Deutsch und Englisch.	Kanúri.	Tédā.	Hausa.	Fulfúlde.
Sünder — *sinner* . . .	(kāmkendōdibbi)	. . . . . .	mai-lōifi[6] . .	aribe . . . / džom-gātše .
Dieb, Gauner — *thief, rogue*	bérbo[1] . . .	udē . . . . / borōmi . .	barāu fm. barau-nia / mai-sāta	gūdāo Pl. wālbe
Räuber — *robber* . . .	gendē-ma[2] .	barka barām[5]	mai-fašī[7] . .	pasotōdo[10] . / tēto džubtōwo / džensido datti
Strassenräuber — *highway-robber*	ngúdī-degél .	erdē (trīe yekóppi-dē)		
Mörder — *murderer* . .	nišotsōma . / debāte-ma?	. . . . . .	mai-kašē mutanē[8]	bār-óndune .
Hurer, Ehebrecher — *adulterer*	kōa dūnyā-ma[3] / kōa zāni (Arb.)	. . . . . .	mai-nēma . .	. . . . . .
Hure — *whore*	kāmo zāni . / kāmo balbi[4] . / kāmo mai-būši	kezíndō . . . / ogī	farka[9] . . . . / mai-nēma . .	dženōwo[11] . .

[1] bérbo. Koelle bárbū. Sowohl das entsprechende Tédā- (burō-mi), wie das Hausa-Wort (barāu) scheint anzuzeigen, dass das zweite b ursprünglich nicht zum Stamme gehörte, sondern vielleicht einer Pluralform seinen Ursprung verdankt. — Koelle hat noch ein anderes Wort für „Dieb", nämlich ádáltema und ein besonderes Wort nányēma für „Taschendieb". — Für „Sünder" gibt er yitumma.

[2] gendē-ma fehlt bei Koelle, der dafür bátalma von bátal hat, das an den bekannten altarabischen Ausdruck erinnert. — ngúdī degél ma, wenn richtig, etwa die Bedeutung haben „verzweifelter Lump". Koelle hat dafür den ganz verschiedenen Ausdruck kambéda. — debātema erklärt Koelle als „executioner by the sword", während er für „Mörder" dátēbama gibt.

[3] kōa dūnyā-ma, wörtlich „der weltliche Mann", wie kāmo dūnyā-ma „die weltliche Frau", beides sich beziehend auf lose, liederliches Leben. — Das zāni hat dann im Kanúri, wie in den übrigen Sprachen, besonders in Bezug auf die Frau den ursprünglichen Begriff der Ehebrecherin gegen den der feilen Hure vertauscht.

[4] balbi fehlt bei Koelle, so auch mai-būši; dagegen hat er den mir völlig unbekannten Ausdruck watsedála. mai-būši (eine ungewöhnliche Zusammensetzung) bedeutet eigentlich „die Herrin der Matte" (bei Koelle búši), die gemeinste Klasse öffentlicher Frauen bezeichnend. — Koelle hat noch einen ganz besonderen Ausdruck, nämlich égaiem mit der Bedeutung „Buhler oder Buhlerin". Diesem Wort legt er auch die neutrale Bedeutung „Ehebruch" bei. — Die Kanúri haben ausserdem den noch viel stärkeren Ausdruck ngelčen, der so ziemlich unserem Worte „Auswurf" zu entsprechen scheint.

[5] barka barám ist ein unbeholfener, dem vulgärsten Arabisch entlehnter Ausdruck. Dagegen ist erdē (er-dē) wol identisch mit dem allgemeineren irdi oben S. [illegible], hier mit dem Zusatz trīe yekóppi-de, „der die Strasse abschneidet", ein echtes Tédā-Wort, das so wie erdē und [illegible] zu der Einleitung S. LXXX, 10. besprochenen Klasse gehört.

[6] mai-lōifi. Ich will hier noch den besonderen Ausdruck für „Heuchler" anführen, oft auch noch mit der allgemeineren Bedeutung „Gauner": H. munáfeki (neben munafutši und wol irrthümlich selbst für Lust, Schön, Job. [illegible]), F. munáfeki-dāo; und „Betrüger, hinterlistiger Fuchs", H. mai-sámba-tšī, F. džom-hīla, halb Arabisch. Ich führe hier auch noch an, dass für „Hure" Koelle im Kanúri karawa angiebt. — Die genaue Bedeutung eines anderen Wortes ma-yiageli in Hausa, entsprechend dem Fulfúlde-Ausdruck džantšo, habe ich nicht erfahren.

[7] mai-fašī. Da [illegible] heisst „ich zerschmettere", so ist es auffallend, dass das davon abgeleitete Substantiv ohne jeglichen Beisatz diese bestimmte Bedeutung von „Räuber" erhalten hat.

[8] mai-kašē mutanē, wörtlich „der Tödter von Menschen". Eine ähnliche Bedeutung scheint das Hausa-Wort māya zu haben, F. māyō-dīō.

[9] farka. Es ist nicht unmöglich, dass dies dasselbe Wort ist wie farka, „Esel", im Songhai und dass es von den Hausaue der Nachbarsprache entlehnt ist, um diesen anderen Begriff zu bezeichnen. Die anderen, weniger häufig gebrauchten Ausdrücke für „Hure" s. bei da n kerré, S. [illegible], N. 10. Der Ausdruck kakalia, den Schön mit dieser Bedeutung aufführt, ist kein Hausa-Wort, sondern gehört einer anderen Sprache an, wahrscheinlich Nūfe.

[10] pasotōdo ist, wie ich glaube, nur bei den Fulbe von Fúmbina in Gebrauch. — tēto džubtōwo ist mir nicht deutlich — džensido datti, „der Wegelagerer". — Zu bār-óndune, „der Menschentödter" s. Einleitung S. CXXXIV, 6, a).

[11] dženōwo, zu der Ableitung s. Einleitung S. CL. Die Fulbe von Fúmbina haben noch den Ausdruck wol für „Hure" und es ist wahrscheinlich, dass dies die allgemeine Songhai-Bezeichnung für „Frau" ist, obgleich man dann erwarten sollte, dass es auch bei den westlicheren Fulbe so gebraucht würde, die doch mit den Songhai in näherer Berührung geblieben sind.

[12] fondo-dumbu-kel. fondo, „der Weg", dumbu, „verscheuchen, unsicher machen", kel, „der Mann von", „der Herr von", also „der Mann, der den Weg unsicher macht", vgl. Einleitung S. CLXXXIV, c).

[13] arō-bāude l. a. a-nō-bé-ade, „er, der Krieg gegen das Menschenleben führt", Einleitung S. CLXXXII, a).

[14] mō-ne ranar. auwar mit dieser Bedeutung ist auffallend. Über die Zusammensetzung s. Einleitung S. CCXXIV, f, b). — muskaura bei greém muskauen scheint Participialform; vgl. Einleitung S. CCVIII, f).

[15] gindá, offenbar von derselben Wurzel, wie ted-alé, „Hyäne", eigentlich wol „Raubthier", wie hier gindé, „Räuber".

[16] mála-hing-déha, „Herr des Abschneidens der Strasse". Einleitung S. CCLXXIV, f).

[17] nēga manda. nē, Plur. nēga, heisst „die Frau"; nēga könnte also wol Pluralform scheinen. Dann ist aber der Zusatz im Sing.: manda, „Jungfrau, Mädchen", unrichtig und die ganze Zusammensetzung auffallend; ich habe daher an das Arabische [illegible] („Beischlaf") gedacht.

[18] gō-melék ist entweder abgeleitet vom Arabischen gōm, قوم, „der Heerhaufen", in der Wüste besonders „Räuberzug", in welchem Fall wir gōm-melék schreiben müssten, oder, was wahrscheinlicher, von gō, „rauben" und von melék, „Herr von"; vgl. Einleitung S. CCCX, m). — Für „Mörder" gibt Seetzen kántsah.

Sońyai.	Lógonē.	Wándalā.	Bágrimma.	Mába.
. . . .	. . . .	. . . . . .	. . . . . .	. . . . . .
. . . .	mus-χoi Pl. mézoχoi	ailō	bōgo	nénik Pl. oenni
fondo-dumbu-koi [12]	bille fé-zijffulo .	gindū [15] . . .	mála-kiṅg-debe [16]	gō-meléh [18]
azō-húnde [13] . .	. . . .	. . . . . .		
. . . .	mó-ne zauar [14] .	zāni múkse-na	. . . . . .	
. . . .	genéuo-o zauar . / geném mus-kauen	mukse zāni .	nēga manda [17] / nēga zāni . . / nēga n kodúpke	ázeba

[1] bérbo: Koelle writes bárbū. As well the corresponding Tēda- (buro-mi), as the Hausa-term (barāo), seem to indicate, that the second b does not originally belong to the root, but may possibly owe its origin to a plural-form. Koelle has, besides, another term for „thief", via ádállima, and also a particular term for „pickpocket" via sānyéma, while for „sinner" he gives ꞌlímma.

[2] gendō-ma is wanting in Koelle, who instead has bátalma from batal which reminds of the identical Arabic term. — ígūdi degéi, if correct, seems to have some such meaning as „desperate wretch". Koelle has for „highway-robber" the term bambáda, which I have never heard. For „murder" also he gives a different term dátybauma, while dabátema he explains by „executioner by the sword".

[3] kós duṅyá-ma means verbally „the worldly man", and kámo duṅyá-ma „the worldly woman", both terms referring to a loose mode of life. — The term záui, especially with regard to the woman, has exchanged its original meaning of „adulteress" against that of a common wench.

[4] balhi, as well as mal-házi is wanting in Koelle, who, instead, has the term walaudála, unknown to myself; the latter term means originally „the mistress of the mat" (Koelle hútái) and indicates the vilest sort of women of the town. Koelle has still another term via ágáatem with the meaning „paramour, a male or female living in a state of adultery" and even attributes to this term the neutral notion of „adultery" itself. — The Kanúri-language, besides, possesses the still stronger term ágeldas, which seems to be identical with the term „outcast".

[5] barka harám is an awkward term, borrowed from the most vulgar Arabic. But, as for erdō, with the distinct explanation of tris ye-kóppi-dē, „he who cuts off the road", it is most probably identical with irdi, „enemy" p. 232 and a pure Tēda-term, which like kealūdē belongs to that class of nouns treated Introductory Remarks, p. LXXXI, 10.

[6] mal-irífi: I here shall adduce the peculiar term for „concealer, pander", frequently used also with a wider sense, as meaning „rogue", in general, H. munafeki (Schön munafuki, to which he wrongly attributes the meaning „fraud, cunning", Schön, Joh. I, v. 48 (47)), F. munafeki-djo; and „cheater, deceiver", H. mai-samba-tái, F. djambila (b. A. „master of cunning"). I here also adduce the Kanúri-term for „witch" according to Koelle, via kárama; see p. 237. — The Hausa-language has another term ma-plegeli, corresponding to the Fulfúlde-term djantlo, but I am not aware of its original meaning.

[7] mai-fázi: as the verb fan-fázé has the general meaning of crushing or shattering to pieces, it is remarkable, that the simple noun, which has been thence derived, should imply the distinct meaning of murdering, which in the verbal phrase is expressed by adding kansa, „his head".

[8] mai-kašō mótané „the killer of men"; a similar meaning seeming to be implied by máyu, in F. mayō-djō.

[9] farka: it is not impossible, that this term is identical with farka, meaning „ass" in Sońyai, and that it has been adopted by the Hausa-people, in order to express this other meaning. The term čakália, given by Schön with this notion, appears to be wrong; at least it does not belong to the Hausa-idiom.

[10] pasuotéda, I presume, is not but used by the Fúlbe settled in Fúmbina. — této djahtówe I am not able to analyse. — djčeualdo dafli means „the cutter of roads". As for bár-óndona, see Introductory Remarks p. CXXXV, 8, a).

[11] djenówe: as for the mode of derivation of this term see Introductory Remarks p. CLI. The Fúlbe settled in Fúmbina employ also the term wai in this sense of „whore"; and it is probable, that this is nothing else but the general Sońyai-word for „woman", although in this case we should expect, that it were generally employed also by the Fúlbe settled near the Niger, who are in constant contact with the Sońyai.

[12] fondo-dumbu-koi: fondo, „road, track", dumbu, „to cut, infest", koi, „man of", „master of"; thus, the meaning is „the man, who infests the road"; compare Introductory Remarks p. CLXXXV, c).

[13] azō-húnde i. q. azō-hú-nde, „he who wages war against the life of man", compare Introd. Rem. p. CLXXXIII, a).

[14] mó-ne zauar: the word zauar with this meaning is curious. As for muskauen further on, it seems to be the particip. act.; compare Introductory Remarks p. CCIX, f).

[15] gindú, is evidently derived from the same root as the term ind-aiā meaning „beast of prey, hyena" p. 195.

[16] mála-kiṅg-débe, „master of cutting off the road", Introductory Remarks p. CCLXXV, f).

[17] nēga manda: nē, plur. nēga, meaning „wife", nēga would seem to be identical with this nēge, but in that case the adding of manda, „virgin, maid", would be grammatically wrong, and moreover curious.

[18] gō-meléh is either derived from the Arabic gōm, قوم, „populus, bostes", especially in the Desert „a predatory expedition", in which case we ought to write gōm-meléh, or, what is rather more probable, from the verb gō, „to plunder", and from meléh, „master of". — For „murderer" in Mába, Seetzen gives the term kástšāh.

Deutsch und Englisch	Kanúri	Tédā	Hausa	Fulfúlde
weltliche, buhlerische Frau — *worldly-minded, amorous woman*	kámo dunyāma	adī zúntu [4] .	kárua [9] . . .	dóbo kállado, karuádžo . . , dertöre worbe [14]
Moslim — *Moslem* . . .	músulmu . .	ńáselum [5] . . , Muslim . .	músleml Pl. músleml	džūl-do [13] Plur. džūl-be
Heide — *heathen, pagan*	kérdi [1] [6]. . .	ráfera [6] . . , erdi . . .	ázena . . . , ba-mágodši [10] Pl. magozaua	kádo Pl. hābe, magddžo Plur. mágui, kéfero Pl. héfer-be
Araber — *Arab* . . .	wáseri [2] . . , šūn	yógo-dē [7] . . , menémenē [8] . , erdi mādé .	ba-tūre [11], ba-túra-n-tši, Plur. turaua	túra-džo Pl. túra-in
Targi (Amóšay) — *Targi*	kindin [3]. . .	yóbur-dē . .	ba-ásben-tši [12] Pl. ásbenaua, ábsenaua	fólo [18] Pl. pelli, tšapāto Pl. sa-pāle, bodedžo Plur. wodébe

[1] kérdi, Koelle kérdi, wird durch die ursprünglichere Tédā-Form in Ursprung und Bedeutung erläutert (s. Einleitung S. LXXXVIII, 6.) und als von den südlichen Völkerschaften aufgenommen dargethan. „Christ" habe ich im Text fortgelassen, weil es in diesen Sprachen eine unsichere Variation des Wortes našāra ist, der Plural vom Arabischen نصراني.

[2] wáseri, Koelle wasili (was sich also der Logoné-Form, woher diese Benennung unzweifelhaft stammt, ursprünglich ba-sili, noch enger anschliesst), bedeutet den Araber oder Weissen von der Küste, šūa den vor Jahrhunderten aus Arabien über die Nilländer in die Negerländer eingewanderten Araber; jedoch scheint letzterer Ausdruck mit dem Namen des Abessinischen Landes Šóa durchaus nichts gemein zu haben. In Dar-Für heissen die Letzteren angeblich Sallúnge.

[3] kíndin. Dieser Name fehlt in Koelle's Kanúri-Wörterbuch, erscheint aber in hervorragender Stellung unter der Form Kándin unter C, 1 seiner Polyglotta, als eine neue Sprache vertretend, die aber keineswegs die reine Tawareg-Sprache darstellt, sondern den buntgemischten Jargon eines in Bórnu eingebürgerten Hausa-Sklaven; s. Reisen I, S. 374 Note.

[4] adī zúnto, wörtlich „schlechte Frau".

[5] ńáselum scheint eine vulgäre Form zu sein.

[6] ráfera ist eine verdorbene, stark veränderte Form von káfir. — Die Beziehung des Tédā-Wortes erdi, „Feind" (oben S. 231) und „Heide" zur Kanúri-Form kérdi ist sprachlich und sachlich höchst interessant; vgl. S. 249, N. 2.

[7] yógo-dē. Der Ursprung dieses eigenthümlichen Ausdruckes ist mir noch unbekannt, während ich das ganz ähnlich gebildete und offenbar zu jenem in lebendigem Gegensatz gebildete yóbur-dē Einleitung S. LXXXII als „der Mann vom Kriege", „der Freibeuter" vollständig erklärt habe. — Zu erdi mādé, „rother Feind" vgl. Reisen, Th. III, S. 461 Note.

[8] menémenē, zuweilen wie mínueminne klingend, ist eigentlich kein so genereller Name, sondern bezeichnet die räuberischen Araber-Stämme, besonders die Uelād-Slimān; s. Reisen, Th. III, S. 60.

[9] kárua ist wol dasselbe Wort wie das für „Wind" und nur metaphorisch auf einen „Windbeutel" von Frau übertragen.

[10] ba-mágodši hängt unzweifelhaft auf das Engste mit dem entsprechenden Fulfúlde-Ausdruck magúdžo zusammen, dessen Plural mágui wieder auf Verbindung mit Hausa mayī, „Zauberer" (oben S. 218, N. 10) schliessen lässt, wir dem auch die nähere Bedeutung des ba-mágodši von einem Heiden, der mit allen Abzeichen des Heidenthums geschmückt Vorstellungen giebt und besonders den dódo-Tanz ausführt (s. Reisen, Th. I, S. 522), eben dahin führt.

[11] ba-túre. Über dieses merkwürdige Wort s. Reisen, Th. I, S. 516, N. ***, zu welcher Bemerkung ich hinzuzufügen habe, dass im Fulfúlde mo-túra-tē heisst „ich werfe mich im Gebet auf den Boden nieder". Auch will ich hier ganz nebenher anführen, ohne darauf besonderes Gewicht zu legen, dass nach Müller (der Ugrische Stamm 1837, Th. I, S. 27?) das Wort túra bei den Kirghisen „Herren" bedeutet und dass túreh in Khokand, Chiwa u. s. w. der Titel von „Häuptling, Richter" ist. túra-n-tši ist die Wesenheit, der Charakter des ba-túre, erhält dann aber durch den Vorsatz von ba wieder die Bedeutung der Persönlichkeit selbst.

[12] ba-ásben-tši. Siehe über den Namen Ásben, Ásben, Reisen, Th. I, S. 340, Note.

[14] dertöre worbe heisst offenbar „Männer suchend", obgleich die Ableitung von dertöre mir unbekannt ist.

[13] džūl-do von mé-dú-džūlo, „ich bete".

[15] tšapāto, „der Vogel", wegen der eiligen Märsche und unerwarteten Überfälle des räuberischen Tawareg-Stammes; bodédžo, „der Rothe". Die letztere Bezeichnung ist sehr bemerkenswerth, weil in Beziehung auf die eigentlichen Negerstämme die Fúlbe selbst „die Rothen" sind. Wegen der genauen Bedeutung von fólo bin ich nicht ganz sicher.

[16] kéfer. Vielleicht giebt es daneben noch einen nationalen Ausdruck, da Kaffenel im verwandten Arama für („Heide") „païen" saúbaú (saúbú) hat.

[17] džáugar. Von diesem džáugar wird „Heidenland" džáugar-tong genannt, entsprechend dem Fertit der Furaua.

[18] áram. Dieser Ausdruck, obgleich ursprünglich eine verdorbene Form des Wortes عرب, bezeichnet doch ganz vorzüglich die in Wádāi einheimische Arabische Bevölkerung und wird wol nie zur Bezeichnung der anderen Araber gebraucht. — Letztere hat noch einen besonderen Mába-Ausdruck für „Weisser", pfefférta(?).

Sónyai.	Lógoné.	Wándalá.	Bágrimma.	Mába.
	genóm e zawar .	mukse záni .	n'ga záni . .	ámba
mislim	mislim	mislim . . .	mislim . . .	mislema
kêfer (Arb.)[16] .	kirdi	kirdi	kirdi	džungur[17] Plur. džunguri
Harab	wásell (s. n. 2) .	Šiwa	minnemínne .	áram[18] Pl. arám-ka
Surgu	kindin	kindîn . . .	kinding . . .	kinun

[1] kérdi: Kotlie kérdi. By means of comparison with the corresponding Tédá-term we have now obtained the true origin of this term, which from Bornu has spread also over the Eastern countries; see Introductory Remarks p. LXXXIX, n. — The term for „Christian" in these different languages I do not adduce in the text, because it is nothing but a slightly changed and very uncertain form of nasára, the original plural-form of نصراني.

[2] wásari (Koelle wásili), most probably of Lógoné origin, designates the Arab or white men from the Northern coast; Šûa the Arab, who, several centuries ago, has immigrated into Negroland from the countries of the Upper Nile, although this name has scarcely any thing in common with the name of the Abyssinian country Šóa. Comp. Tr., vol. III, p. 135 f.

[3] kindin: this name is wanting in Koelle's vocabulary, while under the form Kándin it appears in a conspicuous position in his Polyglotta (C, 1), as representing a peculiar idiom, which ought to be the Tarki-dialect of the Kél-owi, but is nothing else, but the corrupted jargon of a Hausa-slave brought up in Asben. See Travels and Disc., vol. I, p. 342 note.

[4] adi nánin means verbally „a bad woman".

[5] ndacinam seems to be rather a vulgar form.

[6] káfera is a corrupted form of the Arabic káfir, while ordi, meaning properly „enemy" (p. 221) in reference to the closely related Kanúri-word kérdi, is highly interesting and appears to be the primitive form; compare p. 248, note 5.

[7] yógo-dé: the origin of this peculiar national term is as yet unknown to me, while its mode of derivation evidently classes it with the terms treated Introductory Remarks p. LXXXIII; and we may thence conclude, that it forms a sort of opposition to yóhar-dô, which latter term indicates „the man of war", „the freebooter".

[8] monémenô, at times sounding like minnemínne, properly is not a generic name, but serves to indicate the predatory Arab tribes on the Southern border of the desert, especially the Welád Slimán. See Travels, vol. III, p. 66, where in the footnote the term ordi míde also has been explained.

[9] hérna seems to be the very identical term for „wind", being employed in a metaphorical sense, in order to denote the swaggering woman.

[10] ba-mágodži: this term, no doubt, is most intimately connected with the corresponding Fulfúlde-term magádio, the plural-form of which, viz mágui, again closely resembles Hausa mayi, meaning „sorcerer" (p. 248), just as the proper meaning of ba-magoddi, as conveying the notion of a person decked out with all emblems of paganism and as such exhibiting the dance called dódo, refers to the same source of superstition. See Travels, vol. I, p. 531.

[11] ba-túre: with regard to this remarkable word, see Travels, vol. I, p. 471, to which remark I have to add, that also the verb mo-tóre-tó in Fulfúlde means „I throw myself down in prayer". I must also mention, without, however, laying much stress upon that circumstance, that with the Kirghis tûra means „master" and tôreh in the dialect of Khokand Khiva etc. designates the „chief" and „judge"; túra-n-tší is „the nature or character of a ba-túre", whence ba-túra-ntši.

[12] ba-áshen-tši: see with regard to the name A'shen, A'bsen, Travels, vol. I, p. 336.

[13] dertére warbe means evidently „looking after men", although the derivation of dertére is unknown to me.

[14] dájl-do from mé-dô-dájio, „I pray".

[15] šápâto means „bird" in reference to the swift marches and sudden attacks of that roving tribe; hodêdžo, „the red", a signification rather remarkable from the point of view of the Fúlbe, whose name from a comparison with the neighbouring Negro-tribes implies that very colour. As for the meaning of fédo, I am not quite certain.

[16] kêfer: perhaps there may exist another more national term besides this one, Dahruel in the closely related Arama-dialect giving the term soâbeš i. q. sâbâ with this notion („pains").

[17] džungur: from this term džungar the country of the pagans is called džungúr-tang, identical with the term Fertit applied to it by the Furawa.

[18] áram: this term, although originally nothing but a corrupted form of the word عرب, nevertheless designates especially the Arabic population settled in Negroland, and never is used to designate a pure Árab. — I here mention, that Bornu has a particular term for „white man", viz pirffórin[?].

Deutsch und Englisch.	Kanúri.	Tédā.	Haúsa.	Fulfúlde.
Tebu — Tebu	tébū[1] .	tédā[6] . . .	. . . . .	. . . . . .
Bornauer — Bórnu-man	Kanúri[2] . . / kām Bórnu-bé	Túgubā . . . / anna Bórno[7] .	ba-bérbertšē[9] Pl. beréberē	berberēdžo Plur. bérberai
Hausaner — Hausa-man	áfnuó[3] . . .	anna áfnuó .	ba-hauše Plur. hausaua	hausa-nkē-džo Pl. hausa-nkoï
Pullo oder Fūla — Pullo, Fūla, Fellatah	folāta[4] . . .	. . . . . .	ba-féllantšē[10] Pl. féllani	pūlo Pl. fulbe[11]
Kopf — head	kéla[5] . . .	dāho[8] Plur. kōë	kai Plur. kauna	hōre[12] . . .
Vorderkopf, Stirn — fore-head, front	ūgúm . . .	fóufoní . . .	goši	tindo . . .

[1] tébū. Diese umgewandelte Namensform (mit b) dieses grossen, in ihrem nationalen Zusammenhange bisher so räthselhaften Wüstenvolkes ist offenbar eben von der Kanúri-Sprache ausgegangen und war wol ursprünglich nur eine Pluralform, indem der Kern des ursprünglichen nationalen Namens te („Jäger"? vgl. kédedé) war; s. Einleitung S. XLVI, vgl. N. 6 unten. Die älteste davon abgeleitete Arabische Form [illegible] scheint tubu zu sein, mit kurzem u in beiden Silben.

[2] Kanúri. Ich wiederhole hier meine bestimmteste Überzeugung, dass der Name Kanúri nichts in aller Welt mit dem Namen der Stadt oder Landschaft Kanó gemein haben kann, s. Einleitung S. VIII, vgl. S. XL. Der Name war in Gebrauch, ehe die Bornauer irgend eine Beziehung zu jenem Lande hatten, viel weniger zur gleichnamigen Stadt, deren Gründung erst in spätere Zeit fällt, vgl. Reisen, Th. II, S. 136; vgl. „Tabellarisches Verzeichniss der Könige von Bórnu" S. 330. — Bórnu (bei Koelle Bóṙnu, aber in Zusammensetzungen macht er das u lang, wie Bóṙnūma), obgleich vielleicht mit den Berbern am Nil nicht ohne Zusammenhang, ist mehr ein politischer Begriff, im Gegensatz gegen die Bulāla und erscheint gleichzeitig zuerst in dem Bericht des berühmten und für die Kulturgeschichte so wichtigen Reisenden Ebn Batúta, ed. Defrémery tom. IV, p. 441. Siehe über die historische Entwickelung dieses Namens Reisen, Th. II, S. 304, vgl. mit S. 315.

[3] áfnuó wird von Einigen für „schwarz" erklärt, aber ich bezweifle die Richtigkeit dieser Erklärung sehr, da die Hausaua im Gegentheil eine viel hellere Hautfarbe haben, als die Kanúri.

[4] folāta. Das aus u umgewandelte o haben die Kanúri von den Hausaua aufgenommen. — Koelle schreibt Fulāta und macht den Schluss-a in Zusammensetzungen lang, wie Fulātāwa.

[5] kéla. Koelle kalā. Merkwürdig ist es, zu diesem Namen für „Kopf" im Lógoné, Hausa und Kanúri die völlig analogen und sachlich entsprechenden Formen in den beiden Dialekten des ferner [illegible] anzuführen, im Dāza S. kala, im Kéda S. kae.

[6] tédā. Über diese einzig echte einheimische Namensform vgl. Einleitung S. LXVI, 1. — Um die Gesammtheit ihres ausgebreiteten und in viele kleine Abtheilungen zerrissenen Volksstammes zu bezeichnen, bedienen sich die Tédā des Ausdruckes kuhri oder kohrí, wie tarde kuhri tédā, „das gesammte Gebiet der Tédā", und so kommt es, dass dieses blosse Adjektiv von einigen älteren Reisenden irrthümlich als Eigenname der Nation aufgefasst worden ist.

[7] anna Bórno. Vielleicht ging der Name Bórnu oder Bórno eben von den Tédā aus, die es eben mit den Bulāla hielten; s. N. 2. In ähnlicher Weise nennen sie die Leute von Wadāi anna Murba oder Kóga. — Zu der Form Túgubā vgl. Reisen, Th. III, S. 445, Einleitung S. LXVI, 1.

[8] dāho. Hodgson giebt dafür d'aoa, das vielleicht nur dialektisch verschieden ist.

[9] ba-bérbertšē, offenbar „ein Mann aus dem Berberstamme" (vgl. Reisen, Th. II, S. 294), obgleich es auffallend bleibt, dass der Name „Berber" zu den Hausaua gekommen und dann von ihnen auf diesen dem [illegible] doch ganz fernstehenden Stamm der Kanúri bezogen worden ist. Der Name bera-barata erscheint schon in den Völkerlisten von Kazwini.

[10] ba-féllantšē. Ganz ebenso werden andere Singularformen von Völkernamen gebildet; so „ein Toro" F. toró-d'do, Plur. torá-de (s. Reisen, Th. IV, S. 146), H. ba-téro-nkē, Plur. tóro-nkaua; „Einer aus dem Stamme der Zoromaua" F. džaua-nde, Plur. džauamba (s. Reisen, Th. IV, S. 147), H. ba-zóromé, Plur. zóromaua; „Einer der Sulláhma" F. siselli-bo, Plur. sisallibe (s. Reisen, Th. IV, S. 178), H. ba-sulliabē, Plur. sullabaua. — Anführen will ich hier noch, dass die Hausaua den Songai den Namen Yammataua, „Westleute" geben, wenigstens an der Grenze.

[11] pūlo, Plur. fúlbē, ist regelmässig gebildet: pul-o, „er Rother" (pul-gō, „ein Rother") (s. Einleitung S. CXI), in der Mehrheit, da das folgende b das vorhergehende p erweicht, fúl-bē, eigentlich pūl-bē; bē, „sie" 3te Pers. Plur. Pron. pers.

[12] hōre erinnert an das Altegyptische ra, Koptisch or, das ebenfalls „Kopf" und „Fürst" heisst. — Anstatt tindo hat Koelle Polyglotta tiblade.

[13] báli(e) A'ngára, „Mann von A'ngára" oder Ngíre = Garamanta (s. weiter unten) in Zusammenhang mit Ngarú, dem Sitze des früher so mächtigen Ghaladi-ma von Bórnu (s. Reisen, Th. II, S. 304, N. *). Die Leute von Lógoné haben auch sonst noch eigenthümliche Bezeichnungen für ihre Nachbarn; so nennen sie die Bewohner von Bagirmi: Méhodé, die Leute von Gulfé: Ngólahé, und die von Mákari: Méhbatē, welche letztere Form wol der einheimische Name ist.

[14] méttahē bezeichnet wahrscheinlich eine eigenthümliche Individualität der Kanúri, indem es entschieden mit me (Einleitung S. CCXII, f, β) componirt ist. Anführen will ich hier noch, dass die Wándalá die Ghamergú mit Muko' Awélgua bezeichnen.

[15] yíre schliesst sich eng an das gleichbedeutende yira in der Sprache von Kanem.

[16] bío ist in der Sprache und dem Ideenkreise von Bagirmi das Gegentheil von bóla, welcher Name die Leute von Mákari und Kótokó bezeichnet, und die bío begreifen auch die Dynastie von Fittri in sich, als bio bulāla, da diese als ein Zweig der Bórnu-Dynastie von Kánem ausging (s. Reisen, Th. III, S. 381 f.). — Dass die Bagirmaner die Musgu Máua Móochō nennen, hat seinen ethnographischen Grund; s. Reisen, Th. III, S. 361.

[17] guránoh. Das Land der Tédā führt in der Mába-Sprache den besonderen Namen bar-anu, dessen Ableitung oder ethnologischer Zusammenhang mir noch unbekannt ist.

Sonγai.	Lógoné.	Wándalá.	Bagrimma.	Mába.
. . . . . .	tibbo Plur. tibboyê	tibbo . . .	tibbo . . .	guránek [17] Pl. gu-ráni
. . . .	bill(e) A'ngāre [13]	mó'eakē [14] . .	bîo [16] . . .	. . . . . .
?	. . . .	. . . . . .	. . . . .	. . . . . .
?	. . . .	fellâta . . .	fellâta . . .	
boúgo	kā-a	yîre [15] . . .	{dūdžo . . . / {dála . . . }	kēdži
tendžo	kulúm	wofke . . .	netna . . .	dîdi

[1] têbū: this form of that name of the great tribe of the Eastern half of the Desert, the origin and national connection of which was so entirely unknown before the time of my researches, evidently proceeded from the Kanúri-language, and as the form in bu seems to argue, originally was only used for the plural-number. The oldest Arabic form, thence derived, seems to be tubu, with a short vowel.

[2] Kanúri: I here give once more utterance to my most positive conviction, that the name Kanúri has nothing whatever to do with the name of the town or province of Kanó. For the name Kanúri was long employed, before the Bórnu-people had any relation whatever to that country. — Bórnu (with Koelle Bórnu, but in composite words, such as Bórnûma, with a long u) properly is not a national, but a political or dynastical term, used in opposition to the Bulála since the middle of the XIVth century, when Ebn Batútah performed his remarkable journey (ed. Defrémery vol. IV, p. 441). Compare with regard to its historical development Travels, vol. II, p. 253, 266.

[3] áfunō by some authorities is explained as meaning originally „black", but the correctness of that opinion I doubt very much on account of the Hausa-people, in general, having a much lighter colour, than the Kanúri.

[4] feláta: the Kanúri have adopted from the Hausawa the change of the u in the first syllable into an e. Koelle writes Puláta, and, as usual with him, makes the final a long in compositions, such as Fulátōva.

[5] kéla: Koelle kélà. It is rather remarkable to find, that the very same variation of form with regard to this very identical term, which we find in Kanúri compared with Hausa and Lógoné, we find also in the two dialects of the Sonγay-idiom, in Dîara Sonγay bala, in Koda Sonγay kal.

[6] tédà: see Introductory Remarks p. LXXVII, f. as to this being the only true national form of that name. In order to designate the totality of the numerous sections and subdivisions of their nation, the Tédà employ the additional adjective kubri or tubri, as in the phrase torde kubri tédà, „the whole territory of the Tédà", and that is the reason, why this simple adjective has been misunderstood by certain travellers as being by itself a national term.

[7] anna Bórnu: I here remark, that it is not improbable, that the name Bórnu or Bórnu proceeded from the Tédà, who sided with the Bulála (see note 2); as for the form Tūguhū, see Travels and Disc., vol. III, p. 494, Introductory Remarks p. LXVII, f. As for the people of Wádái the Tédà call them anna Marka or Kôga.

[8] dûbe: Hodgson duna, which may be a mere dialectical variation.

[9] ba-bérbertšē appears to mean „an individual of the Berber-tribe", although it is difficult to explain, how the name „Berber" became so generally employed by the Hausa-tribe, as it is not used by the tribes of the Desert themselves, but only by the Moγrebine-Arabs, and was transferred by them to the Kanúri-tribe. Compare Travels, vol. II, p. 269.

[10] ba-félloatšē: just in the same manner the singular modes of other national names are formed, as that of „a Toro" F. torō-dho, plur. torō-de (see Travels, vol. IV, p. 145), H. ba-tóro-ūkē, plur. tóro-ābawa; „one of the tribe of the Zoromawa" F. dīanámde, plur. dīanámbe (see Travels, vol. IV, p. 146), H. ba-zóromē, plur. zóromawa; „one of the Sγillebawa" F. ciseilbe, plur. cisellibe (see Travels, vol. IV, p. 170), H. ba-sγillebē, plur. sγillebawa.

[11] pûlo, plur. fûlbē, is quite regularly formed: pûl-o, „he (one) red man" (see Introductory Remarks p. CXI), in the plural-form, the following b softening the preceding sound of p, fûl-bē or properly pûl-bē, „they red men".

[12] bōre reminds of the ancient Egyptian ro, in Coptic or, meaning likewise both „head" and „prince". — Instead of tinde Koelle in his Polyglotta has tiblada.

[13] bill(e) A'ngāre, „a man from (or of the tribe of) A'ngāre"; with regard to the origin of the latter name I am not certain, although, I think, it may be identical with Ngaru, the former residence of the Ghaladi-ma of Bórnu (see Travels, vol. II, p. 192 but see also vol. III, p. 484, note †). — The Lógoné-people, besides this one, have other very remarkable names for their neighbours, as they call the inhabitants of Bagirmi: Mákodē, the people of Gulfē: Ŋgótakē, and those of Mafalē: Mábbotē.

[14] mó'eakē probably characterises some individual trait of the Kanúri, the way of composition of that term by means of me (see Introductory Remarks p. CCXIII, f. β) being placed beyond a doubt. — I have still also mention, that the Wándalá call the Gámergū by the name of Muha' Amálgua.

[15] yîre closely approaches the identical yîru in the language of Kanem.

[16] bîo in the political terminology of the Bagrimma-language is strictly opposed to the term bála, the latter name comprising the people of Mafalē and Kótokō, and originally in all probability also the whole tribe of the Mása, which at present has been shattered into so many fragments; just as the Musgu are designated by them as Mása Módoko, while the bîo comprise even the dominating tribe of Fitri, the Bulála, which, as has been exposed in my Travels, vol. III, p. 280, proceeded from Kánem as a revolutionary branch of the Bórnu-dynasty.

[17] guránek: the country of the Tédà in the Mába-language is called by the peculiar name har-ūna.

Deutsch und Englisch.	Kanúri.	Tédā.	Hausa.	Fulfúlde.
Hinterkopf — *occiput* . .	būdi [1] . . .	girti	. . . . . .	. . . . . .
Gehirn — *brains* . . .	kirgin kéla-bē [2]	áli	[11]	. . . . . .
Schläfe — *temple* . . .	. . . . . .	. . . . . .	koñs	hódyodu . .
Auge — *eye*	sim, šim . .	{ san S. . . . / sámo N. . . }	idu Pl. idanū .	{ hite-re Pl. gite / yltere . . . }
Pupille — *pupil*	šilògo sim-bū [3]	čžikenāde [8] . .	matsókatšī n idu [12]	darōde gite .
Augenbraue — *eye-brow*	ugamāšu [4] . .	kábsa . . .	{ gerō n bisa.	waiwāko . .
Augenwimper — *eye-lash*			gérarē (Pl.) . }	{ timēlo . . . / waiwāko gite }
Ohr — *ear*	{ símo . . . / sýmo . . . / súmo [5] . . . }	{ ši [9] S. . . . / súmo N. . . }	kunē Pl. kúnne	nófuru Pl. noppi
Ohrlappen — *flaps of the ear*	tentél-lam sýmo-bē [6]		banta n kúnne [13]	nénnebe [15] . .
Ohröffnung — *ear-hole* .	kul sýmo-bē .	. . . . . .	kōfa n kúnne [14]	búde noppi .
Nase — *nose*	ken-tsā [7] . .	{ tšā [10] . . . / kya . . . . }	hantši Pl. hántsoši	hinnere Pl. kinne [16]

[1] būdi. Koelle bódi.

[2] kirgin kéla-bē. Koelle kérgen ohne Zusatz.

[3] šilògo fehlt bei Koelle. Vielleicht ist sillógo richtiger, „das, was (aus dem Auge gleichsam) hervortritt", von lúgtskin, „ich gehe hinaus, trete hervar".

[4] ugamāšu. Koelle schreibt ágamā-šim, aber das ist wol nicht richtig, da ágamā allein kein Wort ist, und wäre es eins und šim stände in Genitivform dann, so müsste es heissen ágamā šim-be.

[5] súmo. Koelle sámō. Für die Ohrrändung haben die Kanúri den besonderen Ausdruck ágona símo-bē, eigentlich „der Schild des Ohres", auf Begriums gáde imbi-sa. — Ich will hier anführen, dass Koelle a. v. árgalam irrthümlich behauptet, dass sámō nur vom Ohr des Pferdes gebraucht werde, sondern dass stets árgalam pérbē (fír-bē) gesagt werde.

[6] tentél-lam sýmo-bē fehlt bei Koelle, es kommt unzweifelhaft von téntel, „Ohrbehang" (bei Koelle téntel, aber nur von den grösseren, den Kameelen angehängten Glocken erklärt), daher jeder „klingende Schmuck", der im Ohrläppchen befestigt wird, das Wort bedeutet also eigentlich nicht das letztere selbst.

[7] ken-tsā. Koelle kéntsā und kántsā.

[8] čžikenāde ist unzweifelhaft ein aus verschiedenen Elementen zusammengesetzter Ausdruck.

[9] ši. Diese kürzeren und älteren Tédā-Formen sind sehr merkwürdig, besonders wenn sich in der Folge herausstellen sollte, wie ich kaum bezweifle, dass sie auch bei den anderen östlichen Stämmen in Gebrauch sind.

[10] tšā, kyā ist interessant, wenn man es mit dem zusammengesetzten Kanúri-Wort ken-tsā zusammenhält, s. Einleitung S. XCII, N. 8.

[11] Während mir im Hausa der entsprechende Ausdruck fehlt, habe ich einen anderen begriffsverwandten Ausdruck, nämlich dákkošī, F. kahánge, dessen genaue Bedeutung mir unbekannt ist.

[12] matsókatšī n idu, wörtlich „der Spiegel des Auges".

[13] banta n kúnne. Der Ausdruck ist hergenommen von dem Leibschurz, bante, weil die Ohrlappen in ähnlicher Weise herabhängen.

[14] kōfa n kúnne, wörtlich „das Thor der Ohren".

[15] nénnebe scheint vulgäre Form, in deren letzterem Theil unzweifelhaft noppi steckt.

[16] hinnere Plur. kinne. Koelle in seiner Polyglotta hat eine andere Form kinol, die mir nicht vorgekommen.

[17] mà-sibu, mà-bē-ri. Raffenel in Arbeo gibt für „paupières", mbo-koara; für „sourcils", mbo-koaahoa.

[18] ki-sāō heisst wol unzweifelhaft „mein Kopf".

[19] wáforol semf. Das soml zeigt wol die Grundform von šémayè an. — Das folgende yaaūl ist vielleicht eigentlich ágaœ ol.

[20] mafulīdīs ist mir undeutlich und ungewiss.

[21] itše steht dem ódoi in Afadu und den entsprechenden Ausdrücken in verwandten Sprachen (bei Koelle Gruppe I.) sehr nahe. — sé itše, eigentlich „die Kugel des Auges". — Auch bel-tši ist ohne Zweifel ähnlich zusammengesetzt.

[22] wá-tlemā. S. Einleitung S. CCXXVIII, wo ich über die Verwechselung des *tl* und *l* gesprochen habe; denn wá-tleme ist entschieden „das Äussere des Ohres", wo ganz wie in wa-harā S. 151, „das Äussere des Feuers, die Flamme", wa-gue, „Rand des Flusses, Ufer", S. 165 und Ähnliches.

[23] ter(i) imbi habe ich mit vollem Vertrauen diese Bedeutung zugewiesen, „Mund des Ohrs", obgleich ich es für „Ohrlappen" niedergeschrieben hatte.

[24] kātih. Burckhardt hat kopak, wenn das nicht Druck- oder Schreibfehler ist. — Statt koyè hat er konah.

Sonyai.	Lógonē.	Wándalā.	Bágrimma.	Mába.
. . . .	úgae kā(-nāū[18] .	godžō . . .	met-gōso . .	kákedē
. . . .	indúnnul káa . .	mafaθēle[20] .	. . . .	. . . .
. . . .	. . . .	. . . . . .	. . . . . .	. . . .
mō Plur. mōēō .	aī	ítše[21] . . .	kamī . . . / kamē . . .	hásik Pl. háse[24]
mō-yé	yomm(a)al aī . .	sō-ítše . . .	ńgán-kamī .	. . . .
mō-sābu . . / mō-bē-ri[17] . .	θalle θē . . .	bél-tši . . .	bī-kamī . .	amnúngo / reārē
haṅga Pl. haṅgalō	šémayē	šemā . . .	imbī	koyē Pl. kondži
haṅga gande . .	wúrorai semī[19] .	wá-θemā[22] .	. . . . . .	. . . .
. . . .	. . . .	. . . . . .	tar(i) imbī[23] .	. . . .
nīne	χae-nī	é-tarē . . .	ēmi	bóū

1 būdi: Koelle bádi.

2 kirgin hola-bē: Koelle kirgen without any addition. It is evidently „seat of the will", from the root rag.

3 Sīlége is wanting in Koelle. It may originally be allēge, „that which starts forth (from lúg-lobin, „I come forth") from the eye".

4 ágamáđu: Koelle writes ágámá-šim, but that can scarcely be right, as there is no such word as ágamá or ágámá, and if there were, it ought to be ágámá šim-be, not ágámā-šim.

5 sémo: Koelle sémé. For the „lobe of the ear", the Kanúri have the particular term ágana sémo-bē, meaning properly „shield of the ear", in Bágrimma gáda imbī-na. — I here will mention, that Koelle erroneously states s. v. árgalam, that sémé is never used of the ear of the horse, but that in this case always argalam (i. e. al bolem, „the pen"[?], one lower down] pérbī (fír-bē) is used.

6 tantál-lam sémo-bē is wanting in Koelle; it, no doubt, is derived from tántal, in Koelle ṭantal, meaning not only, as he says, „the bells tied to the necks of horses or camels", but any thing tinkling, and, therefore, also pieces of brass or coral used as pendants of the ear. Thus, only second-hand it seems to mean the flaps of the ear themselves.

7 kam-teá: Koelle kéntaš and kéntel.

8 álibenáde, no doubt, does consist of different elements of speech, as yet to be analyzed.

9 bī: these short monosyllabic forms in the Tédā-language are very remarkable, and will be more so, if it be proved in course of time, that they are also employed by the Eastern subdivisions of this tribe, which have not been influenced by the intercourse with the Kanúri.

10 tšā, hyā is remarkable, if compared with the Kanúri-term ben-tšā; see Introductory Remarks p. XCIII, note 3.

11 In Hausa I have written down another term dákkoki, corresponding to the Fulfúlde-term kobángo, the exact meaning of which I do not now recollect.

12 matsóhatši n idu means verbally „mirror of the eye".

13 banta n kúnne: it is not impossible, that this term derives its origin from a comparison of the pendants of the ear with the banta or small apron hanging down in similar manner, to cover the shame.

14 kófa n kúnne means verbally „the gate of the ears".

15 námnebe may be a corrupted or vulgar form, the latter part of which, no doubt, contains nopp[?], „ear".

16 hinnere plur. hinne: Koelle in his Polyglotta, as in most similar cases, has a different form in i, via hinei.

17 mō-sébu, mō-bē-ri: Rafenel in Aruma gives a different term for „pupil", via mōe-honra (i. e. mō-húra); for „eyebrow", mōe-hombon (mō-kombu).

18 kā-nāū means „my hand", áyae, „extremity".

19 wúrorai semī: semī, as a sort of genitive, if compared with the fuller nominative form šémayē, which exhibits the same yē, which we find in Kanúri (Koelle K. gr. § 190), is of great linguistic interest. As for the following χae-nī, it is an abbreviation of áyae-nī.

20 mafaθēle is a composite term, yet to be analyzed.

21 ítše resembles very much the ídaṭ in Afadé, and the corresponding terms in other related languages (Koelle's first group). — sō-ítše, properly, means „ball of the eye", and bél-tši seems to be composed in a similar manner.

22 wá-θemā: see Introductory Remarks p. CCXXIX, where I have treated of the change of θ and š; for wá-θemā is certainly „extremity of the ear": wá, just so in wá-kará p. 151, „extremity of the fire, the flame", wá-gaá, „edge of the river, shore", p. 165.

23 tar(i) imbī I have adopted with full conviction, as meaning originally „mouth of the ear" = „ear-hole", although I had written it down with the meaning of „flap of the ear".

24 kásik: Burckhardt has kopak, and instead of my koyē he has konah.

Deutsch und Englisch.	Kanúri.	Tédā.	Hausa.	Fulfúlde.
Nasenlöcher — *nostrils* .	tsorō kin-tsá-bē [1]	. . . . . .	kófofi n hantši [6]	būde hinnere .
Nasenbein — *bridge of the nose*	mañge [2] . . .	. . . . . .	kára n hantši	ðirgel . . .
Mund — *mouth*	tšī	tšī . . . . / kai	bākí Pl. bákona [7]	hónduko . .
Oberlippe — *upper-lip* .	ká-tšī-bē fūri-bē [3]	katrēbu [5] . .	lēbo [8] . . .	tondu Pl. tondi
Unterlippe — *under-lip*	ká-tšī-bē tsidi-ga-bē		dābre . . .	tondu les . .
Schnurrbart — *whiskers* .	kúnduri tšī-bē [4]	burrn S. . . / kása N. . . .	gāši n bākí .	gāsa hónduko [9] / sunsúñko . .

[1] tsorō kin-tsā-bē fehlt bei Koelle, der doch unter tsorō (tsorē) mehrere Zusammensetzungen mit diesem Worte giebt; er hat dafür tsāguli kēntsābē; es ist eigentlich „die Leibhöhle der Nase".

[2] mañge fehlt bei Koelle, wenigstens in dieser Form.

[3] ká-tšī-bē (Koelle kā tšībē). kā ist die ursprünglich kurze Form von kēla, „der Kopf", und hat nichts mit kā, „Spazierstock" [illegible] T. aká, „Holz", zu thun, mit dem Koelle es zusammenordnet, sondern ist ein grundverschiedenes Wort. — fūri-bē ist substantivisch gedacht, obgleich fūri allein, so viel ich weiss, nicht substantivisch gebraucht wird; doch führt Koelle fúri, púri mit der Bedeutung „Höhe", „Gipfel" als ein besonderes Substantiv an. Ebenso wenig ist taldúga oder taldíga eine Substantivform, s. S. 28, N. 1. Ähnlich werden andere Adverbialformen oft gebraucht.

[4] kúnduri tšī-bē, bei Koelle kúnduli kā tšībē. Dem ersten Augenblicke nach ist es sehr bezeichnend für das Haar dieser Völker, dass kúnduri zugleich „Haar" und „Wolle" bedeutet, aber das ist mehr scheinbar, als wirklich, da die Grundbedeutung von dūr-gskin, „ich falle", sehr allgemein ist, „das was fällt, abfällt", also kein dauernder Bestandtheil des Körpers ist; zu derselben Wurzel gehört Koelle's kúndulō, „Karrenmatte"; s. weiter unten.

[5] katrēbu zeigt wieder ein auffallendes Verhältniss zu ká-tšī-bē, aber um dasselbe richtig zu verstehen, müssten wir erst in diesem, wie in so vielen anderen Fällen, die Form des Wortes in [illegible] ganz reinen und unbeeinflussten Tedā-Dialekten erhalten.

[6] kófofi n hantši, wörtlich „die Thüren der Nase".

[7] bākí. Schön schrieb früher bakhi; allerdings ist das Wort in meiner Schreibweise weniger leicht von bakí, „schwarz", zu unterscheiden. Dass dies aber thatsächlich der Fall ist, zeigt das Beispiel von bakí n rūa (s. S. 164, N. 9). — bākí wird übrigens auch für „Sprache" gebraucht.

[8] lēbo. Schön lebob mit dem allgemeinen Begriff von „Lippe" (den es allerdings im Plural hat), und daher hat er dābre mit dem besonderen Begriff „Unterlippe" nicht.

[9] gāsa hónduko ist kein reiner Fulfúlde-Ausdruck, da gāsa wol sicher der Hausa-Sprache entnommen ist.

[10] ni-mē hamba, „Haare der Lippe". Übrigens steht ni-mē, „Lippe" in wahrscheinlicher äusserer Beziehung der Bildung zu nīne, „Nase".

[11] kalgē. Hier erklären und verbessern wir die S. 73 nicht analysirte Phrase: Gada-ni wa-ef-na lagá kalgē nái, „ich bringe eine Hemd (Gada) an meinen Mund".

[12] Gudge kalgē genim heisst offenbar „die weibliche Lippe", genim, genám, „Frau", „weiblich" S. 214, ganz so Gudge kalgē billam die „männliche Lippe" heisst, wol wegen der grösseren Dicke.

[13] hodóh-tarō ist wol zusammengezogen aus hodē kik-tarē, „Leib des Nasenbeins".

[14] sádawa. Wir sehen, dass bei den meisten dieser Völker die Oberlippe als die eigentliche Lippe angesehen und nicht weiter unterschieden, die Unterlippe aber durch ein Nebenwort bezeichnet wird. Übrigens ist es wahrscheinlich eigentlich sáda-wuē (wuē, „Mund") und dann sáda-wuē-domá; ob aber domā eine Beziehung zu „unter" hat, weiss ich nicht.

[15] ugdla-wūā bedeutet „die Haare des Mundes", wie ugdō-yira weiterhin das „Kopfhaar".

[16] hartūm kōya gomák ist mir im Einzelnen unverständlich, obgleich hartūm entschieden an Burckhardt's jar-i- für „Nase" erinnert.

[17] tal-ná, offenbar aus tāl-hanā durch Synkope entstanden, wie lal-nā aus lāl-hanā.

[18] tefē allein kann nicht richtig sein, da es die allgemeine Bedeutung „Haar" hat, der Begriff der Lippe muss wol hinzukommen.

Sonrhay.	Lógoné.	Wándalā.	Bágrimma.	Mába.
nīne funne . .	bulúk ɣaenī . .	hodók-tarē [13].	fūlo émi . .	. . . . . .
nīne bēri . . .	šīek ɣaenī . .	hík-tarē . .	tšungo émi .	hartūm hōya gemák [16]
mē	kalgé [11]	wuē	tarí	kanā
nī-mē béne . .	Ɵuēge kalgē genim [12]	zádawe [14] . .	dīdžo tarin .	tal-nā [17]
nī-mē gande . .	Ɵuēge kalgē billam	zádav wúdomā	mō tarín . .	lul-nā
nī-mē hambe [10].	imisále ge kalgē	ugdža-wūē [15].	bī-tari . . .	tefē [18]

[1] teorá kin-teš-hé is wanting in Koelle, although under teará (teorá) he mentions several other terms connected with this word, while he has a somewhat different term teágulī kéntedbē; it means properly „the belly of the nose".

[2] muhge is wanting in Koelle.

[3] hé-tši-hē (Koelle hé tšíhē); hé is evidently the short original form of hóin, „head", and has scarcely any thing to do with hé, „walking-stick" (identical with ehí, „wood" in Tédā), to which Koelle subordinates our term. — fárihē is constructed, as if fári were a substantive, although, as far as I am aware, it is never used so, as I never heard the term fári or pári mentioned by Koelle meaning „top", „summit". Neither is teidága or teidiga a substantive (see p. 29, note 1), although we have here the form teidéga-hē; but several other adverbial forms are used in a similar manner.

[4] hánduri tši-hē, with Koelle hándulí hé tšíhē. At first sight it looks rather characteristic of the sort of hair of the negroes, that this word designates „wool" as well, as „the woolly hair" of these people; but, if we take into account the root, and original meaning of the term, we see, that it has been derived from dár-uskin, „I fall", conveying the notion of anything which falls of and does not from an integrant portion of the body, the term hándulé, „excrements" (Koelle), belonging to the very same root.

[5] hatrého again shows some curious relation to the K. hé-tši-he, but in order to understand its import fully, we ought first to be acquainted with the form of the word in those dialects of the Tédā-language, which have been totally removed beyond the range of the influence of the Kanúri-idiom.

[6] hófofi n hontši means verbally „the gates, openings of the nose".

[7] bāki: Schön wrote formerly bakki, but in his more recent translations he does not distinguish this word from bakí, „black", and how easily both are in reality confounded, shows the term baki n rba, which by some is explained as „black water", by others „mouth of the water"; see p. 145, note 8. — bākí, however, is also used for „language, idiom".

[8] lébe: Schön formerly wrote lebeb, attributing to it the general notion of „lip", which in the plural-form it really has; as for dēbre he has it not.

[9] gásu hónduke does not seem to be a pure Fulfulde-term, the term gisa evidently being borrowed from the Hausa-language.

[10] nī-mé hambe, „hair of the lip". As for nī-mē, „lip", however, it seems to bear some relation of organical development to nīne, „nose".

[11] kalgē: I will here correct and explain the phrase adduced p. 73 Ɵudá-ni wa-ni-na lagá kalgé nñū, „I bring his hand (Ɵudá) to my mouth".

[12] Ɵuēge kalgé genim means evidently „the female lip", genim, genim meaning „woman, female" p. 211, just as Ɵuēge kalgé billam means „the manly lip", probably on account of its great size and prominent feature.

[13] hodók-tarē appears to be a contracted form of hodé hík-tarē, „belly of the bridge of the nose".

[14] zádawe probably zádo-wūē, so we may have to write the following term more correctly zádo-wūē-domā, although I am not aware of the proper meaning of domā. We see, however, that almost all these peoples regard the upper-lip as the lip in a proper sense, while they distinguish the under-lip either by adding an adjective or by giving to it a term of its own.

[15] ugdža-wūē evidently means „the hair of the mouth", just as ugdā-yire, further on, means „the hair of the head".

[16] hartūm hōya gemák is not quite intelligible to me, although hartūm reminds strongly of Burckhardt's yaraūma, „nose".

[17] tal-nā has evidently been formed from tál-kanā by syncope, just as lul-nā from lúl-kanā.

[18] tefē, without any other term in reference to the lip being added, can scarcely be right, as it means „hair" in general.

Deutsch und Englisch.	Kanúri.	Tēda.	Hausa.	Fulfúlde.
Zahn — *tooth*	tími [1]	{ tōa [9] S. . . / tomaī N. . . }	hákkori Pl. hákkora [11]	ńīre Plur. ńīdže
Zahnfleisch — *gum* . .	kelín [2] . . .	tínteni . . .	angógi [12] . .	gagítte . . .
Zunge — *tongue* . . .	télam [3] . . .	{ tir-bē [10] . . / tir-mēen . . }	halšï [13] . . .	demgal Pl. demde [16]
Gaumen — *palate* . . .	kangáni [4] . .	. . . . . .	dáhori . . .	dasasēhi . .
Schlund — *throat* . . .	kerī-kerī [5] .	kórekū . . .	makógorō [14] .	kónnodol [17] .
Wange, Backe — *cheek*	pǟli [6] . . .	inkéka . . .	sādde [15] . . .	{ gegeauel . . / sādžeol (H.) . }
Backenknochen — *jawbone*	búggo kim-bē [7]	. . . . . .	kúmmatu . .	{ golle . . . / galánge Fmb. }
Wangengrübchen — *dimple*	segári [8] . . .	. . . . . .		. . . . . .

[1] tími. Koelle tími, dem er aber nur die Bedeutung „Vorderzahn“ giebt, während er für „Backenzahn“ den besonderen, von mir nicht gehörten und von ihm vielleicht missverstandenen (vgl. T. kórekū, „Schlund“), Ausdruck kárgā, kárngā, kárgū hat.

[2] kelín scheint bei Koelle zu fehlen.

[3] télam. Koelle télam; im Fūr dáli, wenn ich als blosse äussere Ähnlichkeit dila im Sŏnyo auf Bornu anführe.

[4] kangáni fehlt bei Koelle.

[5] kerī-kerī desgleichen. Er hat dafür ágárguia, das sich entschieden an das entsprechende T. kórekū anlehnt. Vgl. „Kehle“ auf S. 1..

[6] pǟli. Koelle pǟli.

[7] búggo kim-bē heisst wol wörtlich „die Kraft, der Schutz des Auges“; es fehlt bei Koelle, obgleich er das Adverb bug, buggó hat, mit der Bedeutung „heftig, gewaltig“, mit dem es in Verbindung zu stehen scheint. Die Bedeutung von „Backenknochen“ giebt er auch dem vorhergehenden Worte pǟli, hat ausserdem aber noch die beiden Wörter párma und ágeldō mit diesen verschiedenen Bedeutungen.

[8] segári, Koelle tsegári. Die eigentliche Bedeutung, so wie Ableitung unsicher. Koelle erklärt es übrigens minder richtig als den Theil des Mundes zwischen den Zähnen und den Backen, denn für die Backe selbst.

[9] tōa. In diesem Worte haben wir allem Anscheine nach wieder eine leichte Abwandlung der ursprünglicheren Form ti des Kanúri-Ausdruckes: auch im folgenden tinteni für „Zahnfleisch“ möchte die ursprüngliche, einfache Form ti für „Zahn“ liegen.

[10] tir-bē, tir-mēen. Das tir in diesen beiden Wörtern ist allem Anscheine nach mit der einsilbigen Wurzel von télam, nämlich tel, identisch. S. Einleitung S. XC, N. 6.

[11] hákkori. Schön hat hakkore oder hakore im Singular und hauri im Plural; das ist aber entschieden falsch und es wird die zusammengezogene Form hauri, so viel ich weiss, nur vom Elephantenzahn oder Elfenbein gebraucht.

[12] angógi fehlt bei Schön. Ich habe auch noch den begriffsverwandten Ausdruck dásaši (vielleicht verwandt mit dasasēhi im Fulfúlde), S. mohám, dessen genaue Bedeutung ich jedoch augenblicklich vergessen.

[13] halšï, bei Schön halšï, Plur. harusé. Den Plural habe ich nie gehört, wie er natürlicher Weise selten oder nie gebraucht wird.

[14] makógorō. Schön hat neben makogoru noch den mir unbekannten Ausdruck maködi.

[15] sādde bei Schön nicht. — kúmmatu fehlt bei Schön.

[16] demgal. Reichardt dengel, welche Form auch bei Koelle im Timbo erscheint. — Anstatt Pl. dĕdde hat Koelle dēyo.

[17] kónnodel. Koelle hat im Dialekt von Salum die ganz ähnliche Form kónondel, in Kano aber hódánde. — Das folgende gegeauel, fürchte ich, ist wieder nicht reines F., ebenso wenig wie sādžeol, sondern möchte, wie jenes mit H., so seinerseits mit K. gégi, gigi S. 260 zusammenhängen.

[18] koiméle erscheint in Raffenel's Arama in der Form kolo-málel.

[19] Orn nähert sich dem Arabischen [illegible], aber ein solches Zusammentreffen ist zu vereinzelt, um in Rechnung gebracht zu werden als Beweis ursächlicher Verwandtschaft.

[20] wāyăĕ ist in dieser Form sehr zweifelhaft, da yĕĕ der Plur. pron. pers. 3te Person ist, Einleitung S. CC; vgl. übrigens nyee) kōyaé S. 163. — Auch das folgende nyee-sata ist mir nicht deutlich, obgleich nyee, „Ende, Äusseres“ ein so gewöhnliches Element in dieser Zusammensetzung ist. S. 161 hatten wir nyee-el, „Ende des Auges“ für „Schatten“.

[21] hūrati-hūrati habe ich so niedergeschrieben, ist aber unsicher, vgl. iddho kōra für „Kehldeckel“.

[22] sīta. Burckhardt hat santeni und ausserdem noch margāh für „Backenzahn“. — Für „Zahnfleisch“ hat er (anstatt sindi) ombuing.

[23] delmih oder délemih zeigt Verwandtschaft mit dem entsprechenden Kanúri-Ausdruck télam. Burckhardt delmek.

[24] hangar-ili, „Ort des Backenzahnes“. Anstatt dessen hat aber Burckhardt und Seetzen Jeder ein verschiedenes Wort, Ersterer ghombilinsek, Letzterer jiineh.

Sonγai.	Logoné.	Wándalá.	Bágrimma.	Mába.
híñe Plur. híñeö	θan[19]	sarĕ	gangi	sâte[22]
gō Plur. göëö .	dágadĕ	birge	dál n guaé . .	sindir
dēne	nθī	ăra	ĭnyolo	delmik[23]
danka	hirnă	hóda-wuĕ . .	kerre	šokál kană-nak
kolmélo[18] . . .	wáyäu[20]	kúraθ-kúreθĕ[21]	korbo	sángalák
. . . .	uγae-san	urko	gál-kamĕ . .	kungur-íñi[24]
	radágarĕ . . .	ingaida . . .	tšungo gál-kamĕ	
	bágamĕ	gĕla	ñárima	

¹ timi: Koelle timi, to which term, however, he attributes only the meaning of „fronttooth", while he expresses the term „grinder" by the word kergú, kérngă or kérgă.

² kalla seems to be wanting in Koelle.

³ télam: Koelle télam, besides the affinity with the corresponding Tédă-term (see note 10), bears also much resemblance to Fŭr dáli; dila in Sabaye (Bornu) I mention merely as a curiosity.

⁴ kedgàsi is wanting in Koelle.

⁵ koril-koril likewise wanting, while he has, instead, the term ŋgárgale; compare „throat" p. 262.

⁶ pöli: Koelle pöli.

⁷ bággo šim-bö seems to mean originally „the protection of the eye"; it is wanting in Koelle, although he has an adverbe bag, baggĕ with the meaning „violently, vehemently, with force", with which, I have no doubt, our term is intimately connected. Koelle attributes also the meaning of „jawbone" to the term pöli, although he gives, besides, two other terms pármú and ŋgeidĕ with both these meanings.

⁸ segàri, Koelle teggĕli. The original meaning of this term, as well as its mode of derivation, is unknown to me. Koelle explains it as „the part of the mouth between the teeth and the cheeks", and further attributes to it the general meaning of „cheek".

⁹ tös: in this word again, according to all appearance, we have a slight variation of the original form ti of the Kanúri-term timi, „tooth", and in like manner the following tíntemi seems to contain the same.

¹⁰ tir-bö, tir-mósu: I have no doubt, that here again the form tir, being the original part of the Tédă-word, is identical with the original form of K. télam, via tel; see Introductory Remarks p. XCI, note 8.

¹¹ bákkori: Schön has hakkora and hakora as the forms of the singular, and haœri as that of the plural; but that is no doubt wrong, the popular and contracted form haœri being used in the singular as well, but, as far as I know, only with regard to the elephant-tooth or ivory.

¹² sagôgi is wanting in Schön's vocabulary. Besides this term I have another one of related import, viz dásaši, which may be related to dasanëbi in Fulfúlde, but the exact meaning of which I do not now remember, S. mehám.

¹³ baiši, Schön baiŝi, plur. barasa. The plural-form I have never heard, as it is very natural, that it is rarely or never used.

¹⁴ mohógeré: Schön, besides makogara, as he writes this word, has another term unknown to me, viz makoši.

¹⁵ sâdle is wanting in Schön, as well as hóweein.

¹⁶ dengal: Reichardt, as well as Koelle in Timbo, write deŋgal. Instead of sîdle plur. of sîre Koelle writes sîye.

¹⁷ kónnodol: Koelle in the dialect of Salum has the almost identical form kónondol, while in that of Kanó he has kóddóndo. — As for the following term gegesuel, I apprehend, it is not pure F., but derived from K. gógi, gigi p. 260, just as sédšeol is evidently derived from H. sâdle.

¹⁸ kolmélo in Raffenel's Arama appears in the form kolo-mélel.

¹⁹ θan resembles rather closely the Arabic term [illegible], but such a coincidence in original words is very rare, and of no consequence for deciding the question of a Semitic character of these languages.

²⁰ wayău in this form seems doubtful to me, yău being the plural-form of the 1st person poss. pronoun (Introductory Remarks p. CCI); but compare also uγae) kóyaŭ p. 263. The following term uγae-san also is not quite clear to me, although, we may compare I think, uγae-ef, „shadow" i. e. properly „limit, extremity of the eye" p. 151.

²¹ kúraθ-kúreθĕ, as written down, is rather uncertain; compare lŏka kŏra for „epiglottis".

²² sâte: Burckhardt has santeni, and, besides, margah for „grinder, molar teeth". — For „gum", instead of my sindir, he gives ómbaing.

²³ delmik or délemik (Burckhardt dalmek) shows some kind of relation with the corresponding Kanúri-term télam.

²⁴ kungur-íñi, „place of the beard". I have, however, to remark, that Burckhardt as well as Seetzen has a different term, the former ghambiliasch, the latter ĭálnsh.

Deutsch und Englisch.	Kanúri.	Tédā.	Hausa.	Fulfúlde.
Backenbart — *whiskers*	gigi [1] . . .	kĕša . . . gigi . . .	gēme . . .	wâharē . . .
Einschnitte — *incisions, tattooing*	bĕli [2]	tšauna . . .	lašana [9] . .	yarōde [12] . . yāre . . .
Antlitz, Züge, Gesicht — *face, features*	fuska [3] . . .	beri	fuska Pl. fuskoki	yēso Pl. gēne .
Kinn — *chin*	ṅgǵumnu [4] . .	gíidomō (s. N. 4)	hába [10] . . .	kōbel . . . wókude . .
Kinnbart — *beard of the chin*	odžiti [5] . . .	kása	. . . . . .	. . . . . .
Haar — *hair*	kúnduri [6] (kélabē)	tšuso . . . Kuso . . .	gáši Pl. gasúsuka	gāsa Pl. gasādži [13]
Haarbüschel — *tuft of hair*	kógió [7] . . .	kēki	zańko [11] . . .	mordi . . . tóberu . . . sāṅgo . . .
Helmtracht des Frauenhaars — *female mode of wearing the hair in the shape of a helmet*	kótoli [8] . . .	. . . . . .		. . . . . .

[1] gigi. Koelle gégó und gémē, das wol dem Hausa entborgt ist.

[2] bĕli scheint mit dieser Bedeutung bei Koelle ganz zu fehlen; er hat nur bĕli, „Rasirmesser", und unter ógantšī führt er an wu ágantšīni bĕliwa, was er übersetzt „I am tattooed (lit. razored) on my chest". Es fragt sich aber sehr, ob der Name für „Rasirmesser" irgend etwas mit dem für „Hauteinschnitte" zu thun hat, oder ob nicht vielmehr beli identisch ist mit póli S. 258. Das Légané bei ist jedenfalls sehr zu beachten. Übrigens haben die Kanúri 91 Einschnitte im Ganzen, nämlich 20 auf jeder Seite des Gesichts, einen in der Mitte der Stirn, sechs an jedem Arme, sechs an jedem Bein und Schenkel, vier an jeder Brust und neun auf jeder Seite. Ungeachtet der nationalen Bedeutung der Einschnitte übrigens gibt es viele Stämme im Innern, die sich nicht tattowiren, z. B. die Fúlbe.

[3] fiska, Koelle pfoga, ist kein ursprüngliches Kanúri-Wort, sondern dem Hausa entnommen; ursprünglich hatte wol das oben S. 258 aufgeführte póli auch diese Bedeutung.

[4] ṅgómmu, Koelle ṅgámi; offenbar ist es eine Ableitung von ágóm, unzweifelhaft im Grundbegriff verwandt mit ngim, „Hülle", das die obere Ecke des Kopfes, „den Vorderkopf", bedeutet, so hier die untere Ecke, „das Kinn". Auch hörte ich gewöhnlich das Wort wiederholen: ógúmmu-ngúmmu. Zu dem entsprechenden Tédā gódomó vgl. Lyon's euguddi für „Gesicht", vielleicht aus Misverständniss.

[5] oddíti hat Koelle in der sehr verschiedenen Form aiadži.

[6] kúnduri hat Koelle, wie ich schon S. 256, N. 4 bemerkte, in der Form kóndulí.

[7] kógib hat Koelle nicht in dieser Bedeutung, sondern nur in der von Haberstroh[?].

[8] kótoli fehlt bei Koelle; die Kanúri haben dafür eine eigenthümliche ironische Redensart, nämlich ealle dúṅu-num dütši, d. h. „mit deinem Liebste (oder deinem Seelenfrieden) ist es vorbei". dúṅu möchte hier doch wol gewiss eine andere Bedeutung haben als „Leude".

[9] Šakana fehlt bei Schön. Das Wort hängt wol mit dem entsprechenden Tédā tšauna zusammen.

[10] hába, Schön happa, Plur. happuóhi. Das Wort scheint übrigens nicht allein das Kinn zu bedeuten, sondern auch den ganzen unteren Theil des Gesichtes, ja oft auch „Wange".

[11] zańko. Ich will hier einige begriffsverwandte Ausdrücke anführen: eine bei Knaben übliche Haartracht, ganz wie ein Hahnenkamm von dem sonst rasirten Kopf emporstarrend, H. zákara (d. h. eigentlich „Hahn"), F. tumbe und yóbul; eine andere Mode, wo die eine Seite des Kopfes geschoren wird, H. askí ndé déa (wörtlich „das Rasirmesser, die Schur auf einer Seite", deshalb nicht aski n), F. lababāge, loddīs oder lutudógo, S. bongo dāŕe; „Haarflechte", H. dóka, Plur. dókoki, F. tšókol, Plur. tšókoli, das entschieden an Tigre tsequro, Amhara und Harar tsequr, „Haar" erinnert; „Locken", wie sie eigentlich eben nur das mehr seidenartige Haar der reinen Fúlbe gestattet, F. bedžádži oder mordi (ob identisch mit mordi im Text?).

[12] yarode. Daher heisst der „durch Einschnitte gezeichnete" Eingeborene, mai-šašana in Hausa, in Fulfúlde yaróde.

[13] gāsa ist gewiss nicht das ursprüngliche Fulfúlde-Wort, hat aber eine nationale Pluralform erhalten. Reichardt hat sukundu, was mit meinem sonsoṅko, „Schnurrbart" S. 256, verwandt zu sein scheint.

[14] kábe soffe scheint mehr „Kinnbart" als „Backenbart" zu bezeichnen (kábe, „Kinn"). soffe (Arb. súf, vgl. S. 20) scheint hier gleichbedeutend mit bambe gebraucht zu sein, obgleich es mir in keiner anderen Zusammenstellung als dieser vorgekommen ist. Anstatt des folgenden dīanna hat Hafferd im Arama die dialektisch verschiedene Form hienosa

[15] ódlebe. Anstatt dieses Fremdwortes gibt es wol einen eigenthümlichen Songai-Ausdruck und Koelle gibt zwei, nigina und mó, wovon das letztere aber eigentlich „Auge" bedeutet.

[16] bongo mūso bambe, „das Haar des mittleren Kopfes"; übrigens ist bambe entschieden verwandt mit hābe, „Wolle".

[17] imbil demi kann ich nicht im Einzelnen erklären, aber ich vermuthe, dass in diesem Fall der Mágrimma-Ausdruck von den Bewohnern von Logone aufgenommen ist, die jene Nachbar-Sprache überhaupt in so weiter Ausdehnung sprechen, dass hauptsächlich beide Sprachen verwechselte. S. Reisen Th. III, S. 274.

[18] kógló-kokó ist der durch Wiederholung korrumpirte Kanúri-Ausdruck.

[19] mot-ten dáthau-dáthbo ist allem Anschein nach eine gründlich humoristische Umschreibung des Kinns.

[20] kommur, Burckhardt gamur; anstatt tefé, „Haar": senfa. Anstatt biye, „Gesicht" hat Seetzen ajo (adšo).

Sońyai.	Lógoné.	Wándalá.	Bágrimma.	Mába.
kābe soffo[14] . .	imbīl demá[17] .	gegī	bīa gúgurī . .	kuṅgur / kommur[20]
džanaa . . . . . / síri(?)	bel (s. N. 2) . .	. . . . . .	sídžana . . .	. . . . . .
údžebe[15] (Arb.) .	bél-ulái . . .	efke	kát-kamē . .	bīyo
kābe	ugse kumtū . .	kuınma . . .	mol-ten džūhan-džıjbbo[19]	. . . . . .
kābe soffo (s. N. 14)	kúmuté	wūma . . .	imbīa . . .	kuṅgur {affer / áxo
boṅgo hambe .	imtsāle kāa . .	ugdž-yīre . .	bī-džīldāoi .	tefe
boṅgo māso hambe[16] / zúkate zorro (?) .	metaál	kógiō-kokó[18] .	gōlo . . . / dákulók . .	güdže
. . . .	turkú	dagáli . . .	muskun . . .	šūša

[1] gīgī: Koelle gīgē, besides gémē, which seems to have been borrowed from the Hausa.

[2] bēli with this meaning is wanting in Koelle, and he attributes to it only the meaning of „razor", while under the term ágántšī he has the phrase wu ágántšīni bélíwa, explaining it „I am tattooed (lit. razored) on my chest", but as to me it seems very doubtful, whether the meaning of „tattooings" could be attributed to the word, if it meant originally only „razor", and, no doubt, these peoples long practised that custom, before they knew, what a razor was. On the contrary, the identity with the corresponding Lógoné-term bal is of great importance, and Kanúri bēli may be identical with pēli, „face, features", the various modes of tattooing vary the constituting characteristic features of each tribe. For although, there are several tribes in the interior of Africa which use no incisions whatever, the Kanúri have even as many as 91 incisions on the whole of their body, 20 on each side of the face, 1 in the middle of the front, 6 on each arm, 8 more on each leg and thigh, 4 on each part of the chest, and 9 on each side of the body.

[3] fiaka (Koelle pēsgu), probably, is not an original Kanúri-term, but has been borrowed from the Hausa-idiom, the other term pēli originally conveying this notion.

[4] ágúmmu (Koelle ágúmi) evidently has been developed from ágúm, meaning the upper end of the head, „the forehead", while here the lower end, „the chin", is meant. I also heard the term sometimes used by repetition in the form agúmmu-ágúmmu.

[5] ndšīti appears in Koelle in the very different form of nindīl.

[6] kánduri, as observed p. 256, note 4, appears in Koelle in the form kándulí.

[7] kógiō by Koelle is explained as meaning only „the bunch or tuft of feathers on the head of certain birds".

[8] kōteli also is wanting in Koelle; besides this common term the Kanúri-people possess also a peculiarly ironical term, viz nalla dúnu-nuw dātši, „thy prayer is at an end", although I do not understand the exact meaning of dúnu (Koelle dunō) in this phrase, as it can scarcely mean „lots".

[9] kaīana is wanting in Koelle. It seems to have some affinity with the Tédā-term tšaunsa.

[10] hába: Schön habpa, plur. habpuóhi. However, the term according to all appearance not only means „the chin", but also the whole lower portion of the face, nay even „cheek".

[11] suōke: I shall here adduce a few other terms of a related meaning, such as H. sáhara (that is properly „cock"), F. tumbe and yōbal, a custom of wearing the hair in the shape of a cock's comb, usual with boys; another fashion, when the hair is shaved on one side of the head only, being left on the other, H. áski sāē dōa (verbally „the razor", „the shaving on one side", therefore not sabi n), F. labsháuge, leddūe or lataděge, S. boṅgo dīrea; „braid of hair", H. dóka, plur. dúkoki, F. tšókal, plur. tšókeli, a term resembling very closely laéqura in Tigre, taquar in Amhara and Ilorur, meaning „hair"; „curls" such as among the tribes of Central Africa they are only possible for the rather silken hair of the Fúlbe, F. hedāddāl or mardi.

[12] yaráde: thence is formed the adjective paráde, which designates the „tattooed" native, H. mal-Kašuna.

[13] gōan is not an original Fulfúlde word. Reichardt has sáheudu, which seems to have some connection with my suusáhho, „whiskers" p. 256.

[14] kábe soffo: soffo in this instance seems identical with the term hambe, although I have not heard it used in any other case, but this one; but hába meaning „chin", it seems rather to mean „the beard on the chin", than „the whiskers".

[15] údžeba: instead of this foreign term Koelle (Polyglotta) has two original ones nigine and mō, of which the latter, however, means rather „eye", than „face".

[16] boṅgo máso hambe, „the hair on the middle of the head". However, as for hambe, it, no doubt, is intimately connected with hába meaning „wool".

[17] imbil demá I am not able to analyse, but I suspect the Bágrimma-term imbía, imbi having been adopted in this case by the neighbouring people of Lógoné, who use the Bágrimma-idiom to such an extent, that Capt. Denham mistook the latter for their own idiom; see Travels and Disc., vol. III, p. 309.

[18] kógiō-kokō is the Kanúri-term in a corrupted form.

[19] mol-ten dūhan-dūgbbo according to all appearance is a jolly mode of description of the chin.

[20] kommur, Burckhardt gamur, while instead of tefō he has aoufa (aūfa). Instead of hīyo Seetzen has ajo (addo).

Deutsch und Englisch.	Kanuri.	Tédā.	Hausa.	Fulfulde.
Nacken, Hals — *neck*	dábu, débu[1]	tai	wuya	dāode
Kehle — *throat*	gogâlin[2]		makógorō (?)	
Luftröhre — *trachea, wind-pipe*	lulódirám			
Lunge — *lung*	fúfu[3]	errō[9]	fofō	pöfde[12], fóftoki
Athem — *breath*	yinte[4]	. . . . .	. . . . .	. . . . .
Herz — *heart*	kárge[5]	suar	mitšia[11]	bérendē
Galle — *gall*	komâten[6]	máhenu	séfa	dāmul
Leber — *liver*	sonimâten	kómelo[10]	ants, komillo	bēre
Milz — *milt*	tšim-rám	erū	zarma	katkángel Plur. hathánde
Brust — *breast*	ŋgándžī[7]	kuntšu	kirdži	gūru, bibul, wībere, yēso
weibliche Brust — *female breast*	tégam[8], tiggam	tongwa	nóno	yendu Pl. yendi, endi-bálidī[13]

[1] débu, bei Koelle dibū und döbū, der in dieser Bedeutung auch noch, aber mehr für den „Nacken", bádī hat.
[2] gogâlin und lulódirám fehlen bei Koelle, er hat aber, wie S. 255, N. 5 angeführt, ŋgárgalâ, „the head of the wind-pipe".
[3] fúfu fehlt bei Koelle wol nur zufällig, da es im Zusammenhang mit dem entsprechenden Worte der anderen Sprachen eines der charakteristischsten Worte ist, Altegyptisch nöf, Barabra äffefi, auch im Ibo fu, „blasen", wozu vgl. die schönen Bemerkungen von Colenso, Hausa p. 68 und p. 317 über die entsprechenden Kafer-Bezeichnungen.
[4] yinte heisst ursprünglich mehr das Athemholen, als der Athem, von yi-nichin, yi-ŋgin.
[5] kárge, Koelle kárge. Der Ausdruck, ursprünglich unzweifelhaft identisch mit kirgie oder kergen, „Gehirn", der Sitz des Gedankens, wird in vielen Beziehungen gebraucht und bekommt oft die Bedeutung von „Muth, Sinn, Stimmung". Vgl. S. 40 kárge-ni kelši, kárge-ni kulta.
[6] komâten fehlt bei Koelle, gleichwie auch sonimâten. Mit der ersten Bedeutung gibt er tšim-rám, wofür er auch die Form tšimtšimgáram hat.
[7] ŋgándžī. Koelle schreibt ŋgántšī, und allerdings ist das wol Dialektverschiedenheit, da auch das ursprünglichere Tédā-Wort das tš hat. Koelle giebt dem Worte verschiedene Bedeutungen, die mir nicht vorgekommen sind; so habe ich es als von der weiblichen Brust gebraucht gefunden, auch weniger vom Euter der Thiere; dass es dagegen in gewissen Beziehungen die Bedeutung „vor, gegenüber" bekommt, ist ganz natürlich. Das Wort „Klafter" scheint allerdings auf den ersten Blick nichts mit Brust zu thun zu haben, aber der mit den beiden ausgestreckten Armen gemessene Gegenstand, besonders ein Strick oder dergleichen, berührt doch eben die Brust. So erkläre ich es mir auch, dass es zuweilen von der Spur der Schlangen gebraucht wird, ŋgándžī hádi-bē, da dieses Thier eben sein Vordertheil, gleichsam die Brust, über den Erdboden hinzieht und dessen Eindruck hinterlässt.
[8] tégam (Koelle tégam; tšī tégam-bē fehlt bei ihm) steht in ganz enger Bildungsverwandtschaft mit télam, und wir haben hier wieder von derselben Wurzel teg oder tog eine ganz verschiedene Formbildung im Tédā, nämlich tongwa. — Zu der Bedeutung „Euter" s. oben S. 200.
[9] errō hängt offenbar innig zusammen mit rā, „Seele", „Leben".
[10] kómelo ist, wenn richtig, in seiner nahen Berührung mit Hausa auffallend.
[11] nátšia. Schön schreibt es fälschlich mit e, nétšia. Der Plural nátoší wird kaum je gebraucht, noch weniger aber gebräuchlich ist ein Plural ántoíší von ante (Schön früher anteh). — séfa fehlt bei Schön, gleichwie zarma. — nóno heisst eigentlich „Milch", s. weiter unten.
[12] pöfde (vgl. über diese Form Einleitung S. CXXXIV, d) und fóftoki sehen ungleich origineller aus, als Reichardt's döēpe.
[13] endi-bálidī. bálidī bezieht sich wol auf die volle Brust; auch Reichardt hat die Form ende ohne y im Anfang.
[14] gindi erscheint unten noch einmal als „Arm", aber auch im Kugideni ist das der Fall.
[15] ŋgguiral, vielleicht nágu ai roī (reel), „Leib, Ort des Halses", und ähnlich auch wol das folgende eilroel, „Auge (el) des Halses".
[16] afadšákia. Der erste Theil dieses Wortes hängt wol unterschieden mit yo-fúdg, „ich blase", á-fu-pā, „Wind" zusammen (vgl. oben N. 3), ebenso wie das folgende pöfifā.
[17] erváŋgde, „Herz", steht ganz fest, aber ist wahrscheinlich mit erva, „Hand" etymologisch verbunden.
[18] gau mandu an dieser Stelle ist mehr als unwahrscheinlich, vgl. S. 264 „Titi". Ebenso ist kokómakī unzweifelhaft nicht das eigentliche Wort für „Herz", sondern bedeutet etwas Anderes, vielleicht „Luftröhre".
[19] hólik. Burckhardt bilik, während Seetzen für „Nacken" das ganz verschiedene domát gibt. Ebenso gibt Seetzen für „Herz", wo Burckhardt sein hóli als goly hat, kellikhlinge, wol ein Kompositum; für „Galle", edalégge.

[illegible]	Lógoné	Wándalá	Bágrimma	Mába
gindi, dãimdi .	oχse kóya-ũ . .	yẽ	mindi . . .	bõtik
. . . .	ángulrai . .	bokúlalã(?) .	gán manda(?)	. . . . . .
	ailroaĩ	idka kõra . / ag-idka kõra	. . . . . .	. . . . . .
hunde	nefũ	ufodžókia .	ibte . . . / efte(?) . . .	kókʼa
. . . .	ále-kálgehõ . .	póšifã . . .	misma . . .	. . . . . .
bina	. . . . . .	ervángde .	kokúmaki . .	kõli
. . . .	χuantín	ugfeléldža . .	séiti	muñik
tessa	tsokĩ	berávdže . .	kégangri . .	merãrek (Arb.)
. . . .	dézalán	deguhãre . .	belábori? . .	ávsik
gandé . . . / túguri ñẽ [?] . .	welẽ	áksuõ . . .	kadžĩ	kusso
faffa Plur. ifáffayõ	íwayó	wũbe . . .	mbã	ángoñl

1 dóbe with Koelle dóbã and dóbõ, besides hádi (rather with the notion of „back part of the neck").
2 gogálte, as well as inlódirám, are wanting in Koelle, who, however, as mentioned p. 255, note 5, has another term, viz ágárgalã, „the head of the wind-pipe".
3 fáfu is wanting in Koelle, probably by mere accident, it being one of the most characteristic terms, if compared with the corresponding terms in other African languages, in ancient Egyptian nóf, in Berebra áffeli, in Ibo fu, „to blow" (K. fatẽ, „West"). Compare Colenso, Remarks p. 57 „fu, the breath escapes from the mouth"; and p. 317 „the movements of aerial bodies are represented by f. fofa, „to fly", fuko, „to blow", fefula, „to carry away", in speaking of the wind".
4 yínte, originally, means rather the act of respiring, breathing, from yi-nichin, yi-ágin, than the breath itself.
5 kárge, Koelle kárge, originally, no doubt, is identical with kirgin or kergen, „brain", as the seat of thought and will and is used in various relations, often being employed with the notion of „mind, courage". Compare p. 40 kárge-ni kelli, kárge-ni kattu.
6 hemóteu is wanting in Koelle's vocabulary, as well as senimáteu, while he attributes the notion of „gall" to tšimrám, or a fuller form of the same, tšimtšimgóram.
7 agándši: Koelle writes agantši, and attributes to the term various notions, which have not come under my observation; thus I have never found it used of the female breast, much less of the udder of animals. On the other side it is very natural, that the term in certain connections means „(in) front". As for the meaning „fathom", at first sight it seems to have nothing to do with the notion of „breast, chest", but with people, who have no line or chain, the fathom is in reality measured over the chest, so that we see, how this term may obtain also that notion. In the same manner I explain, how it is sometimes used of the track of snakes, agándši kãdi-bõ, the snake, while dragging itself along the ground, leaving there, indeed, the very impression of its fore part or breast.
8 tégam (Koelle tégam; tši tégam-bõ is wanting with him) is formed in the very same manner as tõlam, and we have here again from the same root tag or tog the Tédã tobgwa. As for the notion „udder", see p. 202.
9 orrõ, so totally different from the corresponding terms in the other languages, is derived from rõ, „soul, life".
10 hómolo, if right, is remarkable on account of its close resemblance to the corresponding Ilaasa-term.
11 sálšia: Sebön writes this word wrongly by an s, sátšia. The plural-form sátošĩ is scarcely ever used, as likewise the plural ántolši from onta (Sebön formerly antab). — séfe is wanting in Sebön, as well as serma. — As for uóno, it properly means „milk", just as W. wũbe is identical or closely allied with ũba, „milk".
12 pãfde (compare Introductory Remarks p. CXXXV, d) as well as fóftoki, no doubt, exhibit a much more original character, than the dšápe of Reichardt.
13 endi-bálidi; bálidi seems to refer to the full breast (sing. bálide, read bal); Reichardt also has endo without y.
14 gindi on p. 261 will appear once more with the notion of „arm", if we have not there to read ginde; but in Kungédari also both parts of the body have one and the same name.
15 ángalrai (unga ai rai, roai), properly „belly (inside) of neck", just as ailroaĩ seems to mean „eye (ai) of neck".
16 ufodžókia, as well as the following póšifã, is certainly connected with yo-fóng, „I blow", é-fu-nã, „wind"; see note 3.
17 ervángde, „heart", is, no doubt, right, although it has evidently some connection with erve, „band".
18 gan manda in this place can scarcely be right, while on p. 264 it seems to be in its right place. Thus also kokómaki, no doubt, is not the proper term for „heart", but may mean „air-pipe", or something like it.
19 bõtik: Burckhardt has bitik, while Seetzen for „neck" gives the totally different term domát. Thus for „heart" also (with B. goly, almost identical with my kõli) Seetzen gives kullikiingo, which probably is nothing, but a composite term, derived from the same word; for „gall" he has ndoldgge.

Deutsch und Englisch.	Kanúri.	Tédā.	Hausa.	Fulfúlde.
Brustwarze — teat . . .	tši tégam-bū .	. . . . . .	. . . . . .	. . . . . .
Nabel — navel	dábu[1] . . . / dábu bödi .	débo	tšíbia . . .	wúdu Pl. gúdi
grosser Nabel — large navel	dábua[2] . . .	. . . . . .	mara ? . . . / tšíbia maigirma	kenno? . . .
Leib — body . . . . . / Magen — stomach . . .	tsorò[3] . . .	kešē[8] . . .	tšeki[9] . . . / tšēkí[10] Pl. tšíkona	bandu . . . / rēdu Pl. dédi .
Eingeweide — bowels . .	kálem . . .	kišegal . . .	handži[11] . .	téteke . . . / titékki . . .
männliches Glied — man's privy member	ngeri[4] . . . / kadúgu . .	wo S. . . . / fudi N. . . .	búra	solde . . . / guráku . . / basu[12] . .
Vorhaut — foreskin, prepuce	katšá[5] (Arb.) / tši kadúgu-bū	. . . . . .	. . . . . .	. . . . . .
Hodensack — scrotum, purse	ngirko[6] . . .	. . . . . .	tsnanu . . .	džōke . . .
Hode — testicle	ngúr[7] . . .	. . . . . .	. . . . . .	. . . . . .

[1] dábu. „Nabel" ist der Grundbegriff dieses Wortes, erst metaphorisch „Mitte". Was bödi bedeutet, weiss ich nicht; es erinnert aber in auffallender Weise an das oben bei „Nacken", dábu (bei Koelle geschrieben dábū, also auf das Leichteste mit unserem Ausdruck zu verwechseln und wol von derselben Wurzel abgeleitet) S. 263, N. 1 angeführte bödi Koelle's.

[2] dábua. Dieser Auswuchs eines unnatürlich grossen, bisweilen die Grösse einer Straussenuss erreichenden, Nabels ist in den Negerländern etwas sehr Gewöhnliches, besonders bei Kindern, und ist deshalb von allen Reisenden vielfach erwähnt worden.

[3] tsorò, Koelle tsurò. Sowohl dies Wort, als auch das entsprechende Hausa-Wort tšeki hat in weiterer Entwickelung die allgemeinere Bedeutung „Inneres" erhalten und ist dann auch adverbial gebraucht worden. Koelle hat auch noch támbi für Magen (stomach), das mir aber eher „Gebärmutter" zu heissen scheint. Dann hat er bombon für „Abdomen".

[4] ngeri (eigentlich „das Leben Gebende", wie von ganz ähnlichem Standpunkt aus im Tédā wo, „Blüthe", Einleitung S. ☉) fehlt bei Koelle, aber das Adjektiv kéngeri oder, wie er schreibt, kéngeli ist eben davon abgeleitet, „mit dem Leben gebenden Gliede", daher „männlich", ganz identisch mit dem Arabischen mesakker, im Gegensatz zu kérgeri, „weiblich". — Anstatt des zweiten, so grundverschiedenen, von einem gewissen Schamhaftigkeitsgefühl eingegebenen Ausdrucks kadúgu, „das Hintere" (vom Schamschurz Verdeckte, vgl. S. 80 „der Hintermann") schreibt er kádugū.

[5] katšá; Koelle kátšā, bedeutet nicht nur „Beschneidung", sondern auch das, was beschnitten wird. Übrigens ist die Beschneidung unter Afrikanischen Stämmen auch ohne Islam verbreitet. Vgl. Burton, Journal Geogr. Soc. XXIV, p. 310.

[6] ngirko erscheint hier offenbar in seiner ursprünglichen Bedeutung als das, was das Lebende Gebende, den Samen enthält, „Hodensack", und in ganz entsprechender Weise hat es mit dem Zusatz kámo-bū, „von der Frau" die Bedeutung von „Mutterleib". Erst übertragen hat es dann die allgemeine Bedeutung „Ledersack" erhalten, mit der Koelle es uns anführt.

[7] ngúr ist wieder ein von derselben Wurzel abgeleiteter Begriff „Lebenskeim", der dann auch die Bedeutung von „Kern", „Stein der Frucht" erhalten hat. Koelle hat es wieder aus Mangel tieferer Einsicht in die Sprache der Naturvölker, nicht in unserem Sinn aufgefasst; und doch welche Fülle von Naturwahrheit schliesst sich in diesen drei Wörtern auf, ngúr, ngeri, ngirko; und so erklärt sich uns in lebensvollster, unzweideutiger Klarheit, wie es kommt, dass „männliches Glied" und „Regenzeit" (ba-ngeri, „Zeitraum der Belebung, der Schöpfung") bei diesem Volke fast denselben Namen haben kann; ist doch der Phallus, wie bei den Völkern des Alterthums überhaupt, so ganz besonders in den Altegyptischen Darstellungen eben das Princip des Lebens. Auch wird es so völlig erklärlich, wie die Gazelle, „das lebendigste, schnellste Geschöpf", fast denselben Namen führen kann. S. 196. — Von unserem ngeri übrigens, in materiellstem Sinne, ist unzweifelhaft abgeleitet ngerifō, „Hurensohn".

[8] kešē. Es ist auffallend, dass, während die vorhergehenden Ausdrücke von Theilen des menschlichen Körpers im Tédā sich an die entsprechenden im Kanúri eng anschliessen, wir hier den Hausa-Ausdruck mit umgestalteten Konsonanten finden. Von kešē ist wahrscheinlich das folgende kišegal abgeleitet.

[9] tšeki, Schön tšiki. Über die eigentliche Bedeutung von tšeki übrigens bin ich nicht ganz sicher; denn dass es, obgleich zuweilen so gebraucht, als wenn es „Haut" bedeutete, diese Bedeutung doch nicht ganz habe, zeigt der Ausdruck tšeki n fata.

[10] tšēki. Daran habe ich den bei Schön fehlenden Ausdruck tšikanna für „Magenhöhle", V. [illegible].

[11] handži hat Schön in seinem Vokabular (1843) in der seltsamen Form haganei oder hanatši.

[12] basu. Diesen Ausdruck gebrauchen die Fúlbe Adamaua's.

[13] bi-me, eigentlich „Mund (me) der Geburt".

[14] kolg(o) lwayé, „der Mund der Brust".

[15] [illegible] ([illegible]), „grosser Nabel, Nabelschnur", ngán, „Leib" und ngunán, „Ei", als Samenkeim der Geburt, hängen in ihrer Bildung doch wol zusammen.

[16] [illegible] hängt wol eng mit rammi, „Hodensack", zusammen; dehi ergibt sich aus genim dehi S. 267.

[17] gan mandaine, so ganz ohne Zusammenhang mit dem vorhergehenden Ausdruck, ist auffallend; mande, „die Jungfer". Vgl. S. 266, N. 16.

[18] [illegible], eigentlich gon mina.

[19] kúlik für „Nabel" ist mir sehr zweifelhaft, besonders wegen der Redensart kúlik [illegible] barma (S. 45) für „ich breche mich", weniger wegen da-ring kulék für „Rückgrat" (S. 267). Auch hat Seetzen das ganz verschiedene dummeh. — Für „Brustwarze" hat Burckhardt angoun (angún). — Für „Bauch" haben Beide, Seetzen und Burckhardt, dasselbe Wort, wie ich (B. tabok); für „Magen" aber gibt S. ugál. — Anstatt kuál hat B. kenny; anstatt gubál, gomlou.

Sónyai.	Lógoné.	Wándalá.	Bágrimma.	Mába.
. . . .	kalg(e) iwayō [14] .	?	gan mandaine [17]	. . . . . .
{ dūūla? . . . / hi-me [13] . . . }	ikenhī uńgún . .	otōbe . . .	komī . . .	kūlik? [19]
. . . .	únkonē [15] . . .	žamba . . .	sē-komī . . .	. . . . . .
{ gāda . . . . . / guńgu . . . . . }	uńgún	hodē	gāla	tabúk
ldana	nčšantlo . . .	andžē . . .	lítigi	kuńi
. . . .	rúmninzēn [16] . .	kudá . . .	{ dīdī . . . / dīdīdi . . . }	gubúl
. . . .	kóšia	tōčdo? . . .	kálsiā . . .	. . . . . .
. . . .	{ rummi . . . . / dehī(?) . . . }	. . . . . .	múbula . . .	šekāl (Arb.)
. . . .	úńgukán . . .	. . . . . .	gómmina [18] .	ganrinklo

[1] dábu: I am not quite sure, whether „navel" or „centre" be the primitive meaning of this word; but the former seems to be the case. I do not know, what bōdi means; although it reminds in very remarkable manner of bādī mentioned on p. 263, note 1, as given by Koelle in connection with dábu, „neck", written by him dóbā, and therefore most easily to be confounded with our term.

[2] díbun: this excrescence of a navel of most unnatural size is very common in Negroland, at least with children.

[3] teorā: Koelle tourō. As well this term, as the corresponding Hausa-word čiki in the natural development of the language have received the more general meaning of „the inside", and in consequence are also used adverbially; see p. 25.

[4] āgeri, no doubt, „that which gives life" (āgu), just as the corresponding Tēdā wo seems to be identical with bo, „blossom" (Introductory Remarks p. CI); compare below note 7; it is wanting in Koelle, but the adjective kéngeri or, as he writes it, kéngeli has been thence derived, the original meaning of the latter term being „with a membrum virile", in complete parallelism to the term kérgeri, „female". As for the other very different kadágu (Koelle kádugū), it properly means „that which is behind" (the apron); compare p. 20 „the next man in rank".

[5] katšā: Koelle attributes to this term, which he writes kátšā, only the meaning of „circumcision", and, no doubt, that is the primitive notion, but then it means also that part of the body, on which circumcision is practised.

[6] ágirke (Koelle ágérge) in this place evidently appears with its original meaning, as „that which contains the element of life" (see note 4), and on this account with regard to the woman, by adding kāmo-bē, it means „womb"; and it is not but by mistake, that it has received the general meaning of „leather-bag" mentioned alone by Koelle, who, altogether, has entered very little into the anthropological views of these people, and into the natural development of their language.

[7] ágér, „sperm of life", again, is a term derived from the same root, and thence meaning in general „kernel, stone of fruit", while Koelle does not even mention the notion here given. But what instructive instances of the organical development of language are exhibited by these three terms ágér, āgeri, ágirke, speaking loudly for a systematical arrangement of these vocabularies, instead of a mere alphabetical one. Here, indeed, we find a fresh source of the richest anthropological science, and we now understand clearly, how the rainy season (ne-ágeri, „the seat, the season of life"), as well as the antilope (ágeri p. 196 „the beast of life and animation"), could be called by the same name as the membrum virile, the latter in the pictorial representations of ancient Egypt being the very emblem of life and the creating power.

[8] hešē: it is remarkable, that, while the preceding terms of the Tēdā-idiom, describing parts of the human body, are closely allied by origin with the corresponding Kanúri-terms, we have here a word resembling rather the Hausa-term, the consonants having changed place. From hešē the following hīšegel has probably been derived.

[9] žeki in Schön's vocabulary appears under the form žiki; the term is often employed in a sense approaching to „skin", but that it does not really mean „skin", is shown by the composite term žeki n fáta.

[10] čéki: derived from this term is another one čīkānne, „the pit of the stomach", V. déda.

[11] bendšī appears in Schön's vocabulary (1843) in the remarkable form haganei or bevatšī, but I have no doubt, that he has since relinquished that mode of writing.

[12] bacca, at least, is used by the Fúlbe settled in Adamawa.

[13] hi-me properly „mouth of birth", i. q. „womb".

[14] kalg(e) iwayō, „mouth of the female breast".

[15] úńkonē (uńkn-nē?), „large navel, navel-lace", uńgún, „body", and úńgukán, „testicle" (as containing the sperm of human life) probably are etymologically connected with each other.

[16] rúmninzēn seems to be connected with rummi, „pure".

[17] gan mandaine, as a term independent from the former one mbī, „breast", seems suspicious, and may rather indicate, exclusively the round breast of the virgin (mande); compare p. 263, note 18.

[18] gómmina, properly gou mina.

[19] kūlik with the notion „navel" is very doubtful, especially if we consider the phrase kūlik omdúng burma (p. 45) with the meaning „I vomit", and de-ríng kulék (p. 267) for „back-bone". Besides, Seetzen gives the totally different term dummuk. — As for „foot", Burckhardt has engona (uńgún). — For „body, belly", both as well Seetzen as Burckhardt have my very term (B. taboh); but for „stomac" Seetzen gives the different term agúi. — Instead of kuńi Burckhardt has henny, and instead my gubúl, gomlen.

Deutsch und Englisch.	Kanúri.	Tédā.	Hausa.	Fulfúlde.
weibliche Scham — *privy parts, pudenda of female*	kúrugù? . . . / fúregi[1] (Arb.)	kōgi	dūri[9] . . .	dūaku . . .
Clitoris — *tickler* . . .	kalál[2]	. . . . . .	gōlo	gūlol . . .
Schamhaar — *pubes* . .	tebši	. . . . . .	. . . . .	. . . . . .
Gebärmutter — *womb* . .	táta-ram[3] . / ngirke kámo-bē	. . . . . .	. . . . .	. . . . . .
Taille, Weiche — *waist* .	duwi fúregi-bē[4]	kolt	. . . . .	. . . . . .
der Hintere, Gesäss — *breech, fundament*	ngōlu[5]	lūma	dīwa	hōbe . . . / fúngudù . . / fóruru Fumb.
Rücken — *back*	ngáfo	kusar . . . / fusar; fesár .	bāyo	bāo[11] . . .
Schulter — *shoulder* . . .	gómunu[6] . . .	. . . . .	káfada[10] Pl. káfadu	walauu[12] Pl. baládie
Rückgrat — *back-bone* .	karēre	. . . . . .	. . . . .	. . . . . .
Armhöhle — *pit of the arm*	tillebu[7]	killekilli . .	. . . . . .	. . . . . .
Oberarm — *upper part of the arm*	bibi	nāsu	demtše . . .	tembáhkol[13] Pl. témbide
Unterarm — *lower part of the arm*	déba músko-bē[8]	kobē		

[1] fúregi fehlt bei Koelle, wenn nicht sein Wort fárga, „waist" („Taille") damit zusammenfällt; dies entspricht dem meinem dúwi fúregi-bē. — Dieses fremde und erst später aufgenommene Fremdwort aber hat unzweifelhaft das gröbere und ursprünglichere kúrugū, „Öffnung, Schlund, Kehle, vagina" (vgl. oben S. 25[illegible], N. 1), wovon das Adjektiv kúrguri (eigentlich kurúguri), „weiblich" abgeleitet ist, wenigstens in der höheren Sprache verdrängt.

[2] kalál und tebši fehlen bei Koelle, das letztere ist wahrscheinlich dem Lógonē entlehnt.

[3] táta-ram, eigentlich die „Kinderstätte", fehlt bei Koelle, der aber neben ngérge kāmābē, wie er schreibt, und wenn vgl. S. 264, N. 6, [illegible] kára hat, eigentlich „grosse Mutter", vgl. oben S. 21[illegible] yá, „Mutter", das wol unzweifelhaft etymologisch verwandt ist mit Wándalá ya, „gebären", oben S. 36.

[4] dúwi fáregi-bē, s. N. 1.

[5] ngōlo. Koelle ngólā.

[6] gámanu (kábanu bei Burckhardt), ngáfunu bei Koelle, der mit dieser Bedeutung auch noch einen anderen, mir ganz unbekannten aber um so merkwürdigeren, und meine Ansicht vom gewaltigen Einfluss des Lógonē auf das Kanúri (Einleitung S. CCXXIV) in auffallender Weise bestätigenden Ausdruck, hambélāte, anführt, der unzweifelhaft dem entsprechenden Lógonē-Worte entlehnt ist.

[7] tillebu. Koelle télebē; anstatt karēre schreibt er kárēre.

[8] débu músko-bē (Koelle dábē múskobē), eigentlich „der Hals oder Nacken der Hand". Anstatt bibi accentuirt Koelle bíbi.

[9] dūri. Schön dūli.

[10] káfada. Schön kafata, Plur. kafata.

[11] bāo ist der reine Fulfúlde-Ausdruck, der auch bei Koelle erscheint, sogar in dem Kompositum bāo dánngo statt meines gádo dánngo S. 2[illegible]; sogar im Bonyai finden wir hier einen dem Hausa in der Wurzel so sehr homogenen Ausdruck, banda.

[12] walauu, bei Reichardt balawal, bei Koelle im Timbo Plur. baládue, dagegen im Kano-Dialekt nāfhi, Plur. nāfde; das Letztere mir sehr zweifelhaft.

[13] tembáhkol. Koelle hat ein verschiedenes sēmde für „Oberarm", neben wókude für „Unterarm".

[14] giudi, s. oben S. 26[illegible], N. 1[illegible]. Doch hat Baffreel im Aruma-Dialekt kamba gumme für „Oberarm", kamba banda für „Unterarm", hat aber dann für „Ellbogen" eben meinen Ausdruck, kamba giuda.

[15] genim debi, „weiblicher Sack", s. S. 264, N. 16; vgl. N. 6.

[16] kani m pála vielleicht kin n pála; vgl. N. 4.

[17] áyes yabē habe ich aus Kosjehtur geschrieben, da ich áyer kenkā notirt hatte; aber das nāū, „mein", gehört natürlich nicht zum Worte selbst und ya war wahrscheinlich in der Rede verschluckt worden, wo dann das e in der zweiten Silbe durch das folgende a umgewandelt wurde; vgl. yohá-tadē, „Rücken der Hand" S. 269.

[18] ole tadē, eigentlich „Kind der Hand".

[19] ákyié kann mit dem vorhergehenden Worte zusammenzufallen scheinen, aber man wenigstens hat es ganz unabhängig davon erfragt und niedergeschrieben.

[20] yerwá. Es fragt sich, ob dieses Wort von erwá, „Hand", in Wirklichkeit verschieden ist; ist es das, so ist es zusammengezogen aus ye und erwá.

[21] gaún, bei Burckhardt gouyah.

[22] da-yiág kuléh. kuléh kann nichts mit dem obigen kúlúh zu thun haben (s. S. 264, N. 10).

[23] gelme, bei Burckhardt galma.

Sonγai.	Lógoné.	Wándalá.	Bágrimma.	Mába.
. . . .	mahásso	éktšia [bík-tšia ?]	mogdo . . .	fárig (Arb.)
. . . .	tumbū	. . . .	kálina . . .	guña [21]
. . . .	teresi	. . . . . .	bī naina . .	. . . . . .
bī-ya?	genim debī [15] .	hág-zerē . .	. . . . . .	. . . . . .
. . . .	bírda-ū	ukóþ	dīunō . . .	. . . . . .
koraī	pāse	úkγiē [19] . . .	polá, pelá . .	konték
banda	yahē	yīga	gadī	da-ríñg
džemse	kaui m pála [16] .	áγepē γapē .	tár-damī . .	kórkora
. . . .	úγse yahē [17] . .	irbā	tšuñgo dá n gadī	da-ríñg kulék [22]
. . . .	úγse m pála . .	úktokō . . .	móulkomō . .	kábkabē
gindi [14]	pála	bottaus . . / ururā . . .	bōki	gelme [23]
	óle-θadē [18] . .	yerwā [20] . .	kīli . . . . / kám-dži . . .	durra

[1] fáregi is wanting in Koelle, although his farga may be rather identical with it, while Koelle gives it the meaning „waist", which I have expressed by the composite term dāwi fáregi-hā. fáregi evidently is derived from the Arabic فرج while the original Kanúri-term most probably is kárugū, „throat, vagina" (compare p. 269, note 1), the root of kárgari originally karágari.

[2] kulāi, as well as tekāi, is wanting in Koelle, the latter being probably borrowed from the Lógoné temei.

[3] táta-ram originally means „place of the child", and is wanting in Koelle, who besides ágirge kámábē, as he writes, has also yá kára with this meaning, properly „great mother"; see p. 212 „mother".

[4] dāwi fáregi-hā: see note 1.

[5] ágōlu: Koelle ágōlā.

[6] gémana (kámana with Burckhardt), ágáfana with Koelle, who, besides, has the totally different term kamhējiši, which, although I have never heard it, is of the highest interest, as exhibiting another specimen of how much the Kanúri-idiom is indebted to the Lógoné; compare Introductory Remarks p. CCXXV.

[7] tilisha: Koelle tsíphū.

[8] dóbu múoku-bā (Koelle dábā múokōbā) means properly „the neck of the hand"; instead of bīhi Koelle writes bihī.

[9] dūri: Schön writes dūli.

[10] káfada: Schön kafata, plur. kafata.

[11] báo, although it bears such a close resemblance to the corresponding Hausa-term, is evidently the pure Fulfúlde-term, which is also given in Koelle's Polyglotta, where it appears even in the composite term báo dēuñge, „back of hand" instead of my gáda dēuñge p. 766.

[12] walaun with Reichardt balawal, with Koelle in Timbo (plural) baládee, while in Kano he gives the totally different term nófhi, plur. náfde, which appears very doubtful.

[13] tomháhol: Koelle (Polyglotta) gives sémde for „upper part of the arm", wókude for „lower part of the arm".

[14] gindi, see p. 763, note 15. Raffenel, however, in Arama gives kamba gumme for „upper arm", kamba hanñu for „lower arm", while for „elbow" he has kamba ginde.

[15] genim debī, „female bag", „bag of woman"; compare p. 803, note 16, and note 6 ibid.

[16] kaui m pála probably kāu n pála; compare note 6.

[17] úγse yahē I have written from conjecture, having noted down from hearing the form úγse hanūū; but, the nūū being the form of the possessive pronoun n-nū (Introductory Remarks p. CL), the ya in yahē must probably had been elided, while the following a had changed the e of the last syllable into a.

[18] óle θadē properly means „child of hand".

[19] úkγiē, probably, is the very identical term ukθiē which precedes, the sounds of θ and γ in this language being rather difficult to distinguish.

[20] yerwā: it is questionable, whether this word be in reality different from erwā, „hand"; but, if it differs, it must be contracted from ya and erwā.

[21] guña, with Burckhardt gaayah.

[22] da-ríñg kulék; kulék cannot have any connection with the above kúlik (see p. 785, note 19).

[23] gelme, with Burckhardt galma.

Deutsch und Englisch.	Kanúri.	Tédā.	Hausa.	Fulfúlde.
Ellbogen — *elbow* . . .	ngašī [1] . . . sorió . . .	keō . . . . tii	kába da demlšo [7]	sagúrde [10] . . džohúlde . . nónebo . .
Hand — *hand*	músko [2] . . .	dua . . . . kobĕ	hanū Pl. hánua	džungo Pl. džūde
Rückseite der Hand — *back-side of hand*	ngāfo músko-bē	kolĕ inkiakai [6]	báya n hanū .	gáda džungo .
flache Hand — *palm of hand*	karādi [3] . . .	kobĕ ifē béuuā	tāfi n hanū .	nēure (s. N. 10)
Handgelenk — *wrist-bone*	kiāge músko-bē [4]	mekī . . .	. . . . . .	. . . . . .
Finger — *finger*	gólondō [5] . .	abaī	yāsa [8] . . .	húbeadū Pl. kó-beli
Daumen — *thumb* . . .	gólondū kúrā .	abaī boi . .	babá n fartšo	wordu . . .
Zeigefinger — *fore-finger*	feléterām . .	. . . . . .	ma-nūni [9] . .	sapórdu [11] . .

[1] ngašī, sorió fehlen beide bei Koelle, der für „Ellbogen" das mir unbekannte und zweifelhafte ntšīrōmi gibt.

[2] músko wird in Verbindung mit késka, „der Baum", auch für „Zweig" gebraucht, aber für „Menstruation", wie Koelle angibt, habe ich es nie gebraucht gefunden und es ist mir gar nicht zweifelhaft, dass músko nur durch ganz besondere Beziehung solche Bedeutung erhält, wie denn Koelle sogar kéntāga (d. i. kentāko), „Mond, Monat", für „Menstruation" (?) erklärt, während es doch nur in der Redensart vorkommt kámo-ga kentāko tse-lsi, was einfach heisst „der Monat ergreift die Frau, fordert sein Recht von der Frau". Von dergleichen Erklärungen hat die Sprachforschung wenig Nutzen und schöne Missverständnisse können dadurch erzeugt werden.

[3] karādi fehlt bei Koelle; er hat mit dieser Bedeutung tsárā máskōbē, „der Leib (das Innere, s. oben S. 264, N. 5) der Hand".

[4] kiāge [ke-yāge] músko-bē fehlt auch bei Koelle, der mit dieser Bedeutung Ēlm máskōbē hat; ich hatte zuerst auch kintšī músko-bē niedergeschrieben, was mir nachher zweifelhaft erschienen ist.

[5] gólondō. Koelle galóndō, aber dass es ist richtiger, wenn das Wort wirklich von gō-nishin, „ich ergreife", herkommt und nicht vielleicht dem Wándalā entlehnt ist. — Anstatt g. kúrā gibt Koelle g. mbólan („männlicher Finger"), statt g. feléterām g. pulēterām (danach müsste er das Zeitwort felē-nishin, s. oben S. 10, N. 4, anstatt pélēāgin pulēāgin schreiben); anstatt g. endiga-bē, das ich nicht sicher erklären kann, das aber wol mit Mohammedanischen Begriffen zusammenhängt, führt er mit einem Fragezeichen die Ausdrücke g. kimbūtse dābubē oder g. kamūntse gālibē auf; gālī schreibt er bald gātšī, bald gātšī und erklärt es auch für „letztgebornes Kind".

[6] kobē inkiakai, kobē ifē béuuā s. Einleitung S. LXXX. — abaī boi, „grosser Finger".

[7] kába da demlšo, eigentlich „das Knie des Armes"; denn kába ist sicherlich nur andere Form von kóba S. 260.

[8] yāsa. Die Hausa-Sprache hat auch einen Ausdruck für die Gesammtheit der Finger, „Fingerschaft", nämlich yāsotšī, ohne eigentlich der Plural von yāsa zu sein.

[9] ma-nūni von ina nūna, „ich zeige".

[10] sagórde u. s. w. Koelle (Polyglotta) hat sohunde oder soehunde, Plur. soshúlt. — nēure, „flache Hand" erscheint auch bei Koelle (nēūre), während Reichardt nēwe hat, vielleicht Plural.

[11] sapórdu scheint mit dem Begriff „zeigen" nichts zu thun zu haben; wenigstens habe ich für „ich zeige" das Fulfúlde-Wort mó-dē-holli; es steht aber wol entschieden mit dem Zahlwort sapo, „zehn", d. h. die Gesammtzahl der Finger, im organischen Zusammenhang.

[12] kōbe, bei Raffenel kobe ides, und so sogar „Daumen", „der grosse Finger" bei ihm kobe ider bēr, während ich kōbe iddes, eigentlich „Kind des Fingers" viel natürlicher nur für den „kleinen Finger" habe. Kurz, Raffenel hat wol kobe, „Finger" mit kamba, „Hand" verwechselt.

[13] gāli kabén muss wol auf einem Irrthum beruhen, vielleicht nichts Anderes als yāle kabén, „der Nagel"; lpkena scheint der allgemeine Name für „Finger" zu sein. Jedoch ist der Ausdruck ka-kāli aeē für „Zehe" zu berücksichtigen.

[14] ēg-erwā, vielleicht yig(o) erwā.

[15] golónd(o) erwā. Der ganzen Form nach gehört gólondō nicht der Kanúri-, sondern der Wándalā-Sprache an: vgl. N. 5 und golóndo gādšī, „kleiner Finger" S. 271, so wie golóndo gidšī, „kleine Zehe" S. 272, wo die K. golóndo gandi hat, wo man also deutlich sieht, dass auch das gīdšī dem Wándalā eigenthümlich angehört.

[16] erwā wēla kann unmöglich eigentlich „Zeigefinger" heissen, sondern wird die Stellung anzeigen, welche die Hand selbst (daher erwā) annimmt, wenn man mit dem Zeigefinger auf etwas hinweist.

[17] modgān tadšī, wahrscheinlicher mol-gānte dšī.

[18] gadan-dšī, vielleicht richtiger gadī-n-dšī, und so wäre es dem weiter unten folgenden gadī-(l)adšī analoger gebildet, da dies „Rücken des Fusses" bedeutet.

[19] gon-dšī-gi heisst eigentlich „Sohn der Hand", und es ist auffallend, wie dieser Ausdruck dem oben S. 231 aufgeführten von grundverschiedener Bedeutung nahe kommt, gon-dšī-ab, „ein Kind von 4 Händen oder Spannen" (Höhe nämlich), so wie dem darauf folgenden.

[20] gon-dšī indēdše. Die Grundbedeutung von indēdše ist mir nicht bekannt.

[21] kar-n-gelik. Seetzen hat für „Ellbogen" das ganz verschiedene sefrik. — kárringak ist auffallend; vgl. S. 270, N. 21.

[22] kár-tingól. Burckhardt hat ein ganz verschiedenes und sehr zweifelhaftes nynger missy. — Für „Daumen" hat Seetzen kóddumák.

[23] Sehād, eigentlich nicht mit der Bedeutung „Zeigefinger", sondern „Zeugefinger", nämlich der Finger, womit man einen Eid ablegt, stammt aus dem Arabischen.

Sońyai.	Lógoné.	Wándalá.	Bágrimma.	Mába.
(s. S. 267, N. 14) .	údo	wilme . . .	modgán tadži [17]	kar-n-gulih [21]
komba	ɵadē	erwā	dži	kara
komba banda .	yehá-ɵadē . .	ég-erwā [14] . .	gadan-dži [18] .	kár-n-gák
kambe {gunda . / gine . .}	úngu 'l kadá-ɵadē	kúd-erwā . .	deb-dāi . .	kárai
. . . .	wenáγai . . .	fird-erwā . .	gírak-dži . .	. . . . . .
kōbe [12]	gāli bakán [13] . .	golónd(o) erwā [15]	gon-dži-gi [19]	kár-tungól [22]
kōbe a-ga-bûr .	moraī {durmī . / dogún .}	golóndo yekē .	bóger-dži . .	kar-túngolal ko-lák
. . . .	lábedān	erwā wēla [16] .	gon-dži indădžo [20]	šebēd [23] (Arb.)

[1] ágadī, sórlē are both wanting in Koelle, who for „elbow" gives the term ntšīrēmi unknown to myself.
[2] múske in connection with késka, „tree", means „twig", but it can never mean any thing like „menstruation", as Koelle states; and I have no doubt, that such a meaning can only be expressed by some other words connected with múske. Just in the same manner Koelle attributes the notion „menstruation" even to the word kéntāge (kentāke), „moon", „month", although such a meaning is only expressed by the whole phrase kámo-ga kentāke tee-tei, „the month seizes the woman, lays hold of the woman", i.e. „the month starts its tribute from the women", that particular meaning, therefore, being expressed not by the one term, but by means of the whole phrase.
[3] karédi is wanting in Koelle, who gives this notion to the term teúró múskōbē, „the body (inside) of the hand".
[4] kiāge (ke-yāge) múske-bē: I had also taken down the term kintši múske-bē, which afterwards had appeared to me rather doubtful. Koelle gives for „wristbone" the term šim („ear") múskōbē (múske-bē).
[5] gáloadē: Koelle guléndē, while my mode of writing would evidently be more correct, if we were sure, that the term has been derived from gó-nishin, „I write"; but it seems rather to have been borrowed from the Wándalá. — Instead of g. kúrā Koelle gives g. mbélan („manly finger"), instead of g. fulétarám g. pulétyrám (he therefore ought to write the verb folē-nishin p. 70, note 6 pulēngin, instead of pélēngin, as he does; instead of g. sadiga-bē, which seems to be connected with some Mohammedan notion or custom, he adduces with some doubt the terms g. kámántey débabē or g. kámántey gátēlbē; for gádi he writes gátši or gátši, attributing to it also the notion „lastborn child".
[6] kobē lukiskel, kobē ifē kénaā: see Introductory Remarks p. LXXXI.
[7] kába ea demtše means properly „the chin of the arm"; kabe evidently being identical with kába p. 260, although, in general, h and k in Hausa are not interchanged quite so often as they are in Fulfúlde.
[8] yése: the Hausa-idiom possesses also a term yéeetši, indicating the total number of the fingers as a whole, although it is not a regular plural of yése.
[9] me-nūni from ina nūne, „I show".
[10] segérde etc. Koelle (Polyglotta) has sobunda or sosbunda, plur. sosbūli. — nēure with Koelle appears almost in the very same form (néōre), while Reichardt has the different form newe.
[11] sapérdu: this term apparently is not connected with the notion of „indicator", at least for „I indicate" I have the Fulfúlde-term ma-dē-holli, while it is closely akin to sápo, „ten", meaning the total number of fingers of both hands.
[12] kōbe; Raffenel in Aruma gives kobe idso, the very term, which I have only for the little finger, for the general term „finger", and therefore even for „thumb" has the term kobe idso bōr which is an absurdity, as it would mean „the big son of the finger", „the big little finger". Indeed, I think, he has confounded kobe with kamba, as the finger (kobe) may well be called „the child (iddso) of the hand" (kamba).
[13] gāli bakán may contain an error. lakana seeming to be the general Lógoné-term for „finger", and it may be yála bakán, „the nail"; but, on the other side, the term ka-kāli asē for „toe" seems to show, that gāli or kāli is right.
[14] ég-erwā: perhaps yig(a) erwā.
[15] golónd(o) erwā: The whole character of the term golonde seems to show, that it originally belongs to the Wándalá, and not to the Kanúri-idiom; compare above note 5. This priority of the Wándalá-term is also confirmed by comparing the composite term golóndo gádē, „little finger" p. 271, as well as „little toe" p. 272, the Kanúri having preserved only the former of these two terms, while with regard to the toe they say golóndo gand.
[16] erwā wēla can scarcely convey the same meaning as „indicator", but seems to signify the position adopted by the whole hand (erwā) in consequence of the action of the indicator.
[17] modgán tadži, perhaps more correctly mot-gánie-dži.
[18] gadan-dži: perhaps the form gadī-n-dži is more correct, and it would correspond more exactly with the term gadi-(l)ndži, „the back of the foot" following lower down.
[19] gon-dži-gi means originally „son of the hand", but in quite another sense, as the term adduced p. 231 gon-dži-sō, „a child of 4 hands or spans (of height)", and the following term.
[20] gon-dži indădžo: the original meaning of indădžo is not known to me.
[21] kar-n-gulih: Seetzen for „elbow" gives the totally different term saīyih. — kár-n-gák is remarkable. Comp. p. 271, n. 21.
[22] kár-tungól: Burckhardt has a totally different term ayngar miesy, of the correctness of which I rather doubt. — For „thumb" Seetzen has kíddamak.
[23] Šebēd properly does not mean „the indicator", but „the finger, which is used, when taking an oath".

Deutsch und Englisch.	Kanúri.	Tédā.	Hausa.	Fulfúlde.
Mittelfinger — *middle finger*	gólondô dâba-bē		fartăe n tsakka	tšakkáru[10] .
Goldfinger — *fourth finger*	gólondô ardiga-bē	. . . .	mai-bī-ma na tsakka[5]	tšifáturu[11] Plur. tšifáttel
kleiner Finger — *little finger*	gólondô gâši .	. . . . . .	fartăe n kane[6]	gadáru . . .
Nagel — *nail*	firgânî[1] . . .	túrkonō . . .	{ fartăe[7] . . . / akēfa n fartăe }	fedéngo Pl. fedēli
Hüfte — *hip, haunch* . .	kánerge[2] . .	mâterdē . .	kátara[8] . . .	{ kautale . . / hobōnde . . }
Rippe — *rib*	[šite? s. S. 275, N. 6]	. . . . . .	anaza Pl. anazē	bētaal Pl. bētle
Schenkel, Lende — *thigh, loin*	{ dýuu[3] . . . . / dýuu . . . . }	šâye	tšīgnia[9] . . :	{ amángal Pl. ásali / dango . . . }
Bein — *leg*	šī	biddedī [?] . .	káfa Pl. káfafû	koíngel Pl. koide
Knie — *knee*	gorúm-gorúm[4]	tâye	gulva . . .	fófora Pl. kōpi[12]

[1] firgânî. Koelle pergánî, das er in zweiter Bedeutung auch für die Fusspaar von wilden Thieren erklärt; das ist aber nur sehr uneigentlich, da es eigentlich immer nur Nägel oder Klauen (im Hande abgedrückt) bedeutet.

[2] kanerge bei Koelle kántsrgū; dann hat er ausser šīte auch lêgâ für den weichen Theil unterhalb der Rippen.

[3] dýuu. Koelle dúnā. Eben dasselbe Wort bezeichnet in natürlicher Weiterentwicklung zuerst, wo vom Menschen die Rede ist, dann auch in allgemeiner Beziehung „die Kraft" (vgl. S. 264, N. 3 „Leib", S. 264, N. 1 „Nabel"), und es ist bezeichnend für Koelle's, diesen Natursprachen völlig unangemessenen, unnatürlichen Standpunkt, dass er beide Wörter als grundverschieden ansieht. Ausserdem übrigens hat Koelle noch kântî für den inneren Theil des Schenkels, der nach Seiten am Sattel liegt (wol von ta-shin, „ich fasse").

[4] gorúm-gorúm fehlt bei Koelle. Dagegen hat er noch dýngel für „calf of leg".

[5] mai-bī-ma na tsakka, wörtlich „er, der auf den mittleren folgt". Auffallend ist nur und sehr belehrend für die Vergleichung mit Kanúri, dass das Eigenschaftswort zwiefach ausgedrückt ist, durch mai am Anfange und ma am Ende.

[6] fartăe n kane kann ich in Bezug auf die Grundbedeutung von kane nicht erklären; doch möchte das Lógonē helfen.

[7] fartăe, bei Schön fáratăi, Plur. fárata, bedeutet wol ursprünglich nicht „Nagel", aber auch nicht „Finger", da es wol nie in der allgemeinen Bedeutung von yâts gebraucht wird. — Statt akēfa n fartăe schreibt Schön akaifa faritâi; akēfa ist unzweifelhaft „die Schneide" und kommt in anderer Form weiterhin wieder vor.

[8] kátara. Ich habe noch einen anderen Ausdruck, kanfati, der einen anderen benachbarten Theil des Leibes bezeichnet, aber ich weiss nicht mehr genau, welchen.

[9] tšīgnia. Schön tšinya und tšinia. — Zu káfa vgl. Barabra kafa, „Arm", Altegyptisch gáhu, Plur. gâwu.

[10] tšakkáru ist kein eigentliches Fulfúlde-Wort.

[11] tšifáturu scheint ein mehr bezeichnender Ausdruck zu sein, dessen nähere Beziehung ich jedoch noch nicht kenne.

[12] kōpi. Auch hier wieder haben wir bei Reichardt die Pluralform (kope) statt des Singulars, während Koelle im Kano-Dialekt des Fulfúlde das ganz verschiedene ašohhundu (vgl. S. 266, N. 10) hóssēgal hat.

[13] kóhe iddāe, eigentlich „Sohn des Fingers", d. h. „kleiner Finger"; s. S. 265, N. 12.

[14] kóh-ahol, eigentlich zwei Wörter, kóh(o) ahol; bei Raffenel in Aruma kohe-kal.

[15] Für „Rippe" hat Koelle (Polyglotta) in der Sprache von Timbuktu hérō biri und cigere biri; für „Schenkel", maka.

[16] kandāe, kendāe (bei Raffenel kangbé, bei Koelle kanse), vielleicht eigentlich ken-ite.

[17] yaâ domáalaren. yaâ, „Finger", domá, „gross"; ciesen mir ungewiss.

[18] yonám ist entschieden nichts Anderes als yocóm, doch habe ich es als Probe orthographischer Unsicherheit stehen lassen.

[19] golénde de-dakwé. Oben S. 21 habe ich die Form emdakwé für „der mittlere"; wahrscheinlich aber ist dakwé das eigentliche Wort, das je nach der Beziehung die Vorsilbe am oder de erhält.

[20] goléud(o) iha-orwá. Die Hinzufügung von iha ist bezeichnend.

[21] gon-dīi dáne. Oben S. 21 habe ich für „der mittlere" dadán-nahi, richtiger wol de-dánu-hi.

[22] gon-dīi gadā, „der hintere Finger".

[23] bēr-in-dīi, vielleicht zusammengezogen aus hēger-in-dīi, indem der Schenkel in Bezug auf das Bein gleichgestellt ist dem Daumen, besonders dem unteren Daumengelenk in Bezug auf die Hand, wiederum wie in-dīi, „Bein, Fuss", in der Wortbildung in engster Beziehung zu dīi, „Hand" überhaupt, steht.

[24] kárayok ist innig verbunden mit kar, „Hand".

[25] kó kár-m-bok. kár-m-bok ist vielleicht mit kar-a-gák (S. 269) einerlei. Seetzen hat für „Nägel" ujlngah.

[26] kantéh, das völlig identisch mit dem oben S. 266 für „Hintern" aufgeführten kantéh erscheint, wo es gewiss richtig ist, gehört wol hierher nicht. Seetzen hat gindrim für „Hüfte". — Für „Rippe" gibt er dara; für „Schenkel", anaij; Burckhardt für „Lende", gondiai.

Sonyai.	Lógoné.	Wándalā.	Bágrimma.	Māba.
. . . .	inkana mádeséu-degē / χalā demāsimsen [17]	golóndo dá-dnk-wē [19]	gon-dŝī dāna [21]	kar-túŋgolak ŭorok
. . . .	inkana al būtu. / χalā detke . .	golóad(o) iks-erwā [20]		kar-túŋgolak bārik
kōbe iddže [13] . .	inkana tékosē .	golóndo gādži	gon-dŝī gadō [22]	kárayek [24]
kōb-oboī [14] . .	yalā hakán . .	. . . . . .	kokō	ŏč kár-m-bck [25]
. . . .	yosém (nāū) . .	daŋgwoŝē . .	gcble . . .	kuntók (?) [26]
[15]	. . . .	. . . . . .	. . . . . .	. . . . . .
. . . .	rosém [18] . . .	eg-dágnala .	bēr-in-dŝī [23] .	auag
tāō	mágelā	sorā	in-dŝī . . .	. . . . . .
kēndže / kandže [16]	zēzē	wadže . . .	kamkin . . .	tummo

[1] firgāni: Koelle pergāni, to which, in the second place, he attributes also the notion of „the track or footsteps of dogs, lions" etc., although such a notion is only implied, not expressed by the word, which even in such cases does not indicate but the nails or claws (impressed in the sand); compare, what I have said p. 262, note 7 with regard to ogandēl.

[2] hánoəge with Koelle hánloágū; besides lite, „rib", he has also lagà, „the soft part of the human body below the ribs; side".

[3] dŷne: Koelle dúnó. The very same term in the course of very natural development, especially with regard to men, means „strength", and Koelle in this, as in so many other instances, is wrong in giving these two words as distinct terms.

[4] gorám-gorám is wanting in Koelle who, on the other hand, has a peculiar term dingel for „calf of the leg".

[5] mal-bi-ma na lenkha means verbally „he who follows upon the middle one"; but it is remarkable, that the term expressing the quality is repeated twice, by the prefix mal rather characteristic of the Hausa, as well as by the suffix ma proper to the Kanúri.

[6] faride n hano: as for hano, it seems to bear some affinity to the corresponding Lógoné-term hana, inkana.

[7] faride (Schön féraūi, plur. fárata) originally seems to mean something between „nail", and „finger"; at least it never seems to be used with the same general notion, as yāsa. — Instead of akōfa n farīže Schön writes akaifa faritši, as I myself for the blade of the sword or knife have the form kaifa.

[8] kátera: I have another term, viz haafoli, indicating some neighbouring part of the human body, but I do not now know exactly, which.

[9] tšigaia: Schön writes tšinye and tšinia. — As for hāfa, compare Berabra kefa, „arm", ancient Egyptian gáhu, plur. gáwu.

[10] hōnhkara is not an original Fulfúlde-word, but borrowed from the Hausa.

[11] tšīfátere seems to be a significative term, the distinct relation of which, however, has yet to be illustrated.

[12] kōpi: in this instance also, as in so many others, we find with Rev. Reichardt the shorter (plural) form kópe. Koelle in the Fulfúlde-dialect spoken in Kano gives the totally different term sōnbánde (see p. 260, note 10) hóorégal.

[13] kōba iddže means properly „son of the finger", i. e. „little finger"; see p. 269, note 13.

[14] kōb-oboī does consist of two words, kōb(r) and oboī, with Raffenel in Aruma kobe-bol.

[15] For „rip" in the dialect of Timbuktu Koelle (Polyglotta) gives hérā hīri and algere hīri; for „thigh", máka.

[16] kandže, kendže (with Raffenel kanghé, with Koelle kanee) may properly be ken-tšō.

[17] χal demásisen: χal, „finger", demé, „big", sisen not known to me.

[18] rosém is evidently nothing else, but yosém; but I have left it on purpose, as it is, as a specimen of the uncertainty of orthography in these languages.

[19] golóndo dá-dnhwē; p. 32 I have the form amdahwé with the meaning of „the middle", but probably the proper form is dahwé, in which, according to the special meaning of the phrase, the syllable am or da is added.

[20] golóad(o) ike-erwā: the adding of ike is significative, meaning probably „king (of hand)"; compare iskeé, p. 227.

[21] gon-dŝī dāna: this term enables me, to correct a former term given p. 31, and there to write da-dóma-ki instead of dadám-nekí.

[22] gon-dŝī gadō, „the finger (of) behind".

[23] bēr-in-dŝī may be contracted from béger-in-dŝī, the thigh in its relation to the leg being compared with, and expressed by, a corresponding term, just as the thumb, especially the lower part of the thumb, is in relation to the hand, as the term in-dŝī, again, meaning „leg, foot", has been formed with regard to the closest relation of it with dŝī, „hand".

[24] kárayek is intimately connected with kar, „hand".

[25] ŏč kár-m-bck: kár-m-bek may be identical with kár-á-gáh (p. 267). — Seetzen gives ojingáh for „nails".

[26] kuntók does not seem to belong to this place, while above p. 266 kontók seems to be in its right place. — Seetzen gives gindrim for „hip"; for „rib", dára; for „thigh", anéij; while Burckhardt for „loin" has gendini.

Deutsch und Englisch.	Kanúri.	Tédā.	Hausa.	Fulfúlde.
Schienbein — *shin-bone* .	sigél[1] . . .	. . . . . .	dombúhu[7] . .	hólbunde Pl. kól-bulé
Fuss — *foot*	šī	séhene . . / sāye . . .	káfa	koingel . . .
Fusssohle — *sole of the foot, plant*	tsórō šī-bē .	kīši sāye . .	tāfi n káfa .	ndure koingel
Oberseite des Fusses — *upper part of the foot*	ngāfo šī-bē . / felle . . .	sēnsryhfi[6] . .	. . . . .	gáda koingel .
Hacke — *heel*	godū-godū .	yē-debúrti [?] .	dúgduge . . / mai-takaua[8]	tépere[12] . . .
Fussknöchel — *ankle-bone*	šim šī-bē[2] .	. . . . . .	idu n káfa . / digge . . .	bítere koingel
Zehe — *toe*	gúlondō (šī-bē)	abaī	yāsa n káfa .	bóhendu koingel / Pl. kóheli koingel / korle koide[13]
grosse Zehe — *great toe*	gúlondō kúrā	. . . . . .	. . . . . .	. . . . . .
kleine Zehe — *little toe* .	gúlondō ganā	. . . . . .	. . . . . .	. . . . . .
Haut — *skin*	katígi[3] . . .	ēši	fāta[9]	gurū[14] . . .
Nerven — *nerves* . . .	zer bū-bē[4] .	mūkí . . .	džiddžia[10] . .	dádul bandu Pl. dádi bandu[15]
Blut — *blood*	bū	grē	ženī[11]	ïdžam[16] . .
Knochen — *bone* . . .	šilla[5]	sóro . . . / súrki . . .	kaši	dyīal . . .

[1] sigél, felle und godū-godū fehlen bei Koelle.
[2] šim šī-bē, eigentlich „Auge des Fusses".
[3] katígi. Koelle kátigī. — Ich führe hier noch zum Nutzen und zur Kontrole für zukünftige Reisende den Ausdruck an, den Koelle für „Ellbogen", „Hinterhaupt" gibt, nämlich kal und kándubū.
[4] zer bū-bē. Das zer, mir sonst unbekannt, ist vielleicht einerlei mit tsar, das Koelle mit der Bedeutung „Wurzel" anführt. Ebenso hat ja auch im Arabischen das Wort عرق die Bedeutung von „Wurzel" und „Ader" zugleich.
[5] šilla. Koelle šilā.
[6] sēnsryhfi. sēn ist zusammengezogen aus séhene, „Fuss"; aber den zweiten Theil kann ich nicht erklären.
[7] dombúhu. Ich will hier noch den Hausa-Ausdruck für „Wade" anführen, nämlich šaráha, der, glaube ich, dem Fulfúlde-Worte korlel entspricht.
[8] mai-takaua ist ein (von taka) abgeleitetes Wort mit Adjektivbildung.
[9] fāta. Über den Ausdruck š-k-l n fāta s. oben S. 264, N. 9.
[10] džiddžia, bei Schön džīdžia, Plur. džnōdži.
[11] ženī, bei Schön ženī und žinnai.
[12] tépere hat Koelle im Sálum wol fälschlich für „Fusssohle", da er selbst im Kano-Dialekt für „Hacke" téppēre gibt.
[13] korle koide. Das korle ähnelt entfernt dem entsprechenden kóll im Timbo bei Koelle.
[14] garū, offenbar dem Sonyai entborgt. Auch Koelle hat ágúru in den Dialekten von Sókoto und Gober; aber in Kano ïaral Plur. ïarē. Reichardt hat lōbī.
[15] dádul. Koelle dádol und im Kano-Dialekt eádōl.
[16] ïdžam. Reichardt hat einmal ddidžam (A-B-C-Buch S. 5, a) und einmal ïiyam (S. 6, b); meine Form steht also in der Mitte. Auch Koelle (Polyglotta) hat drei verschiedene Formen gidžam, gidyam, yidyam. — Anstatt des folgenden dyīal hat er dann gīal und yīal.
[17] iāgi, Haffossi in Arama ïlaghi, während Koelle (Polyglotta) im Dialekt von Timbúktu neben ïīági ein ganz verschiedenes sianeiba hat.
[18] merá-dromi ist nichts, als eine andere Form des obigen moral-daromi für „Daumen"; sinnbildlich ebenso gebraucht.
[19] hadi yá-nerē ist auffallend, wenn man die Bedeutung von hadi allein vergleicht und auch sieht, dass es in Bezug zu yá-nerē, „Hacke", gesetzt ist. Doch muss man bedenken, dass, während das ya in yá-nerē ein wirklich selbständiges Wort ist (ya, „Hals, Nacken"), es in den beiden Komposita die blosse Genitiv-Verbindung zu vermitteln scheint, obgleich ich in meiner Einleitung diese Form als solche nicht berücksichtigt habe.
[20] dïó. Ich habe hier verschiedene Abweichungen, besonders in Seetzen's Liste, anzugeben: „Schienbein", térmbel; „Fuss", ohko (Burckhardt djaetongoly); „Wade", momádunāb; „Ferse", tïng; „Knöchel", eïlā; „Haut" (Burckhardt) don; „Blut" (Burckhardt) ery. — šehéd für „kleine Zehe" ist auffallend und vielleicht nur Missverständniss, da das Schwören und Zeugniss Ablegen, wovon der entsprechende Finger diese Benennung erhalten hat, auf den Fuss doch keine Anwendung findet. S. oben S. 268, N. 23.

Soṅyai.	Lógonē.	Wándalā.	Bágrimma.	Mába.
. . . .	mágelā	kokīye . . .	hartya . . .	. . . .
tše	asē	serā	in-dža . . .	dža [20]
tše gande . . .	fúgodil kad-ēl-asē	pilla yá-serā .	deb in-džā . / deb in-džaṅgn	džā kolčk
. . . .	ṅúgun-ēl-asē .	kudā yá-serā [19]	ged(ī)-in-džā .	džā dakīk
	inkumat ēl-asē .	yá-serā . .	mot-gamle .	negúru
	gézidē	teká-serā . .	tokólogē . .	márfakák
	ka-kāli asē . .	golóndo (serā)	gon-in-džaī .	džer-túguli
. . . .	merí-drumi [18] .	golóndo yekē .	gon-in-džaī ṅgōlo	kóddumuk
. . . .	lókudi ī-asē . .	golóndo gādži	gon-in-džaī ṅgel-[nā]	šehēd
kúru	inkenhī	gogó (ruā . .	džāro . .	endē
lengi [17]	billē	bokólalā . .	ngírria . . .	suūī
kāri	χal	wūže	mūso . . .	árē
biri Plur. bíriō .	arē	šešē	tšúṅgo . . .	kándži

[1] algél, fello and godá-godá are wanting in Koelle.
[2] Xim ší-hē means properly „eye of the foot".
[3] kotígi: Koelle kātigi. — I have also for the control of future travellers add the terms, which Koelle gives for „joint", viz hal and hondubá.
[4] oer hā-bē: oer, which else is not known to me, may be identical with taer, a term, which Koelle adduces with the meaning of „root", just in the same manner, as the Arabic word عرق conveys both meanings, „root" as well as „vein".
[5] žille: Koelle žilé.
[6] sēeeryāfé: the first portion of this term is undoubtedly formed by contraction from sēhene, but the second part I am not able to explain.
[7] dombúhu: I here also shall adduce the Hausa-term for „calf of the leg", viz žarábo, which, I think, corresponds with the Fulfúlde-term koriel.
[8] mal-tahane is a composite term with the form of an adjective.
[9] fáte: with regard to the term žehi u fíte see above p. 265, note 9.
[10] dkíddēle in Schön's vocabulary appears in the form kišin, plur. šuōšī.
[11] ženi: in Schön's vocabulary šinī and šinaī.
[12] tépere by Koelle in the dialect of Sókoto is given wrongly as meaning „plant of the foot", while in that of Kano he correctly attributes to it (in the form teppēre) the notion of „heel".
[13] herle kolde: the form herle bears some distant resemblance to the corresponding hēli in the Timbo of Koelle.
[14] garā most probably is borrowed from the Soṅyai. Koelle else in the dialects of Sókoto and Gober has ágere, while in that of Kano he has lērbi, plur. lērē. Reichardt has lébi.
[15] dédul: Koelle dádol in the other dialects, and rádōl in that of Kano.
[16] Idžum: Reichardt once has ddíddem (A-B-C-book p. 5, c), and another time tiyam (p. 6, b), so that my form stands in the midst of both. Koelle else has various forms gidžem, gidyam and yidyem, and instead of the following term dylel, he has gial and yial.
[17] leṅgi: Raffenel in Arama linghi, while Koelle (Polyglotta) in the dialect of Timbúktu besides léṅgi has also the totally different term sieeāba.
[18] merá-drami is nothing else, but another form of the term merai-durmi adduced above as meaning „thumb", the two forms exhibiting another instance of the uncertainty of orthography with regard to these languages.
[19] kudá yá-será is remarkable, if we compare the meaning of kudá, and if we see, that it is brought into relation to yá-será, „heel"; although we have to consider, that the ya in yá-será is an independent word by itself (ya, „neck") while in the two composite terms it seems merely to represent the genitive relation.
[20] Isbád with the notion of „little toe" is remarkable and perhaps due to a misunderstanding, the reason, why the corresponding finger has obtained this appellation, having no application whatever to the foot; see above p. 269, note 23.

Deutsch und Englisch.	Kanúri.	Tédā.	Hausa.	Fulfúlde.
Mark — *marrow* . . .	sóbbio[1] . . .	{šówōš . . . / asrāno[?] . .}	bargō . . .	mbūsam[14] . .
Excremente — *excrements*	billi[2] . . .	ftān	kāši[12] . . .	{būe . . . . / tšille . . . .}
Urin — *urine*	bōbul[3] . . .	gúmsu . . .	fitsarē . . .	tšalbe . . .
Menstruation — *menstruation*	{yila kāmo-bē[4] / bu kāmo-bē}	. . . . . .	yeul n māla .	. . . . .
Schweiss — *perspiration*	zungo[5] . . .	yeski[?][11] . .	{žibi . . . . / zuffa . . .}	{zúrune . . . / asaure . . .}
Schmutz — *dirt* . . .	kadābu[6] . .	. . . . . .	danda[13] . .	tāndi . . .
Augenwasser — *humidity in eye*	kelālu[7] . . .	. . . . . .	konitsa . .	katálti . . .
Thräne — *tear, larm* .			hausi . . .	gondi . . .
Nasenschleim, Rotz — *mucus, snivel*	tillin[8] . . .	sūsu	torōso . . .	. . . . .
Auswurf, Speichel — *saliva, spittle*	{tšelēla[9] . . / belgam . . / kerān . . .}	kāzo[12] . . .	kazámta . .	tútuki džōdi[15]
Embryo — *embryo* . . .	tāta tsórō-bē[10]	lēmi	. . . . . .	. . . . . .
Leichnam — *dead body* .	kabín . . .	agūfir . . .	mátatše[13] . .	mai-do . . .

[1] sóbbio. Koelle söbē.
[2] billi fehlt bei Koelle in dieser Form, aber er hat dafür andere Wörter, nämlich aozāva für „Excremente von Menschen und Affen" und kandulē für „Excremente von Rindern", das aber wol, wenn überhaupt in Gebrauch, auch allgemeiner angewandt werden kann, da es eigentlich, seiner Ableitung nach, „Abfall" bezeichnet; s. oben S. 360, N. 6.
[3] bōbul. Die feineren Ausdrücke, die Koelle neben diesem Wort aufführt, digam und nāmaso, habe ich nicht gehört.
[4] yila kāmo-bē fehlt bei Koelle, der diese Bedeutung fälschlich dem Ausdruck kintāgo (bei ihm kəntāgə) beilegt, wie ich oben S. 96, N. 7 gezeigt habe, und selbst dem Wort mdeko.
[5] zungo. Koelle tsóngu. zungo gō-niskin, „ich schwitze", eigentlich „ich fasse Schweiss".
[6] kadābu. Koelle kádáfū.
[7] keilālu fehlt bei Koelle, wenn es nicht identisch ist mit seinem člmalē, „Thräne".
[8] tillin. Koelle tšlin.
[9] tšelēla. Koelle tšilēle und tšillile. belgam und kerāu fehlen bei ihm.
[10] tāta tsórō-bē, wörtlich „Kind des Leibes" — kabin. Koelle kābin.
[11] yeski hatten wir oben S. 150 für „Dunkelheit".
[12] kāzo nähert sich wieder mehr dem entsprechenden Hausa-Wort, als dem Kanúri-Ausdruck. Grund deren aber ist wol das gleichbedeutende Altegyptische kao; s. die folgende Note.
[12] kāši, Altegyptisch kes. Die Hausa-Sprache gebraucht auch mit dieser Bedeutung terōso, F. dúbude und filāl, und dann für Diarrhöe, eigentlich „Rotz des Leibes", H. mālina n tšeki, F. šilbe rēdo.
[13] denda in Verbindung mit „Ohr", dende n kunne, auch für „Ohrenschmalz" F. tšādi noppi.
[13] mátatše ist mir in seiner Ableitung nicht ganz sicher, hängt aber wahrscheinlich mit mútua, „Tod", matáe, „Sterblicher", zusammen.
[14] mbúsam heisst wahrscheinlich, nicht „Mark" überhaupt, sondern „mein Mark", mbūs(e) am; Reinhardt buse.
[15] tútuki džōdi kann ich nicht nach seiner Entstehung erklären.
[16] fondo heisst „Strasse", und scheint daher mit unserer Bedeutung etwas zweifelhaft, obgleich der Begriff von „Koth" und „Weg" in manchen Beziehungen zusammenfallen mag.
[17] sungol. Raffenel in Arama „Schweiss", tahaoun; „schwitzen", tahasse agonige.
[18] ani scheint mit dieser Bedeutung vorzukommen in der Phrase wa soko ani, „ich lasse Wasser".
[19] ani al il, „Wasser des Auges". il, „Auge" habe ich übrigens selbst, doch wol ganz sicherer Konjektur, hinzugefügt, da in meinem Manr. nur ani al stand.
[20] atšū mágerá. Ich weiss nicht genau, was atšū heisst; indessen so viel ist klar, dass es etwas wie „Lungen" (arfū S. 785) bezeichnen muss.
[21] yole angón, „Kind des Leibes"; bilir mēf, eigentlich „der gestorbene Mensch".
[22] semenšára ist eine mehr als unsichere Form; der letzte Theil šra ist wahrscheinlich 3te Person pron. und das Ganze aufzulösen in semo-wōl el-šrā.
[23] igenrány-bodé hängt unzweifelhaft zusammen mit bodé, „Magen", und vielleicht auch mit báganra, „vulva"; im ersten Theil aber steckt vielleicht edse, „Kind".
[24] mteš von mēl, ein interessanter Zusammenhang.
[25] moo-nē, entweder „das weibliche (nē in gon-nē, „Mädchen") Blut" (mōso, moo), oder „Blut der Frau".
[26] gon etgāligi. gon, „das Kind"; der zweite Theil mir unsicher.
[27] arē tše-era. arē, „das Blut"; tše-erā mir unbekannt.
[28] tle erscheint mir in seiner Eigenschaft als Substantiv mehr als zweifelhaft, da es ganz zusammenfällt mit der 3ten Person Sing. des Präteritums; s. S. 37.

Sonyai.	Lógoné.	Wándalá.	Bágrimma.	Mába.
lundi	besippo	zibba . . .	šúffo	kafãl
fondo[18] [?] . . .	ungũ	ugwe . . .	džong	eñi
tõso	{kunõ . . . . / ami[20] . . . . .}	kurõ	ſdži	kai
. . . . . .	genim dókifnõ .	semsoižára[24] [?]	mus-nẽ[27] . .	árẽ tús-erõ[29]
suńgol[19] . . .	metfũ	berã	. . . . .	. . . . . .
. . . . . .	. . . .	. . . . . .	. . . . .	. . . . . .
mande	ami al si[21] . .	kól-dambẽ .	man kãmi . .	. . . . . .
	. . . .	. . . . . .	. . . . .	. . . . . .
. . . . . .	mágarã	múkodžẽ . .	bãni	. . . . . .
tuffo	{nahẽ . . . . / aifũ mágarã[22] .}	{ñebẽ . . . . / adžã-korã . .}	bòro	yéilik
. . . . . .	yole ungún[23] . .	igsoráńy-bodẽ[25]	gon eigáligi[28]	. . . . . .
bun-koi . . .	bille miĩ	mtoi[26]	gò	tio[30]

[1] eġbbio: Koelle eábä.

[2] billi in this form is wanting in Koelle, who has other terms instead, viz. neaden as meaning „excrements of men and monkeys", and kánduló, to which latter term he gives the restricted notion of „excrements of cattle", while from what I have said p. 261, note 6 it is evident, that originally it must have conveyed a by far more general notion.

[3] böbul: the more delicate terms digow and námsos mentioned by Koelle besides this word are not known to me.

[4] yila kámo-bã is wanting in Koelle, who wrongly attributes this notion to the term kintàge (with him kéntàge), nay even to that of máoko (see p. 265, note 2).

[5] anàgo: Koelle tsnàgu. anàgo gá-nishin, „I transpire", properly „I catch perspiration".

[6] hadàbu: Koelle hádáfá.

[7] kelàla is wanting in Koelle, if it be not identical with his žimaló, „arm".

[8] tilliu: Koelle télia.

[9] tšelàla: Koelle tšilišlo and tšilile. belgam and korán are wanting in his vocabulary.

[10] kàta tsórá-bé means verbally „child of the body". — kabin: Koelle kábin.

[11] yoski seems rather a little doubtful, as we had it above, p. 150, with the notion „darkness".

[12] kèuo approaches the corresponding Haussa-term closer than the Kanúri-word, the reason of this resemblance being probably the ancient Egyptian term kes, which is also represented by Haussa kàši.

[13] kàši; the Haussa-idiom has still another term, viz. toróso, F. dàbudó and filiki, and, besides, for „nurse of the bowels" the term màlinna tšoki, F. àlibe rédu.

[14] dauda: this general term in the composition, dauda n hause, F. ihudi noppi, is also used of the „serwal".

[15] màlatže: I am not quite certain as to the origin of this term; although, according to all probability, it is closely related to mata, „die", matúm, „mortal", mútua, „death".

[16] mhàsam most probably means „my marrow", mhũe(s) am; Reichardt has huse.

[17] tàtahl dàãdi; the origin of this word I am not able to explain

[18] fando means „road, path, track", and may, therefore, seem rather doubtful with our meaning „excrements".

[19] anàgol: Raffenel in Aramu for „perspiration" gives takasen, for „to perspire", takasen agonige.

[20] aul with this notion seems to appear in the phrase wu ache aul, „I make water".

[21] ami al si; al, „eye" I have added myself from most plausible conjecture, my Mscr. exhibiting only ami al, „water of".

[22] aifũ mágarã: I do not know the exact meaning of aifũ; however thus much is clear, that it must signify something like „lungs", for which p. 263 I have nefũ.

[23] yole ngún, „child of body"; bille mil means properly „the dead man".

[24] semsoižára is a rather uncertain form, and probably has to be written soma-wäž(s)-árã, árã being the 3rd pers. pron. pers.

[25] igsoráńy-bodė is probably connected with hágara, „veins", and hadė, „stomach", and possibly odar, „child" may be contained in the first portion of the term.

[26] mtoi may be derived from mil, „dead".

[27] mus-nẽ appears to be composed of mùso, mus, „blood", and nẽ, „female" (in gon-nẽ, „the girl").

[28] gon eigáligi: gon, „the child", the second word being rather uncertain.

[29] árã tús-erõ: árã, „the blood"; tús-erõ unknown to myself.

[30] tio in its character as a substantive is more than doubtful to me, as it coincides exactly with the 3rd person sing. of the past tense, see p. 37.

Deutsch und Englisch.	Kanúri.	Tédā.	Hausa.	Fulfúlde.
Leben — *life*	nebgā [1] . . .	rōn ?	rai [10]	yoaki [12] . . .
Geburt — *birth*	támbō(-ni) [2] .	intu-fúsni [?] .	haifua . . .	džibiógol . .
Geburtstag — *birth-day* .	yim támbō(-ni)-bē	. . . . . .	rāna n haifuá-ta	ðellomāre džibiógol
Name — *name*	tsū	kū	sūna [11] . . .	inde . . . .
was ist dein Name? — *what is thy name?*	á-fi tsu-num [3]	[kunúm onā? [4]]	mē-nēne) sunáoka	nō inde mā .
Tod — *death*	kirmu [4] . . .	kúrmo . . .	mútua . . .	mai-de . . .
Leichenbegängniss — *funeral*	šitra [5] (Arb.) .	. . . . . .	gaus	gauāre . . .
Grab — *grave, sepulcre* .	kabbar [6] (Arb.)	kōbu	košéwa . . .	yenānde Pl. genále
Trauergesang — *dirge, mourning-song, funeral wail*	burgu kirmu-bē [7]	kōbe turkínti [9]		. . . . . .

[1] neágā, eigentlich ne-ágā, „Zustand des Lebendigseins" (vgl. né-ágeri, „Zustand des Bleibens", „Regenzeit" oben S. 264, N. 4 und !) und daher gewiss der Schreibweise Koelle's, némgā, vorzuziehen.

[2] támbō(-ni), „(mein) Geburt". Die Form támbō ist nämlich einfacher und origineller, als die von Koelle angeführte Form kentsámbi, vgl. Koelle's tumbi oben S. 264, N. 3 („Mutterleib"!), und ist eben auch der einzige Ausdruck für „Geburt", den ich kennen lernte, wie der folgende zusammengesetzte Ausdruck seine allgemeine Anwendung beweist, da kentsámbi dagegen kaum haben kann, da es fast unzweifelhaft nur von dem aktiven Gebären der Frau selbst gebraucht wird; kentsámbi nämlich ist das aktive Nennwort von i-s-ambiskin, „ich zeuge, bringe hervor", támboni das passive von ku)-tamb-ó-sko, „ich bin geboren" S. 34.

[3] a-fi tsū-num. Koelle hat dafür ndā tsúnom.

[4] kirmu fehlt bei Koelle, und auch ich kann seine Ableitung nicht angeben (yeremi?), obgleich es ganz allgemein in Gebrauch ist und durch das entsprechende kúrmo im Tédā in interessantester Weise bestätigt wird.

[5] šitra. Koelle šitirā.

[6] kabbar. Koelle kábar und káfer.

[7] burgu in der Form búrgō hat Koelle allerdings eigentlich nur mit der Bedeutung „Hülferuf", dann aber doch auch in weiterem Sinn als Schmerzensausdruck.

[8] kunúm onā ist wahrscheinlich falsch, indem die einheimisch grammatische Form des Tédā durch das Kanúri uns verdunkelt ist.

[9] kōbe turkínti ist wahrscheinlich Verbalform.

[10] rai, „Leben", könnte wol mit Egyptischen Begriffen zusammenhängen, ebenso wie der Ausdruck für „Sonne", „Tag", rāna, das vielleicht richtiger rā-na zu schreiben ist. Ich führe hier das für den eigentlich feigen Charakter des Volkes bezeichnende Hausa-Sprichwort an, sò da rai asámo girma, „nur so lange das Leben dauert, findet man Grösse", d. h. „es ist verkehrt, das Leben zu opfern, um etwas zu erreichen"; F. aotto yoaki kebba mango.

[11] sūna. Hierbei will ich den Hausa-Ausdruck für „Namenstag" (Tag der Taufe) erwähnen, ranasūna, zusammengezogen aus rāna n sūna, F. bellomāre inde.

[12] yoaki. Reichardt hat für „Leben" wurde.

[13] ahre bōho, bei Raffenel aarale fabon, doch ist das l wol nur Schreib- oder Druckfehler.

[14] āgákili ist mir verdächtig und ist offenbar zusammengezogen aus āgā und kilia, „Mensch".

[15] sāni ane-sā. ane scheint das eigentliche Wurzelwort für „Geburt" zu sein. yane-b, d. i. y(e)-ane-b, „ich bin geboren", s. S. 35. — sāni kann ich nicht erklären, da ich für „Tag" eben ságeli habe.

[16] meli. In Bezug auf Übereinstimmung der Hausa- und Lógoné-Sprache in diesem Falle vgl. Einleitung S. CXCVIII.

[17] gal-iksaore hängt doch wol sicherlich mit skešia (šikšia), „weibliche Scham" (S. 196) zusammen. Den folgenden Ausdruck kann ich nicht erklären, ausser dass yorka mit dem Zeitwort yorgom, „ich bin geboren", unzweifelhaft zusammenhängt.

[18] ke-dšā. Wir sehen hieraus, dass das Wurzelwort von man a-dšēdšoma, „ich bin geboren" (S. 85) dšā ist: aber auch in dem folgenden zusammengesetzten Ausdruck tritt die Reduplikation ein. In letzterem haben wir die in ihrer Grundbedeutung identischen Ausdrücke dša, „Sonne, Tageslicht" und dšā, „Geburt" in interessanter Zusammenstellung.

[19] yō, „der Tod", so wie gō, „der Leichnam", von mak-oiga, „ich sterbe", a(ō) oiga; „er ist gestorben" (s. S. 37): also Wurzel oi oder vielmehr yō.

[20] lulúllō, onomatopoetisches Wort vom Ruf lull.

[21] nāo. Hier haben wir die reine Wurzel des Zeitworts „gebären", und ich habe danach die Schreibweise desselben S. 35 zu verbessern, nämlich am-b-nāō-ro, „ich bin geboren", a-nāō, „ich zeuge".

[22] mēli nentas bahámbaro. bahámbarō kann ich nicht analysiren.

Sonyai.	Lógone.	Wandala.	Bágrimma.	Mába.
âhona	ŏgáblil [14] . . .	bamba . . .	kolška . . .	. . . . . .
almúdu (Arb.) .	. . . . . .	gai-fktsere [17] .	ko-džŏ [18] . .	uña [21]
almūdu han . .	sūni ane-aĭ [15] .	ámmoro yerka	dža-džodžo-(a)-ma	. . . . .
. . . .	θemâ	džīra . . .	rī	mēli
. . . .	θemâ-mī bakŏ . .	ázera džirám-ma	rī naŏga . .	mēlj nenēno ña-ñámbarē [22]
bun	motī [16]	amtsa	yŏ [19]	. . . . . .
sâre	šitra	šitra	sítera . . .	. . . . . .
sâre bōbo [13] . .	káberi	irχe	kábberi . . .	turba (Arb.)
. . . .	χsē mli	dohúl-amtsá .	lulálio [20] . .	. . . . . .

[1] naágâ, properly na-ágâ, „state of life", just as ad-ágari (compare p. 264, note 4 and 7) means „state, period of life giving", i. q. „time of creation", „rainy season", and therefore, no doubt, infinitely more correct than Koelle's nfángī.

[2] támbü(-nī), „my) birth". támbü is the only term, which I learnt, and which according to its intrinsic character and derivation (compare the verb ha)-tamb-á-the, „I am born" p. 34, and the tambī of Koelle which, as noted p. 264, note 8, probably means „vulva", and not „woman") can alone convey the passive notion of „birth", while hantsámbī, the form given by Koelle, according to the spirit of the Kanúri-idiom, can only be used of the act of giving birth with regard to the woman; compare the verb t-a-ambiskin, „I procreate, give birth" p. 34.

[3] á-fī taú-nam: Koelle has, instead, adú-tsánym.

[4] kirma is wanting in Koelle, and, although it is a term generally employed, and, no doubt, of indigenous origin, as is shown by the corresponding and nearly identical Tédā-word kárme, I myself am not able to say, whence it may be derived, the root, probably yerem, or something like it, having become obsolete.

[5] Kitra: Koelle Kitçri.

[6] kabbar: Koelle kábar and káfar.

[7] burgu, in the form of búrgū, appears in Koelle only with the notion of „cry for help", while with regard to the verbal form he gives also the general notion of „I cry out aloud".

[8] kūndm ená is not clear to me, nam, the 2nd person pron. pers., belonging to the Kanúri, not to the Tédā-idiom, while ñā, no doubt, is the proper term for „name".

[9] bōbo tarkinti appears to be a verbal form.

[10] rai may well have some connection with Egyptian idrae, as well as the term for „sun", „day", rāna (perhaps more correctly rī-na). As characteristic of the tenacious love of life, which is exhibited by these people, I here adduce the Hausa-proverb sé da rai ndámo girma, „greatness is only won as long as life lasts", i. q. „it is not worth while obtaining a victory, while you lose your life", F. nelle yeáki hebba maágo.

[11] súna: I here mention the Hausa-term for „name-day", ranañna, formed by contraction from rána n súna, F. ñellemāre inda.

[12] yeákī: Reichardt has for „life" wurda; compare note 10.

[13] sâre bōbo: Raffenel sereis iahos, the i probably being a mere lapse of the pen or a misprint.

[14] ŏgáblil is, no doubt, composed of ŏgā and hille, „person".

[15] súni ane-aĭ: ane seems to be the root of the word expressing „birth"; yane-ê i. e. y(e)-ane-ê, „I am born", p. 35. — súni I am not able to explain, although it seems to be another popular form of ságoli, „day".

[16] motī: here we have another instance of some affinity between the Hausa- and Lógone-idiom, of which I have said more in the Introductory Remarks p. CXCIX.

[17] gai-fktserer the íktsere most surely is related to akšīla (hikšīla), „privy parts of female" p. 266. As for the following term, I am not able to explain it, except, that yerka is undoubtedly connected with the verb yergem, „I am born".

[18] ko-džŏ: from this form we see, that the root of the phrase man e-džŏdžema, „I am born" (p. 35), is džŏ; but even in the following term we have another instance of the reduplication, džŏdžo. This composite term is further interesting as exhibiting a combination of the two closely related roots dža, „daylight, sun", and džŏ, „birth".

[19] yŏ, „death", as well as gŏ, „corpse", from mah-oiga, „I die", a(e)-oiga, „he died" (p. 37); the root, therefore, appears to be oi, or rather yŏ.

[20] lulálio is a term belonging to the class of onomatopoetic terms, from the call lulū.

[21] uña: we have here the pure root of the verb, and I have thereto to correct the way, in which I have written it p. 35, writing instead am-b-nāē-re, „I am born", a-ñāó, „I beget, procreate".

[22] mēli nenēno ñañámbarē: I am not able to analyse the word ñañámbarē.

Deutsch und Englisch.	Kanuri.	Tédā.	Hausa.	Fulfulde.
Gesundheit, Wohlsein — *health*	neṅgā [1] / kálaña (h. Arb.)	. . . . . .	láfia (Arb.) .	džam [13] . . .
Krankheit — *sickness* . .	kásua [2] Pl. kasu-sua	kézil . . . / kezēno . . . / gúur . . .	tšiūta	ñau . . . . / bōna (Mas.) .
Husten — *cough* . . .	kásagē [3] . .	zugti	todria . . .	doire . . .
Katarrh — *catarrh* . .	tántanē [4] . .	mor	mážina [9] . .	múra . . . / ñilbe . . .
Fieber — *intermittent) fever*	hangē [5] . . .	keṅgē . . . / gigge [7] . . .	masásera [10] . / zezébbi . . .	yóntare . . . / diltāre [14] . .
Leberkrankheit — *liver-complaint*		. . . . .	tšīo n séfa [11] .	ñau dāmol . .
Nierenkrankheit — *disease of the kidney, renal disease* / Seitenstechen — *pleurisy*	šitíma [6] . . .	erñ tigdžēnni [8]	ágana [12] . . / zánzana . .	gaya maude [15]

[1] neṅgā, eigentlich „Leben" überhaupt, S. 276; für den Ausdruck „Besserung", „Genesung", merā (H. dāma) u. auch noch am Ende der Zeitwörter „es ist besser geworden". — Anstatt kaláña schreibt Koelle kaláña und haláña.

[2] kásua. Koelle kásua und daneben kásk@u und kasúa. — Für „Schmerzen" hat Koelle das mir unbekannte sérṇa, z. B. sírṇa kólábā, „Kopfschmerzen".

[3] kásagē, offenbar von saágin, „ich erschüttere, werde erschüttert" (also die passive Bedeutung von kasáha, „Lanze" s. weiter unten), fehlt bei Koelle; er hat dafür ntsásarel.

[4] tántanē. Koelle tántánē. Andere hier einschlägige Ausdrücke für Unpäßlichkeiten siehe unter den Verbalformen. S. 196.

[5] hangē fehlt auffallender Weise bei Koelle.

[6] šitíma fehlt ebenfalls bei Koelle, aber ich glaube, dass das Wort in engem Zusammenhang mit šite steht, welches Koelle hat, allerdings mit der wol unrichtigen Bedeutung „Rippe" anstatt „Niere".

[7] gigge ist wol nicht eine ganz reine, sondern eine populär verdorbene Form.

[8] erñ tigdžēnni. Die genaue Übereinstimmung dieses Ausdruckes mit šitíma ist nicht deutlich; vgl. oben erñ.

[9] mážina. Ich will hier noch einige andere Ausdrücke anführen, die ich nicht in allen Sprachen vergleichend vorführen kann: „Erkältung", H. sahi, F. pōol, peori oder peodu, daher das Fulfulde-Adjektiv pewādo, „der von Erkältung Befallene", auf H. wo-ne sahi ya-kāma-ni. Übrigens muss ich zu dem Ausdruck sahi bemerken, dass er in der Folge eine sehr weite Bedeutung erhalten hat, besonders auch in Beziehung auf Krankheiten der Geschlechtstheile, wie denn auch Burton bemerkt (Journal der Londoner kgl. Geogr. Ges. Bd. XXIX, S. 387), dass in den von ihm bereisten Gegenden Ost-Afrika's sehr viele ganz andere organisirte Krankheiten auf Erkältung zurückgeführt werden. — So wird selbst die tšīo n māra, „die Leberkrankheit", im Hausa oft als ein tšīo n sahi aufgefasst, F. ñaha.

[10] masásera. Schön masasesara. — zezébbi hat er nicht und es hat auch ein fremdländisches Aussehen.

[11] tšīo n séfa, verwandt ist die N. 9 erwähnte tšīo n māra.

[12] ágana. Auf diese Krankheit, die so ziemlich dem Europäischen Ausdruck entspricht, pflegt die Nervenkrankheit zu folgen, Namens dáldáina (von dálidāla, „Nerven", abgeleitet), weshalb die Hausa-Leute sagen: ágana ta-kāre, dáldálnia ta-na tafōa, ta-na kaṡēna mutám dóna, „wenn die agana nachgelassen, komme die dáldálnia und martert oder schwächt (eigentlich „tödtet") den Menschen sehr". Vgl. hierzu v. Humboldt, Reise in die Äquinoctial-Gegenden, Ausg. von Hauff, Th. 1, S. 392.

[13] džam ist als sehr ursprüngliches Wort Substantiv- und Adverbialform zugleich.

[14] diltāre. Ob der Fúmbina-Ausdruck dumbí auch sonst dem Fulfulde eigen ist, weiss ich nicht.

[15] gaya. Koelle gāya im Sūlum-, gāe im Góber- und Kano-Dialekt.

[16] gande dor, mit dem weiter unten folgenden hende dor verglichen, lässt einigen Zweifel zurück, ob es wirklich „Leberkrankheit" heissen kann.

[17] sāba. „Viele Krankheiten", sāho ñya.

[18] haṅgē. Es wäre auffallend, wenn im Lógoné der Kanúri-Ausdruck für diese doch so gewöhnliche Krankheit aufgenommen wäre; noch auffallender aber ist es, dass wir ihm auch im Bágrimma mit leicht veränderter Form begegnen. Dass das der Ausdruck der Kanúri-Sprache ursprünglich angehörte, scheint doch das entsprechende Tédā-Wort zu zeigen.

[19] hauš annéwuá soll wahrscheinlich heissen hauš owa nah, „die Krankheit schmerzt".

[20] lodēda wāra ist vielleicht lodēda ana-(ārā, ārā 3te Person pron. pers., obgleich ich lodēda nicht erklären kann.

[21] buglēa kann ich nicht mit Sicherheit ableiten: ob mit hauš zusammenhängend (S. 45 am andār hauš)?

[22] haṅgala. Fast scheint auch dieser Ausdruck, wenn wir ihn mit der im Bágrimma üblichen Form haṅgala vergleichen, mit dem Kanúri zusammenzuhängen.

Sońyai.	Lógoné.	Wándalá.	Bágrimma.	Mába.
al áfia (Arb.) . .	. . . . . .	. . . . . .	. . . . . .	. . . . . .
wurki	sáke[17]	kurá amnówuá[19]	mōyo . . .	bagíña[21]
kotókotō . . .	mágara	aw yō múkodžē	kasō	tulda tūulda
durma	mágara ʼl ám . kalár el asen .	múkodžē . .	bāni	bońgo
tōre . . . . . másа-mása . .	kangē[18] . . .	ledēda wāra[20]	kańgais . . .	bańgais[22] nakāb
gande dor[16] . .	. . . . . .	. . . . . .	. . . . . .	. . . . . .
bádani	dézalán	zumba . . .	serāpi . . .	arkšō

[1] nedgá means „life", in general, p. 276; as for the term „improvement", „recovery", K. merō, see the phrase „it has become better", at the end of the verbs. — kolāfia with Koelle kolāfia and kalláfia.

[2] háaso: Koelle hásūo, besides which he has the forms hácāwo and hácōa. Moreover, he has the term eírra, „pain, ache", as, for instance, eíren kolóbó, „hand-ache", which I have not learnt.

[3] hásagé evidently from eságin, „I shake", and therefore, originally, the very same term as heséka, „that which is shaken, the spear", is wanting in Koelle, who, has, instead, ntsáeerei; (Pol.) he gives háságé and bérū for „smallpox".

[4] tántonō: Koelle tántānī. As for other names of various kinds of sickness or disease, see among the verbal forms.

[5] kaságé is wanting in Koelle.

[6] šiltima is also wanting in Koelle, but the term most probably is derived from the word šilt, which appears in Koelle's vocabulary, but with the wrong notion, as it seems, of „rib", instead of „kidney".

[7] gigge does not seem to be a pure form, and may be simply owing to popular corruption.

[8] erfi tigdáfeni: the identity of the notion of this term with that of šiltima is not quite clear; compare above erfi.

[9] máŝino: I have added a few other terms: „a cold, catching cold", H. sośi, F. pēni, pēori or pōedu, from which latter form the adjective powódo has been formed „he who has caught a cold", or rather, in order to imitate the passive form, „he who has been caught by a cold", in H. we-ne sośi ya-kāme-ši. However, with regard to the term sośi, I must remark, that in consequence of peculiar circumstances it has received a wider notion, comprising most of the lighter affections of the urinary organs and the sexual parts, as we know also from Capt. Burton's report (published in the Journal of the R. Geogr. Soc., vol. XXIX, p. 387), that in those regions of Eastern Africa explored by himself many kinds of disease, which in reality have no connection whatever with cold, by the natives are referred to that origin. Thus even the tšīo n móra, „liver-complaint", is often represented in the Hausa-idiom as atšīo n sośi, F. fonbe.

[10] masiccere: Rev. Schön writes mosacacare. sondbbi is wanting in his vocabulary and has, no doubt, a foreign appearance.

[11] tšīo n séfo: compare tšīo n móre note 9.

[12] ágona: this kind of disease, just as is the case in the Equatorial Region of South-America, is generally succeeded by another one, the disease of the nerves, or nervous debility, called dšīdšīnie (from dšīdšīe, „nerves"), wherefore the Hausa-people use to say: ágona ta-káre, dšīdšīnie ta-na tof-ōa, ta-na kaše-wa mutúm déna meaning „when the ágona-sickness has passed by, the dšīdšīnie comes on and distresses and weakens (properly „kills") greatly the person". ágona by Schön is wrongly explained as meaning „itch", for which Koelle (Pol.) gives kaešo.

[13] dšam as a very original term represents at the same time the form of the substantive, and that of the adverb.

[14] dilšáre: the Fúlbe of Fúmbina have yet another term, viz dambi, but I do not know, whether it be a mere provincialism, or whether it may belong to the Fulfúlde-idiom, in general.

[15] geyo: Koelle has the form gáye in Sókoto, gáo in Góber and Kano with the notion of „itch" = Kanúri kásgan.

[16] gande dor compared with bonde dor lower down leaves some doubt, whether it can possibly mean „liver-complaint".

[17] sáke: „many diseases", sáke flya.

[18] kańgē: according to all appearance we have here one of the most generally prevalent terms to denote such a common disease as the fever; for, that the term originally belonged to the Kanúri-idiom, we see clearly from the corresponding Téda-term; nay, even in Bágrimma we meet with the same term in a slightly changed form; root ńgē.

[19] kurá amnówuá probably is not quite correct, and may have to be corrected into kurá owo ná, „the disease where".

[20] ledēda wāra also is not quite certain, and may have to be written ledēda ana-(árá, árá being 3rd person pron. pers.

[21] bagíña: I am not able to give the root of this term with certainty, but it may be connected with bońē (p. 65 and under bańē).

[22] bańgais: even this term, if compared with the Bágrimma-form kańgais, appears to be intimately connected with the Kanúri-idiom; see note 18.

Deutsch und Englisch.	Kanúri.	Tédā.	Hausa.	Fulfúlde.
Dysenterie — *dysentery* .	(s. S. 46) . . .	. . . . . .	ánago [7] . . .	bútšiko rēdu .
Würmer (im Magen — *worms (in the bowels*		. . . . . .	sūtsa n tšeki / māza . . .	gilli rēdu . . / tande rēdu . / dāslbi . . .
offenes Geschwür — *open sore*	tunū [1] . . .	šiegē . . . / farkai . . .	mīki [8] . . .	fūire . . . .
Kropf — *goitre, struma* .	[tunū láfia? s. N. 1]	. . . . . .	makōko . .	yokōde . . .
Pocken — *smallpox* . .	bārū [2] . . .	barma . . .	amáuni . .	bulle bandu [10]
Masern, Krätze — *measles, itch (?)*	tinínim [3] . .	tiríníma . .	misírta . . .	kimodōdo . .
syphilitisch. Ausschlag; Aussatz — *siphilitic sores, leprosy*	džedām . . / bārus [4] (Arb.)	. . . . . .	kutúrta [?] . .	. . . . . .
Syphilis — *siphilis* . .	dun [5] . . .	yákali . . .	temžēre . . / tšiāta n birni [9]	yórendē . . / ñau birni . .
Entzündung der Harnröhre, Tripper — *inflammation of the urethra, clap*	war [6] . . .	. . . . . .	. . . . . .	. . . . . .

[1] tunū wird neben seiner generellen Bedeutung ganz besonders gebraucht von den offenen Hautwunden am Ende der Regenzeit, bei Reisenden, die viel zu Pferde sind, nur am Bein unterhalb des Knie's, die eine grosse schwarze Narbe zurücklassen und daher in Süd-Afrika, am Kap, populärer Weise „schwarze Lache" (black lake) genannt werden. Den Ausdruck tunū láfia (tunū láfia), den Koelle für „Kropf" („king's evil") anführt, habe ich nie gehört.

[2] bārū ist vielleicht dasselbe Wort wie das S. 282 nachfolgende bāle, bei Koelle bálē, dem er auch die allgemeine Bedeutung „Narbe" gibt, selbst mit Einschluss der durch Tättowiren erzeugten Einschnitte (bēli, s. oben S. 260), aber allerdings nicht die Bedeutung „Pocken". Auch könnte mag der Begriff „Narbe" die Grundbedeutung sein, da die Eingeborenen eben das Narbenhafte einer mit Pocken behafteten Person als das Charakteristische der Krankheit ansahen.

[3] tinínim fehlt bei Koelle. Über den genauen Charakter der Krankheit bin ich unsicher.

[4] bārus, das Arabische, „lepra alba"; aber auch džedām ist Arabisch. Beide Ausdrücke fehlen bei Koelle, der seinerseits ein mir unbekanntes, einheimisches dōli für „Aussatz", dōlima für den mit dem Aussatz Behafteten hat. Auch die von ihm erwähnte Krankheit ngǝǝǝ gehört hierher, wo der ganze Körper wie mit Kröpfen bedeckt wird, ganz so wie zwei Bewohner der Carolinen in Dumont D'Urville's Atlas dargestellt sind.

[5] dun fehlt bei Koelle.

[6] war, das Wurzelwort vom Zeitwort war-ǝskin, „ich brenne", entspricht Koelle's warwár, das er jedoch nur für „Striktur in der Harnröhre" erklärt. Die Leiden der Harnröhre sind übrigens bei diesen Völkern überaus umfassend, zumal bei den sieggewohnten Arabern und Halb-Arabern, und zwar nicht eben durch Ausschweifung, sondern durch Abkühlen der geneigten Hitze bei anstrengenden Märschen. — Vgl. S. 214, N. 13 „Diarrhöe".

[7] ánagō. Ich setze hier eine kurze Beschreibung der ánagō auf Hausa, deren Richtigkeit ich aus eigener Erfahrung während meines [illegible] Krankenlagers in Sókoto bezeugen kann: tšeki ši-na fitta kāši kàrami, ka-sáme ya-kāma da yasa, „der Leib gibt von sich kleine (trockene) Exkremente (ähnlich dem Kameeldünger), und (sobald) du dich hinsetzest, erfasst es (den Leib) mit grossen Schmerzen".

[8] mīki. Eine besonders grosse Wunde der Art heisst, H. mīki babá, F. būre mawnde; ein anderes verwandtes Übel, H. giembo, F. (wenigstens in Sókoto) gambōre; eine Entzündung im Allgemeinen H. kāba, und eine Geschwulst mit Entzündung kumberi, beides in F. bádi, Plur. balle.

[9] tšiāta n birni, „die Krankheit der grossen Stadt", ganz ebenso wie das Fulfúlde-Wort. kutúrta vom Adjektiv kúturu scheint den venerischen Aussatz zu bedeuten.

[10] bulle bandu, wörtlich „die Geschwüre (balle Plur. von bádi) des Leibes".

[11] wurki gámo, wurki fátu, „die grosse Krankheit, die schlechte Krankheit".

[12] kūan mawnn: ob „die böse Krankheit" oder „die Krankheit des Feindes"? mawnel, „der Feind".

[13] tánn(-gō. Das gō gehört vielleicht nicht zum Worte selbst; doch darüber später.

[14] dāidden ethkéamà. ethkéamà besteht wahrscheinlich aus drei Redetheilen, et („ist"), kéea und mà, obgleich mir die genaue Bedeutung jedes einzelnen nicht ganz klar ist.

[15] Ich führe hier drei begriffsverwandte Wörter auf, die Seetzen gibt, erstens „Kolik", angatenpéij; dann „Durchlauf", tabāchtennéh und drittens „Ruhr", arrijéterih. Von diesen sind die beiden ersten ganz gleichbedeutend, nur dass das eine Mal anga, das zweite Mal tabāh für „Leib" gebraucht ist; das dritte aber heisst nichts Anderes als „das Blut fliesst", ārō yāterō.

[16] berihōng. Seetzen „Pocken", bórrinjengáb; „Krätze", njiegáb; „Aussatz", hémdi.

[17] Für „venerische Krankheit" hat Seetzen dejiggēl.

Sonyai.	Lógoné.	Wándalá.	Bágrimma.	Mába.
tótoni[?] . . .	. . . .	. . . . . .	. . . . . .	[16]
farka-sdra . .	. . . .	. . . . . .	. . . . . .	
bende dor . . .	añwa	wúyigē . . .	túnu(-gō[13] .	fú
. . . .	. . . .	. . . . . .	. . . . . .	. . . .
. . . .	ul-rétetē . . .	barū džengē .	ktaímazā . .	šálaga
. . . .	wáyelē gadē . .	azaumde . .		boriñōng[16]
. . . .	nadá n kúlfā . fúndoma . . .	abka-dáhdže .		džedām mik
wurki gúmo[11] . wurki fútu . .	dala	kúzu manzau[12]	kello	[17]
. . . .	imánahán . .	tōbe	džidden elkésa-mā[15]	badžang

[1] tonō: this term, besides its general meaning, is particularly applied to the black open wounds of the skin especially of Europeans, caused at the end of the rainy season, leaving behind them a black scar, and on this account called popularly „black lake" at the Cape. As for the composite term tunū láfia (tunū lafia) given by Koelle with the notion of „king's evil", I have never heard it and recommend it to the control of future travellers.

[2] hāru may be the very identical word as bile, which I give p. 282, the bālé of Koelle, to which he attributes the general notion of „scar", including even the marks of tattooing (with me bēll p. 260), and if he does not expressly mention the meaning of „smallpox", we can easily imagine, how a term meaning scar may serve also to indicate this disease, which is especially characterised by the scars, it leaves behind.

[3] sinisim is wanting in Koelle, and I myself am uncertain with regard to the distinct character of the disease.

[4] bárse is the Arabic برص, „lepra alba", the term džedim likewise having been derived from the Arabic; both terms are wanting in Koelle, who, instead, has another indigenous term viz dōll for „leprosy", dálima for „leper", while his ágēnp also belongs to this place „a cutaneous disease, resembling struma, consisting in protuberances, often of a very large size, on any part of the body", and, as I remember myself, resembling very much the two frightful figures of the inhabitants of the Carolines represented in Dumont d'Urville's Atlas.

[5] dua is wanting in Koelle.

[6] wer, identical with the root wer in the verb wer-nishin, „I burn", is the warwáy of Koelle, which he interprets as meaning a „stricture in the urethra", these kind of diseases being extremely common with the inhabitants of these hot Regions, especially with the Arab immigrants, not only in consequence of excess and debauchery, but very often from over-exertion on a long journey.

[7] šnagō: I here give a short Hausa description of this disease, of which I myself suffered very severely during my second stay in Sókoto: tčeki Il-sa fitle kāši kárami, ka-sīma ya-kāma da yans, „the bowels give forth small excrements (similar to the dung of camel), and (as soon as) you sit down, it seizes (the bowels) with violent (pains)".

[8] miki: a peculiarly large sore of the kind is called miki babá, F. hūre maunde; another evil of a related kind H. giembo, F. (at least in Sókoto) gumbáre, and an inflammation in general H. kába; an inflammated sore kúmbori, both kinds being called hádi in F., plur. bulle.

[9] tšiūte a birni, „the disease of the large town or capital", just as in Fulfúlde. As for the term kaldria, I am not quite sure, but it seems to mean „leprosy".

[10] bulle bandu: verbally „the sores (bulle, plural of hádi) of the skin".

[11] wurki gúmo, wurki fúto, „the mighty disease", „the bad disease".

[12] kúzu manzau means either „the bad disease", or „the disease of the enemy"? manzal, „enemy".

[13] túnu(-gō: as for the termination gō, it scarcely does belong to the word.

[15] džidden elkésamā; elkésamā probably does consist of three distinct words, viz el („it is"), késa and mā, although I am not able to explain each single part.

[16] I here adduce and explain three terms of a related kind, given by Seetzen, viz first „colic", angalsbaélj; secondly „diarrhoea", tahachiensch, and finally „bloody flux", arrijáterih. Of these three terms the first two, according to all appearance are perfectly identical, with the sole difference of the term „bowels" being expressed by means of sēga in the one, by tahák in the other, while the third and last one means nothing but „the blood is running", ārē yátera.

[16] boriñōng: Seetzen for „smallpox" gives bérrinjongáh; for „itch", ujingáh; „leprosy", hāmdi.

[17] For „venereal disease" Seetzen gives the term dejiggál, i. q. džiggál.

Deutsch und Englisch.	Kanúri.	Tédâ.	Hausa.	Fulfúlde.
Guineawurm — *Guinea-worm*	ngúdī [1] . . .	íngadī . . .	kúrkonô . .	brâti . . .
Wasser im Knie — *water in the knee*	ngorga [2] . .	. . . . . .	. . . . . .	. . . . . .
Wurm im Kopfe — *worm in the head*	dībugo [3] . .	. . . . . .	. . . . . .	. . . . . .
Wunde — *wound* . . .	kuńgu [4] . . .	úngo [8] . . . / úngul . . .	yańki [10] . . .	pedyŏkki . .
Narbe — *scar*	bálo [5]	. . . .	tombo [11] . . .	batâre [12] . .
Mittel, Heilmittel — *remedy, specific, medicine*	kurgún [6] . . / kúska [7] . .	suru . . . . / sōro [9] . . .	mágani [13] Pl. ma-gúngúna	safaro . . . / lekki . . .

[1] ngúdī. Vgl. über die doppelte charakteristische Bedeutung dieses Wortes S. 266, N. 4. In Betreff der Sache führe ich hier noch in Zusatz zu dem in meinem Reisewerk Gesagten folgende Stelle aus der Mission de Ghadamès an (p. 119): „on nous a assuré, que les nègres et les blancs qui avaient séjourné à Ghat, étaient seuls sujets à l'invasion du ver de Guinée".

[2] ngorga fehlt mit dieser Bedeutung bei Koelle; dagegen hat er den sehr ähnlich klingenden Ausdruck ngérdeu mit der Bedeutung „Kniefleckus". — Die ngorga ist eine in den feuchteren Gegenden der Afrikanischen Tropen ziemlich häufige Krankheit.

[3] dibugo fehlt bei Koelle.

[4] kungu. Koelle kúngû; die Wurzel ist allerdings wol eigentlich dieselbe, wie in kangê, „Farbe".

[5] bálo, s. S. 280, N. 2. — Koelle hat ausserdem noch birti für „Schwiele", birti kâbô für die von Stockschlägen erzeugten Stellen.

[6] kurgún als geistige Medizin bedeutet dann auch „Zauber". Koelle, der kárgun und kórgun schreibt, führt von letzterer geistigen Bedeutung einige Modifikationen an, wie k. dágelbê, k. kársmabâ, hat aber nicht die viel gewöhnlicheren und für den Gebrauch des Europäers unendlich wichtigeren Komposita, wie k. ngúte-bê (s. S. 284), obgleich er tedate und tedata hat. Ich muss hier bemerken und zu S. 44, N. 2 nachtragen, dass wol des harten Zusammenstosses der beiden te wegen die Form mit n im Anfange auch beim Zeitwort, besonders in der 3ten Person, durchaus vorwaltend ist, also öfter ruu-têin oder nge-têin; übrigens ist das Substantiv tenete oder ngete, ngate, erst wieder von dem Zeitwort tenze- oder tenze-niskin abgeleitet, das selbst schon von dem Substantiv tenen hergenommen ist. — Ebenso wenig hat Koelle den ganz gewöhnlichen Ausdruck k. tedrá ken-tá-bê, obgleich er ken-tá (das unzweifelhaft von tá-skin, „ich ergreife" [s. S. 66] kommt), in der Form kéntá hat. — Auch den folgenden Ausdruck kurgún tsoré ke-sé-bê hat Koelle nicht, wie auch das Wort ke-sé allein bei ihm fehlt, das ich mit voller Sicherheit abzuleiten allerdings selbst nicht im Stande bin, obgleich ich überzeugt bin, dass es für ken-se steht (se, „die Kreuzlähmung", in se-niskin, se-ngin, vgl. kaengê S. 278, N. 3).

[7] kúska, eigentlich „der Baum", „das Holz", kann, gleichwie das entsprechende lekki im Fulfúlde, natürlich nicht in allen Beziehungen für das Wort „Medizin" gebraucht werden, aber doch in allen solchen, wo es sich um Wurzeln oder ähnliche Pflanzenstoffe handelt, was bei den einheimischen Medizinen meist der Fall ist.

[8] úngo. Wir haben hier wiederum ein deutliches Beispiel von der Bildung der meisten Kanúri-Wörter durch Vorsetzung eines [illegible] vor die Wurzel, worauf ich noch einmal ausführlich zurückkommen werde.

[9] sōro im Tédâ, safaro im Fulfúlde und sáferi im Songhai sind wol alle drei aus derselben Quelle abgeleitet, vielleicht vom Arabischen [illegible], da f blosse Dialektverschiedenheit von h ist und beide als Sibilanten leicht verschluckt werden.

[10] yanki, eigentlich nur „Schnittwunde", von yanke, „schneiden".

[11] tombo. Ein begriffsverwandtes Wort, dessen genaue Bedeutung mir jedoch unbekannt ist, ist oékos, P. likira.

[13] magani, eigentlich má-gani, ist vielleicht von einem jetzt nicht mehr gebrauchten Zeitwort gani, „helfen", abgeleitet, indem die Grundbedeutung geistiger Art ist, in enger Verbindung mit Zauber; doch macht die Lágané-Form zweifelhaft.

[12] batâre ist wol, wie die meisten auf die Endung re ausgehenden Wörter der Fulfúlde-Sprache, kein einheimisches Wort, sondern von einem Fremdwort abgeleitet.

[14] ipia von fipo, „schlagen", Einleitung S. CCX.

[15] moyón ist wahrscheinlich richtiger als morán; vgl. auch dana moyán, „Färberei". Dieses moyún ist doch wol mit Hausa magani eng verwandt.

[16] wárwerá-wigé. Das wigé hängt wol mit dem S. 281 aufgeführten wáyigê eng zusammen.

[17] náfa. Ich hatte Ölma ge-náfa hingeschrieben, das bezeichnet aber wol eher den Arzt oder Quacksalber, und ich habe daraus náfe für „Heilmittel" abstrahirt. náfa kann möglicher Weise mit dem Worte monbe (mo-nafa?) zusammenhängen, das ich S. 47 für „ich genese" habe, das aber in dieser Form kaum richtig sein kann.

[18] mude. Über die verwandte, an den Quellflüssen des Schiri im Negerlande fast ausschliesslich eigenthümliche Krankheit des Wurmes, der den kleinen Zeh abfrisst, die bei der eingewanderten Arabischen Bevölkerung érûk oder férantit, im Bagirmi mukárdom heisst, s. Reisen. Th. III, S. 305.

[19] yum étan-gengele ist mir in den einzelnen Theilen noch unverständlich. — Statt berdandaba ist vielleicht berdandele zu schreiben.

[20] nd-koré: nd ist wol die Wurzel von mok-ol, „ich schneide", während ich für „ich verwunde" den ganz verschiedenen Ausdruck mok-adhâ habe; jedenfalls bleibt koré unerklärt und gehört kaum zum Worte. Das Ganze ist also zweifelhaft.

[21] fô ist wol nichts Anderes als fô.

[22] féttengé, bei Seetzen in der Form wyftengah. Die Ableitung ist mir unsicher; denn mit dem Zeitwort ttámes hat es doch wol nichts zu thun.

Sonyai.	Lógoné.	Wándalá.	Bágrimma.	Mába.
húmburi . . .	taazō	tiža	mōdu [18] . . .	fō [21]
. . . .	áaanī yíχdegē .	ṅgorga . . .	rum éten-génge-la [19]	díggeri
. . . .	swásuan	uχēša	bardándaba .	. . . . . .
džeffa	ſpia [14]	wérwerē . . .	ol-korō [20] . . .	féttengā [22]
. . . .	megū	wérwerā-wigē [16]	goddu-ebna .	. . . . . .
séferi . . . . . súfarj	morún (moyún?) [15]	kurgún . . . nāfa[?] [17] . . .	kurgún . . .	daua (Arb.)

[1] ágddi: with regard to the original meaning of this term see p. 217, note 4. With regard to the circumstances of the disease itself, I here, in addition to what I have said in the Narrative of my Travels, still adduce the following remark from the French Mission de Ghadamès (p. 117) „on nous a assuré, que les nègres et les blancs qui avaient sejourné à Ghat, étaient seuls sujets à l'invasion du ver de Guinée".

[2] ṅgorga with this notion is wanting in Koelle, while he has a somewhat similar term ágérdon with the meaning „hamstring", „tendon of the ham". — As for the disease itself, it is rather common in the more humid portions of the Tropical Regions of Africa.

[3] dibuge is wanting in Koelle.

[4] kuágu: Koelle káágē.

[5] bále, see p. 281, note 7. Besides this term Koelle has another one for „wale, the mark of a stripe", viz birti, and birti kábé for „the wale caused by a stick".

[6] kurgán, considered as a spiritual medicine, has also the meaning of „charm"; and Rev. Koelle, who writes kárgan and kérgan, mentions several modifications of this latter notion, such as k. dágelbé, k. káramabē, while he has not the very common composite terms here adduced (see p. 284), indicating the various kinds of bodily medicine so important for the European traveller, such as k. aṅate-bé, although he has this latter word in the form toásig and taṅeté; and I must here remark, in addition to what I have said p. 45, note 2, that even the verb, at least in some forms, is generally pronounced with a a in the beginning instead of te, such as ana-téla or aṅe-téla instead of tene-téla, which would sound rather hard to the ear; it cannot be doubted, however, that the substantive tenate, anata or aṅate has been derived in its turn from the verb tanee-niskin or tanee-niskin, which again has been taken from a substantive form tene, tanee, tanee. — Neither has Koelle the equally common term k. teéré ken-tā-bé, although he has ken-té (which undoubtedly is derived from tá-skin, „I seize", p. 64) in the form kénté. — The following term, also k. teéré ka-zá-bē, is wanting in Koelle, as well as the word ka-zé alone, which I myself am not able to explain with certainty, although I think, that it has been derived from ze, „convulsion", in ze-niskin, ze-ágin; compare káangé p. 279, note 3.

[7] késka, properly „the wood, the tree", like the corresponding Fulfúlde-term lekki, cannot be used in all cases to express the notion of medicine, especially when it is a fluid, while it is most fitly applied to all medicines consisting in roots and such like sort, although the original meaning occasionally is lost sight of altogether.

[8] ńágo: we have here again a plain proof of the mode of formation of the Kanúri-terms by means of prefixing to the root the sign of individuality ka, ke.

[9] sáre in Tédā, as well as seféra in Fulfúlde and séferi in Sonyai are derived from the same source, perhaps Arabic sihrien.

[10] yakki properly means nothing but „a cut", a wound produced by „cutting", from the verb yakka.

[11] tembo: a term of a similar notion, but with the exact meaning of which I am not acquainted, is céhus, F. lihfre.

[12] mágani, properly má-gani, seems to have been derived from a verb gani, which, however, is not now used in this sense.

[13] batáre, like most of the Fulfúlde-terms terminating in re, does not seem to be an indigenous word, but derived from a foreign source.

[14] ſpia from the verb ſiye, „beat", Introductory Remarks p. CCXI.

[15] morún, probably more correctly moyún, which resembles very much the corresponding Hausa-term mágani. Compare the composite Lógoné-term dens moyún, „the art of dying".

[16] wérwerā-wigē: wigē seems to be closely allied to the wáyigē mentioned p. 281.

[17] nāfa: I had written down ūima ge-nāfe, and I have thence deducted the term nāfa for „medicine" alone. nāfe may possibly be connected with the verb meabe (perhaps me-afe), which I have adduced p. 47 with the notion „I recover", but which can scarcely be right in this form.

[18] mōdu: with regard to the related kind of disease called árúk or férentit, in Bágrimma mahárdom, viz that of a peculiar kind of worm destroying the little toe, and which in the whole extent of Negroland is almost exclusively restricted to this country, see Travels, vol. III, p. 365.

[19] ram éten-géngela as yet is not intelligible to me in its various elements.

[20] ol-korō: mok-ol, „I cut", while for „I wound" I have among the verbal forms the totally different term mok-adéā. As for korō, however, its meaning here seems rather uncertain.

[21] fō, according to all appearance, is nothing but fū, adduced a few lines before.

[22] féttengā in Seetzen's list appears in the form wgftengâh. As for the root, from whence it is derived, I am uncertain, as it can scarcely be connected with etámae.

Deutsch und Englisch.	Kanúri.	Tédā.	Hausa.	Fulfúlde.
Brechmittel — *vomitive* .	kurgún ntsle-bē (s. S. 282, N. 5)	kómolō sōro .	mágani n komílo .	safāre dāne-dzam[6] / safāre kēfam
adstringirendes Mittel — *astringent remedy*	kurgún tsórō ken-lā-lē (s. S. 282, N. 5)	. . . . .	mágani mai-kāma n tārki[3]	safāre lekki rēdu .
Purganz — *purgative* . .	kurgún tsórō ka-só-lē (s. S. 282, N. 5)		mágani n gúdo n daua[4]	safāre dóggoru rēdu[7]
Gift — *poison*	.		deffi	tōke . . . .
Gegengift — *counter-poison*	. . . . . .		mákari n deffi[5]	. . . . .
Hunger — *hunger* . . .	kanā[2] . . .	(s. S. 36)	yunγwa . . .	wēlo[8] . . .

[1] Koelle gibt für „Gift" im Kanúri den Ausdruck hēll an, den ich nicht erfahren habe und der mit dem S. 260, N. 2 besprochenen hēli doch eine verfängliche Ähnlichkeit hat.

[2] kanā heisst allerdings auch „Hungersnoth", aber doch erst in zweiter Bedeutung, während Koelle, der kānā schreibt, das als die einzige Bedeutung angibt.

[3] mágani mai-kāma n tārki, „ein Heilmittel, das den Leib erfasst". Da das mai-kāma adjektivischer Zusatz zum Hauptwort ist, so ist das oft bisher magani angefügte, die Genitivbeziehung ausdrückende n ungrammatisch. Ein solches adstringirendes Mittel ist übrigens besonders die im H. máge n bagga-rūa, im F. safāre gabāre genannte schleimige Substanz vom Samen der Mimosa Nilotica.

[4] mágani n gúdo n daua, in Betreff des Ausdruckes gúdo n daua s. S. 46, N. 18.

[5] mákari n deffi. mákari, richtiger vielleicht ma-kāri, muss von der Wurzel kara herkommen „zerbrechen", dann „hemmen, entgegenwirken, aufhören machen". Mit makeri, „Schmied", S. 236 kann es wol nichts zu thun haben, obgleich ich es zuweilen mit einem e aussprechen hörte.

[6] safāre dānedzam. Das zweite Wort kann ich nicht erklären. Für „ich breche" habe ich mé-dā tāta. — Auch kēfam ist mir in seiner Ableitung nicht ganz klar.

[7] safare dóggoru rēdu. Vgl. die Phrasen rēdu-am hi-dogga und mé-dā dogga rēdu S. 46.

[8] wēlo. Die in Bogirmi angesiedelten Fulbe haben auch den eigenthümlichen Ausdruck raffo, der aber wol der Fulfúlde-Sprache im Allgemeinen nicht angehört.

[9] menāhere (sēferi) scheint gar keinen Zusammenhang zu haben mit éga-yēri, „ich breche", S. 46 und ist mir in seiner Ableitung noch unklar, wie auch die Stellung der Wörter dem Gesetz der Sońγai-Sprache nicht ganz zu entsprechen scheint.

[10] sēferi kah-āga-halnde gungu. kah-āga-halnde kann ich nicht erklären, ausser dass āga unzweifelhaft die (Einleitung S. CLXXVI, a) besprochene Verbalform ist; gúngu, „der Leib".

[11] sēferi kah-ōhuru gongu. Auch für kah-ōhuru fehlt mir das Zeitwort. Statt gúngu hatte ich wol unzweifelhaft irrthümlicher Weise gundam niedergeschrieben.

[12] ulgi. Bafiruel im eng verwandten Arama hat das ganz verschiedene horté für „Gift" (poison).

[13] mórune winhanen. Das zweite, auf Brechen sich beziehende Wort scheint anzuzeigen, dass der S. 46 für „ich breche mich" angeführte Ausdruck nefa-ū (besser nef-āū) abraya nicht das eigentliche Brechen bezeichnet, sondern vielleicht heisst „mir (eigentlich „meiner Seele") ist übel".

[14] mórune da-ungún kodām. Da ungún „der Leib" bedeutet (s. oben S. 285), so muss da wol in Verbindung mit dem nachfolgenden, mir sonst unbekannten kodām die Bedeutung „anziehen, schliessen" haben. — Die folgende Phrase, mórune ungún, möchte unvollständig scheinen, aber es ist möglich, dass unter einem „Mittel für den Leib" ganz vorzugsweise, und ohne nähere Bezeichnung, eine Purganz verstanden wird.

[15] kurgún abēzāa abāzūa von yē-beza (fuá) S. 45.

[16] kurgún nā bodē heisst nur „Mittel des Leibes" (bodē), bildet also mit seiner hineingetragenen Bedeutung als „adstringirendes Mittel" den geraden Gegensatz von dem, was wir in N. 14 in der Lógoné-Sprache sehen, wo das allgemeine „Leibmittel" die Purganz bedeutet. Das bodē, in der Form fodē mit elidirtem o, scheint mir auch in der folgenden Redensart zu stecken, vielleicht „Mittel des Leibschmerzens".

[17] kurgún t-ōme ist offenbar von wak-ōme, „ich breche mich", obgleich die Genitivverbindung vermittelst t ungewöhnlich und auffallend ist.

[18] kurgún bēra. mam-bré-nekō (S. 47) „ich habe Durchfall".

[19] dúna wange langérka diūkēne. wange langérka heisst wol „welches heilen mag" und kann so das S. 12 fehlende Zeitwort für „heilen" ergänzen. Was heisst aber diūkēne?

[20] dune wange langérka tābuga duāga-yiāgol. tābuga, „der Leib", duāga, „abführen"; yiāgol oder vielleicht e-yiāgol ist mir unbekannt. Was gúnde in der folgenden Phrase bedeutet, weiss ich auch nicht.

Sonyai.	Lógoné.	Wándalá.	Bágrimma.	Mába.
mezákare séferi [9]	mórune winhanen [13]	kurgún aháčša [15]	kurgún t-ômo [17]	dana wañgo lañgérka diñkésno [19]
séferi kak-ága-kainde guñgu [10]	mórune ás-nñgún kadám [14]	kurgún ná bodé [16]	kurgún galbára	dana wañgo lañgérka tábogo duñga-yíñgni [20]
séferi kak-ókuru guñgu [11]	mórune nñgún	kurgún wúwofdé	kurgún béra [18]	daua wañgo lañgérka gúndo doñgne
nâgi [12]		. . . . . .	. . . . . .	. . . . . .
. . . .		. . . . . .	. . . . . .	. . . . . .
hêre	(s. 8. 36)	. . . . . .	bô	. . . . . .

[1] Koelle gives the Kanúri-term bóli for „poison", which I have never heard, but which may possibly be right, although it rather resembles a little too closely the term bóli spoken of p. 760, note 2.

[2] kend, no doubt, means also „famine", which Koelle gives as the only notion of the term (kéné), but, no doubt, it is to be regarded only as a farther amplification of the original meaning of „appetite", „hunger".

[3] mágani mai-kéme a tšehi, „a remedy capable of raising the stomach": mai-kéme is an adjective defining a quality of mágani, but nevertheless an a, expressive of the genitive relation, is sometimes added to the latter. — I will here add, that an astringent remedy used especially in the Hausa-countries is the ruáye a bagga-rúa, F. safáre gawire, the slimy substance extracted from the seeds of the Mimosa Nilotica which, in connection with curled milk and raw pounded rice, I have used myself with success on the occasion.

[4] mágani a gúdu a dawa; as for the term gúdu a dawa see p. 47, note 13.

[5] mákari a daffi: mákari, properly ma-kári, is derived from a root kare, which originally means „break, stop, abrogate, resort"; I have often heard the word pronounced with an e, mákeri (compare p. 236 mákeri, „the smith"), but that seems to be less correct.

[6] safáre dámadám: the second word I am not able to explain; as for the verb „I vomit" I have mé-dô tútu. — The term héfam also is not clear to me in its derivation.

[7] safáre dóggaru ródu: compare the phrases róda-em hi-dogga and mé-dô dogga ródu p. 46.

[8] wálo: that section of the Fúlbe-nation, which is settled in Bagirmi, has still the peculiar term caffo, which, however, does not seem to belong to the Fulfúlde-idiom.

[9] mezákare (séferi) appears to have no connection whatever with the term ága-yéri, „I vomit", mentioned p. 45, and exhibits various points of uncertainty in derivation as well as in syntax.

[10] séferi kak-ága-kainde guñgu: kak-ága-kainde I cannot explain with the exception of the auxiliary verb ága, Introductory Remarks p. CLXXVII, a); guñgu means „the belly, bowels".

[11] séferi kak-ókuru guñgu: also for kak-ókuru the verb is wanting in my list; instead of guñgu I had erroneously written gundam.

[12] nâgi: Raffenel in the closely related Arama-dialect has the totally different term korté for „poison".

[13] mórune winhanen: the second term, which, no doubt, expresses the notion of vomiting, seems to indicate, that the phrase adduced p. 45 nafe-ñ (more correctly naf-kû?) ahraye does not express the proper act of vomiting, but rather the nauseous state, in general, „my soul is sickly"(?).

[14] mórune ás-nñgún kadám: nñgún meaning „the body" (see p. 265), we must conclude, as in connection with the succeeding term kadám, which in other respects has remained unknown to me, to convey the notion of „to astringe". — The following term, mórune nñgún, might seem to be incomplete, but it is possible, that by „the remedy for the stomach", in this case, a purgative is emphatically implied.

[15] kurgún aháčša: aháčša from yé-heen (fuš) p. 45.

[16] kurgún ná bodé means only „remedy of the bowels" (bodé), thus exhibiting the very contrary view of the similar term in Lógoné, which signifies the purgative. The bodé in the form fodé, with the e thrown off, seems to be contained also in the following phrase kurgún wúwofdé.

[17] kurgún t-ômo has evidently been derived from mak-ômo, „I vomit", although the form of the genitive relation by means of t is rather uncommon and remarkable.

[18] kurgún béra: mam-bra-nobô (p. 47), „I have diarrhoea".

[19] daua wañgo lañgérka diñkésno: wañgo lañgérka means probably „which may cure", and may thus serve to minister to us the verb wanting p. 137. But what diñkésno means, I do not know.

[20] dana wañgo lañgérka tábogo duñga-yíñgni: tábogo, „the belly, bowels", duñgo, „to be lax", „have diarrhoea"; but what yíñgni or perhaps a-yíñgni means, I do not know, nor what gúndo in the following phrase may mean.

Deutsch und Englisch.	Kanúri.	Tédā.	[illegible]	Fulfúlde.
Durst — *thirst*	gúdu[1] . . .	(s. S. 30)	ki-ší n rúa[9]	donka . . .
Feistheit, Beleibtheit — *corpulence, plumpness*	. . . . .	. . . . .	ózia . . . / kitše . . .	délere . . .
Magerkeit — *leanness* . .	[děri?][2] . .	. . . . .	rāma . . .	poire . . . .
Schlaf — *sleep*	kenām . . . / kánim . . .	úneši[?] . .	kwāna . . .	. . . . .
Traum — *dream* . . .	kánnōlm[3] . .	. . . . .	méfalki . . .	koidul . . .
Beischlaf — *cohabitation*	ṅgélikté[4] . .	(s. S. 34)	(s. S. 34)	(s. S. 34)
Hochzeit — *wedding* . .	larúsa[5] (Arb.)	názonō[7] . .	amrē[10] . . .	těgel Pl. těle / kōgel Pl. kōle
Spiel — *play*	biskē[6] . . .	aua . . . . / abī kenáke[8]	urgī, wargī[11]	bělbelo . . / wǔlwelo . .

[1] gúdu wird sehr selten gebraucht, ausser wol in der Phrase „ich werde, er wird durstig", gúdu ñ-ga (ši-ga) ten-tei; es fehlt bei Koelle. In vielen der anderen Sprachen konnte ich nur das Adjektiv erfahren, dasselbe mag aber auch da in vielen Fällen Substantiv-Bedeutung haben, wie ja bei diesen einfachen Sprachen beide Bedeutungen so oft zusammenfallen.

[2] Ein eigentliches Substantiv für „Magerkeit" habe ich im Kanúri nicht erfahren, obgleich děri in děri-niskin (S. 234, N. 1) ziemlich substantivisch gedacht ist.

[3] kánnōlm. Koelle schreibt einmal kanāllm und das andere Mal (unter nálim) kąnnalle.

[4] ṅgélikté hängt unzweifelhaft mit ṅgeli, ngeri, „das Lebende, das männliche Glied", zusammen, s. S. 764, N. 4. — Hier will ich auch das Wort ṅgáng anführen, womit die Kanuri ein Mittel zur Erhöhung männlicher Kraft bezeichnen und das wahrscheinlich mit Koelle's Wort ṅgantęm, „Unzucht", „Buhle, Buhlerin", etymologisch zusammenhängt.

[5] larúsa. Koelle larsā, „the act of marrying a virgin". Es ist aber kaum wahrscheinlich, dass bei diesem Fremdwort, wie das bei anderen die Verheirathung betreffenden Wörtern allerdings der Fall ist, irgend ein Unterschied in Bezug auf die Jungfräulichkeit der Angeheiratheten gemacht wird.

[6] biskē. Koelle bāsgē; vgl. S. 60, N. 3. Ich will hier nebenbei einen Irrthum Koelle's berichtigen, der in die Volksredensart kām kélé-ntsen niganwa biskē-rō lā-tšin bigo, „ein Mann, der (eigentlich „sein Kopf") verheirathet ist, geht nicht zur Tanzpartie", etwas von 3 Jahren (one who has been married for three years) hineinbringt, wo kein Silbe darin ist.

[7] názonō ist bemerkenswerth und noch zu erklären.

[8] abī kenáke ist eine zusammengesetzte Redensart und scheint ein Spiel mit Pfeilen zu bezeichnen.

[9] ki-ší n rúa. Bei ki-ši, „Begierde zu trinken" (ša), ist es bemerkenswerth, wie ki zu dieser Bedeutung gekommen ist, wol als das Positive des negativen nš-ki, „ich will nicht", da wir doch wol nicht auch hier im Hausa eine Bildung vermittelst eines vorgesetzten allgemein substantivischen ke annehmen dürfen.

[10] amrē. Ich führe hier auch den auch in die Fulfúlde-Sprache übergegangenen Ausdruck bahī, „Hochzeitsschmause", an.

[11] wargī. Als besondere Arten von wargī führe ich an: „das Spiel mit den Erdnussteln", da n tšālša in Kánem, da n gāžia in Gōber genannt, auf F. bilbe berēdši; dann den wargī n dáwaki, „das Spiel der Pferde", F. putši lōpr, und endlich eine andere Art genannt šāra, auf F. danderāgo.

[12] bánderi. Wir haben hier einmal ein Beispiel eines vollkommen identischen Ausdruckes in zwei grundverschiedenen Sprachen, aber mit vollkommen verschiedenen Bedeutungen, im Sonyai „Traum", im Tédā „Waldthal".

[13] bigni steht im engsten Zusammenhang mit am-bék (am-béy?), „ich heirathe", S. 34.

[14] pisko. Hieraus kann man sich das S. 35 fehlende Zeitwort einigermassen ergänzen.

[15] nalla-kásko. Wir sehen hier eine sonderbare und wol sehr zweifelhafte scheinbare Verschmelzung eines Kanúri-Wortes mit einer einheimischen Form.

[16] yé-šolá ist unzweifelhaft kein Substantiv, besonders da ich S. 35 neben yé-šola als Verbalform yé-šota gášaie habe.

[17] semenšse larúsa. Das erste Wort kann ich nicht analysiren.

[18] džīā-gabgo. Da ich für „ich beschlafe" S. 35 das ganz verschiedene Zeitwort mat-edi habe, so möchte wol entweder hier oder dort ein Irrthum sein. — Chrigwun bezeichnet, wie bekannt, eigentlich das Arabische nika, das hier in Folge der Einführung des Islams die Bedeutung von „Hochzeit" erhalten hat, ursprünglich nichts als „Beischlaf".

[19] flya. Der fortwährende Wechsel zwischen p und f zeigt sich auch hier, da ich unter den Zeitwörtern für „ich spiele" mam-á-plya habe mit p.

[20] bisni scheint in gar keinem Zusammenhange zu stehen mit der Redensart am heddu kaiini für „ich beschlafe", S. 35. Dagegen möchte bisni mit á-bi, „ich schlafe" (S. 39) verwandt zu sein scheinen.

Sonyai.	Lógonē.	Wándalā.	Bágrimma.	Māba.
far	. . . .	. . . . . .	kundžō . . .	. . . . . .
. . . . . .	. . . .	. . . . . .	. . . . . .	. . . . . .
. . . . . .	. . . .	. . . . . .	. . . . . .	. . . . . .
. . . . . .	. . . .	báre [?] . . .	bī	. . . . . .
hénderi [12] . . .	swāne	nešin-kásko [?] [15]	nī	. . . . . .
. . . . . .	yíska [14]	[yé-šelā? [16]] .	džiú-gungo [18]	binni [20]
hīgai [13]	larúsna	semenāse larúsna [17]	nika (Arb.) .	woñing gilte
fīdže	tōli šobba . . .	gúsa	fīya [19] . . .	kūle

[1] gádu, as a substantive, is very rarely, if ever, used, except perhaps in the phrase gádu k-ga (ši-ge) tan-tef, „thirst catches me, him", „I become, he becomes thirsty"; it is wanting in Koelle. In most of the corresponding languages I have only been able to learn the form of the adjective expressing this meaning, to which I, therefore, must refer the reader.

[2] A proper substantive expressing „hunger" in Kanúri I have not learnt, although the root dēri in dēri-nískin p. 235, note 1 is much like a substantive.

[3] kénušin: Koelle once writes kenéšin, and another time (under néšin) kennášin.

[4] ágelíkté most probably is connected with the term ágeli, ágari, „veratrum"; see p. 265, note 4. This place I also think fit to adduce the term ágúág, by which the Kanúri denote a means to increase the conjugal vigour of a man, and which appears to be etymologically connected with the term ágenlym mentioned by Koelle as meaning „adultery" (lowdness!), „paramour".

[5] laráose; Koelle láreá, „the act of marrying a virgin", while this foreign term seems be rather applied to a marriage, in general, without any regard being taken to the former state of the spouse.

[6] bískō: Koelle bégō; compare p. 60, note 3. I must here also correct an error of Koelle's, who in the vulgar maxim or dictum kōm kélā-ntsen nigewa biskó-ré lé-tšin bige meaning „a man, who (properly „his head") is married, does not go to a dancing (or playing) party", explains the first part wrongly „one who has been married for three years".

[7] néonó is a remarkable term yet to be explained.

[8] ebl kenóko does not seem to be a simple term, but rather to mean the playing with arrows.

[9] ki-šī n fūn: ki-šī evidently means „the wish to drink (šo)", where we must suppose, that ki, which in nó-ki means „I will eat", „I detest", does convey this notion of wish, will.

[10] amrē: I here mention the Hausa-term bukí meaning „wedding-meal", which has also been adopted by the Fulfúlde-language.

[11] wargī: As peculiar kinds of wargī I here mention the play with „ground-nuts", called da n tšótka in the Hausa-dialect of Kátsena, da n gošla in that of Góber, in F. bíibe harédši; further the wargī e dakubi, verbally „the play of horses", F. putši lópe; and finally another play called šára, in F. danderāge.

[12] héndari: we have here again an instance of a perfect identity of a term in two languages, while conveying a totally different meaning, héndari meaning „dream" in Sonyai, but „wooded valley" in Tēdā.

[13] hīgai is most intimately connected with the verb am-hék (am-héyē), „I marry", p. 35.

[14] yíska: from this term we may deduce with some degree of accuracy the corresponding verb wanting p. 35.

[15] nešin-kásko, we see here an instance of a remarkable composition of a Kanúri-term (nešin) with an indigenous form.

[16] yé-šelā can by no means be the form of the noun, especially as (p. 35), besides yé-hela, I have the verbal form yé-šelo gášelā.

[17] semenāse most probably does not belong to the term itself, and is not clear to me.

[18] džiú-gungo seems doubtful on account of the verb mat-odī, which I have p. 35 for „I sleep with", but I rather think, the latter has only the meaning „I sleep", and therefore our word in this place may be right. — As for the following term nīke, it was originally the real term for cohabitation, but with these people, in general, has received the notion of marriage.

[19] fīya: we have here another instance of the perpetual change of p and f, as for „I play" I have among the verbs mam-á-pīya.

[20] binni appears to be in no way connected with the term am budda halloi, which I have p. 35 for „I cohabit", but on the contrary it may seem to have some relation to á-bī, „I am sleepy", p. 39.

Deutsch und Englisch.	Kanúri.	Tédā.	Hausa.	Fulfúlde.
Gesang — *song*	kaiga [1] . . .	debòna	wāsa	fidžo Pl. fidžō-dži
Tanz — *dance*	fartu [2] . . .	[búrkintí [11]] .	rana	gammul . .
Musik — *music*	folāni [3] . . .	. . . . . .	gogē	gogēru [15] . .
Händeklatschen — *clapping of hands*	kabélo [4] . .	éferi	tāfi	kéle . . . bóluki . . .
Freudengeschrei der Frauen — *shouts of women*	wulúli [5] (Arb.)	ulūl	. . . . .	. . . . . .
Sklaverei — *slavery* . .	nem-kindži [6] nem-dží . .	. . . . . .	bauta . . .	džága . . .
Freiheit — *freedom* . .	nem-kām-bē [7]	. . . . . .	diantši . . .	dimāku . . .
Lohn — *salary, fee* . . .	lāda [8] . . .	égeri [12] . . .	ladá . . .	géuengel . . genāri . . .
Miethe — *hire*	ágeri [9] . . .		súfuri (Arb.).	gēngel . . .
Geschenk — *gift, present*	segōge [10] . .	kófolō [13] . . .	kiautá . . . túkotší . . . báko-ntši [14].	mótyero . . tāšhu . . . yúloki . . . kodāko . . ko-tšāri . .

[1] kaiga, s. oben S. 60 kaiga gá-nískin.

[2] fartu, ein vom Zeitwort far-nískin (s. S. 60, N. 5) gebildetes Substantiv, fehlt bei Koelle.

[3] folāni ist identisch mit pólānyō bei Koelle, mit der irriger Weise beschränkten Bedeutung „Trommel".

[4] kabélo fehlt bei Koelle.

[5] wulūli, bei Koelle wúlwuli.

[6] nem-kindži. Diese ursprüngliche Form des abgekürzten nem-dží habe ich niemals im Gebrauch gefunden, aber sie mag vorkommen. Koelle schreibt népdži mit der Phrase wu népdžiliu, „ich bin in Sklaverei"; Gr. §. 77 nem-népdži.

[7] nem-kām-bē, wörtlich „der Zustand des freien Mannes"; über nem s. Einleitung S. LX, vgl. S. 60, N. 5, kām-bē oben S. 224, N. 1. Koelle hat némbērem, aber die lokale Endung rem hat hier wol keine Beziehung.

[8] lāde fehlt bei Koelle. Das Wort ist allerdings wol nur aus der Hausa-Sprache entlehnt und es gibt gewiss dafür noch einen anderen einheimischen Ausdruck.

[9] Für „Miethe" habe ich kein eigentliches Substantiv im Kanúri erfahren, aber wie das Zeitwort ágeri-nískin S. 102 zeigt, muss ágeri, vom Arabischen أجر, einmal in dieser Bedeutung gebraucht worden sein, und daran lässt das entsprechende Tédā-Wort nicht den allergeringsten Zweifel. Es ist wol auch noch im Gebrauch.

[10] segōge fehlt bei Koelle; seine Ableitung ist mir undeutlich.

[11] búrkintí ist mir als Substantiv mehr als zweifelhaft, sowol seiner Form wegen überhaupt, als auch, weil ich ausser den von ganz anderer Wurzel abgeleiteten und S. 40 angeführten Verbalformen auch das dort nicht angeführte búrkinti als 3te Person Plur. habe.

[12] égeri, s. N. 9; jedoch ist hier zu bemerken, dass dieses Fremdwort neben dem äusserlich gleichlautenden, aber eigenthümlichen und grundverschiedenen égeri mit der Bedeutung „Amboss" im Tédā auffallend ist.

[13] kófolō ist interessant, wenn wir den Ausdruck kófole, „(allgemeine) Abgabe" in Wádáï vergleichen; s. Reisen, Th. III, S. 514, vgl. unten S. 295.

[14] báko-ntši, so wie kodáko und ko-tšāri im Fulfúlde, 16 im Sońyai bezeichnen nicht das Geschenk im Allgemeinen, sondern das Gastgeschenk.

[15] gogēru, kein nationales Fulfúlde-Wort, sondern nur durch Einfluss der Hausa gebildet.

[16] yāre, „Freiheit", scheint von einer Wurzel yō abgeleitet, das vielleicht S. 125 neben borkin, „freier Mann" (H. dá) zu setzen wäre.

[17] el hedíye. Vielleicht gibt es auch im Sońyai ein national-einheimisches Wort, wie im verwandten Arama nach Raffenel mareégé.

	Sonyai.	Lógoné.	Wándalā.	Bágrimma.	Māba.
	don	talī-kan-halgē	lahē	kā	orū
	agānī	talī-konán	ka-šíkla	ndáme	bégu
	—	musko-liyē	azag-džīre	kálkona(?)	kēlo
	okōbi	tíye ŏéŋadā [ŋadē. „Hand" p. 309, Pl. méŋadā?]	kupála	tófa-džī	tagda
	—	lululū	yéri-yéri	džīri / lūlu	—
	—	—	—	—	—
	yāre[16]	—	—	—	—
	—	—	tilelúñg	girte	mókeru
	súfure	—	—	—	—
	el hadīye[17] (Arb.) / el bāšāra (Arb.) / lō	kāsí	kāši	lée	mundo

[1] halga: compare the phrase halga gō-niekin p. 60.

[2] farta, a verbal substantive from far-niekin (see p. 61, note 5); it is wanting in Koelle.

[3] folānī is identical with Koelle's pēlānyē, to which he wrongly attributes the confused meaning of „drum".

[4] kabéle is wanting in Koelle.

[5] walāli: with Koelle wélwalī.

[6] nem-kindāl, by abbreviation nem-dāl (Koelle néntāl with the phrase wa néntālian, „I am in slavery", besides nem-néntāl (and nemnéli(a) gr. § 78), is not frequently used, although correctly formed.

[7] nem-bām-bō, verbally „the state of the free man"; with regard to nem, the same as in the preceding phrase, see Introductory Remarks p. LXI compare with p. 68, note 5, and, as for bām-bō see p. 225, note 1. Koelle has another term nembēram, but the local termination ram does not seem to be here in its right place.

[8] léde is wanting in Koelle. The word appears to be borrowed from the Hausa-language, and the Kanúri-idiom probably possesses, besides, a totally different indigenous term.

[9] As for the term ágorī meaning „hire, rent", derived from the Arabic كرا, and which is distinctly contained in the verbal form ágori-niekin (see p. 102), I have never heard it used as a distinct substantive, although it must have been so formerly, and is perfectly born out by the corresponding Tédā-term ágorī.

[10] aegége is wanting in Koelle; its mode of derivation is not clear to me.

[11] bárhimlī certainly is not to be regarded as a substantive, but is the 3rd person plur. of the verb, as I have written it down in my collectanea in the right place besides the other terms adduced among my list of verbs p. 60.

[12] ágori: see note 9. — However, it is rather remarkable that, besides this foreign term, we have an almost identical indigenous one in Tédā with the totally different meaning „envii".

[13] héfulē is not without interest if compared with the term háfele designating „tribute" in Wádāi; see below p. 295.

[14] báhe-ntāl in Hausa, as well as hedáke and ke-tšāri in Fulfúlde, lā in Sonyai, do not designate the present in general, but rather the present made to a stranger and a guest in particular.

[15] gogéru is not a national Fulfúlde-term, but entirely due to the influence of the Hausa.

[16] yáre, „freedom", appears to be derived from a term yá, which perhaps has to be placed side by side with bor kin, „free man" (H. dá) p. 225.

[17] el hadīye: possibly the Sonyai-idiom also may possess another indigenous and national term, perhaps the very marenga given with this notion by Raffenel in the closely related Azena-dialect.

Deutsch und Englisch.	Kanúri.	Tédā.	Haussa.	Fulfúlde.
Arbeit, Geschäft — *labour, work, business*	kí-da [1] . . .	ke-dā [6] . . .	aiki	kūgel . . .
Geschäft, Gewerbe — *industry, handicraft*	ken-dō			
Gewerbe eines Webers, Färbers — *handicraft of a weaver, dyer*	kí-da tsāga; kí-da aliu-be	. . . . . .	aiki n mai-saki; aikin mai-rini	. . . . . .
Handel — *trade, commerce*	libaia, libáya [2] (Arb.)	. . . . . .	tšineki . . . / talla [9] . . . / karha . . .	tšoggu . . . / yaúnuki . . . / džábere . . .
Lohn, Anleihe — *loan*	tégeri . . . / kusu(?) . . .		ramtše, ramta	damtšenáya, damtšāka / yamlāki [11] .
baare Bezahlung — *prompt payment*	alūa [3] . . .	. . . . . .	bāši [10] . . .	ñamānde . .
Schuld — *debt*	kūsu [4] . . .	yaúkai [7] . . .	bīa	yólold . . .
Pfand — *pledge, pawn* .	. . . . . .	. . . . . .	žingína . . .	tolmē . . . / bakāhi . .
Preis, Werth — *price, worth*	témman [5] . .	déberi [8] . .	témmane . .	fundi . . . / džaudi [12] . .
was ist der Preis? — *what is its worth?*	áfi témman-tsē	indi déberi .	. . . . . .	. . . . . .
Vortheil, Verdienst, Gewinn — *gain, profit*	faida (Arb.) .	riba (Arb.) .	riba	ñāmi lūmo [13] / héberi lūmo

[1] kí-da. S. oben S. 56 die Phrase kí-da-ni mbé-dilia. Was kí-da tsāga, „das Gewerbe des Webers", und kí-da aliu-bé, „das Gewerbe des Färbers", angeht, so ist tsāga von unbestimmter Ableitung, und vielleicht nicht verbunden mit dem Zeitwort tsa-ágin, tsá-ágin, sondern mit H. saki, noch näher mit W. tsāka zusammenhängend (ob verwandt mit Koelle's tsāgō, „Frucht, feine, kostbare Kleidung"?); aliu, bei Koelle éliu, „die Indigopflanze", s. oben S. 174. — Die vornehmere Klasse gebraucht für kí-da auch das aus dem Arabischen entlehnte sányā, wenn vgl. Koelle s. v.

[2] libáya, libaia, über die Ableitung s. oben zu S. 100, N. 1 libáya di-skin.

[3] alūa kann ich nicht ableiten; es ist wahrscheinlich ein Wándalā-Fremdwort; vgl. „ich bezahle", alū-niskin S. 107.

[4] kūsu. Koelle kásū.

[5] témman. Dieses témman, das bei Koelle fehlt, hängt möglicherweise mit dem entsprechenden Wort im Sebuhn zusammen, das 10 bedeutet. Dann müssten wir annehmen, was allerdings sehr wahrscheinlich ist, dass das entsprechende Haussa-Wort témmane erst von diesem Kanúri abgeleitet sei. Auf eine derartige Berührung des Kanúri mit jener Abessinischen Gruppe komme ich an anderer Stelle zurück. témman, wie das folgende faida fehlt bei Koelle.

[6] ke-dā im Tédā ist auffallend, weil ich für das Zeitwort „thun" ganz andere Wurzelwörter habe, und nur zwei Folgerungen bleiben übrig: entweder gibt es auch ein einheimisches Zeitwort von dieser Wurzel oder das Substantiv ke-dā wird nur von denjenigen Tédā gebraucht, die mit Bornu viel verkehren. S. Einleitung S. XC, N. 5.

[7] yaúkai wird bestätigt durch die verbale Phrase meré yaúkai bódi ya-tí S. 107 „er ist schuldig".

[8] déberi hängt vielleicht mit dob, dobu, höchstes Zahlwort, zusammen und ist dem éferi, égeri und anderen Tédā-Nennwörtern analog gebildet.

[9] talla, so wie das entsprechende Fulfúlde-Wort yaúnuki, bezeichnet eigentlich nicht den ganzen Handel, sondern den Handel im Kleinen, das Krämergeschäft. — karba dagegen, wie džábere im Fulfúlde, bedeutet den Verkauf auf Kredit.

[10] bāši ist ursprünglich eine Verbalform (eigentlich „gib es"), die dann aber allgemein substantivisch gebraucht wird. — Das folgende bīa kommt von bī, „folgen". Beide Ausdrücke sind in lehrreicher Weise verbunden in der Phrase ina bī-nan bāši, „ich bin ihm schuldig", S. 102.

[11] yamlāki ist allem Anschein nach das eigentliche nationale Wort, die beiden anderen nur vom Haussa abgeleitete Formen.

[12] džaudi heisst sonst „Reichthum" und wird wol nur uneigentlich in dieser Bedeutung gebraucht.

[13] ñāmi lūmo, eigentlich „der Fraß des Marktes" (daher auch ñamānde), héberi lūmo „der Fund des Marktes".

[14] ya n dāsu gehört wol kaum hierher: dāsu allein heisst „verschlüsselter Orbes".

[15] dana aliube. Die durchaus dem Kanúri eigenthümliche Genitivform aliube erklärt sich aus dem natürlichen Verhältniss, dass die Färberei von Bornu aus nach Bagirmi verpflanzt ist.

[illegible]	Lógonē.	Wándalā.	Bágrimma.	Mába.
ya n dásu(?)[14] .	merán dana . .	ferā	kida . . . / dana . . .	ɣiddeme
. . . . . .	dana sáka; dana morún	ferā tsáka; ferā ávmie	dana n tšékum; dana alinbe[15]	. . . . . .
taifa(?) . . . . / hebbi	kas-kū	ganē	giana . . .	
garan	. . . . . .	. . . . . .	. . . . . .	. . . . . .
. . . . . .	wāre-nā . . .	(megín mágin) alūa-rā	dugō	galua
garau	muslim	gimo	kedā	. . . . . .
tolma . . . . / árrebān (Arb.) .	. . . . . .	. . . . . .	. . . . . .	. . . . . .
. . . . . .	kas kolle dékemē	gáne	. . . . . .	tamman
. . . . . .	. . . . . .	ázere gán(e)-āra	témman ané dia	. . . . . .
el faida . . .	faide	faida	faida . . .	

[1] ki-da see above p. 86 the phrase ki-da-ni mbé-dāin. As for the technical terms ki-da tedge, „the handicraft of the weaver", and ki-da aliu-bō, „the handicraft of the dyer", tedge (perhaps identical or closely related with Koelle's tedgé, „pomp, fine, costly clothes") may seem to be connected with the verb tes-ágin, teš-ágin but is more probably borrowed from H. séki, W. teáka; alin, the âlin of Koelle, „the indigo-plant", see p. 174.

[2] libáye, libaie: see above p. 101, note 1 the phrase libáye di-ekin.

[3] alūa seems to be a foreign term and is probably borrowed from the Wándalā; compare the verbal term alū-niekin p. 102.

[4] kāua: Koelle kāuā.

[5] témman: this term may possibly be connected with the identical Shoho term meaning „ten", in which case we must look upon the corresponding Hausa-form témmanne as derived from the Kanúri. For, as far some kind of connection of the Kanúri-idiom with the Abyssinian group of languages, it is proved by several instances and will be spoken of in another place. The term is wanting with Koelle, as well as the following faida.

[6] ko-dā in Tédā is remarkable, as I have no root in that idiom, from whence to derive it, and either, therefore, we must suppose, that there is, or has been in use such a verb, or that the term ko-dā has been borrowed from the Kanúri by that section of the Tédā-nation, which has the closest intercourse with Bornu. Compare Introductory Remarks p. XCI, note 5.

[7] yaskai is confirmed by means of the verbal phrase morē yaskai kádi ye-ië adduced p. 102.

[8] déberi has been formed in a perfectly analogous manner with the nouns éferi, égeri and so on, although I have no distinct root, from which to derive it, if we have not to look as such upon dab, deba, the highest numerical unity.

[9] taila, as well as the corresponding Fulfúlde-term yeéaaki, properly does not express the commerce in general, but rather the retail-business, while karba in Hausa, as well as dīāhere in Fulfúlde, means the selling on credit.

[10] bāšī, originally, in a verbal form meaning „give it", which only by abuse has become to be used as a substantive, and that a very common one. — As for the next following term bia, it is formed from bi, „to follow", which in the phrase ina bi-nua bāšī p. 107 is joined to bāšī in a very instructive manner.

[11] yamlāki seems to be the proper national term, the two forms of the other term being borrowed from the Hausa.

[12] dūnudi in most other cases means „wealth, riches", and in this place seems rather to be used improperly.

[13] kásuk lúmo properly means „the food of the market", from má-dō nyámu, „I eat", whence also the term bamánde, béberi lúmo „the thing found in the market".

[14] ya n dásu seems to be a composite term which scarcely belongs to this place; dásu alone by itself meaning „castrated ox".

[15] dana alinbe: As for the genitive form alinbe, which belongs exclusively to the grammar of the Kanúri-idiom, its appearance in this Bágrimma-term is fully explained by means of the fact of the art of dying having been introduced into Bagirmi from the part of Bornu and through Bornu-men.

Deutsch und Englisch.	Kanúri.	Tédā.	Hausa.	Fulfúlde.
Verlust — *loss, damage* .	hasár[1] (Arb.) .	hasár-kíbu .	χasāra (Arb.)	χasāra . . .
Bewegung — *motion* . .	. . . . .	. . . . .	motši . . .	sōño . . . .
Marsch — *march* . . .	lē-tu . . .	. . . . .	fataulši . . .	tigu . . . .
Reise — *journey* . . .	lē-tu . . .	tori . . . ; tíria . . .	tafia	yādu; yēdu . ; džibángel . . ; džahále . .
Zerüstung zum Marsch — *a journey's outfit*	. . . . .	sǎan-tira (?) .	šōri n tafia .	hábuke yādu .
Austreiben des Viehs auf ferne Weiden — *the driving out the cattle to far-distant pastures*	. . . . .	. . . . .	mazūtši n rāni	bertōdži . .
früher Aufbruch — *early start*	taušin . . .		düdlšefi . .	dadaure . .
Rast, Ruhe — *repose* . .	uem-te . . ; lúsu, tuste .	. . . . .	zāma . . .	džonde . . ; džodāki . .
mittägliche Rast — *repose during the midday heat*	débdö, díbdu[2]	duskwi . . .	ēni	yalde (?) . .
Ermüdung — *fatigue, exhaustion*	ógenlfu[3] . .	nolōbu . . .	gažia . . .	tiómmeri . .
Thronbesteigung, Einsetzung eines Königs — *installation of a king*	kir-mai[4] . .	. . . . .	sarauta[7] . .	. . . . .
Einsetzung eines Gouverneurs — *installation of a governor*	ka-gálā[5] . .	tegē (? comp. p. 78)		. . . . .
Regierung — *government*	hókum[6] (Arb.)	diyór . . . ; hokkum . .		lāmu . . .

[1] hasár, Koelle ašár; anstatt lē-tu hat er létṛ.

[2] débdö, díbdu. Koelle schreibt débdö, erklärt es aber irrthümlich als den wirklichen Tag von Sonnenaufgang bis Untergang, da es selbst nur die Mittagszeit erst in zweiter Instanz bedeutet, einzig weil da die Mittagsruhe Statt findet. Siehe die S. 90, N. 4 gemachte Bemerkung.

[3] ógenlfu ist von unsicherer Ableitung, hängt aber wol in der Grundbedeutung des verwahrlosten Zustandes mit ógenl, „Waise" zusammen. Koelle hat dafür das von mir nie gehörte Substantiv kémbárö von mbárgskin.

[4] kir-mai. Koelle kermai; aber das i ist bedeutungsvoll und charakteristisch. kir-mai ist nämlich zusammengesetzt aus ka, „was", ir, „machen", der Wurzel des sonst im Kanúri verloren gegangenen Zeitwortes erik im Tédā (s. Einleitung S. LXXIV, 6, vgl. damit kir, „die Sklavin", d. h. ursprünglich „das Factotum des einfachen Hausstandes"), und mai, „König".

[5] ka-gálā. Koelle (kágalla) erklärt es nicht ganz richtig als das Amt oder den Rang der höheren Behörden. S. über den möglichen Zusammenhang dieser Kanúri-Form mit dem entsprechenden Bagrimma-Wort Einleitung S. XLVI.

[6] hókum, obgleich Fremdwort, ist doch ganz in den Geist der Sprache übergegangen, wie die alltägliche Redensart Allá hegimtsia, „wenn Gott es so fügen sollte", S. 58, N. 9 zeigt. Sollen wir aber danach hier die Orthographie ändern? — In Bezug auf Privatpersonen gebraucht man im Hausa für „Herrschaft, Befehl" den Arabischen Ausdruck el ámeri, wie z. B. in der Phrase el ámeri-nsa dawya, „sein Befehl (ist) schwer", d. h. „er ist streng".

[7] sarauta bedeutet „Thronbesteigung" so gut wie „Regierung", aber im ersteren Falle wird ihm die nähere Angabe des Besteigenden hinzugefügt. — Ich führe hier noch den Hausa-Ausdruck gangame für „öffentlichen (von der Trommel begleiteten) Ausruf" an.

[8] ne-miagsī ist wol die richtige Form, während ich erst nim-migraī geschrieben hatte, in der Voraussetzung, dass nim im Lógoné identisch wäre mit nem im Kanúri.

[9] ingenlfu ist entschieden nicht ursprüngliches Wándalā-Wort, sondern hier wol nur im Drange des Augenblickes dem Kanúri entlehnt; el deié, „den Menschen" ist echtes Wándalā.

[10] iškelrā. Über diese Form s. Einleitung S. CCXL, 4, a).

[11] kyōge. Über die Bildung dieses Nennwortes s. Einleitung S. CCCVIII, a, α).

Sonyai.	Lógoné.	Wándalá.	Bágrimma.	Mába.
. . . . . .	hasár (kaskū . .	ásarē	kásarē	. . . . . .
. . . . . . sette	lóana . . . . . náasgir (verb. ? s. p. 91)	dalā	kabē	gûai, gîai
. . . . . .	. . . .		. . . . .	
. . . . . .	. . . .	. . . . . .	. . . . .	
. . . . . .	. . . .	. . . . . .	. . . . .	. . . . . .
gōro	sin-wāten . . .	džā	indžīra . . .	ŋyōgo [11]
. . . . . .	wogūnbe	wā	wáya . . .	. . . . . .
farga	ínkibā	ingenīfu 'ldalā [9] kodē (?) . .	ingenīfu . .	tāb (Arb.)
. . . . . .	ne-míayaī [8] . .	tékairē [10] . .	kindži n bańge	
. . . . . .	tsiikín	gala-urā . .	garē . . . garā . . .	
el hokm . . .	bunkum . . .	bókunm . .	bókum . . .	bókum

[1] hasár: Koelle writes asár.

[2] dōbdō, dibdu: Koelle, who writes dśbdó, explains it wrongly as „the actual day from sunrise to sunset", while originally it does not even mean the time of midday, the original meaning being that of „repose during the heat of the sun". See what I have said p. 91, note 4.

[3] ágenīfu: the derivation of this term is doubtful, but it seems to have some relation to the term ágeni meaning „orphan", both indicating a state of destitution. Koelle instead of this very common term has kémbárē from the verb mbárgekin.

[4] kir-mai: Koelle kermai, but the i is important and characteristic; kir-mai being composed of three elements, viz ke, „what of", ir, „make", the root of the auxiliary verb erik in the closely related Tedā-tongue, which in the Kanúri-idiom has been nearly lost and obliterated (see Introductory Remarks p. LXXV, 8), and mai, „king".

[5] ka-gáli: Koelle, who writes kágalle, is not quite right, when he attributes to this term the meaning „rank, office of higher charges". As for the relation of this term to the corresponding Bágrimma-term, see Introductory Remarks p. XLVII.

[6] hókum, although originally a foreign term, yet has been perfectly appropriated to the spirit of the language, as is sufficiently proved by the phrase Alle hugímisio p. 58, note 9. But as for the orthography, we need not to change it in consequence of this verbal form. — As for the term el ámeri used with this notion in private affairs, see p. 296, note 7.

[7] sarauta means as well „incoronation, installation", as the government itself, in the former case some further specification having to be added. — Besides, I here adduce the Hausa-term gangamo meaning „public announcement by way of drum".

[8] ne-míayaī seems to me to be the right form, while first I had written nim-miaraī, supposing this nim in Lógoné to be identical with the Kanúri nem.

[9] ingenīfu, no doubt, is not an original Wándalá-term, but has been borrowed from the Kanúri; 'l dalá, el dalá, „of the marsh", is pure Wándalá.

[10] tékairē: as for the form of this term see Introductory Remarks p. CCXLI, 4, a).

[11] ŋyōgo: as for the derivation of this term, see Introductory Remarks p. CCCIX, e, a).

Deutsch und Englisch.	Kanúri.	Tédā.	Hausa.	Fulfúlde.
Tribut — *tribute* . . .	kúntulgū mai-bē	elgésti . . .	gunda[6] . . .	gondal . . .
Abgabe, besonders in Vieh — *tribute, especially in cattle*	džangal[1] . . .		harádži (Arb.)	džangal . . .
Zoll — *toll of different kind*	gábagā mai-bé[2]	. . . . . .	fito	džaindi . . .
Grundsteuer — *ground-rent*	tāïdi-ram mai-bē	. . . . . .	kurdi n kása .	tāēde leadi .
Gericht — *judgement* . .	šérīa[3] . . .	. . . . . .	šerīa . . .	kīta . . . .
Rechtsspruch — *decree of a court of law*			hókkumtāl[7] .	hókkumtāl . .
Geleit — *safe conduct* .	kentaár-dugō .	. . . . . .	rékia[8] . . .	robīīru . . / dóptoki . .
Empfang — *reception* . .	sabāte (?) . .	. . . . . .	tária	tabwāki . .
Krieg, Raubzug — *war, freebooting expedition*	kerígu[4] . . .	wáneerík (? verb.) / yobúr . . .	yāki	kóno[11] Pl. kóni
Galopp, Angriff — *gallop, attack*	ágerémte[5] . .	. . . . . .	súkwa[9] . . .	samgo[12] Plur. samgōdži / sámonki . .
Schlacht — *battle* . . .	libála . . .	túlo	fáda[10]	hábere . . .

[1] Die Übereinstimmung von džangel mit dem entsprechenden Fulfúlde-Ausdruck beruht auf äusseren sachlichen Verhältnissen, da die Fulbe die Hauptviehzüchter in diesen Gegenden sind; es fehlt bei Koelle, wie auch gleicherweise kúntulgū.

[2] gábagā mai-bē, eigentlich „die Baumwollenstreifen des Königs". Von anderen Abgaben führt Koelle noch tilgáram (d. i. dágáram), „Thorzoll, Accise", und tāllirām (offenbar nur dialektisch verschiedene Form meines tāïdiram) oder kissemram, „eine in der kalten Jahreszeit (das soll wol heissen nach völlig abgeschlossener Ernte?) erhobene Taxe", an. — Übrigens ist gábagā und kabagā, „Spanne" wol ein und dasselbe Wort.

[3] šérīa. Koelle hat noch ein besonderes Wort, bérgūram, für das Gericht, wo Fälle von Gewaltthat oder Unterdrückung abgeurtheilt werden.

[4] kerígu. Koelle krigu und kérigu. Wurzel ist wol rí in rí-ischin, rí-sgin, „ich mache Schreck, fürchte mich".

[5] ágerémte hängt eng mit der oben S. 196, N. 5 zu ágari gegebenen Ableitung zusammen und bestätigt den daher abgeleiteten Namen der Gazelle. Koelle hat auch ein Wort kágaraml mit der Bedeutung „Pferderennen", das mir unbekannt geblieben ist, obgleich es von derselben Wurzel abgeleitet ist (ká-ágere-mi), was bei Koelle's Accentuation kaum zu erkennen ist. — Statt libála hat Koelle lębála.

[6] gunda, bei Schön gundu.

[7] hókkumtāl. Ich führe hier das ganz Arabische, aber doch in's gewöhnliche, alltägliche Hausa übergegangene el ámori an, „der Befehl", das besonders gewöhnlich ist in der Redensart el ámori-nsa danya, „sein Gebot ist schwer", d. h. „er ist streng; es ist schwer, ihm zu gehorchen".

[8] rékia und tária scheinen im Hausa keine Verwandtschaft zu haben.

[9] súkwa wird in der Bedeutung eines Angriffs „auf" mit garé konstruirt, wie in der Phrase inuel suái súkwa da derē garé Gissne, sanadaki gerke n šūne hīu, „die Feinde haben in der Nacht einen Angriff auf Gissne gemacht und haben zwei Rinderheerden fortgeführt", was das Fulfúlde in verbaler Form folgendermassen ausdrückt: hābe samai Gissne džemma, kābi hola nai didi.

[10] fáda. So sagt man fáda n birni, im F. hábere hirni, „Schlacht, Kampf um eine Stadt".

[11] kónu. In Timbo (Koelle) ganz ebenso kónu mit dem etwas verschiedenen Plural kóndi, wenn letzterer richtig.

[12] samgo bedeutet den kriegerischen Angriff, sámonki den gewöhnlichen Galopp.

[13] sará-tiye. Daraus ist vielleicht durch Missverständniss der vermeintliche Titel eines Serratik bei den Europäischen Reisenden Senegambiens entstanden, während dieser Name nur das Amt, nicht den Inhaber bezeichnet, welcher letztere vielmehr sará-tiye-hoi heisst. S. oben.

[14] wá miayē. Ich bin etwas unsicher, ob es richtiger ist zu schreiben wa miayōi, „die Sache des Königs", vgl. Einleitung S. CCX, h), oder wa miayē, „was man dem Könige giebt", von wé, „geben".

[15] ih ee gohoin scheint mir zweifelhaft.

[16] hó ee wonī kann ich ebenso wenig analysiren.

[17] miyonō, vielleicht mi-yonā.

[18] moiten hoáhi, vielleicht richtiger moi n hoáhi, wo wir hoáhi wol als Genitivform zu fassen haben. S. Einleitung S. CCLXXII, d) und CCLXXIV, a).

[19] háfain. Hierüber, so wie über dován siehe meinen Reisebericht, Th. III, Anhang, S. 513 flg.; vgl. oben Tédā háfaiá, S. 268, N. 13.

Sónyai.	Lógoné.	Wándalá.	Bágrimma.	Mába.
. . . .	wā miayē [14] . .	sanaál teksē .	bedē n bańga	devān, divān (Arb.)
. . . .	ib se gebaia [15] .	gingle dženǵal	dženǵnl . . .	káfala [19] (Arb.)
. . . .	gábagā miayē .	gébbegā teksē	farda n bańga	. . . . . .
. . . .	bā séwenī [16] . .	áz-abā teksé .	mottien hańki [18]	. . . . . .
sarí	. . . .	. . . . . .	. . . . . .	. . . . . .
sará-tiye [13] . .	. . . .	. . . . . .	. . . . . .	. . . . . .
		. .		
. . . .	. . . .	. . . . . .		
. . . .	. . . .			
wońgu	yanē	uńgwa . . .	wai, waya . .	embéa
. . . .	. . . .	. . . . . .		
dźendži	míyenā [17] . . .	dágala . . .	daue	torre

[1] dženǵal, as well as the preceding kántelgó, are both wanting in Koelle, and as for their mode of derivation I am not certain; but, as for the close identity of the former term both in Kanúri and in Fulfúlde, it is explained by means of the fact of the Fúlbe in these Regions being the cattle breeders par excellence.

[2] gábagā mai-bē properly means „the cottonstripes of (due to) the king". As for other kinds of taxes, Koelle has a distinct term tšigáram (i. e. džegáram) with the meaning „toll, service", and tšilíram (is no doubt nothing but a slightly varied form of my tšiláiram] or binemram, „a tax levied in the cold season [that is to say, after the harvest has been gathered and brought in]". — Koelle also wrongly distinguishes the two terms kábagā as meaning „span" and our gábagā, both being one and the same term.

[3] Férēa: Koelle, besides, has another term bárgārám for the court for criminal causes.

[4] kerige: Koelle kríge and kérige; the root, no doubt, is ri in ri-niskin, ri-ágin, „I fear, become frightened".

[5] Koelle instead of ágorémte has another form kángeramí with the notion „race, horse race", which has remained unknown to me, but which has been derived from the same root ágori spoken of p. 197, note 5.

[6] gunda with Schön in the form gunda.

[7] hókkamtē: I here adduce also another term el ámori, which, although of pure Arab origin, has been received into the daily conversation of the Hausa-language, as for instance in the phrase el ámori-nsa denya, „his commandment is difficult", meaning „his rule is a severe one".

[8] rékie as well as térie are not known to me as for their origin and mode of derivation.

[9] séékwa, if conveying the notion of „attack", is construed with the proposition garé, as, for instance, in the phrase tasal asúl séékwa dé derē garé Ulana, sandanki gerke n šáno bíu, „the enemy in the course of the night has made an attack against Ulana, they have carried off two herds of cattle", a phrase, which the Fúlbe express in a verbal sense in the following manner: hábe samal Ulanu džemma, hōtši kále nai didi.

[10] fáda: thus „a battle for a town" is expressed by means of the composite term fádu n birni, in F. hábere birni.

[11] kûno: in Timbo (Koelle) we have the almost identical form kônu but with the different plural-form kônéli.

[12] samge means the warlike attack, sámaski the ordinary gallop.

[13] sará-tiye: from this term, which means the office itself, not the officer, probably the little Serrotik, common with European travellers in that quarter, has been corrupted, while the proper title of the person is sará-tiye-kei.

[14] wā miayē: I am rather a little uncertain, whether I ought to write wa miayē, „the thing belonging to the king", compare Introductory Remarks p. CCXI, h), or wa miayē, „what has to be given to the king", from wā, „to give".

[15] ib se gebaia seems rather doubtful.

[16] bā se wenī I am not able to analyze at present; it may involve a mistake of some kind.

[17] miyenā: perhaps we ought to write mi-yenā.

[18] mottien hańki: perhaps more correctly to be written mot n hańki, hańki being a sort of general case. See Introductory Remarks p. CCLXXIII, 4) and CCLXXV, g).

[19] káfala, as for the káfala and the devān, see Travels and Disc. vol. III. p. 550 ff. and compare above p. 772, n 13.

www.ingramcontent.com/pod-product-compliance
Lightning Source LLC
Chambersburg PA
CBHW021224300426
44111CB00007B/419
9783741159626